D1587843

Dewey Decimal Classification and Relative Index

Dewey Decimal Classification and Relative Index

Devised by Melvil Dewey

EDITION 21

Edited by

Joan S. Mitchell, Editor

Julianne Beall, Assistant Editor

Winton E. Matthews, Jr., Assistant Editor

Gregory R. New, Assistant Editor

VOLUME 2

Schedules 000-599

FOREST PRESS

A Division of
OCLC Online Computer Library Center, Inc.
ALBANY, NEW YORK
1996

Library of Congress Cataloging-in-Publication Data
Dewey, Melvil, 1851-1931.
    Dewey decimal classification and relative index / devised by
Melvil Dewey. -- Ed. 21 / edited by Joan S. Mitchell, Julianne Beall,
Winton E. Matthews, Jr., Gregory R. New.
    p. cm.
    Contents: v. 1. Introduction. Tables --v. 2-3. Schedules --v. 4. Relative
index. Manual.
    ISBN 0-910608-50-4 (set : alk. paper)
    1. Classification, Dewey decimal. I. Mitchell, Joan S. II. Beall,
Julianne, 1946-   . III. Matthews, Winton, E. IV. New, Gregory R. V.
Forest Press. VI. Title.
Z696.D52   1996   96-7393
025.4'31--dc20   CIP

The paper used in this publication meets the requirements of ANSI/NISO
Z39.48-1992 (Permanence of Paper).

ISBN: (set) 0-910608-50-4; v. 1 0-910608-51-2; v. 2 0-910608-52-0;
v. 3 0-910608-53-9; v. 4 0-910608-54-7

 Recycled paper

Contents

Volume 1

Contents

Summaries

First Summary*
The Ten Main Classes

000	**Generalities**
100	**Philosophy & psychology**
200	**Religion**
300	**Social sciences**
400	**Language**
500	**Natural sciences & mathematics**
600	**Technology (Applied sciences)**
700	**The arts Fine and decorative arts**
800	**Literature & rhetoric**
900	**Geography & history**

*Consult schedules for complete and exact headings

Second Summary*
The Hundred Divisions

000	**Generalities**	**500**	**Natural sciences & mathematics**	
010	Bibliography	510	Mathematics	
020	Library & information sciences	520	Astronomy & allied sciences	
030	General encyclopedic works	530	Physics	
040		540	Chemistry & allied sciences	
050	General serial publications	550	Earth sciences	
060	General organizations & museology	560	Paleontology	Paleozoology
070	News media, journalism, publishing	570	Life sciences	Biology
080	General collections	580	Plants	
090	Manuscripts & rare books	590	Animals	
100	**Philosophy & psychology**	**600**	**Technology (Applied sciences)**	
110	Metaphysics	610	Medical sciences	Medicine
120	Epistemology, causation, humankind	620	Engineering & allied operations	
130	Paranormal phenomena	630	Agriculture & related technologies	
140	Specific philosophical schools	640	Home economics & family living	
150	Psychology	650	Management & auxiliary services	
160	Logic	660	Chemical engineering	
170	Ethics (Moral philosophy)	670	Manufacturing	
180	Ancient, medieval, Oriental philosophy	680	Manufacture for specific uses	
190	Modern western philosophy	690	Buildings	
200	**Religion**	**700**	**The arts Fine and decorative arts**	
210	Philosophy & theory of religion	710	Civic & landscape art	
220	Bible	720	Architecture	
230	Christianity Christian theology	730	Plastic arts Sculpture	
240	Christian moral & devotional theology	740	Drawing & decorative arts	
250	Christian orders & local church	750	Painting & paintings	
260	Social & ecclesiastical theology	760	Graphic arts Printmaking & prints	
270	History of Christianity & Christian church	770	Photography & photographs	
280	Christian denominations & sects	780	Music	
290	Comparative religion & other religions	790	Recreational & performing arts	
300	**Social sciences**	**800**	**Literature & rhetoric**	
310	Collections of general statistics	810	American literature in English	
320	Political science	820	English & Old English literatures	
330	Economics	830	Literatures of Germanic languages	
340	Law	840	Literatures of Romance languages	
350	Public administration & military science	850	Italian, Romanian, Rhaeto-Romanic	
360	Social problems & services; association	860	Spanish & Portuguese literatures	
370	Education	870	Italic literatures Latin	
380	Commerce, communications, transportation	880	Hellenic literatures Classical Greek	
390	Customs, etiquette, folklore	890	Literatures of other languages	
400	**Language**	**900**	**Geography & history**	
410	Linguistics	910	Geography & travel	
420	English & Old English	920	Biography, genealogy, insignia	
430	Germanic languages German	930	History of ancient world to ca. 499	
440	Romance languages French	940	General history of Europe	
450	Italian, Romanian, Rhaeto-Romanic	950	General history of Asia Far East	
460	Spanish & Portuguese languages	960	General history of Africa	
470	Italic languages Latin	970	General history of North America	
480	Hellenic languages Classical Greek	980	General history of South America	
490	Other languages	990	General history of other areas	

*Consult schedules for complete and exact headings

Third Summary*
The Thousand Sections

*Consult schedules for complete and exact headings

Philosophy and psychology

100	**Philosophy & psychology**	**150**	**Psychology**
101	Theory of philosophy	151	
102	Miscellany	152	Perception, movement, emotions, drives
103	Dictionaries & encyclopedias	153	Mental processes & intelligence
104		154	Subconscious & altered states
105	Serial publications	155	Differential & developmental psychology
106	Organizations & management	156	Comparative psychology
107	Education, research, related topics	157	
108	Kinds of persons treatment	158	Applied psychology
109	Historical & collected persons treatment	159	
110	**Metaphysics**	**160**	**Logic**
111	Ontology	161	Induction
112		162	Deduction
113	Cosmology (Philosophy of nature)	163	
114	Space	164	
115	Time	165	Fallacies & sources of error
116	Change	166	Syllogisms
117	Structure	167	Hypotheses
118	Force & energy	168	Argument & persuasion
119	Number & quantity	169	Analogy
120	**Epistemology, causation, humankind**	**170**	**Ethics (Moral philosophy)**
121	Epistemology (Theory of knowledge)	171	Ethical systems
122	Causation	172	Political ethics
123	Determinism & indeterminism	173	Ethics of family relationships
124	Teleology	174	Occupational ethics
125		175	Ethics of recreation & leisure
126	The self	176	Ethics of sex & reproduction
127	The unconscious & the subconscious	177	Ethics of social relations
128	Humankind	178	Ethics of consumption
129	Origin & destiny of individual souls	179	Other ethical norms
130	**Paranormal phenomena**	**180**	**Ancient, medieval, Oriental philosophy**
131	Parapsychological & occult methods	181	Oriental philosophy
132		182	Pre-Socratic Greek philosophies
133	Parapsychology & occultism	183	Sophistic & Socratic philosophies
134		184	Platonic philosophy
135	Dreams & mysteries	185	Aristotelian philosophy
136		186	Skeptic & Neoplatonic philosophies
137	Divinatory graphology	187	Epicurean philosophy
138	Physiognomy	188	Stoic philosophy
139	Phrenology	189	Medieval western philosophy
140	**Specific philosophical schools**	**190**	**Modern western philosophy**
141	Idealism & related systems	191	Philosophy of United States & Canada
142	Critical philosophy	192	Philosophy of British Isles
143	Bergsonism & intuitionism	193	Philosophy of Germany & Austria
144	Humanism & related systems	194	Philosophy of France
145	Sensationalism	195	Philosophy of Italy
146	Naturalism & related systems	196	Philosophy of Spain & Portugal
147	Pantheism & related systems	197	Philosophy of former Soviet Union
148	Eclecticism, liberalism, traditionalism	198	Philosophy of Scandinavia
149	Other philosophical systems	199	Philosophy in other geographic areas

Religion

Social sciences

300	**Social sciences**	**350**	**Public administration & military science**
301	Sociology & anthropology	351	Public administration
302	Social interaction	352	General considerations
303	Social processes	353	Specific fields of public administration
304	Factors affecting social behavior	354	Administration of economy & environment
305	Social groups	355	Military science
306	Culture & institutions	356	Foot forces & warfare
307	Communities	357	Mounted forces & warfare
308		358	Air & other specialized forces
309		359	Sea (Naval) forces & warfare
310	**Collections of general statistics**	**360**	**Social problems & services; association**
311		361	General social problems & welfare
312		362	Social welfare problems & services
313		363	Other social problems & services
314	General statistics of Europe	364	Criminology
315	General statistics of Asia	365	Penal & related institutions
316	General statistics of Africa	366	Associations
317	General statistics of North America	367	General clubs
318	General statistics of South America	368	Insurance
319	General statistics of other areas	369	Miscellaneous kinds of associations
320	**Political science**	**370**	**Education**
321	Systems of governments & states	371	Schools & activities; special education
322	Relation of state to organized groups	372	Elementary education
323	Civil & political rights	373	Secondary education
324	The political process	374	Adult education
325	International migration & colonization	375	Curricula
326	Slavery & emancipation	376	
327	International relations	377	
328	The legislative process	378	Higher education
329		379	Public policy issues in education
330	**Economics**	**380**	**Commerce, communications, transportation**
331	Labor economics	381	Internal commerce (Domestic trade)
332	Financial economics	382	International commerce (Foreign trade)
333	Economics of land & energy	383	Postal communication
334	Cooperatives	384	Communications Telecommunication
335	Socialism & related systems	385	Railroad transportation
336	Public finance	386	Inland waterway & ferry transportation
337	International economics	387	Water, air, space transportation
338	Production	388	Transportation Ground transportation
339	Macroeconomics & related topics	389	Metrology & standardization
340	**Law**	**390**	**Customs, etiquette, folklore**
341	International law	391	Costume & personal appearance
342	Constitutional & administrative law	392	Customs of life cycle & domestic life
343	Military, tax, trade, industrial law	393	Death customs
344	Labor, social, education, cultural law	394	General customs
345	Criminal law	395	Etiquette (Manners)
346	Private law	396	
347	Civil procedure & courts	397	
348	Law (Statutes), regulations, cases	398	Folklore
349	Law of specific jurisdictions & areas	399	Customs of war & diplomacy

Language

400	**Language**		**450**	**Italian, Romanian, Rhaeto-Romanic**
401	Philosophy & theory		451	Italian writing system & phonology
402	Miscellany		452	Italian etymology
403	Dictionaries & encyclopedias		453	Italian dictionaries
404	Special topics		454	
405	Serial publications		455	Italian grammar
406	Organizations & management		456	
407	Education, research, related topics		457	Italian language variations
408	Kinds of persons treatment		458	Standard Italian usage
409	Geographic & persons treatment		459	Romanian & Rhaeto-Romanic
410	**Linguistics**		**460**	**Spanish & Portuguese languages**
411	Writing systems		461	Spanish writing system & phonology
412	Etymology		462	Spanish etymology
413	Dictionaries		463	Spanish dictionaries
414	Phonology & phonetics		464	
415	Grammar		465	Spanish grammar
416			466	
417	Dialectology & historical linguistics		467	Spanish language variations
418	Standard usage Applied linguistics		468	Standard Spanish usage
419	Verbal language not spoken or written		469	Portuguese
420	**English & Old English**		**470**	**Italic languages Latin**
421	English writing system & phonology		471	Classical Latin writing & phonology
422	English etymology		472	Classical Latin etymology
423	English dictionaries		473	Classical Latin dictionaries
424			474	
425	English grammar		475	Classical Latin grammar
426			476	
427	English language variations		477	Old, Postclassical, Vulgar Latin
428	Standard English usage		478	Classical Latin usage
429	Old English (Anglo-Saxon)		479	Other Italic languages
430	**Germanic languages German**		**480**	**Hellenic languages Classical Greek**
431	German writing system & phonology		481	Classical Greek writing & phonology
432	German etymology		482	Classical Greek etymology
433	German dictionaries		483	Classical Greek dictionaries
434			484	
435	German grammar		485	Classical Greek grammar
436			486	
437	German language variations		487	Preclassical & postclassical Greek
438	Standard German usage		488	Classical Greek usage
439	Other Germanic languages		489	Other Hellenic languages
440	**Romance languages French**		**490**	**Other languages**
441	French writing system & phonology		491	East Indo-European & Celtic languages
442	French etymology		492	Afro-Asiatic languages Semitic
443	French dictionaries		493	Non-Semitic Afro-Asiatic languages
444			494	Altaic, Uralic, Hyperborean, Dravidian
445	French grammar		495	Languages of East & Southeast Asia
446			496	African languages
447	French language variations		497	North American native languages
448	Standard French usage		498	South American native languages
449	Provençal & Catalan		499	Austronesian & other languages

Natural sciences and mathematics

500	**Natural sciences & mathematics**	**550**	**Earth sciences**
501	Philosophy & theory	551	Geology, hydrology, meteorology
502	Miscellany	552	Petrology
503	Dictionaries & encyclopedias	553	Economic geology
504		554	Earth sciences of Europe
505	Serial publications	555	Earth sciences of Asia
506	Organizations & management	556	Earth sciences of Africa
507	Education, research, related topics	557	Earth sciences of North America
508	Natural history	558	Earth sciences of South America
509	Historical, geographic, persons treatment	559	Earth sciences of other areas
510	**Mathematics**	**560**	**Paleontology Paleozoology**
511	General principles of mathematics	561	Paleobotany; fossil microorganisms
512	Algebra, number theory	562	Fossil invertebrates
513	Arithmetic	563	Other fossil invertebrates
514	Topology	564	Fossil Mollusca & Molluscoidea
515	Analysis	565	Fossil Arthropoda
516	Geometry	566	Fossil Chordata
517		567	Fossil cold-blooded vertebrates
518		568	Fossil Aves (birds)
519	Probabilities & applied mathematics	569	Fossil Mammalia
520	**Astronomy & allied sciences**	**570**	**Life sciences Biology**
521	Celestial mechanics	571	Physiology & related subjects
522	Techniques, equipment, materials	572	Biochemistry
523	Specific celestial bodies & phenomena	573	Specific systems in animals
524		574	
525	Earth (Astronomical geography)	575	Specific parts of & systems in plants
526	Mathematical geography	576	Genetics & evolution
527	Celestial navigation	577	Ecology
528	Ephemerides	578	Natural history of organisms
529	Chronology	579	Microorganisms, fungi, algae
530	**Physics**	**580**	**Plants**
531	Classical mechanics Solid mechanics	581	Specific topics in natural history
532	Fluid mechanics Liquid mechanics	582	Plants noted for characteristics & flowers
533	Pneumatics (Gas mechanics)	583	Magnoliopsida (Dicotyledons)
534	Sound & related vibrations	584	Liliopsida (Monocotyledons)
535	Light & paraphotic phenomena	585	Pinophyta (Gymnosperms) Coniferales
536	Heat	586	Cryptogamia (Seedless plants)
537	Electricity & electronics	587	Pteridophyta (Vascular seedless plants)
538	Magnetism	588	Bryophyta
539	Modern physics	589	
540	**Chemistry & allied sciences**	**590**	**Animals**
541	Physical & theoretical chemistry	591	Specific topics in natural history
542	Techniques, equipment, materials	592	Invertebrates
543	Analytical chemistry	593	Marine & seashore invertebrates
544	Qualitative analysis	594	Mollusca & Molluscoidea
545	Quantitative analysis	595	Arthropoda
546	Inorganic chemistry	596	Chordata
547	Organic chemistry	597	Cold-blooded vertebrates Fishes
548	Crystallography	598	Aves (Birds)
549	Mineralogy	599	Mammalia (Mammals)

Technology (Applies sciences)

600	**Technology (Applied sciences)**	**650**	**Management & auxiliary services**
601	Philosophy & theory	651	Office services
602	Miscellany	652	Processes of written communication
603	Dictionaries & encyclopedias	653	Shorthand
604	Special topics	654	
605	Serial publications	655	
606	Organizations	656	
607	Education, research, related topics	657	Accounting
608	Invention & patents	658	General management
609	Historical, geographic, persons treatment	659	Advertising & public relations
610	**Medical sciences Medicine**	**660**	**Chemical engineering**
611	Human anatomy, cytology, histology	661	Industrial chemicals technology
612	Human physiology	662	Explosives, fuels, related products
613	Promotion of health	663	Beverage technology
614	Incidence & prevention of disease	664	Food technology
615	Pharmacology & therapeutics	665	Industrial oils, fats, waxes, gases
616	Diseases	666	Ceramic & allied technologies
617	Surgery & related medical specialties	667	Cleaning, color, coating technologies
618	Gynecology & other medical specialties	668	Technology of other organic products
619	Experimental medicine	669	Metallurgy
620	**Engineering & allied operations**	**670**	**Manufacturing**
621	Applied physics	671	Metalworking & metal products
622	Mining & related operations	672	Iron, steel, other iron alloys
623	Military & nautical engineering	673	Nonferrous metals
624	Civil engineering	674	Lumber processing, wood products, cork
625	Engineering of railroads & roads	675	Leather & fur processing
626		676	Pulp & paper technology
627	Hydraulic engineering	677	Textiles
628	Sanitary & municipal engineering	678	Elastomers & elastomer products
629	Other branches of engineering	679	Other products of specific materials
630	**Agriculture & related technologies**	**680**	**Manufacture for specific uses**
631	Techniques, equipment, materials	681	Precision instruments & other devices
632	Plant injuries, diseases, pests	682	Small forge work (Blacksmithing)
633	Field & plantation crops	683	Hardware & household appliances
634	Orchards, fruits, forestry	684	Furnishings & home workshops
635	Garden crops (Horticulture)	685	Leather, fur goods, related products
636	Animal husbandry	686	Printing & related activities
637	Processing dairy & related products	687	Clothing & accessories
638	Insect culture	688	Other final products & packaging
639	Hunting, fishing, conservation	689	
640	**Home economics & family living**	**690**	**Buildings**
641	Food & drink	691	Building materials
642	Meals & table service	692	Auxiliary construction practices
643	Housing & household equipment	693	Specific materials & purposes
644	Household utilities	694	Wood construction Carpentry
645	Household furnishings	695	Roof covering
646	Sewing, clothing, personal living	696	Utilities
647	Management of public households	697	Heating, ventilating, air-conditioning
648	Housekeeping	698	Detail finishing
649	Child rearing & home care of persons	699	

The arts   Fine and decorative arts

Literature and rhetoric

Geography and history

900	**Geography & history**	**950**	**General history of Asia**	**Far East**
901	Philosophy & theory	951	China & adjacent areas	
902	Miscellany	952	Japan	
903	Dictionaries & encyclopedias	953	Arabian Peninsula & adjacent areas	
904	Collected accounts of events	954	South Asia	India
905	Serial publications	955	Iran	
906	Organizations & management	956	Middle East (Near East)	
907	Education, research, related topics	957	Siberia (Asiatic Russia)	
908	Kinds of persons treatment	958	Central Asia	
909	World history	959	Southeast Asia	
910	**Geography & travel**	**960**	**General history of Africa**	
911	Historical geography	961	Tunisia & Libya	
912	Graphic representations	962	Egypt & Sudan	
913	Geography of & travel in ancient world	963	Ethiopia & Eritrea	
914	Geography of & travel in Europe	964	Northwest African coast & offshore islands	
915	Geography of & travel in Asia	965	Algeria	
916	Geography of & travel in Africa	966	West Africa & offshore islands	
917	Geography of & travel in North America	967	Central Africa & offshore islands	
918	Geography of & travel in South America	968	Southern Africa	Republic of South Africa
919	Geography of & travel in other areas	969	South Indian Ocean islands	
920	**Biography, genealogy, insignia**	**970**	**General history of North America**	
921		971	Canada	
922		972	Middle America	Mexico
923		973	United States	
924		974	Northeastern United States	
925		975	Southeastern United States	
926		976	South central United States	
927		977	North central United States	
928		978	Western United States	
929	Genealogy, names, insignia	979	Great Basin & Pacific Slope region	
930	**History of ancient world to ca. 499**	**980**	**General history of South America**	
931	China to 420	981	Brazil	
932	Egypt to 640	982	Argentina	
933	Palestine to 70	983	Chile	
934	India to 647	984	Bolivia	
935	Mesopotamia & Iranian Plateau to 637	985	Peru	
936	Europe north & west of Italy to ca. 499	986	Colombia & Ecuador	
937	Italy & adjacent territories to 476	987	Venezuela	
938	Greece to 323	988	Guiana	
939	Other parts of ancient world to ca. 640	989	Paraguay & Uruguay	
940	**General history of Europe**	**990**	**General history of other areas**	
941	British Isles	991		
942	England & Wales	992		
943	Central Europe	Germany	993	New Zealand	
944	France & Monaco	994	Australia	
945	Italian Peninsula & adjacent islands	995	Melanesia	New Guinea
946	Iberian Peninsula & adjacent islands	996	Other parts of Pacific	Polynesia
947	Eastern Europe	Russia	997	Atlantic Ocean islands	
948	Scandinavia	998	Arctic islands & Antarctica	
949	Other parts of Europe	999	Extraterrestrial worlds	

Schedules

Use of the Schedules

Full instructions on the use of the schedules are found in the Introduction to the Dewey Decimal Classification in volume 1.

The first three digits of a DDC number are found in the number column, or at the top of the page.

Numbers in square brackets [ ] are not used. Numbers in parentheses ( ) are options to standard usage.

000

000 Generalities

See Manual at 000

SUMMARY

050	**General serial publications**
.9	Historical, geographic, persons treatment
051	American English-language serial publications
052	General serial publications in English
053	General serial publications in other Germanic languages
054	General serial publications in French, Provençal, Catalan
055	General serial publications in Italian, Sardinian, Dalmatian, Romanian, Rhaeto-Romanic
056	General serial publications in Spanish and Portuguese
057	General serial publications in Slavic languages
058	General serial publications in Scandinavian languages
059	General serial publications in other languages
060	**General organizations and museology**
.1–.9	Standard subdivisions and special topics
061	General organizations in North America
062	General organizations in British Isles In England
063	General organizations in central Europe In Germany
064	General organizations in France and Monaco
065	General organizations in Italy and adjacent territories
066	General organizations in Iberian Peninsula and adjacent islands In Spain
067	General organizations in eastern Europe In Russia
068	General organizations in other geographic areas
069	Museology (Museum science)
070	**Documentary media, educational media, news media; journalism; publishing**
.01–.09	Standard subdivisions of documentary media, educational media, news media; journalism; publishing
.1–.9	Documentary media, educational media, news media; journalism; publishing
071	Journalism and newspapers in North America
072	Journalism and newspapers in British Isles In England
073	Journalism and newspapers in Central Europe In Germany
074	Journalism and newspapers in France and Monaco
075	Journalism and newspapers in Italy and adjacent territories
076	Journalism and newspapers in Iberian Peninsula and adjacent islands In Spain
077	Journalism and newspapers in eastern Europe In Russia
078	Journalism and newspapers in Scandinavia
079	Journalism and newspapers in other geographic areas
080	**General collections**
.9	Historical, geographic, persons treatment
081	American English-language collections
082	General collections in English
083	General collections in other Germanic languages
084	General collections in French, Provençal, Catalan
085	General collections in Italian, Sardinian, Dalmatian, Romanian, Rhaeto-Romanic
086	General collections in Spanish and Portuguese
087	General collections in Slavic languages
088	General collections in Scandinavian languages
089	General collections in Italic, Hellenic, other languages

090	**Manuscripts, rare books, other rare printed materials**
091	**Manuscripts**
092	**Block books**
093	**Incunabula**
094	**Printed books**
095	**Books notable for bindings**
096	**Books notable for illustrations and materials**
097	**Books notable for ownership or origin**
098	**Prohibited works, forgeries, hoaxes**
099	**Books notable for format**

001 Knowledge

Including history, description, critical appraisal of intellectual activity in general; increase, modification, dissemination of information and understanding

Class here discussion of ideas from many fields

Class epistemology in 121. Class a compilation of knowledge in a specific form with the form, e.g., encyclopedias 030

See Manual at 500 vs. 001

.01 Theory of knowledge

Do not use for philosophy of knowledge, philosophical works on theory of knowledge; class in 121

.1 Intellectual life

Nature and value

For scholarship and learning, see 001.2

See also 900 for broad description of intellectual situation and condition

.2 Scholarship and learning

Intellectual activity directed toward increase of knowledge

Class methods of study and teaching in 371.3. Class scholarship and learning in a specific discipline or subject with the discipline or subject, e.g., scholarship in the humanities 001.3, in history 900

For research, see 001.4

See Manual at 500 vs. 001

.3 Humanities

Including relative value of science versus the humanities

.4   **Research; statistical methods**

Class here evaluation research, works discussing what research is

Class research in a specific discipline or subject with the discipline or subject, plus notation 072 from Table 1, e.g., research in linguistics 410.72; class works embodying the results of research with the subject of the research, but without notation 072 from Table 1, e.g., results of research in linguistics 410 (*not* 410.72)

See Manual at 500 vs. 001

.42   Research methods

Class here scientific method

Class operations research in 003; class computer modeling and simulation in 003.3

For historical, descriptive, experimental methods, see 001.43

.422   Statistical methods

See also 310 for collections of general statistical data, notation 021 from Table 1 for statistics on a specific discipline or subject

See Manual at 519.5, T1—015195 vs. 001.422, T1—0727

[.422 2]   Collection of data

Relocated to 001.433

[.422 4–.422 5]   Tabulation and analysis of data

Numbers discontinued; class in 001.422

.422 6   Presentation of statistical data

Class here graphic presentation

.43   Historical, descriptive, experimental methods

.432   Historical method

Including case studies

.433   Descriptive method

Including collection of data [*formerly* 001.4222], field work, questionnaires, surveys

For analysis of statistical data, see 001.422; for presentation of statistical data, see 001.4226

See also 310.723 for methods of collecting general social statistical data

.434   Experimental method

.44   Support of and incentives for research

Standard subdivisions are added for either or both topics in heading

Including awards, certificates, honors, medals, prizes; fellowships, financial patronage, grants-in-aid, scholarships

Class student finance in higher education in 378.3. Class awards granted in a specific discipline with the discipline, plus notation 079 from Table 1, e.g., awards in fine and decorative arts 707.9

See also 929.81 for awards for general achievements

.9   Controversial knowledge

Including well-established phenomena for which explanations are controversial; the end of the world

Class here interdisciplinary works on controversial knowledge and paranormal phenomena

For paranormal phenomena, see 130. For controversial knowledge concerning a specific discipline or subject, see the discipline or subject, e.g., paranormal and legendary as subjects of folklore 398.4, Piltdown man hoax 569.9, controversial medical remedies 615.856, an alleged conspiracy to assassinate John F. Kennedy 973.922

See Manual at 001.9 and 130

.94   Mysteries

Reported phenomena not explained, not fully verified

Including Atlantis, Bermuda Triangle, pyramid power

Class here nonastronomical extraterrestrial influences on earth

See also 900 for Atlantis as a subject of archaeology

.942   Unidentified flying objects (UFOs, Flying saucers)

.944   Monsters and related phenomena

Including abominable snowman, Loch Ness monster

See also 590 for animals whose reality is not controversial

.95   Deceptions and hoaxes

Class a hoax that influenced history with the hoax in 900, e.g., False Dmitri 947.045

.96   Errors, delusions, superstitions

002   The book

Class here historical bibliography, interdisciplinary works on the book

Class comprehensive works on historical and analytical bibliography in 010.42

For book publishing, see 070.5; for rare books, see 090; for social aspects of the book, see 302.232; for book arts, see 686

[.021 6]	Lists, inventories, catalogs
	Do not use; class in 010
[.029 4]	Trade catalogs and directories
	Do not use; class in 010
.074	Museums, collections, exhibits
	Class catalogs and lists in 010

003 Systems

Class here operations research; systems theory, analysis, design, optimization; models (simulation) applied to real-world systems

Unless other instructions are given, class a subject with aspects in two or more subdivisions of 003 in the number coming last, e.g., control of discrete-time linear systems 003.830115 (*not* 003.5 or 003.74)

Class simulation in education in 371.397. Class systems in a specific subject or discipline with the subject or discipline, plus notation 011 from Table 1, e.g., systems theory in the social sciences 300.11

See also 511.8 for mathematical models not applied to real-world systems, 519.7 for mathematical programming not applied to real-world systems

See Manual at 003; also at 003 vs. 004.21; also at 510, T1—0151 vs. 003, T1—011

[.028 5]	Data processing	Computer applications
	Do not use; class in 003.3	

.1 System identification

Determining a mathematical model for a system by observing its input-output relationships

.2 Forecasting and forecasts

Class here interdisciplinary works on forecasting

For forecasting by parapsychological and occult means, see 133.3

See Manual at 003.2

.209   Historical, geographic, persons treatment of forecasting as a discipline

For forecasting and forecasts for specific areas, see 303.491–303.499

.3   **Computer modeling and simulation**

Standard subdivisions are added for either or both topics in heading

Class here data processing and computer science applied to systems, computer implementation of mathematical models of systems, interdisciplinary works on computer modeling and simulation

Add to base number 003.3 the numbers following 00 in 004–006, e.g., computer simulation languages 003.3513

For computer modeling and simulation applied to a specific subject, see the subject plus notation 0113 from Table 1, e.g., computer modeling in economics 330.0113

See Manual at T1—0113 vs. T1—0285

.5   **Theory of communication and control**

In living and nonliving systems

Including bionics

Class here cybernetics, interdisciplinary works on control and stability of systems

Class social aspects of and interdisciplinary works on communication in systems in 302.2

For artificial intelligence, see 006.3; for control theory in automation engineering, see 629.8312. For control and stability of systems in a specific subject, see the subject plus notation 0115 from Table 1, e.g., control and stability of systems in general engineering 620.00115

See Manual at 003.5 vs. 629.8

.52   Perception theory

Class computer vision in 006.37; class psychology of human perception in 153.7; class perception in animals in 573.87

See also 006.4 for computer pattern recognition

.54   Information theory

Theory concerning measurement of quantities of information; accuracy in transmission of messages subject to noise (unwanted, usually random, signals), distortion, and transmission failure; and methods of coding for efficient, accurate transmission

Class here coding theory

Class information theory in communications engineering in 621.3822, without using notation 01154 from Table 1; class coding for purpose of limiting access to information (cryptography) in 652.8. Class information theory in communications engineering of a specific kind of communications with the kind, without using notation 01154 from Table 1, e.g., radio 621.384; class information theory in any other specific subject with the subject, plus notation 01154 from Table 1, e.g., information theory in economics 330.01154

.56   Decision theory

> *See also 153.83 for decision theory in psychology, 511.65 for decision theory in combinatorial analysis, 658.40301 for decision theory in management*

.7   **Kinds of systems**

Including deterministic, hierarchical, lumped-parameter, self-organizing, small-scale systems

> *For systems distinguished in relation to time, see 003.8*
>
> *See Manual at 003.7*

.71   Large-scale systems

Limited to works emphasizing that the systems are large

.74   Linear systems

.75   Nonlinear systems

.76   Stochastic systems

.78   Distributed-parameter systems

.8   **Systems distinguished in relation to time**

Including continuous-time, instantaneous (zero-memory), time-invariant, time-varying systems

.83   Discrete-time systems

.85   Dynamic systems

Systems in which response depends upon past values of excitation as well as current excitation

.857   Chaotic systems

Class here chaotic behavior in systems

004   **Data processing   Computer science**

Class here selection and use of computer hardware; electronic computers; electronic digital computers; computer systems (computers, their peripheral devices, their operating systems); central processing units; computer reliability; interactive, online processing; comprehensive works on hardware and programs in electronic data processing

Unless other instructions are given, class a subject with aspects in two or more subdivisions of 004 in the number coming last, e.g., external storage for microcomputers 004.56 (*not* 004.16)

Class computer modeling and simulation in 003.3. Class data processing and computer science applied to a specific subject or discipline with the subject or discipline, plus notation 0285 from Table 1, e.g., data processing in banking 332.10285

> *For computer programming, programs, data, see 005; for special computer methods, see 006; for engineering of computers, see 621.39*

> *See also 025.04 for automated information storage and retrieval, 303.4834 for computers as a cause of social change, 343.0999 for computer law, 364.168 for financial and business computer crimes, 371.334 for computer-assisted instruction (CAI), 652.5 for word processing, 658.05 for data processing in management, 794.8 for computer games*

> *See Manual at 004–006; also at 004–006 vs. 621.39; also at 004 vs. 004.33; also at 004 vs. 005; also at 510, T1—0151 vs. 004–006, T1—0285*

SUMMARY

004.01–.09	Standard subdivisions
.1	General works on specific types of computers
.2	Systems analysis and design, computer architecture, performance evaluation
.3	Processing modes
.5	Storage
.6	Interfacing and communications
.7	Peripherals
.9	Nonelectronic data processing

.015 1   Mathematical principles

Class here computer mathematics

.019   Psychological principles

Class here human-computer interaction, psychological principles and human factors in data processing and computer science

Apply notation 019 from Table 1 as modified here throughout 004–006, e.g., human factors in user interfaces 005.437019

Class ergonomic engineering of computer peripherals in 621.3984

.028   Auxiliary techniques and procedures; apparatus, equipment, materials

[.028 7]	Testing and measurement

Do not use; class in 004.24

.1 General works on specific types of computers

Class here specific types of processors, computer systems based on specific types of computers

Class specific types of computers, processors, computer systems distinguished by their processing modes in 004.3; class programmable calculators in 510.28541

See Manual at 004.1; also at 004.1 vs. 004.3

> 004.11–004.16 Digital computers

Class comprehensive works in 004

See Manual at 004.11–004.16

.11 *Digital supercomputers

See Manual at 004.11–004.16

.12 *Digital mainframe computers

Class here large-scale digital computers

For supercomputers, see 004.11

See Manual at 004.11–004.16

.125 Specific digital mainframe computers

Arrange alphabetically by name of computer or processor, e.g., IBM System/390®

.14 *Digital minicomputers

Class comprehensive works on digital minicomputers and microcomputers in 004.16

See Manual at 004.11–004.16

.145 Specific digital minicomputers

Arrange alphabetically by name of minicomputer or processor, e.g., VAX 9000®

.16 *Digital microcomputers

Class here laptop, notebook, palmtop, pen, personal, pocket computers; personal digital assistants, workstations, comprehensive works on minicomputers and microcomputers

For minicomputers, see 004.14

See Manual at 004.11–004.16

---

*Use notation 019 from Table 1 as modified at 004.019

.165 Specific digital microcomputers

Arrange alphabetically by name of microcomputer or microprocessor, e.g., Macintosh®

.19 *Hybrid and analog computers

Standard subdivisions are added for hybrid and analog computers together, for hybrid computers alone

For nonelectronic analog computers, see 004.9

.2 ***Systems analysis and design, computer architecture, performance evaluation**

.21 *Systems analysis and design

Standard subdivisions are added for either or both topics in heading

Class here analysis of a user's problem preparatory to developing a computer system to solve it

Class communications network design and architecture in 004.65

For software systems analysis and design, see 005.12; for database design and architecture, see 005.74

See also 003 for interdisciplinary works on systems analysis and design, 658.4032 for management use of systems analysis

See Manual at 004.21 vs. 004.22, 621.392; also at 003 vs. 004.21

.22 *Computer architecture

See Manual at 004.21 vs. 004.22, 621.392

.24 *Performance evaluation

Class here performance measurement and evaluation to aid in designing or improving the performance of a computer system

Class performance evaluation as a consideration in purchasing a specific item with the item in 004, plus notation 0297 from Table 1, e.g., evaluating microcomputers for purchase 004.160297

See also 004.0685 for management techniques to ensure quality control in data processing

See Manual at 004.24

.25 Systems analysis and design, computer architecture, performance evaluation of specific types of electronic computers

Add to base number 004.25 the numbers following 004.1 in 004.11–004.19, e.g., architecture of digital microcomputers 004.256

For systems analysis and design, computer architecture, performance evaluation of specific types of computers distinguished by processing mode, see 004.3

*Use notation 019 from Table 1 as modified at 004.019

.3   ***Processing modes**

Including batch, offline, pipeline processing; CISC (complex instruction set computing), RISC; multiprogramming, time-sharing

Class here computers, processors, computer systems distinguished by their processing modes; centralized processing

Class comprehensive works on multiprogramming, on time-sharing in 005.434

See Manual at 004.1 vs. 004.3

[.32]   Multiprogramming (Multitasking)

Use of this number for hardware aspects of multiprogramming (multitasking) discontinued; class in 004.3

Comprehensive works on multiprogramming (multitasking) relocated to 005.434

.33   ***Real-time processing**

Limited to processing defined by predictability constraints and timing deadlines

Use of this number for interactive, online, real-time data processing in the broad sense of immediate processing of input or an immediate response to a user's action discontinued; class in 004

See Manual at 004 vs. 004.33

.338   ***Systems analysis and design, computer architecture, performance evaluation of real-time computers**

Add to base number 004.338 the numbers following 004.2 in 004.21–004.24, e.g., architecture of real-time computers 004.3382

.35   ***Multiprocessing**

Including array processing, associative processing, dataflow computation

Class here parallel processing

Class comprehensive works on associative processing and memory in 004.5

.357   Specific multiprocessor computers

Arrange alphabetically by name of computer or processor, e.g., Inmos Transputer®

.358   ***Systems analysis and design, computer architecture, performance evaluation of multiprocessor computers**

.358 1–.358 4   ***Comprehensive works on systems analysis and design, computer architecture, performance evaluation of multiprocessor computers**

Add to base number 004.358 the numbers following 004.2 in 004.21–004.24, e.g., architecture of parallel computers 004.3582

For specific multiprocessor computers, see 004.3585

---

*Use notation 019 from Table 1 as modified at 004.019

14

.358 5	Systems analysis and design, computer architecture, performance evaluation of specific multiprocessor computers

> Arrange alphabetically by name of computer or processor, e.g., Inmos Transputer®

.36	*Distributed processing

Class here client-server computer systems

> *See also 004.6 for computer communications networks, 005.758 for distributed databases*

.368	*Systems analysis and design, computer architecture, performance evaluation of distributed computer systems

> Add to base number 004.368 the numbers following 004.2 in 004.21–004.24, e.g., architecture of distributed computer systems 004.3682

.5	***Storage**

Including hardware aspects of virtual memory; comprehensive works on associative (content-addressable) memory and associative processing

Class comprehensive works on virtual memory in 005.435

> *For associative processing, see 004.35*

.53	*Internal storage (Main memory)

Including magnetic-core, metal-oxide-semiconductor (MOS), semiconductor bipolar, thin-film memory; random-access memory (RAM); read-only memory (ROM)

Class CD-ROM (compact disc read-only memory) in 004.565

> *See also 005.6 for microprogramming and microprograms*

[.54]	Virtual memory

Number discontinued; class in 004.5

Comprehensive works on virtual memory relocated to 005.435

.56	*External (Auxiliary) storage

Including magnetic tapes, e.g., cartridges, cassettes, reel-to-reel tapes; tape drives; magnetic bubble memory; punch cards

.563	*Magnetic disks

Including floppy disks, floppy disk drives

Class here hard disks, hard disk drives

.565	*Optical external storage

Including CD-ROM (compact disc read-only memory), WORM (write once read many) discs and drives

---

*Use notation 019 from Table 1 as modified at 004.019

.6   *Interfacing and communications

> Equipment and techniques linking computers to peripheral devices or to other computers
>
> Standard subdivisions are added for either or both topics in heading
>
> Class here interdisciplinary works on computer communications
>
> Interdisciplinary works on telecommunication relocated to 384
>
> Class data, programs, programming in interfacing and communications in 005.7
>
>> *For social aspects of computer communications, see 302.23; for economic and related aspects of providing computer communications to the public, see 384.3*
>>
>> *See also 004.36 for distributed processing*
>>
>> *See Manual at 004.6; also at 004.6 vs. 005.71; also at 004.6 vs. 384.3; also at 004.6 vs. 621.382, 621.3981*

[.602 18]   Standards

> Do not use; class in 004.62

.61   Interfacing and communications for specific types of electronic computers

[.610 1–.610 9]   Standard subdivisions

> Do not use; class in 004.601–004.609

.611–.616   *Digital computers

> Add to base number 004.61 the numbers following 004.1 in 004.11–004.16, e.g., interfacing and communications for microcomputers 004.616

.618   *Computers distinguished by processing modes

> Add to base number 004.618 the numbers following 004.3 in 004.33–004.36, e.g., distributed computers 004.6186

.619   *Hybrid and analog computers

> Standard subdivisions are added for hybrid and analog computers together, for hybrid computers alone

.62   *Interfacing and communications protocols (standards)

> Class protocols for specific aspects of interfacing and communications with the aspect, e.g., protocols for error-correcting codes 005.72

[.620 218]   Standards

> Do not use; class in 004.62

---

*Use notation 019 from Table 1 as modified at 004.019

.64   *Kinds of hardware

Including baseband and broadband equipment, modems, optical-fiber cable, peripheral control units

Class peripheral control units controlling a specific kind of peripheral with the peripheral, e.g., printer controllers 004.77

> 004.65–004.68   Computer communications networks

Class comprehensive works in 004.6

.65   *Communications network architecture

Class here systems analysis, design, topology (configuration) of computer communications networks

.66   *Data transmission modes and data switching methods

Including circuit and packet switching, multiplexing

.67   *Wide-area networks

.678   *Internet

Class a specific regional or national network with the area served, e.g., Janet 004.6780941

See Manual at 004.678 vs. 025.04, 384.33

.68   *Local-area networks

Including baseband and broadband local-area networks, high-speed local networks

.69   Specific kinds of computer communications

.692   *Electronic mail

.693   *Electronic bulletin boards

.696   *Videotex

.7   *Peripherals

Input, output, storage devices that work with a computer but are not part of its central processing unit or internal storage

Class peripheral storage in 004.56

See also 004.64 for communications devices

.71   Peripherals for digital computers

Add to base number 004.71 the numbers following 004.1 in 004.11–004.16, e.g., peripherals for microcomputers 004.716

.718   *Peripherals for computers distinguished by processing modes

*Use notation 019 from Table 1 as modified at 004.019

.719   *Peripherals for hybrid and analog computers

Standard subdivisions are added for hybrid and analog computers together, for hybrid computers alone

.75   *Peripherals combining input and output functions

Class here computer terminals

Class tape and disk devices in 004.56

.76   *Input peripherals

Including card readers, keyboards

Class input devices that utilize pattern recognition methods in 006.4. Class a special-purpose input device with the purpose, e.g., graphics input devices 006.62, game paddles 688.748

See also 005.72 for data entry

.77   *Output peripherals

Including computer output microform (COM) devices, monitors (video display screens), printers

Class output peripherals that utilize computer sound synthesis in 006.5; class computer graphics output devices in 006.62

See also 005.43 for monitors in the sense of software control programs, 005.6 for monitors in the sense of firmware control programs

.9   *Nonelectronic data processing

Automatic and nonautomatic

Including nonelectronic analog computers; nonelectronic punch-card data processing, e.g., pre-computer use of Hollerith cards

Class comprehensive works on analog computers in 004.19

005   *Computer programming, programs, data

Class here text processing; software reliability, compatibility, portability, reusability, usability

Unless other instructions are given, class a subject with aspects in two or more subdivisions of 005 in the number coming last, e.g., designing object-oriented C programs 005.133 (*not* 005.117 or 005.12)

Class computer programming, programs, data for special computer methods in 006

See also 652.5 for word processing

See Manual at 005; also at 004–006; also at 004–006 vs. 621.39; also at 004 vs. 005; also at 510, T1—0151 vs. 004–006, T1—0285

---

*Use notation 019 from Table 1 as modified at 004.019

SUMMARY

\>   **005.1–005.6   Computer programming and programs**

Class comprehensive works in 005

.1   *Programming

Class here application programming, software engineering

Class a specific application of programming within computer science with the application in 005.4–006.7, e.g., programming of computer graphics 006.66

For programming for specific types of computers, for specific operating systems, for specific user interfaces, see 005.2

See Manual at 005.1–005.2 vs. 005.42; also at 005.1 vs. 005.3; also at 005.1 vs. 510

.101   Philosophy and theory

Do not use notation 01 from Table 1 here or with subdivisions of 005.1–005.2 for general discussions of logic in programming

See also 005.131 for the symbolic (mathematical) logic of programming languages

See Manual at 005.101

.102 8   Auxiliary techniques and procedures; apparatus, equipment, materials

Class special techniques in 005.11

[.102 87]   Testing and measurement

Do not use; class in 005.14

[.102 88]   Maintenance and repair

Do not use; class in 005.16

.11   ‡*Special programming techniques

Class real-time programming in 005.273; class parallel programming in 005.275

See Manual at 005.11

---

*Use notation 019 from Table 1 as modified at 004.019

‡Do not add notation 01 from Table 1 for general discussions of logic in programming; see Manual at 005.101

.112	‡*Modular programming
.113	‡*Structured programming
.114	‡*Functional programming
.115	‡*Logic programming
.117	‡*Object-oriented programming
.118	‡*Visual programming
.12	‡*Software systems analysis and design

Former heading: Program design

Standard subdivisions are added for either or both topics in heading

Class here analysis of a user's problem preparatory to developing a software system to solve it

.120 28   Auxiliary techniques and procedures; apparatus, equipment, materials

Including use of flow-charting and flow charts as aids in program design

See also 005.15028 for preparation of flow charts as program documentation

.13   '‡*Programming languages

Including application generators, nonprocedural (declarative) languages, text editors specially designed to assist in coding programs

Class here coding of programs

Class comprehensive works on text editors in 652.5

See also 005.434 for job control languages

See Manual at 652.5: Text editors

[.130 151]   Mathematical principles

Do not use; class in 005.131

.131   ‡*Symbolic (Mathematical) logic

Class here mathematical principles of programming languages, e.g., automata, formal languages, grammars, recursive functions applied to programming languages

Class mathematical principles of programming in 005.10151. Class the mathematical principles of programming languages applied to the development of a programming language translator with the translator in 005.45, plus notation 015113 from Table 1, e.g., theory of formal languages applied to development of compilers 005.453015113

See also 005.1 for general works about logic in programming

*Use notation 019 from Table 1 as modified at 004.019

‡Do not add notation 01 from Table 1 for general discussions of logic in programming; see Manual at 005.101

.133	**Specific programming languages**

Class here comprehensive works on programming with specific programming languages

Arrange alphabetically by name of programming language, e.g., C++

Class specific microprogramming languages in 005.6

> *For specific machine and assembly languages, see 005.2*
>
> *See also 005.45 for programming language translators for specific programming languages*

.136	‡*Machine and assembly languages

Specific machine and assembly languages relocated to 005.2

.14	‡*Verification, testing, measurement, debugging

Including software metrics

Class a specific application of software metrics with the application, plus notation 0285514 from Table 1, e.g., software metrics applied to parallel programming 005.2750285514

.15	‡*Preparation of program documentation

Including development of online help

Class here preparation of software documentation

> *See also 005.12 for preparation of program design specifications and other technical documentation as an aid in program design, 005.3 for program documentation itself, 808.066005 for technical writing in preparation of program documentation*
>
> *See Manual at 005.15 vs. 808.066005*

.16	‡*Program maintenance

Class here software maintenance

.2	**Programming for specific types of computers, for specific operating systems, for specific user interfaces**

Class here specific machine and assembly languages [*formerly* 005.136]

> *See Manual at 005.1–005.2 vs. 005.42*

.21	‡*Programming for digital supercomputers
.22	‡*Programming for digital mainframe computers

Add to base number 005.22 the numbers following 005.26 in 005.262–005.269, e.g., programming for the IBM System/390® 005.225

---

*Use notation 019 from Table 1 as modified at 004.019

‡Do not add notation 01 from Table 1 for general discussions of logic in programming; see Manual at 005.101

.24 ‡*Programming for digital minicomputers

Add to base number 005.24 the numbers following 005.26 in
005.262–005.269, e.g., programming for the IBM AS/400® 005.245

.26 ‡*Programming for digital microcomputers

Class here programming for personal computers, for microcomputer
workstations; comprehensive works on programming for minicomputers
and microcomputers

For programming for minicomputers, see 005.24

.262 Programming in specific programming languages

Arrange alphabetically by name of programming language, e.g., C++

.265 Programming for specific computers

Class here programming for specific processors, for computer systems
based on specific computers

Arrange alphabetically by name of computer, e.g., IBM PC®

See Manual at 005.268 vs. 005.265, 005.269

.268 Programming for specific operating systems

Writing programs that run on specific operating systems

Arrange alphabetically by name of operating system, e.g., OS/2®

Class programming for a specific operating system where the operating
system is the only operating system that runs on a specific computer in
005.265

See Manual at 005.268 vs. 005.265, 005.269

.269 Programming for specific user interfaces

Writing programs that run on specific user interfaces other than the
native interface of the operating system

Arrange alphabetically by name of user interface, e.g., Microsoft
Windows®

Class programming for the native interface of an operating system
(interface bound inseparably with the operating system) in 005.268

*See Manual at 005.268 vs. 005.265, 005.269; also at 005.269 and
005.284, 005.3684, 005.384*

.27 ‡*Programming for processing modes

---

*Use notation 019 from Table 1 as modified at 004.019

‡Do not add notation 01 from Table 1 for general discussions of logic in programming; see
Manual at 005.101

.273 ‡*Programming for real-time computer systems

> Add to base number 005.273 the numbers following 005.26 in 005.262–005.269, e.g., programming in Ada for real-time computers 005.2732

.275 ‡*Programming for multiprocessor computers

> Class here parallel programming

> Add to base number 005.275 the numbers following 005.26 in 005.262–005.269, e.g., programming for Inmos Transputer® 005.2755

.276 ‡*Programming for distributed computer systems

> Add to base number 005.276 the numbers following 005.26 in 005.262–005.269, e.g., programming for Unix client-server computer systems 005.2768

.28 Programming for specific operating systems and for specific user interfaces

> Not limited by type of computer

.282 Programming for specific operating systems

> Arrange alphabetically by name of operating system, e.g., Unix®

.284 Programming for specific user interfaces

> Writing programs that run on specific user interfaces other than the native interface of the operating system

> Arrange alphabetically by name of user interface, e.g., Motif®

> Class programming for the native interface of an operating system (interface bound inseparably with the operating system) in 005.282

> *See Manual at 005.269 and 005.284, 005.3684, 005.384*

.29 ‡*Programming for hybrid computers

---

*Use notation 019 from Table 1 as modified at 004.019

‡Do not add notation 01 from Table 1 for general discussions of logic in programming; see Manual at 005.101

.3   ***Programs**

Software and firmware

Collections of programs, systems of interrelated programs, individual programs having interdisciplinary applications

Including online help

Class here application programs, electronic spreadsheets, integrated programs, software documentation, software packages, comprehensive works on software and firmware, on applications and systems programs

Class programs for a specific application in computer science with the application in 005–006, e.g., programs for computer graphics 006.68; class online help in specific kinds of programs with the kind, e.g., online help in programs for microcomputers 005.36

For systems programs, see 005.43; for firmware, see 005.6

See also 005.15 for preparation of program documentation

See Manual at 005.3; also at 005.3 vs. 005.43–005.45; also at 005.1 vs. 005.3

.302 18   Standards

See also 005.10218 for standards for programming, 005.150218 for standards for preparation of software documentation

.302 87   Testing and measurement

See also 005.14 for testing and measurement in programming

[.302 88]   Maintenance and repair

Do not use; class in 005.16

.302 96   Buyers' guides and consumer reports

See Manual at 011.3 vs. 005.30296, 011.77

.304   Special topics

.304 2   Specific programs

Not limited by type of computer, by operating system, by user interface

Arrange alphabetically by name of program, e.g., SAS®

>   005.31–005.36 Programs for digital computers

Class comprehensive works in 005.3

.31   ***Programs for digital supercomputers**

---

*Use notation 019 from Table 1 as modified at 004.019

.32 *Programs for digital mainframe computers

Add to base number 005.32 the numbers following 005.36 in 005.362–005.369, e.g., programs for IBM ES/9000® 005.325

.34 *Programs for digital minicomputers

Add to base number 005.34 the numbers following 005.36 in 005.362–005.369, e.g., programs for HP 9000® 005.345

.36 *Programs for digital microcomputers

.362 Programs in specific programming languages

Arrange alphabetically by name of programming language, e.g., BASIC

See Manual at 005.362

.365 Programs for specific computers

Class here programs for specific processors, programs for computer systems based on specific computers

Arrange alphabetically by name of computer or processor, e.g., IBM PC®

See Manual at 005.3682 vs. 005.365, 005.3684

.368 Programs for specific operating systems and for specific user interfaces

.368 2 Programs for specific operating systems

Arrange alphabetically by name of operating system, e.g., MS-DOS®

Class programs for a specific operating system where the operating system is the only operating system that runs on a specific computer in 005.365

See Manual at 005.3682 vs. 005.365, 005.3684

.368 4 Programs for specific user interfaces

Programs that run on specific user interfaces other than the native interface of the operating system

Arrange alphabetically by name of user interface, e.g., Microsoft Windows® programs

Class programs that run on the native interface of an operating system (interface bound inseparably with the operating system) in 005.3682

See Manual at 005.269 and 005.284, 005.3684, 005.384; also at 005.3682 vs. 005.365, 005.3684

---

*Use notation 019 from Table 1 as modified at 004.019

.369		Specific programs

Class here specific computer software systems (organized sets of programs that work together), specific software packages

Arrange alphabetically by name of program or software system, e.g., Lotus 1–2–3®

See Manual at 005.369

.37 Programs for specific processing modes

.373 *Programs for real-time computer systems

Add to base number 005.373 the numbers following 005.36 in 005.362–005.369, e.g., programs for the OS/9® operating system 005.37382

.375 *Programs for multiprocessor computers

Add to base number 005.375 the numbers following 005.36 in 005.362–005.369, e.g., programs for Inmos Transputer® 005.3755

.376 *Programs for distributed computer systems

Class here client-server applications, groupware

Add to base number 005.376 the numbers following 005.36 in 005.362–005.369, e.g., Lotus Notes® 005.3769

.38 Programs for specific operating systems and for specific user interfaces

Not limited by type of computer

.382 Programs for specific operating systems

Arrange alphabetically by name of operating system, e.g., Unix®

.384 Programs for specific user interfaces

Programs that run on specific user interfaces other than the native interface of the operating system

Arrange alphabetically by name of user interface, e.g., Motif®

Class programs that run on the native interface of an operating system (interface bound inseparably with the operating system) in 005.382

See Manual at 005.269 and 005.284, 005.3684, 005.384

.39 *Programs for hybrid and analog computers

Standard subdivisions are added for hybrid and analog computers together, for hybrid computers alone

.4 *Systems programming and programs

Class programming and programs for interfacing and data communications in 005.71; class programming and programs for internal management of data files and databases in 005.74

*Use notation 019 from Table 1 as modified at 004.019

.42 *Systems programming

Writing systems programs

Class here programming to produce operating systems

Class programming for specific aspects of operating systems with the aspect, e.g., programming for communications 005.711; class programming for other specific kinds of systems programs with the kind, e.g., programming for compilers 005.453

> *See also 005.43 for systems programming in the sense of system administration (using expertise in systems software to keep a computer system functioning effectively)*

> *See Manual at 005.1–005.2 vs. 005.42*

.422 Systems programming for specific types of computers, for specific operating systems, for specific user interfaces

> Add to base number 005.422 the numbers following 005.2 in 005.21–005.29, e.g., systems programming for Unix-based systems 005.42282

.424 *Process management programming

> Add to base number 005.424 the numbers following 005.2 in 005.21–005.29, e.g., process management programming for Unix-based systems 005.42482

.425 *Memory management programming

> Add to base number 005.425 the numbers following 005.2 in 005.21–005.29, e.g., memory management programming for Unix-based systems 005.42582

.426 *File system management programming

> Add to base number 005.426 the numbers following 005.2 in 005.21–005.29, e.g., file system management programming for Unix-based systems 005.42682

.428 *Programming of user interfaces

> Add to base number 005.428 the numbers following 005.2 in 005.21–005.29, e.g., programming of user interfaces for Unix-based systems 005.42882

---

*Use notation 019 from Table 1 as modified at 004.019

.43 *Systems programs   Operating systems

Class here system administration (using expertise in systems programs to keep computer systems functioning efficiently), utility programs

Class programming for operating systems in 005.42; class text editors in 652.5. Class a specific application of systems programs with the application, e.g., programming language translators 005.45, computer interfacing and device drivers 005.71, computer security 005.8

For comprehensive works on operating systems for specific types of computers, see 005.44

See Manual at 005.3 vs. 005.43–005.45; also at 652.5: Text editors

.432 Specific operating systems

Not limited by type of computer

Arrange alphabetically by name of operating system, e.g., Unix®

> 005.434–005.436 Specific systems functions

Class here specific systems functions of operating systems for specific types of computers [*formerly* 005.44]

Class comprehensive works in 005.43

.434 *Process management programs

Including job control languages

Class here comprehensive works on multiprogramming (multitasking) [*formerly* 004.32]

Add to base number 005.434 the numbers following 005.3 in 005.31–005.39, e.g., task switchers for IBM PC® compatible computers 005.43465

Class job control languages for a specific type of computer with the type, e.g., job control languages for mainframe computers 005.4342

For hardware aspects of multiprogramming (multitasking), see 004.3

.435 *Memory management programs

Including comprehensive works on virtual memory [*formerly* 004.54]

Add to base number 005.435 the numbers following 005.3 in 005.31–005.39, e.g., memory managers for IBM PC® compatible computers 005.43565

For hardware aspects of virtual memory, see 004.5

*Use notation 019 from Table 1 as modified at 004.019

28

.436   *File system management programs

Add to base number 005.436 the numbers following 005.3 in
005.31–005.39, e.g., file system management programs for IBM PC®
compatible computers 005.43665

For data backup and recovery, see 005.86

See Manual at 005.74 vs. 005.436

.437   *User interfaces

Add to base number 005.437 the numbers following 005.3 in
005.31–005.39, e.g., Microsoft Windows® 005.43769; however, for
specific user interfaces not limited by type of computer, see 005.438

.438   Specific user interfaces

Not limited by type of computer

Arrange alphabetically by name of user interface, e.g., Motif®

.44   Operating systems for specific types of computers

Add to base number 005.44 the numbers following 005.3 in 005.31–005.39,
e.g., operating systems for distributed computer systems 005.4476

Specific systems functions of operating systems for specific types of
computers relocated to 005.434–005.436

See Manual at 005.3 vs. 005.43–005.45

.45   *Programming language translators

Class here code generators, macro processors, parsers, translators for
specific programming languages

Class translators for microprogramming languages in 005.6

*See also 418.02028553 for programs to translate natural languages into
other natural languages*

See Manual at 005.3 vs. 005.43–005.45

.452   *Interpreters

.453   *Compilers

.456   *Assemblers

.6   ***Microprogramming and microprograms**

Including firmware viewed as microprograms, firmware development,
microassembly languages, microcode

Class firmware viewed as hardware in 004

See Manual at 005.6

*Use notation 019 from Table 1 as modified at 004.019

.7 ***Data in computer systems**

For data security, see 005.8

.71 *Data communications

Class here device drivers, interfacing

See also 004.6 for hardware for interfacing and data communications

See Manual at 004 vs. 005; also at 004.6; also at 004.6 vs. 005.71

.711 *Programming

For programming for specific types of computers, see 005.712

.712 Programming for specific types of computers, for specific operating systems, for specific user interfaces

Add to base number 005.712 the numbers following 005.2 in 005.21–005.29, e.g., programming digital microcomputers for data communications 005.7126

.713 *Programs

Add to base number 005.713 the numbers following 005.3 in 005.3042–005.39, e.g., communications programs for digital microcomputers 005.7136

See Manual at 005.713

.72 *Data preparation and representation, record formats

Including conversion to machine-readable form, data entry and validation; digital codes, e.g., ASCII; error-correcting codes

Class computer input devices in 004.76; class data validation in file processing in 005.74

For data encryption and ciphers, see 005.82

.73 *Data structures

*Use notation 019 from Table 1 as modified at 004.019

.74	*Data files and databases

Including data validation in file processing

Class here data file processing, data file and database management, database design and architecture

Class comprehensive works on data validation in 005.72; class interdisciplinary works on computer science and information science aspects of databases in 025.04. Class data files and databases related to a specific computer method with the method in 006, e.g., deductive databases 006.33; class data files and databases with regard to their subject content with the subject, e.g., encyclopedic databases 030, nonbibliographic medical databases 610

For specific types of data files and databases, see 005.75

See Manual at 005.74; also at 005.74 vs. 005.436

.740 1–.740 5	Standard subdivisions of data files, of databases
.740 6	Organizations and management of data files, of databases
.740 68	Management of data files, of databases

Do not use notation 068 from Table 1 for file management or database management in the sense of computer programs that enable operation of files or databases; class these programs in 005.74

Class here management of organizations concerned with databases, e.g., firms that create them

.740 7–.740 9	Standard subdivisions of data files, of databases
.741	*File organization and access methods

Standard subdivisions are added for either or both topics in heading

Including sorting and merging [*both formerly* 005.748], hashing, search algorithms, search trees, sort algorithms

Class here data file formats

.742	*Data dictionaries and directories

Standard subdivisions are added for either or both topics in heading

.746	*Data compression (File compression, Data compaction)
[.748]	Sorting and merging

Relocated to 005.741

.75	Specific types of data files and databases

Including centralized files and databases

.752	*Flat-file databases

Class flat-file databases that run in networks in 005.758

*Use notation 019 from Table 1 as modified at 004.019

.752 5   Specific flat-file database management systems

         Arrange alphabetically by name of database management system, e.g., Filemaker Pro®

.754   *Network databases

         Including database management systems that conform to the standards developed by CODASYL (Conference on Data Systems Languages)

         See also 005.758 for databases that run in a network

.755   *Hierarchical databases

         Class hierarchical databases that run in a network in 005.758

.756   *Relational databases

         Class relational databases that run in a network in 005.758

.756 5   Specific relational database management systems

         Arrange alphabetically by name of database management system, e.g., Paradox®

.757   *Object-oriented databases

         Class object-oriented databases that run in a network in 005.758

.757 5   Specific object-oriented database management systems

         Arrange alphabetically by name of database management system, e.g., Versant Object Database Management System®

.758   *Distributed data files and databases

         Class here data files and databases used in client/server computing, data files and databases that run in a network

         See also 004.36 for distributed processing

.758 5   Specific distributed database management systems

         Arrange alphabetically by name of database management system, e.g., Oracle for client/server computing

.759   *Full-text database management systems

         Database management systems designed to manage records consisting largely or exclusively of free-form text

.759 2   *Hypertext databases

         For specific hypertext databases, see 005.7598

.759 8   Specific full-text database management systems

         Arrange alphabetically by name of database management system, e.g., Folio Views®, HyperCard®

*Use notation 019 from Table 1 as modified at 004.019

.8 ***Data security**

Class here access control

See also 658.478 for data security in management

.82 *Data encryption

Class here ciphers

Class interdisciplinary works on cryptography in 652.8

.84 *Computer viruses

Including Trojan horses, worms

.86 *Data backup and recovery

Standard subdivisions are added for data backup and recovery together, for data backup alone

006 *Special computer methods

Not otherwise provided for

Including automatic data collection, virtual reality

Class here programs, programming, selection and use of hardware in relation to special computer methods

Unless other instructions are given, class a subject with aspects in two or more subdivisions of 006 in the number coming last, e.g., natural language processing in expert systems 006.35 (*not* 006.33)

See also 003.3 for computer modeling and simulation; notation 0113 from Table 1 for computer modeling and simulation in a specific discipline or subject; 004.6 for computer communications; 005.74 for file and database management; 005.8 for data security; 629.89 for special methods in automatic control engineering

See Manual at 004–006; also at 004–006 vs. 621.39; also at 510, T1—0151 vs. 004–006, T1—0285

SUMMARY

006.3	**Artificial intelligence**	
.4	**Computer pattern recognition**	
.5	**Computer sound synthesis**	
.6	**Computer graphics**	
.7	**Multimedia systems**	

.3 ***Artificial intelligence**

Class here question-answering systems

See also 006.4 for pattern recognition not used as a tool of artificial intelligence

See Manual at 153 vs. 006.3: Cognitive science

---

*Use notation 019 from Table 1 as modified at 004.019

.31 *Machine learning

Including genetic algorithms

For machine learning in knowledge-based systems, see 006.331

.32 *Neural nets (Neural networks)

Including perceptrons [*formerly* 006.42]

Class here connectionist learning, neural computers

.33 *Knowledge-based systems

Class here deductive databases, expert systems

.331 *Knowledge acquisition

.332 *Knowledge representation

Class here knowledge engineering

.333 *Deduction, problem solving, reasoning

.336 *Programming for knowledge-based systems

For programming for knowledge-based systems for specific types of computers, for specific user interfaces, for specific operating systems, see 006.337

.336 3 *Programming languages for knowledge-based systems

.337 Programming for knowledge-based systems for specific types of computers, for specific operating systems, for specific user interfaces

.338 *Programs for knowledge-based systems

Collections of programs, systems of interrelated programs, individual programs used to create a knowledge-based system

Including expert system shells

.35 *Natural language processing

See Manual at 410.285 vs. 006.35

.37 *Computer vision

See also 006.42 for optical pattern recognition

See Manual at 006.37 vs. 006.42, 621.367, 621.391, 621.399

.4 *Computer pattern recognition

Class pattern recognition as a tool of artificial intelligence in 006.3

*Use notation 019 from Table 1 as modified at 004.019

.42   *Optical pattern recognition

> Class here comprehensive works on optical pattern recognition and computer graphics, interdisciplinary works on bar coding
>
> Perceptrons relocated to 006.32
>
> Class optical engineering aspects of optical pattern recognition in 621.367
>
> > *For computer graphics, see 006.6; for use of bar coding in materials management, see 658.780285642*
> >
> > *See also 006.37 for computer vision*
> >
> > *See Manual at 006.37 vs. 006.42, 621.367, 621.391, 621.399*

.424   *Optical character recognition (OCR)

.425   *Handwriting recognition

.45   *Acoustical pattern recognition

.454   *Speech recognition

> Including speaker recognition
>
> Class here comprehensive works on speech recognition and speech synthesis
>
> > *For speech synthesis, see 006.54*

.5   ***Computer sound synthesis**

> > *See also 786.76 for computer music*

.54   *Speech synthesis

.6   ***Computer graphics**

> Multimedia systems, interactive video, comprehensive works on computer graphics and computer sound synthesis relocated to 006.7
>
> Class use of computers in video production in 778.590285
>
> > *See also 760 for computer graphic art*

.62   *Hardware

> Including digitizer tablets, graphics terminals, plotters
>
> Class here equipment specifically designed for computer graphics and works treating use of equipment for computer graphics even if the equipment was not specifically designed for that purpose
>
> Class works that treat equally the use of equipment for graphics and nongraphics tasks in 004

.66   *Programming

> > *For programming for specific types of computers, for specific operating systems, for specific user interfaces, see 006.67*

---

*Use notation 019 from Table 1 as modified at 004.019

.663	*Programming languages for computer graphics
.663 3	Specific programming languages

Arrange alphabetically by name of programming language, e.g., C++

.67	Programming for specific types of computers, for specific operating systems, for specific user interfaces

Add to base number 006.67 the numbers following 005.2 in 005.21–005.29, e.g., graphics programming for IBM PC® 006.6765

.68	*Programs

Add to base number 006.68 the numbers following 005.3 in 005.3042–005.39, e.g., graphics programs that run on MS-DOS® 006.68682

.69	*Special topics in computer graphics
.693	*Three-dimensional graphics

Including ray tracing

.696	*Computer animation

Including morphing

For a specific product of computer animation techniques, see the product, e.g., animated cartoons 741.58

.7	***Multimedia systems [*formerly* 006.6]**

Including interactive video [*formerly* 006.6]

Class here comprehensive works on computer graphics and computer sound synthesis [*formerly* 006.6]

Class use of computers in video production in 778.590285

For computer sound synthesis, see 006.5; for computer graphics, see 006.6

See also 384.354 for interactive videotex

.72	*Hardware

Including multimedia authoring systems comprising both hardware and software

Class here equipment specifically designed for multimedia systems and works treating use of equipment for multimedia systems even if the equipment was not specifically designed for that purpose

Class works that treat equally the use of equipment for multimedia and non-multimedia tasks in 004

.76	*Programming

For programming for specific types of computers, for specific operating systems, for specific user interfaces, see 006.77

---

*Use notation 019 from Table 1 as modified at 004.019

.77	Programming for specific types of computers, for specific operating systems, for specific user interfaces

Add to base number 006.77 the numbers following 005.2 in 005.21–005.29, e.g., writing multimedia programs for Macintosh® 006.7765

.78	Programs

Collections of programs, systems of interrelated programs, individual programs used to create multimedia systems

Class here multimedia authoring software

Add to base number 006.78 the numbers following 005.3 in 005.3042–005.39, e.g., multimedia authoring software that runs on Macintosh® 006.7865

[007]   [Unassigned]

Most recently used in Edition 16

[008–009][Never assigned]

010   Bibliography

History, identification, description of printed, written, audiovisual, machine-readable records

Class catalogs and lists of art works with the subject, plus notation 074 from Table 1, e.g., a catalog of the prints in the Library of Congress 769.074753

See also 028.1 for reviews

SUMMARY

010.4	**Special topics**
011	**Bibliographies**
012	**Bibliographies and catalogs of individuals**
013	**Bibliographies and catalogs of works by specific classes of authors**
014	**Bibliographies and catalogs of anonymous and pseudonymous works**
015	**Bibliographies and catalogs of works from specific places**
016	**Bibliographies and catalogs of works on specific subjects or in specific disciplines**
017	**General subject catalogs**
018	**Catalogs arranged by author, main entry, date, or register number**
019	**Dictionary catalogs**

[.28]	Auxiliary techniques and procedures; apparatus, equipment, materials

Do not use; class in 010.44

.4	**Special topics**

.42   Analytical (Descriptive) bibliography

Analysis of the structure of books and their bibliographic description

Class here comprehensive works on historical and analytical bibliography

Class descriptive cataloging in 025.32

> *For historical bibliography, see 002*
>
> *See also 070.5 for book publishing*

.44   Systematic bibliography

Preparation and compilation of bibliographies

Class systematic bibliography applied to a specific kind of bibliography with the kind, plus notation 028 from Table 1, e.g., preparation and compilation of biobibliographies 012.028

[.74]   Collections, guidebooks, catalogs of exhibits

Do not use; class in 011–019

011   Bibliographies

Class here general bibliographies (in any form) in which the items are books or other written or printed works

Class bibliographies of visual and audiovisual media in 011.37; class catalogs in 012–019

> *For bibliographies of individuals, of works by specific classes of authors, of anonymous and pseudonymous works, of works from specific places, of works on specific subjects or in specific disciplines, see 012–016*

SUMMARY

011.001–.009	**Standard subdivisions**	
.02–.09	**[Reference works, free materials, works published in specific historical periods]**	
.1	**Universal bibliographies**	
.2	**General bibliographies of works published in specific languages**	
.3	**General bibliographies of works published in specific forms**	
.4	**General bibliographies of works exhibiting specific bibliographic characteristics other than form**	
.5	**General bibliographies of works issued by specific kinds of publishers**	
.6	**General bibliographies of works for specific kinds of users and libraries**	
.7	**General bibliographies of works having specific kinds of content**	

.001–.007   Standard subdivisions

.008   Bibliographies with respect to kinds of persons

Class bibliographies of works for specific kinds of users in 011.6

.009   *Historical, geographic, persons treatment of bibliographies

---

*Do not add notation 091–099 from Table 1 for bibliographies of works from specific places; class in 015

.009 01–.009 05   Historical periods

> Class bibliographies of works published in specific historical periods in 011.09

.009 1–.009 9   Geographic treatment

> Class bibliographies of works from specific places in 015

.02   *Bibliographies of reference works

> Class bibliographies of general encyclopedic works in 016.03; class bibliographies of general collected biographies in 016.92

.03   *Bibliographies of free materials

.09   General bibliographies and catalogs of works published in specific historical periods

> Add to base number 011.09 the numbers following —090 in notation 0903–0905 from Table 1, e.g., 16th century publications 011.0931

> Class bibliographies of works from specific places in 015

> *For bibliographies of incunabula, see 011.42*

> **011.1–011.7   General bibliographies**

> Lists of works not held in a specific collection or group of collections; not offered for sale by specific organizations or at auction; not restricted to specific subjects, to individuals or specific types of authorship, or to specific places of publication

> No matter how arranged

> Unless other instructions are given, class a subject with aspects in two or more subdivisions of 011.1–011.7 in the number coming last, e.g., Russian-language newspapers on microfilm 011.36 (*not* 011.29171 or 011.35)

> Class general bibliographies and catalogs of works published in specific historical periods, but without other specific restriction, in 011.09; class comprehensive works in 011

> *See also 011.02 for bibliographies of reference works, 011.03 for bibliographies of free materials, 017–019 for general catalogs*

.1   ***Universal bibliographies**

.2   ***General bibliographies of works published in specific languages**

> Add to base number 011.2 notation 2–9 from Table 6, e.g., general bibliographies of Russian-language works 011.29171

---

*Do not add notation 091–099 from Table 1 for bibliographies of works from specific places; class in 015

.3   ***General bibliographies of works published in specific forms**

Including bibliographies of CD-ROM, of products of electronic publishing, of other works in machine-readable form

Class bibliographies of music scores in 016.78026; class bibliographies of cartographic materials in 016.912

> *See also 011.4 for general bibliographies of works exhibiting specific bibliographic characteristics other than form, e.g., rare books 011.44; 011.7 for bibliographies of works having specific kinds of content, e.g., theses 011.75, computer programs 011.77*
>
> *See Manual at 011.3 vs. 005.30296, 011.77*

> 011.31–011.35 General bibliographies of works published in written or printed form

Class microform versions of written or printed works in 011.36; class comprehensive works, general bibliographies of books in 011

.31   ***Manuscripts**

.32   ***Paperbound books**

.33   ***Pamphlets**

.34   ***Serial publications**

Class here general indexes to serial publications

> *For newspapers, see 011.35*
>
> *See also 011.48 for works in series*

.35   ***Newspapers**

.36   ***Microforms**

Microreproductions of written and printed media

.37   ***Visual and audiovisual media**

Including filmstrips, motion pictures, pictures, slides, videodiscs, videotapes

Class microforms in 011.36; class bibliographies of dramatic and entertainment motion pictures in 016.79143; class bibliographies of dramatic and entertainment videotapes in 016.79145

> *For sound recordings, see 011.38*
>
> *See also 011.3 for bibliographies of CD-ROM materials*

---

*Do not add notation 091–099 from Table 1 for bibliographies of works from specific places; class in 015

.38	*Sound recordings

           Including talking books

           Class here cassettes, compact discs

           Class sound films in 011.37; class sound recordings of music in 016.780266

.4   ***General bibliographies of works exhibiting specific bibliographic characteristics other than form**

           See also 011.3 for works published in specific forms

.42   *Incunabula

.44   *Rare books

           For incunabula, see 011.42

.47   *Reprints

.48   *Works in series

           See also 011.34 for serial publications

.5   ***General bibliographies of works issued by specific kinds of publishers**

.52   *Publications of international organizations

           Including publications of UNESCO

.53   *Government publications

.532   *Government publications issued by legislative bodies and their committees

.534   *Government publications issued by executive agencies

.54   *Publications of university and college presses

.55   *Publications of private presses

           Presses printing in limited quantities or for limited distribution

.56   *Publications of underground presses

           Class here clandestinely published works

.6   ***General bibliographies of works for specific kinds of users and libraries**

.62   *Works for children and young adults

           Standard subdivisions are added for works for children and young adults together, for works for children alone

.624   *Works for specific sexes

.624 1   *Works for boys and young men

---

*Do not add notation 091–099 from Table 1 for bibliographies of works from specific places; class in 015

.624 2	*Works for girls and young women
.625	*Works for young adults

Aged twelve and above

Class works for young men in 011.6241; class works for young women in 011.6242

.63   *Works for persons with disabilities and illnesses

Including braille, large-type publications

Class here works for persons with physical disabilities

Class talking and cassette books for persons with physical disabilities in 011.38

.67   *Works for specific types of libraries

Including bibliographies of books for public libraries

.7   *General bibliographies of works having specific kinds of content

Including directories, textbooks, translations

Class reference works in 011.02; class general encyclopedic works in 016.03

.73   *Best books

Class best books for specific kinds of users and libraries in 011.6

.75   *Theses and dissertations

General collections of abstracts of theses and dissertations are usually classed here (or in 015), but those giving substantive information are classed in 080

.77   *Computer programs

Add to base number 011.77 the numbers following 005.3 in 005.3042–005.39, e.g., bibliographies of programs for digital microcomputers 011.776

See Manual at 011.3 vs. 005.30296, 011.77

*Do not add notation 091–099 from Table 1 for bibliographies of works from specific places; class in 015

> **012–016 Bibliographies and catalogs of individuals, of works by specific classes of authors, of anonymous and pseudonymous works, of works from specific places, of works on specific subjects or in specific disciplines**

Unless other instructions are given, observe the following table of preference, e.g., scientific works published in France by women 016.5 (*not* 013.042 or 015.44):

Bibliographies and catalogs of works on specific subjects or in specific disciplines	016
Bibliographies and catalogs of individuals	012
Bibliographies and catalogs of anonymous and pseudonymous works	014
Bibliographies and catalogs of works by specific classes of authors	013
Bibliographies and catalogs of works from specific places	015

Class comprehensive works in 011

012 Bibliographies and catalogs of individuals

Works by or about persons not clearly associated with a specific subject

Class here biobibliographies

For biobibliographies of persons associated with a specific subject, see the the biography of the subject, e.g., biobibliographies of psychologists 150.92

013 Bibliographies and catalogs of works by specific classes of authors

Works not dealing with a specific subject

For bibliographies and catalogs of individuals, see 012

.03–.87　Authors with common characteristics other than residence

Add to base number 013 notation 03–87 from Table 7, e.g., women authors 013.042

For authors occupied with geography, history, related disciplines, see 013.89

See also 011.75 for dissertations and theses

.89　Authors occupied with geography, history, related disciplines

Add to base number 013.89 the numbers following —9 in notation 91–99 from Table 7, e.g., archaeologists 013.893

.9   **Authors resident in specific regions, continents, countries, localities**

Add to base number 013.9 notation 1–9 from Table 2, e.g., authors resident in Ireland 013.9415

Class authors resident in specific regions, continents, countries, localities, but having other characteristics in common in 013.03–013.89

014   Bibliographies and catalogs of anonymous and pseudonymous works

Add to base number 014 the numbers following 03 in 031–039 (but not notation 02 for books of miscellaneous facts), e.g., bibliographies and catalogs of anonymous and pseudonymous works in French 014.41

015   Bibliographies and catalogs of works from specific places

Works issued in specific regions, continents, countries, localities, or by specific publishers

Class here bibliographies and catalogs of theses and dissertations for degrees awarded at specific institutions and at institutions in specific places, publishers' catalogs, sales catalogs of specific college and university presses

Add to base number 015 notation 1–9 from Table 2, e.g., works issued in Hong Kong 015.5125; then add 0* and to the result add the numbers following 011 in 011.1–011.7, e.g., bibliographies of theses for higher degrees at the university of Hong Kong 015.5125075

---

*Add 00 for standard subdivisions; see instructions at beginning of Table 1

016 **Bibliographies and catalogs of works on specific subjects or in specific disciplines**

In list or essay form

Class here annotated subject bibliographies with descriptive annotations that do not give substantive information about the subject; indexes

Add to base number 016 notation 001–999, e.g., bibliographies of philosophy 016.1, of novels 016.80883

Add to the various subdivisions of 016 notation 01–09 from Table 1 as required for works listed in the bibliographies and catalogs, but not for the bibliographies and catalogs being classed, e.g., bibliographies of serial publications on philosophy 016.105, but serially published bibliographies on philosophy that include monographs 016.1 (*not* 016.105)

Class bibliographies and catalogs of belles-lettres in more than two languages in 016.8088. Class biobibliographies of persons associated with a specific subject with the biography of the subject, e.g., biobibliographies of psychologists 150.92; class bibliographies with abstracts giving substantive information about the subject with the subject, e.g., bibliographies with substantive abstracts about chemistry 540

See also 011 for general bibliographies arranged by subject, 011.31 for bibliographies of manuscripts, 011.34 for general bibliographies of serial publications, 011.35 for bibliographies of newspapers, 011.37 for bibliographies of visual and audiovisual media, 011.38 for bibliographies of recorded radio programs, 011.42 for bibliographies of incunabula, 011.44 for bibliographies of rare books, 017–019 for general subject catalogs and general catalogs of serial publications, 050 for general indexes of specific serial publications not limited by subject

See Manual at 016 vs. 026, T1—07

(Option: Class with the specific discipline or subject, using notation 016 from Table 1, e.g., bibliographies of medicine 610.16)

> ## 017–019 General catalogs

Lists of works held in a specific collection or group of collections, or offered for sale by specific organizations other than publishers or at auction, and not restricted to specific subjects, to individuals or specific types of authorship, or to specific places of publication

Class here general catalogs of serial publications and their indexes, union catalogs

Add to the notation for each term identified by * the numbers following 011 in 011.1–011.7, e.g., classified sales catalogs of periodicals 017.434

Class general catalogs of works published in specific historical periods in 011.09; class catalogs of individuals, of works by specific classes of authors, of anonymous and pseudonymous works, of works from specific places, of works on specific subjects or in specific disciplines in 012–016; class comprehensive works in 017

See also 011.1–011.7 for general bibliographies

017 †General subject catalogs

Class here comprehensive works on catalogs

For catalogs on specific subjects, see 016. For a specific kind of nonsubject catalog, see the kind of catalog, e.g., catalogs of works by specific classes of authors 013

> ### 017.1–017.4 Classified catalogs

Class comprehensive works in 017

.1 *†Classified catalogs of nonprivate libraries

.2 *†Classified catalogs of private and family libraries

.3 *†Classified auction catalogs

.4 *†Classified sales catalogs

For classified auction catalogs, see 017.3

> ### 017.5–017.8 Alphabetic catalogs

Class comprehensive works in 017

.5 *†Alphabetic subject catalogs of nonprivate libraries

.6 *†Alphabetic subject catalogs of private and family libraries

*Add as instructed under 017–019

†Do not add notation 091–099 from Table 1 for catalogs of works from specific places; class in 015

.7   **†Alphabetic subject auction catalogs**

.8   **†Alphabetic subject sales catalogs**

> *For alphabetic subject auction catalogs, see 017.7*

018   †Catalogs arranged by author, main entry, date, or register number

> Add to base number 018 the numbers following 017 in 017.1–017.4, e.g., author catalogs of private and family libraries 018.2
>
> *See also 012 for catalogs of individuals*

019   †Dictionary catalogs

> Add to base number 019 the numbers following 017 in 017.1–017.4, e.g., dictionary auction catalogs 019.3

020   Library and information sciences

> Standard subdivisions are added for either or both topics in heading
>
> Class here archives and archival techniques
>
> *For bibliography, see 010*
>
> *See also 003.54 for information theory, 651.5 for records management as a managerial service*
>
> *See Manual at 020*

SUMMARY

020.1–.9	**Standard subdivisions**
021	**Relationships of libraries, archives, information centers**
022	**Administration of the physical plant**
023	**Personnel administration**
025	**Operations of libraries, archives, information centers**
026	**Libraries, archives, information centers devoted to specific disciplines and subjects**
027	**General libraries, archives, information centers**
028	**Reading and use of other information media**

[.601]   International organizations

> Do not use; class in 020.621

[.603–.609]   National, state, provincial, local organizations

> Do not use; class in 020.622–020.624

.62   Permanent nongovernment organizations

---

*Add as instructed under 017–019

†Do not add notation 091–099 from Table 1 for catalogs of works from specific places; class in 015

.621   International nongovernment organizations

        Including International Federation of Library Associations and Institutions

.622   National nongovernment organizations

        Add to base number 020.622 notation 3–9 from Table 2, e.g., Indian Library Association 020.62254, American Society for Information Science 020.62273

.623   Regional, state, provincial nongovernment organizations

.623 2   Regional nongovernment organizations

        Add to base number 020.6232 notation 3–9 from Table 2, e.g., New England Library Association 020.623274

.623 4   State and provincial nongovernment organizations

        Add to base number 020.6234 notation 3–9 from Table 2, e.g., Ontario Library Association 020.6234713

.624   Local nongovernment organizations

        Add to base number 020.624 notation 3–9 from Table 2, e.g., New York Library Club 020.6247471

[.68]   Management

        Do not use; class in 025.1

.7   **Education, research, related topics**

.715 5   On-the-job training

        Do not use for in-service training; class in 023.8

.9   **Historical, geographic, persons treatment**

        Class here comparative librarianship; historical, geographic, persons treatment of librarianship

        For historical and persons treatment of libraries, see 027.009; for geographic treatment of libraries, see 027.01–027.09

021   **Relationships of libraries, archives, information centers**

Standard subdivisions are added for any or all topics in heading

Including role as storage centers

Class here libraries, archives, information centers as social forces

See also 025.56 for orientation and instructional manuals for users; 027 for comprehensive works on libraries, archives, information centers

.2   **Relationships with the community**

.24   Educational role

        For relationships with other educational institutions, see 021.3

.26   Cultural role

         Including sponsorship of community cultural programs

.28   Informational role

         Including clearinghouse for information on community action programs

.3   **Relationships with other educational institutions**

         Including relationships with museums

.6   **Cooperation and networks**

         Including centralization of systems

.64   Cooperation

         Including bibliographical centers

         Class cooperation in a specific activity with the activity, e.g., cooperative cataloging 025.35

         For networks, see 021.65

.642   Cooperation through union catalogs

         See also 017–019 for specific union catalogs

.65   Networks, systems, consortia

         Standard subdivisions are added for any or all topics in heading

         Class networks, systems, consortia for a specific kind of institution in 026–027. Class networks, systems, consortia for a specific function with the function, e.g., interlibrary loan networks 025.62

         See also 025.0028546 for computer networks in libraries, e.g., local area networks in libraries 025.00285468

.7   **Promotion of libraries, archives, information centers**

         Standard subdivisions are added for any or all topics in heading

         Including friends of the library organizations

         Class here public relations

         Class advertising in 659.1902

.8   **Relationships with government**

         Regardless of governmental level

         Including library-government aspects of exchanges, gifts, deposits; political pressures

         See also 025.26 for acquisition through exchange, gift, deposit

.82   Commissions and governing boards

         Standard subdivisions are added for either or both topics in heading

.83	Financial support

See also 025.11 for financial administration

022   Administration of the physical plant

Including reading rooms and other special rooms, bookmobiles

Class here library quarters in buildings devoted primarily to other activities, e.g., physical plant of school libraries; maintenance of physical plant

See also 025.82 for physical security of collections

.1	**Location and site**
.3	**Buildings**

Class here planning for buildings

See also 727.8 for library architecture

.31	Buildings for specific kinds of institutions

Add to base number 022.31 the numbers following 027 in 027.1–027.8, e.g., college library buildings 022.317

.4	**Stacks and shelving**

Standard subdivisions are added for either or both topics in heading

See also 025.81 for closed versus open stacks

.7	**Lighting**
.8	**Heating, ventilation, air conditioning**
.9	**Equipment, furniture, furnishings**

Class comprehensive works on computers in libraries, archives, information centers in 025.00285

For stacks and shelving, see 022.4

See also 025.56 for signs

023   Personnel administration

>	**023.2–023.4 Types of positions**

Class here titles and job descriptions for specific types of positions

Class comprehensive works in 023

.2	**Professional positions**

Including librarians, consultants, systems analysts

Class administrative positions in 023.4

.3   **Technician positions**

> Including library aides, assistants, clerks, paraprofessionals, technicians
>
> Class administrative positions in 023.4

.4   **Administrative positions**

.7   **Job description**

> Class a job description for a specific type of position with the position in 023.2–023.4

.8   **In-service training**

> Class here in-house courses and programs
>
> Class in-service training for specific types of positions in 023.2–023.4; class comprehensive works on courses and programs for practicing library personnel in 020.7155

.9   **Elements of personnel administration**

> Including recruitment, selection, supervision, employer-employee relations, performance evaluation, wage and salary administration; staff manuals, rules, codes
>
> Class elements of personnel administration applied to specific types of positions in 023.2–023.4
>
> *For in-service training, see 023.8*

[024]   [Unassigned]

> Most recently used in Edition 18

025   Operations of libraries, archives, information centers

> Standard subdivisions are added for any or all topics in heading
>
> Class here documentation (the systematic collection, organization, storage, retrieval, and dissemination of recorded information)
>
> Class comprehensive works on operations in specific kinds of institutions in 026–027

SUMMARY

025.001–.009	**Standard subdivisions**
.02–.06	**[Technical processes, information storage and retrieval systems]**
.1	**Administration**
.2	**Acquisitions and collection development**
.3	**Bibliographic analysis and control**
.4	**Subject analysis and control**
.5	**Services to users**
.6	**Circulation services**
.7	**Physical preparation for storage and use**
.8	**Maintenance and preservation of collections**

.001–.009   Standard subdivisions

.02   Technical processes

> Class here commercial and noncommercial processing centers
>
> Class a specific technical process with the process, e.g., acquisitions 025.2

.04   Information storage and retrieval systems

> Including recall, precision, relevance
>
> Class here search and retrieval in information storage and retrieval systems; front-end systems; comprehensive works on online catalogs integrated with information storage and retrieval systems, on automated storage, search, retrieval of information; interdisciplinary works on databases
>
> Class information storage in 025.3
>
> > *For computer science aspects of information storage and retrieval systems, of databases, see 005.74; for information storage and retrieval systems devoted to specific disciplines and subjects, see 025.06. For a specific kind of information storage and retrieval system, see the kind, e.g., online catalogs 025.3132*
> >
> > *See also 658.4038011 for management use of information storage and retrieval systems*
> >
> > *See Manual at 004.678 vs. 025.04, 384.33; also at 005.74*

.06   Information storage and retrieval systems devoted to specific disciplines and subjects

> Class here documentation of specific disciplines and subjects

[.060 001–.060 009]   Standard subdivisions

> > Do not use; class in 025.0401–025.0409

.060 01–.069 99   Specific disciplines and subjects

> > Add to base number 025.06 notation 001–999, e.g., MEDLINE 025.0661

.1   Administration

> Class administration of a specific function with the function, plus notation 068 from Table 1, e.g., administration of cataloging 025.3068
>
> > *For administration of the physical plant, see 022; for personnel administration, see 023*

.11   Finance

> Including comprehensive works on user fees
>
> Class government financial support in 021.83
>
> > *For user fees for a specific service, see the service, plus notation 0681 from Table 1, e.g., fees for automated information search and retrieval 025.040681*

.12   Duplication services (Reprography)

Including library procedures to comply with copyright legislation

Class here photoduplication (photocopying) services, printing services

Class publishing by libraries, archives, information centers in 070.594; class interdisciplinary works on photoduplication in 686.4

See also 346.0482 for copyright law, 686.2 for technology of printing

.17   Administration of collections of special materials

Class here nonbook materials, comprehensive works on treatment of special materials

Add to base number 025.17 the numbers following 025.34 in 025.341–025.349, e.g., administration of a map collection 025.176, comprehensive treatment of serials 025.1732

For a specific kind of treatment of special materials, see the kind, e.g., collection development for and acquisition of materials in special forms 025.28

.19   Administration of specific types of institutions

Add to base number 025.19 the numbers following 02 in 026–027, e.g., administration of secondary school libraries 025.1978223

Class administration of a specific function in a specific type of institution with the function, e.g., administration of a map collection in a map library 025.176

.2   **Acquisitions and collection development**

Standard subdivisions are added for acquisitions and collection development together, for acquisitions alone

.21   Collection development

Class here collection analysis, evaluation, management; cooperative collection development; selection policy and procedures

Class collection development for specific types of material in 025.27–025.29

For approval plans, see 025.233

.213   Censorship

Class here comprehensive works on library policies and practices relating to intellectual freedom

Class interdisciplinary works on censorship in 363.31

For policies and practices relating to intellectual freedom in a library operation other than collection development, see the operation, e.g., circulation services 025.6

See also 098.1 for prohibited works, 303.376 for sociological studies of censorship, 323.44 for intellectual freedom as a civil right, 342.0853 for law on intellectual freedom, 344.0531 for laws of censorship

.216   Weeding

Including selection for transfer to storage

.218   Collection development in specific types of institutions

Add to base number 025.218 the numbers following 02 in 026–027, e.g., collection development in academic libraries 025.21877

Class censorship in a specific type of institution in 025.213; class weeding in a specific type of institution in 025.216

.23   Acquisition through purchase

Class acquisition of specific types of material through purchase in 025.27–025.29

.233   Relations with vendors

Including approval plans, blanket orders, vendor selection

.236   Clerical operations

Including claiming

.26   Acquisition through exchange, gift, deposit

Standard subdivisions are added for any or all topics in heading

Including copyright deposits; exchange centers and organizations

Class acquisition of specific types of material through exchange, gift, deposit in 025.27–025.29

>   025.27–025.29 Acquisition of and collection development for specific types of materials

Class comprehensive works in 025.2

.27   Acquisition of and collection development for materials on specific disciplines and subjects

> Add to base number 025.27 notation 001–999, e.g., acquisition of materials in the social sciences 025.273
>
> Subdivisions are added for either or both topics in heading
>
> Class acquisition of and collection development for materials on area studies in 025.29

.28   Acquisition of and collection development for materials in special forms

> Add to base number 025.28 the numbers following 025.34 in 025.341–025.349, e.g., acquisition of maps 025.286
>
> Subdivisions are added for either or both topics in heading
>
> Class acquisition of and collection development for materials in special forms on specific disciplines and subjects in 025.27

.29   Acquisition of and collection development for materials from geographic areas

> Class here acquisition of and collection development for foreign publications, materials for area studies
>
> Add to base number 025.29 notation 1–9 from Table 2, e.g., acquisition of materials from Latin America 025.298
>
> Subdivisions are added for either or both topics in heading
>
> Class acquisition of and collection development for materials on specific disciplines and subjects from geographic areas in 025.27; class acquisition of and collection development for materials in special forms from geographic areas in 025.28

.3   **Bibliographic analysis and control**

> Including cataloging in publication, International Standard Book Numbers (ISBNs)
>
> Class here comprehensive works on cataloging and classification, on indexing, on information storage
>
> *For subject analysis and control, see 025.4. For information storage using a specific system, see the system, e.g., information storage through coordinate indexing 025.484*
>
> *See also 025.04 for comprehensive works on information storage and retrieval systems*
>
> *See Manual at 025.3*

SUMMARY

[.302 18]   Standards

                Do not use; class in 025.3

.302 85   Data processing   Computer applications

.302 855 72   Applications of computer data preparation and representation, record formats

                Class machine-readable catalog record formats in 025.316; class data entry, conversion to machine-readable form in 025.317

.302 855 74   Applications of computer data files and databases

                Class here comprehensive works on computer data files and databases used for cataloging and indexing

                For computer data files and databases used for a specific purpose, see the purpose, e.g., online catalogs 025.3132

.302 855 741   Applications of computer file organization and access methods

                Class computer sorting of catalog records in 025.3177

.31   *The catalog

.313   *Form

                Including book, card, microform catalogs

.313 2   *Online catalogs

                Class comprehensive works on online catalogs integrated with information storage and retrieval systems in 025.04

.315   *Structure

                Including classified, divided, unified catalogs

*Do not add notation 0218 from Table 1; see Manual at 025.3

.316   *Machine-readable catalog record formats

Including Common Communication Format (CCF)

Class here communication and internal formats for machine-readable cataloging records; Machine-Readable Cataloging (MARC); comprehensive works on machine-readable formats for catalog records, on machine-readable formats for catalog and index records

For display formats for catalog records, see 025.313; for input formats for catalog records, see 025.317. For formats for a specific kind of catalog record, see the kind in 025.32–025.49, plus notation 0285572 from Table 1, e.g., name authority formats 025.32220285572, serials formats 025.34320285572, subject authority formats 025.49000285572

.317   *Conversion and maintenance

Including preparing, correcting, updating manual and machine-readable catalog records

Class retrospective conversion combined with recataloging and reclassification in 025.39

.317 3   *Retrospective conversion

.317 7   *Filing

Including computer sorting of cataloging records

Class here filing rules

.32   *Descriptive cataloging

Class here descriptive cataloging codes, e.g., Anglo-American Cataloguing Rules

Class descriptive cataloging of special materials in 025.34; class cooperative descriptive cataloging in 025.35; class recataloging in 025.393

.322   *Choice of entry and form of heading

Including corporate headings, personal name headings, uniform titles

Class here author-title indexing

.322 2   *Authority files

Including syndetic structure

Class here name, title authorities; comprehensive works on authority files

For subject authorities, see 025.49

.324   *Bibliographic description

Class here codes for bibliographic description, e.g., International Standard Bibliographic Description (ISBD)

---

*Do not add notation 0218 from Table 1; see Manual at 025.3

.34	*Cataloging, classification, indexing of special materials

Class here nonbook materials

Class comprehensive works on treatment of special materials in 025.17

.341	*Manuscripts, archival materials, rarities
.341 2	*Manuscripts
.341 4	*Archival materials

Class manuscripts in 025.3412

.341 6	*Rarities

Class rare manuscripts in 025.3412; class archival materials in 025.3414

.342	*Clippings, broadsides, pamphlets

Class here contents of vertical files, printed ephemera

.343	*Serials, government publications, report literature
.343 2	*Serials

Including CONSER (Cooperative Conversion of Serials) Project, International Serials Data Program (ISDP), International Standard Serial Numbers (ISSNs)

.343 4	*Government publications

Class government serials in 025.3432

.343 6	*Report literature

Class serial report literature in 025.3432; class government reports in 025.3434

.344	*Machine-readable materials

Class here CD-ROM, computer software, interactive video, multimedia

.346	*Maps, atlases, globes

Standard subdivisions are added for any or all topics in heading

.347	*Pictures and materials for projection

Class here comprehensive works on audiovisual materials

For multimedia, see 025.344; for maps, atlases, globes, see 025.346; for sound recordings and music scores, see 025.348; for other special materials, see 025.349

.347 1	*Pictures and prints
.347 3	*Motion pictures, filmstrips, slides, videotapes
.348	*Sound recordings and music scores

*Do not add notation 0218 from Table 1; see Manual at 025.3

.348 2	*Sound recordings
	Class here cassettes, compact discs
	Class sound films and videotapes in 025.3473
.348 8	*Music scores
.349	*Other special materials
	Including large-type publications, realia
.349 2	*Publications in raised characters
	Including braille
.349 4	*Microforms
.349 6	*Games, media kits, models, toys
	Standard subdivisions are added for any or all topics in heading
	Including flashcards
.35	*Cooperative cataloging, classification, indexing
	Including cooperative development of name and subject authority files
	Class cooperative cataloging, classification, indexing of special materials in 025.34
.39	*Recataloging, reclassification, re-indexing
	Class recataloging, reclassification, re-indexing of special materials in 025.34
.393	*Recataloging
	Including descriptive and subject
	See also 025.396 for reclassification
.396	*Reclassification
.4	**Subject analysis and control**
	See Manual at 025.3
[.402 18]	Standards
	Do not use; class in 025.4
.402 8	Abstracting techniques; auxiliary techniques and procedures; apparatus, equipment, materials
	Class composition of abstracts in 808.062

*Do not add notation 0218 from Table 1; see Manual at 025.3

.42 *Classification and shelflisting

Standard subdivisions are added for classification and shelflisting together, for classification alone

Class classification of special materials in 025.34; class cooperative classification in 025.35; class reclassification in 025.396

For general classification systems, see 025.43; for classification of specific disciplines and subjects, see 025.46

.428 *Shelflisting

See also 025.3 for International Standard Book Numbers (ISBNs)

.43 *General classification systems

Class parts of general classification systems applied to a specific subject or discipline with the subject or discipline in 025.46, e.g., Library of Congress Classification Class L Education 025.4637

.431 *Dewey Decimal Classification

.432 *Universal Decimal Classification

.433 *Library of Congress Classification

.434 *Bliss's Bibliographic Classification

.435 *Ranganathan's Colon Classification

.46 *Classification of specific disciplines and subjects

Add to base number 025.46 notation 001–999, e.g., classification of education 025.4637

.47 *Subject cataloging

Class subject cataloging of special materials in 025.34; class cooperative subject cataloging in 025.35; class recataloging in 025.393

For controlled subject vocabularies, see 025.49

.48 *Subject indexing

Including citation indexing

Class indexing of special materials in 025.34; class cooperative indexing in 025.35; class re-indexing in 025.39

For controlled subject vocabularies, see 025.49

.482 *Precoordinate indexing

Including chain indexing, PRECIS, relative indexing

See also 025.42 for precoordinate classification, 025.47 for precoordinate subject cataloging

*Do not add notation 0218 from Table 1; see Manual at 025.3

.484   *Coordinate and postcoordinate indexing

>   Standard subdivisions are added for either or both topics in heading

.486   *Title manipulation

>   Including catchword, KWIC (Key Word in Context), KWOC (Key Word Out of Context) indexing

.49   Controlled subject vocabularies

>   Class here descriptors, indexing terms, subject authority files, subject headings, syndetic structure, thesauri

.490 001–.490 009   *Standard subdivisions

.490 01–.499 99   Vocabularies of specific disciplines and subjects

>   Add to base number 025.49 notation 001–999, e.g., subject headings in science 025.495

.5   Services to users

>   Class library services to special groups and organizations in 027.6. Class a specific service not provided for here with the service, e.g., photocopying services 025.12, circulation services 025.6, storytelling for children 027.6251

.52   Reference and information services

>   Standard subdivisions are added for either or both topics in heading

>   Class here information and referral services; services that involve the use or assistance in the use of information tools but not the creation of them

>   Class the use of books and other media as sources of information in 028.7; class comprehensive works on the creation and use of information storage and retrieval systems in 025.04; class comprehensive works on the creation and use of specific tools for bibliographic control in 025.3

.523   Cooperative information services

.524   Information search and retrieval

>   Using multiple kinds of information sources, e.g., the library catalog, reference books, automated information storage and retrieval systems

>   Class here search strategy

>   Class information search and retrieval using a specific system with the system, e.g., searching an information storage and retrieval system devoted to medicine 025.0661

>   *See also 025.04 for information storage and retrieval systems*

.525   Selective dissemination of information (SDI)

>   Class here current awareness services

*Do not add notation 0218 from Table 1; see Manual at 025.3

.527   Reference and information services in specific types of institutions

Add to base number 025.527 the numbers following 02 in 026–027, e.g., reference and information services in college and university libraries 025.52777; however, for reference and information services to special groups and organizations, see 027.6

Class specific aspects of reference and information service in specific types of institutions in 025.523–025.525

.54   Reader advisory services to individuals and groups

See also 028.8 for use of books and other media as sources of recreation and self-development

.56   Orientation and bibliographic instruction for users

Including signs, regulations for use, user manuals

Add to base number 025.56 the numbers following 02 in 026–027, e.g., orientation to public libraries 025.5674; however, for orientation and bibliographic instruction for special groups and organizations, see 027.6

Subdivisions are added for either or both topics in heading

.58   Library use studies

Add to base number 025.58 the numbers following 02 in 026–027, e.g., use of government libraries 025.5875; however, for use studies of libraries for special groups and organizations, see 027.6

Class studies of use of a specific system and service with the system or service, e.g., catalog use studies 025.313, studies of use of interlibrary loans 025.62

.6   **Circulation services**

Lending and renting materials, keeping records of loans and rentals

Class here document delivery

Class circulation services for special groups and organizations in 027.6

.62   Interlibrary loans

Including regulations

.7   **Physical preparation for storage and use**

Including binding, labeling, pocketing, repair and restoration

Class conservation and preservation in 025.84

.8   **Maintenance and preservation of collections**

Class repair and restoration in 025.7

.81   Physical arrangement and access to collections

Including closed and open stacks, integrated shelving of materials in different formats

.82	Security against theft and other hazards

Including disaster preparedness, taking of inventory

.84	Preservation

Including deacidification

Class here conservation

For repair and restoration, see 025.7

> ## 026–027 Specific kinds of institutions

Class here specific libraries, archives, information centers, and their collections; systems and networks for specific kinds of institutions; comprehensive works on operations in specific kinds of institutions

Class comprehensive works in 027. Class a specific operation in a specific kind of institution with the operation, e.g., reference and information services in college libraries 025.52777

See Manual at 026–027

026 Libraries, archives, information centers devoted to specific subjects and disciplines

Class here information organizations and library departments and collections in specific disciplines and subjects; comprehensive works on archives, on special libraries

Class special libraries not devoted to specific disciplines and subjects with the kind of library in 027.6, e.g., general museum libraries 027.68, general libraries in newspaper offices 027.69

See Manual at 016 vs. 026, T1—07; also at 026–027

.000 1–.000 5	Standard subdivisions
.000 6	Organizations
[.000 68]	Management

Do not use; class in 025.19

.000 7–.000 9	Standard subdivisions
.001–.999	Specific subjects and disciplines

Add to base number 026 notation 001–999, e.g., medical libraries 026.61; however, do not add notation 068 from Table 1 for organizations and management; class in 025.19

027 General libraries, archives, information centers

Standard subdivisions are added for any or all topics in heading

In the subdivisions of this number, the term *libraries* is used as a short way of saying libraries, archives, information centers, media centers

Class here comprehensive works on libraries, on information centers, on libraries and information centers devoted to special materials

> For libraries, archives, information centers devoted to specific disciplines and subjects, see 026

> See Manual at 027; also at 026–027

SUMMARY

027.001–.009	**Standard subdivisions**
.01–.09	**Geographic treatment**
.1	**Private and family libraries**
.2	**Proprietary libraries**
.3	**Rental libraries**
.4	**Public libraries**
.5	**Government libraries**
.6	**Libraries for special groups and organizations**
.7	**College and university libraries**
.8	**School libraries**

.001–.005   Standard subdivisions

.006   Organizations

[.006 8]   Management

Do not use; class in 025.19

.007–.008   Standard subdivisions

.009   Historical and persons treatment

Do not use for geographic treatment; class in 027.01–027.09

.01–.09   *Geographic treatment

Add to base number 027.0 notation 1–9 from Table 2, e.g., libraries in France 027.044

.1   *Private and family libraries

Collections not open to general use

Standard subdivisions are added for either or both topics in heading

.109   Historical and persons treatment

Do not use for geographic treatment; class in 027.11–027.19

*Do not add notation 068 from Table 1; class in 025.19

.11–.19   *Geographic treatment

> Add to base number 027.1 notation 1–9 from Table 2, e.g., family libraries in the United Kingdom 027.141

.2   *Proprietary libraries

> Semiprivate libraries requiring subscription or membership fees for general use

.209   Historical and persons treatment

> Do not use for geographic treatment; class in 027.21–027.29

.21–.29   *Geographic treatment

> Add to base number 027.2 notation 1–9 from Table 2, e.g., proprietary libraries in Leeds 027.242819

.3   *Rental libraries

> Libraries whose materials are available for use on a commercial basis

.309   Historical and persons treatment

> Do not use for geographic treatment; class in 027.31–027.39

.31–.39   *Geographic treatment

> Add to base number 027.3 notation 1–9 from Table 2, e.g., rental libraries in United States 027.373

.4   *Public libraries

> Institutions that provide free service to all residents of a community, district, region, usually supported in whole or in part from public funds

> Class here public library branches, the use of bookmobiles (mobile libraries) in public librarianship

> Class physical plant management of bookmobiles (mobile libraries) in 022; class public library units devoted to specific disciplines and subjects in 026; class public library units for special groups and organizations in 027.6

[.409 3–.409 9]   Treatment by specific continents, countries, localities

> Do not use; class in 027.43–027.49

.43–.49   *Treatment by specific continents, countries, localities

> Add to base number 027.4 notation 3–9 from Table 2, e.g., public libraries in France 027.444

.5   *Government libraries

> National, state, provincial, local

> *For government libraries for special groups, see 027.65*

> *See Manual at 027.5*

*Do not add notation 068 from Table 1; class in 025.19

.509 3–.509 9		Treatment by specific continents, countries, localities

Class specific institutions in 027.53–027.59

.53–.59   *Specific institutions

Add to base number 027.5 notation 3–9 from Table 2 for area served, e.g., Library of Congress 027.573

.6   *Libraries for special groups and organizations

Class here library and information services to special groups and organizations, to the socially disadvantaged

Unless other instructions are given, class a subject with aspects in two or more subdivisions of 027.6 in the number coming last, e.g., libraries for children with disabilities 027.663 (*not* 027.625)

Class libraries for special groups and organizations devoted to specific disciplines and subjects in 026

For libraries for educational institutions, see 027.7–027.8

.62   *Libraries for specific age groups

.622   *Libraries for persons in late adulthood

.625   *Libraries for children

To age eleven

.625 1   Storytelling

.626   *Libraries for young people aged twelve to twenty

.63   *Libraries for minorities

.65   *Government libraries for special groups

Including government information agencies for foreign populaces, legislative reference bureaus

.66   *Welfare institution libraries

.662   *Hospital libraries

Class here comprehensive works on patients' and medical libraries

For medical libraries, see 026.61

.663   *Libraries for persons with disabilities

Including libraries for persons with visual impairments

Class here mainstreaming (the provision of library and information services through regular channels to individuals with special needs)

.665   *Prison libraries

.67   *Libraries for religious organizations

*Do not add notation 068 from Table 1; class in 025.19

.68   *Libraries for nonprofit organizations

Including libraries of learned societies, museum libraries, United Nations Library

For welfare institution libraries, see 027.66; for libraries for religious organizations, see 027.67

.69   *Libraries for business and industrial organizations

Standard subdivisions are added for either or both topics in heading

Including reference collections in newspaper offices used in the writing or editing of articles

---

>   **027.7–027.8 Libraries for educational institutions**

Class here instructional media centers

Class comprehensive works in 027.7. Class libraries for educational institutions but devoted to specific disciplines and subjects with the kind of libraries in 026, e.g., university law libraries 026.34

.7   ***College and university libraries**

Standard subdivisions are added for either or both topics in heading

Including comprehensive works on instructional materials centers [*formerly* 027.8, 371.3078]

Class here comprehensive works on libraries for educational institutions, college and university library branches

For branches devoted to specific disciplines and subjects, see 026; for elementary and secondary school libraries, see 027.8

.709 3–.709 9   Treatment by specific continents, countries, localities

Class specific institutions in 027.73–027.79

.73–.79   *Specific institutions

Add to base number 027.7 notation 3–9 from Table 2, e.g., Perkins Library of Duke University 027.7756563

.8   ***School libraries**

Including comprehensive works on school resource centers [*formerly* 371.3078]

Comprehensive works on instructional materials centers relocated to 027.7

.809 3–.809 9   Treatment by specific continents, countries, localities

Class specific institutions in 027.823–027.829

---

*Do not add notation 068 from Table 1; class in 025.19

.82   Specific levels and specific libraries

                 Class libraries in religious schools of specific levels, in specific religious
                 schools in 027.83

.822   Specific levels

                   Class specific libraries of specific levels in 027.823–027.829

.822 2   *Elementary level

.822 3   *Secondary level

.823–.829   *Specific libraries

                 Add to base number 027.82 notation 3–9 from Table 2, e.g., Phillips
                 Exeter Academy Library 027.827426

.83   *Libraries in religious schools

028   Reading and use of other information media

.1   Reviews

                 Class here general collections of book reviews

                 Class reviews of computer programs in 005.30296; class techniques of
                 reviewing in 808.066028. Class reviews of works on a specific subject or in a
                 specific discipline with the subject or discipline, e.g., reviews of works on
                 chemistry 540, reviews of entertainment films 791.43, critical appraisal of
                 literature 800

.12   Reviews of reference works

                 Class reviews of reference works published in specific forms in 028.13;
                 class reviews of reference works for specific kinds of users in 028.16. Class
                 reviews of a specific kind of reference works with the kind, e.g., reviews of
                 encyclopedias 030

.13   Reviews of works published in specific forms

                 Add to base number 028.13 the numbers following 011.3 in 011.31–011.38,
                 e.g., reviews of documentary, educational, and entertainment films 028.137

                 Class general collections of book reviews in 028.1; class reviews of works
                 published in specific forms for specific kinds of users in 028.16

.16   Reviews of works for specific kinds of users

                 Add to base number 028.16 the numbers following 011.6 in 011.62–011.67,
                 e.g., reviews of works for young people 028.162

.5   Reading and use of other information media by young people

                 Standard subdivisions are added for either or both topics in heading

                 See also 028.162 for reviews of materials for young people

*Do not add notation 068 from Table 1; class in 025.19

.53 Reading and use of other information media by specific age groups

Add to base number 028.53 the numbers following —05 in notation 054–055 from Table 7, e.g., reading and use of other information media by young people twelve to twenty 028.535

Subdivisions are added for either or both topics in heading

.55 Reading interests and habits of young people

Standard subdivisions are added for either or both topics in heading

Class reading interests and habits of young people of specific age groups in 028.53

.7 **Use of books and other information media as sources of information**

Standard subdivisions are added for either or both topics in heading

Class here use of reference works

For reading and use of other information media by young people, see 028.5

.8 **Use of books and other information media as sources of recreation and self-development**

Standard subdivisions are added for either or both topics in heading

For reading and use of other information media by young people, see 028.5

.9 **Reading interests and habits**

For reading interests and habits of young people, see 028.55

[029] **[Unassigned]**

Most recently used in Edition 18

030 General encyclopedic works

Class here books of miscellaneous facts (e.g., almanacs), encyclopedia yearbooks, general works about curiosities

.9 **Historical, geographic, persons treatment**

Class historical, geographic, persons treatment of encyclopedic works in specific languages and language families in 031–039

> ### 031–039   General encyclopedic works in specific languages and language families

By language in which originally written

Class here specific encyclopedias and books of miscellaneous facts, works about them

Except for modifications shown under specific entries, add to each subdivision identified by * as follows:
01   Philosophy and theory
02   Books of miscellaneous facts
       Do not use for other types of miscellany; class in base number for the language
       Including almanacs with general information, believe-it-or-not books
03–09   Standard subdivisions

Books of unusual and curious facts are classed in the numbers for books of miscellaneous facts, e.g., American books of unusual and curious facts 031.02

Class comprehensive works, encyclopedic works originally written in two or more languages or language families without any language or language family being preponderant in 030. Class encyclopedic works originally written in two or more languages or language families with one language or language family being preponderant with the preponderant language or language family, e.g., encyclopedic work written in Portuguese with some articles in Spanish 036.9

(Option A: To give local emphasis and a shorter number to encyclopedias in a specific language, place them first by use of a letter or other symbol, e.g., Arabic-language encyclopedias 03A [preceding 031]. Option B is described under 031)

031   *American English-language encyclopedias

English-language encyclopedias and books of miscellaneous facts originating in Western Hemisphere

(Option B: To give local emphasis and a shorter number to encyclopedias in a specific language other than English, class them in this number; in that case class American English-language encyclopedias in 032. Option A is described under 031–039)

032   *General encyclopedic works in English

For American English-language encyclopedias, see 031

*Add as instructed under 031–039

033 General encyclopedic works in other Germanic languages

Class here comprehensive works on Germanic-language encyclopedias

Add to base number 033 the numbers following —3 in notation 31–394 from Table 6, e.g., Dutch-language encyclopedias 033.931; then add further as instructed under 031–039, e.g., Dutch-language books of miscellaneous facts 033.93102

> *For English-language encyclopedias, see 032; for Scandinavian-language encyclopedias, see 038*

034 General encyclopedic works in French, Provençal, Catalan

Add to base number 034 the numbers following —4 in notation 41–49 from Table 6, e.g., French-language encyclopedias 034.1; then add further as instructed under 031–039, e.g., French-language almanacs 034.102

035 General encyclopedic works in Italian, Sardinian, Dalmatian, Romanian, Rhaeto-Romanic

Add to base number 035 the numbers following —5 in notation 51–59 from Table 6, e.g., Italian-language encyclopedias 035.1; then add further as instructed under 031–039, e.g., Italian-language books of miscellaneous facts 035.102

036 General encyclopedic works in Spanish and Portuguese

Add to base number 036 the numbers following —6 in notation 61–69 from Table 6, e.g., Portuguese-language encyclopedias 036.9; then add further as instructed under 031–039, e.g., Portuguese-language books of miscellaneous facts 036.902

037 General encyclopedic works in Slavic languages

.1   ***Russian**

.8   **Other Slavic languages**

> *For Ukrainian-language and Belarusian-language encyclopedias, see 037.9*

.81   Bulgarian and Macedonian

.811   *Bulgarian

.819   *Macedonian

.82   *Serbo-Croatian

.84   *Slovenian

.85   *Polish

.86   *Czech

.87   *Slovak

.88   *Wendish (Sorbian, Lusatian)

---

*Add as instructed under 031–039

.9   **Ukrainian and Belarusian**

.91   *Ukrainian

.99   *Belarusian

038   **General encyclopedic works in Scandinavian languages**

Add to base number 038 the numbers following —39 in notation 396–398 from Table 6, e.g., Swedish-language encyclopedias 038.7; then add further as instructed under 031–039, e.g., Swedish-language books of miscellaneous facts 038.702

039   **General encyclopedic works in Italic, Hellenic, other languages**

Add to base number 039 notation 7–9 from Table 6, e.g., Chinese-language encyclopedias 039.951; then add further as instructed under 031–039, e.g., Chinese-language books of miscellaneous facts 039.95102

[040]   **[Unassigned]**

Most recently used in Edition 16

[041–049][Unassigned]

Most recently used in Edition 16

050   **General serial publications**

Class here periodicals; indexes to general serial publications

Class books of miscellaneous facts (even if published annually, e.g., almanacs), encyclopedia yearbooks, in 030; class administrative reports and proceedings of general organizations in 060. Class indexes that focus on a specific subject or discipline in general serial publications with the subject or discipline in 016, e.g., an index to information on medicine in general serial publications 016.61

For newspapers, see 070

See also 011.34 for bibliographies of general serial publications, 011.7 for bibliographies of directories, 017–019 for catalogs of general serial publications

.9   **Historical, geographic, persons treatment**

Class historical, geographic, persons treatment of serial publications in specific languages and language families in 051–059

*Add as instructed under 031–039

> ### 051–059 General serial publications in specific languages and language families

By language in which originally written

Class here specific serial publications and works about them

Class comprehensive works, serials originally written in two or more languages or language families without any language or language family being preponderant in 050. Class serials originally written in two or more languages or language families with one language or language family being preponderant with the preponderant language or language family, e.g., serial written in Portuguese with some articles in Spanish 056.9

(Option A: To give local emphasis and a shorter number to serial publications in a specific language, place them first by use of a letter or other symbol, e.g., Hindi-language serial publications 05H [preceding 051]

(Option B: Arrange serial publications alphabetically under 050

(Option C is described under 051)

051 American English-language serial publications

English-language serial publications of Western Hemisphere

(Option C: To give local emphasis and a shorter number to serial publications in a specific language other than English, class them in this number; in that case class American English-language serial publications in 052. Options A and B are described under 051–059)

052 General serial publications in English

For American English-language serial publications, see 051

053 General serial publications in other Germanic languages

Class here comprehensive works on general serial publications in Germanic languages

Add to base number 053 the numbers following —3 in notation 31–394 from Table 6, e.g., Dutch-language serial publications 053.931

For English-language serial publications, see 052; for Scandinavian-language serial publications, see 058

054 General serial publications in French, Provençal, Catalan

Add to base number 054 the numbers following —4 in notation 41–49 from Table 6, e.g., French-language serial publications 054.1

055 General serial publications in Italian, Sardinian, Dalmatian, Romanian, Rhaeto-Romanic

Add to base number 055 the numbers following —5 in notation 51–59 from Table 6, e.g., Italian-language serial publications 055.1

056 General serial publications in Spanish and Portuguese

Add to base number 056 the numbers following —6 in notation 61–69 from Table 6, e.g., Portuguese-language serial publications 056.9

057 General serial publications in Slavic languages

Add to base number 057 the numbers following 037 in 037.1–037.9 for language only, e.g., Polish-language serial publications 057.85

058 General serial publications in Scandinavian languages

Add to base number 058 the numbers following —39 in notation 396–398 from Table 6, e.g., Swedish-language serial publications 058.7

059 General serial publications in Italic, Hellenic, other languages

Add to base number 059 notation 7–9 from Table 6, e.g., Chinese-language serial publications 059.951

060 General organizations and museology

General organizations: academies, associations, conferences, congresses, foundations, societies whose activity is not limited to a specific field

Including history, charters, regulations, membership lists, administrative reports and proceedings

Class here interdisciplinary works on organizations; interdisciplinary works on licensing, certification, accreditation by nongovernmental organizations

Class history, charters, regulations, membership lists, administrative reports and proceedings of a specific organization in 061–068; class interdisciplinary works on licensing, certification, accreditation by governmental and nongovernmental bodies in 352.84

> *For interdisciplinary works on international governmental organizations, see 341.2. For organizations devoted to a specific discipline or subject, see the discipline or subject, plus notation 06 from Table 1, e.g., organizations devoted to computer science 004.06*
>
> *See Manual at 338 vs. 060, 381, 382, 670.294, 910, T1—025, T1—0294, T1—0296*

(Option A: To give local emphasis and a shorter number to organizations in a specific country, place them first by use of a letter or other symbol, e.g., organizations in Pakistan 06P [preceding 061]. Option B is described under 061)

.4 **Special topics**

.42 General rules of order (Parliamentary procedure)

Including *Robert's Rules of Order*

> *For rules and procedures of legislative bodies, see 328.1*
>
> *See also 658.456 for conduct of meetings of business organizations*

.9 Historical and persons treatment

Do not use for geographic treatment of general organizations; class in 061–068

> 061–068 General organizations

Class comprehensive works in 060

061 General organizations in North America

Class organizations in Middle America in 068.72

(Option B: To give local emphasis and a shorter number to organizations in a specific country other than the United States and Canada, class them in this number; in that case class organizations in North America in 068.7. Option A is described under 060)

.1 General organizations in Canada

Add to base number 061.1 the numbers following —71 in notation 711–719 from Table 2, e.g., organizations in British Columbia 061.11

.3–.9 General organizations in United States

Add to base number 061 the numbers following —7 in notation 73–79 from Table 2, e.g., general organizations in Ohio 061.71

For organizations in Hawaii, see 068.969

062 General organizations in British Isles In England

.1–.8 General organizations in England

Add to base number 062 the numbers following —42 in notation 421–428 from Table 2, e.g., organizations in London 062.1

.9 General organizations in Scotland, Ireland, Wales

Add to base number 062.9 the numbers following —4 in notation 41–42 from Table 2, e.g., organizations in Scotland and Ireland 062.91

063 General organizations in central Europe In Germany

Add to base number 063 the numbers following —43 in notation 431–439 from Table 2, e.g., organizations in Poland 063.8

064 General organizations in France and Monaco

Add to base number 064 the numbers following —44 in notation 441–449 from Table 2, e.g., organizations in Paris 064.36

065 General organizations in Italy and adjacent territories

Add to base number 065 the numbers following —45 in notation 451–459 from Table 2, e.g., organizations in Rome 065.632

066 General organizations in Iberian Peninsula and adjacent islands   In Spain

Add to base number 066 the numbers following —46 in notation 461–469 from Table 2, e.g., organizations in Portugal 066.9

067 General organizations in eastern Europe   In Russia

Add to base number 067 the numbers following —47 in notation 472–479 from Table 2, e.g., organizations in Moscow 067.31

068 General organizations in other geographic areas

Add to base number 068 notation 1–9 from Table 2, e.g., comprehensive works on general organizations in Europe 068.4, in Middle America 068.72

069 Museology (Museum science)

For museum activities and services limited to a specific subject or discipline, see the subject or discipline, plus notation 075 from Table 1, e.g., activities and services of a clock museum 681.113075

[.068 2]   Plant management

                Do not use; class in 069.2

[.068 3]   Personnel management

                Do not use; class in 069.63

[.068 5]   Organization of production

                Do not use; class in 069.1

[.068 7]   Management of materials

                Do not use; class in 069.5

.09   Historical, geographic, persons treatment

            Class here specific museums not limited to a specific discipline or subject

            Class historical, geographic, persons treatment of museum buildings in 069.209. Class museums devoted to specific disciplines and subjects with the discipline or subject, plus notation 074 from Table 1, e.g., natural history museums 508.074

.1   Museum services to patrons

            Class here organization of production

.13   Circulation services

            Lending and renting materials

            See also 069.56 for lending and rental collections

.132   Museum objects

.134	Representations of museum objects

Including pictures, slides, films; aids to use of representations

.15	Instruction services

Including lectures, classes, field trips

.16	Recreational services

Including musical programs, theatrical presentations

.17	Special services to persons with disabilities
.2	**Management and use of physical plant**

Standard subdivisions are added for either or both topics in heading

For equipment, furniture, furnishings, see 069.3

.21	Location and site

Standard subdivisions are added for either or both topics in heading

.22	Planning for buildings

See also 727.6 for museum architecture

.24	Special rooms
.29	Utilities and related facilities

Standard subdivisions are added for utilities and related facilities together, for utilities alone

Including communication systems, lighting, plumbing, heating, ventilating, air-conditioning

.3	**Equipment, furniture, furnishings**
.31	Exhibit cases, screens, pedestals
.32	Audiovisual apparatus
.33	Furniture
.4	**Collecting and preparing museum objects**

Including equipment, materials, methods

Class here management of collecting and preparing museum objects, interdisciplinary works on collecting objects

Class comprehensive works on management of museum materials, on collecting or preparing museum objects and collections of museum objects, interdisciplinary works on collecting and collections in 069.5. Class collecting a specific kind of object or objects that pertain to a specific subject or discipline with the subject or discipline, plus notation 075 from Table 1, e.g., collecting fossils 560.75

.5 **Collections and exhibits of museum objects**

Standard subdivisions are added for either or both topics in heading

Class here comprehensive works on management of museum materials, on collecting or preparing museum objects and collections of museum objects; interdisciplinary works on collecting and collections together, on collections alone

For collecting and preparing museum objects and for interdisciplinary works on collecting, see 069.4. For collections of a specific kind of object or objects that pertain to a specific subject or discipline, see the subject or discipline, plus notation 074 from Table 1, e.g., collections of fossils 560.74

[.502 88] Maintenance and repair

Do not use; class in 069.53

.502 89 Safety measures

See also 069.54 for prevention of thefts and identification of forgeries

---

> 069.51–069.54 General activities

Class general activities applied to special collections in 069.55–069.57; class comprehensive works in 069.5

.51 Selection, acquisition, disposal

.52 Registration, recording, indexing

Standard subdivisions are added for any or all topics in heading

Class here museum documentation

.53 Maintenance, conservation, preservation, restoration, display, arrangement, storage, transportation

Including museum labels

Class historic preservation in 363.69

.54 Prevention of thefts and identification of forgeries

> 069.55–069.57 Special collections

Including classification, arrangement, housing

Class comprehensive works in 069.5

.55 Study collections

.56 Lending and rental collections

> Standard subdivisions are added for either or both topics in heading

> *See also 069.13 for circulation services*

.57 Collections of secondary materials

> Including brochures, films, motion pictures, photographs, pictures, prints, slides representing museum objects

.6 Personnel management, regulations for patrons, relations with other organizations

.62 Regulations for patrons

> Including regulations for members, for visitors

.63 Personnel management

> Including in-service training, staff manuals

.68 Relations with other organizations

> Class public relations for museums in 659.29069

070 Documentary media, educational media, news media; journalism; publishing

> Standard subdivisions are added for documentary media, educational media, news media; journalism; publishing together; for newspapers and journalism alone

SUMMARY

.01–.08 Standard subdivisions of documentary media, educational media, news media; journalism; publishing

.09 Historical, geographic, persons treatment of documentary media, educational media, news media; journalism; publishing

> Class historical and persons treatment of journalism and newspapers in 070.9; class geographic treatment of journalism and newspapers in 071–079

SUMMARY

.1   **Documentary media, educational media, news media**

Class here comprehensive works on journalism and production of specific kinds of educational, expository, news media

Class interdisciplinary works on mass media in 302.23. Class documentary, educational, news works themselves and discussion of them with the kind of general work or the subject, e.g., general periodicals 050, recorded television programs on investing 332.6

For specific journalistic activities and types of journalism, see 070.4; for expository writing and editorial techniques, see 808.066

.17   Print media

Class the book in 002

.172   Newspapers

Class newspaper publishing in 070.5722; class specific general newspapers in 071–079

See also 011.35 for bibliographies of newspapers

[.172 09]   Historical, geographic, persons treatment

Do not use for historical and persons treatment; class in 070.9. Do not use for geographic treatment; class in 071–079

.175   Periodicals

Including newsletters

Class specific general periodicals in 050. Class periodicals on a specific discipline or subject with the discipline or subject, plus notation 05 from Table 1, e.g., science journals 505

.18   Motion pictures

Including documentary films, educational films, newsreels

Class photography aspects in 778.53; class comprehensive works about documentary, educational, news and dramatic or entertainment films in 791.43; class interdisciplinary works on motion pictures in 384.8

See also 371.33523 for use of motion pictures in teaching

.19   Broadcast media

.194   Radio

Including news programs

Class comprehensive works on documentary, educational, news and dramatic or entertainment radio programs in 791.44; class interdisciplinary works on radio in 384.54

See also 371.3331 for use of radio in teaching

.195   Television

Including news programs

Class photographic aspects in 778.59; class comprehensive works on documentary, educational, news and dramatic or entertainment television programs in 791.45; class interdisciplinary works about television in 384.55

See also 371.3358 for use of television in teaching

.4   Journalism

Collecting, writing, editing information and opinion of current interest for presentation in newspapers, periodicals, films, radio, television

Class journalists whose careers span many activities in 070.92; class journalism of specific kinds of news media in 070.1; class journalistic composition and editorial mechanics in 808.06607; class comprehensive works on journalism and information media in 070. Class persons in a specific type of journalism with the type, e.g., editors 070.41092, foreign correspondents 070.4332092

See also 050 for general periodicals, 070.5722 for newspaper publishing, 071–079 for specific newspapers, 174.9097 for ethics of journalism, notation 05 from Table 1 for journals on a specific discipline or subject

.401–.407   Standard subdivisions

.408   Journalism with respect to kinds of persons

Class journalism directed to special groups in 070.48

[.409]   Historical, geographic, persons treatment

Do not use for historical and persons treatment; class in 070.9. Do not use for geographic treatment; class in 071–079

.41   Editing

Including editorial crusades, policy on editorial cartoons

Class here editorial policy (selection, presentation, display of news; advocacy of specific points of view)

Class editing with respect to features and special topics in 070.44; class editorials in 070.442; class comprehensive works on editing and news gathering or reporting in 070.4

See also 808.06607 for editorial mechanics, e.g., copy editing, Associated Press stylebook

.43   News gathering and reporting

> Class news gathering and reporting with respect to feature and special topics in 070.44; class comprehensive works on editorial policy and news gathering or reporting in 070.4

.431   News sources

.433   Reporting local, foreign, war news

> Broad descriptions of local, foreign, war reporting as types of reporting, not limited to a specific subject or geographic area; how to do the reporting

> Class reporting of specific subjects with the subject in 070.449, e.g., reporting on world-wide energy resources 070.44933379, on Winter Olympics 070.44979698

> *See Manual at 070.433*

.433 2   Foreign news

> Class here international news

> Class foreign war news in 070.4333

.433 3   War news

.435   Wire services

> Including Associated Press, Reuters

>   070.44–070.49   Specific types of journalism

> Class comprehensive works in 070.4

.44   Features and special topics

> Including techniques and procedures for information-gathering, writing, editing for reports, criticisms, opinions

> Class here newspaper columns

> Class reports, criticism, opinions on a specific subject with the subject, e.g., criticisms of theatrical productions 792

.442   Interpretation and opinion

> Standard subdivisions are added for either or both topics in heading

> Including newspaper editorials, radio comment

> Class editorial policy in 070.41

.444	**Miscellaneous information, advice, amusement**

Including humor, general personal advice columns

Class journalistic handling of information, advice, humor on a specific subject with the subject in 070.449, e.g., advice on dating 070.44964677

See also 741.5 for artistic aspects of comics

.444 092	Persons treatment

Class here biographies of journalists specializing in humor, of journalists known for general personal advice columns

Class biographies of cartoonists in 741.5092. Class biographies of a humorous writer with the writer in 800, e.g., a contemporary British writer of humorous essays 824.914

.449	**Specific subjects**

Class here journalists specializing in specific subjects, e.g., sports announcers 070.449796092

Add to base number 070.449 notation 001–999, e.g., health columns 070.449613

Class features and reports themselves with the subject, e.g., health columns 613

See also 070.433 for reporting of local, foreign, war news as general types of news; 070.444 for miscellaneous information, advice, amusements as types of journalism; 070.48 for general journalism directed to special groups

.48	**Journalism directed to special groups**

Class editing in journalism directed to specific groups in 070.41; class news gathering and reporting in journalism directed to specific groups in 070.43; class school journalism in 371.897. Class a feature or a special topic directed to a special group with the feature or topic in 070.44, e.g., news about religion 070.4492 (*not* 070.482)

.482	**Religious groups**
.483	**Groups by age and sex**
.483 2	Children
.483 26	Boys
.483 27	Girls
.483 3	Young adults

Aged twelve and above

.483 36	Young men
.483 37	Young women

.483 4	Adults

For young adults, see 070.4833

.483 46	Men
.483 47	Women
.484	Foreign-language and nondominant racial, ethnic, national groups
.486	Occupational and employee groups

Standard subdivisions are added for either or both topics in heading

General journalism for occupational and employee groups

Including house organs

Class journalism on a specific subject directed to occupational and employee groups in 070.449

.49	Pictorial journalism

Class here photojournalism

.5 Publishing

Class here book publishing; publishers regardless of their field of activity; book clubs, e.g., Book-of-the-Month Club®; comprehensive works on publishing and printing

Class works on desktop publishing that emphasize typography in 686.22

For printing, see 686.2

.502 94	Trade catalogs and directories

Class publishers' catalogs in 015

.509	Historical, geographic, persons treatment

Class here comprehensive works on specific publishers, using the area number for the publisher's main office, e.g., U.S. Government Printing Office 070.509753, University of California Press 070.50979467

Class economic aspects of publishers as business organizations in 338.7610705

.51	Selection and editing of manuscripts

Class editorial techniques in 808.02

.52	Relations with authors

Including literary agents

See Manual at 808.001–808.7 vs. 070.52

.57	Kinds of publications

Class specific publishers in 070.509; class selection and editing of manuscripts for specific kinds of publications in 070.51; class relations with authors of specific kinds of publications in 070.52

.572	Serials

Class comprehensive works on journalism and publishing of serials in 070.17

.572 2	Newspapers
.573	Specific kinds of books

Including limited editions, paperbacks, subscription books

Class serials in book form in 070.572

.579	Special kinds of publications
.579 2	Braille and other raised characters

Standard subdivisions are added for Braille and other raised characters together, for Braille alone

.579 3	Maps
.579 4	Music
.579 5	Microforms
.579 7	Machine-readable publications

Including CD-ROM

.59	Kinds of publishers

Class specific publishers in 070.509; class selection and editing of manuscripts by specific kinds of publishers in 070.51; class relations with authors of specific kinds of publishers in 070.52; class specific kinds of publications of specific kinds of publishers in 070.57

.592	Commercial publishers
.593	Private publishers

Class here self-publishing

Class works on desktop publishing that emphasize typography in 686.22

.594	Institutional publishers

Including archive, church, information center, library, museum, society, university publishers

.595	Governmental and intergovernmental publishers

Standard subdivisions are added for either or both topics in heading

Class U.S. Government Printing Office in 070.509753

.9	**Historical and persons treatment of journalism and newspapers**

Class geographic treatment in 071–079

.92	Persons regardless of area, region, place

> ### 071–079 Geographic treatment of journalism and newspapers

Class here specific general newspapers, indexes to them, other works about them

When adding from Table 2 for a specific newspaper, use the number for the primary area served by the newspaper; for example, a newspaper published in a city but carrying news about and having many subscribers in the surrounding region should be given the Table 2 number for the region

Class comprehensive works in 070

(Option A: To give local emphasis and a shorter number to newspapers and journalism in a specific country, place them first by use of a letter or other symbol, e.g., newspapers and journalism in New Zealand 07N [preceding 071]

(Option B: Arrange newspapers alphabetically under 070

(Option C is described under 071)

071   Journalism and newspapers in North America

Standard subdivisions are added for either or both topics in heading

Class journalism and newspapers in Middle America in 079.72

(Option C: To give local emphasis and a shorter number to journalism and newspapers in a specific country other than the United States and Canada, class them in this number; in that case class journalism and newspapers in North America in 079.7. Options A and B are described under 071–079)

.1   Journalism and newspapers in Canada

Add to base number 071.1 the numbers following —71 in notation 711–719 from Table 2, e.g., journalism and newspapers in British Columbia 071.11

Subdivisions are added for either or both topics in heading

.3–.9   Journalism and newspapers in the United States

Add to base number 071 the numbers following —7 in notation 73–79 from Table 2, e.g., *New York Times* 071.471

Subdivisions are added for either or both topics in heading

For journalism and newspapers in Hawaii, see 079.969

072   Journalism and newspapers in British Isles   In England

.1–.8   Journalism and newspapers in England

Add to base number 072 the numbers following —42 in notation 421–428 from Table 2, e.g., *Times* of London 072.1

Subdivisions are added for either or both topics in heading

.9　　　**Journalism and newspapers in Scotland, Ireland, Wales**

Add to base number 072.9 the numbers following —4 in notation 41–42 from Table 2, e.g., newspapers in Scotland and Ireland 072.91

Subdivisions are added for either or both topics in heading

073　　**Journalism and newspapers in central Europe　　In Germany**

Add to base number 073 the numbers following —43 in notation 431–439 from Table 2, e.g., journalism and newspapers in Austria 073.6

Subdivisions are added for either or both topics in heading

074　　**Journalism and newspapers in France and Monaco**

Add to base number 074 the numbers following —44 in notation 441–449 from Table 2, e.g., journalism and newspapers in Paris 074.36

Subdivisions are added for journalism, newspapers, or both

075　　**Journalism and newspapers in Italy and adjacent territories**

Add to base number 075 the numbers following —45 in notation 451–459 from Table 2, e.g., journalism and newspapers in Rome 075.632

Subdivisions are added for journalism, newspapers, or both

076　　**Journalism and newspapers in Iberian Peninsula and adjacent islands　　In Spain**

Add to base number 076 the numbers following —46 in notation 461–469 from Table 2, e.g., journalism and newspapers in Portugal 076.9

Subdivisions are added for journalism, newspapers, or both

077　　**Journalism and newspapers in eastern Europe　　In Russia**

Add to base number 077 the numbers following —47 in notation 472–479 from Table 2, e.g., journalism and newspapers in Moscow 077.31

Subdivisions are added for journalism, newspapers, or both

078　　**Journalism and newspapers in Scandinavia**

Add to base number 078 the numbers following —48 in notation 481–489 from Table 2, e.g., journalism and newspapers in Sweden 078.5

Subdivisions are added for either or both topics in heading

079　　**Journalism and newspapers in other geographic areas**

Add to base number 079 notation 1–9 from Table 2, e.g., comprehensive works on general newspapers in Europe 079.4, in Middle America 079.72

Subdivisions are added for either or both topics in heading

080 General collections

Class here addresses, lectures, essays, interviews, graffiti, quotations

Class essays as literary form, collections gathered for their literary quality in 800

See Manual at 080; also at 080 vs. 800

.9 Historical, geographic, persons treatment

Class historical, geographic, persons treatment of collections in specific languages and language families in 081–089

> **081–089 General collections in specific languages and language families**

Class comprehensive works in 080

See Manual at 081–089

(Option A: To give local emphasis and a shorter number to collections in a specific language, place them first by use of a letter or symbol, e.g., collections in Urdu 08U [preceding 081]

(Option B: Arrange collections alphabetically under 080

(Option C is described under 081)

081 American English-language collections

English-language collections of Western Hemisphere

(Option C: To give local emphasis and a shorter number to collections in a specific language other than English, class them in this number; in that case class American English-language collections in 082. Options A and B are described under 081–089)

082 General collections in English

For American English-language collections, see 081

083 General collections in other Germanic languages

Class here comprehensive works on Germanic-language collections

Add to base number 083 the numbers following —3 in notation 31–394 from Table 6, e.g., German-language collections 083.1

For English-language collections, see 082; for Scandinavian-language collections, see 088; for Old-English-language (Anglo-Saxon-language) collections, see 089

084 General collections in French, Provençal, Catalan

Add to base number 084 the numbers following —4 in notation 41–49 from Table 6, e.g., French-language collections 084.1

085 General collections in Italian, Sardinian, Dalmatian, Romanian, Rhaeto-Romanic

Add to base number 085 the numbers following —5 in notation 51–59 from Table 6, e.g., Italian-language collections 085.1

086 General collections in Spanish and Portuguese

Add to base number 086 the numbers following —6 in notation 61–69 from Table 6, e.g., Portuguese-language collections 086.9

087 General collections in Slavic languages

Add to base number 087 the numbers following 037 in 037.1–037.9 for language only, e.g., Polish-language collections 087.85

088 General collections in Scandinavian languages

Add to base number 088 the numbers following —39 in notation 396–398 from Table 6, e.g., Swedish-language collections 088.7

089 General collections in Italic, Hellenic, other languages

Including Old English (Anglo-Saxon)

Add to base number 089 notation 7–9 from Table 6, e.g., Chinese-language collections 089.951

090 Manuscripts, rare books, other rare printed materials

Including rare broadsides

Class interdisciplinary works on books in 002. Class a manuscript or rare work on a specific subject with the subject, e.g., a book of hours 242; class an artistic aspect of a manuscript or rare book with the aspect, e.g., illumination 745.67

> *See also 011.31 for bibliographies of both manuscripts and rare books, 011.44 for bibliographies of rare books only*

091 Manuscripts

> *See also 011.31 for bibliographies of manuscripts*

092 Block books

093 Incunabula

Books printed before 1501

> *See also 011.42 for bibliographies of incunabula*

094 Printed books

.2		**Early printed books**

        To 1700

        For block books, see 092; for incunabula, see 093

.4   **Special editions**

        Including first editions, limited editions, typographic masterpieces

095   **Books notable for bindings**

        See also 686.3 for bookbinding

096   **Books notable for illustrations and materials**

.1   **Books notable for illustrations**

        Class illustrated manuscripts in 091

.2   **Books notable for materials**

        Including leaves of vellum and silk, letters of silver and gold

097   **Books notable for ownership or origin**

        Standard subdivisions are added for either or both topics in heading

098   **Prohibited works, forgeries, hoaxes**

.1   **Prohibited works**

.11   Prohibited by religious authorities

.12   Prohibited by civil authorities

.3   **Forgeries and hoaxes**

        Standard subdivisions are added for either or both topics in heading

099   **Books notable for format**

        Including books of unusual shapes, miniature editions

100 Philosophy, paranormal phenomena, psychology

Class philosophy of a specific discipline or subject with the discipline or subject, plus notation 01 from Table 1, e.g., philosophy of history 901

See Manual at T1—01; also at 170; also at 190 vs. 100, 109; also at 200 vs. 100

SUMMARY

140	Specific philosophical schools and viewpoints
141	Idealism and related systems and doctrines
142	Critical philosophy
143	Bergsonism and intuitionism
144	Humanism and related systems and doctrines
145	Sensationalism
146	Naturalism and related systems and doctrines
147	Pantheism and related systems and doctrines
148	Dogmatism, eclecticism, liberalism, syncretism, traditionalism
149	Other philosophical systems and doctrines
150	Psychology
.1–.9	Standard subdivisions and systems, schools, viewpoints
152	Sensory perception, movement, emotions, physiological drives
153	Conscious mental processes and intelligence
154	Subconscious and altered states and processes
155	Differential and developmental psychology
156	Comparative psychology
158	Applied psychology
160	Logic
161	Induction
162	Deduction
165	Fallacies and sources of error
166	Syllogisms
167	Hypotheses
168	Argument and persuasion
169	Analogy
170	Ethics (Moral philosophy)
.1–.9	Standard subdivisions and special topics
171	Ethical systems
172	Political ethics
173	Ethics of family relationships
174	Occupational ethics
175	Ethics of recreation, leisure, public performances, communication
176	Ethics of sex and reproduction
177	Ethics of social relations
178	Ethics of consumption
179	Other ethical norms
180	Ancient, medieval, Oriental philosophy
.01–.09	Standard subdivisions of ancient, medieval, Oriental philosophy
.1–.9	Standard subdivisions of ancient philosophy
181	Oriental philosophy
182	Pre-Socratic Greek philosophies
183	Sophistic, Socratic and related Greek philosophies
184	Platonic philosophy
185	Aristotelian philosophy
186	Skeptic and Neoplatonic philosophies
187	Epicurean philosophy
188	Stoic philosophy
189	Medieval western philosophy

190	**Modern western and other non-Oriental philosophy**
191	**United States and Canada**
192	**British Isles**
193	**Germany and Austria**
194	**France**
195	**Italy**
196	**Spain and Portugal**
197	**Former Soviet Union**
198	**Scandinavia**
199	**Other geographic areas**

101   Theory of philosophy

Class here works on the concept of philosophy, on the nature of the philosophical task, on the method of philosophy

Class schools of philosophical thought in 140; class ancient, medieval, Oriental schools in 180

102–108 Standard subdivisions of philosophy

109   Historical and collected persons treatment of philosophy

Do not use for geographic treatment; class in 180–190

Not limited by period or place

See Manual at 190 vs. 100, 109

.2   **Collected persons treatment**

Do not use for individual persons treatment; class in 180–190

[.22]   Collected persons treatment

Do not use; class in 109.2

110   Metaphysics

For epistemology, causation, humankind, see 120

111   Ontology

.1   **Existence, essence, substance, accidents**

.2   **Universals**

.5   **Nonbeing, nothingness**

.6   **Finite and infinite**

Including the absolute

.8   **Classical properties of being**

Class comprehensive works on truth in 121

.82   Unity

Including part-whole relationships, principle of identity

.84   Goodness and evil

For ethics, see 170

.85   Beauty

Class here interdisciplinary works on aesthetics

For aesthetics of a specific subject, see the subject, e.g., of the fine arts 701.17

[112]   [Unassigned]

Most recently used in Edition 18

113   Cosmology (Philosophy of nature)

Including cosmic harmony, origin of universe (cosmogony)

Class cosmology as a topic in astronomy in 523.1

For specific topics of cosmology not provided for here, see 114–119

.8   Philosophy of life

Origin and nature of life

Class origin and nature of human life in 128

114   Space

Class here relation of space and matter

Class matter in 117

115   Time

Including eternity, space and time, space-time, relation of time and motion

For space, see 114

116   Change

Including becoming, cycles, evolution, motion, process

Class relation of time and motion in 115

117   Structure

Including matter, form, order, chaos

Class relation of space and matter in 114

118   Force and energy

Standard subdivisions are added for either or both topics in heading

119   Number and quantity

120   Epistemology, causation, humankind

SUMMARY

121   Epistemology (Theory of knowledge)

Class here comprehensive works on truth, e.g., coherence, correspondence theories

Class knowledge and its extension in 001

For truth as a classical property of being, see 111.8; for truth in logic, see 160

.2   Possibility and limits of knowledge

Standard subdivisions are added for either or both topics in heading

Including solipsism and problem of other minds

.3   Origin, sources, means of knowledge

Standard subdivisions are added for any or all topics in heading

Including intuition, reason

Class reason as a human attribute in 128.33

.34   Perception

For sensation, see 121.35

.35   Sensation

Including vision

Class here sense knowledge

.4   Structure of knowledge

Subjective and objective components

Including concepts, ideas

.5   Doubt and denial

Standard subdivisions are added for either or both topics in heading

Class comprehensive works on doubt, denial, certainty, probability in 121.63

.6   Nature of inquiry

Including belief

Class faith in 121.7

.63	Certainty and probability

Standard subdivisions are added for either or both topics in heading

Class here comprehensive works on doubt, denial, certainty, probability

For doubt and denial, see 121.5

.65	Evidence and criteria

Standard subdivisions are added for either or both topics in heading

.68	Meaning, interpretation, hermeneutics

Including reference [*formerly* 160], semantics, semiotics

Class here philosophy of language

Class interdisciplinary works on semiotics in 302.2

See also 149.94 for general semantics as a school of linguistic philosophy, 401.41 for semiotics in linguistics, 401.43 for semantics in linguistics

See Manual at 401 vs. 121.68, 149.94, 410.1

.686	Philosophical hermeneutics
.7	**Faith**

Class belief in 121.6; class religious faith in 200

.8	**Worth and theory of values (Axiology)**

Standard subdivisions are added for any or all topics in heading

Class ethical values in 170

122 Causation

Class here chance versus cause

For determinism and indeterminism, see 123; for teleology, see 124

123 Determinism and indeterminism

Standard subdivisions are added for either or both topics in heading

Including contingency

.3	**Chance**

Class chance versus cause in 122

.5	**Freedom**

Including freedom of will

.7	**Necessity**

124 Teleology

Design, purpose, final cause

[125]   **[Unassigned]**

Most recently used in Edition 18

126   **The self**

Class here consciousness, personality

Class the unconscious and the subconscious in 127

127   **The unconscious and the subconscious**

Standard subdivisions are added for either or both topics in heading

128   **Humankind**

Class here philosophical anthropology; comprehensive works on philosophy of human life, on philosophy and psychology of human life

For the self, see 126; for psychology, see 150

See also 599.9 for physical anthropology

.1   **Soul**

For origin and destiny of individual souls, see 129

.2   **Mind**

Including mind-body relationship

.3   **Attributes and faculties**

Standard subdivisions are added for either or both topics in heading

Including imagination, intellect, memory, will

For perception, see 121.34; for sensation, see 121.35; for freedom of will, see 123.5

.33   Reason and rationality

Standard subdivisions are added for either or both topics in heading

Class reason as an instrument of knowledge in 121.3

For science of reasoning (logic), see 160

See also 149.7 for rationalism

.37   Emotion

Class love in 128.46

.4   **Human action and experience**

Standard subdivisions are added for either or both topics in heading

Nature, conditions, origin

.46   Love

For ethics of love, see 177.7

.5   **Human death**

Class interdisciplinary works on death in 306.9

.6   **Body**

129   Origin and destiny of individual souls

Including immortality, incarnation, reincarnation

Class accounts of previous incarnations in 133.9013

See Manual at 133.9013 vs. 129

130   Paranormal phenomena

Class phenomena of religious experience in 200; class interdisciplinary works on controversial knowledge and paranormal phenomena in 001.9

See Manual at 001.9 and 130; also at 133 vs. 130

SUMMARY

131	Parapsychological and occult methods for achieving well-being, happiness, success
133	Parapsychology and occultism
135	Dreams and mysteries
137	Divinatory graphology
138	Physiognomy
139	Phrenology

[.112]   Forecasting and forecasts

Do not use; class comprehensive works on parapsychological and occult forecasting and forecasts in 133.3. Class a specific type of forecasting or forecast with the type, without adding notation 0112 from Table 1, e.g., astrological methods of forecasting 133.5

131   Parapsychological and occult methods for achieving well-being, happiness, success

Standard subdivisions are added for any or all topics in heading

Class interdisciplinary works limited to psychological and parapsychological or occult techniques for achieving personal well-being, happiness, success in 158; class interdisciplinary works on successful living, on management of personal and family living in 646.7. Class specific methods of parapsychology and occultism for achieving well-being with the method in 133–139, e.g., spells and charms 133.44

[132]   [Unassigned]

Most recently used in Edition 16

133 Parapsychology and occultism

Standard subdivisions are added for either or both topics in heading

Class here frauds in occultism

For Rosicrucian, Hermetic, Cabalistic traditions, see 135.4

See Manual at 133 vs. 130; also at 133 vs. 200

SUMMARY

133.1	Apparitions
.2	Parapsychological and occult aspects of specific things
.3	Divinatory arts
.4	Demonology and witchcraft
.5	Astrology
.6	Palmistry
.8	Psychic phenomena
.9	Spiritualism

.1 Apparitions

Class here ghosts

Class folkloristic ghost stories in 398.25; class ghosts as a subject of folklore in 398.47; class literary accounts of ghosts in 808.80375; class interdisciplinary works on spirits (discarnate beings) in 133.9

.109 Historical, geographic, persons treatment

Class here haunted places

For specific haunted places, see 133.129

See Manual at 133.109 vs. 133.129

.12 Haunted places

[.120 9] Historical, geographic, persons treatment

Do not use; class in 133.109

.122 Specific types of haunted places

Including haunted churches, forests, graveyards, houses

Class specific haunted places regardless of type in 133.129

.129 Specific haunted places

Add to base number 133.129 notation 3–9 from Table 2, e.g., the Tower of London 133.1294215

Class general historical and geographic treatment of ghosts in 133.109

See Manual at 133.109 vs. 133.129

.14	Specific kinds of apparitions

Including animal ghosts, hobgoblins, phantasms of the living

Class haunted places regardless of kind of apparition in 133.12; class materialization of spirits as a mediumistic phenomenon in 133.92

.142	Poltergeists

.2	**Parapsychological and occult aspects of specific things**

Specific things used for more than one purpose, in more than one branch of parapsychology and occultism

For a specific parapsychological or occult use of a specific thing, see the use in 131–139, e.g., fortune-telling by crystals 133.322, fortune-telling by cards 133.3242; for a specific thing in a specific branch of parapsychology and occultism, see the branch in 131–139, e.g., use of candles in witchcraft 133.43028, astrological aspects of planets 133.53

See also 001.94 for pyramid power, 135.3 for parapsychological aspects of dreams

.25	Natural things

Add to base number 133.25 the numbers following 5 in 500.2–599, e.g., occult use of crystals for multiple purposes, such as healing, personality analysis, fortune-telling 133.2548

.3	**Divinatory arts**

Including fortune-telling by bones, dice, pendulum

Class here works on the symbolism of divinatory arts and objects, comprehensive works on occult methods of foretelling the future

Class use of extrasensory perception for divination in 133.82–133.86; class interdisciplinary works on forecasting in 003.2

For astrology, see 133.5; for palmistry, see 133.6; for dream books, see 135.3; for divinatory graphology, see 137; for physiognomy, see 138

See also 291.32 for divination as a religious practice, 303.49 for social forecasting

.309 2	Persons

Class here persons known chiefly for their predictions rather than their methods of predicting, e.g., Nostradamus (Michel de Notredame)

.32	Fortune-telling by crystals and stones; dowsing; fortune-telling by cards, tea leaves and coffee grounds, oracles and sibyls

.322	Fortune-telling by crystals and stones

Standard subdivisions are added for crystals and stones together, for crystals alone

.323	Dowsing

Location of living and inert substances through human sensitivity to latent radiations and use of divining rods, pendulums, other devices

Class here radiesthesia

> 133.323 2–133.323 7 Location of specific substances

Class comprehensive works in 133.323

.323 2	Location of water
.323 3	Location of metals
.323 7	Location of petroleum and gases
[.323 9]	Telediesthesia (Distant prospection)

Number discontinued; class in 133.323

.324	Fortune-telling by cards, tea leaves and coffee grounds, oracles and sibyls
.324 2	Fortune-telling by cards (Cartomancy)
.324 24	Fortune-telling by tarot
.324 4	Fortune-telling by tea leaves and coffee grounds

Standard subdivisions are added for either or both topics in heading

.324 8	Fortune-telling by oracles and sibyls

Standard subdivisions are added for either or both topics in heading

.33	Symbolic divination

Including divination with *I Ching,* names, runes

For cartomancy, see 133.3242

.333	Geomancy
.333 7	Feng shui
.334	Divinatory signs and omens

Standard subdivisions are added for either or both topics in heading

.335	Numerology
.335 4	Fortune-telling by numbers

Including fortune-telling by birthdays

See also 133.5 for astrology

.335 9	Symbolism of specific numbers

.4   **Demonology and witchcraft**

Class here black arts

> *For divinatory arts, see 133.3*
>
> *See also 299.675 for voodooism*
>
> *See Manual at 133 vs. 200*

.42   Demonology

> *See also 291.216 for religious beliefs about demons*
>
> *See Manual at 133 vs. 200*

.422   Satanism (Devil worship)

> *See also 299 for Satanic cults regarded as religions by their adherents*
>
> *See Manual at 133 vs. 200*

.423   Evil spirits

Including incubi, succubi, vampires, werewolves

.425   The evil eye

.426   Demoniac possession

.427   Exorcism of demons

.43   Magic and witchcraft

Standard subdivisions are added for either or both topics in heading

Class here magicians' manuals, e.g., grimoire; witch hunting

> *For spells, curses, charms, see 133.44*
>
> *See also 291.33 for witchcraft as a religious practice*
>
> *See Manual at 133 vs. 200*

.430 9   Historical, geographic, persons treatment

Class here history of witch crazes

> *See also 306.4 for social analysis of witch crazes*

.44   Spells, curses, charms

Including amulets, mascots, talismans

.442   Love spells and charms

Standard subdivisions are added for either or both topics in heading

.443   Good luck spells and charms

Standard subdivisions are added for either or both topics in heading

.446		Therapeutic spells and charms

Standard subdivisions are added for either or both topics in heading

.5   Astrology

Class here works on the symbolism of astrology

[.501 12]   Forecasting and forecasts

Do not use; class in 133.5

.508 82   History and description with respect to specific religious groups

Do not use for types or schools of astrology originating in or associated with a specific religious group; class in 133.594

Class here astrology in general with respect to specific religious groups

.508 9   History and description with respect to specific racial, ethnic, national groups

Do not use for types or schools of astrology originating in or associated with a specific racial, ethnic, national group; class in 133.593

Class here astrology in general with respect to specific racial, ethnic, national groups

.509   Historical, geographic, persons treatment

.509 3–.509 9   Treatment by specific continents, countries, localities; extraterrestrial worlds

Do not use for types or schools of astrology originating in or associated with a specific area; class in 133.592

Class here astrology in general in a specific area

> 133.52–133.58 Specific aspects of western astrology

Class specific aspects of nonwestern astrology in 133.59; class comprehensive works in 133.5

.52   Signs of the zodiac

Class planets in 133.53

.526   First six signs

.526 2   Aries

.526 3   Taurus

.526 4   Gemini

.526 5   Cancer

.526 6		Leo
.526 7		Virgo
.527		Second six signs
.527 2		Libra
.527 3		Scorpio
.527 4		Sagittarius
.527 5		Capricorn
.527 6		Aquarius
.527 7		Pisces
.53		Planets, sun, moon

> Standard subdivisions are added for planets, sun, moon together; for planets alone
>
> Class here positions of planets

.530 4		Special topics
.530 42		Houses

> Class houses in relation to the zodiac in 133.52

.530 44		Aspects
.531		Sun
.532		Moon
.533		Mercury
.534		Venus
.535		Mars
.536		Jupiter
.537		Saturn
.538		Uranus
.539		Trans-uranian planets, and asteroids
.539 1		Neptune
.539 2		Pluto
.539 8		Asteroids

> Including Chiron

.54 Horoscopes

> Class works that emphasize parts or aspects of horoscopes with the part or aspect, e.g., houses 133.53042; class horoscopes for persons associated with a particular part or aspect of the horoscope with the part or aspect, e.g., horoscopes for Gemini 133.5264

[.540 112] Forecasting and forecasts

> Do not use; class in 133.54

.540 4 Special topics

.540 42 Daily guides and birthday books

.542 Casting horoscopes

.548 Horoscopes of individuals

> Class horoscopes of individuals connected with specific topics in 133.58

.55 Astrological ephemerides

.56 Horary astrology

.58 Application of astrology to specific topics

> Add to base number 133.58 notation 001–999, e.g., medical astrology 133.5861, astrological guides to dating 133.5864677, astrological analysis and prediction about the United States and its leaders 133.58973; however, do not add notation 0112 from Table 1 for forecasts and forecasting

.59 Types or schools of astrology originating in or associated with a specific area; originating in or associated with a specific racial, ethnic, national group; originating in or associated with a specific religion

> Class here nonwestern types or schools of astrology

> Unless other instructions are given, class a subject with aspects in two or more subdivisions of 133.59 in the number coming last, e.g., Hindu astrology in India 133.594450954 (*not* 133.59254)

.592 Types or schools of astrology originating in or associated with a specific area

> Add to base number 133.592 notation 3–9 from Table 2, e.g., Chinese astrology 133.59251

.593 Types or schools of astrology originating in or associated with a specific racial, ethnic, national group

> Add to base number 133.593 notation 1–9 from Table 5, e.g., Aztec astrology 133.59397452

> Class types or schools of astrology originating in or associated with a racial, ethnic, national group in areas where the group predominates in 133.592

.594   Types or schools of astrology originating in or associated with a specific religious group

> Add to base number 133.594 the numbers following —29 in notation 292–299 from Table 7, e.g., Hindu astrology 133.59445

.6   Palmistry

[.601 12]   Forecasting and forecasts

> Do not use; class in 133.6

.8   Psychic phenomena

Class here psi phenomena, psychic communication, psychic talents and gifts; comprehensive works treating extrasensory perception (ESP), spiritualism, and ghosts together

Class comprehensive works on divination in 133.3

For ghosts, see 133.1; for spiritualism, see 133.9

[.801 12]   Forecasting and forecasts

> Do not use; class in 133.8

>   133.82–133.86   Extrasensory perception

Class extrasensory perception of animals in 133.89; class comprehensive works on extrasensory perception in 133.8

.82   Telepathy

.84   Clairvoyance

[.840 112]   Forecasting and forecasts

> Do not use; class in 133.84

.85   Clairaudience

[.850 112]   Forecasting and forecasts

> Do not use; class in 133.85

.86   Precognition

[.860 112]   Forecasting and forecasts

> Do not use; class in 133.86

.88   Psychokinesis

For levitation as a mediumistic phenomenon, see 133.92

.89   Animal magnetism, hypnosis, extrasensory perception of animals, aura

Class interdisciplinary works on animal magnetism in 154.72; class interdisciplinary works on hypnotism in 154.7

For use of hypnosis for past-life recall, see 133.90135

.892   Aura

Including Kirlian photography of aura

Class human aura when scientifically considered in 612.0142

See also 778.3 for photographic aspects of Kirlian photography

.9   Spiritualism

The phenomena and systems of ideas connected with belief in communication with spirits (discarnate beings)

Class here communication with extraterrestrial spirits, necromancy, interdisciplinary works on spirits (discarnate beings)

For ghosts, see 133.1

See also 291.213 for spiritualism as a religious doctrine, 289.9 for spiritualist Christian sects, 292–299 for other spiritualist sects and religions

See Manual at 133 vs. 200

.901   Philosophy and theory

.901 3   Personal survival, nature of spiritual world and life after death

Do not use for value; class in 133.901

See Manual at 133.9013 vs. 129

.901 35   Reincarnation

Including use of hypnosis for past-life recall

Class here personal recollections of previous incarnations

.91   Mediumship

Nature and practice

Class here channeling, psychic experiences of individual mediums

For specific mediumistic phenomena, see 133.92

.92   Specific mediumistic phenomena

Including ectoplasm, levitation, materialization and dematerialization, rapping, spirit photography, table tipping, transportation

For psychic messages, see 133.93

.93   Psychic messages

> Method and content of communications purporting to come from discarnate entities

> Including psychic messages on specific nonreligious topics not provided for in 130–139, e.g., unidentified flying objects (UFOs)

> *For psychic messages on religious subjects, see 200. For messages on a specific subject in paranormal phenomena, see the subject, e.g., messages concerning nature of spiritual world and life after death 133.9013*

.932   Specific methods

> Including automatic writing and utterance; use of audiotapes

.932 5   Ouija board

.95   Astral projection (Out-of-body experience)

[134]   **[Unassigned]**

> Most recently used in Edition 16

135   **Dreams and mysteries**

> Class mysteries of magic and witchcraft in 133.43; class interdisciplinary works on mysteries in the sense of reported phenomena not explained, not fully verified in 001.94

.3   **Dreams**

> Including dream books

> Class interdisciplinary works on psychological and parapsychological aspects of dreams in 154.63

.4   **Rosicrucian, Hermetic, Cabalistic traditions**

> *See also 133.32424 for tarot*

.43   Rosicrucianism

.45   Hermetism

.47   Cabala

> *See also 296.16 for Cabala in Judaism*

[136]   **[Unassigned]**

> Most recently used in Edition 16

137   **Divinatory graphology**

> Class interdisciplinary works on graphology and use of graphology in analyzing character in 155.282

138   Physiognomy

Class here comprehensive works on determination of character or divination from analysis of physical features

For palmistry, see 133.6; for phrenology, see 139

139   Phrenology

Determination of mental capacities from skull structures

140   Specific philosophical schools and viewpoints

Including the concept of ideology, of a world view, of a system of beliefs

Class development, description, critical appraisal, collected writings, biographical treatment of individual philosophers regardless of viewpoint in 180–190; class comprehensive works on modern western and ancient, medieval, Oriental viewpoints in 100; class comprehensive works on modern western viewpoints in 190. Class a specific topic or branch of philosophy treated from a specific philosophical viewpoint with the topic or branch, e.g., existentialist ontology 111, realist epistemology 121; class ideologies concerning a specific discipline with the discipline, e.g., political ideologies 320.5

For ancient, medieval, Oriental schools, see 180

See also 171 for systems and schools of ethics

See Manual at 140; also at 140 vs. 180–190

SUMMARY

141	**Idealism and related systems and doctrines**
142	**Critical philosophy**
143	**Bergsonism and intuitionism**
144	**Humanism and related systems and doctrines**
145	**Sensationalism**
146	**Naturalism and related systems and doctrines**
147	**Pantheism and related systems and doctrines**
148	**Dogmatism, eclecticism, liberalism, syncretism, traditionalism**
149	**Other philosophical systems and doctrines**

141   Idealism and related systems and doctrines

Standard subdivisions are added for idealism and related systems and doctrines together, for idealism alone

Including panpsychism, spiritualism, subjectivism, voluntarism

.2   Modern Platonism and Neoplatonism

Standard subdivisions are added for either or both topics in heading

Class comprehensive works on Platonism in 184; class comprehensive works on Neoplatonism in 186.4

.3   Transcendentalism

.4	**Individualism**
.5	**Personalism**
.6	**Romanticism**

142   Critical philosophy

Class critical realism in 149.2

.3	**Kantianism**

Class here Neo-Kantianism

.7	**Phenomenology**
.78	Existentialism

143   Bergsonism and intuitionism

144   Humanism and related systems and doctrines

Standard subdivisions are added for humanism and related systems and doctrines together, for humanism alone

.3	**Pragmatism**
.5	**Instrumentalism**
.6	**Utilitarianism**

145   Sensationalism

Class here ideology as the system based on analysis of ideas into their sensory elements

Class works that discuss ideology, not as a specific philosophical school, but as systems of beliefs in general in 140

146   Naturalism and related systems and doctrines

Standard subdivisions are added for naturalism and related systems and doctrines together, for naturalism alone

Including dynamism, energism

.3	**Materialism**
.32	Dialectical materialism

Class philosophic foundations of Marxism in 335.4112

See Manual at 335.4112 vs. 146.32

.4   **Positivism (Comtism) and related systems**

Standard subdivisions are added for positivism (Comtism) and related systems together, for positivism (Comtism) alone

Class here comprehensive works on the analytical movement

For linguistic analysis, see 149.94

.42   Logical positivism (Logical empiricism)

.44   Empiricism

.5   **Atomism**

Including logical atomism

.6   **Mechanism**

.7   **Evolutionism and process philosophy**

147   Pantheism and related systems and doctrines

Standard subdivisions are added for pantheism and related systems and doctrines together, for pantheism alone

Including animism, occasionalism, panentheism, parallelism, vitalism

.3   **Monism**

.4   **Dualism and pluralism**

Standard subdivisions are added for either or both topics in heading

148   Dogmatism, eclecticism, liberalism, syncretism, traditionalism

149   Other philosophical systems and doctrines

Including constructivism, deconstruction, objectivism, relativism

.1   **Nominalism and conceptualism**

Standard subdivisions are added for either or both topics in heading

.2   **Realism**

Class here neorealism, critical realism

.3   **Mysticism**

Class occult mysticism in 130; class religious mysticism in 291.422

.5   **Optimism**

Class here meliorism

.6   **Pessimism**

.7   **Rationalism and related systems and doctrines**

Standard subdivisions are added for rationalism and related systems and doctrines together, for rationalism alone

Including innatism, intellectualism, nativism

.72   Agnosticism

.73   Skepticism

.8   **Nihilism**

Class here fatalism

For existentialism, see 142.78

.9   **Other systems and doctrines**

.91   Neo-Aristotelianism, neo-scholasticism, neo-Thomism

Standard subdivisions are added for any or all topics in heading

Class ancient Aristotelianism in 185; class medieval scholasticism, medieval Thomism in 189.4

.94   Linguistic philosophies

Including ordinary language philosophy

Class here general semantics as a school of linguistic philosophy (e.g, the school of Alfred Korzybski)

Class semantics, semiotics as philosophical topics in 121.68; class comprehensive works on the analytical movement in 146.4

See also 302.2 for interdisciplinary works on semiotics; 401 for philosophy of language

See Manual at 401 vs. 121.68, 149.94, 410.1

.96   Structuralism

.97   Postmodernism

Class postmodernism in relation to a specific discipline with the discipline, e.g., in relation to literary criticism 801.95

150   Psychology

Unless other instructions are given, observe the following table of preference, e.g., emotions of children 155.4124 (*not* 152.4):

Aptitude tests	153.94
Comparative psychology	156
Subconscious and altered states and processes	154
Differential and developmental psychology	155
Sensory perception, movement, emotions, physiological drives	152
Conscious mental processes and intelligence (*except* 153.94)	153
Applied psychology	158

Class testing for aptitude in a specific discipline or subject in 153.94; class social psychology in 302

For psychological principles (other than principles of aptitude testing) of a specific discipline or subject, see the discipline or subject, plus notation 019 from Table 1, e.g., psychological principles of advertising 659.1019

See Manual at 302–307 vs. 150, T1—019

SUMMARY

150.1–.9	Standard subdivisions and systems, schools, viewpoints
152	Sensory perception, movement, emotions, physiological drives
153	Conscious mental processes and intelligence
154	Subconscious and altered states and processes
155	Differential and developmental psychology
156	Comparative psychology
158	Applied psychology

.1   Philosophy and theory

.19   Systems, schools, viewpoints

Standard subdivisions are added for any or all topics in heading

See Manual at 152–158 vs. 150.19

.192   Existential, faculty, phenomenological, rational schools

.193   Functionalism

Including dynamic, holistic, hormic, organismic psychologies

.194   Reductionism

.194 3   Behaviorism

.194 32   Watsonian behaviorism

Including systems of Watson, Spranger, Hunter, Lashley

.194 34   Neobehaviorism (Pragmatic reductionism)

Including systems of Guthrie, Hull, Skinner, Tolman

.194 4		Reflexology (Associationism)

Including systems of Pavlov, Bekhterev, Thorndike

For associative learning, see 153.1526

.195   Psychoanalytic systems

See Manual at 616.89 vs. 150.195

.195 2   Freudian system

.195 3   Adlerian system

.195 4   Jungian system

.195 7   Neopsychoanalytic systems

Including systems of Horney, Fromm, Sullivan

.198   Other systems

Including humanistic psychology, transpersonal psychology

.198 2   Gestalt psychology

.198 4   Field theory

.287   Testing and measurement

Class comprehensive works on intelligence testing and personality testing in 153.93

See also 174.915 for ethics of psychological testing

.724   Experimental research

See also 174.915 for the ethics of research in psychology

.8   **History and description with respect to kinds of persons**

Do not use for psychology of specific kinds of persons; class in 155

.9   **Historical, geographic, persons treatment**

Class national psychology of specific countries in 155.89

[151]   [Unassigned]

Most recently used in Edition 16

>   152–158   Specific topics in psychology

Class comprehensive works in 150

See Manual at 152–158 vs. 150.19

152   Sensory perception, movement, emotions, physiological drives

Class here comprehensive works on psychology and neurophysiology of sensory perception, movement, emotions, physiological drives

For neurophysiology of sensory perception, movement, emotions, physiological drives, see 612.8

See Manual at 612.8 vs. 152

SUMMARY

.1   Sensory perception

Class here receptive processes and functions, discrimination, thresholds

For quantitative threshold and discrimination studies, see 152.82

See Manual at 153.7 vs. 152.1

.14   Visual perception

.142   Spatial perception

Class comprehensive works on spatial perception in 153.752

.142 2   Visual acuity

.142 3   Pattern perception

.142 5   Movement perception

Class comprehensive works on movement perception in 153.754

.143   Brightness perception

.145   Color perception

.148   Optical illusions

Including afterimages

Class here interdisciplinary works on optical illusions

For a specific aspect or use of optical illusions, see the aspect or use, e.g., physiological aspects 612.84, use of optical illusions in art 701

.15   Auditory perception

.152   Pitch perception

.154   Volume perception

.157	Timbre perception (Tone discrimination)
.158	Localization
.16	Chemical sensory perception
.166	Perception of smells
.167	Perception of tastes
.18	Other types of sensory perception
.182	Cutaneous (Tactile) perception
.182 2	Thermal perception
.182 3	Pressure perception

> Including perception of vibration

.182 4	Pain perception
[.182 8]	Itch and tickle

> Number discontinued; class in 152.182

.188	Proprioceptive perceptions

> Class here biofeedback

.188 2	Kinesthetic and vestibular perceptions

> Standard subdivisions are added for kinesthetic and vestibular perception together, for kinesthetic perception alone

.188 6	Visceral perceptions

> Including fatigue, hunger, thirst, well-being

.189	Synesthesia
.3	**Movements and motor functions**

> Standard subdivisions are added for either or both topics in heading

> *For reaction-time studies, see 152.83*

.32	Involuntary movements

> Class here automatic movements

> *For habits and habit formation, see 152.33*

.322	Reflexes

> Class comprehensive works on reflexology as a psychological system in 150.1944

.322 3	Innate reflexes
.322 4	Conditioned reflexes

.324		Instinctive movements

For innate reflexes, see 152.3223

.33		Habits and habit formation

Standard subdivisions are added for either or both topics in heading

Class here comprehensive works on habits

For conscious mental habits, see 153

See also 362.29 for substance abuse

.334		Motor learning
.335		Handedness and laterality
.35		Voluntary movements
.38		Special motor functions
.382		Locomotion
.384		Expressive movements

Class meaning of movements (as in body language) in 153.69

See Manual at 153.69 vs. 152.384

.384 2		Vocal expressions
.384 5		Graphic expressions
.385		Coordination
.4		**Emotions and feelings**

Standard subdivisions are added for either or both topics in heading

Including embarrassment, grief, guilt, shame

Class here affects, attitudes, moods, sentiments; complexes of emotions and feelings

Class character traits such as bashfulness in 155.232; class loneliness in 155.92; class grief associated with bereavement by death in 155.937; class depression in 616.8527

.41		Love and affection

Standard subdivisions are added for love and affection together, for love alone

Including empathy

.42		Pleasure, enjoyment, happiness, joy, ecstasy
.43		Wit and humor

Standard subdivisions are added for either or both topics in heading

.46 Fear

Including anxiety, worry

.47 Anger

Including frustration

Class here aggressive moods and feelings

Class comprehensive works on psychology of aggression in 155.232

.48 Jealousy and envy

Standard subdivisions are added for either or both topics in heading

.5 Physiological drives

Class motivation, comprehensive works on drives in 153.8

.8 Quantitative threshold, discrimination, reaction-time studies

.82 Threshold and discrimination studies

Standard subdivisions are added for either or both topics in heading

.83 Reaction-time studies

153 Conscious mental processes and intelligence

Standard subdivisions are added for conscious mental processes and intelligence together, for conscious mental processes alone

Class here cognitive science, intellectual processes

For artificial intelligence, see 006.3; for emotions and feelings, see 152.4

See also 121 for epistemology, 128.2 for mind-body problem in philosophy

See Manual at 153 vs. 006.3: Cognitive science; also at 153 vs. 153.4

SUMMARY

153.1	**Memory and learning**
.2	**Formation and association of ideas**
.3	**Imagination, imagery, creativity**
.4	**Thought, thinking, reasoning, intuition, value, judgment**
.6	**Communication**
.7	**Perceptual processes**
.8	**Will (Volition)**
.9	**Intelligence and aptitudes**

[.028 7] Testing and measurement

Do not use; class in 153.93

.1 Memory and learning

.12   Memory

Class memory with respect to a specific topic with the topic, e.g., memory and dreams 154.63

For types of memory, see 153.13; for mnemonics, see 153.14

.122   Retention

.123   Recall and reproduction

Standard subdivisions are added for either or both topics in heading

.124   Recognition

.125   Forgetting

.13   Types of memory

.132   Visual memory

.133   Auditory memory

.134   Visual-auditory memory

.14   Mnemonics

.15   Learning

See Manual at 153.15 vs. 370.15; also at 155.4–155.6 vs. 153.15

.152   Methods of learning

.152 2   Rote learning, learning by repetition

Standard subdivisions are added for either or both topics in heading

.152 3   Learning by imitation

.152 4   Trial-and-error learning

.152 6   Associative learning

Including Pavlovian (classical) conditioning, operant conditioning

Class comprehensive works on associationism in 150.1944

.152 8   Discrimination learning

.153   Factors in learning

.153 2   Attention and concentration

Standard subdivisions are added for either or both topics in heading

.153 3   Interest and enthusiasm

Standard subdivisions are added for either or both topics in heading

.153 4   Motivation

.154   Transfer of learning

.158	Learning curves

.2 Formation and association of ideas

.22	Association of ideas
.23	Concepts and concept formation

Standard subdivisions are added for either or both topics in heading

For abstraction, see 153.24

.24	Abstraction

.3 Imagination, imagery, creativity

Standard subdivisions are added for imagination, imagery, creativity together; for imagination alone

Class here daydreams, fantasies, reveries considered as aspects of the imagination

Class comprehensive works on daydreams, fantasies, reveries in 154.3

.32	Imagery

Including visualization

.35	Creativity

Class here interdisciplinary works on creativity

For creativity in a specific field, see the field, plus notation 019 from Table 1, e.g., creativity in the arts 700.19

.4 Thought, thinking, reasoning, intuition, value, judgment

Former heading: Cognition (Knowledge)

For formation and association of ideas, see 153.2

See Manual at 153 vs. 153.4

[.402 87]	Testing and measurement

Do not use; class in 153.93

.42	Thought and thinking

Standard subdivisions are added for either or both topics in heading

For reasoning, see 153.43

.43	Reasoning

Class here problem solving

See Manual at 153.43 vs. 160

.432	Inductive reasoning

Including inference

.433	Deductive reasoning
.44	Intuition
.45	Value
.46	Judgment

> *For moral judgment, see 155.232*

.6 **Communication**

Class here individual aspects of interpersonal communication

Class sociolinguistics in 306.44; class psychology of language and language processing (psycholinguistics) in 401.9; class psychology of reading in 418.4019; class social psychology of, interdisciplinary works on communication in 302.2

.68 Listening

Class speech perception in 401.9

.69 Nonverbal communication

Class here body language

> *See Manual at 153.69 vs. 152.384*

.7 **Perceptual processes**

Perceptual apprehension and understanding

> *For extrasensory perception, see 133.82–133.86; for sensory perception, see 152.1*

> *See Manual at 153.7 vs. 152.1*

.73 Basic elements

Including apperception, preperception

> *See also 155.2844 for thematic apperception tests*

.733 Attention

Including looking, listening

.736 Subliminal perception

.74 Errors (Normal illusions)

.75 Types of perception

Including perception of feelings of others

.752 Spatial perception

Class visual spatial perception in 152.142

.753 Time and rhythm perception

.754	Movement perception

Class visual perception of movement in 152.1425

.8 **Will (Volition)**

Including self-control

Class here intentionality, motivation, comprehensive works on drives

For physiological drives, see 152.5

.83 Choice and decision

Standard subdivisions are added for either or both topics in heading

.85 Modification of will

Class here behavior modification and attitude change when reference is to bending the will or changing conscious intent

See also 155.25 for modification of character and personality

.852 Persuasion

.853 Menticide (Brainwashing)

.854 Conformity

.9 **Intelligence and aptitudes**

Class factors in differential and developmental psychology that affect intelligence and aptitudes in 155

[.902 87] Testing and measurement

Do not use; class in 153.93

.93 Intelligence tests

Class here comprehensive works on testing and measurement of cognition, of conscious mental processes, of intelligence and personality

For aptitude tests, see 153.94; for personality tests, see 155.28; for educational tests and measurements, see 371.26; for tests to diagnose neuropsychiatric conditions, see 616.80475

.932 Individual tests

Individually administered tests in which there is interaction between tester and person tested

.932 3 Verbal tests

Class comprehensive works on verbal intelligence tests in 153.9333

.932 4 Nonverbal tests

Class comprehensive works on nonverbal intelligence tests in 153.9334

.933	Group tests

Class here written tests

.933 3	Verbal tests

Class here comprehensive works on verbal intelligence tests

For individual verbal tests, see 153.9323

.933 4	Nonverbal tests

Class here comprehensive works on nonverbal intelligence tests

For individual nonverbal tests, see 153.9324

.94	Aptitude tests

Individual, group, verbal, nonverbal tests for special abilities

Class here vocational interest tests

Class use of aptitude and vocational interest tests for academic prognosis and placement in 371.264; class comprehensive works on vocational interests in 158.6

See also 371.26 for achievement tests and measurements

See Manual at 153.94

.940 001–.940 009	Standard subdivisions
.940 01–.949 99	Tests for aptitudes in specific fields

Add to base number 153.94 notation 001–999, e.g., tests for musical ability 153.9478

.98	Superior intelligence

154   Subconscious and altered states and processes

.2	**The subconscious**
.22	Id, ego, superego
.24	Activities

Including complexes, conflicts, reasoning, sublimation, transference

.3	**Daydreams, fantasies, reveries**

Standard subdivisions are added for any or all topics in heading

Class here secondary consciousness

For daydreams, fantasies, reveries considered as aspects of imagination, see 153.3

.4	**Altered states of consciousness**

Including altered states due to use of drugs; hallucinations

.6   **Sleep phenomena**

> *See Manual at 612.821 vs. 154.6*

.63   Dreams

Class here interdisciplinary works on dreams

> *For parapsychological aspects of dreams, see 135.3; for physiological aspects of dreams, see 612.821*

.632   Types

.634   Analysis

.64   Sleepwalking (Somnambulism)

.7   **Hypnotism**

Class here interdisciplinary works on hypnotism

> *For psychic aspects of hypnotism, see 133.89; for medical applications of hypnotism, see 615.8512*

.72   Animal magnetism

.76   Induction of hypnosis

.77   Hypnotic phenomena

.772   Phenomena during trance

.774   Posthypnotic phenomena

155   Differential and developmental psychology

Including role of play in development

Unless other instructions are given, observe the following table of preference, e.g., reactions of African American school children to catastrophic fires 155.935 (*not* 155.424 or 155.8496073):

Influence of specific situations	155.93
Psychology of specific ages	155.4–155.6
Ethnopsychology and national psychology	155.8
Evolutional psychology	155.7
Environmental psychology (*except* 155.93)	155.9
Sex psychology and psychology of the sexes	155.3
Individual psychology	155.2

Class role of play in relation to a specific topic with the topic, e.g., role of play in child development 155.418

> *See Manual at 155*

SUMMARY

.2   Individual psychology

Including defense mechanisms

Class here the self; character, identity, individuality, personality

Class general application of topics of individual psychology in 158. Class defense mechanisms in relation to a specific topic with the topic, e.g., defense mechanisms and adaptability 155.24, defense mechanisms and reactions to death 155.937

See Manual at 158 vs. 155.2

[.202 87]   Testing and measurement

Do not use; class in 155.28

.22   Individual differences

.23   Traits and determinants of character and personality

.232   Specific traits

Including altruism, bashfulness, dependence, extroversion, introversion, moral judgment, perfectionism, workaholism; comprehensive works on the psychology of aggression

Class interdisciplinary works on aggression, aggressive social interactions in 302.54. Class a specific aspect of a specific trait with the aspect, e.g., development of moral judgment 155.25

For aggressive emotions and feelings, see 152.47; for aggressive drives, see 153.8

.234   Determinants

Class here environment versus heredity as determinants

Class comprehensive works on environment versus heredity in psychology in 155.7

For environmental determinants, see 155.9

.24   Adaptability and adjustment

Standard subdivisions are added for either or both topics in heading

.25   Development and modification of character and personality

Standard subdivisions are added for any or all topics in heading

Including maturity, development of self-control

See also 153.85 for behavior modification and attitude change when reference is to bending the will or changing conscious intent

.26   Typology

.262   Classical typology (Hippocrates' theory of temperaments)

.264   Modern typology

Including classification schemes of James, Jung, Kretschmer, Rorschach, Sheldon, Stern

.28   Appraisals and tests

Standard subdivisions are added for either or both topics in heading

Class use of personality tests to determine vocational interests in 153.94; class use of personality tests to diagnose psychiatric disorders in 616.89075; class comprehensive works on appraisals and tests for intelligence and personality in 153.93

.282   Diagnostic graphology

Class here interdisciplinary works on graphology

For divinatory graphology, see 137; for handwriting analysis for the examination of evidence, see 363.2565; for handwriting analysis for screening of prospective employees, see 658.3112

.283   Inventories and questionnaires

Standard subdivisions are added for either or both topics in heading

.284   Projective techniques

.284 2   Rorschach tests

.284 3   Szondi tests

.284 4   Thematic apperception tests

.3   Sex psychology and psychology of the sexes

.31   Erogeneity and libido

Standard subdivisions are added for either or both topics in heading

.32   Sex and personality

.33   Sex differences

.332   Masculinity

Presumed distinctive characteristics of males, whether overtly sexual or not

.333	Femininity

Presumed distinctive characteristics of females, whether overtly sexual or not

.334	Bisexuality

Class here ambiguity of sexual orientation, display of behavior characteristics of both sexes (androgynous behavior)

Class bisexuality in the sense of sexual relations with the same as well as with the opposite sex in 155.34

.34	Sexual relations

Including heterosexual, homosexual, bisexual relations

Class interdisciplinary works on and social psychology of sexual relations in 306.7

See Manual at 306.7 vs. 155.34

> **155.4–155.6 Psychology of specific ages**

Class here developmental psychology

Class comprehensive works in 155

See Manual at 155.4–155.6 vs. 153.15

.4	**Child psychology**

Through age eleven

Class interdisciplinary works on child development in 305.231

See also 649.1 for child rearing

.41	General topics

Class general topics applied to specific groupings in 155.42–155.45

.412	Sensory perception, movement, emotions, physiological drives

Add to base number 155.412 the numbers following 152 in 152.1–152.8, e.g., emotions of children 155.4124

.413	Conscious mental processes and intelligence

Standard subdivisions are added for conscious mental processes and intelligence together, for conscious mental processes alone

Add to base number 155.413 the numbers following 153 in 153.1–153.9, e.g., intelligence tests for children 155.41393 (*not* 155.4130287); however, for aptitude tests for children, see 153.9400083

.418　　　　　　　Personal-social behavior

Including play, stress

Class socialization in 303.32

.418 028 7　　　　　　Testing and measurement

For personality tests for children, see 155.41828

.418 2　　　　　　Individual psychology

Add to base number 155.4182 the numbers following 155.2 in 155.22–155.28, e.g., moral development 155.41825, personality tests for children 155.41828

>　　　　155.42–155.45　Specific groupings

Unless other instructions are given, observe the following table of preference, e.g., boys aged three to five 155.423 (*not* 155.432):

Exceptional children	155.45
Children by status, type, relationships	155.44
Children in specific age groups	155.42
Children by sex	155.43

Class comprehensive works in 155.4

.42　　　　　　Children in specific age groups

.422　　　　　　Infants

From birth to age two

Class here comprehensive works on children from birth to age five

Add to base number 155.422 the numbers following 155.41 in 155.412–155.418, e.g., infants at play 155.4228

For children three to five, see 155.423

.423　　　　　　Children three to five

Class here preschool children, comprehensive works on children aged two to six or three to seven

Add to base number 155.423 the numbers following 155.41 in 155.412–155.418, e.g., conscious mental processes and intelligence of preschool children 155.4233

For children aged six and seven, see 155.424

.424   Children six to eleven

          Class here comprehensive works on school children to age fourteen

          Add to base number 155.424 the numbers following 155.41 in 155.412–155.418, e.g., personal-social behavior of school children 155.4248

          For young people twelve to fourteen, see 155.5

.43   Children by sex

          Class here sex psychology of children

.432   Boys

.433   Girls

.44   Children by status, type, relationships

          Class here psychology of temporary or permanent separation from parents

.442   The only child

          Class the adopted or foster only child in 155.445; class the institutionalized only child in 155.446

.443   Siblings

          For brothers and sisters of same birth, see 155.444; for adopted and foster children, see 155.445

.444   Brothers and sisters of same birth

          Standard subdivisions are added for either or both topics in heading

.445   Adopted and foster children

.446   Institutionalized children

          Including children raised in communities that serve as collective parents, e.g., kibbutz children

.45   Exceptional children; children distinguished by social and economic levels, by level of cultural development, by racial, ethnic, national origin

          Standard subdivisions are added for all topics in heading together, for exceptional children alone

.451–.455   Exceptional children

          Add to base number 155.45 the numbers following 371.9 in 371.91–371.95, e.g., psychology of gifted children 155.455

          Class comprehensive works on exceptional children in 155.45

.456   Children distinguished by social and economic levels, by level of cultural development

[.456 2]	Upper classes
	Number discontinued; class in 155.456

.456 7   Socially and culturally disadvantaged children

Including wild children ("wolf children")

Class psychoanalytic principles derived in part from study of wild children in 150.195

[.456 75]   Migrant children

Number discontinued; class in 155.4567

.457   **Children distinguished by racial, ethnic, national origins**

.457 001–.457 009   Standard subdivisions

.457 03–.457 9   Specific racial, ethnic, national groups

Add to base number 155.457 notation 03–9 from Table 5, e.g., Japanese children 155.457956, Japanese-American children 155.457956073

.5   **Psychology of young people twelve to twenty**

Comprehensive works on young adults relocated to 155.65

Class vocational tests for young people twelve to twenty in 153.94000835; class interdisciplinary works on development of young people twelve to twenty in 305.2355

.51   General topics

Add to base number 155.51 the numbers following 155.41 in 155.412–155.418, e.g., individual psychology of young people twelve to twenty 155.5182, personality tests for young people twelve to twenty 155.51828; however, for aptitude tests for young people twelve to twenty, see 153.94000835
     Subdivisions are added for young people of specific ages, e.g., cognitive development of sixteen-year-olds 155.513

Class general topics applied to young people twelve to twenty by sex in 155.53

.53   Young people twelve to twenty by sex

Class here sex psychology of young people twelve to twenty

.532   Males twelve to twenty

.533   Females twelve to twenty

.6   **Psychology of adults**

See Manual at 155

| .63 | Adults by sex |

Class adults of either sex by status, type, relationships in 155.64; class adults of either sex in a specific age group in 155.65–155.67

.632	Men
.633	Women
.64	Adults by status, type, relationships

Class adults in a specific age group regardless of status, type, relationship in 155.65–155.67

.642	Single status
.642 2	Men
.642 3	Women
.643	Divorced status
.643 2	Men
.643 3	Women
.644	Widowed status
.644 2	Men
.644 3	Women
.645	Married status
.645 2	Men
.645 3	Women
.646	Parents

Class unmarried parents in 155.642; class divorced parents in 155.643; class widowed parents in 155.644

| .646 2 | Fathers |
| .646 3 | Mothers |

> 155.65–155.67 Adults in specific age groups

Class comprehensive works in 155.6

| .65 | Young adults |

Aged twenty-one and above

Class here comprehensive works on young adults [*formerly* 155.5]

For young people twelve to twenty, see 155.5

| .66 | Persons in middle adulthood |

.67   Persons in late adulthood

.671   General topics

.671 2   Sensory perception, movement, emotions, physiological drives

> Add to base number 155.6712 the numbers following 152 in 152.1–152.8, e.g., emotions in late adulthood 155.67124

.671 3   Conscious mental processes and intelligence

> Standard subdivisions are added for conscious mental processes and intelligence together, for conscious mental processes alone

> Add to base number 155.6713 the numbers following 153 in 153.1–153.9, e.g., learning in late adulthood 155.671315; however, for aptitude tests for persons in late adulthood, see 153.94000846

.671 8   Personal-social behavior

> Including stress

.671 802 87   Testing and measurement

> > Do not use for personality tests for persons in late adulthood; class in 155.671828

.671 82   Individual psychology

> Add to base number 155.67182 the numbers following 155.2 in 155.22–155.28, e.g., personality in late adulthood 155.61825; however, for adaptability of persons in late adulthood, see 155.672

.672   Adaptability and adjustment

> Standard subdivisions are added for either or both topics in heading

> Including psychological aspects of institutional life

> Class here psychological aspects of retirement, change in status

.7   **Evolutional psychology**

> Evolution of basic human mental and psychological characteristics

> Including behavioral genetics

> Class here comprehensive works on environment versus heredity in psychology

> *For environment versus heredity in determining traits of character and personality, see 155.234; for environmental psychology, see 155.9*

> *See also 304.5 for genetic bases of social behavior*

> *See Manual at 302–307 vs. 150, T1—019*

.8 **Ethnopsychology and national psychology**

Standard subdivisions are added for ethnopsychology and national psychology together, for ethnopsychology alone

Class here cross-cultural psychology

Class studies of cultural influence in 155.92

See Manual at 155

.81 Nonliterate peoples

Class nonliterate peoples of specific ethnic groups in 155.82

.82 Racial and ethnic differences

Standard subdivisions are added for either or both topics in heading

Class here ethnopsychology

For psychology of specific racial and ethnic groups, see 155.84

.84 Specific racial and ethnic groups

Add to base number 155.84 notation 03–99 from Table 5, e.g., ethnopsychology of African Americans 155.8496073

See Manual at 155.89 vs. 155.84

.89 National psychology

Add to base number 155.89 notation 3–9 from Table 2, e.g., Italian national psychology 155.8945

Class psychology of specific racial and ethnic groups regardless of national origin in 155.84

See Manual at 155.89 vs. 155.84

.9 **Environmental psychology**

Unless other instructions are given, observe the following table of preference, e.g., the influence of family, friends, and work associates upon persons coping with a loss through death 155.937 (*not* 155.92):

Influence of specific situations	155.93
Influence of clothing	155.95
Influence of restrictive environments	155.96
Influence of injuries, diseases, physical disabilities, disfigurements	155.916
Influence of community and housing	155.94
Influence of social environment	155.92
Influence of physical environment and conditions (*except* 155.916)	155.91

.904 Special topics

.904 2	Stress

Class here works on how to cope with stress

For job stress, see 158.72

.91	Influence of physical environment and conditions

Standard subdivisions are added for either or both topics in heading

.911	Influence of sensory stimuli

Add to base number 155.911 the numbers following 152.1 in 152.14–152.18, e.g., psychology of color 155.91145

Class sensory influences associated with climate in 155.915; class sensory influences on persons with injuries, diseases, physical disabilities, disfigurements in 155.916

.915	Influence of climate

Class influence of climate on persons with injuries, diseases, physical disabilities, disfigurements in 155.916

.916	Influence of injuries, diseases, physical disabilities, disfigurements
.92	Influence of social environment

Including comprehensive works on loneliness, on solitude

Add to base number 155.92 the numbers following 158.2 in 158.24–158.27, e.g., influence of family members, birth order 155.924

For influence of community and housing, see 155.94; for overcoming loneliness, see 158.2

See Manual at 302–307 vs. 155.92, 158.2

.93	Influence of specific situations

Including influence of divorce, loss of job

.935	Catastrophic disasters

Including behavior patterns during bombings, earthquakes, fires, floods, hurricanes

Class catastrophic accidents in 155.936; class death in catastrophic disasters in 155.937

.936	Accidents

Class death in accidents in 155.937

.937	Death and dying

Standard subdivisions are added for either or both topics in heading

Class here reactions to death of others

Class interdisciplinary works on death in 306.9

.94 Influence of community and housing

> Standard subdivisions are added for influence of community and housing together, for influence of community alone

---

> 155.942–155.944 Specific types of communities

Class housing in specific types of communities in 155.945; class comprehensive works in 155.94

.942 Urban communities

.943 Suburban communities

.944 Rural communities

.945 Housing

.95 Influence of clothing

.96 Influence of restrictive environments

.962 Prisons

.963 Submarine structures

.964 Subterranean structures

> Including behavior patterns in caves, mines, tunnels, underground shelters

.965 Aircraft

> Class here aviation psychology

.966 Spacecraft

> Class here space psychology

156 Comparative psychology

Comparison of human psychology and the psychology of other organisms; study of other organisms to elucidate human behavior

Class behavior of nonhuman organisms in 591.5

See Manual at 302–307 vs. 156

> ## 156.2–156.5 Animals

Class habits and behavior patterns of animals in 591.5; class comprehensive works in 156

.2 **Comparative psychology of sensory perception, movement, emotions, physiological drives of animals**

> Add to base number 156.2 the numbers following 152 in 152.1–152.8, e.g., comparative reaction-time studies 156.283

.3 **Comparative conscious mental processes and intelligence of animals**

> Standard subdivisions are added for comparative conscious mental processes and intelligence together, for comparative conscious mental processes alone

> Add to base number 156.3 the numbers following 153 in 153.1–153.9, e.g., comparative learning curves 156.3158

.4 **Comparative subconscious and altered states and processes of animals**

.5 **Comparative differential and developmental psychology of animals**

.9 **Plants**

> Class plant behavior in 575.9

[157] **[Unassigned]**

> Most recently used in Edition 19

158 **Applied psychology**

> Class here application of individual psychology in general; comprehensive works on how to better oneself and how to get along with other people; comprehensive works on psychological and parapsychological or occult techniques for achievement of personal well-being, happiness, success

> Class aptitude and vocational interest tests (both general and applied to specific subjects) in 153.94; class interdisciplinary works on successful living, on management of personal and family living in 646.7; class interdisciplinary works on success in business and other public situations in 650.1. Class specific applications of psychology with the application, e.g., educational guidance and counseling 371.4; class application of a specific branch of psychology (other than individual psychology in general) with the branch, e.g., how to be creative 153.35, use of personality tests for self-knowledge and self-improvement 155.28

> *For parapsychological and occult techniques for achievement of well-being, happiness, success, see 131*

> *See Manual at 158 vs. 155.2*

.1   **Personal improvement and analysis**

         Standard subdivisions are added for either or both topics in heading

         Including personality analysis and improvement

         Class here works intended to make one a better person or to stave off failure, to solve problems or to adjust to a life that does not meet one's expectations; works on specific systems and schools of applied psychology written for persons who wish to be improved or analyzed

         Class works on how to get along with other people in 158.2; class works on specific systems and schools of applied psychology written for advisors and counselors to help them assist others in 158.9; class comprehensive works on how to better oneself and how to get along with other people in 158

         See Manual at 616.86 vs. 158.1, 248.8629, 291.442, 362.29

.12   Personal improvement and analysis through meditation

         Standard subdivisions are added for either or both topics in heading

.125   Transcendental meditation

.128   Meditations

         Class here collections of thoughts for use in meditation

.2   **Interpersonal relations**

         Relations between an individual and other people

         Class here dominance, intimacy; overcoming loneliness; applications of assertiveness training, sensitivity training, transactional analysis

         Class individual aspects of interpersonal communication in 153.6; class interpersonal relations in counseling and interviewing in 158.3; class interpersonal relations in leadership in 158.4; class interpersonal relations in negotiation in 158.5; class social psychology of communication in 302.2; class interactions within groups in 302.3; class comprehensive works on loneliness in 155.92

         See Manual at 302–307 vs. 155.92, 158.2

.24   Interpersonal relations with family members

.25   Interpersonal relations with friends and neighbors

         Standard subdivisions are added for either or both topics in heading

.26   Interpersonal relations with work associates

         See also 158.7 for psychology of work

.27   Interpersonal relationships with strangers

.3   **Counseling and interviewing**

Standard subdivisions are added for counseling and interviewing together, for counseling alone

Class here helping behavior

Class helpfulness as a personality trait in 155.232; class interdisciplinary works on counseling in 361.06. Class counseling in a specific discipline with the discipline, e.g., pastoral counseling 253.5

See Manual at T1—019

.35   Group counseling

.39   Interviewing

Class interviewing in a specific discipline with the discipline, e.g., employee selection interviewing 658.31124

.4   **Leadership**

.5   **Negotiation**

Use of this number for cooperation discontinued; class in 158

.6   **Vocational interests**

Class aptitudes in 153.9; class interdisciplinary works on choice of vocation in 331.702

[.602 87]   Testing and measurement

Do not use; class in 153.94

.7   **Industrial psychology**

Works focusing on the psychology of the individual employee in relation to work or taking a broad view that encompasses the concerns of individual employees, union leaders, management

Class here psychology of work

Class workaholism as a personality trait in 155.232. Class industrial psychology applied to a specific subject outside psychology with the subject, plus notation 019 from Table 1, e.g., psychological principles of personnel management 658.30019

See also 158.26 for psychology of interpersonal relations with work associates

.72   Job stress

.723   Job burnout

.9   **Systems and schools of applied psychology**

Including transactional analysis

Class here works about founders of systems and schools of applied psychology, works about systems and schools of applied psychology written for advisors and counselors to help them assist others with personal improvement or analysis

Dianetics relocated to 299.936

Class works on systems and schools of applied psychology written for persons who wish to be improved or analyzed in 158.1. Class application of systems and schools of applied psychology with the application, e.g., application of transactional analysis to interviewing 158.39

[159]   **[Unassigned]**

Most recently used in Edition 19

160   Logic

Science of reasoning

Including counterfactuals, negation, question, truth tables

Class here modality, propositions

Reference relocated to 121.68

Class psychology of reasoning in 153.43; class symbolic (mathematical) logic in 511.3

See Manual at 153.43 vs. 160

161   Induction

For hypotheses, see 167; for analogy, see 169

162   Deduction

For syllogisms, see 166

[163]   **[Unassigned]**

Most recently used in Edition 16

[164]   **[Unassigned]**

Most recently used in Edition 17

165   Fallacies and sources of error

Standard subdivisions are added for either or both topics in heading

Including contradictions, fictions, paradoxes

166   Syllogisms

167   **Hypotheses**

168   **Argument and persuasion**

Standard subdivisions are added for either or both topics in heading

169   **Analogy**

170   Ethics (Moral philosophy)

Class here ethics of specific subjects and disciplines, interdisciplinary works on social ethics

For religious ethics, see 291.5; for social ethics as a method of social control, see 303.372. For ethics of a specific religion, see the religion, e.g., Christian moral theology 241

See Manual at 170; also at 170 vs. 303.372

SUMMARY

170.1–.9	**Standard subdivisions and special topics**
171	**Ethical systems**
172	**Political ethics**
173	**Ethics of family relationships**
174	**Occupational ethics**
175	**Ethics of recreation, leisure, public performances, communication**
176	**Ethics of sex and reproduction**
177	**Ethics of social relations**
178	**Ethics of consumption**
179	**Other ethical norms**

.4   **Special topics**

.42   Metaethics

Class bases for specific systems in 171

.44   Normative ethics

[.440 8]   History and description with respect to kinds of persons

Do not use; class in 170.8

.8   **History and description with respect to kinds of persons**

[.88]   Occupational and religious groups

Do not use for ethics of occupational groups; class in 174. Do not use for ethics of religious groups; class in 291.5

.92   Persons

See Manual at 170.92 vs. 171

171 Ethical systems

Regardless of time or place

Class a specific topic in ethics, regardless of the system within which it is treated, with the topic in 172–179, e.g., professional ethics 174

See Manual at 170.92 vs. 171

.1 Systems based on authority

.2 Systems based on intuition, moral sense, reason

Including empiricism, existentialism, humanism, natural law, naturalism, stoicism

For systems and doctrines based on conscience, see 171.6

See also 171.7 for systems based on biology, genetics, evolution; 340.112 for natural law in legal theory

.3 Perfectionism

Systems based on self-realization, personal fulfillment

.4 Hedonism

Systems based on achievement of individual pleasure or happiness

.5 Utilitarianism and consequentialism

Standard subdivisions are added for either or both topics in heading

.6 Systems based on conscience

Including casuistry, conflict of duties

.7 Systems based on biology, genetics, evolution, education, social factors

Including communist ethics, relativism, situation ethics, sociobiological ethics

See also 171.2 for systems based on natural law, naturalism

.8 Systems based on altruism

For utilitarianism, see 171.5

.9 Systems based on egoism

For hedonism, see 171.4

> # 172–179 Applied ethics (Social ethics)

Ethics of specific human qualities, relationships, activities

Class comprehensive works in 170

172 Political ethics

.1		**Relation of individuals to the state**

Including civic and political activity, military service, obedience to law, payment of taxes, resistance, revolution, civil war

.2   **Duties of the state**

Duties of government toward citizens, e.g., education, freedom, personal security, welfare; duties of officeholders and officials

Class here justice

.4   **International relations**

Including conduct of foreign affairs, disarmament, espionage

.42   War and peace

Standard subdivisions are added for either or both topics in heading

Including conscientious objection, just war theory, pacifism, ways and means of conducting warfare

Class occupational ethics of military personnel in 174.9355

For civil war, see 172.1

.422   Nuclear weapons and nuclear war

Standard subdivisions are added for either or both topics in heading

173   Ethics of family relationships

Including ethics of marriage, divorce, separation, parent-child relationships, sibling relationships

Class ethics of sex and reproduction in 176

174   Occupational ethics

Class here economic, professional ethics; ethics of work

.1   **Clergy**

See Manual at 174.1

.2   **Medical professions**

Class medical ethics related to human reproduction in 176

.22   Hippocratic oath

.24   Questions of life and death

For euthanasia, see 179.7; for abortion, see 179.76

.25   Innovative procedures

Including genetic engineering, organ transplants

Class comprehensive works on bioethics in 174.957

.26	Economic questions

Including advertising, fee splitting

.28	Experimentation

Class here experimentation on human subjects

For experimentation on animals, see 179.4

.3	**Legal professions**
.4	**Business ethics**

Including industrial espionage

Class here ethics of finance, manufacturing, trade

.6	**Gambling business**

Including lottery management

See also 175 for gambling

.9	**Other professions and occupations**

Add to base number 174.9 notation 09–99 from Table 7, e.g., ethics of genetic engineering 174.957; however, for ethics of public administration and public office, see 172.2

175 Ethics of recreation, leisure, public performances, communication

Including ethics of dancing, gambling, music, television; fair play, sportsmanship

Ethics of hunting relocated to 179.3

Class occupational ethics for those involved in the recreation industry with the industry in 174, e.g., occupational ethics for professional athletes 174.9796

[.1–.9]	**Ethics of specific types of recreation**

Numbers discontinued; class in 175

176 Ethics of sex and reproduction

Including artificial insemination, celibacy, chastity, contraception, embryo transplant, homosexuality, premarital and extramarital relations, promiscuity, surrogate motherhood

Class abortion in 179.76

See also 177.65 for ethics of courtship, 177.7 for ethics of love

.5	**Prostitution**
.7	**Obscenity and pornography**

Standard subdivisions are added for either or both topics in heading

For obscenity and pornography in literature, see 176.8; for obscenity in speech, see 179.5

.8 **Obscenity and pornography in literature**

Standard subdivisions are added for either or both topics in heading

177 Ethics of social relations

Limited to the topics provided for below

.1 **Courtesy, hospitality, politeness**

Class etiquette in 395

.2 **Conversation**

Including gossip

.3 **Truthfulness, lying, slander, flattery**

.4 **Personal appearance**

Including exposure of person, ostentatious dress

.5 **Slavery and discriminatory practices**

Standard subdivisions are added for either or both topics in heading

.6 **Friendship and courtship**

.62 Friendship

.65 Courtship

Class sexual ethics in courtship in 176

.7 **Love**

Including benevolence, caring, charity, kindness, liberality, philanthropy

See also 128.46 for love as human experience

178 Ethics of consumption

Including abstinence, gluttony, greed, overindulgence, temperance

Class here use of natural resources, of wealth

Class environmental and ecological ethics, respect for nature in 179.1; class consumption of meat in 179.3

.1 **Consumption of alcoholic beverages**

.7 **Consumption of tobacco**

.8 **Consumption of narcotics**

179 Other ethical norms

Class here cruelty

[.01–.09] Standard subdivisions

Do not use; class in 170

.1   **Respect for life and nature**

Standard subdivisions are added for either or both topics in heading

Class here environmental and ecological ethics

For ethics of consumption, see 178; for treatment of animals, see 179.3; for respect for human life, see 179.7

.2   **Treatment of children**

For parent-child relationships, see 173

.3   **Treatment of animals**

Including ethics of hunting [*formerly* 175], vegetarianism

For experimentation on animals, see 179.4

.4   **Experimentation on animals**

Including vivisection

.5   **Blasphemy, profanity, obscenity in speech**

Standard subdivisions are added for any or all topics in heading

.6   **Courage and cowardice**

.7   **Respect and disrespect for human life**

Standard subdivisions are added for either or both topics in heading

Including capital punishment, dueling, euthanasia, genocide, homicide, suicide

Class here comprehensive works on ethics of violence, of nonviolence

Class medical ethics in 174.2; class ethics of contraception in 176

For ethics of violence, of nonviolence in political activity, see 172; for ethics of civil war, see 172.1; for ethics of war, see 172.42; for treatment of children, see 179.2

.76   Abortion

.8   **Vices, faults, failings**

Not otherwise provided for

Including anger, cheating, covetousness, envy, hatred, jealousy, pride, sloth

.9   **Virtues**

Not otherwise provided for

Including cheerfulness, gentleness, gratitude, honesty, humility, modesty, patience, prudence, self-control, self-reliance, toleration

Class here virtue

> ## 180–190   Historical, geographic, persons treatment of philosophy

Class here development, description, critical appraisal, collected writings, biographical treatment of individual philosophers regardless of viewpoint

Class comprehensive works on geographic treatment in 100; class comprehensive works on historical treatment in 109; class comprehensive works on collected persons treatment in 109.2. Class critical appraisal of an individual philosopher's thought on a specific topic with the topic, plus notation 092 from Table 1, e.g., critical appraisal of Kant's theory of knowledge 121.092

See Manual at 140 vs. 180–190; also at 180–190

180   Ancient, medieval, Oriental philosophy

SUMMARY

180.01–.09	**Standard subdivisions of ancient, medieval, Oriental philosophy**
.1–.9	**Standard subdivisions of ancient philosophy**
181	**Oriental philosophy**
182	**Pre-Socratic Greek philosophies**
183	**Sophistic, Socratic, related Greek philosophies**
184	**Platonic philosophy**
185	**Aristotelian philosophy**
186	**Skeptic and Neoplatonic philosophies**
187	**Epicurean philosophy**
188	**Stoic philosophy**
189	**Medieval western philosophy**

.01–.09   Standard subdivisions of ancient, medieval, Oriental philosophy

.1–.8   Standard subdivisions of ancient philosophy

.9   Historical and geographic treatment of ancient philosophy

Do not use for ancient Oriental philosophy; class in 181

Class treatment of specific schools of ancient western philosophy in 182–188

[.938]   Greece

Number discontinued; class in 180

181   Oriental philosophy

Ancient, medieval, modern

.001–.008   Standard subdivisions

.009   Historical treatment

Do not use for geographic treatment; class in 181.1–181.9

.04–.09   Philosophies based on specific religions

> Add to base number 181.0 the numbers following 29 in 294–299, e.g., Jewish philosophy 181.06, comprehensive works on Islamic philosophy 181.07; however, for Confucian philosophy, see 181.112; for Taoist philosophy, see 181.114; for Hindu-Brahmanical philosophy, see 181.41–181.48

> *For Christian philosophy, see 190. For an individual Islamic philosopher associated with a specific area, see the area, e.g., Arabia 181.92*

> *See Manual at 200 vs. 100*

\>   **181.1–181.9   Philosophy of specific places**

> Class comprehensive works in 181

> (Option: To give local emphasis and a shorter number to philosophy of a specific country, use one of the following:

> (Option A: Place it first by use of a letter or other symbol, e.g., philosophy of Lebanon 181.L [preceding 181.1]

> (Option B: Class it in 181.1; in that case class comprehensive works on philosophy of Far East and South Asia in 181.9)

.1   ***Far East and South Asia**

> *For philosophy of India, see 181.4*

> (Option: To give local emphasis and a shorter number to philosophy of a specific country, class it in this number; in that case class comprehensive works on philosophy of the Far East and South Asia in 181.9)

.11   ***China and Korea**

> Standard subdivisions are added for China and Korea together, for China alone

---

\>   181.112–181.115   Schools of Chinese philosophy

> Class Buddhist philosophy in 181.043; class comprehensive works in 181.11

.112   †Confucian philosophy

> Including Neo-Confucian philosophy

> Class here interdisciplinary works on Confucianism [*formerly* 299.512], the Four Books of Confucius

> Class the Five Confucian Classics in 299.51282

.114   †Taoist philosophy

*Do not add notation 09 from Table 1
†Do not add notation 092 from Table 1

.115	†Mohist, Dialecticianist, Legalist philosophies
.119	*Korea
.12	*Japan

Class Shinto philosophy in 181.09561

.15	*Pakistan and Bangladesh
.16	*Indonesia
.17	*Philippines
.19	*Southeast Asia

Add to base number 181.19 the numbers for countries only following —59 in notation 591–597 from Table 2, e.g., philosophy of Thailand 181.193; however, do not add notation 09 from Table 1 for historical, geographic, persons treatment

For Indonesia, see 181.16; for Philippines, see 181.17

.2 ***Egypt**

.3 ***Palestine Israel**

Class Jewish philosophy in 181.06

.4 ***India**

Class here Hindu-Brahmanical philosophy

Class Buddhist philosophy in 181.043; class Jainist philosophy in 181.044

See also 181.15 for philosophy of Pakistan and Bangladesh

.41	†Sankhya
.42	†Mimamsa
.43	†Nyaya
.44	†Vaiśeṣika
.45	†Yoga

Class here interdisciplinary works on the practice of yoga and yoga as a philosophical school

For yoga as a religious and spiritual discipline, see 291.436; for Hindu yoga as a religious and spiritual discipline, see 294.5436; for physical yoga (hatha yoga), see 613.7046

.452	†Patañjali's philosophy
.46	†Lokāyata

Class here Cārvāka school, Indian materialism

*Do not add notation 09 from Table 1
†Do not add notation 092 from Table 1

.48	†Vedanta
.482	†Śaṅkarācārya (Advaita)
.483	†Rāmānujāchārya (Viśiṣṭādvaita)
.484	†Dualistic school
.484 1	†Madhvāchārya (Dvaita)
.484 2	†Bhedabheda
.484 3	†Nimbarka (Dvaitādvaita)
.484 4	†Vallabhācārya (Śuddhādvaita)

.5   *Iran (Persia)

.6   *Iraq

Class here Assyria, Babylonia, Chaldea, ancient Mesopotamia

.8   *Syria and Lebanon

Including ancient Phoenicia

.9   *Philosophy of other areas of Orient

Including former Soviet Asia, Arabic North Africa other than Egypt

.92   *Arabia

Class here individual Arabian Islamic philosophers

Class Islamic philosophy not limited to one country in 181.07. Class an individual Islamic philosopher associated with another area with the area, e.g., Persia 181.5

>   **182–188   Ancient western philosophy**

Class comprehensive works in 180

182   †Pre-Socratic Greek philosophies

.1   †Ionic philosophy

.2   †Pythagorean philosophy

.3   †Eleatic philosophy

.4   †Heraclitean philosophy

.5   †Empedoclean philosophy

.7   †Democritean philosophy

.8   †Anaxagorean philosophy

*Do not add notation 09 from Table 1
†Do not add notation 092 from Table 1

183   †Sophistic, Socratic, related Greek philosophies

.1   †Sophistic philosophy

.2   †Socratic philosophy

.4   †Cynic philosophy

.5   †Cyrenaic philosophy

.6   †Megaric philosophy

.7   †Elian and Eretrian philosophies

184   †Platonic philosophy

> Class here comprehensive works on ancient and modern Platonism
>
> *For modern Platonism, see 141.2*

185   †Aristotelian philosophy

> Class here comprehensive works on Aristotelian and Neo-Aristotelian philosophy
>
> *For Neo-Aristotelianism, see 149.91*

186   †Skeptic and Neoplatonic philosophies

.1   †Pyrrhonic philosophy

.2   †New Academy

.3   †Eclectic philosophy

.4   †Neoplatonic philosophy

> Class here Alexandrian philosophy, comprehensive works on ancient and modern Neoplatonism
>
> *For modern Neoplatonism, see 141.2*

187   †Epicurean philosophy

188   †Stoic philosophy

189   *Medieval western philosophy

> Class here early Christian philosophy

.2   †Patristic philosophy

.4   †Scholastic philosophy

> *For neo-scholasticism, neo-Thomism, see 149.91*

.5   †Mystic philosophy

---

*Do not add notation 09 from Table 1

†Do not add notation 092 from Table 1

190 Modern western and other non-Oriental philosophy

Class here comprehensive works on Christian philosophy, on modern philosophy, on modern western philosophy, on western philosophy, on European philosophy

Modern philosophy of areas not provided for in 180 is classed here, even if not in the western tradition, e.g., North American native philosophy 191.08997, traditional African philosophy 199.6

Class Oriental philosophy in 181

> *For ancient western and European philosophy, see 180; for early and medieval Christian philosophy, medieval western and European philosophy, see 189*

> *See Manual at 190 vs. 100, 109*

(Option: To give local emphasis and a shorter number to philosophy of a specific country, use one of the following:

(Option A: Place it first by use of a letter or other symbol, e.g., philosophy of Mexico 19M [preceding 191]

(Option B: Class it in 191; in that case class philosophy of United States and Canada in 199.7)

[.94–.99]   Treatment by continent, country, locality

> Do not use; class in 191–199

191 *United States and Canada

Standard subdivisions are added for either or both topics in heading

Class here North American philosophy

> *For Middle American and Mexican philosophy, see 199.72*

(Option: To give local emphasis and a shorter number to philosophy of a specific country, class it in this number; in that case class philosophy of United States and Canada in 199.7)

192 *British Isles

193 *Germany and Austria

Standard subdivisions are added for either or both topics in heading

194 *France

195 *Italy

196 *Spain and Portugal

.1   *Spain

.9   *Portugal

*Do not add notation 09 from Table 1

197 *Former Soviet Union

Class philosophy of former Soviet Asia in 181.9

198 *Scandinavia

.1 *Norway

.5 *Sweden

.8 *Finland

.9 *Denmark

199 *Other geographic areas

Add to base number 199 notation 4–9 from Table 2 for continent or country only, e.g., Mexican philosophy 199.72; however, do not add notation 09 from Table 1 for historical, geographic, persons treatment; for Asian philosophy, see 181; for European philosophy, see 190; for comprehensive works on North American philosophy, see 191

*Do not add notation 09 from Table 1

200 Religion

Beliefs, attitudes, practices of individuals and groups with respect to the ultimate nature of existences and relationships within the context of revelation, deity, worship

Including public relations for religion [*formerly* 659.292]

Comprehensive works on Christianity relocated to 230

Class comparative religion, works dealing with various religions in 291. Class public relations for a specific religion or aspect of a religion with the religion or aspect, e.g., local Christian church 254.4

> *See also 306.6 for sociology of religion*
>
> *See Manual at 133 vs 200; also at 200 vs. 100*

(Option: To give preferred treatment or shorter numbers to a specific religion other than Christianity, use one of the five options described at 292–299)

SUMMARY

200.1–.9	**Standard subdivisions of religion**
210	**Philosophy and theory of religion**
.1	**Theory of philosophy of religion**
211	**Concepts of God**
212	**Existence, knowability, attributes of God**
213	**Creation**
214	**Theodicy**
215	**Science and religion**
218	**Humankind**
220	**Bible**
.01–.09	**Standard subdivisions and special topics**
.1–.9	**Generalities**
221	**Old Testament (Tanakh)**
222	**Historical books of Old Testament**
223	**Poetic books of Old Testament**
224	**Prophetic books of Old Testament**
225	**New Testament**
226	**Gospels and Acts**
227	**Epistles**
228	**Revelation (Apocalypse)**
229	**Apocrypha, pseudepigrapha, intertestamental works**

230	Christianity Christian theology	
.002–.007	Standard subdivisions of Christianity	
.01–.09	Standard subdivisions and specific types of Christian theology	
.1–.9	Doctrines of specific denominations and sects	
231	God	
232	Jesus Christ and his family Christology	
233	Humankind	
234	Salvation (Soteriology) and grace	
235	Spiritual beings	
236	Eschatology	
238	Creeds, confessions of faith, covenants, catechisms	
239	Apologetics and polemics	
240	Christian moral and devotional theology	
241	Moral theology	
242	Devotional literature	
243	Evangelistic writings for individuals and families	
246	Use of art in Christianity	
247	Church furnishings and related articles	
248	Christian experience, practice, life	
249	Christian observances in family life	
250	Local Christian church and Christian religious orders	
.1–.9	Standard subdivisions	
251	Preaching (Homiletics)	
252	Texts of sermons	
253	Pastoral office and work (Pastoral theology)	
254	Parish administration	
255	Religious congregations and orders	
259	Pastoral care of families, of specific kinds of persons	
260	Christian social and ecclesiastical theology	
.9	Historical, geographic, persons treatment	
261	Social theology and interreligious relations and attitudes	
262	Ecclesiology	
263	Days, times, places of religious observance	
264	Public worship	
265	Sacraments, other rites and acts	
266	Missions	
267	Associations for religious work	
268	Religious education	
269	Spiritual renewal	
270	Historical, geographic, persons treatment of Christianity Church history	
.01–.09	Standard subdivisions	
.1–.8	Historical periods	
271	Religious congregations and orders in church history	
272	Persecutions in general church history	
273	Doctrinal controversies and heresies in general church history	
274–279	Treatment by continent, country, locality	

154

280	Denominations and sects of Christian church
.01–.09	Standard subdivisions and special topics
.2–.4	Branches
281	Early church and Eastern churches
282	Roman Catholic Church
283	Anglican churches
284	Protestant denominations of Continental origin and related bodies
285	Presbyterian churches, Reformed churches centered in America, Congregational churches
286	Baptist, Disciples of Christ, Adventist churches
287	Methodist churches; churches related to Methodism
289	Other denominations and sects

290	Comparative religion and religions other than Christianity
291	Comparative religion
292	Classical (Greek and Roman) religion
293	Germanic religion
294	Religions of Indic origin
295	Zoroastrianism (Mazdaism, Parseeism)
296	Judaism
297	Islam, Babism, Bahai Faith
299	Other religions

.1   Systems, value, scientific principles, psychology of religion

Philosophy and theory of religion relocated to 210

.11   Systems [*formerly also* 210.11, 291.011]

[.12]   Classification

Relocated to 291.14

.13   Value [*formerly also* 210.13, 291.013]

[.14]   Language and communication

Relocated to 210.14

.15   Scientific principles [*formerly also* 210.15, 291.015]

Class philosophic treatment of the relation of science and religion in 215

.19   Psychology of religion

Class here psychological principles [*formerly also* 210.19, 291.019]

.2–.3   Standard subdivisions [*formerly also* 291.02–291.03]

.5   Serial publications [*formerly also* 291.05]

[.6]   Organizations

Relocated to 291.65

[.68]   Management

Relocated to 291.6

.7   Education, research, related topics [*formerly also* 291.07]

.71 Education

Class here religion as an academic subject

Class religious education for the purpose of encouraging believers in religious life and practice, comprehensive works on religious education in 291.75

See also 379.28 for place of religion in public schools

See Manual at 291.75 vs. 200.71

.8 **History and description with respect to kinds of persons [*formerly also* 291.08]**

.9 **Historical, geographic, persons treatment [*formerly also* 291.09]**

See Manual at 200.9 vs. 294, 299.5

.92 Persons

See Manual at 200.92 and 291–299

[201] Philosophy and theory of Christianity

Relocated to 230.01

[202–203]Standard subdivisions of Christianity

Relocated to 230.002–230.003

[204] Special topics

Provision discontinued because without meaning in context

[.5] Christian mythology

Relocated to 230

[205] Serial publications of Christianity

Relocated to 230.005

[206] Organizations of Christianity

Relocated to 260

[207] Education, research, related topics of Christianity

Relocated to 230.007

[.1] Education

Relocated to 230.071

[.4–.9] Higher education in specific continents, countries, localities in modern world

Relocated to 230.07114–230.07119

[208] **Christianity with respect to kinds of persons**

Relocated to 270.08

[209] **Historical, geographic, persons treatment of Christianity**

Relocated to 270

210 Philosophy and theory of religion [*formerly* 200.1, 291.01]

Religious beliefs and attitudes attained through observation and interpretation of evidence in nature, through speculation, through reasoning, but not through revelation or appeal to authoritative scriptures

Class here natural theology, philosophical theology

Class a specific topic treated with respect to religions based on revelation or authority with the topic in 291, e.g., concepts of God in world religions 291.211; class a specific topic with respect to a specific religion with the religion, e.g., Christian concepts of God 231

(Option: To give local emphasis and a shorter number to a specific religion other than Christianity, class it in this number, and add to base number 21 the numbers following the base number for that religion in 292–299, e.g., Hinduism 210, Mahabharata 219.23; in that case class philosophy and theory of religion in 200, its subdivisions 211–218 in 201–208, standard subdivisions of religion in 200.01–200.09. Other options are described at 292–299)

.1 **Theory of philosophy of religion**

Including methodology of the philosophy of religion

[.11] Systems

Relocated to 200.11

[.12] Classification

Relocated to 291.14

[.13] Value

Relocated to 200.13

.14 Language and communication of religion [*formerly also* 200.14, 291.014]

[.15] Scientific principles

Relocated to 200.15

[.19] Psychological principles

Relocated to 200.19

211 Concepts of God

Including anthropomorphism

Class here comprehensive works on God, on The Holy

For existence, knowability, attributes of God, miracles, see 212

.2 Pantheism

.3 Theism

For pantheism, see 211.2

.32 Polytheism

.33 Dualism

.34 Monotheism

.4 Rationalism (Free thought)

.5 Deism

.6 Humanism and secularism

Standard subdivisions are added for either or both topics in heading

.7 Agnosticism and skepticism

Standard subdivisions are added for either or both topics in heading

.8 Atheism

212 Existence, knowability, attributes of God

Including miracles

.1 Existence

Including proofs

.6 Knowability

Class proofs in 212.1

.7 Attributes

Including love, omniscience

213 Creation

Including creation of life and human life, evolution versus creation, evolution as method of creation

See Manual at 231.7652 vs. 213, 500, 576.8

214 Theodicy

Vindication of God's justice and goodness in permitting existence of evil and suffering

Class here good and evil [*formerly* 216]

.8 Providence

215 Science and religion

Including technology and religion

Class religion and scientific theories of creation in 213

See also 261.55 for Christianity and science, 291.175 for various religions and science

[.1] Mathematics

Number discontinued; class in 215

.2 Astronomy

Including cosmology

[.24–.25] Life on other worlds and space flight

Numbers discontinued; class in 215

.3 Physics

[.4–.5] Chemistry and geology

Numbers discontinued; class in 215

[.6] Paleontology

Relocated to 215.7

.7 Life sciences

Including paleontology [*formerly* 215.6]

Class evolution versus creation, evolution as method of creation in 213

[.72–.74] Anthropology, ethnology, biology, natural history

Numbers discontinued; class in 215.7

[.8–.9] Archaeology and technology

Numbers discontinued; class in 215

[216] Good and evil

Relocated to 214

[217] [Unassigned]

Most recently used in Edition 18

218   Humankind

Including immortality

For creation of humankind, human evolution, see 213

[219]   Unassigned

Most recently used in Edition 19

220   Bible

Holy Scriptures of Judaism and Christianity

Class Christian Biblical theology in 230.041; class Biblical precepts in Christian codes of conduct in 241.52–241.54; class Jewish Biblical theology in 296.3; class Biblical precepts in Jewish codes of conduct in 296.36

See Manual at 220: Biblical theology

(If option A under 292–299 is chosen, class here sources of the specified religion; class Bible in 298)

SUMMARY

220.01–.09	**Standard subdivisions and special topics**
.1–.9	**Generalities**
221	**Old Testament (Tanakh)**
222	**Historical books of Old Testament**
223	**Poetic books of Old Testament**
224	**Prophetic books of Old Testament**
225	**New Testament**
226	**Gospels and Acts**
227	**Epistles**
228	**Revelation (Apocalypse)**
229	**Apocrypha, pseudepigrapha, intertestamental works**

.01–.02   Standard subdivisions

[.03]   Dictionaries, encyclopedias, concordances

> Do not use for dictionaries and encyclopedias; class in 220.3. Do not use for concordances; class in 220.4–220.5

.04   Special topics

.046   Apocalyptic passages

> Class apocalyptic passages in a book or group of books with the book or group of books, plus notation 0046 from add table under 221–229, e.g., apocalyptic passages in the prophets 224.0046, in Book of Daniel 224.50046

> *For Revelation (Apocalypse), see 228*

.05–.08   Standard subdivisions

.09 Historical, geographic, persons treatment of Bible

Class the canon in 220.12

For geography, history, chronology, persons of Bible lands in Bible times, see 220.9

> **220.1–220.9 Generalities**

Class comprehensive works in 220. Class generalities applied to a specific part of the Bible with the part, plus notation 01–09 from add table under 221–229, e.g., a commentary on Job 223.107

SUMMARY

220.1	Origins and authenticity
.3	Encyclopedias and topical dictionaries
.4	Original texts, early versions, early translations
.5	Modern versions and translations
.6	Interpretation and criticism (Exegesis)
.7	Commentaries
.8	Nonreligious subjects treated in the Bible
.9	Geography, history, chronology, persons of Bible lands in Bible times

.1 **Origins and authenticity**

.12 Canon

Class here selection of the books accepted as Holy Scripture

.13 Inspiration

The Bible as revelation (word of God)

Including authority of Bible

.132 Inerrancy

.15 Biblical prophecy and prophecies

Class Christian messianic prophecies in 232.12; class Christian eschatological prophecies in 236; class Jewish messianic and eschatological prophecies in 296.33

See also 224 for prophetic books of Old Testament

.3 **Encyclopedias and topical dictionaries**

For dictionaries of specific texts, see 220.4–220.5

> ### 220.4–220.5 Texts, versions, translations

Class here critical appraisal of language and style; concordances, indexes, dictionaries of specific texts; complete texts; selections from more than one part; paraphrases

Class texts accompanied by commentaries in 220.77; class comprehensive works in 220.4. Class selections compiled for a specific purpose with the purpose, e.g., selections for daily meditations 242.2

.4 Original texts, early versions, early translations

Class here original texts accompanied by modern translations, comprehensive works on texts and versions

For modern versions and translations, see 220.5

.404 Textual criticism and word studies

.404 6 Textual (Lower) criticism

Use of scientific means to ascertain the actual original texts

.404 7 Theological studies of words or phrases

> ### 220.42–220.49 Texts in specific languages

Add to each subdivision identified by † the numbers following 220.404 in 220.4046–220.4047, regardless of specific version, e.g., textual criticism of Bible in Latin, of Vulgate 220.476, of Old Testament in Greek, of Septuagint 221.486

Class comprehensive works in 220.4

.42 †Aramaic versions

.43 †Syriac versions

.44 †Hebrew version

.45 †Samaritan versions

.46 Other Semitic language versions

Including Arabic, Ethiopic

.47 †Latin versions

.48 †Greek versions

.49 Other early versions

Including Armenian, Coptic

.5 Modern versions and translations

†Add as instructed under 220.42–220.49

.51	Polyglot

.52   Versions in English and Anglo-Saxon

Standard subdivisions are added for versions in English and Anglo-Saxon, for English alone

Works containing translations in English and one other modern language are classed with the other language in 220.53–220.59

.520 01–.520 09   Standard subdivisions

> 220.520 1–220.520 9 English

Add to each subdivision identified by * as follows:
01–02	Standard subdivisions
[03]	Dictionaries, encyclopedias, concordances
	Do not use; class in 3
05–08	Standard subdivisions
09	Geographic and persons treatment
	Do not use for historical treatment of the translation; class in 8
2	Standard editions
3	Concordances, indexes, dictionaries
4	Special editions
	Including annotated editions, study editions, editions notable for illustrations
6	Selections
7	Paraphrases
8	History, criticism, explanation of the translation

Class comprehensive works in 220.52

.520 1   English versions before 1582

Including Coverdale, Tyndale, Wycliffe versions

.520 2   *Douay version

Class here Rheims-Douay, Rheims-Douay-Challoner versions

See also 220.5205 for Confraternity-Douay-Challoner version

.520 3   *Authorized (King James) version

.520 4   Revised version

Including English Revised (1881–1885), American Revised (American Standard) (1901) versions

.520 42   *Revised Standard version (1946–1957)

.520 43   *New Revised Standard version (1990)

---

*Add as instructed under 220.5201–220.5209

.520 5	*Confraternity Bible and New American Bible

Class here Confraternity-Douay-Challoner version

Subdivisions are added for either or both topics in heading

See also 220.5202 for Rheims-Douay, Rheims-Douay-Challoner versions

.520 6	*New English Bible and Revised English Bible

Subdivisions are added for either or both topics in heading

.520 7	*Jerusalem Bible and New Jerusalem Bible

Subdivisions are added for either or both topics in heading

.520 8	Other English translations since 1582

Including New King James, New Century versions

For translations by individuals, see 220.5209

.520 81	*New International Version
.520 82	*Today's English Bible (Good News Bible)
.520 83	*Living Bible
.520 9	Translations by individuals

Including Goodspeed, Knox, Moffatt, Phillips

.529	Anglo-Saxon
.53–.59	Versions in other languages

Add to base number 220.5 notation 3–9 from Table 6, e.g., the Bible in German 220.531

Works containing translations in two modern languages other than English are classed with the language coming later in Table 6; in more than two modern languages in 220.51

.6	**Interpretation and criticism (Exegesis)**

Class Christian meditations based on Biblical passages and intended for devotional use in 242.5; class material about the Bible intended for use in preparing Christian sermons in 251; class Christian sermons based on Biblical passages in 252; class material about the Bible for preparation of Jewish sermons and texts of Jewish sermons in 296.47; class Jewish meditations based on Biblical passages and intended for devotional use in 296.72

For textual (lower) criticism, see 220.4046; for commentaries, see 220.7

.601	Philosophy and theory

Class here hermeneutics

.61	General introductions to the Bible

Including isagogics (introductory studies prior to actual exegesis)

*Add as instructed under 220.5201–220.5209

.64	Symbolism and typology

.64 Symbolism and typology

> Standard subdivisions are added for either or both topics in heading

> Class here interpretation of specific symbols

.65 Harmonies

.66 Literary criticism

> Literary examination of the text in order to reach conclusions about its meaning, structure, authorship, date

> Class here higher criticism, internal criticism, redaction criticism

> Class language and style of specific texts in 220.4–220.5

> *See also 809.93522 for the Bible as literature*

.663 Form criticism

> Analysis of preliterary or oral forms and traditions in Biblical text

.67 Historical criticism

> Interpretation of texts in light of the cultural, historical, religious, social milieu in which written

> Class form criticism in 220.663

.68 Mythological, allegorical, numerical, astronomical interpretations

> Including mythology in the Bible, demythologizing

.7 Commentaries

> Criticism and interpretation arranged in textual order

.77 Commentaries with text

.8 Nonreligious subjects treated in Bible

> Class a religious subject treated in Bible with the specific religion and topic, e.g., Christian theology 230, Jewish theology 296.3

.800 01–.800 09 Standard subdivisions

.800 1–.899 9 Specific nonreligious subjects

> Add to base number 220.8 notation 001–999, e.g., natural sciences in Bible 220.85; however, for geography, history, chronology, persons of Bible lands in Bible times, see 220.9

.9 Geography, history, chronology, persons of Bible lands in Bible times

> Class general history of Bible lands in ancient world in 930

.91 Geography

> Class here description and civilization

> Class civilization treated separately from geography in 220.95

| .92 | Collected persons |

Class an individual person with the part of the Bible in which the person is chiefly considered, e.g., Abraham 222.11092

See Manual at at 220.92; also at 230–280: Biography

.93   Archaeology (Material remains)

.95   History

Including civilization treated separately from geography

Class geographic description and civilization treated together in 220.91

.950 01–.950 09   Standard subdivisions

.950 5   Bible stories retold

Including picture books

> ## 221–229   Specific parts of Bible, Apocrypha, pseudepigrapha, intertestamental works

Add to each subdivision identified by * as follows (subdivisions from this table may be added for a part of any work that has its own number):

001–08   Standard subdivisions and generalities
Add to 0 the numbers following 220 in 220.01–220.8, e.g., interpretation of the work or of a part of the work 06

09   Geography, history, chronology, persons
Add to 09 the numbers following 221.9 in 221.91–221.95, e.g., biography 092

Class comprehensive works in 220

221   Old Testament (Tanakh)

Holy Scriptures of Judaism, Old Testament of Christianity

Class Jewish Biblical theology in 296.3; class Biblical precepts in Jewish codes of conduct in 296.36

For historical books, see 222; for Torah, see 222.1; for poetic books, Ketuvim, see 223; for prophetic books, Nevi'im, see 224

See Manual at 220: Biblical theology; also at 221: Optional numbers for books of Tanakh

(Option: To arrange the books of the Old Testament (Tanakh) as found in Jewish Bibles, use one of the following:
(Option A: Use the optional arrangement of 222–224 given in the Manual at 221
(Option B: Class in 296.11

(A table giving the three numbers for each book is given in the Manual at 221)

[.03]	Dictionaries, encyclopedias, concordances

> Do not use for dictionaries and encyclopedias; class in 221.3. Do not use for concordances; class in 221.4–221.5

.04	Special topics

[.042]	Ketuvim (Hagiographa, Writings)

> Relocated to 223

.044	Megillot (Five scrolls)

> *For a specific book of Megillot, see the book, e.g., Ruth 222.35*

.046	Apocalyptic passages

> Class apocalyptic passages in a book or group of books with the book or group of books, plus notation 0046 from add table under 221–229, e.g., apocalyptic passages in the prophets 224.0046, in Book of Daniel 224.50046

.09	Historical, geographic, persons treatment of Old Testament

> Class the canon in 221.12

> *For geography, history, chronology, persons of Old Testament lands in Old Testament times, see 221.9*

.1–.8	**Generalities**

> Add to base number 221 the numbers following 220 in 220.1–220.8, e.g., Targums 221.42, commentaries 221.7

.9	**Geography, history, chronology, persons of Old Testament lands in Old Testament times**

> Class general history of ancient areas in 930

.91	Geography

> Class here description and civilization

> Class civilization treated separately from geography in 221.95

.92	Persons

> *See Manual at 220.92; also at 230–280: Biography*

.922	Collected treatment

.93	Archaeology (Material remains)

.95	History

> Including civilization treated separately from geography

> Class geographic description and civilization treated together in 221.91

.950 01–.950 09	Standard subdivisions

.950 5	Old Testament stories retold
	Including picture books

222 *Historical books of Old Testament

.1 *Pentateuch (Torah)

Class here Hexateuch

For Joshua, see 222.2

.11	*Genesis
.12	*Exodus

For Ten Commandments, see 222.16

.13	*Leviticus
.14	*Numbers
.15	*Deuteronomy

For Ten Commandments, see 222.16

.16   *Ten Commandments (Decalogue)

Class Ten Commandments as code of conduct in Christianity in 241.52; class Ten Commandments as code of conduct in Judaism in 296.36

.2 *Joshua (Josue)

.3 *Judges and Ruth

.32	*Judges
.35	*Ruth

.4 *Samuel

.43   *Samuel 1

Variant name: Kings 1

.44   *Samuel 2

Variant name: Kings 2

.5 *Kings

.53   *Kings 1

Variant name: Kings 3

.54   *Kings 2

Variant name: Kings 4

.6 *Chronicles (Paralipomena)

*Add as instructed under 221–229

| .63 | *Chronicles 1 (Paralipomenon 1) |
| .64 | *Chronicles 2 (Paralipomenon 2) |

.7 *Ezra (Esdras 1)

> See also 229.1 for Esdras 1 (also called Esdras 3) of the Apocrypha

.8 *Nehemiah (Esdras 2, Nehemias)

> See also 229.1 for Esdras 2 (also called Esdras 4) of the Apocrypha

| (.86) | *Tobit (Tobias) |

> (Optional number; prefer 229.22)

| (.88) | *Judith |

> (Optional number; prefer 229.24)

.9 *Esther

> (Option: Class here deuterocanonical part of Esther; prefer 229.27)

223 *Poetic books of Old Testament

Class here Ketuvim (Hagiographa, Writings) [*formerly* 221.042], wisdom literature

> *For Apocryphal wisdom literature, see 229.3. For a specific book of Ketuvim not provided for here, see the book, e.g., Ruth 222.35*

.1	*Job
.2	*Psalms
.7	*Proverbs
.8	*Ecclesiastes (Qohelet)
.9	*Song of Solomon (Canticle of Canticles, Song of Songs)
(.96)	*Wisdom of Solomon (Wisdom)

> (Optional number; prefer 229.3)

| (.98) | *Ecclesiasticus (Sirach) |

> (Optional number; prefer 229.4)

224 *Prophetic books of Old Testament

Class here Major Prophets, Nevi'im

> *For a specific book of Nevi'im not provided for here, see the book, e.g., Joshua 222.2*

| .1 | *Isaiah (Isaias) |
| .2 | *Jeremiah (Jeremias) |

*Add as instructed under 221–229

.3	***Lamentations**
(.37)	***Baruch**
	(Optional number; prefer 229.5)
.4	***Ezekiel (Ezechiel)**
.5	***Daniel**
	(Option: Class here Song of the Three Children, Susanna, Bel and the Dragon; prefer 229.6)
.6	***Hosea (Osee)**
.7	***Joel**
.8	***Amos**
.9	***Minor Prophets**
	For Hosea, see 224.6; for Joel, see 224.7; for Amos, see 224.8
.91	*Obadiah (Abdias)
.92	*Jonah (Jonas)
.93	*Micah (Micheas)
.94	*Nahum
.95	*Habakkuk (Habacuc)
.96	*Zephaniah (Sophonias)
.97	*Haggai (Aggeus)
.98	*Zechariah (Zacharias)
.99	*Malachi (Malachias)
(.997)	*Maccabees 1 and 2 (Machabees 1 and 2)
	(Optional number; prefer 229.73)

225 New Testament

For Gospels and Acts, see 226; for Epistles, see 227; for Revelation, see 228

[.03]	Dictionaries, encyclopedias, concordances
	Do not use for dictionaries and encyclopedias; class in 225.3. Do not use for concordances; class in 225.4–225.5
.04	Special topics

*Add as instructed under 221–229

.046   Apocalyptic passages

Class apocalyptic passages in a book or group of books with the book or group of books, plus notation 0046 from add table under 221–229, e.g., apocalyptic passages in Gospels 226.0046, in Gospel of Mark 226.30046

For Revelation (Apocalypse), see 228

.09   Historical, geographic, persons treatment of New Testament

Class the canon in 225.12

For geography, history, chronology, persons of New Testament lands in New Testament times, see 225.9

.1–.8   Generalities

Add to base number 225 the numbers following 220 in 220.1–220.8, e.g., Authorized Version 225.5203

.9   Geography, history, chronology, persons of New Testament lands in New Testament times

Add to base number 225.9 the numbers following 221.9 in 221.91–221.95, e.g., individual persons 225.92; however, for Jesus Christ, Mary, Joseph, Joachim, Anne, John the Baptist, see 232

See Manual at 220.92; also at 230–280: Biography

226   *Gospels and Acts

Class here synoptic Gospels

Subdivisions are added for Gospels and Acts together, for Gospels alone

See Manual at 230–280: Biography

.095 05   Gospel stories retold

Number built according to instructions under 221–229

Class Jesus as a historical figure, biography and specific events in life of Jesus in 232.9

.1   Harmonies of Gospels

> **226.2–226.5   Specific Gospels**

Class comprehensive works in 226

For miracles, see 226.7; for parables, see 226.8

.2   *Matthew

Class Golden Rule as code of conduct in 241.54

For Sermon on the Mount, see 226.9

*Add as instructed under 221–229

.3   ***Mark**

.4   ***Luke**

> Class Golden Rule as code of conduct in 241.54
>
> *For Sermon on the Mount, see 226.9*

.5   ***John**

> Class here comprehensive works on Johannine literature
>
> *For Epistles of John, see 227.94; for Revelation (Apocalypse), see 228*

.6   ***Acts of the Apostles**

.7   ***Miracles**

> Class miracles in context of Jesus' life in 232.955

.8   ***Parables**

> Class parables in context of Jesus' life in 232.954

.9   ***Sermon on the Mount**

> Class Sermon on the Mount as code of conduct in 241.53

.93   *Beatitudes

.96   *Lord's Prayer

227   ***Epistles**

> Class here comprehensive works on Pauline epistles

.1   ***Romans**

.2   ***Corinthians 1**

> Class here comprehensive works on Epistles to Corinthians
>
> *For Corinthians 2, see 227.3*

.3   ***Corinthians 2**

.4   ***Galatians**

.5   ***Ephesians**

.6   ***Philippians**

.7   ***Colossians**

.8   ***Other Pauline epistles**

.81   *Thessalonians 1

> Class here comprehensive works on Epistles to Thessalonians
>
> *For Thessalonians 2, see 227.82*

*Add as instructed under 221–229

.82	*Thessalonians 2
.83	*Timothy 1

Class here comprehensive works on Epistles to Timothy, on Pastoral Epistles

For Timothy 2, see 227.84; for Titus, see 227.85

.84	*Timothy 2
.85	*Titus
.86	*Philemon
.87	*Hebrews
.9	***Catholic epistles**
.91	*James
.92	*Peter 1

Class here comprehensive works on Epistles of Peter

For Peter 2, see 227.93

.93	*Peter 2
.94	*John 1

Class here comprehensive works on Epistles of John

For John 2, see 227.95; for John 3, see 227.96

.95	*John 2
.96	*John 3
.97	*Jude

228 *Revelation (Apocalypse)

229 *Apocrypha, pseudepigrapha, intertestamental works

Apocrypha: works accepted as deuterocanonical in some Bibles

Pseudepigrapha, intertestamental works: works from intertestamental times connected with the Bible but not accepted as canonical

Subdivisions are added for Apocrypha, pseudepigrapha, intertestamental works together; for Apocrypha alone

---

> **229.1–229.7 Specific books and works of Apocrypha**

Class comprehensive works in 229

*Add as instructed under 221–229

.1   ***Esdras 1 and 2**

        Variant names: Esdras 3 and 4

        See also 222.7 for Ezra, 222.8 for Nehemiah

.2   ***Tobit, Judith, deuterocanonical part of Esther**

.22   *Tobit (Tobias)

        (Option: Class in 222.86)

.24   *Judith

        (Option: Class in 222.88)

.27   *Deuterocanonical part of Esther

        (Option: Class in 222.9)

.3   ***Wisdom of Solomon (Wisdom)**

        Class here Apocryphal wisdom literature

        For Ecclesiasticus, see 229.4

        (Option: Class in 223.96)

.4   ***Ecclesiasticus (Sirach)**

        (Option: Class in 223.98)

.5   ***Baruch and Epistle of Jeremiah**

        Song of the Three Children relocated to 229.6

        (Option: Class Baruch in 224.37)

.6   ***Song of the Three Children [*formerly* 229.5], Susanna, Bel and the Dragon, Prayer of Manasseh**

        (Option: Class Song of the Three Children, Susanna, Bel and the Dragon in 224.5)

.7   ***Maccabees (Machabees)**

.73   *Maccabees 1 and 2 (Machabees 1 and 2)

        (Option: Class in 224.997)

.75   *Maccabees 3 and 4 (Machabees 3 and 4)

>   **229.8–229.9 Pseudepigrapha, intertestamental works**

        Class comprehensive works in 229.9

        For Maccabees 3 and 4, see 229.75

*Add as instructed under 221–229

.8   ***Pseudo gospels**

> Including agrapha (Jesus' words not appearing in canonical Gospels), Gospel of Thomas

> Class comprehensive works on New Testament pseudepigrapha in 229.92

.9   ***Pseudepigrapha**

> *For pseudo gospels, see 229.8*

.91   *Old Testament

> *For Maccabees 3 and 4, see 229.75*

.911   *Historical books

.912   *Poetic books

> Including Odes of Solomon

.913   *Prophetic books

> Including Apocalypse of Elijah, Ascension of Isaiah, Assumption of Moses, Books of Enoch, Jewish apocalypses

.914   *Testaments

> Including Testament of the Twelve Patriarchs

.92   *New Testament

> *For pseudo gospels, see 229.8; for Epistles, see 229.93; for Apocalypses, see 229.94*

.925   *Acts of the Apostles

.93   *Epistles

.94   *Apocalypses

---

*Add as instructed under 221–229

> ## 230–280 Christianity

Unless other instructions are given, observe the following table of preference for the history of Christianity and the Christian church (except for biography, explained in Manual at 230–280: Biography), e.g., Jesuit missions in India 266.254 (*not* 271.53054); persecution of Jesuits by Elizabeth I 272.7 (*not* 271.53042, 274.206, or 282.42):

Specific topics	220–260
Persecutions in general church history	272
Doctrinal controversies and heresies in general church history	273
Religious congregations and orders in church history	271
Denominations and sects of Christian church	280
Treatment of Christianity and Christian church by continent, country, locality	274–279
General historical, geographic, persons treatment of Christianity and Christian church (*except* 271–279)	270

Class comprehensive works in 230

For Bible, see 220

See Manual at 230–280: Biography; also at 280: Biography

(Option: To give local emphasis and shorter numbers to a specific religion other than Christianity, e.g., Buddhism, class it in these numbers, its sources in 220, comprehensive works in 230; in that case class the Bible and Christianity in 298. Other options are described at 292–299)

> ## 230–270 Specific elements of Christianity

Class here specific elements of specific denominations and sects
  (Option: Class specific elements of specific denominations and sects in 280)

Class comprehensive works in 230

230 Christianity [*formerly* 200]   Christian theology

Including Christian mythology [*formerly* 204.5]

Class here contextual theology

Class doctrinal controversies in general church history in 273

For Christian moral and devotional theology, see 240; for local Christian church and Christian religious orders, see 250; for Christian social and ecclesiastical theology, see 260; for historical, geographic, persons treatment of Christianity and Christian church, see 270; for denominations and sects of Christian church, see 280

See Manual at 230: Contextual theology

SUMMARY

[.001]   Philosophy and theory of Christianity

> Do not use; class in 230.01

.002–.003   Standard subdivisions of Christianity [*formerly* 202–203]

.005   Serial publications of Christianity [*formerly* 205]

[.006]   Organizations and management of Christianity

> Do not use; class in 260

.007   Education, research, related topics of Christianity [*formerly* 207]

[.007 1]   Education

> Do not use; class in 230.071

[.008]   Christianity with respect to kinds of persons

> Do not use; class in 270.08

[.009]   Historical, geographic, persons treatment of Christianity

> Do not use; class in 270

.01   Philosophy and theory of Christianity [*formerly* 201], of Christian theology

.02–.03   Standard subdivisions of Christian theology

.04   Specific types of Christian theology

> Class theology of specific denominations and sects in 230.1–230.9
>
> *See Manual at 230.04 vs. 230.092, 230.1–230.9*

[.040 1–.040 9]   Standard subdivisions

> Do not use; class in 230.01–230.09

.041   Biblical theology

Class theology of a specific part of Old or New Testament with the part, e.g., theology of Pauline epistles 227.06; class biblical theology of a specific topic with the topic in 231–260, e.g., New Testament writers' view of war and peace 261.87309015

See Manual at 220: Biblical theology

.041 1   Christian theology of Old Testament

.041 5   Christian theology of New Testament

.042   **Theology of Eastern and Roman Catholic churches**

Class specific schools and systems of theology in 230.046

.044   Protestant theology

Class specific schools of Protestant theology in 230.046

.046   **Specific schools and systems of theology**

Including dominion, existentialist, liberal, neo-orthodox, process theologies

See Manual at 230: Contextual theology

[.046 01–.046 09]   Standard subdivisions

Do not use; class in 230.01–230.09

.046 2   Evangelical and fundamentalist theology

.046 24   Evangelical theology

.046 26   Fundamentalist theology

.046 3   Dispensationalist theology

.046 4   Liberation theology

.05–.06   Standard subdivisions of Christian theology

.07   Education, research, related topics of Christian theology

.071   Education in Christianity [*formerly* 207.1], in Christian theology

Class here Christianity as an academic subject

Class comprehensive works on Christian religious education, religious education to inculcate Christian faith and practice, catechetics in 268

See Manual at 268 vs. 230.071

.071 1	Higher education in Christianity, in Christian theology

Class here Bible colleges, divinity schools, theological seminaries, graduate and undergraduate faculties of theology; education of ministers, pastors, priests, theologians

Class training for clergy in a specialized subject with the subject, e.g., education in pastoral counseling 253.5071

For higher education for specific denominations and sects, see 230.073

See Manual at 268 vs. 230.071

.071 14–.071 19	Higher education in specific continents, countries, localities [*formerly* 207.4–207.9]

Class here nondenominational and interdenominational schools and courses

.073	Higher education for specific denominations and sects

Add to base number 230.073 the numbers following 28 in 281–289, e.g., Roman Catholic seminaries 230.0732, a Roman Catholic seminary in Dublin 230.073241835

.08–.09	Standard subdivisions of Christian theology

See Manual at 230: Contextual theology; also at 230.04 vs. 230.092, 230.1–230.9

.1–.9	**Doctrines of specific denominations and sects**

Add to base number 230 the numbers following 28 in 281–289, e.g., Methodist doctrines 230.7

See Manual at 230.04 vs. 230.092, 230.1–230.9; also at 230.15–230.2

(Option: Class here specific doctrines of specific denominations and sects; prefer 231–236. If option is chosen, add as above, then add 0* and to the result add the numbers following 23 in 231–236, e.g., Methodist doctrines on salvation 230.704)

> ## 231–239   Christian doctrinal theology

Class specific types of Christian doctrinal theology in 230.042–230.046; class comprehensive works on doctrines of specific denominations and sects in 230.1–230.9; class comprehensive works in 230

See Manual at 261.5 vs. 231–239

---

*Add 00 for standard subdivisions; see instructions at beginning of Table 1

> ## 231–236 Specific topics in Christian doctrinal theology

Class here specific doctrines of specific denominations and sects
(Option: Class specific doctrines of specific denominations and sects in
230.1–230.9)

Class comprehensive works in 230

231   God

.04   Special topics

.042   Ways of knowing God

Including faith, reason, tradition

Class proofs of existence of God based on reason alone in 212.1; class
revelation in 231.74

.044   General concepts of God

Including non-Trinitarian concepts

Class here comprehensive works on Holy Trinity

> ### 231.1–231.3 Holy Trinity

Class comprehensive works in 231.044

.1   **God the Father**

.2   **God the Son**

For Jesus Christ, see 232

.3   **God the Holy Spirit**

For gifts of the Holy Spirit, baptism in the Holy Spirit, see 234.13

.4   **Attributes**

Including omnipotence, omnipresence, omniscience, transcendence

*For love and wisdom, see 231.6; for sovereignty, see 231.7; for justice and
goodness, see 231.8*

.5   **Providence**

.6   **Love and wisdom**

.7   Relation to the world

> Including relation to nature, sovereignty
>
> Class here God's relation to individual believers
>
> Class redemption in 234.3; class divine law in 241.2; class believers' experience of God in 248.2; class God's relation to the church in 262.7
>
> > *For Providence, see 231.5*

.72   Kingdom of God

> Class Kingdom of God to come in 236

.73   Miracles

> Class here miracles associated with saints, comprehensive works on miracles
>
> > *For miracles associated with Mary, see 232.917; for miracles of Jesus, see 232.955; for stigmata, see 248.29*

.74   Revelation

> > *For private visions, see 248.29*

.745   Prophecy

> > *For Biblical prophecy and prophecies, see 220.15; for messianic prophecies, see 232.12; for eschatological prophecies, see 236*

.76   Relation to and action in history

> Including covenant relationship, relationship to the Jewish people

.765   Creation

> *For creation of humankind, see 233.11*

.765 2   Relation of scientific and Christian viewpoints of origin of universe

> Class here creationism, creation science, evolution versus creation, reconciliation of evolution and creation
>
> > *See also 379.28 for teaching creationism in public schools*
> >
> > *See Manual at 231.7652 vs. 213, 500, 576.8*

.8   Justice and goodness

> Including good and evil
>
> Class here theodicy (vindication of God's justice and goodness in permitting existence of evil and suffering)
>
> > *For providence, see 231.5; for moral theology, see 241*

232   Jesus Christ and his family   Christology

> *See Manual at 232*

> **232.1–232.8 Christology**

Class life of Jesus in 232.9; class comprehensive works in 232

.1   Incarnation and messiahship of Christ

Including typology

.12   Messianic prophecies

.2   Christ as Logos (Word of God)

.3   Christ as Redeemer

Including atonement

Class comprehensive works on the doctrine of redemption in 234.3

For sacrifice of Christ, see 232.4

.4   Sacrifice of Christ

.5   Resurrection of Christ

.8   Divinity and humanity of Christ

Including Person; offices as Prophet, Priest, King; intercession

Class here hypostatic union

Class non-Trinitarian concepts of Jesus in 232.9

For incarnation, see 232.1; for Christ as Logos, see 232.2; for Christ as Redeemer, see 232.3

.9   Family and life of Jesus

Class here non-Trinitarian concepts of Jesus, rationalistic interpretations of Jesus

For Islamic doctrines about Jesus, see 297.2465

See Manual at 230–280: Biography

.900 1–.900 9   Standard subdivisions

.901   Life of Jesus

For birth, infancy, childhood of Jesus, see 232.92; for adulthood of Jesus, see 232.95–232.97

.903   Character and personality of Jesus

.904   Jesus as teacher and exemplar

Including influence

Class teachings in 232.954

.906   Jewish interpretations of Jesus

.908	Historicity of Jesus
.91	Mary, mother of Jesus

Class here Mariology

Class Mary's husband and parents in 232.93

.911	Immaculate Conception
.912	Annunciation
.913	Virginity
.914	Assumption (Ascent to heaven)
[.915–.916]	Sanctity and virtues, spiritual powers

Numbers discontinued; class in 232.91

.917	Miracles and apparitions
.92	Birth, infancy, childhood of Jesus

Including Holy Family, circumcision, massacre of innocents, flight into Egypt

Class here Christmas story

For Mary, see 232.91; for Joseph, see 232.932

.921	Virgin birth
.922	Adoration of shepherds
.923	Wise men (Magi)
[.924–.926]	Circumcision, massacre of innocents, flight into Egypt

Numbers discontinued; class in 232.92

.927	Childhood of Jesus

For presentation in temple, see 232.928; for Jesus among doctors in temple, see 232.929

.928	Presentation in temple
.929	Jesus among doctors in temple
.93	Mary's husband and parents
.932	Joseph
.933	Joachim and Anne
.94	John the Baptist
.95	Public life of Jesus

Including baptism, temptation, calling of apostles

.954	Teachings

Class texts and interpretations of New Testament passages narrating parables in 226.8

.955	Miracles

Class texts and interpretations of New Testament passages narrating miracles in 226.7

.956	Transfiguration
.957	Last Supper
.958	Last words to disciples
.96	Passion and death of Jesus
.961	Betrayal by Judas
.962	Trial and condemnation
.963	Crucifixion and death
.963 5	Seven last words on cross
.964	Burial
.966	Relics of Passion
.967	Descent into hell
.97	Resurrection, appearances, ascension of Jesus

233 Humankind

Class salvation in 234

.1	**Creation and fall**
.11	Creation

Including relation of human creation and human evolution

Class comprehensive works on creation in 231.765

.14	Original sin and fall

Class sins in 241.3

.4	**Accountability**

Including guilt

.5 **Nature**

Including body, soul, spirit, sexuality; humankind as image and likeness of God, as child of God

Class free will in 233.7

For original sin, see 233.14; for death, see 236.1; for immortality, see 236.22

.7 **Freedom of choice between good and evil**

Class predestination and free will in relation to salvation in 234.9

For accountability, see 233.4

234 Salvation (Soteriology) and grace

Including election, innate virtues, merit, universal priesthood

.1 **Kinds and means of grace**

Including actual and sanctifying grace

[.12] Gifts of and baptism in the Holy Spirit

Relocated to 234.13

.13 Spiritual gifts

Including interpretation of tongues, prophecy, working of miracles, helps, governments, apostleship, teaching, exhortation, speaking words of wisdom and knowledge

Class here gifts of and baptism in the Holy Spirit [*both formerly* 234.12]

For faith, see 234.2

.131 Healing

Spiritual, emotional, or physical

For discussion of whether cures are miracles, see 231.73

See Manual at 615.852 vs. 291.31, 234.131

.132 Speaking in tongues (Glossolalia) [*formerly also* 248.29]

.16 Sacraments

Class liturgy and ritual of sacraments in 265

.161 Baptism

.161 2   Infant baptism

.161 3   Adult baptism

.162 Confirmation

.163 Eucharist (Holy Communion, Lord's Supper)

.164		Holy Orders
.165		Matrimony
.166		Penance

                         Including confession

.167   Anointing of the sick

.2   **Faith and hope**

                  See also 236 for eschatology, 241.4 for virtues

.23   Faith

.25   Hope

.3   **Redemption**

.4   **Regeneration**

.5   **Repentance and forgiveness**

                  Including atonement, reconciliation

.6   **Obedience**

.7   **Justification**

.8   **Sanctification and holiness**

.9   **Predestination and free will**

235   Spiritual beings

                  For Mariology, see 232.91

.2   **Saints**

                  Class miracles associated with saints in 231.73

                        For Joseph, see 232.932; for Joachim and Anne, see 232.933; for John the Baptist, see 232.94

                        See Manual at 230–280: Biography

.24   Beatification and canonization

>   **235.3–235.4 Pure spirits**

                  Class comprehensive works in 235

                  For God, see 231

.3   **Angels**

                  Including archangels, celestial hierarchy, cherubim, seraphim

.4   **Devils (Demons)**

.47   Satan (Lucifer)

236   Eschatology

Including Antichrist

Class here Kingdom of God to come

.1   **Death**

.2   **Future state (Life after death)**

Class resurrection of the dead in 236.8

For intermediate state, see 236.4

.21   Eternity

.22   Immortality

For conditional immortality, see 236.23

.23   Conditional immortality (Annihilationism)

.24   Heaven

.25   Hell

.4   **Intermediate state**

Probation after death

Including limbo of fathers (limbus patrum) [*formerly* 236.6], limbo of infants (limbus infantium) [*formerly* 236.7]

For purgatory, see 236.5

.5   **Purgatory**

[.6]   **Limbo of fathers (Limbus patrum)**

Relocated to 236.4

[.7]   **Limbo of infants (Limbus infantium)**

Relocated to 236.4

.8   **Resurrection of the dead**

.9   **Last Judgment and related events**

Including Armageddon, Day of the Lord, end of the world, Judgment of Christ, millennium, rapture, Second Coming of Christ, tribulation

Class interdisciplinary works on end of the world in 001.9

[237]   **[Unassigned]**

Most recently used in Edition 16

238 Creeds, confessions of faith, covenants, catechisms

Class catechetics in 268. Class creeds and catechisms on a specific doctrine with the doctrine, e.g., attributes of God 231.4

.1 Early and Eastern creeds

.11 Apostles' Creed

.14 Nicene and post-Nicene creeds of Western Church

Including Constantinopolitan Creed

.142 Nicene Creed

.144 Athanasian Creed

.19 Eastern Church

.2–.9 Other denominations

Add to base number 238 the numbers following 28 in 282–289, e.g., Lutheran catechisms 238.41

239 Apologetics and polemics

Apologetics: systematic argumentation in defense of the divine origin and authority of Christianity

Standard subdivisions are added for either or both topics in heading

Class apologetics of specific denominations in 230.1–230.9. Class apologetics and polemics on a specific doctrine with the doctrine, e.g., on doctrine of Holy Trinity 231.044

See also 273 for doctrinal controversies and heresies in general church history

[.001–.009] Standard subdivisions

Relocated to 239.01–239.09

.01–.09 Standard subdivisions [*formerly* 239.001–239.009]

.1 Apologetics and polemics in apostolic times

For polemics against doctrines of specific groups in apostolic times, see 239.2–239.4

> **239.2–239.4 Polemics against doctrines of specific groups in apostolic times**

Class comprehensive works in 239.1

.2 Polemics against Jews in apostolic times

.3 Polemics against pagans and heathens in apostolic times

.4 Polemics against Neoplatonists in apostolic times

[.5]	**Polemics against deists**

Relocated to 239.7

[.6]	**Polemics against encyclopedists**

Relocated to 239.7

.7	**Polemics against rationalists, agnostics, apostates, atheists in postapostolic times**

Including polemics against deists [*formerly* 239.5], against encyclopedists [*formerly* 239.6], against scientists and materialists [*both formerly* 239.8], against secular humanists [*formerly* 239.9]

[.8]	**Polemics against scientists and materialists**

Relocated to 239.7

.9	**Polemics against other groups in postapostolic times**

Polemics against secular humanists relocated to 239.7

Class comprehensive postapostolic defenses of and attacks on doctrines of specific denominations or sects in 230.1–230.9. Class attacks on doctrines of a specific religion with the religion, e.g., doctrines of Judaism 296.3

.93	Polemics against new age groups and doctrines

240 Christian moral and devotional theology

SUMMARY

241 Moral theology

See Manual at 241 vs. 261.8

.04	Specific denominations and sects

Add to base number 241.04 the numbers following 28 in 280.2–289.9, e.g., Protestant moral theology 241.0404

.1	**Conscience**

.2	**Laws and bases of morality**

Including divine law, natural law

Class here relation of law and gospel

For codes of conduct, see 241.5

.3   **Sin and vices**

> Standard subdivisions are added for either or both topics in heading
>
> Including specific vices
>
> Class original sin in 233.14
>
> > *For specific moral issues, see 241.6*
> >
> > *See Manual at 241.3–241.4 vs. 241.6*

.31   Mortal and venial sin

[.32]   Sins against the Holy Spirit

> Number discontinued; class in 241.3

.4   **Virtues**

> Including specific virtues
>
> Class faith and hope as means of salvation in 234.2
>
> > *For specific moral issues, see 241.6*
> >
> > *See Manual at 241.3–241.4 vs. 241.6*

.5   **Codes of conduct**

> > *For specific moral issues, see 241.6*

.52   Ten Commandments

.53   Sermon on the Mount

.54   Golden Rule

[.57]   Precepts of the church

> Number discontinued; class in 241.5

.6   **Specific moral issues**

> Add to base number 241.6 the numbers following 17 in 172–179, e.g., morality of warfare 241.6242, of abortion 241.6976; however, for specific vices, see 241.3; for specific virtues, see 241.4
>
> > *See Manual at 241.3–241.4 vs. 241.6*

242   Devotional literature

Class here texts of meditations, contemplations, prayers for individuals and families, religious poetry intended for devotional use

Unless other instructions are given, observe the following table of preference, e.g., prayers and meditations for daily use based on passages from the Bible 242.2 (*not* 242.5):

Prayers and meditations for use in times of illness, trouble, bereavement	242.4
Prayers and meditations for specific classes of persons	242.6
Prayers and meditations for daily use	242.2
Prayers and meditations for church year, other Christian feast and fast days	242.3
Prayers and meditations based on passages from the Bible	242.5
Specific prayers and groups of prayers	242.7
Collections of prayers	242.8

Class devotional literature on a specific subject with the subject, e.g., meditations on passion and death of Jesus 232.96

For evangelistic writings, see 243; for hymns, see 264.23

.08   History and description with respect to kinds of persons

Do not use for devotional literature for specific classes of persons; class in 242.6

.2   **Prayers and meditations for daily use**

Not limited to saints' days or specific parts of the church year

Including meditations and prayers for Sunday, Sabbath

Prayers and meditations for daily use for specific classes of persons relocated to 242.6

.3   **Prayers and meditations for church year, other Christian feast and fast days**

Prayers and meditations for church year, other Christian feast and fast days for specific classes of persons relocated to 242.6

>   242.33–242.36 Church year

Class comprehensive works in 242.3

For Pentecost and time after Pentecost (Ordinary time), see 242.38

.33   Advent and Christmas

.332   Advent

.335	Christmas season
	Class here Christmas day
.34	Lent
	For Holy Week, see 242.35
.35	Holy Week
.36	Easter season
	Including Ascension Day [*formerly* 242.37]
	Class here Easter Sunday
.37	Other Christian feast and fast days
	Including saints' days
	Ascension Day relocated to 242.36
.38	Pentecost and time after Pentecost (Ordinary time)

.4 Prayers and meditations for use in times of illness, trouble, bereavement

.5 Prayers and meditations based on passages from the Bible

Class interpretation and criticism of Bible passages for other than devotional use in 220.6; class Bible prayers in 242.722

.6 Prayers and meditations for specific classes of persons

Class here prayers and meditations for daily use for specific classes of persons [*formerly* 242.2], prayers and meditations for church year, other Christian feast and fast days for specific classes of persons [*formerly* 242.3]

Add to base number 242.6 the numbers following 248.8 in 248.82–248.89, e.g., prayers and meditations for college students 242.634; however, for prayers and meditations for use in times of illness, trouble, bereavement, see 242.4

Class collections of prayers for specific classes of persons in 242.82–242.89

.7 Specific prayers and groups of prayers

.72	Specific types of prayers
	Including doxologies
	Class here prayers to Father, Son, Holy Spirit
[.721]	Doxologies (Prayers of praise)
	Number discontinued; class in 242.72
.722	Bible prayers
[.723–.726]	Prayers of faith, thanksgiving, penitence, petition
	Numbers discontinued; class in 242.72

> 242.74–242.76 Prayers addressed to spiritual beings other than God

Class comprehensive works in 242.7

.74 Prayers to Mary

Including Ave Maria (Hail Mary), Rosary

. .75 Prayers to Joseph, Joachim, Anne

.76 Prayers to saints and angels

For Joseph, Joachim, Anne, see 242.75

.8 Collections of prayers

Class here prayer books

For specific prayers and groups of prayers, see 242.7

.800 1–.800 7 Standard subdivisions

.800 8 History and description with respect to kinds of persons

Do not use for collections of prayers for specific classes of persons; class in 242.82–242.89

.800 9 Historical, geographic, persons treatment

.801–.809 Collections of prayers by adherents of specific denominations and sects

Add to base number 242.80 the numbers following 28 in 281–289, e.g., collections of private prayers by Methodists 242.807

.82–.89 Collections of prayers for specific classes of persons

Add to base number 242.8 the numbers following 248.8 in 248.82–248.89, e.g., collections of private prayers for college students 242.834

For collections of prayers by adherents of specific denominations and sects, see 242.801–242.809

243 Evangelistic writings for individuals and families

Works designed to convert readers, promote repentance

Class evangelistic sermons in 252.3

[244] [Unassigned]

Most recently used in Edition 15

[245] Texts of hymns for devotional use of individuals and families

Relocated to 264.23

246 Use of art in Christianity

Religious meaning, significance, purpose

Class attitude of Christianity and Christian church toward secular art, the arts in 261.57; class creation, description, critical appraisal as art in 700

For church furnishings and related articles, see 247

> **246.1–246.4 Schools and styles**

Class specific elements by school and style in 246.5–246.9; class comprehensive works in 246; class interdisciplinary works on schools and styles of Christian art in 709.015–709.05

.1 Byzantine and Gothic art

.2 Early Christian and Romanesque art

.4 Renaissance and modern art

Including Protestant art

> **246.5–246.9 Specific elements**

Class comprehensive works in 246

.5 Icons, symbols, insignia

.53 Icons

.55 Symbols

Including banners, emblems, incense, votive offerings

Class here Christian symbolism

For colors and lights, see 246.6

.558 Crosses and crucifixes

Standard subdivisions are added for either or both topics in heading

.56 Insignia

Including insignia of rank

.6 Colors and lights

.7 Dramatic, musical, rhythmic arts

Including dance, liturgical dance

.72 Dramatic arts

.723 Passion plays

.725 Puppetry

.75 Music

Class here comprehensive works on music in Christianity

Class attitude of Christianity and Christian church toward secular music in 261.578; class interdisciplinary works on Christian sacred music in 781.71

For music in public worship, see 264.2

.9 **Architecture**

Add to base number 246.9 the numbers following 726 in 726.4–726.9, e.g., cathedral church buildings 246.96; however, for church furnishings, see 247

247 Church furnishings and related articles

Including paintings, plastic arts, sculpture, structural decoration, textiles

.1 **Furniture**

248 Christian experience, practice, life

Class here spirituality

See Manual at 230–280: Biography

SUMMARY

248.06	**Organizations and management**
.2	**Religious experience**
.3	**Worship**
.4	**Christian life and practice**
.5	**Witness bearing**
.6	**Stewardship**
.8	**Guides to Christian life for specific classes of persons**

.06 Organizations and management

Pious societies, sodalities, confraternities relocated to 267

.2 **Religious experience**

.22 Mysticism

.24 Conversion

For moral renewal and commitment, see 248.25

> 248.242–248.246 Conversion from one system of belief to another

Class comprehensive works in 248.24

For conversion of Christians to another religion, see the religion, e.g., conversion of Christians to Judaism 296.714

.242 Conversion from Protestantism to Roman Catholicism

.244	Conversion from Roman Catholicism to Protestantism
.246	Conversion from non-Christianity to Christianity
.25	Moral renewal and commitment
.29	Other religious experiences

         Including stigmata, private visions

         Speaking in tongues (glossolalia) relocated to 234.132

         Class spiritual gifts in 234.13

.3   **Worship**

         Class here comprehensive works on worship

         Class texts of prayers and devotions in 242

         For observances in family life, see 249; for public worship, see 264

.32	Prayer
.34	Meditation and contemplation

         Standard subdivisions are added for either or both topics in heading

.4   **Christian life and practice**

         Class here Christian marriage and family

         Class guides to Christian life for specific classes of persons in 248.8

         For moral theology, see 241; for worship, see 248.3; for witness bearing, see 248.5; for stewardship, see 248.6; for Christian observances in family life, see 249

.408	History and description with respect to kinds of persons

         Do not use for guides to Christian life for specific classes of persons; class in 248.8

.46	Individual observances

         Including ceremonial and ritual observances, observance of restrictions and limitations

         For asceticism, see 248.47

[.463]	Pilgrimages

         Relocated to 263.041

.47   Asceticism

Attitudes and practices aside from and beyond normal moral duties adopted as aids to moral and spiritual development

Including practice of celibacy, fasting and abstinence, poverty, solitude, other physical austerities, e.g., flagellation

For clerical celibacy, see 253.25; for practices of religious congregations and orders, see 255

.48   Guides to Christian life by or for adherents of specific denominations and sects

Add to base number 248.48 the numbers following 28 in 280.2–289.9, e.g., guides for Roman Catholics 248.482

Class guides to Christian life for specific classes of persons who are adherents of specific denominations and sects in 248.8

.5   Witness bearing

.6   Stewardship

.8   Guides to Christian life for specific classes of persons

Class here guides to Christian life for specific classes of persons who are adherents of specific denominations and sects

Class guides to a specific aspect of Christian life with the aspect, e.g., prayer 248.32

>   248.82–248.85   Guides to Christian life for specific age groups

Class persons of specific ages in specific occupational groups or experiencing illness, trouble, bereavement in 248.86–248.89; class comprehensive works in 248.8

.82   Children

Through age eleven

.83   Adolescents and college students

Standard subdivisions are added for adolescents and college students together, for adolescents alone

.832   Male adolescents

.833   Female adolescents

.834   College students

Male and female

.84   Adults

For persons in late adulthood, see 248.85

.842	Men
.842 1	Fathers

Regardless of marital status

| .842 2–.842 9 | Men by marital status |

Add to base number 248.842 the numbers following —0865 in notation 08652–08659 from Table 1, e.g., guides for husbands 248.8425

Class fathers in 248.8421

.843	Women
.843 1	Mothers

Regardless of marital status

| .843 2–.843 9 | Women by marital status |

Add to base number 248.843 the numbers following —0865 in notation 08652–08659 from Table 1, e.g., guides for wives 248.8435

Class mothers in 248.8431

| .844 | Married couples |

Class husbands in 248.8425; class wives in 248.8435

| .845 | Parents |

Class here Christian child rearing, Christian religious training of children in the home

For fathers, see 248.8421; for mothers, see 248.8431

| .846 | Separated and divorced persons |

For separated and divorced men, see 248.8423; for separated and divorced women, see 248.8433

| .85 | Persons in late adulthood |

> 248.86–248.89 Guides to Christian life for occupational classes; persons experiencing illness, trouble, bereavement

Class comprehensive works in 248.8

.86	Persons experiencing illness, trouble, bereavement
.861–.864	Persons experiencing illness, disability

Add to base number 248.6 the numbers following 362 in 362.1–362.4, e.g., persons experiencing addiction 248.8629

See Manual at 616.86 vs. 158.1, 248.8629, 291.442, 362.29

.866	Persons experiencing bereavement
.88	Occupational classes

For religious groups, see 248.89

.89	Religious groups
.892	Clergy

For persons in religious orders, see 248.894

.894	Persons in religious orders
.894 2	Men
.894 22	Vocation
.894 25	Selection and novitiate
.894 3	Women
.894 32	Vocation
.894 35	Selection and novitiate

249   Christian observances in family life

Class here family prayer; family observance of religious restrictions, rites, ceremonies

> 250–280   Christian church

Class comprehensive works in 260

250   Local Christian church and Christian religious orders

Standard subdivisions are added for local Christian church and Christian religious orders together, for local Christian church alone

Class public worship in 264; class missions in 266; class religious education in 268

SUMMARY

250.1–.9	**Standard subdivisions**
251	**Preaching (Homiletics)**
252	**Texts of sermons**
253	**Pastoral office and work (Pastoral theology)**
254	**Parish administration**
255	**Religious congregations and orders**
259	**Pastoral care of families, of specific kinds of persons**

[.68]	Management

Do not use for management of local church; class in 254

.9   **Historical, geographic, persons treatment**

> Class general historical treatment of local church in specific continents, countries, localities in 274–279; class historical, geographic, persons treatment of specific denominations in 280

>   **251–254   Local church**

> Class here basic Christian communities

> Class the local church in overall church organization in 262.2; class comprehensive works in 250

> *For pastoral care of families, of specific kinds of persons, see 259*

> *See Manual at 260 vs. 251–254, 259*

251   **Preaching (Homiletics)**

> Class texts of sermons in 252; class pastoral methods in 253.7

.001–.009   Standard subdivisions

.01   Preparation

.02   Sermon outlines

.03   Delivery

> Class here voice, expression, gesture

.07   Radio and television preaching

> Class specific aspects of radio and television preaching in 251.01–251.03

.08   Homiletic illustrations

.1–.9   **Material for preparation of sermons for specific occasions, for specific classes of persons**

> Add to base number 251 the numbers following 252 in 252.1–252.9, e.g., material for preparation of sermons arranged for the church year 251.6

252   **Texts of sermons**

> Class sermons on a specific subject with the subject, e.g., God's Providence 231.5

.001–.009   Standard subdivisions

.01–.09   Texts of sermons by specific denominations and sects

> Add to base number 252.0 the numbers following 28 in 281–289, e.g., Anglican sermons 252.03

.1   **Texts of sermons for baptisms, confirmations, funerals, weddings**

> Class sermons for memorial occasions in 252.9

.3		**Texts of sermons for evangelistic meetings**
.5		**Texts of sermons for specific classes of persons**
.53		Children

Through age eleven

.55	Adolescents and young adults

Junior-high-school, high-school, college students

Including academic, chapel, convocation, commencement sermons

.56	Persons in late adulthood, and persons experiencing illness, trouble, bereavement
.58	Occupational classes

For religious groups, see 252.59

.59	Religious groups
.592	Clergy

For persons in religious orders, see 252.594

.594	Persons in religious orders
.6	**Texts of sermons for church year and public occasions**

Standard subdivisions are added for texts of sermons for church year and public occasions together, for church year alone

---

> 252.61–252.64 Church year

Class comprehensive works in 252.6

.61	Advent and Christmas
.612	Advent
.615	Christmas season

Class here Christmas day

.62	Lent
.625	Holy Week
.63	Easter season

Including Ascension Day [*formerly* 252.67]

Class here Easter Sunday

.64	Pentecost and time after Pentecost (Ordinary time)

.67	**Other feast and fast days**

> Including saints' days
>
> Ascension Day relocated to 252.63

.68	**Secular occasions**

> Including elections, holidays, thanksgivings

.7	**Texts of sermons for consecrations, ordinations, installations**
.9	**Texts of sermons for memorial occasions**

253 Pastoral office and work (Pastoral theology)

Class here the work of priests, ministers, pastors, rectors, vicars, curates, chaplains, elders, deacons, assistants, laity in relation to the work of the church at the local level

Class local clergy and laity in relation to the government, organization and nature of the church as a whole in 262.1; class the ordination of women in 262.14; class the role of clergy in religious education in 268

.08	**History and description with respect to kinds of persons**

> Do not use for pastoral care of specific kinds of persons; class in 259
>
> Class here pastoral care performed by kinds of persons

.09	**Historical, geographic, persons treatment**
.092	**Persons treatment**

> Do not use for biography of clergy in the period prior to 1054; class in 270.1–270.3. Do not use for biography of clergy in the period subsequent to 1054; class in 280
>
> *See Manual at 230–280: Biography*

.2	**Life and person**

> Including professional and personal qualifications
>
> Class education of clergy in 230.0711; class guides to Christian life for clergy in 248.892

.22	**Families of clergy**
.25	**Clerical celibacy**

> Add to base number 253.25 the numbers following 28 in 281–289, e.g., clerical celibacy in Roman Catholic church 253.252, in Roman Catholic church in United States 253.25273

>   **253.5–253.7   Pastoral duties and responsibilities**

Class methods for services to families, to specific kinds of persons in 259; class comprehensive works in 253

For preaching, see 251; for parish administration, see 254

.5   Counseling and spiritual direction

Class pastoral counseling, spiritual direction of specific kinds of persons in 259; class premarital, marriage, family counseling in 259.12–259.14

.52   Pastoral psychology

.53   Spiritual direction

.7   Pastoral methods

Including specific types of activity [*formerly* 259.8], group work, telephone work

[.73]   Outdoor pastoral methods

Number discontinued; class in 253.7

.76   Pastoral methods in homes

.78   Use of radio and television

254   Parish administration

.001–.009   Standard subdivisions

.01–.09   Parish administration by specific denominations and sects

Add to base number 254.0 the numbers following 28 in 281–289, e.g., administration of Roman Catholic parishes 254.02

.1   Initiation of new churches

.2   Parish administration in specific kinds of communities

Class a specific activity in a specific kind of community with the activity, e.g., membership promotion 254.5

.22   Urban communities

.23   Suburban communities

.24   Rural communities

.3   Use of communications media

Including use of audiovisual materials

.4   Public relations and publicity

For use of communications media, see 254.3

.5 **Membership**

Promotion and growth

.6 **Programs**

Planning and execution

.7 **Buildings, equipment, grounds**

.8 **Finance**

Including budget, expenditures, income, methods of raising money

255 Religious congregations and orders

Class here monasticism, comprehensive works on Christian religious congregations and orders

When adding from 271 to indicate kinds of orders or specific orders, add only the notation for the kind or order. Do not use the footnote instruction to add as instructed under 271, but add notation from the table under 255.1–255.7 if it applies, or add notation 01–09 from Table 1. For example, the correct number for contemplative orders in the United Kingdom is 255.010941 (*not* 255.01041); for Benedictines in the United Kingdom 255.100941 (*not* 255.1041)

For guides to Christian life for persons in religious orders, see 248.894; for religious congregations and orders in church organization, see 262.24; for religious congregations and orders, monasticism in church history, see 271. For specific types of activity of religious congregations and orders, see the activity, e.g., pastoral counseling 253.5, missionary work 266

.001–.009 Standard subdivisions

.01–.09 Specific kinds

Add to base number 255.0 the numbers following 271.0 in 271.01–271.09 for the kind only, e.g., contemplative orders 255.01; then, for each kind having its own number, add notation 01–09 from Table 1 (*not* as instructed under 271), e.g., contemplative orders in the United Kingdom 255.010941

.1–.7 **Roman Catholic orders of men**

Add to base number 255 the numbers following 271 in 271.1–271.7 for the order only, e.g., Benedictines 255.1; then, for each order having its own number, add further as follows (*not* as instructed at 271), e.g., Benedictines in the United Kingdom 255.100941, the rule of St. Benedict 255.106:

001–009	Standard subdivisions
02	Constitutions
04	Statutes, ordinances, customs
06	Rule

.8 **Non-Roman Catholic orders of men**

.81 Monasticism of Eastern churches

Add to base number 255.81 the numbers following 281 in 281.5–281.9, e.g., Eastern Orthodox monasticism 255.819

.83   Anglican orders of men

.9   Congregations and orders of women

.900 1–.900 9   Standard subdivisions

.901–.909   Specific kinds

> Add to base number 255.90 the numbers following 271.0 in 271.01–271.09 for the kind only, e.g., contemplative orders 255.901; then, for each kind having its own number, add notation 01–09 from Table 1 (*not* as instructed under 271), e.g., contemplative orders in the United Kingdom 255.9010941

.91–.97   Roman Catholic orders of women

> Add to base number 255.9 the numbers following 271.9 in 271.91–271.97 for the order only, e.g., Dominican sisters 255.972; then, for each order having its own number, add further as instructed under 255.1–255.7 (*not* as instructed at 271), e.g., Dominicans in the United Kingdom 255.97200941, the rule of the Dominicans 255.97206

.98   Non-Roman Catholic orders of women

.981   Monasticism of women of Eastern churches

> Add to base number 255.981 the numbers following 281 in 281.5–281.9, e.g., Eastern Orthodox monasticism of women 255.9819

.983   Anglican orders of women

[256–257][Unassigned]

> Most recently used in Edition 14

[258]   [Unassigned]

> Most recently used in Edition 17

259 Pastoral care of families, of specific kinds of persons

Former heading: Activities of the local church

Performed by clergy or laity

Class here pastoral counseling of specific kinds of persons

Unless other instructions are given, observe the following table of preference, e.g., pastoral care of bereaved young people 259.6 (*not* 259.2):

Pastoral care of the bereaved	259.6
Pastoral care of delinquents and criminals	259.5
Pastoral care of persons with disabilities, with physical or mental illnesses	259.4
Pastoral care of families	259.1
Pastoral care of young people	259.2
Pastoral care of persons in late adulthood	259.3

Class comprehensive works on pastoral care of more than one kind of person in 253

See also 253.08 for pastoral care performed by kinds of persons, 361.75 for works limited to social welfare work by religious organizations

See Manual at 260 vs. 251–254, 259

[.01–.07] Standard subdivisions

Do not use; class in 253.01–253.07

.08 History and description with respect to kinds of persons

Do not use for bereaved persons; class in 259.6

[.083] Young people

Do not use; class in 259.2

.084 Persons in specific stages of adulthood

[.084 2] Young adults

Do not use; class in 259.25

[.084 6] Persons in late adulthood

Do not use; class in 259.3

.086 Persons by miscellaneous social characteristics

[.086 92] Antisocial and asocial persons

Do not use; class in 259.5

.087 Gifted persons

Do not use for persons with disabilities and illnesses; class in 259.4

.088 Occupational and religious groups

[.088 375]	Students
	Do not use; class in 259.2
[.09]	Historical, geographic, persons treatment
	Do not use; class in 253.09

.1 Pastoral care of families

.12 Family counseling

> *For premarital counseling, see 259.13; for marriage counseling, see 259.14*

.13 Premarital counseling

.14 Marriage counseling

.2 Pastoral care of young people

.22 Pastoral care of children

> Through age eleven

.23 Pastoral care of adolescents

> Ages twelve through seventeen; junior-high-school and high-school students
>
> Class here comprehensive works on pastoral care of adolescents and young adults
>
> *For pastoral care of young adults eighteen and older, see 259.25*

.24 Pastoral care of college students

> Class here campus ministry

.25 Pastoral care of young adults

> Aged eighteen and above
>
> *For pastoral care of college students, see 259.24*

.3 Pastoral care of persons in late adulthood

.4 Pastoral care of persons with disabilities, with physical or mental illnesses

> Class here programs for visiting the sick
>
> Add to base number 259.4 the numbers following 362 in 362.1–362.4, e.g., pastoral care of those who have attempted suicide 259.428

.5 Pastoral care of delinquents and criminals

> Class here prison chaplaincy, pastoral care of antisocial and asocial persons

.6 Pastoral care of the bereaved

[.8] **Specific types of activity**

Relocated to 253.7

260 Christian social and ecclesiastical theology

Institutions, services, observances, disciplines, work of Christianity and Christian church

Class here organizations of Christianity [*formerly* 206], comprehensive works on Christian church

For local church and religious orders, see 250; for denominations and sects, see 280

See Manual at 260 vs. 251–254, 259

SUMMARY

260.9	Historical, geographic, persons treatment
261	Social theology and interreligious relations and attitudes
262	Ecclesiology
263	Days, times, places of religious observance
264	Public worship
265	Sacraments, other rites and acts
266	Missions
267	Associations for religious work
268	Religious education
269	Spiritual renewal

.9 **Historical, geographic, persons treatment**

Do not use for historical, geographic, persons treatment of Christian church; class in 270

261 Social theology and interreligious relations and attitudes

Attitude of Christianity and Christian church toward and influence on secular matters, attitude toward other religions, interreligious relations

Class here Christianity and culture

Class sociology of religion in 306.6

.1 **Role of Christian church in society**

Class specific socioeconomic problems in 261.8

.2 **Christianity and other systems of belief**

.21 Christianity and irreligion

Including Christianity and communism, Christianity and the apostate and indifferent

.22–.29 Christianity and other religions

Add to base number 261.2 the numbers following 29 in 292–299, e.g., Christianity and Islam 261.27

.5	**Christianity and secular disciplines**

> *See Manual at 261.5; also at 261.5 vs. 231–239*

.51	Philosophy, logic, related disciplines
.513	Paranormal, occult phenomena and arts
.515	Psychology
.52	Communications media

Class here comprehensive works on attitude toward and use of communications media

> *For a specific use of communications media by the church, see the use, e.g., use in parish administration 254.3*

.55	Science

Class the relation of scientific and Christian views on creation in 231.765

.56	Technology
.561	Medicine
.57	The arts
.578	Music
.58	Literature
.7	**Christianity and political affairs**

Including civil war and revolution

Class here Christianity and civil rights

> *For Christianity and international affairs, see 261.87*

> *See Manual at 322.1 vs. 261.7, 291.177*

.72	Religious freedom
.73	Theocracy

Supremacy of church over civil government

.8	**Christianity and socioeconomic problems**

Class here comprehensive works on the Christian view of socioeconomic and political affairs

> *For Christianity and political affairs, see 261.7*

> *See also 361.75 for welfare services of religious organizations*

> *See Manual at 241 vs. 261.8*

.83	Social problems

.832	Social welfare problems and services
.832 1–.832 5	Problems of and services to persons with illnesses and disabilities, the poor

> Add to base number 261.832 the numbers following 362 in 362.1–362.5, e.g., Christian attitude toward alcoholism 261.832292, toward the poor 261.8325

.832 6	Hunger
.832 7	Abuse within the family
.832 71	Child abuse and neglect

> *For sexual abuse, see 261.83272*

.832 72	Sexual abuse
.832 73	Adults who were victims of abuse as children
.832 8	Refugees and victims of political oppression
.833	Crime

> Add to base number 261.833 the numbers following 364 in 364.1–364.8, e.g., Christian attitude toward treason 261.833131, toward capital punishment 261.83366

.834	Relations of age groups, the sexes, social classes, language groups, ethnic groups

> Add to base number 261.834 the numbers following 305 in 305.2–305.8, e.g., Christian attitude toward women 261.8344; however, for Christianity in relation to other religions, see 261.22–261.29; for attitude toward the poor, see 261.8325

.835	Sexual relations, marriage, divorce, family

> Add to base number 261.835 the numbers following 306 in 306.7–306.8, e.g., Christian attitude toward homosexuality 261.835766

> Class abuse within the family in 261.8327

.836	Ecology and population

> Add to base number 261.836 the numbers following 304 in 304.2–304.8, e.g., Christian attitude toward ecology 261.8362

.85	The economic order

> Including management of business enterprises

.87	International affairs
.873	War and peace

> *For civil war and revolution, see 261.7*

.873 2	Nuclear weapons and nuclear war

262 Ecclesiology

Church government, organization, nature

See Manual at 260 vs. 251–254, 259

SUMMARY

.001   Philosophy and theory

.001 1   Ecumenism

>   Do not use for systems; class in 262.001

>   *See Manual at 280.042 vs. 262.0011*

.001 109   Historical, geographic, persons treatment

>   Do not use for history of the ecumenical movement; class in 280.042

.001 7   Church renewal

.002–.005   Standard subdivisions

.006   Organizations and particular aspects of administration

.006 8   Particular aspects of administration

>   Notation 068 from Table 1 is not used by itself in 262; however, add notation 0681–0688 as appropriate for particular aspects of administration, e.g., financial administration of United Methodist Church 262.0760681

.007–.009   Standard subdivisions

.01–.09   Government and organization, ecclesiology of specific denominations and sects

>   Add to base number 262.0 the numbers following 28 in 281–289, e.g., government and organization of the United Methodist Church 262.076

.1   Governing leaders of churches

>   Authority, function, role

[.109 2]   Persons treatment

> Do not use for biography of church leaders; class in 270. Do not use for biography of leaders of specific denominations; class in 280

See Manual at 230–280: Biography

.11   Apostolic succession

>   262.12–262.15 Governing leaders by rank

Class comprehensive works in 262.1

.12   Episcopacy

Class here bishops, archbishops, national conferences of bishops

Add to base number 262.12 the numbers following 28 in 281–289, e.g., episcopacy of Anglican churches 262.123, of Church of England 262.12342

For papacy and patriarchate, see 262.13

.13   Papacy and patriarchate

Standard subdivisions are added for papacy and patriarchate together, for Roman Catholic papacy alone

---

>   262.131–262.136 Specific aspects of Roman Catholic papacy

Class comprehensive works in 262.13

.131   Papal infallibility

.132   Temporal power of the pope

.135   College of Cardinals

.136   Administration

Including congregations, offices of Curia Romana, Synod of Bishops, tribunals

For national conferences of bishops, see 262.12; for College of Cardinals, see 262.135

.14   Local clergy

Class here ordination of women

Add to base number 262.14 the numbers following 28 in 281–289, e.g., local Methodist clergy 262.147

Class works that treat the ordination of women only in relation to its effect on the local church in 253

.15   Laity

Body of church members

Add to base number 262.15 the numbers following 28 in 281–289, e.g., laity of Lutheran church 262.1541, in United States 262.154173

> 262.17–262.19   Governing leaders by system of government

Class leaders by rank in a specific system of government in 262.12–262.15; class comprehensive works in 262.1

.17   Governing leaders in papal and episcopal systems

.18   Governing leaders in presbyterian systems

.19   Governing leaders in congregational systems

.2   **Local church and religious congregations and orders in church organization**

For administration of parishes, see 254; for government and administration of religious congregations and orders, see 255

See Manual at 260 vs. 251–254, 259

.22   Parishes

.24   Religious congregations and orders

.26   Small groups

Including basic Christian communities

> **262.3–262.4   Specific forms of church organization**

Class comprehensive works on government and organization of specific denominations and sects regardless of form of organization in 262.01–262.09; class comprehensive works in 262. Class a specific aspect of government and organization with the aspect, e.g., role of bishops in a system governed by episcopacy 262.12 (*not* 262.3)

.3   **Government and organization of systems governed by papacy and episcopacy**

Including sees, dioceses, cathedral systems

.4   **Government and organization of systems governed by election**

Including congregational systems, presbyteries, synods

.5   General councils

Add to base number 262.5 the numbers following 28 in 281–289, e.g., ecumenical councils of Roman Catholic Church 262.52

Class legal acts of general councils in 262.9. Class nonlegal decrees on a specific subject with the subject, e.g., statements on original sin 233.14

.7   Nature of the church

Including God's relation to the church

.72   Attributes, marks, notes

Including apostolicity, catholicity, credibility, holiness, infallibility, necessity, unity, visibility and invisibility

.73   Communion of saints

.77   Mystical body of Christ

.8   Church and ministerial authority and its denial

Including heresy, schism

.9   Church law and discipline

Class here canon (ecclesiastical) law

Class civil law relating to church or religious matters in 340

See also 364.188 for offenses against religion as defined and penalized by the state

---

>   262.91–262.94   Roman Catholic law

Class comprehensive works in 262.9

.91   Acts of the Holy See

Including apostolic letters, briefs, encyclicals, papal bulls and decrees

Class acts on a specific subject with the subject, e.g., on the nature of the church 262.7

.92   Early Roman Catholic codes

.922   Early codes to Gratian, ca. 1140

.923   Corpus iuris canonici

.924   Quinque compilationes antiquae

.93   Codex iuris canonici (1917)

.931   General principles (Canons 1–86)

.932   Persons (Canons 87–725)

Clergy, religious, laity

.933   Things (Canons 726–1551)

> Including benefices, sacraments, sacred times and places, teaching office, temporal goods, worship

.934   Procedure (Canons 1552–2194)

> Including trials, cases of beatification and canonization

.935   Crimes and penalties (Canons 2195–2414)

.94   Codex iuris canonici (1983)

.98   Branches and other denominations

> Add to base number 262.98 the numbers following 28 in 280.2–289.9, e.g., Anglican ecclesiastical law 262.983

263   Days, times, places of religious observance

.04   Special topics

.041   Pilgrimages [*formerly* 248.463]

[.041 093–.041 099]   Specific continents, countries, localities

> Do not use; class in 263.0423–263.0429

.042   Holy places

> Class here pilgrimages to holy places in specific continents, countries, localities
>
> *For works treating miracles and shrines associated with them, see 231.73; for miracles associated with Mary and shrines associated with them, see 232.917; for miracles of Jesus and shrines associated with them, see 232.955*

[.042 093–.042 099]   Specific continents, countries, localities

> Do not use; class in 263.0423–263.0429

.042 3–.042 9   Specific continents, countries, localities

> Add to base number 263.042 notation 3–9 from Table 2, e.g., Santiago de Compostela 263.0424611

> **263.1–263.3 Sabbath and Sunday**
>
> Class comprehensive works in 263.3

.1   **Biblical Sabbath**

.2   **Observance of the seventh day**

.3   **Sunday**

Class here Sunday observance [*formerly* 263.4], comprehensive works on
Sabbath and Sunday

> *For Biblical Sabbath, see 263.1; for observance of the seventh day, see
> 263.2*

[.4]   **Sunday observance**

Relocated to 263.3

.9   **Church year and other days and times**

Standard subdivisions are added for church year and other days and times
together, for church year alone

See Manual at 263.9, 291.36 vs. 394.265–394.267

> 263.91–263.94 Church year

Class comprehensive works in 263.9

.91   Advent and Christmas

.912   Advent

.915   Christmas season

Class here Christmas day

.92   Lent

.925   Holy Week

.93   Easter season

Including Ascension Day [*formerly* 263.97]

Class here Easter Sunday

.94   Pentecost and time after Pentecost (Ordinary time)

.97   Other feast and fast days

Ascension Day relocated to 263.93

For saints' days, see 263.98

.98   Saints' days

Standard subdivisions are added for individual saint's days

264   **Public worship**

Ceremonies, rites, services (liturgy and ritual)

Class works not limited by denomination or sect about sacraments, other rites and
acts in 265; class Sunday school services in 268.7; class comprehensive works on
worship in 248.3

SUMMARY

264.001–.009	**Standard subdivisions**
.01–.09	**Public worship by denominations and sects**
.1	**Prayer**
.2	**Music**
.3	**Scripture readings and communion sacrament**
.4	**Responsive readings**
.7	**Prayer meetings, Holy Hours, novenas**
.9	**Sacramentals**

.001   Philosophy and theory

Class here liturgical renewal

.002–.009   Standard subdivisions

> 264.01–264.09 Public worship by denominations and sects

Class here works limited by denomination or sect about sacraments, other rites and acts

Class comprehensive works in 264; class comprehensive works on sacraments, other rites and acts in 265

.01   Early and Eastern churches

Add to base number 264.01 the numbers following 281 in 281.1–281.9, e.g., liturgy and ritual of Eastern Orthodox churches 264.019; then add further as instructed under 264.04–264.09, e.g., Eastern Orthodox Mass 264.019036

.02   Roman Catholic Church

.020 01–.020 09   Standard subdivisions

.020 1–.020 9   History, meaning, place of liturgy, ritual, prayers in public worship

Add to base number 264.02 notation 01–09 from the table under 264.04–264.09, e.g., the Mass 264.02036; however, for texts, see 264.021–264.029

> 264.021–264.029 Texts of liturgy, ritual, prayers

Class comprehensive works in 264.02

.021   Texts of calendars and ordos

.022   Texts of ceremonials

Ceremonials: canonization of saints, election and coronation of popes, creation of cardinals, other papal functions and services; instructions for bishops

.023	Texts of missals

Class here sacramentaries

For lectionary, see 264.029

.024	Texts of breviaries

For psalters, see 264.028

.025	Texts of ritual

Class here Pontificale Romanum, Rituale Romanum

Add to base number 264.025 the numbers following 265 in 265.1–265.7, e.g., text of baptism 264.0251

.027	Texts of special books
.027 2	Texts for special times of year

Including Holy Week

.027 4	Texts for special liturgical services

Including funeral services outside the Mass, litanies, novenas, stations of the cross

.028	Texts of psalters
.029	Texts of lectionary
.03	Anglican churches

Including rubrics

Class here Book of Common Prayer

.030 01–.030 09	Standard subdivisions
.030 1–.030 9	History, meaning, place of liturgy, ritual, prayers in public worship

Add to base number 264.03 notation 01–09 from the table under 264.04–264.09, e.g., prayer 264.0301; however, for texts, see 264.031–264.038

>   264.031–264.038 Texts of liturgy, ritual, prayers

Class comprehensive works in 264.03

.031	Texts of calendars, festivals, fasts
.032	Texts of lectionary

Including texts of epistles, Gospels [*formerly also* 264.036]

Use of this number for rubrics discontinued; class in 264.03

.033	Texts of morning prayer and litany

.034   Texts of evening prayer and vespers

.035   Texts of sacraments, ordinances, services

> Add to base number 264.035 the numbers following 265 in 265.1–265.7, e.g., text of baptism 264.0351

> Class texts of morning prayer and litany in 264.033; class texts of evening prayer and vespers in 264.034

.036   Texts of collects

> Texts of epistles, Gospels relocated to 264.032

[.037]   Texts of ordinal, articles, creeds

> Number discontinued; class in 264.03

.038   Texts of psalters

.04–.09   Other specific denominations and sects

> Add to base number 264.0 the numbers following 28 in 284–289, e.g., United Methodist services 264.076; then add further as follows:
>
> 001–009   Standard subdivisions
> 01–07   Specific elements
> History, meaning, place in public worship, texts
> Add to 0 the numbers following 264 in 264.1–264.7, e.g., the Lord's Supper 036, the Lord's Supper in the United Methodist Church 264.076036
> 08   Sacraments
> History, meaning, place in public worship, texts
> Add to 08 the numbers following 265 in 265.1–265.7, e.g., the ceremony of baptism 081, the ceremony of baptism in the United Methodist Church 264.076081; however, for Holy Communion (Eucharist, Lord's Supper, Mass), see 036
> 09   Sacramentals, other rites and acts
> History, meaning, place in public worship, texts
> 091   Sacramentals
> 098–099   Other rites and acts
> Add to 09 the numbers following 265 in 265.8–265.9, e.g., funeral services 0985, United Methodist funerals 264.0760985

>   **264.1–264.9   Specific elements**

History, meaning, place in public worship, texts

Class specific elements in public worship of specific denominations and sects in 264.01–264.09; class use of the arts (except music), of color in public worship in 246; class liturgical year in 263.9; class comprehensive works in 264

Specific elements as part of the Mass are classed in 264.36, e.g., Eucharistic prayers (*not* 264.1)

.1   **Prayer**

> Class prayers for a specific ceremony with the ceremony, e.g., prayers for funerals 265.85

.13   Texts of prayers

> Including litanies
>
> Class comprehensive collections of public and private prayers in 242.8

.15   Liturgy of the hours (Divine office)

> Including psalters
>
> Class here breviaries

.2   **Music**

> Class comprehensive works on music in Christianity in 246.75; class interdisciplinary works on Christian sacred music in 781.71; class interdisciplinary works on sacred vocal music in 782.22

.23   Hymns

> Class here texts of hymns for devotional use of individuals and families [*formerly* 245]
>
> Class hymnals containing both text and music, interdisciplinary works on hymns in 782.27

.3   **Scripture readings and communion sacrament**

.34   Scripture readings

> Class here common lectionary

.36   Holy Communion (Eucharist, Lord's Supper, Mass)

> Including specific elements when part of the Mass
>
> *For viaticum, see 265.7*

.4   **Responsive readings**

[.5–.6]   **Creeds, confessions of faith, sermons, exhortations, instructions**

> Numbers discontinued; class in 264

.7   **Prayer meetings, Holy Hours, novenas**

.9   **Sacramentals**

> *For consecrations and dedications, see 265.92*

265   Sacraments, other rites and acts

Standard subdivisions are added for sacraments and other rites and acts together, for sacraments alone

Not limited by denomination or sect

Class works limited by denomination or sect about sacraments, other rites and acts in 264.01–264.09

> ### 265.1–265.7 Sacraments

Class comprehensive works in 265

For Holy Communion (Eucharist, Lord's Supper, Mass), see 264.36

.1   Baptism

.12   Infant baptism

.13   Adult baptism

Class here Christian initiation (baptism and confirmation) of adults, catechumenate

For confirmation, see 265.2; for religious education for catechumens, see 268.434

.2   Confirmation

.4   Holy Orders

.5   Matrimony

.6   Penance

.61   Contrition

Examination of conscience, prayers preparatory to confession

.62   Confession

.63   Satisfaction

Penitential prayers and acts for the remission of sin

.64   Absolution

.66   Indulgences

.7   Viaticum and anointing of the sick

.8   Rites in illness and death

.82   Religious ceremonies for the afflicted

For viaticum and anointing of the sick, see 265.7

.85 Religious ceremonies for the dead

Class here funeral services

For requiem Mass, see 264.36

.9 Other acts

Including ceremonies of joining a church, foot washing, laying on of hands, love feasts (agapes)

.92 Consecrations and dedications

.94 Exorcism

266 Missions

Class here missionary societies, religious aspects of medical missions

Class medical services of medical missions in 362.1

For mission schools, see 371.071

.001–.008 Standard subdivisions

.009 Historical, geographic, persons treatment

Do not use for foreign missions originating in specific continents, countries, localities; class in 266.023. Do not use for historical, geographic, persons treatment of missions of specific denominations and sects; class in 266.1–266.9

Class here joint and interdenominational missions; foreign missions by continent, country, locality served

.02 Kinds of missions

.022 Home missions

.023 Foreign missions

[.023 091–.023 099] Geographic and persons treatment

Do not use for foreign missions characterized only by place served; class in 266.009. Do not use for foreign missions originating in specific areas; class in 266.0231–266.0239

.023 1–.023 9 Persons treatment and foreign missions originating in specific areas

Add to base number 266.023 notation 1–9 from Table 2, e.g., missions originating in France 266.02344; then add 0* and again add notation 1–9 from Table 2 for place served, e.g., French missions to Africa 266.0234406

.1–.9 Missions of specific denominations and sects

Add to base number 266 the numbers following 28 in 281–289, e.g., Anglican missions 266.3; Anglican missions serving Africa 266.36

---

*Add 00 for standard subdivisions; see instructions at beginning of Table 1

267 Associations for religious work

Class here pious societies, sodalities, confraternities [*all formerly* 248.06]

> *For religious congregations and orders, see 255; for missionary societies, see 266*
>
> *See Manual at 230–280: Biography*

.1 Associations for religious work for both men and women

.13   Interdenominational and nondenominational associations

> *For Moral Rearmament, see 267.16*

.16   Moral Rearmament

.18   Specific branches, denominations, and sects

> Add to base number 267.18 the numbers following 28 in 280.2–289.9, e.g., Baptist Adult Union 267.186132

.2 Men's associations

.23   Interdenominational and nondenominational associations

> *For Young Men's Christian Associations, see 267.3*

.24   Specific branches, denominations, and sects

> Add to base number 267.24 the numbers following 28 in 280.2–289.9, e.g., Baptist societies 267.246

.3 Young Men's Christian Associations

.306   Organizations and management [*formerly also* 267.33]

[.309]   Historical, geographic, persons treatment

> Do not use; class in 267.39

[.31–.32]   Program and objectives, buildings and equipment

> Numbers discontinued; class in 267.3

[.33]   Organization and management

> Relocated to 267.306

[.34–.35]   Staff and departments

> Numbers discontinued; class in 267.3

.39   Historical, geographic, persons treatment

> Add to base number 267.39 notation 01–9 from Table 2, e.g., Young Men's Christian Association in New York City 267.397471

.4 Women's associations

.43   Interdenominational and nondenominational associations

For Young Women's Christian Associations, see 267.5

.44   Specific branches, denominations, and sects

Add to base number 267.44 the numbers following 28 in 280.2–289.9, e.g., Baptist societies 267.446

.5   Young Women's Christian Associations

.506   Organizations and management [*formerly also* 267.53]

[.509]   Historical, geographic, persons treatment

Do not use; class in 267.59

[.51–.52]   Program and objectives, buildings and equipment

Numbers discontinued; class in 267.5

[.53]   Organization and management

Relocated to 267.506

[.54–.55]   Staff and departments

Numbers discontinued; class in 267.5

.59   Historical, geographic, persons treatment

Add to base number 267.59 notation 01–9 from Table 2, e.g., Young Women's Christian Association in New York City 267.597471

.6   Young adults' associations

.61   Interdenominational and nondenominational associations

For Young Men's Christian Associations, see 267.3; for Young Women's Christian Associations, see 267.5

[.613]   Young People's Society of Christian Endeavor

Number discontinued; class in 267.61

.62   Specific branches, denominations, and sects

Add to base number 267.62 the numbers following 28 in 280.2–289.9, e.g., Baptist Young People's Union 267.626132

.7   Boys' associations

For Young Men's Christian Associations, see 267.3

.8   Girls' associations

For Young Women's Christian Associations, see 267.5

268 Religious education

Class here catechetics (the science or art devoted to organizing the principles of religious teaching), curricula, comprehensive works on Christian religious education

Class Christian religious schools providing general education in 371.071; class place of religion in public schools in 379.28. Class textbooks on a specific subject with the subject, e.g., textbooks on missions 266

For religious education at the university level, see 230.0711; for study of Christianity in secular secondary schools, see 230.0712

See Manual at 268 vs. 230.071

[.068]   Management

Do not use; class in 268.1

.08   History and description with respect to kinds of persons

Do not use for education of specific groups; class in 268.4

Class here education, teaching performed by kinds of persons

[.088 2]   History and descriptions with respect to religious groups

Do not use; class in 268.8

[.088 375]   Students

Do not use; class in 268.4

.1   **Administration**

For plant management, see 268.2; for personnel management, see 268.3

.2   **Buildings and equipment**

.3   **Personnel**

Class here preparation, role, training, personnel management

See Manual at 230–280: Biography

.4   **Religious education of specific groups**

Class here curricula, records and rules, teaching methods, services for specific groups

.43   Specific age groups

.432   Children

Through age eleven

See also 372.84 for religion courses in secular elementary schools

(.432 04)   Special topics

| (.432 045) | Textbooks |
| | (Option: Class here religious education textbooks; prefer the specific subject, e.g., textbooks on Christianity 230, textbooks on missions 266) |

.433	Adolescents
(.433 04)	Special topics
(.433 045)	Textbooks
	(Option: Class here religious education textbooks; prefer the specific subject, e.g., textbooks on Christianity 230, textbooks on missions 266)

.434	Adults
(.434 04)	Special topics
(.434 045)	Textbooks
	(Option: Class here religious education textbooks; prefer the specific subject, e.g., textbooks on Christianity 230, textbooks on missions 266)

.5 Records and rules

Including attendance, decorations, honor rolls, prizes, promotion

Class records and rules for specific groups in 268.4

.6 Methods of instruction and study

Class methods for a specific group with the group, e.g., methods for instruction of children 268.432071

[.61–.62] Value and use of textbooks, textbook method

Numbers discontinued; class in 268.6

.63 Lecture and audiovisual methods

.632 Lecture method

.635 Audiovisual methods

.67 Dramatic method

Class use of dramatic arts for religious purposes not limited to religious education in 246.72

[.68] Laboratory methods

Number discontinued; class in 268.6

.7 Services

Including anniversaries, festivals, music, rallies, special days

Class services for specific groups in 268.4

.8   Specific branches, denominations, and sects

Add to base number 268.8 the numbers following 28 in 280.2–289.9, e.g., Presbyterian religious education 268.85

Class a specific element in religious education by specific denominations and sects with the element in 268.1–268.7, e.g., religious education of children in Baptist churches 268.432088261

269   Spiritual renewal

Class history of the pentecostal movement in 270.82

.2   Evangelism

See also 243 for evangelistic writings for individuals and families, 248.5 for witness bearing by individual lay Christians, 252.3 for texts of evangelistic sermons, 266 for missionary evangelization

.24   Revival and camp meetings

.26   Evangelism by radio and television

[.4]   Pentecostalism

Number discontinued; class in 269

.6   Retreats

Add to base number 269.6 the numbers following 248.8 in 248.82–248.89, e.g., retreats for men 269.642

> ## 270–280 Historical, geographic, persons treatment of Christianity; Church history; Christian denominations and sects

Unless other instructions are given, observe the following table of preference for the history of Christianity and the Christian church (except for biography, explained in Manual at 230–280: Biography), e.g., persecution of Jesuits by Elizabeth I 272.7 (*not* 271.53042, 274.206, or 282.42):

Persecutions in general church history	272
Doctrinal controversies and heresies in general church history	273
Religious congregations and orders in church history	271
Denominations and sects of Christian church	280
Treatment of Christianity and Christian church by continent, country, locality	274–279
General historical, geographic, persons treatment of Christianity and Christian church (*except* 271–279)	270

Class comprehensive works in 270

See Manual at 230–280: Biography; also at 280: Biography

270   Historical, geographic, persons treatment of Christianity [*formerly* 209]   Church history

Class here collected writings of apostolic and church fathers (patristics)

Observe table of preference under 230–280

For historical, geographic, persons treatment of specific denominations and sects, see 280

See Manual at 230–280: Biography

SUMMARY

270.01–.09	Standard subdivisions
.1–.8	Historical periods
271	Religious congregations and orders in church history
272	Persecutions in general church history
273	Doctrinal controversies and heresies in general church history
274–279	Treatment by continent, country, locality

.01–.07   Standard subdivisions

.08   Christianity with respect to kinds of persons [*formerly* 208], church history with respect to kinds of persons

See Manual at 230: Contextual theology

.09	Areas, regions, places in general, persons
[.093–.099]	Treatment by continent, country, locality

Do not use; class in 274–279

> **270.1–270.8 Historical periods**

Class historical periods in specific continents, countries, localities in 274–279; class comprehensive works in 270

See Manual at 281.1–281.4

.1 **Apostolic period to 325**

.2 **Period of ecumenical councils, 325–787**

.3 **787–1054**

Class here comprehensive works on Middle Ages

For a specific part of Middle Ages, see the part, e.g., late Middle Ages 270.5

.38 Great schism, 1054

.4 **1054–1200**

.5 **Late Middle Ages through Renaissance, 1200–1517**

.6 **Period of Reformation and Counter-Reformation, 1517–1648**

Including 17th century

For 1648–1699, see 270.7

.7 **Period from Peace of Westphalia to French Revolution, 1648–1789**

.8 **Modern period, 1789–**

.81 1789–1900

.82   1900–1999

Class here comprehensive works on evangelicalism, fundamentalism, pentecostalism, charismatic movement

Add to base number 270.82 the numbers following —0904 in notation 09041–09049 from Table 1, e.g., 1960–1969 in church history 270.826

Ecumenical movement relocated to 280.042

Class pentecostal churches that are independent denominations in 289.94; class evangelical churches, fundamentalist churches that are independent denominations in 289.95

For evangelicalism, fundamentalism, pentecostalism, charismatic movement in the period 2000–   , see 270.83. For evangelicalism, fundamentalism, pentecostalism, charismatic movement in a specific branch or denomination, see the branch or denomination, e.g., Protestant fundamentalism 280.4

.83   2000–

>   **271–273   Special topics of church history**

Class comprehensive works in 270

271   Religious congregations and orders in church history

Class here history of monasticism, history of specific monasteries and convents even if not connected with a specific order

Add to each subdivision identified by * as follows:
```
001–008      Standard subdivisions
[009]        Historical treatment
                 Do not use; class in base number without further addition
[0091–0099]  Geographic and persons treatment
                 Do not use; class in 01–09
01–09     Geographic and persons treatment
                 Add to base number 0 notation 1–9 from Table 2, e.g., collected
                 biography 022, collected biography of Benedictines 271.1022,
                 Benedictines in the United Kingdom 271.1041
```

Class persecutions involving religious congregations and orders in 272; class doctrinal controversies and heresies involving congregations and orders in 273

SUMMARY

.001–.009   Standard subdivisions

> 271.01–271.09 Specific kinds

Class comprehensive works in 271

.01   *Contemplative religious orders

.02   *Eremitical religious orders

.03   *Teaching orders

.04   *Preaching orders

[.05]   Military orders

Relocated to 271.791

.06   *Mendicant religious orders

.07   *Nursing orders

.08   *Canons regular

.09   Other specific kinds

.092   *Brothers

See also 271.093 for lay brothers

.093   *Lay brothers

.094   *Third orders

Secular and regular

.095   *Secular institutes

> 271.1–271.8 Specific orders of men

Class comprehensive works in 271

*Add as instructed under 271

>   **271.1–271.7   Roman Catholic orders of men**

         Class comprehensive works in 271

.1   ***Benedictines**

.11   *Confederated Benedictines

         For Olivetans, see 271.13

.12   *Cistercians (Bernardines)

.125   *Trappists

.13   *Olivetans

.14   *Cluniacs

         Including Camaldolese, Silvestrians, Monks of Saint Paul the Hermit

         For Carthusians, see 271.71

.16   *Celestines

.17   Mechitarists and Basilians

.18   Antonines (Antonians), Maronites, Chaldeans, Syrians

.19   *Canons

         Including Crosier Fathers, Crosiers of the Red Star, Premonstratensians

         Class Augustinians in 271.4

.2   ***Dominicans (Friars Preachers, Black Friars)**

.3   ***Franciscans (Gray Friars)**

         Including Alcantarines, Observants, Recollects

         See also 271.4 for Augustinian Recollects

.36   *Capuchins

.37   *Conventuals

.38   *Third Order Regular

.4   ***Augustinians**

         Including Augustinian Recollects

.42   *Trinitarians

.45   *Mercedarians

.47   *Servites

*Add as instructed under 271

.49	Other Augustinians

Including Brothers Hospitallers of St. John of God, Minims

.5	***Regular clerics**
.51	*Theatines
.52	*Barnabites
.53	*Jesuits (Society of Jesus)
.54	*Somaschi
.55	*Camillians
.56	*Minor Clerks Regular (Caracciolini)
.57	*Clerks Regular of the Mother of God
.58	*Piarists
.6	***Passionists and Redemptorists**
.62	*Passionists
.64	*Redemptorists
.7	**Roman Catholic orders of men not otherwise provided for**
.71	*Carthusians
.73	*Carmelites (White Friars)
.75	*Sulpicians
.76	*Oblates
.77	*Lazarists (Vincentians)
.78	*Christian Brothers (Brothers of the Christian Schools)
.79	Other Roman Catholic orders of men
.791	*Orders of knighthood

Class here military orders [*formerly* 271.05]

.791 2	*Knights of Malta (Knights Hospitalers of St. John of Jerusalem)
.791 3	*Knights Templars
.791 4	*Teutonic Knights
.8	**Non-Roman Catholic orders of men**
.81	Monasteries of Eastern churches

Add to base number 271.81 the numbers following 281 in 281.5–281.9, e.g., Eastern Orthodox monasteries 271.819, on Mount Athos 271.81949565

---

*Add as instructed under 271

.83	Anglican orders of men

.9   **Congregations and orders of women**

.900 01–.900 08	Standard subdivisions
.900 09	Historical treatment
[.900 091–.900 099]	Geographic and persons treatment

> Do not use; class in 271.9001–271.9009

.900 1–.900 9	Geographic and persons treatment

Add to base number 271.900 notation 1–9 from Table 2, e.g., collected biography of women religious 271.90022, congregations and orders of women in France 271.90044

.901–.909	Specific kinds

Add to base number 271.90 the numbers following 271.0 in 271.01–271.09, e.g., contemplative orders 271.901

>   271.91–271.98   Specific orders of women

Class comprehensive works in 271.9

>   271.91–271.97   Roman Catholic orders of women

Class comprehensive works in 271.9

.91	*Sisters of Charity orders
.92	*Sisters of Mercy orders
.93	*Sacred Heart orders
.94	*Sisters of Bon Secours
.95	*Little Sisters of the Poor
.97	Other Roman Catholic orders of women
.971	*Carmelites
.972	*Dominicans
.973	*Franciscan orders

Class here Poor Clares

.974	*Ursulines
.975	*Visitation orders
.976	*Saint Joseph orders

*Add as instructed under 271

.977   *Presentation orders

.98   Non-Roman Catholic orders of women

.981   Women's convents of Eastern churches

> Add to base number 271.981 the numbers following 281 in 281.5–281.9, e.g., Eastern Orthodox convents of women 271.9819

.983   Anglican orders of women

272   Persecutions in general church history

Regardless of denomination

Class here martyrs

Class relation of state to church in 322.1

> *See also 364.188 for offenses against religion as defined and penalized by the state*

.1   Persecutions of Apostolic Church by imperial Rome

.2   Persecutions by Inquisition

.3   Persecutions of Waldenses and Albigenses

.4   Persecutions of Huguenots

.5   Persecutions of Molinists and Quietists

.6   Persecutions of Anglican reformers by Mary I

.7   Persecutions of Roman Church by Elizabeth I and Anglicans

.8   Persecutions of Quakers, Baptists, witches by Puritans and others of Puritan times

.9   Modern persecutions and martyrs

273   Doctrinal controversies and heresies in general church history

Class persecutions resulting from controversies and heresies in 272; class churches founded on specific doctrines in 280

> *See also 239 for apologetics and polemics*

.1   1st–2nd centuries

Class here Christian Gnosticism

Class comprehensive works and non-Christian Gnosticism in 299.932

> *For Gnosticism of 3rd century, see 273.2*

*Add as instructed under 271

.2	**3rd century**

Including Christian Manicheism

Class comprehensive works and non-Christian Manicheism in 299.932

For Sabellianism, see 273.3

.3	**Sabellianism**
.4	**4th century**

Including Arianism, Donatism

.5	**5th century**

Including Pelagianism

.6	**6th–16th centuries**

Including Albigensianism, Catharism, Waldensianism

Class here antinomianism

For later antinomianism, see 273.7–273.9; for Albigensian, Catharist, Waldensian churches, see 284.4

.7	**17th century**

Including Molinism, Pietism, comprehensive works on Jansenism

For Jansenist churches, see 284.84

.8	**18th century**
.9	**19th century and later centuries**

Including modernism

274–279 Treatment by continent, country, locality

Add to base number 27 notation 4–9 from Table 2, e.g., Christianity, Christian church in Europe 274, in France 274.4; then to the result add the numbers following 27 in 270.01–270.8, e.g., Christian church in France during the Reformation 274.406

Class geographic treatment of a specific subject with the subject, plus notation 09 from Table 1, e.g., persecutions in France 272.0944

280 Denominations and sects of Christian church

Including nondenominational and interdenominational churches

Class here general historical and geographic treatment of, comprehensive works on specific denominations and sects and their individual local churches

Class persecution of or by specific churches in 272

> *See also 273 for doctrines of specific churches considered as heresies*

> *See Manual at 230–280: Biography; also at 280: Biography; also at at 291: Denominations and sects*

(Option: Class here specific elements of specific denominations and sects; prefer 230–270. If option is chosen, add to the number for each specific denomination, sect, group as follows:

001–008	Standard subdivisions
[009]	Historical, geographic, persons treatment
	Do not use; class in 07
02	Basic textual sources
	Class Bible in 220
03–06	Doctrinal, moral, devotional, social, ecclesiastical theology
	Add to 0 the numbers following 2 in 230–260, e.g., the denomination and international affairs 06187
07	Historical, geographic, persons treatment
	Add to 07 the numbers following 27 in 270.1–279, e.g., 20th century 07082)

SUMMARY

280.01–.09	**Standard subdivisions and special topics**
.2–.4	**Branches**
281	**Early church and Eastern churches**
282	**Roman Catholic Church**
283	**Anglican churches**
284	**Protestant denominations of Continental origin and related bodies**
285	**Presbyterian churches, Reformed churches centered in America, Congregational churches, Puritanism**
286	**Baptist, Disciples of Christ, Adventist churches**
287	**Methodist churches; churches related to Methodism**
289	**Other denominations and sects**

.01–.03   Standard subdivisions

.04   Special topics

.042   Relations between denominations

Class here ecumenical movement [*formerly* 270.82]

See Manual at 280.042 vs. 262.0011

.05–.09   Standard subdivisions

> ## 280.2–280.4 Branches

Class specific denominations and sects in 281–289; class comprehensive works in 280

.2 Eastern and Roman Catholic churches

Class comprehensive works on Roman Catholic Church and Eastern churches in communion with Rome in 282

For specific denominations and sects, see 281–282

.4 Protestant churches and Protestantism

Standard subdivisions are added for either or both topics in heading

Class here dissenters, free churches, nonconformists (British context); works on Protestant evangelicalism, fundamentalism, pentecostalism, charismatic movement

Class comprehensive works on evangelicalism, fundamentalism, pentecostalism, charismatic movement in general church history in 270.82

For specific Protestant denominations, see 283–289

> # 281–289 Specific denomination

Class comprehensive works in 280

(Option: Class a specific denomination or sect requiring local emphasis in 289.2)

281 Early church and Eastern churches

> ### 281.1–281.4 Early church

Use these subdivisions only for building other numbers in 230–260, e.g., theology in the Ante-Nicene church 230.13; never use these subdivisions by themselves. When building numbers in 230–260 using these subdivisions, use 281.1 for comprehensive works

Class collected writings of apostolic and church fathers (patristics) in 270; class all works on early church in 270.1–270.3. Class a specific work of an apostolic or church father on a specific subject with the subject, e.g., philosophy 189.2

See Manual at 281.1–281.4

.1 Apostolic Church to the time of the great schism, 1054

For Apostolic Church to 100, see 281.2; for Ante-Nicene church, see 281.3; for Post-Nicene church, see 281.4

.2	**Apostolic Church to 100**
.3	**Ante-Nicene church, 100–325**
.4	**Post-Nicene church, 325–1054**
.5	**Eastern churches**

> Including Catholics of Eastern rites (Eastern rite churches in communion with Rome), St. Thomas (Mar Thoma, Syro-Malabar) Christians
>
> *For Monophysite churches, see 281.6; for Coptic and Ethiopian churches, see 281.7; for Nestorian churches, see 281.8; for Eastern Orthodox churches, see 281.9*
>
> *See Manual at 281.1–281.4*

.6	**Monophysite churches**

> Including Eutychian Church
>
> *For Coptic and Ethiopian churches, see 281.7*

.62	Armenian Church
.63	Jacobite Church

> Class here Syrian Orthodox Church, Jacobite Patriarchate of Antioch
>
> *See also 281.95691 for Eastern Orthodox Church in Syria*

.7	**Coptic and Ethiopian churches**
.72	Coptic (Coptic Orthodox) church
.75	Ethiopian (Ethiopian Orthodox) church
.8	**Nestorian churches**
.9	**Eastern Orthodox churches**
.909	Historical, geographic, persons treatment

> *See Manual at 281.1–281.4*

[.909 3]	Geographic treatment in the ancient world

> Do not use; class early church in 270

[.909 4–.909 9]	Treatment by specific continents, countries, localities in the modern world

> Do not use; class in 281.94–281.99

.94–.99	Treatment by continent, country, locality

> Add to base number 281.9 notation 4–9 from Table 2, e.g., Russian Orthodox Church 281.947, Orthodox Church in America 281.97

282 Roman Catholic Church

Class here the Catholic traditionalist movement, comprehensive works on Roman Catholic Church and Eastern rite churches in communion with Rome

Class modern schisms in Roman Catholic Church in 284.8

For Eastern rite churches in communion with Rome, see 281.5–281.8

.09 Historical, geographic, persons treatment

See Manual at 281.1–281.4

[.093] Geographic treatment in the ancient world

Do not use; class early church in 270

[.094–.099] Treatment by specific continents, countries, localities in the modern world

Do not use; class in 282.4–282.9

.4–.9 Treatment by continent, country, locality

Add to base number 282 notation 4–9 from Table 2, e.g., Roman Catholic Church in Latin America 282.8

> ## 283–289 Protestant and other denominations

Class comprehensive works on Protestant churches in 280.4; class comprehensive works on Protestant and other denominations in 280

See Manual at 283–289

283 Anglican churches

[.094–.099] Treatment by specific continents, countries, localities in the modern world

Do not use; class in 283.4–283.9

.3 Branches not in communion with the See of Canterbury

Including Reformed Episcopal Church and its affiliates

See Manual at 280: Biography; also at 283–289

.4–.9 Treatment by continent, country, locality

Class here national churches in communion with the See of Canterbury

Add to base number 283 notation 4–9 from Table 2, e.g., Church of England 283.42, Episcopal Diocese of Long Island 283.74721

284   Protestant denominations of Continental origin and related bodies

For Protestant denominations of Continental origin not provided for here, see the denomination, e.g., Baptists 286

.1   Lutheran churches

[.109 4–.109 9]   Treatment by specific continents, countries, localities in the modern world

> Do not use; class in 284.14–284.19

(.12)   (Permanently unassigned)

> (Optional number used to provide local emphasis or a shorter number for Lutheran church in a specific country other than the United States; prefer 284.14–284.19)

.13   Specific denominations, branches, synods centered in the United States

See Manual at 280: Biography; also at 283–289

[.130 1–.130 9]   Standard subdivisions

> Do not use; class in 284.101–284.109

.131   *The American Lutheran Church

.131 2   *The Evangelical Lutheran Church

.131 3   *United Evangelical Lutheran Church

.131 4   *The Lutheran Free Church

.132   *The Evangelical Lutheran Synodical Conference of North America

For Wisconsin Evangelical Lutheran Synod, see 284.134

.132 2   *The Lutheran Church—Missouri Synod

For Synod of Evangelical Lutheran Churches, see 284.1323

.132 3   *Synod of Evangelical Lutheran Churches (Slovak)

.133   *The Lutheran Church in America

.133 2   *American Evangelical Lutheran Church

.133 3   *Augustana Evangelical Lutheran Church

.133 4   *Finnish Evangelical Lutheran Church

.133 5   *The United Lutheran Church in America

.134   *Wisconsin Evangelical Lutheran Synod

.135   *Evangelical Lutheran Church in America

---

*Do not use notation 094–099 from Table 1; class in 284.14–284.19

.14–.19 Treatment by continent, country, locality

Add to base number 284.1 notation 4–9 from Table 2, e.g., Lutheran Church of Sweden 284.1485, Memorial Evangelical Lutheran Church of Washington, D.C. 284.1753

See Manual at 284.143

(Option: Class Lutheran churches in a specific country other than the United States in 284.12)

.2 **Calvinistic and Reformed churches of European origin**

Standard subdivisions are added for either or both topics in heading

Class here comprehensive works on Calvinistic churches, on Reformed churches

For Huguenot churches, see 284.5; for Presbyterian churches, see 285; for Reformed churches centered in America, see 285.7

See also 285.9 for Puritanism

[.209 4–.209 9] Treatment by specific continents, countries, localities in the modern world

Do not use; class in 284.24–284.29

.24–.29 Treatment by continent, country, locality

Add to base number 284.2 notation 4–9 from Table 2, e.g., Reformed churches in Holland 284.2492, in South Africa 284.268

.3 **Hussite and Anabaptist churches**

Including Lollards, Wycliffites

See also 289.7 for Mennonite churches

.4 **Albigensian, Catharist, Waldensian churches**

.5 **Huguenot churches**

.6 **Moravian churches**

For Hussite churches, see 284.3

[.609 4–.609 9] Treatment by specific continents, countries, localities in the modern world

Do not use; class in 284.64–284.69

.64–.69 Treatment by continent, country, locality

Add to base number 284.6 notation 4–9 from Table 2, e.g., Moravian churches in Germany 284.643

.8 **Modern schisms in Roman Catholic Church**

Including Constitutional Church, Gallican schismatic churches, Liberal Catholic Church, Little Church of France, Old Catholic churches, Philippine Independent Church

.84   Jansenist churches

.9   Arminian and Remonstrant churches

285   Presbyterian churches, Reformed churches centered in America, Congregational churches, Puritanism

Standard subdivisions are added for Presbyterian churches, Reformed churches centered in America, Congregational churches together; for Presbyterian churches alone

---

> **285.1–285.2 Presbyterian churches of United States, of British Commonwealth origin**

Class comprehensive works on Presbyterian churches, Presbyterian churches of other origin in 285

(If option under 280 is followed, use 285.001–285.008 for standard subdivisions, 285.02–285.07 for specific elements of Presbyterian churches)

.1   Presbyterian churches of United States origin

[.109 4–.109 9]   Treatment by specific continents, countries, localities in the modern world

Do not use; class in 285.14–285.19

.13   Specific denominations

See Manual at 280: Biography; also at 283–289

[.130 1–.130 9]   Standard subdivisions

Do not use; class in 285.101–285.109

.131   *United Presbyterian Church in the U.S.A.

.132   *Presbyterian Church in the United States of America

.133   *Presbyterian Church in the United States

.134   *United Presbyterian Church of North America

.135   *Cumberland Presbyterian Church

.136   *Reformed Presbyterian churches

.137   *Presbyterian Church (U.S.A.)

.14–.19   Treatment by continent, country, locality

Add to base number 285.1 notation 4–9 from Table 2, e.g., the Hudson River Presbytery 285.17473

.2   Presbyterian churches of British Commonwealth origin

---

*Do not use notation 094–099 from Table 1; class in 285.14–285.19

[.209 4–.209 9]   Treatment by specific continents, countries, localities in the modern world

        Do not use; class in 285.24–285.29

.23   Specific denominations

    See Manual at 280: Biography; also at 283–289

[.230 1–.230 9]   Standard subdivisions

        Do not use; class in 285.201–285.209

.232   †United Reformed Church in the United Kingdom

    Class Congregational Church of England and Wales in 285.842

.233   †Church of Scotland

.234   †Free Church of Scotland

.235   †Presbyterian Church of Wales (Welsh Calvinistic Methodist Church)

.24–.29   Treatment by continent, country, locality

    Add to base number 285.2 notation 4–9 from Table 2, e.g., Presbyterianism in Ireland 285.2415, a Church of Scotland parish in Edinburgh 285.24134

    Class United Church of Canada in 287.92; class Uniting Church in Australia in 287.93

.7   Reformed churches centered in America

[.709 4–.709 9]   Treatment by specific continents, countries, localities in the modern world

        Do not use; class in 285.74–285.79

.73   Specific denominations

    See Manual at 280: Biography; also at 283–289

[.730 1–.730 9]   Standard subdivisions

        Do not use; class in 285.701–285.709

.731   *Christian Reformed Church

.732   *Reformed Church in America (Dutch)

.733   *Reformed Church in the United States (German)

.734   *Evangelical and Reformed Church

.74–.79   Treatment by continent, country, locality

    Add to base number 285.7 notation 4–9 from Table 2, e.g., First Reformed Church of Schenectady, N.Y. 285.774744

---

*Do not use notation 094–099 from Table 1; class in 285.74–285.79
†Do not use notation 094–099 from Table 1; class in 285.24–285.29

.8   **Congregationalism**

[.809 4–.809 9]   Treatment by specific continents, countries, localities in the modern world

         Do not use; class in 285.84–285.89

(.82)   (Permanently unassigned)

         (Optional number used to provide local emphasis or a shorter number for Congregational churches in a specific country other than the United States; prefer 285.84–285.89)

.83   Specific denominations centered in the United States

         See Manual at 280: Biography; also at 283–289

[.830 1–.830 9]   Standard subdivisions

         Do not use; class in 285.801–285.809

.832   †Congregational Churches of the United States

.833   †Congregational Christian Churches

.834   †United Church of Christ

         For Evangelical and Reformed Church, see 285.734

.84–.89   Treatment by continent, country, locality

         Class here specific denominations centered outside the United States

         Add to base number 285.8 notation 4–9 from Table 2, e.g., Congregational Church of England and Wales 285.842, Congregational churches in New England 285.874

         Class United Church of Canada in 287.92; class Uniting Church in Australia in 287.93

         (Option: Class Congregational churches in a specific country other than the United States in 285.82)

.9   **Puritanism**

286   Baptist, Disciples of Christ, Adventist churches

         Standard subdivisions are added for Baptist, Disciples of Christ, Adventist churches together; for Baptist churches alone

---

>   **286.1–286.5   Baptist churches**

         Class comprehensive works in 286

         (If option under 280 is followed, use 286.001–286.008 for standard subdivisions, 286.02–286.07 for specific elements of Baptist churches)

.1   **Regular (Calvinistic) Baptists**

---

†Do not use notation 094–099 from Table 1; class in 285.84–285.89

[.109 4–.109 9]	Treatment by specific continents, countries, localities in the modern world

> Do not use; class in 286.14–286.19

(.12)   **(Permanently unassigned)**

> (Optional number used to provide local emphasis or a shorter number for Regular Baptist churches in a specific country other than the United States; prefer 286.14–286.19)

.13   **Specific denominations centered in the United States**

> *See Manual at 280: Biography; also at 283–289*

[.130 1–.130 9]   Standard subdivisions

> Do not use; class in 286.101–286.109

.131   *American Baptist Churches in the U.S.A.

> Former name: American (Northern) Baptist Convention

.132   *Southern Baptist Convention

.133   *National Baptist Convention of the United States of America

.134   *National Baptist Convention of America

.135   *Progressive National Baptist Convention

.136   *American Baptist Association

.14–.19   **Treatment by continent, country, locality**

> Class here specific denominations centered outside the United States

> Add to base number 286.1 notation 4–9 from Table 2, e.g., Association of Regular Baptist Churches of Canada 286.171, a Southern Baptist association in Tennessee 286.1768

> (Option: Class Regular Baptist churches in a specific country other than the United States in 286.12)

.2   **Freewill Baptists**

.3   **Seventh-Day Baptists**

.4   **Old School Baptists**

> Including Antimission, Hard-Shell, Primitive Baptists

.5   **Other Baptist churches and denominations**

> Including Baptist General Conference, Church of the Brethren, Dunkers

.6   **Disciples of Christ (Campbellites)**

---

*Do not use notation 094–099 from Table 1; class in 286.14–286.19

[.609 4–.609 9]   Treatment by specific continents, countries, localities in the modern world

Do not use; class in 286.64–286.69

.63   Specific denominations

Including Christian Church (Disciples of Christ), Churches of Christ

See Manual at 280: Biography; also at 283–289

[.630 1–.630 9]   Standard subdivisions

Do not use; class in 286.601–286.609

.64–.69   Treatment by continent, country, locality

Add to base number 286.6 notation 4–9 from Table 2, e.g., the Christian Church (Disciples of Christ) in Florida 286.6759

.7   Adventist churches

[.709 4–.709 9]   Treatment by specific continents, countries, localities in the modern world

Do not use; class in 286.74–286.79

.73   Specific denominations

Including Advent Christian Church, Church of God General Conference

See Manual at 280: Biography; also at 283–289

[.730 1–.730 9]   Standard subdivisions

Do not use; class in 286.701–286.709

.732   Seventh-Day Adventist Church

[.732 094–.732 099]   Treatment by specific continents, countries, localities in the modern world

Do not use; class in 286.74–286.79

.74–.79   Treatment by continent, country, locality

Add to base number 286.7 notation 4–9 from Table 2, e.g., Seventh-Day Adventists in South America 286.78

287   Methodist churches; churches related to Methodism

Standard subdivisions are added for Methodist churches and churches related to Methodism together; for Methodist churches alone

.1   Wesleyan Methodist Church

[.109 4–.109 9]   Treatment by specific continents, countries, localities in the modern world

Do not use; class in 287.14–287.19

.14–.19   Treatment by continent, country, locality

> Add to base number 287.1 notation 4–9 from Table 2, e.g., Wesleyan Methodist Church in New South Wales 287.1944

.2   Miscellaneous Methodist churches

> Including Congregational Methodist Church, Free Methodist Church of North America

.4   Primitive Methodist Church

[.409 4–.409 9]   Treatment by specific continents, countries, localities in the modern world

> Do not use; class in 287.44–287.49

.44–.49   Treatment by continent, country, locality

> Add to base number 287.4 notation 4–9 from Table 2, e.g., Primitive Methodist Church in Kent 287.44223

.5   Methodist churches in British Isles

[.509 41–.509 42]   British Isles

> Do not use; class in 287.54

.53   Specific denominations

> Including Bible Christians, Methodist New Connexion, Protestant Methodists, United Methodist Church (Great Britain), United Methodist Free Churches, Wesleyan Conference, Wesleyan Reformers, Yearly Conference of People Called Methodists

> *For Wesleyan Methodist Church in British Isles, see 287.141; for Primitive Methodist Church in British Isles, see 287.441*

> *See Manual at 280: Biography; also at 283–289*

[.530 1–.530 9]   Standard subdivisions

> Do not use; class in 287.501–287.509

.532   *United Conference of Methodist Churches

.533   *Independent Methodists

.534   *Wesleyan Reform Union

.54   Treatment by country and locality

> Add to base number 287.54 the numbers following —4 in notation 41–42 from Table 2, e.g., Independent Methodists in Wales 287.5429

.6   United Methodist Church

> *See also 287.53 for United Methodist Church (Great Britain)*

---

*Do not use notation 0941–0942 from Table 1; class in 287.54

[.609 4–.609 9]	Treatment by specific continents, countries, localities in the modern world
	Do not use; class in 287.64–287.69
.63	Specific antecedent denominations

> *For Methodist Protestant Church, see 287.7; for Evangelical United Brethren Church, see 289.9*
>
> *See Manual at 280: Biography; also at 283–289*

[.630 1–.630 9]	Standard subdivisions
	Do not use; class in 287.601–287.609
.631	†The Methodist Church (1939–1968)
.632	†Methodist Episcopal Church
.633	†Methodist Episcopal Church, South
.64–.69	Treatment by continent, country, locality

> Add to base number 287.6 notation 4–9 from Table 2, e.g., United Methodist churches in Ohio 287.6771

.7 Methodist Protestant Church

.8 Black Methodist churches of United States origin

[.809 4–.809 9]	Treatment by specific continents, countries, localities in the modern world
	Do not use; class in 287.84–287.89
.83	Specific denominations

> Including African Methodist Episcopal Church, African Methodist Episcopal Zion Church, Christian Methodist Episcopal Church
>
> *See Manual at 280: Biography; also at 283–289*

[.830 1–.830 9]	Standard subdivisions
	Do not use; class in 287.801–287.809
.84–.89	Treatment by continent, country, locality

> Add to base number 287.8 notation 4–9 from Table 2, e.g., Black Methodist churches in Georgia 287.8758, in Liberia 287.86662

.9 Churches related to Methodism

> Limited to those listed below

.92	United Church of Canada
.93	Uniting Church in Australia
.94	Church of South India

†Do not use notation 094–099 from Table 1; class in 287.64–287.69

.95   Church of North India

.96   Salvation Army

.99   Church of the Nazarene [*formerly* 289.9]

[288]   [Unassigned]

Most recently used in Edition 19

289   Other denominations and sects

SUMMARY

289.1	**Unitarian and Universalist churches**
.3	**Latter-Day Saints (Mormons)**
.4	**Church of the New Jerusalem (Swedenborgianism)**
.5	**Church of Christ, Scientist (Christian Science)**
.6	**Society of Friends (Quakers)**
.7	**Mennonite churches**
.8	**Shakers (United Society of True Believers in Christ's Second Appearing)**
.9	**Denominations and sects not provided for elsewhere**

.1   Unitarian and Universalist churches

Class here Anti-Trinitarianism, Socinianism, Unitarianism

[.109 4–.109 9]   Treatment by specific continents, countries, localities in the modern world

Do not use; class in 289.14–289.19

.13   Specific denominations

See Manual at 280: Biography; also at 283–289

[.130 1–.130 9]   Standard subdivisions

Do not use; class in 289.101–289.109

.132   *Unitarian Universalist Association

.133   *Unitarian churches

.134   *Universalist churches

.14–.19   Treatment by continent, country, locality

Add to base number 289.1 notation 4–9 from Table 2, e.g., Unitarianism in Boston 289.174461

(.2)   (Permanently unassigned)

(Optional number used to provide local emphasis or a shorter number for a specific denomination or sect; prefer the number for the specific denomination or sect in 281–289)

.3   Latter-Day Saints (Mormons)

---

*Do not use notation 094–099 from Table 1; class in 289.14–289.19

[.309 4–.309 9] Treatment by specific continents, countries, localities in the modern world

Do not use; class in 289.34–289.39

.32 Sources (Sacred books)

.322 Book of Mormon

.33 Specific branches

See Manual at 280: Biography; also at 283–289

[.330 1–.330 9] Standard subdivisions

Do not use; class in 289.301–289.309

.332 Church of Jesus Christ of Latter-Day Saints

[.332 094–.332 099] Treatment by specific continents, countries, localities in the modern world

Do not use; class in 289.34–289.39

.333 Reorganized Church of Jesus Christ of Latter-Day Saints

[.333 094–.333 099] Treatment by specific continents, countries, localities in the modern world

Do not use; class in 289.34–289.39

.34–.39 Treatment by continent, country, locality

Add to base number 289.3 notation 4–9 from Table 2, e.g., Mormons in Utah 289.3792

.4 Church of the New Jerusalem (Swedenborgianism)

[.409 4–.409 9] Treatment by specific continents, countries, localities in the modern world

Do not use; class in 289.44–289.49

.44–.49 Treatment by continent, country, locality

Add to base number 289.4 notation 4–9 from Table 2, e.g., Swedenborgianism in Europe 289.44

.5 Church of Christ, Scientist (Christian Science)

[.509 4–.509 9] Treatment by specific continents, countries, localities in the modern world

Do not use; class in 289.54–289.59

.52 Sources

Writings by Mary Baker Eddy

.54–.59   Treatment by continent, country, locality

> Add to base number 289.5 notation 4–9 from Table 2, e.g., First Church of Christ, Scientist, Boston 289.574461

.6   Society of Friends (Quakers)

[.609 4–.609 9]   Treatment by specific continents, countries, localities in the modern world

> Do not use; class in 289.64–289.69

.63   Specific denominations

> *See Manual at 280: Biography; also at 283–289*

[.630 1–.630 9]   Standard subdivisions

> Do not use; class in 289.601–289.609

.64–.69   Treatment by continent, country, locality

> Add to base number 289.6 notation 4–9 from Table 2, e.g., Quakers in England 289.642

.7   Mennonite churches

[.709 4–.709 9]   Treatment by specific continents, countries, localities in the modern world

> Do not use; class in 289.74–289.79

.73   Specific branches

> Including Amish, Church of God in Christ, Defenseless Mennonites, General Conference Mennonites, Hutterian Brethren
>
> *See Manual at 280: Biography; also at 283–289*

[.730 1–.730 9]   Standard subdivisions

> Do not use; class in 289.701–289.709

.74–.79   Treatment by continent, country, locality

> Add to base number 289.7 notation 4–9 from Table 2, e.g., Amish churches in Lancaster County, Pennsylvania 289.774815

.8   Shakers (United Society of True Believers in Christ's Second Appearing)

.9   **Denominations and sects not provided for elsewhere**

Including Christian and Missionary Alliance, Churches of God, Dukhobors, Evangelical Congregational Church, Evangelical United Brethren Church, Messianic Judaism (Jewish Christians), Plymouth Brethren, United Brethren in Christ

Church of the Nazarene relocated to 287.99

Class nondenominational and interdenominational churches in 280; class Protestant nondenominational and interdenominational churches in 280.4

See Manual at 291: Denominations and sects

(Option: Class a specific denomination or sect requiring local emphasis in 289.2)

.92   Jehovah's Witnesses

.93   African independent churches

Independent denominations originating in Africa and not connected to another denomination

Including Celestial Church of Christ, Cherubim and Seraphim Church, Eglise de Jésus-Christ sur la terre par le prophète Simon Kimbangu

.94   Pentecostal churches

Including Assemblies of God, United Pentecostal Church

Class comprehensive works on the pentecostal movement in general church history in 270.82

.95   Independent Fundamentalist and Evangelical churches

Including Evangelical Free Church of America, Independent Fundamental Churches of America

Class comprehensive works on fundamentalist, evangelical movements in general church history in 270.82

.96   Unification Church

.97   Unity School of Christianity

.98   New Thought

Class eclectic New Thought, comprehensive works in 299.93

290   Comparative religion and religions other than Christianity

See Manual at 290

SUMMARY

291		**Comparative religion**
	.04	Special topics
	.1	Religious mythology, social theology, interreligious relations and attitudes
	.2	Doctrines
	.3	Public worship and other practices
	.4	Religious experience, life, practice
	.5	Moral theology
	.6	Leaders and organization
	.7	Missions and religious education
	.8	Sources
	.9	Sects and reform movements
292		**Classical (Greek and Roman) religion**
	.001–.009	Standard subdivisions
	.07–.08	Classical religion by specific culture
	.1–.9	Specific elements
293		**Germanic religion**
294		**Religions of Indic origin**
	.3	Buddhism
	.4	Jainism
	.5	Hinduism
	.6	Sikhism
295		**Zoroastrianism (Mazdaism, Parseeism)**
296		**Judaism**
	.01–.09	Standard subdivisions
	.1	Sources
	.3	Theology, ethics, views of social issues
	.4	Traditions, rites, public services
	.6	Leaders, organization, religious education, outreach activity
	.7	Religious experience, life, practice
	.8	Denominations and movements
297		**Islam, Babism, Bahai Faith**
	.1	Sources of Islam
	.2	Islamic doctrinal theology ('Aqā'id and Kalām); Islam and secular disciplines; Islam and other systems of belief
	.3	Islamic worship
	.4	Sufism (Islamic mysticism)
	.5	Islamic moral theology and religious experience, life, practice
	.6	Islamic leaders and organization
	.7	Protection and propagation of Islam
	.8	Islamic sects and reform movements
	.9	Babism and Bahai Faith
299		**Other religions**
	.1–.4	Religions of Indo-European, Semitic, North African, North and West Asian, Dravidian origin
	.5	Religions of East and Southeast Asian origin
	.6	Religions originating among Black Africans and people of Black African descent
	.7	Religions of North American native origin
	.8	Religions of South American native origin
	.9	Religions of other origin

291   Comparative religion

Class here works dealing with various religions, with religious topics not applied to specific religions; syncretistic religious writings of individuals expressing personal views and not claiming to establish a new religion or to represent an old one

Class treatment of religious topics with respect to philosophy of religion, natural theology in 210; class treatment with respect to Christianity in 220–280; class treatment with respect to a specific religion other than Christianity in 292–299

See Manual at at 291; also at 299.93: New Age religions

(Option: To give preferred treatment or shorter numbers to a specific religion other than Christianity, class it in this number, and add to base number 291 the numbers following the base number for that religion in 292–299, e.g., Hinduism 291, Mahabharata 291.923; if the option is followed, class comparative religion in 290, its subdivision 291.04 in 290.04, its subdivisions 291.1–291.9 in 290.1–290.9. Other options are described at 292–299)

SUMMARY

291.04	**Special topics**
.1	**Religious mythology, social theology, interreligious relations and attitudes**
.2	**Doctrines**
.3	**Public worship and other practices**
.4	**Religious experience, life, practice**
.5	**Moral theology**
.6	**Leaders and organization**
.7	**Missions and religious education**
.8	**Sources**
.9	**Sects and reform movements**

[.01]   Philosophy and theory

         Relocated to 210

[.011]   Systems

         Relocated to 200.11

[.012]   Classification

         Do not use; class in 291.14

[.013]   Value

         Relocated to 200.13

[.014]   Language and communication

         Relocated to 210.14

[.015]   Scientific principles

         Relocated to 200.15

[.019]   Psychological principles

         Relocated to 200.19

[.02–.03]	Standard subdivisions
	Relocated to 200.2–200.3
.04	Special topics
.042	Prehistoric religions and religions of nonliterate peoples
.046	Religions of 19th and 20th century origin
[.05]	Serial publications
	Relocated to 200.5
[.06]	Organizations and management
	Do not use for management; class in 291.6
	Organizations relocated to 291.65
[.07–.09]	Standard subdivisions
	Relocated to 200.7–200.9

.1   **Religious mythology, social theology, interreligious relations and attitudes**

.13   Mythology and mythological foundations

Stories of primeval history, beings, origins, and customs archetypally significant in the sacred life, doctrine, and ritual of religions

Class sources in 291.8. Class myths on a specific subject with the subject, e.g., creation myths 291.24

See Manual at 398.2 vs. 291.13

.14   General classes of religions

Including goddess religions; monotheistic, nontheistic, pantheistic, polytheistic religions

Class here classification of religions [*formerly also* 200.12, 210.12]

Class philosophic treatment of concepts of God in 211; class concepts of God or the gods in world religions in 291.211

.144   Shamanism

Class shamanism in a specific religion with the religion, e.g., shamanism in religions of North American native origin 299.7

.17   Social theologies and interreligious relations and attitudes

Attitudes of religions toward and influences on secular matters, attitudes toward other religions, interreligious relations

.171   Role of organized religions in society

Class specific socioeconomic problems in 291.178

.172	Interreligious relations
	Including relations of religions with irreligion
.175	Religions and secular disciplines
	Including communications media, literature, medicine, psychology, science, technology
.177	Religions and political affairs
	Attitudes toward and influences on political activities and ideologies
	Including civil war and revolution
	Class here religions and civil rights
	Class secular view of religiously oriented political theories and ideologies in 320.55; class secular view of relation of state to religious organizations and groups in 322.1

> *For religion and international affairs, see 291.1787*
>
> *See Manual at 322.1 vs. 261.7, 291.177*

.177 2	Religious freedom
.177 3	Theocracy
	Supremacy of organized religion over civil government
.178	Religions and socioeconomic problems

> *For religions and political affairs, see 291.177*
>
> *See also 361.75 for welfare work of religious organizations*

.178 3	Social problems
.178 32	Social welfare problems and services
.178 321–.178 325	Problems of and services to persons with illnesses and disabilities, the poor
	Add to base number 291.17832 the numbers following 362 in 362.1–362.5, e.g., attitude of religions toward alcoholism 291.17832292, toward the poor 291.178325
.178 326	Hunger
.178 327	Abuse within the family
.178 327 1	Child abuse and neglect
	For sexual abuse, see 291.1783272
.178 327 2	Sexual abuse
.178 327 3	Adults who were victims of abuse as children
.178 328	Refugees and victims of political oppression

.178 33		Crime and punishment

Add to base number 291.17833 the numbers following 364 in 364.1–364.8, e.g., attitude of religions toward treason 291.17833131, toward capital punishment 291.1783366

.178 34   Relations of age groups, the sexes, social classes, language groups, ethnic groups

Add to base number 291.17834 the numbers following 305 in 305.2–305.8, e.g., attitude of religions toward women 291.178344; however, for attitudes toward various religions, see 291.172; for attitude toward the poor, see 291.178325

.178 35   Sexual relations, marriage, divorce, family

Add to base number 291.17835 the numbers following 306 in 306.7–306.8, e.g., attitude of religions toward homosexuality 291.17835766

Class abuse within the family in 291.178327

.178 36   Ecology and population

Add to base number 291.17836 the numbers following 304 in 304.2–304.8, e.g., attitude of religions toward ecology 291.178362

.178 5   The economic order

Including management of business enterprises

.178 7   International affairs

.178 73   War and peace

Including attitude of religions toward pacifism, conscientious objectors

.178 732   Nuclear weapons and nuclear war

.2   Doctrines

Class here beliefs, apologetics, polemics, comprehensive works on theology

For social theologies, see 291.17; for moral theology, see 291.5

.21   Objects of worship and veneration

Class here animism, spiritism

.211   God, gods, goddesses, divinities and deities

.211 2   Attributes of God, of the gods

For attributes of male gods, see 291.2113; for attributes of female goddesses, see 291.2114

.211 3   Male gods

.211 4	Female goddesses

See also 291.14 for goddess religions

.211 7	Relation to the world

Including miracles, prophecy, providence, revelation, relation to and action in history

For creation and cosmology, see 291.24

.211 8	Theodicy

Vindication of God's justice and goodness in permitting existence of evil and suffering

.212	Nature

Including fire, sex, sun, trees, water

.213	Persons

Including ancestors, the dead, heroes, monarchs, saints

.214	Personified abstractions

.215	Good spirits

Class here angels

.216	Evil spirits

Class here demons, devils

.218	Images

.22	Humankind

Including atonement, creation of humankind, repentance, salvation, sin, soul

Class here comprehensive works on karma

Class creation of the world in 291.24

For eschatology, see 291.23. For a specific aspect of karma, see the aspect, e.g., karma as a concept in Buddhist moral theology 294.35

See Manual at 291: Common terms

.23	Eschatology

Including death, end of the world, heaven, hell, immortality, other worlds, punishments, purgatory, resurrection, rewards

.237	Reincarnation

.24	Creation and cosmology

For creation of humankind, see 291.22

.3   **Public worship and other practices**

Practices predominantly public or collective in character

Unless other instructions are given, class a subject with aspects in two or more subdivisions of 291.3 in the number coming first, e.g., religious healing and ceremonies connected with it 291.31 (*not* 291.38)

Class comprehensive works on worship in 291.43; class leaders and organization in 291.6; class missions and religious education in 291.7

.31   Religious healing

See Manual at 615.852 vs. 291.31, 234.131

.32   Divination

Including omens, oracles, prophecies

.33   Witchcraft

.34   Offerings, sacrifices, penances

.35   Pilgrimages and sacred places

Including grottoes, holy buildings, pagodas, shrines, temples

Class monasteries in 291.657

.350 93–.350 99   Treatment by specific continents, countries, localities

Class here pilgrimages to specific sacred places

.351   Pilgrimages [*formerly* 291.446]

[.351 093–.351 099]   Treatment by specific continents, countries, localities

Do not use; class in 291.35093–291.35099

.36   Sacred times

Including holy days, liturgical year, religious calendar, religious festivals

See Manual at 263.9, 291.36 vs. 394.265–394.267

.37   Symbolism, symbolic objects, emblems, sounds

Including mandalas, mantras

Class here religious use, significance, purpose of the arts

See Manual at 291: Common terms

.38   Rites and ceremonies

Conduct and texts

Including liturgy, music, processions, public feasts and fasts, public prayer

Class interdisciplinary works on sacred music in 781.7; class interdisciplinary works on sacred vocal music in 782.22

.4   Religious experience, life, practice

Practices predominantly private or individual in character

Class here spirituality

Class moral theology in 291.5

.42   Religious experience

Including conversion, enlightenment

.422   Mysticism

.43   Worship, meditation, yoga

Class here description, interpretation, criticism, history; practical works on prayer, on contemplation; comprehensive works on worship

For public worship, see 291.3

.432   Devotional literature

Including meditations

.433   Prayer books

.435   Meditation

.436   Yoga

Religious and spiritual discipline

Including kundalini yoga

Class interdisciplinary works on yoga in 181.45

For Hindu kundalini yoga, see 294.5436

See also 613.7046 for physical yoga (hatha yoga)

See Manual at 291: Common terms

.44   Religious life and practice

For worship, meditation, yoga, see 291.43; for moral theology, see 291.5

[.440 85]   Relatives   Parents

Do not use; class in 291.441

.440 86   Persons by miscellaneous social characteristics

[.440 865 5]   Married persons

Do not use; class in 291.441

.441   Marriage and family life

   Including religious training of children in the home

   Class here comprehensive works on marriage

   For marriage as a concern in social theology, see 291.1783581; for ethics of marriage, see 291.563

.442   Persons experiencing illness, trouble, addiction, bereavement

   See Manual at 616.86 vs. 158.1, 248.8629, 291.442, 362.29

.446   Individual observances

   Not provided for elsewhere

   Including almsgiving, ceremonial and ritual observances, observance of restrictions and limitations

   Pilgrimages relocated to 291.351

.447   Asceticism

   Including practice of celibacy, fasting and abstinence, poverty, solitude

[.448]   Guides to religious life

   Number discontinued; class in 291.44

.5   **Moral theology**

   Including conscience, sin, vice, virtue

.56   Specific moral issues, sins, vices, virtues

   Add to base number 291.56 the numbers following 17 in 172–179, e.g., morality of discriminatory practices 291.5675

.6   **Leaders and organization**

   Class here management [*formerly also* 200.68]

.61   Leaders and their work

   Variant names: clergy, gurus, messiahs, ministers, pastors, priests, prophets, shamans

   Role, function, duties

   Including pastoral counseling and preaching

   Class here role, function, duties of persons endowed with supernatural power [*formerly* 291.62], divinely inspired persons [*formerly* 291.63], interpreters of religion [*formerly* 291.64]

   Class theologians in 291.2. Class a specific activity of a leader with the activity, e.g., religious healing by shamans 291.31

   For founders of religions, see 291.63

   See Manual at 200.92 and 291–299

[.610 92]		Persons
		Do not use; class as instructed in Manual at 200.92 and 291–299
[.62]		Persons endowed with supernatural power
		Relocated to 291.61
.63		Founders of religions
		Divinely inspired persons relocated to 291.61
[.630 92]		Persons
		Do not use; class as instructed in Manual at 200.92 and 291–299
[.64]		Interpreters of religion
		Relocated to 291.61

.65   Organizations [*formerly also* 200.6, 291.06] and organization

> Including associations, congregations, institutions, orders, parties; exercise of religious authority
>
> Class laws and decisions in 291.84

.657   Monasticism and monasteries

.7   **Missions and religious education**

.72   Missions

.75   Religious education

> Class here comprehensive works on religious education and religion as an academic subject
>
> *For education in and teaching of comparative religion, religion as an academic subject, see 200.71*
>
> *See Manual at 291.75 vs. 200.71*

.8   **Sources**

> Class theology based on sacred sources in 291.2

.82   Sacred books and scriptures

.83   Oral traditions

.84   Laws and decisions

> Class civil law relating to religious matters in 340
>
> *See also 364.188 for offenses against religion as defined and penalized by the state*

.85   Sources of sects and reform movements

.9 **Sects and reform movements**

Class specific aspects of sects and reform movements in 291.1–291.8

See Manual at 291: Denominations and sects; also at 299.93: New Age religions

---

> **292–299 Religions other than Christianity**

Except for modifications shown under specific entries, add to each subdivision identified by † as follows:

01–05   Standard subdivisions
[06]   Organizations and management
           Do not use for management; class in 6
           Organizations relocated to 65
07   Education, research, related topics
071   Education
           Class here the religion as an academic subject
           Class comprehensive works on religious education, religious education to inculcate religious faith and practice in 75
                See Manual at 291.75 vs. 200.71
08–09   Standard subdivisions
1–9   Specific elements
           Add the numbers following 291 in 291.1–291.9, e.g., organizations 65 [*formerly* —06]

Class comprehensive works in 291

See Manual at 291; also at 200.92 and 291–299

(Options: To give preferred treatment or shorter numbers to a specific religion, use one of the following:

(Option A: Class the religion in 230–280, its sources in 220, comprehensive works in 200; in that case class the Bible and Christianity in 298

(Option B: Class in 210, and add to base number 21 the numbers following the base number for the religion in 292–299, e.g., Hinduism 210, Mahabharata 219.23; in that case class philosophy and theory of religion in 200, its subdivisions 211–218 in 201–208, standard subdivisions of religion in 200.01–200.09

(Option C: Class in 291, and add to base number 291 the numbers following the base number for that religion in 292–299, e.g., Hinduism 291, Mahabharata 291.923; in that case class comparative religion in 290, its subdivision 291.04 in 290.04, its subdivisions 291.1–291.9 in 290.1–290.9

(Option D: Class in 298, which is permanently unassigned

(Option E: Place first by use of a letter or other symbol, e.g., Hinduism 2H0 (preceding 220), or 29H (preceding 291 or 292); add to the base number thus derived, e.g., to 2H or to 29H, the numbers following the base number for the religion in 292–299, e.g., Shivaism 2H5.13 or 29H.513)

292　　　Classical (Greek and Roman) religion

See also 299 for modern revivals of classical religions

See Manual at 291; also at 200.92 and 291–299

.001–.005	Standard subdivisions
[.006]	Organizations and management

> Do not use for management; class in 292.6
>
> Organizations relocated to 292.65

.007	Education, research, related topics
.007 1	Education

> Class here classical religion as an academic subject
>
> Class comprehensive works on religious education, religious education to inculcate religious faith and practice in 292.75
>
> *See Manual at 291.75 vs. 200.71*

.008–.009	Standard subdivisions

> ＞　　　292.07–292.08　Classical religion by specific culture
>
> Class specific elements regardless of culture in 292.1–292.9; class comprehensive works in 292

.07	Roman
.08	Greek
.1–.9	**Specific elements**

> Add to base number 292 the numbers following 291 in 291.1–291.9, e.g., organizations 292.65 [*formerly* 292.006], mythology 292.13
>
> Class classical religion as an academic subject in 292.0071

293　　　†Germanic religion

See also 299 for modern revivals of Germanic religion

See Manual at 291; also at 200.92 and 291–299

294　　　Religions of Indic origin

Including Divine Light Mission, Radha Soami Satsang

See Manual at 200.9 vs. 294, 299.5

---

†Add as instructed under 292–299

SUMMARY

294.3	**Buddhism**
.4	**Jainism**
.5	**Hinduism**
.6	**Sikhism**

.3   **Buddhism**

> *See Manual at 291; also at 200.92 and 291–299*

[.306]   Organizations and management

> Do not use for management; class in 294.36
>
> Organizations relocated to 294.365

.307   Education, research, related topics

.307 1   Education

> Class here Buddhism as an academic subject
>
> Class comprehensive works on religious education, religious education to inculcate religious faith and practice in 294.375
>
> *See Manual at 291.75 vs. 200.71*

.33   Mythology, social theology, interreligious relations and attitudes

> Add to base number 294.33 the numbers following 291.1 in 291.13–291.17, e.g., social theology 294.337

.34   Doctrines and practices

.342   Doctrines

> *For social theology, see 294.337; for moral theology, see 294.35*

.342 04   Doctrines of specific branches, sects, reform movements

> Add to base number 294.34204 the numbers following 294.39 in 294.391–294.392, e.g., Zen doctrines 294.3420427

.342 1–.342 4   Specific doctrines

> Add to base number 294.342 the numbers following 291.2 in 291.21–291.24, e.g., reincarnation 294.34237

.343–.344   Public worship and other practices, religious experience, life, practice

> Add to base number 294.34 the numbers following 291 in 291.3–291.4, e.g., religious experience 294.3442

.35–.37   Moral theology, leaders and organization, missions, religious education

> Add to base number 294.3 the numbers following 291 in 291.5–291.7, e.g., organizations 294.365 [*formerly also* 294.306], the Buddha 294.363
>
> *See Manual at 291.75 vs. 200.71*

†Add as instructed under 292–299

.49   Sects and reform movements

               Number built according to instructions under 292–299

               Class specific aspects of sects and reform movements in 294.41–294.48

.492   Svetambara

.493   Digambara

.5   **Hinduism**

               Class here Brahmanism

               See Manual at 291; also at 200.92 and 291–299

SUMMARY

294.501–.509	**Standard subdivisions**
.51–.53	**Mythology, relations, doctrines, public worship**
.54	**Religious experience, life, practice, moral theology**
.55	**Sects and reform movements**
.56–.57	**Leaders, organization, missions, religious education**
.59	**Sources**

[.506]   Organizations and management

               Do not use for management; class in 294.56

               Organizations relocated to 294.565

.507   Education, research, related topics

.507 1   Education

               Class here Hinduism as an academic subject

               Class comprehensive works on religious education, religious education to inculcate religious faith and practice in 294.575

               See Manual at 291.75 vs. 200.71

.509   Historical, geographic, persons treatment

.509 013   3999–1000 B.C.

               Class here religion of Vedic period

.51–.53   Mythology, relations, doctrines, public worship

               Add to base number 294.5 the numbers following 291 in 291.1–291.3, e.g., attitude toward science 294.5175

.54   Religious experience, life, practice, moral theology

               Practices predominantly private or individual in character

               Class here spirituality

.542   Religious experience

               Including conversion, enlightenment

.542 2	Mysticism
.543	Worship, meditation, yoga

Class here description, interpretation, criticism, history, practical works on prayer, on contemplation; comprehensive works on worship

For public worship, see 294.53

.543 2	Devotional literature

Including meditations

.543 3	Prayer books
.543 5	Meditation
.543 6	Yoga

Religious and spiritual discipline

Including bhakti yoga, jnana yoga, karma yoga, kundalini yoga, raja yoga

Class yoga philosophy, raja yoga philosophy, interdisciplinary works on yoga in 181.45

See also 613.7046 for physical yoga (hatha yoga)

See Manual at 291: Common terms

.544	Religious life and practice

Add to base number 294.544 the numbers following 291.44 in 291.441–291.447, e.g., asceticism 294.5447

.548	Moral theology

Including conscience, dharma, sin, vice

.548 6	Specific moral issues, sins, vices, virtues

Add to base number 294.5486 the numbers following 17 in 172–179, e.g., morality of family relationships 294.54863

.55	Sects and reform movements

Class Buddhism in 294.3; class Jainism in 294.4; class Sikhism in 294.6. Class a specific aspect of a Hindu sect or reform movement with the subject, e.g., doctrines of Vishnuism 294.52

.551	Early Hindu sects
.551 2	Vishnuism

Including International Society for Krishna Consciousness

.551 3	Shivaism

Including Lingayats

.551 4	Shaktaism
	Class here Tantric Hinduism
.551 5	Ganapataism
.551 6	Shanmukaism
.551 7	Sauraism
.555	Ramakrishna movement
.556	Reformed Hinduism
.556 2	Brahma Samaj
.556 3	Arya-Samaj

.56–.57   Leaders, organization, missions, religious education

Add to base number 294.5 the numbers following 291 in 291.6–291.7, e.g., organizations 294.565 [*formerly also* 294.506], the role of the guru 294.561

Class Hinduism as an academic subject in 294.5071

See Manual at 291.75 vs. 200.71

.59   Sources

.592   Sacred books and scriptures

Add to each subdivision identified by * as follows:

04   Special topics
041   Sanskrit texts
            Including textual criticism
            Class Sanskrit texts accompanied by translations in 045; class Sanskrit texts accompanied by commentaries in 047
045   Translations
            Class here Sanskrit texts accompanied by translations
            Add to 045 notation 1–9 from Table 6, e.g., translations into English 04521
            Class texts accompanied by commentaries in 047
046   Interpretation and criticism
                For textual criticism, see 041; for commentaries, see 047
047   Commentaries
            Criticism and interpretation arranged in textual order
            Including texts accompanied by commentaries
048   Nonreligious subjects treated in sacred books and scriptures
            Class a religious subject treated in sacred books and scriptures with the subject, e.g., rites and ceremonies 294.538

.592 1   *Vedic literature

*Add as instructed under 294.592

> 294.592 12–294.592 15   The Vedas

Class here Samhitas, Brahmanas, Aranyakas

Class Upanishads in 294.59218; class Vedic religion in 294.509013; class comprehensive works on the Vedas in 294.5921

.592 12	*Rigveda
.592 13	*Samaveda
.592 14	*Yajurveda
.592 15	*Atharvaveda
.592 18	Upanishads
.592 2	*Ramayana
.592 3	*Mahabharata

For Bhagavad Gita, see 294.5924

.592 4	*Bhagavad Gita
.592 5	Puranas
.592 6	Dharmasastras

Including Code of Manu

.593	Oral traditions
.594	Laws and decisions
.595	Sources of sects and reform movements

Including Hindu tantras

.6   †Sikhism

See Manual at 291; also at 200.92 and 291–299

.663   Founders of Sikhism

Number built according to instructions under 292–299

Class here role and function of the ten founding gurus

295   †Zoroastrianism (Mazdaism, Parseeism)

Class Mithraism in 299.15

See Manual at 291; also at 200.92 and 291–299

296   Judaism

*Add as instructed under 294.592
†Add as instructed under 292–299

SUMMARY

296.01–.09	Standard subdivisions
.1	Sources
.3	Theology, ethics, views of social issues
.4	Traditions, rites, public services
.6	Leaders, organization, religious education, outreach activity
.7	Religious experience, life, practice
.8	Denominations and movements

[.06]   Organizations and management

        Do not use for management; class in 296.6

        Organizations relocated to 296.67

.071   Education

        Class here Judaism as an academic subject

        Class comprehensive works on Jewish religious education, religious education to inculcate religious faith and practice in 296.68

        See Manual at 291.75 vs. 200.71

.071 1   Higher education

        Class here Jewish theological faculties, rabbinical seminaries, yeshivot, education of rabbis

.09   Historical, geographic, persons treatment

        Class here history of specific synagogues [*formerly* 296.8]

        See also 320.54095694 for Zionism, 909.04924 for world history of Jews

---

\>   296.090 1–296.090 5   Historical periods

        Add to each subdivision identified by * as instructed under —0901–0905 in Table 1, e.g., museums of ancient Judaism 296.0901074

        Class comprehensive works in 296.09

.090 1   *To 499 A.D.

.090 13   *Earliest Judaism to 586 B.C.

        Including 999–586 B.C. [*formerly* 296.09014]

.090 14   *Second Temple period, 586 B.C.–70 A.D.

        Including 1–70 A.D. [*formerly* 296.09015]

        999–586 B.C. relocated to 296.09013

.090 15   *Early rabbinic period, 70–499

        1–70 A.D. relocated to 296.09014

---

*Add as instructed under 296.0901–296.0905

.090 2–.090 5   6th–21st centuries

> Add to base number 296.090 the numbers following —090 in notation 0902–0905 from Table 1, e.g., Judaism in the Middle Ages 296.0902

.092   Persons

> Class here persons not associated with one activity or denomination

> Class a person associated with one activity or denomination with the activity or denomination with which the person is associated, e.g., a theologian 296.3092, a Reform rabbi 296.8341092

.1   **Sources**

> Class Jewish theology based on these sources in 296.3

> *For Torah and sacred scripture (Tanakh, Old Testament), see 221*

> *See Manual at 221*

SUMMARY

296.12	**Talmudic literature**
.14	**Midrash**
.15	**Sources of specific sects and movements**
.16	**Cabalistic literature**
.18	**Halakhah (Legal literature)**
.19	**Aggadah (Nonlegal literature)**

(.11)   Tanakh

> (Optional number; prefer 221)

> Arranged as found in Jewish Bibles

> *See Manual at 221: Optional numbers for books of Bible*

[.110 3]   Dictionaries, encyclopedias, concordances

> Do not use for dictionaries and encyclopedias; class in 296.1113. Do not use for concordances; class in 296.1114–296.1115

(.111)   Generalities

> (Optional number; prefer 221)

> Add to base number 296.111 the numbers following 221 in 221.04–221.9, e.g., criticism and interpretation 296.1116

(.112)   *‡Torah (Pentateuch)

(.112 1)   *‡Genesis

(.112 2)   *‡Exodus

> *For Ten Commandments, see 296.1126*

*Add as instructed under 221–229

‡(Optional number; prefer 222–224)

(.112 3)	*‡Leviticus
(.112 4)	*‡Numbers
(.112 5)	*‡Deuteronomy

> For Ten Commandments, see 296.1126

(.112 6)	*‡Ten Commandments (Decalogue)
(.113)	*‡Prophetic books (Nevi'im)
(.113 1)	*Former Prophets (Nevi'im rishonim)

> (Optional number; prefer 222)

> For individual books of Former Prophets, see 296.1132–296.1135

(.113 2)	*‡Joshua
(.113 3)	*‡Judges
(.113 4)	*‡Samuel
(.113 41)	*‡Samuel 1
(.113 42)	*‡Samuel 2
(.113 5)	*‡Kings
(.113 51)	*‡Kings 1
(.113 52)	*‡Kings 2
(.113 6)	*Later Prophets (Nevi'im aḥaronim)

> (Optional number; prefer 224)

> For Isaiah, see 296.1137; for Jeremiah, see 296.1138; for Ezekiel, see 296.1139; for Minor Prophets, see 296.114

(.113 7)	*‡Isaiah
(.113 8)	*‡Jeremiah
(.113 9)	*‡Ezekiel
(.114)	*‡Minor Prophets

> For Zephaniah, Haggai, Zechariah, Malachi, see 296.115

(.114 1)	*‡Hosea
(.114 2)	*‡Joel
(.114 3)	*‡Amos
(.114 4)	*‡Obadiah
(.114 5)	*‡Jonah
(.114 6)	*‡Micah

*Add as instructed under 221–229

‡(Optional number; prefer 222–224)

(.114 7)	*‡Nahum
(.114 8)	*‡Habakkuk
(.115)	*‡Zephaniah, Haggai, Zechariah, Malachi
(.115 1)	*‡Zephaniah
(.115 2)	*‡Haggai
(.115 3)	*‡Zechariah
(.115 4)	*‡Malachi
(.116)	*‡Writings (Ketuvim)
(.116 1)	*‡Psalms
(.116 2)	*‡Proverbs
(.116 3)	*‡Job
(.116 4)	*Megillot (Five scrolls)
	(Optional number; prefer 221.044)
(.116 41)	*‡Song of Solomon (Canticle of Canticles, Song of Songs)
(.116 42)	*‡Ruth
(.116 43)	*‡Lamentations
(.116 44)	*‡Ecclesiastes (Kohelet, Qohelet)
(.116 45)	*‡Esther
(.116 5)	*‡Daniel
(.116 6)	*‡Ezra
(.116 7)	*‡Nehemiah
(.116 8)	*‡Chronicles
(.116 81)	*‡Chronicles 1
(.116 82)	*‡Chronicles 2
(.118)	*Apocrypha
	(Optional number; prefer 229)
	For pseudepigrapha, see 229.9
(.118 1)	*Esdras 1 and 2
	(Optional number; prefer 229.1)
	Variant names: Esdras 3 and 4
	See also 296.1166 for Ezra, 296.1167 for Nehemiah

*Add as instructed under 221–229

‡(Optional number; prefer 222–224)

(.118 2)	*Tobit, Judith, Additions to Esther
	(Optional number; prefer 229.2)
(.118 22)	*Tobit
	(Optional number; prefer 229.22)
(.118 24)	*Judith
	(Optional number; prefer 229.24)
(.118 27)	*Additions to Esther
	(Optional number; prefer 229.27)
(.118 3)	*Wisdom of Solomon (Wisdom)
	(Optional number; prefer 229.3)
	Class here Apocryphal wisdom literature
	For Ecclesiasticus, see 296.1184
(.118 4)	*Ecclesiasticus (Sirach)
	(Optional number; prefer 229.4)
(.118 5)	*Baruch and Epistle of Jeremiah
	(Optional number; prefer 229.5)
(.118 6)	*Song of the Three Children, Susanna, Bel and the Dragon
	(Optional number; prefer 229.6)
(.118 7)	*Maccabees (Machabees)
	(Optional number; prefer 229.7)
(.118 73)	*Maccabees 1 and 2 (Machabees 1 and 2)
	(Optional number; prefer 229.73)
(.118 75)	*Maccabees 3 and 4 (Machabees 3 and 4)
	(Optional number; prefer 229.75)
(.118 8)	*Prayer of Manasseh
	(Optional number; prefer 229.6)

*Add as instructed under 221–229

> 296.12–296.14 Talmudic literature and Midrash

Add to each subdivision identified by ‡ as follows:
001–009   Standard subdivisions
04   Hebrew and Aramaic texts
Including textual criticism
Class texts accompanied by modern commentaries since 1500 in 07
05   Translations
Add to 05 notation 1–9 from Table 6, e.g., literature in English 0521
Class texts accompanied by modern commentaries since 1500 in 07
06   Interpretation and criticism (Exegesis)
Add to 06 the numbers following 220.6 in 220.601–220.68, e.g., historical criticism 067
For textual criticism, see 04; for modern commentaries since 1500, see 07
07   Modern commentaries since 1500
Criticism and interpretation arranged in textual order
Including texts accompanied by modern commentaries
Commentaries written before 1500 are classed with the text without addition of 07
See Manual at 296.12–296.14: Add table: 07
08   Nonreligious subjects treated in Talmudic literature and Midrash
Add to base number 08 notation 001–999, e.g., natural sciences in Talmudic literature and Midrash 085
Class a religious subject treated in Talmudic literature and Midrash with the subject, e.g., Jewish ethics 296.36

Class comprehensive works in 296.1

.12   ‡Talmudic literature

.120 092   Persons

Number built according to instructions under 296.12–296.14

Class here Soferim, Tannaim, Amoraim, Geonim

.123   ‡Mishnah

.123 1   ‡Order Zera'im

Including tractates Berakhot, Bikkurim, Demai, Hallah, Kilayim, Ma'aser Sheni, Ma'aserot, Orlah, Pe'ah, Shevi'it, Terumot

.123 2   ‡Order Mo'ed

Including tractates Bezah, Eruvin, Hagigah, Megillah, Mo'ed Katan, Pesahim, Rosh Hashanah, Shabbat, Shekalim, Sukkah, Ta'anit, Yoma

‡Add as instructed under 296.12–296.14

.123 3   ‡Order Nashim

Including tractates Gittin, Ketubbot, Kiddushin, Nazir, Nedarim, Sotah, Yevamot

.123 4   ‡Order Nezikin

Including tractates Avodah Zarah, Bava Batra, Bava Kamma, Bava Mezia, Eduyyot, Horayot, Makkot, Sanhedrin, Shevu'ot

.123 47   ‡Tractate Avot (Pirke Avot)

.123 5   ‡Order Kodashim

Including tractates Arakhin, Bekhorot, Hullin, Keritot, Kinnim, Me'ilah, Menahot, Middot, Tamid, Temurah, Zevahim

.123 6   ‡Order Tohorot

Including tractates Kelim, Makhshirin, Mikva'ot, Nega'im, Niddah, Oholot (Ahilot), Parah, Tevul Yom, Tohorot, Ukzin, Yadayim, Zavim

.123 7   Minor tractates

.124   ‡Palestinian Talmud (Jerusalem Talmud, Talmud Yerushalmi)

.124 1–.124 7   Individual orders and tractates

Add to base number 296.124 the numbers following 296.123 in 296.1231–296.1237, e.g., Order Zera'im in Palestinian Talmud 296.1241

.125   ‡Babylonian Talmud

Often called simply the Talmud

.125 1–.125 7   Individual orders and tractates

Add to base number 296.125 the numbers following 296.123 in 296.1231–296.1237, e.g., tractate Shabbat in Babylonian Talmud 296.1252

.126   Tosefta and Baraita

.126 2   ‡Tosefta

.126 21–.126 27   Individual orders and tractates

Add to base number 296.1262 the numbers following 296.123 in 296.1231–296.1237, e.g., order Nezikin in Tosefta 296.12624

.126 3   ‡Baraita

.127   Specific types of Talmudic literature

.127 4   ‡Halakhah

.127 6   ‡Aggadah

.14   ‡Midrash

‡Add as instructed under 296.12–296.14

.141	‡Midrashic Halakhah
.142	‡Midrashic Aggadah
.15	Sources of specific sects and movements
.155	Writings of Qumran community

> Class here comprehensive works on Dead Sea Scrolls

> > *For Old Testament texts in Dead Sea Scrolls, see 221.44; for pseudepigrapha in Dead Sea Scrolls, see 229.91*

> > *See also 296.815 for comprehensive works on Qumran community*

.16	Cabalistic literature

> Class here interdisciplinary works on cabala

> The texts of religious cabalistic works are classed here even if the editor introduces and annotates them from an occult or Christian point of view

> Class Jewish mystical experience in 296.712; class Jewish mystical movements in 296.8

> > *For cabalistic traditions in occultism, see 135.47*

.162	Zohar
[.17]	Early rabbinical writings to 1400

> Early rabbinical legal writings, comprehensive works on rabbinical writings to 1400 relocated to 296.18

.18	Halakhah (Legal literature)

> Including early rabbinical legal writings, comprehensive works on rabbinical writings to 1400 [*formerly* 296.17]

> Class here commandments (mitzvot) treated as laws, the 613 commandments, comprehensive works on Jewish law

> Class commandments (mitzvot) treated as ethical values in 296.36; class Jewish law relating to secular matters in 340.58

> > *For Torah, see 222.1; for Talmudic Halakhah, see 296.1274; for Midrashic Halakhah, see 296.141. For early rabbinical writings to 1400 on a specific subject, see the subject, e.g., creation 296.34; for laws on a specific religious topic, see the topic, e.g., laws concerning marriage rites 296.444*

> > *See Manual at 296.18 vs. 340.58*

.180 92	Persons

> Class here Rishonim, Aharonim

‡Add as instructed under 296.12–296.14

.181	Legal writings of Maimonides

Class here comprehensive works on writings of Maimonides

For philosophical writings of Maimonides, see 181.06. For writings on a specific religious topic, see the topic, e.g., the Thirteen Articles of Faith 296.3

.181 2   Mishneh Torah

.182   Work of Joseph Caro

Class here Shulḥan 'arukh

.185   Responsa

Class responsa on a specific religious topic with the topic, e.g., responsa concerning marriage rites 296.444

.185 4   Responsa of reform movements

Add to base number 296.1854 the numbers following 296.834 in 296.8341–296.8344, e.g., Reform responsa 296.18541

.188   Nonreligious subjects treated in halakhah

.188 000 1–.188 000 9   Standard subdivisions

.188 001–.188 999   Specific nonreligious subjects treated in halakhah

Add to base number 296.188 notation 001–999, e.g., agriculture in halakhah 296.18863

.19   Aggadah (Nonlegal literature)

Stories, legends, parables, proverbs, anecdotes, ancient or modern, told for religious edification

Class here comprehensive works on Aggadah

Class Jewish folklore in 398.2089924

For Talmudic Aggadah, see 296.1276; for Midrashic Aggadah, see 296.142

See also 296.45371 for Passover Haggadah

.3   Theology, ethics, views of social issues

Standard subdivisions are added for theology, ethics, social issues together; for theology alone

Class here Biblical theology, the Thirteen Articles of Faith

See also 181.06 for Jewish philosophy

See Manual at 100 vs. 200; also at 220: Biblical theology

.31   God and spiritual beings

.311   God

| .311 2 | Attributes and names of God |
| .311 4 | Relation to the world |

For revelation, see 296.3115; for miracles, see 296.3116; for relation to and action in history, see 296.3117; for creation, see 296.34

| .311 5 | Revelation |
| .311 55 | Prophecy |

Class Biblical prophecy and prophecies in 221.15; class the prophetic books of the Bible in 224; class messianic prophecies in 296.336

.311 6	Miracles
.311 7	Relation to and action in history
.311 72	Relationship to the Jewish people (Covenant relationship)
.311 73	Land of Israel
.311 74	Specific historical events

Including the Holocaust

| .311 8 | Theodicy |

Vindication of God's justice and goodness in permitting existence of evil and suffering

.315	Angels
.316	Devils (Demons)
.32	Humankind

Including atonement, creation of humankind, free will, repentance, salvation, sin, soul

For eschatology, see 296.33

| .33 | Eschatology |

Including death, resurrection, immortality

| .336 | Messianism |

See also 232.906 for Jewish interpretations of Jesus

| .34 | Creation |

For creation of humankind, see 296.32

| .35 | Apologetics and polemics |

.36   Ethics [*formerly* 296.385]

Including Biblical precepts, conscience, ethical wills, sin

Class here general works on commandments (mitzvot) treated as ethical values

Add to base number 296.36 the numbers following 17 in 172–179, e.g., morality of family relationships 296.363

Class works on commandments (mitzvot) treated as laws in 296.18; class guides to conduct of life in 296.7

See also 296.12347 for talmudic tractate Avot (Pirke Avot)

.37   Judaism and secular disciplines [*formerly* 296.3875]

Class here attitudes of Judaism toward and influence on secular issues, religious views and teachings about secular disciplines, works treating relation between Jewish belief and a secular discipline

Class Jewish philosophy of a secular discipline and Jewish theories within a secular discipline with the discipline, e.g., Jewish philosophy 181.06

For Judaism and social issues, see 296.38

See also 296.12–296.14 for nonreligious subjects treated in Talmudic literature and Midrash, 296.188 for nonreligious subjects treated in halakhah

.371   Judaism and philosophy, paranormal phenomena, psychology

.375   Judaism and natural sciences, mathematics

.376   Judaism and technology

Including Judaism and medicine

.377   Judaism and the arts

.38   Judaism and social sciences

Attitudes of Judaism toward and influence on social issues

Including Judaism and human ecology

Class here Judaism and socioeconomic problems, Jewish social theology

Class Jewish view of marriage and family in 296.74

.382   Judaism and politics [*formerly* 296.3877]

Attitude toward and influence on political activities and ideologies

Class here Judaism and civil rights

See Manual at 322.1 vs. 261.7, 291.177; also at 322.1 vs. 296.382, 320.54095694

.382 7   International affairs, war and peace [*formerly* 296.38787]

> Including attitude of Judaism toward civil and revolutionary wars, conscientious objectors, pacifism

.383   Judaism and economics [*formerly* 296.38785]

[.385]   Ethics

> Relocated to 296.36

[.387]   Social theology

> Number discontinued; class in 296.38

[.387 2]   Judaism and other systems of belief

> Relocated to 296.39

[.387 5]   Judaism and secular disciplines

> Relocated to 296.37

[.387 7]   Judaism and politics

> Relocated to 296.382

[.387 835]   Social theology of marriage and family

> Relocated to 296.74

[.387 85]   Judaism and economics

> Relocated to 296.383

[.387 87]   International affairs, war and peace

> Relocated to 296.3827

.39   Judaism and other systems of belief [*formerly* 296.3872]

> Including Judaism and atheism, Judaism and irreligion

.396   Judaism and Christianity

.397   Judaism and Islam

.4   **Traditions, rites, public services**

> Class individual observances not provided for here in 296.7

SUMMARY

296.41	**Sabbath**
.43	**Festivals, holy days, fasts**
.44	**Rites and customs for occasions that occur generally once in a lifetime**
.45	**Liturgy and prayers**
.46	**Use of the arts and symbolism**
.47	**Sermons and preaching (Homiletics)**
.48	**Pilgrimages and sacred places**
.49	**Traditions, rites, public services of ancient Judaism to 70 A.D.**

.41	Sabbath

Liturgy and prayers for Sabbath relocated to 296.45

.412 Prohibited activity

[.42] Sermons and preaching (Homiletics)

Relocated to 296.47

> 296.43–296.44 Festivals, holy days, fasts; rites and customs for occasions that occur generally once in a lifetime

Class here personal ritual observances to be performed at specific times or in conjunction with specific rites

Liturgy and prayers for festivals, holy days, fasts; for occasions that occur generally once in a lifetime relocated to 296.453–296.454

Class comprehensive works in 296.43

For specific rites of ancient Judaism to 70 A.D. not provided for elsewhere, see 296.49

.43 Festivals, holy days, fasts

For Sabbath, see 296.41

See Manual at 263.9, 291.36 vs. 394.265–394.267

.431 High Holy Days

For Yom Kippur (Day of Atonement), see 296.432

.431 5 Rosh Hashanah (New Year)

.432 Yom Kippur (Day of Atonement)

.433 Sukkot (Feast of Tabernacles)

.433 9 Simḥat Torah

.435 Hanukkah (Feast of the Dedication)

.436 Purim (Feast of Lots)

.437 Pesach (Passover)

.438 Shavuot (Feast of Weeks, Pentecost)

.439 Other festivals, holy days, fasts

Including Lag b'Omer, Tishah b'Av

.439 1 Festivals, holy days, fasts associated with the land of Israel

Including Sabbatical Year (shemittah)

.44 Rites and customs for occasions that occur generally once in a lifetime

See also 296.7 for rites and customs which continue throughout life

.442	Special rites for male Jews
.442 2	Berit milah (Circumcision)
.442 3	Pidyon haben (Redemption of first-born male)
.442 4	Bar mitzvah
.443	Special rites for female Jews

Including naming ceremonies

For observance of laws of family purity, see 296.742

.443 4	Bat mitzvah
.444	Marriage and divorce rites and traditions

Standard subdivisions are added for marriage and divorce rites and traditions together, for marriage rites alone, for marriage traditions alone

Including issues concerning who may be married, descent of Jewish identity

For guides to marriage and family life, see 296.74

.444 3	Interreligious marriage
.444 4	Divorce rites and traditions

Standard subdivisions are added for either or both topics in heading

.445	Burial and mourning rites and traditions

Standard subdivisions are added for any or all topics in heading

Including memorial services

.446	Synagogue dedication
.45	Liturgy and prayers

Description, interpretation, conduct, texts of rites and public services; private and public prayers, blessings, benedictions

Including prayer at meals

Class here liturgy and prayers for Sabbath [*formerly* 296.41]; comprehensive works on worship [*formerly* 296.72]; prayer books, e.g., siddurim; Ashkenazic liturgy

Class devotional reading for the individual in 296.72

.450 4	Liturgy of specific groups

Including Ari liturgy

Class Ashkenazic liturgy or liturgy of unspecified group in 296.45

[.450 401–.450 409]	Standard subdivisions

Do not use; class in 296.4501–296.4509

.450 42	Sephardic liturgy
.450 44	Hasidic liturgy
.450 46	Reform liturgy
.450 47	Conservative liturgy
.450 48	Reconstructionist liturgy
.452	Piyyutim

> 296.453–296.454 Liturgy and prayers for festivals, holy days, fasts; for occasions that occur generally once in a lifetime [*formerly* 296.43–296.44]

Add to each subdivision identified by * the numbers following 296.45 in 296.4504, e.g., Passover Haggadah of the Sephardic rite 296.45371042

Class comprehensive works in 296.45

.453   *Liturgy and prayers for festivals, holy days, fasts

Class here Mahzorim

.453 1–.453 6   Liturgy and prayers for High Holy Days, Sukkot, Hanukkah, Purim

Add to base number 296.453 the numbers following 296.43 in 296.431–296.436, e.g., liturgy and prayers for High Holy Days 296.4531; then add further as instructed under 296.453–296.454, e.g., Reform prayer books for High Holy Days 296.4531046

.453 7   *Liturgy and prayers for Pesach (Passover)

.453 71   *Passover Haggadah (Seder service)

.453 8–.453 9   Liturgy and prayers for Shavuot, other festivals, holy days, fasts

Add to base number 296.453 the numbers following 296.43 in 296.438–296.439, e.g., prayers for Shavuot 296.4538; then add further as instructed under 296.453–296.454, e.g., prayers for Shavuot of the Sephardic rite 296.4538042

.454   Liturgy and prayers for occasions that occur generally once in a lifetime

Add to base number 296.454 the numbers following 296.44 in 296.442–296.446, e.g., liturgy and prayers for weddings 296.4544; then add further as instructed under 296.453–2296.454, e.g., Reform prayer books for weddings 296.4544046

.46   Use of the arts and symbolism

Including synagogue buildings

.461   Liturgical articles

Including mezuzot, prayer shawls

*Add as instructed under 296.453–296.454

.461 2	Phylacteries (Tefillin)
.461 5	Torah scrolls

> Class here scribes (soferim)

.462 Music

> Class here cantors
>
> Class works containing both text and music, interdisciplinary works on Jewish liturgical music in 782.36

.47 Sermons and preaching (Homiletics) [*formerly* 296.42]

> Add to base number 296.47 the numbers following 296.4 in 296.41–296.44, e.g., High Holy Day sermons 296.4731
>
> Class sermons on a specific subject with the subject, e.g., sermons on social issues 296.38

.48 Pilgrimages and sacred places

[.480 93–.480 99]   Specific continents, countries, localities

> Do not use; class in 296.482–296.489

.481 Pilgrimages

> Class pilgrimages to specific sacred places in 296.482–296.489

.482 Jerusalem

.483–.489 Geographic treatment of sacred places in specific continents, countries, localities

> Add to base number 296.48 notation 3–9 from Table 2, e.g., sacred places in Iraq 296.48567; however, for Jerusalem, see 296.482
>
> Class the Land of Israel as a theme in Jewish theology in 296.31173

.49 Traditions, rites, public services of ancient Judaism to 70 A.D.

> Not provided for elsewhere

.491 The Temple

.492 Sacrifices and offerings

.493 Ark of the Covenant

.495 Ancient priesthood

.6   Leaders, organization, religious education, outreach activity

.61 Leaders and their work

Role, function, duties

Class here ordination, work of rabbis; activities of leaders and other congregational workers designed to promote religious and social welfare of social groups in community, pastoral care; chaplaincy

For ancient priesthood, see 296.495

See also 296.4615 for scribes, 296.462 for cantors

[.610 92] Persons

Do not use for persons treatment of religious leaders primarily associated with a specific religious activity; class in 296.1–296.7, e.g., a theologian 296.3092. Do not use for persons treatment of religious leaders primarily associated with a specific denomination or movement; class in 296.8, e.g., a Reform rabbi 296.8341092. Do not use for persons treatment of other religious leaders; class in 296.092

Use of this number for persons treatment of writers on leaders and their work discontinued; class in 296.61

.65 Synagogues and congregations

Role and function

See also 296.46 for synagogue buildings

.650 9 Historical, geographic, persons treatment

Class history of specific synagogues in 296.09

.67 Organizations [*formerly also* 296.06] and organization

Theory and history of organizations other than synagogues and congregations

Including religious authority, excommunication, schism; sanhedrin

Class laws and decisions in 296.18. Class organizations sponsored by one denomination with the denomination in 296.8, e.g., Union of Orthodox Congregations of America 296.83206073

For synagogues and congregations, see 296.65

See also 369.3924 for Jewish service and fraternal associations, e.g., B'nai B'rith

[.673–.675] Young Men's and Women's Hebrew Associations

Numbers discontinued; class in 296.67

.68 Religious education

Class Judaism as an academic subject in 296.071

For religious education at the level of higher education, see 296.0711

See Manual at 291.75 vs. 200.71

.680 83	History and description with respect to young people

> Class here afternoon weekday schools, Hebrew schools, Jewish religious schools, Sunday schools; religious education in Jewish day schools
>
> Class comprehensive works on Jewish day schools in 371.076

.69	Outreach activity for the benefit of converts and nonobservant Jews
.7	**Religious experience, life, practice**

> Standard subdivisions are added for religious experience, life, practice together; for religious life and practice together
>
> Practices which continue throughout life
>
> Including asceticism
>
> Class here guides to religious life, spirituality
>
> *For ethics, see 296.36; for traditions, rites, public services, see 296.4*

[.708 5]	Relatives Parents

> Do not use; class in 296.74

.708 6	Persons by miscellaneous social characteristics
[.708 655]	Married persons

> Do not use; class in 296.74

.71	Religious experience
.712	Mysticism

> Class cabalistic literature in 296.16; class Jewish mystical movements in 296.8

.714	Conversion

> Class here conversion of non-Jews to Judaism
>
> Class outreach activity for the benefit of converts and nonobservant Jews in 296.69. Class conversion of Jews to another religion with the religion, e.g., conversion of Jews to Christianity 248.246

.715	Return of Jews from non-observance to religious observance
.72	Devotional reading for the individual

> Including meditation and meditations
>
> Worship relocated to 296.45
>
> Class devotional literature in the form of Aggadah in 296.19

.73	Kosher (Kashrut) observance

> Observance of dietary laws
>
> Including ritual slaughter (shehitah)

.74	Marriage and family life

Class here social theology of marriage and family [*formerly* 296.387835], comprehensive works on marriage

Use of this number for religious life and practice discontinued; class in 296.7

> *For ethics of marriage, see 296.363; for marriage and divorce rites and traditions, see 296.444*

.742	Observance of laws of family purity

> *For ritual bath (mikveh), see 296.75*

.75	Ritual bath (Mikveh)
.8	**Denominations and movements**

History of specific synagogues relocated to 296.09

Class specific aspects of denominations and movements in 296.1–296.7

.81	Denominations and movements of ancient origin

Including Hellenistic movement, Karaites, Zealots

.812	Pharisees
.813	Sadducees
.814	Essenes

> *For Qumran community, see 296.815*

.815	Qumran community

> *See also 296.155 for writings of Qumran community*

.817	Samaritans
.82	Medieval and early modern denominations and movements to ca. 1750

Including Sabbatianism

.83	Modern denominations and movements after ca. 1750
.832	Orthodox Judaism
.833	Mystical Judaism
.833 2	Hasidism
.833 22	Habad Lubavitch Hasidism
.834	Reform movements

Including Humanistic Judaism

.834 1	Reform Judaism [*formerly* 296.8346]
.834 2	Conservative Judaism

.834 4	Reconstructionist Judaism
[.834 6]	Reform Judaism
	Relocated to 296.8341

297   Islam, Babism, Bahai Faith

Standard subdivisions are added for Islam, Babism, Bahai Faith together; for Islam alone

SUMMARY

297.01–.09	Standard subdivisions
.1	Sources of Islam
.2	Islamic doctrinal theology ('Aqā'id and Kalām); Islam and secular disciplines; Islam and other systems of belief
.3	Islamic worship
.4	Sufism (Islamic mysticism)
.5	Islamic moral theology and religious experience, life, practice
.6	Islamic leaders and organization
.7	Protection and propagation of Islam
.8	Islamic sects and reform movements
.9	Babism and Bahai Faith

[.06]	Organizations and management
	Do not use for management; class in 297.6
	Organizations relocated to 297.65
.07	Education, research, related topics
.071	Education
	Class here Islamic religion as an academic subject
	Class comprehensive works on Islamic religious education, religious education to inculcate religious faith and practice in 297.77
	See Manual at 291.75 vs. 200.71
.09	Historical, geographic, persons treatment
	Class here comprehensive religious works on Islamic fundamentalism
	Class political science aspects of Islam in 320
	For Islamic fundamentalism in a specific sect or reform movement, see 297.8
	See also 909.097671 for Islamic civilization
	See Manual at 320.55 vs. 297.09, 322.1

.092   Persons

> Class interdisciplinary works on caliphs as civil and religious heads of state with the subject in 940–990, e.g., Abu Bakr 953.02092

> *For Muslims primarily associated with a specific religious activity, see 297.1–297.7; for founders of Sufi orders, see 297.48; for Muhammad the Prophet, see 297.63; for Muhammad's family and companions (including religious biography of the first four caliphs), see 297.64; for Muslims primarily associated with a specific sect or reform movement, see 297.8*

> *See Manual at 297.092*

> **297.1–297.8 Islam**

> Class comprehensive works in 297

> **297.1–297.3 Sources of Islam; Islamic doctrinal theology ('Aqā'id and Kalām); Islam and secular disciplines; Islam and other systems of belief; Islamic worship**

> Specific aspects of Sufism relocated to 297.4

> Class comprehensive works in 297

.1   **Sources of Islam**

SUMMARY

297.12	**Koran and Hadith**
.14	**Religious and ceremonial laws and decisions**
.18	**Stories, legends, parables, proverbs, anecdotes told for religious edification**

.12   Koran and Hadith

> Class theology based on Koran and Hadith in 297.2

.122   Koran

.122 03   Topical dictionaries and encyclopedias

> Do not use for concordances or non-topical dictionaries; class in 297.1224–297.1225

.122 09   Historical, geographic, persons treatment

> Class here geography, history, chronology of the Middle East in Koran times in relation to the Koran

> Class origin of Koran, commentary about historical occasions on which passages of Koran were revealed in 297.1221; class compilation and recording of Koran in 297.1224042; class comprehensive works on geography, history, chronology of the Middle East in Koran times in 939.4

.122 092   Persons

> *For Muḥammad, see 297.63; for Muḥammad's family and companions, see 297.64; for prophets prior to Muḥammad, see 297.246*

.122 1   Origin and authenticity

Including inspiration, revelation, commentary about historic occasions on which passages were revealed; Koranic prophecy and prophecies

Class compilation and recording of Koran in 297.1224042

.122 2   Koran stories retold

Including picture books

>   297.122 4–297.122 5   Texts

Class comprehensive works in 297.122

For texts accompanied by commentaries, see 297.1227

.122 4   Arabic texts

Class here textual criticism

Class Arabic texts accompanied by translations in 297.1225

.122 404   Special topics

.122 404 2   Compilation and recording of Koran

.122 404 5   Recitation and readings

Standard subdivisions are added for either or both topics in heading

Class here art of melodic reading, tajwīd (adornment of recitation); qirā'āt (science of the readings, which treats various renditions of the text according to different oral traditions)

.122 5   Translations

Class here Arabic texts accompanied by translations

Add to base number 297.1225 notation 1–9 from Table 6, e.g., the Koran in English 297.122521

.122 6   Interpretation and criticism (Exegesis)

Class art of recitation in 297.1224045

> *For textual criticism, see 297.1224; for commentaries, see 297.1227*

.122 601	Philosophy and theory
	Class here hermeneutics, principles and methods of Koranic exegesis
.122 61	General introductions to the Koran
	Including general introductions to the sciences necessary to study the Koran
[.122 64–.122 66]	Symbolism, typology, harmonies, literary criticism
	Numbers discontinued; class in 297.1226
.122 67	Historical criticism
.122 68	Allegorical and numerical interpretations
	Use of this number for mythological, astronomical interpretations discontinued; class in 297.1226
.122 7	Commentaries
	Criticism and interpretation arranged in textual order
	Class here texts accompanied by commentaries
.122 8	Nonreligious subjects treated in the Koran
	Class a religious subject treated in the Koran with the subject, e.g., Islamic ethics 297.5
.122 800 01–.122 800 09	Standard subdivisions
.122 800 1–.122 899 9	Specific nonreligious subjects treated in the Koran
	Add to base number 297.1228 notation 001–999, e.g., natural sciences in the Koran 297.12285
.122 9	Individual suras and groups of suras
	Origins, authenticity; geography, history, chronology of Koran lands in Koran times; texts; criticism, interpretation; commentaries; nonreligious subjects treated in the suras
.124	Hadith (Traditions)
	Including collection by Aḥmad ibn Ḥanbal
.124 001–.124 009	Standard subdivisions
.124 01–.124 08	Generalities
	Add to base number 297.1240 the numbers following 297.122 in 297.1221–297.1228, e.g., origins 297.12401

> 297.124 1–297.124 8   Specific Hadith

> Add to each subdivision identified by * as follows:
> 001–009   Standard subdivisions
> 01–08   Generalities
> Add to 0 the numbers following 297.122 in
> 297.1221–297.1228, e.g., criticism 06

Class comprehensive works in 297.124

.124 1   *Al-Bukhārī, Muḥammad ibn Ismā'īl

.124 2   *Abū Dā'ūd Sulaymān ibn al-Ash'ath al-Sijistānī

.124 3   *Muslim ibn al-Ḥajjāj al-Qushayrī

.124 4   *Al-Tirmidhī, Muḥammad ibn 'Īsá

.124 5   *Al-Nasā'ī, Aḥmad ibn Shu'ayb

.124 6   *Ibn Mājah, Muḥammad ibn Yazīd

.124 7   Other Sunni Hadith

.124 8   Hadith of other sects

[.13]   Oral traditions

Number discontinued; class in 297.1

.14   Religious and ceremonial laws and decisions

Class here fiqh in relation to religious and ceremonial laws and decisions
[*formerly also* 340.59], sharia in relation to religious and ceremonial laws
and decisions

Interdisciplinary works on sharia relocated to 340.59

Class Islamic law relating to secular matters, interdisciplinary works on
Islamic law in 340.59. Class religious law on a specific topic with the topic,
e.g., religious law concerning ḥajj 297.352

See Manual at 340.59 vs. 297.14

.18   Stories, legends, parables, proverbs, anecdotes told for religious
edification

Class here comprehensive works on Islamic legends

Class Islamic folklore in 398.20882971

*For Islamic legends on a specific topic, see the topic, e.g., Islamic
legends about pre-Islamic prophets 297.246*

[.19]   Mythology

Provision discontinued because without meaning in context

*Add as instructed under 297.1241–297.1248

[.197] Islam and secular disciplines; Islam and other systems of belief

Relocated to 297.26–297.28

[.197 835 8] Social theology of marriage and family

Relocated to 297.577

.2 Islamic doctrinal theology ('Aqā'id and Kalām); Islam and secular disciplines; Islam and other systems of belief

Standard subdivisions are added for Islamic doctrinal theology, Islam and secular disciplines, Islam and other systems of belief together; for Islamic doctrinal theology alone

Class Islamic moral theology in 297.5; class doctrines concerning Muḥammad the Prophet in 297.63

SUMMARY

297.204	**Doctrines of specific sects**
.21	**God and spiritual beings**
.22	**Humankind**
.23	**Eschatology**
.24	**Other doctrines**
.26	**Islam and secular disciplines**
.27	**Islam and social sciences**
.28	**Islam and other systems of belief**
.29	**Apologetics and polemics**

> 297.204–297.24 Islamic doctrinal theology ('Aqā'id and Kalām)

Class comprehensive works in 297.2

For apologetics and polemics, see 297.29; for shahāda (profession of faith), see 297.34

.204 Doctrines of specific sects

Add to base number 297.204 the numbers following 297.8 in 297.81–297.87, e.g., doctrines of Shiites 297.2042

.21 God and spiritual beings

.211 God

.211 2 Attributes and names of God

Class vindication of God's justice and goodness in permitting existence of evil and suffering in 297.2118

For tawhid (unity of God), see 297.2113

.211 3 Tawhid (Unity of God)

.211 4	Relation to the world
	Including relation to and action in history
	For revelation, see 297.2115; for creation, see 297.242
.211 5	Revelation
	Including prophecy
	Class Koranic prophecy in 297.1221; class prophets and prophethood in 297.246
.211 8	Theodicy
	Vindication of God's justice and goodness in permitting existence of evil and suffering
.215	Angels
.216	Devils
.217	Jinn
.22	Humankind
	Including faith, repentance
	For eschatology, see 297.23
.221	Creation
	Class comprehensive works on creation in 297.242
.225	Nature
	Including soul
	Class free will and predestination in 297.227
.227	Free will and predestination
	Class here freedom of choice between good and evil
.23	Eschatology
	Including day of judgment, death, eternity, future life, heaven, hell, punishment, resurrection, rewards
	Class doctrines of Hidden Imam, of Mahdi in 297.24
.24	Other doctrines
	Including doctrines of Hidden Imam, of Mahdi
	Caliphate and imamate relocated to 297.61
.242	Creation
	Including origin of life
	Class here Islamic cosmology
	For creation of humankind, see 297.221

.246   Prophets prior to Muḥammad

Including Adam, Moses

Class here comprehensive works on prophets and prophethood in Islam

For Muḥammad the Prophet, see 297.63

.246 3   Abraham

.246 5   Jesus, son of Mary

>   297.26–297.28   Islam and secular disciplines; Islam and other systems of belief [*formerly* 297.197]

Class comprehensive works in 297.2

.26   Islam and secular disciplines

Class here attitudes of Islam toward and influence on secular issues, Islamic views and teachings about secular disciplines

Class relation of a specific Islamic doctrine and a secular discipline with the doctrine in 297.2, e.g., relation of Islamic doctrine about creation and scientific theories about creation 297.242; class work influenced by Islam and Islamic theories within a secular discipline with the discipline, e.g., Islamic philosophy 181.07, architecture in the Islamic world 720.917671

For Islam and social sciences, see 297.27

See also 297.1228 for nonreligious subjects treated in Koran, 297.12408 for nonreligious subjects treated in Hadith

See Manual at 297.26–297.27

.261   Islam and philosophy, paranormal phenomena, psychology

.265   Islam and natural sciences, mathematics

.266   Islam and technology

.267   Islam and the arts

.27   Islam and social sciences

Attitudes of Islam toward and influence on social issues

Including war and peace

Class here attitudes of Islam toward and influence on social issues, Islam and socioeconomic problems, Islamic social theology

Class Islamic view of marriage and family in 297.577

See Manual at 297.26–297.27

.272	Islam and politics

Including civil rights, international affairs, nationalism

Class political science view of religiously oriented political theories and ideologies in 320.55; class political science view of relation of state to religious organizations and groups in 322.1; class political science view of religious political parties in 324.2182

See Manual at 320.55 vs. 297.09, 322.1

.273	Islam and economics

Including Islam and communism

See also 297.289 for Islam and atheism

.28	Islam and other systems of belief

Attitudes toward and relations with other systems of belief

Class apologetics and polemics in 297.29

.282	Islam and Judaism

Class Biblical figures as prophets prior to Muḥammad in 297.246

.283	Islam and Christianity

Class Biblical figures as prophets prior to Muḥammad in 297.246

.284	Islam and religions of Indic origin

Add to base number 297.284 the numbers following 294 in 294.3–294.6, e.g., Islam and Hinduism 297.2845

.289	Islam and irreligion

Including Islam and atheism

.29	Apologetics and polemics
[.291]	Polemics against pagans and heathens

Number discontinued; class in 297.29

.292	Polemics against Judaism
.293	Polemics against Christianity
.294	Polemics against religions of Indic origin
[.295]	Polemics against other religions

Number discontinued; class in 297.29

[.297]	Polemics against rationalists, agnostics, atheists

Number discontinued; class in 297.29

.298	Polemics against scientists and materialists

.3 **Islamic worship**

Including use of arts and symbolism in worship

Class here comprehensive works on Islamic worship, on non-Sufi worship, on Islamic private worship, on non-Sufi private worship [*all formerly* 297.43], public worship

Class Pillars of Islam (Pillars of the Faith) in 297.31. Class specific applications of the arts and symbolism in worship with the application in 297.301–297.38, e.g., use of arts and symbolism in mosques 297.351

For Sufi worship, see 297.43

.300 1–.300 9 Standard subdivisions

.301–.307 Specific sects

Add to base number 297.30 the numbers following 297.8 in 297.81–297.87, e.g., Shiite rites 297.302

.31 Pillars of Islam (Pillars of the Faith) [*formerly* 297.5]

Comprehensive works only

For shahāda (profession of faith), see 297.34; for hajj (pilgrimage to Mecca), see 297.352; for sawm Ramadān (annual fast of Ramadan), see 297.362; for salāt (prayer five times daily), see 297.3822; for zakat, see 297.54

See also 297.72 for jihad

[.32–.33] Divination and occultism

Relocated to 297.39

.34 Shahāda (Profession of faith) [*formerly* 297.51]

.35 Sacred places and pilgrimages

Standard subdivisions are added for sacred places and pilgrimages together, for sacred places alone

Including non-Sufi pilgrimages, comprehensive works on Islamic pilgrimages [*both formerly* 297.446]

Class here rites and ceremonies associated with sacred places and pilgrimages [*formerly* 297.38]

Class pilgrimages to specific places in 297.352–297.359

For Sufi pilgrimages, see 297.435

[.350 93–.350 99] Treatment by specific continents, countries, localities

Relocated to 297.353–297.359

.351 Mosques

Class here interdisciplinary works

For organizational role and function of mosques, see 297.65; for architecture of mosques, see 726.2

[.351 093–.351 099] Treatment by specific continents, countries, localities

Do not use; class in 297.352–297.359

.352 Mecca

Class here ḥajj (pilgrimage to Mecca) [*formerly* 297.55]

.353–.359 Treatment by specific continents, countries, localities [*formerly* 297.35093–297.35099]

Add to base number 297.35 notation 3–9 from Table 2, e.g., Medina 297.35538, Jerusalem 297.35569442; however, for Mecca, see 297.352

.36 Special days and seasons

Including Jum'ah (Friday prayer); 'Āshūrā' (Tenth of Muḥarram); Mawlid al-Nabī (Prophet's birthday); 'Īd al-Aḍḥā, 'Īd al-Fiṭr

Class here rites and ceremonies associated with special days and seasons [*formerly also* 297.38], Islamic religious calendar

See also 297.37 for sermons for special days and seasons

.362 Ṣawm Ramaḍān (Annual fast of Ramadan) [*formerly also* 297.53]

Including Laylat al-Qadr

Class comprehensive works on fasting in 297.53

.37 Sermons and preaching

Class sermons on a specific subject with the subject, e.g., sermons on day of judgment 297.23

.38 Rites, ceremonies, prayer, meditation

Conduct and texts

Including ablutions

Rites and ceremonies associated with sacred places and pilgrimages relocated to 297.35; rites and ceremonies associated with special days and seasons relocated to 297.36

Class ablutions associated with prayer and meditations in 297.382; class ablutions associated with burial and mourning in 297.385

See also 297.37 for sermons and preaching

.382	Prayer and meditation

Standard subdivisions are added for prayer and meditation together, for prayer alone

Including dhikr (remembrance), qiblah (direction of prayer)

Class here practical works on prayer and meditation

Class prayer and meditation associated with sacred places and pilgrimages in 297.35; class prayer and meditation associated with special days and seasons in 297.36. Class prayer and meditation associated with specific rites and ceremonies with the rites and ceremonies, e.g., funerals in 297.385; class prayers and meditations on a specific subject with the subject, e.g., unity of God 297.2113

.382 2	Ṣalāt (Prayer five times daily) [*formerly* 297.52]

For texts of prayers, see 297.3824

.382 4	Texts of prayers and meditations

Class here prayer books

.385	Burial and mourning rites
.39	Popular practices

Including controversial practices, e.g., divination and occultism [*both formerly* 297.32–297.33]

Class occult practices not regarded as Islamic practices in 133; class Islamic views of occultism regarded as a secular topic in 297.261; class sociological studies of Islamic popular practices in 306.69739. Class popular practices associated with a topic provided elsewhere with the topic, e.g., popular practices associated with burial and mourning 297.385

.4	**Sufism (Islamic mysticism)**

Class here specific aspects of Sufism [*formerly* 297.1–297.3, 297.5–297.7]

Non-Sufi and comprehensive works on Islamic religious experience, life, practice relocated to 297.57

See Manual at 297.4

.41	Sufi doctrinal theology; Sufism and secular disciplines; Sufism and non-Islamic systems of belief

Standard subdivisions are added for Sufi doctrinal theology, Sufism and secular disciplines, Sufism and non-Islamic systems of belief together; for Sufi doctrinal theology alone

Add to base number 297.41 the numbers following 297.2 in 297.21–297.29, e.g., Sufi concept of God 297.4111

Class Sufi doctrines concerning Muḥammad the Prophet in 297.4; class Sufi moral theology in 297.45

[.42]   Sufi religious experience

       Number discontinued; class in 297.4

.43   Sufi worship

       Add to base number 297.43 the numbers following 297.3 in 297.3001–297.38, e.g., Sufi pilgrimages 297.435 [*formerly* 297.446], Sufi prayer and meditation 297.4382

       Comprehensive works on Islamic worship, on non-Sufi worship, on Islamic private worship, on non-Sufi private worship relocated to 297.3

.44   Sufi religious life and practice

       Class here guides to Sufi religious life

       Class Sufi moral theology in 297.45

       For Sufi worship, see 297.43

.446   Sufi individual observances

       Including Sufi ascetic practices [*formerly* 297.447], dietary laws and observance

       Non-Sufi pilgrimages, comprehensive works on Islamic pilgrimages relocated to 297.35; Sufi pilgrimages relocated to 297.435

       For Sufi fasting, see 297.45

[.447]   Sufi asceticism

       Sufi ascetic practices relocated to 297.446; Sufi fasting relocated to 297.45

[.448]   Guides to religious life

       Use of this number for guides to Sufi religious life discontinued; class in 297.44

       Non-Sufi and comprehensive guides to religious life relocated to 297.57

.45   Sufi moral theology

       Including Sufi fasting [*formerly* 297.447], almsgiving, ṣadaqah, zakat

       For Sufi observance of ṣawm Ramaḍān, see 297.4362

.48   Sufi orders

       Including Bektashi, Naqshabandiyah, Qādirīyah, Tijānīyah

       See also 297.835 for Kadarites (Islamic sect)

.482   Mevleviyeh

> **297.5–297.7 Islamic moral theology and religious experience, life, practice; Islamic leaders and organization; protection and propagation of Islam**

Specific aspects of Sufism relocated to 297.4

Class comprehensive works in 297

.5 Islamic moral theology and religious experience, life, practice

Standard subdivisions are added for moral theology and religious experience, life, practice together; for moral theology alone

Including conscience; general works on duty, sin, vice, virtue

Pillars of Islam (Pillars of the Faith) relocated to 297.31

Class a specific duty, sin, vice, virtue in 297.56

For jihad, see 297.72

[.51] Shahāda (Profession of faith)

Relocated to 297.34

[.52] Ṣalāt (Prayer five times daily)

Relocated to 297.3822

.53 Ṣawm (Fast)

Class here comprehensive works on fasting

Ṣawm Ramaḍān (Annual Fast of Ramadan) relocated to 297.362

.54 Zakat

Class here almsgiving, ṣadaqah

[.55] Ḥajj (Pilgrimage to Mecca)

Relocated to 297.352

.56 Specific vices, virtues, moral issues

Add to base number 297.56 the numbers following 17 in 172–179, e.g., Islamic sexual ethics 297.566; however, for almsgiving, see 297.54

Class comprehensive works on vices, on virtues in 297.5

.57   Religious experience, life, practice

>   Standard subdivisions are added for any or all topics in heading

>   Class here non-Sufi and comprehensive works on Islamic religious experience, life, practice [*all formerly* 297.4]; non-Sufi and comprehensive guides to religious life [*formerly* 297.448]

>   Class moral theology in 297.5

>>   *For worship, see 297.3; for mysticism and Sufi religious experience, see 297.4; for Sufi life and practice, see 297.44*

[.570 85]   Relatives   Parents

>   Do not use; class in 297.577

.570 86   Persons by miscellaneous social characteristics

[.570 865 5]   Married persons

>   Do not use; class in 297.577

.574   Conversion

>   Class here conversion of non-Muslims to Islam

>   Class da'wah in 297.74. Class conversion of Muslims to another religion with the religion, e.g., conversion of Muslims to Christianity 248.246

.576   Individual observances

>   Including ascetic practices, dietary laws and observance, ritual slaughter of animals to conform with dietary laws

>>   *For pilgrimages, see 297.35; for fasting, see 297.53; for almsgiving, see 297.54*

.577   Marriage and family life

>   Class here social theology of marriage and family [*formerly* 297.1978358]; comprehensive works on marriage, on family life

>>   *For ethics of marriage and family, see 297.563*

.6   Islamic leaders and organization

.61   Leaders and their work

>   Role, function, duties

>   Class here caliphate, imamate [*both formerly* 297.24, 297.65]; ayatollahs, caliphs, imams, ulama

>>   *For doctrine of Hidden Imam, see 297.24; for Muhammad the Prophet, see 297.63; for Muhammad's family and companions (including first four caliphs), see 297.64*

[.610 92]   Persons

Do not use for persons treatment of religious leaders primarily associated with a specific religious activity; class in 297.1–297.7, e.g., founders of Sufi orders 297.48. Do not use for persons treatment of Muḥammad; class in 297.63. Do not use for persons treatment of Muḥammad's family and companions (including first four caliphs); class in 297.64. Do not use for persons treatment of Islamic leaders primarily associated with a specific sect or reform movement; class in 297.8. Do not use for persons treatment of other religious leaders; class in 297.092

Use of this number for persons who study and write about the role, function, duties of religious leaders discontinued; class in 297.61

.63   Muḥammad the Prophet

Class here comprehensive works on Muḥammad and his family and companions

Class Hadith in 297.124

For Muḥammad's family and companions, see 297.64

.630 92   Persons

Do not use for Muḥammad the Prophet; class in 297.63

Class here scholars who specialize in the life and works of Muḥammad the Prophet

.632   Period prior to call to prophethood

Including birth, childhood

See also 297.36 for Mawlid al-Nabī (holiday of Prophet's birthday)

.633   Period at Mecca

Including Isrā' (Night Journey to Jerusalem) and Mi'rāj (Ascent to Heaven)

Class comprehensive works on prophetic career in 297.635

For period prior to call to prophethood, see 297.632

.634   Hijrah (Emigration from Mecca)

.635   Period at Medina

For emigration from Mecca to Medina, see 297.634

.64   Muḥammad's family and companions

Standard subdivisions are added for family and companions together, for family alone

Including descendants of Muḥammad

.642   Wives

.644   Daughters

.648   Ṣaḥābah (Companions)

> Including religious biography and theological discussion of the first four caliphs

> Class interdisciplinary biographies of the first four caliphs with the subject in 950, e.g., Abu Bakr 953.02092

.65   Organizations [*formerly also* 297.06] and organization

> Role and function

> Including associations, congregations, mosques

> Caliphate, imamate relocated to 297.61

> Class Islamic organizations in relation to political affairs in 297.272; class a specific organization limited to a specific sect or reform movement in 297.8; class political science view of relation of state to religious organizations and groups in 322.1; class political science view of religious political parties in 324.2182; class interdisciplinary works on mosques in 297.351

.7   **Protection and propagation of Islam**

.72   Jihad

.74   Da'wah

> Class here call to Islam, missionary work

.77   Islamic religious education

> Class Islam as an academic subject in 297.071; class comprehensive works on madrasa education, treating both religious education and other subjects, in 371.077

> *For religious education at the level of higher education, see 297.0711*

> *See Manual at 291.75 vs. 200.71*

.770 83   Young people

> Class here Islamic religious schools, religious education in Islamic schools that teach all subjects

> Class comprehensive works on Islamic schools that teach all subjects in 371.077

.8   **Islamic sects and reform movements**

> Class specific aspects of sects and reform movements in 297.1–297.7; class secular view of relation of state to religious organizations and groups in 322.1; class secular view of religious political parties in 324.2182

> *For Sufism, see 297.4*

.804		Special topics
.804 2		Relations among sects and reform movements

Class here relations between Sunni and Shia Islam

.81   Sunnites

Class relations between Sunnites and Shiites in 297.8042

.811   Hanafites

.812   Shafiites

.813   Malikites

.814   Hanbalites and Wahhābīyah

.82   Shiites

Class relations between Shiites and Sunnites in 297.8042

.821   Twelvers (Ithna Asharites)

.822   Seveners (Ismailites)

Including Mustalians, Nizaris

.824   Zaydites

.83   Other sects and reform movements

Including Kharijites

.833   Ibadites

.834   Motazilites

.835   Kadarites

See also 297.48 for Qādirīyah (Sufi order)

.837   Murjiites

.85   Druzes

.86   Ahmadiyya movement

.87   Black Muslim movement

Including American Muslim Mission, Nation of Islam, World Community of al-Islam in the West

.9   **Babism and Bahai Faith**

.92   Babism

.93   †Bahai Faith

See Manual at 291

†Add as instructed under 292–299

(298)   **(Permanently unassigned)**

(Optional number used to provide local emphasis and a shorter number for a specific religion other than Christianity; prefer the number for the specific religion elsewhere in 292–299; or optional number used for Christianity if option A under 292–299 is chosen. Other options are described at 292–299)

299   **Other religions**

Including Urantia, modern revivals of long dormant religions, religions based on modern revivals of witchcraft

Class syncretistic religious writings of individuals expressing personal views and not claiming to establish a new religion or to represent an old one in 291

If a religion not named in the schedule claims to be Christian, class it in 289.9 even if it is unorthodox or syncretistic

(Options for giving local emphasis and shorter numbers for a specific religion are described at 292–299)

SUMMARY

299.1–.4	**Religions of Indo-European, Semitic, North African, North and West Asian, Dravidian origin**
.5	**Religions of East and Southeast Asian origin**
.6	**Religions originating among Black Africans and people of Black African descent**
.7	**Religions of North American native origin**
.8	**Religions of South American native origin**
.9	**Religions of other origin**

.1–.4   **Religions of Indo-European, Semitic, North African, North and West Asian, Dravidian origin**

Not otherwise provided for

Add to base number 299 the numbers following —9 in notation 91–94 from Table 5, e.g., Druidism 299.16

Class modern revivals of long dormant religions in 299

.5   **Religions of East and Southeast Asian origin**

See Manual at 200.9 vs. 294, 299.5

.51   Religions of Chinese origin

.512   †Confucianism

Interdisciplinary works on Confucianism relocated to 181.112

Class the Four books of Confucius in 181.112

See Manual at 291; also at 200.92 and 291–299

.514   †Taoism

See Manual at 291; also at 200.92 and 291–299

†Add as instructed under 292–299

.54		Religions of Tibetan origin

Class here Bon

.56		Religions of Japanese and Ryukyuan origin
.561		†Shintoism

See Manual at 291; also at 200.92 and 291–299

.57–.59	Other religions of East and Southeast Asian origin

Add to base number 299.5 the numbers following —95 in notation 957–959 from Table 5, e.g., Caodaism 299.592

.6 Religions originating among Black Africans and people of Black African descent

Unless other instructions are given, class a subject with aspects in two or more subdivisions of 299.6 in the number coming first, e.g., rites of the Yoruba 299.64 (*not* 299.68333)

For Black Muslims, see 297.87; for religions originating among Ethiopians, see 299.28; for religions originating among Cushitic and Omotic peoples, see 299.35; for religions originating among the Hausa, see 299.37

[.609 61–.609 69]	Religions in specific areas in Africa

Do not use; class in 299.691–299.699

.62	Mythology and mythological foundations

Class myths on a specific subject with the subject, e.g., on a god 299.63

See Manual at 398.2 vs. 291.13

.63	Doctrines

Including gods, goddesses, other supernatural beings

.64	Practices [*formerly* 299.65], rites, ceremonies

Including divination, religious healing, zombiism

See Manual at 615.852 vs. 291.31, 234.131

[.65]	Practices

Relocated to 299.64

.67	Specific cults
.672	Umbanda
.673	Candomblé
.674	Santeria
.675	Voodooism

Class voodooism as an occult practice without regard to its religious significance in 133.4

†Add as instructed under 292–299

.676   Ras Tafari movement

.68   Religions of specific groups and peoples

.681   Religions of Khoikhoi and San

.683–.685   Religions of peoples who speak, or whose ancestors spoke,
         Niger-Congo, Nilo-Saharan languages

> Add to base number 299.68 the numbers following —96 in notation
> 963–965 from Table 6, e.g., religion of the Yoruba 299.68333

.686–.688   Religions of national groups in Africa

> Add to base number 299.68 the numbers following —6 in notation
> 66–68 from Table 2, e.g., religion of Ugandans 299.68761

> Class national groups that predominate in specific areas in Africa in
> 299.69

.689   Religions of other national groups of largely African descent

> Add to base number 299.689 notation 4–9 from Table 2, e.g., African
> religion of Haitians 299.6897294

> Class religions of such national groups in areas where they predominate
> in 299.609, e.g., African religion of Haitians in Haiti 299.6097294

.69   Religions of specific areas in Africa

> Add to base number 299.69 the numbers following —6 in notation 61–69
> from Table 2, e.g., religions of West Africa 299.696

.7   Religions of North American native origin

> Unless other instructions are given, class a subject with aspects in two or more
> subdivisions of 299.7 in the number coming first, e.g., rites of Hopi 299.74 (*not*
> 299.7845)

[.709 71–.709 79]   Religions in specific areas in North America

> Do not use; class in 299.791–299.799

.72–.77   Specific aspects

> Add to base number 299.7 the numbers following 299.6 in 299.62–299.67,
> e.g., rites and ceremonies 299.74

.78   Religions of specific groups and peoples

> Add to base number 299.78 the numbers following —97 in notation
> 971–979 from Table 5, e.g., Hopi religion 299.7845

.79   Religions of specific areas in North America

> Add to base number 299.79 the numbers following —7 in notation 71–79
> from Table 2, e.g., religions of Indians of Mexico 299.792

.8   **Religions of South American native origin**

Unless other instructions are given, class a subject with aspects in two or more subdivisions of 299.8 in the number coming first, e.g., rites of Guaranís 299.84 (*not* 299.88382)

[.809 81–.809 89]   Religions of specific areas in South America

Do not use; class in 299.891–299.899

.82–.87   Specific aspects

Add to base number 299.8 the numbers following 299.6 in 299.62–299.67, e.g., gods and goddesses 299.83

.88   Religions of specific groups and peoples

Add to base number 299.88 the numbers following —98 in notation 982–984 from Table 5, e.g., religion of Guaranís 299.88382

.89   Religions of specific areas in South America

Add to base number 299.89 the numbers following —8 in notation 81–89 from Table 2, e.g., religions of Indians of the Amazon 299.8911

.9   **Religions of other origin**

.92   Religions of other ethnic origin

Add to base number 299.92 the numbers following —99 in notation 991–999 from Table 5, e.g., religion of Polynesians 299.924

.93   Religions of eclectic and syncretistic origin

Religions and applied religious philosophies of eclectic, syncretistic, universal nature

Including Eckankar, a Course in Miracles, Great White Brotherhood, New Age religions, New Thought, systems of Bhagwan Shree Rajneesh and Meher Baba, United Church of Religious Science

Class syncretistic religious writings of individuals expressing personal views and not claiming to establish a new religion or to represent an old one in 291

See also 289.98 for Christian New Thought

See Manual at 299.93: New Age religions

.932   Gnosticism

Including Manicheism

Class Christian Gnosticism in 273.1; class Christian Manicheism in 273.2

.933   Subud

.934   Theosophy

| .935 | Anthroposophy |
| .936 | Scientology |

Including dianetics [*formerly* 158.9]

300

300 Social sciences

Class here behavioral studies, social studies

Class a specific behavioral science with the subject, e.g., psychology 150; class military, diplomatic, political, economic, social, welfare aspects of a war with the history of the war, e.g., Vietnamese War 959.7043

For language, see 400; for history, see 900

See Manual at 300; also at 150; also at 300 vs. 600

SUMMARY

300.1–.9	**Standard subdivisions**
301–307	**[Sociology and anthropology]**
310	**General statistics**
314–319	**General statistics of specific continents, countries, localities in modern world**
320	**Political science (Politics and government)**
.01–.09	**Standard subdivisions**
.1–.9	**[Structure and functions of government, ideologies, political situation and conditions, related topics]**
321	**Systems of governments and states**
322	**Relation of the state to organized groups and their members**
323	**Civil and political rights**
324	**The political process**
325	**International migration and colonization**
326	**Slavery and emancipation**
327	**International relations**
328	**The legislative process**
330	**Economics**
.01–.09	**Standard subdivisions**
.1–.9	**[Systems, schools, theories, economic situation and conditions]**
331	**Labor economics**
332	**Financial economics**
333	**Economics of land and energy**
334	**Cooperatives**
335	**Socialism and related systems**
336	**Public finance**
337	**International economics**
338	**Production**
339	**Macroeconomics and related topics**

340	Law
.02–.09	Standard subdivisions
.1–.9	[Philosophy and theory of law, comparative law, law reform, legal systems, conflict of laws]
341	International law
342	Constitutional and administrative law
343	Military, defense, public property, public finance, tax, trade (commerce), industrial law
344	Labor, social problems and services, education, cultural law
345	Criminal law
346	Private law
347	Civil procedure and courts
348	Laws (Statutes), regulations, cases
349	Law of specific socioeconomic regions and of specific jurisdictions and areas
350	Public administration and military science
351	Public administration
352	General considerations of public administration
353	Specific fields of public administration
354	Public administration of economy and environment
355	Military science
356	Foot forces and warfare
357	Mounted forces and warfare
358	Air and other specialized forces and warfare; engineering and related services
359	Sea (Naval) forces and warfare
360	Social problems and services; associations
361	Social problems and social welfare in general
362	Social welfare problems and services
363	Other social problems and services
364	Criminology
365	Penal and related institutions
366	Associations
367	General clubs
368	Insurance
369	Miscellaneous kinds of associations
370	Education
.1–.9	Standard subdivisions, education for specific objectives, educational psychology
371	Schools and their activities; special education
372	Elementary education
373	Secondary education
374	Adult education
375	Curricula
378	Higher education
379	Public policy issues in education

380	Commerce, communications, transportation
.01–.09	Standard subdivisions
.1	Commerce (Trade)
381	Internal commerce (Domestic trade)
382	International commerce (Foreign trade)
383	Postal communication
384	Communications Telecommunication
385	Railroad transportation
386	Inland waterway and ferry transportation
387	Water, air, space transportation
388	Transportation Ground transportation
389	Metrology and standardization

390	Customs, etiquette, folklore
.001–.009	Standard subdivisions
.01–.09	Standard subdivisions of customs
.1–.4	Customs of specific economic, social, occupational classes
391	Costume and personal appearance
392	Customs of life cycle and domestic life
393	Death customs
394	General customs
395	Etiquette (Manners)
398	Folklore
399	Customs of war and diplomacy

SUMMARY

300.1–.9	Standard subdivisions
301	Sociology and anthropology
302	Social interaction
303	Social processes
304	Factors affecting social behavior
305	Social groups
306	Culture and institutions
307	Communities

.1 **Philosophy and theory**

.2 **Miscellany**

.21 Tabulated and related materials

   Do not use for statistics; class in 310

.3–.9 **Standard subdivisions**

301 Sociology and anthropology

Standard subdivisions are added for either or both topics in heading

Class here interdisciplinary works on society, humans

Class a specific topic in sociology and anthropology in 302–307; class social problems and social welfare in 361–365. Class a specific aspect of society not provided for in 302–307 with the aspect, e.g., general history 900

For criminal anthropology, see 364.2; for physical anthropology, see 599.9

See Manual at 301–307; also at 301–307 vs. 361–365; also at 301–307 vs. 361.1, 362.042

[.019] Psychological principles

> Do not use; class in 302

.7 **Nonliterate societies**

> **302–307 Specific topics in sociology and anthropology**

Unless other instructions are given, class a subject with aspects in two or more subdivisions of 302–307 in the number coming last, e.g., social deterioration during civil wars 303.64 (*not* 303.45)

Class comprehensive works in 301. Class effect of one factor on another with the factor affected, e.g., effect of climate on social change 303.4

See Manual at 302–307; also at 302–307 vs. 150, T1—019; also at 302–307 vs. 155.92, 158.2; also at 302–307 vs. 156; also at 302–307 vs. 320

302 Social interaction

Class here psychological principles of sociology, interpersonal relations, social psychology

Class social psychology of a specific situation with the situation, e.g., social psychology of ethnic groups 305.8

See also 155.92 for effect of social environment upon individuals, 158.2 for individual aspects of interpersonal relations

See Manual at 302–307 vs. 150, T1—019; also at 302–307 vs. 155.92, 158.2; also at 302–307 vs. 156

SUMMARY

302.01–.09	**Standard subdivisions**
.1	**General topics of social interaction**
.2	**Communication**
.3	**Social interaction within groups**
.4	**Social interaction between groups**
.5	**Relation of the individual to society**

.015 195 Statistical mathematics

> Class here sociometry

> *See Manual at 519.5, T1—015195 vs. 001.422, T1—072*

[.019] Psychological principles

> Do not use; class in 302

.072 Research

[.072 7] Statistical methods

> Do not use; class in 302.015195

.1   **General topics of social interaction**

.12   Social understanding

Including attribution, risk perception

For social learning, see 303.32; for perception of norms, see 303.37

.13   Social choice

Including attraction, influence

.14   Social participation

Including communalism, competition, cooperation, encounter groups, sensitivity training, voluntarism

Class here social acceptance, social adjustment, social skills, success

See also 302.4 for intergroup aspects of participation

.15   Social role (Role theory)

Including role conflict

.17   Social dysfunction

Dysfunction affecting a substantial portion of society, e.g., mass hysteria, crazes

Including apathy, fear, panic

Class here social psychoanalysis

Class dysfunctional responses of individuals to society in 302.542

.2   **Communication**

Including semiotics

Class here interdisciplinary works on communication

For information theory, see 003.54

.22   Kinds of communication

.222   Nonverbal communication

Including drumbeats, smoke signals; body language, gestures; flower language

Class here means of nonverbal communication, interdisciplinary works on nonlinguistic (nonstructured) communication

Class comprehensive works on means of verbal and nonverbal communication in 302.23; class manual language for the deaf in 419

For iconography, see 704.9; for insignia, see 929.9

.222 3	Symbols

Class here interdisciplinary works on symbols, on symbolism

For Christian religious symbols, see 246.55; for religious symbolism, see 291.37. For symbols in a specific subject other than religion, see the subject, plus notation 0148 from Table 1, e.g., symbols in electrical engineering 621.30148

.224	Verbal communication

Class media in 302.23

For language, see 400

.224 2	Oral communication

For conversation, see 302.346

.224 4	Written communication

Class here literacy, illiteracy

See also 301.7 for nonliterate societies

.23	Media (Means of communication)

Including signboards, signs

Class here mass media, sociology of journalism

Interdisciplinary works on a specific medium relocated to the medium, e.g., newspapers 070.172, television 384.55

Class the effect of mass media on a specific subject other than social groups with the subject, e.g., effect on social change 303.4833, on a company's advertising policy 659.111

.230 8	History and description with respect to kinds of persons

Class here effect of mass media on specific groups, on social stratification

See Manual at 302.2308

.232	Print media

Class interdisciplinary works on the book in 002

.232 2	Newspapers
.232 4	Periodicals and journals

Standard subdivisions are added for either or both topics in heading

.234	Motion pictures, radio, television

Class here the electronic media

.234 3	Motion pictures
.234 4	Radio

.234 5	Television
.235	Telephony and telegraphy

Standard subdivisions are added for telephony and telegraphy together, for telephony alone

.24   Content

Including gossip, rumor

See also 070.1 for journalistic aspect of content

.25   Failures and disruptions of communication

Standard subdivisions are added for either or both topics in heading

For censorship, see 303.376

.3   Social interaction within groups

Class here group decision-making processes, group dynamics, negotiation

.33   Social interaction in abstract and temporary groups

Including audiences, crowds, mobs

Class media audiences in 302.23

.34   Social interaction in primary groups

Groups small enough for all members to engage in face-to-face relationships at one time

Including committees, gangs, play groups

Class here friendship

Class family in 306.85

See also 362.74 for predelinquent gangs, 364.1066 for gangs engaging in crime

.346   Conversation

Including conversational rhythm

.35   Social interaction in complex groups

Class here bureaucracies, hierarchically organized groups, organizational behavior

See Manual at 302.35 vs. 658, T1—068

.4   Social interaction between groups

Including ingroups and outgroups

Class social interaction between a specific social group and other social groups in 305

.5 **Relation of individual to society**

> *See also 155.92 for psychological effects of social environment upon the individual*

.52 Relation through reference groups

.54 Response of individuals

> Including ambition

> Class here aggression, dysfunctional responses, individualism

>> *For conformity, see 303.32*

>> *See also 302.17 for mass manifestations of social dysfunction*

.542 Deviation

> Class here madness considered as a form of interaction of individuals with society

.544 Alienation

.545 Isolation

303 Social processes

> *For social interaction, see 302; for factors affecting social behavior, see 304*

SUMMARY

303.3	Coordination and control
.4	Social change
.6	Conflict

.3 **Coordination and control**

> Class here policy formulation, power

> Class coordination and control in and through specific institutions in 306

.32 Socialization

> Including social learning

> Class here conformity

> Class interdisciplinary works on child development in 305.231

>> *For education, see 370*

.323 Socialization by family

.323 1 Socialization by father

.323 2 Socialization by mother

.324 Socialization by school

.325 Socialization by religious organizations

.327	Socialization by other instrumentalities

Including peer group, play groups, recreational agencies

.33	Social control

> *For socialization, see 303.32; for social control through specific means, see 303.34–303.38*

>   303.34–303.38   Social control through specific means

Class socialization through specific means of control in 303.32; class comprehensive works in 303.33

.34	Leadership

Including cooperation, influence

.342	Persuasion

By individuals

Class here interdisciplinary works on persuasion

> *For a specific aspect of persuasion, see the aspect, e.g., individual psychology of persuasion 153.852, persuasion by media 302.23, persuasion by propaganda 303.375*

.35	Utilitarian control

Use of rewards and incentives

.36	Coercion

Including authority, punishment, restraint, threat

> *See also 364.6 for treatment and punishment of offenders*

.37	Normative methods

Including perception of norms

> *For public opinion, see 303.38*

.372	Belief systems and customs

Standard subdivisions are added for either or both topics in heading

Class here social ethics, justice, values

> *See also 361.61 for values in social policy towards welfare problems*

> *See Manual at 170 vs. 303.372*

.375	Propaganda
.376	Censorship

> *See Manual at 363.31 vs. 303.376, 791.4*

.38 Public opinion

Class here attitudes, attitude formation and change

Class propaganda in 303.375. Class public opinion on a specific subject with the subject, e.g., public opinion on racial stereotypes 305.8, on the political process 324

See also 302.12 for social understanding

.385 Prejudice

Class here social stereotypes and stereotyping

Class prejudices held by racial, ethnic, national groups in 303.387; class prejudices held by occupational and miscellaneous social groups in 303.388; class prejudices regarding a specific group in 305

.387 Opinions held by racial, ethnic, national groups

Add to base number 303.387 notation 1–9 from Table 5, e.g., opinions of Canadians 303.38711

.388 Opinions held by occupational and miscellaneous groups

Add to base number 303.388 notation 04–99 from Table 7, e.g., opinions of dentists 303.3886176; then add 0* and to the result add notation 1–9 from Table 2, e.g., the opinions of dentists in France 303.3886176044

.4 Social change

Class social change in a specific aspect of society with the aspect in 302–307, e.g., changes in religious institutions 306.6

[.401 12] Forecasting and forecasts

Do not use; class in 303.49

[.42–.43] Gradual (Evolutionary), abrupt (revolutionary), disruptive changes

Numbers discontinued; class in 303.4

.44 Growth and development

Standard subdivisions are added for either or both topics in heading

Class here progress, specialization

.45 Deterioration and decay

Standard subdivisions are added for either or both topics in heading

.48 Causes of change

.482 Contact between cultures

Globalisation

Class here acculturation, assimilation; social effects of international assistance, of commerce

Class multicultural education in 370.117

*Add 00 for standard subdivisions; see instructions at beginning of Table 1

.482 09	Historical and persons treatment

Do not use for geographic treatment; class in 303.4821–303.4829

.482 1–.482 9	Contact between specific areas

Add to base number 303.482 notation 1–9 from Table 2, e.g., cultural exchanges with China 303.48251; then add 0* and again add notation 1–9 from Table 2, e.g., cultural exchange between China and Japan 303.48251052

Give priority in notation to the nation most affected. If this cannot be determined, give priority to the one coming first in Table 2
(Option: Give priority to the area requiring local emphasis, e.g., in United States class cultural exchange between United States and France in 303.48273044)

.483	Development of science and technology

See Manual at 303.483 vs. 306.45, 306.46

.483 2	Transportation
.483 3	Communication

Class here information technology

.483 4	Computers

Class here automation, microelectronics, robots

.484	Purposefully induced change

Including dissent, radicalism

Class here social innovation, social reform, social reform movements

Class political aspects of reform movements in 322.44; class role of reform movements in addressing social problems in 361–365. Class innovation and reform directed to a specific end with the end, e.g., reform of banking 332.1

.485	Disasters

Including earthquakes, pandemics, wars

.49	Social forecasts

Class here futurology, social forecasting

Class interdisciplinary works on forecasting in 003.2. Class forecasting in and forecasts of a specific subject with the subject, plus notation 0112 from Table 1, e.g., future of U.S. Democratic Party 324.27360112

.490 9	Historical and persons treatment

Do not use for geographic treatment; class in 303.491–303.499

*Add 00 for standard subdivisions; see instructions at beginning of Table 1

| .491–.499 | Forecasts for specific areas |

Add to base number 303.49 notation 1–9 from Table 2, e.g., Eastern Europe in the year 2000 303.4947

.6 Conflict

Class conflict in a specific social relation with the relation, e.g., racial conflict 305.8; class a specific conflict considered an historical event with the the event in 900, e.g., disturbances of May-June 1968 in France 944.0836

.61 Civil disobedience

Including hunger strikes, passive resistance, sit-ins

Class here nonviolence

.62 Civil disorder

For civil war and revolution, see 303.64

.623 Riots

.625 Terrorism

See also 363.32 for prevention of terrorism

.64 Civil war and revolution

Standard subdivisions are added for either or both topics in heading

Class terrorism in 303.625

.66 War

Including pacifism, sociology of war

Class war as a cause of social change in 303.485; class prevention of war in 327.172; class causes of war in 355.027; class the art and science of warfare in 355–359. Class military, diplomatic, political, economic, social, welfare aspects of a specific war with the history of the war, e.g., of World War II 940.53

For civil war, see 303.64

.69 Conflict resolution

Including mediation

Class here conflict management

Class resolution of a specific kind of conflict with the kind of conflict, e.g., resolution of war 303.66

304 Factors affecting social behavior

.2 Human ecology

Class here ecological anthropology, human geography

See Manual at 578 vs. 304.2, 508, 910

.23 Geographic, space, time factors

Including territoriality, time management

Class aspects of time in relation to a specific subject with the subject in 302–307, e.g., time and conversation 302.346, leisure activities 306.4812

.25 Climatic and weather factors

.27 Biological factors

Other than human

.28 Environmental abuse

Including greenhouse effect

Class here social consequences of pollution, of misuse of resources

Class interdisciplinary works on resources in 333.7; class interdisciplinary works on pollution in 363.73

See Manual at 333.72 vs. 304.28, 363.7

.5 Genetic factors

Class here sociobiology (biosociology), study of genetic bases of human social behavior

Class a specific aspect of sociobiology with the aspect in 302–307, e.g., sociobiology of conflict 303.6

For sociobiology of plants and animals, see 577.8

.6 Population

Class here population size and composition [*both formerly also* 307.2]; demography, demographic anthropology, population geography; comprehensive works on population

For movement of people, see 304.8

.61 Population characteristics

Including density

.62 Growth and decline

See also 304.63 for births, 304.64 for deaths, 304.8 for movement of people

.63 Births

Including birth intervals

Class here comprehensive works on births and deaths

For deaths, see 304.64

See also 304.62 for growth and decline of population

.632	Fertility
.634	Family size
.64	Deaths (Mortality)
.645	Life expectancy
.645 09	Historical and persons treatment

> Do not use for geographic treatment; class in 304.6451–304.6459

.645 1–.645 9	Geographic treatment

> Add to base number 304.645 notation 1–9 from Table 2, e.g., life expectancy in Canada 304.64571

.66	Demographic effects of population control efforts

> Class population policy, comprehensive works on population control in 363.9

> *See Manual at 363.9 vs. 304.66*

.663	Genocide

> Class here ethnic cleansing

.666	Family planning

> Class here birth control

> *See also 363.96 for family planning programs, 613.94 for birth control techniques*

.667	Abortion
.668	Infanticide
.8	**Movement of people**

> *For movement to, from, within communities, see 307.2*

.809	Historical, geographic, persons treatment

> Class here internal movement, emigration from specific areas

> *For emigration to specific areas, see 304.83–304.89*

.81	Causes
.82	International movement

> Class international emigration in 304.809; class international immigration in 304.83–304.89

> *See also 325 for political aspects of international movement*

.83–.89   Migration

> Add to base number 304.8 notation 3–9 from Table 2, e.g., migration to
> Australia 304.894; then add 0* and to the result add notation 1–9 from
> Table 2 for the place of origin, e.g., migration from United States to
> Australia 304.894073

305   Social groups

Including interactions, problems, role, social status of social groups;
discrimination against and conflict involving social groups

Class here culture and institutions of specific groups other than indigenous racial,
ethnic, national groups; subcultures of specific groups; consciousness-raising
groups; social stratification, equality, inequality

Unless other instructions are given, observe the following table of preference, e.g.,
black Roman Catholic middle-class male youths 305.235 (*not* 305.31, 305.55,
305.62, or 305.896):

Persons by physical and mental characteristics	305.908
Age groups	305.2
Groups by sex	305.3–305.4
Social classes	305.5
Religious groups	305.6
Racial, ethnic, national groups	305.8
Language groups	305.7
Occupational and miscellaneous groups (*except* 305.908)	305.9

Class effect of mass media on specific groups, on social stratification in
302.2308; class opinions of specific groups in 303.38; class interactions,
problems, role, social status of specific social groups, discrimination against and
conflict involving specific social groups in 305.2–305.9; class specific problems
of, welfare services to social groups in 362. Class role of a specific group in a
specific institution with the institution in 306, e.g., women in political
institutions 306.2082; class a specific aspect of discrimination with the aspect,
e.g., discrimination in housing 363.51

See Manual at 305; also at 305 vs. 306, 909, 930–990

SUMMARY

305.2	Age groups	
.3	Men and women	
.4	Women	
.5	Social classes	
.6	Religious groups	
.7	Language groups	
.8	Racial, ethnic, national groups	
.9	Occupational and miscellaneous groups	

.2   Age groups

Class here comprehensive works on generation gap

For generation gap within families, see 306.874

*Add 00 for standard subdivisions; see instructions at beginning of Table 1

.23		Young people

Through age twenty

Class here interdisciplinary works on children

For a specific aspect of children, see the aspect, e.g., social welfare of children 362.7

.231 Child development

Class here interdisciplinary works on child development

Class socialization in 303.32

For psychological development of children, see 155.4; for physical development of children, see 612.65

.232 Infants

Children from birth through age two

.233 Children three to five

Class here preschool children

.234 Children six to eleven

Class here school children

For school children over eleven, see 305.235

.235 Young people twelve to twenty

Variant names: adolescents, teenagers, young adults, youth

Comprehensive works on young adults relocated to 305.242

Class young people twenty-one and over in 305.242

.235 5 Development

Class here interdisciplinary works on development of young people twelve to twenty

For psychological development, see 155.5; for physical development, see 612.661

.24 Adults

Class adults of specific sexes in 305.3–305.4

For late adulthood, see 305.26

.242 Young adults

Aged twenty-one and above

Class here comprehensive works on young adults [*formerly* 305.235]

For young adults under twenty-one, see 305.235

.244	Persons in middle adulthood

Class here middle age

.26   Persons in late adulthood

Class sociology of retirement in 306.38

See also 646.79 for guides to retirement

.3   **Men and women**

Class here interdisciplinary works on sex role, the sexes, gender identity; adult men and women

Class sex psychology and psychology of the sexes in 155.3; class the relations between the sexes and within the sexes in 306.7–306.8. Class the relation of a specific sex to a specific subject with the subject, plus notation 081–082 from Table 1, e.g., women in U.S. history 973.082

For men and women in late adulthood, see 305.26; for women, see 305.4. For a specific aspect of sex role and gender identity, see the aspect, e.g., psychology of gender identity 155.33

.31   Men

Class here interdisciplinary works on men, on males

For specific aspects of sociology of men, see 305.32–305.38. For a specific aspect of men not provided for in 305.3, see the aspect, e.g., legal status of men 346.013

[.310 8]   History and description with respect to kinds of men

Do not use; class in 305.33–305.38

.32–.38   Specific aspects of sociology of men

Add to base number 305.3 the numbers following 305.4 in 305.42–305.48, e.g., widowers 305.389654

Class comprehensive works in 305.31

.4   **Women**

Class here interdisciplinary works on women, on females

For a specific aspect of women not provided for here, see the aspect, e.g., women's suffrage 324.623, legal status of women 346.0134

[.408]   History and description with respect to kinds of women

Do not use; class in 305.43–305.48

.42   Social role and status of women

> Standard subdivisions are added for either or both topics in heading
>
> Class here discrimination against women, women's movements
>
> Class social role and status of specific kinds of women with the kind of women in 305.43–305.48, e.g., role of women with physical disabilities 305.489816 (*not* 305.42087)

.43   Women's occupations

> Add to base number 305.43 notation 09–99 from Table 7, e.g., female physicians 305.4361
>
> *See also 331.4 for economic aspects of women's occupations*

.48   Specific kinds of women

> Class kinds of women defined by occupation in 305.43

[.480 1–.480 9]   Standard subdivisions

> Do not use; class in 305.401–305.409

.486–.488   Women belonging to specific religious, language, racial, ethnic, national groups

> Add to base number 305.48 the numbers following 305 in 305.6–305.8, e.g., English-speaking women of South Africa 305.48721068

.489   Miscellaneous groups

> Limited to groups provided for here
>
> Add to base number 305.489 the numbers following 305.90 in 305.904–305.906, e.g., widows 305.489654

.5   **Social classes**

> Class here class struggle
>
> *For theory of class struggle in Marxism, see 335.411*
>
> *See Manual at 305.9 vs. 305.5*

.51   General principles of social classes

.512   Principles of stratification

.512 2   Caste systems

.513   Social mobility

.52   Upper classes

> Class here aristocracy, elites
>
> Class intellectual elites in 305.552

.522   Upper classes by birth

> Class here prominent families

.522 2	Royalty	
.522 3	Nobility	
.523	Upper classes by economic status	
.523 2	Landowners with large estates and landed gentry	
.523 4	Wealthy	

For landowners with large estates, see 305.5232

.524	Upper classes by political status

Including cabinet ministers, commissars, judges, legislative representatives

.55	Middle classes (Bourgeoisie)

Class here moderately well-to-do

Class laboring classes in 305.562

.552	Intelligentsia

Class here intellectual elites

.553	Professional classes
.554	Managerial and entrepreneurial classes

Standard subdivisions are added for either or both topics in heading

Class farmers in 305.555

.555	Farmers

Worker-managers of their own land

Class agricultural labor in 305.563

.556	White collar classes

Including clerks, office workers

.56	Lower, alienated, excluded classes

Class here minorities, nondominant groups

Class a specific minority or nondominant group with the group, e.g., nondominant ethnic groups 305.8

.562	Laboring classes (Proletariat)

Including blue collar workers

Class agricultural workers in 305.563; class slaves in 305.567

.563	Agricultural lower classes

Including agricultural workers, serfs, sharecroppers

.563 3	Peasants

.567	Slaves
.568	Alienated and excluded classes

> Including hippies, hoboes, tramps, untouchables

.569	The poor

> Including homeless persons

> Class here destitute, impoverished persons

.6 Religious groups

Add to base number 305.6 the numbers following —2 in notation 21–29 from Table 7, e.g., Christian Scientists 305.685; then add 0* and to the result add notation 1–9 from Table 2, e.g., Christian Scientists in France 305.685044

.7 Language groups

Add to base number 305.7 notation 1–9 from Table 6, e.g., English-speaking people 305.721; then add 0* and to the result add notation 1–9 from Table 2, e.g., English-speaking people of South Africa 305.721068

Racial, ethnic, national groups associated with a specific language relocated to 305.8

.8 Racial, ethnic, national groups

Class here racial, ethnic, national groups associated with a specific language [*formerly* 305.7]; ethnology, cultural ethnology, ethnography; race relations

Class unassimilated indigenous racial, ethnic, national groups in 306.08; class physical ethnology in 599.97

> *See also 909.04 for the comprehensive history of specific racial, ethnic, national groups*

> *See Manual at 305.8 vs. 306.089*

.800 1–.800 9	Standard subdivisions
.803–.899	Specific racial, ethnic, national groups

> Add to base number 305.8 notation 03–99 from Table 5, e.g., Chinese 305.8951, Chinese in United States 305.8951073

.9 Occupational and miscellaneous groups

Unless other instructions are given, class a subject with aspects in two or more subdivisions of 305.9 in the number coming last, e.g., unemployed bibliographers 305.9091 (*not* 305.906941)

Class here occupational mobility

> *See Manual at 305.9 vs. 305.5*

.900 1–.900 9	Standard subdivisions

*Add 00 for standard subdivisions; see instructions at beginning of Table 1

.904   Persons by kinship characteristics

Add to base number 305.904 the numbers following —04 in notation 043–046 from Table 7, e.g., grandchildren 305.90442

.906   Persons by cultural level, marital status, sexual orientation, special social status

Add to base number 305.906 the numbers following —086 in notation 0863–0869 from Table 1, e.g., gays (including gay liberation movement) 305.90664, veterans 305.90697; however, for members of nondominant socioeconomic groups, see 305.56; for members of nondominant religious groups, see 305.6; for members of nondominant racial, ethnic, national groups, see 305.8; for offenders, see 364.3; for inmates of penal institutions, see 365.6

.908   Persons by physical and mental characteristics

Add to base number 305.908 the numbers following —08 in notation 081–082 from Table 7, e.g., gifted persons 305.90829

.909–.999   Persons by occupation

Add to base number 305.9 notation 09–99 from Table 7, e.g., persons occupied with religion 305.92, postal workers 305.9383

Class men's occupations in 305.33; class women's occupations in 305.43

306   Culture and institutions

Culture: the aggregate of a society's beliefs, folkways, mores, science, technology, values, arts

Institutions: patterns of behavior in social relationships

Including the roles, functions, and patterns within which the groups and members of a society conduct their lives

Class here mass culture (popular culture), cultural and social anthropology

Class cultural exchange in 303.482; class physical anthropology in 599.9; class history of a specific ethnic group in 900

For customs and folklore, see 390

See Manual at 305 vs. 306, 909, 930–990

SUMMARY

306.08	**Indigenous racial, ethnic, national groups**	
.1	**Subcultures**	
.2	**Political institutions**	
.3	**Economic institutions**	
*.4	**Specific aspects of culture**	
.6	**Religious institutions**	
.7	**Institutions pertaining to relations of the sexes**	
.8	**Marriage and family**	
.9	**Institutions pertaining to death**	

.08   Indigenous racial, ethnic, national groups

> Do not use for culture and institutions of a specific kind of person not provided for here; class in 305. Do not use for nonindigenous racial, ethnic, national groups; class in 305.8

> Class here culture and institutions, ethnology, race relations of indigenous groups living in distinct communities not integrated in the economic and social life of a nation

.089   Specific indigenous racial, ethnic, national groups

> Add to base number 306.089 notation 03–99 from Table 5, e.g., Inuit 306.0899712, Inuit in Canada 306.0899712071

> *See Manual at 305.8 vs. 306.089*

.1   **Subcultures**

> Including counterculture, drug culture

> Use of this number for popular culture discontinued; class in 306

> Class subcultures of specific groups in 305; class drug usage considered as a social problem in 362.29

.2   **Political institutions**

> Institutions maintaining internal and external peace

> Class here political sociology; comprehensive works on patronage, on client relationships

> Class political science in 320; class law in 340; class public administration and military science in 350

> *For patronage and client relationships in a specific institution, see the institution, e.g., in systems of production 306.34, in art 306.47*

> *See Manual at 320 vs. 306.2*

> 306.23–306.25   Governmental institutions

> Class comprehensive works in 306.2

.23   Legislative institutions

.24   Executive institutions

> Class military institutions in 306.27; class police in 306.28

.25   Judicial institutions

.26   Political parties

.27   Military institutions

> Class here military sociology

> *See also 355 for military science*

.28   Police institutions

See also 363.2 for police services

.3   **Economic institutions**

Social arrangements for production, distribution

Class here economic anthropology; economic sociology; sociology of economic development, of consumption

Class specific occupational groups in 305.9

For economic institutions relating to housing, see 307.336

See also 305.5 for social classes, 330 for economics

.32   Property systems

Including kinds of land tenure

For agricultural land tenure systems, see 306.349

.34   Systems of production and exchange

Standard subdivisions are added for either or both topics in heading

Class here sociology of industrial conflict and relations

See also 302.35 for organizational behavior, 303.482 for commerce (trade) as agent of social change

.342   Capitalism (Free enterprise)

See also 330.122 for economic aspects

.344   Cooperation

See also 334 for economic aspects of cooperatives

.345   Socialism

Class interdisciplinary works on socialism in 335

See Manual at 335 vs. 306.345, 320.53

.347   Syndicalism

Class interdisciplinary works on syndicalism in 335.82

See Manual at 335 vs. 306.345, 320.53

.349   Agricultural systems

Including plantation as a system of production

Class here agricultural sociology, land tenure systems

For agricultural production systems not involving ownership of land, see 306.364

.36	Systems of labor

Class here industrial sociology, sociology of work

Class sociology of industrial conflict and relations in 306.34; class economic aspects of work in 331

.361   General aspects of systems of labor

Including absenteeism, quality of work life, unemployment

.361 3   Work ethic

See also 174 for philosophical aspects of ethics of work

.361 5   Sexual division of labor

.362   Slavery

See also 305.567 for slaves as a social group

.363   Contract and indentured labor

Standard subdivisions are added for either or both topics in heading

.364   Agricultural systems of labor

Class here agricultural occupations in general; systems of agricultural production not involving ownership of land, e.g., fishing, hunting, gathering systems

Class agricultural slavery in 306.362; class contract and indentured labor in agriculture in 306.363

For agricultural shared return systems, see 306.365

.365   Agricultural shared return systems

Class here serfdom, sharecropping

.366   Free labor systems

Class free labor in agricultural systems in 306.364

.368   Nonagricultural occupations

Class here division of labor

Class social groups defined by occupation in 305.909–305.999

For sexual division of labor, see 306.3615; for agricultural occupations in general, see 306.364

.38   Retirement

See also 646.79 for guides to retirement

.4 **Specific aspects of culture**

Not provided for elsewhere

Including body shape, eating habits, magic, symbols; sociology of witch crazes

Use of this number for popular culture, for comprehensive works on cultural institutions discontinued; class in 306

Class interdisciplinary works on witch crazes in 133.43

.42 Sociology of knowledge

Class here sociology of intellectual life, of information

Class specific instances of sociology of knowledge in 306.43–306.48

.43 Education [*formerly* 370.19]

Class here educational anthropology

See also 370.115 for education for social responsibility

.432 School and society

Including interdisciplinary works on relations of teachers and society [*formerly* 371.104], on relations of colleges and universities with society [*formerly* 378.103]

For community-school relations in education, see 371.19; for community-school relations in higher education, see 378.103

.44 Language

Including pragmatics

Class here sociolinguistics

See Manual at 401.43 vs. 306.44, 401.9, 412, 415

.440 89 History and description with respect to racial, ethnic, national groups

Class here ethnolinguistics

.446 Bilingualism and multilingualism

Standard subdivisions are added for either or both topics in heading

Class here biculturalism and multiculturalism among residents in an area of divergent cultural traditions centered upon different languages

Class treatment of biculturalism and multiculturalism in which difference in language is not a central element in 306; class treatment of bilingualism and multilingualism in context of language planning and policy formulation in 306.449

See also 404.2 for linguistic aspects of bilingualism

.449 Language planning and policy

Class here development of policies on language to solve communication problems of a community that uses more than one language

[.449 094–.449 099]	Treatment by specific continents, countries, localities in modern world

Do not use; class in 306.4494–306.4499

.449 4–.449 9	Treatment by specific continent, country, locality in modern world

Add to base number 306.449 notation 4–9 from Table 2, e.g., language policy of India 306.44954

.45	Science

Class here works contrasting scientific and humanistic cultures

See Manual at 303.483 vs. 306.45, 306.46

.46	Technology

See Manual at 303.483 vs. 306.45, 306.46

.461	Medicine

Class here sociology of health, of illness

Class social aspects of medical welfare problems and services in 362.1042

.47	Art

Class sociology of arts and crafts in 306.489

.48	Recreation
.481	General topics of recreation

Including play, pleasure, wit and humor

.481 2	Leisure

Class here free time

.482	Gambling
.483	Sports

Class gambling on athletic events in 306.482

.484	Music, dance, theater
.485	Motion pictures, radio, television
.487	Games and hobbies

Class gambling on games in 306.482; class sports in 306.483

.488	Reading
.489	Arts and crafts

.6   **Religious institutions**

> Religious institutions considered from a secular, nonreligious viewpoint
>
> Class here sociology of religion
>
> Add to base number 306.6 the numbers following 2 in 230–290, e.g., Sunday school as a social institution 306.668, synagogue as a social institution 306.69665
>
> Class comprehensive works on Christian institutions in 306.63
>
> *See also 261 for Christian social theology, 291.17 for social theology*

.7   **Institutions pertaining to relations of the sexes**

> Class here interdisciplinary works on sex, sexual love, sexual relations
>
> *For sexual ethics, see 176; for problems and controversies concerning various sexual relations, see 363.4; for sex offenses, see 364.153; for customs pertaining to relations between the sexes, see 392.6; for sexual hygiene, see 613.95; for sexual techniques, see 613.96*
>
> *See Manual at 306.7 vs. 155.34*

.73   General institutions

> Class here dating behavior
>
> *For marriage, see 306.81*
>
> *See also 646.77 for practical guidance on dating behavior*

.732   Celibacy

.734   Courtship

> *See also 392.4 for customs of courtship*

.735   Cohabiting

> Including free love, ménage à trois

.736   Extramarital relations

[.738]   Gay marriage

> Relocated to 306.848

.74   Prostitution

> *See also 331.76130674 for prostitution as an occupation, 363.44 for prostitution as a social problem, 364.1534 for prostitution as a crime*

.740 81   History and description with respect to kinds of men

> Do not use for prostitution by males; class in 306.743

.740 82   History and description with respect to kinds of women

> Do not use for prostitution by females; class in 306.742

.740 83	History and description with respect to kinds of young people
	Do not use for prostitution by children; class in 306.745
.742	Prostitution by females
	Class child prostitution in 306.745
.743	Prostitution by males
	Class child prostitution in 306.745
.745	Prostitution by children
.76	Sexual orientation
	Class practices associated with specific orientations in 306.77
.762	Neutral sexual orientation
.764	Heterosexuality
.765	Bisexuality
.766	Homosexuality
.766 2	Male homosexuality
.766 3	Lesbianism
.77	Sexual practices
	Including fetishism, group sex, transvestism
	For sexual practices viewed as medical disorders, see 616.8583
	See also 363.47 for pornography as a social problem, 364.174 for pornography as an offense against public morals, 364.153 for sex crimes
.772	Masturbation
.773	Sodomy
	For oral sex, see 306.774
.774	Oral sex
.775	Sadism
	Class here sado-masochism
	For masochism, see 306.776
.776	Masochism
.8	**Marriage and family**
	See also 362.8286 for premarital and marriage counseling

.81   Marriage

        Class here interdisciplinary works on marriage

        Class patterns of mate selection in 306.82; class alteration of marriage arrangements in 306.88

        For types of marriage, see 306.84. For other aspects of marriage, see the aspect, e.g., sexual techniques 613.96

.82   Patterns in mate selection

        Including endogamy, exogamy

        Class courtship in 306.734

        See also 392.4 for the customs of mate selection, 646.77 for practical guidance on choosing a mate and dating behavior

.83   Types of kinship systems

        Including matrilineal, patrilineal, totemic systems

.84   Types of marriage

        Including common-law marriage, remarriage

.842   Marriage by number of spouses

.842 2   Monogamy

.842 3   Polygamy and polyandry

        Standard subdivisions are added for either or both topics in heading

.843   Interreligious marriage

        Marriage in which the spouses belong to different religions or different branches of same religion

.845   Intercultural marriage

        Class here marriage between citizens of different countries

.846   Interracial marriage

        Class here miscegenation

.848   Gay marriage [*formerly* 306.738]

.85	Family

Including nonconsanguinal family

Class here interdisciplinary works on family

For kinship systems, see 306.83; for intrafamily relationships, see 306.87; for alteration of family arrangements, see 306.88. For a specific aspect of family, see the aspect, e.g., achieving harmonious family relations 646.78

See also 155.924 for psychological influence of family on individual members

.852	Rural family

See also 307.72 for rural sociology

.853	Suburban family

See also 307.74 for suburban communities

.854	Urban family

See also 307.76 for urban sociology

.855	Nuclear family

Class the single-parent family in 306.856

.856	Single-parent family

Class here divorced families with single-parent custody, unwed parenthood

For unwed fatherhood, see 306.8742; for unwed motherhood, see 306.8743

.857	Extended family

Class kinship systems in extended family in 306.83

.858	Patriarchal family
.859	Matriarchal family
.87	Intrafamily relationships

Including abuse within family; birth order; childlessness; dysfunctional relationships; in-law relationships

Class incest in 306.877. Class abuse in specific family relationship with the relationship, e.g., 306.872 spouse abuse

For alteration of family arrangements, see 306.88

See also 362.82 for social services to families, 646.78 for practical guides to harmonious family relationships

.872   Husband-wife relationship

Class sexual practices in 306.77

See also 613.96 for sexual techniques

.874   Parent-child relationship

Including adopted children, children born out of wedlock, only child, youngest child; stepparent-stepchild relationship

Class here generation gap within families

Class comprehensive works on generation gap in 305.2

See also 649.1 for child rearing (parenting)

.874 2   Father-child relationship

Including teenage fatherhood, unwed fatherhood

Class here sociology of fatherhood

.874 3   Mother-child relationship

Including surrogate motherhood, teenage motherhood, unwed motherhood

Class here sociology of motherhood

.874 5   Grandparent-child relationship

.875   Sibling relationships

.875 2   Brother-brother relationship

.875 3   Brother-sister relationship

.875 4   Sister-sister relationship

.877   Incest

.88   Alteration of family arrangements

Including desertion, death

For separation and divorce, see 306.89

.89   Separation and divorce

Standard subdivisions are added for either or both topics in heading

Including binuclear family, shared custody

Class divorced families with single-parent custody in 306.856; class parent-child relationship in divorced families in 306.874

.9   Institutions pertaining to death

Class here interdisciplinary works on death

For a specific aspect of death, see the aspect, e.g., psychology of death 155.937, funeral rites and ceremonies 393.9

307   Communities

See Manual at 307

> ### 307.1–307.3 Specific aspects of communities

Add to each subdivision identified by * as follows:
1   Specific kinds of communities
              Add to 1 the numbers following 307.7 in 307.72–307.77, e.g.,
              cities 16

Class comprehensive works in 307

.1   ***Planning and development**

.12   *Planning

> *See also 711 for the physical aspect of area planning*
>
> *See Manual at 307.12 vs. 711*

.14   *Development

> Class here human settlement
>
> Class resettlement in 307.2; class redevelopment in 307.34

.2   ***Movement of people to, from, within communities**

> Including decentralization, resettlement
>
> Population size and composition relocated to 304.6
>
> Class comprehensive works on population in 304.6

.24   *Movement from rural to urban communities

> Class here rural exodus

.26   *Movement from urban to rural communities

> Class here urban exodus

.3   ***Structure**

> Class movement within communities in 307.2

.32   *Physical setting

.33   *Patterns of use

.332   *Industrial use

.333   *Commercial use

.334   *Recreational use

---

*Add as instructed under 307.1–307.3

.336	*Residential use

Including housing succession

Class here housing patterns, sociology of housing

See also 363.58 for housing programs

See Manual at 363.5 vs. 307.336, 307.34 ·

.336 2	*Neighborhoods

Class ghettos in 307.3366

.336 4	*Slums
.336 6	*Ghettos
.34	*Redevelopment

Class community planning in 307.12

See Manual at 363.5 vs 307.336, 307.34

.342	*City core
.344	*Slum clearance
.346	*Parks and recreational facilities
.7	**Specific kinds of communities**

Class specific aspects of specific kinds of communities in 307.1–307.3

.72	Rural communities

Including plantations considered as communities

Class here rural sociology, rural villages

Class agricultural sociology, the plantation considered as a system of production in 306.349

.74	Suburban communities
.740 9	Historical and persons treatment

Do not use for geographic treatment; class in 307.7609

.76	Urban communities

Class here urban sociology, interdisciplinary works on cities

For suburban communities, see 307.74. For a specific aspect of cities, see the aspect, e.g., public administration of cities 352.16

.760 9	Historical, geographic, persons treatment

Class here specific suburban communities, specific urban communities regardless of size or kind

*Add as instructed under 307.1–307.3

>   307.762–307.764   Urban communities by size

           Class specific urban communities regardless of size in 307.7609; class comprehensive works in 307.76

.762   Small urban communities

              Class here comprehensive works on villages

              For rural villages, see 307.72

.763   Medium-sized urban communities

.764   Large urban communities

              Class here metropolitan areas as communities

              For medium-sized communities, see 307.763

>   307.766–307.768   Urban communities by kind

           Class specific urban communities regardless of kind in 307.7609; class comprehensive works in 307.76

.766   Mining and industrial towns

              Class company towns in 307.767

.767   Company towns

.768   New towns

.77   Self-contained communities

.772   Tribal communities

              Class tribal communities considered in context of culture and institutions of indigenous racial, ethnic, national groups in 306.08

.774   Communes

              Class kibbutzim in 307.776

.776   Kibbutzim

[308]   **[Unassigned]**

           Most recently used in Edition 16

[309]   **[Unassigned]**

           Most recently used in Edition 18

310   Collections of general statistics

Class works on collecting statistical data in 001.433. Class statistics of a specific subject, other than general statistics of a place, with the subject, plus notation 021 from Table 1, e.g., statistics on deaths by crimes of violence 364.15021

> *See also 001.422 for analysis of statistical data, 001.4226 for methods of presenting statistical data*

[.94–.99]   Treatment by specific continents, countries, localities in modern world

> Do not use; class in 314–319

[311]   [Unassigned]

Most recently used in Edition 17

[312]   [Unassigned]

Most recently used in Edition 19

[313]   [Unassigned]

Most recently used in Edition 14

314–319 General statistics of specific continents, countries, localities in modern world

Add to base number 31 notation 4–9 from Table 2, e.g., statistics of France 314.4

320   Political science (Politics and government)

Class sociology of political institutions and processes in 306.2

> *For law, see 340; for public administration and military science, see 350*

> *See Manual at 320: The state and government; also at 302–307 vs. 320; also at 320 vs. 306.2; also at 324 vs. 320; also at 909, 930–990 vs. 320*

SUMMARY

320.01–.09	**Standard subdivisions**
.1–.9	**[Structure and functions of government, ideologies, political situation and conditions, related topics]**
321	**Systems of governments and states**
322	**Relation of the state to organized groups and their members**
323	**Civil and political rights**
324	**The political process**
325	**International migration and colonization**
326	**Slavery and emancipation**
327	**International relations**
328	**The legislative process**

SUMMARY

320.01–.09	**Standard subdivisions**
.1	**The state**
.3	**Comparative government**
.4	**Structure and functions of government**
.5	**Political ideologies**
.6	**Policy making**
.8	**Local government**
.9	**Political situation and conditions**

.01   Philosophy and theory

Class general theory in 320.011

.011   General theory; systems

Including theory of liberty

Class here nature, legitimacy, role of government; political change, political justice

Class systems in 320.0113; class persons treatment of general theory in 320.092; class specific theories in the sense of ideologies in 320.5; class personal liberty in 323.44. Class theories on a specific aspect of political science with the aspect, e.g., social contract as a theory of origin of the state 320.11

See Manual at 320.011 vs. 320.5

.011 3   Systems

The word "systems" here refers only to concepts derived from 003, e.g., systems theory, models

Add to base number 320.0113 the numbers following 003 in 003.1–003.8, e.g., forecasting and forecasts 320.01132, computer modeling and simulation 320.01133,; however, for forecasting and forecasts for a specific period or area, see 320.9

Class systems of governments and states in 321

.014   Language and communication

Class here political persuasion and propaganda

Class interdisciplinary works on persuasion in 303.342; class interdisciplinary works on propaganda in 303.375

.019   Psychological principles

Including political decision making

Class political persuasion and propaganda in 320.014

.02–.08   Standard subdivisions

.09   Historical, geographic, persons treatment

Do not use for political situation and conditions, for forecasting and forecasts in a specific period or area; class in 320.9

.092	Persons

Do not use for persons treatment of political thinkers identified with specific ideologies; class in 320.5

Class here political philosophers and scientists

.1 The state

Class systems by which states are organized in 321

See Manual at 320: The state and government

.101 Philosophy and theory

Do not use for theories of origin of the state; class in 320.11

.101 1 Systems

The word "systems" here refers only to concepts derived from 003, e.g., systems theory, models

Class systems of governments and states in 321

.11 Theories of origin

Class here social contract

.12 Territory

Including boundaries

Class here geopolitics

Class acquisition of territory in 325.32; class territory in international law in 341.42; class history of territorial changes in 911

For geopolitics in international relations, see 327.101

.15 Sovereignty

Class here national self-determination

Class states with restricted sovereignty in 321.08

.3 Comparative government

Class comparison of a specific aspect of government with the aspect, e.g., comparison of committee systems in different legislatures 328.365

.4 Structure and functions of government

Class here civics

Class analysis of systems by which government is structured in 321

For comparative government, see 320.3

See Manual at 320.9, 320.4 vs. 351; also at 909, 930–990 vs. 320.4, 321, 321.09: Change of government

.404 Separation of powers

Class here interdisciplinary works on branches of government

Class systems of selecting chief executives in 321; class legislative control and oversight of executive branch in 328.3456

For separation of powers in specific areas, see 320.41–320.49; for legislative branch, see 328; for judicial branch, see 347; for executive branch, see 351

.404 9 Vertical separation of powers

Class here relation of central governments with regional and local jurisdictions

For relation of local government to higher levels of government, see 320.8; for relation of federal to state and provincial governments, see 321.023

.409 Historical and persons treatment

Do not use for geographic treatment; class in 320.41–320.49

.41–.49 Geographic treatment

Class here systems of state and government in specific countries

Add to base number 320.4 notation 1–9 from Table 2, e.g., structure of government in Cuba 320.47291; then to the result add standard subdivisions as modified under 320.4, e.g., separation of powers in Cuba 320.4729104

.5 Political ideologies

Except as provided under 320.53209, use notation 09 from Table 1 for variants of basic ideologies formulated and practiced in specific nations, e.g., Titoism 320.532309497, apartheid 320.560968

Class ideologies with respect to a specific aspect of political science with the aspect, e.g., ideologies with respect to revolution 321.094

See Manual at 320.011 vs. 320.5; also at 324 vs. 320.5, 320.9: Political movements

.51 Liberalism

.512 Traditional liberalism

Ideologies and theories stressing rationalism, individualism, limited government

Including libertarianism

See also 320.52 for conservatism

.513 Modern liberalism

Ideologies and theories stressing responsibility of the state for welfare of its citizens

.52   Conservatism

> Ideologies and theories stressing limits of human reason and virtue, value of tradition, caution in effecting social change
>
> *See also 320.512 for traditional liberalism*

.53   Collectivism and fascism

> Standard subdivisions are added for collectivism and fascism together, for collectivism alone
>
> Class here new left, radicalism, totalitarianism, comprehensive works on authoritarianism
>
> *For religiously oriented authoritarianism, see 320.55*
>
> *See Manual at 335 vs. 306.345, 320.53*

>   320.531–320.532   Specific collectivist ideologies

> Class comprehensive works in 320.53

.531   Socialism

> Nonauthoritarian systems
>
> Class authoritarian systems of socialism in 320.532; class interdisciplinary works on socialism in 335

.531 2   Non-Marxian and quasi-Marxian socialism

> Including Christian socialism, Fabian socialism

.531 5   Marxian socialism (Democratic socialism, Social democracy)

> Class comprehensive political works on Marxian systems of collectivism in 320.532

.532   Communism

> Class here authoritarian systems of socialism, comprehensive political works on Marxian systems of collectivism
>
> Class interdisciplinary works on Marxism in 335.4
>
> *For nonauthoritarian Marxian socialism, see 320.5315*

.532 093–.532 099   Treatment by specific continents, countries, localities

> Class communism as formulated and practiced in former Soviet Union in 320.5322; class systems of communism as formulated and practiced in specific nations outside of former Soviet Union in 320.5323093–320.5323099, e.g., Maoism 320.53230951

.532 2	Marxism-Leninism

Class here communism as formulated and practiced in former Soviet Union

For variant forms of Marxism-Leninism, see 320.5323

.532 3	Variant forms of communism

Systems of communism, of Marxism-Leninism, other than ones accepted in former Soviet Union

Including Trotskyism

.533	Fascism

Including falangism, national socialism

Class interdisciplinary works on fascism in 335.6

.54	Nationalism

Class here ethnic nationalism, "pan" movements

.540 956 94	Palestine Israel

Class here Zionism

See Manual at 322.1 vs. 296.382, 320.54095694

.549	Regional nationalism

Nationalism not centered around either a single language or a single existing state, e.g., Pan-Slavism (320.5490947)

.55	Religiously oriented ideologies

Including theocracy

Class Zionism in 320.54095694

For Christian socialism, see 320.5312

.56	Racism

Ideologies based on assumptions of racial superiority

Class Nazism in 320.533

.57	Anarchism

Class interdisciplinary works on anarchism in 335.83

.6 **Policy making**

Class here planning, formulation of programs and proposals, policy studies, public policy

Class a specific aspect of policy making with the aspect, e.g., formulating political party programs 324.23, legislative lobbying 328.38, policy making in public administration 352.34

> *For policy making in a specific subject, see the subject, e.g., policy making for economic development 338.9, social welfare policy studies 361.61*

> *See Manual at 300, 320.6 vs. 352–354: Public policy*

.8 **Local government**

Including boundaries and forms of local government

Class here relation of local government to higher levels of government

Class boundaries and forms of specific kinds of local governments in 320.83–320.85; class comprehensive works on relation of parts of a state to the whole in 321.01

> *For local administration, see 352.14*

.83 Intermediate levels

Government levels between national, state, or large provincial government and local municipalities

Including counties, districts, arrondissements, Landkreise, provinces

> *For provinces as state-level units, see 321.023*

> *See Manual at 352.13 vs. 352.15*

.84 Rural government

.85 City government

Including incorporation

Class here urban government

> *See also 321.06 for city-states*

.854 Forms of city government

Including city manager, commission, mayor-council government

.859 Annexation

.9 **Political situation and conditions**

Class here historical and geographic treatment of politics and government

Class general political history in 900

> *See Manual at 320; also at 320.9, 320.4 vs. 351; also at 324 vs. 320.5, 320.9: Political movements; also at 909, 930–990 vs. 320*

.900 1–.900 8   Standard subdivisions

[.900 9]   Historical, geographic, persons treatment

            Do not use; class in 320.901–320.99

.901–.99   Historical, geographic, persons treatment

            Add to base number 320.9 notation 01–9 from Table 2, e.g., political conditions in Egypt 320.962

321   Systems of governments and states

Including heads of state and administration

Class here kinds of states

Unless other instructions are given, use 321 only for considerations of "system" or "kind," and only for areas broader than a specific state. Use 320.4 for structure and functions of governments of any system or kind, and for the system or systems of any specific state

Selecting chief executives relocated to 324

Class a kind of head of state or administration characteristic of a specific system of government with the system, e.g., prime ministers responsible to legislatures 321.8043, constitutional monarchs 321.87

See Manual at 909, 930–990 vs. 320.4, 321, 321.09: Change of government

SUMMARY

321.001–.009	**Standard subdivisions**
.01–.09	**[Systems of relating parts of a state to the whole, kinds of states, change in system of government]**
.1	**Family-based government**
.3	**Feudalism**
.5	**Elitist systems**
.6	**Absolute monarchy**
.8	**Democratic government**
.9	**Authoritarian government**

.001–.008   Standard subdivisions

.009   Historical, geographic, persons treatment

.009 02   Medieval systems of government [*formerly* 321.14]

.009 3   Ancient systems of government [*formerly* 321.14]

.01   Systems of relating parts of a state to the whole

            Including unitary states (states in which full control is vested in central governments)

            Class systems of relating parts of a state to the whole in specific kinds of states (other than unitary states) in 321.02–321.08

>   321.02–321.08   Kinds of states

Class kinds of states in specific jurisdictions in 320.43–320.49; class comprehensive works in 321

For unitary states, see 321.01; for kinds of states defined by source or exercise of governmental authority, see 321.3–321.9

.02   Federations

Class here confederations

For proposed regional and world federations, see 321.04

.023   Relation of federal to state, regional, provincial governments

Standard subdivisions are added for any or all topics in heading

Class here states and provinces in federal systems

Class relation of federal to state, regional, provincial governments in specific nations in 320.43–320.49

.03   Empires

Systems in which a group of states are governed by a single sovereign power

Class specific empires in 321.0309

See also 325.32 for imperialism

.04   Proposed regional and world unions

Unitary or federal

Class here specific proposed world unions, interdisciplinary works on supranational states

Class specific proposed regional unions in 321.0409

For empires, see 321.03

.05   Nation-states

States considered as political embodiments of racial or ethnic groups

Class a national state or nation in the sense of a sovereign state in 320.1

.06   Small states

Including city-states, ministates

See also 320.85 for cities as local governments, 327.101 for international role of small states

.07   Ideal states (Utopias)

Including anarchy as an ideal system

Class proposed regional and world unions in 321.04

.08	States with restricted sovereignty and non-self-governing territories

Including colonies, mandates, protectorates

.09	Change in system of government

Including coups d'état

Class change in system of government in specific nations in 321.09093–321.09099

See Manual at 909, 930–990 vs. 320.4, 321, 321.09

.094	Revolution

Class interdisciplinary works on revolution in 303.64

.1	**Family-based government**

Ancient and modern

Class here government in nonliterate societies

Class government in nonliterate societies in specific areas in 321.109

[.12]	Systems of government among nonliterate peoples

Number discontinued; class in 321.1

[.14]	Ancient and medieval systems of government

Ancient systems of government relocated to 321.0093, medieval systems of government relocated to 321.00902

> **321.3–321.9 Systems of government defined by source or exercise of authority**

Class here kinds of states defined by source or exercise of governmental authority

Class systems of government in specific jurisdictions regardless of source or exercise of authority in 320.43–320.49; class comprehensive works in 321

.3	**Feudalism**
[.4]	**Pure democracy**

Relocated to 321.8

.5	**Elitist systems**

Including aristocracy, oligarchy, plutocracy, theocracy

.6	**Absolute monarchy**

Including divine right of kings

Class here autocracy

.8 **Democratic government**

Including pure democracy [*formerly* 321.4]

.804 Systems defined by method of selecting chief executives

.804 2 Presidential government

Government by a chief executive selected independently of a legislature

[.804 209 73] Selecting presidents and governors in United States

Relocated to 324.630973

[.804 209 74–.804 209 79] Selecting governors in specific states of United States

Relocated to 324.630974–324.630979

[.804 209 969] Selecting governors in Hawaii

Relocated to 324.6309969

.804 3 Cabinet government

Government by a cabinet of ministers (including a chief executive) responsible to a legislature

.86 Republics

Class republics defined by method of selecting chief executives in 321.804

.87 Limited monarchy (Constitutional monarchy)

Class cabinet government in limited monarchies in 321.8043

.9 **Authoritarian government**

Class here dictatorship, totalitarian government

For elitist systems, see 321.5; for absolute monarchy, see 321.6

.92 Communist government

Class here proletarian dictatorship

Class interdisciplinary works on communism in 335.4

.94 Fascist government

Including Nazi system

Class interdisciplinary works on fascism in 335.6

322 **Relation of the state to organized groups and their members**

Relation of the state to groups other than regular political parties

For groups organized for a specific purpose not provided for here, see the purpose, e.g., groups organized to promote political rights 323.5

.1   Religious organizations and groups

Class here church and state, religion and state

See Manual at 322.1 vs. 261.7, 291.177; also at 322.1 vs. 296.382, 320.54095694

.2   Labor movements and groups

Including general strikes

For general strikes directed primarily toward employers or focused upon limited economic objectives, see 331.8925

See also 323.3223 for relation of the state to the working class

.3   Business and industry

.4   Political action groups

Class here protest groups; nonelectoral tactics used by political action groups, e.g., civil disobedience; specific kinds of conflicts between political action groups and constituted authorities, e.g., riots

Class political action committees (United States fund-raising groups) in 324.4; class interdisciplinary works on conflicts and their resolution in 303.6

.42   Revolutionary and subversive groups

Class here revolutionary and subversive activities and branches of political parties

Class comprehensive works on parties and international party organizations engaged in both nonviolent political activity and revolutionary activity in 324.2

.420 93–.420 99   Treatment in specific continent, country, locality

Class here specific revolutionary and subversive groups irrespective of political persuasion or stated goals, e.g., Palestine Liberation Organization 322.42095694, Ku Klux Klan 322.420973

Class impact of specific revolutionary and subversive groups on general history in 930–990

.43   Pressure groups

Groups striving for immediate and relatively limited goals

Class a pressure group working for a specific goal with the goal, e.g., a group working for better law enforcement 363.23

.44   Reform movements

Groups seeking to change a substantial social function

Class interdisciplinary works on social reform in 303.484. Class a movement seeking to reform a specific social function with the function, e.g., women's suffrage movement 324.623, welfare reform 361.68

.5   **Armed services**

323   Civil and political rights

Standard subdivisions are added for civil and political rights together, for civil rights alone

Class here civil liberties, human rights, individual freedom, rights of mankind; relations of the state to its residents

Class welfare aspects of human rights in 361.614

> *For relation of the state to organized groups other than political parties and related organizations, see 322; for relation of the state to political parties and related organizations, see 324; for civil rights law, see 342.085*

SUMMARY

323.01–.09	Standard subdivisions, citizen participation, resistance and repression
.1	Civil and political rights of nondominant groups
.3	Civil and political rights of other social groups
.4	Specific civil rights; limitation and suspension of civil rights
.5	Political rights
.6	Citizenship and related topics

.01   Philosophy and theory

Class here natural rights

.04   Citizen participation; resistance and repression

.042   Participation of citizens in governmental processes

Class here participatory democracy

Class citizen participation in a specific issue with the issue, e.g., participation in public school evaluation 379.158

.044   Resistance; repression and persecution

Class limitation and suspension of civil rights in 323.49

[.08]   History and description with respect to kinds of persons

Do not use for civil and political rights of nondominant groups; class in 323.1. Do not use for civil and political rights of other social groups; class in 323.3

.1 Civil and political rights of nondominant groups

Standard subdivisions are added for either civil or political rights or both

Class specific civil rights of nondominant groups in 323.4; class specific political rights of nondominant groups in 323.5; class interdisciplinary works on nondominant groups in 305.56. Class interdisciplinary works on a specific nondominant group with the group in 305, e.g., nondominant ethnic groups 305.8

> *For specific nondominant groups other than members of racial, ethnic, national groups, see 323.3*

> *See also 305.5 for interdisciplinary works on social aspects of nondominant groups*

[.109 3–.109 9]   Treatment in specific continents, countries, locations

> Do not use; class in 323.13–323.19

.11 Racial, ethnic, national groups

Standard subdivisions are added for either civil or political rights or both

> *See also 305.8 for interdisciplinary works on social aspects of racial, ethnic, national groups*

[.110 93–.110 99]   Treatment in specific continents, countries, localities

> Do not use; class in 323.13–323.19

.111–.119 Specific racial, ethnic, national groups

Add to base number 323.11 notation 1–9 from Table 5, e.g., civil rights of Jews 323.11924, of African Americans 323.1196073
Subdivisions are added for either civil or political rights or both
(Option: Class civil and political rights of North American native races in 970.5, of South American native races in 980.5; prefer 323.1197 and 323.1198, respectively)

Class members of specific racial, ethnic, national groups who are also members of other social groups in 323.3

.13–.19 Comprehensive treatment of nondominant groups, of racial, ethnic, national groups in specific continents, countries, localities

Add to base number 323.1 notation 3–9 from Table 2, e.g., civil rights of national minorities in China 323.151
Subdivisions are added for either civil or political rights or both

Class treatment of specific racial, ethnic, national groups in specific continents, countries, localities in 323.111–323.119; class treatment of other specific nondominant groups in specific continents, countries, localities in 323.3

.3 **Civil and political rights of other social groups**

Groups other than racial, ethnic, national groups

Class a specific civil right of social groups in 323.4; class a specific political right of social groups in 323.5

See also 305 for interdisciplinary works on social aspects of specific groups, e.g., 305.4 for women

[.301–.309] Standard subdivisions

Do not use; class in 323.01–323.09

.32 Groups identified by miscellaneous social characteristics

Add to base number 323.32 the numbers following —086 in notation 0862–0869 from Table 1, e.g., laboring classes 323.3223, intellectuals 323.3231

Subdivisions are added for either civil or political rights or both

.34 Women

Standard subdivisions are added for either civil or political rights or both

Class women identified by miscellaneous social characteristics in 323.32

.35 Age groups

Standard subdivisions are added for either civil or political rights or both

Class age groups identified by miscellaneous social characteristics in 323.32; class women regardless of age group in 323.34

.352 Young people

Standard subdivisions are added for either civil or political rights or both

Class here children

.353 Young and middle-aged adults ·

Standard subdivisions are added for either civil or political rights or both

Class comprehensive works on adults in 323

.354 Persons in late adulthood

Standard subdivisions are added for either civil or political rights or both

.4 **Specific civil rights; limitation and suspension of civil rights**

[.401–.409] Standard subdivisions

Do not use; class in 323.01–323.09

.42 Equal protection of law

[.422]	Procedural rights

Use of this number for comprehensive works on procedural rights discontinued; class in 323.42

Specific procedural rights relocated to the subject in 340, e.g., habeas corpus, trial by jury in criminal cases 345.056

.43	Personal security

Including right to bear arms, right to life

Class right to privacy in 323.448; class legal aspects of right to life in 342.085

.44	Freedom of action (Liberty)

Class here intellectual freedom

For rights of assembly and association, see 323.47; for right of petition, see 323.48

.442	Freedom of conscience and religion
.443	Freedom of speech
.445	Freedom of publication

Class here freedom of information, freedom of the press

.448	Right to privacy
.448 2	Freedom from government surveillance

Surveillance by interception of mail, electronic monitoring, other means

Class governmental databases in 323.4483

.448 3	Freedom from misuse of information in databases
.46	Property rights

Including freedom of contract

Interdisciplinary works on economic rights relocated to 330; employment rights relocated to 331.011

.47	Rights of assembly and association
.48	Right of petition

Class here comprehensive works on rights of petition and assembly

For right of assembly, see 323.47

.49	Limitation and suspension of civil rights

Including harassment through abuse of power, e.g., detention of dissidents for alleged mental health problems

Class limitation and suspension of specific rights in 323.42–323.48

| [.490 8] | History and description with respect to kinds of persons |

Do not use for limitation and suspension of rights of nondominant groups; class in 323.1. Do not use for limitation and suspension of rights of other social groups; class in 323.3

.5 Political rights

Including right to hold office, right to representation

Class right of assembly in 323.47; class right of of petition in 323.48; class exercise of political rights in 324

For citizenship and related rights, see 323.6; for voting rights, see 324.62

| [.508] | History and description with respect to kinds of persons |

Do not use for political rights of nondominant groups; class in 323.1. Do not use for political rights of other social groups; class in 323.3

.6 Citizenship and related topics

Standard subdivisions are added for citizenship and related topics together, for citizenship alone

| .607 15 | Adult education and on-the-job training |

Class here citizenship programs [*formerly also* 374.012]

| .62 | Acquisition of citizenship |

For acquisition of citizenship by marriage, see 323.636

.622	Citizenship by birth
.623	Naturalization
.629	Other ways of acquiring citizenship

Including citizenship by adoption, investments, length of residence

| .63 | Relation of the state to aliens and persons with citizenship problems |
| .631 | Aliens |

Including asylum

Class naturalization of aliens in 323.623

.632	Stateless persons
.634	Persons with dual nationality
.636	Married people of differing nationality

Including acquisition of citizenship by marriage

| .64 | Expatriation and repatriation |

Class comprehensive works on refugees in 325.21

.65   Duties and obligations of citizens

        Including loyalty

.67   Passports and visas

324   The political process

Including termination of tenure of chief executive before expiration of term [*formerly* 351.0036]

Class here selecting chief executives [*formerly also* 321, 351.0034], elections

See Manual at 324 vs. 320; also at 324 vs. 320.5, 320.9: Political movements; also at 909, 930–990 vs. 320

SUMMARY

324.09	**Historical, geographic, persons treatment**
.1	**International party organizations, auxiliaries, activities**
.2	**Political parties**
.3	**Auxiliary party organizations**
.4	**Interest and pressure groups**
.5	**Nominating candidates**
.6	**Election systems and procedures; suffrage**
.7	**Conduct of election campaigns**
.9	**Historical and geographic treatment of elections**

.09   Historical, geographic, persons treatment

        Do not use for historical and geographic treatment of elections; class in 324.9

.1   **International party organizations, auxiliaries, activities**

        Not directly controlled by specific national parties

        Class revolutionary and subversive activities and branches of party organizations in 322.42

        See Manual at 324.2 vs. 324.1

>   324.13–324.17 International organizations, auxiliaries, activities of parties identified primarily by position on right-to-left spectrum

        Class organizations, auxiliaries, activities of parties not primarily identified by position on right-to-left spectrum in 324.18; class comprehensive works in 324.1

.13   International organizations of rightist parties

        Including international anticommunist leagues and their activities, monarchist parties

.14   International organizations of conservative parties

.15   International organizations of centrist parties

.16 International organizations of liberal parties

> *For international organizations of social democratic parties, see 324.172*

.17 International organizations of leftist and labor-oriented parties

> Including First International

.172 International organizations of social democratic parties

.174 International organizations of nonauthoritarian socialist parties

> Including Second and Socialist Internationals
>
> > *For international organizations of social democratic parties, see 324.172*

.175 International organizations of communist parties

> Including Third (Communist) and Fourth (Trotskyist) Internationals, Cominform

.18 International organizations of other parties

> Not primarily identified by position on right-to-left spectrum
>
> Including libertarian parties
>
> Add to base number 324.18 the numbers following 08 in notation 082–087 from table under 324.24–324.29, e.g., international organizations of religious parties 324.182

.2 **Political parties**

> *For revolutionary and subversive activities and branches of parties, see 322.42; for international organizations and activities of parties, see 324.1; for auxiliary organizations, see 324.3*
>
> *See Manual at 324.2 vs. 324.1*

SUMMARY

324.201–.09	**Standard subdivisions**
.21	**Kinds of parties**
.22	**Leadership**
.23	**Programs and ideologies**
.24–.29	**Parties in specific countries in modern world**

[.202 3] Politics as a profession, occupation, hobby

> Do not use; class in 324.22

.204 Relation of political parties to state and government

> Including political patronage

.209 4–.209 9   Treatment in specific continents, countries, localities in modern world

>Do not use for parties in specific countries and localities; class in 324.24–324.29

>*See Manual at 324.2094–324.2099 and 324.24–324.29*

.21   Kinds of parties

Class here party finance, membership, organization; political machines

.210 94–.210 99   Treatment in modern world

>Do not use for kinds of parties in specific countries and localities; class in 324.24–324.29. Do not use for party finance, membership, organizations of parties in specific countries and localities; class in 324.24–324.29, plus notation 011 from table under 324.24–324.29

.212–.218   Specific kinds of parties

>Add to base number 324.21 the numbers following 0 in notation 02–08 from table under 324.24–324.29, e.g., centrist parties 324.215

>*For leadership of specific kinds of parties, see 324.22; for programs and ideologies of specific kinds of parties, see 324.23; for specific parties and kinds of parties in a specific country or part of a country in modern world, see 324.24–324.29; for campaign finance of specific kinds of parties, see 324.78*

.22   Leadership

Including selection of leaders

Class here politicians as a type of person; politics as a profession, occupation, hobby

>*For nominating candidates, see 324.5*

.220 94–.220 99   Treatment in modern world

>Do not use for party leadership in specific countries and localities; class in 324.24–324.29, plus notation 012 from table under 324.24–324.29

.23   Programs and ideologies

Standard subdivisions are added for either or both topics in heading

Class here platforms, campaign literature

>*For campaign literature on a specific subject, see the subject, e.g., campaign literature on United States participation in Vietnamese War 959.7043373*

.230 94–.230 99   Treatment in modern world

>Do not use for party programs and ideologies in specific continents and localities; class in 324.24–324.29, plus notation 013 from table under 324.24–324.29

.232–.238   Programs and ideologies of specific kinds of parties

Add to base number 324.23 the numbers following 0 in notation 02–08 from table under 324.24–324.29, e.g., programs of centrist parties 324.235

For programs and ideologies of specific parties and kinds of parties in a specific country or part of a country in modern world, see 324.24–324.29

.24–.29   Parties in specific countries in modern world

Except where specifically instructed to the contrary below, for a country or for localities within a country add to base number 324.2 notation 4–9 from Table 2 for the specific country, e.g., parties of France 324.244; then add to the number according to the table below, e.g., parties in Paris 324.24400944361, Communist Party of France 324.244075, Communist Party in Paris 324.2440750944361:

001–009   Standard subdivisions
01   General topics
    Class general topics of specific parties in 02–08
011   Organization, membership, finance
    Class here political machines
    Class leadership in 012; class comprehensive works on party organization, membership, finance in 324.21
012   Leadership
    Including selection of leaders
    Class nominating candidates in 015; class comprehensive works on party leadership in 324.22
013   Programs and ideologies
    Standard subdivisions are added for either or both topics in heading
    Class here platforms, campaign literature
    Class comprehensive works on party programs and ideologies in 324.23
    For campaign literature on a specific subject, see the subject, e.g., campaign literature on United States participation in Vietnamese War 959.7043373
014   Auxiliary party organizations [*formerly* 324.3094–324.3099]
015   Nominating party candidates [*formerly* 324.5094–324.5099]
    Class here nomination campaigns; results of campaigns, e.g., delegate counts
    Class comprehensive works on nominating candidates in 324.5; class comprehensive works on nomination and election campaigns in 324.9
0152   Nominating by caucuses and co-optation [*formerly* 324.52094–324.52099]
0154   Nominating by primaries [*formerly* 324.54094–324.54099]
0156   Nominating by conventions [*formerly* 324.56094–324.56099]

(continued)

.24–.29 Parties in specific countries in modern world (continued)

    02 Historical parties
        Parties existing prior to 1945 and no longer in existence
        Class comprehensive works on historical parties in 324.212

    >03–08 Recent parties
        Parties founded or remaining in existence since 1945
        Class comprehensive works on recent parties in specific countries in base number for the country in 324.24–324.29; class comprehensive works on specific kinds of recent parties in 324.21

    >03–07 Recent parties identified primarily by position on right-to-left spectrum
        Class recent parties not primarily identified by position on right-to-left spectrum in 08; class comprehensive works in base number for the country in 324.24–324.29
        See Manual at 324.24–324.29: Parties in right-to-left spectrum vs. Other parties

    03 Rightist parties
        Including monarchist parties
    038 Fascist and Nazi parties
        Standard subdivisions are added for either or both topics in heading
    04 Conservative parties
    05 Centrist parties
    06 Liberal parties
        For social democratic parties, see 072
    07 Leftist and worker parties
    072 Social democratic parties
    074 Nonauthoritarian socialist parties
        For social democratic parties, see 072
    075 Communist parties
    08 Other recent parties
        Not primarily identified by position on right-to-left spectrum
        Including libertarian parties
        See Manual at 324.24–324.29: Parties in right-to-left spectrum vs. Other parties
    082 Religious parties
    083 Nationalist parties
    084 Sectionalist and separatist parties
        Standard subdivisions are added for either or both topics in heading
    087 Environmentalist parties

(Option: Arrange specific parties of a specific country alphabetically, e.g., Labour Party of United Kingdom 324.241)

Class comprehensive works on parties in 324.2; class comprehensive works on specific kinds of parties in 324.21

See Manual at 324.2094–324.2099 and 324.24–324.29

Special developments follow for selected specific countries whose party systems deviate from the above pattern

SUMMARY

324.241	**Parties of United Kingdom**
.271	**Parties of Canada**
.273	**Parties of United States**
.274–.279	**Parties of states of United States and District of Columbia**
.294	**Parties of Australia**
.296 9	**Parties in Hawaii**

.241	**Parties of United Kingdom**
.241 001–.241 009	Standard subdivisions
.241 01	General topics

Add to base number 324.24101 the numbers following 01 in notation 011–015 from table under 324.24–324.29, e.g., campaign literature of parties of United Kingdom 324.241013

Class general topics of specific parties of United Kingdom in 324.24102–342.24109

.241 02	Historical parties

Parties existing prior to 1945 and no longer in existence

Class here parties of Great Britain before union with Ireland, of England and Wales before union with Scotland

.241 04	Conservative Party
.241 06	Liberal Party
.241 07	Labour Party
.241 09	Other parties

Add to base number 324.24109 the numbers following 0 in notation 03–08 from table under 324.24–324.29, e.g., Communist Party 324.2410975

.271	**Parties of Canada**
.271 001–.271 009	Standard subdivisions
.271 01	General topics

Add to base number 324.27101 the numbers following 01 in notation 011–015 from table under 324.24–324.29, e.g., campaign literature of parties of Canada 324.271013

Class general topics of specific parties of Canada in 324.27102–342.27109

.271 02	Historical parties
	Parties existing prior to 1945 and no longer in existence
.271 04	Progressive Conservative Party
	Former name: Conservative Party of Canada
.271 05	Social Credit Party
.271 06	Liberal Party
.271 07	New Democratic Party
.271 09	Other parties

Add to base number 324.27109 the numbers following 0 in notation 03–08 from table under 324.24–324.29, e.g., nationalist parties 324.2710983

.271 1–.271 9	Parties of provinces and territories of Canada

Add to base number 324.271 the numbers following —71 in notation 711–719 from Table 2 for province or territory, e.g., parties in Quebec 324.2714; then to the result add the numbers following 324.271 in 324.271001–324.271009, e.g., Parti québécois 324.27140984

.273	**Parties of United States**

For parties in specific states and District of Columbia, see 324.274–324.279

.273 01–.273 09	Standard subdivisions
.273 1	General topics

Add to base number 324.2731 the numbers following 01 in notation 011–015 from table under 324.24–324.29, e.g., campaign literature of parties of United States 324.27313

Class general topics of specific parties of United States in 324.2732–342.2738

.273 2	Historical parties
	Parties existing prior to 1945 and no longer in existence
	Including American ("Know-Nothing") Party, Free Soil Party
.273 22	Federalist Party
.273 23	Whig Party
	Including National Republican Party
.273 26	Jeffersonian Republican Party
	Variant name: Anti-federalist Party

.273 27	Populist and progressive parties

Including Progressive ("Bull Moose") Party

See also 324.2737 for the Progressive Party (1948)

.273 3	Nationalist parties of the right

Including American Independent Party; sectionalist parties, e.g., States' Rights Party (Dixiecrats)

.273 38	National Socialist White People's Party

Former name: American Nazi Party

.273 4	Republican Party
.273 6	Democratic Party

Including Democratic-Republican Party

.273 7	Leftist and worker parties

Including Progressive Party (1948), Socialist Labor Party, Socialist Workers Party

See also 324.27327 for Progressive ("Bull Moose") Party

.273 75	Communist Party
.273 8	Other recent parties

Including environmentalist, libertarian, prohibitionist, religious, separatist parties

See also 324.2733 for sectionalist parties

.274–.279	**Parties of states of United States and District of Columbia**

Add to base number 324.27 the numbers following —7 in notation 74–79 from Table 2 for state or District of Columbia, e.g., parties in California 324.2794; then add 0*, and to the result, except for New York, add the numbers following 324.273 in 324.2731–324.2738, e.g., Republican Party in California 324.279404

Class comprehensive works in 324.273

For parties in Hawaii, see 324.2969

A special development for New York follows

.274 7	Parties in New York
.274 700 1–.274 700 9	Standard subdivisions

---

*Add 00 for standard subdivisions; see instructions at beginning of Table 1

.274 701	General topics

Add to base number 324.274701 the numbers following 01 in notation 011–015 from table under 324.24–324.29, e.g., campaign literature of parties of New York 324.2747013

Class general topics of specific parties of New York in 324.274702–342.274709

.274 702	Historical parties

Add to base number 324.274702 the numbers following 324.2732 in 324.27322–324.27327, e.g., Whig Party 324.2747023

.274 703	Conservative Party
.274 704	Republican Party
.274 706	Democratic Party
.274 707	Liberal Party
.274 709	Other parties

Add to base number 324.274709 the numbers following 0 in notation 03–08 from table under 324.24–324.29, e.g., Communist Party 324.27470975

.294	Parties of Australia
.294 001–.294 009	Standard subdivisions
.294 01	General topics

Add to base number 324.29401 the numbers following 01 in notation 011–015 from table under 324.24–324.29, e.g., campaign literature of parties of Australia 324.294013

Class general topics of specific parties of Australia in 324.29402–342.29409

.294 02	Historical parties

Parties existing prior to 1945 and no longer in existence

.294 04	Country Party
.294 05	Liberal Party
.294 06	Democratic Labor Party
.294 07	Labor Party
.294 09	Other parties

Add to base number 324.29409 the numbers following 0 in notation 03–08 from table under 324.24–324.29, e.g., Communist Party 324.2940975

.294 1–.294 8   Parties in states and territories of Australia

> Add to base number 324.294 the numbers following —94 in notation 941–948 from Table 2 for state or territory, e.g., parties in New South Wales 324.2944; then to the result add the numbers following 324.294 in 324.294001–324.29409, e.g., Labor Party in New South Wales 324.294407

.296 9   Parties in Hawaii

.296 900 1–.296 900 9   Standard subdivisions

.296 901–.296 908   Parties in Hawaii

> Add to base number 324.29690 the numbers following 324.273 in 324.2731–324.2738, e.g., Democratic Party in Hawaii 324.296906

.3   Auxiliary party organizations

Organizations attached to political parties, e.g., political clubs, women's organizations, youth groups, front organizations

Class revolutionary and subversive branches of political parties in 322.42

For auxiliary organizations of international party organizations, see 324.1

.309 4–.309 9   Treatment in modern world

> Auxiliary party organizations in specific countries and localities relocated to 324.24–324.29, plus notation 014 from table under 324.24–324.29

.4   Interest and pressure groups

Class here influence and activities of groups in extragovernmental processes; political action committees (PACs, United States fund-raising groups); comprehensive works on lobbying

Class comprehensive works on interest groups, political action groups in 322.4; class comprehensive works on pressure groups in 322.43

For legislative-branch lobbying, see 328.38. For lobbying for a specific goal, see the goal, e.g., lobbying for penal reform 364.6

.5   Nominating candidates

Class here campaigns for nomination; results of campaigns, e.g., delegate counts

Class comprehensive works on nomination and election campaigns in 324.9

.509 4–.509 9   Treatment in modern world

> Nominating party candidates in specific countries and localities relocated to 324.24–324.29, plus notation 015 from table under 324.24–324.29

.52   Nominating by caucuses and co-optation

.520 94–.520 99	Treatment in modern world

Nominating party candidates by caucuses and co-optation in specific countries and localities relocated to 324.24–324.29, plus notation 0152 from table under 324.24–324.29

.54	Nominating by primaries
.540 94–.540 99	Treatment in modern world

Nominating party candidates by primaries in specific countries and localities relocated to 324.24–324.29, plus notation 0154 from table under 324.24–324.29

.56	Nominating by conventions

For selecting delegates to nominating conventions by caucuses and co-optation, see 324.52; for selecting delegates to nominating conventions by primaries, see 324.54

See also 324.21 for convention finance

.560 94–.560 99	Treatment in modern world

Nominating party candidates by conventions in specific countries and localities relocated to 324.24–324.29, plus notation 0156 from table under 324.24–324.29

.6	**Election systems and procedures; suffrage**

Class here comprehensive works on systems and procedures for nominations and elections

Class conduct of election campaigns in 324.7

For nominating candidates, see 324.5

See Manual at 342.07 vs. 324.6

.62	Suffrage

Class here qualifications for voting, voting rights

Class comprehensive works on political rights in 323.5

.623	Women's suffrage
.63	Electoral systems

Including direct and indirect elections, electoral colleges

Proportional representation relocated to 328.3347

For electoral basis of representation in legislative bodies, see 328.3347

.630 973	Electoral systems in United States

Class here selecting presidents and governors in United States [*formerly also* 321.80420973]

For selecting governors in specific states of United States, see 324.630974–324.630979

.630 974–.630 979	Electoral systems in specific states of United States

Class here selecting governors in specific states of United States [*formerly also* 321.80420974–321.80420979]

For electoral systems in Hawaii, see 324.6309969

.630 996 9	Electoral systems in Hawaii

Class here selecting governors in Hawaii [*formerly also* 321.804209969]

.64	Registration of voters
.65	Voting procedures

Including absentee voting, ballots and ballot systems, counting and certification of votes, election officials, procedures for contested elections, voting machines

.66	Election fraud

Class irregularities in campaign finance in 324.78

.68	Recall

Removal of an official from office by popular vote

.7	**Conduct of election campaigns**

Variant name: practical politics

Class conduct of campaigns for nomination in 324.5

.72	Strategy

Including citizen participation

For use and effect of media, see 324.73

.73	Use and effect of media
.78	Campaign finance

Class party finance in 324.21

.9	**Historical and geographic treatment of elections**

Class here campaigns, election returns and results, studies of voting behavior

Class platforms, campaign literature in 324.23; class nomination by primary elections in 324.54

.900 1–.900 8	Standard subdivisions
[.900 9]	Historical, geographic, persons treatment

Do not use for comprehensive works on historical treatment; class in 324.9. Do not use for geographic treatment; class in 324.91–324.99

[.900 901–.900 905]	Historical periods

Do not use; class in 324.901–324.905

[.900 92]	Persons

Do not use; class in 324.092

.901–.905 Historical periods

Add to base number 324.90 the numbers following —090 in notation 0901–0905 from Table 1, e.g., election campaigns in 19th century 324.9034

.91–.99 Geographic treatment

Add to base number 324.9 notation 1–9 from Table 2, e.g., political campaigns in the United Kingdom 324.941; then to the result add historical period numbers from appropriate subdivisions of 930–990, e.g., election campaign of 1966 in United Kingdom 324.9410856. In all cases use one 0* except 00† for North America and South America, e.g., the election of 1964 in United States 324.9730923, elections in South America between World Wars 324.980033

325 International migration and colonization

Standard subdivisions are added for international migration and colonization together, for international migration alone

Including involuntary population transfer, population exchange

Class movement of people associated with a specific event in history with the event in 909 or 930–990; class interdisciplinary works on international movement of people in 304.82

[.094–.099] Treatment by specific continent, country, locality in modern world

Do not use; class in 325.4–325.9

.1 Immigration

[.109 4–.109 9] Treatment of immigration by specific continent, country, locality in modern world

Do not use; class in 325.4–325.9

.2 Emigration

[.209 3–.209 9] Treatment of emigration by specific continent, country, locality

Do not use; class in 325.23–325.29

.21 Refugees

Class here displaced persons, political refugees

.210 93–.210 99 Historical, geographic, persons treatment

Refugees from one country in another country are classed in country of origin, e.g., Polish political refugees in Canada 325.21094380971

---

*Add 00 for standard subdivisions; see instructions at beginning of Table 1

†Add 000 for standard subdivisions; see instructions at beginning of Table 1

.23–.29   Emigration from specific continents, countries, localities

> Add to base number 325.2 notation 3–9 from Table 2, e.g., emigration from Japan 325.252, emigration from Japan to United States 325.2520973

.3   Colonization

> Class here exercise of political dominion over distant territories

.309 3   Treatment in ancient world

> Do not use for colonization by specific countries in ancient world; class in 325.33

.309 4–.309 9   Treatment by specific continents, countries, localities in modern world

> Do not use for colonization by specific countries in modern world; class in 325.34–325.39. Do not use for colonization in specific places in modern world; class in 325.4–325.9

[.31]   Colonial administration and policy

> Use of this number for colonial policy discontinued; class in 325.3

> Colonial administration relocated to 353.15

.32   Imperialism

> The policy, practice, or advocacy of acquiring political dominion over territories outside the natural boundaries of a country

> Class comprehensive works on foreign policy in 327.1

.33–.39   Colonization by specific countries

> Add to base number 325.3 notation 3–9 from Table 2, e.g., colonization by United Kingdom 325.341, colonization by United Kingdom in West Africa 325.3410966

> Class imperialism of specific countries in 325.32093–325.32099

.4–.9   International migration to and colonization in specific continents, countries, localities in modern world

> Add to base number 325 notation 4–9 from Table 2, e.g., migration to Israel 325.5694
> Subdivisions are added for either or both topics in heading

> Class emigration from specific continents, countries, localities in modern world to specific continents, countries, localities in 325.24–325.29; class colonization by specific countries in modern world in specific continents, countries, localities in 325.34–325.39; class comprehensive works on colonization by and in specific continents, countries, localities in modern world in 325.3094–325.3099

326   Slavery and emancipation

Standard subdivisions are added for slavery and emancipation together, for slavery alone

Class interdisciplinary works on slavery in 306.362

.8   Emancipation

Class here abolitionism, antislavery movements

327   International relations

Class military science in 355; class interdisciplinary works on relations among countries in 303.482

For international relations with respect to a specific subject, see the subject, e.g., trade negotiations between Germany and Japan 382.0943052

See Manual at 341 vs. 327

SUMMARY

327.02–.09	**Standard subdivisions**
.1	**Foreign policy and specific topics of international relations**
.2	**Diplomacy**
.3–.9	**Foreign relations of specific nations**

[.01]   Philosophy and theory

Do not use; class in 327.101

.06   Organizations

For international governmental organizations, see 341.2

[.068]   Management

Do not use; class in 353.13

.09   Historical, geographic, persons treatment

Class here diplomatic history, international relations of or in specific areas or blocs, e.g., international relations in Middle East 327.0956, foreign relations of former Communist bloc 327.091717

.092   Persons

Do not use for diplomats; class in 327.2092

.093–.099   Treatment by specific continents and localities

Do not use for international relations and diplomatic history of specific nations; class in 327.3–327.9

.1   **Foreign policy and specific topics in international relations**

Standard subdivisions are added for foreign policy

Class here imperialism in international relations, international politics, power politics

Class comprehensive works on imperialism, imperialism as national policy in 325.32

.101   Philosophy and theory of international relations, of foreign policy

Including role and position of small states, economic bases of international relations

Class here geopolitics in international relations, nature of power in international relations

Class comprehensive works on geopolitics in 320.12

.102–.108   Standard subdivisions of foreign policy

.109   Historical, geographic, persons treatment of foreign policy

.109 2   Persons

Do not use for diplomats; class in 327.2092

.109 3–.109 9 Treatment by specific continents and localities

Do not use for foreign policy of specific nations; class in 327.3–327.9

>   327.11–327.17 Specific topics of international relations

Class here specific topics in international relations of specific nations [*formerly* 327.3–327.9]

Class comprehensive works in 327

For diplomacy, see 327.2

.11   Specific means of attaining foreign policy goals

Including government information services

For espionage and subversion, see 327.12; for propaganda and war of nerves, see 327.14

.111   Economic activities

Including foreign aid

Class boycotts and sanctions in 327.117

.112   Balance of power

.114   Spheres of influence

.116   Alliances

Class here collective security

.117	Use of force and threats of force

Including boycotts and sanctions

Class war of nerves in 327.14; class war in 355.02

.12	Espionage and subversion

Standard subdivisions are added for either or both topics in heading

Class here interdisciplinary works on espionage, subversion, intelligence gathering

For military espionage, see 355.3432; for military subversion, see 355.3437

.120 93–.120 99	Treatment by specific continents, countries, localities

Do not use for espionage and subversion by specific nations; class in 327.123–327.129

.123–.129	Espionage and subversion by specific nations

Add to base number 327.12 notation —3–9 from Table 2, e.g., espionage by France 327.1244; then for espionage and subversion by that country in another area add 0* and to the result add notation 1–9 from Table 2, e.g., espionage by France in Communist bloc 327.124401717
Subdivisions are added for either or both topics in heading

.14	Propaganda and war of nerves

Including disinformation activities

Class comprehensive works on political propaganda in 320.014; class comprehensive works on use of force and threats of force in 327.117; class interdisciplinary works on propaganda in 303.375

.16	International conflict

Class war in 355.02; class conflict involving specific means of attaining foreign policy goals in 327.11

See also 327.17 for peaceful resolution of international conflict

.17	International cooperation

Class here internationalism, conflict resolution

Class international governmental organizations in 341.2

For law of international cooperation, see 341.7

.172	Promotion of peace and international order
.174	Disarmament [*formerly also* 355.03] and arms control

Class here problems of arms limitation and of verifying arms-control treaty provisions for specific kinds of weapons [*formerly* 355.82]

---

*Add 00 for standard subdivisions; see instructions at beginning of Table 1

.174 3	Conventional weapons limitation

Including problems of arms limitation and of verifying arms-control treaty provisions for specific kinds of naval weapons [*formerly* 359.82]

.174 5	Chemical and biological disarmament

Standard subdivisions are added for either or both topics in heading

Class here disarmament of specific chemical and biological weapons

.174 7	Nuclear disarmament

Class here strategic arms limitation, limitation of specific nuclear weapons

.2   Diplomacy

Including protocol

Use 327.2 for methods and style of diplomacy; 327 for substance and content of diplomatic relations

For law of diplomacy, see 341.33

.209 2	Persons treatment

Do not use for persons treatment of diplomats of specific nations; class in 327.3–327.9

.3–.9   Foreign relations of specific nations

Add to base number 327 notation 3–9 from Table 2, e.g., foreign relations of Brazil 327.81; then, for relations between that nation and another nation or region, add 0* and to the result add notation 1–9 from Table 2, e.g., relations between Brazil and France 327.81044, between Brazil and Arab world 327.810174927

Give priority in notation to the nation emphasized. If emphasis is equal, give priority to the nation coming first in Table 2
 (Option: Give priority in notation to the nation requiring local emphasis, e.g., libraries in the United States class foreign relations between the United States and France in 327.73044)

Specific topics in international relations of specific nations relocated to 326.11–327.17

328   The legislative process

Class here legislative branch, legislative bodies

See Manual at 909, 930–990 vs. 320

*Add 00 for standard subdivisions; see instructions at beginning of Table 1

SUMMARY

328.01–.09	**Standard subdivisions**
.1	**Rules and procedures of legislative bodies**
.2	**Initiative and referendum**
.3	**Specific topics of legislative bodies**
.4–.9	**The legislative process in specific jurisdictions in modern world**

.060 1   International organizations

Class here interparliamentary unions [*formerly* 328.30601]

.068   Management

Class here public administration of legislative branch

Do not use for management of members' offices; class in 328.331068. Do not use for public administration of legislative branch of specific jurisdiction; class in 328.4–328.9, plus standard subdivision notation 0068 from table under 328.4–328.9

.094–.099   Treatment in specific continents and localities in modern world

Do not use for legislative process in specific jurisdictions in modern world; class in 328.4–328.9

.1   Rules and procedures of legislative bodies

Including rules and procedures for reporting legislative sessions, e.g., television coverage

Class comprehensive rules of order in 060.42

For rules and procedures of committees of legislative bodies, see 328.3653

.109 4–.109 9   Treatment in specific continents and localities in modern world

Do not use for rules and procedures of specific legislative bodies in modern world; class in 328.4–328.9, plus notation 05 from table under 328.4–328.9, e.g., rules of Canadian Parliament 328.7105

.2   Initiative and referendum

.209 4–.209 9   Treatment in specific continents and localities in modern world

Do not use for treatment in specific jurisdictions in modern world; class in 328.24–328.29

.22   Initiative

.220 94–.220 99   Treatment in specific continents and localities in modern world

Do not use for initiative in specific jurisdictions in modern world; class in 328.24–328.29

.23   Referendum

.230 94–.230 99   Treatment in specific continents and localities in modern world

Do not use for referendum in specific jurisdictions in modern world; class in 328.24–328.29

.24–.29   Initiative and referendum in specific jurisdictions in modern world

> Add to base number 328.2 notation 4–9 from Table 2, e.g., initiative in California 328.2794
>> Subdivisions are added for either or both topics in heading

.3   **Specific topics of legislative bodies**

> Use of this number for legislative bodies discontinued; class in 328

> Class specific topics of legislative bodies of specific jurisdictions in modern world in 328.4–328.9, plus notation 07 from table under 328.4–328.9, e.g., specific committees of Canadian Parliament 328.7107658

> *For rules and procedures of legislative bodies, see 328.1*

SUMMARY

328.304		**Legislative reform**
	.31	**Upper houses**
	.32	**Lower houses**
	.33	**Members and membership**
	.34	**Powers, privileges, restrictions**
	.35	**Sessions**
	.36	**Internal organization and discipline**
	.37	**Enactment of legislation**
	.38	**Lobbying**
	.39	**Forms of legislative bodies**

[.301–.303]   Standard subdivisions

> Do not use; class in 328.01–328.03

.304   Legislative reform

> Use of this number for special topics discontinued; class in 328.3

>> *For reform of basis of representation, see 328.334; for reform of internal organization, see 328.36*

[.304 2]   Legislative reform

> Number discontinued; class in 328.304

[.305]   Serial publications

> Do not use; class in 328.05

[.306]   Organizations and management

> Do not use; class in 328.06

[.306 01]   Interparliamentary unions

> Relocated to 328.0601

[.307–.309]   Standard subdivisions

> Do not use; class in 328.07–328.09

.31   **Upper houses**

Class comprehensive works on upper and lower houses in 328.39. Class a specific aspect of upper houses with the aspect, e.g., treaty making power of upper houses 328.346

.32   **Lower houses**

Class a specific aspect of lower houses with the aspect, e.g., basis of representation of lower houses 328.334

.33   **Members and membership**

Including qualifications, term of office, term limitation

Class comprehensive persons treatment of members in 328.092; class persons treatment of members of specific legislative bodies in modern world in 328.4–328.9, plus notation 092 from table under 328.4–328.9

.331   **Work and activity of individual members**

Class here constituency services, work of members' offices

.333   **Compensation**

.334   **Basis of representation**

.334 5   Election districts

Class here apportionment and reapportionment, redistricting

For districts used in proportional representation, see 328.3347

.334 55   Gerrymandering

.334 7   Proportional representation [*formerly also* 324.63]

.34   **Powers, privileges, restrictions**

Class here legislative duties

Class enactment of legislation in 328.37

.341   **General powers**

For treaty and war powers, see 328.346

.341 2   Financial power

Power over appropriation, borrowing and lending, currency, taxation

.341 3   General economic and public welfare powers

.345   **Extralegislative powers**

Including control and oversight of judicial branch

Class here hearings

For hearings on a specific subject, see the subject, e.g., hearings on laws 348.01

.345 2	Investigative power
	Including ombudsman role
	Class interdisciplinary works on ombudsmen in 352.88
.345 3	Judicial power
	Including power to impeach
.345 4	Electoral power
.345 5	Power over appointments
.345 6	Control and oversight of executive branch
	Class here general relations with executive branch
	Class cabinet system of executives in 321.8043; class control of foreign relations in 328.346
	For ombudsman role, see 328.3452
.346	Treaty and war powers
	Class here control of foreign relations
.347	Personal privileges of legislators
	For legislative immunity, see 328.348
.348	Legislative immunity
.349	Restrictions on legislative power
	Including constitutional restrictions, checks exercised by other branches and by the electorate
.35	Sessions
	Class a specific aspect of legislative sessions with the aspect, e.g., internal organization of a session 328.36
.36	Internal organization and discipline
	Class legislative reference bureaus in 027.65; class comprehensive works on rules and procedures in 328.1
[.361]	Auxiliary organizations
	Number discontinued; class in 328.36
.362	Officers and leaders
	Class party organization in legislative bodies in 328.369
.365	Committees
	Class committee hearings and reports on a specific subject that emphasize proposed legislation with the subject in 340, e.g., hearing on bills governing armed services 343.013; class committee hearings and reports on a specific subject that do not emphasize proposed legislation with the subject in 001–999, e.g., general reports on military affairs 355

.365 3	Rules

Including rules of specific committees, of specific types of committees

.365 7	Specific types of committees

Including conference, joint, select committees

Class rules of specific types of committees in 328.3653; class specific types of committees with specific subject jurisdiction in 328.3658

.365 8	Committees of specific subject jurisdiction

Including rules committees

Class rules of committees of specific subject jurisdiction in 328.3653

.366	Discipline of members
.369	Party organization in legislative bodies

Including opposition, opposition parties, party caucuses

.37	Enactment of legislation

Including repeal of legislation

See also 328.365 for committee procedures

.372	Origin of legislation

Submission by members, by executive, by outside interests

.373	Drafting legislation
.375	Passage of legislation

Including votes and voting procedures

.377	Enactment of resolutions
.378	Enactment of special types of legislation

Including procedures for legislative enactment of budgets [*formerly* 351.7223], private bills

Use of this number for enacting public laws discontinued; class in 328.37

For enactment of resolutions, see 328.377; for enactment of budgets, see 352.48

.38	Lobbying
.39	Forms of legislative bodies

Unicameral, bicameral, multicameral

Do not use for description of various legislatures that happen to be of one form or another

For upper houses, see 328.31; for lower houses, see 328.32

.4–.9   The legislative process in specific jurisdictions in modern world

Class here legislative branch, legislative bodies

Add to base number 328 notation 4–9 from Table 2, e.g., the legislative process in Canada 328.71; then add further as follows:

001–008	Standard subdivisions
[009]	Historical and persons treatment
	Do not use; class in 09
01	Journals and calendars
02	Debates
	Including collections of speeches by individual members
03	Abstracts
04	Other documents
	Class here series of miscellaneous parliamentary papers and documents
05	Rules and procedures
	Including legislative manuals
	Class committee rules in 07653
07	Specific topics of legislative bodies
	Add to 07 the numbers following 328.3 in 328.304–328.39, e.g., specific committees 07658
	For rules and procedures, see 05
09	Historical and persons treatment
092	Persons treatment
	Class here biography

For initiative and referendum in specific jurisdictions in modern world, see 328.24–328.29

[329]   [Unassigned]

Most recently used in Edition 18

330   Economics

Including interdisciplinary works on economic rights [*formerly* 323.46]

Class here comprehensive works on economics and management

Unless other instructions are given, observe the following table of preference, e.g., finance as an economic factor in international economics 332.042 (*not* 337):

Cooperatives	334
Public finance	336
Economics of labor, finance, land, energy	331–333
Production, Commerce (381–382), Communications (383–384), Transportation (385–388)	338
Macroeconomics and related topics	339
International economics	337
Socialism and related systems	335

For management, see 658. For a specific kind or aspect of economic rights, see the kind or aspect, e.g., political aspects of property rights 323.46

See Manual at 330 vs. 650; also at 361.614 vs. 330

SUMMARY

335		Socialism and related systems
	.001–.009	Standard subdivisions
	.02	Utopian systems and schools
	.1	Systems of English origin
	.2	Systems of French origin
	.3	Systems of American origin
	.4	Marxian systems
	.5	Democratic socialism
	.6	Fascism
	.7	Christian socialism
	.8	Other systems
	.9	Voluntary socialist and anarchist communities
336		Public finance
	.001–.008	Standard subdivisions
	.01–.09	[Public finance by governmental level; revenue; historical, geographic, persons treatment; associations of sovereign states]
	.1	Nontax revenues
	.2	Taxes and taxation
	.3	Public borrowing, debt, expenditure
	.4–.9	Public finance of specific continents, countries, localities in modern world
337		International economics
	.1	Multilateral economic cooperation
	.3–.9	Foreign economic policies and relations of specific jurisdictions and groups of jurisdictions
338		Production
	.001–.009	Standard subdivisions
	.01–.09	[General topics]
	.1	Agriculture
	.2	Extraction of minerals
	.3	Other extractive industries
	.4	Secondary industries and services
	.5	General production economics
	.6	Organization of production
	.7	Business enterprises
	.8	Combinations
	.9	Economic development and growth
339		Macroeconomics and related topics
	.01	Philosophy and theory
	.2	Distribution of income and wealth
	.3	National product, wealth, income accounts and accounting
	.4	Factors affecting national product, wealth, income
	.5	Macroeconomic policy

.01   Philosophy and theory

Do not use for theories; class in 330.1

.015 1   Mathematical principles

> *See also 330.1543 for mathematical economics as a school of thought*

.015 195		Statistical mathematics

Class here econometrics

See Manual at 519.5, T1—015195 vs. 001.422, T1—0727

.02–.08 Standard subdivisions

.09 Historical, geographic, persons treatment of economics as a discipline

For economic situation and conditions, see 330.9

.1 Systems, schools, theories

.12 Systems

.122 Free enterprise economy

Usually synonymous with capitalism

Including open economy (the economy of an area in which trade with other areas is unrestricted)

Class laissez-faire economic theory in 330.153

See also 382.7 for trade barriers and restrictions

.124 Planned economies

For socialism and related systems, see 335

.126 Mixed economies

Including interventionism, welfare state systems

See also 330.1556 for welfare economics as a school of economic thought

.15 Schools of economic thought

Including Chicago school of economics, supply-side economics

.151 Pre-classical schools

For physiocracy, see 330.152

.151 2 Ancient and medieval theories

.151 3 Mercantilism

.152 Physiocracy

Class here school of Quesnay

.153 Classical economics

Class here school of Smith, Ricardo, Malthus, Mill, Say; laissez-faire economic theory

See also 330.157 for neoclassical school

.154	Methodological schools

Schools based on employment of specific methods of analysis

.154 2	Historical school

Class here the school of Roscher, Knies, Hildebrand, Schmoller, Bücher, Knapp

.154 3	Mathematical economics

Class here the schools of Cournot, Dupuit, Pareto

Class mathematics applied to economics as a whole in 330.0151

See also 330.157 for the marginal utility school

.155	Miscellaneous schools

Only those named below

Including ethical, institutional, romantic, single-tax, social justice schools; universalism

.155 6	Welfare economics school
.156	Keynesianism
.157	Marginal utility school

Variant names: Austrian, neoclassical school

Class here the school of W. S. Jevons, Menger, Walras, Wieser, Böhm-Bawerk, Von Mises

See also 330.1543 for the mathematical economics school of Cournot, Dupuit, Pareto

(.159)	Socialist and related schools

(Optional number; prefer 335)

Add to base number 330.159 the numbers following 335 in 335.1–335.9, e.g., Marxian systems 330.1594

.16	Theories of wealth

For macroeconomic aspects of wealth, see 339

.17	Theories of property
.9	**Economic situation and conditions**

Standard subdivisions are added for either or both topics in heading

Class here works describing situation and conditions at both the macroeconomic (aggregate) level and the microeconomic level (level of the individual unit, such as the household or firm)

Class policies to promote economic growth and development in 338.9; class macroeconomic policies in 339.5

.900 1–.900 8	Standard subdivisions

.900 9   Historical and persons treatment

[.900 901–.900 905]   Historical periods

> Do not use; class in 330.901–330.905

[.900 91]   Treatment by areas, regions, places in general

> Do not use; class in 330.91

[.900 93–.900 99]   Treatment by specific continents, countries, localities

> Do not use; class in 330.93–330.99

.901–.905   Historical periods

> Add to base number 330.90 the numbers following —090 in notation 0901–0905 from Table 1, e.g., economic situation in 1960–1969 330.9046

.91   **Geographic treatment (Economic geography) by areas, regions, places in general**

> Add to base number 330.91 the numbers following —1 in notation 11–19 from Table 2, e.g., economic situation and conditions in developing countries 330.91724; then add 0* and to the result add the numbers following 909 in 909.1–909.8, e.g., economic situation and conditions in developing countries in 1980–1989 330.917240828
>> Use 0 plus standard subdivision —0112 for forecasting and forecasts, e.g., forecasting and forecasts of economic situation and conditions in developing countries 330.9172400112. Do not use historical periods for forecasting and forecasts
>
> (Option: Class in 910.13301)

.93–.99   **Geographic treatment (Economic geography) by specific continents, countries, localities**

> Add to base number 330.9 notation 3–9 from Table 2, e.g., economic situation and conditions in France 330.944; then to the result add historical period numbers from appropriate subdivisions of 930–990, e.g., economic situation and conditions in France under Louis XIV 330.944033. In all cases use one 0* except 00† for North and South America, e.g., economic situation in the United States during Reconstruction period 330.97308, in South America in 20th century 330.980033
>> Use 0 or 00 plus standard subdivision —0112 for forecasting and forecasts, e.g., forecasting and forecasts of economic situation and conditions in France 330.94400112. Do not use historical periods for forecasting and forecasts
>
> (Option: Class in 910.13303–910.13309)

---

*Add 00 for standard subdivisions; see instructions at beginning of Table 1

†Add 000 for standard subdivisions; see instructions at beginning of Table 1

> ## 331–333   Economics of labor, finance, land, energy

Class comprehensive works on economics of labor, finance, land, energy in 330; class comprehensive works on labor, capital, land considered as factors of production in 338.01

331   Labor economics

Class here industrial relations, interdisciplinary works on labor

Unless other instructions are given, observe the following table of preference, e.g., compensation of women in banking 331.42813321 (*not* 331.2813321 or 331.7613321):

Choice of vocation	331.702
Labor force by personal characteristics	331.3–331.6
Labor force and market	331.1
Conditions of employment	331.2
Labor unions (Trade unions), labor-management (collective) bargaining and disputes	331.8
Labor by industry and occupation (*except* 331.702)	331.7

Class economic conditions of laboring classes in 330.9; class full employment policies in 339.5

> *For noneconomic aspects of labor, see the aspect, e.g., relation of labor movements to the state 322.2, managerial views of labor 658.3*

> *See also 305.562 for sociology of laboring classes, 306.36 for sociology of labor*

> *See Manual at 331 vs. 331.8; also at 331 vs. 658.3*

SUMMARY

331.01–.09	**Standard subdivisions and industrial relations by industry and occupation**
.1	**Labor force and market**
.2	**Conditions of employment**
.3	**Workers by age group**
.4	**Women workers**
.5	**Special categories of workers other than by age or sex**
.6	**Categories of workers by racial, ethnic, national origin**
.7	**Labor by industry and occupation**
.8	**Labor unions (Trade unions), labor-management (collective) bargaining and disputes**

.01   Philosophy and theory

.011   **Rights and position of labor**

> Do not use for systems analysis applied to labor economics; class in 331.01. Do not use for systems of labor; class in 331.117
>
> Standard subdivisions are added for either or both topics in heading
>
> Including relation of labor to capital, right of labor to what it produces, right to earn a living
>
> Class here employment rights [*formerly* 323.46]
>
> *For open shop, right to work, see 331.8892*

.011 2   Industrial democracy

> Determination of a company's policies affecting the welfare of its workers by joint action of management and worker representatives
>
> Class producer cooperatives in 334.6; class guild socialism in 335.15; class syndicalism in 335.82; class worker control of industry in 338.6; class employee representation in management discussed from the managerial viewpoint in 658.3152
>
> *For role of labor unions in industrial democracy, see 331.88*

.012   **Satisfactions and dissatisfactions of labor**

> Do not use for classification of occupations; class in 331.70012
>
> Standard subdivisions are added for either or both topics in heading

.013   **Freedom, dignity, value of labor**

.04   **Industrial relations by industry and occupation**

> Standard subdivisions are added for either or both topics in heading

.041   **Industrial relations in industries and occupations other than extractive, manufacturing, construction**

> Standard subdivisions are added for industries, occupations, or both
>
> Class here industrial relations in service industries and occupations

.041 000 1–.041 000 9   Standard subdivisions

.041 001–.041 999   Subdivisions for industrial relations in industries and occupations other than extractive, manufacturing, construction

> Add to base number 331.041 notation 001–999, e.g., industrial relations in clerical occupations 331.04165137
>   Subdivisions are added for industries, occupations, or both

.042–.049   **Industrial relations in extractive, manufacturing, construction industries and occupations**

> Add to base number 331.04 the numbers following 6 in 620–690, e.g., industrial relations in chemical industries 331.046
>   Subdivisions are added for industries, occupations, or both

[.08]	History and description with respect to kinds of persons

Do not use for comprehensive works; class in 331.1143. Do not use for labor force by specific personal characteristics; class in 331.3–331.6

.1 Labor force and market

See Manual at 331.1 vs. 331.11, 331.12

SUMMARY

331.11	Labor force
.12	Labor market
.13	Maladjustments in labor market

.11	Labor force

All who are employed or available for employment

Class here human resources, manpower and womanpower, labor supply, size of labor force

See also 331.123 for demand (need, requirements) for labor, 331.8732 for union membership

See Manual at 331.1 vs. 331.11, 331.12

.110 9	Historical, geographic, persons treatment

Class here geographic distribution [*formerly also* 331.111]

[.111]	Geographic distribution

Relocated to 331.1109

.114	Qualifications and personal characteristics

.114 2	Qualifications

Including innate physical and mental capacity

.114 22	Qualifications by level of skills

Including skilled, semiskilled, unskilled workers

.114 23	Qualifications by level of education
.114 24	Qualifications by level of experience
.114 3	Personal characteristics

Class here comprehensive works on labor force by personal characteristics

For workers with specific characteristics, see 331.3–331.6

.117	Systems of labor

See also 306.36 for social aspects of systems of labor

.117 2	Free labor

.117 3	Compulsory labor
.117 32	State labor (Drafted workers)
.117 34	Slave labor

.118   **Labor productivity**

Class industrial productivity in 338.06

.119   **Labor force by industry and occupation**

Standard subdivisions are added for either or both topics in heading

Class qualifications and personal characteristics of labor force by industry and occupation in 331.114; class systems of labor by industry and occupation in 331.117; class labor productivity by industry and occupation in 331.118; class comprehensive works on labor by industry and occupation in 331.7

.119 04   Special topics

.119 042   Labor force in general categories of occupations

Including blue collar, civilian, governmental (public service), nongovernmental, nonagricultural, service, white collar occupations

.119 1   Labor force in industries and occupations other than extractive, manufacturing, construction

Standard subdivisions are added for industries, occupations, or both

.119 100 01–.119 100 09   Standard subdivisions

.119 100 1–.119 199 9   Subdivisions for labor force in industries and occupations other than extractive, manufacturing, construction

Add to base number 331.1191 notation 001–999, e.g., labor force in stenography 331.11916513741; however, for labor force in general categories of occupations, e.g., governmental (public service) occupations, see 331.119042
Subdivisions are added for industries, occupations, or both

.119 2–.119 9   Labor force in extractive, manufacturing, construction industries and occupations

Add to base number 331.119 the numbers following 6 in 620–690, e.g., labor force in automotive manufacturing 331.119292
Subdivisions are added for industries, occupations, or both

.12   **Labor market**

The activities of and opportunities for buying and selling labor

Class here supply of labor in relation to demand

For maladjustments in labor market, see 331.13

See Manual at 331.1 vs. 331.11, 331.12

SUMMARY

331.120 4		Special topics
	.123	Demand (Need, Requirements) for labor
	.124	Job vacancies (openings, opportunities)
	.125	Labor actively employed
	.126	Turnover
	.127	Mobility of labor
	.128	Placement
	.129	Labor market by industry and occupation

.120 4   Special topics

.120 42   Government policy on the labor market

Including developing, utilizing, employing needed labor

Class policies designed to secure full employment through fiscal and monetary policy in 339.5

For policy with respect to a specific aspect of labor force and market, see the aspect, e.g., assistance in finding jobs 331.128

See also 362.85 for social programs for laboring classes, 370 for education

See Manual at 331.12042 vs. 331.1377

.123   Demand (Need, Requirements) for labor

For job vacancies (openings, opportunities), see 331.124; for shortages and surpluses, see 331.136

.123 1   Demand for labor in industries and occupations other than extractive, manufacturing, construction

Standard subdivisions are added for industries, occupations, or both

Class here demand (need, requirements) for labor in service industries and occupations

.123 100 01–.123 100 09   Standard subdivisions

.123 100 1–.123 199 9   Subdivisions for demand for labor in industries and occupations other than extractive, manufacturing, construction

Add to base number 331.1231 notation 001–999, e.g., demand for teachers 331.12313711
Subdivisions are added for industries, occupations, or both

.123 2–.123 9   Demand for labor in extractive, manufacturing, construction industries and occupations

Add to base number 331.123 the numbers following 6 in 620–690, e.g., demand for carpenters 331.12394
Subdivisions are added for industries, occupations, or both

.124   Job vacancies (openings, opportunities)

.124 1	Job vacancies in industries and occupations other than extractive, manufacturing, construction

Standard subdivisions are added for industries, occupations, or both

Class here job vacancies (openings, opportunities) in service industries and occupations

.124 100 01–.124 100 09	Standard subdivisions

.124 100 1–.124 199 9	Subdivisions for job vacancies in industries and occupations other than extractive, manufacturing, construction

Add to base number 331.1241 notation 001–999, e.g., opportunities in librarianship 331.124102
Subdivisions are added for industries, occupations, or both

.124 2–.124 9	Job vacancies in extractive, manufacturing, construction industries and occupations

Add to base number 331.124 the numbers following 6 in 620–690, e.g., opportunities in paper manufacture 331.12476
Subdivisions are added for industries, occupations, or both

.125	Labor actively employed

That portion of the total available supply of labor employed at any given time

Including types of employment

Class here utilization of human resources, employment, comprehensive works on employment and compensation

For compensation, see 331.21

See also 331.126 for turnover, 331.137 for unemployment

See Manual at 331.1 vs. 331.11, 331.12

.125 1	Labor actively employed in industries and occupations other than extractive, manufacturing, construction

Class here labor actively employed in service industries and occupations

Standard subdivisions are added for industries, occupations, or both

.125 100 01–.125 100 09	Standard subdivisions

.125 100 1–.125 199 9	Subdivisions for labor actively employed in industries and occupations other than extractive, manufacturing, construction

Add to base number 331.1251 notation 001–999, e.g., labor actively employed in education 331.125137
Subdivisions are added for industries, occupations, or both

.125 2–.125 9	Labor actively employed in extractive, manufacturing, construction industries and occupations

> Add to base number 331.125 the numbers following 6 in 620–690, e.g., labor actively employed in the plumbing industry 331.125961
>> Subdivisions are added for industries, occupations, or both

.126	Turnover
.127	Mobility of labor
.127 09	Historical and persons treatment

> Do not use for geographic treatment; class in 331.1279

.127 2	Interoccupational mobility
.127 9	Geographic mobility
.127 91	International mobility

> Including brain drain

.127 93–.127 99	Geographic mobility within specific countries and lesser areas

> Add to base number 331.1279 notation 3–9 from Table 2, e.g., mobility of labor within Canada 331.127971

> Class mobility between countries and continents in 331.12791

.128	Placement

> Formal and informal arrangements for matching people and jobs

> Class here employment agencies, job banks, labor exchanges, sources of job information

> Class lists of job openings in 331.124

>> *See also 362 for employment services viewed as a solution to social problems; 650.14 for success in, techniques of job hunting*

.129	Labor market by industry and occupation

> Standard subdivisions are added for either or both topics in heading

>> *For specific aspects of labor market by industry and occupation, see 331.123–331.128*

.129 04	Special topics
.129 042	Labor market by general categories of occupations

>> Including blue collar, civilian, governmental (public service), nongovernmental, nonagricultural, service, white collar occupations

.129 1	Labor market by industries and occupations other than extractive, manufacturing, construction

> Standard subdivisions are added for industries, occupations, or both

.129 100 01–.129 100 09	Standard subdivisions
.129 100 1–.129 199 9	Subdivisions for labor market by industries and occupations other than extractive, manufacturing, construction

> Add to base number 331.1291 notation 001–999, e.g., labor market in stenography 331.12916513741; however, for labor market in general categories of occupations, e.g., governmental (public service) occupations, see 331.129042
>> Subdivisions are added for industries, occupations, or both

.129 2–.129 9	Labor market by extractive, manufacturing, construction industries and occupations

> Add to base number 331.129 the numbers following 6 in 620–690, e.g., labor market in automotive manufacturing 331.129292
>> Subdivisions are added for industries, occupations, or both

.13   Maladjustments in labor market

> Including underemployment, underemployed

.133   Discrimination in employment

> Class here equal employment opportunity programs

> Class personnel aspects of discrimination in government employment in 352.608; class comprehensive works about personnel policies on discrimination in 658.3008

>> *For discrimination in relation to a specific aspect of industrial relations, see the aspect, e.g., discrimination as a factor affecting compensation 331.2153, discrimination by unions 331.8732*

.136   Labor shortages and surpluses

>> *For unemployment, see 331.137*

.137   Unemployment

> Class here unemployed persons

.137 04   Kinds of unemployment

>> *See Manual at 331.1372 vs. 331.13704*

.137 041   Structural unemployment

> Unemployment resulting from changes in the overall environment, principally changes in population, government policies, technology, and consumer tastes, but not from a general economic recession

>> *For technological unemployment, see 331.137042*

.137 042   Technological unemployment

> Including unemployment due to automation

.137 044	Seasonal unemployment
.137 045	Frictional unemployment
	Irreducible minimum of people out of work because of need or desire to change jobs
.137 047	Cyclical unemployment
	Unemployment due to economic fluctuations
[.137 09]	Historical, geographic, persons treatment
	Do not use; class in 331.1379

>   331.137 2–331.137 7 Specific elements of unemployment

Class comprehensive works in 331.137

.137 2	Causes of unemployment
	For macroeconomic causes, see 339
	See Manual at 331.1372 vs. 331.13704
.137 3	Effects of unemployment
.137 4	Distribution and incidence of unemployment
	Standard subdivisions are added for either or both topics in heading
.137 7	Prevention and relief of unemployment
	Standard subdivisions are added for either or both topics in heading
	For a specific measure of prevention or relief, see the measure, e.g., work sharing 331.2572, economic stabilization 339.5, welfare 362.85
	See Manual at 331.12042 vs. 331.1377
.137 8	Unemployment among general classes of labor, unemployment by industry and occupation
	Class specific elements regardless of class, industry, occupation in 331.1372–331.1377
.137 804	General classes of unemployed persons
	Persons with various degrees of education, skill, experience
	Class unemployed persons having specific personal characteristics in 331.3–331.6
.137 81	Unemployment in industries and occupations other than extractive, manufacturing, construction
	Standard subdivisions are added for industries, occupations, or both
	Class here unemployment in service industries and occupations

.137 810 001–.137 810 009   Standard subdivisions

.137 810 01–.137 819 99   Subdivisions for unemployment in industries and occupations other than extractive, manufacturing, construction

> Add to base number 331.13781 notation 001–999, e.g., unemployment in clerical occupations 331.1378165137
>> Subdivisions are added for industries, occupations, or both

.137 82–.137 89   Unemployment in extractive, manufacturing, construction industries and occupations

> Add to base number 331.1378 the numbers following 6 in 620–690, e.g., unemployment in the automotive industry 331.1378292
>> Subdivisions are added for industries, occupations, or both

.137 9   Historical, geographic, persons treatment

> Add to base number 331.1379 notation 001–9 from Table 2, e.g., unemployment in the United States 331.137973

> Class historical and geographic treatment of specific elements of unemployment in 331.1372–331.1377; class historical, geographic, persons treatment of unemployment among general classes of labor and by industry and occupation in 331.1378

.2   Conditions of employment

> Class conditions of employment discussed from the managerial viewpoint in 658.312

> *See Manual at 331.2 vs. 331.89*

SUMMARY

331.204	**Conditions of employment by industry and occupation**
.21	**Compensation**
.22	**Compensation differentials**
.23	**Guaranteed-wage plans**
.25	**Other conditions of employment**
.28	**Compensation by industry and occupation**
.29	**Historical, geographic, persons treatment of compensation**

.204   Conditions of employment by industry and occupation

> Standard subdivisions are added for either or both topics in heading

.204 1   Conditions of employment in industries and occupations other than extractive, manufacturing, construction

> Standard subdivisions are added for industries, occupations, or both

> Class here conditions of employment in service industries and occupations

.204 100 01–.204 100 09   Standard subdivisions

.204 100 1–.204 199 9	Subdivisions for conditions of employment in industries and occupations other than extractive, manufacturing, construction

> Add to base number 331.2041 notation 001–999, e.g., conditions of employment in clerical occupations 331.204165137
>> Subdivisions are added for industries, occupations, or both

.204 2–.204 9	Conditions of employment in extractive, manufacturing, construction industries and occupations

> Add to base number 331.204 the numbers following 6 in 620–690, e.g., conditions of employment in chemical industries 331.2046
>> Subdivisions are added for industries, occupations, or both

.21 Compensation

Class here wages, comprehensive works on wage-price policy

For compensation differentials, see 331.22; for fringe benefits, see 331.255; for compensation by industry and occupation, see 331.28; for wage-price controls to combat inflation, see 332.415; for price policy, see 338.52; for wage-price policy as a factor in economic stabilization, see 339.5

.210 1	Philosophy and theory

Including bargain theory, marginal productivity theory, national income theory, subsistence theory ("iron law"), wages fund theory

[.210 9]	Historical, geographic, persons treatment

Do not use; class in 331.29

.215 Factors affecting compensation

Including methods of determination, e.g., intraindustry and interindustry comparison; criteria used in determination, e.g., cost of living as a compensation determinant

For minimum-wage policies, see 331.23

See also 332.415 for wage-price controls to combat inflation, 339.5 for wage control as a factor in economic stabilization

.215 3	Discrimination and anti-discrimination policies

Standard subdivisions are added for either or both topics in heading

Class here equal pay for equal work, pay equity

.216 Methods of compensation

Class fringe benefits in 331.255

.216 2	Time payments

Including hourly, weekly, monthly, annual periods

Class guaranteed-wage plans in 331.23

.216 4	Incentive compensation

Including bonuses; piecework, combined timework and piecework; stock ownership and purchase plans, profit-sharing

Class tips in 331.2166

.216 6	Other compensation

Including professional and subcontracting fees, tips, weighting

Class paid leave in 331.2576

.22	Compensation differentials

Differences among industries, occupations, regions

Including comparison among firms in the same industry

Class determination of compensation, factors affecting compensation in 331.215

See Manual at 331.29 vs. 331.22

.220 9	Historical, geographic, persons treatment

Class geographic treatment of compensation not emphasizing differentials in 331.29

.23	Guaranteed-wage plans

Including minimum wage

Class guaranteed minimum income in 362.582

.25	Other conditions of employment

Including economic aspects of physical working conditions, e.g., space, ventilation, working facilities; quality of work life; telecommuting

.252	Pensions

Including retirement age

Class here retirement benefits, interdisciplinary works on pensions

Class pensions for government (public service) employees in 331.2529135

For pensions provided by unions, see 331.8735; for annuities resulting from retirement and estate planning, see 332.02401; for public administration of pensions for government workers, see 353.549; for pensions (annuities) provided through insurance, see 368.37; for government pension plans for the population at large, see 368.43; for comprehensive works on administration of pensions, see 658.3253

.252 2	Pension reform

Including preservation and transfer of vested rights in pensions

.252 9   Pensions by industry and occupation

Standard subdivisions are added for either or both topics in heading

.252 91   Pensions in industries and occupations other than extractive, manufacturing, construction

Standard subdivisions are added for industries, occupations, or both

Class here pensions in service industries and occupations

.252 910 001–.252 910 009   Standard subdivisions

.252 910 01–.252 919 99   Subdivisions for pensions in industries and occupations other than extractive, manufacturing, construction

Add to base number 331.25291 notation 001–999, e.g., pensions for government employees 331.2529135
Subdivisions are added for industries, occupations, or both

.252 92–.252 99   Pensions in extractive, manufacturing, construction industries and occupations

Add to base number 331.2529 the numbers following 6 in 620–690, e.g., pensions in construction trades 331.252924
Subdivisions are added for industries, occupations, or both

.255   Fringe benefits

Including health and employee assistance programs, insurance, unemployment compensation

Class here interdisciplinary works on fringe benefits

For stock ownership and purchase plans, see 331.2164; for pensions, see 331.252; for fringe benefits provided by unions, see 331.8735; for fringe benefits for veterans of military service and their survivors, see 362.86; for benefits provided through insurance, see 368.3; for benefits provided through government-sponsored social insurance, see 368.4; for comprehensive works on administration of employee benefits, see 658.325

.257   Hours

.257 2   Work day and week

Including job sharing, work sharing, part-time employment

Class here flexible working hours, shift work

.257 22   Work week

Including compressed work schedules, e.g., four-day forty-hour week

.257 23	Work day

Including eight-hour day

For rest periods, see 331.2576

.257 4	Night, holy day, Sunday, holiday work

See also 331.2572 for shift work

.257 6	Leave and rest periods (breaks)

Standard subdivisions are added for leave and rest periods together, for leave alone

Including paid vacations and holidays

.257 62	Sick leave
.257 63	Special-purpose leave

Including educational, paternity, sabbatical leave

For maternity leave, see 331.44

.259	Training, worker security, regulation of worker conduct
.259 2	Training

Class here interdisciplinary works on on-the-job vocational training, on vocational training provided by industry

Class interdisciplinary works on vocational education conducted by an educational institution in 370.113

For managerial aspects of training by the employer, see 658.3124. For on-the-job training in a specific occupation, see the occupation, plus notation 07155 from Table 1, e.g., on-the-job apprenticeship of plumbers 696.107155

.259 22	Apprenticeship

Class apprentices as a special class of workers in 331.55; class work experience as part of education in 371.227

.259 24	Retraining
.259 6	Worker security

Including dismissal of employees; employment security, job tenure; right to organize, rights of transfer and promotion, seniority

.259 8	Regulation of worker conduct

Including absenteeism, discipline

.28	Compensation by industry and occupation

Standard subdivisions are added for either or both topics in heading

Class specific elements of compensation by industry and occupation in 331.21–331.23

.281   **Compensation in industries and occupations other than extractive, manufacturing, construction**

> Standard subdivisions are added for industries, occupations, or both
>
> Class here compensation in service industries and occupations

.281 000 1–.281 000 9   Standard subdivisions

.281 001–.281 999   Subdivisions for compensation in industries and occupations other than extractive, manufacturing, construction

> Add to base number 331.281 notation 001–999, e.g., compensation of bankers 331.2813321
> Subdivisions are added for industries, occupations, or both

.282–.289   **Compensation in extractive, manufacturing, construction industries and occupations**

> Add to base number 331.28 the numbers following 6 in 620–690, e.g., compensation in the mining industry 331.2822, average factory compensation 331.287
> Subdivisions are added for industries, occupations, or both

.29   **Historical, geographic, persons treatment of compensation**

> Add to base number 331.29 notation 001–9 from Table 2, e.g., compensation in Australia 331.2994
>
> Class historical, geographic, persons treatment of specific elements of compensation in 331.215–331.23; class historical, geographic, persons treatment of compensation by industries and occupations in 331.28
>
> *See Manual at 331.29 vs. 331.22; also at 331.29 vs. 339.5*

>   **331.3–331.6   Labor force by personal characteristics**

> Class here labor force and market, conditions of employment, industries and occupations, labor unions, labor-management bargaining with respect to special classes of workers
>
> Unless other instructions are given, class a subject with aspects in two or more subdivisions of 331.3–331.6 in the number coming first, e.g., young North American native women 331.34408997 (*not* 331.408997 or 331.6997)
>
> Class choice of vocation for persons with specific personal characteristics in 331.702; class comprehensive works in 331.1143. Class employment services as a form of social service to persons with specific personal characteristics with the kind of person in 362.6–362.8, e.g., sheltered employment for aged people 362.64

.3   **Workers by age group**

.31   Children

> Through age thirteen

.34   Young people

Through age thirty-five

For children, see 331.31; for young people by industry and occupation, see 331.38

.341–.342   Specific aspects of employment of young people

Add to base number 331.34 the numbers following 331 in 331.1–331.2, e.g., training of young workers 331.342592

Class specific aspects of employment of specific kinds of young people in 331.344–331.346

.344–.346   Employment of specific kinds of young people

Add to base number 331.34 the numbers following 331 in 331.4–331.6, e.g., African American youth 331.346396073; however, for apprentices, see 331.55

.347   Persons aged 14 through 20

Class employment of specific kinds of persons aged 14 through 20 in 331.344–331.346

For specific aspects of employment of persons aged 14 through 20, see 331.341–331.342

.348   Persons aged 21 through 35

Class employment of specific kinds of persons aged 21 through 35 in 331.344–331.346

For specific aspects of employment of persons aged 21 through 35, see 331.341–331.342

.38   Young people by industry and occupation

Standard subdivisions are added for either or both topics in heading

Children and young adults

Class employment of specific kinds of young people by industry and occupation in 331.344–331.346

For specific aspects of employment of young people by industry and occupation, see 331.341–331.342

.381   Young people in industries and occupations other than extractive, manufacturing, construction

Standard subdivisions are added for industries, occupations, or both

Class here young people in service industries and occupations

.381 000 1–.381 000 9   Standard subdivisions

.381 001–.381 999   Subdivisions for young people in industries and occupations other than extractive, manufacturing, construction

> Add to base number 331.381 notation 001–999, e.g., young people in clerical occupations 331.38165137
> Subdivisions are added for industries, occupations, or both

.382–.389   **Young people in extractive, manufacturing, construction industries and occupations**

> Add to base number 331.38 the numbers following 6 in 620–690, e.g., young textile workers 331.3877
> Subdivisions are added for industries, occupations, or both

.39   **Other age groups**

.394   **Middle-aged workers**

.398   **Older workers**

.398 8   Older workers by industry and occupation

> Standard subdivisions are added for either or both topics in heading

.398 81   Older workers in industries and occupations other than extractive, manufacturing, construction

> Standard subdivisions are added for industries, occupations, or both

> Class here older workers in service industries and occupations

.398 810 001–.398 810 009   Standard subdivisions

.398 810 01–.398 819 99   Subdivisions for older workers in industries and occupations other than extractive, manufacturing, construction

> Add to base number 331.39881 notation 001–999, e.g., older workers in clerical occupations 331.3988165137
> Subdivisions are added for industries, occupations, or both

.398 82–.398 89   Older workers in extractive, manufacturing, construction industries and occupations

> Add to base number 331.3988 the numbers following 6 in 620–690, e.g., older agricultural workers in 331.39883
> Subdivisions are added for industries, occupations, or both

.4 **Women workers**

Unless other instructions are given, observe the following table of preference, e.g., women clothing workers in labor unions 331.478187 (*not* 331.4887):

Working mothers	331.44
Married women	331.43
Labor unions (trade unions) and labor-management (collective) bargaining and disputes	331.47
Specific aspects of employment of women	331.41–.42
Women workers by industry and occupation	331.48

See also 305.43 for sociological aspects of women's occupations

.41–.42 **Specific aspects of employment of women**

Add to base number 331.4 the numbers following 331 in 331.1–331.2, e.g., discrimination against women 331.4133, compensation of women in banking 331.42813321

.43 **Married women**

.44 **Working mothers**

Including expectant mothers, maternity leave

.47 **Labor unions (trade unions) and labor-management (collective) bargaining and disputes**

Add to base number 331.47 the numbers following 331.8 in 331.87–331.89, e.g., women in labor unions 331.478

.48 **Women workers by industry and occupation**

Standard subdivisions are added for either or both topics in heading

.481 **Women workers in industries and occupations other than extractive, manufacturing, construction**

Standard subdivisions are added for industries, occupations, or both

Class here women in service industries and occupations

.481 000 1–.481 000 9 Standard subdivisions

.481 001–.481 999 Subdivisions for women workers in industries and occupations other than extractive, manufacturing, construction

Add to base number 331.481 notation 001–999, e.g., women in advertising 331.4816591
Subdivisions are added for industries, occupations, or both

.482–.489 **Women workers in extractive, manufacturing, construction industries and occupations**

Add to base number 331.48 the numbers following 6 in 620–690, e.g., women clothing workers 331.4887
Subdivisions are added for industries, occupations, or both

.5   **Special categories of workers other than by age or sex**

> *For categories of workers by racial, ethnic, national origin, see 331.6*

.51   Prisoners and ex-convicts

> Standard subdivisions are added for either or both topics in heading
>
> Including political and war prisoners

.52   Veterans

> Class here nonmilitary labor of former members of the armed forces
>
> > *See also 331.25291355 for pensions received because of military service, 331.761355 for military labor*

.53   Gays

.54   Workers in special economic situations

> Class here economically disadvantaged workers not provided for elsewhere

.542   Contract workers

.544   Migrant and casual workers

> Standard subdivisions are added for migrant and casual workers together, for migrant workers alone
>
> Class here migrant agricultural laborers
>
> > *See also 331.62 for immigrant and alien workers*

.55   Apprentices

> Class training of apprentices in 331.25922

.59   Workers with disabilities and illnesses

> Class here workers with physical disabilities
>
> Add to base number 331.59 the numbers following —087 in notation 0871–0877 from Table 1, e.g., workers with impaired vision 331.591

.6   **Categories of workers by racial, ethnic, national origin**

.62   Immigrants and aliens

> Standard subdivisions are added for either or both topics in heading
>
> > *See also 331.544 for migrant workers*

.620 9   Historical, geographic, persons treatment

> Class here immigrant and alien workers in specific areas, e.g., immigrant workers in Canada 331.620971
>
> > *For immigrant and alien workers from specific jurisdictions, see 331.621–331.629*

>   **331.621–331.629 Immigrants and aliens by place of origin**

Class comprehensive works in 331.62

See also 331.6209 for immigrant and alien workers in specific areas

.621   **Immigrants and aliens from areas, regions, places in general**

Add to base number 331.621 the numbers following — 1 in notation 11–19 from Table 2, e.g., immigrant workers from developing regions 331.621724; then, for area located, add 0* and to the result add notation 1–9 from Table 2, e.g., immigrant workers from developing regions in California 331.6217240794

Subdivisions are added for either or both topics in heading

.623–.629   **Immigrants and aliens from specific continents, countries, localities**

Add to base number 331.62 notation 3–9 from Table 2 for place of origin, e.g., immigrant workers from China 331.6251; then, for area located, add 0* and to the result add notation 1–9 from Table 2, e.g., immigrant workers from China in California 331.62510794

Subdivisions are added for either or both topics in heading

.63   **Native-born nonindigenous ethnic groups**

.630 01–.630 07   Standard subdivisions

.630 08   History and description with respect to kinds of persons

[.630 089]   Racial, ethnic, national groups

Do not use for comprehensive works on native-born nonindigenous ethnic groups; class in 331.63. Do not use for specific native-born nonindigenous ethnic groups; class in 331.6303–331.6399

.630 09   Historical, geographic, persons treatment

.630 3–.639 9   Specific native-born nonindigenous ethnic groups

Add to base number 331.63 notation 03–99 from Table 5, e.g., African Americans 331.6396073, African American workers in Alabama 331.63960730761

.69   **Indigenous ethnic groups**

.690 01–.690 07   Standard subdivisions

.690 08   History and description with respect to kinds of persons

[.690 089]   Racial, ethnic, national groups

Do not use for comprehensive works on indigenous ethnic groups; class in 331.69. Do not use for specific indigenous ethnic groups; class in 331.6903–331.6999

.690 09   Historical, geographic, persons treatment

---

*Add 00 for standard subdivisions; see instructions at beginning of Table 1

.690 3–.699 9   Specific indigenous ethnic groups

Add to base number 331.69 notation 03–99 from Table 5, e.g., North American native peoples in North America 331.6997

.7   Labor by industry and occupation

Standard subdivisions are added for either or both topics in heading

Including professional relationships

For professional relationships in a specific industry or occupation, see the industry or occupation, plus notation 023 from Table 1, e.g., professional relationships in accounting 657.023

.700 1–.700 9   Standard subdivisions

.702   Choice of vocation

Class here choice of vocation for persons with specific personal characteristics, e.g., veterans; interdisciplinary works describing vocations and occupational specialties; interdisciplinary works on career opportunities and vocational counseling

Class studies of vocational interest in 158.6; class job hunting in 650.14

For vocational counseling in schools, see 371.425. For descriptions of, career opportunities in, choice of vocation with regard to specific vocations and occupational specialties, see the vocation or specialty, plus notation 023 from Table 1, e.g., career opportunities in accounting 657.023

.702 3   Choice of vocation for persons at specific educational levels

[.702 301–.702 309]   Standard subdivisions

Do not use; class in 331.70201–331.70209

.702 33   Choice of vocation for high school graduates

.702 35   Choice of vocation for college graduates

.71   Professional and managerial occupations

For specific professional and managerial occupations, see 331.761

.712   Professional occupations

.714   Managerial occupations

.76   Specific industries and occupations

Class specific groups of occupations in 331.79

[.760 1–.760 9]   Standard subdivisions

Do not use; class in 331.7001–331.7009

.761   Industries and occupations other than extractive, manufacturing, construction

Standard subdivisions are added for industries, occupations, or both

.761 000 1–.761 000 9	Standard subdivisions
.761 001–.761 999	Subdivisions for industries and occupations other than extractive, manufacturing, construction

Add to base number 331.761 notation 001–999, e.g., labor in the banking industry 331.7613321; however, for governmental (public service) occupations, see 331.795
Subdivisions are added for industries, occupations, or both

.762–.769	**Extractive, manufacturing, construction industries and occupations**

Add to base number 331.76 the numbers following 6 in 620–690, e.g., food processing 331.7664
Subdivisions are added for industries, occupations, or both

.79	Specific groups of occupations

Unless other instructions are given, class a subject with aspects in two or more subdivisions of 331.79 in the number coming last, e.g., white collar governmental (public service) occupations 331.795 (*not* 331.792)

For professional and managerial occupations, see 331.71; for agricultural occupations, see 331.763

[.790 1–.790 9]	Standard subdivisions

Do not use; class in 331.7001–331.7009

.792	White collar occupations
.793	Service occupations
.794	Industrial occupations

Including the work of artisans and supervisors; skilled, semiskilled work

For unskilled work, see 331.798

.795	Governmental (Public service) occupations

Occupations of elected and appointed civil servants

.798	Unskilled work
.8	**Labor unions (Trade unions), labor-management (collective) bargaining and disputes**

Class here interdisciplinary works on labor movements

Class comprehensive works on industrial democracy in 331.0112

For a specific aspect of labor movements, see the aspect, e.g., political activities of labor movements 322.2

See Manual at 331 vs. 331.8

SUMMARY

331.87	**Labor union organization**
.88	**Labor unions (Trade unions)**
.89	**Labor-management (Collective) bargaining and disputes**

.87   Labor union organization

Class comprehensive works about labor unions in 331.88

.871   Constitutions, bylaws, rules

.872   Levels of organization

Including locals, nationals, federations

.873   Specific aspects of union organization

Including discipline of members

[.873 01–.873 09]   Standard subdivisions

Do not use; class in 331.8701–331.8709

.873 2   Membership

Including discrimination by unions

Class here membership policies

Class discrimination by unions against workers with specific personal characteristics with the characteristic in 331.3–331.6, e.g., discrimination against women 331.47732

.873 3   Officers

Class here union leaders, shop stewards

.873 5   Benefits, funds, property

.874   Union elections and conventions

.88   Labor unions (Trade unions)

Class here unions organized along religious lines, e.g., Christian trade unions

Class managerial viewpoint on labor unions in 658.3153

For labor union organization, see 331.87

See also 322.2 for political activities of labor unions

.880 1   Philosophy and theory

Including anti-union theories; countermonopoly theory; theories of unions as instruments of class struggle, as instruments of industrial democracy, as instruments for worker control of industry

See also 331.0112 for industrial democracy, 338.6 for worker control of industry

.880 4	Special topics
.880 41	White collar unions
.880 42	Blue collar unions
.880 9	Historical, geographic, persons treatment of labor unions
.880 91	Treatment by areas, regions, places in general

Class here international unions

Class international unions with members from only two countries in 331.88094–331.88099, using the comprehensive notation from Table 2 for the two countries, e.g., unions with United States and Canadian workers 331.880973

.881	**Labor unions (Trade unions) by industry and occupation**

Standard subdivisions are added for either or both topics in heading

.881 1	Labor unions (Trade unions) in industries and occupations other than extractive, manufacturing, construction

Standard subdivisions are added for industries, occupations, or both

Class here labor unions (trade unions) in service industries and occupations

.881 100 01–.881 100 09	Standard subdivisions
.881 100 1–.881 199 9	Subdivisions for labor unions (trade unions) in industries and occupations other than extractive, manufacturing, construction

Add to base number 331.8811 notation 001–999, e.g., teachers' unions 331.88113711
  Subdivisions are added for industries, occupations, or both

.881 2–.881 9	Labor unions (Trade unions) in extractive, manufacturing, construction industries and occupations

Add to base number 331.881 the numbers following 6 in 620–690, e.g., garment workers' unions 331.88187
  Subdivisions are added for industries, occupations, or both

.883	**Kinds of unions**

Class specific kinds of unions by industry and occupation in 331.881

For revolutionary unions, see 331.886

.883 2	Craft unions

Unions of workers practicing a specific trade or occupation regardless of the industry in which they are employed

Class semi-industrial unions in 331.8833

.883 3	Industrial unions

Unions in a specific industry or group of industries regardless of craft or occupation practiced

Class here semi-industrial unions (those representing many but not all workers in an industry, e.g., a union that represents all except maintenance workers)

.883 4	Company unions

Unaffiliated labor unions of employees of a single firm

.886	**Revolutionary unions**

Including Industrial Workers of the World (IWW)

.889	**Union security arrangements**
.889 2	Shop arrangements

Including closed, open, union shop; preferential hiring; right to work; sole bargaining rights

Class comprehensive works on rights of labor in 331.011; class right to work as a government measure to deal with labor-management (collective) bargaining and disputes in 331.898

.889 4	Control of hiring and layoffs

Including hiring halls, control of apprenticeships

.889 6	Dues checkoff, make-work arrangements (featherbedding), control of grievance procedures

.89	**Labor-management (Collective) bargaining and disputes**

Standard subdivisions are added for either or both topics in heading

Class works treating collective bargaining from the managerial viewpoint in 658.3154

See Manual at 331.2 vs. 331.89

.890 4	Labor-management (Collective) bargaining and disputes by industry and occupation

Standard subdivisions are added for any or all topics in heading

.890 41	Labor-management (Collective) bargaining and disputes in industries and occupations other than extractive, manufacturing, construction

Standard subdivisions are added for any or all topics in heading

Class here labor-management (collective) bargaining and disputes in service industries and occupations

.890 410 001–.890 410 009	Standard subdivisions

.890 410 01–.890 419 99	Subdivisions for labor-management (collective) bargaining and disputes in industries and occupations other than extractive, manufacturing, construction

> Add to base number 331.89041 notation 001–999, e.g., labor-management bargaining in hospitals 331.8904136211
>> Subdivisions are added for any or all topics in heading

.890 42–.890 49	Labor-management (collective) bargaining and disputes in extractive, manufacturing, construction industries and occupations

> Add to base number 331.8904 the numbers following 6 in 620–690, e.g., labor-management bargaining and disputes in the garment industry 331.890487
> Subdivisions are added for any or all topics in heading

.891 Procedures

Class here labor contracts

.891 2 Preliminaries

Including organizing, winning recognition, negotiation of contract

.891 4 Conciliation measures

.891 42 Mediation

.891 43 Arbitration

.891 5 Negotiation during life of contract

Including cancellation of labor contracts

.892 Strikes

For management measures with respect to strikes, see 331.894; for government measures with respect to strikes, see 331.898

See also 331.8914 for conciliation measures

.892 01 Philosophy and theory

Including right to strike, general theories about effects of strikes

Class effects of strikes on a specific thing with the thing, e.g., effect of strikes on profitability of mining industries 338.23

[.892 09] Historical, geographic, persons treatment

Do not use; class in 331.8929

.892 1 Strike votes

>   331.892 2–331.892 6   Kinds of strikes

Unless other instructions are given, observe the following table of preference, e.g., union-authorized general strikes 331.8925 (*not* 331.8922):

General strikes	331.8925
Sympathetic strikes	331.8923
Protest stoppages, sit-down strikes	331.8926
Unauthorized (Wildcat) strikes	331.8924
Union-authorized strikes	331.8922

Class specific kinds of strikes by industry and occupation in 331.8928; class comprehensive works in 331.892

.892 2   Union-authorized strikes

Not otherwise provided for

Including economic, jurisdictional strikes

Class here official strikes

.892 3   Sympathetic strikes

.892 4   Unauthorized (Wildcat) strikes

Not provided for elsewhere

Class here unofficial strikes

.892 5   General strikes

Work stoppages throughout an area

Class interdisciplinary works on general strikes in 322.2

.892 6   Protest stoppages, sit-down strikes

Standard subdivisions are added for either or both topics in heading

.892 7   Picketing

.892 8   Strikes by industry and occupation

Standard subdivisions are added for either or both topics in heading

.892 81   Strikes in industries and occupations other than extractive, manufacturing, construction

Standard subdivisions are added for industries, occupations, or both

Class here strikes in service industries and occupations

.892 810 001–.892 810 009   Standard subdivisions

.892 810 01–.892 819 99   Subdivisions for strikes in industries and occupations other than extractive, manufacturing, construction

Add to base number 331.89281 notation 001–999, e.g., teachers' strikes 331.892813711
Subdivisions are added for industries, occupations, or both

.892 82–.892 89   Strikes in extractive, manufacturing, construction industries and occupations

Add to base number 331.8928 the numbers following 6 in 620–690, e.g., strikes of rubber workers 331.8928782
Subdivisions are added for industries, occupations, or both

.892 9   Historical, geographic, persons treatment

Add to base number 331.8929 notation 001–9 from Table 2, e.g., strikes in Great Britain 331.892941

Class strikes by industry and occupations in specific periods and places in 331.8928

For specific aspects of strikes in specific periods and places, see 331.8921–331.8927

.893   Other labor measures

Including boycotts, injunctions, sabotage

Class here comprehensive works on labor violence

For violence in strikes, see 331.892

.894   Management measures

Including blacklisting, white-listing, injunctions, labor espionage, lockouts, strikebreaking, yellow-dog contracts

Class comprehensive works on strikes in 331.892

.898   Government measures

Including right-to-work policy

Class comprehensive works on right to work in 331.8892; class comprehensive works on strikes in 331.892

For conciliation measures, see 331.8914

.898 2   Strike requirements

Including purpose, notice, cooling-off periods, exhaustion of other means

.898 4   Use of troops

332   Financial economics

For public finance, see 336

See Manual at 332, 336 vs. 339; also at 332 vs. 338, 658.15

SUMMARY

332.01–.09	Standard subdivisions, personal finance, special topics
.1	Banks
.2	Specialized banking institutions
.3	Credit and loan institutions
.4	Money
.5	Other mediums of exchange
.6	Investment and investments
.7	Credit
.8	Interest and discount
.9	Counterfeiting, forgery, alteration

.024   Personal finance

Do not use for works on financial economics for persons in specific occupations; class in 332.02

For management of personal expenditure, see 640.42. For a specific aspect of personal finance not provided for here, see the aspect, e.g., investing in stocks 332.6322, consumer information 381.33

See Manual at 332.024 vs. 640.42

.024 001–.024 007   Standard subdivisions

.024 008   Personal finance with respect to groups of persons

[.024 008 1–.024 008 8]   Personal finance with respect to specific miscellaneous kinds of persons

      Do not use; class in 332.02403–332.02499

.024 009   Historical, geographic, persons treatment

.024 01   Increasing income, net worth, financial security

Including financial independence; estate planning; planning for retirement, e.g., annuities, individual retirement accounts (IRAs), Keogh plans

[.024 010 81–.024 010 88]   Specific miscellaneous kinds of persons

      Do not use; class in 332.02403–332.02499

.024 02   Personal financial problems

Including debt management; coping with depression, inflation

[.024 020 81–.024 020 88]   Specific miscellaneous kinds of persons

      Do not use; class in 332.02403–332.02499

.024 03–.024 99   Personal finance for specific classes of persons

Add to base number 332.024 notation 03–99 from Table 7, e.g., personal finance for single people 332.0240652

.04   Special topics

.041	Capital

For international aspects of capital, see 332.042

.041 2	Working capital

Including cash, short-term money claims, inventories

.041 4	Fixed (Investment) capital

Instruments of production with economic life span measured in years, e.g., factories, machinery; and funds invested in them

For land, see 333

.041 5	Capital formation and saving

Standard subdivisions are added for either or both topics in heading

Class here interdisciplinary and general economic studies of the ways, means, and problems of raising money for investment in capital assets

For capital formation discussed in relation to production in specific kinds of industries, see 338.1–338.4; for financing of firms, see 338.6041; for savings and investment as a factor affecting national income, see 339.43

[.041 506 8]	Management

Do not use; class in 658.1522

.041 52	Self-financing

Use by an individual of his own savings, or by an enterprise of its retained profits, for investment in own business

Class here procurement of capital from internal sources

Class managerial aspects of self-financing in 658.15226

.041 54	External sources of capital
.042	International finance

Including international capital transactions [*formerly* 382.173], international currency movements [*formerly* 382.174], international capital movements

Class comprehensive works on international economics in 337

For international banks and banking, see 332.15; for exchange of currencies, see 332.45; for international exchange of securities, see 332.65; for international investment, see 332.673; for balance of payments, see 382.17

.06	Organizations and management

Do not use for financial institutions and their management; class in 332.1

.1 **Banks**

Class here banking; bank failures; government guaranty of deposits; comprehensive works on money and banking, on financial institutions and their functions

> *For specialized banking institutions, see 332.2; for credit and loan institutions, see 332.3; for money, see 332.4; for credit, see 332.7; for credit unions, see 334.22*

> *See Manual at 332.7 vs. 332.1*

.11 Central banks

Specific central banks are classed here, e.g., the U.S. Federal Reserve System 332.110973

.112 Relation to monetary policy

Including issuance of bank notes

Class role of central bank in carrying out macroeconomic policy in 339.53

> *For interest rates, reserve requirements, see 332.113; for open-market operations, see 332.114*

.113 Relation to private banks

Including clearance, interest (discount) rates, loans, reserve requirements

.114 Open-market operations

Including purchase of government securities

.12 Commercial banks

Class here clearing banks, clearing houses

Class clearing services in 332.178

> *For international banking, see 332.15; for multiple banking, see 332.16; for banking services of commercial banks, see 332.17*

> *See Manual at 658.15 and T1—0681*

.122 Incorporated banks

Class here chartered banks

.122 3 National banks

> *See also 332.11 for central banks*

.122 4 State and provincial banks

.123 Unincorporated (Private) banks

.15	**International banks**

Class here international operations of commercial and other banks, the role of banks in international borrowing and debt

Class comprehensive works on international borrowing and debt in 336.3435

.152	**International banks for monetary stabilization and balance of payments**

Standard subdivisions are added for either or both topics in heading

Including International Monetary Fund

Class comprehensive works on balance of payments in 382.17

.153	**International banks for development of resources and production**

Standard subdivisions are added for either or both topics in heading

Including International Development Association, International Finance Corporation

Class here comprehensive works on development banks

For development banks serving one country, see 332.28

.153 2	International Bank for Reconstruction and Development (World Bank)
.153 4	European Investment Bank
.153 8	Inter-American Development Bank
.154	**International banks for promotion and facilitation of trade**

Standard subdivisions are added for either or both topics in heading

.155	**International banks for international settlements**

Including Bank for International Settlements

.16	**Multiple banking**

Including branch, chain, group, interstate banking; bank mergers, syndicates, holding companies

.17	**Banking services of commercial banks**

Class here comprehensive works on services of banks

For international operations, see 332.15; for services of specialized banking institutions, see 332.2

See also 332.7 for credit functions not limited to a specific type of financial institution

.175	**General banking services**

.175 2	Deposits

Including demand deposits (checking accounts); time deposits, e.g., certificates of deposit, savings accounts; NOW (negotiable order of withdrawal) accounts; savings departments

.175 3	Loans
.175 4	Investments

See also 332.66 for investment banks

.178	Special banking services

Including clearing services; credit cards; debit and smart cards; safe-deposit services; trust services

See also 332.765 for credit cards offered by multiple types of institutions or without regard to type of institution

.2	**Specialized banking institutions**

For international banks, see 332.15; for agricultural institutions, see 332.31; for investment banks, see 332.66; for banking cooperatives, see 334.2

.21	Savings banks

Including government and stock savings banks

Class here mutual savings banks

Class comprehensive works on thrift institutions in 332.32

For postal savings banks, see 332.22

.22	Postal savings banks
.26	Trust companies
.28	Development banks serving one country

Class banks for development of agriculture in 332.31

See also 332.153 for international development banks

.3	**Credit and loan institutions**

Standard subdivisions are added for either or both topics in heading

Including credit and loan functions of enterprises whose primary function is not credit and loan, e.g., credit function of retail stores, travel agencies

Class credit and loan functions of insurance companies in 332.38

.31	Agricultural institutions

Including land banks

.32   Savings and loan associations

Variant names: building and loan associations, home loan associations, mortgage institutions

Class here comprehensive works on thrift institutions

For savings banks, see 332.21; for credit unions, see 334.22

.34   Loan brokers

Class here pawnbrokers

.35   Consumer and sales finance institutions

Standard subdivisions are added for either or both topics in heading

.37   Industrial banks

Financial institutions organized to extend loans to employees

Class here labor banks

For credit unions, see 334.22

See also 332.35 for banks specializing in consumer loans

.38   Insurance companies

Credit and loan functions

Class interdisciplinary works on insurance companies in 368.0065

.4   Money

Class here comprehensive works on mediums of exchange

Class monetary policy in 332.46; class comprehensive works on money and banking in 332.1

For mediums of exchange other than money, see 332.5

SUMMARY

332.401–.408	**Standard subdivisions and forms and units of money**
.41	**Value of money**
.42	**Monetary standards**
.45	**Foreign exchange**
.46	**Monetary policy**
.49	**Historical, geographic, persons treatment of money and monetary policy**

.401   Philosophy and theory

Including circulation and velocity theory, equation of exchange theory, income and cash balance theories, quantity theory, supply and demand theory

.404   Forms and units of money

.404 2	Gold and silver coins

.404 2   Gold and silver coins

Class here interdisciplinary works on coins

For token coins, see 332.4043. For aspects of coins not provided for here, see the aspect, e.g., coins as an investment 332.63, artistic aspect of coins 737.4

.404 3   Token coins

Coins with an intrinsic value less than their nominal value

Class here coins made of nonprecious metals

.404 4   Paper money

.404 8   Decimalization of currency

[.409]   Historical, geographic, persons treatment

Do not use; class in 332.49

.41   Value of money

Class here inflation, stagflation, deflation

Class the personal financial problem of coping with changing value of money in 332.02402

See also 331.1372 for effects of inflation on unemployment

See Manual at 339.41, 339.42 vs. 332.41

.414   Factors affecting fluctuations in value

Including devaluation, variations in quantity

For stabilization measures, see 332.415

.415   Stabilization measures

Including wage-price controls to combat inflation

Class monetary policy in 332.46; class fiscal policy in 336.3; class comprehensive works on wage-price policy in 331.21; class comprehensive works on economic stabilization policies in 339.5

.42   Monetary standards

.420 4   Special topics

.420 42   Official status of money

Including credit money

Class here legal tender

See also 343.032 for monetary law

> 332.422–332.425   Commodity standards

Systems in which value of monetary unit is kept equal to value of a designated quantity of a particular commodity or group of commodities

Class comprehensive works in 332.42

.422   Monometallic standards

.422 2   Gold standards

                Including gold coin, gold bullion, gold exchange standards

.422 3   Silver standards

.423   Bimetallic standards

                Free concurrent coinage of two metals, without limitation as to quantity or ratio of the metals

                Class here bimetallic standards based on gold and silver

.424   Symmetallic standards

                Coinage from an amalgam of two or more metals in a required proportion

.425   Composite commodity standards

                Staple commodities in predetermined proportions

.427   Fiat money

                Controlled and free forms of nonredeemable (inconvertible) currencies not kept equal to units of any commodity or group of commodities

.45   Foreign exchange

                Exchange of one country's currency for another's

                Including Eurocurrency and Eurodollar market, special drawing rights

                Class here currency convertibility, forward exchange, international monetary systems

                Class investment in Eurobonds in 332.6323; class government Eurobonds in public finance in 336.31; class comprehensive works on international finance in 332.042; class comprehensive works on financial futures in 332.632; class comprehensive works on speculation in 332.645; class comprehensive works on balance of payments in 382.17

.452   **Foreign exchange with a gold standard**

Monetary units of exchanging countries defined in terms of gold, currencies freely convertible into gold, full freedom to import and export gold

Including devaluation

Class effect of devaluation on internal economy of devaluing country in 332.414

.454   **Foreign exchange with a paper standard**

Monetary units of exchanging countries not defined in terms of gold or any other item of intrinsic value

Class regulation of exchange in 332.4564

.456   **Exchange rates**

Class here determination of exchange rates

.456 01–.456 08   Standard subdivisions

Class standard subdivisions of specific currencies and groups of currencies in 332.45609

.456 09   Historical, geographic, persons treatment

.456 091   Exchange rates of specific currencies and groups of currencies in areas, regions, places in general

Add to base number 332.45609 the numbers following — 1 in notation 11–19 from Table 2, e.g., exchange rates of currencies of developing countries 332.456091724; then add 0* and to the result add notation 1 or 3–9 from Table 2, e.g., exchange rate between currencies of developing countries and Europe 332.45609172404
Do not follow add instructions under —091 in Table 1

Give priority in notation to the currency of a jurisdiction or group of jurisdictions coming first in Table 2
(Option: Give priority in notation to the currency of the jurisdiction requiring local emphasis, e.g., libraries in Europe class exchange rate between currencies of Europe and developing countries in 332.45609401724)

*Add 00 for standard subdivisions; see instructions at beginning of Table 1

.456 093–.456 099		Exchange rates of specific currencies and groups of currencies in specific continents, countries, localities

Add to base number 332.45609 notation 3–9 from Table 2, e.g., exchange rates of currency of United Kingdom 332.4560941; then add 0* and to the result add notation 1 or 3–9 from Table 2, e.g., exchange rate between currencies of United Kingdom and United States 332.4560941073
Do not use add table under —093–099 in Table 1

Give priority in notation to the currency of a jurisdiction or group of jurisdictions coming first in Table 2
(Option: Give priority in notation to the currency of the jurisdiction requiring local emphasis, e.g., libraries in United States class exchange rate between currencies of United States and United Kingdom in 332.4560973041)

.456 2   Determination by supply and demand

Standard subdivisions are added for either or both topics in heading

Class here floating exchange rates

.456 4   Determination by government regulation of exchange rates

For determination by international agreement, see 332.4566

.456 6   Determination by international agreement

Class here international monetary policy, international monetary reform

Class comprehensive works on monetary policy in 332.46

For International Monetary Fund, see 332.152

.46   **Monetary policy**

Including minting policies and practices

Class here managed currency

For relation of central banks to monetary policy, see 332.112; for international monetary policy, see 332.4566; for use of monetary policy for economic stabilization, see 339.53

[.460 9]   Historical, geographic, persons treatment

Do not use; class in 332.49

.49   **Historical, geographic, persons treatment of money and monetary policy**

Add to base number 332.49 notation 001–9 from Table 2, e.g., money and monetary policy in India 332.4954
Subdivisions are added for money, monetary policy, or both

.5   **Other mediums of exchange**

Including barter instruments

*Add 00 for standard subdivisions; see instructions at beginning of Table 1

.55   Commercial paper

> Class comprehensive works on commercial paper, commercial paper as a credit instrument in 332.77

.56   Social credit money

.6   Investment and investments

> Standard subdivisions are added for either or both topics in heading
>
> Class here investment prospectuses, portfolio analysis and management
>
> Class description and analysis of business enterprises issuing securities in 338.7–338.8

SUMMARY

332.604	**Special topics**
.62	**Brokerage firms**
.63	**Forms of investment**
.64	**Exchange of securities and commodities**
.65	**International exchange of securities**
.66	**Investment banks**
.67	**Investments by field of investment, kind of enterprise, kind of investor; investment guides**

[.601 12]   Forecasting and forecasts

> Do not use; class in 332.678

.604   Special topics

.604 2   Investment for specific purposes

> Including investment for tax advantages

[.604 201–.604 209]   Standard subdivisions

> Do not use; class in 332.601–332.609

.62   Brokerage firms

> Including discount brokers, investment counselors
>
> Class real estate brokerage in 333.33

.63   Forms of investment

> Including art, coins, stamps
>
> Class here speculation in specific forms of investment
>
> Class speculation in multiple forms of investment in 332.645; class investment in specific kinds of businesses regardless of form in 332.67
>
> *See also 332.0414 for comprehensive works on fixed (investment) capital, 332.62 for brokerage firms*

.632   Securities, real estate, commodities

Standard subdivisions are added for securities, real estate, commodities together; for securities alone

Class here evaluation of growth potential, safety features, yield; speculation in securities; comprehensive works on financial futures

Class buying and selling procedures for securities and commodities in 332.64; class buying and selling procedures for real estate in 333.33; class comprehensive works on speculation in 332.645

For foreign exchange futures, see 332.45

.632 04   Special topics

.632 042   Evaluation techniques for securities, real estate, commodities

Standard subdivisions are added for securities, real estate, commodities together; for securities alone

Including analyzing corporate balance sheets, reading financial pages and ticker tapes

.632 044   General types of securities

Including corporate securities; fixed rate, variable rate securities; gilt-edged securities

Class stocks (shares) in 332.6322; class bonds in 332.6323

See Manual at 332.632044 vs. 332.6323: Gilt-edged securities

.632 2   Stocks (Shares)

Including rights and warrants

See Manual at 332.6322 vs. 332.6323

.632 21   Valuation

Including dividends paid, price-earnings ratio

For prices, see 332.63222

.632 22   Prices

.632 220 21   Tabulated and related materials

Do not use for statistics; class in 332.63222

.632 23   Common stock

Class valuation in 332.63221; class prices in 332.63222; class speculation, works about penny stocks that emphasize speculation in 332.63228

.632 25   Preferred stock

Class valuation in 332.63221; class prices in 332.63222; class speculation in 332.63228

.632 28	Speculation

Including buying on margin, put and call transactions for stock, stock index futures, stock options

.632 3	Bonds

Class here interest rate futures and options, mortgage bonds and certificates

See Manual at 332.632044 vs. 332.6323: Gilt-edged securities; also at 332.6322 vs. 332.6323

.632 32	Government bonds, notes, certificates, bills

Including treasury bills

For municipal bonds, see 332.63233

.632 33	Municipal bonds
.632 34	Corporate bonds
.632 4	Real estate

See also 332.72 for real estate finance, 333.33 for real estate business, 332.0414 for comprehensive works on fixed (investment) capital

---

> 332.632 42–332.632 44 Types of investment in real estate

Class comprehensive works in 332.6324

.632 42	Land

Class sale of real estate in 333.333

.632 43	Buildings and other fixtures

Standard subdivisions are added for buildings and other fixtures, for buildings alone

Class sale of buildings and other fixtures in 333.338

See also 643.12 for how to select a home, 647.92–647.94 for management of multiple dwellings

.632 44	Mortgages

See also 332.6323 for mortgage bonds and certificates

.632 47	Real estate investment trusts

Including real estate syndication

.632 7	Investment company securities

Including investment trusts, money market funds, mutual funds, unit trusts

For real estate investment trusts, see 332.63247

.632 8	Commodities

Class here commodity futures and options, speculation in commodities

See also 332.644 for exchange of commodities and commodities exchanges

.64	Exchange of securities and commodities

Class here buying and selling of securities and commodities; organization, procedures, activities of organized exchanges

See also 332.632 for advice on investing in specific forms of securities and commodities, 332.678 for general investment guides

.642	Exchange of securities and securities exchanges

Standard subdivisions are added for either or both topics in heading

Class here stock exchanges

Class brokerage firms in 332.62; class speculation in 332.632

For over-the-counter market, see 332.643; for international exchange of securities, see 332.65

[.642 094–.642 099]	Geographic treatment in modern world

Do not use; class in 332.6424–332.6429

.642 4–.642 9	Exchange of securities and securities exchanges in the modern world

Add to base number 332.642 notation 4–9 from Table 2, e.g., exchange of securities in the Netherlands 332.642492
Subdivisions are added for either or both topics in heading
When adding from Table 2 for a specific exchange, use the number for the primary area served by the exchange, e.g., New York Stock Exchange 332.64273, Pacific Stock Exchange 332.64279

.643	Over-the-counter market
.644	Exchange of commodities

Class here commodity exchanges, commodity futures and options markets

Class speculation in 332.6328

.644 1	Products of agriculture

Add to base number 332.6441 the numbers following 63 in 633–638, e.g., soybeans 332.6441334

.644 2	Products of mineral industries

Add to base number 332.6442 the numbers following 553 in 553.2–553.9, e.g., copper 332.644243

.645   **Speculation**

Speculation in multiple forms of investment

Including arbitrage, buying on margin, futures, hedging, put and call transactions

Class speculation in specific forms of investment in 332.63; class guides to speculation in 332.678

See also 332.45 for speculation in foreign exchange

.65   **International exchange of securities**

Sale and purchase of securities offered by nationals of one jurisdiction to nationals of another jurisdiction

Class comprehensive works on international investment in 332.673

.66   **Investment banks**

Class here investment banking (underwriting and sale of security issues), issuing houses

For international investment banks, see 332.15

See also 332.1754 for investment services of commercial banks

.67   **Investments by field of investment, kind of enterprise, kind of investor; investment guides**

Class investment in specific forms of securities with the form in 332.63, e.g., investment in railroad stocks 332.6322 (*not* 332.6722); class a specific aspect of investment with the aspect in 332.64–332.66, e.g., speculation by pension funds 332.645 (*not* 332.67254)

.671   **Investment in specific kinds of enterprises and by specific kinds of investors**

For domestic investment, see 332.672; for international investment, see 332.673

[.671 01–.671 09]   Standard subdivisions

Do not use; class in 332.6701–332.6709

.671 2–.671 5   Subdivisions for investment in specific kinds of enterprises and by specific kinds of investors

Add to base number 332.671 the numbers following 332.672 in 332.6722–332.6725, e.g., investments by government agencies 332.67152

.672   **Domestic investment**

.672 08   History and description with respect to kinds of persons

Class here domestic investment by specific kinds of individuals [*formerly* 332.67255]

.672 2	Domestic investment in specific kinds of enterprises

Including insurance companies, petroleum industry, railroads; investment in small business

Class investment in specific kinds of enterprises by specific kinds of investors in 332.6725

See Manual at 332 vs. 338, 658.15

[.672 201–.672 209]	Standard subdivisions

Do not use; class in 332.67201–332.67209

.672 5	Domestic investment by specific kinds of investors
[.672 501–.672 509]	Standard subdivisions

Do not use; class in 332.67201–332.67209

.672 52	Domestic investment by governments and their agencies
.672 53	Domestic investment by private investors

For domestic investment by specific kinds of individuals, see 332.67208; for domestic investment by specific kinds of institutions, see 332.67254

.672 54	Domestic investment by specific kinds of institutions

Including life insurance companies, pension funds

Class investments by banks in 332.1754

[.672 540 1–.672 540 9]	Standard subdivisions

Do not use; class in 332.67201–332.67209

[.672 55]	Domestic investment by specific kinds of individuals

Relocated to 332.67208

.673	International investment

Class international investment banking in 332.15; class specific forms of international investment in 332.63; class history and description of international business ventures and subsidiaries in 338.88; class initiation of international business enterprises (including subsidiaries) in 658.1149

For international exchange of securities, see 332.65

.673 09	Historical, geographic, persons treatment

Class here the advantages and disadvantages of establishing businesses in specific areas, investment in specific areas not originating in other specific areas

Class the advantages and disadvantages of establishing businesses in specific areas resulting from government policy in 332.6732

> *See also 338.09 for works describing where in fact industry is located*

> *See Manual at 338.09 vs. 332.67309, 338.6042, 346.07, 658.11, T1—0681, 658.21, T1—0682*

.673 093–.673 099	Specific continents, countries, localities

> *For investment originating in specific continents and countries, see 332.6733–332.6739*

.673 1	International investment by specific kinds of investors
[.673 101–.673 109]	Standard subdivisions

Do not use; class in 332.67301–332.67309

.673 12	International investment by governments
.673 14	International investment by private investors

Institutional and individual

.673 2	Government policy

Including international control

.673 22	Incentives and obstacles in country of investment

Add to base number 332.67322 notation 3–9 from Table 2, e.g., incentives and obstacles in Brazil 332.6732281
Subdivisions are added for either or both topics in heading

.673 24	Incentives and obstacles in country of investor

Add to base number 332.67324 notation 3–9 from Table 2, e.g., incentives and obstacles to overseas investment by British citizens 332.6732441
Subdivisions are added for either or both topics in heading

.673 3–.673 9	Investment originating in specific continents and countries

Add to base number 332.673 notation 3–9 from Table 2 for origin of investment, e.g., British foreign investments 332.67341; then, for place of investment, add 0* and to the result add notation 1 or 3–9 from Table 2, e.g., British foreign investments in Brazil 332.67341081

Class policies of specific governments in 332.6732

---

*Add 00 for standard subdivisions; see instructions at beginning of Table 1

.678	Investment guides

Including forecasting, formula plans, speculation

Class guides to specific forms of investment in 332.63; class guides to investment by type of investor, type of enterprise, field of investment in 332.671–332.673

.7   Credit

Class here specific types of credit

Class credit functions of banks in 332.1; class credit functions of specialized banking institutions in 332.2; class credit functions of credit and loan institutions in 332.3; class interest and discount in 332.8

See Manual at 332.7 vs. 332.1

.71	Agricultural credit
.72	Real estate finance and mortgages

Standard subdivisions are added for either or both topics in heading

Class here discrimination in mortgage loans; mortgage delinquencies and defaults

Class finance on farm real estate in 332.71

See also 332.32 for mortgage institutions, 332.6323 for mortgage bonds and certificates, 332.63244 for mortgages as an investment

.722	Home (Residential) finance
.74	Other forms of credit
.742	Commercial, mercantile, industrial credit

Including export credit, small business loans

.743	Personal loans

Including consumer credit

.75	Credit restrictions and collapse

Class here bankruptcy

.76	Credit instruments

Including checks, debit cards, money orders

Class certificates of deposit in 332.1752

For commercial paper, see 332.77

.765	Credit cards

Class here comprehensive works on credit cards

For credit cards issued by a specific type of financial institution, see the type in 332.1, e.g., commercial banks 332.178

.77 Commercial paper

Including acceptances, drafts, letters of credit, promissory notes

Class here comprehensive works on commercial paper

For commercial paper as an exchange medium, see 332.55

.8 Interest and discount

.82 Interest

For usury, see 332.83

See also 332.6323 for interest rate futures

.83 Usury

.84 Discount

Including rediscount

.9 Counterfeiting, forgery, alteration

See also 364.133 for counterfeiting as a crime, 364.163 for forgery as a crime, 737.4 for counterfeit coins, 769.55 for counterfeit paper money, 769.562 for counterfeit stamps

333 Economics of land and energy

Land: all natural and man-made resources over which possession of the earth gives control

Class here land as a factor of production

See Manual at 333.7–333.9 vs. 333; also at 333.73–333.78 vs. 333, 333.1–333.5

SUMMARY

333.001–.009	**Standard subdivisions**
.01–.08	**[Theories and land surveys]**
.1	**Public ownership of land**
.2	**Ownership of land by nongovernmental groups**
.3	**Individual (Private) ownership of land**
.4	**Absentee ownership**
.5	**Renting and leasing land**
.7	**Natural resources and energy**
.8	**Subsurface resources**
.9	**Other natural resources**

.001 Philosophy and theory

Do not use for theories; class in 333.01

.001 2 Classification

For land classification, see 333.73012

.002–.009 Standard subdivisions

.01	Theories

.012	Rent

Return produced by ownership of land after deduction of all outlays for labor and capital

Including Ricardo's theory of earning power of land in terms of its marginal productivity

See also 333.5 for renting and leasing land and natural resources

.08	Land surveys

Class here work of chartered surveyors (United Kingdom)

For land surveying techniques, see 526.9. For specific kinds of land surveys, see the kind, e.g., public land surveys 333.18, land use surveys 333.7313

See also 631.47 for surveys that focus on agricultural use of soils

---

> ### 333.1–333.5 Ownership of land

Ownership: right to possession and use; right to transfer of possession and use

Land: all natural and man-made resources over which possession of the earth gives control

Class here the kind of control that stems from ownership; ownership of natural resources

Class comprehensive works in 333.3

See also 333.7–333.9 for usage of natural resources, for control of such usage not stemming from ownership

See Manual at 333.73–333.78 vs. 333, 333.1–333.5; also at 346.043 vs. 333.1–333.5

.1	**Public ownership of land**

Land: all natural and man-made resources over which possession of the earth gives control

Class public control of privately owned lands in 333.717; class comprehensive works on land policy in 333.73

See also 333.2 for ownership and control of land by peoples subordinate to another jurisdiction, 343.02 for law of public property

.11	Acquisition and disposal of specific kinds of lands

Including forests, highways and streets, recreational lands

[.110 1–.110 9]	Standard subdivisions

Do not use; class in 333.101–333.109

.13   Acquisition

   Including eminent domain, expropriation, purchase

   Class here evaluation of lands for government acquisition

   Class acquisition of specific kinds of land in 333.11

   For nationalization, see 333.14

.14   Nationalization

.16   Disposal

   Including grants, leases, sale

   Class disposal of specific kinds of land in 333.11

.18   Public land surveys

   Class surveys of public land use in 333.7313; class interdisciplinary works on land surveys in 333.08

   See also 526.9 for surveying techniques

.2   Ownership of land by nongovernmental groups

   Land: all natural and man-made resources over which possession of the earth gives control

   Including common lands; enclosure of common lands; open-field system; ownership and control of land by peoples subordinate to another jurisdiction, e.g., Amerindian lands in the United States

   For corporate ownership, see 333.324

.3   Individual (Private) ownership of land

   Land: all natural and man-made resources over which possession of the earth gives control

   Including subdivision of private land

   Class here comprehensive works on ownership of land

   For public ownership, see 333.1; for ownership by nongovernmental groups, see 333.2; for absentee ownership, see 333.4

.31   Land reform

   Class here land redistribution, settlement and resettlement of people on the land

   See also 333.2 for enclosure of common lands

[.310 94–.310 99]   Treatment by specific continents, countries, localities of modern world

   Do not use; class in 333.314–333.319

.314–.319	Land reform in specific continents, countries, localities of modern world

Add to base number 333.31 notation 4–9 from Table 2, e.g., land reform in Latin America 333.318

.32	Types of tenure

.322	Feudal tenure

.323	Individual tenure

For corporate ownership, see 333.324

.323 2	Complete ownership (Fee simple)

Full right to possession, use, transfer of possession and use

.323 4	Qualified ownership

Ownership with restrictions on use or transfer

Including entails, life estates, time-sharing

.324	Corporate ownership

.33	Transfer of possession and of right to use

Standard subdivisions are added for either or both topics in heading

Including consolidation of holdings

Class here comprehensive works on real estate business

Class land reform in 333.31

For government acquisition and disposal, see 333.1; for renting and leasing, see 333.5; for real estate development, see 333.7315

See also 332.6324 for real estate investment, 332.72 for real-estate finance

.332	Value and price of land

Standard subdivisions are added for value and price together, for value alone

Class here valuation (appraisal)

Class valuation for government acquisition and disposal in 333.11–333.16; class value and price of specific kinds of land in 333.335–333.339; class valuation for tax purposes in 352.44

.332 2	Real estate market

Class here economic and social factors affecting exchange of real estate

Class price in 333.3323

.332 3	Price

.332 302 1   Tabulated and related materials

> Do not use for statistics; class in 333.3323

.333   Sale and gift

Standard subdivisions are added for sale and gift together, for sale alone

Class sale and gift of specific kinds of land in 333.335–333.339

> 333.335–333.339   Transfer of possession and use of specific kinds of land

Class here transfer of possession and use of specific kinds of real estate, of specific kinds of natural resources

Except for modifications shown under specific entries, add to each subdivision identified by * as follows:

2   Value and price

> Standard subdivisions are added for value and price together, for value alone
>
> Class here valuation (appraisal)

22   Real estate market

> Class here economic and social factors affecting exchange of real estate
>
> Class price in 23

23   Price

3   Sale and gift

> Standard subdivisions are added for sale and gift together, for sale alone

5   Renting and leasing

> Standard subdivisions are added for renting and leasing together, for renting alone
>
> Add to 5 the numbers following 333.5 in 333.53–333.56, e.g., share renting 563

Class comprehensive works in 333.33

.335   *Rural lands   Agricultural lands

.335 7   *Forest lands

.336   *Industrial lands

Including transportation space, e.g., airport space, railroad rights-of-way

Class works that emphasize buildings in 333.338

.337   *Urban lands

Residential and commercial lands

Class works that emphasize buildings in 333.338

For industrial lands, see 333.336

---

*Add as instructed under 333.335–333.339

.338	*Buildings and other fixtures Residential buildings

Including apartments, condominiums, mobile homes

.338 7	*Commercial and industrial buildings

Subdivisions are added for either or both topics in heading

.339	Other natural resources

Appraisal, gift, leasing, renting, sale, market

Including rights to use of minerals, water, air space

.4	**Absentee ownership**
.5	**Renting and leasing land**

Land: all natural and man-made resources over which possession of the earth gives control

Class renting and leasing specific kinds of land in 333.335–333.339

.53	Tenancy

Including tenancy for years (for a specified time period), tenancy from year to year, tenancy at will

For landlord-tenant relations, see 333.54

.54	Landlord-tenant relations
.56	Types of renting
.562	Cash renting
.563	Share renting

Class here percentage renting

For sharecropping, see 333.335563

.7	**Natural resources and energy**

Standard subdivisions are added for natural resources and energy together, for natural resources alone

Aspects other than ownership

Class here raw materials; interdisciplinary works on the environment

Except for modifications shown under specific entries, add to each subdivision identified by * as follows:
01–09   Standard subdivisions

(continued)

---

*Add as instructed under 333.335–333.339

.7   **Natural resources and energy (continued)**

1   General topics

For general topics of a specific kind of resource, see the kind, e.g., control of usage of mountains as recreational areas 333.784 (not 333.7817)

[101–109]   Standard subdivisions

Do not use; class in 01–09

11   Reserves (Stock, Supply)

Quantity available for use

Including shortages

12   Requirements (Need, Demand)

13   Consumption (Utilization)

Class consumption control in 17

Do not add for specific uses (e.g., water for irrigation); class with the subject in 333.7–333.9 without further subdivision

137   Abuse and wastage

Standard subdivisions are added for either or both topics in heading

Class here description of abused resources, consequences of abuse and wastage

Class reclamation, rehabilitation, restoration of abused resources in 153; class prevention of abuse and wastage in 16; class pollution in 363.73

14   Environmental impact studies

Class studies emphasizing abuse and wastage in 137

See Manual at 333.714

>15–17   Management and control

Class here citizen participation, planning, policy.

Class comprehensive works in 333.7–333.9 without adding from this table

15   Development

152   Improvement

153   Reclamation, rehabilitation, restoration

Standard subdivisions are added for any or all topics in heading

Class reclamation that is not restoration to a previous state in 152

158   Subsidies

16   Conservation and protection

Standard subdivisions are added for either or both topics in heading

Class control of usage in 17

17   Control of usage

Including allocation, price control, rationing, ways and means of efficient use

Do not add for specific uses (e.g., water for irrigation); class with the subject in 333.7–333.9 without further subdivision

Class ownership of land in 333.1–333.5; class economic geology in 553; class interdisciplinary works on consumption in 339.47

(continued)

.7   Natural resources and energy (continued)

> *For subsurface resources, see 333.8; for natural resources other than land,
> energy, subsurface resources, see 333.9. For other aspects of the
> environment, see the aspect, e.g., environmental protection 363.7*
>
> *See Manual at 333.7–333.9; also at 333.7–333.9 vs. 333; also at
> 333.7–333.9 vs. 508, 913–919, 930–990: National parks and monuments;
> also at 333.7–333.9 vs. 363.6; also at 363*

SUMMARY

**.701–.71   Standard subdivisions and general topics of natural resources and
              energy**

> Add to base number 333.7 notation 01–1 from table under 333.7, e.g.,
> environmental impact studies 333.714; however, for conservation and
> protection, see 333.72
>> Subdivisions are added for natural resources and energy together, for
>> natural resources alone
>
> *See Manual at 333.714*

.72   Conservation and protection

> Standard subdivisions are added for either or both topics in heading
>
> Class conservation and protection of a specific type of natural resource with
> the resource in 333.73–333.95, plus notation 16 from table under 333.7,
> e.g., conservation of wilderness areas 333.78216
>
> *See Manual at 333.72 vs. 304.28, 363.7*

.73   **Land**

Aspects other than ownership

Including kinds of land by physical condition, e.g., mountainous land, sand dunes

Class here river basins

Class ownership aspects of land in 333.1–333.5; class arid and semiarid lands in 333.736; class comprehensive works on natural areas established for land conservation in 333.7316

For kinds of land by use, see 333.74–333.78; for shorelands and related areas, see 333.917; for submerged lands, wetlands, see 333.918. For specific types of natural areas established for conservation, see the type, e.g., wilderness areas 333.78216

See Manual at 333.73–333.78 vs. 333, 333.1–333.5; also at 333.76 vs. 333.73

.730 1–.731   Standard subdivisions and general topics of land

Add to base number 333.73 notation 01–1 from table under 333.7, e.g., real estate development 333.7315, comprehensive works on soil and water conservation 333.7316

Class soil and water conservation in rural lands in 333.7616; class real estate development in urban lands in 333.7715; class zoning of urban lands in 333.7717; class water conservation in 333.9116; class pollution control in 363.73966; class comprehensive works on real estate business in 333.33

.736   *Arid and semiarid lands

Class here desertification

Subdivisions are added for either or both topics in heading

>   333.74–333.78   Kinds of land by use

Class comprehensive works in 333.73

.74   *Pasture (Grazing) lands

See Manual at 333.73–333.78 vs. 333, 333.1–333.5

.75   *Forest lands

Class here national forests; jungles, rain forests, woodlands; old-growth forests; timber resources

Class parks, recreational, wilderness areas in 333.78

See also 333.95397 for wood as a fuel

See Manual at 333.73–333.78 vs. 333, 333.1–333.5; also at 338.1749 vs. 333.75

*Add as instructed under 333.7

.76   *Rural lands   Agricultural lands

Class rural lands of a specific physical condition not devoted to a specific use in 333.73

For pasture lands, see 333.74; for forest lands, see 333.75; for rural recreational lands, see 333.78

See Manual at 333.73–333.78 vs. 333, 333.1–333.5; also at 333.76 vs. 333.73

.765   *Mined lands   Surface-mined lands

.77   *Urban lands

Including commercial, industrial, residential lands; highways and streets

Class urban mined lands in 333.765; class urban recreational lands in 333.78

See Manual at 333.73–333.78 vs. 333, 333.1–333.5

.78   *Recreational and wilderness areas

Subdivisions are added for recreational and wilderness areas together, for recreational areas alone

Class wildlife in 333.954; class wildlife refuges in 333.95416

See also 363.68 for park and recreation services

See Manual at 333.73–333.78 vs. 333, 333.1–333.5

.782   *Wilderness areas

For specific kinds of wilderness areas, see 333.784

.783   *Parks

.784   Specific kinds of recreational and wilderness areas

Including forests, mountains

[.784 01–.784 09]   Standard subdivisions

Do not use; class in 333.7801–333.7809

>   333.784 4–333.784 6   Recreational use of water

Class here recreational use of land adjoining water, e.g., beaches, shores

Class comprehensive works on recreational use of water in 333.784; class comprehensive works on uses of water and land adjoining it in 333.91

.784 4   Lakes

.784 5   Rivers and streams

Standard subdivisions are added for either or both topics in heading

*Add as instructed under 333.7

.784 6 Reservoirs

See also 333.7844 for lakes

.79 Energy

Class here power resources, production of energy, interdisciplinary works on energy

Class electric power in 333.7932; class extraction of energy resources and comprehensive works on the economics of mineral fuels in 338.2; class interdisciplinary works on mineral fuels in 553

For a specific form of energy, a specific energy resource not provided for here, see the form or resource, e.g., fossil fuels 333.82, geothermal energy 333.88, hydroelectricity 333.914, wind energy 333.92, biomass as an energy resource 333.9539; for a noneconomic aspect of energy, see the aspect, e.g., energy management 658.2, fuel technology 662.6

.790 1–.791 Standard subdivisions and general topics of energy

Add to base number 333.79 notation 01–1 from table under 333.7, e.g., energy development and production 333.7915

Class utilization of waste heat in 333.793

.792 Primary forms of energy

Resources used directly to perform work, to produce other forms of energy

.792 3 Solar energy

Including electricity derived from solar energy, e.g., with photovoltaic cells

Class distribution of electricity derived from solar energy in 333.7932

.792 301–.792 31 Standard subdivisions and general topics of solar energy

Add to base number 333.7923 notation 01–1 from table under 333.7, e.g., development of solar energy and generation of other forms of energy from solar energy 333.792315

.792 33 Financial aspects

Including prices

.792 4 Nuclear energy

Class here electricity derived from nuclear energy

Class distribution of electricity derived from nuclear energy in 333.7932; class nuclear fuels in 333.85

.792 401–.792 41 Standard subdivisions and general topics of nuclear energy

Add to base number 333.7924 notation 01–1 from table under 333.7, e.g., development and generation of nuclear energy 333.792415

.792 43	Financial aspects
	Including prices
.793	Secondary forms of energy

Energy produced through use of other resources

Including cogeneration of electric power and heat, district heating

Class economics of synthetic fuel production in 338.4766266

For secondary forms of energy derived from a specific resource, see the resource, e.g., electricity derived from nuclear energy 333.7924

.793 2	Electrical energy

Including distribution of electrical energy regardless of resource from which the electricity was derived, rural electrification

Class here electricity derived from fossil fuels, electrical utilities, comprehensive works on electrical energy

For electricity derived from a specific resource other than fossil fuels, see the resource, e.g., electricity derived from water 333.914

.793 201–.793 21	Standard subdivisions and general topics of electrical energy

Add to base number 333.7932 notation 01–1 from table under 333.7, e.g., development and generation of electrical energy 333.793215

.793 23	Financial aspects
.793 231	Prices
.793 8	†Energy from waste materials

Class distribution of electricity derived from waste materials in 333.7932; class chemical technology of energy from waste materials in 662.87

For energy from biological wastes, see 333.9539

.794	†Renewable energy resources

Class here alternative energy resources

Class distribution of electricity derived from renewable energy resources in 333.7932

For a specific renewable or alternative energy resource, see the resource, e.g., solar energy 333.7923

†Add as instructed under 333.7, except use 15 for both development and generation of energy

.796   Energy for specific uses

Including energy for military use

Unless other instructions are given, class a subject with aspects in two or more subdivisions of 333.796 in the number coming last, e.g., energy use in school buildings 333.7964 (*not* 333.7962)

Class a specific kind of energy for specific uses with the kind of energy, e.g., energy from petroleum for transportation use 333.8232 (*not* 333.7968)

[.796 01–.796 09]   Standard subdivisions

Do not use; class in 333.7901–333.7909

.796 2   *Energy for use in buildings

Including use in construction

See also 624 for technical aspects of energy use in construction

.796 3   *Energy for residential use

.796 4   *Energy for social service institutions

Including churches, hospitals, prisons, schools

.796 5   *Energy for industrial use

Class here manufacturing use

Class energy use in construction of buildings in 333.7962

For food processing use, see 333.7966

.796 6   *Energy for use in agriculture and food processing

.796 8   *Energy for use in transportation and commerce

Subdivisions are added for transportation and commerce together, for transportation alone

.796 89   *Energy for commercial use

.8   **Subsurface resources**

Class here strategic materials; supply in storage, shortages, surpluses, demand, and projections of these

Class mined lands, including surface-mined lands in 333.765; class extraction of subsurface resources and comprehensive works on the economics of subsurface resources in 338.2; class interdisciplinary works on subsurface resources in 553

For ownership aspects of subsurface resources, see 333.1–333.5; for groundwater, see 333.9104

See Manual at 333.7–333.9; also at 333.7–333.9 vs. 508, 913–919, 930–990: National parks and monuments; also at 553; also at 553 vs. 333.8, 338.2

*Add as instructed under 333.7

.801–.81	Standard subdivisions and general topics of subsurface resources

Add to base number 333.8 notation 01–1 from table under 333.7, e.g., reserves in storage of subsurface resources 333.811; however, for development, see 338.2; for reserves in nature, see 553

.82	Fossil fuels

Class electricity derived from fossil fuels in 333.7932

.820 1–.821	Standard subdivisions and general topics of fossil fuels

Add to base number 333.82 notation 01–1 from table under 333.7, e.g., reserves in storage of fossil fuels 333.8211; however, for development, see 338.272; for reserves in nature, see 553.2

.822	Coal

.822 01–.822 1	Standard subdivisions and general topics of coal

Add to base number 333.822 notation 01–1 from table under 333.7, e.g., reserves in storage of coal 333.82211; however, for development, see 338.2724; for reserves in nature, see 553.24

.823	Oil and natural gas

.823 01–.823 1	Standard subdivisions and general topics of oil and natural gas

Add to base number 333.823 notation 01–1 from table under 333.7, e.g., reserves in storage of oil and natural gas 333.82311; however, for development, see 338.2728; for reserves in nature, see 553.28

.823 2	Oil

Petroleum in its narrow sense

.823 201–.823 21	Standard subdivisions and general topics of oil

Add to base number 333.8232 notation 01–1 from table under 333.7, e.g., reserves in storage of oil 333.823211; however, for development, see 338.27282; for reserves in nature, see 553.282

.823 3	Natural gas

See also 363.63 for gas distribution services of public utilities

.823 301–.823 31	Standard subdivisions and general topics of natural gas

Add to base number 333.8233 notation 01–1 from table under 333.7, e.g., reserves in storage of natural gas 333.823311; however, for development, see 338.27285; for reserves in nature, see 553.285

.85	Minerals

Class comprehensive works on the economics of minerals in 338.2; class interdisciplinary works on nonmetallic minerals in 553; class interdisciplinary works on metals in 669

.850 1–.851   Standard subdivisions and general topics of minerals

> Add to base number 333.85 notation 01–1 from table under 333.7, e.g., reserves in storage of minerals 333.8511; however, for development, see 338.2; for reserves in nature, see 553

.852–.859   Specific minerals

> Add to base number 333.85 the numbers following 553 in 553.2–553.9, e.g., tin 333.85453, uranium 333.854932; however, for fossil fuels, see 333.82; for groundwater, see 333.9104

.88   *Geothermal energy

> Class here electricity derived from geothermal energy, thermal waters

> Class distribution of electricity derived from geothermal energy in 333.7932

.9   **Other natural resources**

> Add to each subdivision identified by * as instructed under 333.7, e.g., conservation and protection of mammals 333.95416

> *For ownership aspects of other natural resources, see 333.1–333.5*

> *See Manual at 333.7–333.9; also at 333.7–333.9 vs. 508, 913–919, 930–990: National parks and monuments*

SUMMARY

333.91	**Water**	
.92	**Air**	
.94	**Space**	
.95	**Biological resources**	

.91   Water

> Class here aquatic resources, land adjoining water, comprehensive works on the economics of aquatic resources

> Class interdisciplinary works on water in 553.7

>> *For a specific aquatic resource, see the resource, e.g., minerals 333.85, fishes 333.956; for a specific aspect of water not provided for here, see the aspect, e.g., recreational use of water and land adjoining it 333.7844–333.7846, regulation and control of distribution of water to consumers 363.61*

>> *See Manual at 363.61; also at 553*

.910 01–.910 09   Standard subdivisions

.910 4   †Groundwater (Subsurface water)

> Class subsurface thermal waters in 333.88

---

*Add as instructed under 333.7

†Add as instructed under 333.7, except use 11 only for reserves in storage; class reserves in nature in 553.7

.911	General topics of water

Class water for specific uses in 333.912–333.915; class comprehensive works on soil and water conservation in 333.7316. Class general topics of a specific kind of water with the kind, e.g., general topics of rivers and streams 331.9162

[.911 01–.911 09]	Standard subdivisions

Do not use; class in 333.91001–333.91009

.911 1–.911 7	Subdivisions for topics of water

Add to base number 333.911 the numbers following 1 in notation 11–17 from table under 333.7, e.g., reserves in storage, as in reservoirs and storage tanks 333.9111; however, for water pollution, see 363.7394; for reserves in nature, see 553.7

>	333.912–333.915 Water for specific uses

Class comprehensive works in 333.91

For recreational use, see 333.7844–333.7846

.912	†Water for domestic (residential) and industrial uses
.912 2	Water for domestic (residential) use

Including drinking and washing

.912 3	Water for industrial use

Class water for generation of energy in 333.914; class water for transportation in 333.915

.913	†Water for irrigation
.914	*Water for generation of energy

Including thermal ocean power conversion

Class here hydroelectricity

Use 11 from table under 333.7 for energy-producing potential of water and use 15 for both development and generation of energy, e.g., potential hydroelectric energy resources of Idaho 333.9141109796, hydropower generation in the Columbia River basin 333.9141509797

.914 11	Energy-producing potential of water
.914 15	Development and generation of energy
.915	†Water for transportation

*Add as instructed under 333.7

†Add as instructed under 333.7, except use 11 only for reserves in storage; class reserves in nature in 553.7

> 333.916–333.918 Specific kinds of water and land adjoining it

Class specific uses of specific kinds of water in 333.912–333.915; class comprehensive works in 333.91

.916   Bodies of water

Class lands adjoining specific kinds of bodies of water in 333.917; class submerged lands and wetlands related to specific types of bodies of water in 333.918

.916 2   †Rivers and streams

Subdivisions are added for either or both topics in heading

Class river basins in 333.73

.916 3   †Lakes and ponds

Subdivisions are added for either or both topics in heading

For saltwater lakes, see 333.9164

.916 4   Oceans and seas

Including bays, gulfs, estuaries, saltwater lakes

.916 401–.916 41   Standard subdivisions and general topics of oceans and seas

Add to base number 333.9164 notation 01–1 from table under 333.7, e.g., conservation and protection of seas 333.916416; however, for reserves in nature, see 551.46
Subdivisions are added for oceans, seas, or both

.917   *Shorelands and related areas

Including beaches, tidelands in the sense of lands that are overflowed by the tide but exposed by low water

Subdivisions are added for shorelands and related areas, for shorelands alone

Class river basins in 333.73; class recreational use of shorelands and related areas in 333.784; class comprehensive works on tidelands in 333.918

---

*Add as instructed under 333.7

†Add as instructed under 333.7, except use 11 only for reserves in storage; class reserves in nature in 553.7

.918   *Submerged lands and wetlands

Class here continental shelves, tidelands in the sense of lands underlying the ocean beyond the low tidemark but within a nation's territorial waters, comprehensive works on tidelands

Subdivisions are added for either or both topics in heading

Class recreational use in 333.784

For tidelands in the sense of lands that are overflowed by the tide but exposed by low water, see 333.917

See also 333.916 for works focusing on bodies of water rather than the land they submerge

.92   *Air

Class here wind energy, use of wind for generation of electricity

Class distribution of wind-generated electricity in 333.7932

.94   Space

See Manual at 333.94 vs. 338.0919

.95   *Biological resources

Class here biodiversity, biosphere

Unless other instructions are given, class a subject with aspects in two or more subdivisions of 333.95 in the number coming last, e.g., game birds 333.95829 (*not* 333.9549)

SUMMARY

333.952	**Specific kinds of biological resources**
.953	**Plants**
.954	**Animals**
.955	**Invertebrates**
.956	**Fishes**
.957	**Reptiles and amphibians**
.958	**Birds**
.959	**Specific kinds of mammals**

.952   Specific kinds of biological resources

Not limited by kind of organisms

Marine biological resources relocated to 333.956

For genetic and germ plasm resources, see 333.9534; for biomass energy, see 333.9539

[.952 01–.952 09]   Standard subdivisions

Do not use; class in 333.9501–333.9509

---

*Add as instructed under 333.7

.952 2	*Rare and endangered species
	Class here extinction, threatened species, vanishing species
	Subdivisions are added for either or both topics in heading
.952 8	*Aquatic biological resources
	Class here freshwater biological resources
	For marine biological resources, see 333.956
.952 88	*Wetland biological resources
.953	*Plants
	Class forests, comprehensive works on timber resources in 333.75
	See also 333.82 for peat
.953 2	*Rare and endangered plants
	Class here threatened, vanishing plants
	Subdivisions are added for either or both topics in heading
.953 3	*Native plants
	Class rare and endangered native plants in 333.9532
.953 4	*Germ plasm resources
	Class here plant varieties; interdisciplinary works on genetic resources, on germ plasm
	For animal genetic resources, germ plasm, see 333.954; for germ plasm, plant varieties in agriculture, see 631.523
.953 8	*Seaweeds
	Class here algae, kelp
.953 9	Plants as sources of energy
	Class here interdisciplinary works on biomass energy
	For animal biomass as an energy resource, see 333.954; for biomass fuel engineering, see 662.88
.953 901–.953 91	Standard subdivisions and general topics of plants as sources of energy
	Add to base number 333.93591 notation 01–1 from table under 333.7, except use 15 for both development and generation of energy, e.g., generation of energy from biomass 333.953915
.953 97	*Fuelwood

*Add as instructed under 333.7

.954   *Animals

                Including biomass energy, genetic resources, germ plasm

                Class here comprehensive works on mammals [*formerly* 333.959], on
                vertebrates; wildlife

                   For invertebrates, see 333.955; for fishes, see 333.956; for reptiles
                   and amphibians, see 333.957; for birds, see 333.958; for specific
                   kinds of mammals, see 333.959

                   See Manual at 338.37 vs. 333.954

.954 2   *Rare and endangered animals

                Class here threatened, vanishing animals

                Subdivisions are added for either or both topics in heading

.954 8   *Aquatic animals

                   For marine animals, see 333.956

.954 88   *Wetland animals

.954 9   *Game animals

                Class economics of hunting in 338.3729

                   For big game animals, see 333.9596

>   **333.955–333.959   Specific taxonomic groups of animals**

                Class comprehensive works in 333.954

                   See Manual at 333.955–333.959 vs. 639.97: Conservation and management

.955   *Invertebrates

                Class here marine invertebrates, shellfish

>   **333.955 3–333.955 5   Marine invertebrates**

                Class comprehensive works in 333.955

.955 3   *Coral reefs

>   **333.955 4–333.955 5   Shellfish**

                Class comprehensive works in 333.955

.955 4   *Mollusks

                Class here Bivalvia

                Class comprehensive works on shellfish in 333.955

---

*Add as instructed under 333.7

.955 41–.955 48   Specific kinds of mollusks

> Add to base number 333.9554 the numbers following 639.4 in 639.41–639.48, e.g., scallops 333.95546; then for each kind of mollusk having its own number, add further as instructed under 333.7 (*not* under 592–599), e.g., supply of scallops 333.9554611

.955 5   *Crustaceans

> Class here Decapoda

.955 54–.955 58   Specific kinds of crustaceans

> Add to base number 333.9555 the numbers following 595.38 in 595.384–595.388, e.g., lobsters 333.95554; then for each kind of crustacean having its own number, add further as instructed under 333.7 (*not* under 592–599), e.g., consumption of lobsters 333.9555413

.955 7   *Insects

.956   *Fishes

> Class here marine biological resources [*formerly* 333.952], comprehensive works on finfish and shellfish
>
> *For shellfish, see 333.955. For a specific kind of marine biological resource not provided for below, see the kind, e.g., marine algae 333.9538, marine mammals 333.9595*

.956 2–.956 7   Specific kinds of fishes

> Add to base number 333.956 the numbers following 597 in 597.2–597.7, e.g., salmons 333.95656; then for each kind of fish having its own number, add further as instructed under 333.7 (*not* under 592–599), e.g., restoration of salmon fisheries 333.95656153

.956 8   *Rare and endangered fishes

> Subdivisions are added for either or both topics in heading
>
> Class specific kinds of rare and endangered fishes in 333.9562–333.9567

.956 9   *Game fishes

> Class specific kinds of game fishes in 333.9562–333.9567; class game fishes in the sense of salmon, trout, graylings in 333.95655; class economics of fishing in 338.3727

.957   *Reptiles and amphibians

> Subdivisions are added for reptiles and amphibians together, for reptiles alone

.957 2   *Rare and endangered reptiles and amphibians

> Subdivisions are added for all topics in heading together, for rare reptiles alone, for endangered reptiles alone

*Add as instructed under 333.7

.957 8–.957 9   Amphibians, specific reptiles

Add to base number 333.957 the numbers following 597 in 597.8–597.9, e.g., turtles 333.95792; then for each kind of reptile or amphibian having its own number, add further as instructed under 333.7 (*not* under 592–599), e.g., protection of turtles 333.9579216; however, for comprehensive works on reptiles, on reptiles and amphibians, see 333.957

.958   *Birds

.958 2   Specific nontaxonomic kinds of birds

[.958 201–.958 209]   Standard subdivisions

Do not use; class in 333.9501–333.9509

.958 22   *Rare and endangered birds

Class here threatened, vanishing birds

Subdivisions are added for either or both topics in heading

.958 28   *Aquatic birds

Class here water birds

Class waterfowl in 333.95841

.958 287   *Sea birds

.958 29   *Game birds

Class lowland game birds in 333.95841; class upland game birds in 333.9586

.958 3–.958 9   Specific kinds of birds

Add to base number 333.958 the numbers following 598 in 598.3–598.9, e.g., wild turkeys 333.958645; then for each kind of bird having its own number, add further as instructed under 333.7 (*not* under 592–599), e.g., demand for wild turkeys 333.95864513

.959   Specific kinds of mammals

Comprehensive works on mammals relocated to 333.954

[.959 01–.959 09]   Standard subdivisions

Do not use; class in 333.95401–333.95409

.959 2–.959 8   Subdivisions for specific kinds of mammals

Add to base number 333.959 the numbers following 599 in 599.2–599.8, e.g., marine mammals, whales 333.9595, big game animals, ungulates 333.9596, carnivores, fur-bearing animals 333.9597; then for each kind of mammal having its own number, add further as instructed under 333.7 (*not* under 592–599), e.g., supply of big game 333.959611

*Add as instructed under 333.7

334 Cooperatives

Voluntary organizations or enterprises owned by and operated for the benefit of those using the services

.060 1 International organizations

Class here international associations of cooperatives [*formerly* 334.0919]

.091 9 Cooperatives in space

International associations of cooperatives relocated to 334.0601

.1 Housing cooperatives

Class here building cooperatives

See also 334.2 for cooperative building associations that are cooperative savings and loan associations

.2 Banking and credit cooperatives

Standard subdivisions are added for either or both topics in heading

.22 Credit unions

Class comprehensive works on thrift institutions in 332.32

.5 Consumer cooperatives

Class consumer housing cooperatives in 334.1; class comprehensive works on cooperative marketing in 334.6813801

[.506 8] Management of consumer cooperatives

Do not use; class in 658.8707

.6 Production cooperatives

.68 Production cooperatives by industry

.681 Production cooperatives in industries other than extractive, manufacturing, construction

Class here service industries

.681 000 1–.681 000 9 Standard subdivisions

.681 001–.681 999 Subdivisions for production cooperatives in industries other than extractive, manufacturing, construction

Add to base number 334.681 notation 001–999, e.g., cooperative marketing by producers and comprehensive works on cooperative marketing 334.6813801, cooperative legal services 334.68134; however, for banking and credit, see 334.2; for consumer cooperatives, see 334.5

.682–.689   Production cooperatives in extractive, manufacturing, construction industries

> Add to base number 334.68 the numbers following 6 in 620–690, e.g., cooperative cattle production 334.68362; however, for building cooperatives, see 334.1; for kibbutzim and moshavim in Israel, see 335.95694; for Communist collective farms, see 338.763

> Cooperative marketing by producers is classed in 334.6813801, e.g., cooperative domestic marketing of cattle by producers 334.6813814162

.7   **Benefit societies**

> Including benevolent, friendly, mutual-aid, provident societies

> *See also 368 for insurance*

335   **Socialism and related systems**

> Standard subdivisions are added for socialism and related systems together, for socialism alone

> Class here state socialism, interdisciplinary works on socialism and related systems

> Class socialism in the sense of communism in 335.43; class comparisons of Communism (Marxism-Leninism) with other systems in 335.437; class socialism in the sense of democratic socialism in 335.5

> *For socialism and communism as political ideologies, see 320.53; for socialist and communist political parties, see 324.217. For a specific topic of economics treated from a socialist or communist point of view, see the topic in economics, e.g., interest 332.82*

> *See Manual at 335 vs. 306.345, 320.53*

> (Option: Class in 330.159)

.001–.009   Standard subdivisions

.02   Utopian systems and schools

> Standard subdivisions are added for either or both topics in heading

> *For specific utopian systems, see 335.1–335.3*

> *See also 301 for ideal societies, 321.07 for ideal states*

> **335.1–335.3 Non-Marxian and quasi-Marxian socialism**

> Class comprehensive works in 335

> *For national socialism, see 335.6; for Christian socialism, see 335.7; for voluntary socialist communities, see 335.9*

.1   **Systems of English origin**

.12	Utopian socialism
	Including Owenism
.14	Fabian socialism
.15	Guild socialism
.2	**Systems of French origin**
	Including Babouvism, Icarianism
.22	Saint-Simonism
.23	Fourierism (Phalansterianism)
.3	**Systems of American origin**
.4	**Marxian systems**
	Class here Marxism
	For democratic Marxian systems, see 335.5
	See Manual at 335.4 vs. 335.401, 335.411
.401	Philosophy
	Do not use for philosophic foundations; class in 335.411. Do not use for comprehensive works on theory of Marxian systems; class in 335.4
	See Manual at 335.4 vs. 335.401, 335.411
.41	Philosophic foundations, economic concepts, aims
	Including social ownership of means of production
.411	Philosophic foundations
	Including theory of class struggle
	For the philosophic foundations of Marxian economics, see 335.412
	See Manual at 335.4 vs. 335.401, 335.411
.411 2	Dialectical materialism
	See Manual at 335.4112 vs. 146.32
.411 9	Historical materialism
.412	Economic concepts
	Including labor theory of value

>   335.42–335.43   Marxian doctrines and systems characteristic of specific historical periods and regions

       Class comprehensive works in 335.4

.42	Early period
.422	Communism (1848–1875)

Period of Communist manifesto

.423	Scientific socialism (1875–1917)

For democratic socialism, see 335.5

.43   Communism (Marxism-Leninism)

Communism of post-1917 period

Class here former Soviet communism, communist theory and practice of democratic centralism

For communism as a political ideology, see 320.532

.433   Trotskyist doctrines

.434   National variants as schools of thought

Use 335.4309 for communism in specific nations viewed as actual economic systems rather than schools of thought, e.g., Cuban communism as an existing system 335.43097291 (*not* 335.4347)

Soviet communism as a school of thought is classed in 335.43, as the economic system of the former Soviet Union in 335.430947

.434 4   Communism of former Yugoslavia

Class here Titoism

.434 5   Chinese communism

Class here Maoism

.434 7   Cuban communism (Castroism)

Including ideas of Che Guevara

.437   Comparative studies

Comparison of communism with capitalism, cooperation, democratic socialism, other forms of collectivism

.5   Democratic socialism

Marxian and non-Marxian socialism pursued through persuasion and consent of the electorate in a nonauthoritarian state

Class Christian socialism in 335.7; class voluntary socialist communities in 335.9

For Fabian socialism, see 335.14

.6   Fascism

Including falangism, national socialism

For fascism as a political ideology, see 320.533

.7 **Christian socialism**

Class voluntary Christian socialist communities in 335.9

For Christian socialism as a political ideology, see 320.5312

.8 **Other systems**

.82 Syndicalism

Class here anarcho-syndicalism

.83 Anarchism

For anarchism as a political ideology, see 320.57; for anarcho-syndicalism, see 335.82; for voluntary anarchist communities, see 335.9

.9 **Voluntary socialist and anarchist communities**

Standard subdivisions are added for either or both topics in heading

Class interdisciplinary studies of communes in 307.774; class interdisciplinary studies of kibbutzim in 307.776

See Manual at 338.7 vs. 335.9

[.909 3–.909 9] Treatment by specific continents, countries, localities

Do not use; class in 335.93–335.99

.93–.99 Voluntary socialist and anarchist communities in specific continents, countries, localities

Add to base number 335.9 notation 3–9 from Table 2, e.g., kibbutzim and moshavim in Israel 335.95694, voluntary socialist communities in the United States 335.973
Subdivisions are added for either or both topics in heading

336 Public finance

Class here intergovernmental fiscal relations, comprehensive works on public finance and financial administration of governments

For financial administration and budgets, see 352.4

See Manual at 336 vs. 352.4; also at 332, 336 vs. 339

SUMMARY

336.001–.008	**Standard subdivisions**	
.01–.09	**[Public finance by governmental level; revenue; historical, geographic, persons treatment; associations of sovereign states]**	
.1	**Nontax revenues**	
.2	**Taxes and taxation**	
.3	**Public borrowing, debt, expenditure**	
.4–.9	**Public finance of specific continents, countries, localities in modern world**	

.001–.005 Standard subdivisions

.006	Organizations and management
.006 01	International organizations

Class associations of sovereign states in 336.0916

.007–.008	Standard subdivisions
[.009]	Historical, geographic, persons treatment

Do not use for treatment by governmental level; class in 336.01. Do not use for historical and persons treatment, for treatment by areas, regions, places in general, for ancient world; class in 336.09

[.009 4–.009 9] Treatment by continents, countries, localities in modern world

Do not use; class in 336.4–336.9

.01 Public finance by governmental level

Multiple jurisdictions at the same level

See Manual at 336.093, 336.4–336.9 vs. 336.01

.012 Public finance at national level

[.012 091] Treatment by areas, regions, places in general

Do not use; class in 336.0121

[.012 093–.012 099] Treatment by specific continents, countries

Do not use for specific continents; class in 336.0123–336.0129. Do not use for specific countries in ancient world; class in 336.093. Do not use for specific countries in modern world; class in 336.4–336.9

.012 1 Public finance at national level in areas, regions, places in general

Add to base number 336.0121 the numbers following —1 in notation 11–19 from Table 2, e.g., national public finance in developing countries 336.0121724

.012 3–.012 9 Public finance at national level in specific continents

Add to base number 336.012 notation 3–9 from Table 2, e.g., national public finance in Europe 336.0124

.013 Public finance at state and provincial level

[.013 091] Treatment by areas, regions, places in general

Do not use; class in 336.0131

[.013 093–.013 099] Treatment by specific continents, countries, localities

Do not use for specific continents, countries; class in 336.0133–336.0139. Do not use for specific localities in ancient world; class in 336.093. Do not use for specific localities in modern world; class in 336.4–336.9

.013 1	Public finance at state and provincial level in areas, regions, places in general

Add to base number 336.0131 the numbers following — 1 in notation 11–19 from Table 2, e.g., state and provincial public finance in developing countries 336.0131724

.013 3–.013 9   Public finance at state and provincial level in specific continents, countries

Add to base number 336.013 notation 3–9 from Table 2, e.g., provincial public finance in Canada 336.01371

.014   Public finance at local level

[.014 091]   Treatment by areas, regions, places in general

Do not use; class in 336.0141

[.014 093–.014 099]   Treatment by specific continents, countries, localities

Do not use; class in 336.0143–336.0149

.014 1   Public finance at local level in areas, regions, places in general

Add to base number 336.0141 the numbers following — 1 in notation 11–19 from Table 2, e.g., local public finance in developing countries 336.0141724

.014 3–.014 9   Public finance at local level in specific continents, countries, localities

Add to base number 336.014 notation 1–9 from Table 2, e.g., local public finance in Pennsylvania 336.014748

.02   Revenue

For specific forms of revenue, see 336.1–336.2

[.020 91]   Treatment by areas, regions, places in general

Do not use; class in 336.021

[.020 93–.020 99]   Treatment by specific continents, countries, localities

Do not use; class in 336.023–336.029

.021   Revenue in areas, regions, places in general

Add to base number 336.021 the numbers following — 1 in notation 11–19 from Table 2, e.g., revenue in developing countries 336.021724

.023–.029   Revenue in specific continents, countries, localities

Add to base number 336.02 notation 3–9 from Table 2, e.g., revenue in France 336.0244

.09   Historical, geographic, persons treatment; associations of sovereign states

Class continents, countries, localities in modern world in 336.4–336.9

.090 1–.090 5	Historical periods

Add to base number 336.090 the numbers following —090 in notation 0901–0905 from Table 1, e.g., public finance in the 19th century 336.09034

.091	Areas, regions, places in general; associations of sovereign states

.091 6	Associations of sovereign states

.091 62	League of Nations

.091 63	United Nations

.091 68	Regional associations

Including League of Arab States

Class regional associations limited to specific continents in 336.4–336.9

.091 7	Socioeconomic regions

Add to base number 336.0917 the numbers following —17 in notation 171–177 from Table 2, e.g., public finance in developing countries 336.091724; however, for public finance in socioeconomic regions by governmental level, see 336.01

Class regional associations of sovereign states in 336.09168

.092	Persons

.093	The ancient world

Add to base number 336.093 the numbers following —3 in notation 31–39 from Table 2, e.g., public finance in Roman Empire 336.0937; however, for public finance in ancient world by governmental level, see 336.01

See Manual at 336.093, 336.4–336.9 vs. 336.01

> **336.1–336.2 Specific forms of revenue**

Class comprehensive works in 336.02

.1   **Nontax revenues**

For public borrowing, see 336.34

> 336.11–336.15 Commercial revenues

Class comprehensive works in 336.1

For revenue from public industries and services, see 336.19

.11	Commercial revenues from rents and franchises

Standard subdivisions are added for either or both topics in heading

.12	Commercial revenues from public lands

Including mineral rights

Class income from rental of land and leasing of mineral rights in 336.11

.15	Commercial revenues from deposits, investments, loans
.16	Administrative revenues

Including fees for services rendered, for licenses; fines; gifts; profits on coinage

For franchises, see 336.11

.17	Revenues from lotteries
.18	Intergovernmental and intragovernmental revenues

Standard subdivisions are added for intergovernmental and intragovernmental revenues together, for intergovernmental revenues alone

.182	Revenues from reparations and interest on war loans
.185	Revenues from one government unit to another

Including grants from higher units, payment in lieu of taxes, technical assistance funds

.188	Revenues from international grants
.19	Revenue from public industries and services

Standard subdivisions are added for either or both topics in heading

.2	**Taxes and taxation**

Standard subdivisions are added for either or both topics in heading

Class here interdisciplinary works on taxes and taxation

For tax law, see 343.04; for tax administration, see 352.44

See Manual at 343.04 vs. 336.2, 352.44

SUMMARY

336.200 1–.200 9	**Standard subdivisions**
.201–.207	**General topics of taxes and taxation**
.22	**Real property taxes**
.23	**Personal property taxes**
.24	**Income taxes**
.25	**Poll taxes**
.26	**Customs taxes (Customs duties)**
.27	**Other taxes**
.29	**Principles of taxation**

.200 1–.200 8	Standard subdivisions

.200 9   Historical, geographic, persons treatment

                 Do not use for treatment by governmental level; class in 336.201

                 See Manual at 336.2009 vs. 336.201

>   336.201–336.207   General topics of taxes and taxation

         Unless other instructions are given, observe the following table of preference,
         e.g., reform of business taxes 336.207 (*not* 336.205):

Business taxes	336.207
Provisions that allow tax avoidance	336.206
Taxes by governmental level	336.201
Tax reform	336.205

         Class comprehensive works in 336.2

.201   Taxes by governmental level

                 Multiple jurisdictions at the same level

                 See Manual at 336.2009 vs. 336.201

.201 2   National taxes

[.201 209 1]   Treatment by areas, regions, places in general

                         Do not use; class in 336.20121

[.201 209 3–.201 209 9]   Treatment by specific continents, countries

                         Do not use for specific continents, class in
                         336.20123–336.20129. Do not use for specific countries;
                         class in 336.20093–336.20099

.201 21   National taxes in areas, regions, places in general

                 Add to base number 336.20121 the numbers following —1 in
                 notation 11–19 from Table 2, e.g., national taxes in developing
                 countries 336.20121724

.201 23–.201 29 National taxes in specific continents

                 Add to base number 336.2012 notation 3–9 from Table 2, e.g.,
                 national taxes in Europe 336.20124

.201 3   State and provincial taxes

[.201 309 1]   Treatment by areas, regions, places in general

                         Do not use; class in 336.20131

[.201 309 3–.201 309 9]   Treatment by specific continents, countries, localities

                         Do not use for specific continents, countries; class in
                         336.20133–336.20139. Do not use for specific localities;
                         class in 336.20093–336.20099

.201 31	State and provincial taxes in areas, regions, places in general

Add to base number 336.20131 the numbers following —1 in notation 11–19 from Table 2, e.g., provincial taxes in developing countries 336.20131724

.201 33–.201 39	State and provincial taxes in specific continents, countries

Add to base number 336.2013 notation 3–9 from Table 2, e.g., provincial taxes in Canada 336.201371

.201 4	Local taxes

[.201 409 1]	Treatment by areas, regions, places in general

Do not use; class in 336.20141

[.201 409 3–.201 409 9]	Treatment by specific continents, countries, localities

Do not use; class in 336.20143–336.20149

.201 41	Local taxes in areas, regions, places in general

Add to base number 336.20141 the numbers following —1 in notation 11–19 from Table 2, e.g., local taxes in developing countries 336.20141724

.201 43–.201 49	Local taxes in specific continents, countries, localities

Add to base number 336.2014 notation 3–9 from Table 2, e.g., local taxes in Pennsylvania 336.2014748

.205	Tax reform

Class here proposals and innovations

.206	Provisions that allow tax avoidance

Including tax credits, deductions, incentives, loopholes, rebates

Class here tax expenditure (tax deductions, exemptions, credits, by which a government "spends" revenue by not collecting it)

.207	Business taxes

Including taxes on industry, manufacturing, small business, international business

.22	Real property taxes

Class here rates (United Kingdom), comprehensive works on property taxes

Class comprehensive works on taxes on personal wealth in 336.24

For personal property taxes, see 336.23

.222	Rates, assessment, valuation

Class rates (percentages), assessment, valuation of specific kinds of real property in 336.225

.225	Specific kinds of real property

Including commercial, farm, residential property

[.225 01–.225 09]	Standard subdivisions

Do not use; class in 336.2201–336.2209

.23	Personal property taxes

On tangible and intangible property

Including mobile homes

Class comprehensive works on property taxes in 336.22

.24	Income taxes

Class here comprehensive works on taxes on personal wealth

For property taxes, see 336.22; for estate, inheritance, gift taxes, see 336.276

.241	General topics of income taxes

Class general topics applied to personal income tax in 336.242; class general topics applied to corporate income tax in 336.243

[.241 01–.241 09]	Standard subdivisions

Do not use; class in 336.2401–336.2409

.241 5	Reform

Class reform of taxes on business income in 336.2417

.241 6	Provisions that allow tax avoidance

Class provisions allowing avoidance of taxes on business income in 336.2417

.241 7	Taxes on business income

.242	Personal (Individual) income taxes

See also 362.582 for negative income tax

.242 1	General topics of personal income taxes

Class general topics applied to taxes on specific kinds of personal income in 336.2422–336.2428

[.242 101–.242 109]	Standard subdivisions

Do not use; class in 336.24201–336.24209

.242 15	Reform
.242 16	Provisions that allow tax avoidance
.242 2	Income from wages

Including withholding tax

.242 3	Self-employment income
	Including income from individual proprietorships, from partnerships
.242 4	Income from property transfers
	Capital gains and losses
	Class here comprehensive works on taxation of individual and corporate capital gains and losses
	For taxation of corporate capital gains, see 336.243
.242 6	Interest income
	Class here comprehensive works on taxation of individual and corporate interest income
	For taxation of corporate interest income, see 336.243
.242 8	Retirement income
.243	**Corporate income taxes**
	Including capital gains taxes, interest income
	Class comprehensive works on business taxes in 336.207
.243 1	General topics of corporate income taxes
	Class general topics applied to profits taxes in 336.2432
[.243 101–.243 109]	Standard subdivisions
	Do not use; class in 336.24301–336.24309
.243 15	Reform
.243 16	Provisions that allow tax avoidance
	Including oil depletion allowance
.243 2	Profits taxes
	Including excess and undistributed profits taxes
.249	**Social security taxes**
	See also 368.4 for social security benefits
	See Manual at 336.249 vs. 368.401, 368.4011
.25	Poll taxes
.26	Customs taxes (Customs duties)
	Class interdisciplinary works on tariff policy in 382.7
.263	Export and transit taxes
	Standard subdivisions are added for export and transit taxes together, for export taxes alone

.264 Import taxes

For import tax schedules, see 336.265; for import taxes on specific products, see 336.266

.265 Import tax schedules

For import tax schedules on specific products, see 336.266

.266 Import taxes and tax schedules on specific products

[.266 000 1–.266 000 9] Standard subdivisions

Do not use for import taxes; class in 336.26401–336.26409. Do not use for import tax schedules; class in 336.26501–336.26509

.266 001–.266 9 Subdivisions of import taxes and tax schedules on specific products

Add to base number 336.266 notation 001–999, e.g., import taxes on paintings 336.26675
Subdivisions are added for either or both topics in heading

.27 Other taxes

.271 Excise, sales, value-added, related taxes

Including luxury, use taxes

.271 3 Sales taxes

.271 4 Value-added taxes

.271 6 Severance taxes

.272 Stamp taxes and revenue stamps

Standard subdivisions are added for either or both topics in heading

.276 Estate, inheritance, gift taxes

Class comprehensive works on taxes on personal wealth in 336.24

.278 Taxes on products, services, industries

Standard subdivisions are added for any or all topics in heading

Class a specific kind of tax on a product, service, industry with the kind of tax, e.g., import taxes on coal 336.26655324, severance taxes on coal 336.2716

.278 000 1–.278 000 9 Standard subdivisions

.278 001–.278 9 Taxes on specific products, services, industries

Add to base number 336.278 notation 001–999, e.g., coal industry taxes 336.2783382724
Subdivisions are added for any or all topics in heading

.29   Principles of taxation

               Class principles of specific kinds of taxes in 336.22–336.27

.291   General principles

               Including adequacy (yield), certainty, diversity, economy and
               convenience of collection, justice

.293   Kinds of rate

               Including progressive, proportional, regressive rates

.294   Incidence

               The final burden of tax payment and the people on whom it falls

               Including direct, indirect, double taxation

               Class incidence of a specific tax with the tax, e.g., incidence of income
               tax 336.24

.3   Public borrowing, debt, expenditure

               Class here fiscal policy, comprehensive works on monetary and fiscal policy

               *For monetary policy, see 332.46; for use of fiscal and monetary policy in
               economic stabilization, see 339.5*

.31   Public (Government) securities

               Including government Eurobonds

               Class investment in government securities in 332.63232

               For short-term securities, see 336.32

.32   Short-term securities

               Including certificates of indebtedness, treasury bills and notes

.34   Public debt

               Class here public borrowing

               For public securities, see 336.31; for debt management, see 336.36

.340 9   Historical, geographic, persons treatment

               Do not use for treatment by governmental level; class in 336.343

               See Manual at 336.3409 vs. 336.343

.343   Public debt by governmental level

               Multiple jurisdictions at the same level

               Class flotation of loans regardless of level in 336.344; class limitation of
               indebtedness regardless of level in 336.346

               See Manual at 336.3409 vs. 336.343

.343 1   Local level

[.343 109 1]   Treatment by areas, regions, places in general

        Do not use; class in 336.34311

[.343 109 3–.343 109 9]   Treatment by specific continents, countries, localities

        Do not use; class in 336.34313–336.34319

.343 11   Local public debt in areas, regions, places in general

        Add to base number 336.34311 the numbers following — 1 in notation 11–19 from Table 2, e.g., local public debt in developing countries 336.34311724

.343 13–.343 19   Local public debt in specific continents, countries, localities

        Add to base number 336.3431 notation 3–9 from Table 2, e.g., local public debt in Pennsylvania 336.3431748

.343 2   State and provincial level

[.343 209 1]   Treatment by areas, regions, places in general

        Do not use; class in 336.34321

[.343 209 3–.343 209 9]   Treatment by specific continents, countries, localities

        Do not use for specific continents, countries; class in 336.34323–336.34329. Do not use for specific localities; class in 336.34093–336.34099

.343 21   State and provincial public debt in areas, regions, places in general

        Add to base number 336.34321 the numbers following — 1 in notation 11–19 from Table 2, e.g., state and provincial public debt in developing countries 336.34321724

.343 23–.343 29   State and provincial public debt in specific continents, countries

        Add to base number 336.3432 notation 3–9 from Table 2, e.g., provincial public debt in Canada 336.343271

.343 3   National level

        Class borrowing by one nation from another nation in 336.3435

[.343 309 1]   Treatment by areas, regions, places in general

        Do not use; class in 336.34331

[.343 309 3–.343 309 9]   Treatment by specific continents, countries, localities

        Do not use for specific continents; class in 336.34333–336.34339. Do not use for specific countries; class in 336.34093–336.34099

.343 31   National public debt in areas, regions, places in general

        Add to base number 336.34331 the numbers following — 1 in notation 11–19 from Table 2, e.g., national public debt in developing countries 336.34331724

.343 33–.343 39		National public debt in specific continents

Add to base number 336.3433 notation 3–9 from Table 2, e.g., national public debt in Europe 336.34334

.343 5   International level

Borrowing by one nation from another, public debts owed by one nation to another

Class here comprehensive works on international borrowing and debts

> *For role of banks in international borrowing and debts, see 332.15*

.344   Flotation of loans

Including allotments, compulsory loans, subscriptions; marketability

Class government securities in 336.31

.346   Limitation of public indebtedness

.36   Debt management

Class debt limits (ceilings) in 336.346

> *See also 339.523 for deficit financing in macroeconomic policy*

.363   Repayment and redemption

Standard subdivisions are added for either or both topics in heading

Including sinking funds

.368   Repudiation

Class here public insolvency

.39   Expenditure

Class tax expenditure in 336.206

> *For expenditure in macroeconomic policy, see 339.522*

> *See Manual at 336 vs. 352.4*

.4–.9   **Public finance of specific continents, countries, localities in modern world**

Add to base number 336 notation 4–9 from Table 2, e.g., public finance of Australia 336.94; however, for public finance by governmental level, see 336.01

> *See Manual at 336.093, 336.4–336.9 vs. 336.01*

337   International economics

Class here international economic planning; comprehensive works on international economic relations, on international economic cooperation

International development and growth relocated to 338.91

For a specific aspect of international economics not provided for here, see the aspect, e.g., international (multinational) business enterprises 338.88, international economic law 341.75, foreign trade 382

[.093–.099]   Treatment by specific continents, countries, localities

Do not use; class in 337.3–337.9

.1   Multilateral economic cooperation

Class here economic integration, multilateral agreements and multistate organizations for economic cooperation

Class bilateral economic cooperation in 337.3–337.9; class interdisciplinary works on international governmental organizations in 341.2

For trade agreements, see 382.9

See Manual at 337.3–337.9 vs. 337.1

.109   Historical and persons treatment

Do not use for geographic treatment; class in 337.11–337.19

.11   Multilateral economic cooperation in areas, regions, places in general

Add to base number 337.11 the numbers following — 1 in notation 17–18 from Table 2, e.g., multilateral economic cooperation in the Western Hemisphere 337.11812

.14   European multilateral cooperation

.142   European Union

Class here European Common Market, European Community, European Economic Community

.143   European Free Trade Association (EFTA)

.147   Council for Mutual Economic Assistance (COMECON)

.15–.19   Multilateral cooperation in continents other than Europe

Add to base number 337.1 notation 5–9 from Table 2, e.g., Andean Group 337.18

.3–.9 **Foreign economic policies and relations of specific jurisdictions and groups of jurisdictions**

Class here bilateral economic cooperation

Add to base number 337 notation 3–9 from Table 2, e.g., economic policy of United Kingdom 337.41; then, for foreign economic relations between two jurisdictions or groups of jurisdictions, add 0* and to the result add notation 1 or 3–9 from Table 2, e.g., economic relations between United Kingdom and France 337.41044

Give priority in notation to the jurisdiction or group of jurisdictions emphasized. If the emphasis is equal, give priority to the one coming first in Table 2

(Option: Give priority in notation to the jurisdiction or group of jurisdictions requiring local emphasis, e.g., libraries in the United States class foreign economic relations between the United States and France in 337.73044)

Class multilateral economic cooperation in 337.1

See Manual at 337.3–337.9 vs. 337.1

338 **Production**

Class here interdisciplinary works on industry, on production

For specific factors of production, see 331–333; for production economics of financial industries, see 332; for production economics of real estate business, see 333.33; for production of energy, see 333.79; for economics of cooperative production, see 334; for production economics of insurance industry, see 368; for commerce, communications, transportation, see 380. For noneconomic aspects of industry and production, see the aspect, e.g., law of industry 343.07, production technology 620–690

See Manual at 332 vs. 338, 658.15; also at 338 vs. 060, 381, 382, 670.294, 910, T1—025, T1—0294, T1—0296; also at 363.5, 363.6, 363.8 vs. 338

SUMMARY

338.001–.009	**Standard subdivisions**
.01–.09	**[General topics]**
.1	**Agriculture**
.2	**Extraction of minerals**
.3	**Other extractive industries**
.4	**Secondary industries and services**
.5	**General production economics**
.6	**Organization of production**
.7	**Business enterprises**
.8	**Combinations**
.9	**Economic development and growth**

.001 Philosophy and theory

For a specific theory, see the theory, e.g., law of diminishing marginal utility 338.5212

---

*Add 00 for standard subdivisions; see instructions at beginning of Table 1

.001 12	Forecasting and forecasts

> Do not use for forecasting and forecasts of products and services; class in 338.020112. Do not use for general production forecasting and forecasts; class in 338.544

.002–.008	Standard subdivisions
.009	Historical, geographic, persons treatment of general principles and theories

> Do not use for historical, geographic, persons treatment of production; class in 338.09

.01	Factors of production

Class here comprehensive and theoretical works on factors of production

Class factors of production as part of industrial conditions and situation in 338.09; class factors of production as costs of production in 338.512

For labor, see 331; for capital, see 332; for land, see 333

.02	Products and services

Standard subdivisions are added for either or both topics in heading

Class general production economics in 338.5; class consumption in 339.47; class shipments and sales in 380.1–382

.020 12	Classification

Class here standard industrial classifications

Add to base number 338.02012 notation 4–9 from Table 2, e.g., standard industrial classifications of Canada 338.0201271

.04	Entrepreneurship
.06	Production efficiency

Including cost-output ratio

Class here industrial productivity [*formerly* 338.09]

Class conservation of energy in 333.7916

For labor productivity, see 331.118

.064	Effect of technological innovations

Class here effect of automation, comprehensive works on effect of technological innovations on the economy

For effect of technological innovations on a specific aspect of the economy, see the aspect, e.g., effect on working conditions 331.25, effect on banking 332.1

See also 303.483 for effect of technological innovation on society

.09   Historical, geographic, persons treatment of production

Class here existing and potential resources for production, industrial conditions and situation, industrial surveys, location of industry

Add to base number 338.09 notation 001–9 from Table 2, e.g., industrial surveys of Canada 338.0971

Industrial productivity relocated to 338.06

Class a specific resource with the resource, e.g., water for power 333.914

> *See also 338.6042 for the rationale for and process of locating business enterprises*

> *See Manual at 333.94 vs. 338.0919; also at 338.09 vs. 332.67309, 338.6042, 346.07, 658.11, T1—0681, 658.21, T1—0682; also at 338.092*

>   338.1–338.4   Specific kinds of industries

Class here finance, general production economics of specific kinds of industries

Class results of market surveys; supply and demand in relation to trade, to marketing opportunities in 380.1–382; class comprehensive works in 338; class interdisciplinary works on capital formation in 332.0415

> *For financial industries, see 332; for credit for specific kinds of industries, see 332.7; for real estate business, see 333.33; for energy production, see 333.79; for cooperatives in specific kinds of industries, see 334; for organization of production in specific kinds of industries, see 338.6; for business enterprises other than cooperatives in specific kinds of industries, see 338.7–338.8; for commerce, communications, transportation, see 380. For biographies of entrepreneurs in a specific kind of industry, see the kind of industry in 338.6–338.8, e.g., biographies of small-business owners 338.642092, biographies of entrepreneurs in textile manufacturing 338.76770092; for biographies of people known for their contributions in a specific type of technology, see the type of technology in 600, e.g., biographies of mining engineers 622.092*

>   338.1–338.3   Primary (Extractive) industries

Class comprehensive works in 338

.1   **Agriculture**

Class agricultural cooperatives in 334.683; class government farm policies in 338.18

> *See Manual at 338.1 vs. 631.558*

.13   Financial aspects

> Class here capital formation and other investment in agriculture, costs, prices received by farmers, farm income

> Add to base number 338.13 the numbers following 63 in 633–638, e.g., prices of rice 338.13318

> Class government policies that affect financial aspects in 338.18; class food prices in 338.19

> *For agricultural credit, see 332.71*

> *See also 338.16 for production efficiency*

> *See Manual at 332 vs. 338, 658.15*

.14   Factors affecting production

> Including drought, plant and animal diseases, shortages of materials and equipment used in farming

> *For financial factors, see 338.13; for production efficiency, see 338.16; for surpluses and shortages of farm products, see 338.17; for government policies, see 338.18*

.16   Production efficiency

> Including cost-output ratio, size of farm, use of labor

> Class here agricultural productivity; science, technological innovation in agriculture

> Class energy conservation in agriculture in 333.7966; class comprehensive works on factors affecting production in 338.14

> *For labor productivity, see 331.118*

.161   Mechanization

> Class here automation

> Class mechanization of harvesting methods in 338.163

.162   Agricultural methods

> Including crop rotation; use of plant nutrients, of insecticides

> *For harvesting methods, see 338.163*

.163   Harvesting methods

.17 Products

Including the seed industry as a whole

Class here surpluses and shortages of farm products, forecasts and projections of supply and demand

Add to base number 338.17 the numbers following 63 in 633–638, e.g., rice or seed rice 338.17318, forestry 338.1749, forest products 338.17498; however, for supply of timber in nature, see 333.7511; for demand for timber, see 333.7512

Class specific elements of production applied to specific products and groups of products in 338.13–338.16; class government farm policies applied to specific products and groups of products in 338.18; class supply, surpluses, shortages of food in 338.19; class specific producers in 338.763. Class specific kinds of seeds with the kind, e.g., corn (maize) seed 338.17315

.174 9 Products of forestry

Number built according to instructions under 338.17

See Manual at 338.1749 vs. 333.75

.18 Government farm policies

Including acreage allotments, agricultural credit, drought relief, price supports, subsidies

Class government policies with respect to food supply in 338.19

[.180 93–.180 99] Treatment by specific continents, countries, localities

Do not use; class in 338.183–338.189

.181 International policies

Policies and programs of international bodies

.183–.189 Treatment by specific continents, countries, localities

Add to base number 338.18 notation 3–9 from Table 2, e.g., government farm policies of India 338.1854; however, for international policies, see 338.181

.19 Food supply

Class here economic causes and effects of, economic remedies for maladjustments in food supply; measures for attaining and maintaining adequate amounts of food; food requirements (demand); reserves (stocks, supply) of food; prices of food to the consumer; comprehensive works on the economics of production, storage, distribution of food

Class interdisciplinary works on food supply in 363.8

For production of food, see 338.13–338.18; for supply of specific food commodities, see 338.17; for food processing, see 338.47664; for distribution of food, see 380.141

See Manual at 363.5, 363.6, 363.8 vs. 338; also at 363.8 vs. 338.19

[.190 91]	Treatment by areas, regions, places in general

Do not use; class in 338.191

[.190 93–.190 99]	Treatment by specific continents, countries, localities

Do not use; class in 338.193–338.199

.191   Food supply in areas, regions, places in general

Add to base number 338.191 the numbers following — 1 in notation 11–19 from Table 2, e.g., food supply in developing countries 338.191724

.193–.199   Food supply in specific continents, countries, localities

Add to base number 338.19 notation 3–9 from Table 2, e.g., food supply in Africa 338.196

.2   **Extraction of minerals**

Class here extraction of energy resources, comprehensive works on the economics of extraction and processing of minerals and energy resources

Class conservation of mineral and energy resources in 333.7–333.9; class mined lands, surface-mined lands in 333.765

For processing of minerals and raw materials of energy, see 338.47

See Manual at 553 vs. 333.8, 338.2

.23   Financial aspects

Class here capital formation and other investment in industries engaged in extraction of minerals; costs, income, prices

Add to base number 338.23 the numbers following 553 in 553.2–553.9, e.g., prices of tin 338.23453

Class industrial credit in 332.742; class production efficiency in 338.26

See Manual at 332 vs. 338, 658.15

.26   Production efficiency

Including automation, cost-output ratio, effect of technological innovation, factors of production

Class here industrial productivity

Class energy conservation in mineral extraction industries in 333.7965

For labor productivity, see 331.118

.27 Products

> Add to base number 338.27 the numbers following 553 in 553.2–553.9, e.g., coal 338.2724

> Class supply in storage, shortages, surpluses, demand, and projections of these in 333.8; class specific elements of production applied to specific products in 338.23–338.26; class specific producers doing extraction only in 338.7622; class specific producers doing both extraction and processing in 338.766; class supply in nature in 553.2–553.9

.3 Other extractive industries

> Including financial aspects, production efficiency

> *See Manual at 332 vs. 338, 658.15*

.37 Products

> Class specific producers in 338.763

> *See Manual at 338.37 vs. 333.954*

.371 Products of culture of invertebrates and cold-blooded vertebrates

> Add to base number 338.371 the numbers following 639 in 639.3–639.7, e.g., culture of oysters 338.37141; however, for insect culture, see 338.178

> Class comprehensive works on fishing and the culture of fishes and other water animals in 338.3727

.372 Products of fishing, whaling, hunting, trapping

> Add to base number 338.372 the numbers following 59 in 592–599, e.g., sponges 338.37234

> Class the culture of invertebrates and cold-blooded vertebrates in 338.371

> *See Manual at 338.372*

.4 Secondary industries and services

> Standard subdivisions are added for either or both topics in heading

> Class government policies in 338.48

> *See Manual at 338.4 vs. 338.47*

.43 Financial aspects

> Class here capital formation and other investment in secondary industry and services; costs, income, prices

> Class industrial credit in 332.742; class production efficiency in 338.45

> *See Manual at 332 vs. 338, 658.15*

.430 001–.430 009 Standard subdivisions

.430 01–.439 99   Specific industries and services

> Add to base number 338.43 notation 001–999, e.g., automobile
> prices 338.43629222; however, for financial aspects of financial
> industries, see 332; for financial aspects of real estate, see 333.33;
> for financial aspects of energy production, see 333.79; for
> financial aspects of cooperative production, see 334; for financial
> aspects of insurance industry, see 368.01; for financial aspects of
> commerce, communications, transportation, see 380
>> Subdivisions are added for either or both topics in heading

.45   Production efficiency

> Including cost-output ratio, factors of production (land, labor, capital),
> production capacity

> Class here industrial productivity

> Class energy conservation in secondary industries in 333.7916

> *For labor productivity, see 331.118*

.454   Automation

> *For automation in specific industries, see 338.456*

.456   Production efficiency in specific industries and groups of industries

> Class here automation in specific industries

[.456 01–.456 09]   Standard subdivisions

> Do not use; class in 338.4501–338.4509

.456 1   Production efficiency in industries other than extractive, manufacturing, construction

> Class here service industries

.456 100 01–.456 100 09   Standard subdivisions

.456 100 1–.456 199 9   Subdivisions for production efficiency in industries other than extractive, manufacturing, construction

> Add to base number 338.4561 notation 001–999, e.g.,
> production efficiency in hospital services 338.456136211;
> however, for production efficiency in financial industries,
> see 332; for production efficiency in real estate business,
> see 333.33; for production efficiency in cooperative
> enterprises, see 334; for production efficiency in the
> insurance industry, see 368; for production efficiency in
> commerce, communications, transportation, see 380

.456 2–.456 9   Production efficiency in manufacturing and construction industries

> Add to base number 338.456 the numbers following 6 in 620–690,
> e.g., power equipment in textile manufacture 338.456770285;
> however, for production efficiency in energy production, see 333.79;
> for production efficiency in cooperative enterprises, see 334

.46   Professional services

> Class specific elements of production applied to professional services in 338.43–338.45; class specific professional services in 338.47

.47   Goods and services

> Standard subdivisions are added for either or both topics in heading

> Class here quantities produced, shortages, surpluses, stockpiles, forecasts and projections of supply and demand

> Class specific elements of production applied to specific goods and services in 338.43–338.45; class specific producers in 338.76; class comprehensive works on professional services in 338.46

> *See Manual at 338.4 vs. 338.47*

.470 001–.470 009   Standard subdivisions

.470 01–.479 99   Subdivisions for goods and services

> Add to base number 338.47 notation 001–999, e.g., the product gasoline 338.4766553827, tourist industry 338.4791; however, for production economics of financial industries, see 332; for production economics of real estate business, see 333.33; for production economics of energy production, see 333.79; for production economics of cooperative enterprises, see 334; for production economics of commerce, communications, transportation, see 380
>> Subdivisions are added for either or both topics in heading

.48   Government policies

> Class government policies with respect to a specific aspect of secondary industries and services in 338.43–338.47

.5   **General production economics**

> Including risk

> Class here microeconomics (economics of the firm)

> Class production economics of specific kinds of industries in 338.1–338.4

> *For organization of production, see 338.6*

[.501 12]   Forecasting and forecasts

> Do not use; class in 338.544

.51   Costs

.512   Factors of production as costs of production

> Including law of diminishing marginal returns, of factor proportions

> Class comprehensive works on factors of production in 338.01

.514   Elements in cost calculation

.514 2		Kinds of cost

Including average, fixed, marginal, variable costs

.514 4		Size of enterprise

Including economies and diseconomies of scale, use of technology

.516		Profit

Including relation of marginal cost to marginal revenue

.52	Prices

Including price determination in international markets [*formerly* 382.1044]

Class here price determination, effects of changes, comprehensive works on prices

Class effect of money on prices in 332.41; class effect of costs on prices in 338.516; class effects of prices on the whole economy in 339.42

.520 1		Philosophy and theory

Do not use for theories; class in 338.521

.520 2		Miscellany
.520 21		Tabulated and related materials

Do not use for statistics; class in 338.528

.521	Price theories

Class here law of supply and demand, theories of value

For supply and demand for natural resources and energy, see 333.7; for Marxian labor theory of value, see 335.412; for supply and demand for specific products, see 338.1–338.4

.521 2		Theory of demand

Including law of diminishing marginal utility, price-demand relationship

.521 3		Theory of supply

Including price-supply relationship

\>   **338.522–338.526 Price determination**

Class comprehensive works in 338.52

.522	**Price determination in free markets**

Including determination in market for brand-name products; interproduct competition, e.g., butter versus margarine

.523	Price determination in controlled markets

        Determination by oligopolies, monopolies

        Including price leadership

.526	Prices determination by government regulation
.528	Price levels

        Class here statistics, indexes

.528 021	Tabulated and related materials

        Do not use for statistics; class in 338.528

.54	Economic fluctuations

        Including seasonal variations, secular trends

[.540 112]	Forecasting and forecasts

        Do not use; class in 338.544

.542	Business cycles

        Including prosperity, recession, depression, recovery; panics

        Class remedial and preventive measures in 338.543

.543	Remedial and preventive action

        Standard subdivisions are added for either or both topics in heading

        Class comprehensive works on economic stabilization in 339.5

.544	General production forecasting and forecasts

        Class forecasting as a technique of managerial decision-making in 658.40355

.544 2	Methods of forecasting

        Class comprehensive works on economic forecasting in 330.0112

.544 3	Forecasts

        Class forecasts of economic situation in 330.900112

.6	**Organization of production**

Including worker control of industry

Class here organization of production in specific kinds of industries

For the role of unions in achieving worker control of industry, see 331.8801; for guild socialism, see 335.15; for syndicalism, see 335.82; for business enterprises and their structure, see 338.7

See Manual at 338.092

.604	Special topics

.604 1	Finance

Class finance of specific kinds of industries in 338.1–338.4; class interdisciplinary works on capital formation in 332.0415

.604 2	Location

Class here proximity to sources of power, raw materials, labor supply, transportation, markets

See Manual at 338.09 vs. 332.67309, 338.6042, 346.07, 658.11, T1—0681, 658.21, T1—0682

.604 6	Specialization and comparative advantage

Standard subdivisions are added for either or both topics in heading

Class works on specialization and comparative advantage that emphasize international commerce in 382.1042

.604 8	Competition and restraint

Standard subdivisions are added for either or both topics in heading

Class monopoly and monopolies in 338.82

.61	Private enterprise

Class specific systems of private enterprise in 338.63; class specific sizes of private enterprise in 338.64

.62	Public enterprise

.63	Systems of production

For factory system, see 338.65

.632	Guild system

.634	Domestic system

Class here cottage industry

.64	Size of enterprises

Class relation of size of enterprise to cost of production in 338.5144; class specific types of enterprises of specific sizes in 338.7–338.8

.642	Small business

Including custom production

Class here small industries

.642 089	Racial, ethnic, national groups

Class minority enterprises in 338.6422

.642 2	Minority enterprises

Class handicraft industries operated by minorities in 338.6425

.642 5	Handicraft industries
.644	Big business

Class here large industry

Class monopoly and monopolies in 338.82

.65	Factory system
.7	**Business enterprises**

Not limited to private or capitalist enterprises

Class here structure of business enterprises; interdisciplinary works on business enterprises, on organizations for production

For cooperatives, see 334; for combinations, see 338.8

See Manual at 338.7 vs. 335.9; also at 338.092

.71 Formation and dissolution of business enterprises

> 338.72–338.74 Specific kinds of business enterprises

Class specific kinds of business enterprises in specific industries and groups of industries in 338.76; class comprehensive works in 338.7

.72	Individual proprietorships
.73	Partnerships
.74	Corporations

Open and closed

Class government corporations as part of the public administrative process in 352.266

.76 Business enterprises by industry

Class here specific individual business enterprises, biographies of entrepreneurs in specific fields

Class business enterprises engaged in trade in 380.1

For biographies of people known for their contribution to technology, see the kind of contribution in 600, plus notation 092 from Table 1, e.g., biographies of mining engineers 622.092

See Manual at 338 vs. 060, 381, 382, 670.294, 910, T1—025, T1—0294, T1—0296

.761 Business enterprises in industries other than extractive, manufacturing, construction

Class here service industries

.761 000 1–.761 000 9   Standard subdivisions

.761 001–.761 999   Subdivisions for business enterprises in industries other than extractive, manufacturing, construction

> Add to base number 338.761 notation 001–999, e.g., law firms 338.76134; however, for financial institutions, see 332.1–332.6; for real estate business enterprises, see 333.33; for cooperative enterprises, see 334; for insurance companies, see 368.0065; for enterprises engaged in commerce, communications, transportation, see 380

.762–.769   **Business enterprises in extractive, manufacturing, construction industries**

> Add to base number 338.76 the numbers following 6 in 620–690, e.g., agriculture 338.763; however, for enterprises engaged in production of energy, see 333.79; for cooperative enterprises, see 334.682–334.689

.8   **Combinations**

> Organization and structure for massive production and control of production

> Class here antitrust policies, economic concentration, comprehensive works on combinations and their practices

> To be classed here, works about specific individual enterprises must stress that they are combinations; otherwise, the works are classed in 338.76

> *See Manual at 338.092*

SUMMARY

338.804	**Special topics**
.82	**Restrictive practices**
.83	**Mergers**
.85	**Trusts**
.86	**Holding companies**
.87	**Informal arrangements**
.88	**International (Multinational) business enterprises**

.804   **Special topics**

.804 2   Kinds of combinations

> Including horizontal, vertical, conglomerate

.82   **Restrictive practices**

> Class here monopoly and monopolies, oligopoly and oligopolies

> Class price determination in 338.523; class restrictive practices of international (multinational) business enterprises in 338.884

.826   **Restrictive practices in specific industries, groups of industries, fields of enterprise**

[.826 01–.826 09]   Standard subdivisions

> Do not use; class in 338.8201–338.8209

.826 1   Restrictive practices in industries and fields of enterprise other than extractive, manufacturing, construction

Class here service industries

.826 100 01–.826 100 09   Standard subdivisions

.826 100 1–.826 199 9   Subdivisions for restrictive practices in industries and fields of enterprise other than extractive, manufacturing, construction

Add to base number 338.8261 notation 001–999, e.g., restrictive practices in publishing 338.82610705; however, for restrictive practices by combinations in the financial industries, see 332.1–332.6; for restrictive practices by combinations in real estate business, see 333.33; for restrictive practices by combinations in cooperative enterprise, see 334; for restrictive practices by combinations in the insurance industry, see 368; for restrictive practices by combinations in commerce, communications, transportation, see 380

.826 2–.826 9   Restrictive practices in extractive, manufacturing, construction industries and fields of enterprise

Add to base number 338.826 the numbers following 6 in 620–690, e.g., restrictive practices by combinations engaged in computer engineering 338.8262139; however, for restrictive practices by combinations engaged in energy production, see 333.79; for restrictive practices by cooperatives, see 334

>   338.83–338.87   Specific forms of combinations and their practices

Class international combinations regardless of form in 338.88; class comprehensive works in 338.8

.83   Mergers

Class here amalgamations

.836   Mergers in specific industries, groups of industries, fields of enterprise

[.836 01–.836 09]   Standard subdivisions

Do not use; class in 338.8301–338.8309

.836 1   Mergers in industries and fields of enterprise other than extractive, manufacturing, construction

Class here service industries

.836 100 01–.836 100 09   Standard subdivisions

.836 100 1–.836 199 9	Subdivisions for mergers in industries and fields of enterprise other than extractive, manufacturing, construction

> Add to base number 338.8361 notation 001–999, e.g., mergers of publishers 338.83610705; however, for mergers of financial institutions, see 332.1–332.6; for mergers of real estate business enterprises, see 333.33; for mergers of cooperatives, see 334; for mergers of enterprises in the insurance industry, see 368.0065; for mergers of enterprises engaged in commerce, communications, transportation, see 380

.836 2–.836 9	Mergers in extractive, manufacturing, construction industries and fields of enterprise

> Add to base number 338.836 the numbers following 6 in 620–690, e.g., mergers of automotive companies 338.836292; however, for mergers of enterprises engaged in energy production, see 333.79; for mergers of cooperatives, see 334

.85	Trusts
.86	Holding companies
.87	Informal arrangements

> Including cartels, interlocking directorates, pools

.88	**International (Multinational) business enterprises**
.880 9	Historical and persons treatment

> Do not use for geographic treatment; class in 338.888–338.889

> 338.881–338.884 Specific aspects of international (multinational) business enterprises

> Class specific aspects of international enterprises engaged in specific fields in 338.887; class specific aspects of foreign-owned enterprises in specific areas in 338.888–338.889; class comprehensive works in 338.88

.881	Growth, expansion, power

> Standard subdivisions are added for any or all topics in heading

> *See also 322.3 for political influence*

.883	Role in international economic development
.884	Restrictive practices and their control

> Standard subdivisions are added for either or both topics in heading

> International monopoly, oligopoly

.887	Multinational business enterprises in specific industries, groups of industries, fields

[.887 01–.887 08]   Standard subdivisions

Do not use; class in 338.8801–338.8808

[.887 09]   Historical and persons treatment

Do not use for geographic treatment; class in 338.888–338.889

.887 1   Multinational business enterprises in industries and fields of enterprise other than extractive, manufacturing, construction

Class here service industries

.887 100 01–.887 100 09   Standard subdivisions

.887 100 1–.887 199 9   Subdivisions for multinational business enterprises in industries and fields of enterprise other than extractive, manufacturing, construction

Add to base number 338.8871 notation 001–999, e.g., multinational enterprises engaged in advertising 338.88716591; however, for multinational enterprises in financial industries, see 332.1–332.6; for multinational enterprises in real estate business, see 333.33; for multinational cooperatives, see 334; for multinational enterprises in the insurance industry, see 368.0065; for multinational enterprises in commerce, communications, transportation, see 380

.887 2–.887 9   Multinational business enterprises in extractive, manufacturing, construction industries and fields of enterprise

Add to base number 338.887 the numbers following 6 in 620–690, e.g., multinational enterprises engaged in mining petroleum and natural gas 338.88722338; however, for multinational enterprises engaged in energy production, see 333.79; for multinational cooperatives, see 334

.888   Foreign-owned enterprises by location of operations

Class foreign-owned enterprises in specific industries and groups of industries in 338.887; class enterprises owned by inhabitants of one nation in another nation in 338.889

See Manual at 338.888–338.889

[.888 09]   Historical treatment

Do not use; class in 338.8809

[.888 091]   Treatment by areas, regions, places in general

Do not use; class in 338.8881

[.888 092]   Persons

Do not use; class in 338.88092

[.888 093–.888 099]   Treatment by specific continents, countries, localities

Do not use; class in 338.8883–338.8889

.888 1   Foreign-owned enterprises in areas, regions, places in general

> Add to base number 333.8881 the numbers following —1 in notation
> 11–19 from Table 2, e.g., foreign-owned enterprises in developing
> countries 338.8881724

.888 3–.888 9   Foreign-owned enterprises in specific continents, countries, localities

> Add to base number 338.888 notation 3–9 from Table 2, e.g.,
> foreign-owned enterprises in Europe 338.8884

.889   Foreign-owned enterprises by owner

> Class foreign-owned enterprises in specific industries or groups of
> industries in 338.887; class foreign-owned enterprises in a specific area
> without regard to area of ownership in 338.888

> *See Manual at 338.888–338.889*

[.889 09]   Historical treatment

> Do not use; class in 338.8809

[.889 091]   Treatment by areas, regions, places in general

> Do not use; class in 338.8891

[.889 092]   Persons

> Do not use; class in 338.88092

[.889 093–.889 099]   Treatment by specific continents, countries, localities

> Do not use; class in 338.8893–338.8899

.889 1   Foreign-owned enterprises by owner in areas, regions, places in general

> Add to base number 338.8891 the numbers following —1 in notation
> 11–19 from Table 2, e.g., foreign enterprises owned by citizens of
> developing countries 338.8891724; then, for area in which enterprise
> is located, add 0* and to the result add notation 1–9 from Table 2,
> e.g., foreign enterprises owned by citizens of developing countries
> and located in Africa 338.889172406

.889 3–.889 9   Foreign-owned enterprises by owner

> Add to base number 338.889 notation 3–9 from Table 2, e.g., foreign
> enterprises owned by United States nationals 338.88973; then, for
> area in which enterprise is located, add 0* and to the result add
> notation 1–9 from Table 2, e.g., enterprises owned by United States
> nationals in Canada 338.88973071

---

*Add 00 for standard subdivisions; see instructions at beginning of Table 1

.9   **Economic development and growth**

> Standard subdivisions are added for either or both topics in heading
>
> Including autarky and interdependence
>
> Class here economic planning, government policies and programs
>
> *For economic development and growth with respect to specific kinds of industries, see 338.1–338.4. For economic development and growth with respect to a specific subject not provided for here, see the subject, e.g., international development banks 332.153*

.900 1–.900 8   Standard subdivisions

.900 9   Historical, geographic, persons treatment

[.900 93–.900 99]   Treatment by specific continents, countries, localities

> Do not use; class in 338.93–338.99

.91   **International development and growth [*formerly also* 337]**

> Standard subdivisions are added for either or both topics in heading
>
> Foreign economic assistance (foreign aid)
>
> Class here assistance (aid) by international organizations, technical assistance
>
> Class foreign economic policies and relations of specific jurisdictions and groups of jurisdictions in 337.3–337.9

.910 91   Treatment by areas, regions, places in general

> Do not use for assistance given by specific jurisdictions and groups of jurisdictions to other jurisdictions; class in 338.911
>
> Class here assistance to specific jurisdictions and groups of jurisdictions

.910 93–.910 99   Treatment by specific continents, countries, localities

> Do not use for assistance given by specific jurisdictions and groups of jurisdictions to other jurisdictions; class in 338.913–338.919
>
> Class here assistance to specific jurisdictions and groups of jurisdictions

.911   International assistance (aid) by specific groups of jurisdictions in areas, regions, places in general

> Add to base number 338.911 the numbers following —1 in notation 11–19 from Table 2, e.g., assistance by countries where Arabs predominate 338.91174; then, for assistance by a specific group of jurisdictions to another group of jurisdictions or to a specific jurisdiction, add 0* and to the result add notation 1 or 3–9 from Table 2, e.g., assistance by Arab countries to Africa 338.9117406

---

*Add 00 for standard subdivisions; see instructions at beginning of Table 1

.913–.919   International assistance (aid) by specific jurisdictions and groups of jurisdictions in specific continents, countries, localities

> Add to base number 338.91 notation 3–9 from Table 2, e.g., assistance by United Kingdom 338.9141; then, for assistance by a specific jurisdiction or group of jurisdictions to another jurisdiction or group of jurisdictions, add 0* and again add notation 1 or 3–9 from Table 2, e.g., assistance by United Kingdom to Nigeria 338.91410669

.92   Specific policies

> Class specific policies in specific continents, countries, localities in 338.93–338.99

[.920 1–.920 8]   Standard subdivisions

> Do not use; class in 338.9001–338.9008

[.920 9]   Historical, geographic, persons treatment

> Do not use; class in 338.9009

[.920 93–.920 99]   Treatment by specific continents, countries, localities

> Do not use; class in 338.93–338.99

.922   Subsidies and grants

> Standard subdivisions are added for either or both topics in heading

.924   Nationalization

.925   Privatization

.926   Information policy

> Class here science policy, technology transfer
>
> *See Manual at 338.926 vs. 352.745, 500*

.927   Appropriate technology

> Class here alternative technology

.93–.99   Economic development and growth in specific continents, countries, localities

> Add to base number 338.9 notation 3–9 from Table 2, e.g., economic policies of United Kingdom 338.941; then add 0* and to the result add the numbers following 338.92 in 338.922–338.927, e.g., subsidies in United Kingdom 338.94102
>
> Subdivisions are added for either or both topics in heading

338.941

PF1

*Add 00 for standard subdivisions; see instructions at beginning of Table 1

339   Macroeconomics and related topics

Standard subdivisions are added for macroeconomics and related topics together, for macroeconomics alone

For economic fluctuations, see 338.54

See Manual at 332, 336 vs. 339

SUMMARY

339.01	**Philosophy and theory**
.2	**Distribution of income and wealth**
.3	**National product, wealth, income accounts and accounting**
.4	**Factors affecting national product, wealth, income**
.5	**Macroeconomic policy**

.01   Philosophy and theory [*formerly* 339.3]

.2   Distribution of income and wealth

Standard subdivisions are added for either or both topics in heading

Class national wealth and income accounts and accounting in 339.3; class specific aspects of income distribution in 339.4; class transfer payments, redistribution of income in 339.52

.21   Functional distribution of income and wealth

Functional distribution of income: division of nation's income among factors of production: land (rent, rental income), labor (wages, salaries), capital (interest), entrepreneurship (proprietor's income), corporate profits

Standard subdivisions are added for either or both topics in heading

.22   Personal distribution of income and wealth

Division of nation's income and wealth among families and individuals

Standard subdivisions are added for either or both topics in heading

Including consumer income, household income

Class income-consumption relations (household budget) in 339.41; class poverty in 339.46

See Manual at 339.32 vs. 339.22

.23   Input-output accounts (Interindustry accounts)

Accounts and analysis of goods and services provided by each industry for all other industries and consuming units

Including data on specific industries

.26   Flow-of-funds accounts

Sources of funds paid to and use of funds by various sectors of the economy

.3   **National product, wealth, income accounts and accounting**

Standard subdivisions are added for accounts, accounting, or both

Class here product, wealth, income accounts and accounting of other types of areas, e.g., states, provinces; interdisciplinary works on national product, wealth, income

Philosophy and theory of macroeconomics relocated to 339.01

Class macroeconomic policy in 339.5

> *For distribution of income and wealth, see 339.2; for factors affecting national product, wealth, income, see 339.4*

.309 3–.309 9   Treatment by specific continents

Do not use for treatment by specific countries and localities; class in 339.33–339.39

.31   Gross product accounts and accounting

Standard subdivisions are added for either or both topics in heading

Class here gross domestic product (GDP), gross national product (GNP)

> *See also 339.32 for net national product (NNP)*

.310 93–.310 99   Treatment by specific continents

Do not use for treatment by specific countries and localities; class in 339.33–339.39

.32   Other kinds of national accounts and accounting

Including net national product (NNP), national income (NI), personal income (PI), disposable personal income (DPI)

> *See Manual at 339.32 vs. 339.22*

.320 93–.320 99   Treatment by specific continents

Do not use for treatment by specific countries and localities; class in 339.33–339.39

.33–.39   Product, wealth, income accounts and accounting of specific countries and localities

Add to base number 339.3 notation 3–9 from Table 2, e.g., gross national product of the United States 339.373

.4   **Factors affecting national product, wealth, income**

Standard subdivisions are added for any or all topics in heading

> *For economic stabilization, see 339.5*

.41 Income in relation to consumption

Including consumer responses to decreases and increases in income, the effect of consumption on income (the accelerator), household budgets as a measure of relation of income to consumption

Class effects of prices on consumption in 339.42; class the multiplier, the relation of consumption and savings in 339.43

See also 658.834 for consumer research in marketing management

See Manual at 339.41, 339.42 vs. 332.41

.42 Cost of living (Prices)

Including effect of prices on consumption; the total effects of rising costs of a commodity on the consumer, e.g., the total effects of rising energy costs on the consumer

Class price statistics and indexes in 338.528

See Manual at 339.41, 339.42 vs. 332.41

.43 Savings and investment

Standard subdivisions are added for either or both topics in heading

Including effect of investment on income (the multiplier), relation of consumption and savings

Class here capital formation

Class interdisciplinary works on capital formation and saving in 332.0415

.46 Economic causes and effects of poverty

See also 362.51 for social causes of poverty, 362.53 for social effects of poverty

.47 Consumption (Spending)

Class here standard of living, interdisciplinary works on consumption

Class consumption in relation to income in 339.41; class consumption in relation to cost of living in 339.42; class consumption in relation to savings and investment in 339.43; class consumption in relation to poverty in 339.46; class government spending in 339.522

For social aspects of consumption, see 306.3; for consumption viewed in light of its effect on the future supply of natural resources and energy, see 333.7–333.9, plus notation 13 from the add table under 333.7; for consumption as a factor in shortages and surpluses of products, see 338; for consumption of specific products and services, of specific groups of products and services, see 339.48; for works discussing consumption as sales or marketing opportunities (e.g., results of market studies) or as a measure of the volume, value, or kind of trade, see 380.1–382

See also 658.834 for consumer research in marketing management

.48   Consumption of specific products and services, of specific groups of
               products and services

[.480 001–.480 009]   Standard subdivisions

                           Do not use; class in 339.4701–339.4709

.480 01–.489 99   Subdivisions for consumption of specific products and services, of
                           specific groups of products and services

                           Add to base number 339.48 notation 001–999, e.g., consumption
                           of agricultural products 339.4863

.49   Conservation of national resources

               National resources: natural resources; human resources; resources that result
               from human activities, e.g., housing

               For conservation of natural resources, see 333.72

[.490 91]   Treatment by areas, regions, places in general

                           Do not use; class in 339.491

[.490 93–.490 99]   Treatment by specific continents, countries, localities

                           Do not use; class in 339.493–339.499

.491   Conservation of national resources in areas, regions, places in
               general

                           Add to base number 339.491 the numbers following — 1 in notation
                           11–19 from Table 2, e.g., conservation of the national resources of
                           developing countries 339.491724

.493–.499   Conservation of national resources in specific continents, countries,
               localities

                           Add to base number 339.49 notation 3–9 from Table 2, e.g.,
                           conservation of national resources of India 339.4954

.5   **Macroeconomic policy**

               Class here economic stabilization and growth, equilibrium, full employment
               policies, incomes policies

               Class comprehensive works on wage-price policy in 331.21

               *For measures to combat inflation, see 332.415; for measures to control
               economic fluctuations, see 338.543; for measures to promote growth and
               development, see 338.9*

               See Manual at 331.29 vs. 339.5

.52   Use of fiscal policy

               Class here income redistribution

.522   Government spending

               Including transfer payments

.523	Budget surpluses and deficits
.525	Taxation
.53	Use of monetary policy

Including discount rates offered by central banks, reserve requirements imposed on banks, open-market operations, regulation of bank credit

Class comprehensive works on relation of central banks to monetary policy in 332.112; class comprehensive works on monetary policy in 332.46

340 Law

Class here jurisprudence

Instructions for building classification numbers for works on law of a jurisdiction or area are found at 342–349

See Manual at 340; also at 340 vs. 808.06634; also at 342–349; also at 363 vs. 340, 353–354

SUMMARY

340.02–.09	**Standard subdivisions**
.1	**Philosophy and theory of law**
.2	**Comparative law**
.3	**Law reform**
.5	**Legal systems**
.9	**Conflict of laws**
341	**International law**
.01–.09	**Standard subdivisions; treaties and cases; relation of international and domestic law**
.1	**Sources of international law**
.2	**The world community**
.3	**Relations between states**
.4	**Jurisdiction and jurisdictional relations of states**
.5	**Disputes and conflicts between states**
.6	**Law of war**
.7	**International cooperation**
342	**Constitutional and administrative law**
.001–.009	**Standard subdivisions; laws, regulations, cases, procedure, courts**
.02	**Basic instruments of government**
.03	**Revision and amendment of basic instruments of government**
.04	**Structure, powers, functions of government**
.05	**Legislative branch of government**
.06	**Executive branch of government**
.07	**Election law**
.08	**Jurisdiction over persons**
.09	**Local government**
.1	**Socioeconomic regions**
.3–.9	**Specific jurisdictions and areas**

343	**Military, defense, public property, public finance, tax, trade (commerce), industrial law**
.001–.009	Standard subdivisions; laws, regulations, cases, procedure, courts
.01	Military, defense, veterans' law
.02	Law of public property
.03	Law of public finance
.04	Tax law
.05	Kinds of taxes by base
.06	Kinds of taxes by incidence
.07	Regulation of economic activity
.08	Regulation of trade (commerce)
.09	Control of public utilities
.1	Socioeconomic regions
.3–.9	Specific jurisdictions and areas
344	**Labor, social service, education, cultural law**
.001–.009	Standard subdivisions; laws, regulations, cases, procedure, courts
.01	Labor
.02	Social insurance
.03	Social service
.04	Miscellaneous social problems and services
.05	Police services, other aspects of public safety, matters concerning public morals and customs
.06	Public works
.07	Education, schools, students
.08	Educational and cultural exchanges
.09	Culture and religion
.1	Socioeconomic regions
.3–.9	Specific jurisdictions and areas
345	**Criminal law**
.001–.009	Standard subdivisions; laws, regulations, cases, procedure, courts
.01	Criminal courts
.02	Crimes (Offenses)
.03	Criminals (Offenders)
.04	Liability, responsibility, guilt
.05	Criminal procedure
.06	Evidence
.07	Trials
.08	Juvenile procedure and courts
.1	Socioeconomic regions
.3–.9	Specific jurisdictions and areas
346	**Private law**
.001–.009	Standard subdivisions; laws, regulations, cases, procedure, courts; equity
.01	Persons and domestic relations
.02	Contracts and agency
.03	Torts (Delicts)
.04	Property
.05	Inheritance, succession, fiduciary trusts, trustees
.06	Organizations (Associations)
.07	Commercial law
.08	Banking and insurance
.09	Securities and negotiable instruments
.1	Socioeconomic regions
.3–.9	Specific jurisdictions and areas

347		**Civil procedure and courts**
	.001–.009	**Standard subdivisions; laws, regulations, cases, procedure, courts**
	.01	**Courts**
	.02	**Courts with general original jurisdiction**
	.03	**Appellate courts**
	.04	**Courts with specialized jurisdiction**
	.05	**Procedure**
	.06	**Evidence**
	.07	**Trials**
	.08	**Appellate procedure**
	.09	**Dispute resolution**
	.1	**Socioeconomic regions**
	.3–.9	**Specific jurisdictions and areas**
348		**Laws (Statutes), regulations, cases**
	.001–.009	**Standard subdivisions and codification**
	.01	**Preliminary materials**
	.02	**Laws (Statutes) and regulations**
	.04	**Cases**
	.05	**Advisory opinions of attorneys-general (ministers of justice)**
	.1	**Socioeconomic regions**
	.3–.9	**Specific jurisdictions and areas**
349		**Law of specific socioeconomic regions and of specific jurisdictions and areas**
	.1	**Law of specific socioeconomic regions**
	.4–.9	**Law of specific jurisdictions and areas**

[.01]   Philosophy and theory

> Do not use; class in 340.1

>   340.02–340.09   Standard subdivisions

Class comprehensive works in 340

See Manual at 340.02–340.09 vs. 349

.02   Miscellany

.023   Law as a profession, occupation, hobby

See Manual at 340.023 vs. 347.0504

.03–.08   Standard subdivisions

.09   Historical, geographic, persons treatment of law

Do not use for historical and geographic treatment of law of traditional societies; class in 340.52. Do not use for comprehensive works on law of specific jurisdictions and areas in modern world; class in 349

[.091 7]   Socioeconomic regions

Relocated to 349.1

.092   Persons treatment

Do not use for theorists; class in 340.1092

[.093]	Treatment in the ancient world
	Do not use; class in 340.53
.1	**Philosophy and theory of law**
	For theory of specific legal systems, see 340.5
.109	Historical, geographic, persons treatment of legal theories and schools
.11	Special topics of philosophy and theory of law
	Do not use for systems; class in 340.1
	Including origin, sources, nature, limits of law; rule of law; legal reasoning; justice, injustice; equal protection of the law
	Class interdisciplinary works on equal protection of the law in 323.42
.112	Law and ethics
	Class here human rights, law and morality, legal positivism, natural law
.115	Law and society
	Including distributive justice
	Class here sociological jurisprudence
.12–.19	Specific aspects of philosophy and theory
	Add to base number 340.1 the numbers following —01 in notation 012–019 from Table 1, e.g., classification of law 340.12
.2	**Comparative law**
	Class comparison of specific branches of law in 342–347
	(If option A under 342–349 is chosen, class comparative law in 349
	(If option B under 342–349 is chosen, class comparative law in 342)
.3	**Law reform**
.5	**Legal systems**
	History and theory
	Class here customary law
	Class a specific subject in specific systems of law with the subject in 340.9–347, e.g., juristic persons in Islamic law 346.1671013, in ancient Roman law 346.37013, in Byzantine law 346.495013, in civil law 346.013; class religious and ceremonial laws of a specific religious body with the body, e.g., Christian canon law 262.9
.52	Law of traditional societies
	Class here ethnological jurisprudence

| [.520 93] | Law of traditional societies in ancient world |
| | Do not use; class in 340.53 |

| [.520 94–.520 99] | Law of traditional societies in modern world |
| | Relocated to 340.524–340.529 |

.524–.529   Law of traditional societies in modern world [*formerly also* 340.52094–340.52099]

> Add to base number 340.52 notation 4–9 from Table 2, e.g., traditional law of the Sahara 340.5266

.53   Ancient law

> Add to base number 340.53 the numbers following —3 in notation 31–39 from Table 2, e.g., law of ancient Greece 340.538; however, for Roman law, see 340.54; for ancient Oriental law, see 340.58

.54   Roman law

> Including Byzantine law

> Class comprehensive works on Roman-derived law in specific jurisdictions and areas in modern world in 349

> *For medieval Roman law, see 340.55*

>   340.55–340.59   Medieval, modern, Oriental systems of law

> Class comprehensive works in 340.5; class comprehensive works on law of specific jurisdictions and areas in modern world in 349

.55   Medieval European law

> Including feudal law, medieval Roman law

> Class medieval civil law in 340.56; class medieval common law in 340.57

.56   Civil law systems

> Systems of law derived from Roman law

> Including Roman-Dutch law

> *See Manual at 340.56 vs. 342–347*

.57   Common law systems

> *See Manual at 340.57 vs. 342–347*

.58 Oriental law

Indigenous systems

Class systems of law in Oriental countries derived from a European system with the system from which they are derived, e.g., civil law 340.56

For Islamic law, see 340.59

See Manual at 296.18 vs. 340.58

.59 Islamic law

Class here sharia [*formerly* 297.14], fiqh

Fiqh in relation to religious and ceremonial laws and decisions relocated to 297.14

For religious and ceremonial law of Islam, see 297.14

.9 **Conflict of laws**

Body of rules governing choice of jurisdiction in cases in private law that fall under laws of two or more such jurisdictions

Class here private international law

Add to base number 340.9 the numbers following 346.0 in 346.01–346.09, e.g., conflict of divorce laws 340.9166

For domestic conflict of laws, see 342.042

See Manual at 340.9

341 **International law**

Class comprehensive works on public law in 342

See also 340.9 for private international law

See Manual at 341 vs. 327

(Option: Class international law of a specific discipline or subject with the discipline or subject, plus notation 026 from Table 1, e.g., international transportation law 388.026, *not* 341.756)

SUMMARY

.02 Miscellany

.026   Treaties and cases

Texts of treaties and judicial decisions; guides

Class here conventions, protocols

Text of treaties limited to termination of war relocated to 341.66026

Class treaties as a source of international law in 341.1; class comprehensive works on treaties in 341.37. Class treaties and cases on a specific subject with the subject in 341.2–341.7, plus notation 026 from add table under 341.2–341.7, e.g., collections of treaties on air transportation 341.7567026

See Manual at 341.37

\>   341.026 1–341.026 6   Texts of treaties

Class comprehensive works in 341.026

\>   341.026 1–341.026 3   Series of treaties compiled by international organizations

Class specific kinds of treaties regardless of the organization compiling them in 341.0265–341.0266; class comprehensive works in 341.026

.026 1   League of Nations series of treaties

Class a League of Nations series relating to a specific area in 341.0264

.026 2   United Nations series of treaties

Class a United Nations series relating to a specific area in 341.0264

.026 3   Series of treaties compiled by regional organizations

Add to base number 341.0263 the numbers following 341.24 in 341.242–341.249, e.g., a series compiled by Organization of American States 341.02635

.026 4   Collections of treaties by area

Add to base number 341.0264 notation 1–9 from Table 2, e.g., treaties on Philippines 341.0264599

Class collections of treaties relating to a specific area compiled by regional organizations in 341.0263; class collections of specific kinds of treaties by area in 341.0265–341.0266

\>   341.026 5–341.026 6   Kinds of treaties

Collections and individual treaties

Class comprehensive works in 341.026

.026 5	Multilateral treaties

Class an agreement between an international organization and a specific country in 341.026

.026 6	Bilateral treaties

Add to base number 341.0266 notation 3–9 from Table 2, e.g., treaties of the United Kingdom 341.026641; then add 0* and again add notation 3–9 from Table 2, e.g., treaties between United Kingdom and France 341.026641044

Give priority in notation to the country coming first in Table 2
(Option: Give priority in notation to the country requiring local emphasis, e.g., libraries in United States class treaties between United Kingdom and the United States in 341.026673041)

.026 7	Codification
.026 8	Cases

Decisions and reports

Class here general collections of cases on international matters tried in any court system

Add to base number 341.0268 notation 4–9 from Table 2, e.g., cases brought by United Kingdom 341.026841; then, for cases brought by that nation against another nation, add 0* and again add notation 4–9 from Table 2, e.g., cases brought by United Kingdom against United States 341.026841073
(Option: Give priority in notation to the nation requiring local emphasis, e.g., libraries in United States class all cases involving United States and United Kingdom in 341.026873041)

.04	Relation of international and domestic law

Class here works on whether domestic or international law prevails in a certain situation

Class the law of a nation or lesser jurisdiction that carries out the provisions of an international agreement in 342–347

.092	Persons treatment

For critical works on individual publicists, see 341.1

.1	**Sources of international law**

Treaties, judicial decisions, custom, general principles of law, works of publicists (theorists)

Class here critical works on individual publicists (theorists)

Class texts of treaties and reports of judicial decisions in 341.026; class comprehensive works on treaties in 341.37. Class writings of publicists on a specific subject with the subject in 341.2–341.7, e.g., international rivers 341.442

*Add 00 for standard subdivisions; see instructions at beginning of Table 1

> ### 341.2–341.7 Specific topics

Add to each subdivision identified by † as follows:

01	Philosophy and theory
02	Miscellany
026	Treaties and cases

Texts of treaties and judicial decisions; guides, e.g., checklists, citators, digests, indexes

Do not use for discussions, commentaries, or popular works; class with the subject in 341.2–341.7 without further subdivision

Class here conventions, protocols

Add to base number 026 the numbers following 341.026 in 341.0261–341.0268, e.g., multilateral treaties 0265

See Manual at 341.37

03–08	Standard subdivisions
09	Historical, geographic, persons treatment

See Manual at 342–349

Class comprehensive works in 341

.2 The world community

Class here international persons and personality

.21 World government

Proposals and schemes

> ### 341.22–341.24 International governmental organizations

Class here legal responsibilities of officials, privileges and immunities, interdisciplinary works on international governmental organizations

Personnel administration in international governmental organizations relocated to 352.6211

Class comprehensive works on international governmental organizations in 341.2; class interdisciplinary works on international organizations in 060

For administration of international governmental organizations, see 352.11. For a specialized international governmental organization, see the subject with which it deals, plus notation 0601 from Table 1, e.g., Interpol 363.20601; for legal aspects of a specialized international governmental organization, see the subject with which it deals in 341.2–341.7, e.g., Interpol 341.77

See Manual at 341.22–341.24

.22	League of Nations

Add to base number 341.22 the numbers following 341.23 in 341.2301–341.239, e.g., Covenant of the League 341.222; however, management relocated from 341.22068 to 352.112; management relocated from 341.223 to 352.112

.23	United Nations
.230 13	Value

Evaluation of and opinions about the effectiveness and worth of the United Nations

[.230 68]	Management

Do not use; class in 352.113

.231	†Functions and activities

Class functions and activities of specific branches of the United Nations in 341.232. Class a specific function or activity with the function or activity in 341.2–341.7, e.g., role in the peaceful settlement of disputes 341.523

.232	†Organization

Including charter

Class here rules of procedure

For legal responsibility of officials, see 341.233

.232 2	†General Assembly
.232 3	†Security Council
[.232 4]	Secretariat

Relocated to 352.113

.233	†Admission and membership

Management relocated to 352.113

For organization, see 341.232

.234–.239	General relations with specific nations

Add to base number 341.23 notation 4–9 from Table 2, e.g., relations with United States 341.2373

Class relations dealing with a specific subject with the subject in 341.2–341.7, e.g., United Nations peacekeeping operations 341.584

.24	Regional associations and organizations
.242	European regional associations and organizations

†Add as instructed under 341.2–341.7

.242 2	†European Union

Class here European Common Market, European Community, European Economic Community

Class laws promulgated by European Union with the subject in 341.2–341.7, e.g., economic enactments 341.750614

For European Parliament, see 341.2424

.242 4	European Parliament

For legislative process in European Parliament, see 328.4

.242 7	Council for Mutual Economic Assistance
.243	Atlantic regional associations and organizations
.245	Western Hemisphere regional associations and organizations

Including Organization of American States

.246	Pacific regional associations and organizations
.247	Asian regional associations and organizations
.247 3	Far East regional associations and organizations

Including ASEAN (Association of East Asian Nations)

.247 7	Western Asia regional associations and organizations

Including League of Arab States

Class here Middle East organizations

.249	African regional associations and organizations

For League of Arab States, see 341.2477

.26	†States

Including recognition of states and governments; mergers, self-determination, sovereignty, succession of states

Class here liability of states

Class liability of states with respect to a specific subject with the subject in 341.2–341.7, e.g., liability for the safety of diplomatic personnel 341.33, liability for damages caused by testing nuclear weapons 341.734

For semisovereign states, see 341.27; for relations between states, see 341.3; for jurisdiction of states, see 341.4

.27	†Semisovereign states

Including mandates, protectorates, trusteeships

.28	†Non-self-governing territories

Class here colonies

†Add as instructed under 341.2–341.7

.29 †Areas having special status in international law

    Including partitioned areas, e.g., Antarctica, Cyprus

.3 **†Relations between states**

    For jurisdictional relations, see 341.4; for disputes and conflicts, see 341.5; for international cooperation, see 341.7

.33 †Diplomatic law

    Including legal aspects of functions, immunities, privileges, status of diplomatic personnel and agencies; delegations to international organizations and their staffs

    Class officials and employees of international organizations in 341.22–341.24; class interdisciplinary works on diplomacy in 327.2

    For consular law, see 341.35

.35 †Consular law

    Including legal aspects of function, immunities, privileges, immunities, status of consular personnel

.37 Treaties

    Including negotiation and ratification, validity and binding force, termination, interpretation

    Class treaties on a specific subject with the subject in 341.2–341.7, plus notation 026 from add table under 341.2–341.7, e.g., a disarmament treaty between Russia and the United States 341.733026647073

    For texts of treaties, see 341.026; for treaties as sources of international law, see 341.1

    See Manual at 341.37

.4 **†Jurisdiction and jurisdictional relations of states**

    Class here extraterritoriality, servitudes and easements, right of innocent passage

    Subdivisions are added for either or both topics in heading

---

> 341.42–341.47 Jurisdiction over physical space

    Class comprehensive works in 341.4

.42 †Territory

    Including acquisition, boundaries, border disputes

    Class mergers of states in 341.26; class boundary rivers in 341.442

.44 †Bodies of water

    For high seas, see 341.45

†Add as instructed under 341.2–341.7

.442	†Rivers

National, semi-national, boundary, internationalized rivers

Including combined river, lake, canal systems, e.g., Saint Lawrence Seaway

Class canalized rivers in 341.446

.444	†Lakes and landlocked seas

Subdivisions are added for either or both topics in heading

Class combined river, lake, canal systems in 341.442

.446	†Canals and straits

Class combined river, lake, canal systems in 341.442

.448	†Territorial waters

Including bays, continental shelves

Class access to the sea, comprehensive works on ocean and sea waters in 341.45

.45	†High seas

Class here comprehensive works on international law of ocean and sea waters

For territorial waters, see 341.448; for development and conservation of sea resources, see 341.762; for oceanographic research, see 341.76755

.46	†Airspace

Class meteorological research in 341.76755

.47	†Extraterrestrial space

Including the moon, planets

Class space research in 341.76752

.48	†Jurisdiction over persons

Including jurisdiction of the state over its nationals in other areas

Class here jurisdiction over personal property

Class private international law in 340.9

.481	†Human rights

Class here civil rights

.481 01	Philosophy and theory

Class here natural rights

See also 340.112 for natural law

†Add as instructed under 341.2–341.7

.482	†Nationality and citizenship

Subdivisions are added for either or both topics in heading

.484	†Jurisdiction over aliens and alien property

> *For liability of states for aliens, see 341.26; for stateless persons and refugees, see 341.486; for criminal jurisdiction over aliens, see 341.488; for enemy aliens and their property, see 341.67*

.484 2	†Immigration, passports, visas
.484 4	†Double taxation
.484 6	†Nationalization (Expropriation) of alien property
.486	†Jurisdiction over stateless persons and refugees
.488	†Criminal jurisdiction

Including extradition, right of asylum

Class international crimes in 341.77

.5	**†Disputes and conflicts between states**

Class disputes on a specific subject with the subject in 341.2–341.7, e.g., jurisdictional disputes 341.4

> *For law of war, see 341.6*

.52	†Peaceful settlement

Including mediation

> *For adjudication, see 341.55*

.522	†Arbitration
.523	†Role of international organizations

Class peace conferences in 341.73

.55	†Adjudication

Courts and court procedure

Including role of domestic courts in adjudicating matters of public international law, interpretation of general international law in courts, adjustment of nonwar claims

Class interpretation of a specific subject with the subject in 341.2–341.7, e.g., interpretation of human rights 341.481

.552	†International Court of Justice (World Court)
.58	†Coercive methods of settlement short of war

Including ultimatums

---

†Add as instructed under 341.2–341.7

.582	†Sanctions

Including boycotts, embargoes, reprisals

.584	†Intervention

Including blockades, deploying peacekeeping forces

.6	**†Law of war**
.62	†Initiation of war

Including aggression, legality, justification, opening of hostilities

.63	†Conduct of war

Including intercourse between belligerents, prize law

.64	†Neutrality and neutral states

Class status of nationals of neutral nations in 341.67

.65	†Treatment of prisoners

Including granting of quarter

.66	Termination of war

Including indemnification, reparations, restitution; laws of occupation

Class here military government of occupied countries

Class texts of treaties that are signed at termination of a war but cover topics other than termination of the war in 341.026

For war claims by private individuals of one country against another country, see 340.9

.660 2	Miscellany
.660 26	Treaties and cases

Class here text of treaties limited to termination of war [*formerly* 341.026]

Add to base number 341.66026 the numbers following 341.026 in 341.0261–341.0268, e.g., text of multilateral treaties 341.660265

.67	†Individuals

Including status of enemy aliens and their property, nationals of neutral nations, combatants, noncombatants, war victims

For treatment of prisoners, see 341.65

.68	†International law and civil war

Including responsibility of the state for acts of unsuccessful insurgent governments

†Add as instructed under 341.2–341.7

.69 †War crimes

> Class here trials of war criminals, e.g., Tokyo war crime trials 341.690268

.7 †International cooperation

SUMMARY

341.72	**Defense and mutual security**
.73	**Peace and disarmament**
.75	**International economic law**
.76	**Social law and cultural relations**
.77	**International criminal law**
.78	**International judicial cooperation**

.72 †Defense and mutual security

> Including civil defense, international security forces

> Class here legal aspects of international mutual security pacts, e.g., NATO (North Atlantic Treaty Organization)

> Subdivisions are added for either or both topics in heading

> Class interdisciplinary works on international mutual security pacts in 355.031

.722 †Peaceful (Friendly) occupation

.725 †Military bases and installations

> Subdivisions are added for either or both topics in heading

.728 †Military missions and assistance

> Subdivisions are added for either or both topics in heading

.73 †Peace and disarmament

> Class here peace conferences, general efforts to gain acceptance of renunciation of war as an instrument of national policy

> Subdivisions are added for peace and disarmament together, for peace alone

> Class peaceful settlement of disputes in 341.52

.733 †Disarmament

> Including suspension of weapons testing

> Class the abolition and control of specific kinds of weapons in 341.734–341.738

.734 †Control of nuclear weapons

.735 †Control of chemical and biological weapons

.738 †Control of strategic weapons during time of peace

> Class control of nuclear strategic weapons in 341.734; class control of chemical and biological strategic weapons in 341.735

†Add as instructed under 341.2–341.7

.75	†International economic law

For double taxation, see 341.4844; for fisheries, see 341.7622; for labor, see 341.763

.750 6	International economic organizations
.750 61	Permanent government organizations
.750 614	European Union

Economic functions

Class here European Common Market, European Community, European Economic Community

Class comprehensive works in 341.2422

.751	†International financial law

Class here international fiscal law

.751 1–.751 6	Special topics of international financial law

Add to base number 341.751 the numbers following 332 in 332.1–332.6, e.g., banking for international economic and social development 341.751153 [*formerly* 341.759], foreign loans 341.75115, foreign exchange 341.75145; then add further as instructed under 341.2–341.7, e.g., multilateral treaties on foreign exchange 341.751450265; however, for investment and investments, see 341.752

[.751 9]	Counterfeiting, forgery, alteration

Number discontinued; class in 341.751

.752	†Investment and investments

Class comprehensive works on business investment by foreign nationals in 346.07; class comprehensive works on foreign investments in 346.092

.752 2–.752 7	Special aspects of investment and investments

Add to base number 341.752 the numbers following 332.6 in 332.62–332.67, e.g., exchange of securities 341.75242; then add further as instructed under 341.2–341.7, e.g., multilateral treaties on exchange of securities 341.7542420265

.753	†Organization and conduct of business

Including combinations, monopoly, restraint of trade; contracts

.754	†Trade (Commerce)

Including standardization, tourism

†Add as instructed under 341.2–341.7

.754 3 †Tariffs

> Class here free trade

> Class tariffs on specific commodities and specific groups of commodities in 341.7547

.754 7 Trade in specific commodities and specific groups of commodities

[.754 701–.754 709] Standard subdivisions

> Do not use; class in 341.75401–341.75409

.754 71–.754 75 Subdivisions for trade in specific commodities and specific groups of commodities

> Add to base number 341.7547 the numbers following 380.14 in 380.141–380.145, e.g., agricultural products 341.75471, rice 341.75471318; then add further as instructed under 341.2–341.7, e.g., multilateral treaties on trade in rice 341.754713180265

.755 †Power and power resources

> Subdivisions are added for either or both topics in heading

.756 †Transportation

> *See also 341.754 for tourism*

.756 5–.756 7 Railroad, water, air, space transportation

> Add to base number 341.756 the numbers following 343.09 in 343.095–343.097, e.g., air traffic control 341.75676; then add further as instructed under 341.2–341.6, e.g., multilateral treaties on air traffic control 341.756760265

> Class right to use territorial waters, ports, roadsteads, harbors, other bodies of water in 341.44; class right to overfly, to use airports and landing fields in 341.46

> *See also 341.63 for prize law*

.756 8 †Road and highway transportation

> Subdivisions are added for either or both topics in heading

.756 82–.756 88 Specific aspects of road and highway transportation

> Add to base number 341.7568 the numbers following 343.094 in 343.0942–343.0948, e.g., bus services 341.756882; then add further as instructed under 341.2–341.7, e.g., multilateral treaties on bus services 341.7568820265

.756 9 †Transportation of specific goods

> Class transportation of a specific good by a specific mode of transportation in 341.7565–341.7568

.756 92 †Transportation of hazardous materials

†Add as instructed under 341.2–341.7

.757	†Communications
.757 3	†Postal communications
.757 7	†Telecommunications

Including communication satellites

.758	†Intangible property

Class here intellectual property, industrial property (intangible property of an industrial nature, e.g., business names, licensing, franchising, goodwill)

.758 2	†Copyright
.758 4	†Design protection
.758 6	†Patents
.758 8	†Trademarks
.759	†Economic and social development

Including economic and technical assistance, technology transfer

Banking for international economic and social development relocated to 341.751153

Class conservation and development of natural resources in 341.762. Class technology transfer in a specific industry with the industry, e.g., technology transfer in telecommunications 341.7577

.759 2	†Food and agricultural assistance

See also 341.766 for food relief

.76	†Social law and cultural relations

Including social security, UNICEF

Subdivisions are added for social law and cultural relations together, for social law alone

For economic and social development, see 341.759

.762	†Conservation and development of natural resources

Including weather control

Class here environmental protection

Subdivisions are added for either or both topics in heading

.762 1	†Seabed (Ocean bottom)
.762 2	†Fisheries

Including whaling, sealing, fishery of invertebrates

.762 3	†Pollution control

Class pollution control of specific resources in 341.7625

†Add as instructed under 341.2–341.7

.762 5	Protection of specific resources

For protection of marine life, see 341.7622

.762 52	†Air pollution
.762 53	†Water pollution
.763	†Labor
.763 2	†Labor conditions

Class wages in 341.7636

.763 6	†Wages
.765	†Public health
.766	†Welfare services

Class public health in 341.765

.767	†Educational, scientific, technological, cultural relations

Subdivisions are added for two or more topics in heading, for educational relations alone, for cultural relations alone

.767 2	†Exchanges of information

Class exchanges of information in specific fields in 341.7675–341.7677

.767 3	†Exchanges of persons

Including exchanges of students and teachers

Class exchanges of persons in research in 341.7675; class exchanges of persons in art and archaeology in 341.7677

.767 5	†Cooperation in scientific and technological research

Subdivisions are added for either or both topics in heading

.767 52	†Astronomical and space research

Subdivisions are added for either or both topics in heading

.767 53	†Physical sciences and technology

Including nuclear research

.767 54	†Chemical sciences and technology
.767 55	†Geological, meteorological, oceanographic sciences
.767 57	†Biological and agricultural research
.767 7	†Cooperation in arts and archaeology

Including preservation of antiquities

†Add as instructed under 341.2–341.7

.77	†International criminal law

Class criminal jurisdiction in 341.488

For war crimes, see 341.69

.772	†Hijacking

Class here piracy

.773	†Terrorism
.775	†Drug traffic
.778	†Genocide
.78	†International judicial cooperation

Including judicial assistance, letters rogatory, status of judgments of foreign courts

For extradition, see 341.488

> ## 342–349 Branches of law; laws (statutes), regulations, cases; law of specific jurisdictions, areas, socioeconomic regions

Classification numbers for law of specific jurisdictions and areas are built from five elements:

(1)	34, the base number, indicating law	
(2)	A digit indicating specific branch of law, original materials, or comprehensive works as follows:	
	2	Constitutional and administrative law
	3	Military, defense, public property, public finance, tax, trade (commerce), industrial law
	4	Labor, social service, education, cultural law
	5	Criminal law
	6	Private law
	7	Civil procedure and courts
	8	Laws (Statutes), regulations, cases not limited to a specific branch
	9	Comprehensive works
(3)	The facet indicator 0*	
(4)	One or more digits indicating a subject subordinate to specific branch of law or type of original material	
	Example: 1 Courts (from 345.01 under 345 Criminal law)	
(5)	Notation from Table 2 indicating the jurisdiction or area	
	Example: —94 Australia	

(continued)

---

*Add 00 for standard subdivisions; see instructions at beginning of Table 1

†Add as instructed under 341.2–341.7

> ## 342–349 Branches of law; laws (statutes), regulations, cases; law of specific jurisdictions, areas, socioeconomic regions (continued)

To show comprehensive works on a specific jurisdiction or area in modern world, arrange the elements as follows, using law of Australia as an example:
Base number: 34
Digit indicating comprehensive works: 9
Jurisdiction or area: Australia, 94
The complete number is 349.94

To show a specific branch, a specific subject, or a kind of original material, arrange the elements as follows, using criminal courts of Australia as an example:
Base number: 34
Branch of law: Criminal law, 5
Jurisdiction or area: Australia, 94
Facet indicator: 0*
Subordinate subject in branch of law: Courts, 1
The complete number is 345.9401

Class comprehensive works in 340; class comprehensive works on law of specific ancient jurisdictions, areas, socioeconomic regions in 340.53; class comprehensive works on law of specific jurisdictions, areas, socioeconomic regions in 349

See Manual at 342–349

(Option: To give preferred treatment to the law of a specific jurisdiction, to jurisdictions in general, to branch of law and its subordinate subjects, or to discipline or subject, use one of the following options or the option at 342–347:

(Option A: To give local emphasis and a shorter notation to law of a specific jurisdiction or area, e.g., Australia, arrange the elements as follows, using criminal courts of Australia as an example:
Base number: 34
Branch of law: Criminal law, 5
Facet indicator: 0*
Subordinate subject in the branch of law: Courts, 1
The complete number is 345.01

(For law of a jurisdiction subordinate to the emphasized jurisdiction or area, insert between the branch of law and facet indicator the notation indicating the subordinate jurisdiction

(continued)

*Add 00 for standard subdivisions; see instructions at beginning of Table 1

> ### 342–349 Branches of law; laws (statutes), regulations, cases; law of specific jurisdictions, areas, socioeconomic regions (continued)

(To show subordinate jurisdictions of an area with regular notation from Table 2, derive the notation by dropping from the area number for subordinate jurisdiction all digits that apply to preferred jurisdiction. For example, drop area number for Australia —94 from area number for Tasmania —946 to obtain notation 6, which is used for Tasmania. Thus, the number for criminal procedure of Tasmania is 345.605

(To show subordinate jurisdictions of an area with irregular notation from Table 2, i.e., with numbers for subdivisions that are coordinate with the number for the entire area, derive notation by dropping the digits from area number that all subdivisions have in common. For example, Sudan's area number is —624, while the numbers for its regions and provinces are —625–629. Drop —62 from full area number for Darfur region —627 to obtain the notation 7, which is used for Darfur region. Thus, the number for criminal procedure of the Darfur region is 345.705

(Class comprehensive works on law of the preferred jurisdiction or area in 342; class comparative law and law of other jurisdictions and areas in 349

(Option B: To give preferred treatment to jurisdictions in general, arrange elements as follows, using criminal courts of Australia as an example:
    Base number: 34
    Jurisdiction or area: Australia, 94
    Facet indicator: 0*
    Branch of law: Criminal law, 5
    Subordinate subject in branch of law: Courts, 1
    The complete number is 349.4051. Other examples: criminal courts of Tasmania 349.46051, texts of welfare laws of Hobart 349.4610430263

(Class comparative law in 342 where full instructions are given

(Option C: To give preferred treatment to branch of law and its subordinate subjects, arrange elements as follows, using criminal courts of Australia as an example:
    Base number: 34
    Branch of law: Criminal law, 5
    Subordinate subject in branch of law: Courts, 1
    Facet indicator: 0*
    Jurisdiction or area: Australia, 94
    The complete number is 345.1094

---

*Add 00 for standard subdivisions; see instructions at beginning of Table 1

> ## 342–347   Branches of law

Class here comprehensive works on specific subjects of law

Except for modifications shown under specific entries, add to each subdivision identified by * as follows:

01	Philosophy and theory
02	Miscellany
026	Laws, regulations, cases, procedure, courts

Standard subdivisions may be added to 026 and its subdivisions

(Option: Class laws, regulations, cases on specific subjects in law in 348)

0262	Preliminary materials

Including bills, hearings, reports, executive messages, statements of witnesses, legislative histories, slip laws

Do not use for commentaries and critical works; class with the subject in 342–347 without further subdivision

See Manual at 350 vs. 342–347

0263	Laws and regulations

Do not use for commentaries and criticism; class with the subject in 342–347 without further subdivision

02632	Individual and collected laws

Including proposed, uniform, model codes

02636	Administrative regulations

Collections and individual regulations

02638	Guides to laws and regulations

Digests, citators, checklists, tables, indexes

0264	Cases

Do not use for casebooks, for popular works; class with the subject in 342–347 without further subdivision

02642	Reports
02643	Court decisions

Class here official court decisions

Do not use for treatises on court decisions and popular treatment of cases; class with the subject in 342–347 without further subdivision

02646	Decisions (Rulings) of regulatory agencies
02648	Guides to cases

Including digests, citators, checklists, tables, indexes, loose-leaf services

Class here guides to laws, regulations, cases

For guides to laws and regulations, see 02638

0265	Advisory opinions of attorneys-general (ministers of justice)
0269	Courts and procedure

Including administrative courts, regulatory agencies; practice, rules, form books

(Option: Class courts and procedure in specific fields in 347)

(continued)

> ## 342–347 Branches of law (continued)

03–05   Standard subdivisions
06   Organizations and management
                 Class regulation of associations engaged in a specific type of
                 enterprise with the enterprise in 343.076–343.078, e.g.,
                 regulation of law partnerships 343.07834; class organization of
                 associations engaged in specific types of enterprises with the
                 kind of association in 346.06, e.g., laws for forming a law
                 partnership 346.0682
07–08   Standard subdivisions
09   Historical, geographic, persons treatment
[0917]   Socioeconomic regions
                 Law limited to a specific socioeconomic region
                 relocated from the subject before the region to the
                 region before the subject, e.g., criminal courts in
                 Communist bloc countries relocated from
                 345.01091717 to 345.11701
093–099   Treatment by limited area within a jurisdiction
                 Law limited to a specific jurisdiction or area is classed
                 under the jurisdiction before indicating the subject of a
                 branch of law, e.g., criminal courts of Australia 345.9401,
                 not 345.01094. Further instructions are given under
                 342–349
                 See Manual at 342–349

Class general laws, regulations, cases in 348; class comprehensive works in
340

*For a specific subject in international law, see the subject in 341, e.g.,
international criminal law 341.77*

See Manual at 340.56 vs. 342–347; also at 340.57 vs. 342–347

(Option: Class the law of a specific discipline or subject with the discipline or
subject, plus notation 026 from Table 1, e.g., law of education 370.26, *not*
344.07)

342   Constitutional and administrative law

Standard subdivisions are added for constitutional and administrative law together, for constitutional law alone

Class here comprehensive works on public law

> *For international law, see 341. For constitutional law on a specific subject not provided for here, see the subject in 343–347, e.g., criminal law 345*

(If Option A under 340 is chosen, class here comprehensive works on the law of preferred jurisdiction, e.g., [assuming Australia to be preferred jurisdiction] comprehensive works on law of Australia 342, on law of Tasmania 342.6. Class specific branches of the law of preferred jurisdiction in 342–348

(If Option B under 340 is chosen, class here comparative law and law without jurisdiction by adding to base number 342 the numbers following 34 in 342–348, but omitting the first 0 after decimal point, e.g., comparative criminal procedure 342.55 [*not* 342.505])

SUMMARY

342.001–.009		**Standard subdivisions; laws, regulations, cases, procedure, courts**
	.02	**Basic instruments of government**
	.03	**Revision and amendment of basic instruments of government**
	.04	**Structure, powers, functions of government**
	.05	**Legislative branch of government**
	.06	**Executive branch of government**
	.07	**Election law**
	.08	**Jurisdiction over persons**
	.09	**Local government**
	.1	**Socioeconomic regions**
	.3–.9	**Specific jurisdictions and areas**

.001–.008   Standard subdivisions

> Notation from Table 1 as modified under 342–347, e.g., cases 342.00264

.009   Historical, geographic, persons treatment

[.009 17]   Socioeconomic regions

> Relocated 342.1

[.009 3–.009 9]   Specific continents, countries, localities

> Do not use; class in 342.3–342.9

\>   342.02–342.09 Specific subjects in constitutional and administrative law

Specific subjects in specific socioeconomic regions relocated to 342.1

Class comprehensive works in 342

.02	*Basic instruments of government

Class here constitutions, municipal charters

For revision and amendment, see 342.03. For constitutional provisions dealing with a specific subject, see the subject in 342–347, e.g., individual rights 342.085

[.020 9]	Historical, geographic, persons treatment

Do not use; class in 342.029

.023	Texts of constitutions

Including texts of proposed constitutions

.024	Sources

Class commentary on source documents without text in 342.0292

.024 2	Convention proceedings

Including debates, journals, minutes

.024 3	Other convention documents

Including enabling acts, memoranda, proposals, rules

.029	Constitutional history

For sources, see 342.024

.029 2	History of conventions

Class proceedings and documents of conventions in 342.024; class constitutional conventions dealing with revision and amendment of constitutions in 342.03

.03	Revision and amendment of the basic instruments of government

Class here constitutional reform

Class proposals for and formation of new constitutions in 342.02

For amendments dealing with a specific subject, see the subject in 342–347, e.g., an amendment establishing an income tax 343.052

[.030 9]	Historical, geographic, persons treatment

Do not use; class in 342.039

.032	*Amendment procedure
.035	Proposed and pending amendments

Class here collected texts of constitutional amendments

Class texts of proposed constitutions in 342.023

.039	History of amendments

Including defeated amendments not limited to a specific subject

*Add as instructed under 342–347

.04   *Structure, powers, functions of government

                 Class government corporations in 346.067

.041   *Powers and functions of government

                 For jurisdiction over persons, see 342.08

.041 2   *Conduct of relations with foreign governments

                 Including annexation of territory [*formerly* 342.0413]; military assistance; power to acquire territory from and cede it to other jurisdictions, to regulate foreign diplomatic and consular personnel, to wage war

                 Class military and defense law in 343.012–343.019

                    See also 342.0418 for police powers, 342.062 for war and emergency powers of executives

.041 3   *Jurisdiction over territory, dependencies, colonies

                 Annexation of territory relocated to 342.0412

                 Class the power to acquire territory from and cede it to foreign jurisdictions in 342.0412

.041 8   *Police powers

                 Powers to exercise control in interests of general security, health, safety, morals, welfare

                 Class individual rights in 342.085. Class the exercise of a specific police power with the power in 342–347, e.g., exclusion of undesirable aliens 342.082, regulation of public health 344.04

                    See also 342.062 for war and emergency powers of executives

.042   *Levels of government

                 Including federal structure; relations between levels, relations among subordinate units of same level; domestic conflict of laws; home rule; interstate compacts

                 Class levels of government with respect to a specific subject with the subject in 342–347, e.g., interstate compacts on seaports and their facilities 343.0967

                    See also 342.09 for local governments

.044   *Branches of government

                 Including distribution and separation of powers, relations between branches

                 Class relations of a specific branch of government with government institutions at a different level in 342.042

                    For legislative branch, see 342.05; for executive branch, see 342.06; for judicial branch, see 347

*Add as instructed under 342–347

.05	*Legislative branch of government

Class here lobbying

Class relations of legislative branch with government institutions at a different level in 342.042

.052	*Duties, functions, powers

.053	*Basis of representation

Including apportionment, districting

.055	*Membership

Including modes of selection, e.g., election; terms of office; immunities, privileges, qualifications; conduct and discipline of members; salaries, expenses, retirement

.057	*Organization and procedure

.06	*Executive branch of government

Class here administrative law

Class relations of executive branch with governmental institutions at a different level in 342.042. Class administrative law on a specific subject with the subject in 342–347, e.g., air traffic control 343.0976

See Manual at 342.06

.062	*Chief and deputy chief executives

Including modes of selection; terms of office; duties, functions, powers; immunities, privileges, qualifications; personal liability; war and emergency powers

Subdivisions are added for either or both topics in heading

Provisional courts relocated to 342.0664

.062 8	*Martial law

.064	*Executive departments (Ministries) and agencies

Class departments and agencies dealing with a specific subject with the subject in 342–347, e.g., revenue agencies 343.036

.066	*Administrative procedure

Class maintenance of privacy in 342.0858

See also 344.0531 for information control laws

.066 2	*Public records

Class here privacy of government records, right to information, sunshine laws

*Add as instructed under 342–347

.066 4	*Administrative courts and regulatory agencies

Including provisional courts [*formerly* 342.062], hearing examiners

Class executive function of administering and enforcing the law in 351–354. Class administrative courts, regulatory agencies dealing with a specific subject with the subject in 342–347, plus notation 0269 from table under 342–347, e.g., agencies regulating civil aeronautics 343.0970269

.066 7	*Ombudsmen
.068	*Officials and employees

Including impeachment [*formerly* 351.993]; modes of selection; terms of office; duties, functions, powers; immunities, privileges, qualifications; personal liability

Class here civil service

Class labor-management bargaining in government service in 344.018904135

For chief and deputy chief executives, see 342.062; for official and employees involved with administrative procedure, see 342.066

.068 4	*Employee rights and discipline

Including conflict of interest, loyalty oaths, political activity of employees, security measures

.068 6	*Conditions of employment

Including pay, fringe benefits, retirement, tenure, leave, job classification, training

.07	*Election law

Class apportionment, districting in 342.053

For electing legislators, see 342.055; for electing executives, see 342.068

See Manual at 342.07 vs. 324.6

.072	*Voting rights and qualifications for voting

Subdivisions are added for either or both topics in heading

.075	*Voting procedures

Including absentee voting, voter registration

Use of this number for election procedures discontinued; class in 342.07

.078	*Campaign practices

Including finance

*Add as instructed under 342–347

.08   *Jurisdiction over persons

Including census law

.082   *Entrance to and exit from national domain

Including immigration, emigration, passports, visas

Class entry and exit of diplomatic and consular personnel in 342.0412

.083   *Citizenship and nationality

Including right of asylum, status of aliens

Subdivisions are added for either or both topics in heading

Class status of diplomatic and consular personnel in 342.0412

.084   *Abortion

Class here comprehensive works

For rights of fetuses, see 342.085; for rights of women, see 342.0878; for medical aspects, see 344.04192; for abortion for population control, see 344.048; for abortion control, see 344.0546; for criminal abortion, see 345.0285

.085   *Rights and activities of individuals

Including individual rights of servicemen, rights of fetuses

Class here civil rights; comprehensive works on individual rights

Class constitutional rights of aliens in 342.083; class constitutional rights of specific social groups in 342.087; class comprehensive works on abortion in 342.084; class interdisciplinary works on civil rights, on individual rights in 323

For a specific right not provided for here, see the right, e.g., right to vote 342.072, right to education 344.079

.085 2   *Religious activities

.085 3   *Freedom of information and opinion

Including freedom of speech, freedom of the press

Subdivisions are added for either or both topics in heading

Academic freedom relocated to 344.078

Class fairness doctrine in 343.09945; class censorship and information control laws in 344.0531; class relation of freedom of the press to the judicial process in 347.05

For freedom of political opinion, see 342.0854

See also 342.0662 for access to public records, 344.0547 for obscenity and pornography laws

*Add as instructed under 342–347

.085 4   *Political activity

> Including civil disobedience and dissent, rights of assembly and petition
>
> Class election law in 342.07

.085 8   *Maintenance of privacy

> Class privacy of government records in 342.0662

.087   *Social groups

> Including slaves
>
> Class here affirmative action, legal status
>
> Class disabilities and restrictions of a specific group in 342.0872–342.0878
>
> *See also 342.085 for rights and activities of individuals*

[.087 08]   History and description with respect to kinds of persons

> Do not use; class in 342.087

.087 2   *Indigenes and aborigines

> Subdivisions are added for either or both topics in heading
>
> Class women in 342.0878

.087 3   *Racial, ethnic, national groups

> Class indigenes and aborigines of specific racial, ethnic, national groups in 342.0872; class women of specific racial, ethnic, national groups in 342.0878

.087 8   *Women

> Including abortion rights
>
> Class comprehensive works on abortion in 342.084

.088   *Government liability

> Including liability for abuse of power, corruption, denial of civil rights
>
> Class liability in a specific field with the field in 342–347, e.g., liability of military units 343.013, liability of schools, school officials, school districts 344.075

.09   *Local government

> Including municipal corporations, municipal governments
>
> Class home rule in 342.042; class specific local governments in 342.3–342.9. Class a specific aspect of local government with the aspect in 342–347, e.g., local real estate taxation 343.054

*Add as instructed under 342–347

.1 Socioeconomic regions

> [*Formerly* 342.00917 and with the subject in law plus notation 0917 from table under 342–347]
>
> Class here specific subjects in specific socioeconomic regions [*formerly* 342.02–342.09]
>
> Add to base number 342.1 the numbers following —17 in notation 171–177 from Table 2, e.g., constitutional and administrative law of developing countries 342.124; then to the result add the numbers following 342 in 342.001–342.09, e.g., election law of developing countries 342.12407, administrative regulations for elections in developing countries 342.1240702636
>
> Class socioeconomic regions of a specific jurisdiction or area in 342.3–342.9

.3–.9 Specific jurisdictions and areas

> Add to base number 342 notation 3–9 from Table 2, e.g., constitutional and administrative law of Australia 342.94, of New South Wales 342.944, of African states 342.6; then to the result add the numbers following 342 in 342.001–342.09, e.g., election law of Australia 342.9407, of New South Wales 342.94407, of African states 342.607, administrative regulations for elections in Australia 342.940702636
>
> *See Manual at 342–349*

343 Military, defense, public property, public finance, tax, trade (commerce), industrial law

SUMMARY

343.001–.009	**Standard subdivisions; laws, regulations, cases, procedure, courts**
.01	**Military, defense, veterans' law**
.02	**Law of public property**
.03	**Law of public finance**
.04	**Tax law**
.05	**Kinds of taxes by base**
.06	**Kinds of taxes by incidence**
.07	**Regulation of economic activity**
.08	**Regulation of trade (commerce)**
.09	**Control of public utilities**
.1	**Socioeconomic regions**
.3–.9	**Specific jurisdictions and areas**

.001–.008 Standard subdivisions

> Notation from Table 1 as modified under 342–347, e.g., cases 343.00264

.009 Historical, geographic, persons treatment

[.009 17] Socioeconomic regions

> Relocated to 343.1

[.009 3–.009 9]   Specific continents, countries, localities

               Do not use; class in 343.3–343.9

>   **343.01–343.09 Specific subjects in military, defense, public property, public finance, tax, trade, industrial law**

        Specific subjects in specific socioeconomic regions relocated to 343.1

        Class comprehensive works in 343

.01   ***Military, defense, veterans' law**

        Class here national security, war and emergency legislation

        Subdivisions are added for two or more topics in heading, for military law alone, for defense law alone

        For war claims, see 341.66; for martial law, see 342.0628

.011   ***Veterans' law**

        Class here veterans' welfare law

        Class veterans' insurance claims in 346.086364

.011 2   ***Veterans' pensions**

        Including benefits to survivors of veterans

.011 3   ***Education and training for veterans**

        Subdivisions are added for either or both topics in heading

.011 4   ***Employment for veterans**

.011 5   ***Health care and rehabilitation for veterans**

        Subdivisions are added for either or both topics in heading

        Class disability compensation in 343.0116

.011 6   ***Disability compensation for veterans**

>   **343.012–343.019 Military and defense law**

        Class military assistance to foreign nations in 342.0412; class civilian employees of military services in 342.068; class comprehensive works in 343.01. Class a specific aspect of military or defense law not provided for here with the aspect in 342–347, e.g., regulation of industry 343.07

.012   ***Manpower procurement**

        Including voluntary enlistment

        Class reserve officers' training corps and military academies in 344.0769

---

*Add as instructed under 342–347

.012 2	*Draft and selective service

Including draft resistance

Subdivisions are added for either or both topics in heading

Class individual rights of servicemen in 342.085; class treatment of conscientious objectors in 343.0126

.012 6	*Conscientious objectors

Including amnesty

.013	*Military services

Including organization, training, rank, pay, promotion, demotion, leave, allowances, living conditions

Class individual rights of servicemen in 342.085

For discipline and conduct, see 343.014; for specific military services, see 343.015–343.019

.014	*Discipline and conduct

Including awards and incentives, enforcement, medals, offenses

Subdivisions are added for either or both topics in heading

.014 3	*Military legal procedure and courts

Including procedural rights of servicemen in military courts

Subdivisions are added for either or both topics in heading

Class international war crime trials in 341.69; class procedural rights in nonmilitary courts in 347

See also 342.085 for general rights of servicemen

.014 6	*Military penology

For military prisons, see 344.03548

.015–.019	Specific military services

Add to base number 343.01 the numbers following 35 in 355–359, e.g., naval law 343.019; then add further as instructed under 342–347, e.g., cases involving naval law 343.0190264; however, for manpower procurement, see 343.012; for discipline and conduct, see 343.014

Class comprehensive works in 343.013

.02	*Law of public property
.023	*Personal property
.025	*Real property

*Add as instructed under 342–347

.025 2	*Acquisition

Including condemnation, eminent domain (expropriation), nationalization

For acquisition of territory from other jurisdictions, see 342.0412

.025 3	*Disposal

See also 342.0412 for cession of territory to other jurisdictions

.025 6	*Control and use

Including construction and maintenance of government buildings

Subdivisions are added for either or both topics in heading

Class regulation of construction of government buildings in 343.07869051; class comprehensive works on control and use of public and private real property, control of natural resources in 346.044

.03	*Law of public finance

For government securities, see 346.0922

.032	*Monetary law

Currency, coinage, foreign exchange

Including commemorative medals and coins that are legal tender

Class here monetary policy

Class international law of monetary exchange in 341.75145; class comprehensive works on commemorative medals in 344.091; class comprehensive works on central banks and banking in 346.0821

.034	*Budgeting and expenditure

Including accounting and auditing, economic stabilization, fiscal policy, grants-in-aid, intergovernmental financial relations, revenue sharing

Subdivisions are added for either or both topics in heading

Class revenue law, revenue sharing as revenue in 343.036; class budgets and their preparation in 352.48. Class bills for authorization of expenditure for a specific purpose with the purpose in 342–347, e.g., price supports 343.0742

See also 343.083 for regulation of prices, 346.063 for public accounting

.036	*Revenue law

For public borrowing and debt, see 343.037; for tax law, see 343.04

.037	*Public borrowing and debt

*Add as instructed under 342–347

.04   *Tax law

Class here internal revenue law; tax auditing, avoidance, planning

Class fiscal policy in 343.034; class tax planning applied to a specific kind of tax in 343.05–343.06; class tax evasion in 345.0233; class interdisciplinary works on taxes in 336.2

For specific kinds of taxes, see 343.05–343.06

See Manual at 343.04 vs. 336.2, 352.44

.042   *Assessment and collection

Including tax accounting, tax appeals

Class assessment and collection of taxes at specific levels in 343.043; class assessment and collection of specific kinds of taxes in 343.05–343.06

.043   Taxes by level

National, state and provincial, local

Class here only comprehensive works and comparisons, e.g., national taxes in North America 343.7043, state taxes in the United States 343.73043, local taxes of the jurisdictions of Pennsylvania 343.748043

Class a specific kind of tax regardless of level with the kind in 343.05–343.06, e.g., income tax law of Michigan 343.774052

Taxes of a specific jurisdiction are classed in 343.3–343.9, plus notation 04 from 343.04, e.g., United States taxes 343.7304

>   343.05–343.06   Specific kinds of taxes

Class comprehensive works in 343.04

.05   Kinds of taxes by base

.052   *Income tax

Class internal revenue law in 343.04

.052 04   Special topics

.052 042   *Assessment of income taxes

.052 044   *Preparation of returns

.052 3   *Provisions that allow tax avoidance

.052 304   *Tax incentives

.052 32   *Charitable deductions

.052 33   *Individual retirement accounts

Including Keogh plans

*Add as instructed under 342–347

.052 34	*Depreciation and depletion allowances

Subdivisions are added for either or both topics in heading

.052 36   *Business losses

Including bad debts

.052 37   *Tax credits

.052 38   *Tax shelters

.052 4   Taxes on specific types of income

Including proceeds from insurance, retirement income

Class reductions in taxes on specific types of income in 343.0523

.052 42   *Wages and salaries

Including social security taxes [*formerly* 344.02], payroll taxes

Subdivisions are added for either or both topics in heading

.052 424   *Withholding tax

.052 44   *Profits

.052 45   *Capital gains

.052 46   *Investment income

Including income from bonds, deposits, stocks

For taxes on capital gains, see 343.05245; for taxes on real estate transactions, see 343.0546

.052 48   *Foreign income

Class taxes on specific types of foreign income in 343.05242–343.05246

.052 6   Income taxes by incidence

Including taxes on citizens resident in foreign countries, on self-employed persons, on the aged

Class here double taxation

Add to base number 343.0526 the numbers following 343.06 in 343.062–343.068, e.g., corporation income taxes 343.05267; then add further as instructed under 342–347, e.g., cases involving corporation income taxes 343.052670264; however, for reduction in taxation regardless of incidence, see 343.0523; for taxes on specific types of income regardless of incidence, see 343.0524

For international double taxation, see 341.4844

.053   *Estate, inheritance, gift taxes

Class here estate planning

For taxes on fiduciary trusts, see 343.05264

*Add as instructed under 342–347

.053 2	*Inheritance taxes
.053 5	*Gift taxes
.054	*Property taxes

                 Real and personal property

.054 2	*Assessment
.054 3	*Exemptions
.054 6	*Taxes on real estate transactions

                 Including real estate sales tax

                 Class aspects of real estate tax not provided for here with the aspect in 342–347, e.g., tax assessment 343.0542

.055   *Excise and transaction taxes

                 Including luxury, severance, transfer, turnover, use, value-added taxes; user fees

                 For taxes on real estate transactions, see 343.0546

.055 2   *Sales taxes

                 Class sales taxes on specific commodities and services in 343.0558

.055 3   *Excise taxes

                 Class excise taxes on specific commodities and services in 343.0558

.055 8   Taxes on specific commodities and services

                 Class comprehensive works on sales taxes in 343.0552; class comprehensive works on excise taxes in 343.0553

[.055 801–.055 809]   Standard subdivisions

                 Do not use; class in 343.05501–343.05509

.055 81–.055 85   Subdivisions for taxes on specific commodities and services

                 Add to base number 343.0558 the numbers following 380.14 in 380.141–380.145, e.g., taxes on products of secondary industries 343.05585, on cigarettes 343.0558567973; then add further as instructed under 342–347, e.g., cases involving taxes on cigarettes 343.0558679730264

.056	*Customs taxes (Tariff)
.057	*Stamp taxes and duties

                 Subdivisions are added for either or both topics in heading

.06   Kinds of taxes by incidence

                 Class taxes on specific bases regardless of incidence in 343.05

*Add as instructed under 342–347

.062	*Taxes on individuals

Class here poll tax

.064	*Taxes on fiduciary trusts

Including pension trusts

.066	*Taxes on organizations

Class here tax-exempt organizations

For taxes on corporations, see 343.067

.066 2	*Partnerships
.066 8	*Charitable foundations and trusts

Subdivisions are added for either or both topics in heading

.067	*Taxes on corporations
.068	*Taxes on business enterprises

Including small business taxes

Class taxes on individuals engaged in business in 343.062; class taxes on specific types of business organizations in 343.066

.07	*Regulation of economic activity

Including daylight saving time, nationalization of industry, rationing

Class here comprehensive works on regulation of small business, licensing, industry and trade

Class regulation of the practice of specific occupations in 344.01; class public health in 344.04; class safety measures in 344.047; class regulation of organizations in 346.06

For regulation of trade, see 343.08

See also 346 for impact of economic activity upon private persons and corporate bodies

.071	*Consumer protection

Class a specific aspect of consumer protection with the aspect in 342–347, e.g., protection against misleading advertising 343.082

> 343.072–343.075 Specific aspects of regulation

Class regulation of specific industries and services regardless of aspect in 343.076–343.078; class regulation of public utilities regardless of aspect in 343.09; class comprehensive works in 343.07. Class a specific aspect of industrial regulation not provided for here with the aspect in 342–347, e.g., wages 344.0121

*Add as instructed under 342–347

.072   **Unfair practices**

                   Including industrial espionage

.072 1   **Antitrust law**

                   Class here competition law

.072 3   **Restraint of trade**

.072 5   **Price fixing and discrimination**

                   Subdivisions are added for either or both topics in heading

.074   **Economic assistance**

                   Class here technology transfer

                   Class assistance to specific industries and services in 343.076–343.078

>   343.074 2–343.074 6 Domestic assistance

                   Class comprehensive works in 343.074

.074 2   Specific kinds of assistance

                   Including loans, mortgage insurance, price supports, subsidies

.074 5   **Rural development**

                   Class specific kinds of assistance to rural areas in 343.0742; class assistance to agriculture in 343.076

.074 6   **Regional development**

                   Class specific kinds of assistance in 343.0742; class development of rural regions in 343.0745

.074 8   **Foreign assistance**

.075   **Production controls**

                   Including weights and measures, packaging (containers)

                   See also 344.042 for product control

>   343.076–343.078 Regulation of specific industries and services

                   Class here regulating the production of and trade in specific goods and services

                   Class comprehensive works in 343.07

                   For trade in specific goods and services, see 343.085; for public utilities, see 343.09; for regulation of labor of specific occupations, see 344.0176

                   See also 346.07 for commercial law

*Add as instructed under 342–347

.076	*Agriculture and agricultural industries

.076   *Agriculture and agricultural industries

Class here comprehensive works on primary industries

Subdivisions are added for either or both topics in heading

For mineral industries, see 343.077

See also 344.049 for veterinary public health

.076 1   Specific production controls

Including acreage allotments, price supports, production quotas

Class controls of specific commodities in 343.0763–343.0769

.076 3–.076 9   Specific commodities

Add to base number 343.076 the numbers following 63 in 633–639, e.g., forest products 343.076498; then add further as instructed under 342–347, e.g., cases involving forest products 343.0764980264

.077   *Mineral industries

See also 346.043 for mineral rights, 346.04685 for conservation of minerals

.077 2   *Oil, oil shales, tar sands, natural gas

.077 5   *Mining of coal and nonfuel minerals

Use of this number for comprehensive works on mining discontinued; class in 343.077

.077 52   *Coal

.077 55   *Nonfuel minerals

.078   Secondary industries and services

See Manual at 343.078 vs. 343.08

.078 000 1–.078 000 9   Standard subdivisions

Notation from Table 1 as modified under 342–347, e.g., cases 343.078000264

.078 001–.078 999   Specific secondary industries and services

Add to base number 343.078 notation 001–999, e.g., regulation of shipbuilding industry 343.07862382; then add further as instructed under 342–347, e.g., cases involving shipbuilding industry 343.078623820264; however, for regulation of advertising industry, see 343.082; for regulation of marketing, see 343.084; for regulation of closely regulated industries, such as transportation and communication, see 343.09; for regulation of health services, see 344.0321

*Add as instructed under 342–347

.08   *Regulation of trade (commerce)

Including guarantees, warranties

Class here commodity exchanges and exchange transactions

Class regulation of real estate business in 346.0437; class regulation of banks in 346.082; class regulation of insurance companies and agencies in 346.086; class regulation of organizations engaged in marketing securities in 346.0926; class comprehensive works on regulation of industry and trade in 343.07

See Manual at 343.078 vs. 343.08

>   343.082–343.084   Advertising, labeling, prices, marketing

Class advertising, labeling, prices, marketing of specific commodities in 343.085; class advertising, labeling, prices, marketing in specific kinds of trade in 343.087–343.088; class comprehensive works in 343.08

.082   *Advertising and labeling

Class restrictions on posting advertisements in 346.045

.083   *Prices

Class price supports in 343.076–343.078

.084   *Marketing

Class law of sale in 346.072

.085   Specific commodities

Class a specific kind of trade in a specific commodity in 343.087–343.088

[.085 01–.085 09]   Standard subdivisions

Do not use; class in 343.0801–343.0809

.085 1–.085 5   Specific commodities

Add to base number 343.085 the numbers following 380.14 in 380.141–380.145, e.g., agricultural commodities 343.0851, rice 343.0851318; then add further as instructed under 342–347, e.g., cases involving rice 343.08513180264

>   343.087–343.088   Specific kinds of trade

Class comprehensive works in 343.08

---

*Add as instructed under 342–347

.087	*Foreign (International) trade

Class here general customs law; combined treatment of trade, tariffs, and general shipping

For tariffs, see 343.056; for shipping, see 343.096

.087 1–.087 5	Specific commodities

Add to base number 343.087 the numbers following 380.14 in 380.141–380.145, e.g., agricultural commodities 343.0871, rice 343.0871318; then add further as instructed under 342–347, e.g., cases involving rice 343.08713180264

.087 7	*Imports

Class imports of specific commodities in 343.0871–343.0875

.087 8	*Exports

Class exports of specific commodities in 343.0871–343.0875

.088	*Domestic trade

Including trade on days of religious observance, e.g., on Sunday

.088 1–.088 5	Specific commodities

Add to base number 343.088 the numbers following 380.14 in 380.141–380.145, e.g., agricultural commodities 343.0881, rice 343.0881318; then add further as instructed under 342–347, e.g., cases involving rice 343.08813180264

.088 7	*Retail trade

Class retail trade in specific commodities in 343.0881–343.0885

.088 8	*Wholesale trade

Class wholesale trade in specific commodities in 343.0881–343.0885

.09	*Control of public utilities

Class here closely regulated industries

SUMMARY

343.091	General considerations of control of public utilities
.092	Water and power supply
.093	Transportation
.094	Road and highway transportation
.095	Railroad transportation
.096	Water transportation
.097	Air and space transportation
.098	Local transportation
.099	Communications

*Add as instructed under 342–347

.091   *General considerations of control of public utilities

Including rates, operations, facilities, services

Class general considerations applied to specific utilities in 343.092–343.099

>   343.092–343.099   Specific utilities

Class comprehensive works in 343.09

.092   *Water and power supply

Subdivisions are added for water and power supply together, for power supply alone

.092 4   *Water

.092 5   *Nuclear energy

.092 6   *Oil and gas

Class extraction in 343.0772; class processing in 343.0786655–343.0786657

.092 7   *Coal

Class extraction in 343.07752; class processing in 343.07866262

.092 8   *Solar energy

.092 9   *Electric power

Including cogeneration of heat and electricity

Class a specific source of electric power with the source in 342–347, e.g., nuclear power 343.0925

.093   *Transportation

Including pipelines

Class here comprehensive works on the law of carriers

Class transportation insurance in 346.0862

For specific kinds of transportation, see 343.094–343.098

.093 2   *Freight

.093 22   *Hazardous materials

.093 3   *Passenger

Class here mass transportation

.093 8   *Transportation safety

Class private law of transportation accidents in 346.0322

*Add as instructed under 342–347

>   343.094–343.098 Specific kinds of transportation

Class comprehensive works in 343.093

.094   *Road and highway transportation

Class here ground transportation

Subdivisions are added for either or both topics in heading

For railroad transportation, see 343.095; for local ground transportation, see 343.098

.094 2   *Roads and highways

Subdivisions are added for either or both topics in heading

.094 4   *Vehicles

Including inspection, product recall; licensing, registration; safety devices

Class vehicle operation in 343.0946; class commercial vehicular services in 343.0948; class vehicle product liability in 346.038; class property laws relating to vehicles in 346.047

See also 346.043 for mobile homes

.094 6   *Vehicle operation and traffic control

Including drivers' licenses, speed limits, traffic signals

Subdivisions are added for either or both topics in heading

Class police traffic services in 344.052332; class traffic offenses in 345.0247

.094 8   *Commercial services

Class commercial vehicles in 343.0944; class operation of commercial vehicles in 343.0946

.094 82   *Bus

.094 83   *Truck

.095   *Railroad transportation

.095 2   *Stationary facilities

Including signals, stations, tracks, yards

.095 5   *Rolling stock

Including cars, locomotives

.095 8   *Services

Passenger, freight

*Add as instructed under 342–347

.096   *Water transportation

Including prize law

Class here maritime, admiralty law

Class international maritime law in 341.7566. Class a specific subject of maritime or admiralty law not provided for here with the subject in 342–347, e.g., maritime contracts 346.02

>   343.096 2–343.096 4   Specific kinds of water transportation

Class facilities, operations, services of specific kinds of transportation in 343.0965–343.0968; class comprehensive works in 343.096

.096 2   *Ocean transportation

Class interoceanic waterways in 343.0964

.096 4   *Inland waterway transportation

Including interoceanic canals

>   343.096 5–343.096 8   Facilities, operations, services

Class comprehensive works in 343.096

.096 5   *Ships

Including papers, registry; qualifications of officers and crew

.096 6   *Navigation and rule of the road

Subdivisions are added for either or both topics in heading

.096 7   *Ports and harbors

Including piloting, tug services

Subdivisions are added for either or both topics in heading

.096 8   *Services

Including freight, passenger services; salvage operations

Class services of ports and harbors in 343.0967

.097   *Air and space transportation

Subdivisions are added for air and space transportation together, for air transportation alone

>   343.097 5–343.097 8   Air transportation

Class comprehensive works in 343.097

*Add as instructed under 342–347

.097 5	*Aircraft

.097 5   *Aircraft

Including papers, registry; qualifications of officers and crew

.097 6   *Air navigation and traffic control

Subdivisions are added for either or both topics in heading

.097 7   *Airports and landing fields

Subdivisions are added for either or both topics in heading

For traffic control, see 343.0976

.097 8   *Air transportation services

Including freight, passenger services

Class services of airports and landing fields in 343.0977

.097 9   *Space transportation

.098   *Local transportation

Class police traffic services in 344.052332; class traffic offenses in 345.0247

For local water transportation, see 343.096; for local air transportation, see 343.097

.098 1   *Pedestrian traffic

.098 2   *Street traffic

.098 3   *Rail transit systems

Surface, subsurface, elevated

.099   *Communications

Class here mass media law

Class censorship in 344.0531; class criminal libel in 345.0256; class libel as a tort in 346.034

.099 2   *Postal service

Class postal offenses in 345.0236

.099 23   *Postal rates

.099 25   *Postal organization

Including routes

.099 4   *Telecommunication

.099 42   *Telegraph

.099 43   *Telephone

.099 44   *Computer communications

Class comprehensive works on computer law in 343.0999

*Add as instructed under 342–347

.099 45   *Radio

Including comprehensive works on fairness doctrine

For fairness doctrine related to television, see 343.09946

.099 46   *Television

Including cable television (CATV)

.099 8   *Press law

Class here publishing law

Class freedom of the press in 342.0853

.099 9   *Information storage and retrieval

Class here comprehensive works on computer law

For a specific aspect of computer law, see the aspect in 342–347, e.g., invasion of privacy 342.0858

.1   Socioeconomic regions

[*Formerly* 343.00917 and with the subject in law plus notation 0917 from table under 342–347]

Class here specific subjects in specific socioeconomic regions [*formerly* 343.01–343.09]

Add to base number 343.1 the numbers following — 17 in notation 171–177 from Table 2, e.g., miscellaneous public law of developing countries 343.124; then to the result add the numbers following 343 in 343.001–343.09, e.g., tax law of developing countries 343.12404, administrative regulations on taxes of developing countries 343.1240402636

Class socioeconomic regions of a specific jurisdiction or area in 343.3–343.9

.3–.9   Specific jurisdictions and areas

Add to base number 343 notation 3–9 from Table 2, e.g., miscellaneous public law of Australia 343.94, of New South Wales 343.944, of African states 343.6; then to the result add the numbers following 343 in 343.001–343.09, e.g., tax law of Australia 343.9404, of New South Wales 343.94404, of African states 343.604, administrative regulations on taxes of Australia 343.940402636

See Manual at 342–349

344   Labor, social service, education, cultural law

---

*Add as instructed under 342–347

SUMMARY

.001–.008   Standard subdivisions

Notation from Table 1 as modified under 342–347, e.g., cases 344.00264

.009   Historical, geographic, persons treatment

[.009 17]   Socioeconomic regions

Relocated to 344.1

[.009 3–.009 9]   Specific continents, countries, localities

Do not use; class in 344.3–344.9

> 344.01–344.09   Specific subjects in labor, social service, education, cultural law

Specific subjects in specific socioeconomic regions relocated to 344.1

Class comprehensive works in 344

.01   *Labor

.010 1   Philosophy and theory

Including job and labor rights

.011–.018   Specific aspects of labor

Add to base number 344.01 the numbers following 331 in 331.1–331.8, e.g., child labor law 344.0131; then add further as instructed under 342–347, e.g., cases involving child labor law 344.01310264; however, for government officials and employees, see 342.068; for military personnel, see 343.013–343.019; for medical personnel, see 344.041; for certification and licensing of teachers, see 344.078

---

*Add as instructed under 342–347

.02   *Social insurance

   Social security taxes relocated to 343.05242

   Class comprehensive works on insurance in 346.086

   See also 344.03 for social service law

.021   *Workers' (Workmen's) compensation insurance

   Class disability compensation for veterans in 343.0116

.021 7   Occupations and industries

   Class disabilities and injuries in specific occupations and industries in 344.0218

.021 8   Disabilities and injuries

.022   *Accident and health insurance

   Class health benefits for veterans in 343.0115

   For workers' (workmen's) compensation insurance, see 344.021

[.022 084 6]   Insurance for persons in late adulthood

   Do not use; class in 344.0226

.022 4   *Maternity insurance

.022 6   *Accident and health insurance for the aged

.023   *Old age and survivors' insurance

   Class accident and health insurance for the aged in 344.0226

.024   *Unemployment insurance

.028   *Insurance against crimes of violence

.03   *Social service

   For social insurance, see 344.02; for miscellaneous social problems and services, see 344.04; for police services, other aspects of public safety, matters concerning public morals and customs, see 344.05; for public works, see 344.06; for insurance, see 346.086

.031   Specific topics of social service in general

   Class specific topics of a specific social problem or service in 344.032–344.035

[.031 001–.031 009]   Standard subdivisions

   Do not use; class in 344.0301–344.0309

*Add as instructed under 342–347

.031 02–.031 8   Subdivisions for specific topics of social service in general

> Add to base number 344.031 the numbers following 361 in 361.02–361.8, e.g., laws governing charitable trusts 344.0317632; then add further as instructed under 342–347, e.g., cases involving charitable trusts 344.03176320264

.032   Social welfare problems and services

.032 02   Miscellany

.032 026   Laws, regulations, cases, procedure, courts

> Add to base number 344.032026 the numbers following 026 in notation 0262–0269 from table under 342–347, e.g., cases 344.0320264

.032 04–.032 8   Specific social welfare problems and services

> Add to base number 344.032 the numbers following 362 in 362.04–362.8, e.g., child welfare law 344.0327; then add further as instructed under 342–347, e.g., cases involving child welfare 344.03270264; however, for veterans' welfare, see 343.011; for comprehensive works on public health, see 344.04; for medical personnel and their activities, see 344.041; for mental and emotional illnesses and disturbances, see 344.044; for adoption, see 346.0178

.033   *Food supply

.035   *Penal institutions

.035 3–.035 7   Specific aspects of penal institutions

> Add to base number 344.035 the numbers following 365 in 365.3–365.7, e.g., law governing convict labor 344.03565; then add further as instructed under 342–347, e.g., cases involving convict labor 344.035650264

.04   Miscellaneous social problems and services

> Only those named below

> Class here comprehensive works on public health

> Class an aspect of public health not provided for here with the aspect, e.g., community health services 344.03212

SUMMARY

344.041	Medical personnel and their activities
.042	Product control
.043	Control of disease
.044	Mental health services and services to substance abusers
.045	Disposal of dead
.046	Environmental protection
.047	Safety
.048	Population control
.049	Veterinary public health

*Add as instructed under 342–347

.041   *Medical personnel and their activities

> Subdivisions are added for either or both topics in heading
>
> Class military medicine in 343.013; class medical institutions and their services in 344.03211–344.03216
>
> *For control of disease, see 344.043*

.041 1   *Medical malpractice [*formerly* 346.0332]

> Class medical malpractice by a specific kind of medical personnel in 344.0412–344.0416; class medical malpractice related to a specific medical problem in 344.0419
>
> *See also 344.03211 for malpractice by hospitals and other medical institutions*

> 344.041 2–344.041 6   **Specific medical personnel and their activities**

> Class a specific type of medical personnel involved with specific problems in 344.0419; class comprehensive works in 344.041

.041 2   *Physicians and their activities

> Including informed consent

.041 21   *Malpractice

> Works specifically emphasizing physicians

.041 3   *Dentists and dentistry

> Including dental assistants, dental technicians
>
> Subdivisions are added for either or both topics in heading

.041 4   *Nurses and nursing

> Subdivisions are added for either or both topics in heading

.041 5   *Midwives and midwifery

> Subdivisions are added for either or both topics in heading

.041 6   *Pharmacists and pharmacy

> Subdivisions are added for either or both topics in heading

.041 9   Problems in medical practice

.041 92   *Abortion

> Class comprehensive works in 342.084

.041 94   *Oversight of the human body and its parts

> Including blood transfusion, organ donation, transplants
>
> Class rights regarding frozen embryos in 346.017

*Add as instructed under 342–347

.041 96	*Human experimentation
	Including medical genetics
.041 97	*Terminal care
	Class here euthanasia, right to die
.042	*Product control
	Including recall of unsafe products
	For motor vehicle recall, see 343.0944
.042 3	*Food, drugs, cosmetics, clothing, toys
.042 32	*Food
	Including food additives
.042 33	*Drugs
.042 35	*Clothing and toys
.042 4	*Chemicals
	Class food additives, drugs, cosmetics in 344.0423
.043	*Control of disease
	Including control of carriers, quarantine, immunization measures
	Class control of carriers, quarantine, immunization measures of a specific disease in 344.0436–344.0438
.043 6–.043 8	Control of specific diseases
	Add to base number 344.043 the numbers following 61 in 616–618, e.g., control of AIDS 344.04369792; then add further as instructed under 342–347, e.g., cases involving control of AIDS 344.043697920264; however, for control of mental diseases, see 344.044
.044	*Mental health services and services to substance abusers
	Class capacity and status of persons with mental illness and disabilities in 346.0138
.044 6	*Services to substance abusers
	Class here addiction
.044 61	*Alcoholics
	Class control of trade in alcoholic beverages in 344.0541

*Add as instructed under 342–347

.044 63–.044 69	Other kinds of substance abusers

Add to base number 344.0446 the numbers following 362.29 in 362.293–362.299 for the substance only, e.g., heroin abusers 344.04463; then add further as instructed under 342–347, e.g., cases involving heroin abusers 344.044630264

Class control of drug traffic in 344.0545

.045	*Disposal of dead
.046	*Environmental protection

Class conservation of natural resources in 346.044

.046 2	*Wastes

Including recycling

Class here waste disposal, management

.046 22	Kinds of waste

Including sewage; animal, chemical, solid wastes

Class disposal of specific kinds of wastes into specific environments in 344.04626

.046 26	Disposal into specific environments

Including dumping into rivers, oceans

.046 3	*Pollution and noise
.046 32	*Pollution

Class waste disposal in 344.0462

For pollutants, see 344.04633; for pollution of specific environments, see 344.04634

.046 33	*Pollutants

Class here pollution of specific environments by specific pollutants [*formerly* 344.04634]

.046 332	*Oil
.046 334	*Pesticides
.046 335	*Asbestos
.046 336	*Acid rain [*formerly* 344.04634]
.046 34	Pollution of specific environments

Including soil pollution

Pollution of specific environments by specific pollutants relocated to 344.04633; acid rain relocated to 344.046336

.046 342	*Air pollution

*Add as instructed under 342–347

.046 343	*Water pollution
.046 38	*Noise
.046 4	*Sanitation in places of public assembly

        Including hotels

        For industrial sanitation, see 344.0465

.046 5	*Industrial sanitation and safety
.047	*Safety

        Class here comprehensive works on public safety [*formerly also* 344.05]

        For transportation safety, see 343.0938; for product safety, see 344.042; for industrial safety, see 344.0465; for other aspects of public safety, see 344.053

.047 2	*Safety in use of hazardous materials and devices

        Class safety in use of hazardous materials in industry in 344.0465

.047 6	*Safety in recreation
.048	*Population control

        Class here birth control

.049	*Veterinary public health

        Including animal welfare, humane law

.05	Police services, other aspects of public safety, matters concerning public morals and customs

        Add to base number 344.05 the numbers following 363 in 363.2–363.4, e.g., fire protection 344.0537, smoking laws 344.054; then add further as instructed under 342–347, e.g., cases involving fire protection 344.05370264; however, comprehensive works on gambling relocated from 344.0542 to 344.099; for criminal investigation and law enforcement, see 345.052

        Comprehensive works on public safety relocated to 344.047

.06	Public works

        Class here public programs not provided for elsewhere

.060 001–.060 009	Standard subdivisions

        Notation from Table 1 as modified under 342–347, e.g., cases 344.06000264

.060 01–.069 99	Specific kinds of public works

        Add to base number 344.06 notation 001–999, e.g., public housing 344.063635; then add further as instructed under 342–347, e.g., cases involving public housing 344.0636350264

*Add as instructed under 342–347

.07   *Education, schools, students

Subdivisions are added for two or more topics in heading, for education alone, schools alone

Unless other instructions are given, class a subject with aspects in two or more subdivisions of 344.07 in the number coming last, e.g., finance of elementary public schools by local governments 344.07682 (*not* 344.074, 344.073, or 344.071)

For educational exchanges, see 344.08

> 344.071–344.074 Kinds of education and schools

Class comprehensive works in 344.07

.071   *Public education and schools

Subdivisions are added for either or both topics in heading

.072   *Private education and schools

Subdivisions are added for either or both topics in heading

.073   Education by level of government

National, state, local

.074   Education by level of education

Elementary, secondary, higher, adult

.075   *Liability of schools, school officials, school districts

.076   *Finance of public and private education

Class financial aid to students in 344.0795

.076 2   *Financial resources

Including investments, natural resources, tax receipts

For aid to education, see 344.0763

.076 3   *Aid to education by higher levels of government

.076 5   *Expenditure

.076 7   Kinds of schools

Including trade, vocational schools

.076 8   Levels of education and schools

.076 82   *Preschool and elementary education

Subdivisions are added for preschool and elementary education together, for elementary education alone

*Add as instructed under 342–347

.076 83	*Secondary education
.076 84	*Higher education
.076 85	*Adult education
.076 9	Educational programs

Including medical and public health education; schools devoted to specific educational programs, e.g., military, merchant marine academies

Programs for exceptional students relocated to 344.0791

.077	*Curriculums and educational materials
.078	*Teachers and teaching

Including academic freedom [*formerly* 342.0853], examination, certification, registration, appointment of teachers

Subdivisions are added for either or both topics in heading

Class employment rights in 344.0101

.079	*Students

Including authority of the law over students, compulsory education, right to education, testing

.079 1	*Education of students belonging to specific groups

Class here programs for exceptional children [*formerly also* 344.0769], special education

Class finance in 344.0769

.079 11–.079 15	Students belonging to a specific group

Add to base number 344.0791 the numbers following 371.9 in 371.91–371.95, e.g., education of students with visual impairments 344.079111; then add further as instructed under 342–347, e.g., cases involving education of students with visual impairments 344.0791110264

.079 2	*Attendance

Including school year and day, truancy

.079 3	*Discipline and student rights

See also 342.085 for general rights of students

.079 4	*Student services

Including counseling

.079 42	*School lunch programs
.079 5	*Financial aid to students

Including loans, scholarships

*Add as instructed under 342–347

.079 6	*Religion and the student
	Including prayer in public schools
.079 8	*Segregation and discrimination
.08	*Educational and cultural exchanges
.09	*Culture and religion

Including flag code, language code (the official language or languages of a specific jurisdiction)

Subdivisions are added for culture and religion together, for culture alone

.091	*Historic commemoration and patriotic events

Subdivisions are added for either or both topics in heading

Class commemorative medals and coins that are legal tender in 343.032

.092	*Libraries and archives

Subdivisions are added for either or both topics in heading

.093	*Museums and galleries

Subdivisions are added for either or both topics in heading

.094	*Historic preservation and monuments

Including antiquities, historical buildings, historical parks

Class historic commemoration and patriotic events in 344.091

.095	*Science and technology

Subdivisions are added for either or both topics in heading

.095 2–.095 7	Specific sciences and technologies

Add to base number 344.095 the numbers following 341.7675 in 341.76752–341.76757, e.g., astronomical law 344.0952; then add further as instructed under 342–347, e.g., cases involving astronomical law 344.09520264

.096	*Religion
.097	*Arts and humanities

For museums and galleries, see 344.093

.099	*Amusements

Including comprehensive works on gambling [*formerly* 344.0542], sports law

Class here recreation law

Class arts and humanities in 344.097

For gambling as a social problem, see 344.0542

*Add as instructed under 342–347

.1 Socioeconomic regions

[*Formerly* 344.00917 and with the subject in law plus notation 0917 from table under 342–347]

Class here specific subjects in specific socioeconomic regions [*formerly* 344.01–344.09]

Add to base number 344.1 the numbers following — 17 in notation 171–177 from Table 2, e.g., social law of developing countries 344.124; then to the result add the numbers following 344 in 344.001–342.09, e.g., labor law of developing countries 344.12401, administrative regulations on labor in developing countries 344.1240102636

Class socioeconomic regions of a specific jurisdiction or area in 344.3–344.9

.3–.9 Specific jurisdictions and areas

Add to base number 344 notation 3–9 from Table 2, e.g., social law of Australia 344.94, of New South Wales 344.944, of African states 344.6; then to the result add the numbers following 344 in 344.001–344.09, e.g., labor law of Australia 344.9401, of New South Wales 344.94401, of African states 344.601, administrative regulations on labor in Australia 344.940102636

See Manual at 342–349

345 Criminal law

Class comprehensive works on civil and criminal procedure and courts in 347; class interdisciplinary works on criminal justice in 364

See Manual at 345

SUMMARY

345.001–.009	**Standard subdivisions; laws, regulations, cases, procedure, courts**
.01	**Criminal courts**
.02	**Crimes (Offenses)**
.03	**Criminals (Offenders)**
.04	**Liability, responsibility, guilt**
.05	**Criminal procedure**
.06	**Evidence**
.07	**Trials**
.08	**Juvenile procedure and courts**
.1	**Socioeconomic regions**
.3–.9	**Specific jurisdictions and areas**

.001–.008 Standard subdivisions

Notation from Table 1 as modified under 342–347, e.g., cases 345.00264

.009 Historical, geographic, persons treatment

[.009 17] Socioeconomic regions

Relocated to 345.1

[.009 3–.009 9]   Specific continents, countries, localities

Do not use; class in 345.3–345.9

\>   345.01–345.08 Specific subjects in criminal law

Specific subjects in specific socioeconomic regions relocated to 345.1

Class comprehensive works in 345

.01   *Criminal courts

Courts specializing in criminal cases, general and other specialized courts considered with respect to their functions in criminal cases

Including public prosecutors, public defenders, legal aid

Class here appellate courts devoted exclusively to criminal cases

Class military courts in 343.0143; class appellate courts hearing both civil and criminal cases in 347.03; class comprehensive works on appellate procedure in 347.08

For juvenile courts, see 345.081

\>   345.02–345.04 General considerations

Class comprehensive works in 345

.02   *Crimes (Offenses)

Class here specific trials of specific crimes and classes of crime, e.g., trials of offenses against the person 345.025, a specific trial for murder 345.02523

See Manual at 345.02 vs. 346.03

.023–.028   Specific crimes and classes of crime

Add to base number 345.02 the numbers following 364.1 in 364.13–364.18, e.g., white collar crime 345.0268; then add further as instructed under 342–347, e.g., court decisions on white collar crime 345.026802643

Class defenses for a specific crime in 345.04

.03   *Criminals (Offenders)

Including juvenile delinquents

.04   *Liability, responsibility, guilt

Including capacity to commit a crime; criminal intent; double jeopardy; defenses, e.g., duress; defenses for a specific crime, e.g., self-defense

Subdivisions are added for any or all topics in heading

See also 345.05044 for defense

---

*Add as instructed under 342–347

.05	*Criminal procedure

Class here administration of criminal justice, court rules

Class procedure in specific courts devoted exclusively to criminal cases in 345.01; class procedure in specific courts hearing both civil and criminal cases in 347.02–347.04

For evidence, see 345.06; for trials, see 345.07; for juvenile procedure, see 345.08

.050 4	Special topics

.050 42	*Prosecution

Class district attorneys, public prosecutors in 345.01

.050 44	*Defense

Class public defenders in 345.01; class defenses in 345.04; class right to counsel in 345.056

.052	*Criminal investigation and law enforcement

Including extradition, judicial assistance

Class here manuals on what police may legally do in course of carrying out their duties

Class rights of suspects in 345.056; class admissibility of evidence in 345.062

.052 2	*Search and seizure

Subdivisions are added for either or both topics in heading

.052 7	*Arrests

Including preventive detention

See also 346.0334 for false arrest

.056	*Rights of suspects

Including habeas corpus, jury trial, protection from self-incrimination, right to counsel

Class legal aid in 345.01

.06	*Evidence

Including confessions

.062–.067	Specific aspects of evidence

Add to base number 345.06 the numbers following 347.06 in 347.062–347.067, e.g., admissibility of evidence 345.062; then add further as instructed under 342–347, e.g., cases involving admissibility of evidence 345.0620264

*Add as instructed under 342–347

.07   *Trials

> Class trials of specific offenses in 345.02; class hearings and trials in juvenile cases in 345.087; class comprehensive works on appellate procedure in criminal cases in 347.08

.072   *Pretrial procedure

> Including arraignment, discovery, grand jury proceedings, indictment, plea bargaining, pleading, preliminary hearings, pretrial release, summons

.075   *Trial (Courtroom) procedure

> Including juries and jury selection, examination of witnesses, instructions to juries, verdicts

> *For final disposition of cases, see 345.077*

.077   *Final disposition of cases

> Including pardon, parole, probation, rehabilitation

.077 2   *Sentencing

> *For penalties, see 345.0773*

.077 3   *Penalties

> Including death penalty

.08   *Juvenile procedure and courts

> Subdivisions are added for procedure and courts together, for procedure alone

> Class juvenile offenders in 345.03; class liability, responsibility, guilt of juveniles in 345.04

.081   *Juvenile courts

.087   *Hearings, trials, disposition of cases

.1   **Socioeconomic regions**

> [*Formerly* 345.00917 and with the subject in law plus notation 0917 from table under 342–347]

> Class here specific subjects in specific socioeconomic regions [*formerly* 345.01–345.08]

> Add to base number 345.1 the numbers following —17 in notation 171–177 from Table 2, e.g., criminal law of developing countries 345.124; then to the result add the numbers following 345 in 345.001–345.08, e.g., the law of evidence in developing countries 345.12406, decisions on evidence in developing countries 345.1240602643

> Class socioeconomic regions of a specific jurisdiction or area in 345.3–345.9

---

*Add as instructed under 342–347

.3–.9 Specific jurisdictions and areas

Add to base number 345 notation 3–9 from Table 2, e.g., criminal law of Australia 345.94, of New South Wales 345.944, of African states 345.6; then to the result add the numbers following 345 in 345.001–345.08, e.g., the law of evidence in Australia 345.9406, in New South Wales 345.94406, in African states 345.606, decisions on evidence in Australia 345.940602643

See Manual at 342–349

Special developments for Scotland and England follow

.411	Criminal law of Scotland
.411 001–.411 009	Standard subdivisions
.411 01	*Criminal courts

Including crown Counsel, Lord Advocate, Solicitor-General; legal aid, procurators fiscal

Class here appellate courts devoted exclusively to criminal cases

Class appellate courts hearing both civil and criminal cases in 347.41103

For Children's Hearings (juvenile courts), see 345.41108

.411 012	*District Court
.411 014	*Sheriff Court
.411 016	*High Court of Justiciary
.411 016 2	*Court of First Instance
.411 016 3	*Court of Appeal
.411 02–.411 07	General considerations and procedure

Add to base number 345.4110 the numbers following 345.0 in 345.02–345.07, e.g., general criminal procedure 345.41105

.411 08	*Juvenile procedure

Including Children's Hearings (juvenile courts)

Class juvenile offenders in 345.41103; class liability, responsibility, guilt of juveniles in 345.41104

.42	Criminal law of England
.420 01–.420 09	Standard subdivisions

---

*Add as instructed under 342–347

.420 1	*Criminal courts

Including Attorney-General, Director of Public Prosecutions; legal aid

Class here appellate courts devoted exclusively to criminal cases

Class appellate courts hearing both civil and criminal cases in 347.4203

For juvenile courts, see 345.42081

.420 12	*Magistrates Court

Comprehensive works

For civil jurisdiction of Magistrates Court, see 347.42023

.420 14	*Crown Court
.420 16	*Divisional Court of Queen's Bench Division of High Court of Justice
.420 18	*Criminal Division of Court of Appeal
.420 2–.420 8	General considerations, procedure, juvenile courts and procedure

Add to base number 345.420 the numbers following 345.0 in 345.02–345.08, e.g., juvenile procedure 345.4208

346 Private law

See also 340.9 for private international law

SUMMARY

346.001–.009	**Standard subdivisions; laws, regulations, cases, procedure, courts; equity**
.01	**Persons and domestic relations**
.02	**Contracts and agency**
.03	**Torts (Delicts)**
.04	**Property**
.05	**Inheritance, succession, fiduciary trusts, trustees**
.06	**Organizations (Associations)**
.07	**Commercial law**
.08	**Banking and insurance**
.09	**Securities and negotiable instruments**
.1	**Socioeconomic regions**
.3–.9	**Specific jurisdictions and areas**

.001	Philosophy and theory
.002	Miscellany
.002 6	Laws, regulations, cases, procedure, courts

Add to base number 346.0026 the numbers following 026 in notation 0262–0269 from table under 342–347, e.g., cases 346.00264

.003	Dictionaries, encyclopedias, concordances

*Add as instructed under 342–347

.004	*Equity

.005–.008   Standard subdivisions

As modified under 342–347

.009   Historical, geographic, persons treatment

[.009 17]   Socioeconomic regions

Relocated to 346.1

[.009 3–.009 9]   Specific continents, countries, localities

Do not use; class in 346.3–346.9

> 346.01–346.09   Specific subjects in private law

Specific subjects in specific socioeconomic regions relocated to 346.1

Class comprehensive works in 346

.01   *Persons and domestic relations

.012   *Persons

For capacity and status of persons, see 346.013

.013   *Capacity and status of persons

Capacity: the attribute of persons (personal or corporate) which enables them to perform civil or juristic acts

Including capacity and status of older persons; of persons with disabilities; of racial, ethnic, national, economic groups; of slaves

Subdivisions are added for either or both topics in heading

Class individual rights in 342.085; class the rehabilitation of a criminal's personal rights lost by judicial sentence in 345.077

[.013 08]   History and description with respect to kinds of persons

Do not use; class in 346.013

.013 4   *Women

.013 5   *Minors

Including age of majority

.013 8   *Persons with mental illness and disabilities

.015   *Domestic relations (Family law)

For marriage, see 346.016; for parent and child, see 346.017

.016   *Marriage

Including prenuptial (antenuptial) contracts, common-law marriage

*Add as instructed under 342–347

.016 3	*Husband and wife

Rights and duties

Including legal status of homemakers

Class legal status of married women in 346.0134

.016 6	*Divorce, annulment, separation

Including marital property [*formerly* 346.04], alimony

Subdivisions are added for divorce, annulment, separation together; for divorce alone

Class child support in 346.0172

.016 65	*Annulment
.016 68	*Separation
.017	*Parent and child

Including illegitimacy, legitimation, visitation rights

Class here parental rights and duties, surrogate parenthood

.017 2	*Child support
.017 3	*Custody of children

Class here joint custody

.017 5	*Paternity
.017 8	*Adoption
.018	*Guardian and ward
.02	*Contracts and agency

Subdivisions are added for contracts and agency together, for contracts alone

See Manual at 346.02

> 346.022–346.025 Contracts

Class here comprehensive works on liability

Class sale in 346.072; class loan in 346.073; class comprehensive works in 346.02. Class contracts dealing with a specific legal aspect not provided for here with the aspect in 342–347, e.g., partnership contracts 346.0682; class contracts concerning a specific nonlegal subject with the subject, plus notation 0687 from Table 1, e.g., roofing contracts 695.0687

For government liability, see 342.088; for liability of schools, of school officials, of school districts, see 344.075; for criminal liability, see 345.04; for extracontractual liability, see 346.03

*Add as instructed under 342–347

.022	*General considerations of contracts

Including breach of contract, parties to contract, rescission, subcontracting

Class general considerations of contracts applied to specific kinds of contracts in 346.023–346.025

.023	*Public (Government) contracts

Including defense, research and development, war contracts

Class governmental contracts themselves in 352.53

.024	*Contracts of service

Including master-servant relationships, mechanics' liens

Class labor contracts in 344.01891; class public contracts of service in 346.023; class contracts of service involving bailments in 346.025; class agency in 346.029

See also 346.074 for liens in secured transactions

.025	*Contracts involving bailments

Including bills of lading, pawnbroking

Class public contracts involving bailments in 346.023

.029	*Agency and quasi contract

Including power of attorney, unjust enrichment

Subdivisions are added for either or both topics in heading

.03	*Torts (Delicts)

Class here liability for the torts of others, e.g., employees

Class remedies in 347.077

See Manual at 345.02 vs. 346.03

.031	Liability of specific classes of persons

Including liability of employers, directors of corporations, hospitals

Class liability of specific classes of persons in specific situations in 346.032–346.038

For personal liability of government officials, see 342.068

.032	*Negligence

Including contributory negligence

Class malpractice in 346.033

*Add as instructed under 342–347

.032 2   *Accidents

Class accidents resulting in personal injury and wrongful death in 346.0323

.032 3   *Personal injury and wrongful death

.033   *Torts against the person

Including assault and battery, invasion of privacy, malpractice (professional liability)

Malpractice pertaining to a specific profession relocated to the profession in 342–347, e.g., malpractice of notaries 347.016, malpractice of lawyers 347.05041

For accidents, see 346.0322; for injury through negligence, see 346.0323; for defamation, see 346.034

[.033 2]   Medical malpractice

Relocated to 344.0411

.033 4   *Malicious prosecution

Class here false arrest and imprisonment

.034   *Libel and slander (Defamation)

Class libel and slander as crimes in 345.0256

.036   *Torts involving property

Including nuisance, trespass, trover and conversion, wrongful entry

Class wrongful entry as invasion of privacy in 346.033

.038   *Product liability

Class here strict liability

.04   *Property

Marital property relocated to 346.0166

For public property, see 343.02

.042   Kinds of interest in property

Including joint tenancy [*formerly also* 346.0432], community and separate property, future interests

.043   *Real property

Land, permanent fixtures, natural resources

Including mobile homes

For government control and regulation of real property, see 346.044

See also 343.0944 for motorized homes

See Manual at 346.043 vs. 333.1–333.5

*Add as instructed under 342–347

.043 2	*Ownership (Land tenure)

Including incidents of ownership, e.g. riparian rights, water rights; recovery, squatter's right; types of estate, e.g., fee simple

Joint tenancy relocated to 346.042

.043 3	*Horizontal property (Condominium) and cooperative ownership

Including time-sharing

.043 4	*Tenancy

Including eviction

Class here landlord and tenant

Class ejectment in 346.0432

.043 44	*Rent

Including rent control

.043 46	*Leases
.043 462	*Commercial leases
.043 48	*Farm tenancy

Class specific aspects of farm tenancy in 346.04344–346.04346

.043 5	*Easements and servitudes

Including right of way

.043 6	*Transfer

Including consolidation of land holdings, restrictions on alienation

Class inheritance and succession in 346.052

For conveyancing, see 346.0438

.043 62	*Acquisition and purchase
.043 63	*Sale

Class real estate business in 346.0437

.043 64	*Mortgages

Class here foreclosure

.043 7	*Real estate business

Including valuation of real property

Class regulation of a specific general administrative function of real estate business with the function in 342–347, e.g., wages 344.0128133333, organization 346.065

*Add as instructed under 342–347

.043 71	*Malpractice

Class malpractice pertaining to closing and settlements in 346.04373; class malpractice pertaining to subdivision in 346.04377

.043 73 *Closing and settlements

Including escrows

.043 77 *Subdivision

.043 8 *Conveyancing

Including deeds, registration and description of land, title examinations, titles

.044 *Government control and regulation of real property

Class here land reform; control and regulation of natural resources; comprehensive works on government control and regulation of public and private real property

Subdivisions are added for either or both topics in heading

Class government as landlord or tenant in 346.0434

For control and use of public real property, see 343.0256; for rent control, see 346.04344; for regional and local community planning, see 346.045; for control of specific kinds of land and natural resources, see 346.046

.045 *Regional and local community (city) planning

Including building codes that relate to regional or city planning or land use; land use; restrictions on posting advertisements; zoning

Class regulations governing construction of buildings in 343.07869

.046 Government control and regulation of specific kinds of land and natural resources

Add to base number 346.046 the numbers following 333 in 333.7–333.9, e.g., control of recreational lands 346.04678

Class comprehensive works in 346.044

.047 *Personal property

Movable property

Including leasing of personal property, e.g., a truck

Class mobile homes in 346.043

For intangible property, see 346.048; for sale, see 346.072

*Add as instructed under 342–347

.048	*Intangible property

Including public lending rights

Class here intellectual property, industrial property (intangible property of an industrial nature, e.g., business names, franchises)

For negotiable instruments, see 346.096

.048 2 *Copyright

.048 4 *Design protection

.048 6 *Patents

.048 8 *Trademarks

.05 *Inheritance, succession, fiduciary trusts, trustees

.052 *Inheritance and succession

Class here estate planning, probate practice

Subdivisions are added for either or both topics in heading

For estate planning to avoid taxes, see 343.053; for wills, see 346.054; for administration of estates, see 346.056

.054 *Wills

.056 *Administration of estates

Including execution of wills

For unclaimed estates, see 346.057

.057 *Unclaimed estates

.059 *Fiduciary trusts and trustees

Subdivisions are added for either or both topics in heading

.06 *Organizations (Associations)

Class here organization of associations engaged in specific types of enterprises, e.g., an organization of railroad companies

Class organization of labor unions in 344.0187. Class operation of organizations engaged in a specific type of enterprise with the type of enterprise, e.g., operation of railroad companies 343.095

.062 *General considerations of organizations

Including meetings, registration

Class general considerations of specific kinds of organizations in 346.064–346.068

*Add as instructed under 342–347

.063   *Accounting

Class accounting for specific kinds of organizations in 346.064–346.068

See also 343.034 for government accounting

.063 1   *Malpractice

.064   *Nonprofit organizations

Including charitable trusts and foundations, trade associations, unincorporated societies

.065   *Business enterprises

Including record requirements, sale, valuation

Class record requirements for a specific kind of organization with the kind in 342–347, e.g., record requirements for a government corporation 346.067; class record requirements for a specific subject with the subject in 342–347, e.g., workers' compensation insurance records 344.021

For corporations, see 346.066; for unincorporated business organizations, see 346.068

.065 2   *Small business

Class small corporations in 346.066

.066   *Corporations (Companies)

Class comprehensive works on corporate and commercial law in 346.07

For government corporations, see 346.067

See also 342.09 for municipal corporations

.066 2   *Organization

Including bylaws, charters, investment banking, liquidation, promotion

.066 22   *Incorporation

.066 26   *Reorganization

Including acquisitions and mergers

.066 4   *Management

Including records

.066 42   *Officers

.066 45   *Meetings

Class shareholders' meetings in 346.0666

.066 48   *Accounting

*Add as instructed under 342–347

.066 6	*Securities and security holders

Including shareholders' voting and meetings

Standard subdivisions are added for either or both topics in heading

Class securities marketing in 346.092. Class tender offers with the subject to which they apply in 342–347, e.g., tender offers for settlement of debts 346.077, for treasury bills 346.0922

.066 8	Kinds of corporations (companies)

Including cooperatives; close corporations; credit unions; holding, limited, public limited companies

Class specific aspects of corporate law applied to specific kinds of corporations in 346.0662–346.0666

For nonprofit corporations, see 346.064; for government corporations, see 346.067

.067	*Government corporations

Including quangos

Class municipal corporations in 342.09

.068	*Unincorporated business enterprises

Including land trusts, sole traders

.068 2	*Partnerships

Class here joint ventures

.07	*Commercial law

Class here laws of a specific jurisdiction governing business investment by foreign nationals, e.g., laws of China governing the conduct of business in China by foreign nationals 346.5107; comprehensive works on business law

For a specific subject of commercial law, of business law not provided for here, see the subject in 342–347, e.g., tax law 343.04, insurance law 346.086

See Manual at 338.09 vs. 332.67309, 338.6042, 346.07, 658.11, T1—0681, 658.21, T1—0682

.072	*Sale

Class sale of real property in 346.04363; class sale of business enterprises in 346.065; class conditional and secured sales transactions in 346.074

.073	*Loan

Including agricultural and consumer credit, interest, truth in lending, usury

Class secured loan transactions in 346.074

*Add as instructed under 342–347

.074   *Secured transactions

                    Including chattel mortgages; conditional, installment sales; guaranty, liens, suretyship

                    Class comprehensive works on mortgages in 346.04364

                    See also 346.024 for mechanics' liens

.077   *Debtor and creditor

                    Including collection of debts, creditors' remedies, debtors' relief

                    For bankruptcy, see 346.078

.078   *Bankruptcy

                    Including receivership

                    Class here insolvency

.08   *Banking and insurance

.082   *Banks and banking

                    Class investment banking in 346.0662. Class regulation of a specific general administrative function with the function in 342–347, e.g., wages 344.012813321, corporate organization 346.0662

                    For loan, see 346.073

.082 1–.082 3   Specific topics of banks and banking

                    Add to base number 346.082 the numbers following 332 in 332.1–332.3, e.g., commercial banks 346.08212; then add further as instructed under 342–347, e.g., cases involving commercial banks 346.082120264

.086   Insurance

                    Class regulation of a specific general administrative function with the function in 342–347, e.g., wages 344.01281368, corporate organization 346.0662

.086 000 1–.086 000 9   Standard subdivisions

                        Notation from Table 1 as modified under 342–347, e.g., cases 346.086000264

.086 01   General principles

                      Add to base number 346.08601 the numbers following 368.01 in 368.011–368.019, e.g., underwriting 346.086012; then add further as instructed under 342–347, e.g., cases involving underwriting 346.0860120264

.086 02   *Malpractice

---

*Add as instructed under 342–347

.086 06–.086 09	Risks and sales groupings

Add to base number 346.0860 the numbers following 368.0 in 368.06–368.09, e.g., automobile insurance 346.086092; then add further as instructed under 342–347, e.g., cases involving automobile insurance 346.0860920264

.086 1–.086 8	Specific topics of insurance

Add to base number 346.086 the numbers following 368 in 368.1–368.8, e.g., fire insurance 346.08611; then add further as instructed under 342–347, e.g., cases involving fire insurance 346.086110264; however, for social insurance, see 344.02

.09	*Securities and negotiable instruments
.092	*Securities

Class initial promotion of securities in 346.0662; class what a corporation must do to make certain a security is valid in 346.0666

See also 346.074 for secured transactions

.092 2	Specific types of securities

Including bonds, government securities, mutual funds, stocks

Class organizations marketing specific types of securities in 346.0926

[.092 201–.092 209]	Standard subdivisions

Do not use; class in 346.09201–346.09209

.092 6	*Marketing agents and arrangements

Including brokers, stock exchanges; par value modification, private placement of securities

Class investment banking in 346.0662. Class regulation of a specific general administrative function of organizations engaged in marketing securities with the function in 342–347, e.g., wages 344.01281332642, organization 346.065

.096	*Negotiable instruments

Including bills of exchange, checks (cheques), promissory notes, trade acceptances, warehouse receipts

For securities, see 346.092

*Add as instructed under 342–347

.1 Socioeconomic regions

[*Formerly* 346.00917 and with the subject in law plus notation 0917 from table under 342–347]

Class here specific subjects in specific socioeconomic regions [*formerly* 346.01–346.09]

Add to base number 346.1 the numbers following —17 in notation 171–177 from Table 2, e.g., private law of developing countries 346.124; then to the result add the numbers following 346 in 346.001–346.09, e.g., property law of developing countries 346.12404, cases involving property law in developing countries 346.124040264

Class socioeconomic regions of a specific jurisdiction or area in 346.3–346.9

.3–.9 Specific jurisdictions and areas

Add to base number 346 notation 3–9 from Table 2, e.g., private law of Australia 346.94, of New South Wales 346.944, of African states 346.6; then to the result add the numbers following 346 in 346.001–346.09, e.g., property law of Australia 346.9404, of New South Wales 346.94404, of African states 346.604, cases involving property law of Australia 346.94040264

See Manual at 342–349

347 Civil procedure and courts

Class here comprehensive works on civil and criminal procedure and courts, judicial branch of government, administration of justice, legal services

For administrative procedure, see 342.066; for criminal procedure and courts, see 345

See Manual at 347: Jurisdiction

(Option: Class here courts and procedure in a specific field of law; prefer specific field in 342–347, plus notation 0269 from table under 342–347)

SUMMARY

347.001–.009	Standard subdivisions; laws, regulations, cases, procedure, courts
.01	Courts
.02	Courts with general original jurisdiction
.03	Appellate courts
.04	Courts with specialized jurisdiction
.05	Procedure
.06	Evidence
.07	Trials
.08	Appellate procedure
.09	Dispute resolution
.1	Socioeconomic regions
.3–.9	Specific jurisdictions and areas

.001–.008 Standard subdivisions

Notation from Table 1 as modified under 342–347, e.g., cases 347.00264

.009	Historical, geographic, persons treatment
[.009 17]	Socioeconomic regions
	Relocated to 347.1
[.009 3–.009 9]	Specific continents, countries, localities
	Do not use; class in 347.3–347.9

> 347.01–347.09 Specific subjects of civil procedure and courts

Specific subjects in specific socioeconomic regions relocated to 347.1

Class comprehensive works in 347

.01 *Courts

Class provisional courts in 342.0664

For juvenile courts, see 345.081; for courts with specific kinds of jurisdiction, see 347.02–347.04

.012 *General considerations of courts

Including judicial discretion, judicial error, judicial review, jurisdiction of courts, contempt power

Class criminal contempt of court in 345.0234; class general considerations of specific aspects of courts in 347.013–347.017

See Manual at 347: Jurisdiction

.013 *Judicial administration (Court management)

Including court calendars, records

For judges, see 347.014; for court officials other than judges, see 347.016

.014 *Judges

Class judges associated with a specific court with the court, e.g., judges of a juvenile court 345.081, judges of the High Court of Justice in England 347.4202534

.016 Other officials

Including clerks, coroners, court reporters, justices of the peace, marshals, notaries, sheriffs

.017 *Legal aid

Interdisciplinary works on legal aid relocated to 362.58

Class legal aid in criminal cases in 345.01; class legal aid as a welfare service in 362.58

---

*Add as instructed under 342–347

>   347.02–347.04   Courts with specific kinds of jurisdiction

Add to each subdivision identified by ‡ as follows:

     01–09   Standard subdivisions
                   Notation from Table 1 as modified under 342–347, e.g., cases 0264
     2   General considerations
                   Including functions, jurisdiction, organization, powers
     3   Judicial administration
     34   Judges
     36   Other officials
     5   Procedure
                   Add to 5 the numbers following 347.05 in 347.0504–347.055, e.g., formbooks 55
                   For evidence, see 347.06; for trials, see 347.07; for appellate procedure, see 347.08

Class comprehensive works in 347.01

>   347.02–347.03   Courts with general jurisdiction

Class procedure in specific levels of courts in 347.05–347.08; class comprehensive works in 347.01

.02   ‡Courts with general original jurisdiction

Class here comprehensive works on courts that have names such as Circuit, District, County, Municipal, Superior Court

.03   ‡Appellate courts

For appellate courts devoted exclusively to criminal cases, see 345.01; for appellate courts with specialized jurisdiction, see 347.04

.033   ‡Intermediate appellate courts

.035   ‡Courts of last resort (Supreme courts)

.04   ‡Courts with specialized jurisdiction

Including admiralty courts, small-claims courts

Class courts dealing with a specific subject with the subject in 342–347, plus notation 0269 from table under 342–347, e.g., tax courts 343.040269

‡Add as instructed under 347.02–347.04

.05	*Procedure

Class here procedure in specific levels of courts, relation of a fair trial to freedom of the press, comprehensive works on procedure

Class procedure in a specific court with the court in 347.02–347.04, plus notation 5 from add table under 347.02–347.04, e.g., practice in supreme courts 347.035504; class procedure with respect to a specific subject with the subject in 342–347, plus notation 0269 from table under 342–347, e.g., court procedure in tax matters 343.040269

For evidence, see 347.06; for trials, see 347.07; for appellate procedure, see 347.08

.050 4	*Practice

Form, manner, order of instituting and conducting a suit, court case, or other judicial proceeding through its successive stages to its end in accordance with rules and principles laid down by law or by regulations and precedents of the courts

See Manual at 340.023 vs. 347.0504

.050 41	*Malpractice

>	347.051–347.055 General considerations of procedure

Class comprehensive works in 347.05

.051	*Court rules

Class rules of specific courts, of courts having specific kinds of jurisdiction in 347.02–347.04

.052	Motions, limitation of actions, parties to trial, jury trial

Class here advocacy

.053	Kinds of actions

Including class actions, lawsuits

.055	Forms and form books

Standard subdivisions are added for either or both topics in heading

Class forms and form books on a specific subject with the subject in 342–347, plus notation 0269 from table under 342–347, e.g., form books on tax matters 343.040269

.06	*Evidence
.062	*Admissibility
.064	Kinds of evidence

For witnesses, see 347.066

---

*Add as instructed under 342–347

.066   *Witnesses

Class examination of witnesses in 347.075

For expert testimony, see 347.067

.067   *Expert testimony

Class forensic science in 363.25; class medical jurisprudence, forensic medicine, forensic psychiatry in 614.1

.07   *Trials

Class a trial dealing with a specific subject with the subject in 342–347, e.g., a product liability trial 346.038; class procedures of trials dealing with a specific subject with the subject in 342–347, plus notation 0269 from table under 342–347, e.g., procedures of product liability trials 346.0380269

.072   *Pretrial procedure

Including discovery, pleading, service of process, summons

.075   *Trial (Courtroom) procedure

Including examination of witnesses, summations, verdicts

.075 2   *Juries

Class here jury selection

Class instructions to juries in 347.0758

.075 8   *Instructions to juries

.077   *Judgments

Including attachment and garnishment, costs, executions of judgment, remedies

.08   *Appellate procedure

Class here comprehensive works on appellate procedure in criminal cases

Class procedure in specific appellate courts hearing both civil and criminal cases, specific appellate courts devoted exclusively to civil cases in 347.03–347.04; class procedure in appellate courts devoted exclusively to criminal cases in 345.01

.09   *Dispute resolution

Class here arbitration, mediation, conciliation

*Add as instructed under 342–347

.1 Socioeconomic regions

[*Formerly* 347.00917 and with the subject in law plus notation 0917 from table under 342–347]

Class here specific subjects in specific socioeconomic regions [*formerly* 347.01–347.09]

Add to base number 347.1 the numbers following — 17 in notation 171–177 from Table 2, e.g., civil procedure and courts of developing countries 347.124; then to the result add the numbers following 347 in 347.001–347.09, e.g., the law of evidence in developing countries 347.12406, court decisions on evidence in developing countries 347.1240602643

Class socioeconomic regions of a specific jurisdiction or area in 347.3–347.9

.3–.9 Specific jurisdictions and areas

Add to base number 347 notation 3–9 from Table 2, e.g., civil procedure and courts of Australia 347.94, of New South Wales 347.944, of African states 347.6; then to the result add the numbers following 347 in 347.001–347.09, e.g., the law of evidence in Australia 347.9406, in New South Wales 347.94406, in African states 347.606; Australian court decisions on evidence in 347.940602643

See Manual at 342–349

Special developments for Scotland, England, the United States follow

.411 Civil procedure and courts of Scotland

.411 001–.411 009 Standard subdivisions

.411 01 *Courts

> For courts with specific kinds of jurisdiction, see
> 347.41102–347.41104

.411 012–.411 017 Specific aspects of courts

Add to base number 347.41101 the numbers following 347.01 in 347.012–347.017, e.g., general considerations 347.411012

> 347.411 02–347.411 04 Courts with specific kinds of jurisdiction

Add to each subdivision identified by ‡ as instructed under 347.02–347.04, e.g., jurisdiction of the Sheriff Court 347.4110212

Class comprehensive works in 347.41101

> 347.411 02–347.411 03 Courts with general jurisdiction

Class procedure in specific levels of courts in 347.41105–347.41108; class comprehensive works in 347.41101

*Add as instructed under 342–347

.411 02	‡Courts with original jurisdiction
.411 021	‡Sheriff Court

Comprehensive works

Class criminal jurisdiction of Sheriff Court in 345.411014; class appellate jurisdiction of Sheriff-Principal in 347.411032

.411 023	‡Court of Session

> *For Outer House, see 347.411024; for Inner House, see 347.411035*

.411 024	‡Outer House of Court of Session
.411 03	‡Courts with appellate jurisdiction

Class here comprehensive works on appellate courts

> *For appellate courts devoted exclusively to criminal cases, see 345.41101; for appellate courts with specialized jurisdiction, see 347.41104*

.411 032	‡Sheriff-Principal
.411 035	‡Inner House of Court of Session
.411 039	‡House of Lords (Court of last resort)
.411 04	‡Courts with specialized jurisdiction

Including Court of the Lord Lyon, Licensing Appeals Courts, Licensing Courts

Class courts dealing with a single specific subject with the subject in 342–347, plus notation 0269 from table under 342–347, e.g., Court of Exchequer 343.411040269

.411 05–.411 09	Procedure and arbitration

Add to base number 347.4110 the numbers following 347.0 in 347.05–347.09, e.g., evidence 347.41106

.42 Civil procedure and courts of England

.420 01–.420 09	Standard subdivisions
.420 1	*Courts

> *For courts with specific kinds of jurisdiction, see 347.4202–347.4204*

.420 12–.420 17	Specific aspects of courts

Add to base number 347.4201 the numbers following 347.01 in 347.012–347.017, e.g., general considerations 347.42012

*Add as instructed under 342–347

‡Add as instructed under 347.02–347.04

>   347.420 2–347.420 4   Courts with specific kinds of jurisdiction

Add to each subdivision identified by ‡ as instructed under 347.02–347.04, e.g., jurisdiction of County Court 347.420212

Class comprehensive works in 347.4201

>   347.420 2–347.420 3   Courts with general jurisdiction

Class procedure in specific levels of courts in 347.4205–347.4208; class comprehensive works in 347.4201

.420 2	‡Courts with original jurisdiction
.420 21	‡County Court
.420 23	‡Domestic Court of Magistrates Court

Class comprehensive works on Magistrates Court in 345.012

.420 25   ‡High Court of Justice

Comprehensive works

For Family Division, see 346.420150269; for Chancery Division, see 347.42026; for Queen's Bench Division, see 347.42027

.420 26   ‡Chancery Division of the High Court of Justice

.420 27   ‡Queen's Bench Division of High Court of Justice

For Divisional Court of Queen's Bench Division, see 345.42016

.420 29   ‡Supreme Court of Judicature

For Crown Court, see 345.42014; for High Court of Justice, see 347.42025; for Court of Appeal, see 347.42032

.420 3   ‡Courts with appellate jurisdiction

Class here comprehensive works on appellate courts

For appellate courts devoted exclusively to criminal cases, see 345.4201; for appellate courts with specialized jurisdiction, see 347.4204

.420 32   ‡Court of Appeal

For Criminal Division, see 345.42018; for Civil Division, see 347.42035

.420 35   ‡Civil Division of Court of Appeal

.420 39   ‡House of Lords (Court of last resort)

Criminal and civil jurisdiction

‡Add as instructed under 347.02–347.04

.420 4   ‡Courts with specialized jurisdiction

   Including Judicial Committee of the Privy Council

   Class courts dealing with a specific subject with the subject in 342–347, plus notation 0269 from table under 342–347, e.g., Lands Tribunal 346.420430269

.420 5–.420 9   Procedure and arbitration

   Add to base number 347.420 the numbers following 347.0 in 347.05–347.09, e.g., evidence 347.4206

.73   Civil procedure and courts of the United States

   Federal procedure and courts; national and regional treatment of state and local procedure and courts

   For civil procedure and courts of specific states and localities, see 347.74–347.79

.730 01–.730 09   Standard subdivisions

.731   *Courts

   For specific court systems, see 347.732–347.734

.731 2–.731 7   Specific aspects of courts

   Add to base number 347.731 the numbers following 347.01 in 347.012–347.017, e.g., judges 347.7314

>   347.732–347.734   Specific court systems

   Class comprehensive works in 347.731

.732   Federal courts

   Add 0 to base number 347.732; then add further as instructed under 347.02–347.04, e.g., periodicals about federal courts 347.732005, federal judges 347.732034

>   347.732 2–347.732 8   Federal courts with specific kinds of jurisdiction

   Class here procedure in specific courts

   Add to each subdivision identified by ‡ as instructed under 347.02–347.04, e.g., Supreme Court rules 347.73265

   Class comprehensive works in 347.732

*Add as instructed under 342–347

‡Add as instructed under 347.02–347.04

> 347.732 2–347.732 6 Federal courts with general jurisdiction

Class procedure in specific levels of courts in 347.735–347.738; class comprehensive works in 347.732

.732 2   ‡District courts

Courts of original jurisdiction

.732 4   ‡Courts of appeal

For Supreme Court, see 347.7326

.732 6   ‡Supreme Court

.732 8   ‡Courts of specialized jurisdiction

Including United States Court of Customs and Patent Appeals

Class courts dealing with a specific subject with the subject in United States law, plus notation 0269 from table under 342–347, e.g., tax courts 343.73040269

.733   *State courts

Class courts of specific states in 347.74–347.79

.733 2–.733 8   Specific aspects of state courts

Add to base number 347.733 the numbers following 347.732 in 347.7322–347.7328, e.g., state supreme courts 347.7336

.734   *Local courts

Class courts of specific localities in 347.74–347.79

.735–.738   Procedure

Class here procedure in specific levels of federal courts

Add to base number 347.73 the numbers following 347.0 in 347.05–347.08, e.g., rules of evidence 347.736

Class procedure in specific courts in 347.732–347.734

.739   *Arbitration, mediation, conciliation

Subdivisions are added for any or all topics in heading

---

*Add as instructed under 342–347

‡Add as instructed under 347.02–347.04

.74–.79 Civil procedure and courts of specific states and localities of the United States

> Add to base number 347 notation 74–79 from Table 2, e.g., civil procedure and courts of Pennsylvania 347.748, of Philadelphia 347.74811; then to the result add the numbers following 347 in 347.001–347.09, e.g., the Supreme Court of Pennsylvania 347.748035, courts of Philadelphia 347.7481101
>
> Class regional treatment of state and local procedure and courts in 347.73; class civil procedure and courts of Hawaii in 347.969

348 Laws (Statutes), regulations, cases

> Original materials and their guides listed here are comprehensive in nature, covering the whole of the law of a specific jurisdiction or a major portion thereof
>
> Class treatises on the whole law of a specific jurisdiction in 349. Class original materials and their guides limited to a specific branch or subject with the branch or subject in 342–347, plus notation 026 from table under 342–347, e.g., a digest of tax laws 343.0402638
>> (Option: Class here laws, regulations, cases covering specific subjects in law; prefer specific subject in 342–347, plus notation 026 from table under 342–347)
>
> *See Manual at 340: Forms of legal material*

SUMMARY

348.001–.009	**Standard subdivisions and codification**
.01	**Preliminary materials**
.02	**Laws (Statutes) and regulations**
.04	**Cases**
.05	**Advisory opinions of attorneys-general (ministers of justice)**
.1	**Socioeconomic regions**
.3–.9	**Specific jurisdictions and areas**

.001–.003 Standard subdivisions of laws, regulations, cases; of laws alone; of regulations alone

.004 Codification

> Class proposed codes in 348.023

.005–.008 Standard subdivisions of laws, regulations, cases; of laws alone; of regulations alone

.009 Historical, geographic, persons treatment

[.009 17] Socioeconomic regions

> Relocated to 348.1

[.009 3–.009 9] Specific continents, countries, localities

> Do not use; class in 348.3–348.9

.01   Preliminary materials

Including bills; legislative hearings, histories; slip laws; statistical reports of bills passed or vetoed, reports on the status of bills

> 348.02–348.05   Specific aspects of laws, regulations, cases

Specific aspects in specific socioeconomic regions relocated to 348.1

Class comprehensive works in 348

.02   Laws (Statutes) and regulations

Including laws arranged in alphabetical order

> 348.022–348.024   Collections of laws

Class comprehensive works and collections in 348

.022   Statutes

Laws arranged in chronological order

Including session laws

(If the option under 348 is chosen, class here individual laws)

.023   Codes

Compilations of statutes in classified order

Including compiled and consolidated statutes

.024   Selected laws

.025   Administrative regulations

> 348.026–348.028   Guides to laws and regulations

Class comprehensive works and guides in 348.026. Class guides to a specific collection of laws with the collection, e.g., a citator to the U.S. Code 348.7323

.026   Digests of laws and regulations

Including summaries of changes

Class here comprehensive guides to laws and regulations

For citators to laws and regulations, see 348.027; for checklists, tables, indexes of laws and regulations, see 348.028

.027   Citators to laws and regulations

.028   Checklists, tables, indexes of laws and regulations

> Standard subdivisions are added for any or all topics in heading

> Class union lists of legal material in 016.34

.04   Cases

> Do not use for casebooks; class with the subject in 342–347 without further subdivision

> Class cases in a specific subject in law with the subject in 343–347, plus notation 0264 from table under 342–347, e.g., cases involving tax law 344.040264

>   348.041–348.043   Reports

> Reports of cases contain a relatively full treatment of each case as well as the ultimate decision

> Class comprehensive works in 348.04

.041   National reports

.042   Regional reports

.043   State and provincial reports

.044   Court decisions

> Texts of decisions with or without accompanying information

.045   Decisions (Rulings) of regulatory agencies

>   348.046–348.048   Guides to cases

> Class here combined guides to laws, regulations, cases

> Class comprehensive works and guides in 348.046. Class guides to a specific set of court reports with the reports, e.g., a citator to U.S. Supreme Court reports 348.73413

> *For guides to laws and regulations, see 348.026–348.028*

.046   Digests of cases

> Class here comprehensive guides to cases

> *For citators to cases, see 348.047; for checklists, tables, indexes of cases, see 348.048*

.047   Citators to cases

.048   Checklists, tables, indexes of cases

> Standard subdivisions are added for any or all topics in heading

.05   Advisory opinions of attorneys-general (ministers of justice)

.1   Socioeconomic regions

[*Formerly* 348.00917 and with the subject in law plus notation 0917 from table under 342–347]

Class here specific subjects in specific socioeconomic regions [*formerly* 348.02–348.05]

Add to base number 348 the numbers following — 17 in notation 171–177 from Table 2, e.g., laws, regulations, cases of developing countries 348.124; then to the result add the numbers following 348 in 348.001–348.05, e.g., selected laws of developing countries 348.124024

Class socioeconomic regions of a specific jurisdiction or area in 348.3–348.9

.3–.9   Specific jurisdictions and areas

Class here general collections of repealed laws

Add to base number 348 notation 3–9 from Table 2, e.g., laws, regulations, cases of Australia 348.94, of New South Wales 348.944, of African states 348.6; then to the result add the numbers following 348 in 348.001–348.05, e.g., selected laws of Australia 348.94024, of New South Wales 348.944024, of African states 348.6024

Class the legislative procedure involved in enacting or repealing a law in 328.37. Class repealed laws on a specific subject with the subject in 342–347, e.g., repeal of a prohibition on the sale and consumption of alcohol 344.0541

See Manual at 342–349

A special development for the United States follows

.73   Federal laws (statutes), regulations, cases of the United States

Including national and regional treatment of state and local laws, regulations, cases

For laws, regulations, cases of specific states and localities, see 348.74–348.79

.730 4   Codification

Class proposed codes in 348.7323

.731   Preliminary materials

Including bills; legislative hearings, histories; slip laws

.732   Federal laws (statutes) and regulations

———

>   348.732 2–348.732 5   Collections of federal laws and regulations

Class comprehensive works and collections in 348.732

.732 2	Federal statutes
	(Option: If the option under 348 is chosen, class here individual laws)
.732 3	United States Code
.732 4	Selected Federal laws
.732 5	Federal administrative regulations

> 348.732 6–348.732 8   Guides to federal laws and regulations

Class comprehensive works and guides in 348.7326

.732 6 Digests of federal laws and regulations

Including summaries of changes

Class here comprehensive guides to federal laws and regulations

For citators to federal laws and regulations, see 348.7327; for checklists, tables, indexes of federal laws and regulations, see 348.7328

.732 7 Citators to federal laws and regulations

.732 8 Checklists, tables, indexes of federal laws and regulations

Standard subdivisions are added for any or all topics in heading

.734 Federal cases

Do not use for casebooks; class with the subject in 342–347 without further subdivision

> 348.734 1–348.734 2   Reports of federal cases

Class comprehensive works and reports in 348.734

.734 1	Federal court reports
.734 13	Supreme Court
.734 15	Lower Federal courts
.734 2	National reporter system
.734 22	Atlantic federal reporter system
.734 23	Northeastern federal reporter system
.734 24	Northwestern federal reporter system
.734 25	Southeastern federal reporter system
.734 26	Southwestern federal reporter system
.734 27	Southern federal reporter system

.734 28	Pacific federal reporter system
.734 4	Court decisions
.734 5	Decisions (Rulings) of regulatory agencies

> 348.734 6–348.734 8   Guides to federal cases

Class here combined guides to federal laws, regulations, cases

Class comprehensive works and guides to federal cases in 348.7346

For guides to federal laws and regulations, see 348.7326–348.7328

.734 6   Digests of federal cases

Class here comprehensive guides to federal cases

For citators to federal cases, see 348.7347; for checklists, tables, indexes of federal cases, see 348.7348

.734 7   Citators to federal cases

.734 8   Checklists, tables, indexes of federal cases

Standard subdivisions are added for any or all topics in heading

.735   Advisory opinions of Attorney-General

.74–.79   Laws, regulations, cases of specific states and localities of the United States

Add to base number 348 notation 74–79 from Table 2, e.g., laws, regulations, cases of Pennsylvania 348.748, of Philadelphia 348.74811; then to the result add the numbers following 348 in 348.001–348.05, e.g., Pennsylvania statutes 348.748022, Philadelphia code of ordinances 348.74811023

Class national and regional treatment of state and local laws, regulations, cases in 348.73; class laws, regulations, cases of Hawaii in 348.969

349   Law of specific jurisdictions, areas, socioeconomic regions

For law of specific ancient jurisdictions, areas, socioeconomic regions, see 340.53; for specific branches of law of a specific jurisdiction, area, socioeconomic region, see 342–347; for original materials on law of a specific jurisdiction, area, socioeconomic region, see 348

See Manual at 340.02–340.09 vs. 349; also at 342–349

(If Option A under 340 is chosen, class here comparative law and law of jurisdictions other than the preferred jurisdiction by adding to base number 349 the numbers following 34 in 342–348, e.g., comparative criminal procedure 349.505, criminal procedure of New Zealand 349.59305. Assuming Australia to be the preferred jurisdiction, criminal procedure of Australia 345.05)

.1   **Law of specific socioeconomic regions [*formerly* 340.0917]**

Add to base number 349.1 the numbers following — 17 in notation 171–177 from Table 2, e.g., works on ordinances from developing countries 349.124; however, for Islamic law, see 340.59

Class law of specific socioeconomic regions of a specific jurisdiction or area in 349.4–349.9

.4–.9   **Law of specific jurisdictions and areas of modern world**

Add to base number 349 notation 4–9 from Table 2, e.g., works on the ordinances of the City of Los Angeles 349.79494

350   Public administration and military science

Except for military science (355–359), this schedule is new and has been prepared with little or no reference to previous editions. Most numbers have been reused with new meanings

A comparative table giving both old and new numbers for a substantial list of topics and equivalence tables showing the numbers in the old and new schedules appear in volume 1 in this edition

In addition, method of selection of chief executive relocated from 351.0034 to 324; termination of tenure of chief executive before expiration of term relocated from 351.0036 to 324; procedures for legislative enactment of budgets relocated from 351.7223 to 328.378; management of police services relocated from 351.74 to 363.2068; impeachment from 351.993 to 342.068

See Manual at 350 vs. 342–347: Preliminary materials on laws and appropriations

SUMMARY

353	Specific fields of public administration
.1	Administration of external and national security affairs
.3	Administration of services related to domestic order
.4	Administration of justice
.5	Administration of social welfare
.6	Administration of health services
.7	Administration of culture and related activities
.8	Administration of agencies supporting and controlling education
.9	Administration of safety, sanitation, waste control Safety administration
354	Public administration of economy and environment
.08	History and description with respect to kinds of persons
.2	General considerations of administration
.3	Administration of environment and natural resources
.4	Administration of energy and energy-related industries
.5	Administration of agriculture
.6	Administration of construction, manufacturing, services
.7	Administration of commerce, communications, transportation
.8	Administration financial institutions, money, credit
.9	Administration of labor and professions
355	Military science
.001–.009	Standard subdivisions
.02–.07	Basic considerations of military science
.1	Military life and customs
.2	Military resources
.3	Organization and personnel of military forces
.4	Military operations
.5	Military training
.6	Military administration
.7	Military installations
.8	Military equipment and supplies (Matériel) Weapons (Ordnance)
356	Foot forces and warfare
.1	Infantry
357	Mounted forces and warfare
.04	General topics
.1	Horse cavalry
.2	Remount services
.5	Mechanized cavalry
358	Air and other specialized forces and warfare; engineering and related services
.1	Missile forces; army artillery and armored forces
.2	Army engineering and related services
.3	Chemical, biological, radiological warfare
.4	Air forces and warfare
.8	Space forces

359		Sea (Naval) forces and warfare
	.001–.009	Standard subdivisions
	.03–.07	[Situation and policy, naval research and development]
	.1–.2	Naval life and resources
	.3	Organization and personnel of naval forces
	.4–.5	Naval operations and training
	.6	Naval administration
	.7	Naval installations
	.8	Naval equipment and supplies (Naval matériel) Naval weapons (Naval ordnance)
	.9	Specialized combat forces; engineering and related services

351 Public administration

Class here executive branch of government, programs administered by executive branch, civil service in the sense of all units of public administration outside armed services

Class relation of executive branch to other branches, works that deal comprehensively with more than one branch of government in 320.404; class civil service in the sense of merit system in 352.63; class interdisciplinary works on management in 658. Class management of government-owned enterprises operating a service with the service, plus notation 068 from Table 1, e.g., management of public hospitals 362.11068, of nationalized railroads 385.068

For administration of legislative branch, see 328.068; for administration of judicial branch, see 347.013; for specific topics of public administration, see 352–354

See Manual at 351; also at T1—068 vs. 353–354; also at 320.9, 320.4 vs. 351; also at 350 vs. 342–347

.025	Directories of persons and organizations

Class directories of elected public officials in 324.025

.05	Serial publications

Class here official gazettes, serial administrative reports of governmental organizations

.06	Nongovernmental organizations

Do not use for governmental organizations; class in 351. Do not use for serial administrative reports of governmental organizations; class in 351.05

See Manual at T1—0601–0609

[.068]	Management

Do not use; class in 351

.07	Education, research, related topics

.076   Review and exercise

Class here interdisciplinary works on civil service examinations

For civil service examinations in a specific subject, see the subject, plus notation 076 from Table 1, e.g., examinations in accounting 657.076

(Option: Class here civil service examinations in specific subjects; prefer the subject in 001–999, plus notation 076 from Table 1. If option is chosen, add to base number 351.076 notation 001–999, e.g., civil service examinations in accounting 351.076657)

.08   History and description with respect to kinds of persons

Do not use for programs directed to kinds of persons; class in 353.53

See Manual at 353.53 vs. 351.08

.09   Historical and persons treatment

Do not use for treatment by areas, regions, places in general; class in 351.1. Do not use for treatment by specific continents, countries, localities; class in 351.3–351.9

.1   Administration in areas, regions, places in general

Not limited by continent, country, locality

Add to base number 351.1 the numbers following 1 in notation 11–19 from Table 2, e.g., administration in developing regions 351.1724; however, for urban administration, see 352.16; for rural administration, see 352.17

.3–.9   Administration in specific continents, countries, localities

Class here administration of specific jurisdictions, practical works on administration of specific subordinate jurisdictions, e.g., provinces

Add to base number 351 notation 3–9 from Table 2, e.g., public administration in Germany 351.43

Class theoretical works on specific kinds of subordinate jurisdictions in 352.13–352.19

> *See Manual at 351.3–351.9 vs. 352.13–352.19: Administration in and of specific subordinate jurisdictions*

(Option A: Class here treatment of specific topics of public administration in specific continents, countries, localities; prefer 352–354, plus notation 09 from table under 352–354. If option is chosen, add to each geographic subdivision as follows:

001–007	Standard subdivisions
	Notation from Table 1 as modified under 351, e.g., serial administrative reports 005
008	History and description with respect to kinds of persons
	Class programs directed to kinds of persons in 0353
009	Historical, geographic, persons treatment
	Use for geographic treatment only when area of interest is narrower than area of jurisdiction, e.g., United States federal administration in Gulf Coast states 351.7300976
02–04	Specific topics of public administration
	Add to base number 0 the numbers following 35 in 352–354, e.g., social welfare administration 035, programs directed to kinds of persons 0353

(Option B: Class here treatment of specific topics of public administration in specific continents, countries, localities not requiring local emphasis; prefer 352–354, plus notation 09 from table under 352–354. If option B is chosen, add to each geographic subdivision as instructed under option A)

> *See Manual at 351: Optional use of 351*

> ## 352–354   Specific topics of public administration

Class here administration of specific departments and agencies

Except for modifications shown under specific entries, add to each subdivision identified by * as follows:

01–07	Standard subdivisions
	Notation from Table 1 as modified under 351, e.g., serial administrative reports 05
08	History and description with respect to kinds of persons
	Class here programs directed to kinds of persons, equal opportunity programs
	See Manual at 353.53 vs. 351.08; also at 353.53 vs. 352.1: Use of table notation for kinds of persons
09	Historical, geographic, persons treatment
093–099	Treatment by specific continents, countries, localities
	(Option A: Class treatment of specific topics of public administration by specific continents, countries, localities in 351.3–351.9
	(Option B: In order to provide local emphasis and shorter notation, class specific topics of public administration treated in jurisdictions requiring local emphasis in 352–354 without adding notation 09 from this table, and class specific topics of public administration in specific continents, countries, localities not requiring local emphasis in 351.3–351.9)
2	General considerations of public administration
21	Jurisdictional levels
	Add to 21 the numbers following 352.1 in 352.105–352.19, e.g., international administration 211
	Class administration at national level, combined treatment of national and other levels (except works that emphasize differences between administration at different levels) in base number without use of notation 21
22–26	Specific topics in management
	Add to 2 the numbers following 352 in 352.2–352.6, e.g., governing boards and commissions 225, contracts and procurement 253
27–28	Administration of supporting and controlling functions of government
	Do not use when redundant
	Add to 2 the numbers following 352 in 352.7–352.8, e.g., promoting and disseminating knowledge 274, regulation 28
	See Manual at 352–353: Add table: 27–28

Unless other instructions are given, class a subject with aspects in two or more subdivisions of 352–354 in the number coming last, e.g., chief executive of a department of agriculture 354.52293 (*not* 352.293)

Class misconduct in office regardless of topic in 353.46; class comprehensive works in 351

See Manual at 352–354; also at 300, 320.6 vs. 352–354

352   General considerations of public administration

Class here general considerations of public administration applying to two or more branches of government, e.g., financial administration of the legislative and judicial branches 352.4

Class general considerations of public administration applied to a specific field with the field in public administration, plus notation 2 from table under 352–354, e.g., local safety administration 353.9214

See Manual at 352; also at 352–354

SUMMARY

352.1	**Jurisdictional levels of administration**
.2	**Organization of administration**
.3	**Executive management**
.4	**Financial administration and budgets**
.5	**Property administration and related topics**
.6	**Personnel administration (Human resource administration)**
.7	**Administration of general forms of assistance**
.8	**Administration of general forms of control**

[.01–.09]   Standard subdivisions

Do not use; class in 351.01–351.09

.1   Jurisdictional levels of administration

Class programs directed to specific kinds of persons at specific levels of administration in 353.5321. Class a specific topic in administrative management, support, control at a specific jurisdictional level of administration with the topic in 352.2–352.8, plus notation 21 from table under 352–354, e.g., financial administration and budgets of international agencies 352.4211, regulation by local government 352.8214

Use 351 for combined treatment of national and other levels of administration except for works that emphasize differences between administration at different levels

For administration at national level, see 351

See Manual at 352; also at 353.53 vs. 352.1: Use of table notation for kinds of persons

SUMMARY

352.101–.109	**Standard subdivisions**
.11	**International administration**
.13	**State and provincial administration**
.14	**Local administration**
.15	**Intermediate units of local administration**
.16	**Urban administration**
.17	**Rural administration**
.19	**Administration of special service districts**

.105	Serial publications

Class here official gazettes, serial administrative reports of governmental organizations

.106	Nongovernmental organizations

Do not use for governmental organizations and management; class in 352.1. Do not use for serial administrative reports of governmental organizations; class in 352.105

.108	History and description in respect to kinds of persons

Do not use for programs at specific levels of administration directed toward kinds of persons; class in 353.5321

.11	International administration

Class here administration of international governmental organizations

Class interdisciplinary works on international governmental organizations in 341.2

.110 5	Serial publications

Class here official gazettes, serial administrative reports of government organizations

.110 6	Nongovernmental organizations

Do not use for governmental organizations and management; class in 351.11. Do not use for serial administrative reports of governmental organizations; class in 352.1105

.110 8	History and description with respect to kinds of persons

Do not use for international programs directed to kinds of persons; class in 353.53211

.110 9	Historical, geographic, persons treatment
[.110 94–.110 99]	Treatment by specific continents, countries, localities in modern world

Do not use; class in 352.114–352.119

.112	League of Nations

Class here management [*formerly also* 341.22068, 341.223]

.113	United Nations

Class here secretariat [*formerly also* 341.2324], management [*formerly also* 341.233]

Class interdisciplinary works on United Nations in 341.23

.114–.119 International administration in specific continents and parts of continents

> Class here administration of international organizations serving continents and parts of continents
>
> Add to base number 352.11 notation 4–9 from Table 2, e.g., international administration in southeast Asia 352.1159, Organization of American States 352.117

> 352.13–352.19 Administration of subordinate jurisdictions

> Except for modifications shown under specific entries, add to each subdivision identified by † as follows:

01–07	Standard subdivisions
	Notation from Table 1 as modified under 351, e.g., serial administrative reports 05
08	History and description with respect to kinds of persons
	Do not use for programs directed to kinds of persons; class in 353.53213
09	Historical, geographic, persons treatment
093–099	Treatment by specific continents, countries, localities
	Limited to comprehensive, theoretical, comparative treatment, e.g. administration of Länder in Germany 352.130943
	Class administration in or of a specific subordinate jurisdiction in 351.3–351.9 (*not* 093–099), e.g., administration of Bavaria 351.433
	See Manual at 351.3–351.9 vs. 352.13–352.19: Administration in and of specific subordinate jurisdictions
3	Administrative cooperation among subordinate jurisdictions
	Class here administrative relations among subordinate jurisdictions that do not involve support and control by a higher jurisdiction, e.g., relations among coordinate city and county governments
	Class comprehensive works on administrative cooperation among subordinate jurisdictions in 352.143
	See also 353.33 for support and control of subordinate jurisdictions by higher jurisdictions
301–308	Standard subdivisions
	Notation from Table 1 as modified under 351, e.g., serial administrative reports 305
309	Historical, geographic, persons treatment

> Class administration of or in specific subordinate jurisdictions in 351.3–351.9, e.g., administration of Bavaria 351.433; class comprehensive works on administration of subordinate jurisdictions in 352.14

> *See Manual at 351.3–351.9 vs. 352.13–352.19: Administration in and of specific subordinate jurisdictions*

.13 †State and provincial administration

States and provinces: regularly constituted territorial subdivisions of large countries, with responsibilities cutting across several fields of administration, and usually encompassing many local units

Subdivisions are added for either or both topics in heading

See Manual at 352.13 vs. 352.15

.14 †Local administration

Limited to comprehensive and comparative treatment, e.g., local administration in Germany 352.140943

Class here comprehensive works on administration of subordinate jurisdictions

Class local government, combined treatment of local government and local administration in 320.8; class regional divisions of administrative agencies in 352.288. Class administration in or of a specific subordinate jurisdiction with the jurisdiction in 351.3–351.9, e.g., administration of Nuremberg 351.43324

For state and provincial administration, see 352.13; for administration of specific kinds of local jurisdictions, see 352.15–352.19; for support and control of subordinate jurisdictions by higher jurisdictions, see 353.33

See Manual at 351.3–351.9 vs. 352.13–352.19: Administration in and of specific subordinate jurisdictions

---

> 352.15–352.19 Administration of specific kinds of local jurisdictions

Class comprehensive works in 352.14

.15 †Intermediate units of local administration

Intermediate units: regularly constituted relatively local territorial subdivisions, with responsibilities cutting across several fields of administration, and usually containing few component units

Class here arrondissements, counties, shires, territorial departments; provinces of small countries

See Manual at 352.13 vs. 352.15

.16 †Urban administration

Class here city administration

See also 354.2793 for administration of urban development

.167 †Administration of metropolitan regions

.169 †Suburban administration

†Add as instructed under 352.13–352.19

.17 †Rural administration

> *See also 354.2794 for administration of rural development*

.19 †Administration of special service districts

> Local districts or authorities established to provide one or a few services
>
> Class regional divisions of state and national agencies in 352.288. Class administration of a specific special service district with the service it administers, e.g., a metropolitan district to coordinate administration of health services 353.6219, a local rail transit authority that operates trains 388.42065

.193 Administrative cooperation among jurisdictions served by special service districts

> Number built according to instructions under 352.13–352.19
>
> Class here control of special service districts by higher jurisdictions and by other local authorities

---

> **352.2–352.6 Specific topics of management in public administration**
>
> Class here specific topics of management in public administration at specific jurisdictional levels, plus notation 211–219 from table under 352–354, e.g., financial administration and budgets of international agencies 352.4211
>
> Class comprehensive works on administrative aspects in 351; class interdisciplinary works on management, on specific topics of management in 658
>
> *See Manual at 352*

.2 *Organization of administration

> Class comprehensive works on executive management in public administration in 352.3; class interdisciplinary works on organization in management in 658.1

.23 *Chief executives

> Class here presidents, prime ministers, monarchs
>
> Class governing boards and commissions in 352.25
>
> *For heads of departments and agencies, see 352.293*

.233 *Heads of state lacking administrative powers

> Presidents in countries where prime ministers are head of administration; constitutional monarchs and their representatives, e.g., governors-general in Commonwealth of Nations countries

.235 *Powers and privileges of chief executives

> Class abuse of power in 353.46

*Add as instructed under 352–354

†Add as instructed under 352.13–352.19

.236	*Leadership role of chief executives
.237	*Office of chief executive
.237 229 3	Chief of staff to chief executive

Number built according to instructions under 352–354

.238	*Executive messages, speeches, writings

Collections, history, description, criticism

For messages, speeches, writings on a specific subject, see the subject, e.g., budget messages of specific jurisdictions 352.493–352.499, messages on German budget 352.4943013, executive messages on economics 330, executive messages on economy of Germany 330.943

.238 4	*Addresses to legislatures
.238 6	*Inaugural addresses
.239	*Deputy chief executives
.24	*Cabinets and cabinet-level committees

Class here councils of ministers, executive councils

Subdivisions are added for either or both topics in heading

For a cabinet-level committee charged with a specific activity, see the activity, plus notation 224 from table under 352–354, e.g., cabinet councils on the economy 354.224

.243	*Cabinet secretariats
.243 229 3	Cabinet secretaries (Ministers with a portfolio of cabinet affairs)

Number built according to instructions under 352–354

.246	*Domestic councils
.25	*Governing boards and commissions

Multimember bodies (other than cabinets and cabinet-level committees) selecting executives and or participating in executive decisions

Subdivisions are added for either or both topics in heading

Class a specific board or commission with the topic it administers, plus notation 09 (*not* 225) from table under 352–354, e.g., United States National Labor Relations Board 354.970973 (*not* 354.972250973)

See also 352.743 for advisory bodies

.26	*Special kinds of agencies

For a special kind of agency not provided for here, see the kind, e.g., cabinets 352.24

*Add as instructed under 352–354

.264   *Independent agencies

> Agencies that are not parts of larger (cabinet-level) departments

> Avoid using notation 2264 from table under 352–354 for specific independent agencies, e.g., independent regulatory agencies 352.8 (*not* 352.82264)

> Class autonomous authorities of local scope in 352.19

.266   *Government corporations (Public enterprises)

> Class government corporations engaged in finance in 332.1–332.6; class government corporations engaged in real estate in 333.33; class government corporations engaged in insurance in 368; class government corporations engaged in specific economic enterprises other than commerce, communication, finance, insurance, real estate, transportation in 338.76. Class a government corporations engaged in commerce, communications, transportations with the subject of its operations in 380, plus notation 065 from table under 380, e.g., government railroad corporation 385.065

.28   *Internal organization

> Class here levels of management

> *For supervision (bottom level of management), see 352.66*

.283   *Distribution and delegation of authority

> Including centralization, decentralization

> Class here line and staff organization

> Subdivisions are added for either or both topics in heading

> *For regional divisions of administrative departments, see 352.288*

.284   *Middle management

.285   *Top management

.288   *Regional divisions of administrative agencies

> Class here field offices, regional offices

.29   *Organization and structure of departments and agencies

> Limited to generalities of organization and structure

> Subdivisions are added for either or both topics in heading

> Class description and purposes of departments and agencies in general in 351. Class organization and structure of a specific kind of department or agency with the kind, plus notation 22 (*not* 229) from table under 352–354, e.g., structure of governing boards 352.2522, structure of governing boards in Germany 352.25220943

> *See Manual at 352.29*

---

*Add as instructed under 352–354

.293   *Heads and deputy heads of departments and agencies

> Class here cabinet officers, ministers of state, secretaries of state
>
> Class cabinet secretaries (ministers with a portfolio of cabinet affairs) in 352.2432293; class secretaries of state of specific states of United States in 352.3870974–352.3870979; class secretaries of state for foreign affairs in 353.132293; class prime ministers, comprehensive works on chief executives in 352.23
>
> > *See also 352.39 for executive development*
> >
> > *See Manual at 352.293*

.3   *Executive management

> Class here interdisciplinary works on public administrators
>
> Class interdisciplinary works on executive management in 658.4
>
> > *For internal organization, see 352.28. For a specific aspect of public administrators, see the aspect, e.g., biography 351.092, law 342.068*

.33   *Decision making

> Class specific means of obtaining guidance for decision making in 352.37

.34   *Planning and policy making

> Subdivisions are added for either or both topics in heading
>
> Class specific means of obtaining guidance for planning and policy making in 352.37

.35   *Internal control

> Including internal inspection, agency ombudsmen
>
> Class here accountability in public administration, administrative responsibility, oversight
>
> Class legislative oversight in 328.3456; class administration of control of society by government in 352.8
>
> > *For oversight by outside agencies, see 352.88*

.357   *Quality control

> Class quality control by managerial accounting in 352.43

.36   *Objectives of administration

> Class here management by objective (MBO)
>
> Class means of obtaining objectives in 352.37

.365   *Project management

.367   *Managing change

> Class here modernization

---

*Add as instructed under 352–354

.37 *Means of obtaining objectives

Class here specific means of obtaining guidance for policy and decision making

Class comprehensive works on decision making in 352.33; class comprehensive works on policy in 352.34; class management by objectives in 352.36

For use of information, see 352.38

.373 *Use of consultants

.375 *Promotion of efficiency

.379 *Intelligence and security

Including computer and office security, security classification

Class military security classification in 355.3433

See also 353.1 for administration of external and national security

.38 *Information management

Class fact-finding and advisory bodies in 352.743

.384 *Communication in management

.387 *Records management

Class here maintaining official records

Class archival treatment of public records in 025.1714; class secretaries of state in specific states of United States in 352.3870974–352.3870979; class programs supporting archives in 352.744

.39 *Managing executive personnel

Class here executive development, leadership, management environment

For leadership role of chief executive, see 352.236; for specific aspects of managing of executive personnel, see 352.6

.4 *Financial administration and budgets

Class here treasury departments and ministries; works covering both government financial administration and administration of financial institutions, money, credit

Subdivisions are added for financial administration and budgets together, for financial administration alone

Class interdisciplinary works on public finance in 336; class interdisciplinary works on financial management in 658.15

For administration of financial institutions, money, credit, see 354.8

See also 332.46 for monetary policy, 336.3 for fiscal policy

See Manual at 336 vs. 352.4

*Add as instructed under 352–354

.43   *Financial control

> Class here managerial accounting (financial and nonfinancial); agencies that perform management, performance, program auditing, e.g., general accounting offices
>
> Class ordinary accounting of government agencies in 657.835

.439   *Management, performance, program audits

> Internal or external audits or comparable reviews to evaluate efficiency, conformance to policies and standards, and effectiveness of expenditures of funds or other administrative activities
>
> Class here reports of general accounting offices
>
> Subdivisions are added for any or all topics named in heading
>
> Class financial auditing of government agencies in 657.835045

.44   *Revenue administration

> Class here tax administration, tax collection
>
> *See also 353.43 for tax litigation*
>
> *See Manual at 343.04 vs. 336.2, 352.44*

.448   *Customs administration

.45   *Debt management

.46   *Public expenditures

> *For payroll administration, see 352.47; for contracts, see 352.53; for financial assistance, see 352.73*

.47   *Payroll administration

> *See also 352.67 for wage and salary scales of government workers, 354.98 for wages and salaries of labor and professions*

.48   *Budgeting

> Including adoption of budgets, budget messages, specific kinds of budgets, e.g., capital, estimated, legislative budgets
>
> Class here comprehensive works on budgets
>
> *For procedures for legislative enactment of budgets, see 328.378; for budgets of specific international organizations and specific jurisdictions, see 352.49*

.49   Budgets for specific international organizations and specific jurisdictions

> Class comprehensive works on budgets in 352.48

[.490 1–.490 9]   Standard subdivisions

> Do not use; class in 352.4801–352.4809

*Add as instructed under 352–354

.491   Budgets for specific international organizations

Add to base number 352.491 the numbers following 352.11 in
352.112–352.119, e.g., budgets for United Nations 352.4913; then add
further as instructed under 352.493–352.499, e.g., proposed budgets for
United Nations 352.491301

.493–.499   Budgets for specific jurisdictions

Add to base number 352.49 notation 3–9 from Table 2, e.g., a budget of
Germany 352.4943; then add further as follows:

001–007	Standard subdivisions	
	Notation from Table 1 as modified under 351, e.g., official serial reports on budgets 005	
008–009	Standard subdivisions	
>01–03	Comprehensive budgets in specific stages of adoption	
	Class here operating budgets	
	Class partial budgets in specific stages of adoption in 04–08; class comprehensive works in 352.493–352.499 without use of notation from this table	
01	Proposed budgets	
	Class here estimated budgets, executive budgets, budget requests from recipient agencies	
	For budgets in legislative process, see 02	
013	Executive budget messages and supporting documents	
02	Budgets in legislative process	
	Class here legislative budgets, legislative authorizations	
023	Legislative hearings and reports on budgets	
	Hearings that concentrate on the objectives that a budget is to achieve are normally classed with the subject outside public administration, e.g., a hearing on the prospect that a budget will help achieve economic stabilization and growth 339.522	
	See Manual at 350 vs. 342–347	
03	Adopted budgets	
>04–08	Partial budgets	
	Class comprehensive works in 352.493–352.499 without use of notation from this table. Class budgets for a specific jurisdiction limited to a specific subject with the subject, plus notation 249 from table under 352–354, e.g., agricultural budgets in specific jurisdictions 354.5249, agricultural budgets for Germany 354.524943	
	For operating budgets, see 01–03	
04	Revenue budgets	
05	Capital budgets	
08	Supplemental budgets	

Class works on budgeting, on budgets in general in 352.48

.5   *Property administration and related topics

Class here general services agencies

Subdivisions are added for property administration and related topics together, for property administration alone

Class records management in 352.387

.53   *Contracts and procurement

Class here procurement of property, comprehensive works on public contracts

Subdivisions are added for either or both topics in heading

> *For procurement of specific forms of property, see 352.55–352.57. For public contracts not related to property, see the subject, plus notation 253 from table under 352–354, e.g., personnel contracts 352.65253*

.538   *Contracting for services

Class here contracting out

Class use of consultants in 352.373

.54   *Maintenance, utilization, disposal of property

Including inventory

> *For maintenance, utilization, disposal of specific forms of property, see 352.55–352.57*

> 352.55–352.57 Specific forms of property

Except for modifications shown under specific entries, add to each subdivision identified by † as follows:
```
01–2      Standard subdivisions and general considerations of
          administration
              Add as instructed under 352–354, e.g., budgets for topic in
              specific jurisdictions 249
3         Contracts and procurement
              Subdivisions are added for either or both topics in heading
              Add to 3 notation 01–2 from table under 352–354 , e.g.,
              procurement in local administration 3214
4         Maintenance, utilization, disposal
              Add to 4 notation 01–2 from table under 352–354, e.g.,
              maintenance, utilization, disposal in local administration 4214
```

Class comprehensive works in 352.5

.55   †Equipment and supplies

Subdivisions are added for either or both topics in heading

Class interdisciplinary works on supply management in 658.7

---

*Add as instructed under 352–354
†Add as instructed under 352.55–352.57

.56	†Buildings and their utilities

Class here plant management

Subdivisions are added for buildings and their utilities, for buildings alone

Class interdisciplinary works on plant management in 658.2

For public land management, see 352.57

.57 †Public lands

Class comprehensive works on land resources in 354.34

.6 *Personnel administration (Human resource administration)

Use subdivisions of 352.6 for specific aspects of management of executive personnel

Class contracting out in 352.538; class interdisciplinary works on personnel management in 658.3

For general management of executive personnel, see 352.39

.602 5 Directories of persons and organizations in personnel administration

Class directories of public officials and employees in 351.025

.608 History and description with respect to kinds of persons

Class here equal employment opportunity programs for government employees

Class comprehensive works on equal employment opportunity programs in 354.908

.621 1 International personnel administration [*formerly also* 341.22–341.24]

Number built according to instructions under 352–354

.63 *Civil service system

Government service in which appointments are determined by merit and examination rather than by political patronage

Including management of office workers

Class here government service, merit system, interdisciplinary works on government workers

Class civil service in the sense of all units of public administration other than armed services in 351; class civil service examinations in 351.076

For specific aspect of government service and government workers, see the aspect, e.g., labor economics 331.795, wage and salary scales 352.67

.64 *Job description

Including job analysis and classification

*Add as instructed under 352–354
†Add as instructed under 352.55–352.57

.65	*Recruiting and selection
.650 8	History and description with respect to kinds of persons

Class here preferential hiring

.66   *Utilization and training

Including discipline, evaluation, motivation, placement, supervision; absenteeism, turnover

Subdivisions are added for utilization and training, for utilization alone

.669   *Training

.67   *Conditions of employment

Including fringe benefits, e.g., counseling, health services; hours of work, work environment

Class here compensation

Class payroll administration in 352.47; class administration of pensions for government workers in 353.549; class comprehensive works on conditions of employment for all workers in 354.98

.68   *Employer-employee relationships

Including labor unions and collective bargaining, other employee organizations, employee participation in management, grievances

Class comprehensive works on grievances against government in 352.885; class comprehensive works on labor unions and collective bargaining for all workers in 354.97

.69   *Separation from service

Including dismissal, layoffs, reduction in force, retirement

Class administration of pensions for government workers in 353.549

> **352.7–352.8 Administration of supporting and controlling functions of government**

Class comprehensive works in 351. Class administration of support and control of a specific topic of management with the topic, plus notation 27–28 from add table under 352–354, e.g., support for commerce and trade 354.7327, advisory bodies in commerce and trade 354.732743

See Manual at 352

---

*Add as instructed under 352–354

.7   *Administration of general forms of assistance

Class here the promotional and supporting role of administration when considered apart from its restraining and limiting role; administration of research and development in noneconomic fields

Class comprehensive works on administration of research and development in 354.27

See also 352.8 for the restraining and limiting role of administration

.73   *Financial assistance

Financial assistance to subordinate jurisdictions or to private parties

Class here grants, grants-in-aid, revenue sharing

Class comprehensive works on support and control of subordinate jurisdictions in 353.33

For price supports, see 352.85

.734   Financial support for specific kinds of subordinate jurisdictions

Add to base number 352.734 the numbers following 352.1 in 352.13–352.19, e.g., grants to states and provinces 352.7343, grants to local governments from either national governments or states and provinces 352.7344

.736   *Loans and loan guarantees

Subdivisions are added for either or both topics in heading

.74   *Promoting and disseminating knowledge

Class here promoting research

Subdivisions are added for either or both topics in heading

Class governmental publishers in 070.595

For census and surveys, see 352.75; for promotion of museums and exhibitions, see 352.76; for administration of agencies supporting and controlling education, see 353.8

.743   *Fact-finding and advisory bodies

Bodies advising the government or the public

Temporary and permanent

Class here counseling bodies, royal commissions

Subdivisions are added for either or both topics in heading

See also 352.25 for governing boards and commissions

*Add as instructed under 352–354

.744   *Promoting libraries and historical research

> Class here programs supporting archives

> Subdivisions are added for either or both topics in heading

> Class library administration in 025.1; class archives administration in 025.1714; class records management in 352.387

>> *For administration of agencies supporting public libraries, see 353.73*

.745   *Promoting general fields of knowledge

> Including natural sciences, social and behavioral sciences, technology; specific field of knowledge not provided for elsewhere, e.g., physics, space

> Class here promoting experimental research

> Class promoting museums and exhibitions in 352.76. Class promoting a specific field of knowledge provided for elsewhere with the field in public administration, plus notation 274 (*not* 2745) from table under 352–354 if not redundant, e.g., promoting environmental knowledge by an environmental protection agency 354.328274, but promoting public libraries 353.73 (*not* 353.73274)

>> *For promoting arts and humanities, see 353.77*

>> *See also 338.926–338.927 for science policy, policies to promote economic development through use of science and technology; 355.07 for military research and development*

>> *See Manual at 338.926 vs. 352.745, 500*

.746   *Consumer information programs

> Class here consumer protection

> Class interdisciplinary works on consumer information in 381.33; class interdisciplinary works on consumer protection in 381.34

>> *For a specific aspect of consumer protection, see the aspect, e.g., price and cost controls 352.85*

.748   *Publicity activities

> Publicity for government's own activities

> Class here public relations [*formerly* 659.2935]

> Class interdisciplinary works on public relations in 659.2

.749   *Protecting intellectual property

> Regardless of subject or field

> Including copyright, patents, trademarks

---

*Add as instructed under 352–354

.75   *Census and surveys

               Class here administration of descriptive research

               Subdivisions are added for either or both topics in heading

.76   *Promoting museums and exhibitions

               Class here government participation in fairs and expositions

               Subdivisions are added for either or both topics in heading

               Class comprehensive works on administration of culture and related
               activities in 353.7

.77   *Public works

               *For a specific program of public works, see the program, e.g.,
               transportation public works 354.76277*

.78   *Sponsorship of volunteers and public service activities

               Subdivisions are added for either or both topics in heading

.79   *Assistance to urban, suburban, rural areas

               Class specific form of assistance to urban and rural areas in 352.73–352.78;
               class comprehensive works on administration of urban and rural
               development in 354.279

               See also 352.7091724 for assistance to underdeveloped areas

.793   *Urban and suburban areas

               Including community planning

               Subdivisions are added for either or both topics in heading

               Class community planning for rural areas in 352.794; class community
               action programs in 353.52793; class comprehensive works on
               administration of community development in 354.2793

               *See also 353.5333 for programs directed to residents of
               disadvantaged urban areas*

.794   *Rural areas

               See also 353.5334 for programs directed to residents of rural areas

.8   *Administration of general forms of control

               Class here the restraining and limiting role of administration when considered
               apart from its promotional and supporting role; regulation, regulatory agencies,
               quasi-judicial agencies

               Class internal control of administrative activities in 352.35; class watchdog
               agencies in 352.88

               See also 352.7 for promotional and supporting role of administration

*Add as instructed under 352–354

.83 ***Setting standards**

> Class here inspection, establishing weights and measures
>
> Class inspection as a form of internal control in 352.35

.84 ***Licensing, accreditation, certification, chartering, registration; incorporation**

> Class here interdisciplinary works on licensing, accreditation, certification, chartering, registration
>
> Subdivisions are added for any or all topics in heading
>
> Class interdisciplinary works on incorporation in 346.06622
>
> > *For licensing, accreditation, certification, chartering by nongovernmental organizations, see 060*

.85 ***Price and cost controls**

> Class here price supports
>
> Subdivisions are added for either or both topics in heading

.86 ***Rationing and allocation**

> Subdivisions are added for either or both topics in heading

.88 ***Use of watchdog and oversight agencies**

> Class here promotion of procedural rights, agencies providing checks and balances to administrative operations, interdisciplinary works on ombudsmen
>
> Subdivisions are added for either or both topics in heading
>
> Class oversight in executive management, ombudsmen within agencies in 352.35; class quasi-judicial agencies in 352.8; class misconduct in office in 353.46
>
> > *For ombudsman role in legislative bodies, see 328.3452*
> >
> > *See also 342.06 for administrative law*

.885 ***Processing claims against government**

> Class here government liability, grievances against government
>
> > *For government-employee grievances and appeals, see 352.68; for international claims, see 353.44*

353 Specific fields of public administration

> *For public administration of economy and environment, see 354*
>
> *See Manual at T1—068 vs. 353–354; also at 352–354; also at 363 vs. 340, 353–354*

---

*Add as instructed under 352–354

SUMMARY

353.1	**Administration of external and national security affairs**
.3	**Administration of services related to domestic order**
.4	**Administration of justice**
.5	**Administration of social welfare**
.6	**Administration of health services**
.7	**Administration of culture and related activities**
.8	**Administration of agencies supporting and controlling education**
.9	**Administration of safety, sanitation, waste control Safety administration**

[.01–.09]   Standard subdivisions

> Do not use; class in 351.01–351.09

.1   *Administration of external and national security affairs

> Subdivisions are added for external and national security affairs together, for national security affairs alone
>
> Class interdisciplinary works on national security in 355.03
>
> *For military and defense administration, see 355.6*
>
> *See also 352.379 for intelligence and security in executive management*

.122 4   Cabinet-level national security councils

> Number built according to instructions under 352–354

.13   *Foreign and diplomatic relations

> Class here departments and ministries of foreign affairs
>
> Subdivisions are added for either or both topics in heading
>
> Class interdisciplinary works on foreign relations in 327

.132 63   Foreign service

> Number built according to instructions under 352–354
>
> Class here consular and diplomatic services

.132 73   Financial assistance

> Number built according to instructions under 352–354
>
> Class here foreign aid
>
> Class use of foreign aid to attain foreign policy objectives in 327.111; class interdisciplinary works on foreign aid in 338.91

.132 74   Promotion and dissemination of knowledge

> Number built according to instructions under 352–354
>
> Class here government information services
>
> Class interdisciplinary works on government information services in 327.11

*Add as instructed under 352–354

.15   *Administration of non-self-governing territories

Class here administration of colonies [*formerly* 325.31], administration of semisovereign states

Class military government of occupied territories in 355.49

.150 93–.150 99   Treatment by specific continents, countries, localities

Do not use for administration of specific non-self-governing territories; class in 351.3–351.9, e.g., British colonial administration in Kenya 351.67620904

Limited to administration of more than one jurisdiction, e.g., British colonial administration 353.150941, British colonial administration in Africa 353.150941096

.159   Administration of territories under international control

.17   *Intelligence and counterintelligence

Limited to administration of operations primarily conducted abroad

Class here espionage, subversion

Subdivisions are added for either or both topics in heading

Class activities of domestic police services relating to intelligence and subversion in 363.23; class interdisciplinary works on intelligence and subversion in 327.12

(.2)   **Military and defense administration**

(Optional number; prefer 355.6)

Class here army administration

For specific topics in military and defense administration, see 355.6

(.25)   Naval administration

(Optional number; prefer 359.6)

For specific topics in naval administration, see 359.6

(.27)   Air forces administration

(Optional number; prefer 358.416)

For specific topics in air forces administration, see 358.416

(.29)   Administration of other military forces

(Optional number; prefer numbers for specific forces in 356–359)

For specific topics in administration of other specific forces, see the specific force, plus notation 6 from table under 356–359, e.g., executive management of marine forces 359.966

---

*Add as instructed under 352–354

> ### 353.3–353.9 Public administration in domestic fields not related to economy and environment

Many works classed here will concern activities of national or state and provincial governments to regulate, control or support services provided by local government agencies. These activities are in contrast to those of local governments which provide the actual services. Works on managing local agencies that directly serve the ultimate recipients are normally classed with the service outside public administration, e.g., management of city police departments 363.2068 (*not* 353.36216), of parole boards 364.62068 (*not* 353.39), of local school systems 371.2 (*not* 353.8215)

Class comprehensive works in 351

See Manual at T1—068 vs. 353–354

.3   *Administration of services related to domestic order

Class here home departments and ministries, European style interior ministries

For administration of justice, see 353.4

See also 354.30973 for United States Department of the Interior

.33   *Support and control of subordinate jurisdictions by higher jurisdictions

Subdivisions are added for either or both topics in heading

Class comprehensive works on administration of subordinate jurisdictions in 352.14

For financial support of subordinate jurisdictions, see 352.73

.332 13–.332 19   Administration by subordinate jurisdictions

Numbers built according to instructions under 352–354

Class support and control of specific kinds of subordinate jurisdictions in 353.333–353.339

.333–.339   Support and control of specific kinds of subordinate jurisdictions

Unless it is redundant, add to base number 353.33 the numbers following 352.1 in 352.13–352.19, e.g., support and control of counties 353.335, but comprehensive works on support and control of local administration by states and provinces or by unitary national administration 353.33 (*not* 353.334); however, for control of special service districts, see 352.193; for support of urban, suburban, rural areas, see 352.79

.36   *Police services

Including control of crowds, explosives, guns; crime prevention

Class operational management of police services in 363.2068; class operational management of bureaus of investigation in 363.25068

For regulating personal conduct, see 353.37

*Add as instructed under 352–354

.37	*Regulating personal conduct

Including administration of censorship; control of alcohol, drugs, gambling, pornography, prostitution, sexual mores and morals

Class personal liberty in 323.44; class police control of personal conduct in 363.23; class censorship in 363.31; class interdisciplinary works on controversies relating to public morals and customs in 363.4

.39	*Corrections

Including parole and probation services

Class here prisons

Class interdisciplinary works on administration of correctional activities in 364.6068; class interdisciplinary works on parole administration in 364.62068; class interdisciplinary works on probation administration in 364.63068; class interdisciplinary works on prison administration in 365.068

.4	***Administration of justice**

Class here administration of criminal justice, departments of justice

For administration of courts, see 347.013; for police services, see 353.36; for correctional activities, see 353.39

.43	*Criminal matters

Including antitrust and tax litigation

Class here criminal prosecution

Class marshals service in 347.016; class criminal litigation to promote civil rights in 353.48; class administration of police services in 363.25068; class interdisciplinary works on criminal procedure in 345.05

.44	*Civil matters

Including international-claims litigation

Class administrative processing of claims against government in 352.885; class civil litigation to promote citizenship and rights in 353.48; class interdisciplinary works on civil procedure in 347.05

.46	*Misconduct in office

Regardless of topic or field

Class here abuse of power, civil rights violations, conflict of interest, corruption, whistle blowing

Class problems resolvable by routine administrative procedures in 352.88; class interdisciplinary works on misconduct in office in 364.132

*Add as instructed under 352–354

.463   *Public investigations and inquiries

Other than normal administrative and legislative oversight

Subdivisions are added for either or both topics in heading

Class legislative oversight hearings on administrative matters with the subject in public administration, e.g., on administration of social welfare 353.5

See also 328.3452 for legislative investigative power, 352.88 for normal administrative oversight and watchdog agencies

.465   Misconduct in specific areas of public administration

Add to base number 353.465 the numbers following 35 in 352–354, e.g., misconduct in treasury departments 353.46524

.48   *Exercise of citizenship and rights

Including litigation

Class here promotion of civil rights

Class election procedures in 324.6

For administration of public defenders, see 345.01; for promotion of procedural rights, see 352.88

.484   *Immigration and naturalization services

Class comprehensive works on activities relating to population and settlement in 353.59

.5   *Administration of social welfare

Class here human services, social security in the sense of social welfare

Class social security in the sense of retirement income in 353.54

For administration of health services, see 353.6

See Manual at 361–365 vs. 353.5

.508   History and description with respect to kinds of persons

Do not use for programs directed to kinds of persons; class in 353.53

See Manual at 353.53 vs. 351.08

*Add as instructed under 352–354

.53   *Programs directed to kinds of persons

Class here equal opportunity programs; programs for minorities, for socially disadvantaged groups; comprehensive works on programs in public administration directed to kinds of persons

Class programs directed to victims of crime and political oppression regardless of other group characteristic in 353.5337–353.5338; class programs directed to ethnic minorities in 353.5339. Class a program directing a specific kind of service to kinds of persons with the kind of service, plus notation 08 from Table 1, e.g., personnel programs directed to minorities 352.608, administrative support for children's recreation 353.78083

For programs directed to labor and professional groups, see 354.9

See Manual at 353.53 vs. 351.08; also at 353.53 vs. 352.1: Use of table notation for kinds of persons

.533   Specific miscellaneous groups

Only those named below

[.533 01–.533 09]   Standard subdivisions

Do not use; class in 353.5301–353.5309

.533 1   *Families

Class here unmarried mothers

See also 353.536 for children

.533 2   *Poor people

Class poor residents of disadvantaged urban and suburban areas in 353.5333; class poor residents of disadvantaged rural and sparsely populated areas in 353.5334

.533 3   *Residents of disadvantaged urban and suburban areas

Class here residents of inner cities, of slums

Subdivisions are added for either or both topics in heading

Class comprehensive works on assistance to urban and suburban areas in 352.793

See also 354.2793 for urban and suburban development

.533 4   *Residents of rural and sparsely populated areas

Subdivisions are added for either or both topics in heading

Class comprehensive works on assistance to rural areas in 352.794

See also 354.2794 for rural development

*Add as instructed under 352–354

.533 7	*Victims of crime
	Regardless of other group characteristics or kind of crime
	Class persons who are victims of both crime and political oppression in 353.5338
.533 8	*Victims of oppression
	Regardless of other group characteristics or of reason for oppression
	Class here refugees, victims of religious persecution
.533 9	*Racial, ethnic, national groups in general
	Class here programs directed to ethnic minorities
	For specific racial, ethnic, national groups, see 353.534
	See Manual at 353.5339 and 353.534
.534	Specific racial, ethnic, national groups
	See Manual at 353.5339 and 353.534
[.534 001–.534 009]	Standard subdivisions
	Do not use; class in 353.533901–353.533909
.534 03–.534 9	Subdivisions for specific racial, ethnic, national groups
	Add to base number 353.534 notation 03–9 from Table 5, e.g., programs for Spanish Americans 353.53468
.535	*Women
.536	*Young people to age twenty
	Class here children
.536 5	Young people twelve to twenty
	Variant names: adolescents, teenagers, young adults, youth
.537	*Persons in late adulthood
.538	*Veterans
.539	*Persons with disabilities and illnesses
	Programs not predominately health related, e.g., access for persons with disabilities
	Subdivisions are added for either or both topics in heading
	Class health programs for persons with disabilities and illnesses in 353.6

*Add as instructed under 352–354

.54	*Income maintenance

Including guaranteed minimum income, unemployment insurance

Class here pensions, social security in the sense of retirement income, comprehensive works on administration of government sponsored insurance

Class social security in the sense of social welfare in 353.5; class comprehensive works on insurance in 354.85

For government-sponsored health insurance, see 353.69

.548	Administration of pensions limited to specific occupations and groups of occupations

Add to base number 353.548 the numbers following 354.9 in 354.93–354.95, e.g., administration of railroad pensions 353.5485385

For pensions of government workers, see 353.549

See also 331.252 for pension benefits

.549	*Administration of pensions for government workers

See also 352.69 for retirement of government workers

.55	*Housing

Including public housing, assistance to home owners

.56	*Nutrition and food

For food purity, designation of nutritional content, see 353.997

.59	*Activities relating to population and settlement

Including birth and death certificates, birth control, population movement

For immigration and naturalization services, see 353.484

.6	***Administration of health services**

Including disposal of the dead

Class here rehabilitation services, services for physical illness

Class comprehensive works on administration of social welfare in 353.5

.627 4	Promoting and disseminating knowledge

Number built according to instructions under 352–354

Class here health promotion, physical fitness programs

.628	General forms of control

Number built according to instructions under 352–354

Class here disease control, medical screening

.63	Specific kinds of physical diseases

Including cancer, contagious diseases

*Add as instructed under 352–354

| .64 | *Mental health services |

Including services for substance abuse

For services for persons with mental retardation, see 353.65

.65	*Services for persons with mental retardation
.66	*Services for persons with physical disabilities
.68	*Health care facilities
.69	*Health insurance

Including workers' compensation insurance

Class here hospital insurance

Class Medicaid and Medicare in 353.690973

.7 ***Administration of culture and related activities**

Including programs to support and control religion, language programs

Subdivisions are added for culture and related activities together, for culture alone

Class administration of communications in 354.75

For promoting museums and exhibitions, see 352.76; for administration of education, see 353.8

See also 353.48 for promotion of religious freedom

| .73 | *Public libraries |

Administration of agencies supporting and controlling public libraries and library systems

Class administration of public libraries and library systems in 025.1974; class support for libraries in general in 352.744

| [.732 25] | Governing boards and commissions |

Do not use; class in 021.82

| .77 | *Arts and humanities |

Including crafts, performing arts, celebrations, historical preservation

For recreation, see 353.78

| .78 | *Recreation |

Including parks, recreational use of environment, sports hunting and fishing

Class here sports

Class comprehensive works on hunting in 354.349; class comprehensive works on fishing in 354.57

For crafts and performing arts, see 353.77

*Add as instructed under 352–354

.8   *Administration of agencies supporting and controlling education

Class here agencies supporting and controlling elementary education, supporting and controlling secondary education

Class school administration and management in 371.2; class public policy issues in education in 379; class comprehensive works on promotion and dissemination of knowledge in 352.74

See Manual at 371 vs. 353.8, 371.2, 379

.822 5   Governing boards and commissions

Number built according to instructions under 352–354

For local school boards, see 379.1531

.824   Financial administration of public education

Number built according to instructions under 352–354

Class here financial administration of agencies supporting public education [*formerly* 379.11]

Class financial management of schools and school systems in 371.206

.84   *Adult education

.88   *Higher education

.882 84   Licensing, accreditation, certification, chartering, registration; incorporation

Number built according to instructions under 352–354

Class here government commissions on standards and accreditation in higher education [*formerly* 379.158]

.89   *Special education

.9   *Administration of safety, sanitation, waste control   Safety administration

.93   *Sanitation and waste control

Including cleanup of pollution, recycling

Subdivisions are added for either or both topics in heading

Class operational management of waste control and disposal services in 363.728068; class comprehensive administrative works on pollution in 354.335

For sanitation in public facilities, see 353.94; for hazardous wastes, see 353.994

---

*Add as instructed under 352–354

.94   *Sanitation in public facilities

Including sanitation in common carriers, eating and drinking places, health facilities, streets, workplaces

Class operational management of sanitary services in 363.72068

> 353.95–353.99 Safety administration

Class here accidents, safety administration of economy and environment

Class comprehensive works in 353.9

For police services, see 353.36; for contagious diseases, see 353.63

.95   *Preparation for disasters

Class here civil defense, emergency planning

Class management of disaster relief in 363.348068

.96   *Occupational (Industrial) safety

Class here workplace safety

Class workplace sanitation in 353.93

.966   Safety in specific extractive, manufacturing, construction occupations

Add to base number 353.966 the numbers following 6 in 620–690, e.g., mine safety 353.96622

.97   *Safety in miscellaneous areas

Including domestic, outdoor, sports safety

Class here safety in public facilities

For workplace safety, see 353.96; for transportation safety, see 353.98

.979   *Fire safety

Class management of fire departments in 363.37068

.98   *Transportation safety

Including space transportation safety

Class here ground-transportation safety

Class comprehensive works on transportation in 354.76

.987   *Water-transportation safety

Class here water safety

For water-sports safety, see 353.97

*Add as instructed under 352–354

.988	*Air-transportation safety

.99   *Hazardous products and materials

Including medical instruments and supplies

Class here hazardous machinery

Subdivisions are added for hazardous products and materials together, for hazardous products alone

.993   *Hazardous materials

Class hazardous wastes in 353.994

For radioactive materials, see 353.999

.994   *Hazardous wastes

For radioactive wastes, see 353.999

.997   *Food safety

Class here food purity, designation of nutritional content

Class comprehensive works on nutrition and food services in 353.56

.998   *Drugs and medicines

Class here drug safety

Subdivisions are added for either or both topics in heading

.999   *Radioactive products

Including radioactive wastes

Class here radiation safety, radioactive materials

354 *Public administration of economy and environment

Subdivisions are added for administration of economy and environment together, for administration of economy

Class administration of safety in economy and environment in 353.95–353.99

See Manual at T1—068 vs. 353–354; also at 352–354; also at 363 vs. 340, 353–354

SUMMARY

354.08	**History and description with respect to kinds of persons**
.2	**General considerations of administration**
.3	**Administration of environment and natural resources**
.4	**Administration of energy and energy-related industries**
.5	**Administration of agriculture**
.6	**Administration of construction, manufacturing, service industries**
.7	**Administration of commerce, communications, transportation**
.8	**Administration of financial institutions, money, banking**
.9	**Administration of labor and professions**

*Add as instructed under 352–354

.08   History and description with respect to kinds of persons

Class here equal economic opportunity programs

.27   General forms of assistance

Number built according to instructions under 352–354

Class here comprehensive works on administration of development, of research and development

Class urban and community development in 354.2793; class rural development in 354.2794; class comprehensive works on administration of research and development in noneconomic fields in 352.7; class interdisciplinary works on research and development in 338.9. Class administration of research and development of a specific economic activity with the activity in 354, plus notation 27 from table under 352–354, e.g., development of agriculture 354.527

.274   Promotion and dissemination of knowledge

Number built according to instructions under 352–354

Class protection of intellectual property in 352.749

.279   Assistance to urban, suburban, rural areas; to small business

Number built according to instructions under 352–354

.279 9   *Assistance to small business

For a specific form of assistance to small business, see the form, e.g., assistance in securing government contracts 352.5327, small business loans 354.2736

>   **354.3–354.8 Administration of specific fields of economic and environmental activity**

Class here industries associated with specific fields of economic and environmental activity

Class administration of labor and professions in specific fields of economic and environmental activity in 354.9; class comprehensive works in 354

.3   ***Administration of environment and natural resources**

Standard subdivisions are added for either or both topics in heading

Class here departments of natural resources, primary industries

For recreational use of environment, see 353.78; for sanitation and waste control, see 353.93; for administration of energy and energy-related resources, see 354.4; for administration of agriculture, see 354.5

*Add as instructed under 352–354

.327   General forms of assistance

       Number built according to instructions under 352–354

       Class here natural resources development

       Class interdisciplinary works on natural resources development in 333.715

.328   General forms of control

       Number built according to instructions under 352–354

       Class here environmental protection

       Class interdisciplinary works on environmental protection in 363.7

       For special forms of environmental protection and control, see 354.33

.33   Special forms of environmental protection and control

       Not provided for in subdivisions of 354.328

       Class comprehensive works on administration of environmental protection and control in 354.328. Class administration of a special form of protection and control relating to a specific environment with the form of control in 354.34–354.37, plus notation 3 from table under 354.34–354.37, e.g., water conservation 354.3634

.333   *Resource use planning

       Class here zoning

       Class urban zoning in 354.353; class interdisciplinary works on zoning in 333.7317

.334   *Conservation

       Class interdisciplinary works on conservation in 333.72

.335   *Prevention and control of pollution

       Class here comprehensive administrative works on pollution

       Class administration of cleanup of pollution in 353.93; class interdisciplinary works on pollution in 363.73

.338   *Noise control

       Regardless of environment

.339   *Pest control

       Regardless of environment

*Add as instructed under 352–354

>   354.34–354.37   Specific environments

Except for modifications shown under specific entries, add to each subdivision identified by † as follows:

01–2   Standard subdivisions and general considerations of administration

         Add as instructed under 352–354, e.g., state and provincial administration of the topic 213

3   Special forms of protection and control

         Add to 3 the numbers following 354.33 in 354.333–354.335, e.g., conservation 34

Class noise control in specific environments in 354.338; class pest control in specific environments in 354.339; class mineral resources derived from a specific environment in 354.39; class comprehensive works on administration of environment in 354.3

.34   †Land and biological resources

Including wetlands

Class here real property

Subdivisions are added for land and biological resources together, for land alone

Class parks in 353.78

For public lands, see 352.57; for urban land, see 354.35

.349   †Biological resources

Including hunting

Class here animal resources

For sports hunting, see 353.78; for forestry, see 354.55; for aquatic biological resources, fishing and fisheries, see 354.57

.35   *Urban land

.353   *Land use planning

Class here city planning, urban zoning

Class comprehensive works on administration of zoning in 354.333; class interdisciplinary works on city planning in 307.1216; class interdisciplinary works on urban zoning in 333.7717

.36   †Water

Including groundwater, estuaries

For aquatic biological resources, fishing and fisheries, see 354.57

*Add as instructed under 352–354

†Add as instructed under 354.34–354.37

.362 7   General forms of assistance

> Number built according to instructions under 354.34–354.37
>
> Class here development of water resources, of electricity from water resources; flood control
>
> Class distribution of electricity derived from water power in 354.49

.366   †Water supply

> *For irrigation projects, see 354.367*

.367   †Irrigation projects

.369   †Oceans

.37   †Air and atmospheric phenomena

> Class here weather bureaus

.39   Mineral resources

> Class here mining bureaus, subsurface resources
>
> Add to base number 354.39 notation 01–3 from table under 354.44–354.49, e.g., conservation of mineral resources 354.393
>
> *For mineral energy resources, see 354.4*

.4   *Administration of energy and energy-related industries

> Class here departments of energy; energy resources, mineral energy resources
>
> Subdivisions are added for either or both topics in heading
>
> *For development of water power, see 354.3627*

.428   General forms of control

> Number built according to instructions under 352–354
>
> Class here control of public utilities supplying energy
>
> Class energy conservation in 354.43; class comprehensive works on control of public utilities in 354.728. Class control of a specific energy utility with the form of energy, plus notation 28 from table under 352–354, e.g., a gas utility 354.4628

.43   *Energy conservation

> Class energy conservation for a specific form of energy with the form, plus notation 3 from the table under 354.44–354.49, e.g., petroleum conservation 354.453

*Add as instructed under 352–354

†Add as instructed under 354.34–354.37

>   354.44–354.49   Specific energy resources and electricity

Except for modifications shown under specific entries, add to each subdivision identified by ‡ as follows:

01–2   Standard subdivisions and general considerations of administration

Add as instructed under 352–354, e.g., budgets for topic in specific jurisdictions 249

3   Conservation

Add to 3 notation 01–2 as instructed under 352–354, e.g., state and provincial administration of conservation 3213

Class comprehensive works in 354.4

>   354.44–354.48   Specific energy resources

Class distribution of electricity derived from specific energy resources in 354.49; class comprehensive works on energy resources in 354.4

.44   ‡Fossil fuels

Including coal

For oil and gas, see 354.45

.45   ‡Oil

Class here comprehensive works on petroleum

For gas, see 354.46

.46   ‡Gas

Natural and manufactured

.47   ‡Nuclear fuels

Class radiation safety, radioactive wastes in 353.999

.472 7   General forms of assistance

Number built according to instructions under 354.44–354.49

Class here development of electricity from nuclear fuels

Class distribution of electricity derived from nuclear fuels in 354.49

.48   ‡Other energy resources

Including geothermal and solar energy

.49   ‡Electricity

‡Add as instructed under 354.44–354.49

.492 7	General forms of assistance

Number built according to instructions under 354.44–354.49

Class here comprehensive works on development of electricity

Class development of electricity from a specific resource with the resource, plus notation 27 from table under 354.44–354.49, e.g., from water power 354.3627, from nuclear fuels 354.4727

.492 8	General forms of control

Number built according to instructions under 354.44–354.49

Class here control of electric utilities, of distribution of electricity regardless of resource from which it is derived

Class development of electricity in 354.4927

.5	***Administration of agriculture**

Class nutrition and food programs in 353.56; class rural development in 354.2794; class soil conservation in 354.3434; class irrigation projects in 354.367; class agricultural price supports in 354.5285; class agricultural credit in 354.86

For hunting, see 354.349

.54	***Plant crops**

For forestry, see 354.55

.55	***Forestry**
.56	***Animal husbandry**
.57	***Fishing and fisheries**

Class here aquatic biological resources, marine biological resources

Subdivisions are added for either or both topics in heading

Class comprehensive works on resources derived from water in 354.36

For sports fishing, see 353.78

.59	***Commodity programs**

Including marketing services

Class here farm produce

Class programs that combine inspection and marketing in 354.59283

For agricultural price supports, see 354.5285

See also 354.88 for commodity exchanges

.6	***Administration of construction, manufacturing, service industries**

Class here administration of secondary industries

*Add as instructed under 352–354

.64 *Construction

Class public works in 352.77

.66 *Manufacturing

.68 *Service industries

> *For commerce, communications, transportation, see 354.7; for financial services, see 354.8*

.7 *Administration of commerce, communications, transportation

.728 General forms of control

Number built according to instructions under 352–354

Class here comprehensive works on control of public utilities

> *For control of a specific public utility, see the utility, plus notation 28 from table under 352–354, e.g., control of electric utilities 354.4928*

.73 *Commerce

Including tourist trade regardless of origin

Class here domestic commerce

> *For foreign commerce, see 354.74*

> *See also 354.76280973 for United States Interstate Commerce Commission*

.74 *Foreign commerce

Class foreign tourism in 354.73

.75 *Communications

Class here telecommunications

Class management, business organizations, and description of facilities, activities, services of a publicly owned communications system in 384, e.g., business organization of a publicly owned telephone system 384.6065

> *See Manual at T1—068 vs. 353–354; also at 380: Add table: 09 vs. 065*

.759 *Postal service

Class operational management of postal service in 383.068; class postal organization in 383.4

.76 *Transportation

Class here ground transportation

Class transportation safety in 353.98

> *For road transportation, see 354.77; for water transportation, see 354.78; for air and space transportation, see 354.79*

*Add as instructed under 352–354

.763   *Passenger services

> *For passenger service in a specific form of transportation, see the form of transportation, plus notation 3 from the table under 354.765–354.79, e.g., rail passenger service 354.7673*

.764   *Freight services

Including pipeline transportation

> *For freight service in a specific form of transportation other than pipelines, see the form of transportation, plus notation 4 from the table under 354.765–354.79, e.g., rail freight service 354.7674*

>   354.765–354.79   Specific forms of transportation

Except for modifications shown under specific entries, add to each subdivision identified by † as follows:

01–2   Standard subdivisions and general considerations of administration
> Add notation 01–2 from table under 352–354, e.g., control of transportation utilities 28

3   Passenger service
> Add to 3 notation 01–2 from table under 352–354, e.g., control of passenger service 328

4   Freight service
> Add to 4 notation 01–2 from table under 352–354, e.g., control of freight service 428

Class transportation safety in 353.98; class comprehensive works in 354.76

.765   †Automotive transportation

Including parking facilities

> *For road transportation, see 354.77*

.765 284   Licensing, accreditation, certification, chartering, registration; incorporation

Number built according to instructions under 354.765–354.79

Class here licensing to drive, registration of passenger automobiles for general use

> *For licensing to drive and registration of passenger automobiles for hire, see 354.7653284*

---

*Add as instructed under 352–354

†Add as instructed under 354.765–354.79

.765 328 4   Licensing, accreditation, certification, chartering, registration; incorporation

> Number built according to instructions under 354.765–354.79

> Class here licensing to drive, registration of passenger vehicles for hire

> *For licensing to drive, registration of passenger automobiles for general use, see 354.765284*

.767   †Railroad transportation

> Class urban rail transportation in 354.769

.769   †Urban mass transportation

> Class here local bus transportation, local rail transportation, comprehensive works on local transportation

> Class a specific form of local transportation not provided for here with the form, e.g., taxi service 354.7653, helicopter service 354.79

.77   †Road transportation

.772 8   General forms of control

> Number built according to instructions under 354.765–354.79

> Class here traffic control, traffic engineering

.78   †Water transportation

> Class here inland water transportation, ocean transportation

.79   †Air and space transportation

> Subdivisions are added for air and space transportation together, for air transportation alone

.8   ***Administration of financial institutions, money, credit**

> Subdivisions are added for financial institutions, money, credit together; for financial institutions alone

> Class works covering administration of both financial system and government finances in 352.4

> *See also 332.46 for monetary policy, see also 336.3 for fiscal policy*

.84   *Money

> Class credit institutions in 354.86

.85   *Insurance

> *For government-sponsored insurance, see 353.54; for government-sponsored health insurance, see 353.69*

---

*Add as instructed under 352–354

†Add as instructed under 354.765–354.79

.86   *Credit institutions

        Class here banks, savings and loan institutions

        Class government loans and loan guarantees in 352.736

.88   *Securities and investments

.9   *Administration of labor and professions

        Class here departments of labor

        Subdivisions are added for labor and professions together, for labor alone

        Class occupational safety in 353.96

.908   History and description with respect to kinds of persons

        Class here affirmative action programs, equal employment opportunity programs

        Class affirmative action programs for a government's own employees in 352.608

.927   General forms of assistance

        Number built according to instructions under 352–354

        Class here job creation

.93   Labor in specific groups of occupations

        Including blue collar, industrial, professional occupations

        Class labor in specific extractive, manufacturing, construction occupations in 354.94; class labor in specific occupations other than extraction, manufacturing, construction in 354.95

        For government workers, see 352.63

.94   Labor in specific extractive, manufacturing, construction occupations

        Add to base number 354.94 the numbers following 6 in 620–690, e.g., miners 354.9422

.95   Labor in other specific occupations

        Add to base number 354.95 notation 001–999, e.g., railroad workers 354.95385

*Add as instructed under 352–354

>   354.96–354.98   Specific programs for labor and professions

Not provided for in subdivisions of 354.927 derived from 352.7

Except for modifications shown under specific entries, add to each subdivision identified by † as follows:

01–2   Standard subdivisions and general considerations of administration
       Add as instructed under 352–354, e.g., state and provincial administration of the topic 213

3   Specific groups of occupations
     Class specific extractive, manufacturing, construction occupations in 4; class other specific occupations in 5
     For government workers, see 352.63

4   Specific extractive, manufacturing, construction occupations
     Add to 4 the numbers following 6 in 620–690, e.g., miners 422

5   Other specific occupations
     Add to 5 notation 001–999, e.g., railroad workers 5385

Class comprehensive works in 354.9

.96   †Employment and related services

Subdivisions are added for employment and related services together, for employment services alone

.968   †Promoting training

Class here promoting apprenticeship

See also 352.669 for training of government's own workers

.97   †Labor unions and collective bargaining

Class here employer-employee relationships

Subdivisions are added for either of both topics in heading

.98   †Compensation and conditions of employment

Class pensions, unemployment insurance in 353.54; class workers' compensation insurance in 353.69

355   Military science

Class here armed forces and services, ground forces and services

For specific kinds of military forces and warfare, see 356–359

See also 306.27 for sociology of military institutions, 322.5 for relation of the state to military organizations, 343.01 for military and defense law

See Manual at 355 vs. 623

†Add as instructed under 354.96–354.98

SUMMARY

.001   Philosophy and theory

.002   Miscellany

[.002 8]   Auxiliary techniques and procedures; apparatus, equipment, materials

> Do not use; class in 355.8

.003–.005   Standard subdivisions

.006   Organizations

[.006 8]   Management

> Do not use; class in 355.6

.007   Education and related topics

.007 1   Education

> Do not use for reserve training; class in 355.2232

.007 11   Higher education

> Class here military colleges and universities

> *See Manual at 355.00711; also at 378 vs. 355.00711: Military schools*

[.007 155]   On-the-job training

> Do not use; class in 355.5

[.007 2]   Research; statistical method

> Do not use for statistical method; class in 355.07

> Research relocated to 355.07

.008   History and description with respect to kinds of persons

.009   Historical, geographic, persons treatment

> Class historical and geographic treatment of military situation and policy in 355.033

> *See Manual at 930–990 vs. 355.009*

.009 3–.009 9   Historical, geographic, persons treatment

Class organization of specific national armies in 355.3093–355.3099

For military history of a specific war, see the war in 930–990, e.g., military history of Vietnamese War 959.70434

>   355.02–355.07   Basic considerations of military science

Class comprehensive works in 355

.02   War and warfare

Class here conventional warfare, total war

Class defense in 355.03

See also 341.6 for law of war

See Manual at 355.02 vs. 355.4: Strategy

.020 11   Systems

Do not use for models; class in 355.48

.021   General topics of war and warfare

[.021 01–.021 09]   Standard subdivisions

Do not use; class in 355.0201–355.0209

.021 3   Militarism

Class here antimilitarism, interdisciplinary works on military-industrial complex

Class relation of military organizations to the state in 322.5; class promotion of peace in 327.172

For economic aspects of military-industrial complex, see 338.47355

.021 5   Limited war

.021 7   Nuclear warfare

Including issues of deterrence

Class here comprehensive works on nuclear forces

For a specific nuclear force and its warfare, see the force, e.g., nuclear missile forces and warfare 358.17

See also 327.1747 for nuclear disarmament

.021 8   Insurgent, resistance, revolutionary warfare

Standard subdivisions are added for any or all topics in heading

Class here civil war, guerrilla warfare

Class guerrilla tactics in 355.425

.027   **Causes of war**

> *For causes of specific wars, see 930–990*

.027 2   Political and diplomatic causes

.027 3   Economic causes

.027 4   Social causes

> *See also 303.66 for sociology of war*

.027 5   Psychological causes

.028   **Aftermath of war**

Including military occupation

Class here dislocation, reconstruction

Class government of occupied territories in 355.49

> *For aftermath of specific wars, see 930–990*

.03   **Military situation and policy**

Class here defense

Disarmament relocated to 327.174

Class defense operations in 355.4

[.030 9]   Historical and geographic treatment

Do not use; class in 355.033

[.030 92]   Persons treatment

Do not use; class in 355.0092

.031   **Military relations**

Class here military alliances, mutual security pacts

> *For military assistance, see 355.032*

.031 09   Historical, geographic, persons treatment

Class here military relations between two regions or countries, e.g., military relations of China 355.0310951, then for relations between that nation and another nation or region add as instructed under —093–099 in Table 1, e.g., military relations between China and Myanmar 355.031095109591

.032   **Military assistance**

Class here military attachés, military missions

.032 093–.032 099   Specific continents, countries, localities

Do not use for military assistance to specific continents, countries, localities; class in 355.0323–355.0329

.032 3–.032 9	Military assistance to specific continents, countries, localities

Add to base number 355.032 notation 3–9 from Table 2, e.g., military assistance to Vietnam 355.032597

.033   General history and description

Class general history and description of military relations in 355.031

.033 000 1–.033 000 8	Standard subdivisions
[.033 000 9]	General historical treatment

Do not use; class in 355.033

[.033 000 901–.033 000 91]   Specific historical periods; areas, regions, places in general

Do not use; class in 355.033001–355.03301

[.033 000 92]   Persons treatment

Do not use; class in 355.0092

[.033 000 93–.033 000 99]   Treatment in specific continents, countries, localities

Do not use; class in 355.03303–355.03309

.033 001–.033 09   Historical and geographic treatment

Add to base number 355.0330 notation 01–9 from Table 2, e.g., military situation and policy in 1930s 355.0330043, military situation of Brazil 355.033081

.033 2   Military capability

Class here combat readiness

Class combat readiness of specific units in 355.3

[.033 209 1–.033 209 9]   Geographic and persons treatment

Do not use; class in 355.03321–335.03329

.033 21–.033 29   Geographic and persons treatment of military capability

Add to base number 355.0332 notation 1–9 from Table 2, e.g., military capability of Sweden 355.0332485

.033 5   Military policy

[.033 509 1–.033 509 9]   Geographic and persons treatment

Do not use; class in 355.03351–355.03359

.033 51–.033 59   Geographic and persons treatment of military policy

Add to base number 355.0335 notation 1–9 from Table 2, e.g., military policy of Italy 355.033545

.07   Military research and development

Limited to military aspects

Class here research [*formerly* 355.0072], comprehensive works on military aspects of research and development of weapons [*formerly* 355.82], relation of military science to science and technology, comprehensive works on military aspects of research and development of supplies and equipment

Class interdisciplinary works on military research and development in 338.4735507

For procurement and contracting aspects of research and development of equipment and supplies, see 355.6212; for military aspects of research and development (other than procurement and contracting) of specific kinds of equipment and supplies, see 355.8

[.072]   Research; statistical method

Do not use; class in 355.07

.1   Military life and customs

Class here conditions of military employment

For social and welfare services provided to soldiers and dependents, see 355.34

.11   Service periods, promotion and demotion, termination

.111   Length of service

.112   Promotion and demotion

.113   Inactive periods

Including furloughs, leaves, missing in action, reserve status, status during captivity or internment

Class reserve training in 355.2232

.114   Termination of service

Including resignation, retirement; reinstatement

.12   Living conditions

Class here living conditions of dependents, comprehensive works on military housing

For quarters for personnel at military installations, see 355.71

.120 68   Management

Class here housing administration [*formerly* 355.67]

.123   Morale and motivation

.129	Living conditions in specific situations
	Class morale in specific situations in 355.123
	For life in military prisons and prison camps (other than prisoner-of-war camps), see 365.48
.129 2	Living conditions in regular quarters
	Including quarters during basic training
.129 3	Living conditions during maneuvers, aboard ship, in transit
.129 4	Living conditions in combat zones
.129 6	Living conditions in prisoner-of-war camps
.13	Conduct and rewards
	Class here discipline, soldierly qualities
	See also 343.014 for law of discipline and conduct
.133	Regulation of conduct
	Class rewards in 355.134
.133 2	Enforcement and punishment
	Class offenses in 355.1334
.133 23	Enforcement
	Including criminal investigation, military police
.133 25	Punishment
	Class military prisons in 365.48
.133 4	Offenses against military discipline
	Including desertion, mutiny
	Class interdisciplinary works on mutinies in 364.131
	See also 364.138 for war crimes
.133 6	Etiquette
	Class dress regulations, etiquette of uniforms in 355.14
.134	Rewards
	Including special privileges
	Class here awards, citations
.134 092	Persons
	See Manual at 355.134092

.134 2   Honorary insignia

> Including badges, decorations, medals
>
> Class here comprehensive works on insignia
>
> Class comprehensive works on insignia and uniforms in 355.14
>
> *For insignia of rank, see 355.14*

.134 9   Gifts and gun salutes

.14   Uniforms

> Including accessories, insignia of rank and service
>
> Class here etiquette of uniforms, comprehensive works on insignia and uniforms
>
> Class issue and use of uniforms in 355.81
>
> *For honorary insignia, comprehensive works on insignia, see 355.1342*
>
> *See Manual at 355.81 vs. 355.14*

.140 9   Historical, geographic, persons treatment

> *See Manual at 355.1409*

.15   Colors and standards

> Standard subdivisions are added for either or both topics in heading

.16   Celebrations and commemorations

> Standard subdivisions are added for either or both topics in heading

.17   Ceremonies

> Class ceremonies for a specific occasion with the occasion, e.g., gun salutes 355.1349

.2   **Military resources**

.21   Preparation, evaluation, preservation

> Class preparation, evaluation, preservation of specific resources in 355.22–355.27

> 355.22–355.27   Specific resources

> Class comprehensive works in 355.2

.22   Human resources

> *For civilian personnel, see 355.23*

[.220 68]	Management

Do not use for management of human resources other than recruiting; class in 355.61. Do not use for recruiting; class in 355.223

.223 Recruiting and reserve training

Standard subdivisions are added for recruiting and reserve training together, for recruiting alone

Class here enlistment

.223 2 Reserve training

.223 207 11 Higher education

Class here reserve training in academic settings, e.g., U.S. Reserve Officers' Training Corps 355.2232071173

.223 4 Qualifications for service

.223 6 Specific methods and procedures of recruiting

Including registration, commissioning

[.223 601–.223 609] Standard subdivisions

Do not use; class in 355.22301–355.22309

.223 62 Voluntary enlistment

Class here all-volunteer army

.223 63 Draft (Conscription)

For universal military service, see 355.225

.224 Conscientious objectors

Class here draft resistance

Class ethics of conscientious objection in 172.1; class techniques for evading draft in 355.22363

.225 Universal military training

Class here universal military service

.23 Civilian workers

[.230 68] Management

Do not use; class in 355.619

.24 Raw materials

Class here strategic materials, comprehensive works on nonhuman resources

For industrial resources, see 355.26; for transportation and communication facilities, see 355.27

.242	Metals
.243	Nonmetallic minerals
.245	Agricultural products
.26	Industrial resources

> Military appraisal and utilization
>
> Class here manufacturing war matériel

.27	Transportation and communications facilities
.28	Mobilization

> Including commandeering, requisition
>
> Class mobilization of specific resources in 355.22–355.27

.29	Demobilization

> Class demobilization of specific resources in 355.22–355.27

.3   **Organization and personnel of military forces**

> Class here organization of national armies, combat readiness of specific units
>
> Class comprehensive works on combat readiness in 355.0332

.31	Kinds of military units

> Including armies, regiments, squads; districts
>
> Class here combat units
>
> Class organization of national armies in 355.3
>
> > *For a specific kind of unit limited to a specific service, see the service, e.g., reserve units 355.37, armored units 358.183*

.33	Personnel and their hierarchy

> Including labor relations and military employee organizations
>
> Class persons treatment of soldiers in 355.0092; class promotion and demotion in 355.112

.330 4	Line and staff organization
.330 41	Line organization

> Including evaluation, leadership, supervision
>
> Class here command and control systems, command functions
>
> > *For motivation, see 355.123*

.330 42	Staff organization

> Class here general staffs, joint chiefs of staff
>
> > *For line functions of chiefs of staff, see 355.33041*

.331	General and flag officers

Officers above rank of colonel (naval rank of captain)

.332	Commissioned and warrant officers

Standard subdivisions are added for commissioned and warrant officers together, for commissioned officers alone

Class officers' manuals in 355

For general and flag officers, see 355.331

.338	Enlisted personnel

Including noncommissioned officers

See also 331.8811355 for military unions

.34	Noncombat services

Including propaganda, social services for dependents, interdisciplinary works on civic action of armed forces

Class here operations of noncombat services, social services for soldiers

For a specific noncombat service not provided for here, see the subject, e.g., housing 355.12, personnel administration 355.61; for a specific civic action of armed forces, see the activity, e.g., civil works program of U.S. Army Corps of Engineers 363.0973

.341	Supply issuing and related services

Including canteens, mess services, post exchanges

Class officers' and noncommissioned officers' clubs in 355.346; class comprehensive works on supply services in 355.621

.342	Public relations [*formerly also* 659.29355]
.343	Unconventional warfare services
.343 2	Intelligence

Including cryptanalysis, mapping, weather forecasting

Class here military espionage

Class counterintelligence in 355.3433; class interdisciplinary works on espionage in 327.12

.343 3	Counterintelligence

Including security classification

.343 4	Psychological warfare
.343 7	Subversion and sabotage

Class interdisciplinary works on subversion in 327.12

.345   Health services

     Including ambulance, sanitation, veterinary services

     Class here medical services

.346   Recreational services

     Including library services, officers' and noncommissioned officers' (NCO) clubs

.347   Religious and counseling services

     Standard subdivisions are added for specific religions, e.g., history of Jewish services 355.34709

.348   Women's units

     Class women in armed forces in 355.0082; class women as a military resource in 355.22082. Class a specific service performed by women with the service, plus notation 082 from Table 1, e.g., women in intelligence services 355.3432082, women in combat 355.4082

.35   Combat units according to field of service

     Class comprehensive works on combat units in 355.31

.351   Units serving wholly within national or local frontiers

     Class here frontier troops, active units called home guards

     Class reserve units called home guards in 355.37

.352   Expeditionary forces

     Class here expeditionary forces of colonies, forces of mother countries dedicated to service in colonies

.354   Mercenary troops

     Class here soldiers of fortune

.356   Allied and coalition forces

     Standard subdivisions are added for either or both topics in heading

     Class here multinational forces

     For multinational forces commanded by international bodies, see 355.357

.357   International forces

     Troops serving under command of international bodies

     Class interdisciplinary works on peaceful resolution of conflict in 327.17

     See also 341.58 for legal aspects of international forces

.359   Foreign legions

Units of national armies consisting primarily of foreign recruits

Class here auxiliaries (troops of foreign countries serving with a state's armies)

.37   Reserves

Class here home guards, home reserves, militia, national guards; military departments devoted to reserve or national guard affairs

Class training of reserves in 355.2232; class active units called home guards in 355.351. Class reserve units of a specific kind of military force with the force, e.g., army engineer reserves 358.223

.4   **Military operations**

Class here attack and defense operations, combat, strategy

See Manual at 355.02 vs. 355.4: Strategy

.409   Historical and persons treatment

Do not use for geographic treatment; class in 355.471–355.479

.41   Support operations

Including camouflage, deception, handling prisoners of war

Class support operations in a specific situation with the situation, e.g., logistics of siege warfare 355.44

.411   Logistics

Including troop movements

For troop support, see 355.415

.412   Encampment

.413   Reconnaissance

Class here patrolling

.415   Troop support

Operations for providing immediate necessities for maintenance of troops

Class comprehensive works on operations for provisioning troops in 355.411

For a specific aspect of troop support, see the aspect, e.g., medical service 355.345

.42   Tactics

For nuclear tactics, see 355.43; for tactics of siege warfare, see 355.44; for tactics of defense of home territory, see 355.45

.422   Specific tactics

> Including antiaircraft defenses, attacks and counterattacks, debarkation and landing, prevention of friendly fire casualties, retreats, skirmishing; mobile (blitz), commando (hit-and-run), infiltration tactics
>
> Class specific tactics in specific conditions in 355.423–355.426

.422 01–.422 09   Standard subdivisions

> Do not use; class in 355.4201–355.4209

>   355.423–355.426 Tactics in specific conditions
>
> Class comprehensive works in 355.42

.423   Tactics in various kinds of terrain, climate, weather

.424   Use of animals

.425   Guerrilla tactics

> Class here tribal fighting
>
> Class guerrilla warfare in 355.0218

.426   Tactics in cities

> Class here house-to-house fighting, street fighting, urban warfare
>
> Class siege warfare in 355.44

.43   Nuclear operations

> Class nuclear warfare in 355.0217

[.430 01–.430 09]   Standard subdivisions

> Relocated to 355.4301–355.4309

.430 1–.430 9   Standard subdivisions [*formerly* 355.43001–355.43009]

.44   Siege and trench warfare, blockades

> Class urban warfare in 355.426; class naval blockades in 359.44

.45   Defense of home territory

> Class defensive forts and installations in 355.7

.46   Combined operations

> Coordination of two or more kinds of military forces
>
> Class here amphibious operations
>
> Class amphibious operations in which marines are main land component in 359.9646

.47   Military geography

[.470 91–.470 99]   Geographic and persons treatment

> Do not use; class in 355.471–355.479

.471–.479   Geographic and persons treatment of military geography

> Class here geographic treatment of military operations

> Add to base number 355.47 notation 1–9 from Table 2, e.g., military geography of Russia 355.4747

.48   Technical analyses of military events

> Including real and imaginary wars, campaigns, battles

> Class here war gaming

> *See also 793.92 for recreational war games*

.49   Occupation of conquered territory

> Including military government

> Class occupation as an aftermath of war in 355.028

.5   Military training

> Training of individuals and units

> *For reserve training, see 355.2232; for universal military training, see 355.225*

.507 1   Education in military training

> Class military training in a specific country with the country in 355.5093–355.5099, e.g., military training in Switzerland 355.509494 (*not* 355.50710494)

.52   Maneuvers

> Including maneuvers involving civil population [*formerly* 355.58]

.54   Basic training

> Including drill, survival training, tactical exercises

.544   Encampment and field training

> Including setting up and dismantling camps, constructing temporary fortifications, running obstacle courses

.547   Small arms and bayonet practice

> Class here manual of arms

> If emphasis is on use by infantry, class in 356.115

.548   Self-defense

> Unarmed combat and combat with knife

> If emphasis is on use by infantry, class in 356.115

.55 Training of officers

Class here mid-career training that is an integral part of an officer's career development, even if conducted at armed forces schools with full academic accreditation

Class university service academies in 355.00711; class training through war games in 355.48

.56 Technical training

[.58] Maneuvers involving civil population

Relocated to 355.52

.6 Military administration

Class here defense administration, departments of defense

Class administration of a function not provided for here with the function, plus notation 068 from Table 1, e.g., administration of installations 355.7068

For organization of military forces, see 355.3

(Option: Class comprehensive works in 353.2. If option is chosen, change heading to "Specific topics in military administration," and do not add standard subdivisions)

[.606 8] Management

Do not use; class in 355.6

.609 1 Treatment by areas, regions, places in general

Class here international military and defense administration

Class administration of international peacekeeping troops in 355.357068

(Option: If option at 355.6 is chosen, class international military and defense administration in 353.2211)

.61 Personnel administration

Class here personnel management of military personnel

For service periods, promotion and demotion, termination, see 355.11; for motivation, see 355.123; for personnel and their hierarchy, see 355.33; for wage and salary administration, see 355.64

.614 Job description for military personnel

Including job analysis and classification

.619 Civilian workers

Add to base number 355.619 the numbers following 352.6 in 352.63–352.69, e.g., recruiting civilian personnel 355.6195

Class civilian workers as a military resource in 355.23

.62	Supply and financial administration and related topics
.621	Supply administration and related topics

Class here administration of specific kinds of equipment and supplies [*formerly* 355.8], supply management [*formerly also* 355.8068], supply management of weapons [*formerly also* 355.82068] comprehensive works on supply services, supply administration of weapons

> *For product development, see 355.07; for supply issuing and related services, see 355.341; for supply depots and installations, see 355.75*

[.621 1]	Contracts

Relocated to 355.6212

.621 2	Contracts [*formerly* 355.6211] and procurement

Standard subdivisions are added for either or both topics in heading

Class here comprehensive works on military contracts

> *For contracts for a specific nonsupply item, see the item, plus notation 068 from Table 1, e.g., contracts for real property 355.7068*

.621 3	Internal control and disposal of supplies

Including warehouse management

.621 32	Inventory control
.621 37	Surplus supplies and their disposal

Standard subdivisions are added for either or both topics in heading

.622	Financial administration

Add to base number 355.622 the numbers following 352.4 in 352.43–352.49, e.g., defense budget 355.6229, defense budget of United States 355.622973

> *For payroll administration, see 355.64*

[.63]	Inspection

Relocated to 355.685

.64	Salary administration

Class here wage and payroll administration

[.67]	Housing administration

Relocated to 355.12068

.68	Executive management

Add to base number 355.68 the numbers following 352.3 in 352.33–352.38, e.g., inspection 355.685 [*formerly* 355.63]; however, for intelligence, see 355.3432; for counterintelligence, see 355.3433

Class command and control systems in 355.33041

For managing executive personnel, see 355.33

.69	Military mail; graves registration and burial services
.693	Military mail
.699	Graves registration and burial services
.7	**Military installations**

Class here military bases, forts, permanent camps, posts, reservations

.709 3–.709 9	Treatment by specific continents, countries, localities

Class here specific forts or systems of fortifications, installations having two or more functions

Use notation for area of installation, not country maintaining it, e.g., United States bases in Panama Canal Area 355.70972875

.71	Quarters for personnel

Housing at military installations

Including barracks, prisoner-of-war camps

Class comprehensive works on military housing in 355.12

.72	Medical installations

Class medical supply depots in 355.75; class veterans' hospitals in 362.11; class comprehensive works on medical services in 355.345

.73	Artillery installations

Class army artillery installations in 358.127

.74	Engineering installations

Class army engineering installations in 358.227

.75	Supply depots and installations

Class comprehensive works on supply services in 355.621

.79	Land

.8   **Military equipment and supplies (Matériel)**   **Weapons (Ordnance)**

Limited to equipment and supplies common to two or more land forces, or to at least two of the three major defense forces, e.g., missiles and tanks, supplies of land and sea forces

Including auxiliary techniques and procedures

Class here apparatus, equipment, materials; military aspects of research and development (other than procurement and contracting) of specific kinds of equipment and supplies

Administration of specific kinds of equipment and supplies relocated to 355.621

Class mobilization of military industrial resources in 355.28; class comprehensive works on military aspects of research and development of equipment and supplies, of weapons in 355.07; class weapons limited to a specific land force in 356–357. Class interdisciplinary works on research and development of a specific kind of supplies and equipment with the kind in 338.47, e.g., small arms 338.4762344

.801–.805   Standard subdivisions

Class here standard subdivisions of weapons [*formerly* 355.8201–355.8205]

.806   Organizations

Class here organizations relating to weapons [*formerly* 355.8206]

[.806 8]   Supply management

Relocated to 355.621

.807   Education and related topics

Class here education and related topics on weapons [*formerly* 355.8207]

[.807 2]   Research; statistical method

Do not use; class in 355.07

.808–.809   Standard subdivisions

Class here standard subdivisions of weapons [*formerly* 355.8208–355.8209]

.81   Clothing, food, camp equipment, office supplies

See Manual at 355.81 vs. 355.14

.82	Specific kinds of weapons (ordnance)

Use of this number for comprehensive works on ordnance discontinued; class in 355.8

Problems of arms limitation and of verifying arms-control treaty provisions for specific kinds of weapons relocated to 327.174; comprehensive works on military aspects of research and development of weapons relocated to 355.07

Class specific kinds of weapons limited to a specific land force in 356–357

For combat vehicles, see 355.83

See Manual at 355 vs. 623

[.820 1–.820 5]	Standard subdivisions of weapons

Relocated to 355.801–355.805

[.820 6]	Organizations relating to weapons

Relocated to 355.806

[.820 68]	Supply management of weapons

Relocated to 355.621

[.820 7]	Education and related topics on weapons

Relocated to 355.807

[.820 72]	Research; statistical method on weapons

Do not use; class in 355.07

[.820 8–.820 9]	Standard subdivisions of weapons

Relocated to 355.808–355.809

.821	Artillery

Class land artillery in 358.1282

For specific pieces of artillery, see 355.822; for artillery projectiles, see 355.82513

.822	Specific pieces of artillery

Class specific pieces of land artillery in 358.1282

.823–.826	Other specific kinds of weapons

Add to base number 355.82 the numbers following 623.4 in 623.43–623.46, e.g., nuclear weapons 355.825119, artillery projectiles 355.82513; however, for comprehensive works on missiles, see 358.17182; for comprehensive works on chemical, biological, radiological weapons, see 358.3; for ordnance of a force dedicated to a specific kind of weapon, see the force in 356–359, e.g., tank ammunition 358.1882

.83   Transportation equipment and supplies

> Including fuel; aircraft used outside air forces, ships used outside naval forces, support vehicles, trains

> Class here combat vehicles

> Class comprehensive works on aircraft in 358.4183; class comprehensive works on ships in 359.83

.85   Communication equipment

> Class army communication equipment in 358.248

.88   Medical supplies

> Class ambulances in 355.83

> ## 356–359   Specific kinds of military forces and warfare

Class here history of specific military forces not limited to any one war, services and units dedicated to specific forces, countermeasures against specific forces

All notes under 355 are applicable here

Except for modifications shown under specific entries, add to each subdivision identified by * as follows:

01–09	Standard subdivisions
	As modified under 355.001–355.009, e.g., management 6 (*not* 068), management of artillery forces 358.126 (*not* 358.12068); however, class research, statistical methods in 072
1	Military life and customs
14	Uniforms
3	Organization and personnel
	Class here units
	For personnel administration, see 6
309	Historical, geographic, persons treatment
	Class here units of specific countries regardless of size of unit
4	Operations
	Class here tactics
5	Training

(continued)

> ## 356–359 Specific kinds of military forces and warfare (continued)

6   Administration
       Including administration of specific kinds of equipment and
       supplies [*formerly* 8], management of equipment and supplies
       [*formerly also* 8068], executive management, financial and
       personnel administration, comprehensive works on supply
       administration
           For administration of a specific topic not provided for here,
           see the topic, plus notation 068 from Table 1, e.g.,
           administration of installations 7068
       (Option: Class comprehensive works on administration in 353.29.
       If option is chosen, change heading to "Specific topics in
       administration," and do not add standard subdivisions)
7   Installations
8   Equipment and supplies (Matériel)
       Class here weapons
       Administration of specific kinds of equipment and supplies
       relocated to 6
[8068]   Management
               Relocated to 6
82   Weapons other than combat vehicles
83   Combat vehicles

Class comprehensive works in 355. Class a specific countermeasure with the
force wielding it, e.g., coast artillery 358.16 (*not* 359)

See Manual at 355 vs. 623

> ## 356–357 Land forces and warfare

Class comprehensive works in 355

For artillery, missile, armored forces, see 358.1; for chemical, biological,
radiological warfare, see 358.3

356   Foot forces and warfare

.1   Infantry

.11   General topics of infantry [*formerly* 356.18]

Motorized infantry relocated to 356.16

Class general topics of irregular troops in 356.15; class general topics of
troops having special combat functions in 356.16

[.110 1–.110 9]	Standard subdivisions	

Do not use; class in 356.101–356.109

.111–.118   Specific topics of infantry

Add to base number 356.11 notation 1–8 from table under 356–359, e.g., infantry training 356.115

.15   *Irregular troops

Including guerrillas, partisans

.16   Troops having special combat functions

Including motorized infantry [*formerly* 356.11]

.162   Troops specializing in specific weapons

Including bazookamen, grenadiers, machine gunners, sharpshooters (snipers)

.164   *Mountain and ski troops

Subdivisions are added for either or both topics in heading

.166   *Paratroops

.167   *Commandos and rangers

Subdivisions are added for either or both topics in heading

[.18]   General topics of infantry

Relocated to 356.11

357   Mounted forces and warfare

.04   General topics of mounted forces and warfare

[.040 1–.040 9]   Standard subdivisions

Do not use; class in 357.01–357.09

.041   Military life and customs

.041 4   Uniforms

.043   Organization and personnel

Class here comprehensive works on units that served as horse cavalry and mechanized or armored cavalry, e.g., U.S. Third Cavalry Division 357.0430973

Class a specific period of service of a unit which changed kinds of mounts with the kind of mount, e.g., U.S. Third Cavalry Division as a horse unit 357.1830973

*Add as instructed under 356–359

.044–.048   Operations, training, administration, installations, equipment and supplies

> Add to base number 357.04 notation 4–8 from table under 356–359, e.g., training mounted forces 357.045

.1   Horse cavalry

> Class here dragoons, lancers
>
> *For remount services, see 357.2*
>
> *See also 358.12 for horse artillery*

.18   General topics of horse cavalry

[.180 1–.180 9]   Standard subdivisions

> Do not use; class in 357.101–357.109

.181–.184   Military life and customs, organization and personnel, operations

> Add to base number 357.18 notation 1–4 from table under 356–359, e.g., uniforms of horse cavalry 357.1814

.185   Training [*formerly also* 357.2]

.186–.188   Administration, installations, equipment and supplies

> Add to base number 357.18 notation 6–8 from table under 356–359, e.g., administration of horse cavalry 357.186

.2   Remount services

> Training relocated to 357.185

.5   Mechanized cavalry

> *For armored cavalry, see 358.18*

.52   *Bicycle troops

.53   *Motorcycle troops

.54   Large motor-vehicle cavalry

> Including jeep and truck cavalry

[.58]   General topics of mechanized cavalry

> Number discontinued; class in 357.5

358   Air and other specialized forces and warfare; engineering and related services

*Add as instructed under 356–359

SUMMARY

358.1	Missile forces; army artillery and armored forces
.2	Army engineering and related services
.3	Chemical, biological, radiological warfare
.4	Air forces and warfare
.8	Space forces

.1 Missile forces; army artillery and armored forces

.12   *Army artillery forces

> Including antitank artillery forces

> Class here field artillery forces

>> *For antiaircraft artillery forces, see 358.13; for coast artillery forces, see 358.16*

.13   *Antiaircraft artillery forces

.16   *Coast artillery forces

.17   Guided missile forces

> Class here strategic missile forces, nuclear missile forces

> Class strategic land missile forces in 358.1754

>> *For air guided missile forces, see 358.42; for naval guided missile forces, see 359.9817*

.171   General topics

> Class general topics of specific missile forces in 358.174–358.176

[.171 01–.171 09]   Standard subdivisions

> Do not use; class in 358.1701–358.1709

.171 1–.171 8   Specific topics of guided missile forces

> Add to base number 357.18 notation 1–8 from table under 356–359, e.g., training of missile forces 357.185

.174   *Antimissile defense forces

> Class here Strategic Defense Initiative (SDI, star wars), surface-to-air missile forces

> Class a specific defense other than surface-to-air missiles with the defense, e.g., beam weapon forces 358.39, air-to-air missile forces 358.43

.175   Specific surface-to-surface missile forces

[.175 01–.175 09]   Standard subdivisions

> Do not use; class in 358.1701–358.1709

*Add as instructed under 356–359

| .175 2 | *Short-range missile forces |

Class here tactical missile forces

| .175 3 | *Intermediate-range missile forces |
| .175 4 | *Long-range missile forces |

Class here strategic land missile forces

| .176 | *Surface-to-underwater missile forces |
| .18 | *Armored forces |

Class here tank forces, armored cavalry

.2   Army engineering and related services

| .22 | *Engineering services |

Including property maintenance

Class here construction engineer services

Class communications services in 358.24; class transportation services in 358.25; class civil activities of army engineering services in 363

| .23 | *Demolition services |

Including bomb disposal units

| .24 | *Communications (Signal) forces |

Including military cryptography services

| .25 | *Transportation services |

.3   Chemical, biological, radiological warfare

Regardless of service or force to which assigned

.34	*Chemical warfare
.38	*Biological warfare
.39	*Radiation and beam warfare

Class here passive defense against nuclear radiation

.4   Air forces and warfare

For naval air forces, see 359.94

| .400 1–.400 6 | Standard subdivisions |

Notation from Table 1 as modified under 355.001–355.009, e.g., air forces administration 358.416 (*not* 358.40068)

| .400 7 | Education and related topics |
| .400 71 | Education |

For reserve training, see 358.412232

*Add as instructed under 356–359

[.400 715 5]	On-the-job training
	Do not use; class in 358.415
[.400 72]	Research; statistical method
	Do not use for statistical method; class in 358.407
	Research relocated to 358.407
.400 8–.400 9	Standard subdivisions
.403	Situation and policy
	Standard subdivisions are added for either or both topics in heading
.407	Research and development

> Limited to air force aspects
>
> Class here research [*formerly* 358.40072], relation of air force and warfare to science and technology, comprehensive works on air force aspects of research and development of equipment and supplies
>
> Class interdisciplinary works on air force research and development in 338.47358407

For procurement and contracting aspects of research and development of supplies and equipment, see 358.416212; for air force aspects of research and development (other than procurement and contracting) of specific kinds of equipment and supplies, see 358.418

.41	General topics of air forces and warfare

Class general topics of specific forces in 358.42–358.47

[.410 1–.410 9]	Standard subdivisions

Do not use; class in 358.4001–358.4009

.411–.415	Air forces life, resources, organization, personnel, operations, training

Add to base number 358.41 the numbers following 355 in 355.1–355.5, e.g., air force uniforms 358.4114

.416	Air forces administration

Add to base number 358.416 the numbers following 355.6 in 355.61–355.69, e.g., executive management 358.4168

(Option: Class comprehensive works in 353.27. If option is chosen, change heading to "Specific topics in air forces administration," and do not add standard subdivisions)

.417–.418	Air forces installations, equipment, supplies

Add to base number 358.41 the numbers following 355 in 355.7–355.8, e.g., comprehensive works on military aircraft 358.4183; however, for aircraft of specific forces, see 358.42–358.47

>   358.42–358.47   Specific forces

> Class chemical, biological, radiological warfare in 358.3; class comprehensive works in 358.4

.42   *Bombing forces

Including air-to-underwater guided missile forces

Class here strategic missions of air forces; air-to-surface guided missile forces; comprehensive works on air guided missile forces, on air nuclear forces

For air-to-air guided missile forces, air-to-air nuclear forces, see 358.43

.43   *Pursuit and fighter forces

Standard subdivisions are added for either or both topics in heading

Including air-to-air guided missile forces, air-to-air nuclear forces, air artillery

Class here tactical missions of air forces

.44   *Transportation services

.45   *Reconnaissance forces and operations

Including antisubmarine reconnaissance

.46   *Communications (Signal) services

.47   *Engineering services

.8   ***Space forces**

See also 358.17 for missile forces when either launch or target is from or to the earth or its atmosphere

359   Sea (Naval) forces and warfare

SUMMARY

359.001–.009	**Standard subdivisions**
.03–.07	**[Situation and policy, naval research and development]**
.1–.2	**Naval life and resources**
.3	**Organization and personnel of naval forces**
.4–.5	**Naval operations and training**
.6	**Naval administration**
.7	**Naval installations**
.8	**Naval equipment and supplies (Naval matériel)** **Naval weapons (ordnance)**
.9	**Specialized combat forces; engineering and related services**

---

*Add as instructed under 356–359

| .001–.006 | Standard subdivisions |

Notation from Table 1 as modified under 355.001–355.006, e.g., naval administration 359.6 (*not* 359.0068)

.007   Education and related topics

.007 1   Education

For reserve training, see 359.2232

[.007 155]   On-the-job training

Do not use; class in 359.5

[.007 2]   Research; statistical method

Do not use for statistical method; class in 359.07

Research relocated to 359.07

.008–.009   Standard subdivisions

.03   Situation and policy

Standard subdivisions are added for either or both topics in heading

Class here naval defense

Class naval defense operations in 359.4

.07   Naval research and development

Limited to naval aspects

Class here research [*formerly* 359.0072], comprehensive works on naval aspects of research and development of weapons [*formerly* 359.82], relation of naval science to science and technology, comprehensive works on naval aspects of research and development of equipment and supplies

Class interdisciplinary works on naval research and development in 338.4735907

For procurement and contracting aspects of research and development of naval equipment and supplies, see 359.6212; for naval aspects of research and development (other than procurement and contracting) of specific kinds of equipment and supplies, see 359.8

.1–.2   Naval life and resources

Add to base number 359 the numbers following 355 in 355.1–355.2, e.g., uniforms 359.14

.3   Organization and personnel of naval forces

.31   Naval units

Including fleets, squadrons, flotillas, divisions

Class noncombat services in 359.34; class reserves in 359.37

For ships as naval units, see 359.32

.32   Ships as naval units

> Class here crews of ships
>
> Class comprehensive works on ships in the navy in 359.83
>
> *See Manual at 359.32 vs. 359.83*

.322   Sailing ships as units

> Class here sailing ships of war

.325–.326   Specific kinds of powered ships as naval units

> Add to base number 359.32 the numbers following 623.82 in 623.825–623.826, e.g., cruisers 359.3253; however, for submarines, see 359.933; for aircraft carriers, see 359.9435; for military supply and transport ships, see 359.9853

.33–.37   Personnel, noncombat services, fields of combat service, reserves

> Add to base number 359.3 the numbers following 355.3 in 355.33–355.37, e.g., noncombat services 359.34

.4–.5   Naval operations and training

> Add to base number 359 the numbers following 355 in 355.4–355.5, e.g., naval blockades 359.44

.6   Naval administration

> Add to base number 359.6 the numbers following 355.6 in 355.61–355.69, e.g., administration of specific kinds of equipment and supplies 359.621 [*formerly* 359.8], supply management 359.621 [*formerly also* 359.8068]
>
> (Option: Class comprehensive works in 353.25. If option is chosen, change heading to "Specific topics in naval administration," and do not add standard subdivisions)

.7   Naval installations

> Add to base number 359.7 the numbers following 355.7 in 355.71–355.79, e.g., quarters for personnel 359.71

.8   **Naval equipment and supplies (Naval matériel)   Naval weapons (Naval ordnance)**

Including auxiliary techniques and procedures

Class here apparatus, equipment, materials; naval aspects of research and development (other than procurement and contracting) of specific kinds of supplies and equipment

Administration of specific kinds of equipment and supplies relocated to 359.621

Class mobilization of naval industrial resources in 359.28; class comprehensive works on naval aspects of research and development of equipment and supplies, of weapons in 359.07. Class interdisciplinary works on research and development of a specific kind of naval supplies and equipment with the kind in 338.47, e.g., warships 338.47623825

.801–.805   Standard subdivisions

Class here standard subdivisions of weapons [*formerly* 359.8201–359.8205]

.806   Organizations

Class here organizations relating to weapons [*formerly* 359.8206]

[.806 8]   Supply management

Relocated to 359.621

.807   Education and related topics

Class here education and related topics on weapons [*formerly* 359.8207]

[.807 2]   Research; statistical methods

Do not use; class in 359.07

.808–.809   Standard subdivisions

Class here standard subdivisions of weapons [*formerly* 359.8208–359.8209]

.81   Clothing, food, camp equipment, office supplies

See Manual at 355.81 vs. 355.14

.82   Specific kinds of weapons (ordnance)

Use of this number for comprehensive works on ordnance discontinued; class in 359.8

Problems of arms limitation and of verifying arms-control treaty provisions for specific kinds of naval weapons relocated to 327.1743; comprehensive works on naval aspects of research and development of weapons relocated to 359.07

For combat vehicles and craft, see 359.83

| [.820 1–.820 9] | Standard subdivisions |

Relocated to 359.801–359.809

.823–.826   Subdivisions for specific kinds of weapons (ordnance)

Add to base number 359.82 the numbers following 623.4 in 623.43–623.46, e.g., small arms 359.824; however, for ordnance on specific kinds of ships, see 359.83; for artillery, see 359.981282; for guided missiles, see 359.981782

.83   Transportation equipment and supplies

Including fuel, support vehicles

Class here comprehensive works on ships in armed forces

For ships as naval units, see 359.32. For ships used outside the naval forces, see the force using them, e.g., coast guard ships 359.9783

See Manual at 359.32 vs. 359.83

.832   Sailing ships as equipment

Class here sailing ships of war

.835–.836   Specific kinds of power-driven warships as equipment

Add to base number 359.83 the numbers following 623.82 in 623.825–623.826, e.g., cruisers 359.8353; however, for submarines, see 359.9383; for aircraft carriers, see 359.94835; for military supply and transport ships, see 359.98583

.85   Communication equipment

.88   Medical supplies

.9   Specialized combat forces; engineering and related services

Class chemical, biological, radiological warfare in 358.3

.93   *Submarine forces

.933   Organization and personnel

Number built according to instructions under 356–359

Class here units, submarines as units

See Manual at 359.32 vs. 359.83

.938   Equipment and supplies (Matériel)

Number built according to instructions under 356–359

.938 3   Ships as equipment

Number built according to instructions under 356–359

Class here submarines as equipment

See Manual at 359.32 vs. 359.83

*Add as instructed under 356–359

.938 32		Conventionally powered submarines
.938 34		Nuclear powered submarines
.94	*Naval air forces	
.943	Organization and personnel	

> Number built according to instructions under 356–359
>
> Class here units

.943 4		Aircraft units

> Including flights, groups, squadrons, wings

.943 5		Aircraft carriers as units

> *See Manual at 359.32 vs. 359.83*

.948		Equipment and supplies (Matériel)

> Number built according to instructions under 356–359

.948 3		Combat vehicles

> Number built according to instructions under 356–359
>
> Class combat vehicles as units in 359.943

.948 34		Aircraft
.948 35		Aircraft carriers as equipment

> *See Manual at 359.32 vs. 359.83*

.96	Marine forces	

> Add to base number 359.96 the numbers following 355 in 355.1–355.8, e.g., training 355.965

.97	*Coast guard	

> As a military service
>
> Class coast guard as a police service, interdisciplinary works on coast guard in 363.286

.98	Artillery and guided missile forces; engineering and related services	
.981	Artillery and guided missile forces	
.981 2	*Artillery services	

> Class artillery units aboard specific kinds of ships in 359.32; class artillery ordnance aboard specific kinds of ships in 359.83

.981 7	*Guided missile forces	

> Class guided missile units aboard specific kinds of ships in 359.32; class guided missile ordnance aboard specific kinds of ships in 359.83

*Add as instructed under 356–359

.982   *Engineering services

.983   *Communications (Signal) services

.984   Special warfare services

> Including frogmen, underwater demolition units, underwater reconnaissance operations; sea, air, land teams

.985   *Transportation services

> Class here military sealift commands

.985 3   Organization and personnel

> Number built according to instructions under 356–359
>
> Including troopships as units
>
> Class here units, military supply ships as units
>
> *See Manual at 359.32 vs. 359.83*

.985 8   Supplies and equipment (Matériel)

> Number built according to instructions under 356–359

.985 83   Military supply ships as equipment

> Number built according to instructions under 356–359
>
> Including troopships
>
> *See Manual at 359.32 vs. 359.83*

360 Social problems and services; associations

SUMMARY

361	**Social problems and social welfare in general**
.001–.008	Standard subdivisions
.02–.06	Specific kinds of assistance
.1	Social problems
.2	Social action
.3	Social work
.4	Group work
.6	Government action
.7	Private action
.8	Community action
.9	Historical, geographic, persons treatment

*Add as instructed under 356–359

362	Social welfare problems and services
.04	Special topics
.1	Physical illness
.2	Mental and emotional illnesses and disturbances
.3	Mental retardation
.4	Problems of and services to people with physical disabilities
.5	Problems of and services to the poor
.6	Problems of and services to persons in late adulthood
.7	Problems of and services to young people
.8	Problems of and services to other groups
.9	Historical, geographic, persons treatment
363	Other social problems and services
.1	Public safety programs
.2	Police services
.3	Other aspects of public safety
.4	Controversies related to public morals and customs
.5	Housing
.6	Public utilities and related services
.7	Environmental problems
.8	Food supply
.9	Population problems
364	Criminology
.01–.09	Standard subdivisions and special topics
.1	Criminal offenses
.2	Causes of crime and delinquency
.3	Offenders
.4	Prevention of crime and delinquency
.6	Penology
.8	Discharged offenders
.9	Historical, geographic, persons treatment of crime and its alleviation
365	Penal and related institutions
.3	Kinds of penal institutions
.4	Institutions for specific classes of inmates
.5	Prison plant
.6	Inmates
.7	Reform of penal institutions
.9	Historical, geographic, persons treatment
366	Associations
.001–.009	Standard subdivisions
.01–.09	Standard subdivisions of esoteric associations and societies
.1	Freemasonry
.2	Knights of Pythias
.3	Independent Order of Odd Fellows
.5	Benevolent and Protective Order of Elks
367	General clubs
.9	Historical, geographic, persons treatment

368	**Insurance**
.001–.009	**Standard subdivisions**
.01–.09	**[General principles, specific forms of risk, sales groupings]**
.1	**Insurance against damage to and loss of property**
.2	**Insurance against damage to and loss of property in transit (Marine insurance, Transportation insurance)**
.3	**Old-age insurance and insurance against death, illness, injury**
.4	**Government-sponsored insurance**
.5	**Liability insurance**
.6	**Glass insurance**
.7	**Insurance against industrial casualties (accidents)**
.8	**Other casualty insurance**
.9	**Insurance by specific continents, countries, localities in modern world**
369	**Miscellaneous kinds of associations**
.1	**Hereditary, military, patriotic societies of United States**
.2	**Hereditary, military, patriotic societies**
.3	**Racial and ethnic clubs**
.4	**Young people's societies**
.5	**Service clubs**

> ## 361–365 Social problems and services

Class here work and policy of government agencies that enforce the law in matters of social problems and services

Class law of social services, including draft laws, enforcement of the law by courts, in 341–346; class the internal administration of governmental agencies dealing with social services, including their administrative annual reports, in 353.5; class insurance in 368; class comprehensive works in 361

> *For social services in armed forces, see 355–359; for school social services, see 371.7; for social services in specific wars, see 900*

> *See Manual at 361–365; also at 301–307 vs. 361–365; also at 361–365 vs. 353.5*

361 Social problems and social welfare in general

Social welfare: social assistance, either free or paid for in part or in full by recipients, to enable individuals to cope with situations usually beyond their individual capacities to overcome

Class here comprehensive works on socioeconomic planning and development, on programs and services encompassing several branches of social sciences, on social problems and services

Class description of present or past social conditions in 930–990

> *For social problems considered purely as social phenomena, see 301–307; for community planning and development, see 307; for economic planning and development, see 338.9; for specific problems and services, see 362–365*

> *See Manual at 361 vs. 362*

SUMMARY

361.001–.008	**Standard subdivisions**
.02–.06	**Specific kinds of assistance**
.1	**Social problems**
.2	**Social action**
.3	**Social work**
.4	**Group work**
.6	**Government action**
.7	**Private action**
.8	**Community action**
.9	**Historical, geographic, persons treatment**

.001–.008   Standard subdivisions

[.009]   Historical, geographic, persons treatment

Do not use; class in 361.9

> 361.02–361.06 Specific kinds of assistance

Class here general discussions covering various problems and client groups, and both governmental and private assistance

Class comprehensive works in 361. Class assistance with respect to a specific problem with the problem, e.g., free assistance to persons in late adulthood 362.6

For governmental assistance, see 361.6; for private assistance, see 361.7

.02   Free assistance

Class specific kinds of free assistance in 361.05–361.06

.04   Paid assistance

Assistance for which the recipient pays all or part of cost

Class specific kinds of paid assistance in 361.05–361.06

.05   Material assistance

Including direct provision of food, clothing, shelter; financial aid; institutional care; recreational activities and facilities; relief

.06   Counseling [*formerly* 361.323], guidance, related services

Standard subdivisions are added for counseling, guidance, related services together; for counseling alone; for guidance alone

Services directed toward enabling individuals and groups to assist themselves

Including citizens advice bureaus; telephone counseling, e.g., hot lines

Class social work in 361.3

.1   **Social problems**

> History, description, appraisal of areas and kinds of social breakdown, of problems endemic to human society
>
> Including risk assessment
>
>> *For specific problems, see 362–363*
>>
>> *See Manual at 301–307 vs. 361.1, 362.042*

.2   **Social action**

> Class change as a social phenomenon in 303.4
>
>> *For a specific aspect of social action not provided for here, see the aspect in 361.3–361.8, e.g., social work 361.3*

.23   Dissent and protest

> Standard subdivisions are added for either or both topics in heading

.24   Reform movements

.25   Action within established social framework

> Class here planning, policy, programs, proposals; citizen participation; comprehensive works on governmental and private action
>
>> *For international action, see 361.26; for social work, see 361.3; for governmental action, see 361.6; for private action, see 361.7; for combined governmental and private community action, see 361.8*

.26   International action

> Class public international action in 361.6; class private international action in 361.77
>
>> *See Manual at 361.6 vs. 361.7, 361.8*

.3   **Social work**   •

.32   Practice of social work

> Class here casework
>
>> *For counseling, see 361.06; for group work, see 361.4*

.322   Interviewing

[.323]   Counseling

> Relocated to 361.06

.37   Volunteer social work

>> *For a specific aspect of volunteer social work, see the aspect, e.g., interviewing 361.322*

.4   **Group work**

> Class counseling in group work in 361.06

.6   **Governmental action**

Class here intergovernmental assistance and planning, governmental international action, interdisciplinary works on government-sponsored socioeconomic planning and development

Class combined public and private action in 361.25; class public social work in 361.3; class combined public and private community action in 361.8

> *For management of public agencies regulating social welfare services, see 353.5*

> *See Manual at 361.6 vs. 361.7, 361.8*

.61   Social policy

Class welfare reform in 361.68

.612   Goals, values, priorities

.613   Relation of politics and social action

Class effect of social action on political structures and values in 320

.614   Relation of welfare and human rights

Including use of compulsory remedial action

Class interdisciplinary works on human rights in 323

> *See Manual at 361.614 vs. 330*

.615   Relation of government and private sectors

Class welfare state in 361.65

.65   Welfare state

Class economics of welfare state in 330.126

.68   Welfare reform

.7   **Private action**

Class combined governmental and private action in 361.25; class private social work in 361.3; class relation of government and private sectors in 361.615; class combined governmental and private community action in 361.8

> *See Manual at 361.6 vs. 361.7, 361.8*

.706   Organizations and management

Do not use for a specific kind of organization; class in 361.75–361.77 with the kind, e.g., nonprofit organizations 361.763

.706 81   Organization and financial management

Class here fund raising

.74	Individual philanthropy

Class an organization that controls the use of the money donated by a philanthropist with the organization, e.g., Rockefeller Foundation 361.7632

.75	Religious organizations
.76	Private organizations

Class religious organizations in 361.75; class private international organizations in 361.77

.763	Nonprofit organizations

Including CARE

.763 2	Charitable foundations and trusts
.763 4	Red cross national societies

Class here affiliated societies, e.g., Red Crescent

Class comprehensive works on the Red Cross in 361.77

.765	Business organizations

Class ways that management can deal with charitable donations in 658.153; class programs of employers for employees in 658.38

.766	Labor unions
.77	Private international organizations

Organizations whose membership is international

Including International Red Cross, comprehensive works on Red Cross and affiliated societies such as Red Crescent

For Red Cross and affiliated societies of a specific nation, see 361.7634

See also 361.76 for local organizations providing services worldwide

.8	**Community action**

Coordination of governmental and private action to promote the welfare of individuals in the community

Including community chests, united givers funds

Class community development in 307.14; class governmental community action in 361.6; class private community action in 361.7

See Manual at 361.6 vs. 361.7, 361.8

.9	**Historical, geographic, persons treatment**

Add to base number 361.9 notation 01–9 from Table 2, e.g., welfare work in Arizona 361.9791

Class historical, geographic, persons treatment of specific kinds of social action in 361.2–361.8

> ## 362–363   Specific social problems and services

Except for modifications shown under specific entries, add to each subdivision identified by * as follows:

01	Philosophy and theory
02	Miscellany
[0218]	Standards
	Do not use; class in 62
[0289]	Safety measures
	Do not use; class in 363.1
03–05	Standard subdivisions
06	Organizations and management
0681	Organization and financial management
	Including managerial cost control
	Class social measures to hold down costs in 5
07	Education, research, related topics
08	History and description with respect to kinds of persons
	See also 3 for persons close to those with a problem
09	Historical, geographic, persons treatment
>1–4	Characteristics of problem
	Class comprehensive works in 362–363, without adding from this table
1	Social causes
	Class here sources
2	Incidence, extent, severity
	Standard subdivisions are added for any or all topics in heading
	Including risk assessment
3	Effects on persons close to those with a problem
	Including effects on co-workers, on neighbors
	Class here families
	Class aftereffects on persons close to those with a problem in 4; class family problems in 362.82
4	Aftereffects on persons with a problem
	Effects that occur either after the problem has ceased or when the person is no longer close to those with the problem
	Class here adult children of persons with the problem
	Class a specific aftereffect with the aftereffect, e.g., social aspects of alcoholism in victims of child abuse 362.292, medical aspects of depression in adult victims of child abuse 616.8527
5	Social action
	Class here social measures to hold down costs
	Add to 5 the numbers following 361 in 361.2–361.8, e.g., international action 526, social work 53, rationing 56
	Class governmental administration of rationing programs in 352.86; class comprehensive works on social action in 361.2
	For specific forms of action, see 6–8

(continued)

>   **362–363 Specific social problems and services (continued)**

>6–8	Specific forms of action
	Class comprehensive works in 5
	Works containing topics from any two of these subdivisions are classed in 5
6	Control
	Elimination and reduction of hazards, of sources and causes of difficulty
	Class measures to protect against and to limit effects of problems in 7
62	Standards
63	Monitoring, surveillance, reporting
	Standard subdivisions are added for any or all topics in heading
64	Inspection and testing
	Standard subdivisions are added for either or both topics in heading
65	Investigation of specific incidents
66	Certification
7	Measures to prevent, protect against, limit effects of problems
	Class here preparedness
	Class measures that both control and prevent problems in 6
	For safety measures, see 363.1
72	Protective measures
	Including design of environments, warning and guidance systems
8	Remedial measures, services, forms of assistance
	Measures applicable primarily to individuals, even if in large groups
	Class here material assistance
	Class remedial measures directed toward altering a social function, e.g., cost control, in 5; class social work in 53; class comprehensive works on material assistance in 361.05
809	Historical, geographic, persons treatment
	Class here the area receiving assistance, e.g., relief to Italy provided by the United States 809450973
	Class the area providing assistance in 8, without adding from Table 1, e.g., relief provided by the United States to many countries 8, not 80973
81	Rescue operations
82	Financial assistance
	Class social insurance in 368.4
83	Provision of food, shelter, household assistance, clothing, other related necessities; recreation

(continued)

> ## 362–363 Specific social problems and services (continued)

84	Employment services
	Including vocational rehabilitation, sheltered employment
85	Residential care
	Care within institutions existing for the purpose
86	Counseling and guidance
	Standard subdivisions are added for either or both topics in heading
	Including legal aid
	Class comprehensive works on counseling and guidance in 361.06

Class discrimination in 305; class comprehensive works in 361

For criminology, see 364

See Manual at 362–363; also at 362–363 vs. 364.1

362   Social welfare problems and services

Class here social security

Unless other instructions are given, observe the following table of preference, e.g., mentally ill veterans 362.208697 (*not* 362.860874):

Physical illness	362.1
Mental and emotional illnesses and disturbances	362.2
Mental retardation	362.3
Problems of and services to people with physical disabilities	362.4
Victims of oppression	362.87
Victims of crimes	362.88
Veterans	362.86
Problems of and services to persons in late adulthood	362.6
Problems of and services to young people	362.7
Laboring classes	362.85
Women	362.83
Members of racial, ethnic, national groups	362.84
Problems of and services to the poor	362.5
Families	362.82
Historical, geographic, persons treatment	362.9

To indicate the relation of a specific kind of problem to a specific kind of person, add notation 08 from Table 1 to the number for the problem, e.g., narcotic addiction among young adults 362.293084

For social security as a form of social insurance, see 368.4

See Manual at 361 vs. 362; also at 362–363 vs. 364.1; also at 362 vs. 368.4

SUMMARY

.04   Special topics

.042   Social problems

> *See Manual at 301–307 vs. 361.1, 362.042*

.042 2   Incidence, extent, severity

> Including social effects

.042 3   Social causes

.042 4   Prevention

.042 5   Social action

> Including remedial measures
>
> Class prevention in 362.0424

[.08]   Social welfare problems and services with respect to kinds of persons

> Do not use; class in 362.1–362.8

[.09]   Historical, geographic, persons treatment

> Do not use; class in 362.9

> **362.1–362.4 Problems of and services to persons with illnesses and disabilities**

Class incidence of and public measures to prevent physical diseases in 614.4–614.5; class comprehensive works in 362.1

See Manual at 362.1–362.4 vs. 610; also at 614.4–614.5 vs. 362.1–362.4

.1   **Physical illness**

Class here interdisciplinary works on illness and disability, on medical care and treatment, on medical missions, on public health

For religious aspects of medical missions, see 266; for sociology of medicine, of health, of illness, see 306.461; for mental and emotional illness, see 362.2; for mental retardation, see 362.3; for problems of and services to persons with a specific physical disability regardless of cause, see 362.4; for technology of medicine, see 610

SUMMARY

.102 3   Services to persons with physical illnesses; as a profession, occupation, hobby

Class here interdisciplinary works on health occupations peripheral to the medical and paramedical professions

Class works covering both the medical and peripheral occupations in 610

For a specific peripheral profession, see the profession, e.g., medical social workers 362.10425, hospital secretaries 651.3741

.104   Special topics

.104 2   Social aspects

Class preventive measures in 614.44–614.48

See Manual at 362.1042 vs. 368.382

.104 22   Social effects

Class incidence in 614.42

.104 25   Forms of assistance

Including medical social work

Class accident and health insurance in 368.38; class government-sponsored accident and health insurance in 368.42

.104 252   Financial assistance

.104 256   Counseling and guidance

Standard subdivisions are added for either or both topics in heading

.104 257   Rural health services

.104 258   Managed care plans

Including health maintenance organizations (HMOs)

.106 8   Management

Class here peer reviews

Class the result of a peer reviews with the result, e.g., the result of the evaluation of New York City hospitals 362.11097471

.108   Services to specific kinds of persons with physical illnesses

Do not use for services rendered by groups of persons to persons with physical illnesses; class in 362.1

Class physical illness among groups of persons in 616.008

.108 3   Services to young people

Do not use for services to infants and children up to puberty; class in 362.19892

.108 4   Services to persons in specific stages of adulthood

[.108 46]   Services to persons in late adulthood

Do not use; class in 362.19897

.109   Historical, geographic, persons treatment

[.109 173 4]   Rural regions

Do not use; class in 362.104257

> 362.11–362.19 Medical services

Free and paid

Class medical treatment in 616; class comprehensive works in 362.1

> 362.11–362.16 Services of specific kinds of institutions

Class services of health maintenance organizations in 362.104258; class specific kinds of services provided by a specific institution in 362.17; class services by a specific institution to patients with specific conditions in 362.19; class comprehensive works in 362.1

.11   Hospitals and related institutions

Standard subdivisions are added for hospitals and related institutions together, for hospitals alone

For clinics and related institutions, see 362.12; for extended care facilities, see 362.16

.12   Clinics and related institutions

Standard subdivisions are added for clinics and related institutions together, for clinics alone

Including dispensaries, health centers, outpatient departments of general hospitals

Class here ambulatory services, community health services

.14 Professional home care

Including visiting nurses' services, services of health visitors

See also 649.8 for home care by family members

.16 Extended care facilities

Institutions rendering medical care for patients requiring long-term or convalescent care

Including convalescent homes, sanatoriums for persons suffering from chronic diseases

Class here extended care facilities for persons in late adulthood, life care communities, nursing and rest homes

[.160 846] Services of extended care facilities for persons in late adulthood

Do not use; class in 362.16

.17 Specific services

Unless other instructions are given, class a subject with aspects in two or more subdivisions of 362.17 in the number coming last, e.g., diagnostic services by doctors 362.177 (*not* 362.172)

Class forms of assistance in 362.10425; class specific kinds of services to patients with specific conditions in 362.19; class technology of the services in 610; class group practice in 610.65

For emergency services, see 362.18; for preventive services, see 614.44

See Manual at 610 vs. 362.17

.172 Services of physicians

Including referral and consulting services

.173 Services of nurses

Class visiting nurses' services in 362.14

.173 068 Management of services of nurses

Class here nonmedical aspects of ward management

.174 Intensive care

.175 Terminal care

.175 6 Hospices

.176 Nutritional services

Class here feeding of sick, comprehensive works on the provision of special diets for various classes of persons with illnesses

Class nutritional programs for the population at large in 363.8

For nutritional services applied to malnutrition disorders, see 362.19639

.177	Diagnostic and screening services
	Including radiology services
.178	Therapeutic services
.178 2	Pharmaceutical services
	Class nutritional services in 362.176
.178 3	Organ and tissue banks
	Standard subdivisions are added for either or both topics in heading
	Including eye banks
	For blood and blood plasma banks, see 362.1784
.178 4	Blood and blood plasma banks
	Standard subdivisions are added for either or both topics in heading
.178 6	Rehabilitation services
.18	Emergency services
	Including trauma centers
.188	Ambulance services
.19	Services to patients with specific conditions
	Class here living with a physical disease
	Class incidence of and public measures to prevent specific diseases in 614.5
	See also 362.10425 for indigent patients, 362.175 for terminal patients
[.190 1–.190 9]	Standard subdivisions
	Do not use; class in 362.101–362.109
.196–.198	Specific conditions

Add to base number 362.19 the numbers following 61 in 616–618 for the condition only, e.g., patients with diabetes 362.196462, dental care 362.1976, maternity hospitals 362.1982; then add further as follows (*not* as instructed under 616.1–616.9, 617, or 618.1–618.8); however, for 362.19892 pediatric care, add 0 before adding further, e.g., periodicals on pediatric care 362.198920005:

    001–009   Standard subdivisions

                Notation from Table 1 as modified under 616.1–616.9, e.g., biography of a person with diabetes 362.1964620092, periodicals on dental care 362.1976005

    02–08   Specific services

                Add to base number 0 the numbers following 362.17 in 362.172–362.178, e.g., intensive care 04

For services to persons with mental illnesses, see 362.2

.2 **Mental and emotional illnesses and disturbances**

Standard subdivisions are added for any or all topics in heading

Class here mental disabilities that consist of mental retardation combined with mental illness

Class life with a psychiatric disorder in 616.890092

For mental retardation, see 362.3

SUMMARY

362.204	**Special topics**
.21	**Mental health facilities**
.22	**Community mental health services**
.23	**Extended care facilities**
.24	**Professional home care**
.25	**Neuroses**
.26	**Psychoses**
.27	**Disorders of personality, intellect, impulse control**
.28	**Suicide**
.29	**Substance abuse**

.204 Special topics

.204 2 Social aspects

.204 22 Incidence, extent, severity

Including social effects

.204 25 Prevention and forms of assistance

Class here psychiatric social work

.204 251 Emergency and rescue operations

Standard subdivisions are added for either or both topics in heading

Class here hot lines

.204 252 Financial assistance

.204 256 Counseling and guidance

Standard subdivisions are added for either or both topics in heading

---

> **362.21–362.24 Medical services**

Class care for specific problems in 362.25–362.29; class medical treatment in 616.8; class comprehensive works in 362.2

.21   **Mental health facilities**

Class here psychiatric hospitals

For psychiatric clinics, see 362.22; for nursing homes and sanatoriums, see 362.23

.22   **Community mental health services**

Class here psychiatric clinics

.223   **Group homes**

.23   **Extended care facilities**

Class here nursing homes, sanatoriums

.24   **Professional home care**

\>   **362.25–362.29   Specific problems**

Class comprehensive works in 362.2

.25   **Neuroses**

Including anorexia nervosa, compulsive gambling, depression

.26   **Psychoses**

Including schizophrenia

.27   **Disorders of personality, intellect, impulse control**

Including food addiction, kleptomania

For suicide, see 362.28; for substance abuse, see 362.29

.28   ***Suicide**

Class here suicidal behavior

.288 1   **Rescue operations**

Number built according to instructions under 362–363

Class here emergency services, hot lines

*Add as instructed under 362–363

.29   Substance abuse

Class here drug abuse; interdisciplinary works on substance abuse, addiction, habituation, intoxication

Class work on "drug abuse" in the sense of only narcotic abuse in 362.293

For subculture of substance abusers, see 306.1; for drug traffic, see 363.45; for illegal sale, possession, use of drugs, see 364.177; for drug use as a custom, see 394.1; for medical aspects of substance abuse, see 616.86

See also 362.27 for food addiction

See Manual at 616.86 vs. 158.1, 248.8629, 291.442, 362.29

.291   Aspects of substance abuse

Class aspects of a specific substance in 362.292–362.299

[.291 01–.291 09]   Standard subdivisions

Do not use; class in 362.2901–362.2909

.291 1–.291 8   Specific aspects of substance abuse

Add to base number 362.291 notation 1–8 from table under 362–363, e.g., prevention of substance abuse 362.2917; however, for control of drug traffic, see 363.45

Notation 1–8 from table under 362–363 is added for both specific aspects of two or more of the substances provided for in 362.292–362.298 and for a combination of substances provided for in 362.292–362.298 and in 362.299, e.g., counseling for alcohol and cocaine abuse, for narcotics and stimulant abuse 362.29186

.292   *Alcohol

Class here interdisciplinary works on alcoholism

For a specific aspect of alcoholism, see the aspect, e.g., medical aspects 616.861

[.292 6]   Control of sale of alcoholic beverages

Do not use; class in 363.41

.292 8   Remedial measures, services, forms of assistance

Number built according to instructions under 362–363

.292 86   Counseling and guidance

Number built according to instructions under 362–363

Class here services of Alcoholics Anonymous

.293   *Narcotics

Opium and its derivatives and synthetic equivalents

Class here specific narcotics, e.g, heroin, morphine

*Add as instructed under 362–363

.294   *Hallucinogens and psychedelics

       Class here specific hallucinogens and psychedelics, e.g., LSD, mescaline, PCP

       Subdivisions are added for either or both topics in heading

       Class cannabis in 362.295

.295   *Cannabis

       Class here specific kinds of cannabis, e.g., hashish, marijuana

.296   *Tobacco

.298   *Cocaine

       Class here specific forms of cocaine, e.g., crack

.299   Other substances

       Including analgesics, depressants, inhalants, sedatives, stimulants

       Class here designer drugs (synthetic drugs of abuse), prescription drugs

       Class alcohol in 362.292; class cocaine in 362.298

       For designer hallucinogens, see 362.294

.299 1   Aspects of more than one substance

[.299 101–.299 109] Standard subdivisions

       Do not use; class in 362.29901–362.29909

.299 11–.299 18 Specific aspects of more than one substance

       Other than alcohol, cannabis, cocaine, hallucinogens, narcotics, psychedelics, tobacco

       Add to base number 362.2991 notation 1–8 from table under 362–363, e.g., prevention of abuse of uppers and downers 362.29917

.3 *Mental retardation

       Class comprehensive works on problems of and services to persons with developmental disabilities (those who have neurological diseases combined with mental retardation and whose problems exhibit themselves before age 18) in 362.1968; class comprehensive works on treatment of mental retardation and mental illness in 362.2

.4 Problems of and services to people with physical disabilities

       Regardless of cause

       Class here comprehensive works on problems of and services to people with disabilities, to people with mental and physical disabilities

       Class comprehensive medical works in 617

       For problems of and services to people with mental disabilities, see 362.3

*Add as instructed under 362–363

.404   Special topics

Add to base number 362.404 notation 1–8 from table under 362–363, e.g., social work with people with physical disabilities 362.40453

.41   *Persons with blindness and visual impairments

Class here blind-deaf persons   (Guide dogs.)

Subdivisions are added for either or both topics in heading

For deaf persons, see 362.42

.42   *Persons with hearing impairments

Class here deaf persons

Class comprehensive works on persons with linguistic and communication disabilities in 362.196855; class blind-deaf persons in 362.41

See also 371.912 for teaching of the deaf

.43   *Persons with mobility impairments

Subdivisions are added for services to persons with specific mobility impairments, e.g., residential care for paraplegics 362.4385

.5   ***Problems of and services to the poor**

Class here services to homeless people

Class economic causes and effects of poverty in 339.46

.57   Measures to prevent, protect against, limit effects of poverty

Number built according to instructions under 362–363

Class economic measures to prevent poverty in 339; class eugenic measures in 363.92

.58   Remedial measures, services, forms of assistance

Number built according to instructions under 362–363

Including interdisciplinary works on legal aid [*formerly* 347.017]

Class birth control as a remedy for poverty in 363.96; class assistance to the poor under social security in 368.4

For law of legal aid, see 347.017; for food stamp programs, see 363.882

.582   Financial assistance

Number built according to instructions under 362–363

Including guaranteed minimum income, negative income tax

Class here supplementary social security for low income people

Class aid to families with dependent children (AFDC) in 362.713

*Add as instructed under 362–363

.583   Provision of clothing, other related necessities; recreation

> Number built according to instructions under 362–363
>
> Do not use for housing; class in 363.5. Do not use for food programs; class in 363.8

.6   Problems of and services to persons in late adulthood

> Including elder abuse
>
> Class here social gerontology
>
> Class parent abuse in 362.8292; class elder abuse as a crime in 364.1555. Class elder abuse in a specific situation with the situation, e.g., elder abuse in nursing homes 362.16

.61   Residential (Institutional) care

> Class here services of homes, institutions providing complete care
>
> Class institutions providing residential care to medical patients in 362.16; class housing in 363.5946

.63   Direct relief

> Including provision of financial aid, food, shelter, household assistance, clothing, recreation
>
> *For residential care, see 362.61; for employment services, see 362.64*

.64   Employment services

> Including sheltered employment, vocational rehabilitation

.66   Counseling and guidance

> Standard subdivisions are added for either or both topics in heading

.7   Problems of and services to young people

> Through age seventeen
>
> Class here children

.708 3   Young people twelve to seventeen [*formerly also* 362.796]

> Do not use for children; class in 362.7
>
> Class here young men and women twelve to seventeen
>
> Comprehensive works on young men and women discontinued; class in 362
>
> Class young people eighteen and over in 362
>
> *See Manual at 362.7083*

[.708 35]   Young people twelve to seventeen

> Do not use; class in 362.7083

.708 69	Persons with special social status
.708 691	Persons with status defined by changes in residence
	Including immigrants [*formerly also* 362.799]
.708 692	Antisocial and asocial persons
[.708 692 3]	Juvenile delinquents and predelinquents
	Do not use for predelinquents; class in 362.74. Do not use for juvenile delinquents; class in 364.36
.708 694	Socially disadvantaged persons
.708 694 5	Children born out of wedlock
	Do not use for abandoned children, orphans; class in 362.73. Do not use for abused children; class in 362.76
.708 9	Racial, ethnic, national groups [*formerly* 362.797]
	Including young people twelve to seventeen [*formerly* 362.796]
.709	Historical, geographic, persons treatment
.709 173 2	Urban youth [*formerly also* 362.799]
.709 173 4	Rural youth [*formerly also* 362.799]

> 362.71–362.73 Specific kinds of services to young people

Class services to maladjusted young people in 362.74; class services to abused and neglected children in 362.76; class comprehensive works in 362.7

.71	Direct relief
	Including recreational services
.712	Day care services
.713	Aid to families with dependent children (AFDC)
.73	Institutional and related services
	Class here abandoned children, orphans
.732	Institutional care
	Including children's homes, orphanages; houseparents
.733	Foster home care
	Class here comprehensive works on foster home care and adoption
	For adoption, see 362.734

.734 Adoption

Including confidentiality of adoption records

Class comprehensive works on the activities of adopted persons seeking their natural parents in 362.8298

> 362.74–362.76 Specific kinds of young people

Class comprehensive works in 362.7

For abandoned children, orphans, see 362.73

.74 *Maladjusted young people

Including predelinquents, runaways

Class here specific services to maladjusted young people, halfway houses for young people who have not committed any crimes

Class young people with mental and emotional illnesses in 362.2083; class families with missing children in 362.8297; class halfway houses for the transition from reform school to society in 365.42

For juvenile delinquents, see 364.36

.76 *Abused and neglected children

Subdivisions are added for either or both topics in heading

Class child abuse as a crime in 364.15554

[.79] Classes of young people

Number discontinued; class in 362.7

[.796] Young people twelve to seventeen

Comprehensive works on young people twelve to seventeen relocated to 362.7083; young people twelve to seventeen of racial, ethnic, national groups relocated to 362.7089

[.797] Young people of racial, ethnic, national groups

Relocated to 362.7089

[.799] Immigrants, urban and rural youth

Immigrants relocated to 362.708691, urban youth relocated to 362.7091732, rural youth relocated to 362.7091734

.8 **Problems of and services to other groups**

.82 *Families

Class here parents

Class family welfare when synonymous with general welfare in 362

---

*Add as instructed under 362–363

.828	Remedial measures, services, forms of assistance

Number built according to instructions under 362–363

Class services and forms of assistance for specific problems in 362.829; class family planning programs in 363.96

.828 2	Financial assistance

Number built according to instructions under 362–363

Class aid to families with dependent children (AFDC) in 362.713

.828 3	Provision of food, shelter, household assistance, clothing, other related necessities; recreation

Number built according to instructions under 362–363

Including visiting housekeepers

Class day care in 362.712

.828 6	Counseling and guidance

Number built according to instructions under 362–363

Including premarital and marriage counseling

.829	Specific problems

Class a problem not provided for here with the the problem, plus notation 3 from the table under 362–363, e.g., alcoholism within the family setting 362.2923

.829 2	*Abuse within the family

Class here parent, spouse abuse

Class abused children in 362.76; class abuse as a crime in 364.1555

.829 4	*Single-parent family

Class here divorce

.829 5	*Parents in prison

.829 7	*Missing children

Class here parental kidnapping

Class runaway children in 362.74

.829 8	*Relationship between adoptees and their biological parents

Class adoption in 362.734. Class a specific aspect of children seeking their biological parents with the aspect, e.g., confidentiality of adoption records 362.734, genealogical searching 929.1

.83	*Women

Class wife abuse in 362.8292; class rape in 362.883

---

*Add as instructed under 362–363

.839	Specific classes of women
.839 2	*Unmarried mothers
.84	Members of racial, ethnic, national groups
.840 01–.840 09	Standard subdivisions
.840 3–.849 9	Specific racial, ethnic, national groups

Add to base number 362.84 notation 03–99 from Table 5, e.g., social services to Italians in United States 362.8451073

Class a social problem of a specific racial, ethnic, or national group in a place where the group predominates with the problem, plus notation 093–099 from Table 1, e.g., poor Italians in Rome 362.50945632; class comprehensive works on the social problems of a specific racial, ethnic, or national group in a place where the group predominates with the place in 362.9, e.g., social problems of Italians in Italy 362.945

.85	*Laboring classes

Including migrant workers

.86	*Veterans

Class here veterans' rights and benefits

.868 2	Financial assistance

Number built according to instructions under 362–363

Veterans' education benefits relocated to 371.223; veterans' higher education benefits relocated to 378.32

Class veterans' pensions in 331.25291355

.87	*Victims of oppression

Class here refugees

.88	Victims of crimes

Including crime prevention for the individual

Class here victimology

Class services to abused family members in 362.8292; class crime prevention for society as a whole in 364.4

For works on why persons become victims of specific crimes, see 364.1

.880 83	Young people

Class services to abused and neglected children in 362.76

.883	Rape

Including rape prevention for individuals

*Add as instructed under 362–363

.9 **Historical, geographic, persons treatment**

Add to base number 362.9 notation 01–9 from Table 2, e.g., social welfare in France 362.944

Class historical, geographic, persons treatment of specific social problems in 362.1–362.8

363 Other social problems and services

Standard subdivisions are added for comprehensive treatment of environmental and safety problems of society, e.g., assuring a safe and secure environment for Japan 363.0952

Class here public works

For communication facilities, see 384; for transportation facilities, see 388

See Manual at 363; also at 362–363 vs. 364.1; also at 363 vs. 340, 353–354

SUMMARY

363.1	**Public safety programs**
.2	**Police services**
.3	**Other aspects of public safety**
.4	**Controversies related to public morals and customs**
.5	**Housing**
.6	**Public utilities and related services**
.7	**Environmental problems**
.8	**Food supply**
.9	**Population problems**

.1 **Public safety programs**

Class here safety measures, interdisciplinary works on safety

Unless other instructions are given, observe the following table of preference, e.g., use of hazardous materials in health care facilities 363.17 (*not* 363.15):

Hazardous materials	363.17
Hazards in sports and recreation	363.14
Transportation hazards	363.12
Hazardous machinery	363.18
Product hazards	363.19
Domestic hazards	363.13
Hazards in health care facilities	363.15
Occupational and industrial hazards	363.11

Class managerial response to safety requirements, comprehensive works on safety management in 658.408. Class safety management in a specific industry with the industry, plus notation 0684 from Table 1, e.g., safety management in petroleum industry 665.50684

For police services, see 363.2; for aspects of public safety not provided for here, see 363.3. For a specific kind of remedial measure other than rescue operations, see the measure, e.g., medical care for the injured 362.1; for safety technology of a specific subject, see the subject, plus notation 0289 from Table 1, e.g., safety technology in hydraulic engineering 627.0289

See Manual at 363.1; also at 333.7–333.9 vs. 363.1, 363.73, 577

SUMMARY

363.100 1–.108		**[Standard subdivisions and general topics of public safety programs]**
	.11	**Occupational and industrial hazards**
	.12	**Transportation hazards**
	.13	**Domestic hazards**
	.14	**Hazards in sports and recreation**
	.15	**Hazards in health care facilities**
	.17	**Hazardous materials**
	.18	**Hazardous machinery**
	.19	**Product hazards**

.100 1–.105   Standard subdivisions and general topics of public safety programs

Add to base number 363.10 notation 01–5 from table under 362–363, e.g., public action to promote safety 363.1056

.106   Public control of safety

.106 2   Standards

.106 3   Monitoring, surveillance, reporting

Standard subdivisions are added for any or all topics in heading

.106 4   Inspection and testing

Standard subdivisions are added for either or both topics in heading

.106 5   Investigation of specific incidents

Class here interdisciplinary works on safety investigation

> *For a technical or engineering aspect of the investigation, see the aspect in 600, e.g., safety engineering 620.86, wreckage studies of automobile accidents 629.2826; for accounts of a specific incident that affected general social life and history, see the incident in 900, e.g., San Francisco earthquake of 1906 979.461051*
>
> *See Manual at 363.1065 vs. 620.86*

.106 6   Certification

.107–.108   Measures to prevent, protect against, limit effects of problems; remedial measures, services, forms of assistance

Add to base number 363.10 notation 7–8 from table under 362–363, e.g., alarm and warning systems 363.1072, counseling 363.1086

.11   *Occupational and industrial hazards

Subdivisions are added for either or both topics in heading

> *See Manual at 363.11 vs. 613.62*

.119   Occupational and industrial hazards in specific industries and occupations

[.119 000 1–.119 000 9]   Standard subdivisions

Do not use; class in 363.1101–363.1109

.119 001–.119 999   Subdivisions for specific industries and occupations

Add to base number 363.119 notation 001–999, e.g., school safety programs 363.119371 [*formerly* 371.77], hazards in coal mining 363.119622334; however, for hazards to transportation workers, see 363.12; for hazards to domestic workers, see 363.13; for hazards to professional athletes, see 363.14; for hazards to workers in health care facilities, see 363.15

.12   Transportation hazards

Class here accidents, fires resulting from accidents

Class comprehensive works on fires in transportation facilities in 363.379

> *See Manual at 900: Historic events vs. nonhistoric events*

.120 01–.120 8   Standard subdivisions and general topics

Add to base number 363.120 notation 01–8 from table under 362–363, e.g., accident prevention 363.1207

.122   *Rail transportation

---

*Add as instructed under 362–363

.123   *Water transportation

Class here water safety

Class safety in water sports in 363.14

.124   *Air and space transportation

Subdivisions are added for either or both topics in heading

.124 1   Causes of air and space accidents

Number built according to instructions under 362–363

.124 12   Natural factors

Including birds, clear-air turbulence (CAT)

.124 14   Operator failures

.124 16   Vehicle failures

.124 18   Failures of traffic control

Class traffic control as a preventive measure in 363.12472

.124 6   Control of air and space transportation

Number built according to instructions under 362–363

.124 65   Investigation of specific air and space accidents

Number built according to instructions under 362–363

Class here general investigations of aircraft accidents

Class wreckage studies in 629.13255

.124 9   Specific types of accidents and accidents in specific types of services

.124 92   Specific types of accidents

Including midair collisions, takeoff accidents

.124 93   Accidents in specific types of services

Including air-taxi services, helicopter services

Class specific types of accidents in specific types of services in 363.12492

.125   *Highway and urban vehicular transportation

Subdivisions are added for either or both topics in heading

.125 1   Causes of accidents

Number built according to instructions under 362–363

Including operator failures and disabilities, vehicle failures, highway and street conditions, weather conditions

See also 364.147 for causes as traffic offenses

*Add as instructed under 362–363

.125 14	Use of drugs
	Class here drunk driving
.125 6	Control of highway and urban vehicular transportation
	Number built according to instructions under 362–363
	Class traffic control by the police in 363.2332
.125 65	Investigation of specific vehicular and highway accidents
	Number built according to instructions under 362–363
	Class here general investigations of automobile accidents
	Class wreckage studies in 629.2826
.125 7	Measures to prevent, protect against, limit effects of problems
	Number built according to instructions under 362–363
	Including school traffic safety programs [*formerly* 371.7752]
.125 9	Hazards in use of specific types of vehicles other than automobiles
	Including bicycles, motorcycles, trucks
.13	*Domestic hazards
.14	*Hazards in sports and recreation
	Subdivisions are added for either or both topics in heading
.147	Measures to prevent, protect against, limit effects of problems
	Number built according to instructions under 362–363
	Including school athletic safety programs [*formerly* 371.7754]
.15	*Hazards in health care facilities
.17	*Hazardous materials
	Manufacture, transportation, use

Class here interdisciplinary works on hazardous materials, works on the control of such materials in their ordinary commercial setting (manufacture, sale, commercial and industrial use, disposal)

For hazardous materials as components of articles that become hazardous products, see 363.19; for hazardous materials as impurities in the water supply, see 363.61; for hazardous wastes, see 363.728; for hazardous materials as environmental pollutants, see 363.738; for hazardous materials technology, see 604.7

See Manual at 363.17

.176	Control

Number built according to instructions under 362–363

See Manual at 363.176 vs. 604.7

*Add as instructed under 362–363

.176 3	Monitoring, surveillance, reporting

> Number built according to instructions under 362–363

> Class here studies on the applicability of both social and technical findings of environmental chemistry and additive toxicology to the monitoring of hazardous materials

.179	Specific hazardous materials

> Including corrosive materials

.179 1	Toxic chemicals

> Including asbestos, lead

> Class toxic agricultural chemicals in 363.1792

.179 2	*Agricultural chemicals

> Class here pesticides

.179 8	Explosives, fuels, related products

> Class here safety considerations with respect to especially flammable materials, control of explosives as ordinary hazardous materials

> Class control of use of explosives by potentially reckless or malign users in 363.33

>> *See also 363.19 for products (e.g., sweaters, mattresses) that might constitute unsuspected fire hazards, 363.377 for measures to control accumulation of ordinary combustible materials*

.179 9	*Radioactive materials

> Class here nuclear accidents

.18	*Hazardous machinery
.189	Specific kinds of hazardous machinery

> Including electrical and x-ray equipment

.19	Product hazards

> Adulteration, contamination, safety, adequacy, effectiveness of products offered for human consumption and use

> Including household appliances, medical instruments and supplies, textiles, toys

> Class here hazards due to containers and applicators that accompany products

.192	*Foods
.192 9	Specific foods

> Including beverages, canned goods, dairy products, meats

*Add as instructed under 362–363

.194	*Drugs and medicines

Subdivisions are added for either or both topics in heading

.196	*Cosmetics

.2   **Police services**

Class police services in control of factors affecting public morals in 363.4. Class a social service function of police with the function in 362, e.g., counseling of rape victims 362.883; class police committing a crime with the crime in 364.1, e.g., police violation of civil rights 364.1322

.206 8	Management [*formerly* 351.74]
.22	Personnel

Duties, functions, activities

Class specific duties, functions, activities in 363.23–363.25

>   363.23–363.25   Specific aspects of police services

Class specific aspects of services of special kinds of security and law enforcement agencies in 363.28; class comprehensive works in 363.2

.23	Police functions

Class here law enforcement, prevention of crime by police

For detection of crime, see 363.25; for control of violence and terrorism, see 363.32

See Manual at 363 vs. 340, 353–354: Law enforcement

.232	Patrol and surveillance

Including pursuit and apprehension of lawbreakers, use of deadly force, undercover work

For highway patrol, see 363.2332

.233	Enforcement of civil laws

Including enforcement of building codes, licensing laws and ordinances, sanitation laws

.233 2	Traffic control

Including highway patrol

Class general investigations of traffic accidents in 363.12565; class investigation of traffic offenses in 363.25; class wreckage studies in 629.2826; class comprehensive works on traffic control in 363.1256

.233 6	Location of missing persons

*Add as instructed under 362–363

.24   Auxiliary services

Including communications services, fingerprint and photograph files, police records

.25   Detection of crime (Criminal investigation)

Class here forensic science (criminalistics); evidence, circumstantial evidence

Class general investigations of transportation accidents in 363.12065

For forensic medicine, see 614.1

See also 364.1 for criminal offenses

> 363.252–363.258 Specific techniques and kinds of evidence

Class comprehensive works in 363.25; class comprehensive works on detection of a specific kind of crime in 363.259. Class detection of a specific crime with the crime in 364.1, e.g., detection of a murder in New York City 364.1523097471

> 363.252–363.256 Procurement and analysis of evidence

Class evidence used in identification of criminals not listed here in 363.258; class comprehensive works in 363.25

.252   Procurement of evidence

Including electronic surveillance, search and seizure, use of informers and secret agents

For interrogation of witnesses, see 363.254

.254   Interrogation of witnesses

Including use of polygraph (lie detector)

.256   Analysis of evidence

Class here laboratories

Class files resulting from criminal investigations in 363.24

.256 2   Physical evidence

Including analysis of blood and hair, use of ballistics

.256 5   Documentary evidence

Including analysis of handwriting and typewriting

.258   Identification of criminals

> Including artists' sketches, fingerprints, lineups, photographs, voice prints

> Class files resulting from criminal investigations in 363.24

.259   Detection of specific types of offenses

> Add to base number 363.259 the numbers following 364.1 in 364.13–364.18, e.g., investigation of murder 363.259523

> Class specific techniques of investigation of specific types of offenses in 363.252–363.258. Class detection of a specific crime with the crime in 364.1, e.g., detection of a murder in New York City 364.1523097471

.28   Services of special kinds of security and law enforcement agencies

> Including park police

> Class agencies to carry out specific police functions in 363.23; class agencies to investigate specific kinds of crime in 363.259

> *For narcotics agents, see 363.45; for postal inspectors, see 383.46*

.282   Marshals and sheriffs

> Standard subdivisions are added for either or both topics in heading

.283   Secret police

.285   Border patrols

.286   Coast guards and harbor patrols

> Standard subdivisions are added for coast guards and harbor patrols together, for coast guards alone

> Class here interdisciplinary works on coast guards

> *For coast guards as a military service, see 359.97*

.287   Transportation security services

> *For automobile traffic control, see 363.2332; for harbor patrols, see 363.286*

> *See also 363.379 for transportation fire hazards*

.287 2   River security services

.287 4   Railway security services

.287 6   Air transportation security services

> Including airport police, sky marshals

.289   Private detective and police services

> Standard subdivisions are added for either or both topics in heading

> Including bodyguards, campus police, store detectives

.3   **Other aspects of public safety**

> *See Manual at 363.1*

.31   Censorship

Class here control of information, press control; censorship as routine governmental function; interdisciplinary works on censorship

> *For a specific aspect of censorship not provided for here, see the aspect, e.g., censorship as social control 303.376, legal aspects of censorship 344.0531*
>
> *See Manual at 363.31 vs. 303.376, 791.4*

.32   Control of violence and terrorism

Standard subdivisions are added for either or both topics in heading

Including crowd and riot control

.33   Control of explosives and firearms

Class here control of use by potentially reckless or malign users, interdisciplinary works on gun control

Class control of explosives as ordinary hazardous materials in 363.1798

> *For gun control as a civil rights issue, see 323.43*

.34   *Disasters

> *See Manual at 900: Historic events vs. nonhistoric events*

.348   Remedial measures, services, forms of assistance

Number built according to instructions under 362–363

Class here disaster relief

Class raising funds for mounting and carrying out disaster relief in 363.34570681. Class disaster relief for a specific type of disasters with the type, plus notation 8 from table under 362–363, e.g., disaster relief for flood victims 363.34938

> *For a specific kind of remedial measure other than those applied immediately at the time and site of the disaster, see the measure, e.g., medical care for the injured 362.1; for a specific form of disaster relief not provided for here, see the form of relief, e.g., long-range planning to replace housing lost due to a volcanic eruption 363.58*

*Add as instructed under 362–363

.348 1	Rescue operations

Number built according to instructions under 362–363

Forms of assistance applied immediately at time and site of disaster

Class here salvage operations; comprehensive works on rescue and salvage operations for disasters in general

Class rescue and salvage operations for a specific type of disaster with the type, plus notation 81 from table under 362–363, e.g., rescue operations for flood victims 363.349381

.349	Specific kinds of disasters

For epidemics and pandemics, see 362.1; for fires, see 363.37. For a disaster resulting from one of the hazards listed in 363.1, see the hazard, e.g., shipwrecks 363.123, nuclear accidents 363.1799

.349 2	Disasters caused by weather conditions

Class here storms

For floods, see 363.3493

.349 21	Aspects of disasters caused by weather conditions

Class an aspect of disasters caused by a specific weather condition in 363.34922–363.34929

[.349 210 1–.349 210 9]	Standard subdivisions

Do not use; class in 363.349201–363.349209

.349 211–.349 218	Specific aspects of disasters caused by weather conditions

Add to base number 363.34921 notation 1–8 from table under 362–363, e.g., rescue operations during storms 363.3492181

.349 22–.349 25	Specific kinds of storms

Add to base number 363.3492 the numbers following 551.55 in 551.552–551.555, e.g., hurricanes 363.34922; then add further as instructed under 363–363, e.g., rescue operations during hurricanes 363.3492281

Class dust storms in 363.34929

.349 29	*Droughts

Including dust storms

.349 3	*Floods
.349 36	Control

Number built according to instructions under 362–363

Class technology of flood control in 627.4

*Add as instructed under 362–363

.349 5	*Earthquakes and volcanoes

Subdivisions are added for earthquakes and volcanoes together, for earthquakes alone

.349 7	Disasters induced by human activity

Including civil disorders, explosions, riots

For transportation accidents, see 363.12; for nuclear accidents, see 363.1799; for war, see 363.3498

.349 8	*War

For civil defense, see 363.35

See also 303.66 for sociology of war

[.349 87]	Measures to prevent, protect against, limit effects of war

Do not use; class in 327.17

.349 88	Remedial measures, services, forms of assistance

Number built according to instructions under 362–363

Class here war relief

Class problems of war refugees when not treated directly in the context of war relief in 362.87. Class war relief during a specific war with the war, e.g., relief work of Switzerland during World War II 940.54778494

.35	Civil defense

Measures to defend civilian populations against war

Class comprehensive works on civil defense and emergency preparedness in 363.347

.37	*Fire hazards

Class fire fighting and fire safety technology in 628.92

.377	Measures to prevent, protect against, limit effects of problems

Number built according to instructions under 362–363

Class here fire prevention, measures to control accumulation of ordinary combustible materials

Class safety considerations with respect to especially flammable materials in 363.1798; class safety of products (e.g., sweaters, mattresses) that might constitute unsuspected fire hazards in 363.19

.378	Remedial measures, services, forms of assistance

Number built according to instructions under 362–363

Class here fire fighting

*Add as instructed under 362–363

.379	**Fire hazards in specific situations**

Including fire safety programs in schools [*formerly* 371.774]; fire hazards in high-rise buildings, schools, transportation; forest fires

For fires resulting from transportation accidents, see 363.12

.4 Controversies related to public morals and customs

Treated as social problems

Class censorship and control of information in 363.31. Class a controversy treated other than as a social issue with the aspect of the controversy, e.g., ethics of gambling 175 (*not* 363.42)

.41 Sale of alcoholic beverages

Class problems of and services to alcoholics in 362.292; class sale of alcoholic beverages as an offense against revenue in 364.133; class public drunkenness as an offense in 364.173

.42 Gambling

Class compulsive gambling in 362.25; class gambling as a crime in 364.172

.44 Prostitution

Class prostitution as a crime in 364.1534

.45 Drug traffic

Class here narcotics agents

Class problems of and services to drug addicts in 362.29; class illegal sale, possession, use of drugs in 364.177

See also 363.41 for sale of alcoholic beverages

.46 Abortion

Class abortion as a crime in 364.185

.47 Obscenity and pornography

Class obscenity and pornography as crimes in 364.174

.48 Premarital and extramarital relations

Class premarital and extramarital relations as crimes in 364.153

For prostitution, see 363.44

.49 Homosexuality

Class interdisciplinary works in 306.766

.5   *Housing

Class here housing as a social problem, interdisciplinary works on housing

For a specific aspect of housing, see the aspect, e.g., sociological aspects 307.336, economic aspects 333.338, provision of temporary housing (shelter) 361.05

See Manual at 363.5, 363.6, 363.8 vs. 338; 363.5 vs. 307.336, 307.34; also at 363.5 vs. 643.1

[.508]   Housing of specific kinds of persons

Do not use; class in 363.59

.51   Social causes

Number built according to instructions under 362–363

Including discrimination in housing

Class here housing conditions

Class housing allocation to relieve discrimination in 363.55

[.52]   Incidence, extent, severity of housing problems

Do not use; class in 363.51

.55   Social action

Number built according to instructions under 362–363

Class here housing allocation to relieve discrimination

.58   Programs and services

Do not use subdivisions of 8 from the table under 362–363

.582   Financial assistance

Class here housing allowances, rental subsidies, subsidized housing

.583   Programs and services for specific objectives

Including home ownership, payment of energy bills, rehabilitation, resettlement, urban homesteading, weatherization

.585   Public operated housing

Class here council housing

*Add as instructed under 362–363

.59   Housing of specific classes of people

Add to base number 363.59 the numbers following —08 in notation 081–089 from Table 1, e.g., housing for persons in late adulthood 363.5946; however, for extended medical care for older adults, see 362.16; for comprehensive works on homelessness, see 362.5; for institutional care for healthy older adults, see 362.61

Class specific aspects of housing the poor, of low-income housing in 363.51–363.58

.6   Public utilities and related services

Standard subdivisions are added for public utilities and related services together, for public utilities alone

Class here problems of allocation among end users, measures to assure abundance of immediately available supplies and services

For communication, see 384; for transportation, see 388

See Manual at 333.7 vs. 363.6; also at 363.5, 363.6, 363.8 vs. 338

.61   Water supply

Class here comprehensive works on water supply, on water-related public works, e.g., a study covering waterworks, treatment plants, canals, flood control, hydroelectric generation

For a specific topic of water supply, see the topic, e.g., flood control 363.34936

See Manual at 363.61

.63   Gas

.68   Park and recreation services

Class here services maintained or proposed after land has been designated for parks, establishment and operation of recreational centers primarily serving the general public

Class park policy and park development in 333.783; class recreational centers in 790.068. Class a specific cultural institution maintained by park and recreation services with the institution, e.g., museums 069, theaters 792

.69   Historic preservation

Including identification and designation of historic buildings and areas

Class here public policies to protect and restore historic buildings and areas and to promote appreciation of them

Class technology of building restoration and preservation in 721.0288

See Manual at 913–919: Historic sites and buildings; also at 930–990: Historic preservation

.7   **Environmental problems**

Class here environmental protection; impact of wastes, of pollution, of actions to control waste and pollution

Class interdisciplinary works on the environment in 333.7

See Manual at 333.714; also at 333.72 vs. 304.28, 363.7

SUMMARY

363.700 1–.707		**Standard subdivisions and general topics**
	.72	**Sanitation**
	.73	**Pollution**
	.74	**Noise**
	.75	**Disposal of the dead**
	.78	**Pest control**

.700 1–.707   Standard subdivisions and general topics

Add to base number 363.70 notation 01–7 from table under 362–363, e.g., international action to protect the environment 363.70526

.72   *Sanitation

.728   Wastes

Do not use for other remedial measures, services, forms of assistance; class in 362.72

Class here industrial, municipal wastes; waste disposal, management

Unless other instructions are given, class a subject with aspects in two or more subdivisions of 363.728 in the number coming last, e.g., recycling scrap metal 363.7288 (*not* 363.7282)

Class dangerous wastes still in hands of processors or users in 363.17; class pollution by waste disposal in 363.73; class dangerous wastes which have escaped both safety and sanitary controls in 363.738

.728 2   Recycling

.728 4   *Liquid wastes

Including combined sewage, sewage sludge, urban water runoff; dredging spoil, water reuse planning

Class here wastewater management

See Manual at 363.61

.728 5   *Solid wastes

.728 7   *Hazardous wastes

.728 8   Specific kinds of wastes

Including agricultural wastes, beverage containers, garbage, household wastes, medical wastes, scrap metal

For radioactive wastes, see 363.7289

*Add as instructed under 362–363

.728 9	*Radioactive wastes
.729	Sanitation in specific environments
.729 1	Streets
.729 2	Recreational areas
	Including swimming pools
.729 3	Common carriers
.729 4	Public toilets
.729 5	Workplaces
.729 6	Food service establishments
.729 7	Health facilities
	Including ambulances
.729 8	Residential buildings
	Other than private family dwellings
.729 9	Barbershops, beauty shops, laundries
.73	*Pollution

Class works that discuss waste and sanitation problems as well as pollution in 363.7; class sanitation in 363.72; class noise in 363.74; class management responsibilities and measures with respect to protection and preservation of the environment in 658.408

See Manual at 333.7–333.9 vs. 363.1, 363.73, 577; also at 363.73 vs. 571.95, 577.27

.731	Social causes

Number built according to instructions under 362–363

Including industrial pollution

Class specific pollutants from specific sources in 363.738

.732	Incidence, extent, severity

Number built according to instructions under 362–363

Class incidence, extent, severity of pollution from specific sources in 363.731

.735	Social action

Number built according to instructions under 362–363

Class here remedial measures

*Add as instructed under 362–363

.737   Measures to prevent, protect against, limit effects of pollution

       Number built according to instructions under 362–363

       Class waste disposal as a method of pollution prevention in 363.728; class technology of pollution prevention in 628.5

.738   Pollutants

       Do not use for remedial measures; class in 363.735

       Class here chemical pollutants

.738 2   *Oil

.738 4   Toxic chemicals

       Including lead emissions, pesticides

.738 6   *Acid rain

.738 7   Fumes, gases, smoke

       Class lead emissions in 363.7384

.738 74   *Greenhouse gases

       Gases contributing to greenhouse effect (global warming)

       Class here interdisciplinary works on greenhouse effect (global warming)

       For a specific aspect of greenhouse effect (global warming) not provided for here, see the aspect, e.g., changes in earth's temperature 551.5253, effect on ecology 577.276

.738 75   *Gases contributing to ozone layer depletion

       Class here interdisciplinary works on ozone layer depletion

       For a specific aspect of ozone layer depletion not provided for here, see the aspect, e.g., chemical changes in earth's ozone layer 551.5142, effect on ecology 577.276

.739   Pollution of specific environments

       Class specific pollutants in specific environments in 363.738

.739 2   *Air pollution

.739 4   *Water pollution

       Class here comprehensive works on water pollution

       For assurance of clean water supply, see 363.61

       See Manual at 363.61

.739 6   *Soil pollution

.74   *Noise

---

*Add as instructed under 362–363

.741   Sources of noise

Number built according to instructions under 362–363

Including forms of transportation, e.g., aircraft, automobile traffic; construction equipment, industry

Class effects of specific sources of noise in 363.742

.742   Incidence, extent, severity

Number built according to instructions under 362–363

Class incidence, extent, severity of noise from specific sources in 363.741

.75   Disposal of the dead

Class here interdisciplinary works on social aspects and services, customs, technology

Class interdisciplinary works on death in 306.9

For death customs, see 393; for technology of disposal of the dead, see 614.6

.78   Pest control

Including dog pounds, rat and mosquito abatement programs, removal of animal carcasses

Class here interdisciplinary works on pest control

For control of disease-carrying pests, see 614.43; for comprehensive works on the technology of pest control, see 628.96; for control of agricultural pests, see 632.9; for control of household pests, see 648.7

.8   *Food supply

Class here famine, hunger; interdisciplinary works on food supply, on nutrition

Class food stamp programs in 363.882; class food relief in 363.883

For economics of food supply, see 338.19; for problems of malnutrition, see 362.19639; for prevention of malnutrition, see 614.5939

See Manual at 363.5, 363.6, 363.8 vs. 338; also at 363.8 vs. 338.19; also at 363.8 vs. 613.2, 641.3

.82   Incidence, extent, severity of food supply problems

Number built according to instructions under 363–363

See Manual at 363.82 vs. 614.5939

.85   Social control

Number built according to instructions under 362–363

*Add as instructed under 362–363

.856   Governmental action

Number built according to instructions under 362–363

Class here food rationing

.9   **Population problems**

Class here interdisciplinary works on population problems

Class interdisciplinary works on population in 304.6

For a specific manifestation of a population problem, see the manifestation, e.g., population growth as a cause of poverty 362.51, pressure on food supply leading to famine 363.8

See Manual at 301–307 vs. 361–365; also at 363.9 vs. 304.66

.91   Population quantity

Overpopulation and underpopulation

Class remedial measures for overpopulation in 363.96

.92   Population quality

Including eugenic measures to control population [*formerly* 363.98]

Class here interdisciplinary works on eugenics

For eugenic measures to reduce crime, see 364.4. For a specific aspect of eugenics, see the aspect, e.g., civil rights 323.4; for application of eugenics to a specific social problem, see the problem, plus notation 6 from table under 362–363, e.g., eugenic measures to reduce mental retardation 362.36

See also 613.94 for family planning techniques

.96   Birth control

Class here remedial measures for overpopulation; interdisciplinary works on birth control, on family planning programs

Class abortion in 363.46

For sterilization, see 363.97; for family planning techniques, see 613.94

.97   Sterilization

Including eugenic and involuntary sterilization

Class here voluntary sterilization

[.98]   Eugenic measures to control population

Relocated to 363.92

364 Criminology

Crime and its alleviation

Class here comprehensive works on criminology and criminal law, on criminal justice that includes criminology, police services, and criminal law

Unless other instructions are given, observe the following table of preference, e.g., punishment of specific types of offenders 364.6 (*not* 364.3):

Penology	364.6
Discharged offenders	364.8
Offenders	364.3
Prevention of crime and delinquency	364.4
Causes of crime and delinquency	364.2
Criminal offenses	364.1
Historical, geographic, persons treatment of crime and its alleviation	364.9

Class social services to victims of crimes and crime prevention for the individual in 362.88

For criminal law, see 345; for police services, see 363.2

SUMMARY

364.01–.09	**Standard subdivisions and special topics**
.1	**Criminal offenses**
.2	**Causes of crime and delinquency**
.3	**Offenders**
.4	**Prevention of crime and delinquency**
.6	**Penology**
.8	**Discharged offenders**
.9	**Historical, geographic, persons treatment of crime and its alleviation**

.019   Psychological principles

For criminal psychology of specific offenses, see 364.1; for criminal psychology of offenders in general, see 364.3

.04   Special topics

.042   Extent and incidence of crime

Criminal offenses and offenders

Class criminal offenses in 364.1; class offenders in 364.3

.08   History and description with respect to kinds of persons

Class works on why persons become victims of specific crimes in 364.1

[.086 923]   Juvenile delinquents and predelinquents

Do not use for predelinquents; class in 362.74. Do not use for juvenile delinquents; class in 364.36

[.086 927]	Offenders

> Do not use for offenders; class in 364.3. Do not use for convicts; class in 365.6

.086 949	Victims of war

> Do not use for victims of crimes; class in 362.88

.09 Historical, geographic, persons treatment of criminology as a discipline

> Do not use for historical, geographic, persons treatment of crime and its alleviation; class in 364.9

.1 **Criminal offenses**

> Class here conspiracy to and incitement to commit an offense, individuals identified with a specific offense or type of offense, investigation of specific crimes, crimes without victims, terrorism as a crime

> Class sociology of terrorism in 303.625; class investigation of specific types of offenses in 363.259; class crime as an event in history in 900

> *See Manual at 362–363 vs. 364.1; also at 900: Historic events vs. nonhistoric events*

SUMMARY

364.101–.109	**Standard subdivisions and organized crime**
.13	**Political and related offenses**
.14	**Offenses against public health, safety, order**
.15	**Offenses against persons**
.16	**Offenses against property**
.17	**Offenses against public morals**
.18	**Other offenses**

.106	Organized crime

> Do not use for organizations dealing with criminal offenses; class in 364.06

> Class here Mafia

[.106 092]	Persons treatment

> Do not use for organized crime figures not associated with a specific offense; class in 364.1092. Do not use for organized crime figures associated with a specific offense; class with the offense, e.g., a hired killer 364.1523092

.106 6	Gangsterism

> Engagement of organized groups in piracy, robbery, theft, hijacking

.106 7	Racketeering

> Engagement of organized groups in extortion from legitimate or illegitimate enterprises through intimidation and force

> Including union racketeering

.106 8	Syndicated crime

Engagement of organized groups in furnishing illegal goods or services

.109 2	Persons treatment

Criminals are classed with the crime for which they are most noted unless they are discussed with relationship to a specific crime, e.g., a general biography of Jesse James, a bank robber, is classed in 364.1552092, but a study of Jesse James' killings is classed in 364.1523092

Class comprehensive works on offenders in 364.3

.13	Political and related offenses
.131	Political offenses

Including espionage, rebellion, seditious libel, subversion, treason

Class genocide in 364.151; class assassination of heads of state and government in 364.1524; class sabotage in 364.164

For war crimes, see 364.138

.132	Offenses against proper government

For offenses against administration of justice, see 364.134

.132 2	Denial and violation of civil rights

Standard subdivisions are added for either or both topics in heading

.132 3	Corruption

Including bribery of officials, graft

.132 4	Electoral offenses

Including bribery of voters, fraudulent reporting of votes, illegal voting, violations of campaign finance laws

.133	Offenses against revenue

Including bootlegging, counterfeiting, illicit distilling, smuggling, tax evasion

See also 363.41 for sale of alcoholic beverages

.134	Offenses against administration of justice

Including collusion, contempt of court, lynching, perjury, subornation of perjury

.135	International offenses

For a specific international offense, see the offense, e.g., piracy 364.164

.136	Offenses against postal laws

.138	War crimes

> *For a specific war crime, see the crime, e.g., genocide 364.151*
>
> *See also 341.69 for war crime trials*

.14   Offenses against public health, safety, order

[.140 01–.140 09]   Standard subdivisions

> Relocated to 364.1401–364.1409

.140 1–.140 9   Standard subdivisions [*formerly* 364.14001–364.14009]

.142   Offenses against public health and safety

> Including adulteration of food and drugs, violations of product and building safety laws

.143   Offenses against public order

> Including carrying concealed weapons, disorderly conduct, rioting, unlawful assembly

.147   Traffic offenses and misuse of communications facilities

> Class offenses against postal laws in 364.136

.148   Vagrancy

.15   Offenses against persons

.151   Genocide

.152   Homicide

> *For lynching, see 364.134; for genocide, see 364.151*

.152 2   Suicide

> Class assisted suicide in 364.1523

.152 3   Murder

> Including assisted suicide
>
> *For assassination, see 364.1524*

.152 4   Assassination

.152 5   Manslaughter

.153   Sex offenses

> Including adultery, indecent exposure, seduction, statutory rape
>
> Class rape in 364.1532; class bigamy in 364.183

.153 2   Rape

> Class social services aspects of rape in 362.883
>
> *See also 364.153 for statutory rape*

.153 4	Prostitution
	See also 363.44 for prostitution as a public morals issue
.153 6	Sexual deviations
	Including incest, sodomy
.154	Abduction, kidnapping, taking and holding of hostages
	Class parental kidnapping in 362.8297
.155	Other violent offenses against persons
.155 2	Robbery
	Thefts including threat of violence or bodily harm, or actual occurrence of violence
	Class here comprehensive works on hijacking
	For a specific type of hijacking, see the type, e.g., taking hostages 364.154
.155 5	Assault and battery
	Standard subdivisions are added for either or both topics in heading
	Including elder abuse
	Class elder abuse as a social problem in 362.6
.155 53	Spouse abuse
	Class social services to battered wives, spouse abuse as a social problem in 362.8292
.155 54	Child abuse
	Class here child neglect
	Class child abuse as a social problem in 362.76
	See also 364.1536 for incest, 364.174 for pornography
.156	Offenses against reputation and honor
	Including defamation, invasion of privacy, libel, slander
	Class seditious libel in 364.131
.16	Offenses against property
.162	Larceny (Theft)
	Including burglary, embezzlement, fencing
	Class robbery in 364.1552; class fraud in 364.163

.163	Fraud

Including forgery, imposture, e.g., literary forgery; welfare fraud, e.g., Medicare fraud

Class mail fraud in 364.136

.164	Violent offenses against property

Including arson, piracy, sabotage, vandalism

Class robbery, comprehensive works on hijacking in 364.1552

.165	Extortion

Including blackmail

.168	Business, financial, professional offenses

Including criminal usury, unfair trade practices; violation of antitrust laws, of laws with respect to securities and their exchange

Class here computer, white collar crime

For embezzlement, see 364.162; for fraud, see 364.163. For a specific type of computer crime not provided for here, see the type, e.g., tax evasion 364.133

.17	Offenses against public morals

For sex offenses, see 364.153

.172	Gambling

See also 363.42 for gambling as a public morals question

.173	Public drunkenness

See also 363.41 for sale of alcoholic beverages

.174	Obscenity and pornography

See also 363.47 for obscenity and pornography as a public morals question

.177	Illegal sale, possession, use of drugs

Standard subdivisions are added for any or all topics in heading

See also 363.45 for drug traffic

.18	Other offenses

Including illegal adoption

.183	Bigamy
.185	Criminal abortion

Class abortion as a public morals question in 363.46

.187	Cruelty to animals
.188	Offenses against religion

      Offenses defined and penalized by the state

      Including blasphemy, heresy, sacrilege

      Class offenses against church law in 262.9

.2   **Causes of crime and delinquency**

      Class here criminal anthropology

      Class victimology in 362.88

.22   Influence of physical environment

      Including climate, seasons, weather

.24   Influence of personal factors

      Including biological factors, e.g., effects of heredity, genetic defects, physical typology; psychological factors

.25   Influence of social factors

      Including leisure and recreation

.253   Influence of family and peer group

.254   Influence of mass media

      Including books, motion pictures, radio, television

.256   Influence of social conflict

      Including class, race, religion, socioeconomic conditions

.3   **Offenders**

      Including recidivists

      Class here criminal psychology

      Class a specific aspect of the justice system for specific types of offenders with the aspect, e.g., determination of sentences for juvenile offenders 364.650835, offenders as prisoners in 365.6

      For individuals chiefly identified with a specific offense or type of offense, see 364.1

[.308 1]   Men

      Do not use; class in 364.373

[.308 2]   Women

      Do not use; class in 364.374

[.308 3]   Young people

      Do not use; class in 364.36

.308 6   Persons by miscellaneous social characteristics

[.308 692 3]   Juvenile delinquents and predelinquents

                            Do not use; class in 364.36

[.308 692 7]   Offenders

                            Do not use; class in 364.3

[.308 74]   Persons with mental illnesses and disabilities

                            Do not use; class in 364.38

[.308 9]   Racial, ethnic, national groups

                            Do not use; class in 364.34

.34   **Members of specific racial, ethnic, national groups**

Add to base number 364.34 notation 03–9 from Table 5, e.g., Germans as offenders 364.3431

Class juvenile delinquents of specific racial, ethnic, national groups in 364.36; class women in 364.374; class offenders with mental illnesses and disabilities in 364.38

.36   **Juvenile delinquents**

Including status offenders (juveniles who have broken laws pertaining only to their age group, e.g., curfew laws, drinking below legal age)

Class here comprehensive works on juvenile delinquency, juvenile delinquents, juvenile justice system

Class comprehensive works on maladjusted young people in 362.74

For legal aspects, see 345

.37   **Adult offenders**

Class adult offenders with mental illnesses and disabilities in 364.38

.373   **Men**

Works specifically emphasizing male sex

.374   **Women**

.38   **Offenders with mental illnesses and disabilities**

Class here offenders with mental retardation

Class juvenile offenders with mental illnesses and disabilities in 364.36

.4	**Prevention of crime and delinquency**

Including curfew, eugenic measures

Class here what society does to prevent crime

Class penalties as a deterrent in 364.601

> For law enforcement, see 363.23. For a specific aspect of prevention by a potential victim, see the aspect, e.g., crime prevention for the individual 362.88, household security 643.16, business intelligence and security 658.47

.404	Special topics
.404 5	Social action

> Add to base number 364.4045 the numbers following 361 in 361.2–361.8, e.g., social policy 364.404561

.41	Identification of potential offenders

Including genetic screening

.43	Citizen participation

Class individual action in 362.88

.44	Welfare services

Including financial assistance; foster home care; recreational services, e.g., camps, playgrounds

Class preventive police work in 363.23

> For counseling and guidance, see 364.48

.48	Counseling and guidance

Standard subdivisions are added for either or both topics in heading

.49	Environmental design
.6	**Penology**

Class here welfare services to offenders, reform of penal system

Class welfare services to prisoners in 365.66; class reform of penal institutions in 365.7

> For discharged offenders, see 364.8; for institutions for correction of offenders, see 365

.601	Philosophy and theory

Class here punishment as retribution, deterrent, protection to society, reformation of offenders

.62   Parole and indeterminate sentence

> Standard subdivisions are added for parole and indeterminate sentence together, for parole alone

> Class services to prisoners to prepare them for parole in 365.66

.63   Probation and suspended sentence

> Standard subdivisions are added for probation and suspended sentence together, for probation alone

> Including reprieve

> Class here comprehensive works on probation and parole

> > *For parole, see 364.62*

.65   Determination of sentence

> Including amnesty, commutation of sentence, pardon

> Class a specific punishment with the punishment, e.g., probation 364.63, imprisonment 365

.66   Capital punishment

.67   Corporal punishment

.68   Noninstitutional penalties

> Including community service, deportation, fines, loss of citizenship, loss of vote

> > *For capital punishment, see 364.66; for corporal punishment, see 364.67*

.8   **Discharged offenders**

.9   **Historical, geographic, persons treatment of crime and its alleviation**

> Add to base number 364.9 notation 01–9 from Table 2, e.g., persons associated with crime and its alleviation 364.92; however, for victims, see 362.88; for police, see 363.2; for criminologists, see 364.092; for offenders associated with specific kinds of crime, see 364.1; for comprehensive works on offenders, see 364.3; for penologists, see 364.6

365   Penal and related institutions

Institutions for correction of offenders and for incarceration of other groups considered socially undesirable

Standard subdivisions are added for penal and related institutions together, for penal institutions alone

Class here imprisonment and detention

Unless other instructions are given, class a subject with aspects in two or more subdivisions of 365 in the number coming last, e.g., maximum security prisons for women 365.43 (*not* 365.33)

Class parole and indeterminate sentence in 364.62; class probation and suspended sentence in 364.63

[.068 2]   Plant management

                  Do not use; class in 365.5

[.09]   Historical, geographic, persons treatment

                  Do not use; class in 365.9

.3   Kinds of penal institutions

Class specific institutions in 365.93–365.99

.32   Institutions by level of government

         National, state or provincial, local

.33   Institutions by degree of security

         Maximum, medium, minimum

.34   Institutions by purpose or type of program

         Including jails, penal colonies, penitentiaries, prerelease guidance centers, prison farms, reformatories, work camps

         Class penal colonies as a part of history of a place with the place in 930–990, e.g., penal colony of Botany Bay as founding settlement of New South Wales 994.402

.4   Institutions for specific classes of inmates

Including debtors' prisons

Class here personal narratives of specific classes of inmates

Class specific institutions in 365.93–365.99; class comprehensive works on inmates in 365.6

.42   Institutions for juveniles

         Including borstals, reformatories; industrial, reform, training schools; halfway houses for the transition from reform school to society

.43	Institutions for adult women
.44	Institutions for adult men

Works specifically emphasizing inmates of the male sex

Class institutions in general, specific kinds of institutions for men in 365.3

.45   Institutions for political prisoners and related classes of persons

Standard subdivisions are added for either or both topics in heading

Class here concentration camps

For concentration camps associated with a specific war, see the war, e.g., World War II concentration camps 940.5317

.46   Institutions for the criminally insane

.48   Military prisons and prison camps

Institutions whose inmates are military personnel

Class institutions for prisoners of war in 355.1296; class military institutions for the insane in 365.46

.5   **Prison plant**

Buildings, equipment, grounds

Class prison architecture in 725.6

.6   **Inmates**

Handling and treatment

Including reception and classification

Class here offenders as inmates; community-based corrections; social aspects of prison life, e.g., conjugal rights, drug abuse

Class institutions for specific classes of inmates, personal narratives of inmates in 365.4

.602 1   Tabulated and related materials

Class statistics of inmates when used to indicate general statistics of offenders in 364.3021

.609 2   Persons

Class a personal narrative of a specific class of inmate with the class of inmate in 365.4, plus notation 092 from Table 1, e.g., a personal narrative of a political prisoner 365.45092

.64   Security, discipline, daily routine, release and discharge

Class here treatment of inmates

.641   Security

Including escapes, riots

.643	Discipline

Rules, rights, privileges

Including furloughs

Class work furloughs in 365.65

For punishments, see 365.644

.644	Punishments for infractions of prison discipline
.646	Daily routine

For labor, see 365.65; for services to prisoners, see 365.66

.647	Release and discharge

Class work release in 365.65; class services to prepare prisoners for release in 365.66

.65	Labor

Including chain gangs, contract system, lease system, work furloughs, work release

.66	Services to prisoners

Including counseling, education, group psychotherapy, health services, prerelease programs, recreational services, rehabilitation, religious services

Class prerelease institutions in 365.34

.7	**Reform of penal institutions**

Class reform of penal system, reform to eliminate prisons as form of punishment for certain types of crimes in 364.6

.9	**Historical, geographic, persons treatment**

Add to base number 365.9 notation 01–9 from Table 2, e.g., prison administrators 365.92; however, for inmates, see 365.6092

Class specific aspects of penal institutions in specific times and places, of specific kinds of institutions in 365.3–365.7

366 Associations

Organizations formed for fraternizing or for mutual assistance

For general clubs, see 367; for miscellaneous kinds of associations, see 369. For associations dealing with a specific subject, see the subject, plus notation 06 from Table 1, e.g., mathematical associations 510.6

See also 200 for religious associations, 368.363 for fraternal insurance

.001–.009	Standard subdivisions
.01–.09	Standard subdivisions of esoteric associations and societies

> **366.1–366.5   Esoteric (Secret and semisecret) associations and societies**

Class comprehensive works in 366

For orders of knighthood, see 929.71

.1   **Freemasonry**

.108 2   Women in Freemasonry [*formerly also* 366.18]

           For Order of the Eastern Star, see 366.18

.108 3   Young people

.108 351   Males twelve to twenty

             Including Order of DeMolay for Boys [*formerly also* 366.17]

.108 352   Females twelve to twenty

             Including International Order of Job's Daughters, International Order of the Rainbow for Girls [*both formerly also* 366.18]

.12   Rituals

.16   Nobles of the Mystic Shrine (Shriners)

[.17]   Order of DeMolay for Boys

         Relocated to 366.108351

.18   Order of the Eastern Star

         Women in Freemasonry relocated to 366.1082; International Order of Job's Daughters, International Order of the Rainbow for Girls relocated to 366.108352

.2   **Knights of Pythias**

.3   **Independent Order of Odd Fellows**

.308 2   Women

           For International Association of Rebekah Assemblies, see 366.38

.38   International Association of Rebekah Assemblies

.5   **Benevolent and Protective Order of Elks**

367   General clubs

Including social clubs, study clubs

Class here social clubs for specific types of people, e.g., social clubs for actors

Class clubs dealing with a specific subject with the subject, plus notation 06 from Table 1, e.g., pinochle clubs 795.41606

[.09]   Historical, geographic, persons treatment

                   Do not use; class in 367.9

.9   **Historical, geographic, persons treatment**

                   Add to base number 367.9 notation 01–99 from Table 2, e.g., The Lamb (social
                   club in New York City composed chiefly of actors, musicians, and playwrights)
                   367.97471

368   Insurance

                   Class here risk, insurance industry

                   Class risk management as part of management in 658.155

                   See also 658.153 for managerial decisions on choosing insurance

                   See Manual at 368 vs. 658.155 : Risk management

                           SUMMARY

368.001–.009	**Standard subdivisions**
.01–.09	**[General principles, specific forms of risk, sales groupings]**
.1	**Insurance against damage to and loss of property**
.2	**Insurance against damage to and loss of property in transit (Marine insurance, Transportation insurance)**
.3	**Old-age insurance and insurance against death, illness, injury**
.4	**Government-sponsored insurance**
.5	**Liability insurance**
.6	**Glass insurance**
.7	**Insurance against industrial casualties (accidents)**
.8	**Other casualty insurance**
.9	**Insurance by specific continents, countries, localities in modern world**

.001   Philosophy and theory

[.001 51]   Mathematical principles

                          Do not use; class in 368.01

.002–.005   Standard subdivisions

.006   Organizations and management

.006 5   Insurance companies

                       For-profit and nonprofit organizations

                       Class here interdisciplinary works on insurance companies

                       Add to base number 368.0065 notation 4–9 from Table 2, e.g.,
                       insurance companies of Texas 368.0065764

                       Class government agencies that provide insurance in 353.54

                          For credit and loan functions of insurance companies, see 332.38

.007–.008   Standard subdivisions

.009   Historical, geographic, persons treatment

[.009 4–.009 9]   Treatment by specific continents, countries, localities in modern world

Do not use; class in 368.9

.01   General principles

Class here actuarial science, finance, mathematical principles

Class investments by insurance companies in 332.67154

.011   Rates

Class here rate making

.012   Underwriting

Risk selection and estimation

.012 2   Reinsurance

.014   Claims

Including adjustment of claims, fraudulent claims, settlement of losses

Class fraudulent claims, insurance fraud as crimes in 364.163

.016   Lapse, persistence, termination

Standard subdivisions are added for any or all topics in heading

.019   Government policies with respect to insurance, insurance industry

---

>   368.06–368.08 Specific forms of risk

Class comprehensive works in 368

.06   Property risks

Risk of loss from impairment or destruction of property

Class risk of consequential loss in 368.08

.062   Risks to tangible property

.063   Risks to intangible property

.07   Personal risks

Risk of loss of income or augmented expenditure due to hazards to the person

.08   Other risks

Including liability risks, risk of consequential loss, risks due to the failure of others, statutory liability risks

.09   Conventional comprehensive sales groupings

Combinations of different lines of insurance, e.g., property-casualty, property-casualty-life and health

Class here all-risk, multiple-line coverage

Class a single line of insurance with the line, e.g., homeowner's liability insurance 368.56

.092   Motor vehicle insurance   Automobile insurance

For motor vehicle transportation insurance as a branch of inland marine insurance, see 368.232; for motor vehicle liability insurance, see 368.572

.093   Aviation insurance

For for air transportation insurance as a branch of inland marine insurance, see 368.24; for aviation liability insurance, see 368.576

.094   Business insurance [*formerly also* 368.81]

Broad property and liability coverage

Class here businessowners insurance, comprehensive business policies; commercial insurance, commercial multi-peril insurance; special multi-peril insurance (SMP)

For a single line of insurance, see the line, e.g., business liability insurance 368.81

.096   Multi-peril real property insurance

Coverage of perils associated with land and whatever is growing on or affixed to it

Class here homeowner's insurance

\> 　　　**368.1–368.8 Specific kinds of insurance**

Add to each subdivision identified by * as follows:
```
001–005      Standard subdivisions
006          Organizations and management
0065    .        Insurance companies
                 For-profit and nonprofit organizations
                 Add to 0065 notation 4–9 from Table 2, e.g., insurance
                 companies in Great Britain 006541
007–009      Standard subdivisions
01      General principles
                 Add to 01 the numbers following 368.01 in 368.011–368.019,
                 e.g., underwriting 012
```

Class comprehensive works in 368

.1 ***Insurance against damage to and loss of property**

Subdivisions are added for either or both topics in heading

Class multi-peril real property insurance in 368.096. Class property damage (liability) insurance as part of a specific type of liability insurance with the type, e.g., property damage insurance as part of public liability 368.56

For insurance against damage to and loss of property in transit, see 368.2; for casualty insurance, see 368.5–368.8

.11 *Fire insurance

For extended coverage endorsement, see 368.129

See also 368.12 for allied fire insurance lines

.12 *Allied fire insurance lines and extended coverage endorsement

Perils and losses traditionally associated with fire insurance

Including explosion, smoke damage, vandalism and malicious mischief (VMM) insurance

Class here commercial property insurance

Subdivisions are added for allied fire insurance lines and extended coverage endorsement together, for allied fire insurance lines alone

Class business interruption insurance in 368.815

See also 368.56 for livestock liability insurance

See Manual at 368.12

.121 *Crop insurance

Class here government-sponsored crop insurance

.122 *Disaster insurance

Including insurance against damage and loss from storms

For insurance for damage to crops from storms and other disasters, see 368.121

.122 2 *Flood insurance

.122 6 *Earthquake insurance

.125 *Civil commotion and riot insurance

Subdivisions are added for either or both topics in heading

.129 *Extended coverage endorsement

.14 *War risk insurance

Class ocean marine war risk insurance in 368.22; class war risk life insurance in 368.364

*Add as instructed under 368.1–368.8

.2 ***Insurance against damage to and loss of property in transit (Marine insurance, Transportation insurance)**

> Including postal and satellite insurance
>
> Class here insurance against damage to and loss of instrumentalities of transportation
>
> Class a combination of transportation property insurance and transportation liability insurance in 368.09

.22 ***Ocean marine insurance**

> Over-the-sea transportation insurance
>
> Including ocean marine war risk insurance

.23 ***Inland marine insurance**

> Land or over-the-land (including over inland waterways) transportation insurance
>
> *For air transportation insurance, see 368.24*

.232 ***Motor vehicle insurance**   Automobile insurance

> Class comprehensive works on all types of motor vehicle insurance in 368.092

.233 ***Railroad insurance**

.24 ***Air transportation insurance**

> Class comprehensive works on all types of air transportation and aviation insurance in 368.093

.3 ***Old-age insurance and insurance against death, illness, injury**

> Class here comprehensive works on private and government-sponsored old-age insurance and insurance against death, illness, injury; comprehensive works on group insurance, on industrial insurance, on old-age and survivors' insurance, on survivors' insurance
>
> Class personnel management of insurance as a fringe benefit in 658.3254; class comprehensive works on insurance as a fringe benefit in 331.255
>
> *For government-sponsored insurance, see 368.4. For a specific type of group insurance, of industrial insurance, of old-age and survivors' insurance, of survivors' insurance not provided for here, see the type, e.g., group credit insurance 368.87*

.32 ***Life insurance**

> *For special fields of life insurance, see 368.36*

.322 ***Endowment insurance**

.323 ***Term life insurance**

---

*Add as instructed under 368.1–368.8

.324	*Universal life insurance
.325	*Variable life insurance
.326	*Whole life insurance
.36	Special fields of life insurance
.362	*Industrial life insurance
.363	*Fraternal insurance
.364	*Life insurance for members of armed services

> Including National Service Life Insurance, veterans' life insurance, war risk life insurance

.366	*Burial insurance
.37	*Annuities

> Class pensions as an element of personnel administration in 658.3253; class comprehensive works on pensions in 331.252

.375	*Variable annuities
.38	*Health insurance, accident insurance, disability income insurance
.382	*Health insurance

> Including disability insurance; health maintenance organizations, preferred provider plans; long-term care insurance, Medigap (Medicare supplement insurance); reimbursement health insurance (insurance in which the insured first pays the bills)

> Class here insurance aspects of managed care, prepaid health insurance (insurance in which the insurer first pays the bills), specific health insurance organizations or plans without regard to type, comprehensive works on health and accident insurance

> Class interdisciplinary works on delivery of health care in 362.1

> *For accident insurance, see 368.384*

> *See also 368.386 for disability income insurance*

> *See Manual at 362.1042 vs. 368.382*

> 368.382 2–368.382 7 Basic health insurance coverage for specific kinds of services

> Class here policies limited to coverage for specific kinds of services, works that focus on specific types of benefits of broader policies

> Class catastrophic health insurance in 368.3828; class comprehensive works in 368.382

*Add as instructed under 368.1–368.8

.382 2	*Medical and surgical insurance
	Subdivisions are added for medical and surgical insurance together, for medical insurance alone
	Class major medical insurance in 368.3828
.382 3	*Dental insurance
.382 4	*Pharmaceutical services insurance
.382 5	*Mental health insurance
	Including coverage for treatment of substance abuse
.382 7	*Hospital insurance
	Class coverage for psychiatric hospitalization in 368.3825; class major medical insurance in 368.3828
.382 8	*Catastrophic health insurance (Major medical insurance)
	Insurance providing protection for potentially large health care expenses after basic health care insurance benefits have been exhausted
.384	*Accident insurance
.386	*Disability income insurance
	See also 368.382 for disability insurance

.4   *Government-sponsored insurance

Class here social insurance, social security as a form of social insurance

For a type of government-sponsored insurance not provided for here, see the type, e.g., crop insurance 368.121, bank deposit insurance 368.854

See Manual at 362 vs. 368.4

.400 68	Management
	Class personnel management of insurance for government employees in 352.67
.400 9	Historical, geographic, persons treatment
.400 973	Treatment in United States
	Do not use for social security in United States; class in 368.4300973
.401	General principles of government-sponsored insurance
	Number built according to instructions under 368.1–368.8
	See Manual at 336.249 vs. 368.401, 368.4011

*Add as instructed under 368.1–368.8

.401 1	Rates

Number built according to instructions under 368.1–368.8

See Manual at 336.249 vs. 368.401, 368.4011

.41	*Workers' (Workmen's) compensation insurance

Protection against losses incurred through disablements caused on the job

Class here comprehensive works on workers' compensation insurance and employers' liability insurance

For employers' liability insurance (insurance of an employer's liability for compensation to his employees in case of accident), see 368.56

.42	*Accident and health insurance

Class comprehensive works on accident and health insurance in 368.382

For workers' (workmen's) compensation insurance, see 368.41

See also 362.1042520973 for United States' Medicaid financial benefits, 362.10973 for United States' Medicaid health services

[.420 084 6]	Accident and health insurance for persons in late adulthood

Do not use; class in 368.426

.420 085 2	Accident and health insurance for mothers

Do not use for maternity insurance; class in 368.424

.424	*Maternity insurance
.426	*Accident and health insurance for persons in late adulthood

Class comprehensive works on accident and health insurance for persons in late adulthood in 368.38200846

.43	*Old-age and survivors' insurance

Class here comprehensive works on government-sponsored old-age and survivors' insurance and government-sponsored accident and health insurance for persons in late adulthood

Class supplementary social security for low-income people in 362.582; class comprehensive works on old-age and survivors' insurance in 368.3

For government-sponsored accident and health insurance for persons in late adulthood, see 368.426

See Manual at 336.249 vs. 368.401, 368.4011

.430 097 3	Treatment in United States

Class here social security in United States

.44	*Unemployment insurance

*Add as instructed under 368.1–368.8

.48   *Insurance against crimes of violence

> Class comprehensive works on crime insurance in 368.82

>   **368.5–368.8   Casualty insurance**

> Class comprehensive works in 368.5

.5   ***Liability insurance**

> Including no-fault insurance, umbrella or excess liability insurance

> Class here comprehensive works on casualty insurance

> Class no-fault insurance, umbrella or excess liability insurance of a specific type with the type, e.g., umbrella personal insurance 368.56, no-fault motor vehicle insurance 368.5728

> *For glass insurance, see 368.6; for insurance against industrial casualties, see 368.7; for other casualty insurance, see 368.8*

.56   Miscellaneous lines of liability insurance

> Only those lines named below

> Including commercial general, contractual, elevator, employers', homeowners', landlords', owners', tenants' liability insurance; livestock liability insurance; personal liability insurance

> Class here public liability insurance

> *See also 368.121 for crop insurance*

.562   *Product liability insurance

.563   *Environmental impairment liability insurance

> Class here pollution liability insurance

.564   *Professional liability insurance

> Class here errors and omissions insurance, malpractice insurance

.564 2   *Medical malpractice insurance

> Class here physicians' liability insurance

.57   *Instrumentalities of transportation

.572   *Motor vehicle liability insurance   Automobile liability insurance

> Class comprehensive works on all types of motor vehicle insurance in 368.092

.572 8   *No-fault motor vehicle insurance

.576   *Aviation liability insurance

> Class comprehensive works on all types of aviation insurance in 368.093

*Add as instructed under 368.1–368.8

.6   *Glass insurance

> Including coverage on plate glass, windows, neon and fluorescent signs and lamps

.7   *Insurance against industrial casualties (accidents)

> Including boiler and machinery, nuclear (nuclear energy, nuclear hazards), power interruption, power plant insurance

.8   Other casualty insurance

.81   *Business liability insurance

> Casualty aspects only
>
> Comprehensive works on business insurance relocated to 368.094

.815   *Business interruption insurance

> Including strike insurance

.82   *Burglary, robbery, theft insurance

> Including extortion, kidnap and ransom insurance
>
> Class here comprehensive works on crime insurance
>
> Subdivisions are added for any or all topics in heading
>
>> *For a specific type of crime insurance not provided for here, see the type, e.g., government-sponsored insurance against crimes of violence 368.48*

.83   *Fidelity bonds

> Guarantee against loss to employers because of dishonesty of employees
>
> Class here comprehensive works on fidelity and surety bonds
>
>> *For surety bonds, see 368.84*

.84   *Surety bonds

> Guarantee against loss due to failure to perform an obligation or fulfill a contract

.85   Guarantees

>> *For a specific guarantee not provided for here, see the guarantee, e.g., surety bonds 368.84*

.852   *Mortgage insurance

.853   *Investment guarantees

.854   *Bank deposit insurance

> Class here government-sponsored bank deposit insurance

*Add as instructed under 368.1–368.8

.87	*Credit insurance

Insurance of creditor against loss due to debtor's insolvency

.88	*Title insurance

.9 **Insurance by specific continents, countries, localities in modern world**

Add to base number 368.9 notation 4–9 from Table 2, e.g., insurance in South America 368.98

For a specific type of insurance in a specific place, see the type, e.g., transportation insurance in South America 368.20098

369 Miscellaneous kinds of associations

.1 **Hereditary, military, patriotic societies of United States**

Standard subdivisions are added for any or all topics in heading

Including state and local societies

(Option: To give local emphasis and a shorter number to hereditary, military, patriotic societies of a specific country, class them in this number; in that case, class hereditary, military, patriotic societies of United States in 369.273)

.11	General societies

Including military and naval orders, Medal of Honor Legion, Military Order of Foreign Wars of the United States, Veterans of Foreign Wars

.12	Colonial America societies

Including General Society of Colonial Wars, General Society of Mayflower Descendants, National Society of the Colonial Dames of America

.13	Revolutionary War societies

Including Society of the Cincinnati, Sons of the American Revolution

.135	Daughters of the American Revolution

.14	Societies commemorating events of 1789–1861

.15	Union Civil War societies

Including Grand Army of the Republic

Class here comprehensive works on societies of Civil War

For Confederate Civil War societies, see 369.17

.17	Confederate Civil War societies

Including United Confederate Veterans, United Daughters of the Confederacy

.18	Societies commemorating wars from 1898 to present

.181	Spanish-American War, 1898

*Add as instructed under 368.1–368.8

.186	World Wars I and II and later wars
.186 1	American Legion
.186 2	American Veterans of World War II, Korea, and Vietnam (AMVETS)
.186 3	Disabled American Veterans

.2   **Hereditary, military, patriotic societies**

> Standard subdivisions are added for any or all topics in heading
>
> Class here nationality clubs
>
> (Option: To give local emphasis and a shorter number to hereditary, military, patriotic societies of a specific country, use one of the following:
>
>> (Option A: Place them first by use of a letter or other symbol, e.g., hereditary, military, patriotic societies of France 369.F [preceding 369.1]
>>
>> (Option B: Class them in 369.1; in that case, class hereditary, military, patriotic societies of United States in 369.273)

[.209 3–.209 9]	Treatment by specific continents, countries, localities
	Do not use; class in 369.23–369.29

.21	International societies

.23–.29	Specific continents, countries, localities

> Add to base number 369.2 notation 3–9 from Table 2, e.g., patriotic societies of Italy 369.245; however, for hereditary, military, patriotic societies of United States, see 369.1
>> Notation 09 from Table 1 is added to indicate nationality clubs not located with the nation of interest, e.g., Order Sons of Italy in America 369.2450973
>
> Class clubs of ethnic groups not defined by specific country or locality in 369.3

.3   **Racial and ethnic clubs**

> Add to base number 369.3 notation 03–9 from Table 5, e.g., B'nai B'rith 369.3924
>
> Class clubs of ethnic groups defined by specific country or locality in 369.23–369.29

.4   **Young people's societies**

> Class a specific aspect of young people's societies with the aspect, e.g., Boy Scout camps 796.5422

.42	Boys' societies

> *For Boy Scouts, see 369.43*

.43	Boy Scouts

> Including Cub Scouts, Explorers

.46	Girls' societies

> *For Explorers, see 369.43; for Camp Fire, see 369.47*

.463	Girl Scouts and Girl Guides
.47	Camp Fire
.5	**Service clubs**

Including Lions International

.52	Rotary International

370   Education

This schedule is extensively revised, 370.1, 370.7, 375–377, and 378.14–378.19 in particular departing from earlier editions

A comparative table giving both old and new numbers for relocated topics, and equivalence tables showing the numbers in the old and new schedules appear in volume 1 of this edition

Class here basic education, public education

Unless other instructions are given, observe the following table of preference, e.g., special education at elementary level 371.90472 (*not* 372):

Public policy issues in education	379
Special education	371.9
Specific levels of education	372–374
Higher education	378
Schools and their activities (*except* 371.9)	371
Education for specific objectives	370.11
Curricula	375
Standard subdivisions, educational psychology (*except* 370.11)	370.1–370.9

Class special education in a specific subject in 371.9; class elementary education in a specific subject in 372.3–372.8. Class comprehensive works on education in a specific subject and on secondary, higher, and adult education in a specific subject with the subject, plus notation 071 from Table 1, e.g., education in science 507.1

See Manual at 370

SUMMARY

370.1–.9	**Standard subdivisions, education for specific objectives, educational psychology**
371	**Schools and their activities; special education**
.001–.009	Standard subdivisions
.01–.07	Specific kinds of schools
.1	Teachers and teaching, and related activities
.2	School administration; administration of student academic activities
.3	Methods of instruction and study
.4	Student guidance and counseling
.5	School discipline and related activities
.6	Physical plant; materials management
.7	Student welfare
.8	Students
.9	Special education
372	**Elementary education**
.01–.08	Standard subdivisions, elementary education for specific objectives
.1	Organization and activities in elementary education
.2	Specific levels of elementary education
.3	Computers, science, technology, health
.4	Reading
.5	Creative and manual arts
.6	Language arts (Communication skills)
.7	Mathematics
.8	Other studies
.9	Historical, geographic, persons treatment of elementary education
373	**Secondary education**
.01–.09	Standard subdivisions, secondary education for specific objectives
.1	Organization and activities in secondary education
.2	Secondary schools and programs of specific kinds, levels, curricula, focus
.3–.9	Secondary education in specific continents, countries, localities
374	**Adult education**
.001–.008	Standard subdivisions
.01	Adult education for specific objectives
.1	Organization and activities in adult education
.2	Groups, media, computers in adult education
.4	Distance education
.8	Specific kinds of institutions and agencies in adult education
.9	Historical, geographic, persons treatment
375	**Curricula**
.000 1–.000 9	Standard subdivisions
.001–.006	[Curriculum development, required and elective courses]
378	**Higher education**
.001–.009	Standard subdivisions
.01–.07	[Higher education for specific objectives, specific kinds of colleges and universities]
.1	Organization and activities in higher education
.2	Academic degrees and related topics
.3	Student aid and related topics
.4–.9	Higher education in specific continents, countries, localities in modern world

379	Public policy issues in education
.1	Specific elements of support and control of public education
.2	Specific policy issues in public education
.3	Public policy issues in private education
.4–.9	Public policy issues in specific continents, countries, localities in modern world

.1 **Philosophy and theory, education for specific objectives, educational psychology**

.11   Education for specific objectives

> Do not use for systems as in systems theory, analysis, design; class in 370.1. Do not use for school systems; class in 371

> Class here curricula directed toward specific educational objectives

.111   Fundamental education

> Preparation of educationally disadvantaged students for participation in community life

> Class here compensatory education

> Class fundamental education of adults in 374.012

.112   Humanistic (Liberal) education

.113   Vocational (Career) education

> Class here occupational training, vocational schools

> Class on-the-job training, vocational training provided by industry in 331.2592

>> *For vocational education at secondary level, see 373.246; for adult vocational education, see 374.013*

>> *See also 331.702 for choice of vocation, 371.425 for vocational guidance in schools*

.114   Moral, ethical, character education

> Standard subdivisions are added for any or all topics in heading

> Class education for social responsibility in 370.115; class moral, ethical, and character training of children at home in 649.7

.115   Education for social responsibility

> Including critical pedagogy, education for democracy, popular education (education for socioeconomic transformation); social education

> Class education for international understanding in 370.116

>> *See also 306.43 for sociology of education*

.116   Education for international understanding

> Class here educational exchanges, foreign study

.116 2	Exchange of students
	Class grants for student exchanges in 371.223
.116 3	Exchange of teachers
.117	Multicultural (Intercultural) and bilingual education
	Multicultural education: programs to promote mutual understanding among cultures
	Standard subdivisions are added for multicultural education and bilingual education together, for multicultural education alone
.117 5	Bilingual education
.118	Education for creativity
.119	Education for effective use of leisure
	Class here education for individual fulfillment
.12	Classification and philosophical foundations
	Including idealism, pragmatism, realism
.13	Value of education
.14	Language and communication
.15	Educational psychology
	Do not use for scientific principles; class in 370.1
	Class here psychology of teaching
	Class interdisciplinary works on psychology in 150. Class psychology of a specific topic in education with the topic, plus notation 019 from Table 1, e.g., psychology of adult education 374.0019
	See Manual at 153.15 vs. 370.15
.151	Differential psychology
	Educational psychology of specific ages and sexes
	Class a specific aspect of psychology of specific kinds of persons in 370.152–370.158
.152	Cognition
	Including critical thinking
	Class here intelligence
	Class perception in 370.155; class creativity in 370.157
.152 2	Memory
.152 3	Learning
	For motivation to learn, see 370.154

.152 4   Reasoning

> Class here problem solving

.153   Emotion and behavior

> Relation of behavior patterns, emotions, feelings to learning, to classroom situation
>
> Including behavior modification, extroversion and introversion, personality, subconscious processes
>
> Class behavior modification methods of instruction in 371.393
>
> *For motivation to learn, see 370.154*

.154   Motivation to learn

.155   Psychomotor and sensory processes in learning

> Including left-handedness, motor skills, perception

[.156]   Psychology of learning specific subjects

> Relocated to specific subject, plus notation 019 from Table 1, e.g., psychology of learning mathematics 510.19

.157   Creativity and imagination

> Standard subdivisions are added for either or both topics in heading
>
> *See also 370.118 for education to promote creativity*

.158   Psychological adjustment to education

> Class here effect of school education and environment on students

[.19]   Sociology of education

> Do not use for psychological principles; class in 370.15
>
> Sociology of education relocated to 306.43

[.284]   Apparatus, equipment, materials

> Do not use; class in 371.67

[.287]   Testing and measurement

> Do not use; class in 371.26

[.288]   Maintenance and repair

> Do not use; class in 371.68

[.68]   Management

> Do not use; class in 371.2

.7 **Education, research, related topics**

> Class here education, research, related topics in teaching
>
> Class education, research, related topics at a specific level with the level, e.g., education for teachers at elementary level 372.071

.8 **History and description with respect to kinds of persons**

> Do not use for students; class in 371.8. Do not use for education of a specific kind of student; class in 371.82, e.g., education of ethnic minorities 371.829

.82 Women in education

> Do not use for education of women; class in 371.822

.9 **Historical, geographic, persons treatment**

> Class here comparative education

371 Schools and their activities; special education

> Standard subdivisions are added for schools and their activities, special education together; for schools and their activities together; for schools alone
>
> Class here school systems, school policy
>
> Class schools and their activities in elementary, secondary, and adult education in 372–374; class schools and their activities in higher education in 378; class public policy issues in education in 379
>
> *For curricula, see 375*
>
> *See Manual at 371 vs. 353.8, 371.2, 379; also at 371 vs. 372–374, 378*

SUMMARY

371.001–.009	Standard subdivisions
.01–.07	Specific kinds of schools
.1	Teachers and teaching, and related activities
.2	School administration; administration of student academic activities
.3	Methods of instruction and study
.4	Student guidance and counseling
.5	School discipline and related activities
.6	Physical plant; materials management
.7	Student welfare
.8	Students
.9	Special education

.001 Philosophy and theory

.001 1 Systems

> Class here systems theory, analysis, design applied to schools and school systems
>
> Class comprehensive treatment of school systems themselves in 371; class specific conventional kinds of school systems in 371.01–371.07

.002	Miscellany
[.002 8]	Auxiliary techniques and procedures
	Do not use; class in 370.28
[.002 84]	Apparatus, equipment, materials
	Do not use; class in 371.67
[.002 88]	Maintenance and repair
	Do not use; class in 371.68
.003–.005	Standard subdivisions
.006	Organizations
[.006 8]	Management
	Do not use; class in 371.2
.007	Education, research, related topics
.008	History and description with respect to kinds of persons

Do not use for schools for specific kinds of persons; class in 371.82

.009	Historical, geographic, persons treatment
.009 4–.009 9	Treatment by continents, countries, localities in modern world

Class here specific all-age schools and school systems

> 371.01–371.07 **Specific kinds of schools**

Class here specific kinds of school systems; types of education characteristic of specific kinds of schools other than public and community schools

Class comprehensive works in 371. Class a specific kind of school defined by characteristics of student body with the kind in 371.82, e.g., schools for ethnic minorities 371.829, schools for African Americans 371.82996073

See Manual at 371 vs. 372–374, 378

.01 Public schools

Class public education in 370; class public community schools in 371.03; class public alternative schools in 371.04; class public policy issues concerning public schools in 379

.02 Private schools

Class here publicly supported private schools, schools not under government control

Class private community schools in 371.03; class private alternative schools in 371.04; class public policy issues in private education in 379.3

For religious schools, see 371.07

.03	Community schools

.04	Alternative schools

Class here experimental schools, free schools

.042	Home schools [*formerly* 649.68]

Class here home schooling [*formerly* 649.68]

See also 371.39 for home instruction by visiting teachers

.07	Religious schools [*formerly* 377]

Class religious education to encourage belief and to promote religious life and practice in 291.7

.071	Christian religious schools

Add to base number 371.071 the numbers following 28 in 281–289, e.g., Catholic schools 371.0712, Catholic schools in Quebec 371.0712714

Class Christian education to encourage belief and to promote religious life and practice in 268

.072–.079	Other religious schools

Add to base number 371.07 the numbers following 29 in 292–299, e.g., Islamic schools 371.077

> **371.1–371.8 Schools and their activities**

Class schools and their activities in special education in 371.9; class public policy issues relating to schools and their activities taken as a whole in 379; class comprehensive works in 371

For specific kinds of schools, see 371.01–371.07

See Manual at 371 vs. 372–374, 378

.1	**Teachers and teaching, and related activities**

Standard subdivisions are added for a combination of two or more topics in heading, for teachers alone

.100 1–.100 6	Standard subdivisions

.100 7	Education, research, related topics

[.100 71]	Education

Do not use; class in 370.71

.100 8–.100 9	Standard subdivisions

.102	Teaching

Class here mentoring

Class substitute teaching in 371.14122; class evaluation of teachers in 371.144; class team teaching in 371.148

For practice teaching, see 370.71; for methods of instruction, see 371.3

[.102 019]	Psychology of teaching

Do not use; class in 370.15

[.102 07]	Education, research, related topics in teaching

Do not use; class in 370.7

.102 2	Communication in teaching
.102 3	Teacher-student relations
.102 4	Classroom management

Class here classroom discipline

Class classroom techniques of instruction in 371.3; class comprehensive works on school discipline in 371.5

.103	Teacher-parent conferences

One-on-one teacher-parent relations

Class comprehensive works on teacher-parent relations in 371.192

.104	Academic status

Privileges, prerogatives, immunities, responsibilities

Including academic freedom, sabbatical leave, tenure

Interdisciplinary works on relations of teachers and society relocated to 306.432

For teacher-community relations, see 371.19

See also 331.2596 for economic aspects of tenure

.106	Relation of teachers to school administration and nonteaching staff

Including teacher participation in management

Class labor unions in 331.88113711; class collective bargaining in 331.89043711

.11	Personal characteristics and qualifications of teachers

Including discrimination because of personal characteristics

.12	Professional qualifications of teachers

Class here teacher certification

.14   Organization of teaching force

> Including teacher turnover
>
> Class performance contracting in 371.15

.141   Staffing and nonteaching activities

.141 2   Staffing

> Including teacher workload
>
> *For team teaching, see 371.148*

.141 22   Substitute teaching

.141 23   Differentiated staffing

> Class use of teacher aides in 371.14124

.141 24   Use of teacher aides (teachers' assistants)

> Paid or volunteer

.141 4   Nonteaching activities

> *For teacher participation in management, see 371.106*

.144   Evaluation of teachers

> Class here accountability, probation
>
> *See also 371.15 for performance contracting, 379.158 for overall educational accountability*

.148   Team teaching

> Two or more people teaching a class

.15   Performance contracting

> *See also 371.144 for teacher accountability*

.19   Community-school relations

> Including teacher-community relations
>
> Class here community involvement in schools, community-school partnerships, school involvement in the community
>
> Class interdisciplinary works on relations of schools and society, teachers and society in 306.432

.192   Parent-school relations

> Class here parent participation in schools; comprehensive works on teacher-parent relations
>
> *For teacher-parent conferences, see 371.103*

.192 06   Organizations and management

> Class here home and school associations, parent-teacher associations

.195 Industry-school relations

Class here industry involvement in schools, industry-school partnerships

See also 370.113 for vocational education, 371.227 for student employment in connection with ongoing academic work

.2 **School administration; administration of student academic activities**

Standard subdivisions are added for either or both topics in heading

See Manual at 371 vs. 353.8, 371.2, 379

SUMMARY

371.200 1–.200 9	**Standard subdivisions**
.201–.207	**School administration**
.21	**Admissions and related topics**
.22	**Student aid and cooperative education**
.23	**School year**
.24	**Schedules and school day**
.25	**Grouping students for instruction**
.26	**Examinations and tests; academic prognosis and placement**
.27	**Classroom and school examinations and tests; marking systems**
.28	**Promotion and failure**
.29	**Student mobility and school attendance**

.200 1 Philosophy and theory

.200 2 Miscellany

[.200 28] Auxiliary techniques and procedures

Do not use; class in 370.28

[.200 284] Apparatus, equipment, materials

Do not use; class in 371.67

[.200 288] Maintenance and repair

Do not use; class in 371.68

.200 3–.200 5 Standard subdivisions

.200 6 Organizations

[.200 68] Management

Do not use; class in 371.2

.200 7–.200 8 Standard subdivisions

.200 9 Historical, geographic, persons treatment

.200 92   Persons

Class here collected persons treatment of school administrators and persons treatment of specific administrators not associated with a specific level of education or school

Class persons treatment of school administrators best known as leaders in education in 370.92; class persons treatment of administrators best known as leaders in elementary education in 372.92; class persons treatment of administrators best known as leaders in adult education in 374.92. Class persons treatment of administrators best known as leaders at a specific level of education other than elementary and adult limited to a specific area or school in the geographic notation for area or school under the specific level, plus notation 092 from Table 1, e.g., a biography of a president of University of California at Berkeley 378.79467092

\>   371.201–371.207   School administration

Class comprehensive works in 371.2. Class management of a specific function with the function in 371, plus notation 068 from Table 1, e.g., management of student welfare 371.7068

For plant management, materials management, see 371.6

.201   Personnel management

Class here staff

For teachers, see 371.1; for support staff, see 371.202

.201 1   School administrators

Role and function

Including school superintendents

Class here leadership, top and middle management

Class education of school administrators in 371.20071; class persons treatment of school administrators in 371.20092

For principals, see 371.2012

.201 2   Principals

.202   Personnel management of support staff

Other than administrators and teachers

Class personnel management of staff providing a specific function with the function, plus notation 0683 from Table 1, e.g., personnel management of school nurses 371.7120683

.202 3   Management of administrative support personnel

.203 **School supervision (Instructional supervision)**

Class here school supervisors

.206 **Financial management**

Including tuition

Class here financial administration of public schools and school systems

Class student aid in 371.22

.207 **Executive management**

Including internal organization

Class here planning

Class government policies in 379

For leadership, school administrators, top and middle management, see 371.2011; for school boards, see 379.1531

> **371.21–371.29 Administration of student academic activities**

Class methods of instruction in 371.3; class student participation in administration in 371.59; class comprehensive works in 371.2

For educational and vocational guidance, see 371.42

.21 **Admissions and related topics**

Class here articulation, matriculation

.216 **Admission procedures**

Class entrance requirements in 371.217

.217 **Entrance requirements**

Class entrance examinations in 371.262; class academic prognosis and placement in 371.264

.218 **Credits**

Class use of credits in placement in 371.264; class use of credits to determine promotion and failure in 371.28

.219 **School enrollment**

.219 09 Historical and persons treatment

Do not use for geographic treatment; class in 371.2191–371.2199

.219 1–.219 9 Geographic treatment of school enrollment

Add to base number 371.219 notation 1–9 from Table 2, e.g., school enrollment in Russia 371.21947

.22	Student aid and cooperative education

Standard subdivisions are added for student aid and cooperative education together, for student aid alone

See also 371.206 for tuition

.223	Scholarships and fellowships

Standard subdivisions are added for either or both topics in heading

Including veterans' education benefits [*formerly also* 362.8682]

Class here grants

.224	Student loans

.225	Student employment

Including employment for service to the community

Class here employment of students by their own school, work-study programs

For employment by industry and nonschool agencies in connection with ongoing academic work (work-study plan), see 371.227

.227	Cooperative education

Student employment by industry and nonschool agencies in connection with ongoing academic work

Class here apprenticeship programs, work-study plan

Class apprenticeship programs without school sponsorship, interdisciplinary works on apprenticeship in 331.25922

.23	School year

Class here school calendar

.232	Summer school

.236	Year-round school

Class here extended school year

.24	Schedules and school day

See also 371.294 for school attendance

.242	Schedules

Including flexible scheduling

Class here scheduling, school week

.244	School day

Class here length of school day

Class scheduling within school day in 371.242

.25   Grouping students for instruction

Including multigraded classes (mixed-level classrooms, combination of grades)

Class here school classes

Class one-room schools in 372.125

.251   Class size

.252   Heterogeneous grouping

Class here mainstreaming outside context of special education

Class comprehensive works on mainstreaming in 371.9046

.254   Homogeneous grouping

Class here ability grouping, streaming

Class mainstreaming for ordinary students in 371.252; class nongraded grouping in 371.255

.255   Nongraded grouping

.256   Open classroom grouping

Class here open plan schools

Class open classroom methods of instruction in 371.3941

.26   Examinations and tests; academic prognosis and placement

Standard subdivisions are added for examinations and tests, academic prognosis and placement together; for examinations alone; for tests alone

Including test-taking skills

Class use of examinations and tests in guidance in 371.42

For classroom and school examinations and tests, see 371.271

.260 13   Value

Including test bias

Class here validity and reliability of tests, of standardized tests

Class validity and reliability of specific kinds of standardized tests in 371.262

.261   Test construction

Class evaluation of tests in 371.26013

.262	Standardized tests

Class here organizations producing standardized tests, comprehensive works on specific kinds of educational tests and their validity

Class interdisciplinary works on intelligence tests in 153.93; class interdisciplinary works on aptitude tests in 153.94. Class standardized tests for a specific subject in elementary school with the subject in 372.3–372.8, plus notation 076 from Table 1, e.g., mathematics tests for elementary school 372.7076; class standardized tests for a specific subject at secondary or higher level with the subject in 001–999, plus notation 076 from Table 1, e.g., mathematics tests for secondary school 510.76

> *For construction of standardized tests, see 371.261; for specific kinds of educational tests devised by individual teachers, see 371.271*

> *See Manual at 371.262 vs. 371.264*

[.262 013]	Value

Do not use; class in 371.26013

.264	Academic prognosis and placement

Including accreditation of prior learning (APL), advanced placement

Class standardized tests, use of specific tests of academic achievement and general education, comprehensive works on specific kinds of educational tests in 371.262

> *See Manual at 371.262 vs. 371.264*

.27	Classroom and school examinations and tests; marking systems
.271	Classroom and school examinations and tests

Tests devised by individual teacher or school

.272	Marking systems

Methods used for recording and reporting students achievement

.28	Promotion and failure

Including educational acceleration, underachievement

.283	Promotion
.285	Failure

Including grade repetition

.29	Student mobility and school attendance
.291	Student mobility
.291 2	School completion

Class here graduation; diplomas, other certificates of completion

.291 3	Dropouts (Early school leavers)

Class student failure in 371.285

.291 4	Transfers
.294	School attendance

Class compulsory education in 379.23

For truancy, school attendance officers, see 371.295

.295	Truancy

Class here school attendance officers, truant officers

Class dropouts in 371.2913

.3	**Methods of instruction and study**

Class here classroom techniques, creative activities, seatwork

Class classroom management in 371.1024; class comprehensive works on teaching in 371.102. Class methods of instruction in a specific subject at elementary level with the subject in 372.3–372.8, plus notation 044 from table under 372.3–372.8, e.g., methods of teaching mathematics in elementary school 372.7044; class methods of instruction in a specific subject at secondary and higher levels with the subject in 001–999, plus notation 071 from Table 1, e.g., methods of teaching mathematics in secondary school 510.712

SUMMARY

371.302 8		**Auxiliary techniques and procedures, techniques of study, lesson plans**
	.32	**Use of textbooks**
	.33	**Teaching aids, equipment, materials**
	.35	**Distance education**
	.36	**Project methods (Cooperative learning)**
	.37	**Recitation and discussion**
	.38	**Methods employed outside classroom**
	.39	**Other methods of instruction**

.302 8	Auxiliary techniques and procedures, techniques of study, lesson plans
.302 81	Techniques of study

Including book reports, homework, note-taking, reading for content, report writing

Class here techniques for parents [*formerly* 649.68], study skills

[.302 84]	Apparatus, equipment, materials

Do not use; class in 371.33

[.302 85]	Data processing Computer applications

Do not use; class in 371.334

[.307 8]	Use of apparatus, equipment, materials in study and teaching

Do not use; class in 371.33

Comprehensive works on instructional materials centers relocated to 027.7; comprehensive works on school resource centers relocated to 027.8

.32	Use of textbooks

Including textbook bias

Class public control of textbooks in 379.156. Class textbooks on a specific subject with the subject in 001–999, e.g., textbooks on mathematics 510

.33	Teaching aids, equipment, materials

Class here educational media, educational technology; use of teaching aids, equipment, materials in study and teaching

Class instructional materials centers in 027.7; class public control of teaching materials in 379.156. Class teaching aids, equipment, materials used in a specific method of instruction with the method, e.g., materials used in Montessori method 371.392

For textbooks, see 371.32

.333	Audio materials and equipment

Standard subdivisions are added for either or both topics in heading

.333 1	Radio
.333 2	Sound recordings and their players

Standard subdivisions are added for either or both topics in heading

.334	Data processing Computer science

Class here computer-assisted instruction (CAI), electronic programmed instruction, teaching machines

Unless it is redundant, add to base number 371.334 the numbers following 00 in 004–006, e.g., instructional use of software 371.33453, use of computer graphics in teaching 371.33466

For computer modeling and simulation, see 371.397

.335	Audiovisual and visual materials and equipment

Standard subdivisions are added for audiovisual and visual materials or equipment together, for audiovisual materials or equipment alone

Class audio materials and equipment in 371.333

See also 371.32 for textbooks

.335 2	Slides and filmstrips, motion pictures and video, pictures

.335 22   Slides and filmstrips

                 Standard subdivisions are added for either or both topics in heading

.335 23   Motion pictures and video recordings

                 Standard subdivisions are added for either or both topics in heading

.335 6   Bulletin boards

.335 8   Television

                 Including videoconferencing

                 Class video recordings in 371.33523

.337   Educational games and toys

                 Standard subdivisions are added for either or both topics in heading

                 Class gaming (simulation) in 371.397

.35   Distance education

                 Class here extension services

.356   Correspondence courses

.358   Electronic distance education

                 Including teleconferencing

                 Class here instructional use of mass media

                 For distance education by radio, see 371.3331; for distance education by computer, see 371.334; for distance education by television, see 371.3358

.36   Project methods (Cooperative learning)

                 Methods that emphasize student direction of group projects

                 Class here group work, unit method

                 Class group teaching (in which class is divided into groups, but activity is still directed by teacher) in 371.395

.37   Recitation and discussion

                 Including seminars

.38   Methods employed outside classroom

.382   Laboratory method

                 Class laboratory method with electronic and visual materials and equipment in 371.33

.384   Outdoor education

                 Class here field trips to indoor locations

.39	Other methods of instruction

Including home instruction by visiting teachers, monitorial system of education, Morrison plan, rote learning, Waldorf method of education

See also 371.042 for home schooling

.392	Montessori method

Montessori method is usually limited to elementary level in 372.1392. Discussion of advancing it to higher grades is classed with higher level

.393	Behavior modification methods

Including student performance contracting

Class use of behavior modification in classroom discipline in 371.1024

.394	Individualized instruction

Class here tutoring

.394 1	Open classroom instruction

Class grouping students for open classroom instruction in 371.256

.394 2	Honors work

.394 3	Independent study

Class independent honors work in 371.3942

For programmed instruction, see 371.3944

.394 4	Programmed instruction

For electronic programmed instruction, see 371.334

.395	Group teaching

Teaching in which class is divided into groups, but activity is still directed by teacher

Class group work that emphasizes student direction of group projects in 371.36

See also 371.148 for team teaching

.396	Lecture method

.397	Gaming and simulation

Class here computer modeling and simulation

Class comprehensive works on instructional use of computers in 371.334

.399	Use of drama (theater)

.4   **Student guidance and counseling**

Standard subdivisions are added for either or both topics in heading

Class here student personnel services, services of deans of students

For a specific student personnel service not provided for here, see the service, e.g., student employment 371.225

.404   Teachers and students in guidance and counseling

.404 6   Role of teachers in guidance and counseling

.404 7   Peer counseling

Counseling by other students

.42   Educational and vocational guidance

.422   Educational guidance

Other than vocational

.425   Vocational guidance

Class interdisciplinary works on vocational guidance in 331.702. Class vocational guidance in a specific occupation with the occupation, plus notation 023 from Table 1, e.g., guidance in law 340.023

.46   Personal counseling

Counseling of students with emotional, personal, social problems by staff other than psychologists and medical personnel

Including school social workers

Class personal counseling by other students in 371.4047; class student welfare programs in 371.7

.5   **School discipline and related activities**

Standard subdivisions are added for school discipline and related activities together, for school discipline alone

For classroom discipline, see 371.1024

.51   General regulations for student conduct

.53   Rewards

Class rewards to discourage specific disciplinary problems in 371.58

.54   Punishments

Class punishments for specific discipline problems in 371.58

.542   Corporal punishment

.543   Probation, suspension, expulsion

.58	Specific discipline problems

Class comprehensive works on crime, delinquency, sexual abuse, substance abuse, vandalism, violence in schools in 371.78

For truancy, see 371.295

.59 Student participation in administration

Including monitors

Class here student government, student participation in maintenance of discipline

See also 371.39 for monitorial system of education

.6 Physical plant; materials management

Standard subdivisions are added for physical plant and materials management together; for physical plant alone

Class here plant management, educational buildings, school facilities

See also 727 for architecture of educational buildings

[.602 84] Maintenance and repair

Do not use; class in 371.67

[.602 88] Maintenance and repair

Do not use; class in 371.68

.61 School grounds, sites, location

.62 Specific kinds of buildings and rooms

Class here furnishings, apparatus, equipment, supplies for specific kinds of buildings and rooms

Class teaching aids, equipment, materials regardless of kind of building or room in 371.33

.621 Instructional spaces

Including study facilities

Class here classrooms

For laboratories, see 371.623

.623 Laboratories

[.623 4] Instructional facilities for teaching specific subjects

Relocated to specific subject, e.g., language laboratories 407.8, chemical laboratories 542.1

[.624] Physical education facilities

Relocated to 796.068

.625	Noninstructional facilities

Class facilities for a specific noninstructional objective with the objective, e.g., cafeterias 371.716

[.629]	Design of educational buildings for noninstructional objectives

Relocated to 727

.63	School furnishings

Class furnishings for specific kinds of buildings and rooms in 371.62

.67	Apparatus, equipment, materials

Class here materials management

Class apparatus, equipment, supplies for specific kinds of buildings and rooms in 371.62

For teaching aids, equipment, materials, see 371.33; for school furnishings, see 371.63

.68	Custodial and maintenance services, renovation

Standard subdivisions are added for a combination of two or more topics in heading, for custodial services alone, for maintenance services alone

Including repair services

For technical maintenance and repair of a specific facility or piece of equipment, see the facility or piece of equipment, plus notation 0288 from Table 1, e.g., repair of educational computers 371.3340288; for custodial and maintenance services, renovation of a specific noninstructional facility, see the facility, plus notation 0682 from Table 1, e.g., maintenance services for school cafeterias 371.7160682

.7	**Student welfare**

Class here school social services

For a specific provision for student welfare not provided for here, see the provision, e.g., personal counseling 371.46, student housing 371.871

.71	Student health and related topics

Standard subdivisions are added for student health and related topics together, for student health alone

.712	School nursing programs

Class use of school nurses in mental welfare programs in 371.713; class use of school nurses in birth control, pregnancy, sex hygiene programs in 371.714

.713	Mental health services

Class here school psychologists

For substance abuse programs, see 371.784

.714	Sex hygiene, birth control, pregnancy programs

Standard subdivisions are added for sex hygiene, birth control, pregnancy programs together; for sex hygiene programs alone

.716   Food services

Including milk programs, nutrition programs

Class here school cafeterias, school lunch programs

[.77]   School safety programs

Relocated to 363.119371

[.774]   Fire safety programs in schools

Relocated to 363.379

[.775 2]   School traffic safety programs

Relocated to 363.1257

[.775 4]   School athletic safety programs

Relocated to 363.147

.78   School programs related to crime, substance abuse, sexual abuse

Class here crime, substance abuse, sexual abuse problems in schools; assistance to victims of crime and abuse

Class crime, substance abuse, sexual abuse as school discipline problems in 371.58

.782   Crime prevention and alleviation

Standard subdivisions are added for either or both topics in heading

Class here delinquency in schools, school violence

Class campus police in 363.289; class prevention and alleviation of crime relating to substance abuse in 371.784; class prevention and alleviation of crime related to sexual abuse in 371.786; class interdisciplinary works on victims of crime in 362.88; class interdisciplinary works on crime prevention in 364.4

.784   Substance abuse programs

.786   Sexual abuse programs

.8   Students

Class here extracurricular activities, student life

For a specific aspect of students not provided for here, see the aspect, e.g., student discipline 371.5

.801 9   Student psychology

Class educational psychology in 370.15

.805   Serial publications

            Limited to serials about students, student life, extracurricular activities

            See also 371.897 for student journalism

.806   Organizations and management

            Do not use for student organizations; class in 371.83

[.808]   History and description with respect to kinds of persons

            Do not use; class in 371.82

.81   Student movements

            Student efforts to achieve reform on campus and social change

            Including student strikes

            Class here student activism, protest, unrest

            Class student movements to achieve a specific objective with the objective, e.g., movements to achieve electoral reform 324.63

.82   Specific kinds of students; schools for specific kinds of students

            Class here comprehensive works on education of specific kinds of students

            Add to base number 371.82 the numbers following —08 in notation 081–089 from Table 1, e.g., education of women 371.822 [*formerly* 376], education of students by racial, ethnic, national origin 371.829; however, for students who are the focus of special education, see 371.9

            For a specific aspect of education of specific kinds of students, see the aspect, e.g., counseling for women students 371.4082

.83   Student organizations

            Class here student clubs

            Class student movements in 371.81

            For Greek-letter societies, see 371.85

[.84]   Student organizations in specific fields

            Relocated to specific field, plus notation 06 from Table 1, e.g., student literary societies 806

.85   Greek-letter societies

            Class here alumni units

.852   Honor societies

            Not in a specific subject field

[.854]   Greek-letter societies in specific fields

            Relocated to specific field, plus notation 06 from Table 1, e.g., Greek-letter medical societies 610.6

.855	Men's Greek-letter social societies
.856	Women's Greek-letter social societies
.87	Housing and transportation of students
.871	Housing
.872	Transportation

Class busing for school integration in 379.263

See also 363.1259 for school bus safety

.89	Miscellaneous student activities

Only those named here or below

Including competitions

Public entertainment activities of students relocated to 790.2088375; intramural sports relocated to 796.042

Class a specific competition with the competition, plus notation 079 from Table 1, e.g., a photographic competition 770.79

.897	Student journalism

Class interdisciplinary student journals in 050. Class a student journal on a specific subject with the subject, plus notation 05 from Table 1, e.g., a journal on student life and extracurricular activities 371.805, a student literary journal 805

.897 4	Producing newspapers
.897 5	Producing magazines
.897 6	Producing yearbooks

Class a yearbook of a specific school with the school, e.g., a yearbook of a prep school in New York city 373.7471

.9 **Special education**

Class here exceptional students, learning disabilities, underachievers in special education; schools and school activities pertaining to special education

Except for modifications shown under specific entries, add to each subdivision identified by * as follows:

[0284]   Apparatus, equipment, materials
            Do not use; class in 5
[0288]   Maintenance and repair
            Do not use; class in 5
[0682]   Plant management
            Do not use; class in 5
3–7 General topics
            Add the numbers following 371.904 in 371.9043–371.9047, e.g.,
            equipment 5, equipment for students with reading disorders
            371.91445

Unless other instructions are given, observe the following table of preference, e.g., emotionally disturbed deaf retarded students 371.928 (*not* 371.912, 371.94):

Gifted students	371.95
Students with mental disabilities	371.92
Students with emotional disturbances	371.94
Students with physical disabilities	371.91
Delinquent and problem students	371.93

Class comprehensive works on underachievers in 371.28

SUMMARY

371.901–.909		**Standard subdivisions**
.91		**Students with physical disabilities**
.92		**Students with mental disabilities**
.93		**Delinquent and problem students**
.94		**Students with emotional disturbances**
.95		**Gifted students**

[.902 84]   Apparatus, equipment, materials

            Do not use; class in 371.9045

[.902 88]   Maintenance and repair

            Do not use; class in 371.9045

.904   Special topics

.904 3   Teaching methods

            Including academic prognosis and placement

            Add to base number 371.9043 the numbers following 371.3 in
            371.3028–371.39, e.g., project methods 371.90436

.904 4	Programs in specific subjects
	Add to base number 371.9044 the numbers following 372 in 372.3–372.8, e.g., mathematics 371.90447
.904 5	Buildings, rooms, furnishings, apparatus, equipment, supplies
	Including maintenance and repair
	Class here plant management
.904 6	Mainstreaming
	Educating exceptional students in regular school programs
	Including identifying students for special education
.904 7	Special education by level
	Class a specific topic in special education at a specific level with the topic, e.g., teaching at elementary level 371.9043
.904 72	Special education at elementary level
.904 73	Special education at secondary level
.904 74	Special education in colleges and universities
	Standard subdivisions are added for either or both topics in heading
.904 75	Adult special education
	Other than in colleges and universities
[.906 82]	Plant management
	Do not use; class in 371.9045

.908   **History and description with respect to kinds of persons**

Do not use for kinds of students requiring special education; class in 371.9

.91   **Students with physical disabilities**

Including general works on students with brain damage

Unless other instructions are given, observe the following table of preference, e.g., students with blindness and mobility impairments 371.916 (*not* 371.911):

Students with linguistic disorders	371.914
Students with mobility impairments	371.916
Students with blindness and visual impairments	371.911
Students with hearing impairments	371.912

Class students with a specific disorder caused by brain damage in 371.911–371.94

.911   *Students with blindness and visual impairments

Subdivisions are added for either or both topics in heading

*Add as instructed under 371.9

.912	Students with hearing impairments
	Class here deaf students
[.912 028 4]	Apparatus, equipment, materials
	Do not use; class in 371.9125
[.912 028 8]	Maintenance and repair
	Do not use; class in 371.9125
[.912 068 2]	Plant management
	Do not use; class in 371.9125
.912 3–.912 6	Teaching methods, specific subjects, facilities, mainstreaming
	Add to base number 371.912 the numbers following 371.904 in 371.9043–371.9046, e.g., teaching methods 371.9123
.912 7	Instruction in lipreading
	Instruction in finger spelling relocated to 419, instruction in sign languages relocated to 419.071
.912 8	Education by level
	Add to base number 371.9128 the numbers following 371.9047 in 371.90472–371.90475, e.g., university education for deaf persons 371.91284
.914	Students with linguistic disorders
.914 2	*Students with speaking disorders
	Including aphasia, stuttering
.914 4	*Students with reading disorders
	Class here dyslexia
	See also 372.43 for remedial reading in elementary education
.916	*Students with mobility impairments
.92	Students with mental disabilities
	Class here students with developmental disabilities
	Class students with mental illness in 371.94
.926	*Slow learners
	Class here students with moderate learning difficulties
.928	Students with mental retardation
	Class here students with severe learning difficulties
.928 001	Philosophy and theory

*Add as instructed under 371.9

.928 002		Miscellany
[.928 002 84]		Apparatus, equipment, materials
		Do not use; class in 371.92805
[.928 002 88]		Maintenance and repair
		Do not use; class in 371.92805
.928 003–.928 005		Standard subdivisions
.928 006		Organizations and management
[.928 006 82]		Plant management
		Do not use; class in 371.92805
.928 007–.928 009		Standard subdivisions
.928 03–.928 07		General topics

Add to base number 371.9280 the numbers following 371.904 in 371.9043–371.9047, e.g., teaching methods 371.92803

.93 *Delinquent and problem students

Not suffering severe emotional disturbances

Including disruptive, hyperactive, maladjusted students

Subdivisions are added for either or both topics in heading

Class delinquent and problem students suffering severe emotional disturbances in 371.94

.94 *Students with emotional disturbances

Including autistic students

Class here students with mental illness

For delinquent and problem students not suffering severe emotional disturbances, see 371.93

.95 Gifted students

[.950 284]		Apparatus, equipment, materials
		Do not use; class in 371.955
[.950 288]		Maintenance and repair
		Do not use; class in 371.955
[.950 682]		Plant management
		Do not use; class in 371.955

.952 Mainstreaming

Educating gifted students in regular school programs

Including identification

*Add as instructed under 371.9

.953   Programs in specific subjects

Class here curricula

Add to base number 371.953 the numbers following 372 in 372.3–372.8, e.g., programs in mathematics 371.9537

.955   Buildings, rooms, furnishings, apparatus, equipment, supplies

Including maintenance and repair

Class here plant management

.956   Teaching methods

Including motivating gifted underachievers

Add to base number 371.956 the numbers following 371.3 in 371.3028–317.39, e.g., use of computers 371.95634

.957   Education by level

Add to base number 371.957 the numbers following 371.9047 in 371.90472–371.90475, e.g., educating gifted students at elementary level 371.9572

> ## 372–374 Specific levels of education

Unless other instructions are given, class works treating two sublevels of education that are not subdivisions of the same number with the higher level, e.g., kindergarten and first grade 372.241 (*not* 372.218)

Class special education at any level in 371.9; class public policy issues relating to a specific level of education taken as a whole in 379; class comprehensive works on education and works dealing comprehensively with elementary and secondary education, with secondary and higher education in 370; class comprehensive works on schools in 371

For higher education, see 378

See Manual at 371 vs. 372–374, 378

372 Elementary education

Class here elementary schools, grade schools, grammar schools (United States), junior schools (United Kingdom), primary schools (United Kingdom); lower sections of all-age schools

For adult elementary education, see 374.012

SUMMARY

.01   Philosophy and theory; elementary education for specific objectives

.011   Elementary education for specific objectives

Do not use for systems as in systems theory, analysis, design; class in 372.01. Do not use for specific kinds of school systems; class in 372.1042

Class here curricula directed toward specific educational objectives

Add to base number 372.011 the numbers following 370.11 in 370.111–370.119, e.g., character education 372.0114

.02   Miscellany

[.028 4]   Apparatus, equipment, materials

Do not use; class in 372.167

[.028 7]   Testing and measurement

Do not use; class in 372.126

[.028 8]   Maintenance and repair

Do not use; class in 372.168

[.068]   Management

Do not use; class in 372.12

.08   History and description with respect to kinds of persons

Do not use for students; class in 372.18. Do not use for education of a specific kind of student; class in 372.182, e.g., education of ethnic minorities 372.1829

[.09]   Historical, geographic, persons treatment

Do not use; class in 372.9

.1   Organization and activities in elementary education

For elementary education for specific objectives, see 372.011; for specific levels of elementary education, see 372.2

[.101–.103]	Standard subdivisions

Do not use; class in 372.01–372.03

.104   Special topics

.104 2   Specific kinds of elementary schools

Class here specific kinds of school systems, kinds of elementary education (other than public elementary education) defined by specific kinds of schools

Add to base number 372.1042 the numbers following 371.0 in 371.01–371.07, e.g., elementary church schools 372.104271, Catholic elementary schools 372.1042712

Class a specific kind of elementary schools at a specific level in 372.2; class specific schools regardless of kind in 372.9

[.105–.108]   Standard subdivisions

Do not use; class in 372.05–372.08

[.109]   Historical, geographic, persons treatment

Do not use; class in 372.9

.11–.18   School organization and activities in elementary education

Add to base number 372.1 the numbers following 371 in 371.1–371.8, e.g., administration 372.12; however, for use of drama as a method of instruction, see 372.66

.19   Elementary education in subject areas

Class here curricula

For elementary education in a specific subject, see 372.3–372.8

.2   **Specific levels of elementary education**

Class specific topics of education at a specific level in 372.1; class specific schools at a specific level in 372.9

[.201–.208]   Standard subdivisions

Do not use; class in 372.01–372.08

[.209]   Historical, geographic, persons treatment

Do not use; class in 372.9

.21   Preschool education

Class here early childhood education, head start programs, preschool education in day-care centers

Class preschool education by parents in the home as part of child-rearing in 649.68

.216	Nursery schools
.218	Kindergarten
.24	Specific levels of elementary school

Class elementary education covering grades 1–4, junior schools (United Kingdom) in 372

See Manual at 372.24 and 373.23

[.240 1–.240 8]	Standard subdivisions

Do not use; class in 372.01–372.08

[.240 9]	Historical, geographic, persons treatment

Do not use; class in 372.9

.241	Lower level

Class here primary grades (1–3), infant schools (United Kingdom), primary schools (United Kingdom)

.242	Upper level

Class here intermediate grades (4–6)

Class middle schools (grades 5–8), junior high schools in 373.236

>   **372.3–372.8   Elementary education in specific subjects**

Add to each subdivision identified by * as follows:
04   Special topics
042   Place of subject in education
043   Curricula
044   Teaching
          Methods, materials, aids, sources
          Class textbooks with the subject in 001–999, e.g., an
          elementary textbook on arithmetic 513
(045)   Textbooks
          (Optional notation; prefer the subject in 001–999, e.g.,
          elementary textbooks on arithmetic 513)
          Including readers (if option at 372.4122 is used)
049   Instruction at specific levels
          Including kindergarten
          Class a specific aspect of instruction at a given level with
          the aspect, e.g., curricula for kindergarten 043

Class comprehensive works in 372.19

.3	**Computers, science, technology, health**
.34	*Computers

Class here computer literacy

---

*Add as instructed under 372.3–372.8

.35   *Science and technology

Including metric system

Subdivisions are added for science and technology together, for science alone

Class computers in 372.34

For mathematics, see 372.7

.357   *Nature study

Class here environmental studies

.358   *Technology

Including robots

For computers, see 372.34; for home economics, see 372.82; for physical education, see 372.86

.37   *Health (Hygiene)

Including diet, food, nutrition

For physical education, see 372.86

.372   *Sex education

Including human reproductive physiology

Class family life education in 372.82

.4   Reading

Class here reading instruction in home schools [*formerly* 649.58]

Unless other instructions are given, class a subject with aspects in two or more subdivisions of 372.4 in the number coming last, e.g., vocabulary building by phonetic methods 372.465 (*not* 372.44)

.402 84   Apparatus and equipment

Do not use for materials; class in 372.412

[.402 87]   Testing and measurement

Do not use; class in 372.48

.41   Instructional materials, reading readiness, methods of instruction and study

.412   Instructional materials

*Add as instructed under 372.3–372.8

(.412 2)	Readers
	(Optional number; prefer specific language in 420–490, plus notation 86 from Table 4, e.g., English-language readers 428.6
	(If this number is used, class readers on a specific subject with the subject in 372.3–372.8, plus notation 045 from table under 372.3–372.8, e.g., science readers 372.35045)
.414	Reading readiness
.416	Methods of instruction and study
	For individualized reading instruction, see 372.417
.416 2	Small-group reading instruction
.416 4	Whole-class reading instruction
.417	Individualized (Personalized) reading instruction
	See also 372.454 for independent reading
.42	Reading motivation
.423	Use of national and commercial programs
	Including Reading is Fundamental
.425	Community-school partnerships
	Class here parent-school partnerships
.427	School-based programs
	Classroom and library programs
.43	Remedial reading
	Including reading failure
	Class reading difficulties treated in special education in 371.9144
.44	Vocabulary development
.45	Reading-skill strategies
	For word-attack strategies, see 372.46; for reading comprehension strategies, see 372.47
.452	Oral reading
.454	Independent reading
	For speed reading, see 372.455
.455	Speed reading
.46	Word-attack (Decoding) strategies
.462	Whole-word (Sight) methods
	Class here word-recognition method

.465	Part-word (Phonetic) methods

Including teaching alphabets

Class here phonetics in elementary education

Class pronunciation in a specific communication skill with the skill, e.g., pronunciation in speech 372.622

.47	Reading comprehension strategies
.472	Strategies using standardized materials

Including cloze procedure, SQ3R technique

Class a strategy using standardized materials in a specific subject with the subject in 372.3–372.8, plus notation 044 from table under 372.3–372.8, e.g., SQ3R in social studies 372.83044

.474	Cognitive strategies

Including critical thinking

.475	Whole-language approach
.476	Reading in content areas
.48	Evaluation of reading skills

Class here testing and measurement

Class evaluation of reading readiness in 372.414

.482	Standardized testing
.484	Classroom and school testing
.486	Diagnostic testing
.5	***Creative and manual arts**

Subdivisions are added for either or both topics in heading

For literature, see 372.64; for theater, see 372.66; for dance, see 372.868

.52	*Drawing, painting, design
.53	*Modeling and sculpture

Subdivisions are added for either or both topics in heading

.54	*Sewing

Including weaving

Class here needlework

.55	*Handicrafts

Including paper work

For needlework, see 372.54

---

*Add as instructed under 372.3–372.8

.6	***Language arts (Communication skills)**

Class here literacy education

For reading, see 372.4

.61	Grammar

Including language usage, word study

.62	Written and spoken expression

Class here whole-language approach

For whole-language approach in reading, see 372.475

.622	Speech

Including pronunciation

Class oral presentations other than public speaking in 372.66

See also 372.465 for phonetic methods of reading instruction, 372.66 for drama

.623	*Composition

Class here comprehensive works on written expression

For spelling and handwriting, see 372.63

.63	Spelling and handwriting
.632	*Spelling (Orthography)
.634	*Handwriting (Penmanship)
.64	*Literature appreciation

Class plays taught as theater in 372.66

.65	*Foreign languages and bilingual instruction

Subdivisions are added for foreign languages and bilingual instruction together, for foreign languages alone

.651	*Bilingual instruction

Class comprehensive works on bilingual education in 370.1175

.652–.659	Specific foreign languages

Add to base number 372.65 notation 2–9 from Table 6, e.g., Spanish 372.6561, English as a second language 372.6521; then add further as instructed under 372.3–372.8, e.g., methods of teaching Spanish 372.6561044

---

*Add as instructed under 372.3–372.8

.66   *Drama (Theater)

Class here school plays, comprehensive works on oral presentations

Class plays taught as literature in 372.64

For public speaking, see 372.622; for other oral presentations, see 372.67. For use of drama as a method of instruction in a specific subject in elementary education, see the subject in 372.3–372.8, plus notation 044 from table under 372.3–373.8, e.g., use of drama in teaching history 372.89044

.67   Other oral presentations

Other than drama and public speaking

Class here activities related to oral presentations

.672   *Media production and presentation

Subdivisions are added for either or both topics in heading

Class media production of a specific dramatic art with the art, e.g., storytelling for media 372.677

.674   *Puppet theater

Limited to instructional use in elementary education

Class here puppetry

Class interdisciplinary works on puppetry in 791.53

.676   *Choral speaking

Class here readers' theater

.677   *Storytelling

.69   *Listening

.7   ***Mathematics**

.72   *Arithmetic

Class here numeracy

.8   **Other studies**

[.801–.809]   Standard subdivisions

Do not use; class in 372.1901–372.1909

.82   *Home economics

Class here family life education, family living

For sewing, see 372.54

*Add as instructed under 372.3–372.8

.83		*Social studies

Class family life education in 372.82

For environmental studies, see 372.357; for history and geography, see 372.89

.832		*Civics (Citizenship)
.84		*Religion

Class religious education of children under church auspices to inculcate Christian faith and practice in 268.432; class religious education of children under auspices of other religious bodies to inculcate religious faith and practice in 291.75

.86		*Physical education and dance

Subdivisions are added for physical education and dance together, for physical education alone

.868		*Dance

Class here movement education

.87		*Music

See also 372.868 for dance

.872		Appreciation
.873		Performance

Including reading music

.874		Composition
.89		History and geography

Standard subdivisions are added for history and geography together, for history alone

Class here civilization

.890 4		Special topics
.890 42–.890 44		Place of history and geography in education; curricula, teaching

Add to base number 372.8904 the numbers following 04 in notation 042–044 from table under 372.3–372.8, e.g., teaching history 372.89044

(.890 45)		Textbooks

(Optional number; prefer 909)

For textbooks on history and civilization of ancient world, of specific continents, countries, localities, see 372.893–372.899

---

*Add as instructed under 372.3–372.8

.890 49	Instruction at specific levels
	Class a specific aspect of instruction at a given level with the aspect, e.g., history curricula for primary grades 372.89043
.891	Geography
.891 04	Special topics
.891 042–.891 044	Place of geography in education; curricula, teaching
	Add to base number 372.89104 the numbers following 04 in notation 042–044 from the table under 372.3–372.8, e.g., using maps in geography 372.891044
(.891 045)	Textbooks
	(Optional number; prefer 910)
	For textbooks on geography of specific places, see 372.8911–372.8919
.891 049	Instruction at specific levels
	Class a specific aspect of instruction at a given level with the aspect, e.g., geography curricula for primary grades 372.891043
(.891 1–.891 9)	Textbooks on geography of specific places
	(Optional number; prefer 910.91, 913–919)
	Add to base number 372.891 notation 1–9 from Table 2, e.g., geography textbooks on Asia 372.8915
(.893–.899)	Textbooks on history and civilization of ancient world, of specific continents, countries, localities
	(Optional number; prefer 930–990)
	Add to base number 372.89 notation 3–9 from Table 2, e.g., textbooks on ancient Egypt 372.8932
	For textbooks on geography of specific places, see 372.8911–372.8919

.9   **Historical, geographic, persons treatment of elementary education**

Class here specific schools and school systems

Add to base number 372.9 notation 01–9 from Table 2, e.g., elementary education in Brazil 372.981

373   Secondary education

Class here upper sections of all-age schools

Class secondary education in a specific subject with the subject, plus notation 0712 from Table 1, e.g., secondary education in agriculture 630.712

SUMMARY

.01   Philosophy and theory, secondary education for specific objectives

.011   Secondary education for specific objectives

> Do not use for systems as in systems analysis and design; class in 373.01. Do not use for specific kinds of school systems; class in 373.21–373.22
>
> Class here curricula directed toward specific educational objectives
>
> Add to base number 373.011 the numbers following 370.11 in 370.111–370.119, e.g., education for social responsibility 373.0115; however, for vocational education, see 373.246

.02   Miscellany

[.028 4]   Apparatus, equipment, materials

> Do not use; class in 373.167

[.028 7]   Testing and measurement

> Do not use; class in 373.126

[.028 8]   Maintenance and repair

> Do not use; class in 373.168

.06   Organizations

[.068]   Management

> Do not use; class in 373.12

.08   History and description with respect to kinds of persons

> Do not use for students; class in 373.18. Do not use for schools and education for a specific kind of student; class in 373.182, e.g., secondary schools for ethnic minorities 373.1829

.082   Women in secondary education

> Do not use for secondary education of young women; class in 373.182352

.09   Historical, geographic, persons treatment

[.093–.099]   Treatment by specific continents, countries, localities

> Do not use; class in 373.3–373.9

.1   **Organization and activities in secondary education**

> *For secondary education for specific objectives, see 373.011; for schools and programs of specific kinds, levels, curricula, focus, see 373.2*

[.101–.109]   Standard subdivisions

> Do not use; class in 373.01–373.09

.11–.18   School organization and activities in secondary education

> Add to base number 373.1 the numbers following 371 in 371.1–371.8, e.g., professional qualifications of teachers 373.112, secondary education of young women 373.182352; however, for cooperative education, see 373.28

.19   Curricula

> Class curricula directed toward specific secondary educational objectives in 373.011; class education in secondary schools identified by specific types of curricula in 373.24–373.26

[.192–.198]   Curricula directed toward specific subject objectives

> Relocated to the subject, plus notation 0712 from Table 1, e.g., ethnic studies curricula 305.80712

.2   **Secondary schools and programs of specific kinds, levels, curricula, focus**

> Class here types of education (other than public education in general) provided by schools and programs of specific kinds, levels, curricula, focus

> Class a specific topic relating to schools and programs of a specific kind, level, curriculum, focus in 373.11–373.18; class a specific school regardless of kind, level, curriculum, focus in 373.3–373.9; class continuation schools in 374.8; class folk high schools in 374.83

[.201–.209]   Standard subdivisions

> Do not use; class in 373.01–373.09

>   **373.21–373.22   Specific kinds of schools**

> Class comprehensive works in 373

.21   Community, alternative, religious secondary schools

> Add to base number 373.21 the numbers following 371.0 in 371.03–371.07, e.g., community schools 373.213

.22   Private and public secondary schools

> Class private and public community, alternative, religious secondary schools in 373.21

.222 **Private secondary schools (Preparatory schools)**

Class here public schools (United Kingdom), comprehensive works on boarding schools

Class private schools (other than modern academic schools) identified by type of curriculum in 373.24–373.26

For a specific kind of boarding school (other than private secondary schools), see the kind, e.g., private elementary boarding schools 372.10422, military boarding schools 373.243

.224 **Public secondary schools**

Class comprehensive works on public secondary education in 373

For specific levels of public secondary schools, see 373.23; for public secondary schools identified by a specific type of curriculum, see 373.24–373.26

.23 **Specific levels of secondary education**

Class private schools regardless of level in 373.222; class schools identified by a specific type of curriculum regardless of level in 373.24–373.26; class comprehensive works on levels of secondary schools, four-year high schools not of a specific type in 373

See Manual at 372.24 and 373.23

[.230 1–.230 9] **Standard subdivisions**

Do not use; class in 373.01–373.09

.236 **Lower level**

Including grades above 6 in elementary schools, forms above the equivalent level in junior schools (United Kingdom)

Class here junior high schools, middle schools

For lower grades of middle schools, see 372.242

.238 **Upper level**

Including high school equivalency programs

Class here senior high schools; high school postgraduate programs; lower years of four-year and three-year junior colleges, of sixth-form colleges

Class comprehensive works on sixth-form colleges in 378.1543

> **373.24–373.26 Secondary schools identified by type of curriculum**

Class here private schools (other than modern academic schools) identified by type of curriculum

Class comprehensive works in 373

.24   Academic, military, vocational schools

.241   Modern academic schools

> Schools emphasizing sciences and modern languages
>
> Class here modern grammar schools (United Kingdom), gymnasiums (Europe), lycées; comprehensive works on magnet schools
>
> Class private modern academic schools in 373.222; class comprehensive works on secondary schools preparing for higher education in 373
>
> > *For classical gymnasiums, see 373.242. For a specific type of magnet school other than modern academic schools, see the type, e.g., magnet public elementary schools 372.10421, magnet secondary schools for science 507.12, magnet secondary schools for arts 700.712*

.242   Classical schools

> Schools emphasizing Latin and Greek
>
> Class here Latin grammar schools

.243   Military schools

> Secondary schools offering professional military education but remaining basically academic in nature .
>
> Class here naval schools
>
> Class schools concentrating on professional military education in 355.0071

.246   Vocational schools

> Class here technical high schools, vocational education
>
> Class comprehensive works on vocational education in 370.113

.25   Comprehensive secondary schools

> Schools offering academic, vocational, general programs when considered distinct from undifferentiated secondary schools

.26   General secondary schools

> Schools offering nonvocational, general terminal education when considered distinct from undifferentiated secondary schools

.27   Apprenticeship programs in secondary education

> Class apprenticeship programs offered by industry in 331.25922; class work-study plan in 373.28; class apprenticeship training as part of personnel management in 658.3124

.28   Cooperative education

> Class here work-study plan

.3–.9   Secondary education in specific continents, countries, localities

Class here specific schools and school systems

Add to base number 373 notation 3–9 from Table 2, e.g., secondary schools of Australia 373.94

374   Adult education

Class here continuing, further, lifelong, permanent, recurrent education

Class on-the-job training in 331.2592; class adult high school equivalency programs in 373.238. Class adult education in a specific subject with the subject, plus notation 0715 from Table 1, e.g., sculpture courses for adults 730.715

.001   Philosophy and theory

.002   Miscellany

[.002 84]   Apparatus, equipment, materials

Do not use; class in 374.167

[.002 87]   Testing and measurement

Do not use; class in 374.126

[.002 88]   Maintenance and repair

Do not use; class in 374.168

.003–.005   Standard subdivisions

.006   Organizations

[.006 8]   Management

Do not use; class in 374.12

.007   Education, research, related topics

.008   History and description with respect to kinds of persons

For students, see 374.18. For education of a specific kind of student, see the kind in 374.182, e.g., adult education of ethnic minority students 374.1829

[.009]   Historical, geographic, persons treatment

Do not use; class in 374.9

.01   Adult education for specific objectives

Class here kinds of agencies promoting specific objectives, curricula

Class specific agencies for adult education regardless of objective in 374.94–374.99

.012   Adult basic education

Class here adult elementary, fundamental, remedial education

Citizenship programs relocated to 323.60715

.012 4   Literacy programs

> Limited to general discussion of programs to promote ability of adults to read and write up to a sixth-grade level

> Class comprehensive works on literacy programs in 379.24; class adult education in effective composition (writing) in 808.00715. Class adult education in standard usage of a specific language with the language, plus notation 800715 from Table 4, e.g., a course in basic English for adults 428.00715

.013–.019   Vocational, moral, ethical, character education; education for social responsibility, for international understanding; multicultural and bilingual education; education for creativity, for effective use of leisure

> Add to base number 374.01 the numbers following 370.11 in 370.113–370.119, e.g., adult education for effective use of leisure 374.019

.1   Organization and activities in adult education

> *For adult education for specific objectives, see 374.01; for groups, media, computers in adult education, see 374.2; for correspondence schools, see 374.4; for specific kinds of institutions and agencies, see 374.8*

[.101–.108]   Standard subdivisions

> Do not use; class in 374.001–374.008

[.109]   Historical, geographic, persons treatment

> Do not use; class in 374.9

.11–.18   School organization and activities in adult education

> Add to base number 374.1 the numbers following 371 in 371.1–371.8, e.g., students 374.18, adult education of women 374.1822; however, for use of media and computers, electronic distance education, see 374.26; for distance education, correspondence schools and courses, see 374.4

.2   Groups, media, computers in adult education

.22   Groups in adult education

> Including discussion, reading, self-help, special-interest, study groups

> *See also 374.182 for specific kinds of persons as students*

.26   Use of mass media and computers

> Standard subdivisions are added for either or both topics in heading

> Class here electronic distance education

.4   Distance education

> Class here correspondence schools and courses, open learning

> *For electronic distance education, see 374.26*

.8   **Specific kinds of institutions and agencies in adult education**

Including community centers for adult education; continuation, evening, vacation schools

Class here specific kinds of schools

Class adult education role of libraries in 021.24; class specific institutions and agencies regardless of kind in 374.94–374.99

For correspondence schools, see 374.4; for alternative colleges and universities as agencies for adult education, see 378.03; for university extension services as agencies for adult education, see 378.175

[.801–.808]   Standard subdivisions

Do not use; class in 374.001–374.008

[.809]   Historical, geographic, persons treatment

Do not use; class in 374.9

.83   Folk high schools

.830 9   Historical, geographic, persons treatment

Class specific folk high schools in 374.9

.9   **Historical, geographic, persons treatment**

Add to base number 374.9 notation 01–9 from Table 2, e.g., adult education in Canada 374.971

375   Curricula

Class curricula of a specific subject at the elementary level in 372.3–372.8. Class curricula of a specific subject for a specific level other than elementary level and for more than one level with the subject, plus notation 071 from Table 1, e.g., curricula for health 613.071; class curricula for a specific level with the level, e.g., secondary-school curricula 373.19

.000 1–.000 9   Standard subdivisions

.001   Curriculum development

For curriculum evaluation and change, see 375.006

.002   Required courses

Class here core curriculum

.004   Elective courses

.006   Evaluation and change

[.008]   Curricula directed toward specific subject objectives

Relocated to the subject, plus notation 071 from Table 1, e.g., ethnic studies curricula 305.8071

(.01–.03)	Curricula and courses in bibliography, library and information sciences, encyclopedias

> (Option: Continue to use 375.01–377.03; prefer 010–039, plus notation 071 from Table 1)

> Add to base number 375 notation 010–039, e.g., curricula in cataloging and classification 375.0253

> Relocated to specific subjects in 010–039, plus notation 071 from Table 1, e.g., curricula in cataloging and classification 025.3071

(.04)	Curricula and courses in knowledge, systems study, data processing, computer science

> (Option: Continue to use 375.04; prefer 001–006, plus notation 071 from Table 1)

> Add to base number 375.04 the numbers following 00 in 001–006, e.g., curricula in computer science 375.044

> Relocated to specific subjects in 001–006, plus notation 071 from Table 1, e.g., curricula in computer science 004.071

(.05–.99)	Curricula and courses of study in other specific subjects

> (Option: Continue to use 375.05–377.99; prefer 050–999, plus notation 071 from Table 1)

> Add to base number 375 notation 050–999, e.g., history curricula 375.9

> Relocated to specific subjects in 050–999, plus notation 071 from Table 1, e.g., history curricula 907.1

[376] Education of women

Relocated to 371.822

[377] Religious schools

Relocated to 371.07

378 Higher education

Class here college education, university education; universities

Class four-year colleges in 378.1542. Class higher education in a specific subject with the subject, plus notation 0711 from Table 1, e.g., medical schools 610.711

See Manual at 371 vs. 372–374, 378; also at 378 vs. 355.00711: Military schools

SUMMARY

.001   Philosophy and theory

.001 1   Systems

Class here systems as in systems analysis and design

Class kinds of college and university systems defined by specific kind of colleges and universities in 378.03–378.07

.002   Miscellany

[.002 84]   Apparatus, equipment, materials

Do not use; class in 378.1967

[.002 87]   Testing and measurement

Do not use; class in 378.166

[.002 88]   Maintenance and repair

Do not use; class in 378.1968

.003–.005   Standard subdivisions

.006   Organizations

[.006 8]   Management

Do not use; class in 378.101

.007   Education, research, related topics

.008   History and description with respect to kinds of persons

Do not use for students; class in 378.198. Do not use for higher education of a specific kind of student; class in 378.1982, e.g., higher education of ethnic minorities 378.19829

.008 2   Women in higher education

Do not use for higher education of women; class in 378.19822. Do not use for higher education of young women; class in 378.1982422

.009   Historical, geographic, persons treatment

.009 2   Persons

Class here administrators

Class persons associated with specific colleges and universities in 378.4–378.9

[.009 4–.009 9]   Treatment by specific continents, countries, localities in modern world

Do not use; class in 378.4–378.9

.01   Higher education for specific objectives

Add to base number 378.01 the numbers following 370.11 in 370.111–370.119, e.g., professional education 378.013

Class professional schools in 378.155

>   378.03–378.07   Specific kinds of colleges and universities

Class here specific kinds of higher education (other than public higher education) characteristic of specific kinds of colleges and universities, specific kinds of college and university systems

Class a specific kind of college and university at a specific level in 378.15; class schools for specific kinds of students in 378.1982; class specific institutions in 378.4–378.9; class comprehensive works in 378

.03   Alternative colleges and universities

Standard subdivisions are added for either or both topics in heading

Class here experimental schools of higher education, free universities, open universities, universities without walls

See also 378.175 for extension services

>   378.04–378.05   Private and public colleges and universities

Class public and private alternative colleges and universities in 378.03; class public and private colleges and universities related to religious bodies in 378.07; class comprehensive works in 378

.04   Private colleges and universities

Standard subdivisions are added for either or both topics in heading

.05   Public colleges and universities

Standard subdivisions are added for either or both topics in heading

Class comprehensive works on public higher education in 378

.052	Municipal colleges and universities

Standard subdivisions are added for either or both topics in heading

Class here county, regional colleges and universities, four-year community colleges

Class two-year community colleges, comprehensive works on community colleges in 378.1543

.053	State and provincial colleges and universities

Standard subdivisions are added for either state or provincial colleges and universities

For municipal colleges supported by state and provincial governments, see 378.052; for land-grant colleges and universities, see 378.054

.054	Land-grant colleges and universities

Standard subdivisions are added for either or both topics in heading

.055	National colleges and universities

Standard subdivisions are added for either or both topics in heading

.07	Colleges and universities related to religious bodies

Add to base number 378.07 the numbers following 371.07 in 371.071–371.079, e.g., church-related universities 378.071, Jewish universities 378.076
Subdivisions are added for either or both topics in heading

.1	**Organization and activities in higher education**

For higher education for specific objectives, see 378.01; for specific kinds of colleges and universities, see 378.03–378.07; for academic degrees and related topics, see 378.2; for student aid and related topics, see 378.3

[.100 1–.100 9]	Standard subdivisions

Do not use; class in 378.001–378.009

.101	College and university administration

Standard subdivisions are added for either or both topics in heading

Class administrators in 378.111

For financial management, see 378.106; for executive management, see 378.107; for personnel management, see 378.11; for plant and materials management, see 378.196

.101 1	Governing bodies
.101 2	Policies and regulations

.103	Community relations

Including volunteer student service (for credit or not for credit)

Interdisciplinary works on relations of colleges and universities with society relocated to 306.432

.104   Cooperation in higher education

Class here consortia in higher education

Class a specific instance of cooperation with the instance, e.g., cooperation in computer networking 004.6

.106   Financial management

Including tuition

Class student aid in 378.3

.107   Executive management

Class here planning

For governing bodies, see 378.1011; for administrators, leadership, top and middle management, see 378.111

.11   Personnel management

Class here staff

For faculty, see 378.12

.111   Administrators

Including leadership, top and middle management

For persons treatment of administrators, see 378.0092. For administrators of a specific function, see the function, e.g., directors of admissions 378.161

.112   Staff personnel

Other than administrators and faculty

For a specific kind of staff personnel, see the kind, e.g., counselors 378.194

.12   Faculty and teaching

Standard subdivisions are added for faculty and teaching together, for faculty alone

[.120 71]   Education of faculty

Do not use; class in 378.0071

.121   Academic status

Privileges, prerogatives, immunities, responsibilities

Including academic freedom, sabbatical leave, tenure

.122   Organization of teaching force

Including hierarchy

Add to base number 378.122 the numbers following 371.14 in 371.141–371.148, e.g., faculty workload 378.12212, evaluation of faculty 378.1224

.124   Personal and professional qualifications

Including discrimination because of personal characteristics

.125   Teaching

For methods of instruction and study, see 378.17

[.125 07]   Education, research, related topics in teaching

Do not use; class in 378.007

.15   Specific levels of higher education, evening school

Class specific institutions in 378.4–378.9. Class a specific topic of higher education regardless of level or school with the topic in 378.1, e.g., teaching in evening school 378.125

.154   Undergraduate colleges

Institutions conferring a bachelor's degree or lower degrees

.154 2   Four-year colleges

Including upper-class (junior-and-senior-year) colleges

Class here three-year institutions conferring the equivalent of a bachelor's degree, undergraduate departments and schools of universities

.154 3   Junior colleges

Class here four-year and three-year junior colleges, sixth-form colleges, two-year community colleges, comprehensive works on community colleges

For lower years of four-year and three-year junior colleges, of sixth-form colleges, see 373.238; for four-year community colleges, see 378.052

.155   Graduate departments and schools

Including postdoctoral programs

Class here independent institutions conferring advanced degrees, comprehensive works on professional schools

Class comprehensive works on professional education in 378.013

For professional schools at undergraduate level, see 378.154

.158   Evening school in higher education

Independent colleges, or departments of larger institutions

.16   Administration of student academic activities

> Add to base number 378.16 the numbers following 371.2 in 371.21–371.29, e.g., admissions and related topics 378.161, college-level examinations 378.1662; however, for academic degrees and related topics, see 378.2; for student aid and related topics, see 378.3
>
> Class methods of instruction in 378.17; class student participation in management in 378.1959

.17   Methods of instruction and study

> Add to base number 378.17 the numbers following 371.3 in 371.3028–371.39, e.g., extension services 378.175, seminars 378.177

.19   Guidance, discipline, physical plant, welfare, students, curricula

.194–.198   Guidance, discipline, physical plant, welfare, students

> Add to base number 378.19 the numbers following 371 in 371.4–371.8, e.g., school discipline 378.195, higher education of specific kinds of students 378.1982

.199   Curricula

> Class curricula directed toward specific educational objectives in 378.01

[.199 2–.199 8]   Curricula directed toward specific subject objectives

> Relocated to the subject, plus notation 0711 from Table 1, e.g., university ethnic studies curricula 305.80711

.2   **Academic degrees and related topics**

> Standard subdivisions are added for academic degrees and related topics together, for academic degrees alone

.24   Requirements for earned degrees

.241   Course, residence, subject requirements

.242   Thesis and dissertation requirements

> Class preparation of theses and dissertations in 808.066378

.25   Honorary degrees

.28   Academic costume

.3   **Student aid and related topics**

> Standard subdivisions are added for student aid and related topics together, for student aid alone
>
> Class student aid in a specific field with the field, plus notation 079 from Table 1, e.g., student aid in medical education 610.79

.32   Veterans' higher education benefits [*formerly* 362.8682]

.33	Fellowships and grants

Including grants for international study (student exchanges)

Class comprehensive works on student exchanges in higher education in 378.0162

.34	Scholarships
.36	Loans and employment
.362	Student loans
.365	Student employment

Including employment for service to the community

Class here employment of students by their own schools, work-study programs

For volunteer student service to community, see 378.103; for employment in connection with fellowships, see 378.33; for employment by industry and nonschool agencies in connection with ongoing academic work (work-study plan), see 378.37

.37	Cooperative education

Student employment by industry and nonschool agencies in connection with ongoing academic work

Class here work-study plan

Class general work-study programs for student employment in 378.365

.38	Costs and expenditures

Standard subdivisions are added for either or both topics in heading

.4–.9   **Higher education in specific continents, countries, localities in modern world**

Class here specific schools

Add to base number 378 notation 4–9 from Table 2, e.g., higher education in Mexico 378.72
(Option: If it is desired to give local emphasis and a shorter number to a specific college or university, place it first by use of a letter or other symbol, e.g., University of South Africa 378.S [preceding 378.4])

Class a school or department of a college or university devoted to a specific subject with the subject, plus notation 0711 from Table 1, e.g., Harvard Law School 340.07117444

379   Public policy issues in education

Class public administration of education in 353.8; class school administration in 371.2

For public policy issues on a topic not provided for here, see the topic, e.g., policy on school admissions 371.21, on medical schools 610.711

See Manual at 371 vs. 353.8, 371.2, 379

SUMMARY

379.1	**Specific elements of support and control of public education**
.2	**Specific policy issues in public education**
.3	**Public policy issues in private education**
.4–.9	**Public policy issues in specific continents, countries, localities in modern world**

[.094–.099]   Treatment by specific continents, countries, localities in modern world

Do not use; class in 379.4–379.9

.1   Specific elements of support and control of public education

Class support and control of activities involved in specific policy issues in public education in 379.2

[.101–.109]   Standard subdivisions

Do not use; class in 379.01–379.09

.11   Support of public education

Class here financial support

Financial administration of agencies supporting public education relocated to 353.824

For support by specific levels of government, international support, see 379.12; for revenue sources, see 379.13

.111   Educational vouchers

Regardless of level of government

Class here school choice

Class educational vouchers for a specific level of education in 379.112–379.118; class educational vouchers for special education in 379.119

For use of educational vouchers in private education, see 379.32

.112   Support of public elementary education

.113   Support of public secondary education

.114   Public support of adult education

.118	Support of public higher education
.119	Public support of special education
.12	Support by specific level of government, international support

Class educational vouchers regardless of level of government providing them in 379.111; class revenue sources of specific levels of government in 379.13

.121	Support by national governments
.121 2	National support of elementary education
.121 3	National support of secondary education
.121 4	National support of higher education
.121 5	National support of adult education
.121 6	National support of special education
.122	Support by state, provincial, regional governments

Add to base number 379.122 the numbers following 379.121 in 379.1212–379.1216, e.g., state support of adult education 379.1225

.123	Local support
.129	International support

Class here international multicultural educational aid

.129 09	Historical, geographic, persons treatment

Do not use for geographic treatment by recipient area; class in 379.1291–379.1299

.129 1–.129 9	Geographic treatment by recipient area

Add to base number 379.129 notation 1–9 from Table 2, e.g., e.g. educational aid to Asia 379.1295; then, for area providing support, add 0*, and again add notation 1–9 from Table 2, e.g., French educational aid to Asia 379.1295044

.13	Revenue sources

Including bond issues

Class here school taxes

Class financial assistance from higher levels of government in 379.12

.15	Control of public education

> 379.151–379.153 Control by specific governmental level

Class control of specific aspects of education regardless of level in 379.155–379.158; class comprehensive works in 379.15

---

*Add 00 for standard subdivisions; see instructions at beginning of Table 1

.151	Control by national governments
.152	Control by state, provincial, regional governments
.153	Control by local governments
.153 1	School boards
.153 5	School districts

> Including centralization and consolidation of schools, changing school attendance boundaries

---

> 379.155–379.158 **Control of specific aspects of education**

Class comprehensive works in 379.15

For control of a specific aspect of education not provided for here, see the aspect, e.g., control of school discipline 371.5

.155	Control of curriculum

See also 379.28 for place of religion in public education

.156	Control of teaching materials

Class here control of textbooks

.157	Control of teachers and administrators

Class control of specific aspects of teachers and teaching in 371.1; class control of specific aspects of school administrators in 371.2011

.158	School standards and accreditation

Class here school accountability, evaluation

Government commissions on standards and accreditation in higher education relocated to 353.88284

.2	**Specific policy issues in public education**

Not otherwise provided for

[.201–.209]	Standard subdivisions

Do not use; class in 379.01–379.09

.23	Compulsory education

Including school-leaving age

.24	Literacy policies

Class here right to read

.26	Educational equalization (Equal educational opportunity)

Class here affirmative action, right to education

.263	School desegregation

Including busing to achieve desegregation

.28	Place of religion in public schools

Regardless of faith or denomination

Including teaching creationism in public schools

.3	**Public policy issues in private education**
.32	Public support of private education

Class here educational vouchers, financial support

.322	Public support of private elementary education
.323	Public support of private secondary education
.324	Public support of private higher education
.326	Public support of private adult education
.328	Public support of private special education
.34	Public control of private education

Add to base number 379.34 the numbers following 379.32 in 379.322–397.328, e.g., public control of private elementary education 379.342

.4–.9	**Public policy issues in specific continents, countries, localities in modern world**

Add to base number 379 notation 4–9 from Table 2, e.g., public educational policies in United States 379.73

380　Commerce, communications, transportation

Except for modifications shown under specific entries, add to each subdivision identified by * as follows:

06	Organization and management
065	Business organizations

Including individual proprietorships, partnerships, companies, public and private corporations, combinations
Add to 065 notation 3–9 from Table 2, e.g., business organizations of France 06544
See Manual at 380: Add table: 09 vs. 065

068	Management

Public and private

09	Historical, geographic, persons treatment

Class specific business organizations in 065
See Manual at 380: Add table: 09 vs. 065

Class public regulation and control in 354.7

See Manual at 380

SUMMARY

380.01–.09	**Standard subdivisions**
.1	**Commerce (Trade)**
381	**Internal commerce (Domestic trade)**
382	**International commerce (Foreign trade)**
383	**Postal communication**
384	**Communications Telecommunication**
385	**Railroad transportation**
386	**Inland waterway and ferry transportation**
387	**Water, air, space transportation**
388	**Transportation Ground transportation**
389	**Metrology and standardization**

.01–.09   Standard subdivisions

.1   *Commerce (Trade)

Class here warehousing, interdisciplinary works on marketing

Class supply and demand in 338.1–338.5; class restrictive practices in business organizations engaged in commerce in 338.82; class comprehensive works on warehousing in 388.044; class interdisciplinary works on consumption in 339.47. Class cooperative, labor, finance, land, energy economics in relation to commerce with the branch of economics in 330, e.g., cooperative marketing 334.6813801

For internal commerce, see 381; for international commerce, see 382; for management of marketing, see 658.8

See Manual at 380.1 and 381, 382; also at 380.1 vs. 658.8

.102 9   Commercial miscellany

Class here interdisciplinary works on commercial miscellany

Notation 029 from Table 1 is seldom used with the subdivisions of 380.1

For commercial miscellany with respect to specific goods and services, see the goods and services, plus notation 029 from Table 1, e.g., buyers guides for tools 621.900296

See Manual at 338 vs. 060, 381, 382, 670.294, 910, T1—025, T1—0294, T1—0296

[.102 97]   Evaluation and purchasing manuals

Do not use; class in 381.33

.13   Commercial policy

Class commercial policy with respect to specific products and services, to specific groups of products and services in 380.14

.14   Specific products and services

.141   *Products of agriculture

*Add as instructed under 380

| [.141 029] | Commercial miscellany |
| | Do not use; class in 630.209 |

| .141 3–.141 8 | Specific products |

Add to base number 380.141 the numbers following 63 in 633–638, e.g., rice 380.141318

| .142 | *Products of mineral industries |

| [.142 029] | Commercial miscellany |
| | Do not use; class in 553.029 |

| .142 2–.142 9 | Specific products |

Add to base number 380.142 the numbers following 553 in 553.2–553.9, e.g., oil 380.142282

| .143 | *Products of other extractive industries |

| [.143 029] | Commercial miscellany |
| | Do not use; class in 639.029 |

| .143 1 | *Products of culture of invertebrates and cold-blooded vertebrates |

Class products of insect culture in 380.1418

| [.143 102 9] | Commercial miscellany |
| | Do not use; class in 639.029 |

| .143 13–.143 17 | Specific products |

Add to base number 380.1431 the numbers following 639 in 639.3–639.7, e.g., oysters 380.143141

| .143 2–.143 9 | Products of fishing, whaling, hunting, trapping |

Add to base number 380.143 the numbers following 59 in 592–599, e.g., fur 380.14397, comprehensive works on products of both finfishing and shellfishing industries 380.1437

| .144 | *Human beings (Slave trade) |

| .145 | Products of secondary industries and services |

| .145 000 1–.145 000 9 | Standard subdivisions |

Notation from Table 1 as modified under 380, e.g., companies 380.14500065

| .145 001–.145 999 | Specific products and services |

Add to base number 380.145 notation 001–999, e.g., clothing 380.145687; then add further as instructed under 380, e.g., clothing stores 380.145687065

See Manual at 709.2 vs. 380.1457092

*Add as instructed under 380

>   ### 381–382   Internal and international commerce (trade)

Class here marketing

Class supply and demand in 338.1–338.5; class comprehensive works in 380.1. Class cooperative, labor, finance, land, energy economics in relation to internal and international commerce with the branch of economics in 330, e.g., retail clerks' unions 331.88113811

381   *Internal commerce (Domestic trade)

Unless other instructions are given, observe the following table of preference, e.g., retail trade in rice 381.41318 (*not* 381.1):

Specific products and services	381.4
Retail and wholesale trade	381.1–381.2
Interregional and interstate commerce	381.5
Commercial policy	381.3

See Manual at 338 vs. 060, 381, 382, 670.294, 910, T1—025, T1—0294, T1—0296; also at 380.1 and 381, 382

[.029 7]   Evaluation and purchasing manuals

Do not use; class in 381.33

.1   *Retail trade

Including exhibit and trade shows, telemarketing, telephone selling, television selling

Class telephone-order houses, telephone selling organizations in 381.142; class consumer problems and their alleviation in 381.3

For consumer cooperatives, see 334.5

See Manual at 381.1 vs. 381.4, 658.87

.12   *Chain stores

Class chain stores with a specific merchandising pattern in 381.14

.13   *Franchise businesses

Class franchise businesses with a specific merchandising pattern in 381.14

.14   Retail channels by merchandising pattern

For factory outlets, see 381.15; for outdoor and street markets, see 381.18

.141   *Department stores

.142   *Mail-order, telephone-order, television selling organizations

.147   *Convenience stores

*Add as instructed under 380

.148	*Supermarkets
.149	*Discount stores
.15	*Factory outlets
.17	*Auctions
.18	*Outdoor and street markets

> Including fairs
>
> Subdivisions are added for either or both topics in heading
>
> Class outdoor and street markets for secondhand goods in 381.19

.19   *Outlets for secondhand goods

> *For auctions, see 381.17*

.192   *Flea markets

.195   Garage, yard, apartment sales

.2   *Wholesale trade

.3   Commercial policy

> Class here consumer problems and their alleviation, consumerism

.32   Consumer movements

> Class specific activities of consumer movements in 381.33–381.34

.33   Consumer information

> Provision of information to consumers by governments and private groups
>
> Including research, testing of products
>
> Class here comprehensive works on evaluation of products and services to be purchased, interdisciplinary evaluation and purchasing manuals
>
> > *For evaluation and purchasing guides and consumer education for household and personal products and services, see 640.73. For evaluation and purchasing manuals for specific products or services, see the product or service, plus notation 0297 from Table 1, e.g., manual on evaluating tools 621.900297*

.34   Consumer protection

> Government and private action directed toward producers and sellers to promote product quality and safety, truth in advertising and labeling
>
> Class product hazards in 363.19; class fraud in 364.163

---

*Add as instructed under 380

.4 **Specific products and services**

Class here works discussing consumption as a measure of the volume, value, or kind of trade in specific products

Add to base number 381.4 the numbers following 380.14 in 380.141–380.145, e.g., domestic trade in products of agriculture 381.41, of rice 381.41318

Class interdisciplinary works on consumption of specific products and services in 339.48

See Manual at 381.1 vs. 381.4, 658.87

.5 ***Interregional and interstate commerce**

Commerce between parts of a single jurisdiction

382 *International commerce (Foreign trade)

Class here trade between nations and their colonies, protectorates, trusts

Unless other instructions are given, observe the following table of preference, e.g., import trade in rice 382.41318 (*not* 382.5):

International commerce by product and service	382.4
Tariff policy	382.7
Import and export trade	382.5–382.6
Generalities of international commerce	382.1
Trade agreements	382.9
Commercial policy	382.3

Class interdisciplinary works on international finance in 332.042; class interdisciplinary works on international economics in 337

See Manual at 338 vs. 060, 381, 382, 670.294, 910, T1—025, T1—0294, T1—0296; also at 380.1 and 381, 382

SUMMARY

382.01–.09	**Standard subdivisions**
.1	**Generalities of international commerce**
.3	**Commercial policy**
.4	**International commerce by product and service**
.5	**Import trade**
.6	**Export trade**
.7	**Tariff policy**
.9	**Trade agreements**

.01 Philosophy and theory

Do not use for theories of international commerce; class in 382.104

.09 Historical, geographic, persons treatment

*Add as instructed under 380

.091   International commerce of areas, regions, places in general

> Add to base number 382.091 the numbers following —1 in notation 11–19 from Table 2, e.g., international commerce of developing countries 382.091724; then, for commerce between an area, region, or place and another area, region, place or a continent, country, locality, add 0† and add notation 1 or 3–9 from Table 2, e.g., commerce between developing countries and United Kingdom 382.091724041
> > Do not follow add instructions under —091 in Table 1

> Give priority in notation to the region, area, place emphasized. If emphasis is equal, give priority to the one coming first in Table 2
> > (Option: Give priority in notation to the region, area, place requiring local emphasis, e.g., libraries in United States class trade between developing nations and United States in 382.097301724)

.093–.099   International commerce in specific continents, countries, localities

> Add to base number 382.09 notation 3–9 from Table 2, e.g., international commerce of United Kingdom 382.0941; then, for commerce between two continents, countries, localities or between a continent, country, locality and a region, area, place, add 0† and add notation 1 or 3–9 from Table 2, e.g., commerce between United Kingdom and communist bloc 382.094101717
> > Do not use add table under —093–099 in Table 1

> Give priority in notation to the continent, country, locality emphasized. If emphasis is equal, give priority to the one coming first in Table 2
> > (Option: Give priority in notation to the continent, country, locality requiring local emphasis, e.g., libraries in United States class trade between United Kingdom and United States in 382.0973041)

.1   **Generalities of international commerce**

.104   Theories

.104 2   Specialization and comparative advantage

> Standard subdivisions are added for either or both topics in heading

> Class comprehensive works in 338.6046

[.104 4]   Price determination in international markets

> Relocated to 338.52

.17   Balance of payments

> Relation between payments and receipts resulting from all commercial and financial transactions carried on between the citizens and government of a country and the citizens and governments of all other countries

> Class here balance of trade

[.173]   International capital transactions

> Relocated to 332.042

---

†Add 00 for standard subdivisions; see instructions at beginning of Table 1

[.174]   International currency movements

> Use of this number for relation of monetary conditions to world trade discontinued; class in 382.17
>
> International currency movements relocated to 332.042

.3   **Commercial policy**

> Class economic imperialism in 337

.4   **International commerce by products and services**

> Standard subdivisions are added for either or both topics in heading
>
> Class here works discussing consumption as a measure of the volume, value, or kind of trade in specific products
>
> Add to base number 382.4 the numbers following 380.14 in 380.141–380.145, e.g., foreign trade in products of agriculture 382.41, of rice 382.41318
>
> Class interdisciplinary works on consumption of specific products and services in 339.48

.5   ***Import trade**

> Class here nontariff barriers to trade
>
> Class the combined import and export trade of a country, the trade between two countries in 382.09; class agreements on nontariff barriers to trade in 382.9

.52   Import quotas

.53   Embargoes on imports

.54   Licensing of imports

.6   ***Export trade**

> Class the combined import and export trade of a country, the trade between two countries in 382.09

.61   Export trade by export market area

.610 9   Historical, geographic, persons treatment

> Class here the area to which goods are being exported
>
> Class the area doing the exporting in 382.609

.63   Export policy

> Including subsidies, services to exporters
>
> *For export controls and restrictions, see 382.64*

.64   Export controls and restrictions

> Standard subdivisions are added for either or both topics in heading
>
> Including licensing, inspection

*Add as instructed under 380

.7   **Tariff policy**

Including drawbacks

Class here comprehensive works on trade barriers and restrictions

Class tax aspects of customs duties in 336.26; class agreements on trade barriers in 382.9

For nontariff barriers to trade, see 382.5

.71   Free trade

.72   Tariff for revenue

.73   Protective and prohibitive tariffs

Standard subdivisions are added for either or both topics in heading

.75   Single and multiple column tariffs

.752   Single column tariffs

Single rates for each product

.753   Multiple column tariffs

Varying rates on the same product designed to favor certain countries of origin

Including generalized system of preference (GSP)

.78   Exemptions

.782   Personal and institutional exemptions

Including products used for educational purposes; privileges for foreign-service personnel, for tourists

.788   Relief supply exemptions

.9   **Trade agreements**

Class here agreements on nontariff barriers to trade, on tariffs

Class general economic cooperation and international arrangements for this purpose in 337; class texts and discussions of treaties in 341.754

.909   Historical, geographic, persons treatment

Do not use for multilateral agreements; class in 382.91. Do not use for bilateral agreements; class in 382.93–382.99

.91   Multilateral agreements

Class here customs unions

Class bilateral agreements in 382.93–382.99; class interdisciplinary works on international governmental organizations in 341.2

For World Trade Organization, see 382.92

[.910 91]   Treatment by area, regions, places in general

                     Do not use; class in 382.911

[.910 93–.910 99]   Treatment by specific continents, countries, localities

                     Do not use; class in 382.913–382.919

.911   Multilateral agreements in areas, regions, places in general

                     Add to base number 382.911 the numbers following — 1 in notation 11–19 from Table 2, e.g., western bloc nations 382.911713

.913   Multilateral agreements in ancient world

                     Add to base number 382.913 the numbers following — 3 in notation 31–39 from Table 2, e.g., ancient Greece 382.9138

\>   382.914–382.919   Multilateral agreements in modern world

                     Class comprehensive works in 382.91

.914   Multilateral agreements in Europe

.914 2   European Union

                     Class here European Common Market, European Community, European Economic Community

.914 3   European Free Trade Association (EFTA)

.914 7   Council for Mutual Economic Assistance (COMECON)

.915–.919   Multilateral agreements in other continents and regions

                     Add to base number 382.91 notation 5–9 from Table 2, e.g., southeast Asia 382.9159

.92   World Trade Organization (WTO)

                     Class here General Agreement on Tariffs and Trade (GATT)

.93–.99   Trade agreements by specific countries

                     Add to base number 382.9 notation 3–9 from Table 2, e.g., trade agreements of United Kingdom 382.941; then, for bilateral agreements, add 0† and again add notation 3–9 from Table 2, e.g., agreements between United Kingdom and France 382.941044
                     Do not use add table under —093–099 in Table 1

                     Give priority in notation to the country emphasized. If emphasis is equal, give priority to the one coming first in Table 2
                     (Option: Give priority in notation to the country requiring local emphasis, e.g., libraries in United States class agreements between United Kingdom and United States in 382.973041)

---

†Add 00 for standard subdivisions; see instructions at beginning of Table 1

> ## 383–388   Communications and transportation

Class comprehensive works on communications in 384; class comprehensive works on communications and transportation together, on transportation alone in 388

Comprehensive works on the activities, services, and facilities of a system are classed in the number for the system, e.g., radio broadcasting activities, services, and facilities 384.54, not 384.544.

See Manual at 383–388

383   Postal communication

Class comprehensive works on communications in 384

See also 769.56 for philately

See Manual at 383–388

.06   Organizations and management

Do not use for postal organizations; class in 383.4

[.09]   Historical, geographic, persons treatment

Do not use; class in 383.49

.1   Mail handling

.12   Classes of mail

Class a specific mode of transportation for a specific class of mail in 383.141–383.144. Class a specific service for a specific class of mail with the service, e.g., special delivery of letters 383.183

.120 01–.120 09   Standard subdivisions

>   383.120 2–383.120 5   Special classes

Class comprehensive works in 383.12

.120 2   Free mail

Including franking privileges

.120 5   Nonmailable matter

Including obscene and subversive material

.122   Letters, postcards, sealed material

Class here first-class mail

.123   Newspapers and periodicals

Class here second-class mail

.124   Printed material

Not provided for elsewhere

Including books, catalogs, circulars; bulk mailings

Class here third-class mail

.125   Parcels

Class here fourth-class mail

Class printed matter in 383.124

.14   Transportation systems, collection, delivery

Standard subdivisions are added for transportation systems, collection, delivery together; for transportation systems alone

---

>   383.141–383.144   Transportation systems

Class comprehensive works in 383.14

.141   Facsimile transmission

.142   Sea mail

.143   Overland mail

Including inland waterway, railroad mail; star routes

.144   Air mail

Including mail carried through space

.145   Collection and delivery

Including postal zones

Class collection and delivery of mail within the military services in 355.69; class star routes in 383.143; class special delivery in 383.183

.145 5   Postal codes

Class here zip code

.18   Other services

Including express mail

.182   Insured and registered mail

Standard subdivisions are added for either or both topics in heading

.183   Special delivery and special handling

Standard subdivisions are added for either or both topics in heading

.184   Cash on delivery (Collect on delivery, COD)

.186   Dead letter services

.2   **Economic aspects of production**

Class economic aspects of mail handling in 383.1

See also 330 for other economic aspects, e.g., postal workers' unions 331.8811383

.23   Rates and costs

Including use of postage stamps

.24   Efficiency of operation

Including use of mechanization and automation

.4   **Postal organization**

[.409]   Historical, geographic, persons treatment

Do not use; class in 383.49

.41   International systems and conventions

.42   Post offices

.46   Internal services

Including dispatching and routing, postal inspection

.49   Historical, geographic, persons treatment of postal communication, of postal organizations and systems

Add to base number 383.49 notation 1–9 from Table 2, e.g., postal communication in Europe 383.494

384   *Communications   Telecommunication

Including recordings, visual signaling

Class here interdisciplinary works on telecommunication [*formerly also* 004.6]

Class comprehensive works on communications and transportation in 388

For postal communication, see 383

See also 302.2 for sociology of communication

See Manual at 383–388

SUMMARY

384.04	Special topics
.1	Telegraphy
.3	Computer communication
.5	Wireless communication
.6	Telephony
.8	Motion pictures

*Add as instructed under 380

.04   Special topics

.041   Economic aspects of production

> Class economic aspects of facilities in 384.042; class economic aspects of activities and services in 384.043
>
> *See also 330 for other economic aspects, e.g., telecommunication workers' unions 331.8811384*

.042   Facilities

> Including stations
>
> Class use of facilities in specific activities and services in 384.043

.043   Activities and services

> Standard subdivisions are added for either or both topics in heading

---

>   **384.1–384.6 Telecommunication**

Class comprehensive works in 384

.1   ***Telegraphy**

> Class here submarine cable telegraphy
>
> *For radiotelegraphy, see 384.52*

.102 84   Materials

> Do not use for apparatus and equipment; class in 384.15

.13   Economic aspects of production

> Class economic aspects of activities and services in 384.14; class economic aspects of facilities in 384.15
>
> *See also 330 for other economic aspects, e.g., telegraphy workers' unions 331.88113841*

.14   ***Activities and services**

> Including Morse and other code telegraphy, printing telegraphy; stock tickers, teletype, telex; comprehensive works on facsimile transmission
>
> Subdivisions are added for either or both topics in heading
>
> Class comprehensive works on electronic mail in 384.34
>
> *For postal facsimile transmission, see 383.141*

.15   Facilities

> Class use of facilities in specific activities and services in 384.14

---

*Add as instructed under 380

.3 ***Computer communication**

Transfer of computer-based information by any of various media (e.g., coaxial cable or radio waves) from one computer to another or between computers and terminals

Class here computer communications networks, links between computers via telephone lines

Class interdisciplinary works on computer communications in 004.6

See Manual at 004.6 vs. 384.3

.302 85 Data processing Computer applications

Class here computer science applied to economic and related aspects of providing computer communication to the public

.31 Economic aspects of production

Class economic aspects of production of computer communication hardware and software and comprehensive works on production and sale in 338.470046; class sale of computer communication hardware and software in 380.1450046; class economic aspects of facilities in 384.32; class economic aspects of activities and services in 384.33

See also 330 for other economic aspects, e.g., computer communication workers' unions 331.88113843

.32 Facilities

Class use of facilities in specific activities and services in 384.33

.33 Activities and services

Standard subdivisions are added for either or both topics in heading

Including services of value-added networks

For electronic mail, see 384.34; for videotex, see 384.35

See Manual at 004.678 vs. 025.04, 384.33

.34 **Electronic mail**

Including teletex

Class here comprehensive works on electronic mail

Class interdisciplinary works on electronic mail in 004.692

For a specific kind of electronic mail, see the kind, e.g., postal facsimile transmission 383.141, telex 384.14

See Manual at 384.34 vs. 384.352

.35 **Videotex**

.352 **Broadcast videotex (Teletext)**

See Manual at 384.34 vs. 384.352

*Add as instructed under 380

.354   *Interactive videotex (Viewdata)

See also 006.6 for interactive video

.5   *Wireless communication

SUMMARY

384.51	**Satellite communication**
.52	**Radiotelegraphy**
.53	**Radiotelephony**
.54	**Radiobroadcasting**
.55	**Television**

.51   *Satellite communication

For a specific form of satellite communication, see the form, e.g., television transmission by satellite 384.552

.52   *Radiotelegraphy

.523–.525   Economic aspects, activities and services, facilities

Add to base number 384.52 the numbers following 384.1 in 384.13–384.15, e.g., apparatus 384.525

.53   *Radiotelephony

Including ship-to-shore communication, citizens band radio

Class here portable telephones

.533–.535   Economic aspects, activities and services, facilities

Add to base number 384.53 the numbers following 384.6 in 384.63–384.65, e.g., transmitting and receiving equipment 384.535

.54   *Radiobroadcasting

Class here public (noncommercial) broadcasting, public aspects of amateur radio, interdisciplinary works on radiobroadcasting and television broadcasting

For television broadcasting, see 384.55

See Manual at 384.54, 384.55, 384.8 vs. 791.4

.540 65   Business organizations

Number built according to instructions under 380

Including network affiliates, public (noncommercial) networks and stations

Class here stations and networks

See Manual at 384.54065 vs. 384.5453, 384.5455; also at 384.54, 384.55, 384.8 vs. 791.4

*Add as instructed under 380

.543	Economic aspects of production

> Class economic aspects of activities and services in 384.544; class economic aspects of facilities in 384.545

> *See also 330 for other economic aspects, e.g., radiobroadcasting workers' unions 331.881138454*

.544	*Activities and services

> Subdivisions are added for either or both topics in heading

.544 2	Scheduling

> Including sale of time

.544 3	Programs

> Class techniques of producing programs in 791.44. Class a specific type of program with the type, e.g., news broadcasts 070.194

.545	Facilities

> Class use of facilities in specific activities and services in 384.544

.545 2	Broadcasting channels

> Class listings of stations by channel (assigned frequency) in 384.5453025

.545 24	Frequency allocation
.545 3	Stations

> Including AM, FM stations

> Class stations as business organizations in 384.54065

> *See Manual at 384.54065 vs. 384.5453, 384.5455*

.545 5	Networks

> Class networks as business organizations in 384.54065

> *See Manual at 384.54065 vs. 384.5453, 384.5455*

.545 6	Satellites
.55	Television

> Including low power television (LPTV) stations (stations that rebroadcast the programs of full-service stations, originate programming that often includes pay television, and are usually limited in power to 10–1000 watts and a 10–mile to 15–mile broadcasting radius)

> Unless other instructions are given, class a subject with aspects in two or more subdivisions of 384.55 in the number coming last, e.g., economic aspects of cable television and controlled transmission television 384.5561 (*not* 384.5551)

> *See Manual at 384.54, 384.55, 384.8 vs. 791.4*

*Add as instructed under 380

.550 65		Business organizations

Number built according to instructions under 380

Organizations engaged in two or more aspects of television, e.g., pay television organizations that produce video products

Including network affiliates; nonaffiliated commercial, private television

Class here stations and networks

Public (Noncommercial) television relocated to 384.554

> *See Manual at 384.55065 vs. 384.5522, 384.5523; also at 384.54, 384.55, 384.8 vs. 791.4*

.551	Economic aspects of production of television in general

> *See also 330 for other economic aspects, e.g., television workers' unions 331.881138455*

.552	Facilities and channels of television in general

Class here direct broadcast satellite (DBS) systems, satellites, satellite dishes

.552 1	Broadcasting channels

Including frequency allocation

.552 2	Stations

Class stations as business organizations in 384.55065

> *See Manual at 384.55065 vs. 384.5522, 384.5523*

.552 3	Networks

Class networks as business organizations in 384.55065

> *See Manual at 384.55065 vs. 384.5522, 384.5523*

.553	*Activities and services of television in general

Subdivisions are added for either or both topics in heading

.553 1	Scheduling

Including sale of time

.553 2	Programs

Class technique of producing programs in 791.45. Class a specific type of program with the type, e.g., news broadcasts 070.195

*Add as instructed under 380

.554	*General broadcasting (Free television)

Transmitting signals over the air for use by the general public

Including translator stations (low-power stations for transmitting the signals of television broadcast stations to areas where reception is unsatisfactory)

Class here public (noncommercial) television [*formerly* 384.55065]

Class works combining both general broadcasting and cable television in 384.55

.554 3	Economic aspects of production

> *See also 330 for other economic aspects, e.g., public television workers' unions 331.8811384554*

.554 4	*Activities and services

Subdivisions are added for either or both topics in heading

.554 42	Scheduling

Including sale of time

.554 43	Programs

Including local programming

Class techniques of producing programs in 791.45. Class a specific type of program with the type, e.g., news broadcasts 070.195

.554 5	Facilities and channels

Class here direct broadcast satellite (DBS) systems, satellites, satellite dishes

Class use of facilities and channels in specific activities and services in 384.5544

.554 52	Broadcasting channels
.554 53	Stations

Class stations as business organizations in 384.554065

> *See Manual at 384.55065 vs. 384.5522, 384.5523*

.554 55	Networks

Class networks as business organizations in 384.554065

> *See Manual at 384.55065 vs. 384.5522, 384.5523*

.554 6	*Community antenna television (CATV) systems

Systems that provide television reception to remote communities, using a tall antenna, usually limited to no more than 12 channels

---

*Add as instructed under 380

.554 61–.554 63   Economic aspects, activities and services, facilities

> Add to base number 384.5546 the numbers following 384.55 in 384.551–384.553, e.g., networks 384.554623

.555   *Pay television

Systems that receive and distribute signals to customers who pay for the service

Class here cable television

Class works combining general broadcasting and cable television in 384.55; class pay television in Canada in 384.5554; class use of cable television in closed-circuit television in 384.556

See Manual at 384.555 vs. 384.5554

.555 1–.555 3   Economic aspects, facilities and channels, activities and services

> Add to base number 384.555 the numbers following 384.55 in 384.551–384.553, e.g., networks 384.55523

.555 4   *Premium (Subscription) television

Systems that scramble signals that are decoded for a fee

Including Cinemax, Home Box Office (HBO), Showtime, The Movie Channel (TMC)

Class here pay-cable, pay television in Canada

See also 384.55 for low power television (LPTV) stations

See Manual at 384.555 vs. 384.5554

.555 41–.555 43   Economic aspects, activities and services, facilities

> Add to base number 384.5554 the numbers following 384.55 in 384.551–384.553, e.g., facilities 384.55542

.556   *Controlled transmission television (Closed-circuit television)

Systems where the signals are carried to a specific audience

Including theater television

Class here industrial uses, e.g., surveillance, monitoring of hazardous industrial processes

.556 1–.556 3   Economic aspects, activities and services, facilities

> Add to base number 384.556 the numbers following 384.55 in 384.551–384.553, e.g., rates 384.5561

*Add as instructed under 380

.558   *Video production

> Including camcorders, video cassette recorders (VCRs), video disc players, videotapes, laser optical discs

> Class video production associated with a specific aspect of television communication with the aspect, e.g., video production in cable television 384.555

.6   ***Telephony**

> Class here comprehensive works on wire and cable communication

> *For telegraphy, see 384.1; for radiotelephony, portable telephones, see 384.53; for cable television, see 384.555*

.602 5   Directories of persons and organizations

> *See also 914–919, plus notation 0025 from table under 913–919, for telephone directories, e.g., New York City telephone directory 917.4710025*

.63   Economic aspects of production

> Class economic aspects of activities and services in 384.64; class economic aspects of facilities in 384.65

> *See also 330 for other economic aspects, e.g., telephone unions workers' 331.88113846*

.64   *Activities and services

> Including caller ID telephone service; conference calls; emergency services; local, long-distance, overseas service

> Subdivisions are added for either or both topics in heading

.646   *Audiotex

> Including dial-a-message telephone calls

.65   Facilities

> Including stations, lines, switchboards, dialing systems, transmitting and receiving equipment

> Class use of facilities in specific activities and services in 384.64

.8   ***Motion pictures**

> *See Manual at 384.54, 384.55, 384.8 vs. 791.4*

.83–.85   Economic aspects, activities and services, facilities

> Add to base number 384.8 the numbers following 384.1 in 384.13–384.15, e.g., activities 384.84

---

*Add as instructed under 380

385 *Railroad transportation

Class here standard-gage and broad-gage railways

Class comprehensive works on transportation, on ground transportation in 388

For local rail transit systems, see 388.42

See Manual at 383–388; also at 629.046 vs. 388

.065   Business organizations

Number built according to instructions under 380

Class here railroad companies

See also 385.5065 for narrow-gage and special-duty railroad companies, 385.6065 for inclined and mountain railroad companies

---

> 385.1–385.3 Specific aspects

Class specific aspects of narrow-gage and special-duty railroads in 385.5; class specific aspects of inclined and mountain railroads in 385.6; class comprehensive works in 385

.1   **Economic aspects of production**

Class economic aspects of activities and services in 385.2; class economic aspects of facilities in 385.3

See also 330 for other economic aspects, e.g., railroad workers' unions 331.8811385

.2   **Activities and services**

Standard subdivisions are added for either or both topics in heading

.204   Special topics

.204 2   Basic activities

Including dispatching, routing, scheduling, traffic control

For operation of rolling stock, see 385.2044

.204 4   Operation of rolling stock

> 385.22–385.24 Transportation activities and services

Class comprehensive works in 385.2

.22   *Passenger services

Including baggage, meal, sleeper services

.23   *Express transportation of goods

*Add as instructed under 380

.24	*Freight services

Class unitized cargo services in 385.72

For express transportation of goods, see 385.23

.26	Activities and services of terminals and stations

Standard subdivisions are added for either or both topics in heading

Including fueling

.262	*Passenger services

Including passenger amenities, reservation systems

.264	*Freight services

Including freight handling, warehousing, storage

For railroad mail, see 383.143

.3	**Facilities**

Class use of facilities in specific activities and services in 385.2

.31	Stationary facilities

.312	The way

Including bridges, grade crossings, tracks, tunnels

.314	Terminals and stations

Including yards, roundhouses, train sheds, shop buildings

.316	Communications facilities

Including signals

.32–.34	Cars

Add to base number 385.3 the numbers following 625.2 in 625.22–625.24, e.g., diners 385.33

Class comprehensive works in 385.37

.36	Locomotives

Add to base number 385.36 the numbers following 625.26 in 625.261–625.266, e.g., steam locomotives 385.361

.37	Rolling stock

For cars, see 385.32–385.34; for locomotives, see 385.36

*Add as instructed under 380

.5   ***Narrow-gage and special-purpose railroads**

Including monorail railroads

Class here interurban railroads

For inclined and mountain railroads, see 385.6; for special-purpose railroads located entirely within a metropolitan region, see 388.42–388.46

.52   ***Narrow-gage railroads**

Class narrow-gage industrial railroads in 385.54

.54   ***Industrial railroads**

Subdivisions are added without regard to the purpose of the railroad, e.g., lumber railroads in Georgia 385.5409758, mine railroads in Colorado 385.5409788

.6   ***Inclined and mountain railroad systems**

Including cable, funicular, rack railroads

.7   **Railroad combined with other transportation systems**

.72   ***Unitized cargo services**

Including piggyback transportation (trucks, trailers, buses, private automobiles on flatcars)

For container-ship operations, see 387.5442

.77   ***Ship railroads**

Rail transportation of vessels overland between bodies of water

386   ***Inland waterway and ferry transportation**

Class comprehensive works on water transportation in 387; class comprehensive works on transportation in 388

See Manual at 383–388; also at 629.046 vs. 388

.1   **Economic aspects of production**

Class economic aspects of facilities in 386.2; class economic aspects of activities and services in 386.24; class economic aspects of specific kinds of inland water and ferry transportation in 386.3–386.6

See also 330 for other economic aspects, e.g., inland-waterway transportation workers' unions 331.8811386

.2   **Activities, services, facilities**

Class activities and facilities (except for ships and ports) of specific types of inland water systems in 386.3–386.6; class activities, services, facilities of ports in 386.8

---

*Add as instructed under 380

.22   Ships

Including air-cushion vehicles

Add to base number 386.22 the numbers following 623.82 in 623.821–623.829, e.g., tugboats 386.2232

Class use of ships in specific activities and services in 386.24

.24   Activities and services

Standard subdivisions are added for either or both topics in heading

.240 4   Special topics

.240 42   Basic activities

Including dispatching, routing, scheduling, traffic control

For operation of ships, see 386.24044

.240 44   Operation of ships

.242   *Passenger services

Including baggage, meal, sleeper services

.244   *Freight services

For inland waterway mail, see 383.143

>   **386.3–386.6 Specific kinds of inland water and ferry transportation**

Class here activities, services, facilities

Class ships for specific kinds of inland water transportation in 386.22; class ports for specific kinds of inland water transportation in 386.8; class comprehensive works in 386

>   **386.3–386.5 Specific kinds of waters**

Class ferry transportation on specific kinds of waters in 386.6; class comprehensive works in 386

.3   ***River transportation**

Class here transportation by canalized rivers

Class combined river, lake, canal systems in 386.5

.32   The way

.35   Activities and services

Standard subdivisions are added for either or both topics in heading

Add to base number 386.35 the numbers following 386.24 in 386.2404–386.244, e.g., freight services 386.354

*Add as instructed under 380

.4   ***Canal transportation**

Class canalized rivers in 386.3; class combined river, lake, canal systems in 386.5

.404   Special topics

.404 2   Activities and services

Standard subdivisions are added for either or both topics in heading

Add to base number 386.4042 the numbers following 386.24 in 386.2404–386.244, e.g., freight services 386.40424

> 386.42–386.48 Specific canals and kinds of canals

Existing and proposed

Class comprehensive works in 386.4

.42   Interoceanic canals

For canals connecting specific oceans, see 386.43–386.45

> 386.43–386.45 Canals connecting specific oceans

Class comprehensive works in 386.42

.43   Canals connecting Indian and Atlantic Oceans

Class here Suez Canal

.44   Canals connecting Atlantic and Pacific Oceans

Class here Panama Canal

.445   Proposed Nicaragua Canal

.447   Proposed Tehuantepec Canal

.45   Canals connecting Pacific and Indian Oceans

.46   Noninteroceanic canals

Including canals connecting parts of one ocean

For kinds of noninteroceanic canals, see 386.47–386.48

> 386.47–386.48 Kinds of noninteroceanic canals

Class here specific canals

Class comprehensive works in 386.46

.47   *Ship canals

*Add as instructed under 380

.48	*Small craft and barge canals

Subdivisions are added for either or both topics in heading

.5	***Lake transportation**

Class here transportation on combined river, lake, canal systems, e.g., Saint Lawrence Seaway 386.509714

.52	The way
.54	Activities and services

Standard subdivisions are added for either or both topics in heading

Add to base number 386.54 the numbers following 386.24 in 386.2404–386.244, e.g., passenger services 386.542

.6	***Ferry transportation**

Oceanic and inland

.8	***Ports**

Add to base number 386.8 the numbers following 387.1 in 387.12–387.16, e.g., freight terminals 386.853

See Manual at 386.8 vs. 387.1

387   Water, air, space transportation

Class here comprehensive works on water transportation

Class comprehensive works on transportation in 388

For inland waterway and ferry transportation, see 386

See Manual at 383–388

SUMMARY

387.001–.009		**Standard subdivisions of water transportation**
	.1	**Ports**
	.2	**Ships**
	.5	**Ocean (Marine) transportation**
	.7	**Air transportation**
	.8	**Space transportation**

.001–.009	Standard subdivisions of water transportation

Notation from Table 1 as modified under 380, e.g., water transportation business organizations 387.0065

.1	**Ports**

For inland ports, see 386.8

See Manual at 386.8 vs. 387.1

**Add as instructed under 380

.12	Physiographic location of ports

Including ports on tidal rivers, roadsteads

Class facilities of specific types of ports in 387.15; class activities and services of specific types of ports in 387.16

.120 9   Historical, geographic, persons treatment

Class a specific port in 387.109

.13   Free ports

Class facilities of free ports in 387.15; class activities and services of free ports in 387.16

.130 9   Historical, geographic, persons treatment

Class a specific free port in 387.109

.15   Port facilities

Including docks, marinas, piers, quays

Class use of port facilities in specific activities and services in 387.16

.152   Passenger terminals

.153   Freight terminals

.155   Navigational aids

Class here lighthouses

Class piloting in 387.166

.16   Activities and services

Standard subdivisions are added for either or both topics in heading

Including port maintenance

.162   *Passenger services

Including booking services

.164   *Freight services

Including freight handling, warehousing, storage, connection with land transportation

.166   Operational services

Including piloting, ship-to-shore communication, towing, tug services

.168   Auxiliary services

Including fueling

*Add as instructed under 380

.2 Ships

Including air-cushion vehicles

Class use of ships in inland waterway transportation in 386.22; class use of ships in specific activities and services in 387.54

See Manual at 629.046 vs. 388

.204 General types

Add to base number 387.204 the numbers following 623.820 in 623.8202–623.8205, e.g., sailing craft 387.2043

.21–.29 Specific types

Add to base number 387.2 the numbers following 623.82 in 623.821–623.829, e.g., cargo ships 387.245

.5 *Ocean (Marine) transportation

For seaports, see 387.1; for ships, see 387.2

See Manual at 629.046 vs. 388

.51 Economic aspects of production

Class economic aspects of ships in 387.2; class economic aspects of routes and kinds of routes in 387.52; class economic aspects of activities and services in 387.54; class economic aspects of facilities in 387.58

See also 330 for other economic aspects, e.g., ocean transportation workers' unions 331.88113875

.52 Routes and kinds of routes

Class here specific routes

Class activities and services on routes and kinds of routes in 387.54; class use of facilities on routes and kinds of routes in 387.58

.522 Intercoastal routes

.523 Auxiliary, irregular, tramp routes

.524 Coastwise routes

.54 Activities and services

Standard subdivisions are added for either or both topics in heading

Class activities and services of ports in 387.16

.540 4 Special topics

.540 42 Basic activities

Including dispatching, routing, scheduling, traffic control

For operation of ships, see 387.54044

*Add as instructed under 380

.540 44		Operation of ships

Including life and activities of marine personnel at sea

.542   *Passenger services

Including baggage, meal, sleeper services

.544   *Freight services

.544 2   *Container-ship operations

Class unitized cargo in 385.72; class carriage of specific kinds of cargo in container-ship operations in 387.5448

.544 8   Carriage of specific kinds of cargo

Including dry cargo, fertilizer, petroleum

For sea mail, see 383.142

.55   *Salvage

.58   Facilities

Class facilities of ports in 387.15; class ships in 387.2; class use of facilities in specific activities and services in 387.54

For lighthouses, see 387.155

.7   *Air transportation

See Manual at 629.046 vs. 388

.71   Economic aspects of production

Class economic aspects of routes in 387.72; class economic aspects of facilities in 387.73; class economic aspects of activities and services in 387.74

See also 330 for other economic aspects, e.g., air transportation workers' unions 331.88113877

.712   Rates and fares

.72   Routes

Including helicopter routes to and from airports

Class use of facilities on routes and kinds of routes in 387.73; class activities and services on routes in 387.74

.73   Facilities

Class here comprehensive works on aircraft

.732–.733   Specific types of aircraft

Add to base number 387.73 the numbers following 629.133 in 629.1332–629.1333, e.g., helicopters 387.73352

Class use of aircraft in specific activities and services in 387.74

*Add as instructed under 380

.736		Airports
		Class here landing fields
.736 2		Facilities
		Including hangars, runways, terminal buildings; access to airports
		Class use of facilities in specific activities and services in 387.7364
.736 4		Activities and services
		Standard subdivisions are added for either or both topics in heading
		Including booking, fueling, passenger services

.74   Activities and services

Standard subdivisions are added for either or both topics in heading

Class activities and services of airports and landing fields in 387.7364

.740 4		Special topics
.740 42		Basic activities
		Including dispatching, routing, scheduling; airport noise and its alleviation

For operation of aircraft, see 387.74044

.740 426   Air traffic control

See Manual at 629.1366 vs. 387.740426

.740 44   Operation of aircraft

Class here operating personnel, flight crews

Class maintenance and maintenance personnel in 387.73

.742   *Passenger services

Including baggage, meal, sleeper services

.742 2   *Reservation systems

.742 8   *Charter services

.744   *Freight services

Including all-cargo plane services

For air mail, see 383.144

.8   *Space transportation

See Manual at 629.046 vs. 388

*Add as instructed under 380

388   *Transportation   Ground transportation

Class here comprehensive works on communications and transportation, interdisciplinary works on transportation

Comprehensive works on the activities, services, and facilities of a system are classed in the number for the system, e.g., seaport activities, services, and facilities 387.1, not 387.15 nor 387.16

Class services designed to facilitate the use of transportation by persons with disabilities in 362.40483; class services designed to facilitate the use of transportation by older persons in 362.63

> *For transportation safety and safety measures, see 363.12; for transportation security, see 363.287; for postal transportation, see 383.14; for communications, see 384; for railroad transportation, see 385; for water, air, space transportation, see 387; for transportation technology, see 629.04*

> *See also 385.7 for railroad combined with other transportation systems*

> *See Manual at 383–388; also at 629.046 vs. 388*

SUMMARY

388.04	**Special topics**	
.1	**Roads**	
.3	**Vehicular transportation**	
.4	**Local transportation**	
.5	**Pipeline transportation**	

.04   Special topics

.041   Activities and services

Standard subdivisions are added for either or both topics in heading

Including routing, scheduling, dispatching, traffic control

Class specific kinds of services in 388.042–388.044

.042   *Passenger services

Including baggage, reservation, meal, sleeper services

Class here mass transportation

.044   *Freight services

Including handling, storage; comprehensive works on warehousing

Class unitized cargo services in 385.72

> *For commerce aspects of warehousing, see 380.1*

.047   Comparative studies of kinds of transportation

Class a comparative study of a specific kind of transportation with the kind, e.g., comparative study of local transportation 388.4

*Add as instructed under 380

.049   Economic aspects of production

> Class economic aspects of activities and services in 388.041; class economic aspects of passenger services in 388.042; class economic aspects of freight services in 388.044

> > *See also 330 for other economic aspects, e.g., transportation workers' unions 331.8811388*

.1   *Roads

Class here highways

> *For highway services and use, see 388.31; for urban roads, see 388.411*

.11   Economic aspects of production

> Class economic aspects of kinds of roads in 388.12; class economic aspects of special road features in 388.13. Class economic effects of roads on a specific aspect of an economic activity with the activity, e.g., effect on business location 338.6042

> > *See also 330 for other economic aspects, e.g., road transportation workers' unions 331.88113881*

.112   Costs

.114   Finance

> Including user charges, tolls

.12   Kinds of roads

> Including primary and secondary roads, bicycle paths, pedestrian paths

> Class special features of kinds of roads in 388.13

> > *For access roads, see 388.13*

.122   Expressways

> Variant names: beltways, freeways, motorways, parkways, throughways, tollways, turnpikes

.13   Special road features

> Including access roads, grade separations, intersections, tunnels

> Class signs and signals for traffic control in 388.3122

.132   Bridges

.3   *Vehicular transportation

Class urban vehicular transportation in 388.41

.31   Traffic flow and maintenance

---

*Add as instructed under 380

.312	Highway services	Traffic control

Including lighting, roadside park facilities, snow removal

For traffic control by police, see 363.2332; for speed limits, see 388.3144

.312 2   Traffic control through signs and signals

Standard subdivisions are added for either or both topics in heading

.312 4   Driver information

Information supplied en route

Including information on traffic patterns via commercial radio

.314   Highway use

.314 2   Traffic volume

Class peak hours in 388.3143

.314 3   Traffic patterns

Including patterns by origin, by destination; peak hours; use by specific kinds of vehicles

.314 4   Speed limits

.32   *Vehicular activities and services

Subdivisions are added for either or both topics in heading

See also 388.34 for vehicles

See Manual at 629.046 vs. 388

.321   *Services of private passenger automobiles

Including limousine services

.322   *Bus services

Class here passenger services

Class services of terminals, stations, stops in 388.33

.322 04   Special topics

.322 042   Basic activities

Including dispatching, routing, scheduling, traffic control

For operation of vehicles, see 388.322044

.322 044   Operation of vehicles

.322 1   Routes

Intercity and trunk

Class services offered on specific routes and kinds of routes in 388.3222

*Add as instructed under 380

.322 2	Types of services

Including charter, baggage, meal, small package and express services; tourism

Use of this number for comprehensive works on passenger services discontinued; class in 388.322

.322 8	*Stagecoach services

Class stagecoach routes in 388.3221

For types of stagecoach services, see 388.3222

.324	*Trucking services

Class services of terminals in 388.33

.324 04	Special topics
.324 042	Basic activities

Including dispatching, routing, scheduling, traffic control

For operation of vehicles, see 388.324044

.324 044	Operation of vehicles
.324 2	Routes

Including long-haul, line-haul, intercity routes

.324 3	Kinds of carriers

Including common (for-hire), contract, private carriers

.33	Terminals, stations, stops

Including activities, services, facilities (e.g., vehicle sheds, docks, booking facilities)

.34	Vehicles

Including natural gas vehicles, snowmobiles

Class use of vehicles in specific services, vehicle operation in 388.32

For air-cushion vehicles, see 388.35

See Manual at 629.046 vs. 388

.341	Carts, wagons, carriages, stagecoaches

Including rickshaws, animal-drawn omnibuses

Class here nonmotor land vehicles

Class cycles in 388.347

*Add as instructed under 380

.342–.348   Gasoline-powered, oil-powered, man-powered vehicles

Add to base number 388.34 the numbers following 629.22 in 629.222–629.228, e.g., buses 388.34233

For rickshaws, see 388.341

.35   Air-cushion vehicles

Class here comprehensive works on air-cushion vehicles

For air-cushion ships for inland waterways, see 386.22; for air-cushion ships for ocean transportation, see 387.2

.4   ***Local transportation**

Class here urban and suburban transportation, rapid transit, mass transit, commuter services

See also 385.5 for interurban railways

.404   Special topics

.404 2   Economic aspects of production

See also 330 for other economic aspects, e.g., local transportation workers' unions 331.88113884

\>   388.41–388.46   Specific kinds of local transportation

Class terminals and parking facilities for specific kinds of transportation in 388.47; class comprehensive works in 388.4

See Manual at 629.046 vs. 388

.41   Vehicular and pedestrian traffic

Including moving sidewalks

Class vehicles in 388.34–388.35

.411   Urban roads

Including parkways, expressways, arterial and side streets, sidewalks, bicycle paths (bikeways); intersections, traffic circles (roundabouts)

Class here streets

Class operation, services, use of urban roads in 388.4131

.413   Activities and services

Standard subdivisions are added for either or both topics in heading

.413 1   Traffic flow and maintenance

Add to base number 388.4131 the numbers following 388.31 in 388.312–388.314, e.g., peak hours 388.413143

---

*Add as instructed under 380

.413 2	Vehicular services
.413 21	*Services by private passenger automobiles
.413 212	*Car and van pools

> Class here ridesharing
>
> Subdivisions are added for either or both topics in heading

.413 214	*Taxicabs and limousines
.413 22	*Bus services

> Including animal-drawn omnibuses

.413 223	*Trolleybuses
.413 24	*Trucking services
.42	*Local rail transit systems

> Including guided-way systems
>
> Class rail terminals and stations in 388.472
>
> *For elevated rail transit systems, see 388.44; for surface rail transit systems, see 388.46*

.428	*Underground (Subway) systems
.44	*Elevated rail transit systems

> Including elevated monorail systems

.46	*Surface rail transit systems

> Class here tramways

.47	Terminals, stations, parking facilities
.472	Rail terminals and stations
.473	Truck and bus stations and terminals

> Including bus stops

.474	Parking facilities

> Including on-street and off-street parking facilities, facilities located above and below street level
>
> Class here interdisciplinary works on parking
>
> *For a specific aspect of parking, see the aspect, e.g., city planning 711.73*

.5	***Pipeline transportation**
.55	*Oil (Petroleum)

*Add as instructed under 380

.56   *Natural gas

.57   *Coal

             Class here coal slurry

389   Metrology and standardization

.1   Metrology

Social use of systems of measurement

Class interdisciplinary works on measurement in 530.8

.109   Historical, geographic, persons treatment [*formerly* 389.15]

.15   Systems of measurement

Including metric system (système international, SI), imperial (British) system

Historical, geographic, persons treatment of metrology relocated to 389.109

Class adoption of metric system in 389.16; class mathematical tables of conversion from one system to another in 530.81

.16   Adoption of metric system (système international, SI)

See also 658.4062 for management measures for coping with conversion to metric system

.17   Time systems and standards

Including conversion tables; daylight saving, standard, universal time; time zones

Class interdisciplinary works on chronology in 529

.6   Standardization

.62   Standardization of quantity and size

Class here standardization for interchangeability

.63   Standardization of quality

Class here performance standards

390   Customs, etiquette, folklore

Class here folkways

For customs of military life, see 355.1

See Manual at 390

*Add as instructed under 380

SUMMARY

.001–.009 Standard subdivisions

.01–.07 Standard subdivisions of customs

.08 History and description of customs with respect to kinds of persons

.084 6 Persons in late adulthood [*formerly also* 392.9]

.086 Persons by miscellaneous social characteristics

[.086 2] Persons by social and economic levels

> Do not use for persons by economic status; class in 390.1. Do not use for persons by social class; class in 390.2

.088 Religious groups

> Do not use for occupational groups; class in 390.4

.09 Historical, geographic, persons treatment of customs

> **390.1–390.4 Customs of specific economic, social, occupational classes**

Class comprehensive works in 390

.1 Customs of people by economic status

Class customs of slaves and serfs in 390.25

.2 Customs of people by social class

.22 Customs of royalty

.23 Customs of nobility

.24 Customs of common people

> Class customs of common people of specific economic statuses in 390.1; class customs of specific occupations in 390.4

.25 Customs of slaves and serfs

.4   **Customs of people by occupation**

Add to base number 390.4 notation 09–99 from Table 7, e.g., customs of lawyers 390.4344; however, for customs of military personnel, see 355.1; for customs of diplomats, see 399

>   **391–394   Customs**

Class comprehensive works in 390

For customs of specific economic, social, occupational classes, see 390.1–390.4; for customs of war and diplomacy, see 399

391   **Costume and personal appearance**

Standard subdivisions are added for costume and personal appearance together, for costume alone

Class here interdisciplinary works on costume, clothing, fashion

Class costumes and clothing associated with a specific occasion with the occasion in 392–394, e.g., wedding apparel 392.54

For fashion design, see 746.92. For a specific aspect of costume and clothing, see the aspect, e.g., stage costuming 792.026, clothing construction 646.4

See Manual at 391 vs. 646.3, 746.92

.001–.007   Standard subdivisions

.008   History and description with respect to kinds of persons

[.008 1–.008 4]   Sex and age groups

         Do not use; class in 391.1–391.3

.008 6   Persons by miscellaneous social characteristics

[.008 62]   Persons by social and economic levels

         Do not use for persons by economic status; class in 391.01. Do not use for persons by social class; class in 391.02

.008 8   Religious groups

         Do not use for occupational groups; class in 391.04

.009   Historical, geographic, persons treatment

.01–.04   Costumes of economic, social, occupational groups

Add to base number 391.0 the numbers following 390 in 390.1–390.4, e.g., costumes of royalty 391.022; however, for military costume, see 355.14

> **391.1–391.3 Costumes of specific ages and sexes**

Class costumes of specific economic, social, occupational classes regardless of age or sex in 391.01–391.04; class auxiliary garments and accessories for specific age and sex groups in 391.4; class comprehensive works in 391

.1 **Costumes of men**

.2 **Costumes of women**

.3 **Costumes of children**

.4 **Auxiliary garments and accessories**

.41 Handwear, footwear, neckwear

Including muffs, scarves, ties

.412 Gloves and mittens

.413 Footwear

Including hosiery

Class here shoes and boots

.42 Underwear and nightclothes

.43 Headwear

Including hats

.434 Masks

.44 Accessories

Including canes, combs, eyeglasses, fans, flowers, parasols

For jewelry, see 391.7

.45 Buttons

.5 **Hair styles**

Including beards, wigs

.6 **Personal appearance**

For hair styles, see 391.5

.62 Body contours

.63 Use of cosmetics and perfume

.64 Personal cleanliness and hygiene

Including bathing

.65 Tattooing and incision

.7   **Jewelry**

Class here interdisciplinary works on jewelry

For jewelry making, see 739.27

392   Customs of life cycle and domestic life

For death customs, see 393

.1   **Customs of birth, puberty, majority**

.12   Birth customs

Including baptism, couvade, infanticide, name giving

.13   Child-rearing customs

.14   Customs relating to attainment of puberty

Including initiation rites

.15   Customs relating to attainment of majority

Including debuts

.3   **Customs relating to dwelling places and domestic arts**

.36   Dwelling places

Class here furnishings, heating, lighting, sanitation

.360 01–.360 07   Standard subdivisions

.360 08   Dwelling places with respect to kinds of persons

.360 086   Persons by miscellaneous social characteristics

[.360 086 2]   Persons by social and economic levels

Do not use for persons by economic status; class in 392.3601. Do not use for persons by social class; class in 392.3602

.360 088   Religious groups

Do not use for occupational groups; class in 392.3604

.360 09   Historical, geographic, persons treatment

.360 1–.360 4   Customs relating to dwelling places of specific economic, social, occupational classes

Add to base number 392.360 the numbers following 390 in 390.1–390.4, e.g., dwelling places of royalty 392.36022

.37   Cooking

Class comprehensive works on food and meals in 394.1

.4   **Courtship and engagement customs**

Including bride purchase, bundling, infant betrothal, matchmaking

.5 **Wedding and marriage customs**

> *See also 395.22 for etiquette of weddings*

.54 Wedding apparel

.6 **Customs of the relations between sexes**

Including chaperonage

> *For courtship and engagement customs, see 392.4; for wedding and marriage customs, see 392.5*

[.9] **Customs relating to the treatment of persons in late adulthood**

Relocated to 390.0846

393 Death customs

Customs relating to disposal of the dead and to mourning

.1 **Burial**

Including entombment

.2 **Cremation**

.3 **Embalming**

.4 **Exposure**

.9 **Mourning**

Including funerals, suttee, wakes

394 General customs

Including kissing, swearing

SUMMARY

394.1	Eating, drinking; using drugs
.2	Special occasions
.3	Recreational customs
.4	Official ceremonies and observances
.5	Pageants, processions, parades
.6	Fairs
.7	Customs of chivalry
.8	Dueling and suicide
.9	Cannibalism

.1 **Eating, drinking; using drugs**

Situations and methods of use, prohibited uses

Class here food and meals

> *For cooking, see 392.37*

.12   Eating and drinking

> Class eating and drinking customs of a specific meal in 394.15; class food taboos in 394.16

> *For drinking of alcoholic beverages, see 394.13*

.13   Drinking of alcoholic beverages

.14   Use of drugs

> Including marijuana, narcotics, tobacco

> *For alcoholic beverages, see 394.13*

.15   Specific meals

[.150 1–.150 9]   Standard subdivisions

> Do not use; class in 394.101–394.109

.16   Food taboos

.2   **Special occasions**

> Including anniversaries, birthdays, celebrations, fast days

> Class official ceremonies in 394.4; class pageants, processions, parades in 394.5

.25   Carnivals

> Including Mardi Gras

.26   Holidays

> Class here festivals; independence days; patriotic, seasonal, secular holidays

> Class a season associated with a holiday with the holiday, e.g., the Christmas season 394.2663; class a technology or craft associated with holidays with the technology or craft, e.g., making fireworks 662.1, decorating Easter eggs 745.5944

> *For Mardi Gras, see 394.25*

[.260 9]   Historical, geographic, persons treatment

> Do not use; class in 394.269

>   394.261–394.264 Secular holidays

> Class here specific patriotic holidays [*formerly* 394.2684], specific seasonal holidays [*formerly* 394.2683]

> Class religious holidays of a specific season in 394.265; class comprehensive works in 394.26

.261	Holidays of December, January, February
	Class here wintertime holidays of the northern hemisphere, summertime holidays of the southern hemisphere
.261 4	New Year
.261 8	Valentine's Day
.262	Holidays of March, April, May
	Including Mother's Day
	Class here springtime holidays of the northern hemisphere, autumn holidays of the southern hemisphere
.262 7	May Day
.263	Holidays of June, July, August
	Class here summertime holidays of the northern hemisphere, wintertime holidays of the southern hemisphere
.263 4	Fourth of July
.263 5	Bastille Day
.264	Holidays of September, October, November
	Class here autumn holidays of the northern hemisphere, springtime holidays of the southern hemisphere
.264 4	Oktoberfest
.264 6	Halloween
.264 9	Thanksgiving
.265	Religious holidays [*formerly* 394.2682]
	Add to base number 394.265 the numbers following 29 in 291–299 for the religion only, e.g., Hindu holidays 394.26545; however, for Jewish holidays, see 394.267
	Class secular holidays with a religious or quasi-religious origin in 394.261–394.264
	For Christian holidays, see 394.266
	See Manual at 263.9, 291.36 vs. 394.265–394.267
.266	Christian holidays [*formerly* 394.26828]
	Holidays of the church year
.266 3	Christmas
.266 7	Easter
.267	Jewish holidays [*formerly* 394.268296]

[.268]	Specific kinds of holidays
	Number discontinued; class in 394.26
[.268 2]	Religious holidays
	Relocated to 394.265
[.268 28]	Christian holidays
	Relocated to 394.266
[.268 296]	Jewish holidays
	Relocated to 394.267
[.268 3]	Seasonal holidays
	Use of this number for comprehensive works on seasonal holidays discontinued; class in 394.26
	Specific seasonal holidays relocated to 394.261–394.264
[.268 4]	Patriotic holidays
	Use of this number for comprehensive works on patriotic holidays discontinued; class in 394.26
	Specific patriotic holidays relocated to 394.261–394.264
.269	Historical, geographic, persons treatment

Add to base number 394.269 notation 01–9 from Table 2, e.g., holidays of Mexico 394.26972

Class historical, geographic, persons treatment of specific holidays and of specific kinds of holidays in 394.261–394.267

.3 Recreational customs

Including dances, gambling, games, toys

.4 Official ceremonies and observances

Including coronations, inaugurations, jubilees, state visits, triumphs

For military ceremonies, see 355.17

.5 Pageants, processions, parades

Class pageants, processions, parades associated with a specific activity with the activity, e.g., Thanksgiving Day parades 394.2649

See Manual at 394.5 vs. 791.6

.6 Fairs

.7 Customs of chivalry

.8 Dueling and suicide

.9 Cannibalism

395   Etiquette (Manners)

Prescriptive and practical works on social behavior

Unless other instructions are given, class a subject with aspects in two or more subdivisions of 395 in the number coming last, e.g., table manners for children 395.54 (*not* 395.122)

Class customs in 391–394

For protocol of diplomacy, see 327.2

See Manual at 395

[.081–.084]   Etiquette with respect to sex and age groups

Do not use; class in 395.1

.1   Etiquette for age groups and sexes

.12   Etiquette for age groups

.122   Children

From birth through age eleven

.123   Young adults

Aged twelve and above

.123 2   Men

.123 3   Women

.126   Adults aged sixty-five and over

.14   Etiquette for sexes

Class etiquette for age groups regardless of sex in 395.12

.142   Male

.144   Female

.2   Etiquette for stages in life cycle

.22   Engagements and weddings

.23   Funerals

.24   Occasions associated with birth, puberty, majority

Including christening, confirmation, bar mitzvah, debut

.3   Etiquette for social occasions

Including dances

Class here hospitality and entertainment

Class etiquette for stages in life cycle in 395.2; class invitations in 395.4

.4 **Social correspondence**

Including invitations and announcements

Class here written and spoken styles and forms of address and greeting

.5 **Etiquette by situations**

Including school, sports etiquette

.52 Business and office etiquette

.53 Public behavior

Including etiquette in church, at theater, in stores and shops

.54 Table manners

.59 Conversation

Class here telephone etiquette

[396–397][Unassigned]

Most recently used in Edition 16

398 Folklore

See also 291.13 for religious mythology, 800 for belles-lettres by identifiable authors, anonymous literary classics

SUMMARY

398.01–.09	**Standard subdivisions**
.2	**Folk literature**
.3	**Natural and physical phenomena as subjects of folklore**
.4	**Paranatural and legendary phenomena as subjects of folklore**
.5	**Chapbooks**
.6	**Riddles**
.8	**Rhymes and rhyming games**
.9	**Proverbs**

[.04] Special topics

Number discontinued; class in 398

[.042] History and criticism

Relocated to 398.09

.09 Historical, geographic, persons treatment of folklore

Class here history and criticism [*formerly also* 398.042]

For historical, geographic, persons treatment of folk literature, see 398.209

.2 Folk literature

Folklore as literature

Class here fairy tales, literary appraisal and criticism of folk literature, interdisciplinary works on mythology

For religious mythology, see 291.13; for minor forms of folk literature, see 398.5–398.9

See Manual at 398.2; also at 398.2 vs. 291.13; also at 398.2 vs. 398.3–398.4; also at 800 vs. 398.2

.204 Folk literature by language

Add to base number 398.204 notation 1–9 from Table 6, e.g., folk tales from French-speaking areas of the world 398.20441; however, for tales of a specific language from an area where that language predominates, see the area in 398.209, e.g., French folk tales from France 398.20944, from Quebec 398.209714

.209 3–.209 9 Treatment by specific continents, countries, localities

Class here collections of tales and lore on a specific topic from a specific continent, country, locality; individual tales and lore [*both formerly* 398.21–398.27]; collections of tales and lore from a specific continent, country, locality; works consisting equally of the tales and lore and criticism of them

Add to base number 398.209 notation 3–9 from Table 2, e.g., folk literature of France 398.20944; then add further as follows:

001	Forecasting and forecasts [*formerly* 01]
002	Statistics and illustrations [*formerly* 02]
0021	Statistics
0022	Illustrations
005	Serial publications [*formerly* 05]
007	Museums, collections, exhibits; collecting objects [*formerly* 07]
0074	Museums, collections, exhibits
	Add to base number 0074 notation 4–9 from Table 2, e.g., museums in Germany 007443
0075	Collecting folk literature
>01–07	Tales and lore on a specific topic

Class here literary criticism

Class comprehensive works in the base number for the continent, country, locality in 398.2093–398.2099. Class comprehensive works on history and criticism of a specific topic with the topic in 398.3–398.4, e.g., history and criticism of tales and lore about witches 398.45

See Manual at 398.2 vs. 398.3–398.4

(continued)

.209 3–.209 9	Treatment by specific continents, countries, localities (continued)

01	Tales and lore of paranatural beings of human and semihuman form

Class here centaurs, fairies, gods and goddesses, mermaids and mermen, ogres, vampires, witches and warlocks, wizards

Forecasting and forecasts relocated to 001

For werewolves, see 0454; for ghosts, see 05

0101–0109	Standard subdivisions of more than one tale

Notation from Table 1 as modified under 398.21–398.27, e.g., literary criticism 0109

02	Tales and lore of legendary or mythological persons

Persons without paranormal powers

Class here heroes, kings, ordinary persons

Statistics and illustrations relocated to 002

0201–0209	Standard subdivisions of more than one tale

Notation from Table 1 as modified under 398.21–398.27, e.g., literary criticism 0209

03–04	Tales and lore of places, times, plants, animals

Add to base number 0 the numbers following 398.2 in 398.23–398.24, e.g., tales about werewolves 0454

05	Ghost stories

Serial publications relocated to 005

0501–0509	Standard subdivisions of more than one tale

Notation from Table 1 as modified under 398.21–398.27, e.g., literary criticism 0509

06	Tales and lore involving physical phenomena

Real and legendary

Class here fire, heavenly bodies, minerals, water, weather

0601–0609	Standard subdivisions of more than one tale

Notation from Table 1 as modified under 398.21–398.27, e.g., literary criticism 0609

07	Tales and lore of everyday human life

Collections of tales relating to a specific aspect of everyday human life; individual tales not provided for elsewhere

Class here historical and quasi-historical events; birth, love, marriage, death; occupations, recreation; dwellings, food

Museums, collections, exhibits; collecting objects relocated to 007

See Manual at 398.27, 398.353 vs. 615.882: Medical folk literature

0701–0709	Standard subdivisions of more than one tale

Notation from Table 1 as modified under 398.21–398.27, e.g., literary criticism 0709

(continued)

.209 3–.209 9   Treatment by specific continents, countries, localities (continued)

> 09   Historical and geographic treatment
> Class here literary criticism
> Add to base number 09 the numbers following —09
> in notation 090–099 from Table 1, e.g., folk
> literature of Middle Ages 0902
> Use 093–099 to add notation for a specific continent,
> country, locality when first area notation is used to
> specify area of origin of the tales and lore, while
> second one identifies area in which the tales and lore
> are discussed or modified, e.g., French tales
> 398.20944, Haitian version of French tales
> 398.20944097294

(Option: Class collections of tales and lore on a specific topic from a specific continent, country, locality; individual tales and lore in 398.21–398.27)

See Manual at 398.2093–398.2099

> 398.21–398.27   Tales and lore on a specific topic

Add to each subdivision identified by * as follows:
01–08   Standard subdivisions
09   Historical, geographic, persons treatment
Class here literary criticism
Class comprehensive works on history and criticism of a specific topic with the topic in 398.3–398.4, e.g., history and criticism of tales and lore about witches 398.45
See Manual at 398.2 vs. 398.3–398.4
[093–099]   Collections of tales and lore from a specific continent, country, locality; individual tales and lore
Relocated to 398.2093–398.2099
(Option: Continue to use 093–099; prefer 398.2093–398.2099)

Class comprehensive works in 398.2

.21   *Tales and lore of paranatural beings of human and semihuman form

Class here witches [*formerly* 398.22], centaurs, fairies, gods and goddesses, mermaids and mermen, ogres, vampires, warlocks, wizards

Use of this number for comprehensive works on fairy tales (tales of paranatural beings) discontinued; class in 398.2

For werewolves, see 398.2454; for ghosts, see 398.25

---

*Add as instructed under 398.21–398.27

.22   *Tales and lore of legendary or mythological persons

    Persons without paranormal powers

    Class here heroes, kings, ordinary persons

    Witches relocated to 398.21; comprehensive works on historical and quasi-historical events relocated to 398.27

.23   *Tales and lore of places and times

    Class historical and quasi-historical events in 398.27

.232   *Real places

    Class tales of real places at special times in 398.236

    See also 398.209 for tales originating in specific places

.232 1–.232 9   Specific places

    Add to base number 398.232 notation 1–9 from Table 2, e.g., tales about India 398.23254; then add further as instructed under 398.21–398.27, e.g., 18th century tales about India 398.2325409033

.234   *Legendary places

    Class here Atlantis

.236   *Times

    Class here holidays, seasons

.24   *Tales and lore of plants and animals

.242   *Plants

    Real and legendary

.245   *Animals

    See Manual at 800 vs. 398.245, 590, 636

.245 2   *Real animals

.245 22–.245 29 Specific animals

    Add to base number 398.2452 the numbers following 59 in 592–599, e.g., cats 398.24529752; then add further as instructed under 398.21–398.27, e.g., 18th century tales about cats 398.2452975209033

.245 4   *Legendary animals

    Class here dragons, phoenixes, unicorns, werewolves

.25   *Ghost stories

*Add as instructed under 398.21–398.27

.26	*Tales and lore involving physical phenomena

Real and legendary

Class here fire, heavenly bodies, minerals, water, weather

.27	*Tales and lore of everyday human life

Collections of tales relating to a specific aspect of everyday human life; tales not provided for elsewhere

Class here comprehensive works on historical and quasi-historical events [*formerly* 398.22]; birth, love, marriage, death; occupations, recreation; dwellings, food

See Manual at 398.27, 398.353 vs. 615.882: Medical folk literature

---

> ### 398.3–398.4 History and criticism of specific subjects of folklore

Limited to works without extended text of folk tales

Class here origin, role, function of themes and subjects of folklore as cultural and social phenomena

Class comprehensive works in 398.09. Class literary criticism of a tale or lore or a collection of tales or lore from a specific continent, country, locality on a specific topic with the topic in 398.2093–398.2099, using the notation for the topic plus notation 09 from table under 398.21–398.27, e.g., literary criticism of French tales and lore about witches 398.209440109; class comprehensive treatment of literary criticism of tales or lore on a specific topic with the topic in 398.2, plus notation 09 from table under 398.21–398.27, e.g., literary criticism of tales and lore about witches 398.2109

See Manual at 398.2 vs. 398.3–398.4

.3	**Natural and physical phenomena as subjects of folklore**
.32	Places
.322	Physiographic regions
.329	Specific places

Class historical and political themes, historical events in specific places in 398.358

[.329 01–.329 09]	Standard subdivisions

Do not use; class in 398.3201–398.3209

.329 3–.329 9	Specific continents, countries, localities

Add to base number 398.329 notation 3–9 from Table 2, e.g., London as a subject for folklore 398.329421

.33	Times

Class here seasons; parts of day, e.g., darkness, dawn; holidays

---

*Add as instructed under 398.21–398.27

.35	Humanity and human existence
.352	Persons without paranormal powers

Class here heroes, kings, ordinary persons

.353 Human body, personality, qualities, activities

Class here chivalry, friendship, insanity, pride, sex, success; medical folklore

For love, see 398.354

See Manual at 398.27, 398.353 vs. 615.882: Medical folk literature

.354 Life cycle

Class here birth, love, marriage, death

.355 Social themes

Class here commerce, crime, dwellings, environment, food, law, occupations, recreation, violence

.356 Technical themes

Class here engineering, flight, ships

For medical folklore, see 398.353

.357 Artistic and literary themes

Class here books, music, painting

.358 Historical and political themes

Class here nationalism, war; historical events in specific places

.36 Scientific themes

Class here physical phenomena

.362 Heavenly bodies

.363 Weather

.364 Fire and water

.365 Minerals

.368 Plants

Add to base number 398.368 the numbers following 58 in 582–588, e.g., flowers 398.368213

.369 Animals

Add to base number 398.369 the numbers following 59 in 592–599, e.g., rabbits 398.369932

.4   Paranatural and legendary phenomena as subjects of folklore

Class here magic

See also 133.43 for magic in occultism

.41   Folk beliefs

Class here superstitions

.42   Legendary places

Class here Atlantis

.45   Paranormal beings of human and semihuman form

Class here centaurs, fairies, gods and goddesses, mermaids and mermen, ogres, vampires, witches and warlocks, wizards

For ghosts, see 398.47

.46   Legendary minerals, plants, animals

.465   Minerals

Class here philosopher's stone

.468   Plants

.469   Animals

Class here dragons, phoenixes, unicorns, werewolves

.47   Ghosts

Class here haunted places

> **398.5–398.9 Minor forms of folk literature**

Class here literary appraisal and criticism

Class comprehensive works in 398.2

.5   Chapbooks

.6   Riddles

Class here interdisciplinary works

For riddles as amusements, see 793.735; for riddles as belles-lettres, see 808.882

.8   Rhymes and rhyming games

Including jump rope rhymes, lullabies, tongue twisters

Class here minor forms of folk poetry, nursery rhymes

Class other forms of folk poetry with the form in 800, e.g., medieval metrical romances 808.813

.84   Counting-out (Counting) rhymes

.87   Street cries and songs

.9   **Proverbs**

Class here folk aphorisms

Add to base number 398.9 notation 1–9 from Table 6, e.g., French proverbs 398.941

399   Customs of war and diplomacy

Including dances, peace pipe

Class protocol of diplomacy in 327.2; class customs of military life in 355.1; class cannibalism in 394.9

400 Language

Class here interdisciplinary works on language and literature

For literature, see 800; for rhetoric, see 808. For the language of a specific discipline or subject, see the discipline or subject, plus notation 014 from Table 1, e.g., language of science 501.4

See Manual at 400 vs. 800; also at 909, 930–990 vs. 400; also at T1—014 vs. T4—864

(Option A: To give local emphasis or a shorter number to a specific language, class in 410, where full instructions appear

(Option B: To give local emphasis or a shorter number to a specific language, place before 420 through use of a letter or other symbol. Full instructions appear under 420–490)

SUMMARY

401–409	Standard subdivisions and bilingualism
410	Linguistics
420	English and Old English (Anglo-Saxon)
430	Germanic (Teutonic) languages German
440	Romance languages French
450	Italian, Sardinian, Dalmatian, Romanian, Rhaeto-Romanic languages
460	Spanish and Portuguese languages
470	Italic languages Latin
480	Hellenic languages Classical Greek
490	Other languages

401 Philosophy and theory

See Manual at 401 vs. 121.68, 149.94, 410.1

.3 International languages

Do not use for value; class in 401

Class here universal languages; general discussions of international languages, e.g., diplomatic languages, lingua francas

Class artificial languages in 499.99. Class a specific international language with the language in 420–490, e.g., Latin as a diplomatic language 470, Swahili as a lingua franca 496.392

.4   **Language and communication**

Class here lexicology, interdisciplinary works on terminology

For dictionaries of linguistics, see 410.3; for general polyglot dictionaries, see 413; for lexicography, see 413.028; for applied linguistics treatment of terminology, see 418. For terminology of a specific subject or discipline, see the subject or discipline, plus notation 014 from Table 1, e.g., terminology of linguistics 410.14, terminology of engineering 620.0014

.41   Semiotics

Class here content analysis, discourse analysis

Class pragmatics in sociolinguistics in 306.44; class pragmatics in psycholinguistics in 401.9; class interdisciplinary works on semiotics in 302.2. Class a semiotic study of a specific subject with the subject, plus notation 014 from Table 1, e.g., a semiotic study of science 501.4

For semantics, see 401.43

See also 121.68 for semiotics as a topic in philosophy

[.42]   Etymology

Do not use; class in 412

.43   Semantics

For history of word meanings, see 412

See also 121.68 for semantics as a topic in philosophy, 149.94 for general semantics as a philosophical school

See Manual at 401.43 vs. 306.44, 401.9, 412, 415

[.48]   Abbreviations and symbols

Do not use for abbreviations and symbols as part of writing systems; class in 411. Do not use for dictionaries of abbreviations and symbols; class in 413.1

.5   **Scientific principles**

.51   Mathematical principles

Mathematical linguistics relocated to 410.151

.9   **Psychological principles**

Class here psycholinguistics

Class psychology of bilingualism in 404.2019

See also 306.44 for sociolinguistics

See Manual at 401.43 vs. 306.44, 401.9, 412, 415

.93	Language acquisition

See also 418.0071 for study and teaching of language, 418.4019 for psychology of reading

See Manual at 407.1, T1—071 vs. 401.93, 410.71, 418.0071, T4—80071

402 Miscellany

.85	Data processing Computer applications

Computational linguistics relocated to 410.285

403 Dictionaries, encyclopedias, concordances

Class here dictionaries, encyclopedias, concordances that treat comprehensively both language and literature

For dictionaries, encyclopedias, concordances of linguistics, see 410.3; for general polyglot dictionaries, see 413; for dictionaries, encyclopedias, concordances of literature, see 803

404 Special topics

.2 Bilingualism

Class here multilingualism

Specific instances of bilingualism are classed with the language dominant in the country in which the linguistic interaction occurs, e.g., a discussion of Spanish-English bilingualism in Los Angeles 420.42610979494. If neither language is dominant, class with the one coming later in 420–490

See also 306.446 for sociology of bilingualism and multilingualism

405–406 Standard subdivisions

407 Education, research, related topics

See Manual at 407.1, T1—071 vs. 401.93, 410.71, 418.0071, T4—80071

408 Treatment of language with respect to kinds of persons

See also 306.44 for sociology of language

.9 Treatment of language with respect to racial, ethnic, national groups

Class ethnolinguistics in 306.44089

409 Geographic and persons treatment

Do not use for language history not limited by area; class in 417.7

Class specific languages and groups of languages in 420–490

See also 410.9 for geographic and persons treatment of linguistics

410   Linguistics

Science and structure of spoken and written language

Class here descriptive, synchronic linguistics; comprehensive works on Eurasiatic languages, on Indo-European languages, on Indo-Germanic languages, on Indo-Hittite languages

Class linguistics of specific languages in 420–490

> *For sociolinguistics, see 306.44; for lexicology, see 401.4; for semiotics, see 401.41; for specific Indo-European languages, see 420–491*

> *See Manual at 410; also at 411–418 and T4—1–8*

(Option A: To give local emphasis and a shorter number to a specific language, e.g., Russian, class it here and add to base number 41 as instructed under 420–490; in that case class linguistics in 400, its subdivisions in 401–409, standard subdivisions of language and of linguistics in 400.1–400.9. Option B is described under 420–490)

SUMMARY

410.1–.9	**Standard subdivisions**
411	**Writing systems**
412	**Etymology**
413	**Dictionaries**
414	**Phonology and phonetics**
415	**Grammar**
417	**Dialectology and historical (diachronic) linguistics**
418	**Standard usage (Prescriptive linguistics)** **Applied linguistics**
419	**Structured verbal language other than spoken and written**

.1   **Philosophy and theory**

Do not use for philosophy and theory of language and languages; class in 401

Class schools and theories of linguistics in 410.18

> *See Manual at 401 vs. 121.68, 149.94, 410.1*

.151   Mathematical principles

Class here mathematical linguistics [*formerly also* 401.51]

.18   Schools and theories of linguistics

Including functionalism, structural linguistics

> *For works on schools and theories of linguistics that stress syntax, or syntax and phonology, see 415*

.19   Psychological principles

Class psycholinguistics in 401.9

.2   **Miscellany**

Do not use for miscellany of language and languages; class in 402

.285   Data processing   Computer applications

Class here computational linguistics [*formerly also* 402.85]

See Manual at 410.285 vs. 006.35

.3–.9   **Standard subdivisions**

Do not use for standard subdivisions of language and languages; class in 403–409

See Manual at 407.1, T1—071 vs. 401.93, 410.71, 418.0071, T4—80071

411   Writing systems

Including alphabets, ideographs, syllabaries; braille; abbreviations, acronyms, capitalization, punctuation, spelling, transliteration

Class manual alphabets, finger spelling in 419

See also 652 for practical works on how to write by hand or machine, e.g., penmanship 652.1

.7   **Paleography**

Study of ancient and medieval handwriting

Class paleography in the broad sense of all aspects of early writings in 417.7

412   Etymology

Class comprehensive works on historical linguistics in 417.7; class interdisciplinary works on onomastics in 929.97. Class a specific aspect of etymology with the aspect, e.g., phonetic development of words 414

See Manual at 401.43 vs. 306.44, 401.9, 412, 415

413   Dictionaries

Class here polyglot dictionaries

.028   Techniques, procedures, apparatus, equipment, materials

Class here lexicography

.1   **Specialized dictionaries**

Including dictionaries of abbreviations and acronyms; picture dictionaries

.2–.9   **Polyglot dictionaries with entry words or definitions in only one language**

Add to base number 413 notation 2–9 from Table 6, e.g., a dictionary with terms in English, French, and German, but with definitions only in English 413.21

414   **Phonology and phonetics**

Standard subdivisions are added for phonology and phonetics together, for phonology alone

Class comprehensive works on phonology and morphology, on phonology and syntax, or on all three in 415

.6   **Suprasegmental features**

Phonology and phonetics of vocal effects extending over more than one sound element

Including juncture (pauses), pitch, stress

Class here intonation

See Manual at 808.1 vs. 414.6

.8   **Phonetics**

For phonetic aspects of suprasegmental features, see 414.6

415   **Grammar**

Descriptive study of morphology and syntax

Including case, categorial, dependency, generative, relational grammar

Class here grammatical relations; parts of speech; comprehensive works on phonology and morphology, on phonology and syntax, or on all three

Class derivational etymology in 412

For phonology, see 414; for prescriptive grammar, including inflectional schemata designed for use as aids in learning languages, see 418

See Manual at 401.43 vs. 306.44, 401.9, 412, 415

[416]   **[Unassigned]**

Most recently used in Edition 18

417   **Dialectology and historical (diachronic) linguistics**

.2   **Dialectology**

Including study of nongeographic language variations, e.g., slang and jargon

Class here study of geographic language variations

.22   **Pidgins and creoles**

Standard subdivisions are added for either or both topics in heading

See Manual at T4—7

.7 **Historical (Diachronic) linguistics**

Study of development of language over time

Class here language history not limited by area, language change, paleography in the broad sense of all aspects of early writings

For change in and history of a specific element of language, see the element, e.g., paleography in the narrow sense of study of ancient and medieval handwriting 411.7, grammar 415

See also 409 for geographic treatment of language history, 410.9 for the history of linguistics

See Manual at 410

418 Standard usage (Prescriptive linguistics) Applied linguistics

Including multilingual phrase books

Class dictionaries in 413; class lexicography in 413.028

.001–.009 Standard subdivisions

See Manual at 407.1, T1—071 vs. 401.93, 410.71, 418.0071, T4—80071

.02 Translation and interpretation

Standard subdivisions are added for either or both topics in heading

.4 **Reading**

419 Structured verbal language other than spoken and written

Including instruction in finger spelling [*formerly also* 371.9127]; finger spelling; specific sign languages, e.g., American Sign Language

Class here sign languages

Class nonlinguistic (nonstructured) communication in 302.222

See Manual at 419 vs. 419.093–419.099

.071 Teaching

Do not use for a specific sign language; class in 419

Class here instruction in sign languages [*formerly also* 371.9127]

See also 371.9127 for instruction in lipreading

.093–.099 Treatment by specific continents, countries, localities; extraterrestrial worlds

Do not use for a specific sign language; class in 419

See Manual at 419 vs. 419.093–419.099

> # 420–490   Specific languages

Class here comprehensive works on specific languages and their literatures

Except for modifications shown under specific entries, add to base number for each language identified by * notation 01–8 from Table 4, e.g., grammar of Japanese 495.65. The base number is the number given for the language unless the schedule specifies a different number

> (Option: For any group of languages, add notation 04 to the base number and then add notation 01–8 from Table 4, e.g., grammar of Celtic languages 491.6045)

The numbers used in this schedule for individual languages do not necessarily correspond exactly with those in 810–890 or with notation in Table 6. Use notation from Table 6 only when so instructed, e.g., at 494

Class comprehensive works in 410

> *For specific sign languages, see 419; for literatures of specific languages, see 810–890*

> *See Manual at 420–490*

(Option B: To give local emphasis and a shorter number to a specific language, place it first by use of a letter or other symbol, e.g., Arabic language 4A0 [preceding 420], for which the base number is 4A. Option A is described under 410)

> # 420–491   Specific Indo-European languages

Class comprehensive works in 410

420   English and Old English (Anglo-Saxon)

> ### 420.1–428   Subdivisions of English language

Class here comprehensive works on English and Old English (Anglo-Saxon)

Except for modifications shown under specific entries, add to base number 42 notation 01–8 from Table 4, e.g., phonology of English language 421.5

Class comprehensive works in 420

> *For Old English (Anglo-Saxon), see 429*

421   Writing system, phonology, phonetics of standard English

Number built according to instructions under 420.1–428

.52   Spelling (Orthography) and pronunciation

> Number built according to instructions under 420.1–428

> Including standard Canadian spelling and pronunciation

> > *For standard American (U.S.) spelling and pronunciation, see 421.54; for standard British spelling and pronunciation, see 421.55*

.54   Standard American (U.S.) spelling and pronunciation

.55   Standard British spelling and pronunciation

422–423   Etymology and dictionaries of standard English

> Numbers built according to instructions under 420.1–428

[424]   [Unassigned]

> Most recently used in Edition 16

425   Grammar of standard English

> Number built according to instructions under 420.1–428

[426]   [Unassigned]

> Most recently used in Edition 18

427   Historical and geographic variations, modern nongeographic variations

> Number built according to instructions under 420.1–428

> *For Old English (Anglo-Saxon), see 429*

.001–.008   Standard subdivisions

.009   Historical, geographic, persons treatment

[.009 02]   6th–15th centuries, 500–1499

> Do not use for Middle English; class in 427.02

[.009 4–.009 9]   Treatment by specific continents, countries, localities in modern world

> Do not use; class in 427.1–427.9

.02   Middle English, 1100–1500

.09   Modern nongeographic variations

> Including ephemera, slang

.1–.8   Geographic variations in England

> Add to 427 the numbers following —42 in notation 421–428 from Table 2, e.g., dialects of London 427.1

> Class geographic variations in Scotland, Wales, and Ireland in 427.941–427.942, e.g., dialects of North Wales 427.94291

.9 **Geographic variations in other places**

Class here pidgins, creoles

Add to 427.9 notation 4–9 from Table 2, e.g., dialects of Canada 427.971, Tok Pisin 427.9953

428 **Standard English usage (Prescriptive linguistics) Applied linguistics**

Number built according to instructions under 420.1–428

Class here Basic English

429 ***Old English (Anglo-Saxon)**

See also 427.02 for Middle English

430 **Germanic (Teutonic) languages   German**

For English and Old English (Anglo-Saxon), see 420

.01–.03 Standard subdivisions of Germanic (Teutonic) languages

Notation from Table 1 as modified under —01–03 in Table 4, e.g., semantics of Germanic languages 430.0143

.04 Special topics of Germanic (Teutonic) languages

Add to base number 430.04 notation 1–8 from Table 4, e.g., grammar of Germanic languages 430.045

.05–.09 Standard subdivisions of Germanic (Teutonic) languages

---

> **430.1–438 Subdivisions of German language**

Except for modifications shown under specific entries, add to base number 43 notation 01–8 from Table 4, e.g., phonology of German language 431.5

Class comprehensive works in 430

431–433 Writing system, phonology, phonetics, etymology, dictionaries of standard German

Numbers built according to instructions under 430.1–438

[434] **[Unassigned]**

Most recently used in Edition 16

435 **Grammar of standard German**

Number built according to instructions under 430.1–438

[436] **[Unassigned]**

Most recently used in Edition 18

*Add to base number as instructed under 420–490

437   Historical and geographic variations, modern nongeographic variations

Number built according to instructions under 430.1–438

Class Low German in 439.4

.001–.008   Standard subdivisions

.009   Historical, geographic, persons treatment

[.009 02]   6th–15th centuries, 500–1499

> Do not use for Old High German; class in 437.01. Do not use for Middle High German and early New High German; class in 437.02

[.009 4–.009 9]   Treatment by specific continents, countries, localities in modern world

> Do not use; class in 437.1–437.9

.01   Old High German to 1100

.02   Middle High German and early New High German, 1100–1500

.09   Modern nongeographic variations

> Including ephemera, slang

.1–.6   Geographic variations in Germany and Austria

Add to 437 the numbers following —43 in notation 431–436 from Table 2, e.g., dialects of Bavaria 437.3

.9   Geographic variations in other places

Add to 437.9 notation 4–9 from Table 2, e.g., German dialects of Alsace 437.944383; however, Yiddish relocated from 437.947 to 439.1

438   Standard German usage (Prescriptive linguistics) Applied linguistics

Number built according to instructions under 430.1–438

439   Other Germanic (Teutonic) languages

.1   *Yiddish [*formerly* 437.947]

> Use of this number for comprehensive works on Old Low Germanic languages discontinued; class in 439
>
> Old Frisian relocated to 439.2; Old Low Franconian relocated to 439.31; Old Low German, Old Saxon relocated to 439.4

---

*Add to base number as instructed under 420–490

> ### 439.2–439.4 Low Germanic languages

Class here West Germanic languages

Class comprehensive works in 439

.2 *Frisian

Including Old Frisian [*formerly* 439.1]

.3 Netherlandish languages

.31 *Dutch

Including Old Low Franconian [*formerly* 439.1]

Class here Flemish

.36 *Afrikaans

.4 *Low German (Plattdeutsch)

Including Old Low German, Old Saxon [*both formerly* 439.1]

.5 Scandinavian (North Germanic) languages

For specific Scandinavian languages, see 439.6–439.8

> ### 439.6–439.8 Specific Scandinavian languages

Class comprehensive works in 439.5

.6 West Scandinavian languages   Old Norse (Old Icelandic)

.600 1–.600 9   Standard subdivisions of West Scandinavian languages

.601–.68   Subdivisions of Old Norse (Old Icelandic)

Add to base number 439.6 notation 01–8 from Table 4, e.g., grammar of Old Norse 439.65

.69 Modern West Scandinavian languages   Modern Icelandic

.690 01–.690 09   Standard subdivisions of modern West Scandinavian languages

.690 1–.698   Subdivisions of Modern Icelandic

Add to base number 439.69 notation 01–8 from Table 4, e.g., grammar of Modern Icelandic 439.695

.699   *Faeroese

> ### 439.7–439.8 East Scandinavian languages

Class comprehensive works in 439.5

*Add to base number as instructed under 420–490

.7	***Swedish**
.8	**Danish and Norwegian**
.81	*Danish

Class Dano-Norwegian in 439.82

.82	*Norwegian (Bokmål, Riksmål)

Class here Dano-Norwegian, comprehensive works on Norwegian

For New Norse, see 439.83

.83	*Norwegian (New Norse, Landsmål)

Class comprehensive works on Norwegian in 439.82

.9	**East Germanic languages**

Including Burgundian, Gothic, Vandalic

440   Romance languages   French

Class comprehensive works on Italic languages in 470

For Italian, Sardinian, Dalmatian, Romanian, Rhaeto-Romanic, see 450; for Spanish and Portuguese, see 460

.01–.03	Standard subdivisions of Romance languages

Notation from Table 1 as modified under —01–03 in Table 4, e.g., semantics of Romance languages 440.0143

.04	Special topics of Romance languages

Add to base number 440.04 notation 1–8 from Table 4, e.g., grammar of Romance languages 440.045

.05–.09	Standard subdivisions of Romance languages

> **440.1–448 Subdivisions of French language**

Except for modifications shown under specific entries, add to base number 44 notation 01–8 from Table 4, e.g., phonology of French language 441.5

Class comprehensive works in 440

441–443 Writing system, phonology, phonetics, etymology, dictionaries of standard French

Numbers built according to instructions under 440.1–448

[444]   [Unassigned]

Most recently used in Edition 16

---

*Add to base number as instructed under 420–490

445 Grammar of standard French

Number built according to instructions under 440.1–448

[446] [Unassigned]

Most recently used in Edition 18

447 Historical and geographic variations, modern nongeographic variations

Number built according to instructions under 440.1–448

See also 449 for Franco-Provençal

.001–.008   Standard subdivisions

.009   Historical, geographic, persons treatment

[.009 02]   6th–15th centuries, 500–1499

> Do not use for Old French; class in 447.01. Do not use for Middle French; class in 447.02

[.009 031]   16th century, 1500–1599

> Do not use; class in 447.02

[.009 4–.009 9]   Treatment by specific continents, countries, localities in modern world

> Do not use; class in 447.1–447.9

.01   Old French to 1400

.02   Middle French, 1400–1600

.09   Modern nongeographic variations

Including ephemera, slang

.1–.8 Geographic variations in France

Add to 447 the numbers following —44 in notation 441–448 from Table 2, e.g., dialects of Picardy 447.26; however, langue d'oc relocated from 447.8 to 449

See also 449 for Provençal and Franco-Provençal

.9 Geographic variations in other places

Class here pidgins, creoles

Add to 447.9 notation 4–9 from Table 2, e.g., dialects of Quebec 447.9714, Haitian Creole 447.97294

448 Standard French usage (Prescriptive linguistics) Applied linguistics

Number built according to instructions under 440.1–448

449   Provençal (Langue d'oc [*formerly also* 447.8]), Franco-Provençal, Catalan

.01–.8   Subdivisions of Provençal (Langue d'oc)

> Add to base number 449 notation 01–8 from Table 4, e.g., grammar of Provençal 449.5
>
> Class Franco-Provençal in 449

.9   *Catalan

450   Italian, Sardinian, Dalmatian, Romanian, Rhaeto-Romanic languages

> Class Sardinian in 457.9; class Dalmatian in 457.994972; class comprehensive works on Romance languages in 440; class comprehensive works on Italic languages in 470

>   **450.1–458 Subdivisions of Italian language**

> Except for modifications shown under specific entries, add to base number 45 notation 01–8 from Table 4, e.g., phonology of Italian language 451.5
>
> Class comprehensive works in 450

451–453 Writing system, phonology, phonetics, etymology, dictionaries of standard Italian

> Numbers built according to instructions under 450.1–458

[454]   [Unassigned]

> Most recently used in Edition 16

455   Grammar of standard Italian

> Number built according to instructions under 450.1–458

[456]   [Unassigned]

> Most recently used in Edition 18

457   Historical and geographic variations, modern nongeographic variations

> Number built according to instructions under 450.1–458

.001–.008   Standard subdivisions

[.009 02]   6th–15th centuries, 500–1499

> Do not use for Old Italian; class in 457.01. Do not use for Middle Italian; class in 457.02

---

*Add to base number as instructed under 420–490

[.009 031]	16th century, 1500–1599

[.009 031]   16th century, 1500–1599

Do not use; class in 457.02

[.009 4–.009 9]   Treatment by specific continents, countries, localities in modern world

Do not use; class in 457.1–457.9

.01   Old Italian to 1300

.02   Middle Italian, 1300–1600

.09   Modern nongeographic variations

Including ephemera, slang

.1–.7   Geographic variations in continental Italy

Add to 457 the numbers following —45 in notation 451–457 from Table 2, e.g., dialects of Lombardy 457.2

.8   Geographic variations in Sicily

Add to 457.8 the numbers following —458 in notation 4581–4582 from Table 2, e.g., dialects of Palermo 457.823

.9   Other geographic variations

.91–.94   Geographic variations in Sardinia

Add to 457.9 the numbers following —459 in notation 4591–4594 from Table 2, e.g., dialects of Cagliari 457.91

Class comprehensive works on Sardinian language in 457.9

.95   Geographic variations in Corsica

.99   Geographic variations in other places

Add to 457.99 notation 4–9 from Table 2, e.g., dialects in Ticino Canton of Switzerland 457.9949478, Dalmatian language 457.994972

**458   Standard Italian usage (Prescriptive linguistics)
Applied linguistics**

Number built according to instructions under 450.1–458

459   Romanian and Rhaeto-Romanic

.01–.8   Subdivisions of Romanian

Add to base number 459 notation 01–8 from Table 4, e.g., grammar of Romanian 459.5

.9   Rhaeto-Romanic languages

Including Friulian, Ladin, Romansh

460   Spanish and Portuguese languages

Class comprehensive works on Romance languages in 440

.01–.09   Standard subdivisions for comprehensive works on Spanish and Portuguese

---

> **460.1–468   Subdivisions of Spanish language**

Except for modifications shown under specific entries, add to base number 46 notation 01–8 from Table 4, e.g., phonology of Spanish language 461.5

Class comprehensive works in 460

461–463 Writing system, phonology, phonetics, etymology, dictionaries of standard Spanish

Numbers built according to instructions under 460.1–468

[464]   [Unassigned]

Most recently used in Edition 16

465   Grammar of standard Spanish

Number built according to instructions under 460.1–468

[466]   [Unassigned]

Most recently used in Edition 18

467   Historical and geographic variations, modern nongeographic variations

Number built according to instructions under 460.1–468

.001–.008   Standard subdivisions

.009   Historical, geographic, persons treatment

[.009 02]   6th–15th centuries, 500–1499

Do not use for Old Spanish; class in 467.01. Do not use for Middle Spanish; class in 467.02

[.009 031]   16th century, 1500–1599

Do not use; class in 467.02

[.009 4–.009 9]   Treatment by specific continents, countries, localities in modern world

Do not use; class in 467.1–467.9

.01   Old Spanish to 1100

.02   Middle Spanish, 1100–1600

.09   Modern nongeographic variations

Including ephemera, slang

.1–.8   **Geographic variations in Spain**

Add to 467 the numbers following —46 in notation 461–468 from Table 2, e.g., dialects of Andalusia 467.8

.9   **Geographic variations in other places**

Class here pidgins, creoles

Add to 467.9 notation 4–9 from Table 2, e.g., Judeo-Spanish (Ladino) 467.9496, Papiamento 467.972986, Latin American dialects 467.98

468   Standard Spanish usage (Prescriptive linguistics) Applied linguistics

Number built according to instructions under 460.1–468

469   *Portuguese

.7   **Historical and geographic variations, modern nongeographic variations**

Number built according to instructions under 420–490

.700 1–.700 8   Standard subdivisions

.700 9   Historical, geographic, persons treatment

[.700 902]   6th–15th centuries, 500–1499

Do not use for Old Portuguese; class in 469.701. Do not use for Middle Portuguese; class in 469.702

[.700 903 1]   16th century, 1500–1599

Do not use; class in 469.702

[.700 94–.700 99]   Treatment by specific continents, countries, localities in modern world

Do not use; class in 469.71–469.79

.701   Old Portuguese to 1100

.702   Middle Portuguese, 1100–1600

.709   Modern nongeographic variations

Including ephemera, slang

.71–.76   Geographic variations in continental Portugal

Add to 469.7 the numbers following —469 in notation 4691–4696 from Table 2, e.g., dialects of Lisbon 469.7425

.78   Geographic variations in Madeira

.79   Other geographic variations

Class here pidgins, creoles

*Add to base number as instructed under 420–490

.791	Geographic variations in Azores
.794	Geographic variations in Spain

Class here comprehensive works on Galician (Gallegan)

For Galician dialects in Portugal, see 469.71–469.72

.798	Geographic variations in Brazil

Add to 469.798 the numbers following —81 in notation 811–817 from Table 2, e.g., dialects of São Paulo 469.79861

.799	Geographic variations in other places

Add to 469.799 notation 4–9 from Table 2, e.g., Crioulo of Guinea-Bissau 469.7996657, Crioulo of Cape Verde Islands and comprehensive works on Crioulo 469.7996658

See also 467.972986 for Papiamento

470   Italic languages   Latin

Class comprehensive works on Latin and Greek in 480

For Romance languages, see 440

.01–.09	Standard subdivisions of Italic languages

>   **470.1–478   Subdivisions of Latin language**

Except for modifications shown under specific entries, add to base number 47 notation 01–8 from Table 4, e.g., phonology of Latin language 471.5

Class comprehensive works in 470

See Manual at 471–475, 478 vs. 477

471–473 Writing system, phonology, phonetics, etymology, dictionaries of classical Latin

Numbers built according to instructions under 470.1–478

[474]   [Unassigned]

Most recently used in Edition 16

475   Grammar of classical Latin

Number built according to instructions under 470.1–478

[476]   [Unassigned]

Most recently used in Edition 18

477   Old (Preclassical), Postclassical, Vulgar Latin

Number built according to instructions under 470.1–478

478   Classical Latin usage (Prescriptive linguistics)   Applied linguistics

Number built according to instructions under 470.1–478

Class here classical-revival Latin usage during medieval or modern times

479   Other Italic languages

.4–.9   Specific languages

Add to 479 the numbers following —79 in notation 794–799 from Table 6, e.g., Umbrian 479.9

480   Hellenic languages   Classical Greek

Classical Greek: the Greek that flourished between 750 and 350 B.C.

Class here comprehensive works on classical (Greek and Latin) languages

For Latin, see 470

.01–.09   Standard subdivisions of classical languages

.1–.9   Standard subdivisions of Hellenic languages, of classical Greek

---

>   481–488   Subdivisions of classical, preclassical, postclassical Greek

Except for modifications shown under specific entries, add to base number 48 notation 1–8 from Table 4, e.g., phonology of classical Greek language 481.5

Dialects of classical Greek are classed in the numbers for classical Greek (480.1–485, 488)

Class comprehensive works in 480

For standard subdivisions of classical Greek, see 480.1–480.9

481–483 Writing system, phonology, phonetics, etymology, dictionaries of classical Greek

Numbers built according to instructions under 481–488

[484]   [Unassigned]

Most recently used in Edition 16

485   Grammar of classical Greek

Number built according to instructions under 481–488

[486]   [Unassigned]

Most recently used in Edition 18

487   Preclassical and postclassical Greek

Number built according to instructions under 481–488

.1   Preclassical Greek

Including paleography of preclassical Greek, Minoan Linear B

See also 492.6 for Minoan Linear A

.3   Postclassical Greek

Including Byzantine Greek

For Koine, see 487.4

.4   Koine (Hellenistic Greek)

Class here Biblical Greek

488   Classical Greek usage (Prescriptive linguistics)   Applied linguistics

Number built according to instructions under 481–488

489   Other Hellenic languages

.3   *Modern Greek

Including Demotic, Katharevusa

490   Other languages

Including language of Indus script

SUMMARY

491   East Indo-European and Celtic languages

*Add to base number as instructed under 420–490

SUMMARY

491.1	**Indo-Iranian languages**	
.2	**Sanskrit**	
.3	**Middle Indic languages**	
.4	**Modern Indic languages**	
.5	**Iranian languages**	
.6	**Celtic languages**	
.7	**East Slavic languages**	**Russian**
.8	**Slavic (Slavonic) languages**	
.9	**Baltic and other Indo-European languages**	

.1   Indo-Iranian languages

> *For Indo-Aryan (Indic) languages, see 491.2–491.4; for Iranian languages, see 491.5*

> **491.2–491.4 Indo-Aryan (Indic) languages**

Class comprehensive works in 491.1

.2   *Sanskrit

.29   Vedic (Old Indic)

.3   Middle Indic languages

Class here comprehensive works on Prakrit languages

For modern Prakrit languages, see 491.4

.37   *Pali

.4   Modern Indic languages

Class here modern Prakrit languages

Class comprehensive works on Prakrit languages in 491.3

.41   Sindhi and Lahnda

.410 1–.418   Subdivisions of Sindhi

> Add to base number 491.41 notation 01–8 from Table 4, e.g., grammar of Sindhi 491.415

.419   *Lahnda

.42   *Panjabi

.43   Western Hindi languages   Hindi

.430 01–.430 09   Standard subdivisions of Western Hindi languages

.430 1–.438   Subdivisions of Hindi

> Add to base number 491.43 notation 01–8 from Table 4, e.g., grammar of Hindi 491.435

---

*Add to base number as instructed under 420–490

.439	*Urdu
.44	*Bengali

Class here comprehensive works on Bengali and Assamese

For Assamese, see 491.451

.45	Assamese, Bihari, Oriya
.451	*Assamese
.454	*Bihari
.454 7	Historical and geographic variations, modern nongeographic variations

Number built according to instructions under 420–490

Including Bhojpuri, Magahi, Maithili

.456	*Oriya
.46	*Marathi
.467	Historical and geographic variations, modern nongeographic variations

Number built according to instructions under 420–490

Including Konkani

.47	Gujarati, Bhili, Rajasthani
.470 1–.478	Subdivisions of Gujarati

Add to base number 491.47 notation 01–8 from Table 4, e.g., grammar of Gujarati 491.475

.479	*Rajasthani
.479 7	Historical and geographic variations, modern nongeographic variations

Number built according to instructions under 420–490

Including Jaipuri, Marwari

.48	Sinhalese-Maldivian languages Sinhalese
.480 1–.488	Subdivisions of Sinhalese

Add to base number 491.48 notation 01–8 from Table 4, e.g., Sinhalese grammar 491.485, Divehi (Maldivian) 491.487

.49	Other Indo-Aryan (Indic) languages

Including Awadhi, Bagheli, Chattisgarhi, Eastern Hindi, Nuristani (Kafiri), Pahari

See also 494.8 for Dravidian languages, 495.4 for Tibeto-Burman languages, 495.95 for Munda languages

---

*Add to base number as instructed under 420–490

.495	*Nepali language
.497	*Romany [*formerly* 491.499]
.499	Dardic (Pisacha) languages

> Including Kashmiri, Khowar, Kohistani, Shina
>
> Use of this number for Nuristani (Kafiri) discontinued; class in 491.49
>
> Romany relocated to 491.497

.5 Iranian languages

.51	*Old Persian

> Class here ancient West Iranian languages
>
> *See also 491.52 for Avestan language*

.52	*Avestan

> Class here ancient East Iranian languages

.53	Middle Iranian languages

> Including Khotanese (Saka), Pahlavi (Middle Persian), Sogdian

.55	*Modern Persian (Farsi)

> Dari relocated to 491.56
>
> Class Tajik in 491.57

.56	*Dari [*formerly* 491.55]
.57	*Tajik [*formerly* 491.59]
.59	Other modern Iranian languages

> Including Pamir languages; Ossetic
>
> Tajik relocated to 491.57

.593	*Pashto (Afghan)

> Use of this number for Pamir languages discontinued; class in 491.59

.597	Kurdish languages Kurdish (Kurmanji)

> Including Kurdi

.597 01–.597 8	Subdivisions of Kurdish (Kurmanji)

> Add to base number 491.597 notation 01–8 from Table 4, e.g., grammar of Kurdish 491.5975

.598	*Baluchi

.6 Celtic languages

> Including Gaulish

*Add to base number as instructed under 420–490

.62	*Irish Gaelic
.63	*Scottish Gaelic
.64	*Manx
.66	*Welsh (Cymric)
.67	*Cornish
.68	*Breton

.7   **East Slavic languages   Russian**

Class comprehensive works on Slavic (Slavonic) languages in 491.8

.700 1–.700 9   Standard subdivisions of East Slavic languages

.701–.75   Standard subdivisions, writing systems, phonology, phonetics, etymology, dictionaries, grammar of Russian

> Add to base number 491.7 notation 01–5 from Table 4, e.g., grammar of Russian 491.75

.77   Historical and geographic variations, modern nongeographic variations of Russian

> Number built according to instructions under 420–490

.770 01–.770 08   Standard subdivisions

.770 09   Historical, geographic, persons treatment

[.770 090 2]   6th–15th centuries, 500–1499

> Do not use; class in 491.7701

[.770 090 31]   16th century, 1500–1599

> Do not use for Old Russian; class in 491.7701. Do not use for Middle Russian; class in 491.7702

[.770 090 32]   17th century, 1600–1699

> Do not use; class in 491.7702

.770 090 33   18th century, 1700–1799

> Do not use for Middle Russian; class in 491.7702

[.770 094–.770 099]   Treatment by specific continents, countries, localities in modern world

> Do not use; class in 491.774–491.779

.770 1   Old Russian to 1550

.770 2   Middle Russian, 1550–1750

.770 9   Modern nongeographic variations

> Including ephemera, slang

*Add to base number as instructed under 420–490

.774–.779	Geographic variations

Add to 491.77 notation 4–9 from Table 2, e.g., dialects of Far Eastern Siberia 491.77577

.78	Standard Russian usage (Prescriptive linguistics)　　Applied linguistics

Add to base number 491.78 the numbers following —8 in notation 8001–86 from Table 4, e.g., reading Russian 491.784

.79	Ukrainian and Belarusian
.790 1–.798	Subdivisions of Ukrainian

Add to base number 491.79 notation 01–8 from Table 4, e.g., grammar of Ukrainian 491.795

.799	*Belarusian
.8	**Slavic (Slavonic) languages**

Including Common Slavic

Class here comprehensive works on Balto-Slavic languages

For East Slavic languages, see 491.7; for Baltic languages, see 491.9

.801–.803	Standard subdivisions

Notation from Table 1 as modified under —01–03 in Table 4, e.g., semantics of Slavic languages 491.80143

.804	Special topics

Add to base number 491.804 notation 1–8 from Table 4, e.g., grammar of Slavic languages 491.8045

.805–.809	Standard subdivisions
.81	South Slavic languages　　Bulgarian

For Serbo-Croatian, see 491.82; for Slovenian, see 491.84

.810 01–.810 09	Standard subdivisions of South Slavic languages
.810 1–.815	Standard subdivisions, writing systems, phonology, phonetics, etymology, dictionaries, grammar of Bulgarian

Add to base number 491.7 notation 01–5 from Table 4, e.g., grammar of Bulgarian 491.815

.817	Historical and geographic variations, modern nongeographic variations of Bulgarian

Number built according to instructions under 420–490

.817 001–.817 008	Standard subdivisions

*Add to base number as instructed under 420–490

.817 009	Historical, geographic, persons treatment	

Do not use for Old Bulgarian; class in 491.81701

.817 01   *Old Bulgarian (Church Slavic)

.818   Standard Bulgarian usage (Prescriptive linguistics)   Applied
linguistics

Add to base number 491.78 the numbers following —8 in notation
8001–86 from Table 4, e.g., reading Bulgarian 491.784

.819   *Macedonian

.82   *Serbo-Croatian

.84   *Slovenian

.85   West Slavic languages   Polish

Including Kashubian

*For Czech, see 491.86; for Slovak, see 491.87; for Wendish, see 491.88;
for Polabian, see 491.89*

.850 01–.850 09   Standard subdivisions of West Slavic languages

.850 1–.858   Subdivisions of Polish

Add to base number 491.85 notation 01–8 from Table 4, e.g.,
grammar of Polish 491.855

.86   *Czech

.867   Historical and geographic variations, modern nongeographic
variations

Number built according to instructions under 420–490

Including Moravian dialects [*formerly* 491.87]

.87   *Slovak

Moravian dialects relocated to 491.867

.88   *Wendish (Lusatian, Sorbian)

.89   *Polabian

.9   Baltic and other Indo-European languages

\>   491.91–491.93   Baltic languages

Class comprehensive works in 491.9

.91   Old Prussian

.92   *Lithuanian

*Add to base number as instructed under 420–490

.93	*Latvian (Lettish)
.99	Other Indo-European languages

Add to 491.99 the numbers following —9199 in notation 91991–91998 from Table 6, e.g., Albanian 491.991, Phrygian 491.993; then to the number given for each language listed below add notation 01–8 from Table 4, e.g., grammar of Albanian 491.9915

491.991 Albanian

491.992 Armenian

491.994 Tocharian

491.998 Hittite

492 Afro-Asiatic (Hamito-Semitic) languages   Semitic languages

For non-Semitic Afro-Asiatic languages, see 493

.01–.03	Standard subdivisions

Notation from Table 1 as modified under —01–03 in Table 4, e.g., semantics of Semitic languages 492.0143

.04	Special topics

Add to base number 491.804 notation 1–8 from Table 4, e.g., grammar of Semitic languages 492.045

.05–.09	Standard subdivisions
.1	**East Semitic languages Akkadian (Assyro-Babylonian)**

For Eblaite, see 492.6

See also 499.95 for Sumerian

.101–.18	Subdivisions of Akkadian (Assyro-Babylonian)

Add to base number 492.1 notation 01–8 from Table 4, e.g., Akkadian grammar 492.15; Assyrian, Babylonian dialects 492.17

>	**492.2–492.9 West Semitic languages**

Class comprehensive works in 492

.2	**Aramaic languages**

For Eastern Aramaic languages, see 492.3

.29	Western Aramaic languages

Including Biblical Aramaic (Chaldee) and Samaritan

*Add to base number as instructed under 420–490

.3   **Eastern Aramaic languages**   **Syriac**

.301–.38   Subdivisions of Syriac

> Add to base number 492.3 notation 01–8 from Table 4, e.g., grammar of Syriac 492.35

.4   ***Hebrew**

.6   **Canaanite languages**

> Including Ammonite, Eblaite, Moabite, Phoenician, language of Minoan Linear A

> Class here comprehensive works on Canaanitic languages

> *For Hebrew, see 492.4*

> *See also 487.1 for Minoan Linear B*

> *See Manual at T6—926: Minoan Linear A*

.67   *Ugaritic

.7   **Arabic**

> Class here Classical Arabic

> *See also 492.9 for South Arabian languages*

.701–.78   Subdivisions of Arabic

> Add to base number 492.7 notation 01–8 from Table 4, e.g., Arabic grammar 492.75; however, Maltese relocated from 492.77 to 492.79

.79   *Maltese [*formerly* 492.77]

.8   **Ethiopian languages**

> Including Gurage, Harari

> Class here comprehensive works on South Semitic languages

> *For South Arabian languages, see 492.9*

.81   *Ge'ez language

.82   *Tigré

.83   *Tigrinya

.87   *Amharic

.877   Historical and geographic variations, modern nongeographic variations

> Number built according to instructions under 420–490

> Use of this number for Argobba discontinued; class in 492.8

---

*Add to base number as instructed under 420–490

.9 **South Arabian languages**

Including Mahri, Sokotri

Class comprehensive works on South Semitic languages in 492.8

See also 492.7 for Arabic

493 Non-Semitic Afro-Asiatic languages

Add to 493 the numbers following —93 in notation 931–937 from Table 6, e.g., Afar 493.5, Oromo 493.55; then to the number for each language listed below add notation 01–8 from Table 4, e.g., grammar of Oromo 493.555

493.1 Egyptian

493.2 Coptic

493.33 Tamazight

493.34 Kabyle

493.38 Tamashek

493.54 Somali

493.55 Oromo

493.72 Hausa

494 Altaic, Uralic, Hyperborean, Dravidian languages

Add to 494 the numbers following —94 in notation 941–948 from Table 6, e.g., Mongolian 494.23, Altai 494.33; then to the number given for each language listed below add notation 01–8 from Table 4, e.g., grammar of Mongolian 494.235

494.23 Mongolian, Khalkha Mongolian

494.315 Chuvash

494.323 Uighur

494.325 Uzbek

494.332 Yakut

494.345 Kazakh

494.347 Kirghiz

494.35 Turkish, Osmanli, Ottoman Turkish

494.361 Azerbaijani

494.364 Turkmen

494.387 Tatar

494.388 Crimean Tatar

494.511 Hungarian (Magyar)

494.541 Finnish (Suomi)

494.545 Estonian

494.55 Sami

494.811 Tamil

494.812 Malayalam

494.814 Kannada (Kanarese)

494.823 Gondi

494.824 Khond (Kandh)

494.827 Telugu

494.83 Brahui

For Japanese, see 495.6; for Korean, see 495.7

See also 497.1 for Inuit (Inuktitut), Yupik, Aleut languages

495   Languages of East and Southeast Asia   Sino-Tibetan languages

Including Karen

Here are classed South Asian languages closely related to the languages of East and Southeast Asia

For Austronesian languages of East and Southeast Asia, see 499.2

.1   *Chinese

Class here Beijing dialect

Base number for Mandarin (Putonghua) (standard written Chinese): 495.1

.17   Historical and geographic variations, modern nongeographic variations of Chinese

Number built according to instructions under 420–490

Including Hakka, Mĭn, Wú, Xiāng, Yuè (Cantonese) dialects

Use of this number for Beijing dialect discontinued; class in 495.1

.4   Tibeto-Burman languages   Tibetan

Including Baric, Bodish, Loloish languages

Class Karen in 495

For Burmese, see 495.8

.400 1–.400 9   Standard subdivisions of Tibeto-Burman languages

.401–.48   Subdivisions of Tibetan

Add to base number 495.4 notation 01–8 from Table 4, e.g., grammar of Tibetan 495.45

.49   Eastern Himalayan languages

Including Chepang, Limbu, Magari, Sunwar; Newari

Use of this number for Himalayan languages other than Kiranti languages and Newari discontinued; class in 495.4

See also 491.495 for Nepali

.6   *Japanese

.7   *Korean

.8   *Burmese

.9   Miscellaneous languages of Southeast Asia; Munda languages

Limited to the languages provided for below

Class Austroasiatic languages in 495.93

For Austronesian languages, see 499.2

*Add to base number as instructed under 420–490

.91	Tai languages Thai (Siamese)

.910 01–.910 09   Standard subdivisions of Tai languages

.910 1–.918   Subdivisions of Thai (Siamese)

> Add to base number 495.91 notation 01–8 from Table 4, e.g., grammar of Thai 495.915

.919   Other Tai languages

> Including Shan

> *For Viet-Muong languages, see 495.92*

.919 1   *Lao

.92–.97   Viet-Muong, Mon-Khmer, Munda, Hmong-Mien (Miao-Yao) languages

> Add to 495.9 the numbers following —959 in notation 9592–9597 from Table 6, e.g., Vietnamese 495.922, Khasi 495.93; then to the number given for each language listed below add notation 01–8 from Table 4, e.g., grammar of Vietnamese 495.225
>
> > 495.922 Vietnamese
> >
> > 495.932 Khmer (Cambodian)
> >
> > 495.972 Hmong (Miao)

496   African languages

Class Afrikaans in 439.36; class Malagasy in 499.3. Class an African creole having a non-African primary source language with the source language plus notation 7 from Table 4, e.g., Krio 427.9664

> *For Ethiopian languages, see 492.8; for non-Semitic Afro-Asiatic languages, see 493*

.1   Khoisan languages

> Including Khoikhoi, San

.3   Niger-Congo languages

> Including Ijoid, Kordofanian languages; Dogon

.32   West Atlantic languages

.321   Senegal group

> Including Serer

> *For Fulani, see 496.322*

.321 4   *Wolof

.322   *Fulani (Fulah)

---

*Add to base number as instructed under 420–490

.33	Igboid, Defoid, Edoid, Idomoid, Nupoid, Oko, Ukaan-Akpes languages; Kwa languages; Kru languages

Igboid, Defoid, Edoid, Idomoid, Nupoid, Oko, Ukaan-Akpes languages, formerly considered Kwa languages, are now considered Benue-Congo languages

Add to 496.33 the numbers following —9633 in notation 96332–96338 from Table 6, e.g., Yoruba 496.333, Baoulé 496.3385; then for each language with a base number listed below, add notation 01–8 from Table 4, e.g., grammar of Yoruba 496.3335

496.332 Ibo (Igbo)

496.333 Yoruba

496.3374 Ewe

496.3378 Gã

496.3385 Akan, Fante, Twi

Class comprehensive works on Benue-Congo languages in 496.36

.34	Mande languages
.345	Mandekan languages
.345 2	*Bambara
.348	Mende-Bandi group Mende
.348 01–.348 8	Subdivisions of Mende

Add to base number 496.348 notation 01–8 from Table 4, e.g., grammar of Mende 496.3485

.35	Gur (Voltaic) languages

Including Dagomba, Moré, Senufo

Class Dogon in 496.3

.36	Benue-Congo and Adamawa-Ubangi languages

Former heading: Benue-Niger languages

Standard subdivisions are added for Benue-Congo and Adamawa-Ubangi languages together, for Benue-Congo languages alone

Including Bamileke

Class here Bantoid languages

For Igboid, Defoid, Edoid, Idomoid, Nupoid, Oko, Ukaan-Akpes languages, see 496.33; for Bantu languages, see 496.39

.361	Adamawa-Ubangi languages

Including Gbaya, Zande

*Add to base number as instructed under 420–490

.361 6	*Sango
.364	Cross River languages
	Including Ibibio
.364 2	*Efik
.39	Bantu languages

Bantu proper (Narrow Bantu)

Including Kari group

With the exception of zone J, groups and zones of Bantu languages are based on Malcolm Guthrie's *Comparative Bantu; an Introduction to the Comparative Linguistics and Prehistory of the Bantu Languages,* 1967–1971

See also 496.36 for Bantoid languages other than Bantu proper

See Manual at T6—9639

.390 1–.390 3	Standard subdivisions

Notation from Table 1 as modified under —01–03 in Table 4, e.g., semantics of Bantu languages 496.390143

.390 4	Special topics

Add to base number 491.804 notation 1–8 from Table 4, e.g., grammar of Bantu languages 496.39045

.390 5–.390 9	Standard subdivisions

*Add to base number as instructed under 420–490

.391–.399   Specific Bantu languages and language families

Add to 496.39 the numbers following —9639 in notation 96391–96399 from Table 6, e.g., Venda 496.397, Zulu 496.3986; then for each language with a base number listed below, add notation 01–8 from Table 4, e.g., grammar of Zulu 496.39865

496.3915 Bemba

496.3918 Nyanja, Chichewa (Chewa)

496.392 Swahili

496.3931 Kongo

496.3932 Kimbundu (Mbundu)

496.39461 Rwanda (Kinyarwanda)

496.39465 Rundi

496.3954 Kikuyu

496.3957 Ganda (Luganda)

496.3962 Duala

496.39686 Lingala

496.3975 Shona

496.39771 Northern Sotho

496.39772 Southern Sotho

496.39775 Tswana

496.3978 Tsonga

496.3985 Xhosa

496.3986 Zulu

496.3987 Swazi (siSwati)

.5   **Nilo-Saharan languages**

Including Nilotic, Nubian languages; Luo, Songhai

Class here Chari-Nile (Macrosudanic) languages

497 North American native languages

Including Tarascan

Class here comprehensive works on North and South American native languages

Add to 497 the numbers following —97 in notation 971–979 from Table 6, e.g., Uto-Aztecan languages 497.45, Nahuatl 497.452; then to the number for each language listed below add notation 01–8 from Table 4, e.g., grammar of Nahuatl 497.4525

497.124 Eastern Canadian Inuktitut

497.19 Aleut

497.4152 Maya, Yucatec Maya

497.452 Nahuatl (Aztec)

For South American native languages, see 498

498 South American native languages

Including Araucanian, Cahuapanan, Mataco-Guaicuru, Tacanan, Uru-Chipaya, Witotoan, Yanomam languages; Hixkaryana, Warao, Yaruro

Add to 498 the numbers following —98 in notation 982–984 from Table 6, e.g., Quechua 498.323, Tucanoan languages 498.35; then to the number for each language listed below add notation 01–8 from Table 4, e.g., grammar of Quechua 498.3235

498.323 Quechua (Kechua)

498.324 Aymara

498.372 Jivaroa proper, Shuar

498.382 Guaraní

498.3829 Tupí (Nhengatu)

499   **Non-Austronesian languages of Oceania, Austronesian languages, miscellaneous languages**

Add to 499 the numbers following —99 in notation 991–999 from Table 6, e.g., Polynesian languages 499.4, Maori 499.442; then to the number for each language listed below add notation 01–8 from Table 4, e.g., grammar of Maori 499.4425

     499.211 Tagalog (Filipino)

     499.221 Indonesian (Bahasa Indonesia)

     499.222 Javanese

     499.28 Malay (Bahasa Malaysia)

     499.3 Malagasy

     499.42 Hawaiian

     499.442 Maori

     499.444 Tahitian

     499.462 Samoan

     499.92 Basque

     499.95 Sumerian

     499.9623 Abkhaz

     499.9625 Adyghe

     499.969 Georgian

     499.992 Esperanto

     499.993 Interlingua

500

500 Natural sciences and mathematics

Natural sciences: sciences that deal with matter and energy, or with objects and processes observable in nature

Class here interdisciplinary works on natural and applied sciences

Class natural history in 508. Class scientific principles of a discipline or subject with the discipline or subject, plus notation 015 from Table 1, e.g., scientific principles of photography 770.15

> *For applied sciences, see 600*
>
> *See Manual at 231.7652 vs. 213, 500, 576.8; also at 338.926 vs. 352.745, 500; also at 500 vs. 001; also at 500 vs. 600*

SUMMARY

500.2–.8	[Physical and space sciences, history and description with respect to kinds of persons]
501–509	Standard subdivisions and natural history
510	Mathematics
.1	Philosophy and theory
511	General principles of mathematics
512	Algebra, number theory
513	Arithmetic
514	Topology
515	Analysis
516	Geometry
519	Probabilities and applied mathematics
520	Astronomy and allied sciences
521	Celestial mechanics
522	Techniques, procedures, apparatus, equipment, materials
523	Specific celestial bodies and phenomena
525	Earth (Astronomical geography)
526	Mathematical geography
527	Celestial navigation
528	Ephemerides
529	Chronology

530	**Physics**
.01–.09	**Standard subdivisions**
.1–.8	**[Theories, mathematical physics, states of matter, instrumentation, measurement]**
531	**Classical mechanics Solid mechanics**
532	**Fluid mechanics Liquid mechanics**
533	**Pneumatics (Gas mechanics)**
534	**Sound and related vibrations**
535	**Light and paraphotic phenomena**
536	**Heat**
537	**Electricity and electronics**
538	**Magnetism**
539	**Modern physics**
540	**Chemistry and allied sciences**
.1–.9	**Standard subdivisions**
541	**Physical and theoretical chemistry**
542	**Techniques, procedures, apparatus, equipment, materials**
543	**Analytical chemistry**
544	**Qualitative analysis**
545	**Quantitative analysis**
546	**Inorganic chemistry**
547	**Organic chemistry**
548	**Crystallography**
549	**Mineralogy**
550	**Earth sciences**
551	**Geology, hydrology, meteorology**
552	**Petrology**
553	**Economic geology**
554–559	**Earth sciences by specific continents, countries, localities in modern world; extraterrestrial worlds**
560	**Paleontology Paleozoology**
.1–.9	**Standard subdivisions; stratigraphic paleontology, paleoecology**
561	**Paleobotany; fossil microorganisms, fungi, algae**
562	**Fossil invertebrates**
563	**Miscellaneous fossil marine and seashore invertebrates**
564	**Fossil Mollusca and Molluscoidea**
565	**Fossil Arthropoda**
566	**Fossil Chordata**
567	**Fossil cold-blooded vertebrates Fossil Pisces (fishes)**
568	**Fossil Aves (birds)**
569	**Fossil Mammalia**
570	**Life sciences Biology**
.1–.9	**Standard subdivisions and microscopy**
571	**Physiology and related subjects**
572	**Biochemistry**
573	**Specific physiological systems in animals, regional histology and physiology**
575	**Specific parts of and physiological systems in plants**
576	**Genetics and evolution**
577	**Ecology**
578	**Natural history of organisms and related subjects**
579	**Microorganisms, fungi, algae**

580	**Plants**	
.1–.9	Standard subdivisions	
581	Specific topics in natural history of plants	
582	Plants noted for specific vegetative characteristics and flowers	
583	Magnoliopsida (Dicotyledons)	
584	Liliopsida (Monocotyledons)	
585	Pinophyta (Gymnosperms)	Coniferales (Conifers)
586	Cryptogamia (Seedless plants)	
587	Pteridophyta (Vascular cryptogams)	
588	Bryophyta	
590	**Animals**	
.1–.9	Standard subdivisions	
591	Specific topics in natural history of animals	
592	Invertebrates	
593	Miscellaneous marine and seashore invertebrates	
594	Mollusca and Molluscoidea	
595	Arthropoda	
597	Cold-blooded vertebrates	Pisces (Fishes)
598	Aves (Birds)	
599	Mammalia (Mammals)	

.2 **Physical sciences**

> *For astronomy and allied sciences, see 520; for physics, see 530; for chemistry and allied sciences, see 540; for earth sciences, see 550*
>
> *See Manual at 530 vs. 500.2*

.5 **Space sciences**

> *For astronomy, see 520; for earth sciences in other worlds, see 550. For space sciences aspects of a specific subject, see the subject, plus notation 0919 from Table 1, e.g., chemical reactions in space 541.390919*
>
> *See Manual at 520 vs. 500.5, 523.1, 530.1, 919.9*

.8 **History and description with respect to kinds of persons**

> Add to base number 500.8 the numbers following —08 in notation 081–089 from Table 1, e.g., women scientists 500.82

501 Philosophy and theory

> Class scientific method as a general research technique in 001.42; class scientific method applied in the natural sciences in 507.2

502 Miscellany

.8 **Auxiliary techniques and procedures; apparatus, equipment, materials**

.82 Microscopy

> Class here microscopes; interdisciplinary works on microscopy
>
> *For manufacture of microscopes, see 681.413*
>
> *See also 570.282 for microscopy in biology*

[.822]	Simple microscopes

Number discontinued; class in 502.82

.823	Compound microscopes

[.824]	Ultramicroscopes

Number discontinued; class in 502.82

.825	Electron microscopes

503–506 Standard subdivisions

507 Education, research, related topics

.2 Research; statistical methods

Class research covering science in general in 001.4; class scientific method as a general research technique in 001.42

See Manual at 500 vs. 001

.8 Use of apparatus and equipment in study and teaching

Class here science fair projects, science projects in schools

508 Natural history

Do not use for history and description of natural sciences and mathematics with respect to groups of persons; class in 500.8

Class here description and surveys of phenomena in nature

Class natural history of organisms in 578

See Manual at 333.7–333.9 vs. 508, 913–919, 930–990; also at 578 vs. 304.2, 508, 910

.09 Historical and persons treatment

Do not use for geographic treatment; class in 508.3–508.9

.2 Seasons

Class here interdisciplinary works on seasons

For a specific aspect of seasons, see the aspect, e.g., effect of seasons on organisms 577.23

.3 Treatment by areas, regions, places in general; by specific continents, countries, localities in the ancient world

.31 Treatment by areas, regions, places in general

Add to base number 508.31 the numbers following —1 in notation 11–19 from Table 2, e.g., natural history of the sea 508.3162

.33   Treatment by specific continents, countries, localities in the ancient world

> Add to base number 508.33 the numbers following —3 in notation 31–39 from Table 2, e.g., natural history of ancient Greece 508.338

.4–.9   **Treatment by specific continents, countries, localities in the modern world**

> Add to base number 508 notation 4–9 from Table 2, e.g., natural history of Brazil 508.81

509   Historical, geographic, persons treatment

> Class historical, geographic, persons treatment of natural phenomena in 508

510   Mathematics

> Class here finite mathematics

> *See Manual at 510; also at 005.1 vs. 510; also at vs. 510, T1—0151 vs. 003, T1—011; also at 510, T1—0151 vs. 004–006, T1—0285*

SUMMARY

510.1	Philosophy and theory
511	General principles of mathematics
512	Algebra, number theory
513	Arithmetic
514	Topology
515	Analysis
516	Geometry
519	Probabilities and applied mathematics

.1   **Philosophy and theory**

> Including metamathematics

> Class mathematical logic in 511.3

511   General principles of mathematics

> Class general principles applied to a specific branch of mathematics with the branch, e.g., arithmetic approximation 513.24

.2   **Mathematical systems**

.22   Inductive mathematics

> Class here intuitive mathematics

.24   Deductive mathematics

.3   **Mathematical (Symbolic) logic**

> Including automata theory, formal languages, machine theory; sequential and Turing machines; categories, completeness theorem, decidability, Gödel's theorem, Petri nets
>
> Class here axioms, hypotheses, postulates, proof theory; logic operators; predicate calculus, propositional calculus
>
> Class proof for inductive mathematics in 511.22

.32   Sets

> Including partially ordered sets
>
> *For point sets, see 511.33*

.322   Set theory

> Including combinatorial set theory; continuum hypothesis, transfinite numbers; fuzzy sets

.324   Set algebra

> Class here Boolean algebra

.33   Relations, lattices, ordered algebraic structures

> Standard subdivisions are added for any or all topics in heading
>
> Including equations, functions, mappings, point sets, transformations
>
> *See also 515 for theory of functions*

.35   Recursion theory

> Including recursive functions

.4   **Approximations and expansions**

.42   Methods

> Including curve fitting, interpolation, least squares, splines

.43   Error analysis

.5   **Theory and construction of graphs**

> Including nomography

.52   Trees

.6   **Combinatorial analysis**

> Including combinatorial configurations and designs
>
> Class graph theory in 511.5

.62   Enumeration

.64   Permutations and combinations

> Including Latin and magic squares

.65	Choice

See also 519.3 for decision making in game theory

.66	Maxima and minima

Standard subdivisions are added for either or both topics in heading

.8	**Mathematical models (Mathematical simulation)**

Including algorithms

512 Algebra, number theory

Standard subdivisions are added for algebra and number theory together, for algebra alone

Including numerical algebra

Class here universal algebra, modern algebra (abstract algebra combined with number theory)

Class foundations of algebra in 512.9

.001–.009	Standard subdivisions
.02	Abstract algebra

For subdivisions of abstract algebra, see 512.2–512.5

.1	**Algebra combined with other branches of mathematics**

For arithmetic and algebra, see 513.12

See Manual at 510: Combination of topics

.12	Algebra and Euclidean geometry
.13	Algebra and trigonometry
.14	Algebra and analytic geometry
.15	Algebra and calculus

>	**512.2–512.5 Subdivisions of abstract algebra**

Class comprehensive works in 512.02

.2	**Groups and group theory**

Standard subdivisions are added for either or both topics in heading

Including representations of groups

Class here cosets, semigroups, subgroups; Abelian (commutative), Brauer, cyclic, permutation groups

For topological and related algebras and groups, see 512.55; for algebraic topology, see 514.2

.24   Algebras based on group properties

> Including associative, nonassociative, commutative, flexible, free, Jordan algebras
>
> Class algebras defined by dimension of space in 512.5; class topological algebras in 512.55

.3   **Fields**

> Class here field theory, Galois theory
>
> Class linear algebra in 512.5; class number theory in 512.7

.4   **Rings**

> Including subrings, extension theory
>
> Class here ideals, integral domains, modules, radical theory
>
> *For fields, see 512.3*

.5   **Linear, multilinear, multidimensional algebras**

> Standard subdivisions are added for linear, multilinear, multidimensional algebras together; for linear algebra alone
>
> Including Cayley algebra, quaternions
>
> Class here vector algebra, linear algebra combined with analytic geometry
>
> Class foundations of algebra in 512.9; class analysis combined with linear algebra in 515.14

.52   Vector spaces

> Class bilinear forms in 512.944; class topological vector spaces in 515.73

[.53]   Algebras defined by dimension of space and other geometric algebras

> Number discontinued; class in 512.5

.55   Topological and related algebras and groups

> Standard subdivisions are added for topological and related algebras and groups together, for topological algebras alone, for topological groups alone
>
> Including algebraic k-theory, homological algebra, categories, functors, morphisms; toposes; Banach, Fréchet, Hopf, Lie, operator (e.g., C*, Von Neumann, W*), reductive, Stein, uniform algebras and their groups
>
> *For differential algebras, see 512.56; for factor algebras, see 512.57*
>
> *See also 514.2 for algebraic topology*

.56   Differential algebras

> Class here difference algebras

.57   Factor algebras

> Including Clifford, exterior, spinor, tensor algebras

.7	**Number theory**

Class here lattices

For theory of equations, see 512.94

.72	Elementary number theory

Including combinations, congruence, continued fractions, Diophantine equations, divisibility, Fibonacci numbers, natural numbers, operations, power residues, prime numbers, quadratic residues, representations, residues, roots, sequences of integers, sieves, transformations

.73	Analytic number theory

Including additive properties, Diophantine approximations, distribution theory of prime numbers, functions, modular forms, multiplicative properties, number theoretic functions, partitions, Riemannian hypothesis, transcendental numbers

.74	Algebraic number theory

Including algebraic function theory, class groups, class numbers, discriminants, factorization, Fermat's last theorem, field extensions, fields, ideals, p-adic numbers, quadratic forms, reciprocity, rings, unit theory

.75	Geometry of numbers

Class here geometry of rational numbers

.76	Probabilistic number theory
.9	**Foundations of algebra**

Class algebra combined with other branches of mathematics in 512.1

.900 1–.900 9	Standard subdivisions
.92	Algebraic operations

Class here addition, subtraction, multiplication, division

.922	Exponents and logarithms
.923	Root extraction

Including factoring

.924	Approximation, ratio, proportion
.925	Combinations, permutations, distributions
.93	Simple algebraic and geometric progressions
.94	Theory of equations
.942	Specific types and systems of equations

Including binomial, polynomial, quadratic, cubic, quartic equations

Mixed equations relocated to 515.38

.943	Determinants and matrices
.943 2	Determinants
	Class determinants of matrices in 512.9434
.943 4	Matrices
	Including eigenvalues and eigenvectors
.944	Theory of forms and algebraic invariant theory
	Standard subdivisions are added for either or both topics in heading
.96	Algebra of non-equation functions
	Including rational functions
	For inequalities, see 512.97
.97	Inequalities

513　Arithmetic

Including numeracy

.1　Arithmetic combined with other branches of mathematics

See Manual at 510: Combination of topics

.12	Arithmetic and algebra
[.122–.123]	Separate and combined treatment
	Numbers discontinued; class in 513.12
.13	Arithmetic and geometry
[.132–.133]	Separate and combined treatment
	Numbers discontinued; class in 513.13
.14	Arithmetic, algebra, geometry
[.142–.143]	Separate and combined treatment
	Numbers discontinued; class in 513.14

.2　Arithmetic operations

.21	Basic operations
.211	Addition
	Including counting
.212	Subtraction
.213	Multiplication
.214	Division

.224	Structures and spaces

Standard subdivisions are added for either or both topics in heading

Including braids, fiber bundles (fiber spaces), knots, links, path spaces, sheaves

.23	Homology and cohomology theories

Standard subdivisions are added for either or both topics in heading

Including K-theory

See also 512.55 for topological groups

.24	Homotopy theory

Including retracts, shape theory

.3	**Topology of spaces**

Class here topological manifolds [*formerly also* 514.233], manifold topology, metric topology

.32	Systems and spaces

Standard subdivisions are added for either or both topics in heading

.320 01–.320 09	Standard subdivisions
.320 2	Uniform spaces
.320 3	Derived spaces
.322	Point set topology (General topology)
.323	Proximity topology
.7	**Analytic topology**
.72	Differential topology

Including foliations

.74	Global analysis

Including catastrophes, Hamiltonian systems, index theorems

Class here global analysis in analysis and comprehensive works on global analysis [*formerly also* 515]

.742	Fractals

515 Analysis

Class here calculus; numerical analysis; comprehensive works on the theory of functions

Global analysis and comprehensive works on global analysis relocated to 514.74

Class probabilities in 519.2. Class the theory of a specific function or group of functions with the function or group of functions, e.g., analysis of continued fractions 512.72

For applied numerical analysis, see 519.4

SUMMARY

.1 Analysis and calculus combined with other branches of mathematics

For algebra and calculus, see 512.15

See Manual at 510: Combination of topics

.13 Analysis and topology

.14 Analysis and linear algebra

.15 Calculus and analytic geometry

.16 Calculus and trigonometry

.2 General aspects of analysis

Class a specific application with the application, e.g., expansion of functions of real variables 515.8234

.22 Properties of functions

.222 Continuity, dimension, limit

.223 Uniformity and multiformity

Standard subdivisions are added for either or both topics in heading

Class here uniform and multiform functions

Riemann surfaces relocated to 515.93; analytic spaces (generalization of Riemann surfaces to n-dimensional spaces) relocated to 515.94

.23 Operations on functions

For differentiation, see 515.33; for integration, see 515.43

.232	Determination of functions
.234	Expansion of functions
.235	Evaluation of functions
.24	Sequences and series

Standard subdivisions are added for sequences and series together, for sequences alone

Class here infinite processes

.243	Series

Including summability

Class here infinite series

Class number theory of continued fractions in 512.72

.243 2	Power series
.243 3	Fourier and harmonic analysis

Standard subdivisions are added for either or both topics in heading

Including wavelets

Class Fourier transforms in 515.723

For abstract harmonic analysis, see 515.785

.25	Equations and functions

Standard subdivisions are added for either or both topics in heading

.252	Equations and functions by degree

Including linear, nonlinear, quadratic equations

.253	Equations and functions by property

Including homogeneous, indeterminate, reciprocal equations

.254	Equations and functions by origin

Including conditional equations

.26	Inequalities
.3	**Differential calculus and equations**

Class differential topology in 514.72; class differential operators in 515.7242; class differential geometry in 516.36

.33	Differential calculus

Including ordinary, partial, total differentiations; total and directional derivatives, differentials, mean value theorems

Class numerical differentiation in 515.623; class vector differentiation in 515.63; class probability differentiation in 519.2

.35	Differential equations

Class here bifurcation, perturbation, stability theories; Cauchy problem; orders, degrees; comprehensive works on boundary-value problems

Class mixed equations in 515.38

For boundary-value problems of finite differences, see 515.62

.352	Ordinary differential equations

Class here dynamical systems

.353	Partial differential equations

Including elliptic, hyperbolic, parabolic equations

.354	Linear differential equations

Class linear ordinary differential equations in 515.352; class linear partial differential equations in 515.353

.355	Nonlinear differential equations

Class nonlinear ordinary differential equations in 515.352; class nonlinear partial differential equations in 515.353

.36	Differential inequalities
.37	Differential forms
.38	Mixed equations [*formerly also* 512.942]

Including difference-differential and integro-differential equations

.4	**Integral calculus and equations**

Class special functions in 515.5; class integral transforms in 515.723; class integral geometry in 516.362

.42	Theory of measure and integration

Standard subdivisions are added for either or both topics in heading

Including ergodic theory

For functionals, see 515.74

.43	Integral calculus

Including integration, summation, arc length, cubature, quadrature; Cauchy, definite, Denjoy, Green, Haar, improper, Lebesgue, line, Poisson, Poisson-Stieltjes, proper, Riemann, Stokes', surface integrals

Class numerical integration in 515.624; class vector integration in 515.63; class probability integration in 519.2

.45	Integral equations

Class mixed equations in 515.38

.46	Integral inequalities

.5 **Special functions**

.52	Eulerian integrals

Including beta and gamma functions

.53	Harmonic functions

Including Bessel, Hankel, Laplace, Legendre, Neumann functions

.54	Mathieu functions
.55	Orthogonal polynomials

Including Chebyshev, Hermite, hypergeometric, Jacobi, Lagrange, Laguerre, Legendre polynomials

.56	Zeta function

Class application of Riemann zeta function with respect to prime number theory in 512.73

.6 **Other analytic methods**

For functional analysis, see 515.7

.62	Calculus of finite differences

Class here boundary-value problems when either limit has a numerical value

.623	Numerical differentiation
.624	Numerical integration
.625	Difference equations

Class difference-differential equations in 515.38

.63	Vector, tensor, spinor analysis

Standard subdivisions are added for vector, tensor, spinor analysis together; for vector analysis alone; for tensor analysis alone

Including vector and tensor calculus

Class algebraic vector analysis in 512.52; class geometric vector analysis in 516.182

.64	Calculus of variations

Including control theory

See also 003.5 for interdisciplinary works on control theory, 629.8312 for control theory in engineering

.7   **Functional analysis**

Class here comprehensive works on real-valued, complex-valued, vector-valued functions

Abstract potential theory relocated to 515.9

Class theory of measure and integration in 515.42; class potential theory in 515.9

For topological algebras, see 512.55; for functions of real variables, see 515.8; for functions of complex variables, see 515.9

.72   Operational calculus

Class a specific application with the application, e.g., differential operators in topological vector spaces 515.73

.722   Spectral and representation theories

.722 2   Spectral theory

.722 3   Representation theory

Including forms

Class abstract harmonic analysis in 515.785

.723   Transforms (Integral operators)

Including Fourier, Hilbert, Laplace, Legendre, Z transforms

.724   Operator theory

For integral operators, see 515.723

.724 2   Differential operators

Including elliptic operators

.724 6   Linear operators

Class linear integral operators in 515.723; class linear differential operators in 515.7242

.724 8   Nonlinear operators

Class nonlinear integral operators in 515.723; class nonlinear differential operators in 515.7242

.73   Topological vector spaces

Including spaces of analytic functions; spaces of continuous functions; spaces of measurable functions, e.g., L^p spaces, Orlicz spaces; Hermitian (unitary) and Riesz spaces

Class here linear topological spaces

For functionals, see 515.74

.732	Banach spaces

Class here normed linear spaces

For Hilbert spaces, see 515.733

.733	Hilbert spaces

Class here inner product spaces

.74	Functionals
.78	Special topics
.782	Distribution theory

Including duality, Sobolev spaces

Class here generalized functions

.783	Abstract measure theory
.784	Valuation theory
.785	Abstract harmonic analysis

Including Fourier analysis on groups

.8	**Functions of real variables**

Class combined treatment of functions of real and complex variables in 515.9

.82	General aspects of functions of real variables

Add to base number 515.82 the numbers following 515.2 in 515.22–515.26, e.g., expansion of functions 515.8234

Class a specific application with the application, e.g., expansion of functions of several real variables 515.84

.83	Functions of one real variable

Including fractional calculus

.84	Functions of several real variables
.88	Specific types of real variable functions

Including real variable analytic functions

.9	**Functions of complex variables**

Class here abstract potential theory [*formerly also* 515.7], automorphic functions, conformal mapping, potential theory

For a specific application of potential theory, see the application, e.g., harmonic analysis and potential theory 515.2433

.92   General aspects of functions of complex variables

> Add to base number 515.92 the numbers following 515.2 in 515.22–515.26, e.g., expansion of functions 515.9234

> Class a specific application with the application, e.g., expansion of functions of several complex variables 515.94

.93   Functions of one complex variable

> Including Riemann surfaces [*formerly* 515.223]

.94   Functions of several complex variables

> Including analytic spaces (generalization of Riemann surfaces to n-dimensional spaces) [*formerly* 515.223], Teichmüller spaces

.98   Specific types of complex variable functions

> Including entire and pseudoanalytic functions

.982   Meromorphic functions

.983   Elliptic functions

> Class special elliptic functions in 515.5

.984   Theta function

516   Geometry

Class here geometry combined with topology

Class algebra combined with geometry in 512.1; class arithmetic combined with geometry in 513.13; class analysis combined with geometry in 515.1; class geometric probability in 519.2

For topology, see 514

SUMMARY

516.001–.009	Standard subdivisions
.02–.08	[Classical and modern geometry; planes, solids, manifolds, convex sets]
.1	General aspects of geometry
.2	Euclidean geometry
.3	Analytic geometries
.4	Affine geometry
.5	Projective geometry
.6	Abstract descriptive geometry
.9	Non-Euclidean geometries

.001–.009   Standard subdivisions

.02   Classical geometry

.04   Modern geometry

.05   Planes

.06	Solids
.07	Manifolds
.08	Convex sets

.1 General aspects of geometry

Class here automorphisms, metric geometry, transformations

Class general aspects applied to a specific geometry with the geometry, e.g., angles in Euclidean geometry 516.215

.12	Incidence geometry
.13	Combinatorial geometry

Use of this number for constructive geometry discontinued; class in 516

.15   Geometric configurations

Including angles, circles, conic sections, cubes, curves, polyhedrons, spheres, spirals, squares, surfaces; patterns, sizes, space

Class here measures, shapes

Class geometric configurations in a specific subject with the subject, e.g., measuring the sphere in solid geometry 516.23

.16   Coordinate systems

Including Cartesian, curvilinear, homogeneous systems

.17	Geometry of inequalities
.18	Nonpoint base geometries
.182	Vector geometry
.183	Line geometry
.184	Circle geometry
.185	Modular geometry
.186	Geometries over algebras, groups, rings

.2 Euclidean geometry

Including the imbedding of Euclidean spaces in other geometries

Class here congruences, similarity, metric geometry

Class a specific type of Euclidean geometry with the type, e.g., Euclidean analytic geometry 516.3

.200 1–.200 9	Standard subdivisions
.204	Famous problems

Including trisecting an angle, squaring the circle, doubling the cube

.21	General aspects of Euclidean geometry

> Add to base number 516.21 the numbers following 516.1 in 516.12–516.18, e.g., angles 516.215
>
> Class a specific application with the application, e.g., angles in plane geometry 516.22

.22	Plane geometry

> Including Pythagorean theorem

.23	Solid geometry
.24	Trigonometry
.242	Plane trigonometry
.244	Spherical trigonometry
.3	**Analytic geometries**

> Class linear algebra combined with analytic geometry in 512.5; class analytic affine geometry in 516.4; class analytic projective geometry in 516.5

.32	Plane analytic geometry
.33	Solid analytic geometry
.34	Analytic trigonometry

> Plane and spherical

.35	Algebraic geometry

> Geometries based on linear algebra
>
> Including enumerative geometry, lattice point geometry
>
> Class here abstract algebraic geometry, birational and conformal transformations, connections, dual geometries, intersections; bilinear and sesquilinear forms; polytopes; complex multiplication

.352	Curves and surfaces on projective and affine planes

> Standard subdivisions are added for either or both topics in heading
>
> Including Mordell conjecture
>
> Class here theory of curves

.353	Algebraic varieties of higher dimensions
.36	Differential and integral geometry

> Standard subdivisions are added for differential and integral geometry together, for differential geometry alone
>
> Class here curves, differentiable manifolds, surfaces, torsion
>
> *For metric differential geometries, see 516.37*

| .360 01–.360 09 | Standard subdivisions |

.362   Integral geometry (Global differential geometry)

Including arc length, curvature, evolutes, fiber spaces (fiber bundles), geodesics, involutes, tangent space at a point; analytic, convex, developable, minimal, ruled surfaces; analytic, asymptotic, minimal curves

Class here modern differential geometry

[.363]   Local and intrinsic differential geometry

Number discontinued; class in 516.36

.37   Metric differential geometries

.372   Euclidean geometry

.373   Riemannian geometry

Including Sasakian geometry

.374   Minkowski geometry

Including Einstein geometry

.375   Finsler geometry

.376   Cartan geometry

.4   **Affine geometry**

Class affine differential geometry in 516.36

.5   **Projective geometry**

Class projective differential geometry in 516.36

.6   **Abstract descriptive geometry**

See also 604.2015166 for descriptive geometry in technical drawing

.9   **Non-Euclidean geometries**

Including Bolyai, Gauss, hyperbolic, inversive, Lobachevski geometries; imbeddings of non-Euclidean spaces in other geometries

Class a specific type of non-Euclidean geometry with the type, e.g., non-Euclidean analytic geometries 516.3

[517]   **[Unassigned]**

Most recently used in Edition 17

[518]   **[Unassigned]**

Most recently used in Edition 15

519 Probabilities and applied mathematics

Class a specific application with the application, e.g., game theory in gambling 795.01

.2 Probabilities

Class here conditional probabilities, independent and dependent trials, games of chance, geometric probability, probability calculus

Class probabilities applied to statistical mathematics in 519.5

See Manual at 795.015192 vs. 519.2

.23 Random (Stochastic) processes

.232 Stationary processes

Including time series

.233 Markov processes

Including Markov chains

.234 Branching processes

.24 Probability distribution

Class here descriptive probabilities

[.26] Probabilities over rings, algebras, other algebraic structures

Number discontinued; class in 519.2

.28 Special topics

.282 Random walks

Class here Monte Carlo method

.287 Expectation and prediction

Standard subdivisions are added for either or both topics in heading

Including estimation, reliability, renewal theories; martingales; Markov risk

.3 Game theory

Class here mathematical optimization

Class control theory in 515.64; class games of chance in 519.2

For a specific mathematical optimization technique, see the technique, e.g., mathematical programming 519.7

See also 511.65 for choice and decision making in combinatorial analysis

.4 Applied numerical analysis

.5   **Statistical mathematics**

           Class here numerical data, parametric and nonparametric methods

           See Manual at 519.5, T1—015195 vs. 001.422, T1—072

.52   Theory of sampling

.53   Descriptive statistics, multivariate analysis, analysis of variance and covariance

           Including cluster analysis

.532   Frequency distributions

.533   Measures of central tendency

           Including median, mean, mode

.534   Measures of deviation

           Including standard deviation

.535   Multivariate analysis

           Including latent structure analysis

           For regression analysis, see 519.536; for correlation (association) analysis, see 519.537

.535 4   Factor analysis

           Including principal components analysis

.536   Regression analysis

.537   Correlation (Association) analysis

.538   Analysis of variance and covariance

           Standard subdivisions are added for either or both topics in heading

.54   Statistical inference

           Including expectation, nonparametric statistics, prediction, sequential analysis

.542   Decision theory

           Including Bayesian statistical decision theory

.544   Estimation theory

.55   Time-series analysis

.56   Hypothesis testing

           Including chi-square test

.7   **Programming**

.700 1–.700 9		Standard subdivisions
.702		Single-stage programming
.703		Multistage programming
		Including dynamic programming
.72		Linear programming
.76		Nonlinear programming
		Including convex and quadratic programming
		Class integer programming in 519.77
.77		Integer programming
.8		**Special topics**
.82		Queuing
		Including congestion
.83		Inventory and storage
.84		Success runs
.85		Epidemics and fluctuations
.86		Quality control

520 Astronomy and allied sciences

See Manual at 520 vs. 500.5, 523.1, 530.1, 919.9: Outer space; also at 520 vs. 523.1, 523.112, 523.8

SUMMARY

521	Celestial mechanics
522	Techniques, procedures, apparatus, equipment, materials
523	Specific celestial bodies and phenomena
525	Earth (Astronomical geography)
526	Mathematical geography
527	Celestial navigation
528	Ephemerides
529	Chronology

[.153]	Physical principles
	Do not use; class in 523.01
[.154]	Chemical principles
	Do not use; class in 523.02
[.28]	Auxiliary techniques and procedures; apparatus, equipment, materials
	Do not use; class in 522

> ### 521–525 Astronomy

Class comprehensive works in 520

For geodetic astronomy, see 526.6

521 Celestial mechanics

Including equilibrium, problems of three and *n* bodies

Class here motion

Class applications to specific celestial bodies and phenomena in 523

.1 **Gravitation**

.3 **Orbits**

Class here Kepler's laws

.4 **Perturbations**

.9 **Precession**

Including nutation

Class corrections of precession in 522.9

522 Techniques, procedures, apparatus, equipment, materials

Class here astrometry, positional and practical astronomy

Class positional astronomy as an aspect of mathematical geography in 526.6

[.028] Auxiliary techniques and procedures; apparatus, equipment, materials

Do not use for general works; class in 522. Do not use for specific auxiliary techniques and procedures; class in 522.8

> ### 522.1–522.6 Practical astronomy

Class comprehensive works in 522

For corrections, see 522.9; for practical astronomy of specific celestial bodies and phenomena, see 523

.1 **Observatories**

.109 Historical and persons treatment

Do not use for geographic treatment; class in 522.19

.19 Geographic treatment

Add to base number 522.19 notation 01–9 from Table 2, e.g., space observatories 522.1919, observatories in China 522.1951

.2   Astronomical instruments   Telescopes

Class here movable nonspace telescopes

For meridional instruments, see 522.3; for extrameridional instruments, see 522.4; for auxiliary instruments, see 522.5; for astronomical instruments in nonoptical astronomy, see 522.68

.29   Fixed-location and space telescopes

.290 9   Historical and persons treatment

Do not use for geographic treatment; class in 522.291–522.299

.291–.299   Geographic treatment

Add to base number 522.29 notation 01–9 from Table 2, e.g., fixed-location telescopes in Chile 522.2983

.3   Meridional instruments

For zenith telescopes, see 522.4

.4   Extrameridional instruments

Including astrolabes, quadrants, reflecting circles, sextants, zenith and equatorial telescopes

.5   Auxiliary instruments

Including chronographs, chronometers

For auxiliary instruments in special methods of observation, see 522.6

.6   Special methods of observation

.62   Photometry

.622   Photographic photometry

.623   Photoelectric photometry

.63   Photography

For photographic photometry, see 522.622

.65   Polarimetry

.67   Spectroscopy

Class spectroscopy of a specific celestial body with the body, plus notation 0287 from Table 1, e.g., spectroscopy of planets 523.40287

.68   Nonoptical astronomy

.682   Radio astronomy

.683   Infrared astronomy

[.684]   Radar astronomy

Number discontinued; class in 522.68

.686	Particle methods of observation
.686 2	Gamma-ray astronomy
.686 3	X-ray astronomy

.7   Spherical astronomy

Including celestial reference systems

Class comprehensive works on geodetic coordinates in 526.6

.8   Specific auxiliary techniques and procedures

Add to base number 522.8 the numbers following —028 in notation 0285–0289 from Table 1, e.g., testing and measurement 522.87

Class spectroscopy in 522.67

.9   Corrections

Corrections of aberration, astronomical refraction, parallax, precession; of instrumental errors

523   Specific celestial bodies and phenomena

Including zodiac

Class phenomena of celestial bodies directly comparable to terrestrial phenomena with the terrestrial phenomena in 550, e.g., volcanic activity on Mars 551.21099923

SUMMARY

523.01–.02	[Astrophysics and cosmochemistry]
.1	The universe, galaxies, quasars
.2	Solar system
.3	Moon
.4	Planets
.5	Meteors, solar wind, zodiacal light
.6	Comets
.7	Sun
.8	Stars
.9	Satellites (Moons) and rings; eclipses, transits, occultations

[.001–.009]   Standard subdivisions

Do not use; class in 520.1–520.9

.01   Astrophysics

For celestial mechanics, see 521

.013   Heat

Add to base number 523.013 the numbers following 536 in 536.1–536.7, e.g., heat transfer 523.0132

.015	Light and paraphotic phenomena

Add to base number 523.015 the numbers following 535 in 535.01–535.8, e.g., ultraviolet radiation 523.015014

.018	Electricity and magnetism

Add to base number 523.018 the numbers following 53 in 537–538, e.g., magnetism 523.0188

.019	Molecular, atomic, nuclear physics

Add to base number 523.019 the numbers following 539 in 539.1–539.7, e.g., cosmic rays 523.0197223

.02	Cosmochemistry
.1	**The universe, galaxies, quasars**

Standard subdivisions are added for the universe, galaxies, quasars together; for the universe alone

Class here cosmology

See also 523.8875 for black holes

See Manual at 520 vs. 500.5, 523.1, 919.9: Outer space; also at 520 vs. 523.1, 523.112, 523.8

.11	Galaxies and quasars
[.111]	Space

Number discontinued; class in 520

.112	Galaxies

For Milky Way, see 523.113

See Manual at 520 vs. 523.1, 523.112, 523.8: Stars and galaxies

.112 5	Interstellar and intergalactic matter

Standard subdivisions are added for interstellar and intergalactic matter together, for interstellar matter alone

Class here cosmic dust

Dark matter relocated to 523.1126

.112 6	Dark matter [*formerly* 523.1125]
.113	Milky Way
.113 5	Interstellar matter

Including diffuse and planetary nebulas

For dark matter, see 523.1126

.115	Quasars

.12	Cosmogony

> *For expanding universe theories, see 523.18*

.18	Expanding universe theories
.19	End of universe theories
.2	**Solar system**

> *For specific parts, see 523.3–523.7*

> **523.3–523.7 Specific parts of solar system**

Class comprehensive works in 523.2

.3	**Moon**
.31	Constants and dimensions

Including size, mass

.32	Optical, electromagnetic, radioactive, thermal phenomena

Including phases

.33	Orbit and motions

Including librations, sidereal month

.38	Eclipses
.4	**Planets**

Class here comprehensive works on planets, satellites, rings

Add to notation for each number identified by * the numbers following 523.3 in 523.31–523.33, e.g., orbit of Jupiter 523.453

> *For satellites and rings, see 523.98; for transits, occultations, see 523.99; for earth, see 525*

.41	*Mercury
.42	*Venus
.43	*Mars
.44	Asteroids (Planetoids)

Class comprehensive works on meteors and asteroids in 523.5

.45	*Jupiter
.46	*Saturn
.47	*Uranus

*Add as instructed under 523.4

.48	Trans-Uranian planets
.481	*Neptune
.482	*Pluto

.5   Meteors, solar wind, zodiacal light

Class here interplanetary matter, comprehensive works on meteors and asteroids

For asteroids, see 523.44

.51	Meteors

Class here meteoroids, meteorites

For meteor showers, see 523.53

.53	Meteor showers

Including radiant points

.58	Solar wind
.59	Zodiacal light

Including counterglow (gegenschein)

.6   Comets

.63	Motion and orbits

Class motion and orbits of specific comets in 523.64

.64	Specific comets
[.640 1–.640 9]	Standard subdivisions

Do not use; class in 523.601–523.609

.642	Halley's comet
.66	Physical phenomena and constitution

Class physical phenomena and constitution of specific comets in 523.64

.7   Sun

.702 1	Tabulated and related materials

Class sun tables indicating orbits and motions of earth in 525.38

.71	Constants and dimensions

Including size, mass

*Add as instructed under 523.4

.72   Optical, electromagnetic, radioactive, thermal phenomena

Class here solar energy, solar radiation

For phenomena of photosphere, see 523.74; for phenomena of chromosphere and corona, see 523.75

See also 523.59 for zodiacal light

.73   Motions

Including apparent motion, rotation

.74   Photosphere

Including faculae, solar granulation, sunspots

.75   Chromosphere and corona

Including solar flares and prominences

See also 523.58 for solar wind

.76   Solar interior

.78   Eclipses

.8   **Stars**

Class here comprehensive works on stars and galaxies

For galaxies, see 523.112; for sun, see 523.7

See also 523.115 for quasars

See Manual at 520 vs. 523.1, 523.112, 523.8: Stars and galaxies

.802 12   Formulas and specifications

Star catalogs relocated to 523.80216

.802 16   Lists, inventories, catalogs

Class here star catalogs [*formerly* 523.80212]

[.802 87]   Testing and measurement

Do not use; class in 523.87

>   523.81–523.83   Properties and phenomena

Class comprehensive works in 523.8

For physical constitution, see 523.86. For properties and phenomena of a specific kind of star or aggregation of stars, see the kind or aggregation, e.g., properties of supernovas 523.84465, properties of of spectral types 523.87

.81   Constants and dimensions

Including size, mass, parallax

.82	Optical, electromagnetic, radioactive, thermal phenomena

Class here stellar radiation

.822	Magnitudes
.83	Motion

Including velocity

.84	Aggregations and variable stars

Standard subdivisions are added for aggregations and variable stars together, for aggregations alone

Class here comprehensive works on binary stars and clusters

For clusters, see 523.85

See also 523.112 for galaxies

.841	Binary and multiple stars

Standard subdivisions are added for binary and multiple stars together, for binary stars alone

Including optical and visual binaries

Class here astrometric binaries [*formerly* 523.843]

For spectroscopic binaries, see 523.842; for eclipsing binaries, see 523.8444

.842	Spectroscopic binaries
[.843]	Astrometric binaries

Relocated to 523.841

.844	Variable stars
.844 2	Intrinsic variables

For eruptive variables, see 523.8446

.844 25	Pulsating variables

Class here Cepheids

For long-period and semiregular variables, see 523.84426; for pulsars, see 523.8874

.844 26	Long-period and semiregular variables
.844 4	Eclipsing binaries (Extrinsic variables)
.844 6	Eruptive variables

Including flare stars, novas

.844 65	Supernovas

.85	Clusters
.852	Open clusters
.855	Globular clusters
.86	Physical constitution

Class physical constitution of a specific kind or aggregation of star with the kind or aggregation, e.g., constitution of neutron stars 523.8874

.87	Spectral types

Class here spectroscopy, testing and measurement

Class spectral types representative of specific stages in the evolution of stars in 523.88. Class spectroscopy of a specific kind or aggregation of star with the kind or aggregation, plus notation 0287 from Table 1, e.g., spectroscopy of neutron stars 523.88740287

.88	Kinds of stars characteristic of stages of stellar evolution

Including giant (R, N, or S spectral type), main sequence, red dwarf, Wolf-Rayet stars; star formation

Class here stellar evolution

For intrinsic variables, see 523.8442

.887	Terminal stages

Including white dwarfs

.887 4	Neutron stars

Class here pulsars

.887 5	Black holes
.9	**Satellites (Moons) and rings; eclipses, transits, occultations**
.91	Transits of Mercury
.92	Transits of Venus
.98	Satellites (Moons) and rings

Add to base number 523.98 the numbers following 523.4 in 523.43–523.48, e.g., satellites of Jupiter 523.985, orbits of Jovian satellites 523.9853

Subdivisions are added for either or both topics in heading

For earth's moon, see 523.3

.99	Eclipses, transits, occultations

For transits of Mercury, see 523.91; for transits of Venus, see 523.92. For eclipses of a specific celestial body, see the body, e.g., eclipses of the moon 523.38

[524] **[Unassigned]**

Most recently used in Edition 14

525 **Earth (Astronomical geography)**

For magnetic properties, see 538.7

.1 **Constants and dimensions**

Including size, shape

Class determination of size and shape in 526.1

.2 **Optical, radioactive, thermal properties**

.3 **Orbit and motions**

.35 Rotation

.36 Foucault's pendulum

.38 Sun tables

.5 **Seasons and zones of latitude**

Standard subdivisions are added for seasons and zones of latitude together, for seasons alone

Limited to astronomical causes of seasons and zones of latitude

Class climatology in 551.6; class interdisciplinary works on seasons in 508.2

.7 **Twilight**

Class here dawn

526 **Mathematical geography**

Class here cartography (map making)

Class map making for a specific purpose with the purpose, e.g., military map making 623.71

For astronomical geography, see 525

See also 912.014 for map reading

.022 1 Drafting illustrations

Class here map drawing

.1 **Geodesy**

For geodetic surveying, see 526.3; for geodetic astronomy and geographical positions, see 526.6; for gravity determinations, see 526.7

.3 **Geodetic surveying**

Surveying in which curvature of earth is considered

.31	Reconnaissance (Preliminary surveys)
.32	Bench marks
.320 9	Historical and persons treatment

> Do not use for geographic treatment; class in 526.321–526.329

.321–.329   Geographic treatment

> Add to base number 526.32 notation 1–9 from Table 2, e.g., bench marks in California 526.32794

.33   Triangulation, trilateration, traversing

> Standard subdivisions are added for triangulation, trilateration, traversing together; for triangulation alone

> Including base lines, nets

.36   Leveling

> Class here spirit leveling

> *For bench marks, see 526.32; for barometric leveling, see 526.37; for trigonometric leveling, see 526.38*

.37   Barometric leveling

.38   Trigonometric leveling

.6   Geodetic astronomy and geographical positions

> Standard subdivisions are added for geodetic astronomy and geographical positions together, for geodetic astronomy alone

> Class here geodetic aspects of positional astronomy; comprehensive works on geodetic coordinates

> Class comprehensive works on positional astronomy in 522

> *For coordinates in spherical astronomy, see 522.7*

.61   Latitude

> *For latitude in celestial navigation, see 527.1*

.62   Longitude

> *For longitude in celestial navigation, see 527.2*

.63   Azimuth

.64   Geographical positions

> Including effect of irregularities of earth's surface on determining geographical positions

.7   Gravity determinations

.8	**Map projections**

Class map reading in 912.014

.82	Conformal (Orthomorphic) projections
.85	Equal-area (Equivalent) projections
.9	**Surveying**

Class here plane surveying (surveying in which curvature of earth is disregarded), land surveying

Class work of chartered surveyors (United Kingdom), interdisciplinary works on land surveys in 333.08; class engineering surveys in 622–629

For geodetic surveying, see 526.3

[.92]	Land (Boundary) surveying

Number discontinued; class in 526.9

.98	Topographic surveying
.981	Contour surveying
.982	Photogrammetry

Class here aerial and space surveying

.982 5	Ground (Terrestrial) photogrammetry
.99	Hydrographic surveying

527 Celestial navigation

For celestial navigation of specific craft, see the craft, e.g., navigation of nautical craft 623.89

.1	**Latitude**
.2	**Longitude**
.3	**Position determination**

Including Sumner's method

For determination of latitude, see 527.1; for determination of longitude, see 527.2

[.5]	**Direction and course**

Number and its subdivisions discontinued; class in 527

528 Ephemerides

Variant names: astronomical and nautical almanacs

Class tables of specific celestial bodies in 523

.093–.099	Treatment in ancient world, treatment by specific continent

Do not use for treatment by specific country or locality; class in 528.1–528.8

.1–.8 **Ephemerides of specific countries and localities**

Add to base number 528 the numbers following 06 in 061–068, e.g., ephemerides of England 528.2

.9 **Ephemeris making**

529 Chronology

.1 **Days**

Including apparent and mean days, equation of time, sidereal and solar days

.2 **Intervals of time**

Including years, months, weeks

For sidereal month, see 523.33; for days, see 529.1

See also 525.5 for seasons

.3 **Calendars**

For western calendars, see 529.4; for calendar reform, see 529.5

.32 Calendars of specific religions and traditions

Add to base number 529.32 the numbers following 29 in 292–299, e.g., Jewish calendar 529.326; however, for Julian calendar, see 529.42

For Christian calendars, see 529.4

.4 **Western calendars**

Class here Christian calendars

.42 Julian calendar

.43 Gregorian calendar

.44 Christian church calendar

Including determination of movable feasts and fast days

.5 **Calendar reform**

.7 **Horology**

Finding and measuring time

530   Physics

Class here energy, matter, antimatter, classical physics; comprehensive works on classical and quantum mechanics

Class quantum mechanics, energy in quantum mechanics in 530.12; class classical mechanics in 531; class energy in classical mechanics in 531.6; class physical chemistry in 541.3

For astrophysics, see 523.01

See Manual at 530 vs. 500.2; also at 530 vs. 540; also at 530 vs. 621

SUMMARY

530.01–.09	**Standard subdivisions**
.1–.8	**[Theories, mathematical physics, states of matter, instrumentation, measurement]**
531	**Classical mechanics Solid mechanics**
532	**Fluid mechanics Liquid mechanics**
533	**Pneumatics (Gas mechanics)**
534	**Sound and related vibrations**
535	**Light and paraphotic phenomena**
536	**Heat**
537	**Electricity and electronics**
538	**Magnetism**
539	**Modern physics**

SUMMARY

530.01–.09	**Standard subdivisions**
.1	**Theories and mathematical physics**
.4	**States of matter**
.7	**Instrumentation**
.8	**Measurement**

.01   Philosophy and theory

          Do not use for theories; class in 530.1

[.015 1]   Mathematical physics

          Do not use; class in 530.15

.02   Miscellany

.028 4   Materials

          Do not use for apparatus and equipment; class in 530.7

[.028 7]   Testing and measurement

          Do not use; class in 530.8

.03–.09   Standard subdivisions

.1   **Theories and mathematical physics**

Standard subdivisions are added for theories and mathematical physics together, for theories alone

Including space

Class applications to specific states of matter in 530.4

See Manual at 520 vs. 500.5, 523.1, 530.1, 919.9

.11   Relativity theory

Including fourth dimension

Class here conservation of mass-energy [*formerly also* 531.62], equivalence of mass-energy (E=mc²), space-time

Class specific relativistic theories in 530.12–530.14

.12   Quantum mechanics (Quantum theory)

Class here relativistic, nonrelativistic quantum mechanics

For quantum statistics, see 530.133; for quantum kinetic theories, see 530.136; for quantum field theory, see 530.143; for quantum electronics, see 537.5; for quantum electrodynamics, see 537.67

See Manual at 530.12 vs. 531; also at 530.475 vs. 530.12, 531.16: Brownian motion and particle mechanics

.122   Matrix mechanics (Heisenberg representation)

.124   Wave mechanics

Waves considered as a fundamental property of matter

Class here Schrödinger wave mechanics

See also 530.141 for waves in electromagnetic theory, 531.1133 for waves in classical physics

.13   Statistical mechanics

Class here relativistic, nonrelativistic statistical mechanics

Including percolation theory

.132   Classical statistical mechanics (Boltzmann statistics)

.133   Quantum statistics (Quantum statistical mechanics)

[.133 2–.133 4]   Bose-Einstein and Fermi-Dirac statistics

Numbers discontinued; class in 530.133

.136   Kinetic theories

Class here quantum, combined quantum-classical kinetic theories

For classical kinetic theory, see 531.113

.138	Transport theory
.14	Field and wave theories

Theories accounting for fundamental particles and interactions

Standard subdivisions are added for field and wave theories together, for field theories alone

Including problem of few bodies, theory of continuum physics

Class here quantum, classical, relativistic, nonrelativistic field and wave theories

For wave mechanics, see 530.124

.141	Electromagnetic theory

Electromagnetic fields and waves considered in terms of fundamental structure of matter

Including Maxwell's equations

Class electromagnetic spectrum and waves in 539.2

See also 537.1 for theories of electricity, 538.01 for theories of magnetism

.142	Unified field theory

Class here grand unified theory

.142 3	Supergravity

Class here comprehensive works on supergravity and supersymmetry

For supersymmetry, see 539.725

.143	Quantum field theory
.143 5	Gauge fields
.144	Problem of many bodies
.15	Mathematical physics

Add to base number 530.15 the numbers following 51 in 511–519, e.g., statistics 530.1595

Class mathematical description of physical phenomena according to a specific theory with the theory in 530.1, e.g., statistical mechanics 530.13

[.16]	Measurement theory

Relocated to 530.801

.4   **States of matter**

Class here quantum mechanics of specific states of matter; sound, light, heat, electricity, magnetism as properties of a specific state of matter

Unless other instructions are given, class a subject with aspects in two or more subdivisions of 530.4 in the number coming last, e.g., tunneling in thin films 530.4175 (*not* 530.416)

For superconductivity and superconductors, see 537.623

.41   Solid-state physics

Class here physics of condensed matter

For liquid-state physics, see 530.42; for crystallography, see 548

See Manual at 548 vs. 530.41

.411   Structure

Including electron arrangement, lattice dynamics

.412   Properties

Including elastic, electrical, magnetic, optical, thermal properties

.413   Kinds

Including amorphous, crystalline and noncrystalline, metallic and nonmetallic, ordered and disordered, organic, porous solids; polymers; solid particles

For dielectric matter, see 537.24; for semiconductors, see 537.622; for crystals, see 548

.414   Phase transformations

Transformations between different phases of condensed matter, between solid and gas phases

.415   Diffusion and mass transfer

Standard subdivisions are added for either or both topics in heading

Class transport theory in 530.138

.416   Responsive behavior and energy phenomena

Including bombardment, collisions, emission, excitation, excited states, excitons, field effects, internal friction, ion implantation, Jahn-Teller effect, Josephson effect, oscillation, phonons, radiation effect, relaxation, scattering, sputtering, tunneling, vibration

Class responsive behavior and energy phenomena in semiconductors in 537.622

See Manual at 530.416 vs. 539.75

.417	Surface physics

Class here interface with other states of matter

Class surface physics of semiconductors in 537.622

.417 5	Thin films

Class comprehensive works on thin films in 530.4275

.42	Liquid-state physics

Including superfluidity

Class here fluid-state physics

.424	Phase transformations

Transformations between different fluid phases

Including critical points

Class phase transformations between fluids and solids in 530.414

.425	Diffusion and mass transfer

Standard subdivisions are added for either or both topics in heading

Including Brownian motion in liquids, osmosis

> *See Manual at 530.475 vs. 530.12, 531.16: Brownian motion and particle mechanics*

.427	Surface physics

Including capillarity, drops, surface tension

Class here interface with gases

Class interface with solids in 530.417; class surface tension of thin films in 530.4275

.427 5	Thin films

Class here bubbles

.429	Liquid crystals

Including liquid polymers

.43	Gaseous-state physics

Ionization of gases relocated to 530.444

Class interface with solids in 530.417; class interface with liquids in 530.427

> *For plasma physics, see 530.44*

.435	Diffusion and mass transfer

Standard subdivisions are added for either or both topics in heading

.44 Plasma physics

Physics of ionized gases

Add to base number 530.44 the numbers following 530.41 in 530.412–530.416, e.g., ionization of gases 530.444 [*formerly also* 530.43], optical properties of plasmas 530.442

See also 537.532 for ionization of gases in electronics

.47 Generalities of states of matter

For generalities of specific states of matter, see 530.41–530.44

.474 Phase transformations

Variant names: phase changes, phase transitions

Including critical phenomena, e.g., critical points; phase diagrams, equilibria, stability; triple points

Class phase transformations between different phases of condensed matter, between solids and gases in 530.414; class phase transformations between fluid phases in 530.424; class phase transformations between plasmas and other states of matter in 530.444

See Manual at 536.4 vs. 530.474

.475 Diffusion and mass transfer

Standard subdivisions are added for either or both topics in heading

Variant name for mass transfer: mass transport

Class here Brownian motion

For heat transfer, see 536.2

See Manual at 530.475 vs. 530.12, 531.16: Brownian motion and particle mechanics

.7 **Instrumentation**

Instrumentation for measurement, control, recording

.8 **Measurement**

Including dimensional analysis, testing

Class here interdisciplinary works on measurement, on mensuration

Class instrumentation for measurement in 530.7

For horology, see 529.7. For measurement, mensuration in a specific subject, see the subject, plus notation 0287 from Table 1, e.g., psychological measurement 150.287

See also 516.15 for geometric mensuration

.801 Philosophy and theory

Class here measurement theory [*formerly* 530.16]

.802	Miscellany
[.802 1]	Tabulated and related material
	Relocated to 530.81

.81 **Physical units and constants**

Standard subdivisions are added for physical units and constants together, for physical units alone

Including dimensions, interdisciplinary works on size

Class here tabulated and related materials [*formerly also* 530.8021], systems of measurement, conversion tables between systems

Class units of dimension and size in metric system in 530.812; class units of dimension and size in British system in 530.813

> *For social aspects of systems of measurement, see 389.1. For a specific aspect of size, see the aspect, e.g., size of business enterprise 338.64*

[.810 21] Tabulated and related material

Number discontinued; class in 530.81

.812 **Metric system (Système international, SI)**

.813 **British system**

Variant names: English, Imperial system

Class here United States customary units

531 Classical mechanics   Solid mechanics

Variant names for classical mechanics: mechanics, continuum mechanics

> *For fluid mechanics, see 532*

> *See Manual at 530.12 vs. 531*

.015 195 Statistical mathematics

Class classical statistical mechanics in 530.132

.1 Dynamics, statics, mass and gravity, particle mechanics

Including pressure, mechanics of points

[.101–.109] Standard subdivisions

Do not use; class in 531.01–531.09

.11 Dynamics

> *For particle dynamics, see 531.163; for solid dynamics, see 531.3*

.112 Kinematics

Motion considered apart from mass and force

Including linear and relative motion, velocity, acceleration, vector quantities; search for a moving target

.113 Kinetics

Including centrifugal and centripetal forces, rotational motion

Class comprehensive works on motion in 531.11

.113 3 Waves

Waves observable in matter of classical physics

Including shock waves

See also 530.124 for waves considered as a fundamental property of matter

.113 4 Rheology (Deformation and flow)

Including viscosity and friction

Most works on deformation are limited to solids and are classed in 531.38; most works on flow are limited to fluids and are classed in 532.051

.12 Statics

Including graphic statics

For particle statics, see 531.16; for solid statics, see 531.2

.14 Mass and gravity

Including density, gravity of earth, specific gravity

Class geodetic gravity determinations in 526.7

For gravity in celestial mechanics, see 521.1

See also 539.754 for fundamental gravitational interaction

.16 Particle mechanics

Class here mechanics of solid particles

Class mechanics of molecular, atomic, and subatomic particles (quantum mechanics) in 530.12

See also 620.43 for fine particle technology

See Manual at 530.475 vs. 530.12, 531.16: Brownian motion and particle mechanics

[.162] Statics

Number discontinued; class in 531.16

.163   Dynamics

>   **531.2–531.5   Mechanics of solids**

      Class here mechanics of rigid bodies

      Class comprehensive works in 531

      For mechanics of solid particles, see 531.16

.2   **Solid statics**

      Including graphic statics

.3   **Solid dynamics**

      Including solid kinematics

      Class here solid kinetics

      For friction and viscosity, see 531.4; for ballistics, see 531.55

[.31]   Trajectories

      Relocated to 531.55

.32   Vibrations

      Class here oscillations

.324   Pendulum motion

.33   Waves

      Including shock waves

.34   Rotational motion (Spin)

      Class here gyrodynamics

      For centrifugal and centripetal forces, see 531.35

.35   Centrifugal and centripetal forces

      Standard subdivisions are added for either or both topics in heading

.38   Deformation; stresses and strains

      Standard subdivisions are added for deformation, stresses, strains together; for deformation alone

.381   Stresses and strains

      Standard subdivisions are added for for either or both topics in heading

      Including elastic constants, Poisson's ratio, yield point

      Class application to elasticity in 531.382; class application to plasticity in 531.385

.382	Elasticity
	Variant names: elastic, temporary deformation
	Including elastic limit, coefficient of restitution
	Class here Hooke's law
	Class elastic vibrations in 531.32
.385	Plasticity
	Variant names: permanent, plastic deformation

.4 Friction and viscosity of solids

Standard subdivisions are added for either or both topics in heading

.5 Mass and gravity of solids; projectiles

Including laws of falling bodies

.54 Density and specific gravity

Standard subdivisions are added for either or both topics in heading

.55 Projectiles

Including trajectories [*formerly* 531.31]

Class here ballistics

.6 Energy

Including momentum, work

Class comprehensive works on energy in physics in 530; class interdisciplinary works on energy in 333.79

.62 Conservation of energy

Conservation of mass-energy relocated to 530.11

See also 333.7916 for programs to conserve energy

.68 Transformation

Change in form of energy

For a specific transformation, see the resultant form, e.g., transformation of light to heat 536

532 Fluid mechanics   Liquid mechanics

Class here hydraulics (hydromechanics)

For pneumatics, see 533

.001–.009 Standard subdivisions

> 532.02–532.05 Fluid statics and dynamics

Class comprehensive works in 532

.02 Statics

Including buoyancy

For liquid statics, see 532.2

[.04] Mass, density, specific gravity

Number discontinued; class in 532

.05 Dynamics

Including kinematics, vibrations

Class here kinetics

For liquid dynamics, see 532.5

.051 Flow

Including boundary layers

Class waves and vortex motion in 532.059

For types of flow, see 532.052; for flow properties, see 532.053

.052 Types of flow

Rotational flow relocated to 532.0595

Class properties of specific types of flow in 532.053

For viscous flow, see 532.0533

.052 5 Laminar flow

.052 6 Transitional flow

.052 7 Turbulent flow

.053 Flow properties

.053 2 Velocity

.053 3 Viscosity and friction

Standard subdivisions are added for either or both topics in heading

Class here viscous flow

.053 5 Elasticity and compressibility

Standard subdivisions are added for either or both topics in heading

.059 Waves and vortex motion

.059 3	Waves
	Including shock waves
.059 5	Vortex motion
	Including centrifugal and centripetal forces
	Class here rotational flow [*formerly* 532.052]
	Cavitation relocated to 532.597

> **532.2–532.5 Hydraulics**

In sense of liquid mechanics

Class comprehensive works in 532

.2   **Hydrostatics**

In sense of liquid statics

Class hydrostatics in sense of fluid statics in 532.02

.25   Buoyancy

Class here floating, sinking

.4   **Mass, density, specific gravity of liquids**

.5   **Hydrodynamics**

In sense of liquid dynamics

Including kinematics

Class here kinetics

Class hydrodynamics in sense of fluid dynamics in 532.05

.51   Flow

Rotational flow relocated to 532.595

Class waves and vortex motion in 532.59

For flow variations, see 532.52–532.56; for flow properties, see 532.58

.515   Laminar flow

.516   Transitional flow

.517   Turbulent flow

> **532.52–532.56 Flow variations**

Class comprehensive works in 532.51

.52   Flow through openings

.53   Flow over and around obstacles

> Standard subdivisions are added for either or both topics in heading

.54   Flow through open and closed channels

> Standard subdivisions are added for either or both topics in heading

.55   Flow through bends and irregular enclosures

> Standard subdivisions are added for either or both topics in heading

.56   Flow when pressure is variable

> Including flow over and around submerged bodies, multiphase flow

.57   Flow velocity

.58   Flow properties

> Including elasticity and compressibility, viscosity and friction, viscous flow
>
> *For flow velocity, see 532.57*
>
> *See also 536.413 for expansion and contraction of liquids as a result of heating and cooling*

.59   Waves, vortex motion, cavitation

.593   Waves

> Including shock waves

.595   Vortex motion

> Class here rotational flow [*formerly* 532.51]
>
> Cavitation relocated to 532.597

.597   Cavitation [*formerly* 532.0595, 532.595]

533   Pneumatics (Gas mechanics)

>   **533.1–533.5   Specific aspects of pneumatics (gas mechanics)**

Class comprehensive works in 533

.1   **Statics; mass, density, specific gravity**

> *For vacuums, see 533.5*

.12   Statics

> Including buoyancy
>
> *For aerostatics, see 533.61*

.15	Mass, density, specific gravity
.2	**Dynamics**
	Including kinematics
	Class here kinetics
	For aerodynamics, see 533.62; for kinetic theory of gases, see 533.7
.21	Flow
	Rotational flow relocated to 533.295
	Class waves and vortex motion in 533.29
	For flow at specific speeds, see 533.27; for flow properties, see 533.28
.215	Laminar flow
.216	Transitional flow
.217	Turbulent flow
.27	Flow at specific speeds
	Class here velocity
.273	Subsonic flow
.274	Transonic flow
.275	Supersonic flow
	For hypersonic flow, see 533.276
.276	Hypersonic flow
.28	Flow properties
	Including elasticity and compressibility, viscosity and friction, viscous flow
	Class flow properties at specific speeds in 533.27
	See also 536.412 for expansion and contraction of gases resulting from heating and cooling
.29	Waves and vortex motion
.293	Waves
	Including shock waves
.295	Vortex motion
	Class here rotational flow [*formerly also* 533.21]
	Provision for cavitation discontinued because without meaning in context
.5	**Vacuums**

.6   **Aeromechanics**

Including mass, density, specific gravity of air

For vacuums, see 533.5

.61   Aerostatics

Including buoyancy

.62   Aerodynamics

.7   **Kinetic theory of gases**

> # 534–538   Specific forms of energy

Class here transformation into specific forms of energy

Class specific forms of energy as properties of specific states of matter in 530.4; class comprehensive works in 530; class comprehensive works on transformation of energy in 531.68

For mechanical energy, see 531.6

534   Sound and related vibrations

Standard subdivisions are added for sound and related vibrations together, for sound alone

---

> ### 534.1–534.3   Sound

Class comprehensive works in 534

.1   **Generation of sound**

.2   **Transmission of sound**

.200 1–.200 9   Standard subdivisions

.202   Velocity

.204   Reflection (Echoes)

.208   Absorption (Damping)

.22   Transmission in solids

.23   Transmission in liquids

.24   Transmission in gases

.3   **Characteristics of sound**

Including Doppler effect

| [.32] | Frequency and pitch |
| | Number discontinued; class in 534.3 |

.5　　　**Vibrations related to sound**

Class here vibrations that can not be heard by the human ear

.52　　　Subsonic vibrations

.55　　　Ultrasonic vibrations

535　　Light and paraphotic phenomena

Standard subdivisions are added for light and paraphotic phenomena together, for light alone

Class here optics

See also 537.56 for electron and ion optics

.01　　　Spectral regions; philosophy and theory of light and paraphotic phenomena

Class here paraphotic phenomena, radiations of nonvisible spectral regions

Class a specific element of a specific spectral region, of radiation from a specific nonvisible spectral region in 535.2–535.6

.010 1–.010 9　　　Standard subdivisions of spectral regions

.012　　　Infrared region

Class heat radiation in 536.3

.013　　　Visible region

Class comprehensive works on visible light in 535

.014　　　Ultraviolet region

.019　　　Philosophy and theory of light and paraphotic phenomena

Add to base number 535.019 the numbers following —01 in notation 011–019 from Table 1, e.g., abbreviations and symbols in optics 535.01948

Class theories in 535.1

.028　　　Auxiliary techniques and procedures; apparatus, equipment, materials

Class spectroscopy in 535.84

.1　　　**Theories**

See also 539.7217 for photons

.12　　　Corpuscular theory

.13　　　Mechanical wave theory

.14	Electromagnetic theory
.15	Quantum theory

> **535.2–535.6   Specific elements of light**

Class comprehensive works in 535

For spectroscopy, see 535.84

.2   Physical optics

Including coherent and nonlinear optics

For dispersion of light, see 535.4; for beams, see 535.5

.22	Intensity of light
.220 287	Testing and measurement
	Class here photometry
.24	Velocity of light

.3   Transmission, absorption, emission of light

.32	Geometrical optics
[.322]	Rectilinear propagation
	Number discontinued; class in 535.32
.323	Reflection
.324	Refraction
.326	Absorption
.35	Luminescence
.352	Fluorescence

            Class fluorescence by source of exciting energy in 535.355–535.358

.353	Phosphorescence

            Class phosphorescence by source of exciting energy in 535.355–535.358

> 535.355–535.358   Luminescence by source of exciting energy

Class comprehensive works in 535.35

For chemiluminescence, see 541.35; for bioluminescence, see 572.4385

.355	Photoluminescence
.356	Thermoluminescence

.357	Electroluminescence

.4 **Dispersion of light**

Including shadows

Holography relocated to 774.0153

Class comprehensive works on beams and their dispersion in 535.5

.42	Diffraction
.420 284	Apparatus, equipment, materials

Class here interdisciplinary works on prisms

For a specific aspect of prisms, see the aspect, e.g., geometry of prisms 516.15

.43	Scattering
.47	Interference

.5 **Beams**

.52	Polarization
[.523–.524]	Plane and rotary polarization

Numbers discontinued; class in 535.52

.6 **Color**

.8 **Special developments**

.84	Optical and paraphotic spectroscopy

Class here comprehensive works on spectroscopy in physics

Class interdisciplinary works on spectroscopy in 543.0858

For a specific kind of spectroscopy in physics other than optical and paraphotic, see the kind, e.g., radiofrequency spectroscopy 537.534

.842	Infrared spectroscopy
.843	Light spectroscopy
.844	Ultraviolet spectroscopy
.845	Vacuum ultraviolet spectroscopy
.846	Raman spectroscopy

Including Raman effect

536 **Heat**

.01	Philosophy and theory

Do not use for theories; class in 536.1

.1 **Theories**

.2 **Heat transfer**

For radiation, see 536.3

.200 1–.200 9   Standard subdivisions

.201   Heat-transfer properties of matter

Class specific heat in 536.6

For heat-transfer properties of matter at low temperatures, see 536.56; for heat-transfer properties of matter at high temperatures, see 536.57

See also 620.11296 for thermal properties of engineering materials

.201 2   Thermal conductivity

.201 4   Thermal diffusivity

.23   Conduction

Class here heat transfer in solids

Class thermal conductivity in 536.2012

For conduction in fluids, see 536.25

.25   Convection

Class here heat transfer in fluids

.3 **Radiation**

Class here absorption, scattering

[.31–.34]   Reflection, refraction, radiation, absorption

Numbers discontinued; class in 536.3

.4 **Effects of heat on matter**

See Manual at 536.4 vs. 530.474

[.400 1–.400 9]   Standard subdivisions

Relocated to 536.401–536.409

.401–.409   Standard subdivisions [*formerly* 536.4001–536.4009]

.41   Expansion and contraction

Class here coefficients of expansion

Class expansion and contraction in fusion and solidification in 536.42; class expansion and contraction in vaporization and condensation in 536.44

.412   Gases

For liquefaction and solidification of gases at low temperatures, see 536.56

.413   Liquids

.414   Solids

.42   Fusion (Melting) and solidification

Including freezing and melting points, latent heat of fusion and solidification

Class comprehensive works on fusion and solidification (536.42) and vaporization and condensation (536.44) in 536.4

.44   Vaporization and condensation

Including boiling points, dew points, latent heat of evaporation and condensation, liquefaction of gases

For liquefaction of gases at low temperatures, see 536.56

[.445]   Sublimation

Number discontinued; class in 536.44

[.45]   Incandescence

Number discontinued; class in 536.4

.5   Temperature

Class here absolute temperature

.502 87   Testing and measurement

Including resistance thermometry [*formerly* 536.53]

Class here thermometry

For measurement at a specific range of temperature, see 536.51–526.54

>   536.51–536.54 Measurement at a specific range of temperature

Class comprehensive works in 536.50287

.51   Measurement of normal-range temperatures

Including liquid-in-glass thermometry

.52   Measurement of high temperatures (Pyrometry)

Including thermocouples

[.53]   Resistance thermometry

Relocated to 536.50287

.54   Measurement of low temperatures (Cryometry)

.56	Cryogenics and low temperatures

Standard subdivisions are added for either or both topics in heading

Including liquefaction and solidification of gases at low temperatures, properties of matter at low temperatures

Class a specific property of matter at low temperature with the property, e.g., conduction of electricity at low temperatures 537.62

.560 287	Testing

Do not use for measurement; class in 536.54

.57	High temperatures

Including properties of matter at high temperature

Class a specific property of matter at high temperature with the property, e.g., conduction of electricity 537.62

.570 287	Testing

Do not use for measurement; class in 536.52

.6	**Specific heat**

Class here calorimetry, heat capacity

Class heat of transformation in fusion and solidification in 536.42; class heat of transformation in vaporization and condensation in 536.44

.63	Solids and liquids
.65	Gases
.7	**Thermodynamics**
.701	Philosophy and theory

Do not use for theories; class in 536.71

.71	Theories

Including Carnot cycle, Joule's law, Maxwell's thermodynamic formulas

Class here laws of thermodynamics

.73	Entropy
537	**Electricity and electronics**

Standard subdivisions are added for electricity and electronics together, for electricity alone

Class here electromagnetism

Class interdisciplinary works on electricity in 333.7932

For magnetism, see 538

.01   Philosophy and theory

> Do not use for theories; class in 537.1

.1   **Theories**

.12   Wave theories

> Class electromagnetic theory of matter in 530.141

[.123–.125]   Specific wave theories

> Numbers discontinued; class in 537.12

[.14]   Corpuscular theory

> Number discontinued; class in 537.1

.2   **Electrostatics**

.21   Electric charge and potential

> Standard subdivisions are added for either or both topics in heading
>
> Including triboelectricity

.24   Dielectrics

> Including electrets, electrocapillarity, electrostriction

.243   Dipole moments

.244   Piezoelectricity and ferroelectricity

> *See also 548.85 for electrical properties of crystals*

[.244 2]   Pyroelectricity

> Number discontinued; class in 537.24

.244 6   Piezoelectricity

.244 8   Ferroelectricity

.5   **Electronics**

> Including exploding wire phenomena
>
> Class here quantum electronics
>
> *For semiconductors, see 537.622*

.52   Disruptive discharges

> Including coronas, electric arcs
>
> Class discharge through rarefied gases and vacuums in 537.53

.53   Discharge through rarefied gases and vacuums

.532   Ionization of gases

> Class comprehensive works on ionization of gases in 530.444

[.533]	Thermionic emission
	Number discontinued; class in 537.53
.534	Radio wave and microwave electronics
	Standard subdivisions are added for radio wave and microwave electronics together, for radio wave electronics alone
	Class here spectroscopy
.534 2	Long waves
.534 3	Short waves
.534 4	Microwaves and ultrahigh-frequency waves
.535	X-ray and gamma-ray electronics
.535 2	Spectroscopy
	Including Mössbauer spectroscopy and effect
	Class a specific application of spectroscopy with the application, e.g., X-ray spectroscopy in qualitative analysis 544.66
.54	Photoelectric phenomena
	Including photoconductivity, photoemission, photovoltaic effect
.56	Electron and ion optics
	Standard subdivisions are added for electron and ion optics together, for electron optics alone
.6	**Electrodynamics (Electric currents) and thermoelectricity**
	Standard subdivisions are added for electrodynamics and thermoelectricity together, for electrodynamics alone
[.61]	Direct currents
	Number discontinued; class in 537.6
.62	Electric conductivity and resistance
	For dielectrics, see 537.24
.622	Semiconductivity
	Class here solid-state physics of semiconductors
.622 1	Structure of semiconductors
	Class structure of specific kinds of semiconductors in 537.6223
.622 3	Kinds of semiconductors
	Class diffusion and mass transfer in specific kinds of semiconductors in 537.6225; class interactions in and specific properties of specific kinds of semiconductors in 537.6226

.622 5	Diffusion and mass transfer in semiconductors
	Standard subdivisions are added for either or both topics in heading
.622 6	Interactions in and specific properties of semiconductors
	Including effects of beams and electromagnetic fields, Hall effects; adsorption, instabilities, resistivity, tunneling
.623	Superconductivity
	Class here solid-state physics of superconductors
	Add to base number 537.623 the numbers following 537.622 in 537.6221–537.6226, e.g., ternary superconductors 537.6233
.624	Thermal effects of currents
.65	Thermoelectricity
.67	Quantum electrodynamics
	Class application of quantum electrodynamics to electric conductivity and resistance in 537.62

538 Magnetism

.3	**Magnetic properties and phenomena**
	Standard subdivisions are added for either or both topics in heading
	Including hysteresis, magnetic moment and relaxation
	Class specific magnetic substances and their characteristic phenomena in 538.4
.36	Magnetic resonance
.362	Nuclear magnetic resonance (NMR)
	Including nuclear quadrupole resonance (NQR), electron-nuclear double resonance (ENDOR)
.364	Electron paramagnetic resonance (EPR)
	Variant name: electron spin resonance (ESR)
.4	**Magnetic substances and their characteristic phenomena**
	Standard subdivisions are added for either or both topics in heading
	Class here magnetic induction, natural magnets
	Class comprehensive works on specific magnetic phenomena in 538.3
.42	Diamagnetism
.43	Paramagnetism
.44	Ferromagnetism
.45	Ferrimagnetism

.6   **Magnetohydrodynamics**

.7   **Geomagnetism and related phenomena**

> Standard subdivisions are added for geomagnetism and related phenomena together, for geomagnetism alone

.709   Historical, geographic, persons treatment

> Do not use for geographic treatment of magnetic surveys; class in 538.78. Do not use for geographic treatment of magnetic observations at observatories; class in 538.79

.72   Magnetic fields of solid earth

> Class here secular variations

> Observations of magnetic fields of solid earth at observatories relocated to 538.79

> Class transient variations in magnetism of solid earth in 538.74

> *For magnetic surveys, see 538.78*

.727   Paleomagnetism

> Class here paleomagnetic surveys [*formerly* 538.78], geomagnetic reversals, paleomagnetic observations at observatories

.74   *Transient magnetism

> *For auroras, see 538.768*

.742   *Diurnal variations

.744   *Magnetic storms

> Use of this number for pulsations discontinued; class in 538.74

.746   *Sunspot effects

.748   *Earth currents

.76   Magnetosphere, ionosphere, auroras

.766   Magnetosphere

> Including Van Allen radiation belts

> Class transient magnetism of magnetosphere in 538.74

.767   Ionosphere

> Class here atmospheric ionization

.767 2   D region

.767 3   E region

> Variant name: Kennelly-Heaviside layers

---

*Do not use notation 09 Table 1 for magnetic observations at permanent observatories; class in 538.79

.767 4		F region
		Variant name: Appleton layers
.768		Auroras
		Class here northern lights
.78		Magnetic surveys
		Paleomagnetic surveys relocated to 538.727
.780 9		Historical and persons treatment
		Do not use for geographic treatment; class in 538.781–537.789
.781–.789		Geographic treatment
		Add to base number 538.78 notation 1–9 from Table 2, e.g., surveys of Ireland 538.78415
.79		Magnetic observations at observatories
		Class here observations of magnetic fields of solid earth at observatories [*formerly also* 538.72]
		For paleomagnetic observations at observatories, see 538.727
.790 9		Historical and persons treatment
		Do not use for geographic treatment; class in 538.791–538.799
.791–.799		Geographic treatment
		Add to base number 538.79 notation 1–9 from Table 2, e.g., findings from observatories in Russia 538.7947

539 Modern physics

Class here quantum physics

For theories of modern physics, see 530.1; for states of matter, see 530.4; for modern physics of specific forms of energy, see 534–538

See Manual at 530 vs. 500.2

SUMMARY

539.01	**Philosophy and theory**
.1	**Structure of matter**
.2	**Radiation (Radiant energy)**
.6	**Molecular physics**
.7	**Atomic and nuclear physics**

.01	Philosophy and theory
	Class theories in 530.1
[.015 1]	Mathematical principles
	Do not use; class in 530.15

.1   **Structure of matter**

For structure of specific states of matter, see 530.4

.12   Molecular structure

Use 539.12 only for studies of molecular structure without reference to chemical characteristics. Prefer 541.22 if there is discussion of chemical phenomena

.14   Atomic structure

For nuclear structure, see 539.74

.2   **Radiation (Radiant energy)**

Class here electromagnetic radiation, spectrum, waves

For a specific kind of radiation, see the kind, e.g., ultraviolet radiation 535.014, ionizing radiation 539.722

.6   **Molecular physics**

Atom-atom and molecule-molecule relationships

Including molecular and vibrational spectra

For molecular structure, see 539.12

.602 87   Testing and measurement

Class here comprehensive works on mass spectrometry in physics

Class interdisciplinary works on mass spectrometry in 543.0873

For spectrometry of a specific nonmolecular particle, see the particle, e.g., atomic spectrometry 539.7

.7   **Atomic and nuclear physics**

Standard subdivisions are added for either or both topics in heading

For atomic structure, see 539.14

SUMMARY

539.72	**Particle physics; ionizing radiations**
.73	**Particle acceleration**
.74	**Nuclear structure**
.75	**Nuclear activities and interactions**
.76	**High-energy physics**
.77	**Detecting and measuring particles and radioactivity**

.72 Particle physics; ionizing radiations

Standard subdivisions are added for particle physics and ionizing radiations together, for particle physics alone

Class here antiparticles, relativistic particles

For field and wave theories accounting for fundamental particles, see 530.14; for particle acceleration, see 539.73; for nuclear activities and interactions, see 539.75; for detection and measurement of particles and radioactivity, see 539.77

[.720 287] Testing and measurement

Do not use; class in 539.77

.721 Specific kinds of subatomic particles

Including bosons, fermions, Regge poles

Class subatomic particles considered as a cosmic ray in 539.7223

[.721 01–.721 09] Standard subdivisions

Do not use; class in 539.7201–539.7209

.721 1 Leptons

For neutrinos, see 539.7215; for photons, see 539.7217

.721 12 Electrons

Including beta particles

For beta positrons, see 539.7214

See also 537.5 for electronics

.721 14 Muons (Mu-mesons)

.721 2 Nucleons

For neutrons, see 539.7213

.721 23 Protons

Class here antiprotons

Class protons considered as cosmic rays in 539.7223

.721 3 Neutrons

.721 4 Positrons

.721 5 Neutrinos

.721 6 Hadrons

Class here strange particles and strangeness

.721 62	Mesons
	Including pions (pi-mesons), kaons (K-mesons)
	For mu-mesons, see 539.72114
.721 64	Baryons
	Including hyperons
	For nucleons, see 539.7212
.721 67	Quarks
	Including quantum flavor
	See also 539.7548 for quantum chromodynamics
.721 7	Photons
	See also 539.756 for photonuclear reactions
.722	Ionizing radiations
	For a specific kind of ionizing radiation not provided for here, see the kind, e.g., alpha particles 539.7232
	See also 537.532 for ionization of gases by electron discharge
.722 2	X and gamma rays
	Including bremsstrahlung (secondary X rays), gamma particles
	See also 537.535 for X-ray and gamma-ray electronics
.722 3	Cosmic rays
	Class here any particle considered as a cosmic ray
.723	Nuclei and atoms considered as particles
.723 2	Nuclei
	Including alpha particles, deuterons
	Class component particles of nuclei in 539.721; class nuclei considered as cosmic rays in 539.7223; class nuclear structure in 539.74
.723 4	Heavy ions
.725	Particle characteristics
	Including angular momentum, charge, energy levels, orbits, spin, symmetry, supersymmetry
	Class characteristics of a specific particle with the particle, e.g., orbits of electrons 539.72112, strangeness of strange particles 539.7216
	For supergravity, comprehensive works on supergravity and supersymmetry, see 530.1423; for magnetic properties, see 538.3
.725 8	Superstring theory

.73   Particle acceleration

             Including bombardment, particle beams

.732   High-voltage accelerators

             Including Van de Graaff electrostatic generators

.733   Resonance accelerators

             Including cyclotrons, linear accelerators

.734   Induction accelerators

             Including betatrons

.735   Synchronous accelerators

             Including synchro-cyclotrons and synchrotrons (betatron-synchrotrons)

.736   Supercolliders

             Class here superconducting supercolliders

.737   Acceleration of specific particles

             Class acceleration of specific particles in specific accelerators in
             539.732–539.736

[.737 01–.737 09]   Standard subdivisions

             Do not use; class in 539.7301–539.7309

.737 1–.737 7   Specific particles

             Add to base number 539.737 the numbers following 539.721 in
             539.7211–539.7217, e.g., proton acceleration 539.73723

.74   Nuclear structure

             Class here isotope and nuclide structure, nuclear models

.742   Liquid-drop model

.743   Shell model

.744   Interpretation through spectroscopy

.75   Nuclear activities and interactions

             Standard subdivisions are added for either or both topics in heading

             Including annihilation, capture, coupling, creation

             *For ionizations of gases, see 530.444; for high energy physics, see
             539.76*

             See Manual at 530.416 vs. 539.75

.752	Natural radioactivity
	Including half-life
	Class here decay schemes, radioactive substances (radioelements), radioisotopes, radionuclides; comprehensive works on radioactivity
	For artificial radioactivity, see 539.753
[.752 028 7]	Testing and measurement
	Do not use; class in 539.77
.752 2	Alpha decay
.752 3	Beta decay
.752 4	Gamma decay
.753	Artificial radioactivity
	Including radioactive fallout
	See also 363.738 for pollution from radioactive fallout
[.753 028 7]	Testing and measurement
	Do not use; class in 539.77
.754	Fundamental interactions
	Including gravitational interaction
	Class field theories covering fundamental interactions in 530.14
	See also 531.14 for gravity
.754 4	Weak interaction
	For beta decay, see 539.7523
.754 6	Electromagnetic interaction
.754 8	Strong interaction
	Including quantum chromodynamics
.756	Photonuclear reactions
.757	Collision
.758	Scattering
.76	High-energy physics
	Class high-energy levels of particles in 539.725
[.761]	Chain reactions
	Number discontinued; class in 539.76
.762	Nuclear fission

| .764 | Nuclear fusion (Thermonuclear reaction) |
| .77 | Detecting and measuring particles and radioactivity |

Class here radiation measurement

.772	Ionization chambers
.773	Proportional counters
.774	Geiger-Müller counters
.775	Scintillation counters
.776	Crystal conduction counters
.777	Wilson cloud chambers
.778	Photography

540 Chemistry and allied sciences

Standard subdivisions are added for chemistry and allied sciences together, for chemistry alone

Class cosmochemistry in 523.02

See Manual at 530 vs. 540

SUMMARY

540.1–.9	Standard subdivisions
541	Physical and theoretical chemistry
542	Techniques, procedures, apparatus, equipment, materials
543	Analytical chemistry
544	Qualitative analysis
545	Quantitative analysis
546	Inorganic chemistry
547	Organic chemistry
548	Crystallography
549	Mineralogy

| .1 | Philosophy and theory |

Do not use for theoretical chemistry; class in 541.2

| .11 | Ancient and medieval theories |

Do not use for systems; class in 540.1

| .112 | Alchemy |

Including philosopher's stone

| .118 | Phlogiston theory |
| [.28] | Auxiliary techniques and procedures; apparatus, equipment, materials |

Do not use; class in 542

.72   Research; statistical methods

Do not use for laboratories; class in 542.1

> ## 541–547 Chemistry

Class comprehensive works in 540

> ## 541–545 General topics in chemistry

Inorganic and combined inorganic-organic

Class comprehensive works in 540

For general topics of specific inorganic chemicals and groups of chemicals, see 546; for general topics in organic chemistry, see 547

541 Physical and theoretical chemistry

Class physical and theoretical chemistry of specific elements, compounds, mixtures, groupings in 546; class physical and theoretical crystallography in 548

See Manual at 541 vs. 546

SUMMARY

541.04	**Special topics**
.2	**Theoretical chemistry**
.3	**Physical chemistry**
.7	**Optical activity**

.04   Special topics

.042   Chemistry of states of matter

Add to base number 541.042 the numbers following 530.4 in 530.41–530.44, e.g., solid-state chemistry 541.0421

.2 Theoretical chemistry

.22   Molecular structure

Class molecular structure studied without reference to chemical characteristics in 539.12

For quantum chemistry, see 541.28

.221   Structural formulas

.222   Molecular weights

.223   Stereochemistry

Comprehensive works on stereochemistry relocated to 547.1223

For structural variations, see 541.225

.224   **Chemical bonds, valences, radicals**

Standard subdivisions are added for chemical bonds, valences, radicals together; for chemical bonds alone; for valences alone

Including atomic bonds and interatomic forces [*formerly* 541.244–541.246]

Class bond angles and distances in 541.223

.224 2   Coordination chemistry

Including ligands

Class chelates in 547.59044242

.225   Structural variations

.225 2   Isomers

Class here tautomerism

Comprehensive works on isomers relocated to 547.12252

[.225 3]   Chelates

Relocated to 547.59044242

.225 4   Polymers

Class comprehensive works on polymerization in 547.28; class comprehensive works on polymers in 547.7

.226   Intermolecular forces

.24   Atomic structure

Class here periodic law, periodicity

Class periodic table in 546.8

.242   Atomic weights

Class here atomic mass and numbers

[.243]   Spatial atomic arrangements

Number discontinued; class in 541.24

[.244–.246]   Atomic bonds and interatomic forces

Relocated to 541.224

.26   Stoichiometry

.28   Quantum chemistry

Including molecular and atomic orbitals

Class radiochemistry in 541.38

.3   **Physical chemistry**

For optical activity, see 541.7

SUMMARY

541.33	**Surface chemistry**
.34	**Solution chemistry**
.35	**Photochemistry**
.36	**Thermochemistry and thermodynamics**
.37	**Electrochemistry and magnetochemistry**
.38	**Radiochemistry**
.39	**Chemical reactions**

.33   Surface chemistry

Including absorption, adhesion, adsorption, bubbles, capillarity, chemisorption, cohesion, surface tension

Class here chemistry of interfaces

.34   Solution chemistry

For electrolytic solutions, see 541.372

.341   Properties of solutions

.341 3   Mechanical properties

.341 4   Optical properties

.341 5   Colligative properties

Including effect on osmotic pressure

.341 6   Thermal properties

.342   Solutions by type of solvent

Class here solubility

Class properties of specific type of solvent in 541.341

.342 2   Aqueous solutions

.342 3   Nonaqueous solutions

.345   Colloid chemistry

.345 1   Specific types of colloids

[.345 101–.345 109]   Standard subdivisions

Do not use; class in 541.34501–541.34509

.345 13   Matter dispersed in solids

Including gels, solid foams

.345 14   Hydrosols

Including emulsions, foams, froths, lathers

Class solid foams in 541.34513

.345 15	Aerosols
	Including fogs, mists, smokes
.348	Solution components
.348 2	Solvents
.348 3	Solutes
.348 5	Precipitates
	Including Liesegang rings
.35	Photochemistry
	Including chemiluminescence
	For bioluminescence, see 572.4385
.351	Energy transformations
.353	Photochemical reactions due to specific radiations
[.353 01–.353 09]	Standard subdivisions
	Do not use; class in 541.3501–541.3509
.353 2	Infrared radiations
.353 3	Visible light
.353 4	Ultraviolet radiations
.36	Thermochemistry and thermodynamics

                 Standard subdivisions are added for thermochemistry and thermodynamics together, for thermochemistry alone

---

>	541.361–541.368 Thermochemistry
	Class comprehensive works in 541.36
.361	Combustion
	Including explosion, flame, ignition
.362	Exothermic and endothermic reactions
	Including latent heat
	For combustion, see 541.361
.363	Changes of state (Phase transformations)
	Including Gibb's phase rule
	Class interdisciplinary works on phase transformations in 530.474
	For latent heat, see 541.362
	See also 541.042 for chemistry of specific states of matter

.364	Thermal dissociation
.368	Reactions under temperature extremes
.368 6	Low temperatures
	Reactions below -100° C
.368 7	High temperatures
.369	Thermodynamics
.37	Electrochemistry and magnetochemistry

Standard subdivisions are added for electrochemistry and magnetochemistry together, for electrochemistry alone

---

> 541.372–541.377 Electrochemistry

Class comprehensive works in 541.37

.372	Electrolytic solutions

Including electrodialysis, electrolyte conductivity, electrophoresis

Class here ions

For nonelectrical properties, see 541.374

.372 2	Ionization (Electrolytic dissociation)
.372 3	Ion exchange and ionic equilibriums

Standard subdivisions are added for either or both topics in heading

.372 4	Electrodes and electrode phenomena

Standard subdivisions are added for either or both topics in heading

.372 8	Hydrogen-ion concentration

Class here pH

.374	Nonelectrical properties of electrolytic solutions

Add to base number 541.374 the numbers following 541.341 in 541.3413–541.3416, e.g., optical properties 541.3744

.377	Semiconductors
.378	Magnetochemistry
.38	Radiochemistry

Class here nuclear chemistry

Class quantum chemistry in 541.28

.382	Radiolysis

Class here radiation chemistry

.388	Isotopes
.388 4	Radioisotopes
.39	Chemical reactions

Class here synthesis

Class thermochemistry of reactions in 541.36

.392	Chemical equilibrium

Including law of mass action

Class here Le Chatelier's principle

.393	Specific reactions

Including addition, condensation, hydrolysis, oxidation, polymerization, reduction, substitution; chain, heterogeneous, homogeneous, irreversible, reversible reactions

Class comprehensive works on polymerization in 547.28

[.393 01–.393 09]	Standard subdivisions

Do not use; class in 541.3901–541.3909

.394	Reaction kinetics

Class kinetics of specific reactions in 541.393

For catalysis, see 541.395

.395	Catalysis
.7	**Optical activity**

Including mutarotation, racemization

Class here optical rotation

542   Techniques, procedures, apparatus, equipment, materials

Standard subdivisions are added for any or all topics in heading

Class techniques, procedures, apparatus, equipment, materials used in a specific application with the application, e.g., techniques and equipment for chemical analysis 543

.1   Laboratories

Class receptacles and accessory equipment in 542.2; class specific techniques and procedures of laboratories in 542.3–542.8

.2   **Receptacles and accessory equipment**

Standard subdivisions are added for receptacles and accessory equipment together, for receptacles alone

Including crucibles, test tubes

Class receptacles and accessory equipment for specific techniques and procedures in 542.3–542.8

>   **542.3–542.8 Specific techniques and procedures**

Class here apparatus, equipment, materials used in specific techniques and procedures

Class comprehensive works in 542

.3   **Testing and measuring**

Standard subdivisions are added for either or both topics in heading

For gas measuring, see 542.7; for analytical chemistry, see 543

.4   **Heating and distilling**

Standard subdivisions are added for heating and distilling together, for heating alone

Including blowpipes [*formerly* 542.5]

[.5]   **Blowpipes**

Relocated to 542.4

.6   **Filtering and dialysis**

Standard subdivisions are added for either or both topics in heading

Class dialysis in qualitative analysis in 544.5

.7   **Gas production, processing, measuring**

.8   **Auxiliary techniques and procedures, electrical and electronic equipment**

Add to base number 542.8 the numbers following —028 in notation 0284–0289 from Table 1, e.g., electrical and electronic equipment 542.84; however, for comprehensive works on apparatus, equipment, materials, see 542; for testing and measurement, see 542.3

543   **Analytical chemistry**

Class analytical chemistry of specific elements, compounds, mixtures, groupings in 546

For qualitative analysis, see 544; for quantitative analysis, see 545

See Manual at 543 vs. 544–545

.001	Philosophy and theory
.002	Miscellany
.002 84	Materials

Do not use for reagents; class in 543.01. Do not use for apparatus and equipment; class in 543.07

.003–.009	Standard subdivisions
.01	Reagents
.02	Sample preparation
.07	Instrumentation
.08	Specific methods

Including gas analysis

.081	Microanalysis and semimicroanalysis

Standard subdivisions are added for microanalysis and semimicroanalysis together, for microanalysis alone

.081 2	Microscopic analysis
.081 3	Microchemistry
.081 32	Systematic analysis
.081 34	Spot tests
.081 5	Semimicroanalysis

Small-scale adaptations of existing macroanalytic methods

.083	Mechanical methods

Including gravimetric analysis

.085	Optical methods
.085 2	Photometry

Including colorimetry

.085 3	Refractometry and interferometry
.085 6	Polarimetry (Polariscopic analysis)
.085 8	Spectroscopy (Spectrum analysis)

Class here interdisciplinary works on spectroscopy

For spectroscopy in physics, see 535.84; for spectroscopic interpretation of chemical structure, see 541.2. For a specific kind of spectrum analysis not provided for here, see the kind, e.g., mass spectrometry 543.0873

.085 82	Microwave spectroscopy

.085 83	Infrared spectroscopy
.085 84	Visible light spectroscopy
	Including fluorescence, luminescence, Raman spectroscopy
.085 85	Ultraviolet spectroscopy
.085 86	X-ray and gamma-ray spectroscopy
	Including Mössbauer spectroscopy
.086	**Thermal analysis**
	Including thermogravimetry
.087	**Electromagnetic methods**
.087 1	Electrochemical analysis
	For polarography, see 543.0872; for coulometry, see 543.0874
.087 11	Conductometric analysis
.087 12	Potentiometry
.087 2	Polarography
.087 3	Mass spectrometry (Mass spectroscopy)
.087 4	Coulometry
	Including electrodeposition analysis
.087 7	Magnetic spectroscopy
	Including nuclear magnetic resonance spectroscopy, nuclear spectroscopy
	For mass spectrometry, see 543.0873
.088	**Radiochemical analysis**
.088 2	Nuclear activation (Radioactivation) analysis
.088 4	Radioactive tracer techniques
.089	**Chromatographic analysis**
.089 2	Separation by specific types of interaction
	Including adsorption, molecular sieve, partition separations
	Class specific types of interaction applied to liquid chromatography in 543.0894; class specific types of interactions applied to gas chromatography in 543.0896
	For ion-exchange separations, see 543.0893

.089 3	Ion-exchange chromatography

Class here ion-exchange separations

Class ion-exchange separations in liquid chromatography in 543.0894; class ion-exchange separations in gas chromatography in 543.0896

.089 4	Liquid chromatography

Including column chromatography

Class supercritical fluid chromatography in 543.0896

For paper and thin-layer chromatography, see 543.0895

.089 5	Paper and thin-layer chromatography
.089 52	Paper chromatography
.089 56	Thin-layer chromatography
.089 6	Gas chromatography

Including supercritical fluid chromatography

544 Qualitative analysis

Class qualitative analysis of specific elements, compounds, mixtures, groupings in 546

See Manual at 543 vs. 544–545

.001	Philosophy and theory
.002	Miscellany
.002 84	Materials

Do not use for reagents; class in 544.01. Do not use for apparatus and equipment; class in 544.07

.003–.009	Standard subdivisions
.01	Reagents
.02	Sample preparation
.07	Instrumentation
.1	**Systematic separations**

Including decomposition analysis

.12	Cation separation
.13	Anion separation
.2	**Thermal analysis**

For blowpipe analysis, see 544.3

.3	**Blowpipe analysis**
.4	**Gas analysis**
.5	**Diffusion analysis**

Including ultrafiltration (dialysis)

.6 **Spectroscopy (Spectrum analysis)**

Add to base number 544.6 the numbers following 543.0858 in 543.08582–543.08586, e.g., infrared spectroscopy 544.63

.8 **Microanalysis and semimicroanalysis**

Standard subdivisions are added for microanalysis and semimicroanalysis together, for microanalysis alone

Add to base number 544.8 the numbers following 543.081 in 543.0812–543.0815, e.g., microchemical analysis 544.83

.9 **Other methods**

.92 Chromatographic analysis

Add to base number 544.92 the numbers following 543.089 in 543.0892–543.0896, e.g., liquid chromatography 544.924

.93 Mechanical methods

Including gravimetric analysis

.94 Biochemical methods

Including identification by means of microorganisms

.95 Optical methods

For spectroscopy, see 544.6

.952 Photometry

Including colorimetry

[.953] Refractometric and interferometric analysis

Number discontinued; class in 544.95

.956 Polarimetry (Polariscopic analysis)

.97 Electromagnetic methods

Add to base number 544.97 the numbers following 543.087 in 543.0871–543.0877, e.g., mass spectrometry 544.973

.98 Radiochemical analysis

.982 Nuclear activation (Radioactivation) analysis

.984 Radioactive tracer techniques

545   Quantitative analysis

Class quantitative analysis of specific elements, compounds, mixtures, groupings in 546

See Manual at 543 vs. 544–545

.001	Philosophy and theory
.002	Miscellany
.002 84	Materials

Do not use for reagents; class in 545.01. Do not use for apparatus and equipment; class in 545.07

.003–.009	Standard subdivisions
.01	Reagents
.02	Sample preparation
.07	Instrumentation
.08	Mechanical methods
.1	**Gravimetric analysis**

For thermogravimetric methods, see 545.4

.2	**Volumetric analysis**
.22	Neutralization methods
.23	Oxidation-reduction methods

Including iodometry

.24	Precipitation methods

Class gravimetric analysis of precipitates in 545.1

.3	**Electromagnetic methods**

Add to base number 545.3 the numbers following 543.087 in 543.0871–543.0877, e.g., mass spectroscopy 545.33

.4	**Thermal analysis**

Class here thermogravimetry

[.42–.43]	Combustion and blowpipe analysis; pyrolysis

Numbers discontinued; class in 545.4

.46	Volatilization analysis
.7	**Gas analysis**
.8	**Other methods**

.81	Optical methods

For spectroscopy, see 545.83

.812	Photometry
[.813]	Refractometric and interferometric analysis

Number discontinued; class in 545.81

.816	Polarimetry (Polariscopic analysis)
.82	Radiochemical analysis
.822	Nuclear activation (Radioactivation) analysis
.824	Radioactive tracer techniques
.83	Spectroscopy (Spectrum analysis)

Add to base number 545.83 the numbers following 543.0858 in 543.08582–543.08586, e.g., x-ray spectroscopy 545.836

.84	Microanalysis and semimicroanalysis

Standard subdivisions are added for microanalysis and semimicroanalysis together, for microanalysis alone

Add to base number 545.84 the numbers following 543.081 in 543.0812–543.0815, e.g., semimicroanalysis 545.845

.89	Chromatographic analysis

Add to base number 545.89 the numbers following 543.089 in 543.0892–543.0896, e.g., gas chromatography 545.896

546   Inorganic chemistry

Class here general topics of chemistry applied to specific elements, compounds, mixtures, groupings; comprehensive works on inorganic and organic chemistry of specific elements, compounds, mixtures, groupings

Specific compounds are classed with the first element named, except that hydrogen is disregarded for acids

Add to each subdivision identified by * as follows:

>1–3		The element, compounds, mixtures
		Class theoretical, physical, analytical chemistry of the element, compounds, mixtures in 4–6; class comprehensive works in base number for the element in 546.3–546.7
1		The element
2		Compounds
		Names of compounds usually end in -ide or one of the suffixes listed in 22 and 24 below
		For organo compounds, see 547.01–547.08
22		Acids and bases
		Names of acids usually end in -ic or -ous
24		Salts
		Names of salts frequently end in -ate or -ite
25		Complex compounds
3		Molecular and colloidal mixtures
		Class here alloys
4		Theoretical chemistry
		Add to 4 the numbers following 541.2 in 541.22–541.28, e.g., molecular structure 42
5		Physical chemistry
		Add to 5 the numbers following 541.3 in 541.33–541.39, e.g., radiochemistry 58
6		Analytical chemistry
64		Qualitative analysis
65		Quantitative analysis

Class general topics of chemistry applied to inorganic chemistry as a whole in 541–545

For organic chemistry of specific elements, compounds, mixtures, groupings, see 547

See Manual at 541 vs. 546; also at 549 vs. 546

SUMMARY

546.2	**Hydrogen and its compounds**
.3	**Metals, their compounds and mixtures**
.4	**Group 3B**
.5	**Groups 4B, 5B, 6B, 7B**
.6	**Groups 8, 1B, 2B, 3A, 4A**
.7	**Groups 5A, 6A, 7A, O**
.8	**Periodic table**

.2   **Hydrogen and its compounds**

Standard subdivisions are added for hydrogen and its compounds together, for hydrogen compounds alone

Class here hydrogen chemistry

Class the element hydrogen studied by itself in 546.21

.21   The element

.212   Deuterium

.213   Tritium

>   546.22–546.24 Hydrogen compounds

Class comprehensive works in 546.2

For bases, see 546.32

.22   Water

Including deuterium oxide (heavy water)

.224   Theoretical chemistry

Add to base number 546.224 the numbers following 541.2 in 541.22–541.28, e.g., quantum chemistry 546.2248

.225   Physical chemistry

Add to base number 546.225 the numbers following 541.3 in 541.33–541.39, e.g., thermochemistry 546.2256

.226   Analytical chemistry

.24   Acids

For a specific acid, see the distinguishing element, plus notation 22 from table under 546, e.g., hydrochloric acid 546.73222

.25   Theoretical chemistry of hydrogen

Add to base number 546.25 the numbers following 541.2 in 541.22–541.28, e.g., chemical bonds 546.2524

.26   Physical chemistry of hydrogen

Add to base number 546.26 the numbers following 541.3 in 541.33–541.39, e.g., thermochemistry 546.266

.3 Metals, their compounds and mixtures

Standard subdivisions are added for metals, their compounds and mixtures together; for metal chemistry alone; for metallic compounds alone

Class here metal chemistry

Class metallic elements studied collectively in 546.31; class physical and chemical metallurgy in 669.9; class interdisciplinary works on metals in 669

> *For metals of groups other than 1A and 2A, see 546.4–546.7; for organometallic compounds, see 547.05*

.31 Metallic elements

> 546.32–546.34 Metallic compounds

Class comprehensive works in 546.3

> *For compounds of a specific metal, see the metal, plus notation 2 from table under 546, e.g., compounds of ammonium 546.7112*

.32 Bases

.34 Salts

.342 Simple salts

Salts formed by union of two elements

See also 546.3824 for table salt

.343 Double salts

Salts formed by union of two simple salts

For complex salts, see 546.345

.345 Complex salts

Double salts that do not form their component salts on solution

---

> 546.38–546.39 Alkali and alkaline-earth metals

Class comprehensive works in 546.38

.38 Alkali metals (Group 1A)

Class here comprehensive works on alkali and alkaline-earth metals

For alkaline-earth metals, see 546.39

.381 *Lithium

.382 *Sodium

*Add as instructed under 546

.383	*Potassium
.384	*Rubidium
.385	*Cesium
.386	*Francium
.39	Alkaline-earth metals (Group 2A)
.391	*Beryllium
.392	*Magnesium
.393	*Calcium
.394	*Strontium
.395	*Barium
.396	*Radium
.4	**Group 3B**
.400 1–.400 9	Standard subdivisions
.401	*Scandium
.403	*Yttrium
.41	Rare earth elements (Lanthanide series)
.411	*Lanthanum
.412	*Cerium
.413	Praseodymium and neodymium
.414	*Promethium
.415	Samarium and europium
.416	Gadolinium and terbium
.417	Dysprosium and holmium
.418	Erbium and thulium
.419	Ytterbium and lutetium
.42	Actinide series

> For uranium, see 546.431; for transuranium elements, see 546.44

.421	*Actinium
.422	*Thorium
.424	*Protactinium

*Add as instructed under 546

.43	Uranium, neptunium, plutonium
.431	*Uranium
.432	*Neptunium
.434	*Plutonium
.44	Transuranium elements

> *For neptunium, see 546.432; for plutonium, see 546.434; for rutherfordium, see 546.51; for hahnium, see 546.52*

[.440 01–.440 09]	Standard subdivisions
	Relocated to 546.4401–546.4409
.440 1–.440 9	Standard subdivisions [*formerly* 546.44001–546.44009]
.441	Americium
.442	Curium
.444	Berkelium
.448	Californium
.449	Other transuranium elements

> Including einsteinium, fermium, lawrencium, mendelevium, nobelium

.5	**Groups 4B, 5B, 6B, 7B**
.51	Titanium group (Group 4B)

> Including rutherfordium

.512	*Titanium
.513	*Zirconium
.514	*Hafnium
.52	Vanadium group (Group 5B)

> Including hahnium

.522	*Vanadium
.524	*Niobium (Columbium)
.526	*Tantalum
.53	Chromium group (Group 6B)
.532	*Chromium
.534	*Molybdenum
.536	*Tungsten

*Add as instructed under 546

.54	Manganese group (Group 7B)
.541	*Manganese
.543	*Technetium
.545	*Rhenium

.6 **Groups 8, 1B, 2B, 3A, 4A**

Class here comprehensive works on transition metals

For group 3B, see 546.4; for groups 4B, 5B, 6B, 7B, see 546.5

.62	Group 8

For platinum metals, see 546.63

.621	*Iron
.623	*Cobalt
.625	*Nickel
.63	Platinum metals

For osmium, iridium, platinum, see 546.64

.632	*Ruthenium
.634	*Rhodium
.636	*Palladium
.64	Osmium, iridium, platinum
.641	*Osmium
.643	*Iridium
.645	*Platinum

Class comprehensive works on platinum metals in 546.63

.65	Group 1B
.652	*Copper
.654	*Silver
.656	*Gold
.66	Group 2B
.661	*Zinc
.662	*Cadmium
.663	*Mercury

*Add as instructed under 546

.67	Group 3A
.671	*Boron
.673	*Aluminum
.675	*Gallium
.677	*Indium
.678	*Thallium
.68	Group 4A
.681	*Carbon
.681 2	Carbon compounds

> Number built according to instructions under 546

> Use this number for carbon oxides, carbonates, metal carbonyls, carbon halides when treated as inorganic compounds. Class other carbon compounds in 547

.683	*Silicon
.684	*Germanium
.686	*Tin
.688	*Lead

.7 Groups 5A, 6A, 7A, O

Class here nonmetals

> *For a specific nonmetallic element not provided for here, see the element, e.g., silicon 546.683*

.71	Group 5A
.711	*Nitrogen
.712	*Phosphorus
.715	*Arsenic
.716	*Antimony
.718	*Bismuth
.72	Group 6A
.721	*Oxygen
.723	*Sulfur
.724	*Selenium
.726	*Tellurium

*Add as instructed under 546

.728	*Polonium
.73	Halogens (Group 7A)
.731	*Fluorine
.732	*Chlorine
.733	*Bromine
.734	*Iodine
.735	*Astatine
.75	Noble gases (Group 0)

> Variant names: inert, rare gases

.751	*Helium
.752	*Neon
.753	*Argon
.754	*Krypton
.755	*Xenon
.756	*Radon
.8	**Periodic table**

Class specific elements, groups, series in 546.2–546.7

547   Organic chemistry

Class here biochemicals when not considered in their biological context

Add to each subdivision identified by * as follows:
04	Special topics
044	Theoretical chemistry
	Add to 044 the numbers following 541.2 in 541.22–541.28, e.g., molecular structure 0442
045	Physical chemistry
	Add to 045 the numbers following 541.3 in 541.33–541.39, e.g., radiochemistry 0458
046	Analytical chemistry
0464	Qualitative analysis
0465	Quantitative analysis

Class interdisciplinary works on biochemicals in 572

For biochemistry, see 572

*Add as instructed under 546

SUMMARY

547.001–.009	**Standard subdivisions**
.01–.08	**Kinds of compounds identified by component elements**
.1	**Physical and theoretical chemistry**
.2	**Synthesis and miscellaneous reactions**
.3	**Analytical chemistry**
.4	**Aliphatic compounds**
.5	**Cyclic compounds**
.6	**Aromatic compounds**
.7	**Macromolecular and related compounds**
.8	**Other organic substances**

.001   Philosophy and theory

> Do not use for theoretical organic chemistry; class in 547.12

.002–.009   Standard subdivisions

>   547.01–547.08   Kinds of compounds identified by component elements

> Unless other instructions are given, class a compound with components in two or more subdivisions of 547.01–547.08 in the number coming last, e.g., sulfonamides 547.067 (*not* 547.042)

> Class kinds of compounds identified by structure and function in 547.4–547.8; class comprehensive works in 547. Class the reaction producing a kind of compound identified by a component element with the reaction in 547.2, e.g., halogenation 547.223

.01   *Hydrocarbons

.02   *Halocarbons

> Class halogenation in 547.223

.03   *Oxy and hydroxy compounds

> Class oxidation and reduction reactions in 547.23

.031   *Alcohols

.035   *Ethers

.036   *Aldehydes and ketones

> Subdivisions are added for either or both topics in heading

.037   *Acids

.038   *Esters

> Class esterification in 547.24

.04   *Organonitrogen compounds

> Class nitration in 547.26

*Add as instructed under 547

.041	*Nitro and nitroso compounds
	Class nitrosation in 547.26
.042	*Amines and amides
	Subdivisions are added for either or both topics in heading
	Class amination in 547.25
.043	*Azo compounds
	Class diazotization in 547.25
.044	*Nitriles and isonitriles
	Subdivisions are added for either or both topics in heading
.05	*Organometallic compounds
.053–.057	Specific organometallic compounds

Add to base number 547.05 the numbers following 546 in 546.3–546.7 for the element only, e.g., organozinc compounds 547.05661; then add further as instructed under 547, e.g., analytical chemistry of organozinc compounds 547.05661046; however, for organophosphorus compounds, see 547.07; for organosilicon compounds, see 547.08

.06	*Organosulfur compounds
.061	*Sulfites (Thioethers)
.063	*Hydrosulfites (Thioalcohols)
.064	*Thioacids
.065	Oxy derivatives of thioethers
	Including sulfones, sulfoxides, thioaldehydes, thioketones
.066	*Sulfinic acids
.067	*Sulfonic acids
	Class sulfonation in 547.27
.07	*Organophosphorus compounds
.071	*Phosphonium compounds and phosphines
	Subdivisions are added for either or both topics in heading
.073	*Phosphoalcohols
.074	*Phosphoacids
.075	*Phosphoaldehydes and phosphoketones
	Subdivisions are added for either or both topics in heading

*Add as instructed under 547

.076	*Phosphinic acids
.077	*Phosphonic acids
.08	*Organosilicon compounds

.1   Physical and theoretical chemistry

Add to base number 547.1 the numbers following 541 in 541.2–541.7, e.g., comprehensive works on stereochemistry 547.1223 [*formerly* 541.223], comprehensive works on isomers 547.12252 [*formerly* 541.2252], specific reactions 547.1393; however, for synthesis (e.g., addition, condensation, hydrolysis, oxidation, polymerization, reduction) and miscellaneous reactions, see 547.2

Class physical and theoretical chemistry of specific kinds of compounds identified by component elements in 547.01–547.08; class physical and theoretical chemistry of kinds of compounds identified by structure and function in 547.4–547.8

For inorganic isomers, see 541.2252

.2   Synthesis and miscellaneous reactions

Standard subdivisions are added for either or both topics in heading

Limited to reactions named below

Class here reactions producing kinds of compounds identified by component element; addition

Class comprehensive works on specific reactions not named below in 547.1393

For synthesis and miscellaneous reactions in specific kinds of compounds identified by structure and function, see 547.4–547.8

.21	Acylation, alkylation, aromatization

Including Friedel-Crafts, Würtz-Fittig reactions

Class aromatic compounds in 547.6

.22	Halogenation, hydroxy addition and substitution
.223	Halogenation

Class halocarbons in 547.02

.225	Hydrolysis and saponification

Standard subdivisions are added for hydrolysis and saponification together, for hydrolysis alone

Comprehensive works on saponification relocated to 547.7704593

.23	Oxidation and reduction

Including hydrogenation, dehydrogenation, peroxidation, quinonization

Class oxy and hydroxy compounds in 547.03

*Add as instructed under 547

.24 Esterification

> Class esters in 547.038

.25 Amination and diazotization

> Class amines in 547.042; class azo compounds in 547.043

.26 Nitration and nitrosation

> Class organonitrogen compounds in 547.04; class nitro and nitroso compounds in 547.041

.27 Sulfonation

> Class sulfones in 547.065

.28 Polymerization and condensation

> Standard subdivisions are added for polymerization and condensation together, for polymerization alone
>
> Including copolymerization, addition and condensation polymerization
>
> Class polymers in 547.7

.29 Fermentation

.3 **Analytical chemistry**

.300 1–.308 Standard subdivisions, general topics and methods

> Add to base number 547.30 the numbers following 543.0 in 543.001–543.08, e.g., reagents 547.301

.34 Qualitative analysis

> Add to base number 547.34 the numbers following 544 in 544.001–544.98, e.g., qualitative organic chromatographic analysis 547.3492

.35 Quantitative analysis

> Add to base number 547.35 the numbers following 545 in 545.001–545.89, e.g., volumetric analysis 547.352

> **547.4–547.8 Kinds of compounds identified by structure and function**

> Class comprehensive works in 547

.4 ***Aliphatic compounds**

> Unless other instructions are given, class a subject with aspects in two or more subdivisions of 547.4 in the number coming last, e.g., aliphatic sulfonamides 547.467 (*not* 547.442)
>
> Class aliphatic macromolecular compounds in 547.7

.41 *Hydrocarbons

---

*Add as instructed under 547

.411		*Paraffins (Alkanes)

> See also 547.77 for paraffin wax

.412		*Olefins (Alkenes)
.413		*Acetylenes (Alkynes)
.42–.48		Other compounds

Add to base number 547.4 the numbers following 547.0 in 547.02–547.08, e.g., carboxylic acids 547.437

For proteins, see 547.75

.5   *Cyclic compounds

Class here alicyclic compounds

For aromatic compounds, see 547.6

> 547.51–547.58   Alicyclic compounds

Unless other instructions are given, class a subject with aspects in two or more subdivisions of 547.51–547.58 in the number coming last, e.g., alicyclic sulfonamides 547.567 (*not* 547.542)

Class comprehensive works in 547.5

.51	*Alicyclic hydrocarbons
.511	*Cycloparaffins
.512	*Cycloolefins
.513	*Cycloacetylenes
.52–.58	Other alicyclic compounds

Add to base number 547.5 the numbers following 547.0 in 547.02–547.08, e.g., alicyclic halocarbons 547.52

.59	Heterocyclic compounds
.590 4	Special topics

Add to base number 547.5904 the numbers following 04 in notation 044–046 from table under 547, e.g., chelates 547.59044242 [*formerly* 541.2253]

.592	*Hetero oxygen compounds

Including furans, oxazoles, pyrans

.593	*Hetero nitrogen compounds

Including chlorophylls, diazines, imidazoles, porphyrins, pyrazoles, pyridines, pyrroles

*Add as instructed under 547

.594	*Hetero sulfur compounds

Including thiazoles, thiophenes

.595	Compounds with two or more different hetero atoms

Including oxazines, oxdiazines, oxdiazoles

.596	*Fused heterocyclic compounds

Including purines, quinolines

.6	***Aromatic compounds**

Unless other instructions are given, class a subject with aspects in two or more subdivisions of 547.6 in the number coming last, e.g., aromatic sulfonamides 547.667 (*not* 547.642)

Class aromatization in 547.21

.61	*Hydrocarbons
.611	*Benzenes
.613	*Polyphenyl hydrocarbons

Including diphenyl hydrocarbons

.615	*Fused hydrocarbons

Including naphthalenes

For anthracenes, see 547.616

.616	*Anthracenes
.62	*Halogenated compounds
.63	*Oxy and hydroxy compounds

Subdivisions are added for either or both topics in heading

.631	*Alcohols

Class phenols in 547.632

.632	*Phenols

Including monohydric hydroxy aromatics

.633	*Polyhydroxy aromatics

Including dihydroxy and trihydroxy aromatics, catechols, hydroquinones, resorcinols

.635	*Ethers
.636	*Aldehydes and ketones

Subdivisions are added for either or both topics in heading

*Add as instructed under 547

.637	*Acids
.638	*Esters
.64–.68	Other aromatic compounds

Add to base number 547.6 the numbers following 547.0 in 547.04–547.08, e.g., aromatic amines 547.642

.7 *Macromolecules and related compounds

Subdivisions are added for macromolecules and related compounds, for macromolecules alone

Class here macromolecules when not considered in their biological context; comprehensive works on polymers

Class polymerization in 547.28; class interdisciplinary works on macromolecules in 572

For inorganic polymers, see 541.2254; for fossil substances, see 547.82; for comprehensive works on high polymers, see 547.84; for dyes and pigments, see 547.86

| .71 | Terpenes and essential oils |

Including camphors

| .72 | *Alkaloids |

See also 615.7 for pharmacodynamics of alkaloids

| .73 | *Steroids and hormones |

Subdivisions are added for steroids and hormones together, for steroids alone

| .731 | *Sterols |

Including cholesterol, ergosterol

| .734 | *Hormones |

Class here steroid hormones

| .734 2 | *Auxins |

Including gibberellins

| .734 3 | *Sex hormones |
| .734 5 | Nonsteroid hormones |

Including adrenalin, cortin, insulin, oxytocin, thyroxine, vasopressin

| .737 | *Bile acids (Cholic acids) |
| .74 | *Vitamins |

*Add as instructed under 547

.75   *Proteins

> Class here amino acids
>
> Class protein hormones in 547.7345

>   547.752–547.756   Proteins identified by structure
>
> Class comprehensive works in 547.75

.752   Simple proteins

> Including albumins, globulins, histones

.753   Scleroproteins

> Including collagen, keratin

.754   Conjugated proteins

> Including chromoproteins, hemoglobin, lipoproteins, nucleoproteins, phosphoproteins

.756   Derived proteins

> Including peptides, peptones

.758   *Enzymes

> Class here coenzymes

.76   *Antibiotics

.77   *Lipids

> Class here fats, fatty acids
>
> Including waxes
>
> *For steroids, see 547.73*
>
> *See also 547.411 for paraffin hydrocarbons*

.770 459 3   Specific reactions

> Number built according to instructions under 547
>
> Including comprehensive works on saponification [*formerly* 547.225]

.78   *Carbohydrates

> Class here saccharides

.781   *Sugars

.781 3   *Monosaccharides

> Including fructose, glucose (dextrose), ribose

*Add as instructed under 547

.781 5		*Oligosaccharides

Including lactose, maltose, sucrose (common sugar)

.782		*Polysaccharides

Including cellulose, chitin, dextrans, glycogen, pectins, starches

Class conjugated carbohydrates in 547.783

.783		*Conjugated carbohydrates

Including glycosides, gums

For glycoside pigments, see 547.869

.79		*Nucleic acids
.8		**Other organic substances**
.82		*Fossil substances

Including coal tar

Class a specific compound derived from a fossil substance with the compound, e.g., synthetic rubber 678.72

For petroleum, see 547.83

.83		*Petroleum
.84		*High polymers

Class high polymers of a specific chemical group with the group, e.g., polysaccharides 547.782

.842		*Elastomers
.842 5		*Latexes
.842 6		*Rubber
.843		*Flexible polymers
.843 4		*Resins
.86		*Dyes and pigments

Standard subdivisions are added for dyes and pigments together, for dyes alone

.869		*Pigments

548 Crystallography

Class crystallographic mineralogy in 549.18; class comprehensive works on solid state physics in 530.41

See Manual at 548 vs. 530.41; also at 549 vs. 548

*Add as instructed under 547

.015 1   Mathematical principles

> Do not use for mathematical crystallography; class in 548.7

.3   Chemical crystallography

Relationship between structure and bonding

Including isomorphism, polymorphism, pseudomorphism

.5   Crystallization and crystal growth

Standard subdivisions are added for either or both topics in heading

.7   Mathematical crystallography

Measurement and calculation of angles

Class geometric crystallography in 548.81

.8   Physical and structural crystallography

Standard subdivisions are added for physical and structural crystallography together, for physical crystallography alone

.81   Structural crystallography

Class here crystal lattices, geometrical crystallography

Class structural crystallography of a specific substance with the substance, e.g., structural chemistry of silicates 549.6

For diffraction methods, see 548.83

.810 151   Mathematical principles

> Do not use for mathematical crystallography; class in 548.7

.83   Diffraction crystallography

Including crystallograms

Class optical methods of crystal study in 548.9

>   548.84–548.86   Physical properties of crystals

Class comprehensive works in 548.8

For optical properties, see 548.9

.84   Mechanical properties

.842   Stresses, deformation, strength properties

Including elasticity, plasticity; dislocation, fracture, hardness

[.843–.845]   Cleavage, cohesion, density, specific gravity

Numbers discontinued; class in 548.84

.85	Electrical, electronic, magnetic properties

Including conductivity, dielectricity

.86	Thermal properties

Including fusibility

.9   Optical crystallography

Optical properties of crystals and optical methods of crystal study

549   Mineralogy

Occurrence, description, classification, identification of naturally occurring minerals

Class crystallography in 548; class economic geology in 553

See Manual at 549 vs. 546; also at 549 vs. 548; also at 552 vs. 549

SUMMARY

549.09	Historical, geographic, persons treatment
.1	Determinative mineralogy
.2	Native elements
.3	Sulfides, antimonides, arsenides, selenides, tellurides; sulfosalts
.4	Halides
.5	Oxides
.6	Silicates
.7	Other minerals
.9	Geographic treatment of minerals

.09	Historical, geographic, persons treatment

Do not use for geographic treatment of minerals; class in 549.9

.1   Determinative mineralogy

Class determinative mineralogy of specific minerals in 549.2–549.7

See Manual at 549.1

.11	Minerals in specific kinds of formations
.112	Meteorite minerals

Class here petrology of meteorites

[.113]	Minerals in placers

Number discontinued; class in 549.11

.114	Minerals in rocks

Add to base number 549.114 the numbers following 552 in 552.1–552.5, e.g., determinative mineralogy in sedimentary rocks 549.1145

.116	Minerals in pegmatite dikes

[.119]	Minerals in veins and lodes
	Number discontinued; class in 549.11
.12	Physical mineralogy
.121	Mechanical properties
	Including cleavage, fracture, hardness
.125	Optical properties
	Including color, fluorescence, luminescence
.127	Electrical, electronic, magnetic properties
.13	Chemical mineralogy
.131	Composition, properties, reactivity
.133	Analysis
.18	Crystallographic mineralogy
	Study of crystalline structure and properties of minerals

> **549.2–549.7 Specific minerals**

Class comprehensive works in 549

.2 **Native elements**

Use 549.7 for mineral compounds of specific elements not provided for elsewhere in 549.3–549.7

.23 Metals

Native metals only

Class interdisciplinary works on physico-chemical characteristics of metals in 669.9

.25 Semimetals

Including antimony, arsenic, bismuth, boron, selenium, tellurium

.27 Nonmetals

Including graphite (carbon)

.3 **Sulfides, antimonides, arsenides, selenides, tellurides; sulfosalts**

Class sulfates in 549.75

.32 Sulfides, antimonides, arsenides, selenides, tellurides

Including chalcocite, cinnabar, galena, molybdenite, pyrite, sphalerite

.35 Sulfosalts (Double sulfides)

Including tetrahedrite

.4	**Halides**
	Including carnallite, cryolite, fluorite (fluorspar), halite, rock salt
.5	**Oxides**
.52	Simple and multiple oxides
	Standard subdivisions are added for either or both topics in heading
.522	Cuprite, ice, zincite
.523	Hematite group
	Including corundum, ilmenite
.524	Rutile group
	Including cassiterite
.525	Goethite group
	Including diaspore
.526	Spinel group
	Including chromite, magnetite
.528	Other groups of oxides
	Including uraninite
.53	Hydroxides
	Including bauxite, limonite
.6	**Silicates**
	Class here clay
.62	Nesosilicates
	Including andalusite, cyanite, garnet, kyanite, sillimanite, staurolite, topaz, zircon
.63	Sorosilicates
	Including epidote
.64	Cyclosilicates
	Including beryl, chrysocolla, cordierite, tourmaline
.66	Inosilicates
	Including amphiboles, pyroxenes, spodumene, wollastonite
.67	Phyllosilicates
	Including chlorite, glauconite, kaolinite, mica, pyrophyllite, serpentine, talc

.68	Tectosilicates

Including feldspar, leucite, opal, quartz, scapolite, zeolite

.7 Other minerals

[.701–.709] Standard subdivisions

Do not use; class in 549.01–549.09

.72 Phosphates, arsenates, vanadates

Including apatite, monazite, turquoise

.73 Nitrates and borates

.732 Nitrates

Including saltpeter (niter), Chile saltpeter (soda niter)

.735 Borates

Including borax, colemanite

.74 Molybdates and tungstates

Including scheelite, wolframite

.75 Sulfates and chromates

Standard subdivisions are added for sulfates and chromates together, for sulfates alone

.752 Chromates and anhydrous sulfates

Including anhydrite, barite, celestite

.755 Hydrous and basic sulfates

Including alunite, gypsum

.78 Carbonates

.782 Calcite group

Including dolomite, magnesite, siderite

.785 Aragonite group

Including malachite

.9 Geographic treatment of minerals

Add to base number 549.9 notation 1–9 from Table 2, e.g., minerals of Greenland 549.9982

550 Earth sciences

Class here geophysics; phenomena of celestial bodies directly comparable to terrestrial phenomena, e.g., volcanic activity on Mars 551.21099923

Use 550 and its standard subdivisions for works that deal comprehensively with geology, hydrology, and meteorology; for works on geology in the sense of all earth sciences. Use 551 and its standard subdivisions for works on geology in the sense limited to properties and phenomena of the solid earth

See Manual at 550 vs. 910; also at 559.9

SUMMARY

551	**Geology, hydrology, meteorology**
552	**Petrology**
553	**Economic geology**
554–559	**Earth sciences by specific continents, countries, localities in modern world; extraterrestrial worlds**

[.154]   Chemical principles

Do not use; class in 551.9

[.94–.99]   Treatment by specific continents, countries, localities in modern world; extraterrestrial worlds

Do not use; class in 554–559

551 Geology, hydrology, meteorology

Geology: science that deals with properties and phenomena of the solid earth (lithosphere)

Use 550 and its standard subdivisions for works that deal comprehensively with geology, hydrology, and meteorology; for works on geology in the sense of all earth sciences. Use 551 and its standard subdivisions for works on geology in the sense limited to properties and phenomena of the solid earth

For astronomical geography, see 525; for geodesy, see 526.1; for petrology, see 552; for economic geology, see 553; for physical geography, see 910.02

SUMMARY

551.01–.09	**Standard subdivisions of geology**
.1	**Gross structure and properties of the earth**
.2	**Volcanoes, earthquakes, thermal waters and gases**
.3	**Surface and exogenous processes and their agents**
.4	**Geomorphology and hydrosphere**
.5	**Meteorology**
.6	**Climatology and weather**
.7	**Historical geology**
.8	**Structural geology**
.9	**Geochemistry**

.01   Philosophy and theory of geology

[.015 4]	Chemical principles
	Do not use; class in 551.9
.02–.08	Standard subdivisions of geology
.09	Historical, geographic, persons treatment of geology
[.091 62–.091 68]	Treatment in oceans and seas
	Do not use; class in 551.4608
[.094–.099]	Geology by specific continents, countries, localities in modern world; extraterrestrial worlds
	Do not use; class in 554–559

.1   **Gross structure and properties of the earth**

         For geomagnetism, see 538.7

.11   Interior

         For properties, see 551.12

.112   Core

[.115]   Gutenberg discontinuity

         Number discontinued; class in 551.11

.116   Mantle

[.119]   Mohorovicic discontinuity

         Number discontinued; class in 551.11

.12   Properties of interior

         Including heat, temperature ranges

.13   Crust

         Including magma

         For properties, see 551.14; for structural geology, see 551.8

.136   Plate tectonics (Continental drift)

         Including sea-floor spreading

         Class comprehensive works on tectonics in 551.8

.14   Properties of crust

         Including elasticity, heat, temperature ranges

.2   **Volcanoes, earthquakes, thermal waters and gases**

         See also 363.3495 for volcanic and earthquake disasters

.21   Volcanoes

> Class here comprehensive works on craters
>
> Class volcanic thermal waters and gases in 551.23; class petrology of volcanic rocks in 552.2
>
> *For meteorite craters, see 551.397*

.22   Earthquakes

> Class here seismology
>
> Class seismic sea waves in 551.47024

.220 287   Testing and measurement

> Class here seismography

.23   Thermal waters and gases

> Standard subdivisions are added for thermal waters and gases together, for thermal waters alone
>
> Including volcanic volatiles [*formerly* 552.2]
>
> Class here surface manifestations, e.g., fumaroles, hot springs

.3   **Surface and exogenous processes and their agents**

> Standard subdivisions are added for any or all topics in heading
>
> Class here sedimentology as study of surface processes
>
> Class comprehensive works on landforms in 551.41; class comprehensive works on sedimentology in 552.5

.300 1–.300 9   Standard subdivisions

>   551.302–551.307   Erosion and weathering, sediments and sedimentation, soil formation, mass movement

> Class comprehensive works in 551.3
>
> *See Manual at 551.302–551.307 vs. 551.35*

.302   Erosion and weathering

> Class here soil erosion, interdisciplinary works on erosion
>
> Class role of weathering in soil formation in 551.305
>
> *For a specific aspect of erosion, see the aspect, e.g., erosion engineering 627.5, control of agricultural soil erosion 631.45*

.303   Transporting and depositing of materials

> Standard subdivisions are added for either or both topics in heading
>
> Class here sedimentation

.304	Transported materials (Sediments)
.305	Soil formation

Class here role of water in soil formation

| .307 | Mass movement (Mass wasting) |

Including avalanches, creep, mud flows, rockfalls; subsidence

Class here landslides, slope failure, work of water in mass movement

See also 363.349 for disasters resulting from avalanches and other mass movements

| .31 | Geologic work of ice   Glaciology |

Class here interdisciplinary works on ice

For ice in water and other forms of ice, see 551.34; for geologic work of frost, see 551.38. For a specific aspect of ice, see the aspect, e.g., ice manufacture 621.58

| .312 | Glaciers |

For icebergs, shelf ice, growlers, see 551.342

| .313 | Glacial action |

Including work of glaciers in erosion, soil formation, weathering

| .314 | Material transported by glaciers |

Class here glacial drift and till, moraines regarded as materials

Class glacial drift and till, moraines regarded as landforms in 551.315

| .315 | Landforms created by glaciers |

Including cirques, drumlins, kames, kettles, roches moutonnées

Class here glacial drift and till, moraines regarded as landforms

| .34 | Ice in water and other forms of ice |

Standard subdivisions are added for ice in water and other forms of ice together, for ice in water alone

For snow, see 551.5784

| .342 | Ice in the sea |

Including icebergs, shelf ice, growlers

For sea ice, see 551.343

.343	Sea ice (Frozen seawater)
.344	Anchor and frazil ice

.345   **Lake and river ice**

Class here ice cover

For anchor and frazil ice, see 551.344

.35   **Geologic work of water**

Work of precipitation, of surface and subsurface waters

For role of water in soil formation, see 551.305; for geologic work of marine waters, see 551.36

See Manual at 551.302–551.307 vs. 551.35

.352   **Erosion and weathering**

Standard subdivisions are added for erosion and weathering together, for erosion alone

.353   **Transporting and depositing materials**

Standard subdivisions are added for either or both topics in heading

Class here sedimentation in water

For role of water in mass movement, see 551.307

.354   **Transported materials (Sediments)**

.355   **Landforms created by water**

For specific landforms created by water, see 551.42–551.45

.36   **Geologic work of marine waters**

Including wave action, beach erosion

For specific landforms created by marine waters, see 551.42–551.45

.37   **Geologic work of wind**

.372   **Erosion**

Class here weathering

.373   **Transporting and depositing materials**

Standard subdivisions are added for either or both topics in heading

.374   **Transported materials**

.375   **Landforms created by wind**

Class here dunes

.38   **Geologic work of frost**

Class here nivation; work of frost in erosion, in soil formation, in weathering; comprehensive works on frost

For frost as a cold spell, see 551.5253; for condensation of frost, see 551.5744

.382	Fragmentation of rocks
[.383]	Nivation

> Number discontinued; class in 551.38

.384	Permafrost
.39	Geologic work of other agents

> Including temperature changes

.397	Meteorites

> Class here meteorite craters

.4 Geomorphology and hydrosphere

SUMMARY

551.41	**Geomorphology**
.42	**Islands and reefs**
.43	**Elevations**
.44	**Depressions and openings**
.45	**Plane and coastal regions**
.46	**Hydrosphere Oceanography**
.47	**Dynamic oceanography**
.48	**Hydrology**
.49	**Groundwater (Subsurface water)**

.41	Geomorphology

> Creation and modification of topographic landforms by erosional and depositional processes

> Class here geomorphology of continents, comprehensive works on landforms

>> *For specific landforms, see 551.42–551.45; for submarine geomorphology, see 551.46084*

>> *See also 551.136 for continental drift*

[.410 916 2–.410 916 8]	Treatment in oceans and seas

> Do not use; class in 551.46084

.415	Arid-land geomorphology

> Class here desert geomorphology

> 551.42–551.45 Specific landforms

Class here specific land formations created by water; comprehensive works on specific kinds of topographical features, on present and past examples of specific landforms

Class comprehensive works in 551.41

For a specific landform created by plutonic action, see the landform in 551.2, e.g., volcanic mountains 551.21; for a specific landform created primarily by exogenous agents other than water or living organisms, see the landform in 551.3, e.g., glacial moraines 551.315; for a specific landform created by tectonic deformations, see the landform in 551.8, e.g., rift valleys 551.872

.42 Islands and reefs

Standard subdivisions are added for islands and reefs together, for islands alone

.423 Barrier islands

Class barrier reefs in 551.424

.424 Reefs

Including atolls

.43 Elevations

Including slopes

Class slopes of specific kinds of elevations in 551.432–551.436; class orogeny in 551.82

.432 Mountains

.434 Plateaus

.436 Hills

Use of this number for comprehensive works on slopes discontinued; class in 551.43

.44 Depressions and openings

For craters, see 551.21

.442 Valleys

Including canyons, gorges, ravines; floodplains; river beds

For deltas, see 551.456; for rift valleys, see 551.872

.447	Caves and related features

Standard subdivisions are added for caves and related features together, for caves alone

Including karst formations, sink holes

.45	Plane and coastal regions

.453	Plane regions

Class here pampas, plains, prairies, steppes, tundras; comprehensive works on grasslands

> *For floodplains, see 551.442; for deltas, see 551.456. For a specific kind of grassland not in a plane region, see the kind, e.g., alpine meadows 551.432*

.456	Deltas

.457	Coastal regions

Including beaches

> *For deltas, see 551.456; for shorelines, see 551.458*

.458	Shorelines

Marine and lake

Class here changes in sea and lake levels

.46	Hydrosphere Oceanography

Class here hydrography, marine science, oceans and seas

Class ice in 551.31; class geologic work of water in 551.35; class ocean-atmosphere interactions in 551.5246; class interdisciplinary works on water in 553.7

> *For dynamic oceanography, see 551.47; for hydrology, see 551.48; for marine ecology, see 577.7; for marine biology, see 578.77*

> *See also 620.4162 for oceanographic engineering*

> *See Manual at 578.76–578.77 vs. 551.46*

.460 01–.460 06	Standard subdivisions
.460 07	Education, research, related topics
.460 072 3	Descriptive research

Do not use for deep-sea surveys and explorations; class in 551.4607

.460 08–.460 09	Standard subdivisions
.460 1	Composition and properties of seawater

Including salinity, temperature

.460 7   Deep-sea surveys and explorations

Standard subdivisions are added for either or both topics in heading

.460 8   Submarine geology

For sea-floor spreading, see 551.136

[.460 809 163–.460 809 168]   Treatment in specific oceans and seas

Do not use; class in 551.4608093–551.4608098

.460 809 3–.460 809 8   Specific oceans and seas

Do not use for treatment in specific continents, countries, localities; class in 551.460809

Add to base number 551.460809 the numbers following — 16 in notation 163–168 from Table 2, e.g., submarine geology of Arctic Ocean 551.46080932

[.460 809 9]   Treatment in other parts of world

Do not use; class in 551.460809

.460 83   Composition of ocean floor, deposits, sediments

Standard subdivisions are added for any or all topics in heading

[.460 830 916 3–.460 830 916 8]   Treatment in specific oceans and seas

Do not use; class in 551.460833–551.460838

.460 833–.460 838   Specific oceans and seas

Add to base number 551.46083 the numbers following — 16 in notation 163–168 from Table 2, e.g., marine sediments of North Sea 551.46083336

.460 84   Submarine geomorphology

Class here topography of ocean floor, comprehensive works on ocean floor

For composition of ocean floor, deposits, sediments, see 551.46083

[.460 840 916 3–.460 840 916 8]   Treatment in specific oceans and seas

Do not use; class in 551.460843–551.460848

.460 843–.460 848   Specific oceans and seas

Add to base number 551.46084 the numbers following — 16 in notation 163–168 from Table 2, e.g., geomorphology of Pacific Ocean floor 551.460844

.460 9   Special saltwater forms

Including coastal pools, estuaries, inland seas, salt lakes, saltwater lagoons

For specific coastal pools, estuaries, saltwater lagoons, see 551.461–551.469

>   **551.461–551.469 Oceanography of specific oceans and seas**

Class submarine geology of specific oceans and seas in 551.4608093–551.4608098; class comprehensive works in 551.46

.461   Atlantic Ocean

For Mediterranean Sea, see 551.462; for Gulf of Mexico, see 551.4634; for Caribbean Sea, see 551.4635; for South Atlantic Ocean, see 551.464

.461 1   North Atlantic Ocean

For northeast and northwest Atlantic Ocean, see 551.4613–551.4614; for Arctic Ocean (North Polar Sea), see 551.468

.461 3–.461 4   Northeast and northwest Atlantic Ocean

Add to base number 551.461 the numbers following —163 in notation 1633–1634 from Table 2, e.g., Chesapeake Bay 551.46147

Class comprehensive works in 551.4611

.462   Mediterranean Sea

Add to base number 551.462 the numbers following —1638 in notation 16381–16389 from Table 2, e.g., Black Sea 551.4629

.463   Gulf of Mexico and Caribbean Sea

.463 4   Gulf of Mexico

Including Yucatán Channel

For Straits of Florida, see 551.46463

.463 5   Caribbean Sea

Including Gulfs of Darien, Honduras, Venezuela

.464   South Atlantic Ocean

Add to base number 551.464 the numbers following —163 in notation 1636–1637 from Table 2, e.g., Sargasso Sea 551.46462; however, for Caribbean Sea and Gulf of Mexico, see 551.463

For Atlantic sector of Antarctic waters, see 551.4693

.465	Pacific Ocean

Add to base number 551.465 the numbers following — 164 in notation 1644–1649 from Table 2, e.g., South China Sea 551.46572

For east Pacific Ocean, see 551.466; for Pacific sector of Antarctic waters, see 551.4694

.466	East Pacific Ocean
.466 1	Southeast Pacific Ocean

American coastal waters from Strait of Magellan to Mexico-United States boundary

Including Gulfs of California, Guayaquil, Panama, Tehuantepec

.466 3	Northeast Pacific Ocean

North American coastal waters from California to tip of Alaska

Add to base number 551.4663 the numbers following — 1643 in notation 16432–16434 from Table 2, e.g., San Francisco Bay 551.46632

.467	Indian Ocean

Add to base number 551.467 the numbers following — 165 in notation 1652–1657 from Table 2, e.g., Red Sea 551.46733

For Indian Ocean sector of Antarctic waters, see 551.4695

.468	Arctic Ocean (North Polar Sea)

Add to base number 551.468 the numbers following — 1632 in notation 16324–16327 from Table 2, e.g., Hudson Bay 551.4687

.469	Antarctic waters

Add to base number 551.469 the numbers following — 167 in notation 1673–1675 from Table 2, e.g., Drake Passage 551.4693

.47	Dynamic oceanography
.470 01–.470 09	Standard subdivisions
.470 1	Ocean currents

For specific ocean currents, see 551.471–551.479

.470 2	Waves

Class here gravity, internal, surface waves

See also 551.36 for geologic work of waves

.470 22	Wind waves

Including storm surges, swell

.470 23	Seiches
	In bays, gulfs, inland seas
	Class seiches in freshwater lakes in 551.482
.470 24	Seismic sea waves
	Variant names: tidal waves, tsunami
.470 8	Tides and tidal currents
	Standard subdivisions are added for either or both topics in heading
	See also 551.36 for geologic work of tides
.471–.479	Specific ocean currents
	Add to base number 551.47 the numbers following 551.46 in 551.461–551.469, e.g., Gulf Stream 551.4711
	Class waves in 551.4702; class comprehensive works in 551.4701
	For tides and tidal currents, see 551.4708
.48	Hydrology
	Class here hydrological cycle, limnology, water balance
	Class comprehensive works on oceanography and hydrology in 551.46; class water resources, interdisciplinary works on water in 553.7
	For fumaroles, see 551.23; for groundwater, see 551.49; for hydrometeorology, see 551.57
.482	Lakes, ponds, freshwater lagoons
	Standard subdivisions are added for any or all topics in heading
	Class inland seas and salt lakes in 551.4609
.483	Rivers and streams
	Standard subdivisions are added for either or both topics in heading
	For waterfalls, see 551.484; for floods, see 551.489
.484	Waterfalls
.488	Runoff
.489	Floods
.49	Groundwater (Subsurface water)
	Class here aquifers
	For thermal waters, see 551.23
.492	Water table

.498   Surface manifestations

Including springs, wells

For hot springs, see 551.23

.5   **Meteorology**

Class forecasting and forecasts of specific phenomena in 551.64; class forecasts of specific phenomena in specific areas in 551.65; class micrometeorology in 551.66

For climatology and weather, see 551.6

See Manual at 551.5 vs. 551.6

SUMMARY

551.51	**Composition, regions, dynamics of atmosphere**
.52	**Thermodynamics, atmosphere interactions with earth's surface, temperatures, radiations**
.54	**Atmospheric pressure**
.55	**Atmospheric disturbances and formations**
.56	**Atmospheric electricity and optics**
.57	**Hydrometeorology**

[.501 12]   Forecasting and forecasts

Do not use; class in 551.63

.51   Composition, regions, dynamics of atmosphere

.511   Composition

Class here chemistry, photochemistry of atmosphere

.511 2   Gases

.511 3   Aerosols and dust

Class dust storms in 551.559

>   551.513–551.514   Atmospheric regions

Class comprehensive works in 551.51. Class a specific aspect with the aspect, e.g., upper-atmosphere temperatures 551.5257

.513   Troposphere

.514   Upper atmosphere

Including magnetosphere, mesosphere

Class magnetic phenomena in magnetosphere, comprehensive works on magnetosphere in 538.766

.514 2   Stratosphere

Class here ozone layer

.514 5	Ionosphere
.515	Dynamics

Class here mechanics

For circulation, see 551.517

.515 1	Kinematics
[.515 2–.515 3]	Statics and dynamics

Numbers discontinued; class in 551.515

.517	Circulation

*For wind, see 551.518; for atmospheric disturbances and formations,
see 551.55*

.518	Wind

Class wind in atmospheric disturbances and formations in 551.55

> 551.518 3–551.518 5 Wind systems in troposphere

Class comprehensive works in 551.518

.518 3	Planetary wind systems

Including jet streams, trade winds, westerlies

.518 4	Monsoons
.518 5	Local wind systems

Including land and sea breezes; mountain and valley winds, e.g.,
chinooks, foehns

.518 7	Winds in upper atmosphere
.52	Thermodynamics, atmosphere interactions with earth's surface, temperatures, radiations
.522	Thermodynamics

Class thermodynamics in microclimatology in 551.66

.523	Land-atmosphere interactions

Class here earth temperatures affecting atmosphere

.524	Atmosphere interactions with earth's surface

Class here water-atmosphere interactions, water temperatures affecting
atmosphere

For land-atmosphere interactions, see 551.523

[.524 091 62–.524 091 68]	Treatment in oceans and seas

Do not use; class in 551.5246

[.524 091 69]	Fresh and brackish waters
	Do not use; class in 551.5248
.524 6	Ocean-atmosphere interactions
[.524 609 163–.524 609 167]	Treatment in specific oceans and seas
	Do not use; class in 551.52463–551.52467
.524 63–.524 67	Specific oceans and seas

Add to base number 551.5246 the numbers following —16 in notation 163–167 from Table 2, e.g., temperatures of Indian Ocean 551.52465

.524 8	Lake and river interactions with atmosphere
.525	Temperatures

Class here air temperatures, energy budget, energy flow

For earth temperatures affecting atmosphere, see 551.523; for water temperatures affecting atmosphere, see 551.524; for radiant energy, see 551.527

See also 333.79 for economic aspects of energy budgets

.525 09	Historical, geographic, persons treatment

Class here geographic distribution at earth's surface [*formerly* 551.5252]

.525 091 732	Urban regions

Class here urban heat islands

For specific urban heat islands, see 551.525093–551.525099

[.525 2]	Geographic distribution at earth's surface
	Relocated to 551.52509
.525 3	Variations over time at earth's surface

Including maximums, minimums, frosts

Class comprehensive works on frost in 551.38

.525 4	Vertical distribution in troposphere
.525 7	Upper-atmosphere temperatures
.527	Radiations

For optical phenomena, see 551.565

.527 1	Solar radiation
.527 2	Terrestrial radiation

For radiation originating in atmosphere, see 551.5273

.527 3	Radiation originating in atmosphere
.527 6	Cosmic radiations

> Including cosmic noise
>
> Class here cosmic rays
>
> Use of this number for corpuscular radiation discontinued; class in 551.527

.54	Atmospheric pressure
.540 9	Historical, geographic, persons treatment

> Class here geographic distribution at earth's surface [*formerly* 551.542]

[.542]	Geographic distribution at earth's surface

> Relocated to 551.5409

.543	Variations over time at earth's surface
.543 09	Historical and persons treatment

> Do not use for geographic treatment; class in 551.5409

.547	Upper-atmosphere pressures
.55	Atmospheric disturbances and formations

> Standard subdivisions are added for atmospheric disturbances and formations together, for atmospheric disturbances alone
>
> Class here storms
>
> Class precipitation from storms in 551.577
>
> *See also 363.3492 for storms as disasters*

.551	Atmospheric formations
.551 2	Air masses and fronts
.551 3	Cyclones

> *See also 551.552 for hurricanes, 551.553 for tornadoes*

.551 4	Anticyclones

> **551.552–551.559 Atmospheric disturbances**
>
> Class comprehensive works in 551.55

.552	Hurricanes

> Variant names: typhoons, baguios, tropical cyclones, willy-willies

.553	Tornadoes
	Variant names: cyclones (Midwest United States), twisters
	Including waterspouts
.554	Thermal convective storms
	Including hailstorms
	Class here thunderstorms
	For tornadoes, see 551.553
.555	Snowstorms
	Including blizzards
[.557]	Upper-atmosphere storms
	Number discontinued; class in 551.55
.559	Other storms
	Including dust and ice storms
.56	Atmospheric electricity and optics
.561	Electricity in stable atmosphere
	Including conductivity, ionization
.563	Atmospheric electricity
	Including electricity of aerosols and dust [*formerly* 551.564]
	Class magnetic phenomena in 538.7
	For electricity in stable atmosphere, see 551.561
.563 2	Lightning
	For ball lightning, see 551.5634
[.563 3]	Saint Elmo's fire
	Number discontinued; class in 551.563
.563 4	Ball lightning
[.564]	Electricity of aerosols and dust
	Relocated to 551.563
.565	Atmospheric optics
	Class here optical phenomena produced by refraction, e.g., mirages, scintillation
	Class visibility in 551.568
	For optical phenomena produced by absorption and scattering, see 551.566; for optical phenomena produced by condensation products, see 551.567

.566	Optical phenomena produced by absorption and scattering
	Including sky color, twilight, night skies
.567	Optical phenomena produced by condensation products
	Including cloud colors, rainbows
.568	Visibility
.57	Hydrometeorology
.571	Humidity
.571 09	Historical, geographic, persons treatment
	Class here geographic treatment in troposphere [*formerly* 551.5712]
[.571 2]	Geographic distribution in troposphere
	Relocated to 551.57109
.571 3	Variations of humidity over time
[.571 4–.571 7]	Vertical distribution in troposphere, humidity in upper atmosphere
	Numbers discontinued; class in 551.571
.572	Evapotranspiration
	Standard subdivisions are added for evapotranspiration, for evaporation alone
.574	Condensation of moisture
	For condensation of moisture in a specific form, see the form, e.g., clouds 551.576
.574 1	Condensation processes
	Class here atmospheric nucleation, formation of particles on which moisture condenses
	Class condensation processes on earth's surface in 551.5744; class comprehensive works on atmospheric aerosols and dust in 551.5113
.574 4	Condensations on earth's surface
	Including dew, glaze, hoarfrost
	Class comprehensive work on frost in 551.38
[.574 7]	Condensations on objects in upper atmosphere
	Number discontinued; class in 551.574
	Formation of hailstones relocated to 551.5787
.575	Fog and mist
	Standard subdivisions are added for fog and mist together, for fog alone

.576	Clouds
	Class cloud colors in 551.567
.577	Precipitation
	Class here liquid precipitation, rain, rainfall
	Class geologic work of precipitation in 551.35
	For frozen precipitation, see 551.578
.577 09	Historical and persons treatment
	Do not use for geographic treatment; class in 551.5572
.577 1	Properties
	Including composition, temperature; meteorology of acid rain
	Class interdisciplinary works on acid rain in 363.7386
.577 2	Geographic distribution of precipitation
	Add to base number 551.5772 notation 1–9 from Table 2, e.g., rainfall in Nigeria 551.5772669
	Class geographic distribution of variations over time in 551.5773
.577 3	Variations over time
	Including droughts, maximums, minimums
	See also 551.489 for floods
.577 5	Factors affecting precipitation
	Including bodies of water, cities, topography, vegetation
	Class comprehensive works on atmosphere interactions with earth's surface in 551.524
.578	Frozen precipitation
.578 4	Snow
.578 409	Historical and persons treatment
	Do not use for geographic treatment; class in 551.57842
.578 41–.578 43	Properties, geographic distribution, variations over time
	Add to base number 551.5784 the numbers following 551.577 in 551.5771–551.5773, e.g., variations in snow and snowfall over time 551.57843
.578 46	Snow cover
	For snow surveys, see 551.579
[.578 461]	Duration
	Number discontinued; class in 551.57846

.578 464	Ablation
	Class here melting
[.578 465–.578 466]	Firnification and stratification
	Number discontinued; class in 551.57846
.578 47	Snow formations
	Including drifts
	For avalanches, see 551.57848
.578 48	Avalanches
.578 7	Hail and graupel

Standard subdivisions are added for hail and graupel together, for hail alone

Including formation of hailstones [*formerly* 551.5747]

.579	Snow surveys
.579 09	Historical and persons treatment

Do not use for geographic treatment; class in 551.5791–551.5799

.579 1–.579 9	Geographic treatment

Add to base number 551.579 notation 1–9 from Table 2, e.g., snow surveys in Nevada 551.579793

.6 Climatology and weather

Standard subdivisions are added for either or both topics in heading

See Manual at 551.5 vs. 551.6

[.601 12]	Forecasting and forecasts

Do not use; class in 551.63

.609	Historical, geographic, persons treatment

Do not use for geographic treatment of weather; class in 551.65. Do not use for geographic treatment of climate, of climate and weather taken together; class in 551.69

.62	General types of climate
.620 9	Historical and persons treatment

Do not use for geographic treatment; class in 551.69

.63	Weather forecasting and forecasts, reporting and reports

Standard subdivisions are added for weather forecasting and forecasts, reporting and reports together; for weather forecasting alone; for weather forecasts alone

For forecasting and forecasts of specific phenomena, see 551.64

.630 284		Materials
		Do not use for apparatus and equipment; class in 551.635
.630 9		Historical and persons treatment
		Do not use for geographic treatment; class in 551.65
.631	Historical methods of forecasting	
	Class here weather lore	
.632	Reporting and reports	
	Standard subdivisions are added for either or both topics in heading	
	Class reports of specific weather phenomena in 551.5	
	For instrumentation in reporting, see 551.635	
.632 09		Historical, geographic, persons treatment
		Do not use for geographic treatment of weather reports; class in 551.65
.633	Statistical forecasting	
.634	Numerical forecasting	
.635	Instrumentation in reporting and forecasting	
	Standard subdivisions are added for either or both topics in heading	
.635 2	Radiosondes	
.635 3	Radar	
.635 4	Weather satellites	
.636	Short-range and long-range forecasts	
	Class a specific aspect of short-range and long-range forecasts with the aspect, e.g., satellites in long-range forecasts 551.6354	
.636 2	Short-range forecasts	
	Forecasts for a maximum of a week	
.636 5	Long-range forecasts	
	Forecasts more than a week in advance	
.64	Forecasting and forecasts of specific phenomena	
[.640 1–.640 9]	Standard subdivisions	
	Do not use; class in 551.6301–551.6309	

.641–.647	Specific meteorological phenomena

Class here methods of forecasting specific phenomena for specific areas

Add to base number 551.64 the numbers following 551.5 in 551.51–551.57, e.g., hurricane warnings 551.6452

Class flood forecasting and forecasts in 551.4890112; class forecasts of specific phenomena for specific areas in 551.65

.65	Geographic treatment of weather

Class here geographic treatment of weather forecasts and reports, of forecasts of specific phenomena

[.650 1–.650 9]	Standard subdivisions

Do not use; class in 551.601–551.609

.651–.659	Specific regions and areas

Class here forecasts of specific phenomena for specific regions and areas

Add to base number 551.65 notation 1–9 from Table 2, e.g., forecasts for South Africa 551.6568

.66	Microclimatology

Small-scale interactions of atmosphere with land and water

Class here micrometeorology

Class specific meteorological phenomena other than thermodynamics in 551.5; class comprehensive works on atmosphere interactions with earth's surface in 551.524

.68	Artificial modification and control of weather

Add to base number 551.68 the numbers following 551.5 in 551.51–551.57, e.g., cloud seeding 551.6876

.69	Geographic treatment of climate

Class here paleoclimatology of specific areas

Add to base number 551.69 notation 1–9 from Table 2, e.g., climate of Australia 551.6994

Class general types of climate in 551.62; class microclimatology of specific areas in 551.66; class comprehensive works on paleoclimatology in 551.60901

.7   **Historical geology**

Class here paleogeography, stratigraphy

Class history of a specific kind of geologic phenomena with the kind of phenomena, e.g., history of Jurassic volcanism in Pacific Northwest 551.2109795, Devonian reefs 551.424, paleozoic orogeny 551.82

For paleontology, see 560

See Manual at 551.7; also at 551.7 vs. 560

.700 1–.700 8   Standard subdivisions

.700 9   Historical, geographic, persons treatment

Do not use for geographic treatment of historical geology during a specific period; class in 551.71–551.79

[.700 94–.700 99]   Historical geology of specific continents, countries, localities in modern world; extraterrestrial worlds

Do not use; class in 554–559

.701   Geologic time and age measurements

Standard subdivisions are added for either or both topics in heading

---

>   **551.71–551.79   Specific geological periods**

Class comprehensive works in 551.7

.71   Precambrian era

Variant name: Cryptozoic eon

.712   Archean era

Variant names: Archeozoic, Lower Precambrian era

.715   Proterozoic era

Variant names: Algonkian, Upper Precambrian eras

.72   Paleozoic era

For Ordovician and Silurian periods, see 551.73; for Devonian period, see 551.74; for Carboniferous and Permian periods, see 551.75

.723   Cambrian period

.73   Ordovician and Silurian periods

.731   Ordovician period

Former name: Lower Silurian epoch

.732   Silurian period

Former name: Upper Silurian epoch

.74	Devonian period
.75	Carboniferous and Permian periods

Standard subdivisions are added for Carboniferous and Permian periods together, for Carboniferous period alone

---

>   551.751–551.752   Carboniferous period

Class comprehensive works in 551.75

.751	Mississippian (Lower Carboniferous) period
.752	Pennsylvanian (Upper Carboniferous) period
.756	Permian period
.76	Mesozoic era

For Cretaceous period, see 551.77

.762	Triassic period
.766	Jurassic period
.77	Cretaceous period
.78	Cenozoic era Tertiary period

For Quaternary period, see 551.79

.782	Paleogene period

For Paleocene epoch, see 551.783; for Eocene epoch, see 551.784; for Oligocene epoch, see 551.785

.783	Paleocene epoch
.784	Eocene epoch
.785	Oligocene epoch
.786	Neogene (Neocene) period

Class Quaternary period in 551.79

For Miocene epoch, see 551.787; for Pliocene epoch, see 551.788

.787	Miocene epoch
.788	Pliocene epoch
.79	Quaternary period
.792	Pleistocene epoch (Ice age)
.793	Recent (Postglacial) epoch

.8   Structural geology

> Class here deformation, diastrophism, epeirogeny, tectonics
>
> Class geomorphology in 551.41
>
> *For plate tectonics, see 551.136*

.81   Stratifications

.810 9   Historical, geographic, persons treatment

> Do not use for geographic treatment of stratifications during a specific geologic period; class in 551.71–551.79

[.810 94–.810 99]   Stratifications by specific continents, countries, localities in modern world; extraterrestrial worlds

> Do not use; class in 554–559

.82   Orogeny

> Class here lateral compression of earth's crust, specific orogenies
>
> Class comprehensive works on elevations (e.g., mountains, plateaus, hills) in 551.43. Class a specific aspect of orogeny with the aspect, e.g., volcanism 551.21

.84   Joints and cleavages

> Standard subdivisions are added for either or both topics in heading

.85   Dips, outcrops, strikes

.86   Anticlines and synclines

.87   Faults and folds

.872   Faults

> Including nappes, rift valleys
>
> Class here dislocations
>
> Class nappes produced by folding in 551.875

.875   Folds

> *For anticlines and synclines, see 551.86*

.88   Intrusions

> Including dikes, laccoliths, necks, sills, veins
>
> Class volcanoes in 551.21

.9   Geochemistry

> *For geochemistry of a specific subject in earth sciences or mineralogy, see the subject, e.g., organic geochemistry 553.2*

552 Petrology

Class here petrography, lithology, rocks

Class structural geology in 551.8

For mineralogy, see 549; for petrology of geologic materials of economic utility other than structural and sculptural stone, see 553

See Manual at 552 vs. 549

.001–.008 Standard subdivisions

.009 Historical, geographic, persons treatment

Do not use for geographic distribution of rocks; class in 552.09

.03 Petrogenesis

Class here diagenesis

.06 Properties, composition, analysis, structure of rocks

Class comprehensive works on geochemistry in 551.9

.09 Geographic distribution of rocks

Add to base number 552.09 notation 1–9 from Table 2, e.g., rocks of Sahara Desert 552.0966

Class rocks studied in their stratigraphic setting in 554–559

> **552.1–552.5 Specific kinds of rocks**

Class comprehensive works in 552

.1 **Igneous rocks**

For volcanic rocks, see 552.2; for plutonic rocks, see 552.3

.2 **Volcanic rocks**

Class here aphanites

Volcanic volatiles relocated to 551.23

.22 Lava

Including felsites, obsidian, rhyolite

Class pyroclastic felsites in 552.23

For basalts, see 552.26

.23 Pyroclastic rocks

Including andesite, pumice, tuff, volcanic ash

Class andesitic lava in 552.22

.26   Basalts

Including pillow lava

Class basaltic pyroclastic rocks in 552.23

.3   **Plutonic rocks**

Including diorites, dolerites, gabbros, granites, norites, peridotites, porphyries, syenites

Class here phanerites

.4   **Metamorphic rocks**

Including serpentinites [*formerly also* 552.58], gneisses, marbles, quartzites, schists, slates

.5   **Sedimentary rocks**

Including gypsum, sandstones, shales, tufa; clay, diatomaceous earth, sand, silt, soil

Class here comprehensive works on sedimentology

Class pyroclastic tufa (tuff) in 552.23

For sedimentology as study of surface processes, see 551.3

.58   Carbonate rocks

Including chalk, dolomites, limestones, oolites

Serpentinites relocated to 552.4

.8   **Microscopic petrology**

Class microscopic petrology of specific kinds of rocks in 552.1–552.5

553   Economic geology

Quantitative occurrence and distribution of geologic materials of economic utility

Class here interdisciplinary works on nonmetallic geologic materials

Class economic aspects other than reserves of geologic materials in 333.7; class interdisciplinary works on metals in 669

For a specific aspect of nonmetallic geologic materials other than economic geology, see the aspect, e.g., prospecting 622.18

See Manual at 553; also at 553 vs. 333.8, 338.2

SUMMARY

.1   Formation and structure of deposits

> Class formation and structure of deposits of specific materials in 553.2–553.9

.13   Placer deposits

.14   Stratified layers and beds

.16   Pegmatite dikes

.19   Veins and lodes

> **553.2–553.9   Specific materials**

> Class comprehensive works in 553

.2   Carbonaceous materials

> Class here fossil fuels, organic geochemistry

> *For diamonds, see 553.82; for jet, see 553.87; for amber, see 553.879*

> 553.21–553.25   Coal

> Class comprehensive works in 553.24

.21   Peat

> Including peat coal

.22   Lignite (Brown coal)

> Jet relocated to 553.87

.23   Cannel coal

.24   Bituminous and semibituminous coal

> Standard subdivisions are added for bituminous and semibituminous coal together, for bituminous coal alone

> Class here comprehensive works on coal

> *For peat, see 553.21; for lignite, see 553.22; for cannel coal, see 553.23; for anthracite, see 553.25*

.25	Anthracite
.26	Graphite

> Variant names: black lead, plumbago
>
> Class graphitic anthracite coal in 553.25

.27	Solid and semisolid bitumens

> Standard subdivisions are added for either or both topics in heading
>
> Including ozokerite
>
> Class here asphalt (pitch)
>
> Class liquid bitumens (oil) in 553.282; class rocks and sands impregnated with solid or semisolid bitumens in 553.283

.28	Oil, oil shales, tar sands, natural gas

> Class here petroleum geology
>
> Use 553.28 for petroleum in the broad sense covering oil and gas, 553.282 for petroleum in the narrow sense limited to oil

.282	Oil
.283	Oil shale and tar sands

> Variant names for oil shale: bituminous shale, black shale; for tar sands: bituminous sands, oil sands

.285	Natural gas
.29	Fossil resins and gums

> Standard subdivisions are added for fossil resins and gums together, for fossil resins alone
>
> Amber relocated to 553.879

.3	**Iron**
.4	**Metals and semimetals**

> Standard subdivisions are added for metals and semimetals together, for metals alone
>
> *For iron, see 553.3*

.41	Gold
.42	Precious metals

> *For gold, see 553.41*

.421	Silver
.422	Platinum

.43	Copper
.44	Lead
.45	Zinc, tin, mercury
.452	Zinc
.453	Tin
.454	Mercury
.46	Metals used in ferroalloys

For cobalt and nickel, see 553.48

.462	Titanium, vanadium, manganese
.462 3	Titanium
.462 6	Vanadium
.462 9	Manganese
.464	Chromium, molybdenum, tungsten
.464 3	Chromium
.464 6	Molybdenum
.464 9	Tungsten
.465	Zirconium and tantalum
.47	Antimony, arsenic, bismuth
.48	Cobalt and nickel
.483	Cobalt
.485	Nickel
.49	Other metals
.492	Light metals
.492 3	Beryllium
.492 6	Aluminum
.492 9	Magnesium
.493	Fissionable metals

Including radium, thorium

.493 2	Uranium
.494	Rare-earth metals

Class here lanthanide series

.494 2	Scandium
.494 3	Cerium group
.494 7	Yttrium group
.495	Platinum metals

> *For platinum, see 553.422*

.499	Metals not provided for elsewhere

> Including barium, indium, lithium, niobium, sodium, tellurium
>
> Class here semimetals
>
> *For antimony, arsenic, bismuth, see 553.47*

.5   Structural and sculptural stone

> Standard subdivisions are added for either or both topics in heading
>
> Class petrology of structural and sculptural stone in 552
>
> *For semiprecious sculptural stone, see 553.87*

.51	Marble and limestone
.512	Marble

> *For verd antique and onyx marble, see 553.55*

.516	Limestone

> Including dolomite, travertine

.52	Granite and syenite

> Standard subdivisions are added for granite and syenite together, for granite alone

.53	Sandstone

> Including bluestone, flagstones
>
> *For flagstones of a specific stone other than sandstone, see the stone, e.g., slate 553.54*

.54	Slate
.55	Serpentine, soapstone (steatite), and their variants

> Including verd antique and onyx marble
>
> *See also 553.87 for onyx*

.6   Other economic materials

> Including diatomaceous earth
>
> Class here earthy materials, industrial minerals
>
> *For soils, see 631.4*

.61	Clay

Including bentonite, diaspore clay, kaolin; fuller's earth

Class here comprehensive works on ceramic materials

> *For fireclay, see 553.67. For a specific nonclay ceramic material, see the material, e.g., glass sands 553.622*

.62	Sand and gravel

Class here aggregates

.622	Sand

Including glass sand

.626	Gravel
.63	Salts

> *For saltpeter, see 553.64; for mineral waters, see 553.73*

.632	Rock salt (Sodium chloride)
.633	Borates

Including borax

.635	Gypsum

Including alabaster

.636	Potash salts

Class here potassium minerals

.64	Nitrates and phosphates

Including apatites, saltpeter

Class here mineral fertilizers

.65	Abrasives

Including corundum, flint, industrial diamonds

Class comprehensive works on abrasives that are also gems in 553.8

> *For sand, see 553.622*

.66	Mineral pigments and sulfur
.662	Mineral pigments

Including barite

.668	Sulfur

.67	Refractory materials

Including alumina, fireclay

For soapstone, see 553.55

.672	Asbestos
.674	Mica
.676	Talc
.678	Vermiculite
.68	Cement materials

Including chalk, lime, marl

For gypsum, see 553.635

.7	**Water**

Including ice

Class interdisciplinary works on thermal waters in 333.88; class interdisciplinary works on ice in 551.31

For geology of thermal waters, see 551.23

See Manual at 363.61

.72	Saline water
.73	Mineral waters

For saline water, see 553.72

.78	Surface water
.79	Groundwater (Subsurface water)
.8	**Gems**

Class here comprehensive works on stones that are both gems and abrasives

For gemstones treated as abrasives, see 553.65

>	553.82–553.86 Precious stones

Class comprehensive works in 553.8

.82	Diamonds

For industrial diamonds, see 553.65

.84	Rubies and sapphires
.86	Emeralds

.87	Semiprecious stones

Including jet [*formerly* 553.22], agates, amethysts, garnet, tourmaline, turquoise

.873	Opals
.876	Jade

Class here jadite, nephrite

.879	Amber [*formerly* 553.29]
.9	**Inorganic gases**
.92	Hydrogen
.93	Nitrogen
.94	Oxygen
.95	Chlorine and fluorine
.97	Noble gases

Variant name: inert, rare gases

Including radon

.971	Helium

554–559 Earth sciences by specific continents, countries, localities in modern world; extraterrestrial worlds

Class here geology, geological surveys, stratifications

Add to base number 55 notation 4–9 from Table 2, e.g., geology of Japan 555.2, of moon 559.91

Class historical geology and stratifications of specific continents, countries, localities during a specific period in 551.71–551.79; class geological surveys of specific areas emphasizing materials of economic importance in 553.094–553.099; class comprehensive works on earth sciences in 550; class comprehensive works on geology in 551. Class a specific geologic topic (other than historical geology taken as a whole) in a specific area with the topic, e.g., volcanoes in Japan 551.210952, geomorphology of Japan 551.410952

See Manual at 559.9

> ## 560–590 Life sciences

Class comprehensive works in 570

See Manual at 560–590

560   Paleontology   Paleozoology

This schedule is extensively revised, 569 in particular having been prepared with little reference to earlier editions

A comparative table giving both old and new numbers for a substantial list of topics and equivalence tables showing the numbers in the old and new schedules appear in volume 1 in this edition

Including organisms of uncertain status as plant or animal, as chordate or invertebrate

Class the analysis of paleontological evidence to determine geological time and age in 551.701; class the analysis of paleontological evidence to determine a specific geological age in 551.71–551.79; class comprehensive works on paleontology and historic geology in 560

> *See Manual at 560: Specific plants and animals; also at 551.7 vs. 560; also at 576.8 vs. 560*

SUMMARY

560.1–.9	**Standard subdivisions; stratigraphic paleontology, paleoecology**
561	**Paleobotany; fossil microorganisms, fungi, algae**
562	**Fossil invertebrates**
563	**Miscellaneous fossil marine and seashore invertebrates**
564	**Fossil Mollusca and Molluscoidea**
565	**Fossil Arthropoda**
566	**Fossil Chordata**
567	**Fossil cold-blooded vertebrates Fossil Pisces (fishes)**
568	**Fossil Aves (birds)**
569	**Fossil Mammalia**

.1   Philosophy and theory; stratigraphic paleontology

.17   Stratigraphic paleontology

Class here stratigraphic paleozoology

Add to base number 560.17 the numbers following 551.7 in 551.71–551.79, e.g., Precambrian paleontology 560.171

Class fossils of specific kinds of organisms in 561–569

.4   Special topics

.45   Paleoecology and fossils of specific environments

Class here zoological paleoecology and fossil animals of specific environments

Add to base number 560.45 the numbers following 577 in 577.01–577.7, e.g., marine paleoecology 577.7

Subdivisions are added for either or both topics in heading

.9   Historical, geographic, persons treatment

Class stratigraphic paleontology and paleozoology in 560.17

[.914–.919]   Treatment by areas, regions, places in general other than polar,
temperate, tropical regions

>   Do not use; class in 560.45

561   Paleobotany; fossil microorganisms

Including plantlike fossils of uncertain taxonomic position

Class here fossil Spermatophyta, Angiospermae

Class fernlike fossils of uncertain taxonomic position in 561.597

.09   Historical, geographic, persons treatment

For geographic treatment of fossil plants, see 561.19

[.091 4–.091 9]   Treatment by areas, regions, places in general other than polar,
temperate, tropical regions

>   Do not use; class in 561.1

.1   **General topics of paleobotany**

Including botanical paleoecology, plant fossils of specific environments,
stratigraphic paleobotany

Class general topics of specific plants and groups of plants in 561.3–561.9

.13   Fossil pollen and spores

Standard subdivisions are added for either or both topics in heading

Class here comprehensive works on paleopalynology

*For physiology of pollen, see 571.845; for physiology of spores, see
571.847*

.14   Fossil fruits and seeds

Standard subdivisions are added for either or both topics in heading

.16   Trees and petrified wood

Standard subdivisions are added for either or both topics in heading

.19   Geographic treatment of fossil plants

Add to base number 561.19 notation 1–9 from Table 2, e.g., plant fossils of
West indies 561.19729; however, class treatment by areas, regions, places
in general other than polar, temperate, tropical regions in 561.1

>   **561.3–561.9 Specific plants and groups of plants**

Class comprehensive works in 561

.3   **Fossil Magnoliopsida (dicotyledons)**

.4   **Fossil Liliopsida (monocotyledons)**

.45	Arecidae

Class here Arecales (Palmales), Arecaceae (Palmae, palm family)

.49	Poales (Graminales, grasses)
.5	**Fossil Pinophyta (gymnosperms) and fernlike fossils of uncertain taxonomic position**

Standard subdivisions are added for fossil Pinophyta and fernlike fossils of uncertain taxonomic position together, for fossil Pinophyta alone

Class here Coniferales (conifers)

.52–.55	Coniferales (Conifers)

Add to base number 561.5 the numbers following 585 in 585.2–585.5, e.g., fossil Pinaceae 561.52

.56	Taxales
.57	Ginkgoales
.58	Gneticae
.59	Cycadales, Cycadeoidales, Pteridospermae, fernlike fossils of uncertain taxonomic position, Cordaitales
.591	Cycadales (True cycads)
.592	Cycadeoidales (Bennettitales)

Including Cycadeoidaceae, Williamsoniaceae

.595	Pteridospermae (Seed ferns)

Including Calamopityaceae, Lyginopteridaceae, Medullosaceae

.597	Fernlike fossils of uncertain taxonomic position

Including Alethopteris, Alliopteris, Archaeopteris, Callipteris, Cyclopteris, Glossopteris, Linopteris, Mariopteris, Megalopteris, Neuropteris, Odontopteris, Pecopteris, Rhacopteris, Sphenopteris, Taeniopteris

.6	**Fossil Cryptogamia**

For Pteridophyta, see 561.7; for Bryophyta, see 561.8; for microorganisms, fungi, algae, see 561.9

.7	**Fossil Pteridophyta**

Class fernlike fossils of uncertain taxonomic position in 561.597

.72	Sphenopsida

Including Calamitales, Equisetales, Hyeniales, Pseudoborniales, Sphenophyllales

.73   Polypodiopsida (Filicopsida)

> Including Coenopteridales, Filicales, Marattiales, Ophioglossales

.74   Psilopsida

> Including Psilophytales, Psilotales

.79   Lycopsida (Club mosses)

> Including Isoetales, Lepidodendrales, Pleuromeiales, Protolepidodendrales

.8   Fossil Bryophyta

.9   Fossil microorganisms, fungi, algae

.91   Prokaryotes

> Class here bacteria

.92   Fungi

.93   Algae

.99   Protozoa

.992   Zoomastigophorea

.994   Foraminifera

.995   Radiolaria

> **562–569   Specific taxonomic groups of animals**

> Class here taxonomic paleozoology
>
> Class comprehensive works in 560

562   Fossil invertebrates

> *For Protozoa, see 561.99; for miscellaneous marine and seashore invertebrates, see 563; for Mollusca and Molluscoidea, see 564; for Arthropoda, see 565*

.2   Conodonts

.3–.7   Worms and related animals

> Add to base number 562 the numbers following 592 in 592.3–592.7, e.g., annelida 562.6
>
> Class comprehensive works in 562.3

563   Miscellaneous fossil marine and seashore invertebrates

[.01–.09]   Standard subdivisions

> Do not use; class in 562.01–562.09

.4   **Porifera (Sponges) and Archaeocyatha**

Standard subdivisions are added for Porifera and Archaeocyatha together, for Porifera alone

Class here Parazoa

.47   Archaeocyatha

.5   **Cnidaria (Coelenterata)**

Including Scyphozoa

For Anthozoa, see 563.6

.55   Hydrozoa

Including Graptolitoidea

.58   Stromatoporoidea

.6   **Anthozoa**

Class here corals

Class Archaeocyatha in 563.47

.8   **Ctenophora**

.9   **Echinodermata and Hemichordata**

Standard subdivisions are added for Echinodermata and Hemichordata together, for Echinodermata alone

---

>   563.92–563.96   Echinodermata

Class comprehensive works in 563.9

.92   Crinozoa, Blastozoa, Homalozoa

Standard subdivisions are added for Crinozoa, Blastozoa, Homalozoa together; for Crinozoa alone

Including Camerata, Flexibilia, Inadunata; carpoids

.93   Asterozoa (Starfish)

For Ophiuroidea, see 563.94

.94   Ophiuroidea

.95   Echinozoa

Including Cystoidea

For Holothurioidea, see 563.96

.96   Holothurioidea

Including Arthrochirotida

.99   Hemichordata

> Including Enteropneusta, Planctosphaeroidea
>
> Class here Pterobranchia

564   Fossil Mollusca and Molluscoidea

> ### 564.2–564.5 Mollusca (Mollusks)
>
> Class comprehensive works in 564

.2–.4   **Specific Mollusca other than Cephalopoda**

> Add to base number 564 the numbers following 594 in 594.2–594.4, e.g., Bivalvia 564.4

.5   **Cephalopoda**

.52   Nautiloidea

.53   Ammonoidea

.56   Octopoda

.58   Decapoda

.6   **Molluscoidea**

> Including Entoprocta

.67   Bryozoa

.68   Brachiopoda (Lamp shells)

565   Fossil Arthropoda

.3   **Crustacea and Trilobita**

> Standard subdivisions are added for Crustacea and Trilobita together, for Crustacea alone

.32–.38   Specific kinds of Crustacea

> Add to base number 565.3 the numbers following 595.3 in 595.32–595.38, e.g., Ostracoda 565.33

.39   Trilobita

.4   **Chelicerata**

> Including Architarbi
>
> Class here Arachnida

.49   Merostomata and Pycnogonida

> Standard subdivisions are added for Merostomata and Pycnogonida together, for Merostomata alone

.492   Xiphosura (Horseshoe crabs)

.493   Eurypterida

.6   Myriapoda

.7   Insecta

Class here Uniramia, Hexapoda, Pterygota

Add to base number 565.7 the numbers following 595.7 in 595.72–595.79, e.g., Coleoptera 565.76

For Myriapoda, see 565.6

566   Fossil Chordata

Including Cephalochordata, Urochordata (Tunicata)

Class here Vertebrata (Craniata, vertebrates), Tetrapoda (land vertebrates)

For fossil cold-blooded vertebrates, see 567; for fossil Aves, see 568; for fossil Mammalia, see 569

567   Fossil cold-blooded vertebrates   Fossil Pisces (fishes)

Including Leptolepis

Class here Actinopterygii, Osteichthyes, Teleostei

Class specific kinds of Actinopterygii, Osteichthyes, Teleostei in 567.4–567.7

\>   **567.2–567.7   Fossil Pisces (fishes)**

Class comprehensive works in 567

.2   Agnatha, Acanthodii, Placodermi

Including Cyclostomata

.3   Chondrichthyes and Sarcopterygii

Standard subdivisions are added for Chondrichthyes and Sarcopterygii together, for Chondrichthyes alone

Including Bradyodonti, Cladoselachii, Pleuracanthodii

Class here Elasmobranchii, Selachii; sharks

Add to base number 597.3 the numbers following 597.3 in 597.33–597.39, e.g., Sarcopterygii 567.39

.4–.7   Specific fossil Actinopterygii

Class here Osteichthyes, Teleostei

Add to base number 567 the numbers following 597 in 597.4–597.7, e.g., Salmoniformes 567.5

Class fossil Actinopterygii not traceable to surviving superorders, e.g., Leptolepis; comprehensive works on Actinopterygii, Osteichthyes, Teleostei in 567

For Sarcopterygii, see 567.39

.8   Amphibia

Including Anura, Gymnophiona, Labyrinthodontia, Lepospondyli, Urodela

.9   Reptilia

Class here Archosauria, Diapsida, Dinosaurs

.91   Specific dinosaurs and other Archosauria

Including Thecodontia

For Crocodilia, see 567.98. For a "dinosaur" of an order not assigned to Archosauria, see the order, e.g., Ichthyosauria 567.937

[.910 1–.910 9]   Standard subdivisions

Do not use; class in class in 567.901–567.909

>   567.912–567.915   Specific dinosaurs

Class comprehensive works in 567.9

.912   Saurischia

Including Allosaurus, Baryonyx, Coelophysis, Deinonychus, Oviraptor

Class here Theropoda (carnivorous dinosaurs)

For Sauropodomorpha, see 567.913

.912 9   Tyrannosaurus

.913   Sauropodomorpha (Herbivorous Saurischia)

Including Diplodocus, Seismosaurus

.913 8   Apatosaurus (Brontosaurus)

.914   Ornithischia

Including Hadrosauridae (duck-billed dinosaurs); Anatosaurus, Corythosaurus, Hypsilophodon, Iguanodon, Maiasaura, Pachycephalosaurus, Parasaurolophus

Class here Ornithopoda

For Stegosauria, Ankylosauria, Ceratopsia, see 567.915

.915   Stegosauria, Ankylosauria, Ceratopsia (horned dinosaurs)

Including Protoceratops

Class here armored dinosaurs

.915 3   Stegosaurus

.915 8   Triceratops

.918   Pterosauria (Flying reptiles)

Including Pteranodon, Pterodactylus

Class comprehensive works on flying and marine reptiles in 567.937

.92   Anapsida

Including Cotylosauria, Chelonia (Testudines)

For Mesosauria, see 567.937

.93   Euryapsida, Synapsida; Mesosauria

Including Araeoscelidia, Pelycosauria, Placodontia, Pelycosauria, Therapsida

.937   Marine reptiles

Including Ichthyosauria, Mesosauria, Sauropterygia (Nothosauria and Plesiosauria)

For Mosasauridae, see 567.95

.94   Lepidosauria

Including Eosuchia

Class here Squamata

For Sauria, see 567.95; for Serpentes, see 567.96

.945   Rhynchocephalia

.95   Sauria

Including Mosasauridae (marine lizards)

Class comprehensive works on Sauria and Serpentes in 567.94

.96   Serpentes

.98   Crocodilia

568   Fossil Aves (birds)

Class here Neornithes

.2   Archaeornithes, Hesperornithiformes, Ichthyornithiformes

.22   Archaeornithes

.23   Hesperornithiformes and Ichthyornithiformes

.3   **Charadriiformes, Ciconiiformes, Diatrymiformes, Gruiformes, Phoenicopteriformes**

.4   **Water birds**

> Including Anseriformes, Gaviiformes, Pelecaniformes, Podicipediformes, Procellariiformes, Sphenisciformes
>
> *For Charadriiformes, Ciconiiformes, Diatrymiformes, Gruiformes, Phoenicopteriformes, see 568.3*

.5   **Palaeognathae**

> Including Aepyornithiformes, Apterygiformes, Caenagnathiformes, Casuariiformes, Dinornithiformes, Rheiformes, Struthioniformes, Tinamiformes
>
> Class here ratites

.6   **Galliformes and Columbiformes**

> Standard subdivisions are added for Galliformes and Columbiformes together, for Galliformes alone

.7   **Miscellaneous land birds**

> Limited to those named herein
>
> Including Apodiformes, Coliiformes, Coraciiformes, Cuculiformes, Piciformes, Psittaciformes, Trogoniformes
>
> Class comprehensive works on land birds in 568

[.701–.709]   Standard subdivisions

> Do not use; class in 568.01–568.09

.8   **Passeriformes**

.9   **Falconiformes, Caprimulgiformes, Strigiformes**

> Standard subdivisions are added for Falconiformes, Caprimulgiformes, Strigiformes, together; for Falconiformes alone

569   Fossil Mammalia

.2   **Metatheria and Prototheria**

> Standard subdivisions are added for Metatheria and Prototheria together, for Metatheria alone
>
> Including Trituberculata
>
> Class here Marsupialia

.29   Prototheria

> Including Allotheria, Eotheria
>
> Class here Monotremata

> **569.3–569.9 Eutheria**

Class comprehensive works in 599

.3 **Miscellaneous orders of Eutheria**

Limited to those named below

[**.301–.309**] Standard subdivisions

Do not use; class in 569.01–569.09

.31 Edentata, Palaeanodonta, Pholidota, Taeniodontia, Tillodontia, Tubulidentata

.32–.37 Dermoptera, Insectivora, Lagomorpha, Macroscelidea, Rodentia, Scandentia

Add to base number 569.3 the numbers following 599.3 in 599.32–599.37, e.g., Insectivora 569.33

.4 **Chiroptera (Bats)**

Including Megachiroptera

Class here Microchiroptera

.5 **Cetacea, Desmostylia, Sirenia**

Standard subdivisions are added for Cetacea and Sirenia together, for Cetacea alone

Including Archaeoceti

Class here Mysticeti, Odontoceti; marine mammals, whales

For Pinnipedia, see 569.79

.6 **Ungulates**

Class Desmostylia, Sirenia in 569.5

.62 Extinct orders of ungulates

Including Astrapotheria, Condylarthra, Dinocerata, Embrithopoda, Litopterna, Notoungulata, Pantodonta, Pyrotheria, Xenungulata

Class extinct members of surviving orders in 569.63–569.68

.63–.68 Surviving orders of ungulates

Add to base number 569.6 the numbers following 599.6 in 599.63–599.68, e.g., Proboscidea 569.67

.7   **Carnivores**

Including Creodonta

Class here Fissipedia

Add to base number 569.7 the numbers following 599.7 in 599.74–599.79, e.g., Pinnipedia 567.79

.8   **Primates**

Class here Anthropoidea, monkeys

Add to base number 569.8 the numbers following 599.8 in 599.83–599.88, e.g., Pongidae 569.88

Class Tupaiidae in 569.338

For Hominidae, see 569.9

.9   **Hominidae (Humans and forebears)**

Including Australopithicus; Cro-Magnon, Heidelberg, Java, Neanderthal, Peking, Piltdown, Rhodesian men

Class here prehistoric humans, genus Homo [*formerly* 573.3]

Class progenitors of contemporary races in 599.972

570   Life sciences   Biology

This schedule is new and has been prepared with little or no reference to previous editions. Most numbers have been reused with new meanings

A comparative table giving both old and new numbers for a substantial list of topics and equivalence tables showing the numbers in the old and new schedules appear in volume 1 in this edition

In addition, human races relocated from 572 to 599.97; specific races relocated from 572.8 to 599.98; physical anthropology relocated from 573 to 599.9; prehistoric humans (paleozoology of Homo) relocated from 573.3 to 569.9; behavior relocated from 574.5 to 591.5; genetic engineering relocated from 575.10724 to 660.65; sexual selection relocated from 575.5 to 591.562; food microbiology relocated from 576.163 to 664.001579; microscopy of plants relocated from 578 to 580.282; microscopy of animals relocated from 578 to 590.282; collecting of botanical specimens relocated from 579 to 580.75; preserving botanical specimens relocated from 579 to 580.752; collecting zoological specimens relocated from 579 to 590.75; preserving zoological specimens relocated from 579 to 590.752

For paleontology, see 560; for plants, see 580; for animals, see 590; for medical sciences, see 610

See Manual at 560–590; also at 570–590: Number building; also at 578 vs. 304.2, 508, 910

SUMMARY

578		**Natural history of organisms and related subjects**
	.01–.09	**Standard subdivisions**
	.4	**Adaptation**
	.6	**Miscellaneous nontaxonomic kinds of organisms**
	.7	**Organisms characteristic of specific kinds of environments**
579		**Microorganisms, fungi, algae**
	.01–.09	**Standard subdivisions**
	.1	**Specific topics in natural history of microorganisms, fungi, algae**
	.2	**Viruses and subviral organisms**
	.3	**Prokaryotes (Bacteria)**
	.4	**Protozoa**
	.5	**Fungi Eumycophyta (True fungi)**
	.6	**Mushrooms**
	.7	**Lichens**
	.8	**Algae**

.1   Philosophy and theory

Class here nature of life, differences between living and nonliving substances

Class origin of life, conditions needed for life to begin in 576.83

.12   Classification

Class taxonomic classification in 578.012

.15   Scientific principles

.151 95   Statistical mathematics

Class here biometrics, biostatistics

See Manual at 519.5, T1—015195 vs. 001.422, T1—0727

.2   Miscellany

.28   Auxiliary techniques and procedures; apparatus, equipment, procedures; microscopy

.282   Microscopy

Including photomicrography

Class here microscopes

Class interdisciplinary works on microscopy in 502.82

.282 3   Compound microscopes

.282 5   Electron microscopes

.282 7   Slide preparation

Including fixation, staining; microtomy

.7   Education, research, related topics

.72   Research; statistical methods

.724   Experimental research

Class here experimental biology

Class tissue and organ culture in 571.538; class cell culture in 571.638

.75   Museum activities and services   Collecting

.752   Preserving biological specimens

.753   Organizing and preparing collections and exhibits

For preserving biological specimens, see 570.752

.9   Historical, geographic, persons treatment

For geographic treatment of organisms, see 578.09

.919   Space

Class space biology in 571.0919

.999   Extraterrestrial worlds

Do not use for extraterrestrial life; class in 576.83

> **571–575 Internal biological processes and structures**

Class here internal biological processes and structures in plants and animals [*formerly* 580–590]

Unless other instructions are given, class a subject with aspects in two or more subdivisions of 571–575 in the number coming last, e.g., cytology of animal circulatory system 573.136 (*not* 571.1 or 571.6)

Class comprehensive works in 571

See Manual at 571–575; also at 570–590: Add instructions in 571–575; also at 571–575 vs. 630; also at 571–573 vs. 610

> **571–572 General internal processes common to all organisms**

Add to each subdivision identified by * the numbers following 571 in 571.01–571.2, e.g., the subject in animals 1, the subject in plants and microorganisms 2

Class comprehensive works in 571

See Manual at 571–573 vs. 610

571   Physiology and related subjects

Standard subdivisions are added for physiology and related subjects, for physiology alone

Class here comprehensive works on internal biological processes

For biochemistry, see 572; for specific physiological systems in animals, regional histology and physiology, see 573; for specific parts of and physiological systems in plants, see 575; for genetics, see 576.5

See Manual at 571–575 vs. 630

SUMMARY

571.01–.09	**Standard subdivisions**	
.1	**Animals**	
.2	**Plants and microorganisms**	
.3	**Anatomy and morphology**	
.4	**Biophysics**	
.5	**Tissue biology and regional physiology**	
.6	**Cell biology**	
.7	**Biological control and secretions**	
.8	**Reproduction, development, growth**	
.9	**Diseases Pathology**	

.01–.08   Standard subdivisions

Notation from Table 1 as modified under 570.1–570.8, e.g., microscopy in physiology 571.0282

.09   Historical, geographic, persons treatment

.091 9   Space

Class here space biology

.099 9   Extraterrestrial worlds

Class extraterrestrial life in 576.83

.1   Animals

Class here comparative physiology

Add to base number 571.1 the numbers following 59 in 590.1–599, e.g., marine animals 571.1177, mammals 571.19; however, for physiology and related subjects in humans, see 612; for physiology and related subjects in domestic animals, see 636.0892

Class comprehensive works on animals in 590

For comparative physiology of plants and microorganisms, see 571.2; for Protozoa, see 571.294

See Manual at 570–590: Notation for specific organisms in 571–575

.2   **Plants and microorganisms**

> Standard subdivisions are added for plants and microorganisms together, for plants alone
>
> Class here comparative physiology of plants and microorganisms, physiology of agricultural plants
>
> Class comprehensive works on plants in 580
>
> > *See Manual at 570–590: Notation for specific organisms in 571–575*

.201–.28   Standard subdivisions and specific plants

> > Add to base number 571.2 the numbers following 58 in 580.1–588, e.g., aquatic plants 571.2176, monocotyledons 571.24
> >
> > *For fungi, see 571.295; for algae, see 571.298*

.29   Microorganisms, fungi, algae

> > Add to base number 571.29 the numbers following 579 in 579.01–579.8, e.g., marine microorganisms 571.29177, Protozoa 571.294
> >
> > Subdivisions are added for microorganisms, fungi, algae together, for microorganisms alone
> >
> > Class comprehensive works on microorganisms, fungi, algae in 579
> >
> > > *See Manual at 571.629 vs. 571.29*

.3   ***Anatomy and morphology**

> Class here comparative anatomy
>
> Subdivisions are added for either or both topics in heading
>
> > *For anatomy and morphology of microorganisms, see 571.63329*

.4   ***Biophysics**

> Class here effects of physical forces on organisms
>
> Class comprehensive works on biophysics and biochemistry in 572
>
> > *For bioenergetics, physical biochemistry, see 572.43*

.43   *Biomechanics and effects of mechanical forces

> Class here biodynamics, solid biomechanics
>
> Subdivisions are added for either or both topics in heading
>
> Class biomechanics of locomotion in 573.79343

.435   *Gravity

.437   *Pressure

.44   *Effects of mechanical vibrations, sound, related vibrations

---

*Add as instructed under 571–572

.443	*Mechanical vibrations

Class here subsonic vibrations

.444	*Sound
.445	*Ultrasonic vibrations
.45	*Radiobiology
.453	*Radio waves and microwaves

Subdivisions are added for either or both topics in heading

.454	*Infrared radiation
.455	*Light
.456	*Ultraviolet radiation
.457	*X rays
.459	*Particle radiations

Including beta, gamma, neutron radiations; cosmic rays

For X rays, see 571.457

.46	*Effects of low and high temperatures
.464	*Low temperatures
.464 5	*Cryogenic temperatures (Cryobiology)
.467	*High temperatures
.47	*Effects of electricity and magnetism

Subdivisions are added for effects of electricity and magnetism together, for effects of electricity alone

.49	*Environmental biophysics

Effects of combinations of physical forces characteristic of unusual environments

Including effects of climate, high altitudes

Class effects of a specific physical force with the force in 571.43–571.47

.499	*Extraterrestrial biophysics

Class here bioastronautics

*Add as instructed under 571–572

> **571.5–571.9 Tissue biology, regional physiology, cell biology, biological control and secretions, reproduction, development, growth, diseases**

> Except for modifications shown under specific entries, add to each subdivision identified by † as follows:
>
> 01–2   Standard subdivisions and specific kinds of organisms
>   Add the numbers following 571 in 571.01–571.2, e.g., the subject in animals 1, the subject in plants 2
> 3   Anatomy and application of processes to other processes
> [301–309]   Standard subdivisions
>   Do not use; class in 01–09
> 33–38   Anatomy and application of specific processes to other processes
>   Add to 3 the numbers following 571 in 571.3–571.8, e.g., anatomy 33, biophysics 34, cell biology 36

> Class comprehensive works in 571.5

.5   ***Tissue biology and regional physiology**

> Class here histology, histophysiology; comprehensive works on tissue and cell biology

> Subdivisions are added for tissue biology and regional physiology together, for tissue biology alone

> Class biophysics of tissues in general in 571.4; class biophysics of specific tissues in 571.55–571.58

> *For cell biology, see 571.6; for histogenesis, see 571.835*

.53   Tissue anatomy, morphology, culture

[.530 1–.530 9]   Standard subdivisions

> Do not use; class in 571.501–571.509

.533   *Tissue anatomy and morphology

> Subdivisions are added for either or both topics in heading

.538   *Tissue culture

> Class here organ culture, comprehensive works on tissue and cell culture

> *For cell culture, see 571.638*

> **571.55–571.57 Specific tissues in animals**

> Class comprehensive works in 571.51

> *For tissues of a specific physiological system, see the system in 573, plus notation 35 from table under 573, e.g., tissues of circulatory system 573.135*

*Add as instructed under 571–572

.55	†Epithelial tissues
.555	†Endothelium
.56	†Connective tissues

For adipose tissues, see 571.57

.57	†Adipose tissues
.58	Specific tissues in plants

Class comprehensive works in 571.52

For tissues of a specific part or physiological system, see the part or physiological system in 575, plus notation 35 from table under 575, e.g., tissues of leaves 575.5735

[.580 1–.580 9]   Standard subdivisions

Do not use; class in 571.5201–571.5209

.585   †Parenchyma

Class here pith, sclerenchyma

.59   Regional histology and physiology

Standard subdivisions are added for either or both topics in heading

For regional histology and physiology of animals, see 573.99; for regional physiology of plants, see 575.4; for regional histology of plants, see 575.4359

.590 1–.590 9   Standard subdivisions

Notation from Table 1 as modified under 570.1–570.9, e.g., microscopy in regional physiology 571.590282

.592   Fungi and algae

.592 9   Specific fungi and algae

Add to base number 571.5929 the numbers following 579 in 579.5–579.8, e.g., regional physiology of mushrooms 571.59296

.6   *Cell biology

Class here cell physiology, cytology, eukaryotic cells, protoplasm

For reproduction and growth of cells, see 571.84; for cytopathology, see 571.936; for cytochemistry, see 572; for cell digestion, metabolism, nutrition, see 572.4; for cell respiration, see 572.47

.629   Microorganisms, fungi, algae

Number built according to instructions under 571–572

See Manual at 571.629 vs. 571.29

---

*Add as instructed under 571–572

†Add as instructed under 571.5–571.9

.63	Cell anatomy, morphology, biophysics, culture
[.630 1–.630 9]	Standard subdivisions

          Do not use; class in 571.601–571.609

.633	*Cell anatomy and morphology

          Subdivisions are added for either or both topics in heading

.634	Cell biophysics

          Add to base number 571.63 the numbers following 571 in 571.401–571.49, e.g., effect of high temperatures on cells 571.63467

.638	*Cell culture

          Class comprehensive works on tissue and cell culture in 571.538

.64	†Membranes

          Class here biological transport, ion transport

          For membranes of specific cellular components, see 571.65–571.68

.65	†Cytoplasm

          Class here endoplasmic reticulum, organelles

.654	†Cytoskeleton

          Class here microfilaments, microtubules

.655	†Vacuoles

          Including peroxisomes

          Class here lysosomes, vesicles

.656	†Golgi apparatus
.657	†Mitochondria
.658	†Ribosomes
.659	†Plastids
.659 2	Plants and microorganisms

          Number built according to instructions under 571.5–571.9

          Class here chloroplasts

.66	†Nucleus

          Including linin network, nuclear envelope, nuclear membrane, nucleolus

          Class here nucleoplasm

          Class nucleic acids in 572.8

          For chromosomes, see 572.87

*Add as instructed under 571–572

†Add as instructed under 571.5–571.9

.67	†Cell movement
	Including basal body
	Class here cilia, flagella, irritability, pseudopoda
.68	†Cell walls

.7 †Biological control and secretions

Biological control: control of an organism's own physiological processes

Subdivisions are added for biological control and secretions together, for biological control alone

> *See also 632.96 for biological control of agricultural pests*

.71	Animals
	Number built according to instructions under 571.5–571.9
	Class here comprehensive works on endocrine and nervous systems

> *For endocrine system, see 573.4; for nervous and sensory systems, see 573.8*

| .72 | Plants and microorganisms |
| | Number built according to instructions under 571.5–571.9 |

> *See also 575.9 for animal-like physiological processes in plants*

| .74 | †Biochemistry of control |
| | Class here comprehensive works on hormones |

> *For animal hormones, see 573.44*
>
> *See Manual at 573.44 vs. 571.74: Hormones*

.75	†Homeostasis and physiological balance
	Subdivisions are added for either or both topics in heading
.76	†Body temperature
	Class here homoiothermy, poikilothermy
.77	†Periodicity
	Class here biorhythms, chronobiology
.78	†Dormancy
.785	†Diapause
.786	†Aestivation
.787	†Hibernation
	Class comprehensive works on hibernation in 591.565

†Add as instructed under 571.5–571.9

.79	†Secretions

Other than hormones

Class here exocrine secretions, comprehensive works on glands

Class excretory system of animals in 573.49

> *For endocrine glands, see 573.4. For secretions of a specific organ or system, or ones related to a specific process, see the organ, system or process, plus notation 379 from add tables under 571.5–571.9, 573, 575, e.g., digestive secretions 573.3379*

.8 **†Reproduction, development, growth**

Class here life cycle, sexual reproduction

Subdivisions are added for any or all topics in heading

> *See Manual at 571.8 vs. 573.6, 575.6*

.81 Animals

Number built according to instructions under 571.5–571.9

> *For reproduction, sexual reproduction in animals, see 573.6*

.82 Plants and microorganisms

Number built according to instructions under 571.5–571.9

> *For reproduction, sexual reproduction in plants, see 575.6*

.829 Fungi and algae

Number built according to instructions under 571.5–571.9

Class reproduction and development of unicellular microorganisms in 571.8429; class sexual reproduction of unicellular microorganisms in 571.84529

.835 Histogenesis

Number built according to instructions under 571.5–571.9

Class here cell differentiation, tissue differentiation

[.836] Cell biology

Do not use for cell differentiation; class in 571.835. Do not use for cell reproduction and growth; class in 571.84

.84 †Reproduction and growth of cells

Subdivisions are added for reproduction and growth together, for reproduction alone

Class chromosome recombination in 572.877

> *For cell differentiation, see 571.835*

†Add as instructed under 571.5–571.9

.844	†Cell division
	Including centromeres, chromatids
	Class here mitosis
.845	†Gametogenesis
	Including egg cells, megaspores, pollen (microspores), sperm
	Class here meiosis; germ, haploid, sex cells
	Class comprehensive works on palynology, pollen in 561.13
	For maturation and fertilization of gametes, see 571.864
.847	†Reproduction by asexual spores
	Class here spores, sporulation
	Class comprehensive works on spores in 561.13
.849	†Cell growth
	Class cell differentiation in 571.835
.85	†Developmental genetics
.86	†Embryology
	Class comprehensive works on developmental biology in 571.8
.864	†Fertilization
	Including maturation of gametes
	Class here zygotes
.864 2	Fertilization in plants and microorganisms
	Number built according to instructions under 571.5–571.9
	Class here pollination
	For coevolution of pollination, see 576.875
.865	†Early cell division
	Class here blastulas, gastrulation
.87	†Development after embryo
	Class here maturation
	Class comprehensive works on development in 571.8
.876	†Development in distinct stages
	Class here comprehensive works on metamorphosis
	For embryo stage, see 571.86

†Add as instructed under 571.5–571.9

.878	†Aging	

Class pathological aging and death in 571.939

.879	†Longevity
.88	Miscellaneous topics in reproduction

Limited to topics named below

[.880 1–.880 9]	Standard subdivisions

Do not use; class in 571.801–571.809

.882	†Sex differentiation

For gametogenesis, see 571.845

.882 157 9   Sex differentiation in Hymenoptera

Number built according to instructions under 571.5–571.9

Class here physiology of caste differentiation among social insects

.884	†Alternation of generations (Metagenesis)
.886	†Hermaphroditism
.887	†Parthenogenesis

Class comprehensive works on asexual reproduction in 571.89

.889	†Regeneration
.89	†Vegetative reproduction

Class here asexual reproduction

For asexual reproduction of microorganisms, see 571.8429; for parthenogenesis, see 571.887

.892	Microorganisms, fungi, algae

Number built according to instructions under 571.5–571.9

Do not use for vegetative reproduction of plants; class in 575.49

.892 9	Specific microorganisms, fungi, algae

Number built according to instructions under 571.5–571.9

Add to base number 571.8929 the numbers following 579 in 579.2–579.8, e.g., vegetative reproduction of fungi 571.89295

†Add as instructed under 571.5–571.9

.9 ***Diseases** **Pathology**

Class here histopathology, pathogenicity, pathophysiology

For human diseases, results of experimental research on human diseases in animals, see 616. For diseases of a specific physiological system in animals, see the system in 573, plus notation 39 from table under 573, e.g., bone diseases 573.7639; for diseases of specific parts of and physiological systems in plants, see the part or system in 575, plus notation 39 from table under 575, e.g., diseases of leaves 575.5739

.93 Generalities of diseases

[.930 1–.930 9] Standard subdivisions

Do not use; class in 571.901–571.909

.933–.938 General topics of disease

Add to base number 571.93 the numbers following 571 in 571.3–571.8, e.g., pathological anatomy 571.933, physical causes of diseases 571.934, radiation injury 571.9345, tissue degeneration 571.935, cytopathology 571.936, developmental disorders 571.938; however, for pathological aging, see 571.939

Class comprehensive works in 571.9

.939 †Pathological aging and death

Subdivisions are added for either or both topics in heading

.94 Pathological biochemistry

Add to base number 571.94 the numbers following 572 in 572.01–572.8, e.g., metabolic diseases 571.944, protein deficiency 571.946, genetic diseases 571.948

.95 †Toxicology

Class here diseases and stress caused by pollutants, by water pollution; ecotoxicology, environmental diseases, poisons

For environmental diseases induced by physical stresses, see 571.934

See Manual at 363.73 vs. 571.95, 577.27

.954 Specific elements and groups of elements

[.954 01–.954 09] Standard subdivisions

Do not use; class in 571.9501–571.9509

.954 3–.954 7 Specific elements and groups of elements

Add to base number 571.954 the numbers following 546 in 546.3–546.7 for the element or group of elements only, e.g., metal toxicology 571.9543, mercury toxicology 571.954663

*Add as instructed under 571–572

†Add as instructed under 571.5–571.9

.956	†Air pollutants
	Class here products of combustion
.957	†Organic compounds
	Class organic pesticides in 571.959
.959	†Pesticides
.96	†Immunity

Class here disease resistance, immune system, immunology, leukocytes, lymphocytes

Class allergies in 571.972; class autoimmunity in 571.973; class immune deficiency diseases in 571.974

See Manual at 616.079 vs. 571.96

.964	†Immunochemistry and immune response

Subdivisions are added for immunochemistry and immune response together, for immunochemistry alone

.964 4	†Interferons
.964 5	†Antigens
.964 6	†Immune response

Including clonal selection

Class here antigen recognition

Class antigen-antibody reactions in 571.9677

.964 8	†Immunogenetics

Including transduction, transfection, transformation

.966	†T cells (T lymphocytes)

Class here cell-mediated (cellular) immunity, cytotoxic T cells

See also 571.968 for killer cells

.967	†B cells (B lymphocytes)

Class here antibodies (immunoglobulins)

For maternally acquired antibodies, see 571.9638; for antibody-dependent immune mechanisms, see 571.968

.967 7	†Antigen-antibody reactions

†Add as instructed under 571.5–571.9

| .968 | †Phagocytes and complement |

Including granulocytes, killer cells

Class here antibody-dependent immune mechanisms

Subdivisions are added for phagocytes and complement together, for phagocytes alone

See also 571.966 for cytotoxic T cells

| .968 5 | †Macrophages |
| .968 8 | †Complement |

Class activation of macrophages by complement in 571.9685

| .97 | Miscellaneous diseases |

Limited to those named below

| [.970 1–.970 9] | Standard subdivisions |

Do not use; class in 571.901–571.909

| .972 | †Allergies |
| .973 | †Autoimmunity |

Class here autoimmune diseases

| .974 | †Immune deficiency diseases |
| .976 | †Deformities |

Class here teratology

| .978 | †Tumors |

Class here cancer

| .98 | †Communicable diseases |

Class here diseases caused by living organisms, by microorganisms

Class poisons in 571.95; class comprehensive works on immunity to communicable diseases in 571.96

For specific communicable diseases, see 571.99

.986	†Disease vectors
.99	Specific communicable diseases
[.990 1–.990 9]	Standard subdivisions

Do not use; class in 571.9801–571.9809

†Add as instructed under 571.5–571.9

.992–.995   Diseases caused by microorganisms and fungi

> Add to base number 571.99 the numbers following 579 in 579.2–579.5, e.g., protozoan diseases 571.994
>
> Class comprehensive works in 571.98

.999   †Parasitic diseases

> Class here diseases caused by animals, by endoparasites, by worms
>
> *For protozoan diseases, see 571.994*

572   *Biochemistry

> Class here cytochemistry, histochemistry; comprehensive works on biochemistry of nonmetallic elements and their compounds; comprehensive works on biochemistry and biophysics; interdisciplinary works on biochemicals, on macromolecules
>
> *For chemistry of biochemicals, see 547; for chemistry of macromolecules, see 547.7; for biophysics, see 571.4; for biochemistry of control processes, see 571.74; for pathological biochemistry, see 571.94; for immunochemistry, see 571.964; for biogeochemistry, see 577.14; for industrial biochemistry, see 660.63. For biochemistry of a specific physiological system in animals, see the system in 573, plus notation 4 from table under 573, e.g., chemistry of circulatory fluids in animals 573.154; for biochemistry of a reproductive organ or physiological system in plants, see the organ or system in 575.6–575.9, plus notation 4 from table under 575.6–575.9, e.g., chemistry of circulatory fluids in plants 575.754*

SUMMARY

572.3	**General topics of biochemistry**
.4	**Metabolism**
.5	**Miscellaneous chemicals**
.6	**Proteins**
.7	**Enzymes**
.8	**Biochemical genetics**

.3   **General topics of biochemistry**

[.301–.309]   Standard subdivisions

> Do not use; class in 572.01–572.09

.33   *Molecular structure

> Class here bonds, conformation, sequences of polymers and other component units of large molecules, theoretical chemistry
>
> Class structure-activity relationships in 572.4; class molecular biology (biochemical genetics) in 572.8

.36   *Analytical biochemistry

---

*Add as instructed under 571–572

†Add as instructed under 571.5–571.9

.38   *Biochemical evolution

> Class comprehensive works on molecular evolution in 572.838

> *For biochemistry of origin of life, see 576.83*

.39   *Nutritional requirements

> Class conditions needed for life to begin in 576.83

> *For a specific kind of chemical requirement, see the chemical in 572.5–572.8, plus notation 39 from table under 572.5–572.8, e.g., vitamin requirements 572.5839*

.4   *Metabolism

> Class here cell digestion and metabolism, structure-activity relationships, comprehensive biological works on nutrition

> Class molecular structure in 572.33; class interdisciplinary works on human nutrition in 363.8

> *For metabolism of a specific chemical, see the chemical in 572.5–572.8, plus notation 4 from table under 572.5–572.8, e.g., metabolism of enzymes 572.74, enzyme kinetics 572.744; for a specific aspect of biology of nutrition, see the aspect, e.g., nutritional requirements 572.39, digestive system 573.3*

.41   Animal metabolism

> Number built according to instructions under 571–572

> Class comprehensive works on animal digestion in 573.3

.43   *Energy metabolism

> Class here biochemical interactions, reactions, reactivity; bioenergetics, energy phenomena in organisms, physical biochemistry

> Class effects of physical agents on organisms, comprehensive works on biophysics in 571.4

.435   *Photobiochemistry and bioluminescence

> Subdivisions are added for photobiochemistry and bioluminescence together, for photobiochemistry alone

> *For photosynthesis, see 572.46*

.435 8   *Bioluminescence

> *For bioluminescent organs, see 573.95*

.436   *Thermodynamics

> Class here thermochemistry

.437   *Bioelectrochemistry

> *For electric organs, see 573.97*

*Add as instructed under 571–572

.44   *Reaction kinetics

.45   *Biosynthesis (Anabolism)

> For photosynthesis, see 572.46

.46   *Photosynthesis

> Class here chlorophylls

.47   *Cell respiration

> Class here tissue respiration, comprehensive works on respiration

.471   Cell respiration in animals

> Number built according to instructions under 571–572
>
> Class comprehensive works on respiration in animals in 573.2

.472   Cell respiration in plants and microorganisms

> Number built according to instructions under 571–572
>
> For gas exchange from surface tissues of plants, see 575.8

.475   *Tricarboxylic acid cycle

> Variant names: citric acid cycle, Krebs cycle
>
> Class here adenosine triphosphate

.478   *Anaerobic respiration

.48   *Catabolism

.49   *Fermentation

> **572.5–572.8   Specific biochemicals and biochemical genetics**

> Except for modifications shown under specific entries, add to each subdivision identified by † as follows:
>
> 01–2   Standard subdivisions and specific kinds of organisms
> > Add the numbers following 571 in 571.01–571.2, e.g., the subject in animals 1, the subject in plants 2
>
> 3   General topics in biochemistry
> > Add to 3 the numbers following 572.3 in 572.33–572.39, e.g., molecular structure 33, nutritional requirements 39
>
> 4   Metabolism and genetic aspects
> > Add to 4 the numbers following 572.4 in 572.401–572.49, e.g., biosynthesis 45
> > Subdivisions are added for either or both topics in heading
>
> Class comprehensive works in 572

.5   **Miscellaneous chemicals**

> Not provided for elsewhere

---

*Add as instructed under 571–572

[.501–.509]	Standard subdivisions

> Do not use; class in 572.01–572.09

.51	†Bioinorganic chemistry

Class here biomineralization, coordination biochemistry, metals in biochemistry

> *For bioinorganic chemistry of metals other than calcium, iron, copper, see 572.52; for bioinorganic chemistry of nonmetallic elements, see 572.53–572.55*

.511	Animals

Number built according to instructions under 572.5–572.8

> *For biomineralization in animals, see 573.76451*

.515	†Trace elements

Class here micronutrients

> *For a specific trace element, see the element in 572.51–572.55, e.g., iron 572.517*

.516	†Calcium
.517	†Iron
.518	†Copper
.52	Bioinorganic chemistry of metals other than calcium, iron, copper
[.520 1–.520 9]	Standard subdivisions

> Do not use; class in 572.5101–572.5109

.523–.527	Specific metals

Add to base number 572.52 the numbers following 546 in 546.38–546.72, e.g., magnesium 572.52392, nickel 572.52625; however, for calcium, see 572.516; for iron, see 572.517; for copper, see 572.518

>	572.53–572.55 Nonmetallic elements and their compounds in biochemistry

Class comprehensive works in 572

.53	†Oxygen

> *For oxygen in respiration, see 572.47*

.539	†Water
.54	†Nitrogen

> *For biogeochemical nitrogen cycle, see 577.145*

---

†Add as instructed under 572.5–572.8

.545	†Nitrogen fixation
.548	†Amines

> *For alkaloids, see 572.549; for amino acids, see 572.65*

.549	†Alkaloids
.55	Other nonmetallic elements and their compounds in biochemistry

Class carbon, hydrogen in 572

[.550 1–.550 9]	Standard subdivisions

Do not use; class in 572.01–572.09

.553	†Phosphorus
.554	†Sulfur
.555	†Selenium
.556	†Halogens
.56	†Carbohydrates

Class here saccharides

.565	†Sugars

Including insulin

Class here monosaccharides, oligosaccharides

[.565 49]	Fermentation

Do not use; class in 572.49

.566	†Polysaccharides
.566 8	†Structural polysaccharides

Class cellulose in 572.56682; class chitin in 573.774

.567	†Conjugated carbohydrates

Including glycosides

.567 2	Plants and microorganisms

Number built according to instructions under 572.5–572.8

Including gums

.57	†Lipids

Including waxes

Class here fats, fatty acids

.579	†Steroids

†Add as instructed under 572.5–572.8

.579 5   †Sterols

                Class here cholesterol

.58   †Vitamins

.59   †Pigments

                Class chlorophyll in 572.46

.6   †Proteins

For hormones, see 571.74; for immunoglobulins, see 571.967; for enzymes, see 572.7; for nucleoproteins, see 572.84

.633   Molecular structure

            Number built according to instructions under 572.5–572.8

            Class here amino acid sequence

.645   Biosynthesis (Anabolism)

            Number built according to instructions under 572.5–572.8

            Class here genetic translation

.65   †Components of proteins

            Class here amino acids, peptides, polypeptides

            Class amino-acid sequence in 572.633

.66   †Simple proteins

            Including albumins, globulins, histones

.67   †Structural proteins

            Class here collagen, scleroproteins

.68   †Conjugated proteins

            Including cromoproteins, glycoproteins, lipoproteins, phosphoproteins

.69   †Carrier proteins

            Class here comprehensive works on bioactive proteins

For hormones, see 571.74; for immunoglobulins, see 571.967; for enzymes, see 572.7; for prions, see 579.29

.7   †Enzymes

            Class here coenzymes, cofactors

For enzymes performing a specific physiological function, see the physiological function, e.g., enzymes in cellular respiration 572.47, digestive enzymes 573.347

†Add as instructed under 572.5–572.8

.75–.78   Enzymes catalyzing reactions of specific chemicals

> Add to base number 572.7 the numbers following 572 in 572.5–572.8, e.g., proteolytic enzymes 572.76; however, for oxidases, see 572.791

> Class comprehensive works on classes of enzymes named according to the reaction they catalyze in 572.79

.79   Classes of enzymes named according to specific kind of reaction they catalyze

> Including isomerases, ligases, lyases

> *For enzymes catalyzing specific kinds of chemicals, see 572.75–572.78*

[.790 1–.790 9]   Standard subdivisions

> Do not use; class in 572.701–572.709

.791   †Oxidoreductases

> Oxidizing and reducing enzymes

> Including catalases, dehydrogenases, oxidases, zymases

> Class cellular respiration in 572.47

.792   †Transferases

.793   †Hydrolases

.8   †Biochemical genetics

> Class here cytogenetics, molecular biology, molecular genetics, physiological genetics, nucleic acids

> Class developmental genetics in 571.85; class comprehensive works on genetics in 576.5. Class genetic aspects of a specific biochemical with the specific biochemical in 572.5–572.7, plus notation 4 from table under 572.5–572.8, e.g., genetic regulation of enzymes 572.74

> *See Manual at 572.8; also at 576.5 vs. 572.8*

.838   Molecular evolution

> Number built according to instructions under 572.5–572.8

> Class here evolutionary genetics, genetic evolution

> Class molecular evolution of a specific biochemical with the biochemical, plus notation 38 from table under 572.5–572.8, e.g., biochemical evolution of enzymes 572.738

> *For molecular evolution during origin of life, see 576.83*

†Add as instructed under 572.5–572.8

.84   Metabolism

Number built according to instructions under 572.5–572.8

Class here nucleic-acid hybridization, nucleic acid-protein interactions, comprehensive works on nucleoproteins

For nucleoproteins in a specific situation, see the situation, e.g., nucleoproteins in chromosomes 572.87

.85   †Nucleotides

Class here nucleosides

.86   †DNA (Deoxyribonucleic acid)

Class here chromosomal DNA, codons, genes, genomes

Class genetic transfection and transformation in 571.9648; class DNA as a component of chromosomes in 572.87

.863 3   Molecular structure

Number built according to instructions under 572.5–572.8

Class here DNA topology, double helix, genetic code; chromosome, gene, genome mapping; base, gene, nucleotide sequences

Class amino acid sequence in 572.633

For base and nucleotide sequence in RNA, see 572.8833

.864 5   Biosynthesis

Number built according to instructions under 572.5–572.8

Class here DNA replication

Class genetic transcription in 572.8845

.864 59   *DNA repair

.865   †Gene expression

Class here genetic regulation, regulation of gene expression

.869   †Extrachromosomal DNA

Including plasmid DNA, plasmids, transposons

Class here chloroplastic DNA, cytoplasmic inheritance, mitochondrial DNA

Class viruses in 579.2

For transduction, transfection, transformation, see 571.9648

See also 572.877 for genetic recombination

.87   †Chromosomes

Class here chromatin, chromosome numbers, nucleosomes

*Add as instructed under 571–572
†Add as instructed under 572.5–572.8

.873 3　　　　　　Molecular structure

Number built according to instructions under 572.5–572.8

For chromosome mapping, nucleotide sequences in chromosomes, see 572.8633

.877　　　　　†Genetic recombination

Including aneuploidy, crossing over, inversion, translocation

Class somatic variation resulting from genetic recombination in 576.54; class recombinant DNA in 660.65

.88　　　　　†RNA (Ribonucleic acid)

For viroids, see 579.29

.884 5　　　　　Biosynthesis

Number built according to instructions under 572.5–572.8

Class here genetic transcription

Class genetic translation, protein synthesis in 572.645

.886　　　　　†Transfer RNA

573　Specific physiological systems in animals, regional histology and physiology

Class here comprehensive works on specific physiological systems

Except for modifications shown under specific entries, add to each subdivision identified by * as follows:

01–1　　Standard subdivisions; comparative physiology; the system in specific kinds of animals
　　　　Add the numbers following 571 in 571.01–571.1, e.g., comparative physiology of the system 1, the system in mammals 19

2　　Operation of one physiological system within another system
　　　Class hormones in 374

21　　Circulation in the system

2101–211　　Standard subdivisions; comparative physiology; circulation in specific kinds of animals
　　　　Add to 21 the numbers following 571 in 571.01–571.1, e.g., circulation in the system in mammals 2119

213　　Anatomy and general biological processes of circulation
　　　Add to 213 the numbers following 571 in 571.3–571.9, e.g., anatomy of circulation 2133, development of circulation 2138

(continued)

†Add as instructed under 572.5–572.8

573   Specific physiological systems in animals, regional histology and physiology (continued)

25	Integument of the system
	Class here membranes enveloping an organ even if not an integral part of the organ, e.g., pericardium 573.1725
	Add to 25 the numbers following 21 in 2101–213, e.g., cytology of integument of an organ 2536
27	Muscles of the system
	Add to 27 the numbers following 21 in 2101–213, e.g., biophysics of muscles 2734
28	Innervation of the system
	Add to 28 the numbers following 21 in 2101–213, e.g., innervation of the system in mammals 2819
3	Anatomy and general biological processes of the system or region
	Class anatomy of, or a specific biological process within, a specific physiological subsystem in 2
[301–309]	Standard subdivisions
	Do not use; class in class in 01–09
33–39	Anatomy and specific biological processes of the system or region
	Add to 3 the numbers following 571 in 571.3–571.9, e.g., anatomy 33, biophysics 34, cell biology 36
4	Biochemistry
	Add to 4 the numbers following 572 in 572.01–572.8, e.g., biochemistry of the system in mammals 419, enzymes 47, biochemical genetics 48

Class comprehensive works on physiological systems in 571

For specific physiological systems in plants, see 575; for specific physiological systems in humans, see 612; for specific physiological systems in domestic animals, see 636.0892

See Manual at 571–573 vs. 610

SUMMARY

573.1	**Circulatory system**
.2	**Respiratory system**
.3	**Digestive system**
.4	**Endocrine and excretory systems**
.5	**Integument**
.6	**Reproductive system**
.7	**Musculoskeletal system**
.8	**Nervous and sensory systems**
.9	**Miscellaneous systems and organs, regional histology and physiology**

[.01–.09]   Standard subdivisions

Do not use; class in 571.101–571.109

.1   ***Circulatory system**

Class here cardiovascular system

For circulation in a specific system or organ, see the system or organ, plus notation 21 from table under 573, e.g., circulation in brain 573.8621

.15   *Circulatory fluids

Class here blood

For lymph, see 573.16

.153 6   Cell biology

Number built according to instructions under 573

Class here blood cells, erythrocytes

For leukocytes, see 571.96; for platelets, see 573.159

.155   *Hematopoiesis

Class here blood-forming system

.155 5   *Spleen

.155 6   *Bone marrow

.156   *Plasma

.159   *Blood coagulation

Class here blood coagulation factors, platelets

.16   *Lymphatic system

Class here lymph

For role of lymphatic system in immunity, see 571.96; for spleen, see 573.1555

.163 6   Cell biology

Number built according to instructions under 573

For leukocytes, lymphocytes, see 571.96

>   573.17–573.18 Circulatory organs

Class comprehensive works in 573.1

.17   *Pumping mechanisms

Class here heart

.18   *Blood vessels

.185   *Arteries

---

*Add as instructed under 573

.186	*Veins
.187	*Capillaries

.2   *Respiratory system

Class here aerobic respiration, comprehensive works on respiration in animals

For cell and tissue respiration in animals, see 572.471

.25	*Lungs
.26	*Organs accessory to lungs

Including diaphragm, nasal sinuses, nose, trachea

Class olfactory nerves in 573.877; class use of accessory respiratory organs in vocal communication in 573.92

For larynx, see 573.925

.28   *Gills

.3   *Digestive system

Class here digestion

Class comprehensive works on biology of nutrition in 572.4; class interdisciplinary works on human nutrition in 363.8

For cellular digestion, see 572.4

.35   *Mouth and esophagus

Class here physiology of eating, ingestion

Subdivisions are added for mouth and esophagus together, for mouth alone

.355   *External mouth parts

Class here beak, bill, cheeks, lips; feeding appendages and tentacles

.356	*Teeth
.357	*Tongue
.359	*Esophagus
.36	*Stomach

Including pylorus

.37   *Intestine

.377   *Pancreas

Including islands of Langerhans

Class insulin in 572.565

*Add as instructed under 573

.378   *Small intestine

Including duodenum, ileum, jejunum

.379   *Large intestine

Including colon, rectum

.38   *Biliary tract

Including bile ducts, gallbladder

Class here liver

.4   *Endocrine and excretory systems

Class here endocrinology

Subdivisions are added for endocrine and excretory systems together, for endocrine system alone

Class comprehensive works on endocrine and nervous systems in 571.71

.44   Biochemistry

Number built according to instructions under 573

Class here comprehensive works on animal hormones

> *For hormones of a specific endocrine gland, see the gland, plus notation 4 from table under 573, e.g., pituitary hormones 573.454, estrogen 573.6654; for hormones controlling a specific function in 571.5–571.9, see the function, plus notation 374 from tables under 571.5–571.9, e.g., growth hormones 571.8374; for hormones controlling a specific animal physiological system, see the function in 573, plus notation 374 from table under 573, e.g., gastrointestinal hormones 573.3374*

> *See Manual at 573.44 vs. 571.74: Hormones*

>   573.45–573.47 Specific endocrine glands

Class comprehensive works in 573.4

> *For islands of Langerhans, see 573.377; for testes, see 573.655; for ovaries, see 573.665; for nervous system, see 573.8*

.45   *Pituitary gland and hypothalamus

Subdivisions are added for pituitary gland and hypothalamus together, for pituitary gland alone

Class comprehensive works on neurohormones in 573.8374

.459   *Hypothalamus

.46   *Adrenal glands

*Add as instructed under 573

.47	*Thyroid and parathyroid glands

Subdivisions are added for thyroid and parathyroid glands together, for thyroid gland alone

.478	*Parathyroid glands
.49	*Excretory system

Class here excretion, urinary system

.496	*Kidneys
.5	***Integument**

Including color

Class here hide, skin

Class color of hair, fur, scales, feathers, horns, related topics in 573.58–573.59; class exoskeleton in 573.77

For integument of a specific system or organ, see the system or organ, plus notation 25 from table under 573, e.g., pericardium 573.1725, meninges 573.8625

.58	*Hair and fur

Subdivisions are added for either or both topics in heading

.59	*Scales, feathers, horns, related topics

Including claws, nails

.595	*Scales
.597	*Feathers
.6	***Reproductive system**

Class here genital organs, reproduction, sexual reproduction, comprehensive works on urogenital system

Class comprehensive works on reproduction, development, growth of animals in 571.81

For urinary system, see 573.49

See Manual at 571.8 vs. 573.6, 575.6

.65	*Male reproductive system
.655	*Testes

Class sperm in 571.845

.656	*Penis
.658	*Prostate

*Add as instructed under 573

.66	*Female reproductive system

Class pregnancy and lactation in 573.67

.665	*Ovaries

Class egg cells in 571.845; class eggs in 573.68; class plant ovaries in 575.665

.667	*Uterus
.67	*Pregnancy and lactation

Subdivisions are added for pregnancy and lactation together, for pregnancy alone

.679	*Lactation

Class here mammary glands

.68	*Eggs

For embryology of animals, see 571.861

.7 *Musculoskeletal system

Class here physiology of movement

.735 6	Connective tissues

Number built according to instructions under 573

For tendons, see 573.75356; for cartilage, see 573.76356; for ligaments, see 573.78356

.75	*Muscles

For muscles of a specific system or organ, see the system or organ, plus notation 27 from table under 573, e.g., heart muscles 573.1727

.76	*Bones

Class here comprehensive works on skeleton

For bone marrow, see 573.1556; for horns, see 573.59; for exoskeleton, see 573.77

.764 51	Bioinorganic chemistry

Number built according to instructions under 573

Class here comprehensive works on biomineralization in animals

For biomineralization in a specific system or organ, see the system or organ, plus notation 451 from table under 573, e.g., biomineralization in teeth 573.356451, biomineralization in horns 573.59

.77	*Exoskeleton

*Add as instructed under 573

.78   *Joints

.79   *Locomotion and related activities

> Including rest
>
> Class here crawling, running, walking, work
>
> Subdivisions are added for locomotion and related activities together, for locomotion alone
>
> Class behavioral aspects of locomotion in 591.5

.798   *Flying

> Class here physiology of wings
>
> Class comprehensive works on wings in 591.479

.8   *Nervous and sensory systems

> Subdivisions are added for nervous and sensory systems together, for nervous system alone
>
> Class comprehensive works on regulation and control in animals, on endocrine and nervous systems in 571.71

.85   *Nerves and nerve fibers

> Class here irritability, peripheral nerves
>
> Subdivisions are added for either or both topics in heading
>
> Class comprehensive works on nerves, nerve fibers, central nervous system in 573.8
>
> > *For cell irritability, see 571.67; for nerves and nerve fibers in central nervous system, see 573.86. For innervation of a specific system or organ, see the system or organ, plus notation 28 from table under 573, e.g., innervation of muscles 573.7528*

.86   *Central nervous system

> Class here brain

.868   *Physiology of sleep

> Class sleep behavior in 591.56; class interdisciplinary works on sleep in 154.6

.869   *Spinal cord

.87   *Sense organs

> Including physiology of navigation
>
> Class here sensation, senses
>
> Class migration in 591.568
>
> > *For eyes, see 573.88; for ears, see 573.89*

*Add as instructed under 573

.875		*Touch
.877		*Chemical senses

Class here olfaction, olfactory nerves, smell

For taste, see 573.878

.878 *Taste

Class here taste buds

.88 *Eyes

Including light sensing by pineal gland

Class here sight, vision

.89 *Ears

Class here hearing

.9 Miscellaneous systems and organs, regional histology and physiology

Limited to topics named below

[.901–.909] Standard subdivisions

Do not use; class in 571.101–571.109

.92 *Communication systems

Class here vocal communication

Class comprehensive works on animal communication in 591.59

For receiving sensory systems, see 573.87; for bioluminescent communication, see 573.95; for communication involving electric organs, see 573.97

.925 *Larynx

Class here vocal cords

.927 *Nonvocal sound communication

Class here physiology of stridulation

.929 *Chemical communication

Production of chemicals that arouse behavioral responses

.95 *Bioluminescent organs

Class here bioluminescent communication

.97 *Electric organs

.99 *Regional histology and physiology

Subdivisions are added for either or both topics in heading

*Add as instructed under 573

.995	*Head
.996	*Thorax
.997	*Abdomen
.998	*Appendages

> Class locomotor functions of appendages in 573.79

[574] [Unassigned]

> Most recently used in Edition 20

575 Specific parts of and physiological systems in plants

> Except for modifications shown under specific entries, add to each subdivision identified by † as follows:
>
> 01–09 Standard subdivisions
>> Notation from Table 1 as modified under 570.1–570.9, e.g., microscopy 0282
>
> 2 Specific kinds of plants
>> Class here comparative physiology, evolution of the part or system
>> Add to 2 the numbers following 58 in 581–588, e.g., monocotyledons 24
>>
>> *For physiological systems in fungi and algae, see 571; for specific parts of fungi and algae, see 571.5929*
>
> 3 Generalities of parts or processes
> [301–309] Standard subdivisions
>> Do not use; class in 01–09
>
> 33–39 Generalities of specific parts or processes
>> Add to 3 the numbers following 571 in 571.3–571.9, e.g., histology 35, pathology 39
>
> *For external description of parts and organs and their configurations, see 581.4*

SUMMARY

575.4	Stems	
.5	Roots and leaves	
.6	Reproductive organs	Flowers
.7	Circulation, food storage, excretion	
.8	Transpiration	
.9	Animal-like physiological processes	

[.01–.09] Standard subdivisions

> Do not use; class in 571.201–571.209

.4 †Stems

> Class here comprehensive works on regional physiology, on shoots
>
> *For regional physiology of roots, see 575.54; for leaves, see 575.57*

---

*Add as instructed under 573

†Add as instructed under 575

.435 9   Regional histology

                 Number built according to instructions under 575

                 Class here comprehensive works on regional histology of plants

                     For regional histology of roots, see 575.54359; for regional histology of leaves, see 575.57359

.45   Special features of stems

                 Limited to those named below

[.450 1–.450 9]   Standard subdivisions

                 Do not use; class in 575.401–575.409

.451   †Primary epidermis

                 Class here comprehensive works on epidermis of plants

                     For bark, see 575.452; for transpiration from primary epidermis, see 575.8

.452   †Bark

                 Class here phloem

                 For circulation in phloem, see 575.7

.454   †Nodes

.457   †Thorns

.46   †Wood

                 Class here xylem

                 For circulation in phloem, see 575.7

.48   †Growing points and layers

                 Class here meristem

                 Subdivisions are added for either or both topics in heading

.485   †Apical meristem

.486   †Buds

.488   †Cambium

.49   †Stems specialized for reproduction

                 Class here asexual reproduction, vegetative reproduction, underground stems

                 Class food storage in specialized stems in 575.78; class comprehensive works on reproduction of plants in 575.6

.495   †Bulbs

†Add as instructed under 575

.496	†Corms
.497	†Rhizomes
.498	†Tubers
.499	†Stolons (Runners)
.5	**Roots and leaves**
.54	Roots

> Add to base number 575.54 the numbers following 575.4 in
> 575.401–575.48, e.g., xylem in roots 575.546
>
> *For absorption of water and nutrients by roots, see 575.76*
>
> *See also 575.49 for underground stems*

.57	†Leaves

> *For transpiration from leaves, see 575.8*

> **575.6–575.9 Reproductive organs and physiological systems in plants**

Except for modifications shown under specific entries, add to each subdivision
identified by * as follows:

    01–3   Standard subdivisions, specific kinds of plants, generalities of
            organs and systems
                Add as instructed under 575, e.g., the organ or process in
                monocotyledons 24, histology 35
    4   Biochemistry
                Add to 4 the numbers following 572 in 572.01–572.8, e.g.,
                biochemistry of the organ or process in monocotyledons 424,
                enzymes 47, biochemical genetics 48

Class comprehensive works in 575

.6	***Reproductive organs Flowers**

Class here reproduction, sexual reproduction, sporangia

Class pollination in 571.8642; class comprehensive works on reproduction,
development, growth of plants in 571.82; class interdisciplinary works on
flowers in 582.13

> *For asexual reproduction, vegetative reproduction, see 575.49*
>
> *See Manual at 571.8 vs. 573.6, 575.6*

.65	*Male reproductive organs

Class here anthers, microsporangia, stamens

Class pollen (microspores) in 571.845

---

*Add as instructed under 575.6–575.9
†Add as instructed under 575

.66	*Female reproductive organs

Class here pistils

Class fruits in 575.67

.665	*Ovaries

Class here carpels, megasporangia

Class egg cells (megaspores) in 571.845; class seeds in 575.68

.67	*Fruits

For seeds, see 575.68

.68	*Seeds

For embryology of plants (including germination of seeds), see 571.862

.69	*Other flower parts

Class here petals, sepals

.7	***Circulation, food storage, excretion**

Subdivisions are added for circulation, food storage, excretion together; for circulation alone

Class transpiration in 575.8

For a specific circulatory tissue, see the tissue, e.g., phloem 575.452, xylem 575.46

.75	*Circulatory fluids

Class here sap

.76	*Absorption of water and nutrients

Subdivisions are added for either or both topics in heading

.78	*Food and water storage

Subdivisions are added for food and water storage together, for food storage alone

.79	*Excretion

Class here internal isolation of unusable substances

.8	***Transpiration**

Class here gas exchange from surface tissues

For a specific tissue or organ of transpiration, see the tissue or organ, e.g., leaves 575.57

.9	***Animal-like physiological processes**

Class here behavior of plants

*Add as instructed under 575.6–575.9

.97   *Movement

> *For movement that is a direct result of growth, see 571.82*

.98   *Sensitivity

.99   *Physiology of predatory activity

Trapping mobile organisms

Class comprehensive works on carnivorous plants in 583.75

> ## 576–578 General and external biological phenomena

Class general and external biological phenomena of specific kinds of organisms in 579–590; class comprehensive works in 578

576   Genetics and evolution

Except for modifications shown under specific entries, add to each subdivision identified by † as follows:
01–09   Standard subdivisions
Notation from Table 1 as modified under 570.1–570.9, e.g., microscopy 0282

.01–.09   Standard subdivisions

Notation from Table 1 as modified under 570.1–570.9, e.g., microscopy in study of genetics and evolution 576.0282

.5   †**Genetics**

Class here heredity, experimental works on genetics of specific organisms, interdisciplinary works on genetics

> *For biochemical, molecular, physiological genetics; cytogenetics, see 572.8; for genetics of microorganisms, fungi, algae, see 579.135; for genetics of plants, see 581.35; for genetics of animals, see 591.35. For a specific aspect of genetics, see the aspect, e.g., eugenics 363.92, medical genetics 616.042, genetic engineering, gene cloning 660.65*

> *See Manual at 576.5 vs. 572.8*

.52   †Laws of genetics

Class here Mendel's laws

.53   †Genetic makeup

Class here genotypes, phenotypes

Class biochemical aspects of genetic makeup in 572.8

---

*Add as instructed under 575.6–575.9

†Add standard subdivisions as instructed under 576

.54	†Variation

Class here factors affecting heredity and variation

For genetic recombination as a factor affecting heredity and variation, see 572.877

See also 571.9648 for transduction, transformation; 572.869 for transposons

.542	†Environmental factors (Mutagens)

Including radiogenetics

Class here chemical mutagens

Class toxic aspects of mutagens in 571.95; class biochemical action of mutagens in 572.8

.544	†Breeding patterns

Class here inbreeding

.549	†Mutation
.58	†Population genetics

Class here ecological genetics; gene pools; role of populations, species as vehicles of evolution

Class comprehensive works on population biology in 577.88

.8	**†Evolution**

Class creationism in 231.7652

For evolution of microorganisms, see 579.138; for evolution of plants, see 581.38; for evolution of animals, see 591.38. For evolution of a specific internal process or structure, see the process or structure, e.g., molecular evolution 572.838, evolution of circulatory system 573.1

See Manual at 231.7652 vs. 213, 500, 576.8; also at 560 vs. 576.8

.801	Philosophy and theory

Do not use for theories; class in 576.82

.82	†Theories of evolution

Including punctuated equilibrium

Class here Darwinism, natural selection

Class sexual selection in 591.562

.827	†Lamarckian theories

Class here inheritance of acquired characteristics

†Add standard subdivisions as instructed under 576

.83   †Origin of life

Including spontaneous generation

Class here conditions needed for life to begin, biochemistry of forms of life before achievement of full self-replication

Class comprehensive works on molecular evolution in 572.838

.839   †Extraterrestrial life

Including theory of extraterrestrial origin of life on earth

Class here astrobiology

Class extraterrestrial civilization, extraterrestrial intelligence in 999

See also 571.0919 for space biology

.84   †Evolutionary cycles

Class here catastrophes, extinction, radiation

.85   †Factors affecting evolution

Including symbiosis

Class comprehensive works on symbiosis in 577.85

For role of genetics in evolution, see 576.5; for natural selection, see 576.82

.855   †Sexual factors

Class here evolution of sexes

Class sexual selection in 591.562

.86   †Speciation

Class here role of species in evolution

Class comprehensive works on species in 578.012

.87   †Coevolution

Class symbiosis as a factor affecting evolution in 576.85

.875   †Coevolution of flowering plants and insects

Class here coevolution of flowering plants with insect-like pollinators

.88   †Phylogeny

†Add standard subdivisions as instructed under 576

577　　Ecology

Including aerial ecology, ecotones

Class here biomes, ecosystems, terrestrial ecology

Except for modifications shown under specific entries, add to each subdivision identified by * as follows:

01–08　　　Standard subdivisions
　　　　　　Notation from Table 1 as modified under 570.1–570.8, e.g.,
　　　　　　microscopy 0282
09　　　　　Historical, geographic, persons treatment
[0914–0919]　　　Treatment by areas, regions, places in general other than polar,
　　　　　　temperate, tropical regions
　　　　　　Do not use; class in 577.3–577.7

Unless other instructions are given, class a subject with aspects in two or more subdivisions of 577 in the number coming last, e.g., grassland swamps 577.684 (*not* 577.4)

> *For paleoecology, see 560.45; for ecology of microorganisms, fungi, algae, see 579.17; for ecology of plants, see 581.7; for ecology of animals, see 591.7*

> *See Manual at 333.7–333.9 vs. 363.1, 363.73, 577; also at 577 vs. 578.7: Ecology and biology of specific environments*

SUMMARY

577.01–.09	**Standard subdivisions**
.1	**Specific ecosystem processes**
.2	**Specific factors affecting ecology**
.3	**Forest ecology**
.4	**Grassland ecology**
.5	**Ecology of miscellaneous environments**
.6	**Aquatic ecology　　　Freshwater ecology**
.7	**Marine ecology**
.8	**Synecology and population biology**

.01–.08　　　Standard subdivisions

　　　　　　Notation from Table 1 as modified under 570.1–570.8, e.g., microscopy
　　　　　　577.0282

.09　　　　　Historical, geographic, persons treatment

[.091 4–.091 9]　　　Treatment by areas, regions, places in general other than polar,
　　　　　　temperate, tropical regions

　　　　　　Do not use; class in 577.3–577.7

.1　　　　Specific ecosystem processes

[.101–.109]　　　Standard subdivisions

　　　　　　Do not use; class in 577.01–577.09

.13　　　　　*Ecological bioenergetics

　　　　　　Class here energy budget, energy flow, physics in ecology

*Add standard subdivisions as instructed under 577

.14   *Environmental chemistry

>   Class here biogeochemical cycles, biogeochemistry
>
>   Class eutrophication in 577.63158; class comprehensive works on biochemistry and biogeochemistry in 572
>
>>   *For ecological bioenergetics, see 577.13; for environmental chemistry of pollution, see 577.27*

.144   *Carbon cycle

>   Including carbon dioxide sinks

.145   *Nitrogen cycle

.15   *Biological productivity

>   Class here primary productivity
>
>   Class eutrophication in 577.63158

.16   *Food chains

>   Class here ecological pyramids

.18   *Ecological succession

>   Including biological invasions

.2   Specific factors affecting ecology

>   Including fire ecology

[.201–.209]   Standard subdivisions

>>   Do not use; class in 577.01–577.09

.22   *Biometeorology (Bioclimatology)

>   Including micrometeorology
>
>   Class acclimatization and temperature adaptation in 578.42

.23   *Seasons

>   Class seasonal adaptation in 578.43

.26   *Autecology

>>   *For autecology of a specific kind of organism, see the kind of organism in 579–590, plus notation 17 from tables at 579.2–579.8, 583–588, and 592–599, e.g., autecology of insects 595.717*
>>
>>   *See Manual at 577.26 vs. 579–590*

*Add standard subdivisions as instructed under 577

.27   *Effects of humans on ecology

Class here effects of pollution on ecology

Class comprehensive works on ecotoxicology, on environmental toxicology in 571.95

For soil pollution, see 577.5727; for water pollution, see 577.627

See also 577.55 for ecology of environments made by humans

See Manual at 363.73 vs. 571.95, 577.27

.272   *Engineering works

Including dams, land reclamation, roads

.272 6   *Thermal pollution

Thermal pollution is primarily about water pollution; class comprehensive works in 577.62726

Class interdisciplinary work on thermal pollution in 363.7394

.273   *Agricultural pollution

.274   *War

Including nuclear winter

.275   Pollution by acids, by specific elements and groups of elements

[.275 01–.275 09]   Standard subdivisions

Do not use; class in 577.2701–577.2709

.275 2   *Pollution by acids

Class here acidification

.275 3–.275 7   Pollution by specific elements and groups of elements

Add to base number 577.275 the numbers following 546 in 546.3–546.7 for the element or group of elements only, e.g., influence of metals on ecology 577.2753, influence of mercury 577.275663; then to the result add standard subdivision notation as modified under 577.01–577.09, e.g., microscopy in study of pollution by metals 577.27530282

Class comprehensive works in 577.27

.276   *Air pollution

Including pollution by gases contributing to greenhouse effect (global warming), to ozone layer depletion

Class here pollution by products of combustion

.277   *Radioactive pollution

Class here radioecology

*Add standard subdivisions as instructed under 577

| .278 | *Pollution by organic compounds |
| .279 | *Pesticide pollution |

> **577.3–577.6 Ecology of specific nonmarine environments**

Add to each subdivision identified by † the numbers following 577 in 577.01–577.2, e.g., food chains 16, effects of pollution 27; however, do not add notation 26 derived from 577.26 for autecology; class in number for the environment in 577.3–577.6 without notation 26

Class terrestrial ecology, comprehensive works on ecology in 577; class comprehensive works on biology of specific environments in 578.7

.3   †Forest ecology

Class here ecology of exploited forests, of woodlands

For forest wetland ecology, see 577.683

| .309 13 | Torrid zone (Tropics) |

Class tropical rain forest ecology in 577.34

.34   †Rain forest ecology

Class here ecology of jungles, tropical rain forests

| [.340 913] | Torrid zone (Tropics) |

Do not use; class in 577.34

.37   †Taiga ecology

Class here ecology of boreal forests, taiga wetlands

.38   †Shrubland ecology

Class here chaparral, heath (dry moor) ecology

Class bog ecology, comprehensive works on moor ecology in 577.687

.4   †Grassland ecology

Class here ecology of agricultural grasslands, of rangelands, of temperate zone grasslands

Class alpine grassland ecology in 577.538

See also 333.74 for management of grasslands and rangelands by society

| [.409 12] | Temperate zones (Middle latitude zones) |

Do not use; class in 577.4

| [.409 13] | Torrid zone (Tropics) |

Do not use; class in 577.48

*Add standard subdivisions as instructed under 577
†Add as instructed under 577.3–577.6

.44 †Prairie ecology

[.440 912] Temperate zones (Middle latitude zones)

Do not use; class in 577.44

.46 †Meadow ecology

[.460 912] Temperate zones (Middle latitude zones)

Do not use; class in 577.46

.48 †Savanna ecology

Class here tropical grassland ecology

[.480 913] Torrid zone (Tropics)

Do not use; class in 577.48

.5 Ecology of miscellaneous environments

Limited to those named below

[.501–.509] Standard subdivisions

Do not use; class in 577.01–577.09

.51 †Coastal ecology

For ecology of a specific environment in coastal zone, see the environment, e.g., coastal forest ecology 577.3, saltwater wetland ecology 577.69, sublittoral ecology 577.78

.52 †Island ecology

Class island forest ecology in 577.3; class island grassland ecology in 577.4

.53 †Mountain ecology

Class mountain forest ecology in 577.3; class mountain grassland ecology other than alpine grassland ecology in 577.4

.538 †Alpine ecology

Ecology above timber line

Including alpine grassland ecology

.54 †Desert ecology

Class here ecology in arid lands, in semiarid lands

For sand dune ecology, see 577.583

†Add as instructed under 577.3–577.6

.55	†Ecology of environments made by humans

Including roadside ecology

Class here agricultural ecology

Class meadow ecology in 577.46

> *For ecology of exploited forests, see 577.3; for ecology of agricultural grasslands, of rangelands, see 577.4; for urban ecology, see 577.56*
>
> *See also 577.27 for effects of humans on ecology*

.554	†Garden and household ecology

Class here backyard ecology

Subdivisions are added for garden and household ecology together, for garden ecology alone

.555	†Hedgerow ecology
.56	†Urban ecology
.57	†Soil ecology

Class sand dune ecology in 577.583

.58	†Ecology of hostile land environments

Not provided for elsewhere

.583	†Sand dune ecology

Desert or seashore dune ecology

.584	†Cave ecology
.586	†Tundra, glacier, snow cover ecology

Subdivisions are added for tundra, glacier, snow cover ecology together; for tundra ecology alone

.6	**†Aquatic ecology Freshwater ecology**

Class here biological limnology

Class interdisciplinary works on limnology in 551.48

> *For marine ecology, see 577.7*

.63	†Lake and pond ecology

Class here ecology of freshwater lagoons, reservoirs

Subdivisions are added for lake and pond ecology together, for lake ecology alone

Class comprehensive works on ecology of lakes, ponds, rivers, streams in 577.6

†Add as instructed under 577.3–577.6

.631 5	Biological productivity
	Number built according to instructions under 577.3–577.6
.631 58	*Eutrophication
	Class social measures to control eutrophication in 363.73946; class engineering measures to control eutrophication in 628.112
.636	†Pond ecology
.639	†Salt lake ecology
	Class here ecology of inland seas
.64	†River and stream ecology
	Subdivisions are added for either or both topics in heading
.66	†Floodplain ecology
	Class ecology of a specific environment on a floodplain with the specific environment, e.g., ecology of floodplain grasslands 577.4
.68	†Wetland ecology
	Including riparian ecology
	Class here marsh, swamp ecology
	For saltwater wetland ecology, see 577.69
.683	†Forest wetland ecology
	For taiga, see 577.37
.684	†Grass wetland ecology
.687	†Peat bog ecology
	Class here bog, peatland, wet moor ecology; comprehensive works on moor ecology
	For heath (dry moor) ecology, see 577.38
.69	†Saltwater wetland and seashore ecology
	Class here ecology of coastal wetlands, salt and tide marshes
	Subdivisions are added for saltwater wetland and seashore ecology together, for saltwater wetland ecology alone
.694	†Sea grass wetland ecology
.697	†Forest saltwater wetland ecology
[.697 091 3]	Torrid zone (Tropics)
	Do not use; class in 577.698

*Add standard subdivisions as instructed under 577

†Add as instructed under 577.3–577.6

.698	†Mangrove swamp ecology

Class here tropical saltwater wetland forest ecology

.699	†Seashore ecology

Including ecology of rock pools, sea caves, tidal flats, tide pools

For sand dune ecology, see 577.583

.7	**Marine ecology**

Class here saltwater ecology

Class comprehensive works on marine biology in 578.77

> *For salt lake ecology, see 577.639; for saltwater wetland and seashore ecology, see 577.69*

.701–.708	Standard subdivisions

Notation from Table 1 as modified under 570.1–570.8, e.g., microscopy in marine ecology 577.0282

.709	Historical, geographic, persons treatment
[.709 162]	Oceans and seas

Do not use; class in 577.7

[.709 163–.709 165]	Atlantic, Pacific, Indian Oceans

Do not use; class in 577.73–577.75

.71–.72	Specific ecosystem processes; specific factors affecting marine ecology

Add to base number 577.7 the numbers following 577 in 577.1–577.2, e.g., marine food chains 577.716, marine pollution 577.727; however, class autecology in 577.7

.73–.75	Ecology of specific oceans and seas

Add to base number 577.7 the numbers following — 16 in notation 163–165 from Table 2, e.g., Atlantic Ocean ecology 577.73; then add 0, and to the result add the numbers following 577 in 577.01–577.2, e.g., food chains in Atlantic Ocean 577.73016; however, for Sargasso Sea ecology, see 577.76362

For Antarctic Ocean, see 577.709167

>   577.76–577.79   Specific kinds of marine environments

Add to each subdivision identified by ‡ the numbers following 577.7 in 577.701–577.75, e.g., food chains 16, pollution 27, the environment in Atlantic Ocean 3

Class comprehensive works in 577.7

---

†Add as instructed under 577.3–577.6

.76 ‡Surface regions

Class here ecology of plankton

For freshwater plankton ecology, see 577.6

.763 62 Sargasso Sea

Number built according to instructions under 577.76–577.79

.77 ‡Marine benthic ecology

.78 ‡Nearshore ecology

Class here sublittoral ecology

For saltwater wetland and seashore ecology, see 577.69

.786 ‡Estuarine ecology

.789 ‡Reef ecology

Class here coral reef ecology

.79 ‡Ecology of abyssal zone

.8 Synecology and population biology

Standard subdivisions are added for synecology and population biology together, for synecology alone

Class here ecological aspects of sociobiology

Except for modifications shown under specific entries, add to each subdivision identified by † as follows:
01–09 Standard subdivisions
Notation from Table 1 as modified under 570.1–570.9, e.g., microscopy 0282

Class ecological succession in 577.18; class behavioral aspects of sociobiology in 591.5; class predation in 591.53; class interdisciplinary works on sociobiology in 304.5

.801–.809 Standard subdivisions

Notation from Table 1 as modified under 570.1–570.9, e.g., microscopy in study of synecology 577.80282

.82 †Ecological communities

Including ecological niches

Class biomes in 577. Class plant associations characteristic of a specific environment with the environment in 577.3–577.7, e.g., prairie grass associations 577.44

.83 †Competition

---

†Add standard subdivisions as instructed under 577.8

‡Add as instructed under 577.76–577.79

.85   †Symbiosis

Class symbiosis as a factor affecting evolution in 576.85; class symbiosis in the sense limited to mutually beneficial relationships in 577.852

.852   †Mutualism

Including commensalism

.857   †Parasitism

Class parasites in 578.65; class pathology of parasitism, comprehensive works on parasitism in 571.999

When classifying parasitism of specific kinds of organisms in 579–590, prefer the number for the parasite. Emphasis on the host organism usually indicates that the work should be classed as a disease in 571.999

.88   †Population biology

Class here population dynamics

See also 576.58 for population genetics

578   Natural history of organisms and related subjects

Standard subdivisions are added for natural history of organisms and related subjects together, for natural history of organisms alone

Class here descriptive biology, specific nontaxonomic kinds of organisms, comprehensive works on general and external biological phenomena

Except for modifications shown under specific entries, add to each subdivision identified by ‡ as follows:

01–08   Standard subdivisions
        Notation from Table 1 as modified under 578.01–578.08, e.g., microscopy 0282

09   Historical, geographic, persons treatment

For genetics and evolution, see 576; for ecology, see 577; for natural history of microorganisms, fungi, algae, see 579; for natural history of plants, see 580; for natural history of animals, see 590

See Manual at 578 vs. 304.2, 508, 910

.012   Classification

Including chemotaxonomy, cladistic analysis, cytotaxonomy, numerical taxonomy, species

Class here systematics, taxonomy

Class speciation in 576.86; class taxonomic nomenclature in 578.014

.028   Auxiliary techniques and procedures; apparatus, equipment, materials

Notation from Table 1 as modified under 570.28, e.g., microscopy in descriptive biology 578.0282

---

†Add standard subdivisions as instructed under 577.8

.07	Education, research, related topics

.073   Collections and exhibits of living organisms

> Class here history and description, guidebooks

> To show area in which collections, exhibits are found, add to base number 578.073 notation 1–9 from Table 2, e.g., collections of living plants and animals in China 578.07351

.074   Museums, collections, exhibits

> Do not use for collections and exhibits of living organisms; class in 578.073

.075   Museum activities and services   Collecting

.075 2   Preserving biological specimens

.075 3   Organizing and preparing collections and exhibits

> *For preserving biological specimens, see 578.0752*

.09   Historical, geographic, persons treatment

[.091 4–.091 9]   Treatment by areas, regions, places in general other than polar, temperate, tropical regions

> Do not use; class in 578.7

.099 9   Extraterrestrial worlds

> Class extraterrestrial life in 576.839

.4   **‡Adaptation**

> Class here organisms illustrating specific kinds of adaptation

> Class adaptation of miscellaneous nontaxonomic kinds of organisms in 578.6

.41   ‡Size, weight, shape of organisms

.42   ‡Acclimatization and temperature adaptation

> Standard subdivisions are added for acclimatization and temperature adaptation together, for acclimatization alone

> Including phenology

> Class climate and weather as factors influencing ecology in 577.22

> *For seasonal adaptation, see 578.43*

.43   ‡Seasonal adaptation

> Class seasonal variation as a factor influencing ecology in 577.23

.46   ‡Reproductive adaptation

> Class reproductive physiology in 571.8

‡Add standard subdivisions as instructed under 578

.47   ‡Protective adaptation

Including camouflage

.6   ‡Miscellaneous nontaxonomic kinds of organisms

Not provided for elsewhere

Class here economic biology

.63   ‡Beneficial organisms

See Manual at 630 vs. 579–590, 641.3

.65   ‡Harmful organisms

Including parasites

When classifying parasites under a specific kind of organism in 579–590, prefer number for the parasite. Emphasis on the host organism usually indicates that the work should be classed as a disease in 571.999

.68   ‡Rare and endangered species

Standard subdivisions are added for either or both topics in heading

Including recently extinct species

.7   Organisms characteristic of specific kinds of environments

Class here biology of specific kinds of environments

Class specific kinds of adaptation characteristic of specific kinds of environment in 578.4; class miscellaneous nontaxonomic kinds of organisms characteristic of specific kinds of environments in 578.6

For ecology of specific kinds of environments, see 577

See Manual at 577 vs. 578.7

[.701–.709]   Standard subdivisions

Do not use; class in 578.01–578.09

.73–.75   Specific kinds of nonaquatic environments

Add to base number 578.7 the numbers following 577 in 577.3–577.5 for the environment only, e.g., organisms characteristic of grasslands 578.74; then to the result add standard subdivisions as instructed under 578.01–578.09, e.g., collections of living grassland plants and animals 578.74073

Class comprehensive works on terrestrial organisms in 578

For space biology, see 571.0919; for extraterrestrial life, see 576.839

‡Add standard subdivisions as instructed under 578

.76–.77   Aquatic environments

Add to base number 578.7 the numbers following 577 in 577.6–577.7 for the environment only, e.g., marine organisms, marine biology 578.77; then to the result add standard subdivisions as instructed under 578.01–578.09, e.g., collections of living marine plants and animals 578.77073

See Manual at 578.76–578.77 vs. 551.46

> ## 579–590   Natural history of specific kinds of organisms

Class here comprehensive works on biology of specific kinds of organisms

Class comprehensive works on biology in 570; class comprehensive works on natural history of organisms in 578

See Manual at 579–590; also at 577.26 vs. 579–590; also at 630 vs. 579–590, 641.3

579   Microorganisms, fungi, algae

Standard subdivisions are added for microorganisms, fungi, algae together; for microorganisms alone

Class here Thallobionta (Thallophyta) [*formerly* 589], microbiology, Protista, protophytes; natural history and descriptive biology of microorganisms, fungi, algae; interdisciplinary works on microorganisms, fungi, algae

For internal biological processes of microorganisms, fungi, algae, see 571.29. For a specific aspect of microorganisms, fungi, algae, see the aspect, e.g., cooking mushrooms 641.658

SUMMARY

579.01–.09	**Standard subdivisions**
.1	**Specific topics in natural history of microorganisms, fungi, algae**
.2	**Viruses and subviral organisms**
.3	**Prokaryotes (Bacteria)**
.4	**Protozoa**
.5	**Fungi Eumycophyta (True fungi)**
.6	**Mushrooms**
.7	**Lichens**
.8	**Algae**

.01–.08   Standard subdivisions

Notation from Table 1 as modified under 578.01–578.08, e.g., collections of living microorganisms 579.073

.09   Historical, geographic, persons treatment

For historical, geographic, persons treatment in specific kinds of environment, see 579.17

[.091 4–.091 9]   Treatment by areas, regions, places in general other than polar,
                    temperate, tropical regions

                    Do not use; class in 579.17

.1   Specific topics in natural history of microorganisms, fungi, algae

Class here specific nontaxonomic kinds of microorganisms, fungi, algae

Except for modifications shown under specific entries, add to each subdivision
identified by † as follows:
    01–08   Standard subdivisions
             Notation from Table 1 as modified under 578.01–578.08, e.g.,
             microscopy 0282
    09   Historical, geographic, persons treatment

Unless other instructions are given, observe the following table of preference,
e.g., beneficial marine microorganisms 579.163 (*not* 579.177):

Miscellaneous nontaxonomic kinds of organisms	579.16
Adaptation	579.14
Genetics and evolution	579.13
Organisms characteristic of specific environments, ecology	579.17

[.101–.109]   Standard subdivisions

                Do not use; class in 579.01–579.09

.13   †Genetics and evolution

.135   †Genetics

         Class here works on genetic constitution of microorganisms, fungi, algae
         that elucidate their total function

         Class experimental works on genetics of microorganisms, fungi, algae;
         comprehensive works on genetics in 576.5

         For biochemical genetics in microorganisms, fungi, algae, see
         572.829

.138   †Evolution

         Class here phylogeny

.14   Adaptation

         Add to base number 579.14 the numbers following 578.4 in
         578.401–578.47, e.g., seasonal adaptation 579.143

.16   †Miscellaneous nontaxonomic kinds of organisms

         Not provided for elsewhere

         Class here economic microbiology

         Class food microbiology in 664.001579

---

†Add standard subdivisions as instructed under 579.1

.163   †Beneficial organisms

Including edible microorganisms, fungi, algae

.165   †Harmful organisms

Class here pathogenic and poisonous microorganisms, fungi, algae

See Manual at 579.165 vs. 616.01

.17   Organisms characteristic of specific environments, ecology

Standard subdivisions are added for either or both topics in heading

Class here autecology

.170 1–.170 8   Standard subdivisions

Notation from Table 1 as modified under 578.01–578.08, e.g., microscopy in study of ecology of microorganisms 579.170282

.170 9   Historical, geographic, persons treatment

[.170 914–.170 919]   Treatment by areas, regions, places in general other than polar, temperate, tropical regions

Do not use; class in 579.173–579.177

.173–.177   Specific kinds of environments

Add to base number 579.17 the numbers following 577 in 577.3–577.7 for the environment only, e.g., marine botany 579.177; then to the result add standard subdivisions as modified under 578.01–578.09, e.g., collections of living marine microorganisms and algae 579.177073

Class comprehensive works on terrestrial microorganisms, fungi, algae in 579

.178   Synecology and population biology

Add to base number 579.178 the numbers following 577.8 in 577.801–577.88, e.g., population dynamics of microorganisms 579.1788

>   **579.2–579.8 Specific taxonomic groups of microorganisms, fungi, algae**

Add to each subdivision identified by * the numbers following 579 in 579.01–579.1, e.g., poisonous organisms 165

Class comprehensive works in 579

See Manual at 579–590: When subdivisions are added for individual species

†Add standard subdivisions as instructed under 579.1

.2 ***Viruses and subviral organisms**

Class here animal viruses, vertebrate viruses, virology

Subdivisions are added for viruses and subviral organisms together, for viruses alone

See also 579.327 for rickettsias

.23 *Invertebrate viruses

For specific kinds of invertebrate viruses, see 579.24–579.25

\> 579.24–579.25 Specific kinds of viruses

Class comprehensive works in 579.2

For specific kinds of bacterial viruses, see 579.26; for specific kinds of fungal viruses, see 579.27; for specific kinds of plant viruses, see 579.28

See Manual at 579.24–579.25

.24 *DNA viruses

.243 *Double-stranded, enveloped DNA viruses

.243 2 *Poxviridae

.243 4 *Herpesviridae

.243 6 *Baculoviridae

.244 *Double-stranded, nonenveloped DNA viruses

.244 3 *Adenoviridae

.244 5 *Papovaviridae

Including Papillomavirus, Polyomavirus, SV40

.247 *Single-stranded, nonenveloped DNA viruses

Class here Parvoviridae

.25 *RNA viruses

.254 *Double-stranded, nonenveloped RNA viruses

Including Reoviridae

.256 *Single-stranded, enveloped RNA viruses

Including Arenaviridae, Paramyxoviridae

.256 2 *Togaviridae

Class here arboviruses

.256 6 *Rhabdoviridae

Including Lyssavirus

*Add as instructed under 579.2–579.8

.256 9		*Retroviridae

Class here oncoviruses, comprehensive works on oncogenic viruses

For a specific nonretrovirus oncogenic virus, see the virus, e.g., oncogenic papovaviruses 579.2445

.257	*Single-stranded, nonenveloped RNA viruses
.257 2	*Picornaviridae

Including Poliovirus

.26	*Bacterial viruses (Bacteriophages)
.27	*Fungal viruses
.28	*Plant viruses
.29	*Subviral organisms

Including prions

Class here viroids

.3   *Prokaryotes (Bacteria) [*formerly* 589.9]

Variant names: Monera, Schizomycetes, Schizophyta

Class here bacteriology, Eubacteriales, comprehensive works on bacteria and viruses

Class bacteria culture for biological research in 571.638293

For viruses, see 579.2

See Manual at 579.3

.314	Adaptation

Number built according to instructions under 579.2–579.8

.314 9	†Anaerobic bacteria
.32	Minor kinds of bacteria

Not provided for elsewhere

Including chemolithotrophic bacteria, colorless sulfur bacteria, Myxobacteria, Spirochetes

Class comprehensive works on minor kinds of bacteria in 579.3

See Manual at 579.32

[.320 1–.320 9]	Standard subdivisions

Do not use; class in 579.301–579.309

.321	*Archaeobacteria

Including methanogenic bacteria, Halobacteriaceae, halophilic bacteria

*Add as instructed under 579.2–579.8
†Add standard subdivisions as instructed under 579.1

.323　　　*Aerobic-microaerophilic, motile, helical-vibrioid gram-negative bacteria

　　　　　Including Aquaspirillum, Azospirillum

.325　　　*Anaerobic gram-negative straight, curved, and helical rods

　　　　　Including Bacteroides

.327　　　*Rickettsias and Chlamydias

.328　　　*Mycoplasmas

　　　　　Variant names: Mollicutes, Tenericutes

.33　　　*Gram-negative aerobic rods and cocci

　　　　　Including Acetobacter, Brucella, Legionella, Neisseria

　　　　　For Halobacteriaceae, see 579.321

.332　　　*Pseudomonas

　　　　　Subdivisions are added for the genus as a whole and for individual species

.334　　　*Rhizobium

　　　　　Subdivisions are added for the genus as a whole and for individual species

.34　　　*Facultatively anaerobic gram-negative rods

　　　　　Including Erwinia, Pasteurella, Photobacterium, Shigella, Yersinia

　　　　　Class here Enterobacteriaceae

.342　　　*Escherichia

　　　　　Subdivisions are added for the genus as a whole and for individual species

.344　　　*Salmonella

　　　　　Subdivisions are added for the genus as a whole and for individual species

.35　　　*Gram-positive cocci

.353　　　*Staphylococcus

　　　　　Subdivisions are added for the genus as a whole and for individual species

.355　　　*Streptococcus

　　　　　Class here Lactococcus (lactic acid Streptococcus)

　　　　　Subdivisions are added for the genus as a whole and for individual species

*Add as instructed under 579.2–579.8

.36   *Endospore-forming gram-positive rods and cocci

.362   *Bacillus

               Subdivisions are added for the genus as a whole and for individual
               species

.364   *Clostridium

               Subdivisions are added for the genus as a whole and for individual
               species

.37   *Actinomycetes and related bacteria

               Including Frankia, Lactobacillus, Listeria, Nocardia

               Subdivisions are added for Actinomycetes and related bacteria together, for
               Actinomycetes alone

               See Manual at 579.37

.373   *Irregular, nonsporing, gram-positive rods

               Including Arthrobacter, Bifidobacterium, Corynebacterium

.374   *Mycobacteria

.378   *Streptomycetes and related genera

               Class here Streptomyces

.38   *Anoxygenic phototrophic bacteria

               Including green bacteria

               Class here purple bacteria; comprehensive works of photosynthetic bacteria,
               on sulfur bacteria

               *For colorless sulfur bacteria, see 579.32; for oxygenic photosynthetic
               bacteria, see 579.39*

.385   *Purple nonsulfur bacteria

               Including Rhodobacter, Rhodopseudomonas

.39   *Cyanobacteria and Prochlorales

               Oxygenic photosynthetic bacteria

               Variant name for Cyanobacteria: Cyanophyta, blue-green algae

               Including Chroococcales, Nostocales, Oscillatoriales

               Subdivisions are added for Cyanobacteria and Prochlorales together, for
               Cyanobacteria alone

---

*Add as instructed under 579.2–579.8

.4 ***Protozoa [*formerly* 593.1]**

Class here Sarcomastigophora

For a specific group or organism that may be regarded as either protozoa or algae, see the group or organism in 579.8, e.g., Euglenophyta (Euglenida) 579.84

> 579.42–579.45 Sarcomastigophora

Class comprehensive works in 579.4

.42 ***Zoomastigophorea (Zooflagellates)**

Class phytoflagellates, comprehensive works on flagellates in 579.82

.43 ***Rhizopodea**

Including Arcellinida

Class here Sarcodina

For Foraminifera, see 579.44

.432 ***Amoebida (Amoebas)**

.44 ***Foraminifera**

.45 ***Actinopoda**

Class here Radiolaria

The term Radiolaria is sometimes limited to one of several subtaxa of Actinopoda

.47 ***Sporozoa**

.48 ***Cnidospora**

.49 ***Ciliophora (Ciliates)**

Class here Ciliatea

.495 ***Hymenostomatida**

Including Paramecium

.5 ***Fungi   Eumycophyta (True fungi)**

Class here mycology

Class comprehensive works on molds, on mildew in 579.53

For lichens, see 579.7; for comprehensive works on mushrooms, see 579.6

*Add as instructed under 579.2–579.8

.52   *Myxomycotina (Slime molds)

Variant names: Mycetozoa, Myxomycetes, Myxomycophyta, Myxomycota

Including Acrasia (cellular slime molds), Physarales, Stemonitales, Trichiales

Class here Myxogastromycetidae

For Plasmodiophoromycetes, see 579.53

\>   579.53–579.59   Eumycophyta (True fungi)

Class comprehensive works in 579.5

.53   *Miscellaneous fungi

Not provided for elsewhere

Including Chytridiomycetes, Hyphochytridiomycetes, Plasmodiophoromycetes, Trichomycetes, Zygomycetes; Rhizopus (bread molds), uniflagellate molds

Class here Mastigomycotina, Phycomycetes; comprehensive works on molds, on mildew

Class slime molds in 579.52

For Oomycetes, see 579.54; for ascomycete molds and mildew, see 579.56

.54   *Oomycetes

Former name: Biflagellates

.542   *Saprolegniales

.546   *Peronosporales (Downy mildew)

Including Phytophthora

.55   *Deuteromycotina (Deuteromycetes, Fungi Imperfecti)

Including Coelomycetes, Hyphomycetes; Melanconiales, Moniliales, Mycelia Sterilia, Sphaeropsidales

When sexual reproduction of some members of a specific genus of imperfect fungi has been established, class the genus with the kind of fungi of the sexually reproducing members, e.g., Penicillium 579.5654, Fusarium 579.5677

.56   *Ascomycotina (Ascomycetes)

For Discomycetes, see 576.57

---

*Add as instructed under 579.2–579.8

.562   *Hemiascomycetes

> Including Protomycetales, Taphrinales; comprehensive works on Saccharomycetaceae, on yeasts

> Class here Endomycetales

>> *For Saccharomyces (common yeasts), see 579.563. For a specific kind of yeasts not in family Saccharomycetaceae, see the kind, e.g., basidiomycete yeasts 579.59*

.563   *Saccharomyces (Common yeasts)

> Subdivisions are added for the genus as a whole and for individual species

> Class comprehensive works on Saccharomycetaceae in 579.562

.564   *Loculoascomycetes

> Including Asterinales, Dothideales, Melanommatales, Mycrothyriales, Myriangiales, Pleosporales

.565   *Plectomycetes

> Including Gymnascales, Microascales, Onygenales

> Class here Eurotiales

.565 4   *Penicillium

> Subdivisions are added for the genus as a whole and for individual species

.565 7   *Aspergillus

> Subdivisions are added for for the genus as a whole and for individual species

.567   *Pyrenomycetes

> Including Chaetomiales, Claricipitales, Diaporthales, Erysiphales, Laboulbeniales, Sordariales, Xylariales

.567 7   *Hypocreales

> Including Fusarium, Nectria, Trichoderma

.57   *Discomycetes (Cup fungi)

> Including Helotiales, Ostropales, Phacidiales, Tuberales (truffles)

.578   *Pezizales

> Including Ascobolus, morels, saddle fungi

*Add as instructed under 579.2–579.8

.59	*Basidiomycotina (Basidiomycetes)

Including Exobasidiales, Tremellales (jelly fungi); basidiomycete yeasts

Class here Heterobasidiomycetes, Homobasidiomycetes

For Agaricales, comprehensive works on mushrooms, see 579.6

.592	*Uredinales (Rusts)
.593	*Ustilaginales (Smuts)
.597	*Polyporales

Variant name: Aphyllophorales

Including club, coral, pore (bracket, shelf) fungi

.599	*Gastromycetes

Including Lycoperdales (puffballs), Nidulariales (bird's-nest fungi), Phallales (stinkhorns)

.6	***Mushrooms**

Including Boletaceae (boletes), Hydnaceae (spine fungi), Thelephoraceae (leather fungi)

Class here Agaricales (Agaricaceae, gill fungi), toadstools

Class comprehensive works on Basidiomycotina in 579.59

For mushrooms of a specific order other than Agaricales, see the order in 579.5, e.g., morels 579.578

.7	***Lichens**
.8	***Algae**

Class here algology, phycology

For blue-green algae, see 579.39; for lichens, see 579.7

.82	*Minor divisions of algae

Including Chloromonadophyta, Cryptophyta, Xanthophyta (yellow-green algae)

Class here Phytomastigophorea (phytoflagellates); comprehensive works on flagellates, on organisms that may be regarded as either protozoa or algae

For a specific kind of flagellate, see the kind, e.g., Zoomastigophorea 579.42, Oomycetes 579.54, dinoflagellates 579.87; for a specific organism that may be regarded as either protozoa or algae, see the kind in 579.8, e.g., euglenoids 579.84

.83	*Chlorophyta (Green algae)

Including Prasinophyceae; Chaetophorales, Siphonocladales

Class here Chlorophyceae, green seaweeds

*Add as instructed under 579.2–579.8

.832	*Volvocales
	Including Chlamydomonadaceae, Dunaliellaceae
.833	*Chlorococcales
.835	*Caulerpales
	Variant names: Bryopodales, Codiales, Siphonales
.836	*Dasycladales
	Including Acetabularia
.837	*Zygnematales
	Variant name: Conjugales
	Including Desmidiaceae (desmids)
.839	*Charophyceae
	Class here Charales, stoneworts
.84	*Euglenophyta (Euglenoids)
	Variant name: Euglenida
.85	*Bacillariophyceae (Diatoms)
.86	*Chrysophyta (Golden algae)
	Including Haptophyceae
	Class here Chrysophyceae
.87	*Pyrrophyta (Dinoflagellates)
	Including Desmophyceae, red tide
	Class here Dinophyceae
.88	*Phaeophyta (Brown algae)
	Class here Phaeophyceae, comprehensive works on seaweeds
	For green seaweeds, see 579.83; for red seaweeds, see 579.89
.887	*Laminariales
	Including Macrocystis, Saccorhiza, Undaria
	Class here comprehensive works on kelps
	For kelps of order Fucales, see 579.888
.888	*Fucales
	Including Ascophyllum, Fucus, Sargassum
	Class here rockweeds

*Add as instructed under 579.2–579.8

.89   *Rhodophyta (Red algae)

Including Bangiophycideae, red seaweeds

Class here Florideophycideae, Rhodophyceae

Class red tide in 579.87

>   # 580–590   Plants and animals

Internal biological processes and structures relocated to 571–575

Class comprehensive works on biology of plants and animals in 570; class comprehensive works on natural history of plants and animals in 578

580   Plants

This schedule is extensively revised, 581, 583, and subdivisions built on zeros in particular having been prepared with little reference to earlier editions, and 589 having been relocated to 579

A comparative table giving both old and new numbers for a substantial list of topics and equivalence tables showing the numbers in the old and new schedules appear in volume 1 of this edition

Class here botany; Embryophyta, vascular plants (tracheophytes), Spermatophyta (seed plants), Angiospermae (flowering plants); natural history and descriptive biology of plants; interdisciplinary works on plants

Class interdisciplinary works on food from plants in 641.303

For paleobotany, see 561; for internal biological processes and structures of plants, see 571.2; for fungi, see 579.5; for algae, see 579.8. For a specific aspect of plants, see the aspect, e.g., plant cultivation 631.5

See Manual at 560–580; also at 577.26 vs. 579–590; also at 579–590; also at 580 vs. 582.13; also at 630 vs. 579–590, 641.3

SUMMARY

580.1–.9	**Standard subdivisions**
581	**Specific topics in natural history of plants**
582	**Plants noted for specific vegetative characteristics and flowers**
583	**Magnoliopsida (Dicotyledons)**
584	**Liliopsida (Monocotyledons)**
585	**Pinophyta (Gymnosperms)** **Coniferales (Conifers)**
586	**Cryptogamia (Seedless plants)**
587	**Pteridophyta (Vascular seedless plants)**
588	**Bryophyta**

.1–.6   **Standard subdivisions**

Notation from Table 1 as modified under 578.01–578.06, e.g., microscopy of plants 580.282 [*formerly* 578]

---

*Add as instructed under 579.2–579.8

.7	**Education, research, related topics**
.724	Experimental research

Class tissue and organ culture in 571.5382

.73	Collections and exhibits of living plants

Class here botanical gardens

To show area in which collections and exhibits are found, add to base number 580.73 notation 1–9 from Table 2, e.g., botanical gardens of Germany 580.7343

.74	Museums, collections, exhibits

Do not use for collections and exhibits of living plants; class in 580.73

Class here herbariums, collections of dried plants

.75	Museum activities and services Collecting

Class here collecting botanical specimens [*formerly* 579]

.752	Preserving botanical specimens [*formerly* 579]
.753	Organizing and preparing collections and exhibits

For preserving botanical specimens, see 580.752

.8	**History and description with respect to kinds of persons**
.9	**Historical, geographic, persons treatment**
[.914–.919]	Treatment by areas, regions, places in general other than polar, temperate, tropical regions

Do not use; class in 581.73–581.76

.93–.99	Treatment of botany as a discipline by specific continents, countries, localities

Class treatment of plants by specific continents, countries, localities in 581.9

581   Specific topics in natural history of plants

Class here specific nontaxonomic kinds of plants

Except for modifications shown under specific entries, add to each subdivision identified by † as follows:

01–08   Standard subdivisions
               Notation from Table 1 as modified under 580.1–580.8, e.g., preservation of botanical specimens 0752
09   Historical, geographic, persons treatment

Unless other instructions are given, observe the following table of preference, e.g., beneficial aquatic plants 581.63 (*not* 581.76):

Miscellaneous nontaxonomic kinds of plants	581.6
Adaptation	581.4
Genetics and evolution	581.3
Plants characteristic of specific environments, plant ecology	581.7
Treatment of plants by specific continents, countries, localities	581.9

Class a specific topic in natural history of plants with respect to a specific taxonomic group with the group, plus notation 1 from table under 583–588, e.g., useful monocotyledons 584.163

For plants noted for specific vegetative characteristics and flowers, see 582

[.01–.09]   Standard subdivisions

Do not use; class in 580.1–580.9

.3   †Genetics and evolution

.35   †Genetics

Class here works on genetic constitution of plants that elucidate their total function

Class experimental works on plant genetics, comprehensive works on genetics in 576.5

For biochemical genetics in plants, see 572.82

.38   †Evolution

Class here phylogeny

.4   †Adaptation

Class here plants noted for specific kinds of adaptation

.41   †Size, weight, shape

Including silhouettes

---

†Add standard subdivisions as instructed under 581

.42 †Acclimatization and temperature adaptation

> Standard subdivisions are added for acclimatization and temperature adaptation together, for acclimatization alone

> *For seasonal adaptation, see 581.43*

.43 †Seasonal adaptation

> 581.46–581.49 Adaptation of specific parts of plants

> Class comprehensive works in 581.4

> *For physiology of specific parts of plants, see 575*

.46 †Reproductive adaptation

> Including buds, stems specialized for reproduction

> *For flowers, see 582.13*

.464 †Fruits

> *For seeds, see 581.467*

.467 †Seeds

.47 †Protective adaptation

> Including thorns

> Class here bark

.48 †Leaves and fronds

> Standard subdivisions are added for either or both topics in heading

> Including tendrils

.49 †Stems and roots

.495 †Stems

> *For stems specialized for reproduction, see 581.46*

.498 †Roots

.6 **†Miscellaneous nontaxonomic kinds of plants**

> Not provided for elsewhere

> Class here economic botany

> Class carnivorous plants in 583.75

> *See Manual at 583–585*

.63 †Beneficial plants

> Class here herbs

---

†Add standard subdivisions as instructed under 581

.632	†Edible plants
.634	†Medicinal plants
.636	†Plants of industrial and technological value

> Other than medicinal plants

.65	†Harmful plants
.652	†Weeds

> *For agricultural weeds, see 632.5*

.657	†Allergenic plants
.659	†Poisonous plants
.68	†Rare and endangered plants

> Standard subdivisions are added for either or both topics in heading
>
> Including recently extinct species

.7   Plants characteristic of specific environments, plant ecology

> Standard subdivisions are added for either or both topics in heading
>
> Class here autecology
>
> Class plants characteristic of specific environments noted for specific vegetative characteristics and flowers, ecology of such plants in 582

.701–.708   Standard subdivisions

> Notation from Table 1 as modified under 580.1–580.8, e.g., microscopy 581.70282

.709   Historical, geographic, persons treatment

[.709 14–.709 19]   Treatment by areas, regions, places in general other than polar, temperate, tropical regions

> Do not use; class in 581.73–581.76

.73–.76   Specific kinds of environments

> Class here botany of specific kinds of environments
>
> Add to base number 581.7 the numbers following 577 in 577.3–577.6 for the environment only, e.g., aquatic plants 581.76; then to the result add standard subdivisions as modified under 578.01–578.09, e.g., aquatic gardens 581.76073
>
> Class marine botany in 579.177

.78   Synecology and population biology

> Add to base number 581.78 the numbers following 577.8 in 577.801–577.88, e.g., parasitism 581.7857

†Add standard subdivisions as instructed under 581

.9   Treatment of plants by specific continents, countries, localities

> Add to base number 581.9 notation 3–9 from Table 2, e.g., plants in Argentina
> 581.982

582   Plants noted for specific vegetative characteristics and flowers

> Class genetics and evolution, adaptation and parts other than flowers,
> miscellaneous kinds of plants noted for vegetative characteristics and flowers in
> 581

> *For a specific taxonomic group of plants noted for either specific vegetative
> characteristics or flowers, see the group in 583–588, e.g., lilies noted for their
> flowers 584.3*

[.01–.09]   Standard subdivisions

> Do not use; class in 580.1–580.9

.1   Herbaceous and woody plants, plants noted for their flowers

> Except for modifications shown under specific entries, add to each subdivision
> identified by ‡ as follows:
> 01–08   Standard subdivisions
>   Notation from Table 1 as modified under 580.1–580.8, e.g.,
>   botanical gardens 073
> 09   Historical, geographic, persons treatment
> [0914–0919]   Treatment by areas, regions, places in general other than
>   polar, temperate, tropical regions
>   Do not use; class in 7
> 7   The kind of plant in specific environments
>   Add to base number 7 the numbers following 577 in 577.3–577.6,
>   e.g., aquatic plants 76; then to the result add standard subdivisions
>   as modified under 578.01–578.09, e.g., aquatic gardens 76073

> *See Manual at 635.9 vs. 582.1*

[.101–.109]   Standard subdivisions

> Do not use; class in 580.1–580.9

.12   ‡Herbaceous plants

> Including biennials

> Class here annuals

> Class herbaceous plants noted for their flowers in 582.13

> *For herbaceous vines, see 582.189*

‡Add as instructed under 582.1

.13   ‡Plants noted for their flowers

Class here wild flowers, interdisciplinary works on flowers

Class woody plants noted for their flowers in 582.16; class vines noted for their flowers in 582.18; class comprehensive works on Angiospermae (flowering plants) in 580

For physiology of flowers, see 575.6. For a specific aspect of flowers, see the aspect, e.g., flower gardening 635.9, flower arrangement 745.92

See Manual at 580 vs. 582.13

.16   ‡Trees

Class here dendrology; comprehensive works on perennials, on woody plants

Class forest ecology in 577.3

For herbaceous perennials, see 582.12; for shrubs, see 582.17; for woody vines, see 582.18

See Manual at 577.26 vs. 579–590

.17   ‡Shrubs

.18   ‡Vines

Class here woody vines

.189   ‡Herbaceous vines

> ### 583–588 Specific taxonomic groups of plants

Except for modifications shown under specific entries, add to each subdivision identified by * as follows:
01–08   Standard subdivisions
                    Notation from Table 1 as modified under 580.1–580.8, e.g., collections of living plants 073
09   Historical, geographic, persons treatment
[0914–0919]   Treatment by areas, regions, places in general other than polar, temperate, tropical regions
                    Do not use; class in 173–176
1   General topics of natural history of plants
                    Add to base number 1 the numbers following 581 in 581.3–581.7, e.g., aquatic plants 176

Class comprehensive works in 580

See Manual at 579–590: When subdivisions are added for individual species

---

‡Add as instructed under 582.1

> ## 583–584 Angiospermae (Flowering plants)

Class comprehensive works in 580

See Manual at 583–584

583 *Magnoliopsida (Dicotyledons)

See Manual at 583–585: Interdisciplinary works; also at 583–584

SUMMARY

583.2	Magnoliidae
.3	Ranunculidae
.4	Hamamelididae
.5	Caryophyllidae
.6	Dilleniidae
.7	Rosidae
.8	Other orders of Rosidae
.9	Asteridae

.2 *Magnoliidae

Including Rafflesiales; Rafflesiaceae (Cytinaceae); monster flower

.22 *Magnoliales

Including Magnoliaceae (magnolia family), Annonaceae (custard apple family), Myristicaceae (nutmeg family), Winteraceae (Winter's bark family)

Including cherimoya, cucumber tree, lancewoods, mace, michelias, papaws, tulip tree (yellow poplar), wild cinnamon

See also 583.626 for papaws of family Caricaceae

.23 *Laurales

Including Chloranthaceae, Hernandiaceae, Monimiaceae

Including avocados, cinnamon, Oregon myrtle (California laurel), sassafras, sweet bay (bay laurel); comprehensive works on laurels

Class here Lauraceae (laurel family)

Class comprehensive works on myrtles in 583.765

For laurels of Ericaceae family, see 583.66; for spurge laurel, see 583.67; for hedge laurels, see 583.72

See Manual at 579–590: Nomenclature

.25 *Piperales

Including Saururaceae (lizard's-tail family); black pepper, peperomias

Class here Piperaceae (pepper family)

Class peppers of Solanaceae family, comprehensive works on peppers in 583.952

*Add as instructed under 583–588

.26   *Aristolochiales

>   Class here Aristolochiaceae (birthwort family)

.29   *Nymphaeales

>   Including Ceratophyllaceae (hornworts)
>
>   Class here Nymphaeaceae (water lilies)
>
>   Class Nelumbo in 583.3
>
>> *See also 588.3 for hornworts of subclass Anthocerotidae (horned liverworts)*

.3   *Ranunculidae

>   Including Illiciales, Nelumbonales (lotuses); magnolia vine, star anise

.34   *Ranunculales (Ranales)

>   Including Ranunculaceae (buttercup family), Berberidaceae (barberry family), Menispermaceae (moonseed family), Podophyllaceae
>
>   Including aconites, anemones, Christmas rose, clematises, columbines, delphiniums (larkspurs), hellebores, lesser celandine, mayapple (mayflower, mandrake), monkshoods (wolfsbanes)
>
>> *See also 583.952 for mandrakes of family Solanaceae*

.35   *Papaverales (Rhoeadales)

>   Including Papaveraceae (poppy family), Fumariaceae (fumitory family); bleeding hearts, bloodroot, celandines, Dutchman's breeches
>
>> *See also 583.34 for lesser celandine*

.36   *Sarraceniales

>   Class here Sarraceniaceae (New World pitcher plant family)
>
>   Class comprehensive works on carnivorous plants, on pitcher plants in 583.75

.4   *Hamamelididae

.43   *Minor orders of Hamamelididae

>   Including Balanopales (Balanopsidales), Barbeyales, Casuarinales (beefwood order), Cercidiphyllales (katsura tree), Didymelales, Eucommiales, Eupteleales, Leitneriales, Myricales (wax myrtle order), Trochodendrales
>
>   Including bayberries, candleberry, sweet gale (bog myrtle)
>
>   Class Jamaica bayberry, comprehensive works on myrtles in 583.765
>
>> *See also 583.93 for bog myrtle (buckbean)*

*Add as instructed under 583–588

.44   *Hamamelidales

> Including Platanaceae (sycamore family); ironwood, plane trees, sweet gums

> Class here Hamamelidaceae (witch hazel family)

> Class comprehensive works on ironwoods in 583.48

.45   *Urticales

> Including Urticaceae (nettle family), Cannabaceae (hemp family), Moraceae (mulberry family), Ulmaceae (elm family)

> Including banyan, breadfruits, figs, hackberries, hops, marijuana, osage orange, pileas, ramie (China grass plant), rubber plant (India rubber tree), West Indian boxwood; comprehensive works on hemps

>> *For hemps of a specific family other than Cannabaceae, see the family, e.g., aloe and sisil hemps 584.352*

>> *See also 583.69 for boxwoods of family Buxaceae, 583.96 for dead nettles*

.46   *Fagales

> Including Castaneoideae (chestnuts), Fagoideae (beeches), Quercoideae (oaks); chinquapin, cork oak

> Class here Fagaceae

.48   *Betulales

> Including alders, filberts (hazelnuts), hornbeams; comprehensive works on ironwoods

> Class here Betulaceae (birch family)

>> *For ironwoods of a specific family other then Betulaceae, see the family, e.g., ironwoods of family Rhamnaceae 583.86*

.49   *Juglandales

> Including butternuts, hickories, pecans

> Class here Juglandaceae (walnut family)

.5   *Caryophyllidae

> Including Plumbaginales (leadwort order), Theligonales (Cynocrambales); sea lavenders, thrifts

.53   *Caryophyllales

> Including Caryophyllaceae (pink family), Aizoaceae (carpetweed family), Amaranthaceae (amaranth family), Chenopodiaceae (goosefoot family), Nyctaginaceae, Phytolaccaceae (pokeweed family), Portulacaceae (purslane family)

> Including beets, bougainvilleas, carnations, four-o'clock, ice plants (sea figs), lithops (living stones), Madeira vine, spinach

*Add as instructed under 583–588

.56 *Cactales

    Class here Cactaceae (cactus family)

.57 *Polygonales

    Including dock, rhubarbs, sorrel

    Class here Polygonaceae (buckwheat family)

.6 ***Dilleniidae**

.62 *Miscellaneous orders of Dilleniidae

    Limited to orders named here and below

    Including Dilleniales, Paeoniales (peony order)

.624 *Theales

    Including Theaceae (Ternstroemiaceae, tea family), Clusiaceae (Guttiferae), Dipterocarpaceae, Elatinaceae, Hypericaceae, Marcgraviaceae, Ochnaceae

    Including camellias, garcinias, mammee apple, mangosteen, Stewartia

.625 *Violales

    Including Violaceae (violet family), Bixaceae (annatto tree), Cistaceae (rockrose family), Flacourtiaceae; pansies

    See also 583.95 for African violets

.626 *Passiflorales

    Including Caricaceae (papaya family), Turneraceae; granadillas, maypop, papaws

    Class here Passifloraceae (passionflower family)

    See also 583.22 for papaws of family Annonaceae

.627 *Begoniales

    Class here Begoniaceae, begonias

.628 *Tamaricales

    Including Fouquieriaceae (candlewood family); alkali heath, ocotillo

    Class here Tamaricaceae (tamarisk family)

.63 *Cucurbitales

    Including cucumbers, melons, pepos, pumpkins, squashes, watermelons

    Class here Cucurbitaceae (gourd family)

*Add as instructed under 583–588

1124

.64   *Capparales

Former name: Capparidales

Including Capparaceae (caper family), Resedaceae (mignonette family)

Including alyssums, cabbages, candytufts, cresses, crucifixion thorns, Nasturtium genus, radishes, rapes, rutabagas, shepherd's purse, spiderflowers, stocks (Matthiola), turnips, wallflowers, watercresses

Class here Brassicaceae (Cruciferae, mustard family)

See also 583.76 for Brazilian spiderflowers, 583.79 for nasturtiums of family Tropaeolaceae

.65   *Salicales

Including Populus (poplars and aspens), cottonwoods

Class here Salicaceae (willow family), salix

See also 583.22 for yellow poplar

.66   *Ericales

Including Clethraceae (pepperbush family), Epacridaceae, Monotropaceae (Indian pipe family), Pyrolaceae, Saurauiaceae

Including azaleas, blueberries, cranberries, crowberries, heather, huckleberries, kalmias, kiwi (Chinese gooseberry), mountain laurel, rhododendrons, sourwood, wintergreens

Class here Ericaceae (heath family)

Class comprehensive works on laurels in 583.23

.67   *Ebenales, Primulales, Diapensiales, Thymelaeales (mezereum order)

Including daphnes, galax, spurge laurel

.674   *Ebenales

Including Ebenaceae (ebony family), Sapotaceae, Styracaceae (storax family), Symplocaceae (sweetleaf family)

Including persimmons, sapodilla, star apples

.675   *Primulales

Including Primulaceae (primrose family), Myrsinaceae, Theophrastaceae

Including auriculas, coralberry, cyclamens, loosestrife, primulas, shooting stars

Class evening primroses in 583.76

.68   *Malvales

Including Bombacaceae (silk cotton tree family), Elaeocarpaceae, Sterculiaceae (cacao family), Tiliaceae (linden family)

Including balsa, baobabs, basswood, jute, kapok, kola nuts, lime trees

*Add as instructed under 583–588

.685   *Malvaceae (Mallow family)

> Including cotton, hibiscuses, hollyhock, okra, rose of Sharon

.69   *Euphorbiales

> Including Buxaceae (boxwood family), Dichapetalaceae
>
> Including cassavas (maniocs), castor-oil plant, copperleaves, crotons, crown of thorns, heveas, manchineels, mercuries, poinsettias, rubber tree, snow-on-the-mountain, tallow tree, tung tree
>
> Class here Euphorbiaceae (spurge family)
>
> *See also 583.45 for West Indian boxwood*

.7   ***Rosidae**

> *For orders of Rosidae not provided for below, see 583.8*

.72   *Saxifragales

> Including Saxifragaceae (saxifrage family), Brunelliaceae, Bruniaceae, Byblidaceae, Cephalotaceae, Crassulaceae, Cunoniaceae, Escalloniaceae, Grossulariaceae (gooseberry family), Hydrangeaceae (hydrangea family), Parnassiaceae, Pittosporaceae (hedge laurel family)
>
> Including brexias, currants, deutzias, escallonias, houseleeks (live-forevers), mock oranges (syringas), pickaback plants, Ribes, stonecrops (orpines, sedums), Virginia willow
>
> Class comprehensive works on carnivorous plants in 583.75

.73   *Rosales

> Including Chrysobalanaceae
>
> Including almonds, apples, apricots, blackberries, cane fruits, cherries, chokeberries, cinquefoils, dewberries, drupaceous fruits, hawthorns, loquat, medlar, mountain ashes, peaches, pears, plums, pomaceous fruits, pyracanthas (fire thorns), quince, raspberries, Rubus, serviceberries, spireas, strawberries
>
> Class here Rosaceae (rose family)
>
> *See also 583.765 for rose apples, 583.77 for hog plums of family Anacardiaceae*

.734   *Rosa (Roses)

> Subdivisions are added for the genus as a whole and for individual species

---

*Add as instructed under 583–588

.74   ***Fabales (Leguminales)**

Including alfalfa, beans, beggar's lice, bluebonnet, carob, clovers, indigo plants, kudzu, lentils, lespedezas, locoweeds, locusts, peanuts (groundnuts), Scotch broom, shamrocks, smoke tree, soybean (soja, soya), tamarind, vetches, wisterias

Class here Fabaceae (pea family)

> *See also 583.77 for smoke trees of family Anacardiaceae; 583.79 for shamrock of family Oxalidaceae*

.748   ***Mimosaceae (Mimosa family)**

Including acacias, mesquite, sensitive plants, silk tree

.749   ***Caesalpiniaceae (Senna family)**

Including redbuds

.75   ***Nepenthales**

Including Nepenthaceae (Old World pitcher plant family), Droseraceae (sundew family); Venus's flytrap; comprehensive works on pitcher plants

Class here comprehensive works on carnivorous plants

> *For Sarraceniaceae (New World pitcher plants), see 583.36; for Byblidaceae, Cephalotaceae, see 583.72; for Lentibulariaceae, see 583.95*

.76   ***Myrtales**

Including Anisophylleaceae, Combretaceae, Lecythidaceae (Brazil nut family), Lythraceae (loosestrife family), Melastomataceae (meadow beauty family), Onagraceae (evening primrose family), Trapaceae

Including Brazilian spiderflowers, cigar flower, clarkias, crape myrtle, fireweed, fuchsias, pomegranate

Class mangroves of family Combretaceae in 583.763

> *See also 583.64 for spiderflowers of family Capparaceae, 583.675 for loosestrife of family Primulaceae, 583.99 for fireweeds of family Asteraceae*

---

*Add as instructed under 583–588

.763   *Rhizophoraceae and Sonneratiaceae

Including mangroves of family Combretaceae, e.g., button mangrove, white mangrove

Class here comprehensive works on mangroves

Subdivisions are added for Rhizophoraceae and Sonneratiaceae together, for Rhizophoraceae alone

Class mangrove swamp ecology in 577.698

For mangroves of family Verbenaceae, see 583.96; for mangrove of family Arecaceae (nipa palm), see 584.5

See Manual at 577.26 vs. 579–590

.765   *Myrtaceae (Myrtle family)

Including allspice (pimento), clove, guavas, Jamaica bayberry (bay rum tree), rose apples, water chestnuts; comprehensive works on myrtles

For Eucalyptus, see 583.766. For myrtle of a specific family other than Myrtaceae, see the family, e.g., Oregon myrtle 583.23, wax myrtle 583.43, crape myrtle 583.76

See also 583.952 for pimientos (peppers), 584.84 for Chinese water chestnut

.766   *Eucalyptus (Gum trees)

Subdivisions are added for the genus as a whole and for individual species

.77   *Rutales

Including Rutaceae (orange family), Anacardiaceae (mango family), Burseraceae (incense tree family), Coriariaceae, Meliaceae (mahogany family), Simaroubaceae (ailanthus family)

Including cashew, chinaberry tree, citrus fruits, cork trees, hog plums (Spanish plums), hop tree, orange jessamine, pistachio nut, poison ivies, rue, smoke trees, sumacs, tree of heaven, varnish trees; comprehensive works on balms

Class comprehensive works on ivies in 583.84

For balm of a specific family other than Burseraceae, see the family, e.g., bee balms 583.96

See also 583.46 for cork oak, 583.73 for hog plums of family Rosaceae, 583.74 for smoke tree of family Fabaceae

.78   *Sapindales

Including Sapindaceae (soapberry family), Aceraceae (maple family), Hippocastanaceae (horse chestnut family), Sabiaceae, Staphyleaceae (bladdernut family)

Including buckeyes, honey bush, hopbushes, horse chestnuts, litchis

*Add as instructed under 583–588

.79   *Geraniales

Including Geraniaceae (geranium family), Balsaminaceae (balsam family), Erythroxylaceae (coca family), Hugoniaceae, Humiriaceae, Ixonanthaceae, Linaceae (flax family), Malpighiaceae, Oxalidaceae (wood sorrel family), Tropaeolaceae (nasturtium family), Zygophyllaceae (lignum vitae family)

Including creosote bush, erodiums, impatiens, jewelweeds (touch-me-nots), pelargoniums, shamrock, wild mango (dika)

See also 583.64 for Nasturtium genus in family Brassicaceae, 583.74 for shamrocks of family Fabaceae

.8   Other orders of Rosidae

[.801–.809]   Standard subdivisions

Do not use; class in 583.701–583.709

.82   *Minor orders of Rosidae

Including Connarales, Elaeagnales (oleaster order), Hippuridales (Haloragales), Podostemales (riverweed order), Polygalales (milkwort order); Vochysiaceae

Including gunneras, mare's tail

.84   *Cornales

Including Cornaceae (dogwood family), Araliaceae (ginseng family, ivy family)

Including Garrya, tupelos (sour gums), wild sarsaparilla; comprehensive works on ivies

For ivies of a specific family other than Araliaceae, see the family, e.g., poison ivies 583.77

See also 584.356 for sarsaparilla of family Smilacaceae

.849   *Umbelliferae (Apiaceae, Parsley family)

Including anise, caraway, carrots, celery, dills, parsnips, poison hemlocks, Queen Anne's lace

.85   *Celastrales

Including Celastraceae (staff tree family), Aquifoliaceae (holly family), Hippocrateaceae, Icacinaceae; bittersweet, khat, maté

See also 583.952 for bittersweet of family Solanaceae

.86   *Rhamnales

Including Rhamnaceae (buckthorn family), Leeaceae, Vitaceae (grape family); Boston ivy, ironwoods, jujubes, Virginia creeper

Class comprehensive works on ironwoods in 583.48

*Add as instructed under 583–588

.87   *Oleales

Including ashes, forsythias, jasmines, lilacs, privets

Class here Oleaceae (olive family)

.88   *Santalales

Including Santalaceae (sandalwood family), Balanophoraceae, Loranthaceae (mistletoe family), Olacaceae, Opiliaceae, Viscaceae

Class Rafflesiaceae in 583.2

.89   *Proteales

Including banksias, grevilleas, hakeas, macadamias, Persoonia, proteas, Telopea (waratahs)

Class here Proteaceae

.9   *Asteridae

Including Calycerales

.92   *Dipsacales

Including Dipsacaceae (teasel family), Caprifoliaceae (honeysuckle family), Valerianaceae (valerian family)

Including elders, snowballs, viburnums

.93   *Gentianales

Including Gentianaceae (gentian family), Apocynaceae (dogbane family, Indian hemp family), Asclepiadaceae (milkweed family), Loganiaceae, Potaliaceae, Rubiaceae (madder family)

Including bog myrtle, buckbeans, buttonbushes, carrion flowers, cinchonas, coffee, gardenias, Indian sarsaparilla, oleanders, partridgeberry, periwinkles, Plumeria, rauwolfias, stephanotises

See also 583.43 for bog myrtle (sweet gale), 584.356 for carrion flower and sarsaprillas of family Smilacaceae

.94   *Polemoniales

Including Polemoniaceae (phlox family), Boraginaceae (forget-me-not family), Convolvulaceae (morning glory family), Cuscutaceae (dodder family), Hydrophyllaceae (waterleaf family), Loasaceae

Including baby blue-eyes, borage, comfreys, dichondras, heliotropes, honeyworts, hound's-tongues, Jacob's ladders, sweet potatoes (yams), Virginia cowslip (bluebell)

See also 583.98 for bluebells of bellflower family, 584.32 for bluebells of lily family, 584.357 for yams of family Dioscoreaceae

*Add as instructed under 583–588

.95   *Scrophulariales

Including Scrophulariaceae (figwort family, snapdragon family), Acanthaceae (acanthus family), Bignoniaceae (catalpa family), Buddlejaceae, Gesneriaceae, Lentibulariaceae (bladderwort family), Myoporaceae, Nolanaceae, Orobanchaceae (broomrape family), Pedaliaceae (sesame family), Plantaginaceae (plantago family)

Including African violets, butterfly bushes, calabash tree, foxglove, mulleins, Penstemon, plantains, trumpet creepers, unicorn plants

Class here Personales

Class comprehensive works on violets in 583.625; class comprehensive works on carnivorous plants in 583.75

See also 584.39 for plantain of banana family

.952   *Solanaceae (Nightshade family, Potato family)

Including belladonna, bittersweet, butterfly flowers (schizanthuses), capsicums, daturas, eggplants, henbane, jimsonweed, mandrakes, paprika, petunias, pimientos, tobacco, tomatoes; cayenne, red, sweet peppers; comprehensive works on peppers

For pepper of Piperaceae family, see 583.25

See also 583.34 for mandrake of family Podophyllaceae (mayapple), 583.765 for pimento (allspice), 583.85 for bittersweet of family Celastraceae

.96   *Lamiales

Including Verbenaceae (verbena family)

Including basils, bee balms, black mangrove, catnip, Chinese artichoke, dead nettles, ground ivy, horehound, hyssop, lavenders, lopseed, marjorams, rosemary, sage, teak, thymes, vervains

Class here Lamiaceae (Labiatae, mint family)

Class comprehensive works on mangroves in 583.763; class comprehensive works on balms in 583.77

See also 583.99 for sagebrushes

.98   *Campanulales

Including Campanulaceae (bellflower family), Goodeniaceae, Lobeliaceae, Stylidiaceae; bluebells, Campanula, Indian tobacco

See also 583.94 for bluebells of forget-me-not family, 584.32 for bluebells of lily family

*Add as instructed under 583–588

.99 *Asterales

Including artichokes, asters, black-eyed Susans, chamomiles, chicory, chrysanthemums, cornflower, cosmos, dahlias, dandelions, endive, everlastings, fireweeds, fleabanes, gerberas, goldenrods, groundsels (ragworts), guayule, lettuce, marigolds, ragweeds, safflower, sagebrushes, sunflowers, thistles, wormwoods, zinnias

Class here Asteraceae (Compositae)

> *See also 583.76 for fireweed of family Onagraceae, 583.96 for Chinese artichoke*

584 *Liliopsida (Monocotyledons)

See Manual at 583–585: Interdisciplinary works; also at 583–584

SUMMARY

584.3	**Liliaidae**
.4	**Orchidales**
.5	**Arecidae**
.6	**Cyclanthales, Arales, Pandanales, Typhales**
.7	**Alismidae**
.8	**Commelinidae**
.9	**Poales (Graminales, Grasses)**

.3 *Liliidae

Class here Liliales, lilies

For Orchidales, see 584.4

See also 583.29 for water lilies

> 584.32–584.35 Liliales

Class comprehensive works in 584.3

.32 *Liliaceae (Lily family)

Including aloes, bluebells, day lilies, Easter lily, hostas (plantain lilies), hyacinths, lily of the valley, trilliums, tulips

Class comprehensive works on lilies in 584.3

> *See also 583.94 for bluebells of forget-me-not family, 583.98 for bluebells of bellflower family, 584.72 for water hyacynths*

.33 *Alliaceae

Including African lilies, chives, garlics, leeks, onions, shallots

.34 *Amaryllidaceae (Amaryllis family)

Including daffodils, narcissus; atamasco, Peruvian, spider lilies

*Add as instructed under 583–588

.35	Other families of Liliales

Including Cyanastraceae, Philesiaceae, Philydraceae, Pontederiaceae, Taccaceae, Tecophilaeaceae, Xanthorrhoeaceae

Class comprehensive works in 584.3

[.350 1–.350 9]	Standard subdivisions

Do not use; class in 584.301–584.309

.352	*Agavaceae

Including agaves, aloe hemp, aloes (century plants), dracaenas, sansevierias (snake plants), sisal hemp, tequila, yuccas

Class comprehensive works on hemps in 583.45

.353	*Alstroemeriaceae

Including box lily

.354	*Haemodoraceae (Bloodwort family), Hypoxidaceae, Velloziaceae (tree lily family)

.355	*Asparagaceae

Including Ruscaceae, asparaguses

.356	*Smilacaceae

Including cat briers, carrion flower, greenbriers, sarsaparillas

See also 583.84 for wild sarsaparilla of ginseng family; 583.93 for carrion flowers of family Asclepiadaceae, Indian sarsaparilla

.357	*Dioscoreaceae (Yam family)

See also 583.94 for sweet potatoes (yams)

.37	*Triuridales

Class here Triuridaceae

.38	*Iridales

Including Burmanniaceae

Including blackberry lily, crocuses, freesias, gladiolus (sword lilies), saffron, tigerflowers

Class here Iridaceae (iris family)

*Add as instructed under 583–588

.39   *Zingiberales

Including Zingiberaceae (ginger family), Cannaceae (canna family), Costaceae, Heliconiaceae, Marantaceae (arrowroot family), Musaceae (banana family)

Including abaca (Manila hemp), cardamoms, ginger lily, heliconias, plantain, prayer plant, turmerics, zebra plant

Class comprehensive works on hemps in 583.45

See also 583.95 for plantains of plantago family

.4   ***Orchidales**

Including vanillas

Class here Orchidaceae (orchid family)

.5   ***Arecidae**

Including coconuts, dates, nipa palm (mangrove), palmettos, rattans

Class here Arecales (Palmales), Arecaceae (Palmae, palm family)

For Cyclanthales, Arales, Pandanales, Typhales, see 584.6

.6   ***Cyclanthales, Arales, Pandanales, Typhales**

.62   *Cyclanthales

Including jipijapa (Panama hat palm)

Class here Cyclanthaceae

.64   *Arales

Including Lemnaceae (duckweed family)

Including anthuriums, caladiums, calla lilies, Chinese evergreen, dieffenbachias, elephant's ears, jack-in-the-pulpits, monsteras, philodendrons, skunk cabbages, taro, watermeals

Class here Araceae (arum family)

Class comprehensive works on lilies in 584.3

See also 583.64 for cabbages of Brassicaceae family

.66   *Pandanales

Including screw pines

Class here Pandanaceae (hala family)

.68   *Typhales

Including Sparganiaceae, Sparganium (bur reeds)

Class here Typhaceae, Typha (cattails and bulrushes)

Class comprehensive works on bulrushes in 584.84

*Add as instructed under 583–588

.7   ***Alismidae**

.72   *Alismales (Alismatales)

Including Butomaceae (water poppy family), Limnocharitaceae; arrowheads, water hyacinths

Class here Alismaceae (water plantain family)

.73   *Hydrocharitales

Including turtle grass

Class here Hydrocharitaceae (frogbit family)

.74   *Najadales (Potamogetonales)

Including Najadaceae (naiad family), Aponogetonaceae (lattice plant family), Juncaginaceae (arrow grass family), Lilaeaceae, Posidoniaceae, Ruppiaceae (widgeon grass family), Scheuchzeriaceae, Zanichelliaceae, Zosteraceae (eelgrass family)

.742   *Potamogetonaceae (Pondweed family)

.8   ***Commelinidae**

Including Restionales

For Poales, see 584.9

.82   *Juncales

Including Thurniaceae

Class here Juncaceae (rush family), comprehensive works on rushes

For rushes of cattail family, see 584.68; for rushes of sedge family, see 584.84

.84   *Cyperales

Including Chinese water chestnut, cotton grasses, papyrus, umbrella plant; beak, spike rushes; comprehensive works on bulrushes

Class here Cyperaceae (sedge family)

Class comprehensive works on rushes in 584.82

For bulrushes of cattail family, see 584.68

.85   *Bromeliales

Including Bromeliaceae (pineapple family); bromeliads, Spanish moss

.86   *Commelinales

Including Rapateaceae, Xyridaceae (yellow-eyed grass family); boat lily, wandering Jews

Class here Commelinaceae (spiderwort family)

---

*Add as instructed under 583–588

.87   *Eriocaulales

Class here Eriocaulaceae (pipewort family)

.9   *Poales (Graminales, Grasses)

Including Agrosteae, Anomochloeae, Arundineae, Arundinelleae, Aveneae (oat tribe), Bambuseae (bamboo tribe), Chlorideae (gama grass tribe), Eragrosteae, Festuceae (fescue tribe), Hordeeae (barley tribe), Leptureae, Lygeeae, Nardeae, Olyreae, Oryzeae (rice tribe), Pappophoreae, Parianeae, Phalarideae (canary grass tribe), Phareae, Sporoboleae, Stipeae, Streptochaeteae, Thysanolaeneae, Zoysieae

Including bent grasses, bluegrasses, bromegrasses, espartos, orchard grass (cocksfoot), pampas grass, reeds, rye, timothy, wheat

Class here Poaceae (Gramineae), Pooideae

Class comprehensive works on grassland ecology in 577.4; class Cyperaceae in 584.84

See Manual at 577.26 vs. 579–590

.92   *Panicoideae

Including Paniceae (millet tribe), Andropogoneae (sugarcane tribe), Maydeae (maize tribe)

Including citronella, corn, crabgrasses, milos, panic grasses, proso, sorghums, Sudan grass, thatch grasses

585   *Pinophyta (Gymnosperms)   Coniferales (Conifers)

Class here Pinicae

See Manual at 583–585: Interdisciplinary works

>   **585.2–585.5   Coniferales**

Class comprehensive works in 585

.2   *Pinaceae (Pine family)

Including firs, hemlocks, larches, piñons, spruces, tamaracks, true cedars; comprehensive works on cedars, on pines

For Huon, dammar, New Zealand red pines, see 585.3; for cypress pine, cedars of the cypress family, see 585.4; for China fir, Japanese and Tasmanian cedars, see 585.5

.3   *Podocarpaceae, Araucariaceae, Cephalotaxaceae (plum-yew family)

Including Huon pine, kauris (dammar pines), New Zealand red pine, podocarpuses (yellowwoods), Prince Albert's yew

Subdivisions are added for Podocarpaceae, Araucariaceae, Cephalotaxaceae together; for Podocarpaceae alone

---

*Add as instructed under 583–588

.4 ***Cupressaceae (Cypress family)**

Including arborvitaes, cypress pine, junipers; Chilean, incense, red cedars

Class here comprehensive works on cypresses

For bald cypresses, see 585.5

.5 ***Taxodiaceae**

Including bald cypresses, China fir, redwood, sequoias; Japanese, Tasmanian cedars

.6 ***Taxales**

Class here Taxaceae (yew family), comprehensive works on yews

For plum and Prince Albert's yews, see 585.3

.7 ***Ginkgoales**

Class here Ginkgoaceae; ginkgo (maidenhair tree)

.8 ***Gneticae**

Including Gnetales, Ephedrales (ephedras), Welwitschiales (tumboa plant); Gnetum, Mormon tea

.9 ***Cycadales (Cycads)**

Class here Cycadaceae

586 ***Cryptogamia (Seedless plants)**

For fungi , see 579.5; for algae, see 579.8; for Pteridophyta, see 587; for Bryophyta, see 588

587 ***Pteridophyta (Vascular seedless plants)**

Variant name: vascular cryptogams

.2 ***Sphenopsida (Articulatae, Horsetails)**

Class here Equisetales, Equisetaceae, Equisetum

.3 ***Polypodiopsida (Filicopsida, ferns)**

Including Marsiliales (waterclovers), Salviniales

Including bracken, brakes, spleenworts, water spangles; maidenhair, royal, staghorn ferns

Class here Polypodiales (Filicales)

See also 587.4 for whisk ferns

.33 ***Marattiales (Giant ferns) and Ophioglossales**

Including adder's-tongues, moonworts; grape, rattlesnake ferns

*Add as instructed under 583–588

.4   **Psilopsida (Whisk ferns)**

          Class here Psilotales

.9   **Lycopsida**

          Including Lycopodiales (club mosses), Isoetales (quillworts), Selaginellales (spike mosses); resurrection plants

          Class here club mosses in broad sense comprising Lycopsida

588   *Bryophyta

.2   **Bryopsida (Musci, mosses)**

          Including Andreaeales (black mosses, granite mosses)

          Class here Bryales (true mosses)

          See also 587.9 for club and spike mosses, 588.3 for scale mosses

.29   *Sphagnales

          Including Sphagnaceae (peat mosses, bog mosses)

.3   **Hepatopsida (Liverworts)**

          Including Anthocerotidae (horned liverworts, hornworts), Marchantiales (great liverworts)

          Class here Hepatidae (Hepaticae), Jungermanniales, leafy liverworts (scale mosses)

          See also 583.29 for hornworts of family Ceratophyllaceae

[589]   Thallobionta

          Relocated to 579

[.9]   **Prokaryotes (Bacteria)**

          Relocated to 579.3

*Add as instructed under 583–588

590 Animals

This schedule is extensively revised, 591, 597, 599, and subdivisions built on zeros in particular having been prepared with little reference to earlier editions

A comparative table giving both old and new numbers for a substantial list of topics and equivalence tables showing the numbers in the old and new schedules appear in volume 1 of this edition

Class here natural history and descriptive biology of animals, zoology, interdisciplinary works on animals

Class interdisciplinary works on food from animals in 641.306

> *For paleozoology, see 560; for internal biological processes and structures in animals, see 571.1. For a specific aspect of animals, see the aspect, e.g., animal husbandry 636*
>
> *See Manual at 560–590; also at 577.26 vs. 579–590; also at 579–590; also at 630 vs. 579–590, 641.3; also at 800 vs. 398.245, 590, 636*

SUMMARY

596	Chordata
.2	Urochordata (Tunicata)
.4	Cephalochordata (Lancelets)

597	Cold-blooded vertebrates Pisces (Fishes)
.176 36	Pond ecology
.2	Agnatha (Jawless fishes)
.3	Selachii, Holocephali, Sarcopterygii
.4	Miscellaneous superorders of Actinopterygii
.5	Protacanthopterygii Salmoniformes
.6	Scopelomorpha, Paracanthopterygii, Acanthopterygii
.7	Perciformes
.8	Amphibia
.9	Reptilia

598	Aves (Birds)
.072 3	Descriptive research and birdwatching
.163–.176	[Beneficial and aquatic birds]
.3	Gruiformes, Charadriiformes, Ciconiiformes, Phoenicopteriformes
.4	Miscellaneous orders of water birds
.5	Palaeognathae
.6	Galliformes and Columbiformes
.7	Miscellaneous orders of land birds
.8	Passeriformes (Perching birds)
.9	Falconiformes, Strigiformes, Caprimulgiformes

599	Mammalia (Mammals)
.163	Beneficial mammals
.2	Marsupialia and Monotremata
.3	Miscellaneous orders of Eutheria (placental mammals)
.4	Chiroptera (Bats)
.5	Cetacea and Sirenia
.6	Ungulates
.7	Carnivora Fissipedia (Land carnivores)
.8	Primates
.9	Hominidae Homo sapiens

.1–.6   Standard subdivisions

Notation from Table 1 as modified under 578.01–578.06, e.g., microscopy of animals 590.282 [*formerly* 578]

.7   Education, research, related topics

.724   Experimental research

Class tissue and organ culture in 571.5381

.73   Collections and exhibits of living animals

Class here general zoos; zoos limited to vertebrates in general, to land vertebrates in general, to mammals in general

To show area in which collections and exhibits are found, add to base number 590.73 notation 1–9 from Table 2, e.g., zoos of Germany 590.7343

Class zoos limited to other groups of animals with the group, e.g., insect zoos 595.7073, aquariums for marine vertebrates 596.177073

.74	Museums, collections, exhibits

Do not use for collections and exhibits of living animals; class in 590.73

.75	Museum activities and services	Collecting

Class here collecting zoological specimens [*formerly* 579]

.752	Preserving zoological specimens [*formerly* 579]
.753	Organizing and preparing collections and exhibits

For preserving zoological specimens, see 590.752

.8 **History and description with respect to kinds of persons**

.9 **Historical, geographic, persons treatment**

[.914–.919]	Treatment by areas, regions, places in general other than polar, temperate, tropical regions

Do not use; class in 591.73–591.77

.93–.99	Treatment of zoology by specific continents, countries, localities

Class treatment of animals by specific continents, countries, localities in 591.9

591 Specific topics in natural history of animals

Class here specific nontaxonomic kinds of animals

Except for modifications shown under specific entries, add to each subdivision identified by † as follows:
01–08   Standard subdivisions
        Notation from Table 1 as modified under 590.1–590.8, e.g.,
        preservation of zoological specimens 0752
09   Historical, geographic, persons treatment

Unless other instructions are given, observe the following table of preference, e.g., social behavior of beneficial animals 591.56 (*not* 591.63):

Behavior	591.5
Miscellaneous nontaxonomic kinds of animals	591.6
Physical adaptation	591.4
Genetics, evolution, young of animals	591.3
Animals characteristic of specific environments, animal ecology	591.7
Treatment of animals by specific continents, countries, localities	591.9

Class a specific topic in natural history of animals with respect to a specific taxonomic group of animals with the group of animals, plus notation 1 from table under 592–599, e.g., beneficial mammals 599.163

SUMMARY

591.3	**Genetics, evolution, young of animals**
.4	Physical adaptation
.5	Behavior
.6	Miscellaneous nontaxonomic kinds of animals
.7	Animals characteristic of specific environments, animal ecology
.9	Treatment of animals by specific continents, countries, localities

[.01–.09]   Standard subdivisions

> Do not use; class in 590.1–590.9

.3   †Genetics, evolution, young of animals

.35   †Genetics

> Class here works on genetic constitution of animals that elucidate their total function
>
> Class experimental works on animal genetics, comprehensive works on genetics in 576.5
>
> *For biochemical genetics in animals, see 572.81*

.38   †Evolution

> Class here phylogeny
>
> Class sexual selection in 591.562

.39   †Young of animals

.4   †Physical adaptation

> Class here animals noted for specific kinds of physical adaptation, comprehensive works on animal adaptation
>
> *For behavioral adaptation, see 591.5*

.41   †Size, weight, shape

> Including silhouettes

.42   †Acclimatization and temperature adaptation

> Standard subdivisions are added for acclimatization and temperature adaptation together, for acclimatization alone
>
> *For seasonal adaptation, see 591.43*

.43   †Seasonal adaptation

.46   †Reproductive adaptation

> Class here secondary sexual characteristics
>
> Class reproductive physiology in 573.6

.468   †Eggs

> *For physiology of eggs, see 573.68*

†Add standard subdivisions as instructed under 591

.47	†Protective and locomotor adaptations
	Standard subdivisions are added for protective and locomotor adaptations together, for protective adaptation alone
	Including animal weapons, horns, tusks; integument
	Class here animal defenses
	Class physiology of musculoskeletal system in 573.7
	For protective behavior, see 591.566
.472	†Camouflage
	Class here color, protective coloration
	Class physiology of color in 573.5; class mimicry in 591.473
.473	†Mimicry
.477	†Protective covering
	Class here exoskeletons, shells, armored animals
.479	†Locomotor adaptation
	Including legs, tracks, wings
.5	**†Behavior [*formerly also* 574.5]**
	Class here animal psychology, behavioral adaptation, ethology
	Class comparative psychology of humans and animals in 156; class physiology of nervous system in 573.8; class comprehensive works on animal adaptation in 591.4
	See Manual at 302–307 vs. 156
.51	General topics in behavior
	Limited to those named below
	Class general topics related to specific behaviors in 591.53–591.59; class play in 591.563
.512	†Instinct
.513	†Intelligence
.514	†Learning
.518	†Nocturnal behavior
	Class here nocturnal animals
.519	†Sleep
	Class hibernation in 591.565
	For physiology of sleep, see 573.868

†Add standard subdivisions as instructed under 591

>   **591.53–591.54   Feeding behavior**

          Class comprehensive works in 591.53

.53   †Predation

          Including food storing and hoarding

          Class here predator-prey relations, predatory animals; food habits, e.g., hoarding; comprehensive works on feeding behavior

          Class physiology of eating in 573.35

          For herbivorous feeding, see 591.54

.54   †Herbivorous feeding

          Class here browsing, grazing; herbivorous animals

.56   †Behavior relating to life cycle

          Class here reproductive, social behavior

          Class reproductive physiology in 573.6; class physical reproductive adaptation in 591.46; class interdisciplinary works on sociobiology in 304.5

          For communication, see 591.59

.562   †Sexual behavior

          Including sexual selection [*formerly* 575.5]

          Class here courtship, mating

          Class grooming in 591.563

.563   †Family behavior

          Including grooming, kin recognition, play (regardless of kinship)

          Class here maternal behavior, parental behavior

.564   †Making habitations

          Class here nesting, nests

.564 8   †Burrowing

          Class here burrowing animals

          Class comprehensive works on soil animals in 591.757

.565   †Hibernation

          Class physiology of hibernation in 571.787

---

†Add standard subdivisions as instructed under 591

.566 †Territoriality

Class here comprehensive works on fighting, on protective behavior

For fighting during mating, see 591.562; for fighting, protective behaviors during parenting, see 591.563

.568 †Migration

Class here migratory animals

Class physiology of navigation in 573.87

.59 †Communication

For physiology of communication, see 573.92

.594 †Acoustical communication

Class here animal sounds

Class stridulation in 595.71594; class vocalization in 596.1594

.6 †Miscellaneous nontaxonomic kinds of animals

Not provided for elsewhere

Class here economic zoology

See Manual at 630 vs. 579–590, 641.3

.63 †Beneficial animals

Including game animals

For animals as food source, see 641.306

.65 †Harmful animals

Class here dangerous and poisonous animals

.68 †Rare and endangered animals

Standard subdivisions are added for either or both topics in heading

Including recently extinct species

.7 Animals characteristic of specific environments, animal ecology

Standard subdivisions are added for either or both topics in heading

Class here autecology

.701–.708 Standard subdivisions

Notation from Table 1 as modified under 590.1–590.8, e.g., microscopy 591.70282

.709 Historical, geographic, persons treatment

†Add standard subdivisions as instructed under 591

[.709 14–.709 19]   Treatment by areas, regions, places in general other than polar, temperate, tropical regions

Do not use; class in 591.73–591.77

.73–.77   Specific kinds of environments

Class here zoology of specific kinds of environments

Add to base number 591.7 the numbers following 577 in 577.3–577.7 for the environment only, e.g., marine animals 591.77; then to the result add standard subdivisions as modified under 578.01–578.09, e.g., collections of living marine animals 591.77073

Class comprehensive works on terrestrial animals in 590

.78   Synecology and population biology

Add to base number 591.78 the numbers following 577.8 in 577.801–577.88, e.g., parasitism 591.7857

.9   **Treatment of animals by specific continents, countries, localities**

Add to base number 591.9 notation 3–9 from Table 2, e.g., animals in Brazil 591.981

> ## 592–599   Specific taxonomic groups of animals

Except for modifications shown under specific entries, add to each subdivision identified by * as follows:

01–08   Standard subdivisions

Notation from Table 1 as modified under 590.1–590.8, e.g., collections of living animals 073

09   Historical, geographic, persons treatment

[0914–0919]   Treatment by areas, regions, places in general other than polar, temperate, tropical regions

Do not use; class in 173–177

1   General topics of natural history of animals

Add to base number 1 the numbers following 591 in 591.3–591.7, e.g., beneficial animals 163, marine animals 177

Do not add notation from 591.3–591.7 when redundant or nearly so, e.g., marine sponges 593.4 (*not* 593.4177)

Class comprehensive works in 590

See Manual at 579–590: When subdivisions are added for individual species

592   *Invertebrates

For Protozoa, see 579.4; for miscellaneous marine and seashore invertebrates, see 593; for Mollusca and Molluscoidea, see 594; for Arthropoda, see 595

---

*Add as instructed under 592–599

.3   *Worms

> Including Echiurida (spoonworms), Phoronida (horseshoe worms), Pogonophora (beardworms), Priapulida

> Class here helminthology

>> *For Platyhelminthes, see 592.4; for Aschelminthes, see 592.5; for Annelida, see 592.6*

>> *See also 592.7 for oncopods*

.32   *Nemertea (Ribbon worms)

> Variant names: Nemertina, Rhynchocoela; bootlace, proboscis worms

.33   *Acanthocephala (Spiny-headed worms)

.35   *Sipuncula (Peanut worms)

.38   *Chaetognatha (Arrowworms)

> Class here Sagitta

.4   *Platyhelminthes (Flatworms)

> Including Aspidocotylea (Aspidobothria)

.42   *Turbellaria

> Including Acoela, Alloecoela, Rhabdocoela; planarians

.44   *Monogenea

.46   *Cestoda (Tapeworms)

> Class here Eucestoda

.48   *Trematoda (Flukes)

> Including Aspidogastrea

> Class here Digenea

.5   *Aschelminthes (Nemathelminthes)

.52   *Rotifera (Rotifers)

.53   *Gastrotricha

.55   *Kinorhyncha (Echinodera)

>> *See also 593.9 for Echinodermata*

.57   *Nematoda (Nemata, Roundworms)

> Including Adenophorea, Secernentea

.59   *Nematomorpha (Horsehair worms, Hairworms)

> Class here Gordioida

*Add as instructed under 592–599

.6 ***Annelida (Segmented worms)**

.62   *Polychaeta

      Including Archiannelida, Myzostomida, Phyllodocida

.64   *Oligochaeta

      Including Haplotaxia, Lumbriculida, Moniligastrida

      Class here earthworms (night crawlers)

.66   *Hirudinea (Leeches)

      Including Arhynchobdellida, Rhynchobdellida

.7 ***Oncopods (Pararthropoda)**

.72   *Tardigrada (Water bears)

.74   *Onychophora

.76   *Pentastomida

      Including Linguatula

593   Miscellaneous marine and seashore invertebrates

      Limited to phyla provided for below

      See also 592.3177 for marine and seashore worms, 594 for Mollusca and Molluscoidea, 595.3 for Crustacea

[.01–.09]   Standard subdivisions

      Do not use; class in 592.01–592.09

[.1]   **Protozoa**

      Relocated to 579.4

.4   ***Porifera (Sponges)**

      Class here Parazoa

.42   *Calcispongiae (Calcarea)

      Including Calcaronea, Calcinea

.44   *Hyalospongiae (Hexactinellida)

      Class here glass sponges

.46   *Demospongiae

      Including Haplosclerida, Spongillidae

.5   ***Cnidaria (Coelenterata)**

      For Anthozoa, see 593.6

*Add as instructed under 592–599

.53   *Scyphozoa

Including Coronatae, Cubomedusae, Rhizostomeae, Semaeostomeae, Stauromedusae

Class here comprehensive works on jellyfish, medusas

For hydrozoan jellyfish and medusas, see 593.55

.55   *Hydrozoa

Including Chondrophora, Hydroida, Milleporina, Pteromedusae, Siphonophora, Stylasterina, Trachylina

Including hydras, Portuguese man-of-war

Class here hydroids

.6   ***Anthozoa**

Including Alcyonaria, Zoantharia (Hexacorallia); sea anemones, fans, pens

Class here corals

.8   ***Ctenophora (Comb jellies)**

Including Nuda, Tentaculata; sea walnuts

.9   ***Echinodermata and Hemichordata**

Subdivisions are added for Echinodermata and Hemichordata together, for Echinodermata alone

See also 592.55 for Echinodera

> 593.92–593.96   Echinodermata

Class comprehensive works in 593.9

.92   *Crinozoa

Class here Crinoidea (sea lilies), Articulata

.93   *Asterozoa (Starfish)

Including Concentricycloidea, Forcipulata, Phanerozonia, Spinulosa, Stelleroidea

Class here Asteroidea

For Ophiuroidea, see 593.94

.94   *Ophiuroidea

Including Phrynophiurida, basket stars

Class here Ophiurida, brittle stars

*Add as instructed under 592–599

.95   *Echinozoa

        Including Perischoechinoidea; sand dollars, sea urchins

        Class here Echinoidea, Euechinoidea

        For Holothurioidea, see 593.96

.96   *Holothurioidea (Sea cucumbers)

        Including Apodacea, Aspidochirotacea, Dendrochirotacea

.99   *Hemichordata

        Including Enteropneusta, Planctosphaeroidea, Pterobranchia

594   *Mollusca and Molluscoidea

        Class here malacology, comprehensive works on shellfish

        Subdivisions are added for Mollusca and Molluscoidea together, for Mollusca alone

        For crustacean shellfish, see 595.3

>   **594.2–594.5   Mollusca (Mollusks)**

        Class comprehensive works in 594

.2   **ature *Minor classes of Mollusca**

        Including Aplacophora (Solenogastres), Caudofoveata, Monoplacophora

.27   *Polyplacophora (Amphineura, Chitons)

.29   *Scaphopoda (Tooth shells, Tusk shells)

.3   **Gastropoda (Snails and slugs)**

.32   *Prosobranchia (Streptoneura, Sea snails)

        Including Archaeogastropoda, Mesogastropoda, Neogastropoda; abalones, cowries, whelks; comprehensive works on limpets

        For pulmonate limpets, see 594.38

.34   *Opisthobranchia (Sea slugs)

        Including Acochlidacea, Cephalaspidea, Gymnosomata, Notaspidea, Philinoglossacea, Pyramidellacea, Thecosomata

        For Sacoglossa, see 594.35; for Nudibranchia, see 594.36; for Anaspidea, see 594.37

.35   *Sacoglossa

.36   *Nudibranchia

---

*Add as instructed under 592–599

.37   *Anaspidea (Tectibranchia, Sea hares)

Including Pteropoda

.38   *Pulmonata (Land snails and slugs)

Including Basommatophora, Systellommatophora

Class here Stylommatophora

.4   *Bivalvia

Including Protobranchia; mussels, oysters, scallops, shipworms

Class here Lamellibranchia; clams

.5   *Cephalopoda

Class here Coleoidea

.52   *Nautiloidea

.55   *Vampyromorpha

.56   *Octopoda (Octopuses)

.58   *Decapoda

Including Sepioidea, cuttlefish

Class here Teuthoidea, squid

.6   *Molluscoidea

See also 592.3 for Phoronida

.66   *Entoprocta

.67   *Bryozoa (Moss animals)

Variant names: Ectoprocta, Polyzoa

Including Cyclostomata, Stenolaemata

.676   *Gymnolaemata

Including Ctenostomata

Class here Cheilostomata

.68   *Brachiopoda (Lamp shells)

595   *Arthropoda

Class Pararthropoda in 592.7

SUMMARY

595.3	**Crustacea**
.4	**Chelicerata Arachnida**
.6	**Myriapoda**
.7	**Insecta (Insects)**

*Add as instructed under 592–599

.3   ***Crustacea**

.32   *Branchiopoda

Including Anostraca (fairy and brine shrimps), Cladocera (water fleas), Conchostraca (clam shrimps), Notostraca (tadpole shrimps)

.33   *Ostracoda (Mussel shrimps, Seed shrimps)

Including Cladocopa, Myodocopa, Platycopa, Podocopa

.34   *Copepoda (Copepods)

Including Calanoida, Caligoida, Cyclopoida (cyclops), Harpacticoida, Lernaeopodoida, Monstrilloida, Notodelphyoida

.35   *Cirripedia (Barnacles)

Including Acrothoracica, Ascothoracica, Rhizocephala, Thoracica

.36   *Branchiura (Fish lice), Cephalocarida (horseshoe shrimps), Mystacocarida (mustache shrimps)

Including Arguloida

.37   *Malacostraca   Peracarida

For Eucarida, see 595.38

>   595.372–595.378 Peracarida

Class comprehensive works in 595.37

.372   *Isopoda

Including pill and sow bugs, wood lice

.373   *Thermosbaenacea

.374   *Tanaidacea

.375   *Mysidacea (Opossum shrimps)

.376   *Cumacea

.378   *Amphipoda

Including beach hoppers, sand fleas, scuds, well shrimps, whale lice

.379   *Phyllocarida, Hoplocarida, Syncarida

.379 2   *Phyllocarida

Class here Leptostraca (Nebaliacea)

.379 6   *Hoplocarida

Class here Stomatopoda (mantis shrimps)

*Add as instructed under 592–599

| .38 | *Eucarida Decapoda |

Class here Reptantia

---

*Add as instructed under 592–599

| .38 | *Eucarida   Decapoda |
| | Class here Reptantia |

---

*Add as instructed under 592–599

.455	*Ricinulei
.46	*Scorpiones (Scorpions)
.47	*Pseudoscorpiones (Book scorpions)
.48	*Solpugida (Solifugae)

Including sun spiders, weasel spiders, wind scorpions

.49	*Xiphosura and Pycnogonida
.492	*Xiphosura (Horseshoe crabs)
.496	*Pycnogonida (Sea spiders)
.6	***Myriapoda**
.62	*Chilopoda (Centipedes)
.63	*Symphyla
.64	*Pauropoda
.66	*Diplopoda (Millipedes)
.7	***Insecta (Insects)**

Class here Uniramia, Hexapoda, Pterygota, Endopterygota (Holometabola); entomology

For Myriapoda, see 595.6

SUMMARY

595.72	**Apterygota; Orthoptera and related orders**
.73	**Exopterygota (Hemimetabola)**
.74	**Mecoptera, Trichoptera, Neuroptera, Megaloptera, Raphidioda**
.75	**Homoptera, Heteroptera, Anoplura, Mallophaga, Thysanoptera**
.76	**Coleoptera (Beetles)**
.77	**Diptera (Flies) and Siphonaptera**
.78	**Lepidoptera**
.79	**Hymenoptera**

.72	*Apterygota; Orthoptera and related orders

Subdivisions are added for Apterygota, Orthoptera and related orders together; for Apterygota alone

---

> 595.722–595.725 Apterygota

All orders of Apterygota except Thysanura are sometimes regarded as classes coordinate with Insecta

Class comprehensive works in 595.72

.722	*Protura

*Add as instructed under 592–599

.723	*Thysanura (Bristletails)
	Including Microcoryphia, silverfish
.724	*Diplura (Entotrophi)
.725	*Collembola (Springtails)

> 595.726–595.729 Orthoptera and related orders

Class comprehensive works in 595.726

.726	*Orthoptera and Grylloblattodea (ice bugs)

Including crickets, grasshoppers, katydids, locusts

Class here comprehensive works on Orthoptera and related orders

Subdivisions are added for Orthoptera and Grylloblattodea together, for Orthoptera alone

For Mantodea, see 595.727; for Blattaria, see 595.728; for Phasmida, see 595.729

.727	*Mantodea (Mantises)
.728	*Blattaria (Cockroaches)

Class here comprehensive works on Dictyoptera

For Mantodea, see 595.727

.729	*Phasmida (Phasmatodea)

Including leaf insects, stick insects, walkingsticks

.73	*Exopterygota (Hemimetabola)

For Orthoptera and related orders, see 595.726–595.729; for Homoptera, Heteroptera, Anoplura, Mallophaga, Thysanoptera, see 595.75

.732	*Psocoptera (Corrodentia, Book lice)
.733	*Odonata

Including damselflies

Class here dragonflies

.734	*Ephemeroptera (Mayflies)
.735	*Plecoptera (Stone flies)
.736	*Isoptera (Termites)
.737	*Embioptera

*Add as instructed under 592–599

.738   *Zoraptera

.739   *Dermaptera (Earwigs)

.74   *Mecoptera, Trichoptera, Neuroptera, Megaloptera, Raphidiodea

.744   *Mecoptera (Scorpion flies)

.745   *Trichoptera (Caddis flies)

.747   *Neuroptera (Lacewings), Megaloptera (dobsonflies and alderflies), Raphidiodea (snakeflies)

> Including ant lions

> Subdivisions are added for Neuroptera, Megaloptera, Raphidiodea together; for Neuroptera alone

.75   *Homoptera, Heteroptera, Anoplura, Mallophaga, Thysanoptera

.752   *Homoptera

> Including aphids, cicadas, hoppers, plant lice, scale insects, whiteflies

> Class comprehensive works on Homoptera and Heteroptera (sometimes regarded as a single order Hemiptera) in 595.754

.754   *Heteroptera (True bugs)

> Including bedbugs, water striders

> Class here Hemiptera whether regarded as a synonym of Heteroptera or as an order including Homoptera and Heteroptera

> *For Homoptera, see 595.752*

.756   *Anoplura (Siphunculata, Sucking lice)

> Variant name: true lice

> Class here comprehensive works on Phthiraptera (apterous insects)

> *For Mallophaga, see 595.757*

> *See also 595.732 for book lice, 595.752 for plant lice*

.757   *Mallophaga (Bird lice)

> Variant names: biting, chewing lice

.758   *Thysanoptera (Thrips)

>   595.76–595.79   Endopterygota (Holometabola)

Class comprehensive works in 595.7

> *For Mecoptera, Trichoptera, Neuroptera, Megaloptera, Raphidiodea, see 595.74*

*Add as instructed under 592–599

.76	*Coleoptera (Beetles)

Including Strepsiptera

Class here Polyphaga

.762	*Adephaga, Archostemata, Myxophaga

Including Carabidae (ground beetles), Cicindelidae (tiger beetles), Cupesidae (reticulated beetles), Dytiscidae (true water beetles), Gyrinidae (whirligig beetles), Hydroscaphidae (skiff beetles)

Subdivisions are added for Adephaga, Archostemata, Myxophaga together; for Adephaga alone

---

>	595.763–595.769 Polyphaga

Class comprehensive works in 595.76

.763	*Minor superfamilies of Polyphaga

Including Bostrychoidea, Buprestoidea (metallic wood-boring beetles), Byrrhoidea (pill beetles), Cleroidea, Dascilloidea, Dermestoidea, Histeroidea, Hydrophiloidea (water scavenger beetles), Lymexyloidea (ship timber beetles), Rhipiceroidea

Including checkered, death watch, hister, pine, powder post, skin, soft-winged flower, spider beetles

.764	*Staphylinoidea, Cantharoidea, Dryopoidea, Chrysomeloidea, Scarabaeoidea

.764 2	*Staphylinoidea

Including Pselaphidae, Silphidae (burying beetles, carrion beetles); mammal nest beetles

Class here Staphylinidae (rove beetles)

.764 4	*Cantharoidea

Including Cantharidae (soldier beetles), Lampyridae (fireflies and glowworms), Lycidae (net-winged beetles)

.764 5	*Dryopoidea

Including Elminidae (riffle beetles)

.764 8	*Chrysomeloidea

Including Chrysomelidae (leaf beetles), Cerambycidae (wood boring beetles); Diabrotica, flea beetles

.764 9	*Scarabaeoidea (Lamellicornia)

Including Lucanidae (stag and pinching beetles); dung, Japanese, June beetles; chafers, tumble bugs

Class here Scarabaeidae

*Add as instructed under 592–599

.765 ***Elateroidea**

Including wireworms

Class here Elateridae (click beetles)

.768 ***Curculionoidea (Snout beetles)**

Including Anthribidae (fungus weevils), Scolytidae (bark beetles)

Class here Curculionidae (weevils)

.769 ***Cucujoidea**

Including Coccinellidae (ladybugs), Colydiidae (cylindrical bark beetles), Meloidea (blister beetles, oil beetles), Mordellidae (tumbling flower beetles), Nitidulidae (sap beetles), Tenebrionidae (darkling beetles)

Including flour beetles, mealworms

.77 ***Diptera (Flies) and Siphonaptera**

Subdivisions are added for Diptera and Siphonaptera together, for Diptera alone

Class maggots in 595.77139

> **595.772–595.774 Diptera**

Class comprehensive works in 595.77

.772 ***Nematocera (Long horned flies)**

Including Bibionidae (march flies), Cecidomyiidae (gall gnats and midges), Chironomidae, Culicidae (mosquitoes), Psychodidae (moth flies), Sciaridae, Simuliidae (black flies and buffalo gnats), Tipulidae (crane flies)

Including gnats, leatherjackets, midges

See also 595.773 for march flies of Tabanidae family

.773 ***Brachycera**

Variant name: Brachycera-Orthorrhapha

Including Asilidae (robber flies), Bombyliidae (bee flies), Dolichopodidae (long-legged flies), Empididae (dance flies), Rhagionidae (snipe flies), Stratiomyidae (soldier flies), Tabanidae (horse and deer flies), Therevidae (stiletto flies)

Including march flies of Tabanidae family, mydas flies

See also 595.772 for Bibionidae (march flies)

*Add as instructed under 592–599

.774   *Cyclorrhapha

         Variant name: Brachycera-Cyclorrhapha

         Including Agromyzidae (leaf miner flies), Braulidae (bee lice), Calliphoridae (blow flies), Chamaemyiidae (aphid flies), Chyromyiidae, Diopsidae (stalk-eyed flies), Drosophilidae (small fruit flies), Ephydridae (shore flies), Glossinidae, Hippoboscidae (louse flies), Muscidae, Oestridae (bot and warble flies), Phoridae (coffin flies, humpbacked flies), Piophilidae (skipper flies), Sarcophagidae (flesh flies), Scatophagidae (dung flies), Sciomyzidae (marsh flies), Syrphidae (flower flies, hover flies), Tachinidae, Trypetidae (large fruit flies)

         Including bat, beach, house, rust, stable, tsetse, vinegar flies

.775   *Siphonaptera (Fleas)

.78   *Lepidoptera

         Including Bombycoidea, Geometroidea, Noctuoidea, Pyralidoidea, Tineoidea, Tortricoidea

         Including armyworms, budworms, cutworms, Heliothis

         Class here moths

         Class caterpillars in 595.78139

.788   *Hesperioidea (Skippers)

.789   *Papilionoidea (Butterflies)

.79   *Hymenoptera

         Including Chalcidoidea, Ichneumonoidea, Scolioidea, Symphyta (sawflies)

         Class here Apocrita, wasps, social insects

         Class true wasps (Vespoidea) in 595.798

.796   *Formicidae (Ants)

.798   *Vespoidea and Sphecoidea

         Class here true wasps

         Subdivisions are added for Vespoidea and Sphecoidea together, for Vespoidea alone

.799   *Apoidea (Bees)

596   *Chordata

         Class here Vertebrata (Craniata, vertebrates), Tetrapoda (land vertebrates)

         For cold-blooded vertebrates, see 597; for Aves, see 598; for Mammalia, see 599

[.073]   Collections and exhibits of living vertebrates

         Do not use; class in 590.73

*Add as instructed under 592–599

.2 ***Urochordata (Tunicata)**

Including Ascidiacea (sea squirts), Larvacea, Thaliacea

.4 ***Cephalochordata (Lancelets)**

597 *Cold-blooded vertebrates   Pisces (Fishes)

Class here Osteichthyes (bony fishes), Actinopterygii (ray-finned fishes), Teleostei (fully boned fishes); ichthyology

Class specific kinds of Osteichthyes in 597.39–597.7; class specific kinds of Actinopterygii in 597.4–597.7; class specific kinds of Teleostei in 597.43–597.7

SUMMARY

597.176 36	**Pond ecology**
.2	**Agnatha (Jawless fishes)**
.3	**Selachii, Holocephali, Sarcopterygii**
.4	**Miscellaneous superorders of Actinopterygii**
.5	**Protacanthopterygii** **Salmoniformes**
.6	**Scopelomorpha, Paracanthopterygii, Acanthopterygii**
.7	**Perciformes**
.8	**Amphibia**
.9	**Reptilia**

.176 36   Pond ecology

Number built according to instructions under 592–599

Class fishpond ecosystems in 577.636

>   **597.2–597.7 Pisces (Fishes)**

Class comprehensive works in 597

.2 ***Agnatha (Jawless fishes)**

Class here Cyclostomata (hagfishes and lampreys)

.3 ***Selachii, Holocephali, Sarcopterygii**

Class here Chondrichthyes (cartilaginous fishes), Elasmobranchii; sharks

Subdivisions are added for Selachii, Holocephali, Sarcopterygii together; for Selachii alone

Class typical sharks (family Carcharhinidae) in 597.34; class cartilaginous ganoids in 597.42

>   597.33–597.36 Selachii

Class here sharks

Class comprehensive works in 597.3

*Add as instructed under 592–599

.33   *Isuridae

Including mako sharks

Class here Carcharodon carcharias (great white shark); mackerel sharks

.34   *Carcharhinidae

Variant name: typical sharks

Including Australian school, blacktip, bull, great blue, lemon, soupfin, tiger, whitetip sharks; tope

.35   *Rajiformes (Batoidei)

Including guitarfishes, sawfishes, skates, torpedoes

Class here rays

.36   *Dogfishes

Including Oxynotidae, Squalidae, Triakidae

Class here Squaloidei

.38   *Holocephali

Class here Chimaerae (Chimaeriformes, chimeras, ghost sharks)

>   597.39–597.7   Osteichthyes (Bony fishes)

Class comprehensive works in 597

.39   *Sarcopterygii (Fleshy-finned fishes)

Including Crossopterygii (coelacanths), Dipnoi (lungfishes); barramunda

---

>   **597.4–597.7   Actinopterygii (Ray-finned fishes)**

Class comprehensive works in 597

.4   **Miscellaneous superorders of Actinopterygii**

Limited to those named below

Class comprehensive works on Actinopterygii in 597

[.401–.409]   Standard subdivisions

Do not use; class in 597.01–597.09

.41   *Holostei

Including Amiiformes (bowfins and river dogfishes), Semionotiformes (gars)

Class here bony ganoids

See also 597.66 for garfish of order Atheriniformes

*Add as instructed under 592–599

.42   *Chondrostei

Including Polypteriformes (bichirs and reedfishes)

Class here Acipenseriformes (sturgeons and paddlefishes); cartilaginous ganoids, comprehensive works on Ganoidei

For bony ganoids, see 597.41

>   597.43–597.7   Teleostei (Fully boned fishes)

Class comprehensive works in 597

.43   *Elopomorpha

Including Elopiformes, Notacanthiformes; congers, morays, tarpons

Class here Anguilliformes (eels), comprehensive works on eels

For a specific kind of nonanguilliform eel, see the kind, e.g., electric eels 597.48, swamp eels 597.64

.432   *Anguillidae (Freshwater eels)

Class here Anguilla

Subdivisions are added for the family as a whole and for individual species

.45   *Clupeomorpha

Including anchovies, menhadens, pilchards, sardines, shads

Class here Clupeiformes, Clupeidae (herring family)

Class sardines in sense of young bristling and herring in 597.452

.452   *Clupea

Class here bristling (sprat), common herring

Young bristling and common herring are often called sardines

Class true sardine in 597.45

.47   *Osteoglossomorpha

Including Osteoglossiformes, Mormyriformes; elephant fishes, freshwater butterfly fishes

See also 597.72 for marine butterfly fishes

>   597.48–597.49   Ostariophysi

Class comprehensive works in 597.48

---

*Add as instructed under 592–599

.48   *Cypriniformes

Including Characidae (Characins), Citharinidae (moonfishes), Gasteropelecidae (freshwater hatchetfishes); electric eels, headstanders, loaches, pencil fishes, piranhas, suckers, tetras, tigerfishes

Class here Characiformes, comprehensive works on Ostariophysi

For Siluriformes, see 597.49

See also 597.5 for marine hatchetfishes, 597.66 for Cyprinodontoidei, 597.7 for moonfishes of order Perciformes

.482   *Cyprinidae (Carp family)

Including bighead, glass carps; barbs (barbels), bream, chubs, daces, danios, freshwater zebra fishes, roach, shiners, squawfishes, tench

Class here minnows

For Carpio (carp), see 597.483; for Carassius (goldfish), see 597.484

See also 597.68 for saltwater zebra fishes

.483   *Carpio (Carp)

Class koi, interdisciplinary works on carp in 639.37483

.484   *Carassius (Goldfish)

Class interdisciplinary works on goldfish in 639.37484

.49   *Siluriformes (Catfishes)

.492   *Ictaluridae (North American freshwater catfishes)

Including Noturus (madtoms)

Class here Ictalurus; bullheads; blue, channel catfishes

Subdivisions are added for Ictaluridae as a whole and for individual species of Ictalurus

.5   ***Protacanthopterygii   Salmoniformes**

Including Gonorhynchiformes; Sternoptychidae (marine hatchetfishes); milkfish, mudminnows, smelts, stomiatoid dragonfishes, viperfishes

See also 597.48 for freshwater hatchetfishes, 597.64 for dragonfishes of order Pegasiformes

---

>   597.55–597.59 Salmoniformes

Class comprehensive works in 597.5

*Add as instructed under 592–599

.55   *Salmonidae

Including Australian grayling, whitefishes (whitings)

Class brook (speckled), Dolly Varden trout, lake trout in 597.554

For salmon, see 597.56; for trout of genus Salmo, see 597.57

See also 597.633 for whitings of genus Gadus, 597.72 for rock whiting, 597.725 for whiting (kingfish)

.554   *Salvelinus (Chars)

Class here brook (speckled) trout, Dolly Varden trout, lake trout

Subdivisions are added for the genus as a whole and for individual species

.559   *Thymallus (Graylings)

Subdivisions are added for the genus as a whole and for individual species

Class Australian grayling in 597.55

.56   *Salmon

Class here Salmo salar (Atlantic salmon), Oncorhynchus (Pacific salmon)

Subdivisions are added for salmon as a whole and for individual species

See also 597.7 for Australian salmon

.57   *Trout

Species of genus Salmo other than Salmo salar

Class here comprehensive works on Salmo

Subdivisions are added for trout as a whole and for individual species

For Salmo salar, see 597.56

See also 597.554 for brook (speckled), Dolly Varden, lake trout

.59   *Esocidae

Class here Esox; muskellunge (muskie), pickerels, pikes

Subdivisions are added for the family as a whole and for individual species

See also 597.758 for walleyed pike

.6   Scopelomorpha, Paracanthopterygii, Acanthopterygii

Class comprehensive works in 597

[.601–.609]   Standard subdivisions

Do not use; class in 597.01–597.09

*Add as instructed under 592–599

.61 *Scopelomorpha

Including Myctophidae (lantern fishes), Synodontidae (lizard fishes); spiderfishes

Class here Myctophiformes

.62 *Paracanthopterygii

Including Batrachoidiformes (toadfishes), Gobiesociformes (clingfishes), Percopsiformes, Polymixiiformes (beard fishes)

Including anglerfishes, batfishes, cave fishes, frogfishes, goosefishes, trout-perches

Class here Lophiiformes

For Gadiformes, see 597.63

.63 *Gadiformes

Including Carapidae (Carapodidae, pearlfishes), Macrouridae (grenadiers), Moridae (deep sea cods), Ophidiidae (brotulas and cusk eels), Zoarcidae (eelpouts)

.632 *Gadidae

Including arctic cod, burbots, haddocks, hakes, pollocks

For Gadus (cods), see 597.633

.633 *Gadus (Cods)

Class here Atlantic, Greenland, Pacific cods; whitings

See also 597.55 for whitings (whitefishes), 597.63 for deep sea cods, 597.632 for arctic cod, 597.72 for rock whitings, 597.725 for whitings (kingfish)

.64 *Acanthopterygii (Spiny-rayed fishes)

Including Beryciformes, Channiformes (snakeheads), Dactylopteriformes, Lampridiformes, Pegasiformes (dragonfishes), Synbranchiformes (swamp eels), Tetraodontiformes, Zeiformes

Including alfonsinos, boar fishes, boxfishes, cowfishes, filefishes, John Dories, lantern-eyed fishes, oarfishes, ocean sunfishes, opah, orange roughy, pinecone fishes, porcupine fishes, puffer fishes, squirrelfishes (soldierfishes), triggerfishes, unicorn fishes, whale fishes

For Antheriniformes, see 597.66; for Gasterosteiformes, see 597.67; for Scorpaeniformes, see 597.68; for Pleuronectiformes, see 597.69; for Perciformes, see 597.7

See also 597.2 for lampreys, 597.5 for stomiatoid dragonfishes

*Add as instructed under 592–599

.66 ***Atheriniformes**

Including Cyprinodontoidei; flying fishes, garfish, halfbeaks, needlefishes, silversides, topminnows

Class Cyprinodontidae and topminnows of families Cyprinodontidae and Poeciliidae in 597.665–597.667

See also 597.41 for gars of order Semionotiformes, 597.48 for Cypriniformes

.665 ***Cyprinodontidae (Killifishes)**

.667 ***Poeciliidae (Live-bearers)**

Including guppies, mollies, platy, swordtail

.67 ***Gasterosteiformes**

Including ghost pipefishes, trumpet fishes

.672 ***Gasterosteidae (Sticklebacks)**

Subdivisions are added for the family as a whole and for individual genera and species

.679 ***Syngnathidae (Pipefishes and sea horses)**

Subdivisions are added for the family as a whole and for individual species of pipefishes

Class ghost pipefishes in 597.67

.679 8 ***Sea horses**

Class here Hippocampus

Subdivisions are added for sea horses as a whole and for individual genera and species

.68 ***Scorpaeniformes**

Including gurnards, rockfishes, saltwater zebra fishes, scorpion fishes

See also 597.482 for freshwater zebra fishes

.69 ***Pleuronectiformes (Heterosomata, Flatfishes)**

Including California halibut, soles, turbots

Class here flounders

Class turbot of family Pleuronectidae in 597.694

.694 ***Pleuronectidae (Right-eyed flounders)**

Including Greenland halibut, plaice, winter flounder

For Hippoglossus (halibuts), see 597.695

*Add as instructed under 592–599

.695   *Hippoglossus (Halibuts)

             Subdivisions are added for the genus as a whole and for individual
             species

                 *See also 597.69 for California halibut, 597.694 for Greenland
                 halibut*

.7   *Perciformes

             Including Australian salmon, barracudas, betta (Siamese fighting fish), cardinal
             fishes, goatfishes, gobies, grunts, halfmoons, labyrinth fishes, moonfishes,
             mullets, parrotfishes, spiny eels, stargazers, swallowers, wrasses

             Class here Percoidei

                 See also 597.48 for moonfishes of family Citharinidae

.72   *Percoidea

             Including Centropomidae (robalos, snooks), Chaetodontidae (marine
             butterfly fishes), Latidae (giant perches), Lethrinidae, Lutjanidae (snappers),
             Pomacanthidae (angelfishes), Pomacentridae (damselfishes), Sparidae
             (porgies, sea breams)

             Including garibaldi, jacks, rock whiting, scups; comprehensive works on
             angelfishes

                 *For basses and related fishes, see 597.73; for Cichlidae, angelfishes of
                 cichlid family, see 597.74; for Percidae, see 597.75*

                 See also 597.47 for freshwater butterfly fishes

.725   *Sciaenidae (Drums, Croakers)

             Including Sciaenops, red drum (channel bass), weakfish, whiting
             (kingfish)

                 *See also 597.55 for whitings (whitefishes), 597.633 for whitings of
                 genus Gadus, 597.72 for rock whiting*

.73   *Basses and related fishes

             Including Grammatidae (basslets), Percichthyidae (temperate basses, perch
             trout)

             Including Australian bass; macquarie perch

             Subdivisions are added for basses and related fishes together, for basses
             alone

                 For channel bass, see 597.725

.732   *Moronidae

             Class here Morone; striped, white bass; white perch

.736   *Serranidae (Sea basses)

             Including graysby, groupers

---

*Add as instructed under 592–599

.738   *Centrarchidae (Sunfishes and black basses)

         Including crappies; calico, rock basses

         Subdivisions are added for sunfishes and black basses together, for sunfishes alone

.738 8   *Micropterus (Black basses)

         Class here largemouth, smallmouth basses

         Subdivisions are added for the genus as a whole and for individual species

.74   *Cichlidae

         Including Pterophyllum (angelfishes), Symphysodon (discus fishes); tilapias

         Class comprehensive works on angelfishes in 597.72

.75   *Percidae

         Including perches

         Class here darters

         See also 597.72 for giant perches, 597.732 for white perch

.758   *Stizostedion (Lucioperca, pike perches)

         Class here sauger, walleye (walleyed pike), zander

.77   *Blenoidei (Blennies)

.78   *Scombroidei

         Including Gempylidae, Istiophoridae, Trichiuridae (cutlass fishes), Xiphiidae (swordfish)

         Including billfishes, marlins, sailfishes, spearfishes

.782   *Scombridae

         Class here mackerel

         For tunas, see 597.783

.783   *Tunas

         Class here Thunnus; albacore, bonito, skipjack

         Subdivisions are added for tunas as a whole and for individual species

.8   *Amphibia

         Class here Anura (Salientia)

         Class herpetology, comprehensive works on amphibia and reptilia in 597.9

.82   *Gymnophiona (Apoda, Caecilians)

*Add as instructed under 592–599

.85   *Urodela (Caudata)

> Including Sirenidae (sirens); congo eels, hellbender, mud puppies, newts
>
> Class here salamanders

>   597.86–597.89   Anura (Salientia, Frogs and toads)

Class comprehensive works in 597.8

.86   *Discoglossoidea, Pelobatoidea, Pipoidea

Including burrowing, fire-bellied, midwife toads; tongueless frogs, · spadefoots

Class comprehensive works on toads in 597.87; class comprehensive works on frogs in 597.89

.87   *Bufonoidea

Including Centrolenidae (leaf frogs), Dendrobatidae (poison arrow frogs), Hylidae (tree frogs), Leptodactylidae, Rhinodermatidae (mouth-breeding frogs)

Class here Bufonidae, comprehensive works on toads

For burrowing, fire-bellied, midwife toads, see 597.86

.89   *Ranoidea

Including Microhylidae

Class here Ranidae, comprehensive works on frogs

For tongueless frogs, see 597.86; for leaf, mouth-breeding, poison arrow, tree frogs, see 597.87

.9   *Reptilia

Class here herpetology, comprehensive works on Amphibia and Reptilia

For Amphibia, see 597.8

.92   *Chelonia (Testudines, Turtles)

Including tortoises

.94   *Lepidosauria

Including Amphisbaenia

Class here Squamata (scaly reptiles)

For Sauria, see 597.95; for Serpentes, see 597.96

.945   *Rhynchocephalia (Beaked reptiles)

Class here Sphenodontidae, tuataras

*Add as instructed under 592–599

.95	*Sauria (Lizards)

Including chameleons, Gila monsters

Class comprehensive works on Sauria and Serpentes in 597.94

.96	*Serpentes (Snakes)
.98	*Crocodilia (Crocodiles)

Including alligators, gavial

598 *Aves (Birds)

Class here land birds, ornithology

Interdisciplinary works on species of domestic birds relocated to 636.5

Class specific kinds of land birds in 598.5–598.9; class comprehensive works on warm-blooded vertebrates in 599

SUMMARY

598.072 3	**Descriptive research and bird watching**
.163–.176	**[Beneficial and aquatic birds]**
.3	**Gruiformes, Charadriiformes, Ciconiiformes, Phoenicopteriformes**
.4	**Miscellaneous orders of water birds**
.5	**Palaeognathae**
.6	**Galliformes and Columbiformes**
.7	**Miscellaneous orders of land birds**
.8	**Passeriformes (Perching birds)**
.9	**Falconiformes, Strigiformes, Caprimulgiformes**

.072 3	Descriptive research and bird watching
.072 32	Birdbanding and census taking
.072 34	Bird watching
[.072 340 94–.072 340 99]	Treatment by specific continents, countries, localities in modern world

Do not use; class in 598.072344–598.072349

.072 344–.072 349	Treatment by specific continents, countries, localities in modern world

Add to base number 598.07234 notation 4–9 from Table 2, e.g., bird watching in East Africa 598.07234676

.163	Beneficial birds

Number built according to instructions under 592–599

Including game birds, wildfowl

Class lowland game birds, waterfowl in 598.41; class upland game birds in 598.6

*Add as instructed under 592–599

.176 Aquatic birds

Number built according to instructions under 592–599

Class here water birds

Class waterfowl in 598.41

For specific kinds of water birds, see 598.3–598.4

> **598.3–598.4 Water birds**

Class comprehensive works in 598.176

.3 *Gruiformes, Charadriiformes, Ciconiiformes, Phoenicopteriformes

Class here wading birds

.32 *Gruiformes

Including Gruidae (cranes), Otididae (bustards), Psophiidae (trumpeters), Rallidae (rail family), Turnicidae (button quails)

Including coots, gallinules

.33 *Charadriiformes

Including Charadriidae (plovers and lapwings), Alcidae, Haematopodidae (oystercatchers), Jacanidae (jacanas), Phalaropodidae (phalaropes), Scolopacidae

Including auks, murres, puffins, sandpipers, snipes, turnstones, woodcocks

Class here Charadrii, shore birds

.338 *Lari

Including Rynchopidae (skimmers), Stercorariidae (skuas and jaegers)

Class here Laridae (gulls and terns)

.34 *Ciconiiformes

Including Ciconiidae (storks), Ardeidae, Threskiornithidae (ibis and spoonbills)

Including bitterns, egrets, herons

.35 *Phoenicopteriformes (Flamingos)

.4 Miscellaneous orders of water birds

Limited to those named below

Class comprehensive works on water birds in 598.176

[.401–.409] Standard subdivisions

Do not use; class in 598.17601–598.17609

---

*Add as instructed under 592–599

.41	*Anseriformes

Including Anhimidae (screamers)

Class here Anatidae (waterfowl); ducks; comprehensive works on lowland game birds

For a specific kind of lowland game bird, see the kind, e.g., murres 598.33

> 598.412–598.415 Ducks

Class comprehensive works in 598.41

.412	*Aix

Including mandarin duck

.412 3	*Aix sponsa (Wood duck)
.413	*Anas

Including black duck, blue-winged teal

.413 4	*Anas platyrhynchos (Mallard)
.414	*Aythya

Including canvasback

.415	*Mergini

Including eiders, goldeneyes, mergansers

.417	*Anserini (Geese)
.417 3	*Anser

Including greylag, white-fronted geese

.417 5	*Chen

Class here snow, blue goose

.417 8	*Branta

Class here Canada goose

.418	*Cygninae (Swans)

Class here Cygnus

.418 4	*Cygnus buccinator (Trumpeter swan)
.418 7	*Cygnus olor (Mute swan)

*Add as instructed under 592–599

.42	*Procellariiformes
	Including Procellariidae, Diomedeidae (albatrosses), Hydrobatidae (storm petrels), Pelecanoididae (diving petrels)
	Including fulmars, shearwaters
.43	*Pelecaniformes
	Including Pelecanidae (pelicans), Fregatidae (frigate birds), Phaethontidae (tropic birds), Phalacrocoracidae (cormorants), Sulidae (boobies)
.44	*Gaviiformes and Podicipediformes
	Class here Colymbiformes
.442	*Gaviiformes (Loons)
.443	*Podicipediformes (Grebes)
	Class here Podicipedidae
.47	*Sphenisciformes (Penguins)

> ### 598.5–598.9 Land birds

Class comprehensive works in 598

.5 ***Palaeognathae**

Class here ratites

.52	*Rheiformes and Struthioniformes
.522	*Rheiformes (Rheas)
.524	*Struthioniformes (Ostriches)
.53	*Casuariiformes
	Including emu
	Class here Casuariidae (cassowaries)
.54	*Apterygiformes (Kiwis)
.55	*Tinamiformes (Tinamous)

.6 ***Galliformes and Columbiformes**

Class here Galli, poultry, upland game birds

Subdivisions are added for Galliformes and Columbiformes together, for Galliformes alone

Class interdisciplinary works on domestic poultry in 636.5

For a specific kind of upland game bird, see the kind, e.g., crows 598.864

---

*Add as instructed under 592–599

>   598.62–598.64   Galliformes

                  Class comprehensive works in 598.6

.62   *Phasianidae

.623   *Partridges

                  Including francolins

.623 2   *Perdix perdix (Common partridge, Gray partridge, Hungarian partridge)

.625   *Pheasants

                  Including Gallus (chickens, jungle fowl)

                  Class results of experimental studies in internal biological processes
                  using chickens in 571–573, plus notation 18625 from add instructions in
                  571–573, e.g., embryology in domestic chickens 571.8618625; class
                  interdisciplinary works on Gallus (chickens) in 636.5

.625 2   *Phasianus colchicus (Ring-necked pheasant)

.625 8   *Pavo (Peafowl)

.627   *Quails

                  Including Gambel's quail

                  See also 598.32 for button quails

.627 2   *Coturnix

                  Including common quail, Japanese quail

                  See also 598.6273 for bobwhites

.627 3   *Colinus (Bobwhites)

                  Subdivisions are added for the genus as a whole and for individual
                  species

.63   *Tetraonidae (Grouse)

                  See also 598.65 for sand grouse

.633   *Lagopus (Ptarmigans)

.634   *Tetrao

                  Including black grouse, capercaillies

.635   *Bonasa

                  Class here ruffed grouse

.636   *Centrocercus (Sage grouse)

---

*Add as instructed under 592–599

.637	*Tympanuchus
	Class here prairie chickens
.637 8	*Tympanuchus phasianellus (Sharp-tailed grouse)
.64	*Other families of Galliformes

.64 includes:

Including Cracidae, Megapodiidae (brush turkeys, mound builders), Numididae (Guinea fowl), Opisthocomidae (hoatzin)

Including chachalacas, curassows, guans

Opisthocomidae are sometimes regarded as a separate order Opisthocomi

| .645 | *Meleagrididae (Turkeys) |

Class here wild turkeys

Class interdisciplinary works on turkeys in 636.592

| .65 | *Columbiformes |

Including Pteroclididae (sand grouse), dodos

Class here Columbidae (doves, pigeons)

| **.7** | **Miscellaneous orders of land birds** |

Limited to those named below

Class comprehensive works on land birds in 598

| [.701–.709] | Standard subdivisions |

Do not use; class in 598.01–598.09

| .71 | *Psittaciformes |

Including budgerigars, cockatoos, kakapo, lories, macaws, parakeets, parrots, rosellas

Class here Psittacidae

| .72 | *Piciformes |

Including Picidae, Bucconidae (puffbirds), Capitonidae (barbets), Galbulidae (jacamars), Indicatoridae (honey guides), Ramphastidae (toucans); woodpeckers

Class here Pici

| .73 | *Trogoniformes (Trogons) |
| .74 | *Cuculiformes |

Including Cuculidae, Musophagidae (touracos); anis, cuckoos, roadrunners

For Opisthocomidae, see 598.64

| .75 | *Coliiformes |

Class here Coliidae (mousebirds)

*Add as instructed under 592–599

.76   *Apodiformes

.762   *Apodi (Swifts)

              Including Hemiprocnidae (tree swifts)

              Class here Apodidae (true swifts)

.764   *Trochili (Hummingbirds)

              Class here Trochilidae

.78   *Coraciiformes

              Including Corcaciidae (rollers), Alcedinidae (kingfishers), Bucerotidae (hornbills), Meropidae (bee eaters)

.8   ***Passeriformes (Perching birds)**

              Including bell magpies, cuckoo shrikes, honey eaters, magpie larks, vanga shrikes, wattled crows, wood shrikes, wood swallows

              Class here Oscines (Passeres, songbirds)

.82   *Nonoscine Passeriformes, Paridae, Alaudidae, Hirundinidae, Certhiidae, Sittidae

              Including creepers, nuthatches

.822   *Nonoscine Passeriformes

              Including Cotingidae (cotingas), Dendrocolaptidae (woodcreepers), Eurylaimidae (broadbills), Menuridae (lyrebirds), Pipridae (manakins), Pittidae (pittas)

              For Tyrannidae, see 598.823

.822 5   *Furnariidae (Ovenbirds)

.822 6   *Formicariidae (Antbirds)

.823   *Tyrannidae (Tyrant flycatchers, New World flycatchers)

              See also 598.848 for Old World flycatchers

>   598.824–598.88   Oscines (Passeres, Songbirds)

              Class comprehensive works in 598.8

              See Manual at 598.824–598.88

.824   *Paridae (Titmice)

              Including chickadees

.825   *Alaudidae (Larks)

              Class magpie larks in 598.8

              See also 598.874 for meadowlarks

*Add as instructed under 592–599

.826	*Hirundinidae (Martins and swallows)

Class wood swallows in 598.8

.83	*Cinclidae, Troglodytidae, Timaliidae, Chamaeidae
.832	*Cinclidae (Dippers, Water ouzels)
.833	*Troglodytidae (Wrens)
.834	*Timaliidae (Babblers) and Chamaeidae (wren-tit)

Subdivisions are added for Timaliidae and Chamaeidae together, for Timaliidae alone

.84	*Turdidae, Sylviidae, Mimidae, Muscicapidae
.842	*Turdidae (Thrushes)

Including bluebirds, nightingales, robins (American)

.843	*Sylviidae (Old World warblers)

Including kinglets

.844	*Mimidae

Including catbirds, mockingbirds, thrashers

.848	*Muscicapidae (Old World flycatchers)

See also 598.823 for New World flycatchers

.85	*Bombycillidae, Ptilogonatidae, Motacillidae
.852	*Bombycillidae (Waxwings)
.853	*Ptilogonatidae (Silky flycatchers)
.854	*Motacillidae (Pipits and wagtails)
.86	*Laniidae, Sturnidae, Corvidae, Paradisaeidae
.862	*Laniidae (Shrikes)

Class cuckoo shrikes, vanga shrikes, wood shrikes in 598.8

See also 598.878 for pepper-shrikes and shrike-vireos

.863	*Sturnidae (Starlings)

Including mynas, oxpeckers

.864	*Corvidae

Including crows, jays, magpies, ravens, rooks

Class bell magpies, magpie larks, wattled crows in 598.8

.865	*Paradisaeidae (Birds of paradise)

*Add as instructed under 592–599

.87   *Parulidae, Icteridae, Thraupidae, Tersinidae, Vireonidae, Cyclarhidae, Vireolaniidae

.872   *Parulidae (Wood warblers)

.874   *Icteridae

Including blackbirds (American), cowbirds, grackles, meadowlarks, orioles

See also 598.825 for larks of family Alaudidae

.875   *Thraupidae (Tanagers) and Tersinidae (swallow-tanager)

Subdivisions are added for Thraupidae and Tersinidae together, for Thraupidae alone

.878   *Vireonidae (Vireos), Cyclarhidae (pepper-shrikes), Vireolaniidae (shrike-vireos)

Including greenlets

Subdivisions are added for Vireonidae, Cyclarhidae, Vireolaniidae together; for Vireonidae alone

.88   *Finches and related birds

Including Catamblyrhynchidae (plush-capped finch)

Subdivisions are added for finches and related birds together, for finches alone

.883   *Fringillidae (New World seedeaters)

Including Emberizinae (Emberizidae); buntings, cardinals, Darwin's finches, grosbeaks, juncos, towhees, comprehensive works on sparrows

For sparrows of genus Passer, see 598.887

.885   *Carduelidae

Including bullfinches, canaries, crossbills, goldfinches, hawfinches, redpolls, rosefinches, siskins

.886   *Estrildidae (Waxbills)

Including weaver finch

Class comprehensive works on weaver finches in 598.887

.887   *Ploceidae (Weaverbirds, Weavers)

Including queleas; sparrows of genus Passer, e.g., English sparrow, house sparrow

Class here comprehensive works on weaver finches

For weaver finch of family Estrildidae, see 598.886

*Add as instructed under 592–599

.9 ***Falconiformes, Strigiformes, Caprimulgiformes**

Including Sagittariidae (secretary bird)

Class here birds of prey, raptors

Subdivisions are added for Falconiformes, Strigiformes, Caprimulgiformes together; for Falconiformes alone

---

> 598.92–598.96 Falconiformes

Class comprehensive works in 598.9

.92 ***Cathartidae (New World vultures)**

Including condors, king vulture, turkey vulture (turkey buzzard)

Class here comprehensive works on vultures

For Old World vultures, see 598.94

.93 ***Pandionidae (Osprey)**

.94 ***Accipitridae**

Including true buzzards, harriers, Old World vultures

Class comprehensive works on vultures in 598.92

See also 598.92 for turkey buzzard

.942 ***Eagles**

For Haliaeetus leucocephalus (bald eagle), see 598.943

.942 3 ***Aquila chrysaetos (Golden eagle)**

.943 ***Haliaeetus leucocephalus (Bald eagle)**

.944 ***Hawks**

.945 ***Kites**

.96 ***Falconidae (Falcons)**

Including caracaras, kestrels

.97 ***Strigiformes (Owls)**

Including Tytonidae (barn and grass owls)

Class here Strigidae

.99 ***Caprimulgiformes**

Including Nyctibiidae (potoos), Podargidae (frogmouths); oilbird, whippoorwill

Class here Caprimulgidae (goatsuckers, nighthawks, nightjars)

---

*Add as instructed under 592–599

599   *Mammalia (Mammals)

Class here warm-blooded vertebrates, Eutheria (placental mammals)

Interdisciplinary works on species of domestic mammals relocated to 636

For Aves, see 598

See Manual at 599: Sources of taxonomic information

SUMMARY

599.163	**Beneficial mammals**	
.2	**Marsupialia and Monotremata**	
.3	**Miscellaneous orders of Eutheria (placental mammals)**	
.4	**Chiroptera (Bats)**	
.5	**Cetacea and Sirenia**	
.6	**Ungulates**	
.7	**Carnivora**	**Fissipedia (Land carnivores)**
.8	**Primates**	
.9	**Hominidae**	**Homo sapiens**

[.073]   Collections of living mammals

Do not use; class mammalian zoos in 590.73

.163   Beneficial mammals

Number built according to instructions under 592–599

Including game mammals

Class big game animals in 599.6; class fur-bearing animals in 599.7

[.177]   Marine mammals

Do not use; class in 599.5

.2   *Marsupialia and Monotremata

Class here Diprotodonta, Metatheria

Subdivisions are added for Marsupialia and Monotremata together, for Marsupialia alone

---

>   599.22–599.27 Marsupialia

Class comprehensive works in 599.2

>   599.22–599.25 Diprotodonta

Class comprehensive works in 599.2

*Add as instructed under 592–599

.22   *Macropodidae

> Including rat and tree kangaroos
>
> Class here wallabies

.222   *Macropus

> Including gray kangaroos, wallaroos
>
> Class here comprehensive works on kangaroos
>
> Class rat and tree kangaroos in 599.22

.222 3   *Macropus rufus (Red kangaroo)

.23   *Australasian possums

> Including Burramyidae, Petauridae, Tarsipedidae
>
> Class here Phalangeroidea
>
> *For Macropodidae, see 599.22*
>
> *See also 599.276 for American opossums*

.232   *Phalangeridae

> Including brush-tailed and scaly-tailed possums
>
> Class here Phalanger (cuscuses)

.24   *Vombatidae (Wombats)

.25   *Phascolarctidae (Koala)

.26   *Peramelina (Bandicoots)

> Class here Peramelidae

.27   *Marsupicarnivora and Paucituberculata

> Including Caenolestidae (shrew opossums), Dasyuridae; marsupial cats, mice, moles, rats; numbat, Tasmanian devil, thylacine (Tasmanian tiger, Tasmanian wolf)
>
> Subdivisions are added for Marsupicarnivora and Paucituberculata together, for Marsupicarnivora alone

.276   *Didelphidae (American opossums)

> *See also 599.23 for Australasian possums*

.29   *Monotremata

> Including Ornithorhynchidae (platypus), Tachyglossidae (echidnas, spiny anteaters)
>
> Class here Prototheria

*Add as instructed under 592–599

> **599.3–599.9 Eutheria (Placental mammals)**

Class comprehensive works in 599

.3 **Miscellaneous orders of Eutheria (placental mammals)**

Limited to those named below

SUMMARY

599.31	**Edentata (Xenarthra), Pholidota (pangolins, scaly anteaters), Tubulidentata (aardvark, ant bear)**
.32	**Lagomorpha**
.33	**Insectivora and related orders**
.35	**Rodentia (Rodents)**
.36	**Sciuridae (Squirrel family)**
.37	**Castoridae (Beavers)**

[.301–.309]   Standard subdivisions

Do not use; class in 599.01–599.09

.31   *Edentata (Xenarthra), Pholidota (pangolins, scaly anteaters), Tubulidentata (aardvark, ant bear)

Subdivisions are added for Edentata, Pholidota, Tubulidentata together; for Edentata alone

> 599.312–599.314 Edentata (Xenarthra)

Class comprehensive works in 599.31

.312   *Dasypodidae (Armadillos)

Subdivisions are added for the family as a whole and for individual genera and species

.313   *Bradypodidae (Sloths)

Subdivisions are added for the family as a whole and for individual genera and species

.314   *Myrmecophagidae

Class here comprehensive works on anteaters

Class ant bears, scaly anteaters in 599.31

For spiny anteaters, see 599.29

.32   *Lagomorpha

Class here Leporidae; rabbits

Class interdisciplinary works on domestic rabbits in 636.9322

*Add as instructed under 592–599

>   599.322–599.328   Leporidae

        Class comprehensive works in 599.32

.322   *Oryctolagus (Old World rabbit)

.324   *Sylvilagus (Cottontails)

        Subdivisions are added for the genus as a whole and for individual species

.328   *Lepus

        Class here hares, jackrabbits

        Subdivisions are added for the genus as a whole and for individual species

.329   *Ochotonidae (Pikas, Conies)

        Class here Ochotona

        See also 599.68 for conies of order Hyracoidea

.33   *Insectivora and related orders

        Including Dermoptera (Cynocephalidae, colugos, flying lemurs); otter shrews, solenodons, tenrecs

        Class here Lipotyphla

        Subdivisions are added for Insectivora and related orders together, for Insectivora alone

---

>   599.332–599.336   Insectivora

        Class comprehensive works in 599.33

.332   *Erinaceidae

        Including wood shrews

        Class here hedgehogs

.332 2   *Erinaceus

        Class here European hedgehog

        Subdivisions are added for the genus as a whole and for individual species

.335   *Talpidae and Chrysocloridae

        Class here moles

        Subdivisions are added for Talpidae and Chrysocloridae together, for Talpidae alone

---

*Add as instructed under 592–599

| .336 | *Soricidae |

Class here comprehensive works on shrews

Class otter shrews in 599.33

For wood shrews, see 599.332; for elephant shrews, see 599.337; for tree shrews, see 599.338

| .336 2 | *Sorex (Long-tailed shrews) |

Class here pigmy shrew

Subdivisions are added for the genus as a whole and for individual species

| .337 | *Macroscelidea (Macroscelididae, Elephant shrews) |

| .338 | *Scandentia (Tupaiidae, Tree shrews) |

| .35 | *Rodentia (Rodents) |

Including jerboas; harvest, jumping mice; mole rats, swamp rats

Class here Myomorpha; Muridae in the broad sense encompassing Cricetidae, Rhizomyidae, Spalacidae; mice; rats

Class results of experimental studies on internal biological processes using laboratory mice and rats in 571–573, plus notation 1935 from add instructions in 571–573, e.g., circulation in rats 573.11935

For Sciuridae, see 599.36; for Castoridae, see 599.37

| > | 599.352–599.358 Muridae |

Class comprehensive works in 599.35

| .352 | *Rattus (Common rats) |

Class here black rat, Norway (brown) rat

Subdivisions are added for the genus as a whole and for individual species

Class comprehensive works on rats in 599.35

| .353 | *Mus (Common mice) |

Class here house mouse

Subdivisions are added for the genus as a whole and for individual species

Class comprehensive works on mice in 599.35

| .354 | *Voles |

Including Arvicola (water voles)

Class here Microtus (meadow mice)

*Add as instructed under 592–599

.355	*Peromyscus (Deer mice, White-footed mice)
.356	*Hamsters

Class here Cricetus, Mesocricetus (golden hamsters)

Class interdisciplinary works on domestic species of hamsters in 636.9356

.357	Miscellaneous rats of family Muridae

Limited to those named below

[.357 01–.357 09]	Standard subdivisions

Do not use; class in 599.3501–599.3509

.357 2	*Sigmodon (Cotton rats)
.357 3	*Neotoma (Wood rats)
.357 9	*Muskrats

Class here Ondatra, Neofiber

.358	Miscellaneous Muridae

Limited to those named below

[.358 01–.358 09]	Standard subdivisions

Do not use; class in 599.3501–599.3509

.358 2	*Lemmings

Class here Lemmus

.358 3	*Gerbils

Class interdisciplinary works on domestic species of gerbils in 636.93583

.358 5	*Apodemus (Wood and field mice)
.359	*Rodentia other than Castoridae, Muridae, Sciuridae

Including agoutis (pacas), capybaras, coypu (nutria), gundis, hutias, springhaas; African mole rat; cane, rock, spiny rats

Class here Caviomorpha, Hystricomorpha, Phiomorpha

.359 2	*Caviidae

Class here Cavia, cavies, guinea pigs

Class interdisciplinary works on Cavia porcellus (domestic guinea pigs) in 636.93592

.359 3	*Chinchillidae

Class here chinchillas

Class interdisciplinary works on chinchillas in 636.93593

*Add as instructed under 592–599

.359 6   *Gliridae (Myoxidae, Dormice)

.359 7   *Porcupines

                       Including Hystricidae (Old World porcupines)

.359 74   *Erethizontidae (New World porcupines)

.359 8   *Heteromyidae

                       Including pocket mice, kangaroo mice

.359 87   *Dipodomys (Kangaroo rats)

.359 9   *Geomyidae (Pocket gophers)

                       See also 599.365 for gopher of genus Spermophilus

.36   *Sciuridae (Squirrel family)

           Class here squirrels

.362   *Sciurus (Tree squirrels)

           Class here European red squirrel, fox squirrel, gray squirrel

           Subdivisions are added for the genus as a whole and for individual species

.363   *Tamiasciurus (North American red squirrels, Chickarees)

           Class here Douglas squirrel

           Subdivisions are added for the genus as a whole and for individual species

.364   *Chipmunks

           Subdivisions are added for chipmunks as a whole and for individual genera and species

.365   *Ground squirrels

           Including gopher, susliks

           Class here Spermophilus

               See also 599.3599 for pocket gophers, 599.364 for chipmunks

.366   *Marmota (Marmots)

           Class here woodchuck (groundhog)

           Subdivisions are added for the genus as a whole and for individual species

.367   *Cynomys (Prairie dogs)

           Subdivisions are added for the genus as a whole and for individual species

*Add as instructed under 592–599

.369   *Flying squirrels

            Class here Glaucomys; eastern flying squirrel

.37   *Castoridae (Beavers)

            Class here Castor

            Subdivisions are added for the genus as a whole and for individual species

.4   *Chiroptera (Bats)

            Class here Microchiroptera

.45   *Phyllostomidae

            Including neotropical fruit bats, vampire bats

.47   *Vespertilionidae

            Including big brown bats, house bats

.472   *Myotis (Little brown bats)

            Subdivisions are added for the genus as a whole and for individual
            species

.49   *Pteropodidae (Old World fruit bats)

            Including flying foxes

            Class here Megachiroptera

.5   *Cetacea and Sirenia

            Class here marine mammals; whales, great whales; Mysticeti (baleen whales),
            Odontoceti (toothed whales)

            Subdivisions are added for Cetacea and Sirenia together, for Cetacea alone

            For Pinnipedia, see 599.79

>   599.52–599.54 Cetacea

            Class comprehensive works in 599.5

.52   Specific Mysticeti (baleen whales)

            Including pygmy right whale

            Class comprehensive works on Mysticeti in 599.5

[.520 1–.520 9]   Standard subdivisions

            Do not use; class in 599.501–599.509

.522   *Eschrichtidae (Gray whale)

*Add as instructed under 592–599

.524	*Balaenopteridae (Rorquals)

Including Bryde's, minke, sei whales

Class here Balaenoptera

For Megaptera, see 599.525

.524 6	*Balaenoptera physalus (Fin whale, Finback whale)
.524 8	*Balaenoptera musculus (Blue whale)
.525	*Megaptera (Humpback whale)
.527	*Balaenidae
.527 3	*Eubalaena (Right whale)
.527 6	*Balaena (Bowhead whale, Greenland right whale)

> 599.53–599.54 Odontoceti (Toothed whales)

Class comprehensive works in 599.5

.53	*Dolphins and porpoises

Including false killer, pilot whales

Class here Delphinidae

Subdivisions are added for dolphins and porpoises together, for dolphins alone

---

> 599.532–599.536 Delphinidae

Class comprehensive works in 599.53

For river dolphins of family Delphinidae, see 599.538

.532	*Delphinus (Common dolphin)
.533	*Tursiops (Bottle-nose dolphins)

Subdivisions are added for the genus as a whole and for individual species

.534	*Stenella

Including spinner, spotted, striped dolphins

.536	*Orcinus (Killer whale)
.538	*River dolphins

Class here Platanistidae

.539	*Phocoenidae (Porpoises)

*Add as instructed under 592–599

.54   ***Other Odontoceti (toothed whales)**

Other than dolphins and porpoises

Class comprehensive works on Odontoceti in 599.5

> *For false killer, pilot whales, see 599.53; for killer whale, see 599.536*

.542   ***Delphinapterus (Beluga, White whale)**

Class here Monodontidae

> *For Monodon, see 599.543*

.543   ***Monodon (Narwhal)**

.545   ***Ziphiidae (Beaked whales)**

.547   ***Physeteridae**

Including dwarf and pygmy sperm whales

Class here Physeter (sperm whale)

.55   ***Sirenia (Sea cows)**

Class here manatees

.559   ***Dugongidae**

Class here dugong

Class Steller's sea cow in 599.559168

.6   *Ungulates

Class here hoofed mammals, comprehensive works on big game animals

Class Sirenia in 599.55; class big game hunting in 799.26

> *For a specific kind of nonungulate big game animal, see the kind, e.g., bears 599.78*

SUMMARY

599.63	**Artiodactyla (Even-toes ungulates)**	
.64	**Bovidae**	
.65	**Cervidae (Deer)**	
.66	**Perissodactyla (Odd-toed ungulates)**	
.67	**Proboscidea (Elephants)**	
.68	**Hyracoidea (Hyraxes)**	

.63   ***Artiodactyla (Even-toed ungulates)**

Including Tragulidae (chevrotains, mouse deer)

Class here Ruminantia (ruminants)

Class comprehensive works on Artiodactyla and Perissodactyla in 599.6

> *For Bovidae, see 599.64; for Cervidae, see 599.65*

---

*Add as instructed under 592–599

.633	*Suidae (Pigs, Swine)

Including African bush pig, babirusa, giant forest hog, warthog

Class here comprehensive works on Suiformes

For Tayassuidae, see 599.634; for Hippopotamidae, see 599.635

.633 2	*Sus

Including bearded, Javan pigs

Class here wild boars

Class interdisciplinary works on Sus scrofa (domestic swine) in 636.4

.634	*Tayassuidae (Peccaries)
.635	*Hippopotamidae (Hippopotamuses)

Including pigmy hippopotamus

Class here Hippopotamus amphibius

.636	*Camelidae
.636 2	*Camelus (Camels)

Subdivisions are added for the genus as a whole and for individual species

Class interdisciplinary works on camels in 636.295

.636 7	*Lama

Class here guanaco, vicuña

Class interdisciplinary works on guanaco (alpaca, llama) in 636.296

>   599.638–599.65   Ruminantia (Ruminants)

Class comprehensive works in 599.63

.638	*Giraffidae

Including okapi

Class here giraffe

.639	*Antilocapridae (Pronghorn)

Variant name: pronghorn antelope

.64	*Bovidae

Including Cephalophinae (duikers)

Class here antelopes

See also 599.639 for pronghorn antelope

*Add as instructed under 592–599

.642	*Bovinae

Including buffalo, elands, four-horned antelopes

For American buffalo, see 599.643

.642 2	*Bos (Oxen)

Including banteng, gaur, yak

Class interdisciplinary works on Bos taurus (domestic cattle) in 636.2

.642 3	*Tragelaphus

Including bongo, bushbuck, kudus, nyalas

.643	*Bison

Including European bison (wisent)

Class here American bison (American buffalo)

.645	*Hippotraginae

Including addax, hartebeests, oryx, reedbucks, waterbuck; roan, sable antelopes

Class here Alcelaphinae

.645 9	*Connochaetes (Gnus, Wildebeests)
.646	*Antilopinae

Including dik-diks, impala, springbok

.646 9	*Gazella (Gazelles)
.647	*Caprinae

Including chamois, saiga, serows

For Capra, see 599.648; for sheep, see 599.649

.647 5	*Oreamnos (Mountain goat)
.647 8	*Ovibos (Muskox)
.648	*Capra

Including ibexes, turs

Class here goats

Class interdisciplinary works on Capra hircus (domestic goat) in 636.39

See also 599.6475 for mountain goat

.649	*Sheep

Including aoudad (Barbary sheep), bharals (blue sheep)

Class here Ovis

Class interdisciplinary works on Ovis aries (domestic sheep) in 636.3

*Add as instructed under 592–599

.649 7	*Ovis canadensis (Bighorn sheep)
.65	*Cervidae (Deer)

Including chital, muntjacs

See also 599.63 for mouse deer

.652	*Odocoileus

Class here white-tailed (Virginia) deer

For Odocoileus hemionus (mule deer), see 599.653

.653	*Odocoileus hemionus (Mule deer)
.654	*Cervus

Including sambar

.654 2	*Cervus elaphus (American elk, red deer, wapiti)

See also 599.657 for elk of genus Alces

.655	*Dama (Fallow deer)
.657	*Alces (Elk, Moose)

See also 599.6542 for American elk

.658	*Rangifer (Caribou, Reindeer)
.659	*Capreolus (Roe deer)
.66	*Perissodactyla (Odd-toed ungulates)

Including Tapiridae (tapirs)

.665	*Equidae

Including asses

Class here Equus

Class interdisciplinary works on asses in 636.18

.665 5	*Equus caballus (Horse)

Class here mustang, Przewalski's horse, wild horse

Class interdisciplinary works on horses in 636.1

.665 7	*Zebras

Subdivisions are added for zebras as a whole and for individual species

Class quagga in 599.6657168

.668	*Rhinocerotidae (Rhinoceroses)

Subdivisions are added for the family as a whole and for individual genera and species

*Add as instructed under 592–599

.67	*Proboscidea (Elephants)
.674	*Loxodonta (African elephant)
.676	*Elephas (Asiatic elephant, Indian elephant)
.68	*Hyracoidea (Hyraxes)

        Variant names: conies, dassies

        See also 599.329 for conies of order Lagomorpha

.7   ***Carnivora**   **Fissipedia (Land carnivores)**

        Class here comprehensive works on fur-bearing animals

        For a specific kind of noncarnivorous fur-bearing animal, see the kind, e.g., beavers 599.37

SUMMARY

599.74	**Feloidea**
.75	**Felidae (Cat family)**
.76	**Canoidea**
.77	**Canidae (Dog family)**
.78	**Ursidae (Bears)**
.79	**Pinnipedia (Marine carnivores)**

>   599.74–599.78   Fissipedia (Land carnivores)

        Class comprehensive works in 599.7

.74	*Feloidea

        For Felidae, see 599.75

.742	*Viverridae

        Including civets, fossa, genets, linsangs, mongooses

.743	*Hyaenidae

        Including aardwolf

        Class here hyenas

.75	*Felidae (Cat family)

        Including clouded leopard

.752	*Felis

        Including margay, ocelot, serval

        Class genus Lynx in 599.753; class interdisciplinary works on Felis catus (domestic cats) in 636.8

.752 4	*Felis concolor (Cougar, Mountain lion, Panther, Puma)

*Add as instructed under 592–599

.752 6	*Felis silvestris (European wildcat)

See also 599.7536 for bobcat (wildcat)

.753	*Lynx

Subdivisions are added for the genus as a whole and for individual species other than Lynx rufus

.753 6	*Lynx rufus (Bobcat, Wildcat)

See also 599.7526 for European wildcat

.755	*Panthera (Leo)

Including jaguar

Class here big cats

For Panthera tigris (tiger), see 599.756; for Panthera leo (lion), see 599.757. For a specific big cat not provided for here, see the cat, e.g., mountain lion 599.7524

.755 4	*Panthera pardus (Leopard)

Class here comprehensive works on leopards

Class clouded leopard in 599.75

For snow leopard, see 599.7555

.755 5	*Panthera uncia (Ounce, Snow leopard)
.756	*Panthera tigris (Tiger)
.757	*Panthera leo (Lion)
.759	*Acinonyx (Cheetah)
.76	*Canoidea

For Canidae, see 599.77; for Ursidae, see 599.78

.763	*Procyonidae

Including coatis, kinkajou, red (lesser) panda

See also 599.789 for giant panda

.763 2	*Procyon (Racoons)

Subdivisions are added for the genus as a whole and for individual species

.766	*Mustelidae

Including grisons, marbled polecat, wolverine, zorilla (striped polecat)

Class here Mustelinae

For Melinae, see 599.767; for Mephitinae, see 599.768; for Lutrinae, see 599.769

*Add as instructed under 592–599

.766 2	*Mustela
	Including ermine (stoat), comprehensive works on Old World polecats
	Class here weasels
	Class marbled polecat, zorilla (striped polecat) in 599.766; class European polecat in 599.76628
	For weasels in genera other than Mustela, see 599.7663
	See also 599.768 for New world polecats (skunks)
.766 27	*Minks
	Subdivisions are added for minks as a whole and for individual species
.766 28	Mustela putorius (European polecat)
	Class interdisciplinary works on ferrets (domestic European polecat) in 636.976628
.766 29	*Mustela nigripes (Black-footed ferret)
.766 3	*Weasels in genera other than Mustela
	Including Patagonian, striped weasels
.766 5	*Martes
	Including fisher, sable
	Class here martens
.767	*Melinae and Mellivorinae
	Class here badgers
	Subdivisions are added for Melinae and Mellivorinae together, for Melinae alone
.767 2	*Meles (Old World badger)
.768	*Mephitinae (Skunks)
	Variant name: polecats
	See also 599.7662 for Old World polecats
.769	*Lutrinae (Otters)
	Including clawless, giant otters
.769 2	*Lutra (River otters)
	Subdivisions are added for the genus as a whole and for individual species
.769 5	*Enhydra (Sea otter)

*Add as instructed under 592–599

.77   *Canidae (Dog family)

Including dhole; dogs and wolves of genera other than Canis

.772   *Canis

Including dingo, jackals

Class here comprehensive scientific works on dogs

Class dogs of genera other than Canis in 599.77; class interdisciplinary works on dogs in 636.7

For Canis lupus (gray wolf, timber wolf) and Canis rufus (red wolf), see 599.773

.772 5   *Canis latrans (Coyote)

.773   *Canis lupus (Gray wolf, Timber wolf) and Canis rufus (red wolf)

Class here comprehensive works on wolves

Subdivisions are added for either or both topics in heading

Class wolves of genera other than Canis in 599.77

.775   *Vulpes

Class here red fox, comprehensive works on foxes

Subdivisions are added for the genus as a whole and for individual species

For foxes of genera other than Vulpes, see 599.776

.776   *Foxes of genera other than Vulpes

Including fennec, gray foxes

.776 4   *Alopex (Arctic fox)

.78   *Ursidae (Bears)

.784   *Ursus (Grizzly bear, Brown bear)

.785   *Eurarctos (American black bear)

.786   *Thalarctos (Polar bear)

.789   *Ailuropoda (Giant panda)

See also 599.763 for lesser panda

.79   *Pinnipedia (Marine carnivores)

Class here Phocidae (earless seals, hair seals, true seals); seals

---

\>   599.792–599.796 Phocidae (Earless seals, Hair seals, True seals)

Class comprehensive works in 599.79

*Add as instructed under 592–599

.792	*Phoca

Including Baikal, Caspian, ribbon, ringed, spotted seals

.792 3	*Phoca vitulina (Harbor seal)
.792 9	*Phoca groenlandica (Harp seal)
.793	*Halichoerus (Gray seal)
.794	*Mirounga (Elephant seals)

Subdivisions are added for the genus as a whole and for individual species

.795	*Monachus (Monk seals)

Subdivisions are added for the genus as a whole and for individual species

.796	*Other Phocidae

Including bearded, crabeater, hooded, leopard, Ross, Weddell seals

.797	*Otariidae (Eared seals)
.797 3	*Arctocephalinae (Fur seals)

Class here Callorhinus (northern fur seal, Pacific fur seal)

.797 38	*Arctocephalus (Southern fur seals)

Subdivisions are added for the genus as a whole and for individual species

.797 5	*Otariinae (Sea lions)
.799	*Odobenidae (Walrus)
.8	***Primates**

Class here Anthropoidea, monkeys

.83	*Prosimii

Including Lemuridae (lemurs), Lorisidae, Tarsiidae (tarsiers)

Including aye-ayes, bush babies, galagos, indri, lorises, sifakas

Class Tupaiidae in 599.338

>   599.84–599.88 Anthropoidea

Class comprehensive works in 599.8

For Hominidae, see 599.9

*Add as instructed under 592–599

> 599.84–599.86 Monkeys

Class comprehensive works in 599.8

.84 *Callithricidae (Marmosets)

Including tamarins

.85 *Cebidae (New World monkeys)

Class here Platyrrhini

For Callithricidae, see 599.84

.852 *Saimiri (Squirrel monkeys)

Subdivisions are added for the genus as a whole and for individual species

.855 *Alouatta (Howler monkeys)

Subdivisions are added for the genus as a whole and for individual species

.858 *Atelinae

Including spider, woolly monkeys

.86 *Cercopithecidae (Old World monkeys)

Class here Catarrhini

.862 *Cercopithecus (Guenons)

Including blue, green monkeys

.864 *Macaca (Macaques)

.864 3 *Macaca mulatta (Rhesus monkey)

.864 4 *Macaca fuscata (Japanese macaque, Snow monkey)

.865 *Papio (Baboons)

Subdivisions are added for the genus as a whole and for individual species

.88 *Pongidae (Great apes) and Hylobatidae

Class here apes, comprehensive works on Hominoidea

Subdivisions are added for Pongidae and Hylobatidae together, for Pongidae alone

For Hominidae, see 599.9

*Add as instructed under 592–599

.882	*Hylobatidae (Gibbons)
	Including siamang
	Class here Hylobates

>   599.883–599.885 Specific Pongidae (great apes)

Class comprehensive works in 599.88

.883	*Pongo (Orangutan)
.884	*Gorilla
.885	*Pan (Chimpanzees)
.9	**Hominidae Homo sapiens**

Class here physical anthropology [*formerly* 573]

Class social anthropology, interdisciplinary works on social and physical anthropology in 306

> *For psychology, see 150; for prehistoric Hominidae, see 569.9; for medicine, see 610*

.93	Genetics, sex and age characteristics, evolution
.935	Genetics

Class here heredity

> *For variation, see 599.94; for biochemical genetics, see 612.015*

.936	Sex characteristics
.937	Age characteristics

Class longevity in 612.68

.938	Evolution

> *For paleontology of hominidae, see 569.9*

.94	Anthropometry

Class here variation

> *See Manual at 599.94 vs. 611*

.943	Teeth
.945	Skin

Including dermatoglyphics, fingerprints

Class use of fingerprints in criminal investigation in 363.258

---

*Add as instructed under 592–599

.947   Bones

For craniology, see 599.948

.948   Head and face

Standard subdivisions are added for either or both topics in heading

Class here craniology

.949   Somatotypes

Including persons with abnormal dimensions, e.g., dwarfs, giants

Class pathological aspects of abnormal dimensions in 616.043

.95   Environmental effects on physique

Including effect on pigmentation

Class here human biological ecology

Class interdisciplinary works on human ecology in 304.2

.97   Human races [*formerly* 572]

Class here physical ethnology

.972   Origins and causes of physical differences among races

Class nonracial physical characteristics in 599.9; class origins and causes of physical differences of specific races in 599.98

.98   Specific races [*formerly* 572.8]

Add to base number 599.98 notation 03–9 from Table 5, e.g., Celtic race 599.98916

Class extinct races in 569.9

The 21st edition of the Dewey Decimal Classification was designed by Lisa Hanifan of Albany, New York. Edition 21 was generated from an online database. Database design, technical support, and programming for this edition were provided by John Finni and Kurt Lanza from Inforonics, Inc. of Littleton, Massachusetts. Composition was done in Times Roman and Helvetica under the supervision of Inforonics, Inc. and Word Management, Inc. of Albany, New York. The book was printed and bound by Hamilton Printing Company of Rensselaer, New York.